lonely planet

Russia

THIS EDITION WRIT[illegible]

Simon [illegible],

Marc Bennetts, Greg Bloom, Marc Di Duca,

Anthony Haywood, Anna Kaminski, Tom Masters, Leonid Ragozin,

Tamara Sheward, Regis St Louis, Mara Vorhees

PLAN YOUR TRIP

ON THE ROAD

PETE SEAWARD/LONELY PLANET ©

GUM DEPARTMENT STORE P114

PETE SEAWARD/LONELY PLANET ©

GRAND PALACE, PETERHOF P211

OLIVIER RENC/GETTY IMAGES ©

Contents

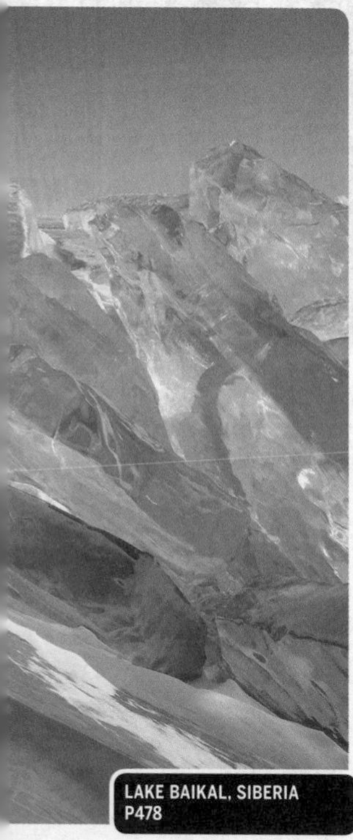

LAKE BAIKAL, SIBERIA
P478

ON THE ROAD

CULTURA TRAVEL/PHILIP LEE HARVEY/GETTY IMAGES ©

BUSKER, TRANS-SIBERIAN RAILWAY P38

Contents

Welcome to Russia

The world's largest country offers it all, from historic cities and idyllic countryside to artistic riches, epic train rides and vodka-fuelled nightlife.

Historic & Contemporary

If ancient walled fortresses, glittering palaces and swirly-spired churches are what you're after, focus on European Russia. Here Moscow and St Petersburg are the must-see destinations, twin repositories of eye-boggling national treasures, political energies and contemporary creativity. Within easy reach of these cities are charming historical towns and villages, such as Veliky Novgorod, Pskov and Suzdal, where the vistas dotted with onion domes and lined with gingerbread cottages measure up to the rural Russia of popular imagination.

Arty & Adventurous

Whether you're a culture vulture in search of inspiration from great artists and writers or an adventure addict looking for new horizons to conquer, Russia amply delivers. Tread in the footsteps of literary greats, including Tolstoy and Pushkin, on their country estates. Arrange a ski holiday in Krasnaya Polyana, newly spruced up for the 2014 Sochi Winter Olympics, go trekking in the Altai, or even climb an active volcano in Kamchatka – the varied possibilities will make your head spin.

Off the Beaten Track

Russia's vast geographical distances and cultural differences mean you don't tick off its highlights in the way you might those of a smaller nation. Instead, view Russia as a collection of distinct territories, each one deserving separate attention.

Rather than transiting via Moscow, consider flying direct to a regional centre such as Irkutsk, Novosibirsk or Yekaterinburg and striking out from there. With a welcome spread of Western-style hostels along the Trans-Siberian route and the ease of booking trains and flights online, it's never been easier to organise this kind of trip.

A Riddle Worth Solving

We won't lie: tolerating bureaucracy, corruption and occasional discomfort, particularly away from the booming urban centres, remains an integral part of the Russian travel experience. However, a small degree of perseverance will be amply rewarded and one of the great joys of travel in Russia is being swept away by the boundless hospitality of the people.

Aleksandr Solzhenitsyn put it best when he talked about Russia's 'ancient, deeply rooted autonomous culture…full of riddles and surprises to Western thinking'. You, too, will be beguiled by the beauty of its arts and the quixotic nature of its people.

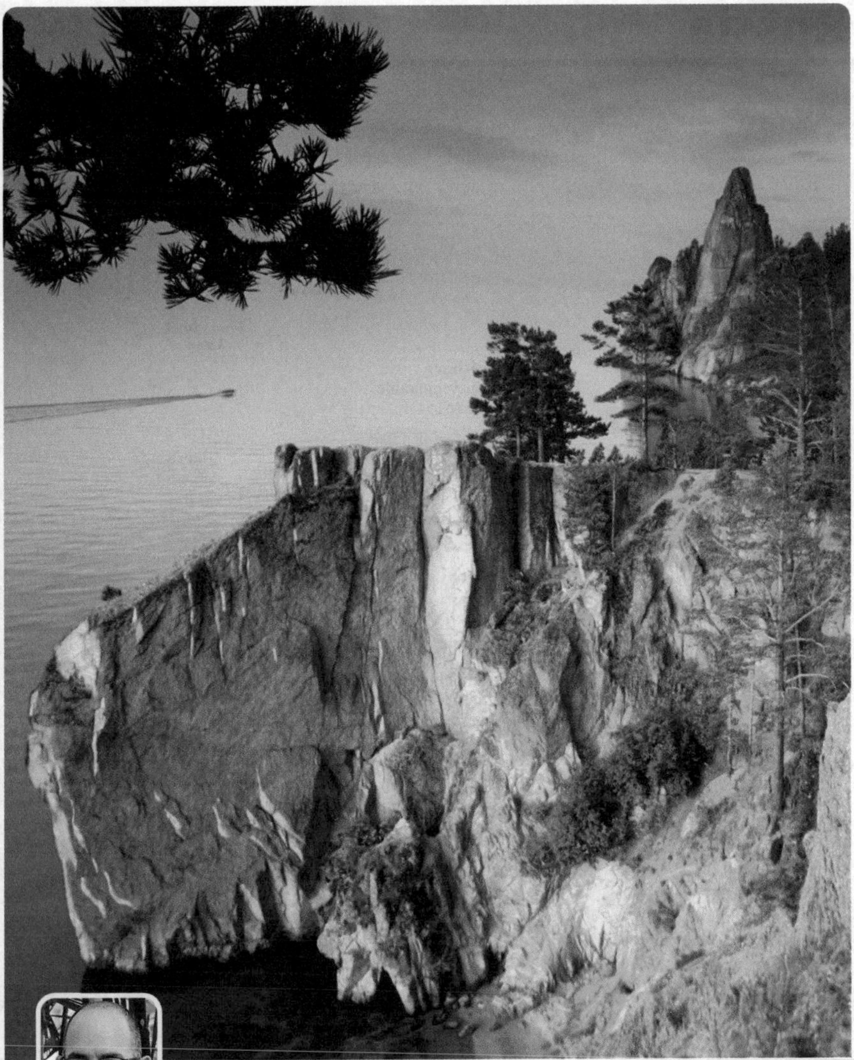

Why I Love Russia

By Simon Richmond, Author

A traveller's relationship with Russia is never an easy one, but over two decades of exploring this multifaceted country, I've yet to tire of it or be disappointed. It's a thrill to discover the latest on the dynamic and liberal art scene in the major cities and I particularly relish the serene countryside, with Lake Baikal a favourite location. Above all, it has been encounters and passionate conversations with warmly welcoming, highly educated and hospitable Russians that have made the most lasting impression on me.

For more about our authors, see page 696.

Above: Lake Baikal (p478), Eastern Siberia

Russia

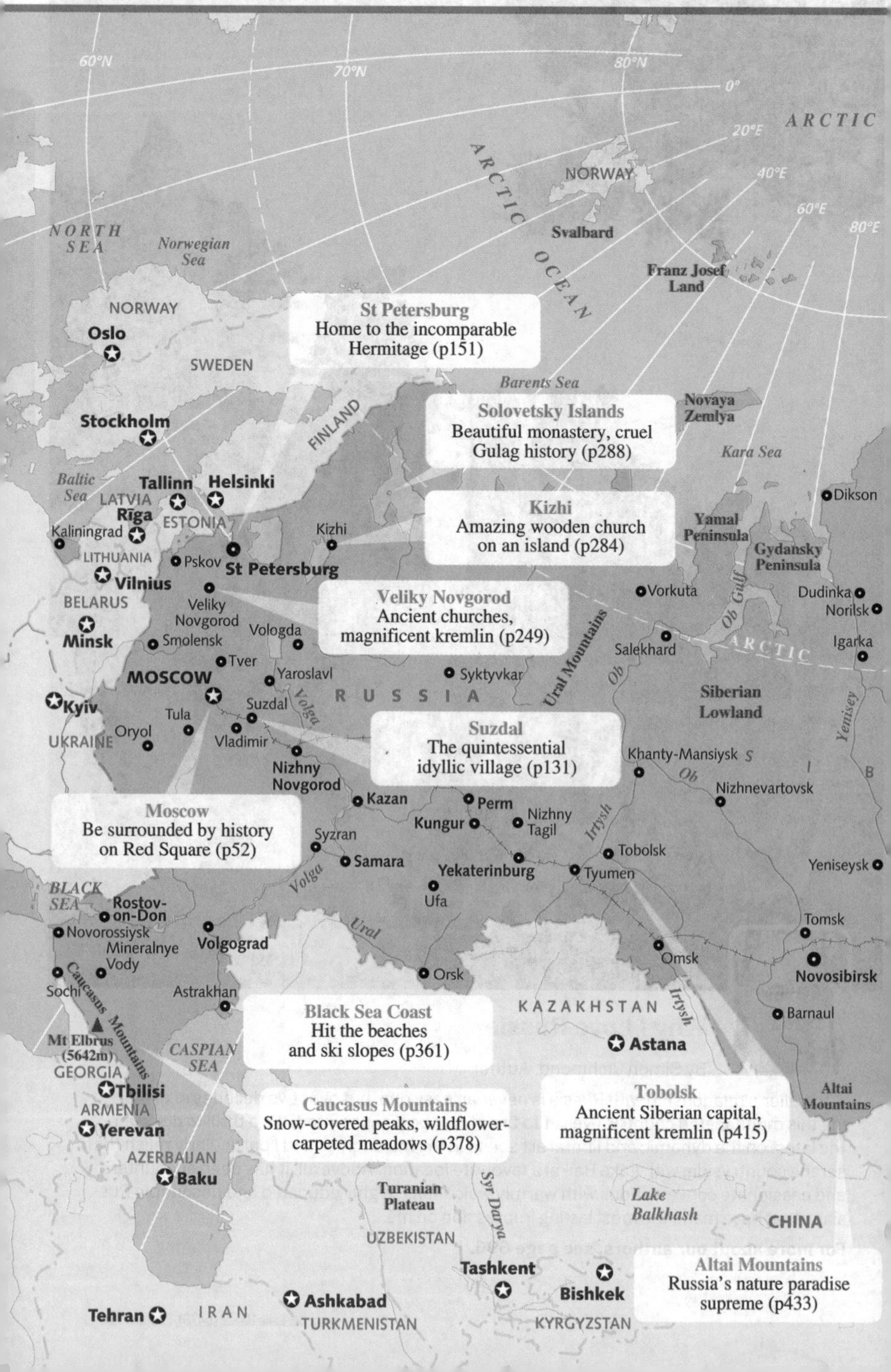

60°N
70°N
80°N
0°
20°E
40°E
60°E
80°E
ARCTIC
ARCTIC OCEAN
NORWAY
Svalbard
Franz Josef Land
NORTH SEA
Norwegian Sea
NORWAY
Oslo
SWEDEN
St Petersburg
Home to the incomparable Hermitage (p151)
Barents Sea
Solovetsky Islands
Beautiful monastery, cruel Gulag history (p288)
Novaya Zemlya
Kara Sea
Stockholm
FINLAND
Baltic Sea
Tallinn
Helsinki
LATVIA
Rīga
ESTONIA
Kaliningrad
LITHUANIA
Kizhi
Kizhi
Amazing wooden church on an island (p284)
Dikson
Yamal Peninsula
Gydansky Peninsula
Pskov
St Petersburg
Vilnius
BELARUS
Minsk
Veliky Novgorod
Smolensk
Vologda
Veliky Novgorod
Ancient churches, magnificent kremlin (p249)
Vorkuta
Ob Gulf
Dudinka
Norilsk
Ural Mountains
Salekhard
ARCTIC
Igarka
Tver
MOSCOW
Yaroslavl
Syktyvkar
Kyiv
Suzdal
Volga
RUSSIA
Ob
Siberian Lowland
Yenisey
Tula
UKRAINE
Oryol
Vladimir
Suzdal
The quintessential idyllic village (p131)
Khanty-Mansiysk
Ob
Nizhny Novgorod
Nizhnevartovsk
Kazan
Perm
Moscow
Be surrounded by history on Red Square (p52)
Kungur
Nizhny Tagil
Irtysh
Syzran
Samara
Tobolsk
Yekaterinburg
Tyumen
Yeniseysk
BLACK SEA
Volga
Ufa
Rostov-on-Don
Ural
Tomsk
Novorossiysk
Mineralnye Vody
Volgograd
Omsk
Novosibirsk
Sochi
Caucasus Mountains
Astrakhan
Orsk
KAZAKHSTAN
Irtysh
Barnaul
Black Sea Coast
Hit the beaches and ski slopes (p361)
Mt Elbrus (5642m)
CASPIAN SEA
Astana
GEORGIA
Tbilisi
ARMENIA
Yerevan
Caucasus Mountains
Snow-covered peaks, wildflower-carpeted meadows (p378)
Tobolsk
Ancient Siberian capital, magnificent kremlin (p415)
Altai Mountains
AZERBAIJAN
Baku
Turanian Plateau
Syr Darya
Lake Balkhash
CHINA
UZBEKISTAN
Tashkent
Bishkek
Altai Mountains
Russia's nature paradise supreme (p433)
Tehran
IRAN
Ashkabad
TURKMENISTAN
KYRGYZSTAN

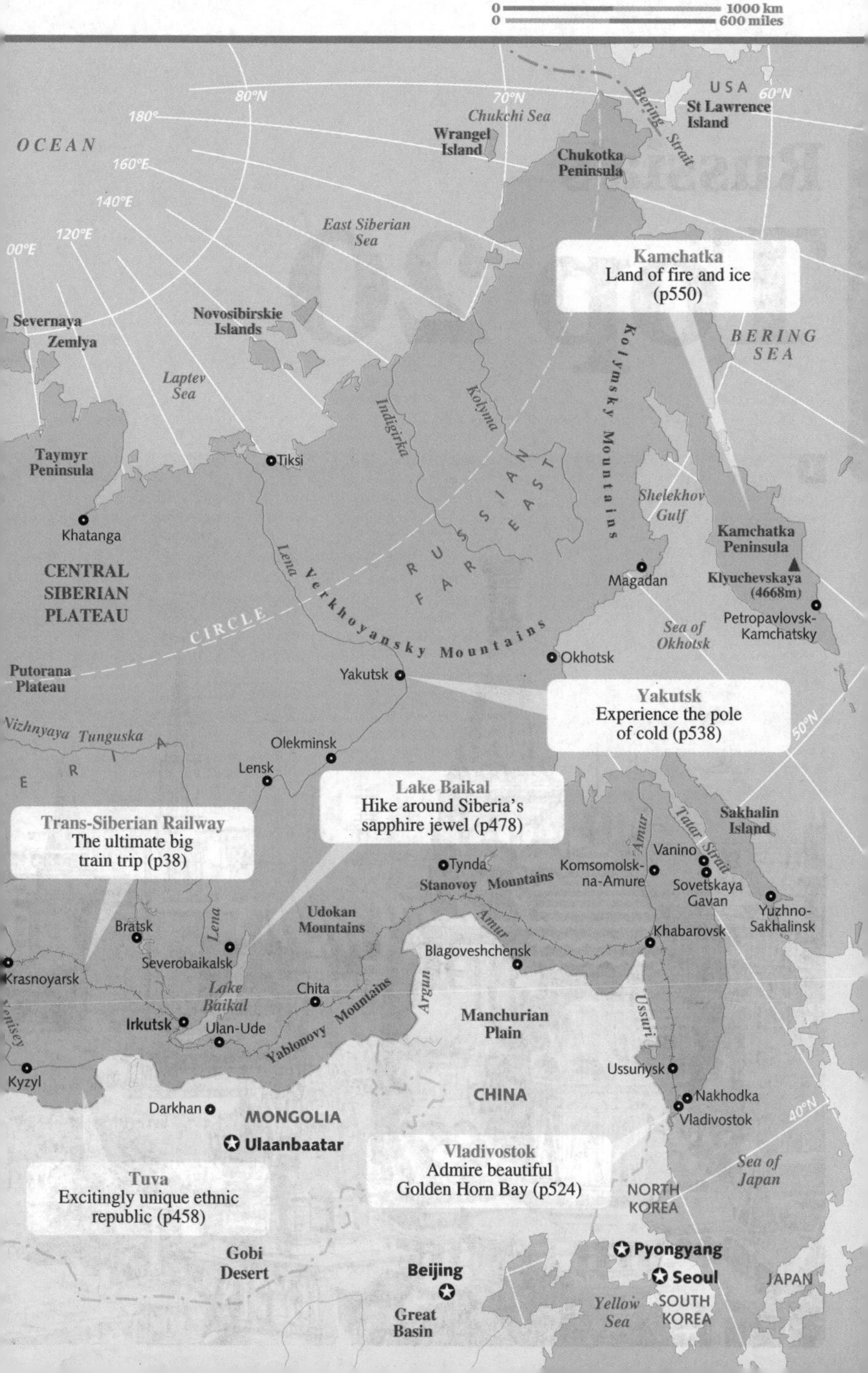

0 1000 km
0 600 miles
OCEAN
80°N
70°N
60°N
50°N
40°N
180°
160°E
140°E
120°E
00°E
USA
St Lawrence Island
Bering Strait
Chukchi Sea
Wrangel Island
Chukotka Peninsula
East Siberian Sea
Kamchatka
Land of fire and ice (p550)
BERING SEA
Severnaya Zemlya
Novosibirskie Islands
Laptev Sea
Indigirka
Kolyma
Kolymsky Mountains
Taymyr Peninsula
Tiksi
RUSSIAN FAR EAST
Shelekhov Gulf
Khatanga
Kamchatka Peninsula
CENTRAL SIBERIAN PLATEAU
Lena
Verkhoyansky Mountains
Magadan
Klyuchevskaya (4668m)
Petropavlovsk-Kamchatsky
CIRCLE
Sea of Okhotsk
Okhotsk
Putorana Plateau
Yakutsk
Yakutsk
Experience the pole of cold (p538)
Nizhnyaya Tunguska
Olekminsk
Lensk
Lake Baikal
Hike around Siberia's sapphire jewel (p478)
Amur
Tatar Strait
Sakhalin Island
Trans-Siberian Railway
The ultimate big train trip (p38)
Tynda
Stanovoy Mountains
Komsomolsk-na-Amure
Vanino
Sovetskaya Gavan
Yuzhno-Sakhalinsk
Udokan Mountains
Bratsk
Severobaikalsk
Khabarovsk
Blagoveshchensk
Krasnoyarsk
Lake Baikal
Chita
Yablonovy Mountains
Argun
Manchurian Plain
Irkutsk
Ulan-Ude
Yenisey
Ussuri
Kyzyl
Ussuriysk
Nakhodka
Vladivostok
Darkhan
MONGOLIA
CHINA
Ulaanbaatar
Vladivostok
Admire beautiful Golden Horn Bay (p524)
Sea of Japan
Tuva
Excitingly unique ethnic republic (p458)
NORTH KOREA
Pyongyang
Gobi Desert
Beijing
Seoul
JAPAN
Yellow Sea
SOUTH KOREA
Great Basin

Russia's Top 20

1

Walking Across Red Square

1 Stepping onto Red Square (p57) never ceases to inspire: the tall towers and imposing walls of the Kremlin, the playful jumble of patterns and colours adorning St Basil's Cathedral, the majestic red bricks of the State History Museum and the elaborate edifice of GUM, all encircling a vast stretch of cobblestones. Individually they are impressive, but the ensemble is electrifying. Come at night to see the square empty of crowds and the buildings awash with lights.

Banya at Sanduny Baths

2 The quintessential Russian experience is visiting a traditional bathhouse, or *banya*. Forget your modesty, strip down and brave the steam room at the likes of Moscow's Sanduny Baths (p52). As the heat hits, you'll understand why locals wear felt hats to protect their hair. A light thrashing with a bundle of birch branches is part of the fun, as is the invigorating blast that follows the post-steam dive into an icy pool or the douse in a frigid shower – as the locals say, *'S lyogkim parom!'* (Hope your steam was easy!).

DE AGOSTINI/D. STAQUET/GETTY IMAGES ©

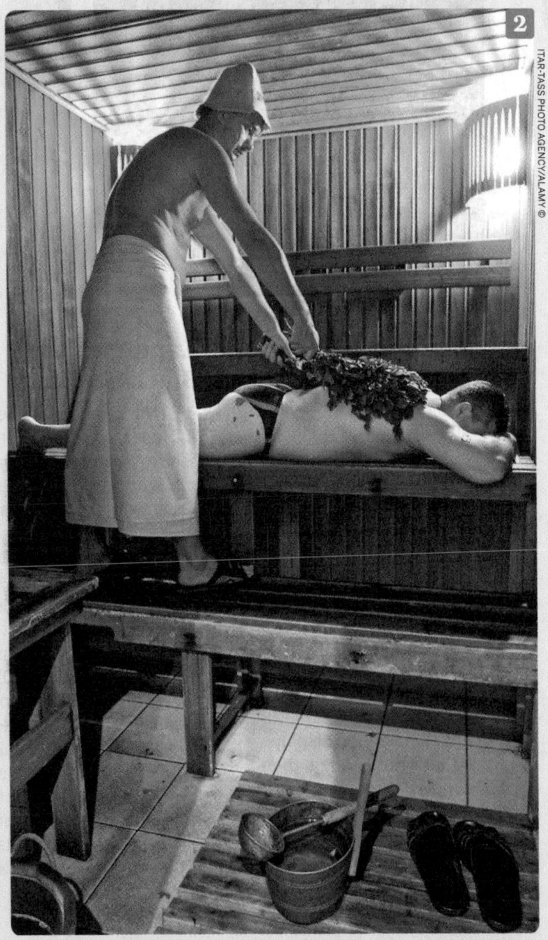

ITAR-TASS PHOTO AGENCY/ALAMY ©

LATITUDESTOCK - STUART COX/GETTY IMAGES ©

The Hermitage

3 Little can prepare most visitors for the scale and quality of the exhibits at the State Hermitage Museum (p185). Comprising an almost unrivalled history of Western art, the collection includes a staggering number of Rembrandts, Rubens, Picassos and Matisses – the latter two now displayed in new galleries in the General Staff Building. In addition, there are superb antiquities, sculpture and jewellery on display. If that's not enough, then simply content yourself with wandering through the private apartments of the Romanovs, for whom the Winter Palace was home until 1917.

Exploring the Black Sea

4 The serene Black Sea coast (p378) has long been a favourite of Russian holidaymakers for its seaside towns, easygoing ambience and magnificent scenery in the nearby Caucasus mountains. The gateway to it all is Sochi, a vibrant city that reinvented itself as a first-rate international resort and host of the 2014 Winter Olympics. The looming peaks of nearby Krasnaya Polyana (p369) make a superb destination for ski lovers, while there's great hiking – past waterfalls and up to eagle's-nest heights – in the Agura Valley. Top middle: Skier, Krasnaya Polyana

Kamchatka

5 It seems almost trite to describe Kamchatka (p550) as majestic. To many Kamchatka is, quite simply, the most beautiful place in the world. It's Yellowstone, Rotorua and Patagonia rolled into one, and it teems with wildlife free to frolic in one of the world's great remaining wildernesses. Traditionally the domain of well-heeled tourists who could afford helicopter rides to view its trademark volcanoes, geysers and salmon-devouring bears, Kamchatka has finally loosened up a bit for the independent traveller. Now if only they could fix that weather... Top right: Maly Semyachik, Kamchatka

DANITA DELIMONT/GETTY IMAGES ©

Veliky Novgorod's Kremlin

6 In the town that considers itself Russia's birthplace stands one of the country's most impressive and picturesque stone fortresses. Within the kremlin's grounds (p226) rise the Byzantine 11th-century Cathedral of St Sophia and a 300-tonne sculpture celebrating 1000 years of Russian history. Climb the Kokui Tower for an overview of the complex, then enter the Novgorod State United Museum to see one of Russia's best collections of iconographic art. A pleasant park and riverside beach also fringe the magnificent brick walls.

Suzdal's Idyll

7 'Ding-dong' ring the bells of a few dozen churches as you ride your bike through the streets of Suzdal (p134), lined with wooden cottages and lush gardens. This is Russia as it would have been, if not for the devastating 20th century – unpretentious, pious and very laid-back. Some of the best religious architecture is scattered around, but you can just as well spend all day lying in the grass and watching the river before repairing to a *banya* for the sweet torture of heat, cold and birch twigs. Top: Cathedral of the Transfiguration of the Saviour (p133)

Overnight Train Through Siberia

8 Daylight gradually fades, light illuminates the carriage, and windows reflect life inside the train. One of the pleasures of travelling Russia is to board an overnight train (p38) and alight in a different city the following morning. This may be inside a deluxe carriage from St Petersburg, but most likely it's in a four-berth compartment as you travel across Siberia on Russia's 'track of the camel', or perhaps hurtle through a Siberian night in third-class to the snores, silences and groans of more than 50 fellow travellers.

Kizhi

9 Old buildings made from logs may not usually be synonymous with heart-stopping excitement, but Kizhi's collection of wooden masterpieces (p307) is enough to spike anyone's blood pressure. The first glimpse of the heavenly Transfiguration Church, viewed from the approaching hydrofoil, causes such a ripple that the boat practically bounces: *is it... it is!* Up close, the church is a miracle of design: legend has it that the unnamed builder destroyed his axe upon its completion, correctly assuming that its glory could not be matched. Top: Transfiguration Church (p285), Kizhi

The Caucasus Mountains

10 Photos simply don't do them justice: the astonishing beauty of the Caucasus mountains (p353) is best appreciated on a trek among the jagged peaks. You can take short hikes through meadows, past waterfalls and up into alpine heights from the villages of Dombay and Arkhyz. Those seeking to conquer Europe's highest mountain set their sights on Elbrus, the twin-peaked overlord that tops out at 5642m – one of Russia's most rewarding mountain adventures. Wherever you plan to go, be sure to arrange permits well in advance. Above: Mountaineers, Garvash Pass, Caucasus Mountains

11

ROBERT JEAN/HEMIS.FR/GETTY IMAGES ©

12

13

Hiking the Great Baikal Trail

11 Already one of Russia's most successful environmental projects, the Great Baikal Trail (p450) has the ambitious aim of encircling Lake Baikal with marked hiking trails. That's still a long way from being achieved, but where trails have been etched into the landscape, donning boots for a trek along Baikal's shores is all the rage. Whichever section you choose, Baikal's gob-smacking vistas and the tough going will leave you breathless as you pass through virgin taiga, along isolated beaches and through cold, flowing rivers. Top left: Hiker crossing frozen Lake Baikal

Tobolsk

12 The former capital of Siberia, Tobolsk (p410) is today renowned across Russia for its magnificent kremlin. Crowds are rare, though, and if you come on a weekday you're likely to have its grounds almost to yourself. The kremlin is perched high above the old town, a part of Tobolsk where you'll lose track of time as you explore the endless wooden buildings and dramatic churches. Tobolsk is off the main Trans-Siberian route, but its charms are well worth the detour. Top right: Carved wooden facade, Tobolsk

Olkhon Island

13 Sacred of the sacred to the shamanist western Buryats, who attach a legend or fable to every rock, cape and hillock, enchanted Olkhon (p478) sits halfway up Lake Baikal's western shore. It's obvious why the gods and other beings from the Mongol *Geser* epic chose to dwell on this eerily moving island, though today it's more likely to be a bunch of backpackers you meet emerging from a cave. The island's landscapes are spellbinding, Baikal's waters lap balmiest on its western shore and if you're after some Siberia-inspired meditation, there's no better spot. Above: Shaman flags, Olkhon Island

A Night at the Mariinsky

14 What could be more Russian than a night at the ballet, dressed to the nines, watching *Swan Lake* or *Romeo and Juliet*? St Petersburg's famed Mariinsky Theatre (p151) offers the ultimate in classical ballet or operatic experiences, and now with a contemporary twist as the Mariinsky's long-awaited second stage has finally opened. Also worth a visit is Moscow's Bolshoi Theatre (p112), looking better than ever after a long renovation. Tickets are no longer cheap, but the experience will stay with you forever.

Exploring the Altai

15 Misty mountain passes, tranquil lakes and empty roads that stretch on forever – welcome to the Altai Republic (p444), Russia's supreme natural paradise, almost twice the size of Wales but with less than one-tenth of the population. You can travel for hours here without seeing anyone – unless you count the wild horses and goats. From snow-capped peaks to the lunar landscapes of Kosh-Agach, desolation has never been quite so appealing. Be warned – the Altai and its mysteries possess a magnetic pull. Bottom: Rope bridge over the Anuy River, Altai Republic

14

15

Tuva

16 Throat singers zing and burp under upturned eaves, nomads' yurts pimple the dust-bare grasslands and a hoard of Scythian gold gleams in the National Museum – this is Tuva (p479), a republic isolated from the rest of Russia by the Yergaki Mountains (at least until the new railway is built), where Slavic influence has all but faded. You'll long remember a tour of this incredible country, not least for its wildernesses peppered with petroglyph-etched standing stones and its excitingly unique traditional music. Below: Tuvan people praying at a shaman ritual

Golden Horn Bay

17 Vladivostok (p524), capital of Russia's east, has a swagger in its step after being remade for an economic summit in 2012. No longer a remote satellite of Moscow, Vladivostok is Asia's rising star, and Golden Horn Bay is its heart and soul. Take it in from one of the city's myriad viewpoints, or join the frenzy of activity on the bay with a ferry cruise. Check out the impressive new suspension bridge spanning the bay. Suddenly those San Francisco comparisons don't seem quite so preposterous.

16

17

VINCENZO LOMBARDO/GETTY IMAGES ©

MORDOLFF/GETTY IMAGES ©

Pole of Cold, Sakha Republic

18 Some people just want cold. Bone-tingling, mind-numbing, nostril-hair-freezing cold. And there's no better place in the world to be cold than in the Sakha Republic (p538), home of the self-proclaimed 'pole of cold'. Yakutsk, the capital, is the world's coldest city of any decent size. But the actual pole of cold – the coldest inhabited place on earth – is in Oymyakon (p545), where temperatures have dropped to -71°C. A festival here celebrates cold every February. Above: Bridge in Yakutsk

Buying Souvenirs at Izmaylovsky Market

19 It's a fine line between shopping and fun at the kremlin in Izmaylovo (p92). Cross the footbridge and walk through the gate to enter a Disney-like medieval village, complete with wooden church, white-washed walls and plenty of souvenir shops. Wander among the sprawling market's stalls to find an endless array of traditional handicrafts, as well as art and antiques, Central Asian carpets, Soviet paraphernalia and more.

Solovetsky Islands

20 Delve into the Gulag past of the Solovetsky Islands (p298) and visit one of Russia's most impressive fortress-monasteries. Some of Stalin's most brutal repressions took place on these remote, forested islands, reachable only by boat and small plane and made infamous by Solzhenitsyn's *Gulag Archipelago*. The monastery, with its sturdy stone walls and powerful cannons, is famous for fighting off the British and withstanding an eight-year siege. Today it's a place of worship once more, the golden iconostases of its churches returned to former glory. Above: Solovetsky Transfiguration Monastery (p289)

Need to Know

For more information, see Survival Guide (p637)

Currency
Russian rouble (₽)

Language
Russian

Visas
Required by all; apply at least a month in advance of your trip.

Money
Credit and debit cards accepted. ATMs plentiful. Euro or US dollars best currencies for exchange.

Mobile Phones
Prepaid SIM cards readily available. International roaming OK.

Time
Moscow/St Petersburg (GMT/USC + four hours)

When to Go

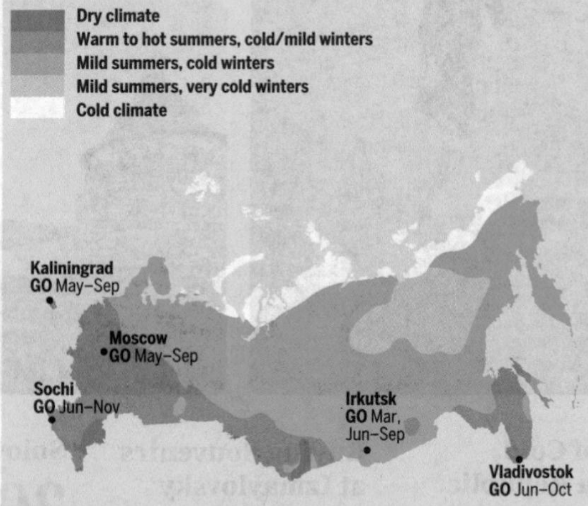

High Season
(Jun–Sep)

➡ Protect against disease-carrying ticks.

➡ Book all forms of transport in advance.

➡ Prices can rise in St Petersburg, particularly during White Nights in June and July.

Shoulder
(May & Oct)

➡ Late spring and early autumn see the country bathed in the fresh greenery or russet shades of the seasons.

➡ Good time for cultural events in cities and major parades on 9 May, Victory Day.

Low Season
(Nov–Apr)

➡ Snow falls and temperatures plummet, creating the wintery Russia of the imagination.

➡ Best time for skiing (although resorts charge higher prices) and visiting museums and galleries.

Useful Websites

Lonely Planet (www.lonelyplanet.com/russia) Greatest website for preplanning.

Way to Russia (www.waytorussia.net) Comprehensive online travel guide.

Moscow Times Guides (www.themoscowtimes.com/guides/index.php) Travel guides and supplements by leading English-language newspaper in Moscow.

Moscow Expat Site (www.expat.ru) Mine expat knowledge of Russia.

Important Numbers

To dial listings in this book from outside Russia, dial your international access code, Russia's country code (☎7), then the number including the full area code.

Ambulance	☎03
Country code	☎7
Fire	☎01
International access code	☎8
Police	☎02

Exchange Rates

Australia	A$1	₽38
Canada	C$1	₽38
Europe	€1	₽54
Japan	¥100	₽38
New Zealand	NZ$1	₽34
UK	UK£1	₽69
US	US$1	₽43

For current exchange rates see www.xe.com.

Safe Travel

Russia is a socially conservative and religious society. LGBT travellers should be mindful that they may offend less-liberal locals but on the whole will be able to travel safely in the country. See p645 for other things to consider to ensure safe travel in Russia.

Daily Costs

Budget: Less than ₽1500

- Dorm bed: ₽700–₽800
- Cafe or street-stall meal: ₽200–₽500
- Travel on buses and metro: ₽30

Midrange: ₽1500–₽4000

- Double room in a midrange hotel: ₽2000–₽3000
- Two-course meal: ₽500–₽1000
- Museum entry fee: ₽100–₽300
- City-centre taxi ride: ₽200–₽300

Top End: More than ₽4000

- Double room in a top-end hotel: ₽5000+
- Two-course meal with wine: ₽2000+
- Ballet tickets: ₽3500
- First-class train ticket, Moscow–St Petersburg: ₽6000

Opening Hours

Banks 9am to 6pm Monday to Friday

Restaurants noon-midnight

Cafes 9am-10pm

Bars and clubs noon-midnight (until 5am on Friday and Saturday)

Shops 10am-8pm

Arriving in Russia

Sheremetyevo Airport (Moscow; p118) Aeroexpress trains (₽400, 30 minutes) run to city every half-hour from 5am to 12.30am. Taxis cost ₽2000 to ₽2500 and take at least an hour.

Domodedovo Airport (Moscow; p118) Aeroexpress trains (₽400, 45 minutes) run every half-hour between 6am and 11.30pm. Taxis cost ₽2000 to ₽2500 and take at least an hour.

Pulkovo Airport (St Petersburg; p208) Frequent buses (₽36) run to Moskovskaya metro station (₽28) for a total journey time to the city centre of around 30 minutes. Taxis charge around ₽800 to the centre and can take up to an hour depending on traffic.

Getting Around

To check train times and make bookings go to the trip-planning section of Russian Railways' website (http://pass.rzd.ru/main-pass/public/en)

Train The extensive network is the best way of getting around, with many comfortable overnight services between far-flung cities.

Air Worth considering if you need to speed up your travels (with online tickets sometimes cheaper than those for trains). Only book airlines with solid safety records.

Bus Useful for getting to places not covered by the train. Sometimes faster than local *elektrichka* (suburban) train services.

Car or Taxi Sometimes the only way to get to really remote destinations.

For much more on **getting around**, see p652

First Time Russia

For more information, see Survival Guide (p637)

Checklist

- Make sure your passport is valid for at least six months beyond the expiry date of your visa.
- Arrange your visa.
- Check airline baggage restrictions.
- Check travel advisory websites.
- Tell banks and credit-card providers your travel dates.
- Organise travel insurance (see p643).

What to Pack

- Good walking shoes – Russian cities are best explored on foot.
- Phrasebook, minidictionary or translation app.
- Earplugs and eye mask for napping on trains, in noisy hotels and during long White Nights.
- Sense of humour and a bucketful of patience.

Top Tips for Your Trip

- Consider using a specialist travel agency to arrange visas, make key transport bookings and hire guides. See our Russian Adventures chapter (p41) for lists of reputable agents.
- Treat yourself to a stay at a business or luxury hotel over the weekend when many often drop their rates substantially to cover the shortfall in business customers. Big discounts can also be had on hotel rack rates (the ones we quote in this guide) for online bookings.
- Rail tickets can be booked online or at stations 45 days in advance. There are discounts for online and advance bookings; see p37.
- Fixed-price business lunches, common in cities, are a great deal and an ideal way to sample the cuisine at fancier restaurants.
- Schedule some time out of the big cities at rural or off-the-beaten track destinations to fully appreciate what is special about Russia.

What to Wear

Russians make an effort when they go to the theatre or a posh restaurant – you should do likewise to fit in. If you're planning on exploring on foot, a comfortable pair of waterproof walking shoes will come in handy, as will an umbrella or rain jacket.

In winter bundle up with several layers before going out and bring a long, windproof coat to stay nicely warm. Hats and coats are always removed on entering a museum or restaurant and left in the cloakroom.

Sleeping

For major cities it's a good idea to book a night or two in advance (especially during the busy summer season in St Petersburg). Elsewhere you can usually just turn up and find a room.

- **Hotels** Range from unreconstructed edifices of the Soviet era to luxurious and contemporary
- **Hostels, B&B and homestays** Plenty of the former in Moscow, St Petersburg and along the Trans-Siberian route; not so many B&Bs or homestays but worth trying for a true experience of Russian hospitality.

Money

➡ If prices are listed in US dollars or euros, you will still be presented with a final bill in roubles.

➡ ATMs, linked to international networks, are common right across Russia – look for signs that say *bankomat* (БАНКОМАТ). Credit cards are commonly accepted in the big cities but don't expect to be able to use them in more off-the-beaten-track spots and rural areas.

➡ Inform your bank or credit-card provider of the dates you'll be travelling in Russia and using your card, to avoid a situation where the card is blocked.

Bargaining

Prices are fixed in shops but at souvenir markets, such as Izmaylovo in Moscow, polite haggling over prices is a good idea.

Tipping

➡ **When to tip** Customary in restaurants, cafes and bars, optional elsewhere.

➡ **Restaurants** Leave small change or about 10%, if the service warrants it.

➡ **Guides** Around 10% of their daily rate; a small gift will also be appreciated.

➡ **Taxis** No need to tip as the fare is agreed either before you get in or metered.

➡ **Hotels** Only in the most luxurious need you tip attendants etc, and only if service is good.

Language

Russian is the common language, although dozens of other languages are spoken by ethnic minorities. It's relatively easy to find English speakers in the big cities, but not so easy in smaller towns and the countryside. Learning Cyrillic and a few key phrases will help you enormously in being able to decode street signs, menus and timetables. See Language (p664) for more info.

1 Is this Moscow or local time?

Это московское или местное время?

e·ta ma·*skof*·ska·ye *i*·li *myes*·na·ye *vryem*·ya

Russia has 11 time zones but the entire country's rail and air networks run on Moscow time. Ask if you're not certain what time zone your transport is running on.

2 I live in Moscow, I won't pay that much.

Я живу в Москве, я не буду платить так много.

ya zhih·*vu* v mask·*vye* ya nye *bu*·du pla·*tit'* tak *mno*·ga

Taxi drivers and market sellers sometimes try to charge foreigners more, so you may want to bargain in Russian.

3 Are you serving?

Вы обслуживаете? vih aps·*lu*·zhih·va·it·ye

It may be hard to attract the attention of workers in the service industry – if you want to get served, use this polite expression.

4 I don't drink alcohol.

Я не пью спиртного.

ya nye pyu spirt·*no*·va

Refusing a drink from generous locals can be very difficult, so if you're really not in the mood you'll need a firm, clear excuse.

5 May I have an official receipt, please?

Дайте мне официальную расписку, пожалуйста.

deyt·ye mnye a·fi·tsi·*yal'*·nu·yu ras·*pis*·ku pa·*zhal*·sta

Russian authorities might expect an unofficial payment to expedite their service, so always ask for an official receipt.

Etiquette

Russians are sticklers for formality. They're also rather superstitious. Follow these tips to avoid faux pas.

➡ **Visiting homes** Shaking hands across the threshold is considered unlucky; wait until you're fully inside. Remove your shoes and coat on entering a house. Always bring a gift. If you give anyone flowers, make sure it's an odd number – even numbers of blooms are for funerals.

➡ **Religion** Women should cover their heads and bare shoulders when entering a church. In some monasteries and churches it's also required for a woman to wear a skirt – wraps are usually available at the door. Men should remove their hats in church and not wear shorts.

➡ **Eating and drinking** Russians eat resting their wrists on the table edge, with fork in left hand and knife in the right. Vodka toasts are common at shared meals – it's rude to refuse to join in and traditional (and good sense) to eat a little something after each shot.

Plan Your Trip

Getting Your Visa

Save for a handful of exceptions, everyone needs a visa to visit Russia. Arranging one is, generally, straightforward but is likely to be time consuming, bureaucratic and – depending on how quickly you need the visa – costly. Start the application process at least a month before your trip.

Visa Agencies

Action-visas.com (www.action-visas.com)

CIBT (http://cibtvisas.co.uk)

Comet Consular Services (https://cometconsular.com)

IVDS (www.visum-ivds.de)

Real Russia (www.realrussia.co.uk)

VisaHQ.com (http://russia.visahq.com)

Visalink.com.au (http://visalink.com.au)

ZVS (http://zvs.com)

Invitations can also be arranged with:

Express to Russia (www.expresstorussia.com)

Visa Able (www.visaable.com)

Way to Russia (www.waytorussia.net)

Main Visa Types

Tourist Valid maximum of 30 days, nonextendable

Business Valid for three months, six months or one year (three years for US citizens)

Transit By air up to 72 hours, by train 10 days

72-Hour On Demand Only for Kaliningrad for citizens of Schengen countries, UK and Japan if travelling with approved agencies

Cruise Ship Passengers

Visa free visits of up to 72 hours for tourists arriving at ports of Anadyr, Kaliningrad, Korsakov, Novorossiysk, Sochi, St Petersburg, Vladivostok and Vyborg

Starting the Process

For most travellers a tourist visa (single- or double-entry and valid for a maximum of 30 days, nonextendable, from the date of entry) will be sufficient. If you plan on staying longer than a month, it's advisable to apply for a business visa, which are available as single, double or multiple entry.

Whatever visa you go for, the process has three main stages: invitation, application and registration.

Note that application and registration rules for trips to sensitive border regions, such as the Altai, Volga Delta, Caucasus and Tuva, are slightly different and processing of your visa can take longer.

Invitation

To obtain a visa, everyone needs an invitation, also known as 'visa support'. Hotels and hostels will usually issue anyone staying with them an invitation voucher free or for a small fee (typically around €20 to €30). If you are not staying in a hotel or hostel, you will need to buy an invitation – this can be done through most travel agents or via specialist visa agencies, also for around €20.

Application

Invitation voucher in hand, you can then apply for a visa. Wherever in the world you are applying you can start by entering

IMMIGRATION FORM

Immigration forms are produced electronically by passport control at airports. Take good care of your half of the completed form as you'll need it for registration and could face problems while travelling in Russia – and certainly will on leaving – if you can't produce it.

details in the online form of the Consular Department of the **Russian Ministry of Foreign Affairs** (https://visa.kdmid.ru/PetitionChoice.aspx).

Take care in answering the questions accurately on this form, including listing all the countries you have visited in the last 10 years and the dates of the visits – stamps in your passport will be checked against this information and if there are anomalies you will likely have to restart the process. Keep a note of the unique identity number provided for your submitted form – if you have to make changes later, you will need this to access it without having to fill the form in from scratch again.

Russian embassies in the UK and US have contracted separate agencies to process the submission of visa applications and check everything is in order; these companies use online interfaces that direct the relevant information into the standard visa application form. In the UK, the agency is **VFS.Global** (http://ru.vfsglobal.co.uk), with offices in London and Edinburgh; in the US it's **Invisa Logistic Services** (http://ils-usa.com), with offices in Washington DC, New York, San Francisco, Houston and Seattle.

Consular offices apply different fees and slightly different application rules country by country. For example, at the time of research a pilot project to collect biometric data via fingerprinting was being run for visa applications in the UK, Denmark, Myanmar and Namibia. Avoid potential hassles by checking well in advance what these rules might be. Among the things that you will need are:

- A print out of the invitation/visa support document
- A passport-sized photograph for the application form
- If you're self employed, bank statements for the previous three months showing you have sufficient funds to cover your time in Russia.
- Details of your travel insurance.

The charge for the visa will depend on the type of visa applied for and how quickly you need it.

We highly recommend applying for your visa in your home country rather than on the road. Trans-Mongolian travellers should note that unless you can prove you're a resident of China or Mongolia, attempting to get visas for Russia in Beijing and Ulaanbaatar can be a frustrating and ultimately fruitless exercise.

Registration

Every visitor to Russia should have their visa registered *within seven days of arrival,* excluding weekends and public holidays. The obligation to register is with the accommodating party – your hotel or hostel, or landlord, friend or family if you're staying in a private residence.

If you're staying at a hotel or hostel, the receptionist will register you for free or for a small fee (typically around €10). Once registered, you should receive a slip of paper confirming the dates you'll be staying at that particular accommodation. Keep this safe – that's the document that any police who stop you will request to see.

If staying in a homestay or rental apartment, you'll either need to make

VISA COSTS

The following are fees for single-entry visas; expect to pay anything up to double/triple these fees for double-/multiple-entry visas.

- **Australia** Both tourist and work visas issued in 10/two working days are $120/240.
- **Most EU countries** Tourist visas issued in 10/four working days are €35/70, work visas €99/136.
- **UK** Tourist and work visas issued in five working days/next working day are £50/100 plus a service charge of £32.40/39.60.
- **USA** Single- or double-entry tourist or work visas issued in 10/three working days are $140/250.

VISA EXTENSIONS & CHANGES

Any extensions or changes to your visa will be handled by Russia's Federal Migration Service (Federalnoy Migratsionnoy Slyzhby), often shortened to FMS. It's possible you'll hear the old acronyms PVU and OVIR used for this office.

Extensions are time consuming and difficult; *tourist visas can't be extended at all*. Avoid the need for an extension by arranging a longer visa than you might need. Note that many trains out of St Petersburg and Moscow to Eastern Europe cross the border after midnight, so make sure your visa is valid up to and including this day.

arrangements with the landlord or a friend to register you through the post office. See http://waytorussia.net/RussianVisa/Registration.html for how this can be done and for more details on the whole process.

Depending on how amenable your hotel or inviting agency is, you can request that they register you for longer than you'll actually be in one place. Otherwise, every time you move city or town and stay for more than seven days, it's necessary to go through the registration process again. There's no need to be overly paranoid about this, but the more thorough your registration record, the less chance you'll have of running into problems. Keep all transport tickets (especially if you spend nights sleeping on trains) to prove to any overzealous police officers exactly when you arrived in a new place.

It's tempting to be lax about registration, and we've met many travellers who were and didn't experience any problems as a result of it; note, you will not be asked to show registration slips when leaving from Moscow and St Petersburg's airports.

However, if you're travelling for a while in Russia and particularly if you're visiting off-the-beaten-track places, it's worth making sure you are registered at each destination, since it's not uncommon to encounter fine-hungry cops hoping to catch tourists too hurried or disorganised to be able to explain long gaps in their registration.

Types of Visa

In addition to the tourist visa, there are other types of useful visas.

Business

Available for three months, six months or one year (or three years in the US), and as single-entry, double-entry or multiple-entry visas, business visas are valid for up to 90 days of travel within any 180-day period. You don't actually need to be on business to apply for these visas (they're great for independent tourists with longer travel itineraries and flexible schedules) but to get one you must have a letter of invitation from a registered Russian company or organisation (these can be arranged via specialist visa agencies); a covering letter stating the purpose of your trip; and proof of sufficient funds to cover your visit.

Transit

For transit by air, a transit visa is usually valid for up to three days. For a nonstop Trans-Siberian Railway journey, it's valid for 10 days, giving westbound passengers a few days in Moscow; those heading east, however, are not allowed to linger in Moscow. Note that transit visas for train journeys are tricky to secure and are usually not that much cheaper than single entry tourist visas (from £40 in the UK, compared to £50 for the tourist visa).

Visa-Free Travel

Only a handful of destinations can be visited without a prearranged visa, and only for up to 72 hours. For St Petersburg and Vyborg you need to enter and exit the city on a cruise or ferry such as that offered by **St Peter Line** (www.stpeterline.com) or **Saimaa Travel** (www.saimaatravel.fi). For Kaliningrad, make arrangements in advance with locally based tour agencies.

If You Like...

Epic Journeys

Trans-Siberian Railway The 9289km trip from Moscow to Vladivostok is the big one to do. (p38)

Baikal-Amur Mainline (BAM) The 'other Trans-Sib' route takes you through very lonely parts of Siberia and the Russian Far East. (p39)

Chuysky Trakt Hop in a shared taxi or hire a car to travel the 600km route through dramatic Altai landscapes, including glimpses of snowy mountain peaks and vertigo-inducing canyons. (p415)

Neryungri to Yakutsk An iron butt is required for this full-day classic jeep ride through the Sakha Republic. (p535)

Frolikha Adventure Coastline Trail Pushed through virgin territory by Great Baikal Trail volunteers, this 100km-long lakeside trail is an eight-day Siberian odyssey. (p505)

Golden Ring Circuit around some of Russia's oldest and cutest towns on a loop that begins and ends in Moscow. (p126)

Majestic Landscapes

Southern Caucasus Home to 200 peaks over 4000m, including Europe's highest mountain. (p361)

Kola Peninsula Spot the northern lights reflecting off snowbound forests and tundra in the Arctic wilderness. (p278)

Tunka Valley A wall of snow-capped peaks sends icy streams murmuring into this broad vale where hot springs gush in mineral-hued pools and Buddhist prayer wheels whirr in the breeze. (p476)

Barguzin Valley Isolated, virtually uninhabited and hemmed by high peaks, this is one of the most stunning Siberian landscapes in which to go astray. (p475)

Kamchatka Frozen peninsula kinglike with its crown of volcanoes. (p550)

Volga Delta Where the mighty river explodes like a firecracker into myriad *raskaty* (channels). (p318)

Arts & Crafts

Russian Museum As well as the country's best collection of works by native artists, this St Petersburg institution has a fantastic folk crafts section. (p164)

Flyonovo Crafts are still produced at the pretty riverside estate of late-19th-century art lover Princess Maria Tenisheva, 18km southeast of Smolensk. (p262)

Novgorod State United Museum Within Veliky Novgorod's kremlin is an incredible collection of iconographic art spanning several centuries. (p251)

Kremlin in Izmaylovo A bustling market for all kinds of handicrafts, but you can also watch them being made or try your hand at making your own. (p92)

Caucasus Crafts In Nalchik you can find Kabardian and Circassian crafts as well as intricate Dagestani silver jewellery. (p376)

Imperial Grandeur

Catherine Palace The vast baroque centrepiece of Tsarskoe Selo is famed for its Amber Room, dazzling Great Hall and beautiful grounds. (p215)

Peterhof Gape at the Grand Cascade fronting Peter the Great's Gulf of Finland crash pad. (p200)

Yusupov Palace A canal-side mansion offering a series of sumptuously decorated rooms culminating in a gilded minitheatre. (p175)

Kolomenskoe Museum-Reserve An ancient royal country seat and Unesco World Heritage Site. (p83)

Tsaritsyno The contemporary manifestation of the exotic summer home that Catherine the Great began but never finished. (p94)

Soviet Relics

Lenin's Mausoleum Soviet relics hardly come more authentic than the embalmed body of VI a fixture of Red Square since 1924. (p68)

VDNKh (All-Russia Exhibition Centre) Filled with grandiose pavilions and fabulous fountains glorifying socialism's economic achievements. (p78)

Alyosha The ever-vigilant, utilitarian concrete statue keeps an eye on Murmansk's wind-whipped and splendidly hideous Soviet architecture. (p302)

Mamaev Kurgan An astounding 72m-tall statue of Mother Russia is the memorial to those who fell in the bloody Battle of Stalingrad. (p342)

Lenin Head Installed to celebrate the commie leader's 100th birthday, this gigantic bust dominates Ulan-Ude's main square. (p498)

Literary Titans

Anna Akhmatova Museum at the Fountain House Celebrating the life and times of the famous 20th-century St Petersburg–based poet. (p170)

Spasskoe-Lutovinovo The family home of Ivan Turgenev, surrounded by beautiful grounds, is a short trip from the literary town of Oryol. (p239)

FM Dostoevsky House Museum The author, famously associated with St Petersburg, lived for many years in this modest, riverside home in sleepy Staraya Russa. (p255)

Top: Grand Cascade (p210), Peterhof

Bottom: Even people conducting a ceremony, Bystrinsky Nature Park (p559), Esso

Pyatigorsk Visit the cottage and adjoining museum where Mikhail Lermontov spent his final days before being killed in a duel. (p358)

Mikhailovskoe Stand in the shade of Pushkin's beloved oak tree on his family's estate near the small town of Pushkinskie Gory. (p258)

Zhivago Restaurant and cafe in the Urals city of Perm that featured as a backdrop to classic works by Boris Pasternak and Anton Chekhov. (p395)

Religious Buildings

St Basil's Cathedral Easily the country's most famous church, its candy coloured domes and swirly spires face the Kremlin across Red Square. (p67)

Grand Choral Synagogue Lavish place of worship indicating the pivotal role played by Jews in imperial St Petersburg. (p178)

Ivolginsk (Ivolga) Datsan The centre of Russian Buddhism continues to expand into its dramatic setting. (p494)

Mystical Islands The vastly different islands of Kizhi (p307), Solovetsky (p298) and Valaam (p297) offer one thing in common: divine (literally) ancient architecture.

Kul Sharif Mosque Dominating Kazan's World Heritage–listed kremlin is this enormous mosque named after the imam who died defending the city against Ivan the Terrible's troops. (p328)

Church of the Intercession on the Nerl Revered for its exemplary perfect proportions and beautiful setting. (p131)

Sergiev Posad Russia's holiest of holies, the beautiful Trinity Monastery of St Sergius. (p131)

Quirky Places & Experiences

Permafrost Kingdom A never-melting pod of elaborate ice sculptures in a cocoon of permafrost and neon. (p543)

Bunker-42 A secret underground Cold War communications centre now open for exploration. (p92)

Sumarokovskaya Moose Farm Meet some friendly moose and drink their milk at this farm-cum-scientific-institute outside Kostroma. (p140)

Dancing Forest Marvel at the twisting and turning pines, sculpted by the winds that whistle across the Kurshskaya Kosa National Park. (p277)

Chess City Sit on the 12 chairs of the Ostap Bender monument in this literary fantasy come to surreal life in Elista. (p351)

Multicultural Encounters

Jewish Museum & Centre of Tolerance Constructivist architect Konstantin Melnikov's bus depot gets a thrilling makeover as one of the country's best museums. (p73)

Tuva With its throat-singing, yurt-building, milk-fermenting traditions, this isolated republic in southern Siberia is a revelation. (p479)

Lovozero This dilapidated outpost is worth the trek for those wanting to come into contact with the reindeer-herding Sami (Lapp) people of the Kola Peninsula. (p308)

Elista The capital of Kalmykia is home to the only Buddhist national group within Europe. (p348)

Esso Make contact with Evenki and Even people in this pretty village in the hinterland of Kamchatka. (p515)

Kosh-Agach With a population made up almost entirely of ethnic Altai and Kazakhs, it's easy to forget you are still in Russia. (p419)

Month by Month

TOP EVENTS

Easter, March/April

Victory Day, 9 May

Sadko Festival, June

White Nights, June/July

Kamwa Festival, September

January

Much of Russia becomes snow- and icebound during this and subsequent winter months, but the weather rarely causes disruption to transport. Book transport tickets well in advance of the busy New Year period.

Russian Orthodox Christmas (Rozhdestvo)

On Christmas Eve (6 January) the religious fast from morning to nightfall, after which they tuck in to a feast that includes roast duck and the porridge *kutya*. Special masses are held in churches at midnight.

Hyperborea Festival

Running into February, this Karelian festival celebrates all that is wonderful about wintertime with parties, exhibitions, and an ice- and snow-sculpture competition that attracts entrants from across Russia and the world. (p281)

March

The devout deny themselves meat, milk, alcohol and sex during Lent's 40-day pre-Easter fasting period. Many restaurants offer special Lenten menus. Come prepared for wet, cold weather.

Pancake Week (Maslenitsa)

The Russian for this Shrovetide festival comes from the word *masla* (butter). Folk shows and games celebrate the end of winter, with lots of pancake eating before Lent (pancakes were a pagan symbol of the sun).

Women's Day

Celebrated on 8 March, this is like St Valentine's Day, with women receiving presents of flowers, chocolates and the like, and a chance to rest up while men take care of the daily chores.

Tibetan Buddhist New Year (Tsagaalgan)

A movable feast lasting 16 days, Tsagaalgan celebrates the lunar new year and hence advances by about 10 days annually. It's mainly celebrated at family level in Buryatiya and Tuva, where it's known as Shagaa.

Golden Mask Festival

This Moscow-based festival (www.goldenmask.ru), usually held in late March and early April, involves two weeks of performances by Russia's premier drama, opera, dance and musical performers, culminating in a prestigious awards ceremony. (p96)

April

In Western European Russia melting snow makes the streets a slushy mess. However, it's a great time to brave Siberia and the far north, where winter still rules but with less savage force.

Festival of the North

A 10-day Arctic funfest kicking off in late March

in Murmansk, replete with reindeer-sled races and snowmobile events. Kola's indigenous Sami (Lapp) people join the celebrations with displays of traditional culture. (p303)

Easter (Paskha)

Easter Sunday begins with midnight services. Afterwards, people eat *kulich* (traditional dome-shaped bread) and *paskha* (cheesecake), and exchange painted wooden Easter eggs. Falls on 12 April 2015, 1 May 2016 and 16 April 2017.

Alexander Nevsky Festival

The second weekend in April sees this celebration in Veliky Novgorod honouring Russia's best-known prince. Members of historical clubs dress up as knights, engage in mock battle and storm the kremlin walls. (p253)

May

The long-awaited arrival of pleasant spring weather makes this one of the best months for travel. Between International Labour Day on 1 May and Victory Day on 9 May some offices and museums have limited hours as people take advantage of the holidays for extended r'n'r.

Victory Day

On 9 May, this Russian public holiday celebrates the end of WWII, which Russians call the Great Patriotic War. Big military parades in Moscow and St Petersburg are well worth attending.

Glinka Festival

The composer Mikhail Glinka is honoured in his home town of Smolensk with this week-long festival of classical music at the end of the month that draws in top talent. (p243)

Cossack Fairs

Held in Starocherkassk on the last Sunday of the month from May to September, with much singing, dancing, horse riding and merrymaking. (p358)

June

Popular month for *den goroda* (city day), when towns celebrate their birthdays with parades and street festivals: Veliky Novgorod has one on 12 June and Tver on 25 June. The weather is hot, but be prepared for rain too.

White Nights

As days lengthen Russia's cultural capital, St Petersburg, hosts a huge party made up of a variety of events including a jam-packed itinerary of shows at the Mariinsky Theatre and Concert Hall. Events run until late July. (p188)

Sadko Festival

Held the first weekend of June in Veliky Novgorod, this event includes traditional dancing, singing and a crafts fair. (p253)

Ysyakh

Held around 21 June near Yakutsk, this celebration of Sakha culture includes the chance to sample traditional eats while watching local sports and spectacular costumed battle reenactments. (p541)

International Platanov Festival

Voronezh hosts this ambitious week-long jamboree of theatre, music and the arts (http://en.platonovfest.com) in memory of local talent Andrei Platanov, a banned Soviet-era writer. (p249)

Moscow International Film Festival

Russia's premier film festival (www.moscowfilmfestival.ru) runs for 10 days at the end of the month and includes retrospective and documentary cinema programs as well as the usual awards. (p96)

Uglich Versta

A few hundred bicyclists meet for three days of riding, singing and drinking at this annual cycle fest (www.velo.uglich.ru) in the Golden Ring town. Expect competitions, kids' events, entertainment and a bicycle parade. (p136)

Perm White Nights

Inaugurated in 2011, Perm's White Nights fest runs through most of June, offering an eclectic mix of contemporary music, street art, theatre, readings and interesting side-festival events. (p393)

Sabantuy

Joking competitions and serious sport events – horse races and *koresh* (wrestling matches) – feature prominently during this holiday celebrated all over Tatarstan and beyond in the middle of June. (p329)

Kinotavr Film Festival

Running for a week in early June, Sochi's Kinotavr Open Russian Film Festival (www.kinotavr.ru/en/) showcases over a dozen feature-length Russian movies, with local filmmakers and actors on hand. Open-air screenings, too. (p364)

July

The best time to visit the Volga Delta is between late July and late September, when lotus flowers blossom. Russians head to the coast and their dachas (summer houses) as the weather really heats up.

Mir Sibiri

Similar to the UK's Womad Festival, this large event (www.festmir.ru; previously known as the Sayan Ring Festival) floods the small Siberian town of Shushenskoe with almost 25,000 visitors. Tuvan throat singers usually steal the show. (p475)

El-Oiyn Festival

Held every two years on the first weekend of July, this 'folk games' festival gathers some 60,000 people for a celebration of Altai culture. (p425)

Solovetsky Islands Herring Festival

Head to Solovki to get your hands on some of Russia's finest fish – literally, in the case of the barehanded catch competition.

August

Train prices can spike during this hot month as many people take holidays – book ahead if you want to travel on particular services along the Trans-Siberian route.

Tuvan Naadym

Naadym offers four wild days of underpants-hoicking *khuresh* wrestling, stern-faced archery contests, gravity-defying feats of steppe horsemanship, lots of croaky throat singing and fireworks bursting over the Tuvan capital Kyzyl. (p459)

Dzhangariada Festival

Held in late August or September, this Kalmyk cultural celebration takes place on the open steppe at a different location every year. It includes wrestling, archery contests and traditional singers. (p349)

September

One of the best months to visit the country as the heat of summer abates, but it's still nice enough to enjoy the outdoors of the countryside and beaches minus the holiday season crowds.

Kamwa Festival

The 'ethno-futuristic' Kamwa Festival (www.kamwa.ru), taking place in early September in Perm and Khokhlovka, brings together ancient ethno-Ugric traditions and modern culture. (p393)

October

Russia's brief, brilliantly colourful autumn is swiftly followed by the onset of winter – at the end of the month come prepared for snow flurries and plummeting temperatures.

Russian Grand Prix

The Formula One caravan hits Sochi for the first time in 2014 with the race taking place in the former Winter Olympic Park.

December

Short days and long nights keep people inside for most of this month. If you're prepared it's the best time to see freshly snow-covered landscapes.

December Nights Festival

Moscow's most prestigious music event, hosted at the Pushkin Fine Arts Museum, features a month of performances by high-profile musicians and accompanying art exhibits. (p96)

New Year's Eve

See out the old year with vodka and welcome in the new one with champagne while listening to the Kremlin chimes on TV.

Itineraries

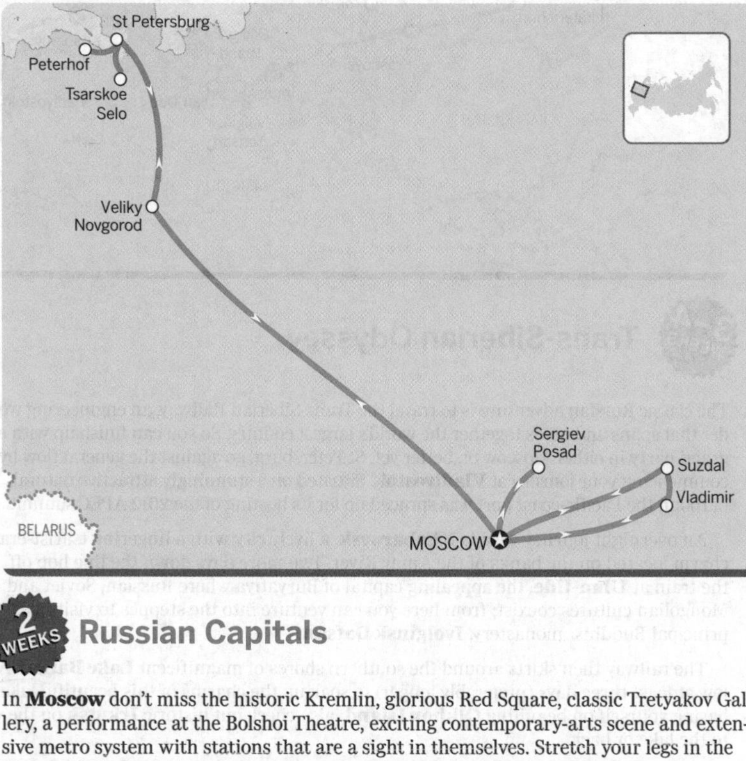

2 WEEKS Russian Capitals

In **Moscow** don't miss the historic Kremlin, glorious Red Square, classic Tretyakov Gallery, a performance at the Bolshoi Theatre, exciting contemporary-arts scene and extensive metro system with stations that are a sight in themselves. Stretch your legs in the revamped Gorky Park and along the embankments of the Moscow River.

From Moscow it's easy to make trips to the historic Golden Ring towns of **Sergiev Posad**, **Suzdal** and **Vladimir**, where you will be rewarded with a serene slice of rural Russian life.

Practically a museum of architecture, the historic heart of St Petersburg offers the incomparable Hermitage and Russian Museum, as well as cruising the city's rivers and canals. Enjoy some of Russia's top restaurants and bars, and attend first-rate performances at the Mariinsky and Mikhailovsky Theatres.

St Petersburg is ringed by grand palaces set in beautifully landscaped grounds, such as **Peterhof** and **Tsarskoe Selo**.

Between the two big cities, tourist-friendly **Veliky Novgorod** deserves a couple of days too. It's home to an impressive riverside kremlin, ancient churches and a wonderful open-air museum of wooden architecture.

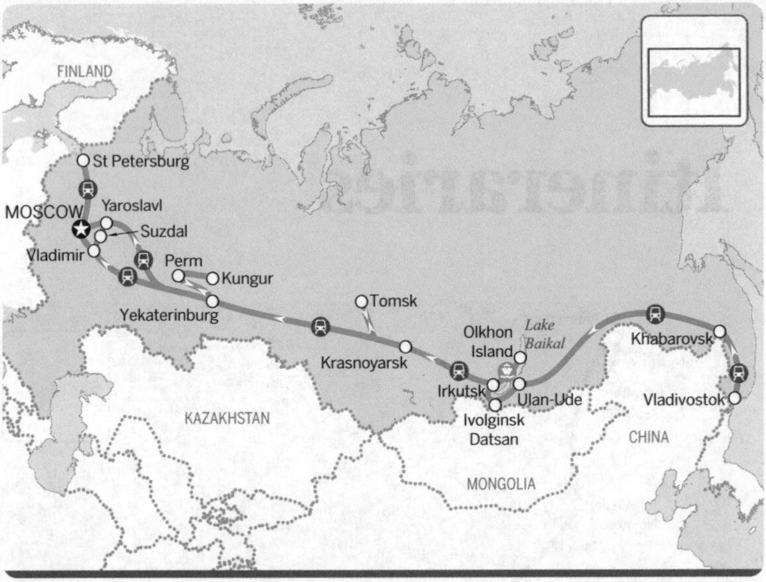

3–4 WEEKS

Trans-Siberian Odyssey

The classic Russian adventure is to travel the Trans-Siberian Railway, an engineering wonder that spans and holds together the world's largest country. So you can finish up with a grand party in either Moscow or, better yet, St Petersburg, go against the general flow by commencing your journey at **Vladivostok**. Situated on a stunningly attractive natural harbour, the Pacific-coast port was spruced up for its hosting of the 2012 APEC summit.

An overnight journey west is **Khabarovsk**, a lively city with a lingering tsarist-era charm located on the banks of the Amur River. Two more days down the line hop off the train at **Ulan-Ude**, the appealing capital of Buryatiya where Russian, Soviet and Mongolian cultures coexist; from here you can venture into the steppes to visit Russia's principal Buddhist monastery, **Ivolginsk Datsan**.

The railway then skirts around the southern shores of magnificent **Lake Baikal**. Allow at least three days (preferably longer) to soak up the charms of this beautiful lake, basing yourself on beguiling **Olkhon Island**; also check out historic **Irkutsk** on the way to the lake or back.

Flush with oil wealth, happening **Krasnoyarsk**, on the Yenisey River, affords the opportunity for scenic cruises along one of Siberia's most pleasant waterways. Detour slightly from the main Trans-Sib line to **Tomsk**, the 'cultural capital of Siberia', to hang with its lively student population and admire the city's treasure trove of wooden architecture.

Crossing the Urals into European Russia, spend a day or so in **Yekaterinburg**, a historic, bustling city well stocked with interesting museums and sites connected to the murder of the last tsar and his family. **Perm** is also doing an excellent job of reinventing itself as a cultural centre; use it as a base from which to make trips to an ice cave at **Kungur** and the Gulag labour camp Perm-36, preserved as a museum.

Finally, fortify yourself for the bustle of **Moscow** or **St Petersburg** by taking a reviving break in the Golden Ring towns of **Yaroslavl** or **Vladimir**, which is also the access point for the idyllic village of **Suzdal**: all are stacked with beautiful, old, onion-domed churches.

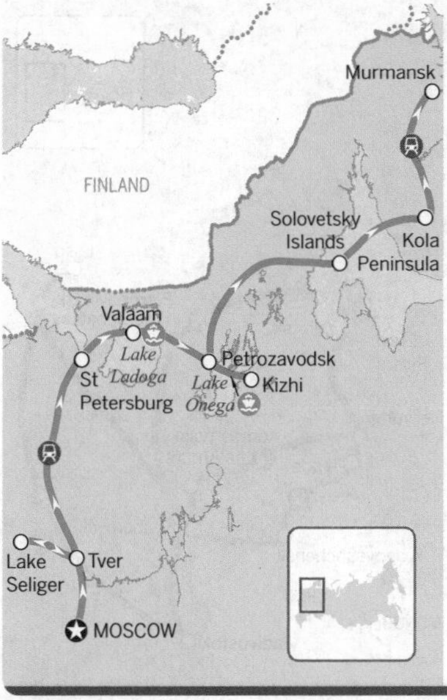

3 WEEKS Lakes of the Russian North

From **Moscow** begin your water-themed journey towards the Arctic Circle by following the Volga River north to **Tver**, an appealing historic town that Catherine the Great used to pause in on her court's cross country journeys. Make a side trip to **Lake Seliger**.

Top up on big-city culture in **St Petersburg** then take the train to **Petrozavodsk** to access **Lake Ladoga** and the island of **Valaam**, home to a beguiling working monastery. Return to Petrozavodsk where you can board a hydrofoil that will zip you across **Lake Onega** to another island – **Kizhi**, an architectural reserve that includes the astounding Transfiguration Church, a symphony of wooden domes, gables and decoration.

The White Sea is the location of the **Solovetsky Islands**; the beautiful landscapes and monastery here were also the setting for some of the most brutal scenes in Solzhenitsyn's *Gulag Archipelago*. More offbeat adventures, including top fishing sites, await in the **Kola Peninsula**.

Finish in **Murmansk** by checking out a decommissioned nuclear icebreaker and the giant concrete soldier 'Alyosha'. In summer the sun never fully sets, while in winter you may witness the amazing northern lights.

3 WEEKS Volga Route to Astrakhan

The mighty Volga flows east from **Moscow** towards **Nizhny Novgorod**, where the major aquatic highway can be viewed from above on a cable-car ride. Spend a day or so here enjoying the town's kremlin, museums and its 'Food and Culture' movement, and making a short trip by hydrofoil to the small town of **Gorodets**, known for its folk arts.

The next major stop is the intriguing Tatarstan capital of **Kazan**. The highlight here is the World Heritage–listed kremlin that includes an enormous mosque and small satellite branch of St Petersburg's Hermitage. The Volga continues to guide you south past Lenin's birthplace of **Ulyanovsk** and **Samara**, from where you could go hiking in the rocky Zhiguli Hills or search out the town's several offbeat design and cultural sights.

An amazing 72m-tall statue of Mother Russia wields her sword over **Volgograd**, a city entirely rebuilt after Russia's bloodiest battle of WWII. The Volga spills into the Caspian Sea at **Astrakhan**, jumping-off point for exploring the glorious natural attractions, including rare flamingos, of the Volga Delta, home to the endangered sturgeon, the source of Beluga caviar.

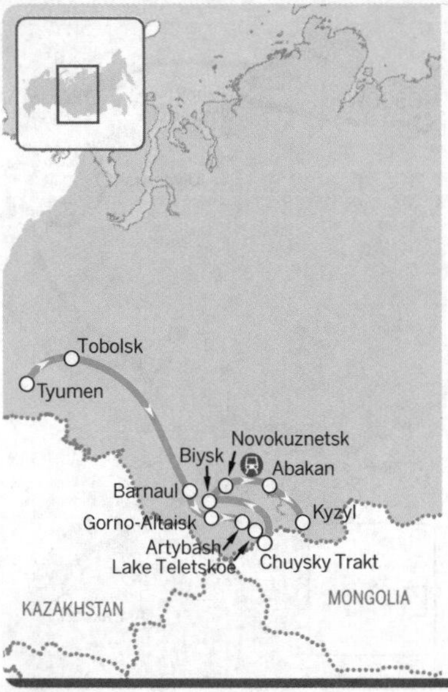

4 WEEKS Siberia's Deep South

For a journey covering some of Siberia's lesser-known locations begin in the oil-rich city of **Tyumen**, which includes several picturesque areas of traditional architecture. Journey northeast in the footsteps of the Siberian conqueror Yermak Timofeevich, the exiled writer Fyodor Dostoevsky and the last tsar to **Tobolsk**, whose splendid kremlin lords it over the Tobol and Irtysh Rivers. Next, head south to **Barnaul**, gateway to the mountainous Altai Republic. Here you can arrange a white-water rafting expedition or plan treks out to beautiful **Lake Teletskoe** and the pretty village of **Artybash**. Drive along the panoramic **Chuysky Trakt**, a helter-skelter mountain road leading to yurt-dotted grasslands, first stopping in **Gorno-Altaisk** to register your visa. Return to **Biysk**, take a bus to **Novokuznetsk** then a train to **Abakan** to arrange onward travel to Tuva. This remote and little-visited region, hard up against Mongolia (with which it shares several cultural similarities), is famed for its throat-singing nomads and mystical shamans. **Kyzyl** has a good new National Museum and Cultural Centre and can be used as a base for expeditions to pretty villages and the vast Central Asian steppes.

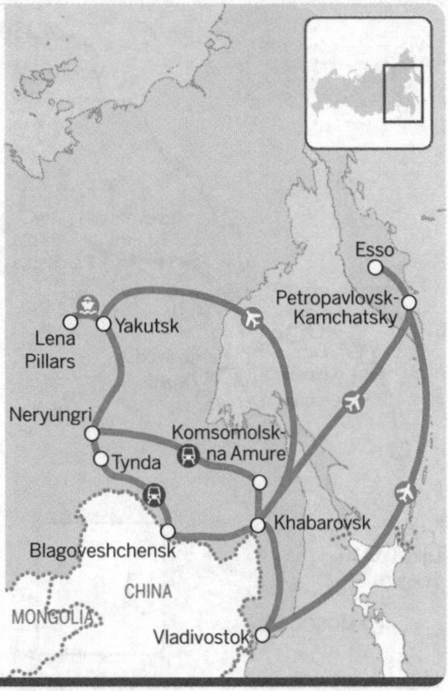

4 WEEKS Russian Far-East Circuit

From the 'wild east' port of **Vladivostok** head via **Khabarovsk** to lively **Blagoveshchensk** with its splendid tsarist architecture. Take the overnight train to **Tynda**, the main hub on the Baikal-Amur Mainline (BAM), from where there's a choice. Tough-travel fanatics can train it to **Neryungri** then endure a very bumpy all-day ride in a Russian UAZ jeep to **Yakutsk**, the extraordinary permafrost-bound capital of the Sakha Republic. Alternatively, board the BAM through to the attractive city of **Komsomolsk-na-Amure** and back to Khabarovsk, from where there are flights to Yakutsk. Once in Yakutsk, visit the city's eccentric Permafrost Kingdom and Mammoth Museum. If it's the summer sailing season, cruise to the scenic **Lena Pillars** on the Lena River. Backtrack to Khabarovsk or Vladivostok from where you can fly to spectacular Kamchatka, to cap off your adventures by climbing one of the snowcapped volcanoes rising behind the rugged peninsula's capital, **Petropavlovsk-Kamchatsky**. Or make your way north to **Esso**, newly friendly to independent travellers with its cheap guesthouses, public hot springs and well-mapped trails for trekking.

Plan Your Trip

Great Train Journeys

One of the best ways to see Russia and connect with locals is to take a train journey. With over 85,200km of track, there's a fair chance that Russian Railways (RZD or РЖД) will have a service to suit your travel plans.

Tickets

Bookings & Costs

You can buy train tickets at stations and online – via **RZD** (rzd.ru) or a host of other online travel agencies – up to 45 days in advance of your planned date of travel. Those selling tickets as agents for RZD will add their own charges to the basic fares. Note when booking that every train in Russia has two numbers: one for eastbound service (even numbers) and one for the westbound (odd numbers).

Unless otherwise specified, we quote *kupe* (2nd-class compartment) fares in this guide. Expect 1st-class fares to be double this and *platskartny* (3rd-class fares) to be about 40% less. Children under five travel free if they share a berth with an adult; otherwise, children under 10 pay a reduced fare for their own berth.

RZD operates 'dynamic pricing' which means fares vary by the season and demand for travel – expect to pay anything up to 20% more at peak travel times, eg early July to early August and around key holidays such as Easter and New Year. The inverse happens at slack times of the year, such as early January to March, when there are discounts on fares.

Discounts are often available for online bookings and if you're prepared to take the upper bunks in *kupe* carriages. It's also

Inspirational Books

The Big Red Train Ride Eric Newby

Through Siberia by Accident and **Silverland** Dervla Murphy

Trans-Siberian Railway Anne and Olaf Meinhardt

The Trans-Siberian Railway: A Traveller's Anthology ed Deborah Manley

Journey into the Mind's Eye Lesley Blanch

To the Edge of the World: The Story of the Trans-Siberian Railway Christian Wolmar

The Great Railway Bazaar, Riding the Iron Rooster, Ghost Train to the Eastern Star Paul Theroux

Useful Websites

RZD (http://rzd.ru) National rail network.

Man in Seat 61 (www.seat61.com) Up-to-date info and links.

Trans-Siberian Railway Web Encyclopaedia (www.transsib.ru) Not updated, but still a mine of useful background detail.

A Journey on the Trans-Siberian Railway (www.trans-siberian-railway.co.uk) Clive Simpson's site, based on his 2006 trip.

Top Trips

Moscow–Vladivostok (p38)

Moscow–Ulaanbaatar & Beijing (p38)

Tayshet–Sovetskaya Gavan (p39)

Murmansk–Adler (p39)

possible to have two grades of *kupe* fare: with or without meals.

Classes

The five classes of ticket are:

➡ Мягкие (*myagkiye;* soft) 1st-class compartment sleeping two with its own toilet and shower; only available on certain *firmeny* (premium class) services.

➡ СВ (SV, standing for *spalny vagon*) Also 1st-class compartment sleeping two, but with shared toilets for the carriage.

➡ Купе (*kupe*) 2nd-class compartment sleeping four, with shared toilets for the carriage.

➡ Плацкарт (*platskart*) Dorm carriage with 54 berths

➡ Общий (*obshchiy*) General or seating class, usually only for day trains.

Trans-Siberian Routes

Extending 9289km from Moscow to Vladivostok on the Pacific, the Trans-Siberian Railway is among the most famous of the world's great train journeys. Rolling out of Europe and into Asia, over vast swaths of taiga, steppe and desert, the Trans-Siberian – the world's longest single-service railway – makes all other train rides seem like once around the block with Thomas the Tank Engine.

Don't look for the Trans-Siberian Railway on a timetable, though. The term is used generically for three main lines and the numerous trains that run on them. For the first four days' travel out of Moscow's Yaroslavsky vokzal (station), the trans-Siberian, trans-Manchurian and trans-Mongolian routes all follow the same line, passing through Nizhny Novgorod on the way to Yekaterinburg in the Ural Mountains and then into Siberia.

Many travellers choose to break their journey at Irkutsk to visit Lake Baikal (we recommend you do) but, otherwise, the three main services continue on round the southern tip of the lake to Ulan-Ude, another possible jumping-off point for Baikal. From here trans-Siberian trains continue to Vladivostok, while the trans-Mongolian ones head south for the Mongolian border, Ulaanbaatar and Beijing. The trans-Manchurian service continues past Ulan-Ude to Chita, then turns southeast for Zabaikalsk on the Chinese border.

For details about the journey, read Lonely Planet's *Trans-Siberian Railway* guide.

Moscow to Vladivostok

The Rossiya (1/2) train is the premier Moscow–Vladivostok service, but tickets on it are more expensive than other services; if you're stopping along the route it will be cheaper to use other trains. For comparison, a *kupe* berth for the whole journey on the 99/100 train which also links Moscow and Vladivostok (via Yaroslavl) costs ₽15,800 compared to ₽24,100 on the Rossiya.

If you'd prefer to skip Moscow in favour of St Petersburg as the start or finish of a trans-Siberian journey, the Demidovsky Express (71/72) between St Petersburg and Yekaterinburg is a recommended option.

And if you'd like to speed things up a little there's also the high-speed Sapsan trains connecting Moscow and Nizhny Novgorod in just under four hours.

Moscow to Ulaanbaatar & Beijing

The more popular of the two options running directly between Moscow and Beijing

BREAKING YOUR JOURNEY

There is no Russian rail pass. Hence, if you are travelling from, say, Moscow to Vladivostok, and plan on spending a night or two in Nizhny Novgorod and Irkutsk, you'll need three separate tickets: Moscow–Nizhny Novgorod, Nizhny Novgorod–Irkutsk and Irkutsk–Vladivostok.

If you're planning to frequently hop on and off trains and want to save some money along the way, it's a good idea to avoid the premium trains and go for the regular services, which offer the cheaper *platskartny* (3rd-class) carriages. Most of these services are perfectly acceptable and take pretty much the same travelling time point to point as the premium trains.

SHE WHO MUST BE OBEYED

On any long-distance Russian train journey you'll soon learn who's in charge: the *provodnitsa*. Though sometimes male *(provodnik)*, carriage attendants are usually women.

Apart from checking your ticket before boarding the train, doling out linen and shaking you awake in the middle of the night when your train arrives, the *provodnitsa*'s job is to keep her carriage spick and span (most are very diligent about this) and to make sure the samovar is always fired up with hot water. They will have cups, plates and cutlery to borrow, if you need them, and can provide drinks and snacks for a small price.

On long journeys the *provodnitsa* works in a team of two; one will be working while the other is resting.

Initially, a *provodnitsa* can come across as quite fearsome. Very few will speak any other language than Russian. Some sport the most distinctive hairdos you'll come across this side of a drag-queen convention. All look as smart as sergeant majors in their Russian Railways (RZD) uniforms – and just as ready to knock you into shape if you step out of line! However, if you're polite and respectful to your *provodnitsa*, and bestow on her plenty of friendly smiles, chances are high that she will do her best to make your journey a very pleasant one.

is the weekly 3/4 trans-Mongolian service, a Chinese train that travels via Ulaanbaatar and the only one to offer deluxe carriages with showers.

If you're planning to stop off in Irkutsk, there's also the less fancy 361/362 service to/from Naushki, with through carriages to/from Ulaanbaatar.

The weekly Vostok (19/20) trans-Manchurian service is a Russian train that crosses the border into China at Zabaikalsk, and passes through Harbin before terminating in Beijing seven days after its initial departure from Moscow.

The BAM: Tayshet to Sovetskaya Gavan

The alternative trans-Sib route is the Baikal-Amur Mainline (Baikalo-Amurskaya Magistral; BAM). It begins at Tayshet (4515km east of Moscow), curls around the top of Lake Baikal, cuts through nonstop taiga, winds around snow-splattered mountains and burrows through endless tunnels on its way east to Sovetskaya Gavan on the Tatar Strait.

The BAM's prime attraction is the incredibly remote and utterly wild scenery viewed from the train window. As well as Lake Baikal's lovely northern lip, adventures on the BAM reach some very out-of-the-way places including Bratsk, Tynda and Komsomolsk-na-Amure.

Other Long-Distance Routes

Other intriguing services that link up far-flung corners of Russia and further afield include the 225/226 Murmansk–Adler train, a 76-hour service that connects the Arctic Circle city with the sun-kissed shores of the Black Sea. The train passes through Kem (jumping-off point for the Solovetsky Islands), Petrozavodsk (for access to Kizhi), Tver, Moscow, Voronezh, Rostov-on-Don and Sochi. If travelling this route in the winter months, apart from the glorious snow-blanketed wilderness (and little snowed-in villages pumping chimney smoke), watch out for little ice-fishing 'cities' that pop up on wide frozen lakes and the occasional glimpse of villagers playing football on said icy expanses. Train breaks are always great for running out to buy huge smoked fish (or more expensive smoked whole eels) from the babushkas on the platforms.

Even on short visits to the country it's possible to squeeze in one overnight train journey, the most popular one being between Moscow and St Petersburg. The high-speed, TGV-standard Sapsan trains may link the two metropolises in under four hours, but they lack the glamour and romance of climbing aboard premium overnight RZD services such as the Krasnaya

Strela (Red Arrow) or the private **Grand Express** (www.grandexpress.ru).

And if you really can't get enough of long-distance trains, the RZD network is just as connected to Europe's networks as it is to those of Asia's, offering direct services to, among other places, Berlin, Nice, Paris and Vienna. The website **Man in Seat 61** (www.seat61.com) has full details.

On the Journey

There is nothing quite like the smell of a Russian train: coal smoke, coffee, garlic, sausage, sweat, vodka and dozens of other elements combine to form an aroma that's so distinctive it will be permanently etched in your sensual memory.

To calculate where you are while on a journey, keep an eye out for the small, black-and-white kilometre posts generally on the southern side of the track. These mark the distance to and from Moscow. In between each kilometre marker are smaller posts counting down roughly every 100m. The distances on train timetables don't always correspond to these marker posts (usually because the timetable distances are the ones used to calculate fares).

Luggage

Russians have a knack of making themselves totally at home on trains. This often means that they'll be travelling with plenty of luggage, causing inevitable juggling of the available space in all compartment classes.

In all but local trains there's a luggage bin underneath each lower berth that will hold a medium-sized backpack or small suitcase. There's also enough space beside the bin to squeeze in another medium-sized bag. Above the doorway (in 1st and 2nd classes) or over the upper bunks (in 3rd class) there's room to accommodate a couple more rucksacks.

Etiquette

➡ Sleeping compartments are mixed sex; when women indicate that they want to change clothing before going to bed or after getting up, men go out and loiter in the corridor.

➡ It's good manners to offer any food or drinks you bring to the fellow passengers in your compartment; Russians will always offer to share their food with you.

➡ Smoking is forbidden anywhere on the train and on the platforms.

Toilets

Located at both ends of each carriage, toilets can be locked long before and after station stops (there's a timetable on the door). Except on a very few premium-service trains there are no shower facilities – improvise with a sponge, flannel or short length of garden hose that you can attach to the tap for a dousing.

Food & Drink

Every sleeping carriage has a samovar filled with boiling water that's safe to drink and ideal for hot drinks, instant noodles or porridge.

The quality of food in dining cars varies widely. Rather than for eating they become the place to hang out, drink beer and play cards, particularly on the long trans-Siberian trip. Note also on the trans-Mongolian and trans-Manchurian trains that the dining cars are changed at each border, so en route to Beijing you get Russian, Chinese and possibly Mongolian versions. Occasionally, between the Russian border and Ulaanbaatar there is no dining car.

A meal in a restaurant car can cost anything from ₽400 to ₽1000. If you don't fancy what's on offer, there's often a table of pot noodles, savoury snacks, chocolate, alcohol, juice and the like being peddled by the staff. They sometimes make the rounds of the carriages too, with a trolley of snacks and drinks. Prices are typically a little more than you'd pay at the kiosks or to the babushkas at the station halts.

Shopping for supplies at the stations is part of the fun of any long-distance Russian train trip. The choice of items is often excellent, with fresh milk, ice cream, grilled chicken, boiled potatoes, home cooking such as *pelmeni* (Russian-style ravioli dumplings) or *pirozhki* (savoury pies), buckets of forest berries and smoked fish all on offer.

Plan Your Trip

Russian Adventures

Russia offers a thrilling and irresistible range of terrain for outdoor adventures. There are majestic mountains to climb and ski down, national parks and wilderness areas to hike through, and fast-flowing rivers for rafting and canoeing. Piloting a supersonic MiG fighter jet or training as a cosmonaut are also possible!

While most specialist operators are professional, this is Russia, so be flexible, patient and prepared for things not to go as smoothly as you may hope. There will often also be a group of enthusiasts more than happy to share their knowledge and even equipment with a visitor; you might also be able to locate guides for trekking and other activities where detailed local knowledge is essential. Provide as much advance warning as possible; even if you can't hammer out all the details, give operators an idea of your interests.

Always check the safety equipment before you set out and make sure you know what's included in the quoted price. Also, make sure you have adequate insurance – many travel insurance policies have exclusions for risky activities, including skiing, diving and even trekking.

Boating, Canoeing & Rafting

Although the pollution of many rivers discourages numerous travellers from even getting near the water, the coasts offer many canoeing and kayaking possibilities. The Altai region's pristine rivers are best for full-blown expedition-grade rafting, as well as easy, fun splashes possible on a 'turn up' basis. Kamchatka's Bystraya River is also recommended.

The Solovetsky Islands in Northern European Russia are an example of the

Top Five Adventures

- Climb mountains in the Caucasus
- Hike the Great Baikal Trail
- Drive across Russia
- Fish for wild salmon in Kamchatka
- Hit the slopes at Krasnaya Polyana or Sheregesh

Inspiring Adventure Tales

Kolyma Diares (Jacek Hugo-Bader) Hitchhiking along the 2025km 'road of bones' from Magadan to Yakutsk.

Barbed Wire and Babushkas (Paul Grogan) Kayaking down the Amur River through China and Siberia.

River of No Reprieve (Jeffrey Tayler) Sailing an inflatable raft along the Lena River, from Lake Baikal to the Arctic Ocean.

Off the Rails (Tim Cope & Chris Hatherly) Cycling 10,000km from Moscow to Beijing.

www.timcopejourneys.com Tim Cope's other Russian expeditions include rowing a boat 4500km down the Yenisey River to the Arctic Ocean.

Cycling Home from Siberia (Rob Lilwall) Rob's website (http://roblilwall.com) features original blog posts and videos.

Consolations of the Forest (Sylvain Tesson) Living for six months as a hermit in a cabin beside Lake Baikal.

remote and fascinating places that can be toured by boat during the summer.

The Volga River Delta, with its fascinating flora and fauna, below Astrakhan is an amazing place to explore by boat. In towns and parks with clean lakes, there are usually rowing boats available for rent during the warmer months. Both Moscow and St Petersburg sport active yacht clubs.

California-based agency **Raft Siberia** (☎1-541 386 2271; www.raftsiberia.com) arranges rafting trips on the Katun, Chuya, Sayan Oka and Chatkal Rivers in Siberia. One of its founders, Vladimir Gavrilov, is the author of *Rivers of an Unknown Land: A Whitewater Guide to the Former Soviet Union,* the only English-language guidebook to include detailed information about rafting rivers in Russia.

Caucasus Mountains Agencies

- Masterskaya Priklucheny (p364), Sochi
- Reinfo (p364), Sochi
- Sphere (p369), Sochi

Russian Far East Agencies

- DVS-Tour (p512), Magadan
- Kamchatintour (p553), Petropavlovsk-Kamchatsky
- Lost World (p553), Petropavlovsk-Kamchatsky
- Nata Tour (p537), Komsomolsk-na-Amure

Siberia Agencies

- Alash Travel (p460), Kyzyl
- **Ak Tur** (Map p436; ☎3852-659 407; www.aktour.ru; Ultra Business Centre, pr Lenina 10, Barnaul; ⊙10am-7pm Mon-Sat), Barnaul
- K2 Adventures (p419), Omsk
- MorinTur (p499), Ulan-Ude

Moscow, St Petersburg & Petrozavodsk Agencies

- **Megatest** (☎499-126 9119; www.megatest.ru), Moscow
- **Solnechny Parus** (Map p172; ☎812 327 3525; www.solpar.ru; ul Vosstaniya 55; ⊙10am-8pm Mon-Fri, 11am-6pm Sat; Ⓜ Chernyshevskaya), St Petersburg
- **Wild Russia** (Map p162; ☎812 313 8030; www.wildrussia.spb.ru; nab reki Fontanki 59; Ⓜ Gostiny Dvor), St Petersburg
- Russia Discovery North-West (p281), Petrozavodsk

Ural Mountains Agencies

- Ekaterinburg Guide Centre (p400), Yekaterinburg
- Krasnov (p392), Perm
- Tengri (p404), Ufa
- Ural Expeditions & Tours (p400), Yekaterinburg

Volga Region Agencies

- Samara Intour (p336), Samara
- Team Gorky (p323), Nizhny Novgorod

Cycling

Russia's traffic-clogged cities are far from a cyclist's nirvana, but off-road cyclists will find plenty of challenging terrain. Rural Russians are quite fascinated with and friendly towards long-distance riders. Just make certain you have a bike designed for the harshest conditions and carry plenty of spare parts.

Bike Rentals

- Moscow (p95)
- St Petersburg (p185)
- Suzdal (p134)
- Svetlogorsk (p275)

Organised Bike Tours

Agencies offering organised bike tours:

- Ekaterinburg Guide Centre (p400), Yekaterinburg
- Kola Travel (p300), Monchegorsk
- Russia Discovery North-West (p281), Petrozavodsk
- Samara Intour (p336), Samara
- Skat Prokat (p185), St Petersburg
- Team Gorky (p323), Nizhny Novgorod

Diving

Fancy diving Lake Baikal, within the Arctic Circle or in the Baltic Sea? Such specialist trips can be arranged. Contact the following agencies:

- Arctic Circle PADI Dive Center (p299), Kola Peninsula
- BaikalExplorer (p484), Irkutsk
- Demersus (p275), Yantarny
- **Nereis** (☎812-103 0518; www.nereis.ru/eng/index.html), St Petersburg. Can arrange ice diving and diving in the White Sea.

ILYA GUREVICH: EXTREME CYCLING

Ilya Gurevich is one of the founders of the St Petersburg–area cycling website **VeloPiter** (www.velopiter.spb.ru), as well as the author of **Towns.ru** (www.towns.ru, mainly in Russian), which carries reviews and pictures of charming off-the-beaten-path places around the country, many of which could be visited on a cycling tour. He talked to us about some of his cycling adventures – most of which have taken place in the depths of winter when freezing conditions have allowed access to places otherwise too wet or infested with insects to visit in the summer.

Tell us about one of your more memorable cycling trips. In March 2001 I cycled with two others across a frozen Lake Baikal. [Ilya's route and a report in Russian is shown at www.velopiter.spb.ru/rep/baikal]. We started the trip by taking the BAM railway to Novy Uoyan, which is north of the lake, and cycling through the forest as far as Ust-Barguzin on the lake's eastern shore. It was very cold, down to -37°C on the lake. Obviously there's no road; we followed the tracks made by lorries that cross through the forest and over the lake in winter. It took us 19 days to travel 1019km.

Is that the coldest place you've cycled? No, that would have to be my trip from Yakutsk to Oymyakon (the Sakha Republic settlement with the lowest recorded temperatures in Russia) in 2004. There were five of us and it took two weeks to make that journey, during which I endured the coldest night of my life: -45°C.

What's the biggest challenge on these trips? Sometimes the conditions make it very difficult to judge how quickly you can go. In 2007 I planned a trip from Amderma (on the Kara Sea within the Arctic Circle) to Vorkuta. However we only managed the first 167km to the village of Ust-Kara, which took us 13 days. One day was so bad we covered just 12km.

Any other Arctic cycling adventures? Yes, in April 2013, together with two other cyclists, I succeeded in cycling the coast of Chukotka from Billings to Pevek along the East Siberian Sea. It took us 16 days to cover 300km using 'fat bikes' with tyres of 4.8 inches. That expedition won an award for the most difficult cycling trip of the year. [You can watch a short video about it at www.youtube.com/watch?v=NfKJLQ2weLY.]

What advice would you have for anyone wanting to undertake a similar bike ride in Russia? Bring the right equipment, especially if you're travelling across ice and snow in winter. Having ice spikes on your wheels is essential. Also do a less ambitious preliminary trip to test out what it's like to cycle in the Russian winter.

Former submarine designer Ilya Gurevich and colleagues lead cycling trips around Russia and beyond.

➡ **RuDive** (☎495-925 7799; www.dive.ru) Moscow. A group of dive companies, with the Diving Club and School of Moscow State University at its core. They offer trips in the White and Barents Seas and the Sea of Japan, including ice diving off the live-aboard boat *Kartesh* (www.barentssea.ru/index/en.htm).

➡ SVAL (p486), Lake Baikal

➡ Three Dimensions (p486), Lake Baikal

Fishing

Serious anglers drool at the opportunity to fish the rivers, lakes and lagoons of Kaliningrad Region, Northern European Russia, the Russian Far East and Siberia. Kamchatka is a particular draw, with steelhead fishing in the peninsula reckoned to be the best in the world.

Start saving up: organised fishing trips in Russia can be heart-stoppingly expensive. While it's possible to go it alone and just head off with rod and tackle, most regions have severe restrictions on fishing, so you'd be wise to at least check these out before departure. A curious alternative is ice fishing for Lake Baikal's unique *omul*.

Hooked: Fly Fishing Through Russia (titled *Reeling in Russia* in the US) by Fen Montaigne charts the former Moscow-based correspondent as he spends a revealing three months casting his rod in the country's largely polluted lakes and rivers.

Fishing agencies:

➡ Arctic Land (p303), Murmansk

➡ Baltma Tours (p272), Kaliningrad

➡ DVS-Tour (p512), Magadan

➡ Explore Kamchatka (p553), Yelizovo

➡ Kamchatintour (p553), Petropavlovsk-Kamchatsky

➡ Lost World (p553), Petropavlovsk-Kamchatsky

➡ Nata Tour (p537), Komsomolsk-na-Amure

➡ Portal Sezonov (p520), Khabarovsk

➡ Sergey Outfitter (p520), Khabarovsk

➡ Yug Kola (p298), Apatity

Flying & Skydiving

Several tour operators can arrange passenger flights in the supersonic MiG-29s that fly out of Nizhny Novgorod's Sokol Airbase to the edge of space where you can view the curvature of the globe. For more details contact:

➡ **Incredible Adventures** (www.incredible-adventures.com) US-based, also offers flight in L39 Albatross out of Vyazma Air Base, three hours southwest of Moscow.

➡ **Skyandspacetravel.com** (www.skyandspacetravel.com) UK-based.

➡ **Country of Tourism** (www.bestrussiantour.com) Russia-based.

The latter two also organise trips to see the launch of the manned Soyuz spacecraft from the Baikonur Cosmodrome in Kazakhstan and a range of activities at Star City.

Helicopter sightseeing flights over St Petersburg can be arranged with **Helitour** (www.helitour.ru/ENG).

➡ **Aerograd Kolomna** (www.aerograd.ru), 100km south of Moscow, is the largest skydiving centre in Russia; a tandem jump costs ₽7500, while a level 1 skydiving course is ₽19,180.

Hiking, Mountaineering & Rock Climbing

Serious hikers and mountain climbers will have the Caucasus mountains topping their wish list, particularly the areas around Mt Elbrus, Dombay, Krasnaya Polyana and Mt Fisht. The Agura Valley is a prime location for rock climbing.

For any trekking in the Caucasus check on the current situation and arrange far in advance any necessary permits – this is best done through local agencies.

In the southern Ural Mountains, Zyuratkul National Park and Taganay National Park are both beautiful places to hike. Siberia also harbours many equally fantastic hiking and mountaineering locations, principally the Altai region (again you will need permits for most climbs in this area, including

SAFETY GUIDELINES FOR HIKING

Before embarking on a hike, consider the following:

➡ Be sure you're healthy and feel comfortable about hiking for a sustained period. The nearest village in Russia can be vastly further away than it would be in other countries.

➡ Get the best information you can about the physical and environmental conditions along your intended route. Russian 'trails' are generally nominal ideas rather than marked footpaths, so employing a guide is very wise.

➡ Walk only in regions, and on trails, within your realm of experience.

➡ Be prepared for severe and sudden changes in the weather and terrain; always take wet-weather gear.

➡ Pack essential survival gear including emergency food rations and a leak-proof water bottle.

➡ If you can, find a hiking companion. At the very least tell someone where you're going and refer to your compass frequently so you can find your way back.

➡ Unless you're planning a camping trip, start early so you can make it home before dark.

➡ Allow plenty of time.

➡ For longer routes, consider renting, or even buying (then later reselling), a pack horse.

Mt Belukha) and around Lake Baikal, where you'll find the Great Baikal Trail. Kamchatka also has plentiful hiking and mountaineering possibilities, including the chance to summit active volcanoes, but you will certainly need to hire guides to avoid danger.

Elsewhere, multiple national parks and state nature reserves exist, but don't expect them to have especially good facilities or even well-marked trails. For this reason, it's especially important to seek out local advice, information and even guides before setting off.

Caucasus Mountains Agencies

➡ Dombay Tourist (p382), Dombay

➡ **Pyatigorsk Intour** (Map p374; ☎8793-349 213; tour@pintour.kmv.ru; pl Lenina 13; ⏰10am-6pm), Pyatigorsk

➡ Reinfo (p364), Sochi

➡ Sphere (p369), Sochi

Siberia Agencies

➡ Ak Tur (p442), Barnaul

➡ Alash Travel (p460), Kyzyl

➡ K2 Adventures (p419), Omsk. Good for tackling Mt Belukha.

➡ **LenAlp Tours** (www.russia-climbing.com) Also specialises in Mt Belukha.

➡ Sibir-Altai (p442), Novosibirsk

➡ Tour Academy (p442), Novosibirsk

Ural Mountains Agencies

➡ Ekaterinburg Guide Centre (p400), Yekaterinburg

➡ Ural Expeditions & Tours (p400), Yekaterinburg

Agencies in Other Regions

➡ Kola Travel (p300), Monchegorsk

➡ Megatest (p42), Moscow

➡ Wild Russia (p42), St Petersburg. Recommended for Mt Elbrus.

Horse Riding

Many of the same areas that offer good hiking and mountaineering also offer horse-riding treks. Try Dombay and Arkhyz in the Caucasus, the Altai region, around Lake Baikal and Kamchatka. There's also the famous Georgenburg Stud Farm in Chernyakhovsk.

Following are specific operators who can arrange horse riding:

➡ Alash Travel (p450), Kyzyl

➡ Baikal Naran Tour (p499), Ulan-Ude

➡ **GTK Suzdal** (ГТК; ☎49231-23 380, 49231-20 908; ul Korovniki 45; ⏰10am-6pm), Suzdal

➡ Krasnov (p392), Perm

➡ Oleg (p380), Teberdinsky State Natural Biosphere Reserve

➡ Ural Expeditions & Tours (p400), Yekaterinburg

Skiing & Winter Sports

The 2014 Winter Olympics in Sochi and Krasnaya Polyana put Russia on winter-sports enthusiasts' radars across the world.

Downhill ski slopes are scattered throughout the country, although cross-country skiing is more common, attracting legions of enthusiasts during the long winters. Given the wealth of open space, you won't have a problem finding a place to hit the trail. For off-piste adventures, try heliskiing and back-country skiing in the Caucasus and Kamchatka.

For further details, go to **World Snowboardguide.com** (www.worldsnowboardguide.com/resorts/russia) or **Onboard.ru** (www.onboard.ru).

Caucasus Mountains Ski Areas

➡ Mt Elbrus (p384)

➡ Mt Cheget (p385)

➡ Dombay (p378)

➡ Krasnaya Polyana (p369)

Siberia Ski Resorts & Areas

➡ Bobrovy Log Ski Resort (p467), Krasnoyarsk

➡ **Gladenkaya** (http://ski-gladenkaya.ru) Sayanogorsk, Khakassia Republic

➡ Lake Manzherok, Altai

➡ **Sheregesh** (www.sheregesh.ru)

Skiing in St Petersburg & Northern European Russia

➡ Kirovsk (p298)

➡ **Krasnoe Ozero** (www.krasnoeozero.ru), near St Petersburg

➡ **Tuutari Park** (www.tyytari.spb.ru), near St Petersburg

➡ **Zolotai Dolina** (www.zoldolspb.narod.ru/business4.html), near St Petersburg

DRIVING THE TRANS-SIBERIAN HIGHWAY

For intrepid souls the challenge of driving across the vast expanse of Russia is irresistible. Ewan McGregor and Charley Boorman wrote about their Russian road adventures in *Long Way Round* (www.longwayround.com); part of their round-the-world route took them from Volgograd all the way to Yakutsk and Magadan via Kazakhstan and Mongolia.

The celebrity bikers had a camera crew and support team following them. For a more accurate view of what to expect read *The Linger Longer* by brothers Chris and Simon Raven, who somehow coaxed a rusty Ford Sierra from the UK to Vladivostok; *One Steppe Beyond* by Thom Wheeler, which covers a similar journey in a VW campervan; *Travels in Siberia* by the humorist Ian Frazier, who was accompanied by two Russian guides on his 2001 drive from St Petersburg to Vladivostok in a Renault van; and *White Fever* by Jacek Hugo-Bader, who drives from Moscow to Vladivostok in the middle of winter.

Whatever your mode of transport, since the full black-top completion in September 2010 of the 2100km Amur Hwy, between Chita and Khabarovsk (previously the rockiest section of the road), driving the 11,000km from St Petersburg to Vladivostok has become a more feasible proposition. Even so, it's worth heeding the words of Prime Minister Vladimir Putin, who, in August 2011, drove a 350km stretch of the Amur Hwy in a bright-yellow Lada Kalina Sport, afterwards commenting: 'It is a dependable, modern farm road, but not the Autobahn.'

For some information in Russian on this section of the road see http://amur-trassa.ru. Also, **National Geographic Adventure** (http://adventure.nationalgeographic.com/2008/06/trans-siberian-highway/mckenzie-funk-text) has a feature article called 'Road-Tripping the Trans-Siberian Highway' about driving the route in 2008.

Ural Mountains Ski Areas

- Abzakovo (p405)
- **Metallurg-Magnitogorsk** (www.ski-bannoe.ru) near Bannoye, Bashkortostan

Snowmobiling & Arctic Adventures

For snowmobile safaris and activities in the Arctic contact the following:

- Kola Travel (p300) in Monchegorsk
- Megatest (p42) in Moscow
- **Vicaar** (812-713 2781; www.northpolextreme.com) in St Petersburg
- Yug Kola (p298) in Apatity

GTK (p45) in Suzdal also offers snowmobile rides.

Cruises in the Arctic region are also popular. See p307 for more details.

Space Adventures

Zvezdny Gorodok (Star City), a once highly classified community of cosmonauts and scientists, around an hour's drive northeast of Moscow, is where those looking to blast off into outer space train for the experience. Since 2001 **Space Adventures** (in USA 888-85-SPACE, outside USA 703-524-7172; www.spaceadventures.com), a US-based company, has arranged for several billionaire civilians to achieve their dream of space flight by training here also.

While you don't need to be filthy rich to sign up for the programs offered by Space Adventures, they are far from your everyday travel adventure both in terms of cost and the amount of serious physical and mental commitment required. Cosmonaut training (US$89,500), for example, takes a week and includes a spacewalk mission simulation in a neutral buoyancy tank. The least costly deal is to train for a spacewalk (US$7650), which still includes visiting Star City, trying on an Orlan spacesuit, meeting with cosmonauts and chowing down at Star City's cafeteria. A feature in *Wired* magazine (http://archive.wired.com/techbiz/people/magazine/16-09/ff_starcity?currentPage=all) gives the inside scoop on training to go into space at Star City.

Moscow-based **Country of Tourism** (www.bestrussiantour.com) can also arrange similar tours to Star City, including zero-gravity flights from €5000. If you just want to visit Star City and have a look around, this is also possible. Tours of the technical area and museum can be arranged through the **Yury Gagarin Russian State Science Research Cosmonauts Training Centre** (495-526 2612; www.gctc.su).

Regions at a Glance

When planning a trip to the largest country in the world, it's best to establish what your travel priorities are. The vast majority of visitors are going to want to spend time in Moscow and St Petersburg; both these historic cities deliver the goods in terms of memorable sights and comfortable facilities, and function as bases for trips further afield to locations in Western European Russia or the Golden Ring. Siberia's splendid natural attractions are pretty irresistible but you're going to need time to see this vast area, which we split into more manageable western and eastern regions. To get fully off the beaten track head to the Russian Far East, Northern European Russia or the Caucasus.

Moscow

Art
History
Performing Arts

Glorious Galleries

The illustrious Tretyakov and Pushkin Galleries are only the beginning of the art in Moscow, where contemporary artists and their patrons are taking over former factories and warehouses to display their works.

Historical Landmarks

The Kremlin shows off the splendour of Muscovy's grand princes. St Basil's Cathedral recounts the defeat of the Tatars. And on Red Square, Lenin lies embalmed.

Performing Arts

The city's classical performing arts are still among the best in the world. Nowadays, even the most traditional theatres are experimenting with innovative arrangements and cutting-edge choreographies.

p52

Golden Ring

Churches & Icons
Country Roads
Village Life

Churches & Icons

Admire the quintessentially Russian images of golden cupolas and whitewashed monastery walls guarding stunning medieval frescoes and icons encased in richly decorated altars.

Country Roads

From Vladimir to Yaroslavl, drive or cycle the picturesque A113, which skirts coniferous forests, sun-filled birch-tree groves and neat villages of brightly painted log houses and dilapidated churches.

Village Life

Wake up in a gingerbread cottage, plunge into the nearby lake or river, savour your breakfast bliny and then take it easy for the rest of the day in a garden chair, with a book and a jar of freshly picked strawberries for company.

p126

St Petersburg

Palaces
History
Art

Imperial Splendour

Grand imperial palaces line the embankments of the Neva River, its tributaries and canals. Restoration over the past two decades has been painstaking; the results are breathtaking.

Revolutions

Everything about St Petersburg is revolutionary: from Peter the Great's determination to forge a new Russia by opening the country to the rest of Europe, to Lenin's 1917 coup, which led to the creation of the world's first communist state.

Staggering Collections

The Hermitage collection is unrivalled anywhere else in the country. The Russian Museum positively groans under the weight of its own unique collection of Russian painting from icons to the avant-garde.

p151

Western European Russia

Kremlins
Architecture
Literary Shrines

Fortresses

The formidable stone fortresses of early Rus trading towns such as Veliky Novgorod, Pskov and Smolensk stand today as majestic backdrops to historical explorations.

Mystical Churches

Enter the ancient monastery at Pechory, or the icon-crammed cathedrals of Veliky Novgorod and Smolensk to witness the revival of Orthodox Christianity in the region where the religion originally took root centuries ago.

Literary Shrines

The family estates of Pushkin, Turgenev and Tolstoy provide insight into the country life of the gentry in the 19th century. In Staraya Russa, Fyodor Dostoevsky's home looks as if the writer has only just popped out for a stroll.

p226

Kaliningrad Region

History
Museums
Beaches

Historical Roots

A rebuilt Gothic cathedral and the city's gates and fortifications are fragments of the time when Kaliningrad was Königsberg in the kingdom of Prussia.

Museums

Learn about maritime history at the Museum of the World Ocean and be dazzled by artworks carved from petrified tree resin at the Amber Museum, both in Kaliningrad. Be charmed by the sculptures and gardens at the Herman Brachert House-Museum near Svetlogorsk.

Beaches

Discover some of Russia's best beaches at Yantarny, Zelenogradsk and in the Kurshskaya Kosa National Park where massive sand dunes and wind-sculpted pines are sandwiched between the Baltic and Curonian Lagoon.

p263

Northern European Russia

Great Outdoors
History
Museums

Great Outdoors

Each season offers its own adventures, from swimming with human 'walruses' in winter to summertime fishing for champion salmon in rugged, yet pristine rivers.

Historical Architecture

From the wooden marvels of Kizhi and the haunting stone edifices of Solovki to the nautically inspired churches of landlocked Totma, the architectural landscape here is as worth traversing as the natural one.

Museums

The mineral-heavy towns of the Kola region rock several highbrow geology repositories, exhibitions in Kargopol and Totma offer unique glimpses into local life, and Arkhangelsk's WWII-centric museum is a destination in itself.

p278

Volga Region

Architecture
Landscapes
Food & Culture

Architecture

Historic kremlins overlook the Volga River in Nizhny Novgorod, Kazan and Astrakhan, monumental Stalinist buildings rise up out of Volgograd, contrasted by simple wood cottages in towns throughout the region.

Mighty Volga

The Volga has many different faces. The Samara Bend is perfect for hiking, and in the Volga Delta this magnificent river culminates in a spectacular wetland where boats are often the only mode of transport.

Food & Culture

Tatar culture dominates Kazan and Astrakhan, where you can best sample Tatar cuisine. Buddhism and a very different culinary culture prevail in Kalmykia, while in Nizhny Novgorod a 'Food and Culture' project is thriving.

p318

Russian Caucasus

Skiing
Trekking
Scenery

Olympic Skiing

From Sochi access the mountain resort of Krasnaya Polyana, which thanks to the Olympics, has scores of memorable runs, with an excellent assortment of cosy guesthouses and revitalising *bani* (hot baths) when the day is done.

Terrific Trekking

The Caucasus are a magnet for adventure seekers. You can summit majestic Mt Elbrus – Europe's highest peak – or go on multiday treks exploring some of Russia's most dramatic scenery.

Idyllic Scenery

Pretty Mineral Waters towns such as Kislovodsk and Pyatigorsk, nestled in the Caucasus foothills, are idyllic settings for scenic walks in the surrounding hills.

p353

The Urals

Landscapes
Cities & Towns
Museums

Diverse Landscapes

The Ural Mountains may only be truly spectacular in the north, but they are a lush, picturesque getaway elsewhere, with Lake Zyuratkul or the ice cave of Kungur.

Cities & Towns

Yekaterinburg, home to a good variety of museums, is the most famous of the region's cities. Chelyabinsk is idiosyncratic beneath its urban grit and Perm lives the eccentric difference.

Gulag & Art

Contrast Perm-36, the once-horrific Gulag camp located outside the city, with the modern and contemporary art space PERMM which offers up the shock of the new.

p389

Western Siberia

Great Outdoors
Winter Sports
Architecture

Nature

The Altai Republic's snow-capped mountains and remote lakes make the region a playground for nature lovers. Tourism is massively underdeveloped here though, so be prepared to rough it.

Winter Sports

Ski resort Sheregesh may be rough around the edges, but at least you won't have to queue long for the lifts. It also enjoys a stunning location in the heart of the Siberian countryside.

Historic Buildings

Tobolsk, Siberia's old capital, sports a handsome kremlin and charmingly decrepit old town. In Siberia's 'cultural capital', Tomsk, it's easy to lose yourself in a wonderland of wooden mansions and log cabins with intricately carved facades.

p410

Eastern Siberia

Great Outdoors
Landscapes
Museums

Great Outdoors

Whether you hike the Great Baikal Trail, discover the impenetrable taiga on horseback, click on skis for a bit of off-piste or kayak Lake Baikal's sapphire waters, Eastern Siberia is outdoorsy bliss.

Stunning Landscapes

Show-stopping vistas are ensured in Tuva's grasslands, Krasnoyarsk's Stolby Nature Reserve, the back country of the Barguzin Valley, and the snow-whipped Eastern Sayan Mountains.

Exceptional Museums

Be rendered speechless by the intricacy of Scythian gold, take a virtual submarine to Lake Baikal's murky depths and peruse a mini Khakassian Stonehenge at the region's intriguing repositories of the past.

p450

Russian Far East

Mountains
Adventures
Indigenous Cultures

Mountainous Scenery

Kamchatka hogs the glory with its volcanoes, but Russia's entire eastern seaboard from Vladivostok to Magadan is a riot of old-growth taiga and icy peaks primed for adventure.

Adventures

In addition to anything mountain-related, you can hitch the Chukotka highway, drive a reindeer sled across the Arctic… you're only limited by your imagination.

Indigenous Cultures

The weak don't survive in the 'pole of cold', and so it is that the Far East's native inhabitants are among the world's heartiest. Journey to their villages, where they fish and herd reindeer, or celebrate the summer solstice with the Sakha at Yakutsk's Ysyakh.

p512

On the Road

Kaliningrad Region p263
St Petersburg p151
Northern European Russia p278
Moscow p52
Golden Ring p126
Western European Russia p226
Volga Region p318
Russian Caucasus p353
The Urals p389
Western Siberia p410
Eastern Siberia p450
Russian Far East p512

Moscow

Includes ➡

Best Places to Eat

- Delicatessen (p103)
- Cafe Pushkin (p104)
- As Eat Is (p104)
- Khachapuri (p104)
- Kitayskaya Gramota (p103)
- Lavka-Lavka (p103)

Best Places to Stay

- Hotel Metropol (p97)
- Hotel de Paris (p100)
- Kitay-Gorod Hotel (p99)
- Blues Hotel (p100)
- Godzillas Hostel (p97)

Why Go?

The state becomes more authoritarian. International relations deteriorate. But Moscow keeps getting cooler, more cosmopolitan and more creative. The capital is bursting with energy, as factories and warehouses are converted into art galleries and post-industrial nightclubs; parks are overrun with healthy, active, sporty types; and chefs experiment with their own interpretations of international cooking.

The ancient city has always been a haven for history buffs – the red-brick towers of the Kremlin occupy the founding site of Moscow (Москва); monuments and churches remember fallen heroes and victorious battles; and remains of the Soviet state are scattered all around. But now museums are broaching subjects long brushed under the carpet.

The capital is even experiencing an unprecedented growth in birth rates. From artistry and history to recreation and procreation, Moscow is a cauldron of creativity.

When to Go

Moscow

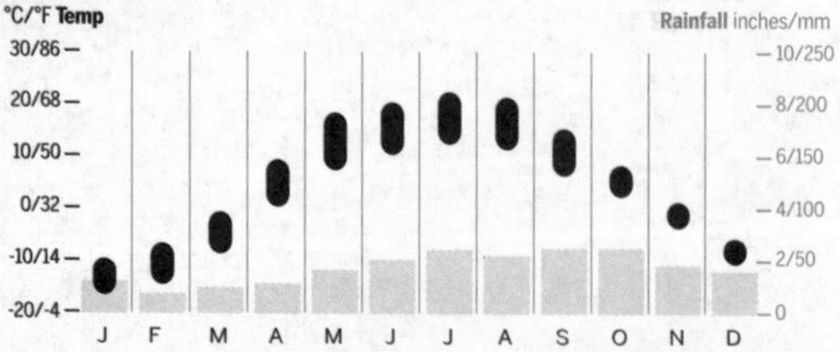

May & Jun Long hours of daylight and mild temperatures entice Muscovites outdoors.

Sep Moscow celebrates City Day, as the foliage turns the capital splendid oranges, reds and yellows.

Dec The snow-covered city hosts its premier cultural event, the December Nights Festival.

Arriving in Moscow

Most travellers arrive by air, flying into one of the city's three airports. The majority of international flights go in and out of Domodedovo and Sheremetyevo international airports. All three airports are accessible by the convenient Aeroexpress train (p121) from the city centre.

If you wish to go by taxi, go to the taxi desk (or straight to the dispatcher) for an official airport taxi, which will charge ₽2000 to ₽2500 to the centre. Note that driving times vary wildly depending on traffic.

Rail riders will arrive at one of the central train stations :Kievsky or Belorussky vokzal if you're coming from Europe; Leningradsky vokzal if you're coming from St Petersburg; and Yaroslavsky or Kazansky vokzal if you're coming from the east. All the train stations are located in the city centre, with easy metro access. Alternatively, most taxi companies offer a fixed rate of ₽400 to ₽600 for a train-station transfer.

GET THE BIG PICTURE

Moscow can be overwhelming for the first-time visitor. An introductory tour can provide an overview of the city, as well as useful advice and information for the rest of your trip.

- Moscow Free Tour (p96) Offers a free walking tour, led by knowledgable and extremely enthusiastic guides. Did we mention it's free?
- Moscow 360 (p96) Four unique and informative walking tours (all free), as well as a big-picture tour by air-conditioned minivan (not free).
- Moscow Bike Tours (p96) Cover more ground and see more sites, while getting fresh air and exercise.
- River Cruises (p96) Two boat-tour companies follow the route from Kievsky vokzal or the former Hotel Ukraine in Dorogomilovo to Novospassky Monastery in Taganka. You can get off and on the boat, but the 90-minute trip is a pleasant way to get the big picture.

New in Moscow

- **Gorky Park** (p92) & **Hermitage Garden** (p73) Moscow's major green spaces have been revamped into vibrant centres of sport and culture.
- **Jewish Museum & Centre of Tolerance** (p73) Excellent, interactive, multimedia presentations at this groundbreaking museum.
- **Moscow Museum** (p87) This city museum has a new location and a new mission.
- **Krymskaya Naberezhnaya** (p91) Closed to car traffic and filled with fountains and art.

NEED TO KNOW

Most Moscow museums are closed on Monday, but the Kremlin and the Armoury are closed on Thursday instead. Many museums also close once a month for 'sanitary day', often during the last week of the month.

Fast Facts

- **Telephone area code** ☎495 or ☎499
- **Population** 12 million
- **Moscow time** (GMT/USC plus four hours)

Where to Stay

Moscow is big and filled with cars. Pay attention to the location of your hotel or hostel so you don't spend all your time commuting. Choose a place that is in the centre (preferably within the Garden Ring) and a short walk from the metro.

Resources

- **Calvert Journal** (www.calvertjournal.com) Excellent articles on Russia's contemporary creative culture.
- **Moscow Times** (www.themoscowtimes.com) Leading English-language newspaper in Moscow.
- **Expat.ru** (www.expat.ru) Run by and for English-speaking expats living in Moscow.

Alternatively, head to **Lonely Planet** (www.lonelyplanet.com/russia/moscow) for planning advice, author recommendations and tips.

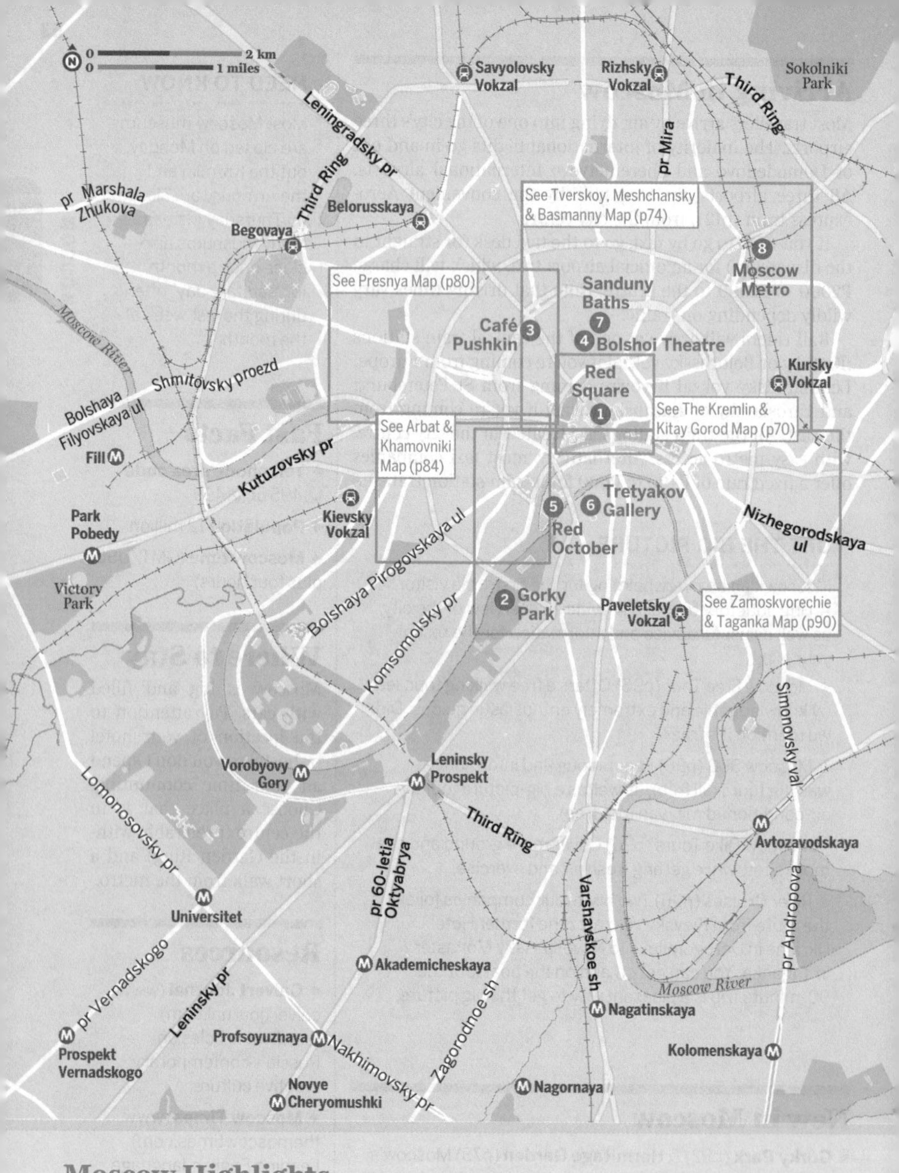

Moscow Highlights

1 Be awestruck by the assemblage of tall towers and onion domes on **Red Square** (p57).

2 Hang out with Moscow's hipsters in **Gorky Park** (p92) – ride bikes, admire art, play ping-pong or dance under the stars.

3 Splurge on a Russian feast amid 18th-century opulence at **Cafe Pushkin** (p104).

4 See the ballerinas slide across *Swan Lake* at the **Bolshoi Theatre** (p109).

5 Explore the former **Red October** (p89) chocolate factory, now filled with art galleries, nightclubs and fashion boutiques.

6 Ogle the icons, peruse the Peredvizhniki and contemplate the avant-garde at the **Tretyakov Gallery** (p89).

7 Steam your cares away at the luxurious **Sanduny Baths** (p94).

8 Ride the Moscow **metro** (p112) for a cheap history lesson and art exhibit all in one.

History

Moscow is first mentioned in the historic chronicles in 1147, when Prince Yury Dolgoruky invited his allies to a banquet: 'Come to me, brother, please come to Moscow'. Moscow's strategic importance prompted Yury to construct a moat-ringed wooden palisade on the hilltop, the first Kremlin. Moscow blossomed into an economic centre, attracting traders and artisans to the merchant rows just outside the Kremlin's walls.

Medieval Moscow

Beginning in 1236, Eastern Europe was overwhelmed by the ferocious Golden Horde, a Mongol-led army of nomadic tribesmen. The Mongols introduced themselves to Moscow by burning the city to the ground and killing its governor. The Golden Horde was mainly interested in tribute, and Moscow was conveniently situated to monitor the river trade and road traffic. As Moscow prospered, its political fortunes rose too. It soon surpassed Vladimir and Suzdal as the regional capital.

Moscow eventually became a nemesis of the Mongols. In the 1380 Battle of Kulikovo, Moscow's Grand Prince Dmitry won a rare victory over the Golden Horde on the banks of the Don River. He was thereafter immortalised as Dmitry Donskoy. From this time, Moscow acted as champion of the Russian cause.

Towards the end of the 15th century, Moscow's ambitions were realised as the once-diminutive duchy emerged as an expanding autocratic state. Under the long reign of Grand Prince Ivan III (the Great), the eastern Slav principalities were consolidated into a single territorial entity. In 1480 Ivan's army faced down the Mongols at the Ugra River without a fight: the 200-year Mongol yoke was lifted.

To celebrate his successes, Ivan III undertook a complete renovation of his Moscow fortress. The Kremlin's famous brick walls and imposing watchtowers were constructed at this time. Next to the Kremlin, traders and artisans set up shop in Kitay Gorod, and a stone wall was erected around these commercial quarters. The city developed in concentric rings outward from this centre.

As it emerged as a political capital, Moscow also took on the role of religious centre. In the mid-15th century, the Russian Orthodox Church was organised, independent of the Greek Church. Under Ivan IV (the Terrible), the city earned the nickname 'Gold-Domed Moscow' because of the multitude of monastery fortresses and magnificent churches constructed within them.

Imperial Moscow

Peter the Great always despised Moscow for its scheming boyars (high-ranking nobles) and archaic traditions. In 1712 he startled the country by announcing the relocation of the capital to a swampland in the northwest (St Petersburg). The spurned ex-capital fell into decline, later exacerbated by an outbreak of bubonic plague.

By the turn of the 19th century, Moscow had recovered from its gloom. By this time, the city hosted Russia's first university, museum and newspaper. Moscow's intellectual and literary scene gave rise to a nationalist-inspired Slavophile movement, which celebrated the cultural features of Russia that were distinctive from the West.

In the early 1800s Tsar Alexander I decided to resume trade with England, in violation of a treaty Russia had made with France. A furious Napoleon Bonaparte set out for Moscow with the largest military force the world had ever seen. The Russian army engaged the advancing French at the Battle of Borodino, 130km from Moscow. More than 100,000 soldiers lay dead at the end of this inconclusive one-day fight. Shortly thereafter, Napoleon entered a deserted Moscow. By some accounts, defiant Muscovites burned down their city rather than see it occupied. French soldiers tried to topple the formidable Kremlin, but its sturdy walls withstood their pummelling.

The city was feverishly rebuilt following Napoleon's final defeat. Monuments were erected to commemorate Russia's hard-fought victory, including a Triumphal Arch and the grandiose Cathedral of Christ the Saviour. Meanwhile, the city's two outer defensive rings were replaced with the tree-lined Boulevard Ring and Garden Ring roads.

By midcentury, industry overtook commerce as the city's economic driving force. With a steady supply of cotton from Central Asia, Moscow became a leader in the textile industry, and was known as 'Calico Moscow'. By 1900, Moscow claimed more than one million inhabitants.

Red Moscow

The Bolshevik coup provoked a week of street fighting in Moscow, leaving more than 1000 dead. Fearing a German assault on St

Petersburg, in 1918 Lenin ordered that the capital return to Moscow.

In the 1930s Josef Stalin launched an industrial revolution, at the same time devising a comprehensive urban plan for Moscow. On paper, it appeared as a neatly organised garden city; unfortunately, it was implemented with a sledgehammer. Historic cathedrals and monuments were demolished, including landmarks such as the Cathedral of Christ the Saviour and Kazan Cathedral. In their place appeared the marble-bedecked metro and neo-Gothic skyscrapers.

When Hitler launched 'Operation Barbarossa' into Soviet territory in June 1941, Stalin was caught by surprise. By December the Nazis were just outside Moscow, within 30km of the Kremlin, but an early winter halted the advance. In the Battle of Moscow, war hero General Zhukov staged a brilliant counteroffensive and saved the city from capture.

Stalin was succeeded by Nikita Khrushchev, a former mayor of Moscow, who introduced wide-ranging reforms and promised to improve living conditions. Huge housing estates grew up round the outskirts of Moscow. The expansion continued under his successor, Leonid Brezhnev. As the Soviet Union emerged as a military superpower, the aerospace, radio-electronics and nuclear weapons ministries operated factories and research laboratories in and around the capital. By 1980 the city's population surpassed eight million.

Transitional Moscow

Mikhail Gorbachev came to power in March 1985 with a mandate to revitalise the ailing socialist system; he promoted Boris Yeltsin as the new head of Moscow. Yeltsin's populist touch made him an instant success with Muscovites and he embraced the more open political atmosphere.

On 18 August 1991 the city awoke to find tanks in the streets. Gorbachev had been arrested and a self-proclaimed 'Committee for the State of Emergency in the USSR' proclaimed itself in charge. Crowds gathered at the White House to build barricades. Yeltsin, from atop a tank, declared the coup illegal. When KGB snipers didn't shoot, the coup – and Soviet communism – was over. By the year's end Boris Yeltsin had moved into the Kremlin.

The first years of transition were fraught with political conflict. In September 1993 Yeltsin issued a decree to shut down the Russian parliament. Events turned violent. The army intervened on the president's side and blasted the parliament into submission. In all, 145 people were killed and another 700 wounded – the worst incident of bloodshed in the city since the Bolshevik takeover in 1917.

Within the Moscow city government, the election of Yury Luzhkov as mayor in 1992 set the stage for the creation of a big-city boss in the grandest of traditions. The city government retained ownership of property in Moscow, giving Luzhkov's administration unprecedented control over would-be business ventures, and making him as much a CEO as a mayor.

While the rest of Russia struggled to survive the collapse of communism, Moscow quickly emerged as an enclave of affluence and dynamism. The new economy spawned a small group of 'New Russians', routinely derided and often envied for their garish displays of wealth.

Terror in the Capital

In September 1999 a series of mysterious explosions in Moscow left more than 200 people dead. It was widely believed, although unproven, that Chechen terrorists were responsible for the bombings. This was the first of many terrorist attacks in the capital that were linked to the ongoing crisis in Chechnya.

In 2002, Chechen rebels, wired with explosives, seized a popular Moscow theatre, holding 800 people hostage for three days. Russian troops responded by flooding the theatre with immobilising toxic gas, resulting in 120 deaths and hundreds of illnesses. Over the next decade, suicide bombers in Moscow made strikes in metro stations, at rock concerts, on trains and aeroplanes, and in the international airport, leaving hundreds of people dead and injured, and reminding Muscovites that the Chechen crisis is not over.

Millennium Moscow

In 2010 long-time mayor Yury Luzhkov lost his job. He was replaced by Sergei Sobyanin, the former head of the presidential administration under Putin. Like other prized possessions in Putin's Russia, Moscow now belongs to the Kremlin.

In the run-up to Putin's reappointment as president in 2012, Moscow's streets and squares saw regular protests 'for fair elections'. The demonstrations morphed into broader antigovernment unrest, sometimes called the 'Snow Revolution'. But this energy fizzled when Putin enacted restrictive legislation and the capital returned to business as usual.

As the economic rhythms of the city seem to be steadying, wealth is trickling down beyond the 'New Russians'. In Moscow, the burgeoning middle class endures a high cost of living, but enjoys unprecedented employment opportunities and a dizzying array of culinary, cultural and consumer choices.

Russia's international exploits have resulted in a renewed sense of patriotism in the capital. The city continues to attract fortune seekers from around the world. And Moscow – political capital, economic powerhouse and cultural innovator – continues to lead the way as the most fast-dealing, freewheeling city in Russia.

Sights

Kremlin & Red Square

Red Square and the Kremlin are the historical, geographic and spiritual heart of Moscow, as they have been for nearly 900 years. The mighty fortress, the iconic onion domes of St Basil's Cathedral and the granite mausoleum of Vladimir Lenin are among the city's most important and iconic historical sights. The surrounding streets of Kitay Gorod are crammed with charming churches and old architecture. This is the starting point for any visit to Moscow.

KREMLIN

The apex of Russian political power and once the centre of the Orthodox Church, the **Kremlin** (Кремль; www.kreml.ru; adult/student ₽350/100; 10am-5pm Fri-Wed, ticket office 9.30am-4.30pm; M Aleksandrovsky Sad) is not only the kernel of Moscow but of the whole country. It's from here that autocratic tsars, communist dictators and modern-day presidents have done their best – and worst – for Russia. These red-brick walls and tent-roof towers enclose some 800 years of artistic accomplishment, religious ceremony and power politics.

Buy your tickets at the **Kremlin ticket office** (Кассы музеев Кремля; Map p70; 9.30am-4pm Fri-Wed; M Aleksandrovsky Sad) in Alexander Garden. Before entering, deposit bags at the **Kremlin left-luggage office** (Map p70; per bag ₽60; 9am-6.30pm Fri-Wed), beneath the Kutafya Tower. The ticket to the 'Architectural Ensemble of Cathedral Square' covers entry to all four churches, as well as Patriarch's Palace. It does not include the Armoury or the Diamond Fund Exhibition. In any case, you can and should buy tickets for the Armoury here. There's also an entrance at the southern **Borovitskaya Tower** (Боровицкая башня), mainly used by those heading straight to the Armoury or Diamond Fund Exhibition.

Inside the Kremlin, police will keep you from straying into the out-of-bounds areas. Photography is not permitted inside the Armoury or any of the buildings on Sobornaya pl (Cathedral Sq).

Visiting the Kremlin buildings and the Armoury is at least a half-day affair. If you intend to visit the Diamond Fund or other special exhibits, plan on spending most of the day here.

To really do the Kremlin justice, let the professionals show you around. Recommended tour companies include **Kremlin Excursion Office** (Map p70; 495-697 0349; www.kremlin.museum.ru; Alexander Garden; 90-min tour ₽2500; M Alexandrovsky Sad) and Capital Tours (p96), departing from Gostinny Dvor every day that the Kremlin is open; the price includes admission. Also **Kremlin Tour with Diana** (916-333 2555; www.kremlintour.com) offers private Kremlin tours, with or without the Armoury.

Book all tours in advance.

Kutafya Tower TOWER

(Кутафья башня; Map p70) The Kutafya Tower, which forms the main visitors entrance today, stands apart from the Kremlin's west wall, at the end of a ramp over the Alexander Garden. The ramp was once a bridge over the Neglinnaya River and used to be part of the Kremlin's defences; this river has been diverted underground, beneath the Alexander Garden, since the early 19th century. The Kutafya Tower is the last of a number of outer bridge towers that once stood on this side of the Kremlin.

Trinity Gate Tower TOWER

(Троицкая башня; Map p70) From the Kutafya Tower, walk up the ramp and pass through the Kremlin walls beneath the 1495 Trinity Gate Tower. At 80m it's the tallest of the Kremlin's towers. Right below your feet were the cells for prisoners in the 16th century.

The Kremlin

A DAY AT THE KREMLIN

Only at the Kremlin can you see 800 years of Russian history and artistry in one day. Enter the ancient fortress through the Trinity Gate Tower and walk past the impressive Arsenal, ringed with cannons. Past the Patriarch's Palace, you'll find yourself surrounded by white-washed walls and golden domes. Your first stop is **Assumption Cathedral** ❶ with the solemn fresco over the doorway. As the most important church in prerevolutionary Russia, this 15th-century beauty was the burial site of the patriarchs. The **Ivan the Great Bell Tower** ❷ now contains a nifty multimedia exhibit on the architectural history of the Kremlin. The view from the top is worth the price of admission. The tower is flanked by the massive **Tsar Cannon & Bell** ❸.

In the southeast corner, **Archangel Cathedral** ❹ has an elaborate interior, where three centuries of tsars and tsarinas are laid to rest. Your final stop on Sobornaya pl is **Annunciation Cathedral** ❺, rich with frescoes and iconography.

Walk along the Great Kremlin Palace and enter the **Armoury** ❻ at the time designated on your ticket. After gawking at the goods, exit the Kremlin through Borovitsky Gate and stroll through the Alexander Garden to the **Tomb of the Unknown Soldier** ❼.

TOP TIPS

» **Lunch** There are no eating options. Plan to eat before you arrive or stash a snack.

» **Lookout** After ogling the sights around Sobornaya pl, take a break in the park across the street, which offers wonderful views of the Moscow River and points south.

Assumption Cathedral

Once your eyes adjust to the colourful frescoes, the gilded fixtures and the iconography, try to locate *Saviour with the Angry Eye*, a 14th-century icon that is one of the oldest in the Kremlin.

BOROVITSKY TOWER

Use the entrance at Borovitsky Tower if you intend to skip the churches and visit only the Armoury or Diamond Fund.

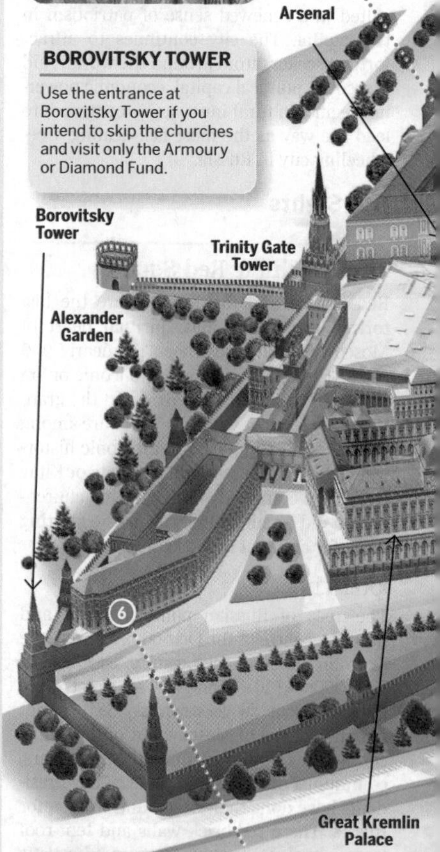

Armoury

Take advantage of the free audio guide to direct you to the most intriguing treasures of the Armoury, which is chock-full of precious metalworks and jewellery, armour and weapons, gowns and crowns, carriages and sledges.

MARTIN CHILD / GETTY IMAGES ©

Tomb of the Unknown Soldier

Visit the Tomb of the Unknown Soldier honouring the heroes of the Great Patriotic War. Come at the top of the hour to see the solemn synchronicity of the changing of the guard.

AVOID CONFUSION

Regular admission to the Kremlin does not include Ivan the Great Bell Tower. But admission to the bell tower does include the churches on the Kremlin grounds.

KEREN SU / GETTY IMAGES ©

Ivan the Great Bell Tower

Check out the artistic electronic renderings of the Kremlin's history, then climb 137 steps to the belfry's upper gallery, where you will be rewarded with super, sweeping vistas of Sobornaya pl and beyond.

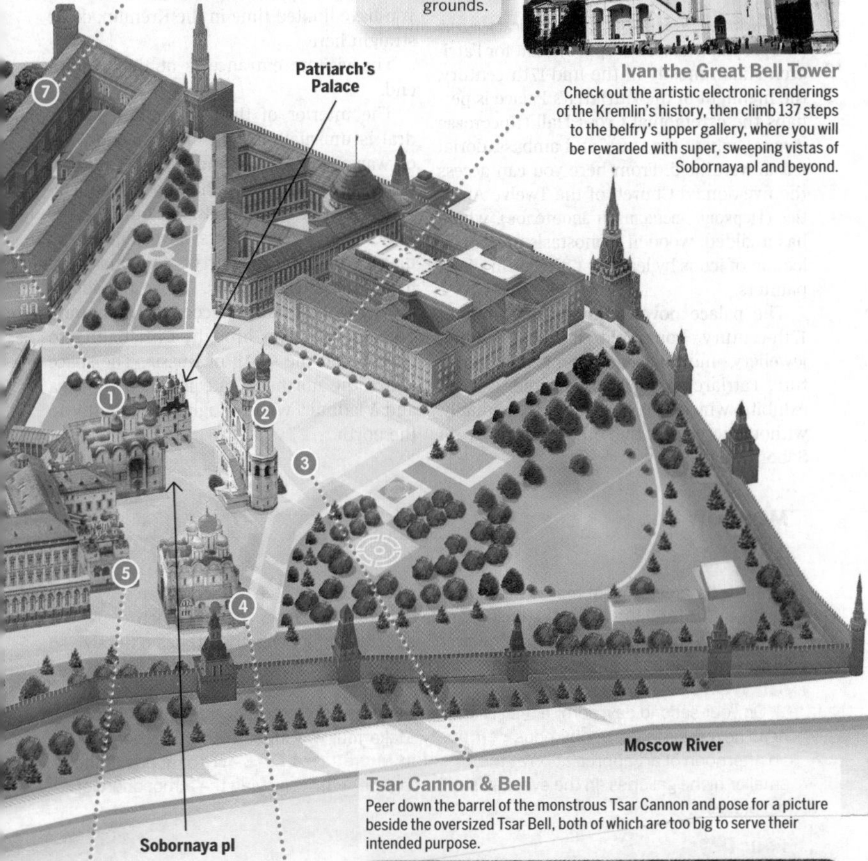

Tsar Cannon & Bell

Peer down the barrel of the monstrous Tsar Cannon and pose for a picture beside the oversized Tsar Bell, both of which are too big to serve their intended purpose.

KEN SCICLUNA / GETTY IMAGES ©

Annunciation Cathedral

Admire the artistic mastery of Russia's greatest icon painters – Theophanes the Greek and Andrei Rublyov – who are responsible for many of the icons in the deesis and festival rows of the iconostasis.

Archangel Cathedral

See the final resting place of princes and emperors who ruled Russia for more than 300 years, including the visionary Ivan the Great, the tortured Ivan theTerrible and the tragic Tsarevitch Dmitry.

Senate NOTABLE BUILDING

(Сенат; Map p70) The offices of the president of Russia, the ultimate seat of power in the modern Kremlin, are in the yellow, triangular former Senate building, a fine 18th-century neoclassical edifice, east of the Arsenal. Built in 1785 by architect Matvei Kazakov, it was noted for its huge cupola. In the 16th and 17th centuries this area was where the boyars lived. Next to the Senate is the 1930s Supreme Soviet building.

Patriarch's Palace HISTORICAL BUILDING

(Патриарший дворец; Map p70) Built for Patriarch Nikon mostly in the mid-17th century, the highlight of the Patriarch's Palace is perhaps the ceremonial Cross Hall (Крестовая палата), where the tsars' and ambassadorial feasts were held. From here you can access the five-domed Church of the Twelve Apostles (Церковь двенадцати апостолов), which has a gilded, wooden iconostasis and a collection of icons by leading 17th-century icon painters.

The palace now contains an exhibit of 17th-century household items, including jewellery, hunting equipment and furniture. Patriarch's Palace often holds special exhibits, which can be visited individually, without access to the other buildings on Sobornaya pl.

Assumption Cathedral CHURCH

(Успенский собор; Map p70) On the northern side of Sobornaya pl, with five golden helmet domes and four semicircular gables facing the square, the Assumption Cathedral is the focal church of prerevolutionary Russia and the burial place of most of the heads of the Russian Orthodox Church from the 1320s to 1700. A striking 1660s fresco of the Virgin Mary faces Sobornaya pl, above the door once used for royal processions. If you have limited time in the Kremlin, come straight here.

The visitors entrance is at the western end.

The interior of the Assumption Cathedral is unusually bright and spacious, full of warm golds, reds and blues. The west wall features a scene of the Apocalypse, a favourite theme of the Russian Church in the Middle Ages. The pillars have pictures of martyrs on them, as martyrs are considered to be the pillars of faith. Above the southern gates there are frescoes of Yelena and Constantine, who brought Christianity to Greece and the south of Russia. The space above the northern gate is taken by Olga and Vladimir, who brought Christianity to the north.

MOSCOW IN...

Two Days

Spend a day seeing what makes Moscow famous: **St Basil's Cathedral**, **Lenin's Mausoleum** and the **Kremlin** (including the bling in the **Armoury**). After lunch, stroll through **Kitay Gorod** discovering the countless 17th-century churches. Dine on trendy ul Petrovka, perhaps at **Lavka-Lavka**, then take in a show at the world-famous **Bolshoi Theatre**.

On your second day, admire the art and architecture at **Novodevichy Convent**, then head next door to the eponymous **cemetery**. Make your way into the Arbat district for an afternoon of art appreciation at the **Pushkin Museum of Fine Arts** or at one of the smaller niche galleries. In the evening, stroll along the **Arbat** enjoying the atmosphere of old Moscow.

Four Days

On your third day, get an early start to beat the crowds to the **Tretyakov Gallery**. Take your time inspecting the icons, examining the Peredvizhniki and marvelling at the Russian Revival. Grab a post-museum lunch in **Red October**, then stroll along Krymskaya naberezhnaya, where you can frolic in fountains and explore the outdoor art gallery at **Art Muzeon**. Then head across the street to **Gorky Park** for bicycle riding or boat paddling. Stay into the evening for drinking and dancing under the stars.

Reserve the morning on your last day for shopping at the **Izmaylovsky Market** crammed with souvenir stalls. On your way back to the centre, make a stop at **Flakon** or **Winzavod** and nearby **Art Play on Yauza** to see what's happening in Moscow's former industrial spaces. Indulge in a farewell feast at **Cafe Pushkin**.

Most of the existing murals on the cathedral walls were painted on a gilt base in the 1640s, with the exception of three grouped together on the south wall: The Apocalypse (*Apokalipsis*), The Life of Metropolitan Pyotr (*Zhitie Mitropolita Petra*) and All Creatures Rejoice in Thee (*O tebe raduetsya*). These are attributed to Dionysius and his followers, the cathedral's original 15th-century mural painters. The tombs of many of the leaders of the Russian Church (metropolitans up to 1590, patriarchs from 1590 to 1700) are against the north, west and south walls.

Near the south wall is a tent-roofed, wooden throne made in 1551 for Ivan the Terrible, known as the Throne of Monomakh. Its carved scenes highlight the career of 12th-century Grand Prince Vladimir Monomakh of Kyiv. Near the west wall there is a shrine with holy relics of Patriarch Hermogen, who was starved to death during the Time of Troubles in 1612.

The iconostasis dates from 1652, but its lowest level contains some older icons. The 1340s Saviour with the Angry Eye (*Spas yaroe oko*) is second from the right. On the left of the central door is the Virgin of Vladimir (*Vladimirskaya Bogomater*), an early-15th-century Rublyov school copy of Russia's most revered image, the Vladimir Icon of the Mother of God (*Vladimirskaya Ikona Bogomateri*). The 12th-century original, now in the Tretyakov Gallery, stood in the Assumption Cathedral from the 1480s to 1930. One of the oldest Russian icons, the 12th-century red-clothed St George (*Svyatoy Georgy*) from Novgorod, is positioned by the north wall.

The original icons of the lower, local tier are symbols of victory brought from Vladimir, Smolensk, Veliky Ustyug and other places. The south door was brought from the Nativity of the Virgin Cathedral in Suzdal.

Church of the Deposition of the Robe — CHURCH

(Церковь Ризположения; Map p70) This delicate single-domed church, beside the west door of the Assumption Cathedral, was built between 1484 and 1486 in exclusively Russian style. It was the private chapel of the heads of the Church, who tended to be highly suspicious of such people as Italian architects.

Ivan the Great Bell Tower — TOWER

(Колокольня Ивана Великого; Map p70) With its two golden domes rising above the eastern side of Sobornaya pl, the Ivan the Great Bell Tower is the Kremlin's tallest structure – a landmark visible from 30km away. Before the 20th century it was forbidden to build any higher in Moscow.

Its history dates back to the Church of Ioann Lestvichnik Under the Bells, built on this site in 1329 by Ivan I. In 1505 the Italian Marco Bono designed a new belfry, originally with only two octagonal tiers beneath a drum and a dome. In 1600, Boris Godunov raised it to 81m. Local legend claims this was a public-works project designed to employ the thousands of people who had come to Moscow during a famine, but historical documents contradict the story.

The building's central section, with guilded single dome and a 65-tonne bell, dates from between 1532 and 1542. The tent-roofed annexe, next to the belfry, was commissioned by Patriarch Filaret in 1642 and bears his name.

Tsar Bell — BELL

(Царь-колокол; Map p70) Beside (not inside) the Ivan the Great Bell Tower stands the world's biggest bell, a 202-tonne monster that has never rung. The bas-reliefs of Empress Anna and Tsar Alexey, as well as some icons, were etched on its sides.

Tsar Cannon — CANNON

(Царь-пушка; Map p70) North of the bell tower is the 40-tonne Tsar Cannon. It was cast in 1586 by the blacksmith Ivan Chokhov for Fyodor I, whose portrait is on the barrel. Shot has never sullied its 89cm bore and certainly not the cannonballs beside it, which are too big even for this elephantine firearm.

Archangel Cathedral — CHURCH

(Архангельский собор; Map p70) The Archangel Cathedral, at the southeastern corner of Soborny pl, was for centuries the coronation, wedding and burial church of tsars. It was built by Ivan Kalita in 1333 to commemorate the end of the great famine, and dedicated to Archangel Michael, guardian of the Moscow princes. By the early 16th century it fell into disrepair and was rebuilt between 1505 and 1508 by the Italian architect Alevisio Novi.

Like the Assumption Cathedral, it has five domes and is essentially Byzantine-Russian in style. However, the exterior has many Venetian Renaissance features, notably the distinctive scallop-shell gables and porticoes.

Moscow Metro Map

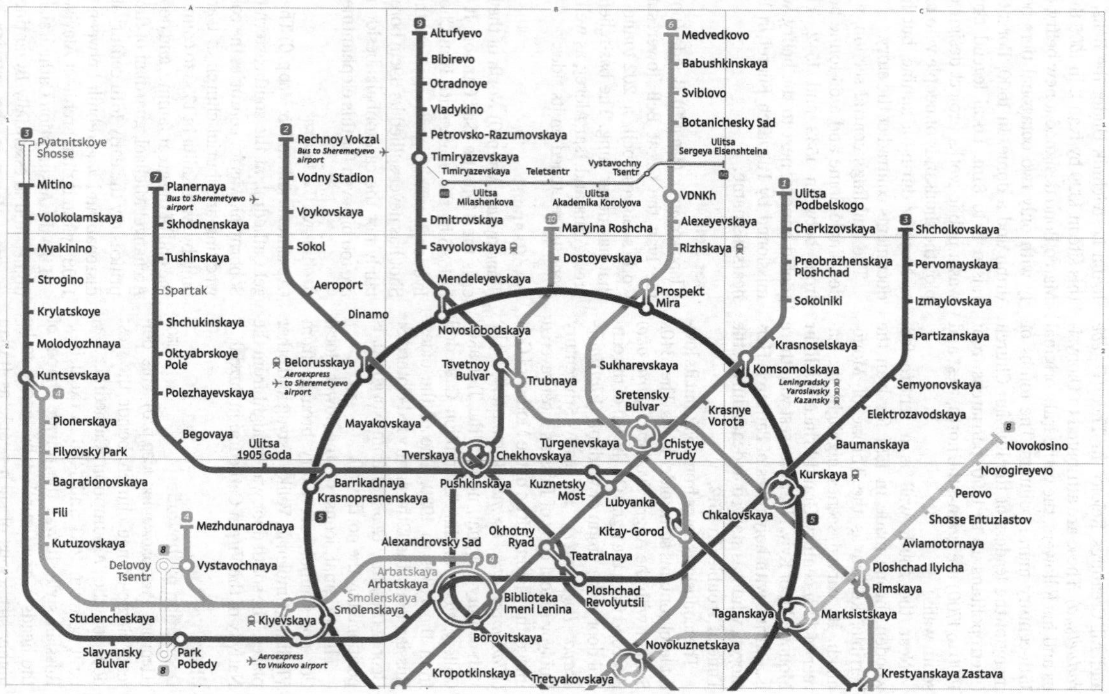

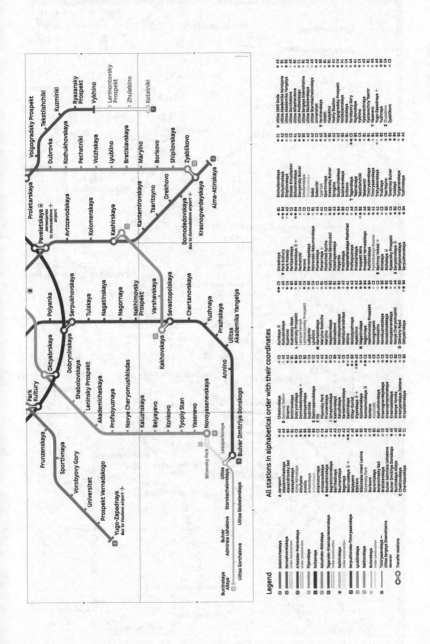

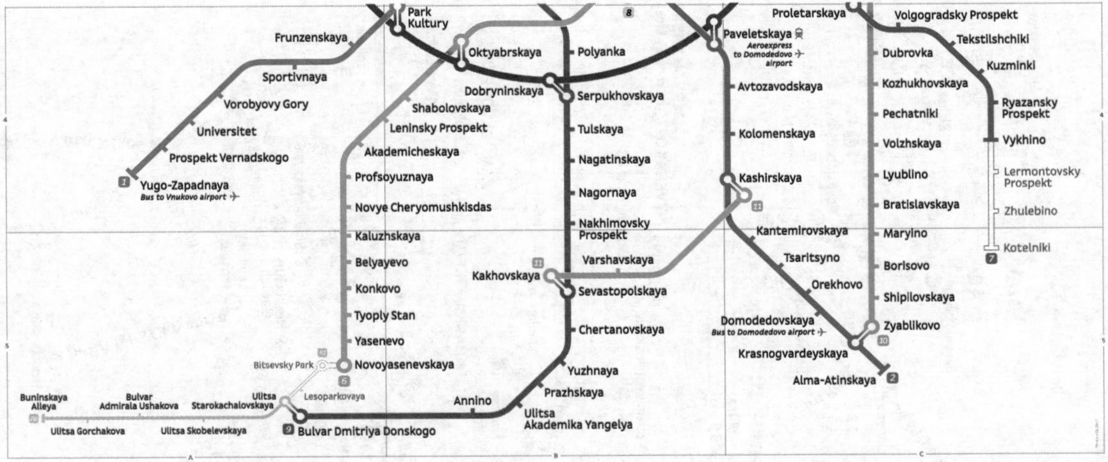

Legend

- 1 Sokolnicheskaya
- 2 Zamoskvoretskaya (Under construction)
- 3 Arbatsko-Pokrovskaya (Under construction)
- 4 Filyovskaya
- 5 Koltsevaya
- 6 Kaluzhsko-Rizhskaya
- 7 Tagansko-Krasnopresnenskaya (Under construction)
- 8 Kalininskaya (Under construction)
- 9 Serpukhovsko-Timiryazevskaya
- 10 Lyublinskaya
- 11 Kakhovskaya
- 12 Butovskaya (Under construction)
- 13 Timiryazevskaya — Ulitsa Sergeya Eisenshteina (Monorail)
- Transfer stations

All stations in alphabetical order with their coordinates

A	Aeroport	A2
	Akademicheskaya	A4
	Alexandrovsky Sad	B3
	Alexeyevskaya	B1
	Alma-Atinskaya	C5
	Altufyevo	B1
	Annino	B5
	Arbatskaya	B3
	Arbatskaya	B3
	Aviamotornaya	C3
	Avtozavodskaya	C4
B	Babushkinskaya	B1
	Bagrationovskaya	A3
	Barrikadnaya	A3
	Baumanskaya	C2
	Begovaya	A2
	Belorusskaya	A2
	Belyayevo	A5
	Bibirevo	B1
	Biblioteka imeni Lenina	B3
	Bitsevsky Park	A5
	Borisovo	C5
	Borovitskaya	B3
	Botanichesky Sad	B1
	Bratislavskaya	C5
	Bulvar Admirala Ushakova	A5
	Bulvar Dmitriya Donskogo	A5
	Buninskaya Alleya	A5
C	Chekhovskaya	B2
	Cherkizovskaya	C1
	Chkalovskaya	C3
D	Delovoy Tsentr	A3
	Dinamo	A2
	Dmitrovskaya	B1
	Dobryninskaya	B4
	Domodedovskaya	C5
	Dostoyevskaya	B2
	Dubrovka	C4
E	Elektrozavodskaya	C2
F	Fili	A3
	Filyovsky Park	A2
	Frunzenskaya	A4
I	Izmaylovskaya	C2
K	Kakhovskaya	B5
	Kaluzhskaya	A5
	Kantemirovskaya	C5
	Kashirskaya	C4
	Kitay-Gorod	B3
	Kiyevskaya	A3
	Kolomenskaya	C4
	Komsomolskaya	C2
	Konkovo	A5
	Kotelniki	C5
	Kozhukhovskaya	C4
	Krasnogvardeyskaya	C5
	Krasnopresnenskaya	A3
	Krasnoselskaya	C2
	Krasnye Vorota	B2
	Krestyanskaya Zastava	C3
	Kropotkinskaya	B3
	Kurskaya	C3
	Kutuzovskaya	A3
	Kuzminki	C4
	Kuznetsky Most	B3
L	Leninsky Prospekt	B4
	Lesoparkovaya	A5
	Lermontovsky Prospekt	C4
	Lubyanka	B3
	Lyublino	C4
M	Marksistskaya	C3
	Maryina Roshcha	B1
	Maryino	C5
	Mayakovskaya	B2
	Medvedkovo	B1
	Mendeleyevskaya	B2
	Mezhdunarodnaya	A3
	Mitino	A1
	Molodyozhnaya	A2
	Myakinino	A2
N	Nagatinskaya	B4
	Nagornaya	B4
	Nakhimovsky Prospekt	B4
	Novogireyevo	C3
	Novokosino	C2
	Novokuznetskaya	B3
	Novoslobodskaya	B2
	Novoyasenevskaya	A5
	Novye Cheryomushki	A4
O	Okhotny Ryad	B3
	Oktyabrskaya	B4
	Otradnoye	B1
P	Park Kultury	B4
	Park Pobedy	A3
	Partizanskaya	C2
	Paveletskaya	B4
	Pechatniki	C4
	Perovo	C3
	Pervomayskaya	C2
	Petrovsko-Razumovskaya	B1
	Pionerskaya	A2
	Planernaya	A1
	Ploshchad Ilyicha	C3
	Ploshchad Revolyutsii	B3
	Polezhayevskaya	A2
	Polyanka	B4
	Prazhskaya	B5
	Preobrazhenskaya Ploshchad	C2
	Profsoyuznaya	A4
	Proletarskaya	C4
	Prospekt Mira	B2
	Prospekt Vernadskogo	A4
	Pushkinskaya	B3
	Pyatnitskoye Shosse	A1
R	Rechnoy Vokzal	A1
	Rimskaya	C3
	Rizhskaya	B2
	Ryazansky Prospekt	C4
S	Savyolovskaya	B2
	Semyonovskaya	C2
	Serpukhovskaya	B4
	Shcholkovskaya	C1
	Shchukinskaya	A2
	Shipilovskaya	C5
	Shosse Entuziastov	C3
	Skhodnenskaya	A1
	Slavyansky Bulvar	A3
	Smolenskaya	B3
	Smolenskaya	A3
	Sokol	A2
	Sokolniki	C2
	Spartak	A2
	Sportivnaya	A4
	Sretensky Bulvar	B2
	Strogino	A2
	Studencheskaya	A3
	Sukharevskaya	B2
	Sviblovo	B1
T	Taganskaya	C3
	Teatralnaya	B3
	Tekstilshchiki	C4
	Teletsentr	B1
	Timiryazevskaya	B1
	Timiryazevskaya	B1
	Tretyakovskaya	B3
	Trubnaya	B2
	Tsaritsyno	C5
	Tsvetnoy Bulvar	B2
	Tulskaya	B4
	Turgenevskaya	B2
	Tushinskaya	A2
U	Ulitsa 1905 Goda	A3
	Ulitsa Akademika Korolyova	B1
	Ulitsa Akademika Yangelya	B5
	Ulitsa Gorchakova	A5
	Ulitsa Milashenkova	B1
	Ulitsa Podbelskogo	C1
	Ulitsa Sergeya Eisenshteina	B1
	Ulitsa Skobelevskaya	A5
	Ulitsa Starokachalovskaya	A5
	Universitet	A4
V	Varshavskaya	B5
	VDNKh	B1
	Vladykino	B1
	Vodny Stadion	A1
	Volgogradsky Prospekt	C4
	Volokolamskaya	A1
	Volzhskaya	C4
	Vorobyovy Gory	A4
	Voykovskaya	A1
	Vykhino	C4
	Vystavochnaya	A3
	Vystavochny Tsentr	B1
Y	Yasenevo	A5
	Yugo-Zapadnaya	A4
	Yuzhnaya	B5
Z	Zhulebino	C4
	Zyablikovo	C5

Greater Moscow

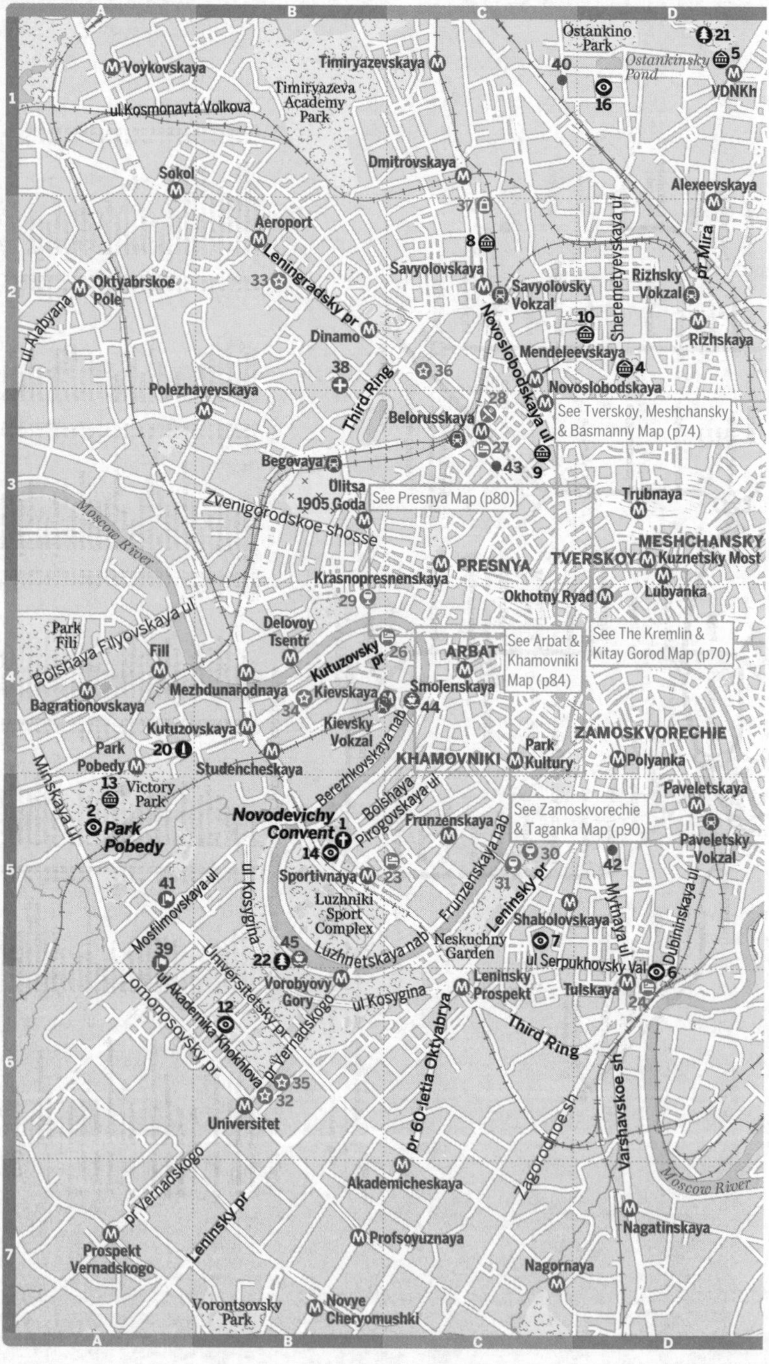

The tombs of all Muscovy's rulers from the 1320s to the 1690s are here, bar one (the absentee is Boris Godunov, whose body was taken out of the grave by the order of a False Dmitry and buried at Sergiev Posad in 1606). The bodies are buried underground, beneath the 17th-century sarcophagi and 19th-century copper covers. Tsarevich Dmitry, a son of Ivan the Terrible who died mysteriously in 1591, lies beneath a painted stone canopy.

It was Dmitry's death that sparked the appearance of a string of impersonators, known as False Dmitrys, during the Time of Troubles. Ivan's own tomb is out of sight behind the iconostasis, along with those of his other sons: Ivan (whom he killed), and Fyodor (who succeeded him). From Peter the Great onwards, emperors and empresses were buried in St Petersburg; the exception was Peter II, who died in Moscow in 1730 and is here.

The 17th-century murals were uncovered during restorations in the 1950s. The south wall depicts many of those buried here; on the pillars are some of their predecessors, including Andrey Bogolyubsky, Prince Daniil and his father, Alexander Nevsky.

Annunciation Cathedral CHURCH

(Благовещенский собор; Map p70; Blagoveshchensky sobor) The Annunciation Cathedral, at the southwest corner of Sobornaya pl, contains the celebrated icons of master painter Theophanes the Greek. They have a timeless beauty that appeals even to those usually left cold by icons.

Many of the murals in the gallery date from the 1560s. Among them are the *Capture of Jericho* in the porch, *Jonah and the Whale* in the northern arm of the gallery, and the *Tree of Jesus* on its ceiling. Other murals feature ancient philosophers Aristotle, Plutarch, Plato, Socrates and others holding scrolls with their own wise words.

The small central part of the cathedral has a lovely jasper floor. The 16th-century frescoes include Russian princes on the north pillar and Byzantine emperors on the south, both with Apocalypse scenes above them. But the chapel's real treasure is the iconostasis, where restorers in the 1920s uncovered early-15th-century icons by three of the greatest medieval Russian artists.

Theophanes likely painted the six icons at the right-hand end of the deesis row, the biggest of the six tiers of the iconostasis. Andrey Rublyov is reckoned to be the artist of the

Greater Moscow

Top Sights

1	Novodevichy Convent	B5
2	Park Pobedy	A5

Sights

3	Ascension Church	E7
4	Central Museum of the Armed Forces	D2
5	Cosmonautics Museum	D1
6	Danilov Monastery	D6
7	Donskoy Monastery	C5
8	Experimentanium	C2
	Exposition of Military Equipment	(see 2)
9	Glinka Museum of Musical Culture	C3
10	Jewish Museum & Centre of Tolerance	D2
11	Kolomenskoe Museum-Reserve	E7
12	Moscow State University (MGU)	B6
13	Museum of the Great Patriotic War	A5
14	Novodevichy Cemetery	B5
15	Old Believers' Community	F4
16	Ostankino TV Tower	D1
17	Proekt_Fabrika	E3
18	Sokolniki	E2
19	Soviet Arcade Games Museum	E3
20	Triumphal Arch	A4
21	VDNKh	D1
22	Vorobyovy Gory Nature Preserve	B5

Sleeping

23	Blues Hotel	C5
24	Danilovskaya Hotel	D6
25	Elokhovsky Hotel	E3
26	Radisson Royal	C4
27	Sleepbox Hotel	C3

Eating

28	Farmer's Diner	C3

Drinking & Nightlife

29	Jagger	B4
30	Le Boule	C5
31	Lebedinoe Ozero	C5

Entertainment

32	Bolshoi Circus on Vernadskogo	B6
33	CSKA Arena	B2
34	Kuklachev Cat Theatre	B4
35	Moscow Children's Musical Theatre	B6
36	Russian Ball at Yar	C2

Shopping

37	Flakon	C2

Information

38	Botkin Hospital	B2
39	Chinese Embassy	A5
40	Expert Collegium	C1
41	German Embassy	A5

Transport

42	Avis	D5
	Europcar	(see 42)
43	Hertz	C3
44	Kievsky Vokzal Landing	C4
45	Vorobyovy Gory Landing	B5

most of the paintings at the left end of the festival row (above the deesis row), while the seven at the right-hand end are attributed to Prokhor of Gorodets.

The basement – which remains from the previous 14th-century cathedral on this site – contains a fascinating exhibit on the archaeology of the Kremlin. The artefacts date from the 12th to 14th centuries, showing the growth of Moscow during this period.

Terem Palace NOTABLE BUILDING

(Теремной дворец; Map p70) The 16th- and 17th-century Terem Palace is the most splendid of the Kremlin palaces. Made of stone and built by Vasily III, the palace's living quarters include a dining room, living room, study, bedroom and small chapel. Unfortunately, the palace is closed to the public, but you can glimpse its cluster of 11 golden domes and chequered roof behind and above the Church of the Deposition of the Robe.

Great Kremlin Palace HISTORICAL BUILDING

(Большой Кремлёвский дворец; Map p70) Between the Armoury and the Annunciation Cathedral stretches the 700-room Great Kremlin Palace, built as an imperial residence between 1838 and 1849. Now it is an official residence of the Russian president and is used for state visits and receptions. Apart from the Armoury, it's not open to the public.

★ Armoury MUSEUM

(Оружейная палата; Map p70; adult/student ₽700/250; 10am, noon, 2.30pm & 4.30pm; M Aleksandrovsky Sad) The Armoury dates back to 1511, when it was founded under Vasily III to manufacture and store weapons, imperial arms and regalia for the royal court. Later it also produced jewellery, icon frames and embroidery. To this day, the Armoury still contains plenty of treasures for ogling, and remains a highlight of any visit to the Kremlin. If possible, buy your

A TOUR OF THE ARMOURY

Your tour of the Armoury starts upstairs, where the first two rooms house gold and silver objects from the 12th to the 17th centuries, many of which were crafted in the Kremlin workshops. In Room 2, you'll find the renowned **Easter eggs** made by St Petersburg jeweller Fabergé. The tsar and tsarina traditionally exchanged these gifts each year at Easter. Most famous is the Grand Siberian Railway egg, with gold train, platinum locomotive and ruby headlamp, created to commemorate the Moscow–Vladivostok line.

The following rooms display armour, weapons and more armour and more weapons. Don't miss the **helmet of Prince Yaroslav**, the **chainmail of Boris Godunov** and the **sabres of Minin and Pozharsky.**

Downstairs in Room 6, you can see the **coronation dresses** of 18th-century empresses (Empress Elizabeth, we're told, had 15,000 other dresses). Other 'secular' dresses are also on display, including an impressive pair of boots that belonged to Peter the Great. The following room contains the **joint coronation throne** of boy tsars Peter the Great and his half-brother Ivan V (with a secret compartment from which Regent Sofia prompted them), as well as the **800-diamond throne of Tsar Alexey**, Peter's father. The gold **Cap of Monomakh**, jewel-studded and sable-trimmed, was used for two centuries at coronations.

End your tour in Room 9, which houses centuries of **royal carriages and sledges**. Look for the sleigh in which Elizabeth rode from St Petersburg to Moscow for her coronation, pulled by 23 horses at a time – about 800 in all for the trip.

time-specific ticket to the Armoury when you buy your ticket to the Kremlin.

Diamond Fund Exhibition MUSEUM

(Алмазный фонд России; Map p70; www.almazi.net; admission ₽500; ⏲10am-1pm, 2-5pm Fri-Wed) If the Armoury hasn't sated your lust for diamonds, there are more in the Diamond Fund Exhibition. The fund dates back to 1719, when Peter the Great established the Russian Crown treasury. These gemstones and jewellery were garnered by tsars and empresses, including the 190-carat diamond given to Catherine the Great by her lover Grigory Orlov. The Great Imperial Crown, encrusted with 4936 diamonds, was the coronation crown of Catherine the Great and successive rulers.

Security is super tight and you are not allowed to bring cameras, phones or bags of any sort.

Alexander Garden GARDEN

(Александровский сад; Map p70; Ⓜ Aleksandrovsky Sad) The first public park in Moscow, Alexander Garden sits along the Kremlin's western wall. Colourful flower beds and impressive Kremlin views make it a favourite strolling spot for Muscovites and tourists alike. Back in the 17th century, the Neglinnaya River ran through the present gardens, with dams and mills along its banks. When the river was diverted underground, the garden was founded by architect Osip Bove, in 1821.

RED SQUARE

Setting foot on Red Square (Krasnaya Ploshchad) for the first time is guaranteed to induce awe. The vast rectangular stretch of cobblestones, surrounded by architectural marvels, is jaw-dropping, gasp-inducing gorgeous. In old Russian '*krasny*' meant 'beautiful', and Krasnaya Pl lives up to its name. Further, it evokes an incredible sense of import to stroll across the place where so much of Russian history has unfolded.

★ St Basil's Cathedral CHURCH

(Покровский собор, Храм Василия Блаженного; Map p70; www.saintbasil.ru; adult/student ₽250/50, audioguide ₽200; ⏲11am-5pm; Ⓜ Ploshchad Revolyutsii) At the southern end of Red Square stands the icon of Russia: St Basil's Cathedral. This crazy confusion of colours, patterns and shapes is the culmination of a style that is unique to Russian architecture. In 1552 Ivan the Terrible captured the Tatar stronghold of Kazan on the Feast of Intercession. He commissioned this landmark church, officially the Intercession Cathedral, to commemorate the victory. Created from 1555 to 1561, this masterpiece would become the ultimate symbol of Russia.

The cathedral's apparent anarchy of shapes hides a comprehensible plan of nine main chapels. The tall, tent-roofed tower in the centre houses the namesake Church of the Protecting Veil of the Mother of God. The four biggest domes top four octagonal-towered chapels: the Church of

DON'T MISS

TOMB OF THE UNKNOWN SOLDIER

At the north end of Alexander Garden, the **Tomb of the Unknown Soldier** (Могила неизвестного солдата; Map p70) is a kind of national pilgrimage spot, where newlyweds bring flowers and have their pictures taken. The inscription reads: 'Your name is unknown, your deeds immortal.' There's an eternal flame, and other inscriptions listing the Soviet hero cities of WWII – those that withstood the heaviest fighting – and honouring 'those who fell for the motherland' between 1941 and 1945. Every hour on the hour, the guards of the Tomb of the Unknown Soldier perform a perfectly synchronized ceremony to change the guards on duty.

Sts Cyprian & Justina, Church of the Holy Trinity, Church of the Icon of St Nicholas the Miracle Worker, and the Church of the Entry of the Lord into Jerusalem. Finally, there are four smaller chapels in between. Each chapel was consecrated in honour of an event or battle in the struggle against Kazan.

Legend has it that Ivan had the architects blinded so that they could never build anything comparable. This is a myth, however, as records show that they were employed a quarter of a century later (and four years after Ivan's death) to add an additional chapel to the structure.

★Lenin's Mausoleum MEMORIAL

(Мавзолей Ленина; Map p70; www.lenin.ru; 10am-1pm Tue-Thu, Sat & Sun; M Ploshchad Revolyutsii) FREE Although Vladimir Ilych requested that he be buried beside his mum in St Petersburg, he still lies in state at the foot of the Kremlin wall, receiving visitors who come to pay their respects. Line up at the western corner of the square (near the entrance to Alexander Garden) to see the embalmed leader, who has been here since 1924. Note that photography is not allowed; and stern guards ensure that all visitors remain respectful and silent.

After trooping past the embalmed figure, emerge from the mausoleum and inspect the Kremlin wall, where other communist heavy hitters are buried:

➡ Josef Stalin

The second general secretary, successor to Lenin.

➡ Leonid Brezhnev

The fourth general secretary, successor to Khrushchev.

➡ Felix Dzerzhinsky

The founder of the Cheka (forerunner of the KGB).

➡ Yakov Sverdlov

A key organiser of the revolution and the first official head of the Soviet state.

➡ Andrei Zhdanov

Stalin's cultural chief and the second most powerful person in the USSR immediately after WWII.

➡ Mikhail Frunze

The Red Army leader who secured Central Asia for the Soviet Union in the 1920s.

➡ Inessa Armand

Lenin's rumoured lover. She was a respected Bolshevik who was the director of Zhenotdel, an organisation fighting for equality for women within the Communist Party.

➡ John Reed

The American author of *Ten Days that Shook the World,* a first-hand account of the October 1917 Revolution.

Saviour Gate Tower TOWER

(Спасская башня; Map p70) The Kremlin's 'official' exit onto Red Square is the stately red-brick Saviour Gate Tower. This gate – considered sacred – has been used for processions since tsarist times. The two white-stone plaques above the gate commemorate the tower's construction in 1491. The current clock was installed in the gate tower in the 1850s. Hauling 3m-long hands and weighing 25 tonnes, the clock takes up three of the tower's 10 levels. Its melodic chime sounds every 15 minutes across Red Square.

State History Museum MUSEUM

(Государственный исторический музей; Map p70; www.shm.ru; Krasnaya pl 1; adult/student ₽300/100, audioguide ₽300; 10am-6pm Wed & Fri-Mon, 11am-9pm Thu; M Okhotny Ryad) At the northern end of Red Square, the State History Museum has an enormous collection covering the whole Russian Empire from the time of the Stone Age. The building, dating from the late 19th century, is itself an attraction – each room is in the style of a different period or region, some with highly decorated walls echoing old Russian churches.

The exhibits about medieval Rus are excellent, with several rooms covering the Mongol invasions and the consolidation of the Russian state. The 2nd floor is dedicated to the Imperial period, with exhibits featuring personal items of the royals, furnishings and decoration from the palace interiors and various artworks and documents from the era. Specific rooms are dedicated to the rule of various tsars. An unexpected highlight is an exhibit addressing the expansion of the Russian Empire by examining the growing network of roads and how people travelled.

Resurrection Gate GATE

(Map p70) At the northwestern corner, Resurrection Gate provides a great vantage point for your first glimpse of Red Square. With its twin red towers topped by green tent spires, the original 1680 gateway was destroyed because Stalin thought it an impediment to the parades and demonstrations held in Red Square. This exact replica was built in 1995. Just outside the gateway is the bright Chapel of the Iverian Virgin, originally built in the late 18th century to house the icon of the same name.

Kazan Cathedral CHURCH

(Казанский собор; Map p70; Nikolskaya ul 3; 8am-7pm; M Okhotny Ryad) FREE The original Kazan Cathedral was founded on this site at the northern end of Red Square in 1636, in thanks for the 1612 expulsion of Polish invaders (for two centuries it housed the Virgin of Kazan icon, which supposedly helped to rout the Poles). Three hundred years later, the cathedral was completely demolished, allegedly because it impeded the flow of celebrating workers during holiday parades. The little church that occupies the site today is a 1993 replica.

War of 1812 Museum MUSEUM

(Музей отечественной войны 1812 года; Map p70; www.1812shm.ru; pl Revolyutsii 2; adult/child ₽300/100; 10am-6pm Wed & Fri-Mon, 11am-9pm Thu; M Ploshchad Revolyutsii) Part Russian Revival, part neo-Renaissance, this red-brick beauty was built in the 1890s as the Moscow City Hall and later served as the Central Lenin Museum. It was converted into the War of 1812 Museum in honor of the war's 200-year anniversary. Artwork, documents, weapons and uniforms are all on display, offering a detailed depiction of the events and effects of the war.

LENIN UNDER GLASS

Red Square is home to the world's most famous mummy, that of Vladimir Lenin. When he died of a massive stroke (on 22 January 1924, aged 53), a long line of mourners patiently gathered in winter's harshness for weeks to glimpse the body as it lay in state. Inspired by the spectacle, Stalin proposed that the father of Soviet communism should continue to serve the cause as a holy relic. So the decision was made to preserve Lenin's corpse for perpetuity, against the vehement protests of his widow, as well as his own expressed desire to be buried next to his mother in St Petersburg.

Boris Zbarsky, a biochemist, and Vladimir Vorobyov, an anatomist, were issued a political order to put a stop to the natural decomposition of the body. The pair worked frantically in a secret laboratory in search of a long-term chemical solution. In the meantime, the body's dark spots were bleached, and the lips and eyes sewn tight. The brain was removed and taken to another secret laboratory, to be sliced and diced by scientists for the next 40 years in the hope of uncovering its hidden genius.

In July 1924 the scientists hit upon a formula to successfully arrest the decaying process, a closely guarded state secret. This necrotic craft was passed on to Zbarsky's son, who ran the Kremlin's covert embalming lab for decades. After the fall of communism, Zbarsky came clean: the body is wiped down every few days, and then, every 18 months, thoroughly examined and submerged in a tub of chemicals, including paraffin wax. The institute has now gone commercial, offering its services and secrets to wannabe immortals for a mere million dollars.

Every so often, politicians express intentions to heed Lenin's request and bury him in St Petersburg, but it usually sets off a furore from the political left as well as more muted objections from Moscow tour operators. It seems that the mausoleum, the most sacred shrine of Soviet communism, and the mummy, the literal embodiment of the Russian revolution, will remain in place for at least several more years.

The Kremlin & Kitay Gorod

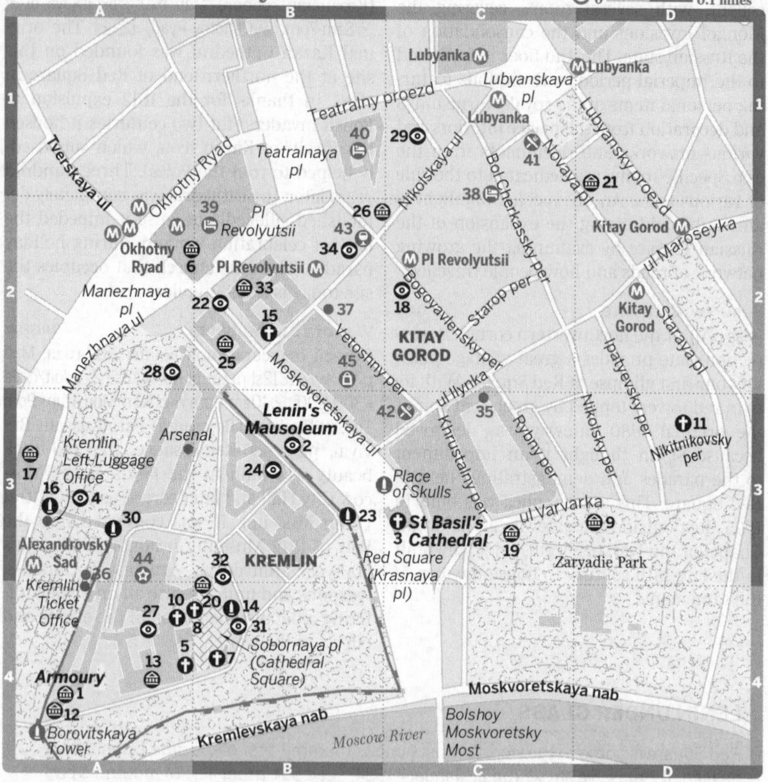

Archaeological Museum MUSEUM
(Музей археологии Москвы; Map p70; www.mosmuseum.ru; Manezhnaya pl 1; M Okhotny Ryad) An excavation of Voskresensky Bridge (which used to span the Neglinnaya River at the foot of Tverskaya ul) uncovered coins, clothing and other artefacts from old Moscow. The museum displaying these treasures is situated in a 7m-deep underground pavilion that was formed during the excavation itself. The entrance is at the base of the Four Seasons Hotel Moskva. It was closed for renovation at the time of writing.

Manege Exhibition Centre ART GALLERY
(Выставочный центр Манеж; Map p70; www.moscowmanege.ru; Manezhnaya pl; exhibits ₽200-300; 11am-8pm Tue-Sun; M Biblioteka Imeni Lenina) The long, low neoclassical building west of Alexander Garden is Moscow Manege, a vast space that is used for art exhibits and other events. The recent 'Golden Age of Russian Avant-Garde' exhibit attracted the attention of art connoisseurs, but it also hosts wide-ranging events such as poetry readings, film screenings and literary festivals.

Kitay Gorod

The narrow old streets east of Red Square are known as Kitay Gorod. It translates as 'Chinatown', but the name actually derives from *kita,* meaning 'wattle', and refers to the palisades that reinforced the earthen ramp erected around this early Kremlin suburb. Kitay Gorod is one of the oldest parts of Moscow, settled in the 13th century as a trade and financial centre.

From the 16th century Kitay Gorod was exclusively the home of merchants and craftsmen, as evidenced by the present-day names of its lanes: Khrustalny (Crystal), Rybny (Fish) and Vetoshny (Rugs). **Ulitsa Varvarka** has Kitay Gorod's greatest concentration of interesting buildings. They were long dwarfed by the gargantuan Hotel Rossi-

The Kremlin & Kitay Gorod

ya, which was finally demolished in 2006, soon to be replaced by **Zaryadie Park**, showing off Russia's four different climate zones.

Tretyakovsky Proezd HISTORICAL SITE

(Третьяковский проезд; Map p70; Ⓜ Teatralnaya) The gated walkway of Tretyakovsky proezd (originally built in the 1870s) leads from Teatralny proezd into Kitay Gorod. Nearby, you can see where archaeologists uncovered the 16th-century fortified wall that used to surround Kitay Gorod, as well as the foundations of the 1493 Trinity Church. There is also a statue of Ivan Fyodorov, the 16th-century printer responsible for Russia's first book.

Synod Printing House HISTORICAL BUILDING

(Печатный двор Синод; Map p70; Nikolskaya ul 15; Ⓜ Ploshchad Revolyutsii) Now housing the Russian State University for the Humanities, this elaborately decorated edifice is where Ivan Fyodorov reputedly produced Russia's first printed book, *The Apostle*, in 1563. (You can see the man himself near Tretyakovsky proezd.) Spiraling Solomonic columns and Gothic windows frame the lion and unicorn, who are facing off in the centre of the facade.

Zaikonospassky Monastery MONASTERY

(Заиконоспасский монастырь; Map p70; Nikolskaya ul 7-9; Ⓜ Ploshchad Revolyutsii) This monastery was founded by Boris Godunov in 1600, although the church was built in 1660. The name means 'Behind the Icon Stall', a reference to the busy icon trade that once took place here. After being closed for more than 90 years, the monastery has recently reopened. The now-functioning, multitiered **Saviour Church** is tucked into the courtyard away from the street.

Monastery of the Epiphany MONASTERY

(Богоявленский монастырь; Map p70; Bogoyavlensky per 2; Ⓜ Ploshchad Revolyutsii) This monastery is the second oldest in Moscow, founded in 1296 by Prince Daniil, son of Alexander Nevsky. The current **Epiphany Cathedral** – with its tall, pink, gold-domed cupola – was constructed in the 1690s in the Moscow-baroque style. If you're lucky, you may hear the bells ringing forth from the old wooden belfry nearby.

Chambers of the Romanov Boyars MUSEUM

(Палаты бояр Романовых; Map p70; www.shm.ru; ul Varvarka 10; admission ₽200; ⏲10am-5pm Thu-Mon, 11am-6pm Wed; Ⓜ Kitay-Gorod) This small but interesting museum is devoted to the lives of the Romanov family, who were mere boyars before they became tsars. The house was built by Nikita Romanov, whose grandson Mikhail later became the first tsar of the 300-year Romanov dynasty. Exhibits show the house as it might have been when the Romanovs lived here in the 16th century. Enter from the rear of the building.

Church of the Trinity in Nikitniki CHURCH

(Церковь Троицы в Никитниках; Map p70; Ipatyevsky per; Ⓜ Kitay-Gorod) This little gem of a church, built in the 1630s, is an exquisite example of Russian baroque. Its onion domes and tiers of red and white spade gables rise from a square tower. Its interior is covered with 1650s gospel frescoes by Simon Ushakov and others. A carved doorway leads into St Nikita the Martyr's Chapel, above the vault of the Nikitnikov merchant family, who were among the patrons who financed the construction of the church.

Old English Court MUSEUM

(Палаты старого Английского двора; Map p70; www.mosmuseum.ru; ul Varvarka 4a; Ⓜ Kitay-Gorod) This reconstructed 16th-century house, white with wooden roofs, was the residence of England's first emissaries to Russia (sent by Elizabeth I to Ivan the Terrible). It also served as the base for English merchants, who were allowed to trade duty free in exchange for providing military supplies to Ivan. Today, it houses a small exhibit dedicated to this early international exchange. It was closed for renovations at the time of writing.

Polytechnical Museum MUSEUM

(Политехнический музей; Map p70; www.polymus.ru; Novaya pl 3/4; Ⓜ Lubyanka) Occupying the entire block of Novaya pl, this giant museum showcases the history of Russian science, technology and industry. Indeed, it has claimed to be the largest science museum in the world. The museum is closed for a long overdue renovation and update, promising a 'fundamentally new museum and education centre' by 2018. In the meantime, a temporary exhibit has been set up at the VDNKh (All Russia Exhibition Centre, p78).

Tverskoy District

The streets around Tverskaya ul comprise the vibrant Tverskoy district, characterised by old architecture and new commerce. Aside from being a cultural centre (home to 20-plus theatres and concert halls, including the world-famous Bolshoi Theatre), Tverskoy is also the city's liveliest commercial district, its streets lined with restaurants, shops and other venues.

MOSCOW'S WHITE-HOT CONTEMPORARY-ART SCENE

The Garage Museum of Contemporary Art (p92) isn't the only place to take the pulse of Moscow's vibrant contemporary-art scene.

➡ The red-brick buildings of former chocolate factory Red October (p89) now host a handful of galleries, as well as the centrepiece **Strelka Institute for Media, Architecture and Design** (www.strelkainstitute.ru).

➡ Former wine factory Winzavod (p78) has morphed into a postindustrial complex of prestigious galleries, shops, a cinema and a trendy cafe.

➡ The still-functioning paper factory **Proekt_Fabrika** (Map p64; www.proektfabrika.ru; 18 Perevedenovsky per; ⏲10am-8pm Tue-Sun; Ⓜ Baumanskaya) FREE is the location for nonprofit gallery and performance spaces enlivened by arty graffiti and creative-industry offices.

➡ The 'design centre' **Art Play on Yauza** (Map p74; ☎495-620 0882; www.artplay.ru; Nizhny Syromyatnichesky per 10; ⏲ noon-8pm Tue-Sun; Ⓜ Chkalovskaya) FREE is home to firms specialising in urban planning and architectural design, as well as furniture showrooms and antique stores.

➡ Former glassworks Flakon (p115) has been turned over to artists and designers.

DON'T MISS

JEWISH MUSEUM & CENTRE OF TOLERANCE

The vast **Jewish Museum & Centre of Tolerance** (Еврейский музей и Центр терпимости; Map p64; www.jewish-museum.ru; ul Obraztsova 11, str 1a; adult/student ₽400/200; ⏲ noon-10pm Sun-Thu; Ⓜ Novoslobodskaya), filled with cutting-edge multimedia technology, tackles the uneasy subject of relations between Jews and the Russian state over centuries. The exhibition tells the stories of pogroms, Jewish revolutionaries, the Holocaust and the Soviet anti-Semitism in a calm and balanced manner. The somewhat limited collection of material exhibits is compensated by the abundance of interactive video displays. We especially like those that encourage visitors to search for answers to dilemmas faced by early-20th-century Jews – to stand up and fight, to emigrate or to assimilate and keep a low profile.

Russia's Jewish population was quite small until the 18th century, when the empire incorporated a vast chunk of Poland then inhabited by millions of Yiddish-speaking Jews. They were not allowed to move into Russia proper until the early 20th century – a policy that became known as the Pale of Settlement. This led to the perception of Jews as an ethnic, rather than religious group, which lingers up until now.

The museum occupies a heritage garage, designed by Konstantin Melnikov and purpose-built to house a fleet of Leyland double-deckers that plied Moscow streets in the 1920s.

Gulag History Museum MUSEUM
(Исторический музей ГУЛАГ; Map p74; ☎495-621 7346; www.gmig.ru; ul Petrovka 16; adult/student ₽150/20; ⏲11am-6pm Tue-Wed & Fri-Sun, noon-8pm Thu; Ⓜ Teatralnaya) Amid all the swanky shops on ul Petrovka, an archway leads to a courtyard that is strung with barbed wire and hung with portraits of political prisoners. This is the entrance to a unique museum dedicated to the Chief Administration of Corrective Labour Camps and Colonies, better known as the Gulag. Guides dressed like guards describe the vast network of labour camps that once existed in the former Soviet Union and recount the horrors of camp life.

Upper St Peter Monastery MONASTERY
(Петровский монастырь; Map p74; cnr ul Petrovka & Petrovsky bul; ⏲8am-8pm; Ⓜ Chekhovskaya) The Upper St Peter Monastery was founded in the 1380s as part of an early defensive ring around Moscow. The main, onion-domed **Virgin of Bogolyubovo Church** dates from the late 17th century. The loveliest structure is the brick Cathedral of Metropolitan Pyotr, restored with a shingle roof. (When Peter the Great ousted the Regent Sofia in 1690, his mother was so pleased she built him this church).

Moscow Museum of Modern Art MUSEUM
(Московский музей современного искусства; MMOMA; Map p74; www.mmoma.ru; ul Petrovka 25; adult/student ₽250/100; ⏲noon-8pm Tue-Wed & Fri-Sun, 1-9pm Thu; Ⓜ Chekhovskaya) A pet project of the ubiquitous Zurab Tsereteli, this museum is housed in a classical 18th-century merchant's home, originally designed by Matvei Kazakov (architect of the Kremlin Senate). It is the perfect light-filled setting for an impressive collection of 20th-century paintings, sculptures and graphics, which includes both Russian and foreign artists. The highlight is the collection of avant-garde art, with works by Chagall, Kandinsky and Malevich.

Unique to this museum is its exhibit of 'nonconformist' artists from the 1950s and '60s – those whose work was not acceptable to the Soviet regime. The gallery also hosts temporary exhibits that often feature contemporary artists. Be sure not to bypass the whimsical sculpture garden in the courtyard. There are additional MMOMA outlets, used primarily for temporary exhibits, on **Tverskoy bul** (MMOMA; Map p80; www.mmoma.ru; Tverskoy bul 9; admission ₽150; ⏲noon-8pm; Ⓜ Pushkinskaya) and **Yermolayevsky per** (MMOMA; Map p80; www.mmoma.ru; Yermolaevsky per 17; adult/student ₽200/100; ⏲noon-8pm; Ⓜ Mayakovskaya).

Hermitage Gardens PARK
(Сады Эрмитажа; Map p74; mosgorsad.ru; ul Karetny Ryad 3; ⏲24hr; Ⓜ Pushkinskaya) FREE All the things that have improved Moscow parks no end in recent years fill this small, charming garden to the brim. Today it is possibly the most happening place in

Tverskoy, Meshchansky & Basmanny

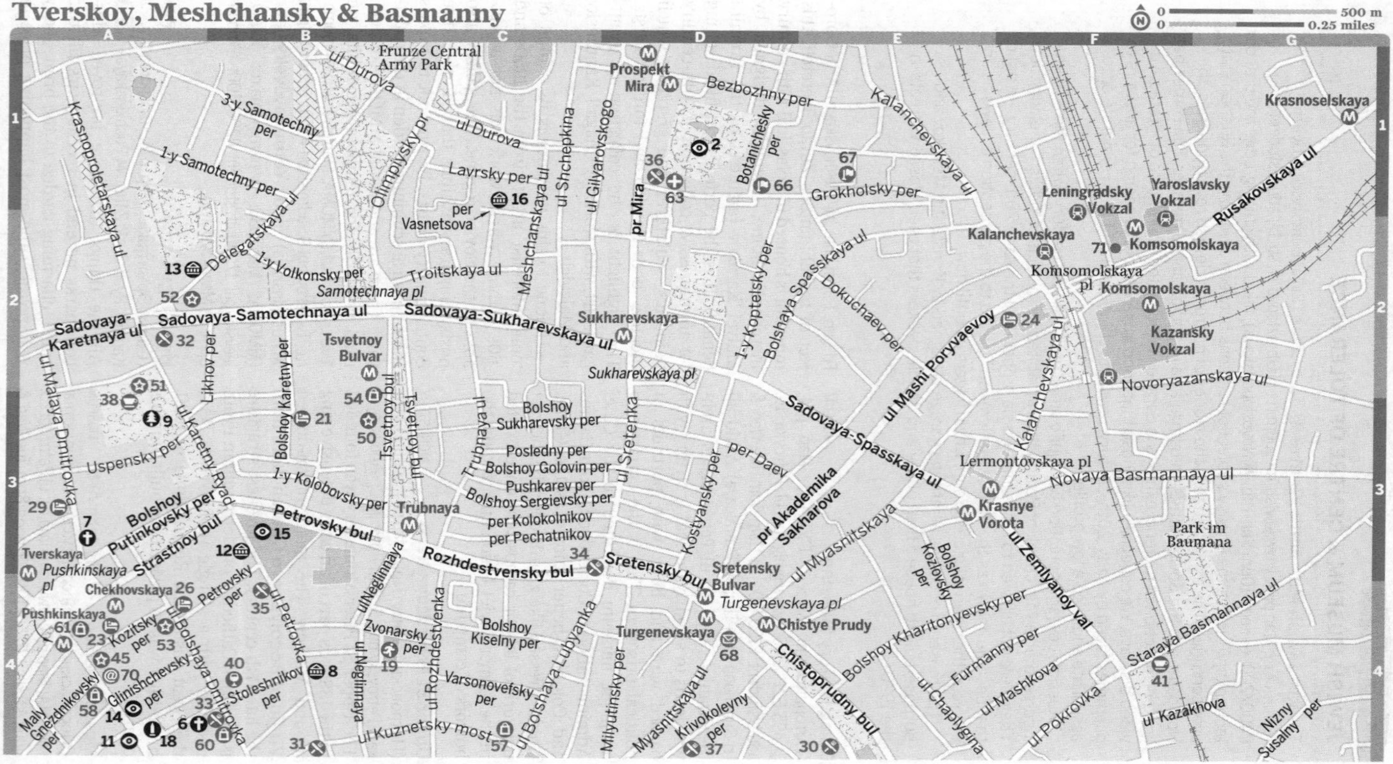
0 500 m
0 0.25 miles
A
B
C
D
E
F
G
1
2
3
4
Frunze Central Army Park
ul Durova
Prospekt Mira
Bezbozhny per
Kalanchevskaya ul
Krasnoselskaya
3-y Samotechny per
1-y Samotechny per
Krasnoproletarskaya ul
Olimpiysky pr
Lavrsky per
16
per Vasnetsova
Meshchanskaya ul
ul Shchepkina
ul Gilyarovskogo
pr Mira
2
36
63
Botanichesky per
66
67
Grokholsky per
Leningradsky Vokzal
Yaroslavsky Vokzal
Rusakovskaya ul
Kalanchevskaya
71
Komsomolskaya
Komsomolskaya pl
Delegatskaya ul
13
1-y Volkonsky per
Samotechnaya pl
Troitskaya ul
52
Sadovaya-Karetnaya ul
Sadovaya-Samotechnaya ul
Sadovaya-Sukharevskaya ul
Sukharevskaya
1-y Koptelsky per
Bolshaya Spasskaya ul
Dokuchaev per
ul Mashi Poryvaevoy
24
Kazansky Vokzal
Novoryazanskaya ul
32
Likhov per
Bolshoy Karetny per
Tsvetnoy Bulvar
54
Tsvetnoy bul
21
50
Sukharevskaya pl
Trubnaya ul
Bolshoy Sukharevsky per
Posledny per
Bolshoy Golovin per
Pushkarev per
Bolshoy Sergievsky per
per Kolokolnikov
per Pechatnikov
ul Sretenka
Kostyansky per
per Daev
Sadovaya-Spasskaya ul
Lermontovskaya pl
Novaya Basmannaya ul
Krasnye Vorota
Park im Baumana
51
38
9
ul Malaya Dmitrovka
Uspensky per
ul Karetny Ryad
1-y Kolobovsky per
Trubnaya
29
7
Bolshoy Putinkovsky per
Strastnoy bul
Petrovsky bul
15
12
Tverskaya
Pushkinskaya pl
Chekhovskaya
26
Petrovsky per
35
ul Petrovka
ulNeglinnaya
Rozhdestvensky bul
34
Sretensky bul
Sretensky Bulvar
pr Akademika Sakharova
ul Myasnitskaya
Bolshoy Kozlovsky per
ul Zemlyanoy val
Pushkinskaya
61
23
Kozitsky per
53
45
70
Glinishchevsky per
Bolshaya Dmitrovka
40
Stoleshnikov per
8
Zvonarsky per
19
ul Neglinnaya
ul Rozhdestvenka
Bolshoy Kiselny per
Varsonofevsky per
ul Bolshaya Lubyanka
Milyutinsky per
Turgenevskaya
68
Turgenevskaya pl
Chistye Prudy
Bolshoy Kharitonyevsky per
Furmanny per
Staraya Basmannaya ul
41
Maly Gnezdnikovsky per
58
14
11
18
6
33
60
31
ul Kuznetsky most
57
Myasnitskaya ul
Krivokoleyny per
37
30
Chistoprudny bul
ul Chaplygina
ul Mashkova
ul Pokrovka
ul Kazakhova
Nizny Susalny per

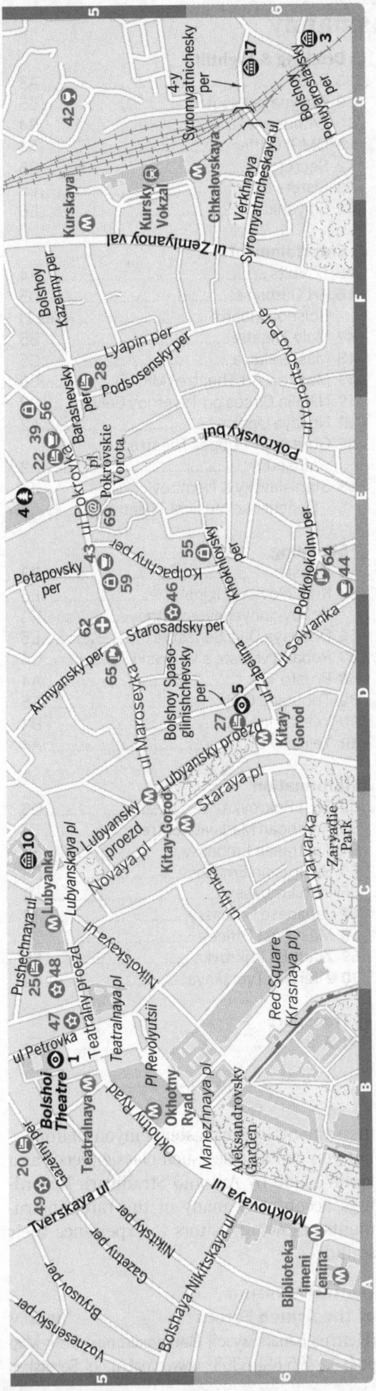

Moscow, where art, food and crafts festivals, and concerts occur almost weekly, especially in summer. Apart from welcoming lawns and benches, it boasts a large playground for children, a summer cinema and a cluster of curious food and crafts kiosks. Come here to unwind and mingle with the coolest Muscovites.

The garden was created in 1894 around a theatre that saw the screening of the Lumiere brothers' first film in 1896 and the 1898 Moscow premiere of Chekhov's *Seagull* performed by the troupe that had just been scrambled together by Stanislavsky and Nemirovich-Danchenko.

Tverskaya ploshchad HISTORICAL SITE

(Тверская площадь; Map p74) A statue of the founder of Moscow, Yury Dolgoruky, presides over this prominent square near the bottom of Tverskaya ul. So does Mayor Sergei Sobyanin, as the buffed-up five-storey building opposite is the Moscow mayor's office. Many ancient churches are hidden in the back streets, including the 17th-century Church of Sts Kosma & Damian.

Church of the Nativity of the Virgin in Putinki CHURCH

(Церковь Рождества Богородицы в Путинках; Map p74; ul Malaya Dmitrovka 4; M Pushkinskaya) When this church was completed in 1652, the Patriarch Nikon responded by banning tent roofs like the ones featured here. Apparently, he considered such architecture too Russian, too secular and too far removed from the Church's Byzantine roots. Fortunately, the Church of the Nativity has survived to grace this corner near Pushkinskaya pl.

Vasnetsov House-Museum ART MUSEUM

(Дом-музей Васнецова; Map p74; 495-681 1329; www.tretyakovgallery.ru; per Vasnetsova 13; adult/student ₽250/100; 10am-5pm Tue-Sat; M Sukharevskaya) Viktor Vasnetsov was a Russian-revivalist painter, who drew inspiration from fairy tales and village mysticism. In 1894 he designed his own house in Moscow, which is now a museum. Fronted by a colourful gate, it is a charming home in neo-Russian style filled with the original wooden furniture, a tiled stove and many of the artist's paintings. The attic studio, where he once worked, is now adorned with paintings depicting Baba Yaga and other characters from Russian fairy tales.

Tverskoy, Meshchansky & Basmanny

Top Sights
1 Bolshoi Theatre B5

Sights
2 Aptekarsky Ogorod D1
3 ArtPlay G6
4 Chistye Prudy E5
5 Choral Synagogue D6
6 Church of Sts Kosma & Damian A4
7 Church of the Nativity of the Virgin in Putinki A3
8 Gulag History Museum B4
9 Hermitage Gardens A3
10 Lubyanka Prison C5
11 Moscow Mayor's Office A4
12 Moscow Museum of Modern Art B3
13 Museum of Decorative & Folk Art A2
14 Tverskaya ploshchad A4
15 Upper St Peter Monastery B3
16 Vasnetsov House-Museum C1
17 Winzavod G6
18 Yury Dolgoruky Statue A4

Activities, Courses & Tours
19 Sanduny Baths B4

Sleeping
20 Anti-Hostel Cosmic B5
21 Godzillas Hostel B3
22 Godzillas Urban Jungle Lodge E5
23 Guest House Amelie A4
24 Hilton Moscow Leningradskaya F2
25 Hotel Savoy C5
26 iVAN Hostel A4
27 Kitay-Gorod Hotel D6
28 Privet Hostel F5
29 Pushkin Hotel A3

Eating
30 Avocado E4
31 Brasserie Most B4
32 Delicatessen A2
33 Fresh B4
34 Kitayskaya Gramota C3
35 Lavka-Lavka B4
36 Madam Galife D1
37 Odessa-Mama D4

Drinking & Nightlife
38 3205 A3
39 Chaynaya Vysota E5
40 Enthusiast B4
41 OMG! Coffee F4
42 Secret G5
43 Sisters Cafe E5
44 Solyanka E6

Entertainment
45 12 Volts A4
46 Art Garbage D5
Bolshoi Theatre (see 1)
47 Maly Theatre B5
48 Masterskaya C5
49 Moscow Art Theatre (MKhT) B5
50 Nikulin Circus on Tsvetnoy Bulvar B3
51 Novaya Opera A2
52 Obraztsov Puppet Theatre & Museum A2
53 Stanislavsky & Nemirovich-Danchenko Musical Theatre A4

Shopping
54 Depst B3
55 Khokhlovka Original E6
Ochevidnoyeneveroyatnoye (see 17)
56 Odensya Dlya Schastya E5
57 Podarki vMeste s Vorovski C4
58 Prosto Tak A4
59 Tricotage Club E5
60 Yekaterina B4
61 Yeliseev Grocery A4

Information
62 36.6 Pokrovka D5
63 American Medical Centre D1
64 Australian Embassy E6
65 Belarusian Embassy D5
66 Irish Embassy D1
67 Japanese Embassy E1
68 Main Post Office D4
69 Ziferblat Pokrovka E5
70 Ziferblat Tverskaya A4

Transport
71 Avis F2

Glinka Museum of Musical Culture MUSEUM
(Музей музыкальной культуры Глинки; Map p64; ☎495-739 6226; www.glinka.museum; ul Fadeeva 4; admission ₽200; ⊙noon-7pm Tue-Sun; Ⓜ Mayakovskaya) This musicologist's paradise boasts over 3000 instruments – handcrafted works of art – from the Caucasus and the Far East. Russia is very well represented – a 13th-century *gusli* (traditional instrument similar to a dulcimer) from Novgorod, skin drums from Yakutia, a balalaika (triangular instrument) by the master Semyon Nalimov – but you can also see such classic pieces as a violin made by Antonio Stradivari. Recordings accompany many of the rarer instruments, allowing visitors to experience their sound.

Central Museum of the Armed Forces MUSEUM
(Центральный музей Вооружённых Сил; Map p64; ☎495-681 6303; www.cmaf.ru; ul Sovetskoy

Armii 2; adult/student ₽120/60; ⏲10am-4.30pm Wed-Sun; Ⓜ Novoslobodskaya) Covering the history of the Soviet and Russian military since 1917, this massive museum occupies 24 exhibit halls plus open-air exhibits. Over 800,000 military items, including uniforms, medals and weapons, are on display. Among the highlights are remainders of the American U2 spy plane (brought down in the Urals in 1960) and the victory flag raised over Berlin's Reichstag in 1945. Take trolleybus 69 (or walk) 1.3km east from the Novoslobodskaya metro.

Museum of Decorative & Folk Art ART MUSEUM
(Всероссийский музей декоративно-прикладного и народного искусства; Map p74; ☎495-609 0146; www.vmdpri.ru; Delegatskaya ul 3 & 5; adult/student ₽200/100; ⏲10am-6pm Wed-Mon; Ⓜ Tsvetnoy Bulvar) Just beyond the Garden Ring, this museum showcases centuries-old arts-and-crafts traditions from around Russia and the former Soviet republics. Of the 40,000 pieces in the collection, you might see painted *khokhloma* woodwork from Nizhny Novgorod, including wooden toys and *matryoshka* dolls; baskets and other household items made from birch bark, a traditional Siberian technique; intricate embroidery and lacework from the north, as well as the ubiquitous Pavlov scarves; and playful Dymkovo pottery and Gzhel porcelain.

Experimentanium MUSEUM
(Экспериментаниум; Map p64; ☎495-789 3658; http://experimentanium.ru; ul Butyrskaya 46/2; ⏲9.30am-7pm Mon-Fri, 10am-8pm Sat, Sun & holidays; Ⓜ Savylovskaya) Travelling with children who ask too many questions about life, the universe and everything? Here is a place that provides answers for them to ponder for a while. Experimentanium is an exciting place where children learn physics, chemistry, mechanics, acoustics, anatomy and whatnot by playing, and indeed experimenting, with a vast number of interactive exhibits.

Meshchansky & Basmanny

Meshchansky and Basmanny districts flank the little Yauza River in the eastern part of the city. The former is a bustling neighbourhood that retains its quaint 19th-century outlook. The latter is largely comprised of old factories, now taken over by hipsters and housing innovative postmodern galleries and clubs.

Lubyanka Prison HISTORICAL BUILDING
(Лубянка; Map p74; Lubyanskaya pl; Ⓜ Lubyanka) In the 1930s Lubyanka Prison was the feared destination of thousands of innocent victims of Stalin's purges. Today the grey building looming on the northeastern side of Lubyanskaya pl is no longer a prison, but is the headquarters of the Federal Security Service, or *Federalnaya Sluzhba Bezopasnosti*. The FSB keeps a pretty good eye on domestic goings on. The building is not open to the public.

Chistye Prudy PARK
(Чистые пруды; Map p74; Chistoprudny bul; Ⓜ Chistye Prudy) Chistye Prudy (Clean Ponds) is the lovely little pond that graces the Boulevard Ring at the ul Pokrovka intersection. The Boulevard Ring is always a prime location for strolling, but the quaint pond makes this a desirable address indeed. Paddle boats in summer and ice skating in winter are essential parts of the ambience. Pick a cafe and sip a beer or a coffee while watching strollers and skaters go by.

Choral Synagogue NOTABLE BUILDING
(Московская Хоральная Синагога; Map p74; Bolshoy Spasoglinishchevsky per 10; ⏲9am-6pm; Ⓜ Kitay-Gorod) Construction of a synagogue was banned inside Kitay Gorod, so Moscow's oldest and most prominent synagogue was built just outside the city walls, not far from the Jewish settlement of Zaryadye. Construction started in 1881 but dragged on due to roadblocks by the anti-Semitic tsarist government. It was completed in 1906 and was the only synagogue that continued to operate throughout the Soviet period, despite attempts to convert it into a workers' club.

Novospassky Monastery MONASTERY
(Новоспасский монастырь; Map p90; ☎495-676 9570; www.spasnanovom.ru; Verkhny Novospassky proezd; ⏲7am-7pm; Ⓜ Proletarskaya) FREE Novospassky Monastery, a 15th-century fort-monastery, is about 1km south of Taganskaya pl. The centrepiece of the monastery, the **Transfiguration Cathedral**, was built by the imperial Romanov family in the 1640s in imitation of the Kremlin's Assumption Cathedral. Frescoes depict the history of Christianity in Russia, while the Romanov family tree, which goes as far back as the Viking Prince Rurik, climbs one wall. The other church is the 1675 **Intercession Church**.

Under the river bank, beneath one of the towers of the monastery, is the site of a mass grave for thousands of Stalin's victims. At

WORTH A TRIP

VDNKH & OSTANKINO

Palaces for workers! There is hardly a better place to see this slogan put into practice than at **VDNKh** (Map p64; Ⓜ VDNKh), which stands for Exhibition of Achievements of the National Economy. This Stalin-era name was being resurrected at the time of writing, replacing the post-Soviet VVTs (All-Russian Exhibition Centre). VDNKh is like a Stalinesque theme park, with palatial pavilions, each designed in its own unique style to represent all Soviet republics and various industries, from geology to space exploration.

The highlights are two opulently decorated fountains. Positioned right behind the main gates, **People's Friendship Fountain** is surrounded by 16 gilded female figures dressed in ethnic costumes representing Soviet republics (the mysterious 16th figure stands for the Karelo-Finnish republic disbanded in 1956). Further on, the jaw-dropping **Stone Flower Fountain**, themed on Urals miners' mythology, is covered in semi-precious stones from the Urals.

On the approach to VDNKh from the metro, the soaring 100m titanium obelisk is a monument 'To the Conquerors of Space', built in 1964 to commemorate the launch of *Sputnik*. In its base is the **Cosmonautics Museum** (Map p64; http://kosmo-museum.ru; admission ₽200; ⏲11am-7pm Tue-Sun, to 9pm Thursday; Ⓜ VDNKh), featuring cool space paraphernalia such as the first Soviet rocket engine and the moon-rover Lunokhod. An inspiring collection of space-themed propaganda posters evokes the era of the space race.

To the west, the **Ostankino TV Tower** (Останкинская башня; Map p64; ☎8-800-100 5553; tvtower.ru; adult/child ₽980/490; ⏲10am-8pm Tue-Sun; Ⓜ VDNKh) looms over the assemblage. From the top, there are 360-degree views. Tours take place hourly and must be booked in advance; bring your passport.

the northern end of the monastery's grounds are the brick Assumption Cathedral and an extraordinary Moscow-baroque gate tower.

Winzavod GALLERY

(Винзавод; Map p74; www.winzavod.ru; 4 Syromyatnichesky per 1; Ⓜ Chkalovskaya) FREE Formerly a wine-bottling factory, this facility was converted into exhibit and studio space for Moscow artists in 2007. The post-industrial complex is now home to Moscow's most prestigious art galleries, including M&J Guelman, Aidan and XL. The complex also contains several photo galleries, a design studio and furniture showroom, and a concept clothing store, as well as a few funky gift shops and boutiques.

Soviet Arcade Games Museum MUSEUM

(Музей советских игровых автоматов; Map p64; www.15kop.ru; ul Baumanskaya 11; ⏲1-8pm; Ⓜ Baumanskaya) Growing up in the 1980s USSR was a peculiar, but not necessarily entirely bleak experience. Here is an example – a collection of about 40 mostly functional Soviet arcade machines. At the entrance, visitors get a paper bag full of 15-kopek Soviet coins, which fire up these recreational dinosaurs that would look at home in the oldest episodes of *Star Trek*. Most of the games test your shooting or driving skills.

Aptekarsky Ogorod GARDEN

(Аптекарский огород; Map p74; www.hortus.ru; pr Mira 26; admission day/evening ₽100/150; ⏲10am-10pm May-Sep, to 5pm Oct-Apr; Ⓜ Prospekt Mira) This lovely, thoroughly revamped garden is Moscow's chief source of flower power and that's a not a cultural metaphor. It really is full of flowers, as well as shade and dozens of inviting benches. Established in 1706, the garden was originally owned by the Moscow general hospital to grow herbs and other medicinal plants – hence the name, which translates as Pharmacy Garden.

Sokolniki PARK

(Сокольники; Map p64; 📶👪; Ⓜ Sokolniki) FREE Changed beyond recognition in recent years, Sokolniki park is criss-crossed by cycling paths, and blends into a proper forest bordering on **Losiny Ostrov national park** (Национальный парк Лосиный остров). The area by the entrance, centred around a fountain, is full of cool eateries and welcoming benches. Further away, to the left of the entrance, is a funfair with rides and carousels. Another attraction is the **Rosarium** (Розариум), a manicured rose garden.

At least three outlets in the central part of the park hire out bicycles and other sporting equipment. In summer, beach bums head to the **Basseyn** (Бассейн) open-air swimming pool, which turns into a party zone in the evening. Come winter, the park opens a skating rink and Moscow's longest (200m) sledding hill. All kinds of urban culture and sport festivals, including the popular **Equestrian Fest** (Конный Фестиваль; 29 Aug-1 Sep), take place year round, with the main events occurring during weekends.

Presnya District

Presnya is Moscow's largest administrative district, encompassing some of the capital's oldest neighbourhoods as well as its newest development. Inside the Garden Ring, Presnya includes lovely residential areas, chock-full of evocative architecture, historic parks, and fantastic drinking and dining spots. The area around Patriarch's Ponds has emerged as a dining hot spot, while the former textile factory at Trekhgornaya is fast becoming a centre for nightlife.

Museum of Oriental Art MUSEUM

(Музей искусства народов востока; Map p80; 495-691 0212; www.orientmuseum.ru; Nikitsky bul 12a; admission ₽300; 11am-8pm Tue-Sun; M Arbatskaya) This impressive museum on the Boulevard Ring holds three floors of exhibits spanning the Asian continent. Of particular interest is the 1st floor, dedicated mostly to the Caucasus, Central Asia and North Asia (meaning the Russian republics of Cukotka, Yakutiya and Priamurie).

But the entire continent is pretty well represented, including the countries that were not part of the Russian or Soviet Empires. The collection covers an equally vast time period, from ancient times through to the 20th century, including painting, sculpture and folk art. One unexpected highlight is a special exhibit on Nikolai Rerikh, the Russian artist and explorer who spent several years travelling and painting in Asia.

Gogol House MUSEUM

(Дом Гоголя; Map p80; www.domgogolya.ru; Nikitsky bul 7; admission ₽100; noon-7pm Wed & Fri, 2-9pm Thu, noon-5pm Sat & Sun; M Arbatskaya) Nineteenth-century writer Nikolai Gogol spent his final tortured months here. The rooms – now a small but captivating museum – are arranged as they were when Gogol lived here. You can even see the fireplace where he famously threw his manuscript of *Dead Souls*.

Churches of the Grand & Small Ascension CHURCH

(Церковь Большого Вознесения и Церковь Малого Вознесения; Bolshaya Nikitskaya ul; M Arbatskaya) In 1831 poet Alexander Pushkin married Natalya Goncharova in the elegant **Church of the Grand Ascension** (Map p80), on the western side of pl Nikitskie Vorota. Six years later he died in St Petersburg, defending her honour in a duel. Such passion, such romance… The celebrated couple is featured in the Rotunda Fountain, erected in 1999 to commemorate the poet's 100th birthday.

Down the street, the festive **Church of the Small Ascension** (Map p80) sits on the corner of Voznesensky per. Built in the early 17th century, it features whitewashed walls and stone embellishments carved in a primitive style.

MAMONTOV'S METROPOL

The **Hotel Metropol** (Гостиница Метрополь), among Moscow's finest examples of art nouveau architecture, is another contribution by Savva Mamontov, famed philanthropist and patron of the arts. The decorative panel on the hotel's central facade, facing Teatralny proezd, is based on a sketch by the artist Mikhail Vrubel. It depicts the legend of the Princess of Dreams, in which a troubadour falls in love with a kind and beautiful princess and travels across the seas to find her. He falls ill during the voyage and is near death when he finds his love. The princess embraces him, but he dies in her arms. Naturally, the princess reacts to his death by renouncing her worldly life. The ceramic panels were made at the pottery workshop at Mamontov's Abramtsevo estate.

The ceramic work on the side of the hotel facing Teatralnaya pl is by the artist Alexander Golovin. The script was originally a quote from Nietzsche: 'Again the same story: when you build a house you notice that you have learned something'. During the Soviet era, these wise words were replaced with something more appropriate for the time: 'Only the dictatorship of the proletariat can liberate mankind from the oppression of capitalism'. Lenin, of course.

Presnya

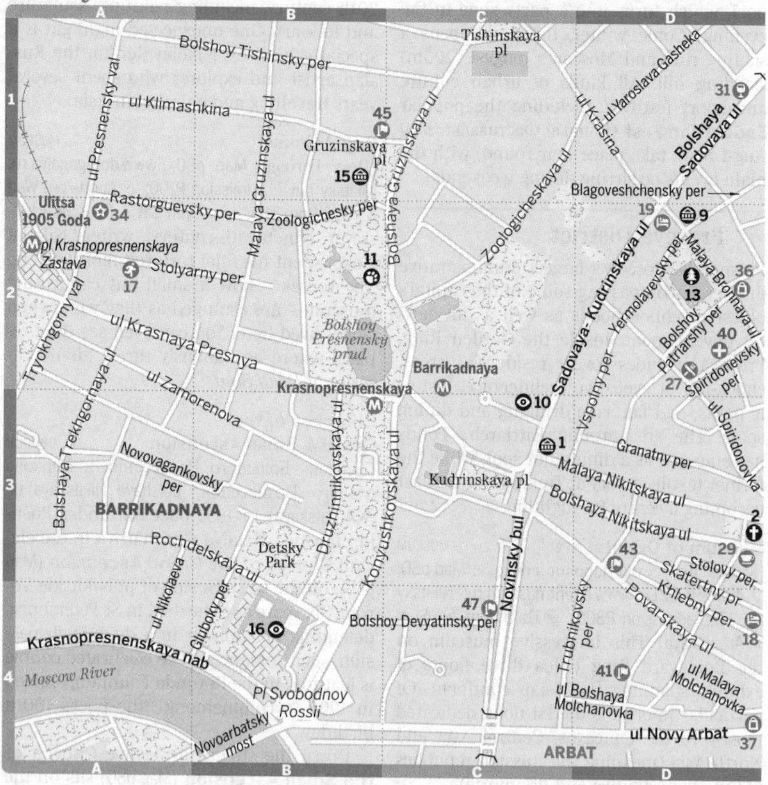

Contemporary History Museum MUSEUM

(Музей современной истории России; Map p80; ☎495-699 6724; www.sovr.ru; Tverskaya ul 21; adult/student ₽250/100; ⊙10am-6pm Tue-Sun; Ⓜ Pushkinskaya) Formerly known as the Revolution Museum, this retro exhibit traces Soviet history from the 1905 and 1917 revolutions up to the 1980s. The highlight is the extensive collection of propaganda posters, in addition to all the Bolshevik paraphernalia. Look for the picture of the giant Palace of Soviets (Дворец Советов) that Stalin was going to build on the site of the blown-up – and now rebuilt – Cathedral of Christ the Saviour.

Ryabushinsky Mansion MUSEUM

(Особняк Рябушинского; Map p80; Malaya Nikitskaya ul 6/2; ⊙11am-5.30pm Wed-Sun; Ⓜ Pushkinskaya) FREE Also known as the Gorky House-Museum, this fascinating 1906 art nouveau mansion was designed by Fyodor Shekhtel and gifted to celebrated author Maxim Gorky in 1931. The house is a visual fantasy with sculpted doorways, ceiling murals, stained glass, a carved stone staircase and exterior tilework. Besides the fantastic decor it contains many of Gorky's personal items, including his extensive library.

Patriarch's Ponds PARK

(Патриаршие пруды; Map p80; Bolshoy Patriarshy per; Ⓜ Mayakovskaya) Patriarch's Ponds harks back to Soviet days, when the parks were populated with children and *babushky*. You'll see grandmothers pushing strollers and lovers kissing on park benches. In summer children romp on the swings, while winter sees them ice skating on the pond. The small park has a huge statue of 19th-century Russian writer Ivan Krylov, known to Russian children for his didactic tales.

Patriarch's Ponds were immortalised by writer Mikhail Bulgakov, who had the devil appear here in *The Master and Margarita*.

The initial paragraph of the novel describes the area to the north of the pond, where the devil enters the scene and predicts the rapid death of Berlioz. Contrary to Bulgakov's tale, a tram line never ran along the pond. Bulgakov's flat, where he wrote the novel and lived up until his death, is around the corner on the Garden Ring.

Lyubavicheskaya Synagogue SYNAGOGUE

(Любавическая синагога; Map p80; Bolshaya Bronnaya ul 6; M Pushkinskaya) Converted to a theatre in the 1930s, this building was still used for gatherings by the Jewish community throughout the Soviet period. Today the building serves as a working synagogue, as well as a social centre for the small but growing Jewish community in Moscow.

Chekhov House-Museum MUSEUM

(Дом-музей Чехова; Map p80; ul Sadovaya-Kudrinskaya 6; admission ₽150; 11am-6pm Tue, Wed & Fri-Sun, 2-8pm Thu; M Barrikadnaya) 'The colour of the house is liberal, ie red', Anton Chekhov wrote of his house on the Garden Ring, where he lived from 1886 to 1890. The red house now contains the Chekhov House-Museum, with bedrooms, drawing room and study all intact. Musical performances are held here several times a week in the late afternoon.

Moscow Planetarium PLANETARIUM

(Московский планетарий; Map p80; www.planetarium-moscow.ru; ul Sadovaya-Kudrinskaya 5; exhibits each ₽300-600; museum 10am-9pm, theatre 10am-midnight Wed-Mon; M Barrikadnaya) The new planetarium shines bigger and brighter than before, expanding in area by more than three times and incorporating all kinds of high-tech gadgetry, interactive exhibits and educational programs. The centrepiece is the **Large Star Hall** (Большой Звездный Зал; ₽550-600, the biggest in Europe!), with its 25m silver dome roof, a landmark which is visible from the Garden Ring. There are two observatories, the larger of which (aka the Big Observatory) employs Moscow's largest telescope.

Moscow Zoo ZOO

(Московский зоопарк; Map p80; www.moscowzoo.ru; Yaroslavskoe shosse; adult weekday/weekend ₽300/500, child free; 10am-8pm Tue-Sun Apr-Sep, to 5pm Oct-Mar; ; M Barrikadnaya) In 2014 the zoo underwent a huge renovation in honour of its 150th anniversary, so it should be in great shape in coming years. Huge flocks of feathered friends populate the central ponds, making for a pleasant stroll for birdwatchers. For a new perspective on Moscow's nightlife, check out the nocturnal animal exhibit. Other highlights include the big cats (featuring Siberian tigers), and the Dolphinarium. For more four-legged fun, follow the footbridge to see exhibits featuring animals from each continent.

Tsereteli Studio-Museum MUSEUM

(Музей-мастерская Зураба Церетели; Map p80; www.mmoma.ru; Bolshaya Gruzinskaya ul 15; admission ₽250; 11am-6pm Fri-Wed, 1-8pm Thu; ; M Belorusskaya) Moscow's most prolific artist, Zurab Tsereteli, has opened up his 'studio' as a space to exhibit his many masterpieces. You can't miss this place – whimsical characters adorn the front lawn. They give just a tiny hint of what's inside: a courtyard crammed with bigger-than-life bronze beauties and elaborate enamelwork.

Presnya

Sights

1 Chekhov House-Museum ... C3
2 Church of the Grand Ascension ... D3
3 Church of the Resurrection ... F3
4 Church of the Small Ascension ... E3
5 Contemporary History Museum ... E1
6 Gogol House ... E4
7 Lyubavicheskaya Synagogue ... E3
8 Moscow Museum of Modern Art Tverskoy ... E3
9 Moscow Museum of Modern Art Yermolaevsky ... D2
10 Moscow Planetarium ... C3
11 Moscow Zoo ... B2
12 Museum of Oriental Art ... E4
13 Patriarch's Ponds ... D2
14 Ryabushinsky Mansion ... E3
15 Tsereteli Studio-Museum ... B1
16 White House ... B4

Activities, Courses & Tours

17 Krasnopresnkiye Bany ... A2

Sleeping

18 Arbat House Hotel ... D4
19 Bear Hostel on Mayakovskaya ... D2
20 Element Hotel ... E3
21 Hotel de Paris ... E2
22 Nikitskaya Hotel ... F3

Eating

23 As Eat Is ... E2
24 Café Pushkin ... F2
25 Cafe Receptor ... E3
26 Cafe Receptor ... E2
27 Favorite ... D2
28 Khachapuri ... F2
Ugolyok ... (see 22)

Drinking & Nightlife

29 Art Lebedev Cafe Studio ... D3
Bar Klava ... (see 36)
30 Noor ... E1
31 Time-Out Bar ... D1

Entertainment

32 Moscow English Theatre ... E3
33 Moscow Tchaikovsky Conservatory ... F4
34 Sixteen Tons ... A2
35 Tchaikovsky Concert Hall ... E1

Shopping

36 Bolshe ... D2
37 Dom Knigi ... D4

Information

38 36.6 Tverskaya ... E1
39 Central Telegraph ... F3
40 European Medical Centre ... D2
41 Mongolian Embassy ... D4
42 Netherlands Embassy ... E4
43 New Zealand Embassy ... D3
44 Norwegian Embassy ... E4
45 Polish Embassy ... B1
46 Ukrainian Embassy ... F3
47 US Embassy ... C4

The highlight is undoubtedly Putin in his judo costume, although the huge tile Moscow cityscapes are impressive. You'll also recognise some smaller-scale models of monuments that appear around town. Indoors, there are three floors of the master's sketches, paintings and enamel arts.

White House NOTABLE BUILDING

(Белый дом; Map p80; Krasnopresnenskaya nab 2; M Krasnopresnenskaya) The White House – officially the House of Government of the Russian Federation – fronts a stately bend in the Moscow River, just north of the Novoarbatsky most.

It was here that Boris Yeltsin rallied the opposition that confounded the 1991 hardline coup, then two years later sent in tanks and troops to blast out conservative rivals, some of them the same people who backed him in 1991. The images of Yeltsin climbing on a tank in front of the White House in 1991, and of the same building ablaze after the 1993 assault, are among the most unforgettable from those tumultuous years.

Arbat & Khamovniki

These two side-by-side districts are rich with culture. Moscow's most famous street, ul Arbat, is something of an art market, complete with portrait painters and soapbox poets, while the nearby streets are lined with museums and galleries, including the world-class Pushkin Museum of Fine Arts. Khamovniki is home to the ancient Novodevichy Convent & Cemetery, as well as several unique newer museums.

★**Pushkin Museum of Fine Arts** MUSEUM

(Музей изобразительных искусств им Пушкина; Map p84; www.arts-museum.ru; ul Volkhonka 12; admission each branch ₽200-300; 10am-7pm Tue-Sun, to 9pm Thu; M Kropotkinskaya) This is Moscow's premier foreign-art museum, showing off a broad selection of European works, including masterpieces

WORTH A TRIP

KOLOMENSKOE MUSEUM-RESERVE

Set amid 4 sq km of picturesque parkland, on a bluff above a bend in the Moscow River, **Kolomenskoe** (Музей-заповедник 'Коломенское'; Map p64; www.mgomz.com; ⌚grounds 8am-9pm; Ⓜ Kolomenskaya or Kashirskaya) FREE is an ancient royal country seat and Unesco World Heritage Site. Shortly after its founding in the 14th century, the village became a favourite destination for the princes of Moscow. The royal estate is now an eclectic mix of churches and gates and other buildings that were added to the complex over the years.

Outside the front gate, overlooking the river, rises Kolomenskoe's loveliest structure, the **Ascension Church** (Map p64; pr Andropova 39; ⌚10am-6pm Tue-Sun; Ⓜ Kolomenskoye) FREE, sometimes called the 'white column'. Built between 1530 and 1532 for Grand Prince Vasily III, it was a revolutionary structure at the time, which experts attribute to Italian masters.

In the mid-17th century, Tsar Alexey built a palace so fab it was dubbed 'the eighth wonder of the world'. This whimsical building was famous for its mishmash of tent-roofed towers and onion-shaped eaves, all crafted from wood and structured without a single nail. Although the legendary building was demolished in 1768, a very kitschy gingerbread replica **Tsar Alexey's palace** (Дворец царя Алексея Михайловича; pr Andropova 39; admission ₽400; ⌚10am-6pm Tue-Sun; Ⓜ Kashirskaya) was built some 230 years later. Come here for the opulent interiors, which allegedly replicate the originals, based on historical records.

Among the other old wooden buildings on the grounds is the **cabin** where Peter the Great lived while supervising ship- and fort-building at Arkhangelsk. The cabin is surrounded by a re-creation of the tsar's orchards and gardens.

from ancient civilisations, the Italian Renaissance and the Dutch Golden Age.

To see the incredible collection of Impressionist and post-Impressionist paintings, visit the Gallery of European & American Art. What's left in the main building is still impressive, especially since the place has been revamped with more modern museum lighting and improved layout. This is only the first phase of a multiyear project that will have the Pushkin expanding into a new complex.

In the meantime, the museum has room to show off some of its paintings that have never been displayed before, including Renaissance masterpieces. Artists such as Botticelli, Tiepolo and Veronese are all represented. The highlight is perhaps the Dutch masterpieces from the 17th century, the so-called Golden Age of Dutch art. Rembrandt is the star of the show, with many paintings on display, including his moving *Portrait of an Old Woman*. The rest of Europe is also well represented from this period.

The Ancient Civilisation exhibits contain a surprisingly excellent collection, complete with ancient Egyptian weaponry, jewellery, ritual items and tombstones. Most of the items were excavated from burial sites, including two haunting mummies.

Another room houses the impressive 'Treasures of Troy' exhibit, with excavated items dating to 2500 BC. A German archaeologist donated the collection to the city of Berlin, from where it was appropriated by the Soviets in 1945.

Museum of Private Collections MUSEUM

(Музей личных коллекций; Map p84; www.artprivatecollections.ru; ul Volkhonka 10; adult/child ₽200/100; Ⓜ Kropotkinskaya) Next door to the Pushkin Fine Arts Museum, this smaller museum shows off art collections donated by private individuals, many of whom amassed the works during the Soviet era. Exhibits are organised around the collections, each as a whole, with the details of collectors displayed alongside the art. The centrepiece is

ⓘ CHANGES IN STORE FOR PUSHKIN MUSEUM OF FINE ARTS

The Pushkin Museum of Fine Arts is supposed to undergo a much-needed renovation and an ambitious expansion of its facilities (scheduled for completion in 2018). The museum is likely to close during this construction.

Arbat & Khamovniki

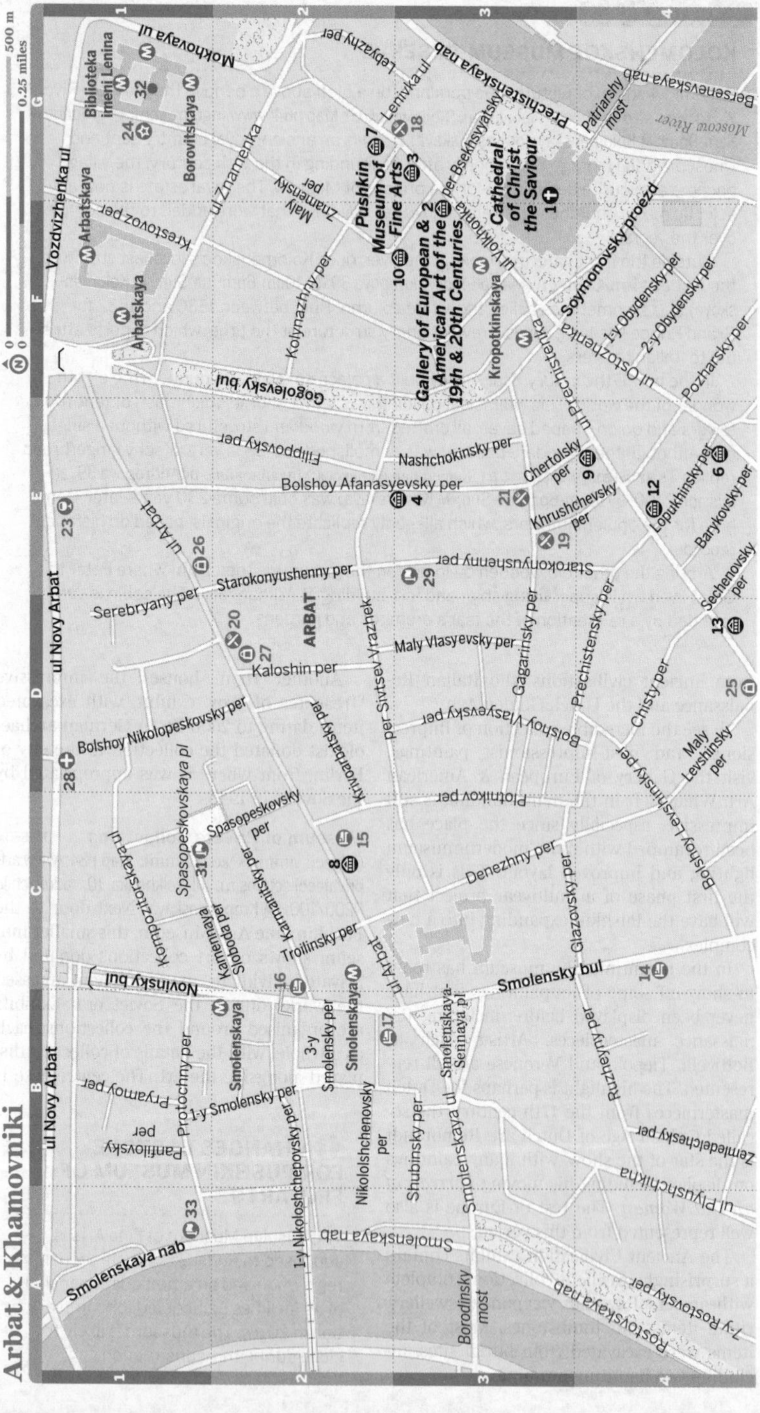

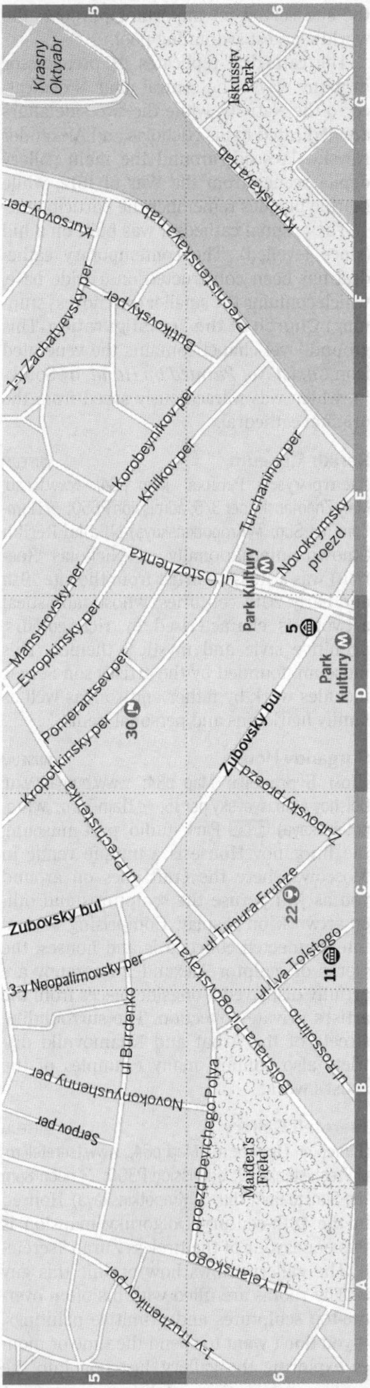

the collection of the museum's founder, Ilya Silberstein, an accomplished historian of Russian literature and art.

Other highlights include a collection of Old Believer icons from the 16th to 20th centuries, the Lemkul room exhibiting fantastic glassworks, and impressive exhibits of 20th-century artists such as Alexander Rodchenko and Barbara Stepanova.

★Gallery of European & American Art of the 19th & 20th Centuries MUSEUM
(Map p84; www.newpaintart.ru; ul Volkhonka 14; adult/child ₽300/150; M Kropotkinskaya) This branch of the Pushkin Museum of Fine Arts contains a famed assemblage of French Impressionist works, based on the collection of two well-known Moscow art patrons, Sergei Shchukin and Ivan Morozov. It includes representative paintings by Degas, Manet, Renoir and Pisarro, with an entire room dedicated to Monet.

Rodin's sculptures include pieces from the *Gates of Hell* and the *Monument to the Townspeople of Calais*. The gallery displays many of the most famous paintings by Matisse, such as *Goldfish*; some lesser-known pieces by Picasso; a few exquisite primitive paintings by Rousseau; and works by Miro, Kandinsky and Chagall. The museum also contains several pieces by Van Gogh, including the scorching *Red Vineyards* and the tragic *Prison Courtyard*, painted in the last year of his life. There is an entire room devoted to works by Gauguin, representing his prime period. The rich collection of 20th-century art continues to grow, with recent additions by Arp and others.

★Cathedral of Christ the Saviour CHURCH
(Храм Христа Спасителя; Map p84; ul Volkhonka 15; ⏲1-5pm Mon, 10am-5pm Tue-Sun; M Kropotkinskaya) FREE This gargantuan cathedral was completed in 1997 – just in time to celebrate Moscow's 850th birthday. It is amazingly opulent, garishly grandiose and truly historic. The cathedral's sheer size and splendour guarantee its role as a love-it-or-hate-it landmark. Considering Stalin's plan for this site (a Palace of Soviets topped with a 100m statue of Lenin), Muscovites should at least be grateful they can admire the shiny domes of a church instead of the shiny dome of Ilyich's head.

The Cathedral of Christ the Saviour sits on the site of an earlier and similar church of the same name, built in the 19th century to commemorate Russia's victory over

Napoleon. The original was destroyed in 1931, during Stalin's orgy of explosive secularism. His plan to replace the church with a 315m-high Palace of Soviets never got off the ground – literally. Instead, for 50 years the site served an important purpose: the world's largest swimming pool.

The cathedral replicates its predecessor in many ways. The central altar is dedicated to the Nativity, while the two side altars are dedicated to Sts Nicholas and Alexander Nevsky. Frescoes around the main gallery depict scenes from the War of 1812, while marble plaques remember the participants.

The original cathedral was built on a hill (since levelled). The contemporary cathedral has been constructed on a wide base, which contains the smaller (but no less stunning) **Church of the Transfiguration**. This ground-level chapel contains the venerated icon *Christ Not Painted by Hand*, by Sorokin, which was miraculously saved from the original cathedral.

Rerikh Museum — MUSEUM

(Центр-музей Рериха; Map p84; www.icr.su; Maly Znamensky per 3/5; admission ₽650; 11am-6pm Tue-Sun; M Kropotkinskaya) Nikolai Rerikh (known internationally as Nicholas Roerich) was a Russian artist from the late 19th and early 20th centuries, whose fantastical artwork is characterised by rich colours, primitive style and mystical themes. This museum, founded by the artist's son Sergei, includes work by father and son, as well as family heirlooms and personal items.

Burganov House — MUSEUM

(Дом Бурганова; Map p84; www.burganov.ru; Bolshoy Afanasyevsky per 15; 11am-7pm; M Kropotkinskaya) FREE Part studio, part museum, the Burganov House is a unique venue in Moscow, where the craft goes on around you as you peruse the sculptures and other artwork on display. Comprising several interconnected courtyards and houses, the works of sculptor Alexander Burganov are artfully displayed alongside pieces from the artist's private collection. The surrounding streets of the Arbat and Khamovniki districts also contain many examples of the artist's work.

Tsereteli Gallery — MUSEUM

(Галерея Церетели; Map p84; www.tsereteli.ru; ul Prechistenka 19; admission ₽300; noon-8pm Tue-Sun, to 9pm Thu; M Kropotkinskaya) Housed in the 18th-century Dolgoruky mansion is this endeavour of the tireless Zurab Tsereteli. The gallery shows how prolific this guy is. The rooms are filled with his often over-the-top sculptures and primitive paintings. If you don't want to spend the time or money exploring the gallery, just pop into the

Galereya Khudozhnikov cafe (Галерея художников; Map p84; ☑ 495-637 2866; www. gal-h.ru; ul Prechistenka 19; mains ₽800-1200; ☺noon-midnight; ☺ 🍴📶; 🅜Kropotkinskaya), which is an exhibit in itself.

Pushkin House-Museum MUSEUM
(Дом-музей Пушкина; Map p84; www.pushkin-museum.ru; ul Arbat 53; admission ₽120; ☺10am-6pm Tue-Sun, noon-9pm Thu; 🅜Smolenskaya) After Alexander Pushkin married Natalya Goncharova at the nearby Church of the Grand Ascension, they moved to this charming blue house on the old Arbat. The museum provides some insight into the couple's home life, a source of much Russian romanticism. (The lovebirds are also featured in a statue across the street.)

Multimedia Art Museum ART GALLERY
(Мультимедиа Арт Музей; Map p84; www. mamm-mdf.ru; ul Ostozhenka 16; admission ₽300; 🅜Kropotkinskaya) This slick, modern gallery is home to an impressive photographic library and archives of contemporary and historic photography. The facility usually hosts several simultaneous exhibits, often featuring works from prominent photographers from the Soviet period, as well as contemporary artists. The complex also hosts several month-long festivals: **Photobiennale** and **Fashion & Style in Photography** (held in alternating years).

Pushkin Literary Museum MUSEUM
(Литературный музей Пушкина; Map p84; www.pushkinmuseum.ru; ul Prechistenka 12/2; admission ₽120; ☺10am-5pm Tue-Sun; 🅜Kro-potkinskaya) Housed in a beautiful Russian Empire–style mansion dating from 1816, this museum is devoted to the life and work of Russia's favourite poet. Personal effects, family portraits, reproductions of notes and handwritten poetry provide insight into the work of the beloved bard. Perhaps the most interesting exhibit is 'Pushkin & His Time', which puts the poet in a historical context, demonstrating the influence of the Napoleonic Wars, the Decembrists' revolt and other historic events.

Tolstoy Literary Museum MUSEUM
(Литературный музей Толстого; Map p84; www.tolstoymuseum.ru; ul Prechistenka 11; adult/student ₽200/100; ☺11am-6pm Tue-Sun; 🅜Kro-potkinskaya) The Tolstoy Literary Museum is supposedly the oldest literary memorial museum in the world (founded in 1911). In addition to its impressive reference library, the museum contains exhibits of manuscripts, letters and artwork focusing on Leo Tolstoy's literary influences and output. Family photographs, personal correspondence and artwork from the author's era all provide insight into his work.

Moscow Museum MUSEUM
(Музей Москвы; Map p84; www.mosmuseum.ru; Zubovsky bul 2; adult/child ₽300/120; ☺10am-8pm Tue-Wed & Fri-Sun, 11am-9pm Thu; 🚻; 🅜Park Kultury) Formerly the Museum of the History of Moscow, this excellent museum has a new name, a new location and a new mission. The permanent history exhibit demonstrates how the city has spread from

ARBAT, MY ARBAT

For Moscow's beloved bard Bulat Okudzhava, the Arbat was not only his home, it was his inspiration. Although he spent his university years in Georgia dabbling in harmless verse, it was only upon his return to Moscow – and to his cherished Arbat – that his poetry adopted the freethinking character for which it is known.

He gradually made the transition from poet to songwriter. While Bulat and his friends enjoyed his songs, other composers, singers and guitarists did not. The ill feeling subsided when a well-known poet announced that they are 'just another way of presenting poetry'.

And so a new form of art was born. The 1960s were heady times – in Moscow as elsewhere – and Okudzhava inspired a whole movement of liberal-thinking poets to take their ideas to the streets. Vladimir Vysotsky and others – some political, some not – followed in Okudzhava's footsteps, their iconoclastic lyrics and simple melodies drawing enthusiastic crowds all around Moscow.

The Arbat today – crowded with souvenir stands and overpriced cafes – bears little resemblance to the hallowed haunt of Okudzhava's youth. But its memory lives on in the bards and buskers, painters and poets who still perform for strolling crowds on summer evenings.

WORTH A TRIP

PARK POBEDY

The Great Patriotic War – as WWII is known in Russia – was a momentous event that is still vivid in the hearts, minds and memories of many Russian citizens. Magnificent **Park Pobedy** (Парк Победы, Victory Park; Map p64; Kutuzovsky pr; ⌚dawn-dusk; Ⓜ Park Pobedy) FREE at Poklonnaya Hill is a huge memorial complex commemorating the sacrifice and celebrating the triumph of the war. Unveiled on the 50th anniversary of the victory, the park includes endless fountains and monuments, as well as the memorial church, synagogue and mosque.

The dominant monument is an enormous **obelisk**, topped with a sculpture of St George slaying the dragon (the work of Zurab Tsereteli). The height of the obelisk is exactly 141.8m, with every 10cm representing one day of the war. At the 60th Victory Day celebrations in 2005, Putin unveiled 15 mighty bronze cannons, symbolic of the war's 15 fronts.

Facing the obelisk, the **Museum of the Great Patriotic War** (Центральный музей Великой Отечественной Войны; Map p64; www.poklonnayagora.ru; ul Bratiev Fonchenko 10; adult/child ₽250/100; ⌚10am-6pm Tue-Sun Nov-Mar, to 8pm Apr-Oct; Ⓜ Park Pobedy) is the centrepiece of Park Pobedy. The museum contains two impressive memorial rooms, as well as hundreds of exhibits, including dioramas of every major WWII battle the Russians fought.

The unique **Exposition of Military Equipment** (Площадка боевой техники; Map p64; www.poklonnayagora.ru; adult/child ₽250/100; ⌚10am-7pm Tue-Sun; Ⓜ Pak Pobedy) – tucked into the southwestern corner of the park – displays more than 300 examples of weapons and military equipment from the WWII era.

its starting point at the Kremlin. It is heavy on artefacts from the 13th and 14th centuries, especially household items and weapons. More exciting, the museum has space to launch thought-provoking temporary exhibits, including artists' and other local perspectives on the city.

It's housed in the former warehouses and garages of the Defense Ministry, with a central courtyard that displays outdoor art and interactive exhibits.

Tolstoy Estate-Museum MUSEUM
(Музей-усадьба Толстого 'Хамовники'; Map p84; www.tolstoymuseum.ru; ul Lva Tolstogo 21; adult/student ₽200/100; ⌚10am-6pm Tue, Wed & Fri-Sun, noon-8pm Thu; Ⓜ Park Kultury) Leo Tolstoy's winter home during the 1880s and 1890s now houses an interesting museum dedicated to the writer's home life. While it's not particularly opulent or large, the building is fitting for junior nobility – which Tolstoy was. Exhibits here demonstrate how Tolstoy lived, as opposed to his literary influences, which are explored at the Tolstoy Literary Museum (p87). See the salon where Rachmaninov and Rimsky-Korsakov played piano, and the study where Tolstoy himself wove his epic tales.

★Novodevichy Convent CONVENT
(Новодевичий монастырь; Map p64; adult/student ₽300/100, photos ₽100; ⌚grounds 8am-8pm, museums 9am-5pm Wed-Mon; Ⓜ Sportivnaya) The Novodevichy Convent was founded in 1524 to celebrate the taking of Smolensk from Lithuania, an important step in Moscow's conquest of the old Kyivan Rus lands. The oldest and most dominant building in the grounds is the white Smolensk Cathedral, with a sumptuous interior covered in 16th-century frescoes. Novodevichy is a functioning monastery. Women are advised to cover their heads and shoulders when entering the churches, while men should wear long pants.

From early on, the 'New Maidens' Convent' was a place for women from noble families to retire – some more willingly than others. The convent's most famous residents included Irina Godunova (wife of Feodor I and sister of Boris Godunov), Sofia Alexeyevna (half-sister of Peter the Great), and Eudoxia Lopukhina (first wife of Peter the Great).

Enter the convent through the red-and-white Moscow-baroque **Transfiguration Gate-Church** (Преображенская надвратная церковь), built in the north wall between 1687 and 1689. All of these striking walls and towers, along with many other buildings on the grounds, were rebuilt around this time, under the direction of Sofia Alexeyevna. The elaborate **bell tower** (Колокольня) against the east wall towers 72m over the rest of the monastery. When it was built in 1690 it was one of the tallest towers in Moscow (second only to the Ivan the Great Bell Tower in the Kremlin).

The centrepiece of the monastery is the white **Smolensk Cathedral** (Смоленский собор), built from 1524 to 1525 to house the precious *Our Lady of Smolensk* icon. Previously surrounded by four smaller chapels, the floorplan was modelled after the Assumption Cathedral in the Kremlin. The sumptuous interior is covered in 16th-century frescoes, which are considered to be among the finest in the city. The huge gilded iconostasis – donated by Sofia in 1685 – includes icons that date from the time of Boris Godunov. The icons on the fifth tier are attributed to 17th-century artists Simeon Ushakov and Feodor Zubov. The tombs of Sofia, a couple of her sisters and Eudoxia Lopukhina are in the south nave.

Sofia Alexeyevna used the convent as a residence when she ruled Russia as regent in the 1680s. During her rule, she rebuilt the convent to her liking – which was fortunate, as she was later confined here when Peter the Great came of age. After being implicated in the Streltsy rebellion, she was imprisoned here for life, primarily inhabiting the **Pond Tower** (Напрудная башня). Sofia was later joined in her enforced retirement by Eudoxia Lopukhina, who stayed in the **Chambers of Tsarina Eudoxia Miloslavkaya** (Палаты царевны Евдокии Милославской).

Novodevichy Cemetery CEMETERY

(Новодевичье кладбище; Map p64; ⏲9am-5pm; Ⓜ Sportivnaya) FREE Adjacent to the Novodevichy Convent, the Novodevichy Cemetery is one of Moscow's most prestigious resting places – a veritable who's who of Russian politics and culture. Here you will find the tombs of Bulgakov, Chekhov, Gogol, Mayakovsky, Prokofiev, Stanislavsky and Eisenstein, among many other Russian and Soviet cultural notables. The most recent notable addition to the cemetery is former President Boris Yeltsin, whose tomb is marked by an enormous Russian flag.

In Soviet times Novodevichy Cemetery was used for eminent people the authorities judged unsuitable for the Kremlin wall, most notably Khrushchev. The intertwined white-and-black blocks round Khrushchev's bust were intended by sculptor Ernst Neizvestny to represent Khrushchev's good and bad sides. The tombstone of Nadezhda Alliluyeva, Stalin's second wife, is surrounded by unbreakable glass to prevent vandalism. If you want to investigate this place in depth, buy the Russian map (on sale at the kiosk), which pinpoints nearly 200 graves.

Zamoskvorechie & Taganka

Zamoskvorechie – which means 'Beyond Moscow River' – stretches south from the bank opposite the Kremlin. This district is the site of Moscow's traditional-art museum, the Tretyakov, as well as the capital's most exciting contemporary-art and entertainment complex in the former Red October chocolate factory. Green Gorky Park lies further south along the Moscow River, while two ancient fortress-monasteries guard the city's southern flank. South of the Yauza, Taganskaya pl is a monster intersection that can be difficult to navigate, but the district is home to a few unusual sights.

★State Tretyakov Gallery Main Branch GALLERY

(Главный отдел Государственной Третьяковской галереи; Map p90; www.tretyakovgallery.ru/en/; Lavrushinsky per 10; adult/student ₽400/250; ⏲10am-6pm Tue, Wed, Sat & Sun, to 9pm Thu & Fri, ticket office closes 1hr before closing; Ⓜ Tretyakovskaya) The exotic *boyar* castle on a little lane in Zamoskvorechie contains the main branch of the State Tretyakov Gallery, housing the world's best collection of Russian icons and an outstanding collection of other prerevolutionary Russian art. Show up early to beat the queues.

The building was designed by Viktor Vasnetsov between 1900 and 1905. The gallery started as the private collection of the 19th-century industrialist brothers Pavel and Sergei Tretyakov. Pavel was a patron of the Peredvizhniki (Wanderers), a group of 19th-century painters who broke away from the conservative Academy of Arts and started depicting common people and social problems. Nowadays, these are among Russia's most celebrated painters, and the Tretyakov boasts some of the most exquisite examples of their work. For more see p92.

Red October ARTS CENTRE

(Завод Красный Октябрь; Map p90; Bersenevskaya nab; Ⓜ Kropotkinskaya) FREE This defiant island of Russian modernity

Zamoskvorechie & Taganka

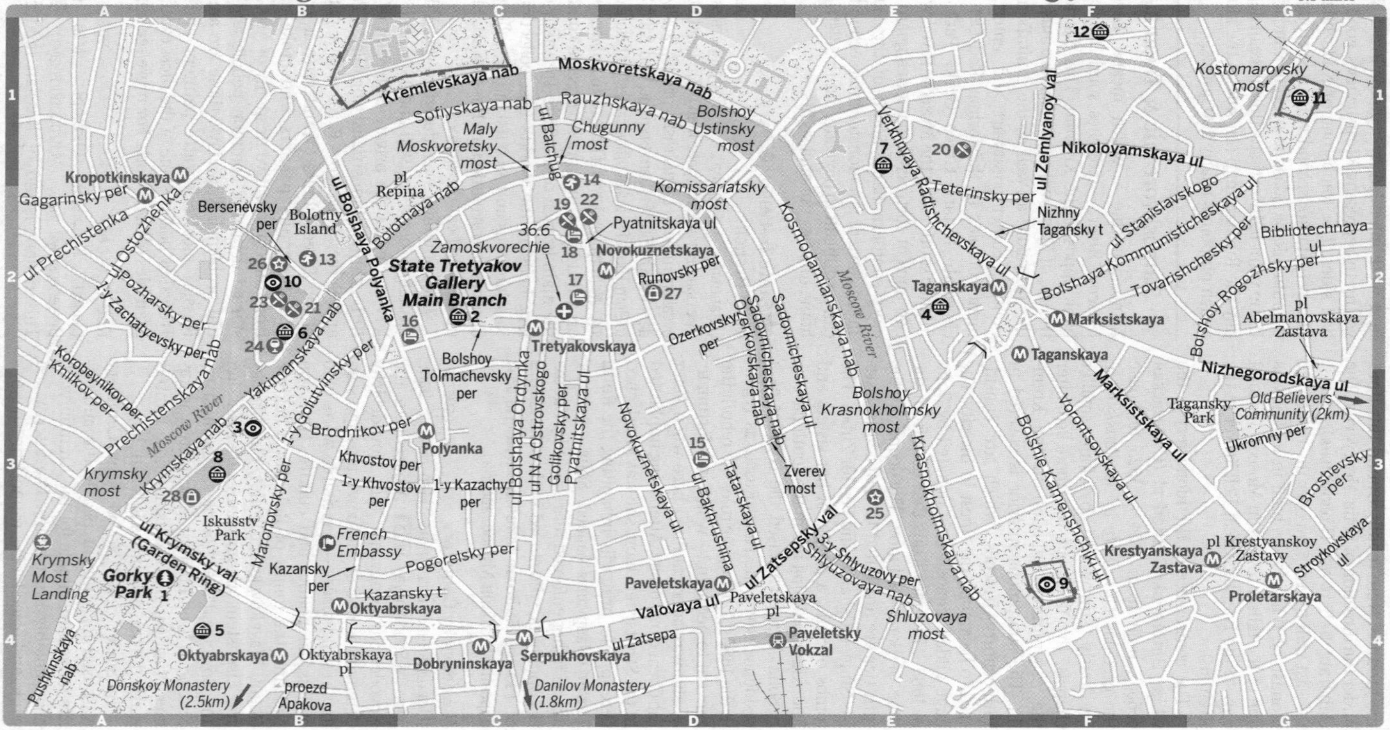
0
1 km
0
0.5 miles
A
B
C
D
E
F
G
1
2
3
4
Kremlevskaya nab
Moskvoretskaya nab
Sofiyskaya nab
Rauzhskaya nab
Bolshoy Ustinsky most
Maly Moskvoretsky most
ul Balchug
Chugunny most
Komissariatsky most
Kosmodamianskaya nab
Moscow River
Kostomarovsky most
11
12
7
20
Verkhnyaya Radishchevskaya ul
Teterinsky per
ul Zemlyanoy val
Nikoloyamskaya ul
Nizhny Tagansky t
ul Stanislavskogo
Bolshaya Kommunisticheskaya ul
Tovarishchesky per
Bibliotechnaya ul
Bolshoy Rogozhsky per
pl Abelmanovskaya Zastava
Taganskaya
4
Marksistskaya
Taganskaya
Nizhegorodskaya ul
Marksistskaya ul
Taganskiy Park
Old Believers' Community (2km)
Ukromny per
Broshevsky per
Vorontsovskaya ul
Bolshie Kamenshchiki ul
Krestyanskaya Zastava
pl Krestyanskoy Zastavy
Stroykovskaya ul
Proletarskaya
9
Kropotkinskaya
Gagarinsky per
ul Prechistenka
ul Ostozhenka
Bersenevsky per
Bolotny Island
26
13
10
23
21
6
24
pl Repina
Bolotnaya nab
ul Bolshaya Polyanka
1-y Pozharsky per
1-y Zachatyevsky per
Korobeynikov per
Khilkov per
Prechistenskaya nab
Moscow River
Yakimanskaya nab
1-y Golutvinsky per
3
Krymskaya nab
8
28
Krymsky most
Iskusstv Park
Maronovsky per
Brodnikov per
Polyanka
Khvostov per
1-y Khvostov per
1-y Kazachy per
French Embassy
Kazansky per
Pogorelsky per
Kazansky t
Oktyabrskaya
Krymsky Most Landing
Gorky Park
1
ul Krymsky val (Garden Ring)
5
Oktyabrskaya
Oktyabrskaya pl
Pushkinskaya nab
Donskoy Monastery (2.5km)
proezd Apakova
Dobryninskaya
Serpukhovskaya
Danilov Monastery (1.8km)
ul Zatsepa
14
19
22
36.6
18
Pyatnitskaya ul
Novokuznetskaya
Runovsky per
27
Zamoskvorechie
17
State Tretyakov Gallery Main Branch
2
16
Tretyakovskaya
Bolshoy Tolmachevsky per
ul Bolshaya Ordynka
ul N A Ostrovskogo
Golikovsky per
Pyatnitskaya ul
Novokuznetskaya ul
Ozerkovsky per
Sadovnicheskaya nab
Ozerkovskaya nab
Sadovnicheskaya ul
Bolshoy Krasnokholmsky most
15
ul Bakhrushina
Tatarskaya ul
Zverev most
25
Krasnokholmskaya nab
ul Zatsepsky val
3-y Shlyuzovy per
Shlyuzovaya nab
Shluzovaya most
Paveletskaya
Paveletskaya pl
Valovaya ul
Paveletsky Vokzal

Zamoskvorechie & Taganka

Top Sights
1 Gorky Park ... A4
2 State Tretyakov Gallery Main Branch ... C2

Sights
3 Art Muzeon & Krymskaya Naberezhnaya ... B3
4 Bunker-42 Cold War Museum ... E2
5 Garage Museum of Contemporary Art ... B4
6 Lumiere Brothers Photography Centre ... B2
7 Museum of the Russian Icon ... E1
8 New Tretyakov Gallery ... B3
9 Novospassky Monastery ... F4
10 Red October ... B2
11 Rublyov Museum of Early Russian Culture & Art ... G1
12 Sakharov Centre ... F1

Activities, Courses & Tours
13 Bersenevskiye Bany ... B2
14 Oliver Bikes ... C1

Sleeping
15 IBIS Bakhrushina ... D3
Mercure Moscow Paveletskaya ... (see 15)
16 Park Inn Sadu ... C2
17 Three Penguins ... C2
18 Weekend Inn Apartments ... C2

Eating
19 Chugunny most ... C2
20 Darbazi ... E1
21 Mizandari ... B2
22 Ochen Domashneye Kafe ... C2
23 Produkty ... B2

Drinking & Nightlife
Bar Strelka ... (see 26)
24 Gipsy ... B2
Rolling Stone ... (see 6)

Entertainment
25 Moscow International House of Music ... E3
26 Strelka Institute for Architecture, Media & Design ... B2

Shopping
27 Bookhunter ... D2
28 Central House of Artists (TsDKh) ... A3

and European-ness is a vibrant arts centre filled with cool bars, restaurants and galleries. With an aptly revolutionary name, the former Red October chocolate factory looks straight into Kremlin's eyes – a vivid reminder that Russia is not all about totalitarian control and persecution.

Made of red brick, like its imperial counterpart across the river, the factory was built by German national Theodor Ferdinand von Einem and proudly bore his name until the Bolshevik takeover. Production was suspended in the noughties when its conversion into Moscow's hottest restaurant and entertainment area began. These days it is a key part of the hipster belt stretching along the river into Gorky Park and beyond. Come here to rub shoulders with Moscow's smart, cool and beautiful in one of the rooftop bars or check out an exhibition at the flagship **Strelka Institute** (Map p90; www.strelkainstitute.ru; Bersenevskaya nab 14/5; Ⓜ Kropotkinskaya) or **Lumiere Brothers Photography Centre** (Map p90; www.lumiere.ru; Bldg 1, Bolotnaya nab 3; ⏲ noon-9pm Tue-Sun).

Sadly, Red October might be losing a part of its pull as the embattled independent Dozhd TV channel (that is, half of the trendy crowd in local bars) is moving out and the pro-Putin LifeNews channel is taking over the premises.

Art Muzeon & Krymskaya Naberezhnaya SCULPTURE PARK
(Map p90; ul Krymsky val 10; Ⓜ Park Kultury) FREE Now fully revamped and merged with the wonderfully reconstructed Krymskaya Naberezhnaya embankment, is this motley collection of (mostly kitschy) sculpture and monuments to Soviet idols (Stalin, Sverdlov, a selection of Lenins and Brezhnevs) that were ripped from their pedestals in the post-1991 wave of anti-Soviet feeling. All of these stand in a lovely garden with boardwalks and many inviting benches.

New Tretyakov Gallery GALLERY
(Новая Третьяковская галерея; Map p90; www.tretyakovgallery.ru/en/; ul Krymsky val 10; adult/student ₽400/250; ⏲ 10am-6pm Tue, Wed, Sat & Sun, 10am-9pm Thu & Fri, ticket office closes 1hr before closing; Ⓜ Park Kultury) The premier venue for 20th-century Russian art is this branch of the State Tretyakov Gallery, better known as the New Tretyakov. This place has much more than the typical socialist realist images of muscle-bound men wielding scythes, and busty women milking cows (although there's

that too). The exhibits showcase avant-garde artists such as Malevich, Kandinsky, Chagall, Goncharova and Popova.

★Gorky Park PARK

(Парк Горького; Map p90; ⏲24hr; 📶 👪; Ⓜ Oktyabrskaya) FREE Moscow's main escape from the city within the city is not your conventional expanse of nature preserved deep inside an urban jungle. It is not a funfair either, though it used to be one. Its official name says it all – Maxim Gorky's Central Park of Culture & Leisure. That's exactly what it provides: culture and leisure in all shapes and forms. Designed by avant-garde architect Konstantin Melnikov as a piece of communist utopia in the 1920s, these days it showcases the enlightened transformation Moscow has undergone in the recent past.

Garage Museum of Contemporary Art ART GALLERY

(Map p90; www.garageccc.com; ul Krymsky val 9; adult/student ₽300/150; ⏲11am-9pm Mon-Thu; Ⓜ Oktyabrskaya) The brainchild of Moscow art fairy Darya Zhukova, incidentally the girlfriend of oligarch Roman Abramovich, has seen better times, but it remains one of the hottest modern-art venues in the capital. Retaining its original name, Garage is now housed in a temporary, though notable, Gorky Park structure – architect Sigeru Ban used recycled paper as the construction material.

Bunker-42 Cold War Museum MUSEUM

(Map p90; ☎495-500 0554; www.bunker42.com; 5-ya Kotelnichesky per 11; admission ₽1300; ⏲by appointment; Ⓜ Taganskaya) On a quiet side street near Taganskaya pl, a nondescript neoclassical building is the gateway to the secret Cold War–era communications centre.

A TOUR OF THE TRETYAKOV GALLERY

The main building of the Tretyakov Gallery (p89) houses the world's biggest collection of Russian icons and prerevolutionary Russian art. Start your tour on the 2nd floor.

Breeze through the first section of the museum, which displays many portraits and landscapes from the 18th and 19th centuries. The real gems of the collection start with room 16. In the 1870s daring artists started to use their medium to address social issues, thus founding the Peredvizhniki (Wanderers).

Room 17 is dedicated to **Vasily Perov**, one of the original founders of the movement. Look for his famous portrait of Dostoevsky and the moving painting *Troika*, with its stark depiction of child labour.

Viktor Vasnetsov (room 26) painted fantastical depictions of fairy tales and historical figures. His painting *Bogatyrs* (Heroes) is perhaps the best example from the revivalist movement, although *A Knight at the Crossroads* is more dramatic.

Vasily Surikov (room 28) excels at large-scale historical scenes. Most famously, *Boyarina Morozova* captures the history of the schism in the Orthodox Church and how it tragically played out for one family.

Ilya Repin (rooms 29 and 30) is perhaps the most beloved Russian realist painter. *Ivan the Terrible and his Son Ivan* is downright chilling. Room 31 has a few masterpieces by **Nikolai Ge**, another founder of the Peredvizhniki movement.

Mikhail Vrubel (rooms 32 to 34) was a symbolist-era artist who defies classification. One entire wall is covered with his fantastic art nouveau mural *The Princess of the Dream*.

Descend to the 1st floor to find a selection of landscapes by **Isaac Levitan** in room 37 and portraits by **Valentin Serov** in rooms 41 and 42. Continue to rooms 43 to 48 to see Russian forays into Impressionism, art nouveau and symbolism. Defying categorisation, **Nikolai Rerikh (Roerich)** shows off his fantastical storytelling style in room 47.

Proceed to the ground floor to peruse the world-class collection of icons, found in rooms 56 to 62. Room 60 contains **Holy Trinity**, Andrei Rublyov's icon from Sergiev Posad, often regarded as Russia's greatest icon.

End your tour at the **Church of St Nicholas in Tolmachi**. The centrepiece is the revered 12th-century *Vladimir Icon of the Mother of God*, protector of all Russia, which was transferred here from the Assumption Cathedral in the Kremlin.

WORTH A TRIP

SPARROW HILLS

The green hills in the south of Moscow are known as Sparrow Hills (Vorobyovy Gory). Running along the south side of the river bank, opposite the tip of the Khamovniki peninsula, there is a pleasant strip of greenery known as **Vorobyovy Gory Nature Preserve** (Воробёвы горы; Map p64; www.vorobyovy-gory.ru; Ⓜ Vorobyovy Gory) FREE. This wooded hillside is a less-developed, less-crowded extension of Gorky Park and Neskuchny Garden. The paved path that originates further north continues along the river for several kilometres, and bikes and skates are available to rent here.

Walking trails from the river bank wind up through the woods to a **lookout point**. From here, most of the city spreads out before you. It is an excellent vantage point to see Luzhniki, the huge stadium complex built across the river for the 1980 Olympics, as well as Novodevichy Convent and the Cathedral of Christ the Saviour.

The Stalinist spire of **Moscow State University** (Московский Государственный Университет; MGU; Map p64; Universitetskaya pl; Ⓜ Universitet) towers over the square. One of the 'Seven Sisters', the building is the result of four years of hard labour by convicts between 1949 and 1953. It boasts an amazing 36 storeys and 33km of corridors. The shining star that sits atop the spire is supposed to weigh 12 tonnes.

The facility was meant to serve as the communications headquarters in the event of a nuclear attack. As such, the building was just a shell, serving as an entryway to the 7000-sq-metre space 60m underground. Now in private hands, the facility has been converted into a sort of a museum dedicated to the Cold War.

Unfortunately, not much remains from the Cold War days. The vast place is nearly empty, except for a few exhibits set up for the benefit of visitors, such as a scale model of the facility. Visitors watch a 20-minute film about the history of the Cold War, followed by a guided tour of the four underground 'blocks'.

Sakharov Centre MUSEUM

(Map p90; ☎495-623 4401; www.sakharov-center.ru; ul Zemlyanoy val 57; ⊙11am-7pm Tue-Sun; Ⓜ Chkalovskaya) FREE South of Kursky vokzal, by the Yauza River, is a small park with a two-storey house containing a human-rights centre named after Russia's most famous dissident. Inside, there is a museum recounting the life of Sakharov, the nuclear-physicist-turned-human-rights-advocate, detailing the years of repression in Russia and providing a history of the courage shown by the dissident movement.

Museum of the Russian Icon ART MUSEUM

(Частный музей русской иконы; Map p90; www.russikona.ru; ul Goncharnaya 3; ⊙11am-7pm Thu-Tue; Ⓜ Taganskaya) FREE This museum houses the private collection of Russian businessman and art patron Mikhail Abramov. He has personally amassed a collection of more than 4000 pieces of Russian and Eastern Christian art, including some 600 icons. The collection is unique in that it represents nearly all schools of Russian iconography. Highlights include Simon Ushakov's 17th-century depiction of the Virgin Odigitria and an icon of St Nikolai Mirlikiisky.

Rublyov Museum of Early Russian Culture & Art ART MUSEUM

(Музей древнерусской культуры и искусства им Андрея Рублёва; Map p90; www.rublev-museum.ru; Andronevskaya pl 10; adult/student ₽350/200; ⊙11am-6pm Mon, Tue, Fri & Sat, 2-9pm Thu; Ⓜ Ploshchad Ilycha) On the grounds of the former Andronikov Monastery, the Rublyov Museum exhibits icons from days of yore and the present. Unfortunately, it does not include any work by its acclaimed namesake artist. It is still worth visiting, not least for its romantic location. Andrei Rublyov, the master of icon painting, was a monk here in the 15th century. He is buried in the grounds, but no one knows quite where.

Danilov Monastery MONASTERY

(Даниловский монастырь; Map p64; msdm.ru; ul Danilovsky val; ⊙7am-7pm; Ⓜ Tulskaya) FREE The headquarters of the Russian Orthodox Church stands behind white fortress walls. On holy days this place seethes with worshippers murmuring prayers, lighting candles and ladling holy water into jugs at the tiny chapel inside the gates. The Danilovsky Monastery was built in the late 13th century

WORTH A TRIP

TSARITSYNO

On a wooded hill in far southeast Moscow, **Tsaritsyno Palace** (Музей-заповедник Царицыно; ☎495-355 4844; www.tsaritsyno-museum.ru; ⏰grounds 6am-midnight, exhibits 11am-6pm Tue-Fri, 11am-8pm Sat & Sun; Ⓜ Tsaritsino) FREE is a modern-day manifestation of the exotic summer home that Catherine the Great began in 1775 but never finished. For hundreds of years, the palace was little more than a shell, until the Russian government finally decided to finish it in 2007.

Nowadays, the **Great Palace** (Большой дворец; admission ₽150) is a fantastical building that combines old Russian, Gothic, classical and Arabic styles. Inside, exhibits are dedicated to the history of Tsaritsyno, as well as the life of Catherine the Great. The nearby kitchen building, or **khlebny dom** (Хлебный дом; admission ₽300), also hosts rotating exhibits, sometimes culinary and sometimes on less-tantalising topics such as icons and art. The *khlebny dom* is a pleasant place to hear classical **concerts** (☎499-725 7291; tickets ₽150-300; ⏰5pm Sat & Sun) in summer.

Tsaritsyno is easy to find: just follow the signs from the eponymous metro station.

by Daniil, the first Prince of Moscow, as an outer city defence.

The monastery was repeatedly altered over the next several hundred years, and served as a factory and a detention centre during the Soviet period. It was restored in time to replace Sergiev Posad as the Church's spiritual and administrative centre, and became the official residence of the Patriarch during the Russian Orthodoxy's millennium celebrations in 1988.

Enter beneath the pink **St Simeon Stylite Gate-Church** on the north wall. The oldest and busiest church is the **Church of the Holy Fathers of the Seven Ecumenical Councils**, where worship is held continuously from 10am to 5pm daily. Founded in the 17th century and rebuilt repeatedly, the church contains several chapels on two floors: the main one upstairs is flanked by side chapels to St Daniil (on the northern side) and Sts Boris and Gleb (south). On the ground level, the small main chapel is dedicated to the Protecting Veil, and the northern one to the prophet Daniil.

The yellow neoclassical **Trinity Cathedral**, built in the 1830s, is an austere counterpart to the other buildings. West of the cathedral are the patriarchate's External Affairs Department and, at the far end of the grounds, the Patriarch's Official Residence. Against the north wall, to the east of the residence, there's a 13th-century **Armenian carved-stone cross** *(khachkar)*, a gift from the Armenian Church. The church guest house, in the southern part of the monastery grounds, has been turned into the elegant Danilovskaya Hotel (p101).

Donskoy Monastery MONASTERY
(Донской монастырь; Map p64; ☎495-952 1646; www.donskoi.org; Donskaya ul; Ⓜ Shabolovskaya) Moscow's youngest monastery, Donskoy Monastery was founded in 1591 as the home of the *Virgin of the Don* icon (now in the Tretyakov Gallery). This icon is credited with the victory in the 1380 battle of Kulikovo; it's also said that, in 1591, the Tatar Khan Giri retreated without a fight after the icon showered him with burning arrows in a dream.

Activities

★ **Sanduny Baths** BATHHOUSE
(Map p74; ☎495-628 4633; www.sanduny.ru; Neglinnaya ul 14; male & female 1st class ₽1500, male 2nd class & female premium ₽1850, male premium class ₽2300; ⏰8am-10pm; Ⓜ Kuznetsky Most) Sanduny is the oldest and most luxurious *banya* in the city. The Gothic Room is a work of art with its rich wood carving, while the main shower room has an aristocratic Roman feel to it. There are several classes, as on trains, though regulars say that, here, second male class is actually better than the premium class.

No matter which class you choose, it will be a costly experience, especially if you rent the essential items – a sheet to wrap yourself into (₽170), a felt hat to avoid burning your hair (₽410) and a pair of slippers.

Bersenevskiye Bany BATHHOUSE
(Берсеневские бани; Map p90; ☎495-281 5086; Bersenevskaya nab 16 str 5; 2hr ₽1200, each subsequent hour ₽600; ⏰8am-11pm, women only Mon-Wed, men only Thu-Sun) Proof that Red October hipsters have no aversion to centuries-old

traditions, this new bathhouse is both elegant and competently run. The vaulted cellars of the former Smirnov distillery (yes, this is the birthplace of Smirnoff vodka) create just the right circulation in the steam room. Unless you are an old Russian *banya* hand, splash some extra money and let them pamper you.

If being beaten with twigs qualifies as pampering, that is.

Krasnopresnkiye Bany BATHHOUSE

(Краснопресненские бани; Map p80; ☎men's banya 495-255 5306, women's banya 495-253 8690; www.baninapresne.ru; Stolyarny per 7; general admission ₽1200-1700; ⏰8am-11pm; Ⓜ Ulitsa 1905 Goda) Lacking an old-fashioned, decadent atmosphere, this modern, clean, efficient place nonetheless provides a first-rate *banya* experience. The facility has a Russian steam room, Finnish sauna, plunge pool and massage services.

Oliver Bikes CYCLING

(Оливер Байкс; Map p90; ☎499-340 2609; www.bikerentalmoscow.com; Pyatnitskaya ul 2; per hour/day from ₽100/500, tours ₽900; ⏰2-10pm Tue-Fri, 11am-10pm Sat & Sun; Ⓜ Novokuznetskaya) Oliver rents all kinds of two-wheeled vehicles, including cruisers, mountain bikes, folding bikes and tandem bikes, all of which are in excellent condition. Its location is convenient for bike rides along the Moscow River. Oliver also offers weekend bike tours, but only occasionally in English.

MOSCOW FOR CHILDREN

Filled with icons and onion domes, the Russian capital might not seem like an appealing destination for kids, but you'd be surprised. In Moscow, little people will find museums, parks, theatres and even restaurants that cater especially to them. Look for the 👪 icon for options that are particularly good for kids.

Sights & Activities

For starters, the city is filled with more than 100 parks and gardens, with plenty of space for kids to let off steam. Many have playgrounds, while larger sites such as Gorky Park (p92) and Izmaylovsky Park offer bicycles, paddle boats and more.

Most sights and museums offer reduced-rate tickets for children up to 12 or 18 years of age. Admission for children under five years old is often free. Look out for family tickets, which allow the whole family to enter for one price.

Eating

Some restaurants have a dedicated play space for children. Many restaurants host 'children's parties' on Saturday and Sunday afternoons, offering toys, games, entertainment and supervision for kids while their parents eat.

Entertainment

Cultural instruction starts at a young age in Moscow, with many companies and performances geared specifically towards young kids.

The country's largest puppet theatre, **Obraztsov Puppet Theatre & Museum** (Театр и музей кукол Образцова; Map p74; ☎495-699 5373; www.puppet.ru; Sadovaya-Samotechnaya ul 3; ⏰box office 11am-2.30pm & 3.30-7pm; Ⓜ Tsvetnoy Bulvar), performs colourful Russian folk tales and adapted classical plays.

At the unusual **Kuklachev Cat Theatre** (Театр кошек Куклачёва; Map p64; ☎495-243 4005; www.kuklachev.ru; Kutuzovsky pr 25; tickets ₽300-2000; ⏰noon, 2pm or 4pm Thu-Sun, daily in summer; 👪; Ⓜ Kutuzovskaya), acrobatic cats do all kinds of stunts for the audience's delight.

Performances at the **Moscow Children's Musical Theatre** (Детский Музыкальный театр им. Н.И.Сац; Map p64; ☎495-930 7021; www.teatr-sats.ru; pr Vernadskogo 5; tickets ₽200-1200; ⏰times vary Wed-Sun Sep-Jun; 👪; Ⓜ Universitet) are highly entertaining and educational.

Transport

The metro might be fun (and free) for kids, but be careful during rush hour, when trains and platforms are packed. Also, be aware that there are no elevators, so you'll face some challenges with your stroller. Detskoe Taxi (p122) company will look out for your kids, offering smoke-free cars and child seats upon request.

Tours

Capital Shipping Co BOAT TOURS
(CCK, Столичная Судоходная Компания; ☎495-225 6070; www.cck-ship.ru; 90min tour adult/child ₽500/300, 24hr pass ₽800/400) Ferries ply the Moscow River from May to September (every 20 minutes); board at any dock along the route. Originally, this was simply a form of transportation, but visitors realised that riding the entire route (1½ hours) was a great way to see the city. Alternatively, buy a full-day pass, which allows you to get on and off at will.

CCK also offers boat excursions out of central Moscow, such as to the Nikolo-Ugreshsky Monastery in the eastern suburb of Dzerzhinsky.

Capital Tours TOUR
(Map p70; ☎495-232 2442; www.capitaltours.ru; Gostiny Dvor, ul Ilynka 4, entry 6; Kremlin tours ₽1600, other tours ₽900; ⏰10am Fri-Wed; Ⓜ Kitay-Gorod) This spin-off of Patriarshy Dom offers a daily Kremlin tour, as well as regularly scheduled tours of the metro and Moscow by night. The guides are well-informed but not super engaging.

Also on offer: a daily four-hour tour of Jewish Moscow, which goes by vehicle to two synagogues and other sites of note.

Moscow 360 WALKING TOURS
(☎8-915-205 8360; www.moscow360.org) FREE This ambitious company offers four – count 'em, four! – different walking tours, all of which are free of charge. They include tours of Red Square, the Cathedral of Christ the Saviour and the Metro, as well as – the most unusual – an AK-47 Tour (the guiding and transport are free, but you'll pay to shoot). Tips are gratefully accepted – obviously.

Moscow Bike Tours CYCLING TOUR
(☎8-916-970 1419; www.moscowbiketours.com; 3hr tour ₽1800) Cover more ground and see more sites, while getting fresh air and a bit of exercise: that's a win-win-win! On the recommended three-hour bike tour, You'll enjoy magnificent views of Moscow from Krymskaya embankment, riding through Gorky Park and all the way down to Sparrow Hills, before crossing into Khamovniki. Day and evening rides offered, with an extended tour available on weekends.

Moscow Free Tour WALKING TOURS
(Map p70; ☎495-222 3466; http://moscowfree-tour.com; Nikolskaya ul 4/5; paid tours ₽950-1550) Every day, these enthusiastic ladies offer an informative, inspired two-hour guided walk around Red Square and Kitay Gorod – and it's completely free. It's so good, that (they think) you'll sign up for one of their excellent paid tours, covering the Kremlin, the Arbat and the Metro, or more thematic tours like communist Moscow or mystical Moscow.

Festivals & Events

Winter Festival CULTURAL
An outdoor fun-fest for two weeks in December and January, for those with anti-freeze in their veins. Admire the elaborate ice sculptures on Red Square, stand in a crowd of snowmen on ul Arbat and ride the troika at Izmaylovsky Park.

Golden Mask Festival THEATRE
(www.goldenmask.ru) This festival involves two months of performances by Russia's premier drama, opera, dance and musical performers, culminating in a prestigious awards ceremony in April.

Moscow International Film Festival FILM
(www.moscowfilmfestival.ru) This 10-day event in June/July attracts filmmakers from the US and Europe, as well as the most promising Russian artists. Films are shown at theatres around the city.

City Day CULTURAL
City Day, or *den goroda* in Russian, celebrates Moscow's birthday on the first weekend in September. The day kicks off with a festive parade, followed by live music on Red Square and plenty of food, fireworks and fun.

Moscow Biennale of Contemporary Art ART FESTIVAL
(www.moscowbiennale.ru) This month-long festival, held in odd-numbered years (and sometimes in different months), has the aim of establishing the capital as an international centre for contemporary art. Venues around the city exhibit works by artists from around the world.

December Nights Festival ART, MUSIC
(www.artsmuseum.ru) Perhaps Moscow's most prestigious music event, this annual festival in December is hosted at the Pushkin Museum of Fine Arts, with a month of performances by high-profile musicians and accompanying art exhibits.

WORTH A TRIP

OLD BELIEVERS' COMMUNITY

One of Russia's most atmospheric religious centres is the **Old Believers' Community** (Старообрядческая Община; Map p64; ul Rogozhsky posyolok 29; ⌚9am-6pm Tue-Sun; Ⓜ Ploshchad Ilycha) at Rogozhskoe, 3km east of Taganskaya pl. The Old Believers split from the main Russian Orthodox Church in 1653, when they refused to accept certain reforms. They have maintained the old forms of worship and customs ever since. In the late 18th century, during a brief period free of persecution, rich Old Believer merchants founded this community, which is among the most important in the country.

The yellow, classical-style **Intercession Church** contains one of Moscow's finest collections of icons, all dating from before 1653, with the oldest being the 14th-century *Saviour with the Angry Eye* (Spas yaroe oko), protected under glass near the south door. The icons in the Deesis row (the biggest row) of the iconostasis are supposedly by the Rublyov school, while the seventh, *The Saviour*, is attributed to Rublyov himself. North of the church is the **Rogozhskoe Cemetery**.

Visitors are welcome at the church, but women should take care to wear long skirts (no trousers) and headscarves. The community is a 30-minute walk from pl Ilycha. Otherwise, take trolleybus 16 or 26, or bus 51, east from Taganskaya pl and get off after crossing a railway.

Sleeping

Moscow is flush with international luxury hotels, but more affordable options are few and far between. Fortunately, a slew of hostels have opened in Moscow, so budget travellers have plenty of options. And, slowly but surely, more midrange options are also appearing, usually in the form of 'minihotels'. Prices usually include the 20% VAT (value-added tax) but not the 5% sales tax that's charged mainly at luxury hotels.

- Budget accommodation is generally less than ₽3000. It is usually dorm-style, although there are a few private rooms available in this range.
- Midrange accommodation falls between ₽3000 and ₽8000 per night. This wide-ranging category includes privately owned minihotels, which usually occupy one or two floors in an apartment building. The rooms have been renovated to comfortably accommodate guests, but the hotel itself (which might have a dozen rooms or less) does not usually offer other facilities. Considering the shortage of midrange options, minihotels are some of the best-value accommodation in the city.
- Top end starts at ₽8000 and goes all the way up.

Kitay Gorod

Capital House HOTEL **$$**
(Map p70; ☎8-968-931 6646; www.capitalhouse.su; Bol Cherkassky per 4, bldg 1; r from ₽4500; Ⓜ Lubyanka) It feels a little sketchy when you enter through the courtyard, off a side street in the heart of Kitay Gorod. The surrounding buildings are rather decrepit, but the interior of this mini-hotel is fresh, with 20 simple rooms on the first two floors. It's nothing fancy, but you'll find acceptable, Ikea-style furnishings, high ceilings and plenty of natural light.

Breakfast is served in the rooms.

★**Hotel Metropol** HISTORIC HOTEL **$$$**
(Map p70; ☎499-501 7800; www.metropol-moscow.ru; Teatralny proezd 1/4; d ₽9930-11,400, breakfast ₽2000; Ⓜ Teatralnaya) Nothing short of an art nouveau masterpiece, the 1907 Metropol brings an artistic, historic touch to every nook and cranny, from the spectacular exterior to the grand lobby, to the individually decorated (but small) rooms. The breakfast buffet is ridiculously priced, but it's served under the restaurant's gorgeous stained-glass ceiling.

The lower end of the price range is available on weekends and during other discounted periods.

Tverskoy District

★**Godzillas Hostel** HOSTEL **$**
(Map p74; ☎495-699 4223; www.godzillashostel.com; Bolshoy Karetny per 6; dm from ₽760, s/d ₽2400/2600; Ⓜ Tsvetnoy Bulvar) Tried and true, Godzillas is Moscow's best-known hostel, with dozens of beds spread out over four floors. The rooms come in various sizes,

but they are all spacious and lightfilled and painted in different colours. To cater to the many guests, there are bathroom facilities on each floor, three kitchens and a big living room with satellite TV.

Anti-Hostel Cosmic HOSTEL **$**
(Map p74; ☎499-390 8132; http://anti-hostel.ru/; ul Bolshaya Dmitrovka 7/5, str 3; capsules from ₽1350; wi-fi; M Teatralnaya) Occupying a converted apartment, this place marries the idea of hostel with that of capsule hotel. The location is hard to beat – Red Square is just a five-minute walk away. Capsules create a tiny, though comfortable universe for guests to enjoy on their own. There is also a nice common area to mingle with fellow capsule-dwellers.

iVAN Hostel HOSTEL **$**
(Map p74; ☎8-916-407 1178; www.ivanhostel.com; per Petrovsky 1/30 apt 23; dm from ₽750, d with shared bathroom from ₽2500; wi-fi; M Chekhovskaya) iVAN consists of two clean and quiet apartments located in the same tsarist-era residential building, a short walk from Pushkin square. Being a hostel, it naturally has dorms – and very nice ones at that; however, its main virtue are several simply furnished but tastefully designed private rooms with whitewashed walls and large windows.

Bathrooms are shared and there is no breakfast, but you can cook it yourself in the fully equipped communal kitchen. Washing machine is available at extra charge.

★ **Sleepbox Hotel** HOTEL **$$**
(Map p64; ☎495-989 4104; www.sleepbox-hotel.ru; ul 1st Tverskaya-Yamskaya 27; s without bathroom from ₽3200, d/q from ₽4700/5500; air-con, wi-fi; M Belorusskaya) It might draw comparisons with capsule hotels, but it is actually better. Think a comfortable train compartment – it's close to what you get in this immaculately clean and unusual hotel, conveniently located for those arriving by train from Sheremetyevo airport. Common showers and toilets are very modern and clean; queues are unusual.

It also has more conventional doubles with bathrooms, and larger family rooms. Bicycles are available for rent.

Guest House Amelie GUESTHOUSE **$$**
(Map p74; ☎495-650 1789; www.hotel-amelie.ru; Strastnoy bul 4, str 3 apt 17; s/d without breakfast from ₽3000/3500; wi-fi; M Chekhovskaya) Amelie benefits from its superb location right by Pushkin Square – it's unlikely you will find a room cheaper than this in the vicinity, and it's a very nicely furnished room, too! On the downside, the hotel is a converted apartment, which means shared bathrooms and an unmarked entrance located on Kozitsky per.

Once you find this lane, look out for the entrance number in the building marked as per Kozitsky 3. Dial 17 and they will let you in.

SERVICED APARTMENTS

Entrepreneurial Muscovites have begun renting out apartments on a short-term basis. Flats are equipped with kitchens and laundry facilities and they almost always offer wi-fi access. The rental agency usually makes arrangements for the flat to be cleaned every day or every few days. Often, a good-sized flat is available for the price of a hotel room, or less. It is an ideal solution for families or travellers in a small group.

Apartments are around ₽4300 to ₽8600 per night. Expect to pay more for fully renovated, Western-style apartments. Although there are usually discounts for longer stays, they are not significant, so these services are not ideal for long-term renters.

Recommended agencies:

Enjoy Moscow (www.enjoymoscow.com; apt per night from US$155; wi-fi) This long-standing rental company has a range of apartments – mostly in the Tverskoy district – starting at US$155 per night. The apartments vary in size and decor, but the company provides responsive, reliable service.

Intermark Serviced Apartments (www.intermarksa.ru; apt per night from ₽6800; wi-fi) Catering mostly to business travellers, Intermark offers four-star accommodation starting at ₽6800 per night.

Moscow Suites (www.moscowsuites.ru; studio per night from US$199; wi-fi) Slick apartments in central locations on Tverskaya or Novy Arbat. Services such as airport pick-up and visa support are included in the price, which starts at US$199 for a studio.

Pushkin Hotel HOTEL $$

(Отель Пушкин; Map p74; ☎495-201 0222; http://otel-pushkin.ru; per Nastasyinsky 5, str 1; s/d from ₽7000/8000; ; M Pushkinskaya) Just off the eponymous square, this hotel strives to fuse 19th-century style with the modern perception of comfort. We'd call it plush, if not for the tiny, B&B-style reception area. There is a restaurant on the premises, but no need to use it since the area is packed with great places to eat and drink.

The entrance was poorly marked when we visited, but it's the only one in the building, so hard to miss. Note huge discounts are available during weekends.

Hotel Savoy BOUTIQUE HOTEL $$$

(Отель Савой; Map p74; ☎495-620 8500; www.savoy.ru; ul Rozhdestvenka 3; s/d from ₽9500/12,600; ; M Lubyanka) Built in 1912, the Savoy maintains an atmosphere of tsarist-era privilege for its guests, and is more intimate and affordable than other luxury hotels. All rooms are equipped with marble bathrooms and Italian fittings and furnishings. The state-of-the-art health club includes a glass-domed 20m swimming pool, complete with geysers and cascades to refresh tired bodies.

Basmanny

Privet Hostel HOSTEL $

(Хостел Привет; Map p74; ☎495-374 5949; www.privethostels.ru; per Podsosensky 3, str 2; dm from ₽800; ; M Kurskaya) Declaring itself the largest hostel in the ex-USSR, Privet occupies a mansion in the sweet and central Chistye Prudy neighbourhood. All painted in deep purple, four- and six-bed dorms have solid wooden bunk beds with orthopaedic mattresses, and some are equipped with smallish working tables. Showers and toilets look almost luxurious by Russian hostel standards.

Also on the premises is a cafe serving breakfasts (at extra charge), a small communal kitchen, a gym and a small cinema showing films in Russian and English. The entrance is on per Barashevsky.

Kitay-Gorod Hotel HOTEL $$

(Отель Китай-Город; Map p74; ☎495-991 9971; www.otel-kg.ru; Lubyansky proezd 25; s ₽3800-5500, d ₽5200-7500; ; M Kitay-Gorod) A rare chance for budget-conscious travellers to stay this close to Red Square, not to mention easy access to the metro and many restaurants in the vicinity. Forty-six small but comfortable rooms are situated on two floors of this residential building. The location can be noisy: it's worth requesting air-con as you'll want to keep your windows closed. Prices are lower on weekends.

AIRPORT ACCOMMODATION

Recommended for transit travellers who need to crash between flights, both hotels listed here operate free shuttle buses from their respective airports.

Aerotel Domodedovo (Аэротель Домодедово; ☎495-795 3868; www.airhotel.ru; Domodedovo airport; s/d from ₽6800/7400;) Small but satisfactory rooms, plus a fitness centre and billiards room.

Atlanta Sheremetyevo Hotel (☎499-647 5947; www.atlanta-hotel.ru; 7 Severnaya ul, Sheremetyevsky; s/d from ₽5100/5400;) Friendly, small and convenient, the Atlanta is an anomaly in the airport world. Reduced rates are available for six- and 12-hour layovers.

Elokhovsky Hotel HOTEL $$

(Отель Елоховский; Map p64; ☎495-632 2300; http://elohotel.ru/; ul Spartakovskaya 24; s/d 3900/4600; ; M Baumanskaya) Admittedly not very central and occupying the top floor of a shopping arcade, this hotel is nevertheless about the best value for money you can find in Moscow. Room themes are based on the world's major cities, and are painted in soothing, homey colours. The coffee machine in the lobby is available 24 hours. Baumanskaya metro and Elokhovsky cathedral are a stone's throw away.

Watching shoppers move four floors below without being able to see you is actually quite meditative.

Godzillas Urban Jungle Lodge GUESTHOUSE $$

(Map p74; ☎8-925-347 4677; www.godzillashostel.com/ujl/; ul Pokrovka 21, 3rd fl; s/d without bathroom ₽2450/₽3150; ; M Chistye Prudy) A branch of Moscow's most popular hostel, this place has about a dozen funky-looking singles and doubles above the popular Coffee Bean cafe in one of the city's loveliest neighbourhoods. Bathrooms are shared, and it's a bit of a walk up a steep and slightly off-putting staircase. But it is about as good as it gets for this price.

Presnya District

Bear Hostel on Mayakovskaya HOSTEL $
(Map p80; ☎495-649 6736; www.bear-hostels.com; ul Sadovaya-Kudrinskaya 32; dm ₽550-1000; 🚭 ❄ @ 📶; Ⓜ Mayakovskaya) A less institutional atmosphere gives this place a leg up. Bold colours and words of wisdom stencilled on the walls lend some lightness and brightness to the otherwise standard place, which offers dorms ranging from four to 14 beds (including one women's dorm). We're fans of the location, just around the corner from Patriarch's Ponds.

Element Hotel HOTEL $$
(Отель Элемент; Map p80; ☎495-988 0064; www.hotel-element.ru; Bolshaya Nikitskaya ul 24/1, bldg 5; d ₽3800-4500; 🚭 ❄ 📶; Ⓜ Arbatskaya) This location on trendy Bol Nikitskaya is prime, and prices are unbeatable; so you'll forgive the side-street entrance and the fact that rooms can be rented by the hour. It's actually a perfectly respectable place, with spotless rooms, pleasant decor and helpful staff. The cheapest rooms are tiny, so unless you're travelling solo, you'll probably want to upgrade.

★ **Hotel de Paris** BOUTIQUE HOTEL $$$
(Map p80; ☎495-777 0052; www.hotel-deparis.ru; Bol Bronnaya ul 23, bldg 3; s/d from ₽9000/9450; 🚭 ❄ 📶; Ⓜ Pushkinskaya) Steps from the madness of Tverskaya, this is a delightfully stylish hotel tucked into a quiet courtyard off the Boulevard Ring. Situated on the lower floors, the rooms do not get much natural light, but they feature king-size beds, Jacuzzi tubs and elegant design. Service is consistently friendly. Prices drop by 40% on weekends, offering terrific value.

★ **Nikitskaya Hotel** BOUTIQUE HOTEL $$$
(Гостиница Никитская ; Map p80; ☎495-933 5001; www.assambleya-hotels.ru; Bolshaya Nikitskaya ul 12; s/d ₽9300/11,300; 🚭 ❄ 📶; Ⓜ Okhotny Ryad) If you like small hotels in quaint neighbourhoods you will love the Nikitskaya Hotel. While the building and rooms are perfectly maintained, the hotel preserves an old-fashioned atmosphere of cosiness and comfort. And you can't beat the location, in the midst of the excellent restaurants and grand architecture of Bolshaya Nikitskaya. Breakfast (₽500) is served in the popular attached restaurant, **Ugolyok** (Уголёк; Map p80; ☎495-629 0504; Bolshaya Nikitskaya 12; 🕐9am-midnight Sun-Wed, to 1.30am Thu-Sat; 🚭; Ⓜ Biblioteka imeni Lenina).

Arbat House Hotel HOTEL $$$
(Отель Арбат Хаус; Map p80; ☎495-643 1910, reservations 495-695 5136; www.arbat-house.ru; Skatertny per 13; s/d from ₽7800/8300; 🚭 ❄ 📶; Ⓜ Arbatskaya) With new management, a new name and new renovations, the Arbat House is still essentially a three-star hotel with four-star prices (but not bad value by Moscow standards). The rooms are small but comfortable places to crash. Service is friendly. The quaint location is not all that close to the Arbat, but tucked into a quiet residential street surrounded by embassies.

Arbat & Khamovniki

Bear Hostel on Smolenskaya HOSTEL $
(Map p84; ☎495-649 6736; www.bear-hostels.com; Smolensky bul 15; dm ₽600-950, breakfast ₽130; 🚭 ❄ @ 📶; Ⓜ Smolenskaya) A smart, no-nonsense hostel with air-conditioned dorms (all co-ed) on the Garden Ring just west of the Arbat. The 50 wide bunk beds have guardrails to protect the young or inebriated. This is the nicest of the reliable Bear hostel chain, which also includes the run-of-the-mill Bear on Mayakovskaya and the larger flagship Bear on Arbatskaya.

★ **Blues Hotel** BOUTIQUE HOTEL $$
(Map p64; ☎495-961 1161; www.blues-hotel.ru; ul Dovatora 8; s/d from ₽5800/6300; 🚭 ❄ 📶; Ⓜ Sportivnaya) The location is not exactly central, but is not a disadvantage. It is steps from the red-line metro (five stops to Red Square) and a few blocks from Novodevichy, with several worthwhile restaurants in the vicinity. Considering that, this friendly, affordable boutique hotel is a gem, offering stylish, spotless rooms with king-size beds and flat-screen TVs.

Further discounts on weekends.

★ **Mercure Arbat Hotel** BOUTIQUE HOTEL $$
(Гостиница Меркурий Арбат; Map p84; ☎495-225 0025; www.mercure.com; Smolenskaya pl 6; d from ₽7000; 🚭 ❄ 📶; Ⓜ Smolenskaya) We're charmed by this sweet boutique hotel. It's not much to look at on the outside, but the rooms are attractive and rather plush to boot. The most affordable ones have queen-size beds, work space, flat-screen TVs and chic bathrooms with basin sinks. It's surprisingly quiet for its location right on the Garden Ring. Excellent value, especially on weekends.

You'll pay extra for the big buffet breakfast.

People Hotel HOTEL $$
(Map p84; ☎495-363 4581; www.hotelpeople.ru; Novinsky bul 11; s/d ₽3890/4290, without bathroom ₽2690/3290; ; Smolenskaya) This delightful option occupies three wings in a stately neoclassical palace, just outside the Garden Ring. Rooms are small and sparse, walls are thin, and house cleaning comes every third day. But the sunlit, modern rooms represent rare good value in Moscow, and there is a nice kitchen and lounge for common use. Summer nights can be hot with no air-con.

Bulgakov Mini-Hotel HOTEL $$
(Map p84; ☎495-229 8018; www.bulgakovhotel.com; ul Arbat 49; d ₽4000; ; Smolenskaya) The classy rooms, graced with high ceilings and Master-and-Margarita-inspired art, are as good as it gets in Moscow for this price, especially considering the primo location. The bathrooms are tiny but they are private. Enter the courtyard from Plotnikov per and use entrance No 2.

Zamoskvorechie & Taganka

Three Penguins HOSTEL $
(Три Пингвина; Map p90; ☎8-910-446 1778; www.3penguins.ru; ul Pyatnitskaya 20, str 2; dm/d ₽750/₽2600; ; Novokuznetskaya) It's a very small hostel located in a converted flat with a comfy (we'd even say intimate) common area in the building best identified by cafe Illarion, just off ul Pyatnitskaya. Apart from the dorms, it features four doubles – two regular and two with bunk beds.

The Penguins scores high on friendliness and has a prime location in Zamoskvorechie's busiest area (also convenient for the Kremlin). Numerous cafes and Tretyakov Gallery are in close proximity.

Weekend Inn Apartments GUESTHOUSE $$
(Map p90; ☎495-648 4047; www.weekend-inn.ru; ul Pyatnitskaya 10, str 1; d/tr from ₽3900/4500; Novokuznetskaya) A short walk from the Kremlin across the river, this modest establishment occupies two upper floors in a 19th-century building. Rooms are spacious, with whitewashed walls and minimalist design. Shared bathrooms are immaculately clean and there is a common kitchen area, but there's honestly no reason to bother cooking – the area is packed with cafes.

Danilovskaya Hotel HOTEL $$
(Даниловская гостиница; Map p64; ☎495-954 0503; www.danilovsky.ru; Bul Starodanilovsky per; s/d incl breakfast ₽6000/6500; ; Tulskaya) Moscow's holiest hotel is on the grounds of the 12th-century monastery of the same name – the exquisite setting comes complete with 18th-century churches and well-maintained gardens. The modern five-storey hotel was built so that nearly all the rooms have a view of the grounds. The recently renovated rooms are simple but

SLEEPING WITH STALIN'S SISTERS

Two of the Stalinist skyscrapers known as the Seven Sisters contain hotels. Both of these have been renovated into four-star facilities with Western management.

Radisson Royal (Радиссон; Map p64; ☎495-221 5555; www.radissonblu.com; Kutuzovsky pr 2/1; r from ₽11,000; ; Kievskaya) Housed in one of Stalin's Seven Sisters, this bombastic beauty sits majestically on the banks of the Moscow River facing the White House. The place has retained its old-fashioned ostentation, with crystal chandeliers, polished marble and a thematic ceiling fresco in the lobby. Heavy drapes, textured wallpaper and reproduction antiques give the guestrooms a similar atmosphere of old aristocracy, but all the modern amenities are here.

Significant discounts are available if you book well in advance or if you're willing to prepay a nonrefundable room.

Hilton Moscow Leningradskaya (Map p74; ☎495-627 5550; www.hilton.com; Kalanchevskaya ul 21/40; d from ₽7000; ; Komsomolskaya) Occupying one of the iconic Stalinist skyscrapers, the old Leningradskaya Hotel has a new life thanks to the Hilton and its upgrade. Hilton has maintained the Soviet grandiosity in the lobby, but has updated the rooms with contemporary design and state-of-the-art amenities.

This is the most convenient option if you are arriving or departing by train, due to its proximity to three stations. This beauty overlooks Komsomolskaya pl, in all its chaotic, commotion-filled glory.

clean, and breakfast is modest: no greed, gluttony or sloth to be found here.

Park Inn Sadu HOTEL $$
(Map p90; ☎495-644 4844; www.parkinn.ru; ul Bolshaya Polyanka 17; s/d from ₽3900/4500; ❄📶; Ⓜ Polyanka) It's a very regular branch of the Park Inn – think slightly impersonal, predictable comforts – which boasts a prime location within walking distance of the Kremlin and the Red October cluster of bars and galleries. Prices fall to a jaw-dropping low in the middle of summer.

IBIS Bakhrushina HOTEL $$
(Map p90; ☎495-720 5301; www.ibis.com; ul Bakhrushina 11; r from ₽3990; ❄📶; Ⓜ Paveletskaya) The IBIS's latest incursion into the city centre has improved the hotel scene here in a big way. Yes, it's just another IBIS; but in Moscow knowing exactly what you're getting is a big deal: affordable, comfortable rooms and professional, reliable service. Spa facilities in the adjacent Mercure hotel are available at extra charge.

Mercure Moscow Paveletskaya HOTEL $$
(Map p90; ☎495-720 5301; www.mercure.com; ul Bakhrushina 11; r from ₽5900; 📶; Ⓜ Paveletskaya) This Mercure branch seems to consist entirely of virtues. Convenient for Domodedovo airport trains and close to Paveletskaya metro station, it is a quality hotel with plush rooms (purple colour prevailing), located in a quiet street of portly 19th-century houses, offering four-start comforts for a price that's hard to come by in Moscow.

The complimentary spa facilities are something you might be thankful for after a sweaty day in Moscow.

ONCE & FUTURE HOTEL MOSKVA

The story goes that Stalin was shown two possible designs for the Hotel Moskva on Manezhnaya pl. Not realising they were alternatives, he approved both. The builders did not dare point out his error, and so built half the hotel in constructivist style and half in Stalinist style. The incongruous result became a familiar and beloved feature of the Moscow landscape, even gracing the label of Stolichnaya vodka bottles.

The infamous Hotel Moskva was finally demolished in 2003, but **Four Seasons** (Map p70; www.fourseasons.com; Okhotny ryad 2; 🚭❄📶🏊👪; Ⓜ Okhotny Ryad) has reconstructed the old exterior, complete with architectural quirks. The updated interior, of course, is contemporary and classy. The new five-star hotel is expected to be open by 2015.

Eating

In recent years Moscow has blossomed into a culinary capital. Foodies will be thrilled by the dining options, from old-fashioned *haute russe* to 'author cuisine'. Daring chefs are breaking down stereotypes and showing the world how creative they can be. They're importing exotic ingredients, rediscovering ancient cooking techniques and inventing new ones. And Moscow diners are eating it up. Literally.

Many restaurants, especially top-end eateries, accept credit cards, and almost all restaurants have English-language menus. Discounted 'business lunch' specials are often available weekdays before 4pm. This is a great way to sample some of the pricier restaurants around town. Most upscale places require booking a table in advance, especially on weekends.

During Lent (the 40-day period before Orthodox Easter), vegetarians will have a plethora of eating options, as many restaurants offer special Lenten menus that feature no meat or dairy products. Only a few restaurants are exclusively vegie all year round.

Kremlin & Kitay Gorod

Stolovaya 57 CAFETERIA $
(Столовая 57; Map p70; 3rd fl, GUM, Krasnaya pl 3; mains ₽200-300; ⏰10am-10pm; 🚭📖; Ⓜ Okhotny Ryad) Newly minted, this old-style cafeteria offers a nostalgic re-creation of dining in post-Stalinist Russia. The food is good – and cheap for such a fancy store. Meat cutlets and cold salads come highly recommended. This is a great place to try 'herring in a fur coat' (herring, beets, carrots and potatoes).

Coffee Mania CAFE $$
(Кофе мания; Map p70; www.coffeemania.ru; Mal Cherkassky per 2; breakfast ₽300-500, mains ₽500-1100; ⏰8am-midnight Mon-Thu, 8am-2am Fri, 10am-2am Sat, 10am-midnight Sun; 🚭❄📶✍📖; Ⓜ Lubyanka) This place has the same overpriced but appetizing fare as other outlets of the ubiquitous chain, but the fabulous 'grand cafe' interior makes this one

a special experience. Marble floors, art deco chandeliers and elaborate lattice work evoke another era. Efficient service and excellent atmosphere.

Bosco Cafe ITALIAN $$$
(Map p70; ☎495-620 3182; www.bosco.ru; GUM, Krasnaya pl 3; pasta ₽500-1000, mains ₽1200-2000; ⊙10am-10pm; ; Ⓜ Ploshchad Revolyutsii) Sip a cappuccino in view of the Kremlin. Munch on lunch while the crowds line up at Lenin's Mausoleum. Enjoy an afternoon aperitif while admiring St Basil's domes. This cafe on the 1st floor of GUM is the only place to sit right on Red Square and marvel at its magnificence.

The menu is wide-ranging, so you don't have to spend a fortune. Reservations recommended for dinner.

Tverskoy District

Farmer's Diner BISTRO $
(Новослободский; Map p64; ul Lesnaya 5; ₽300-450; ⊙11am-11pm; Ⓜ Belorusskaya) This little bistro is run by people obsessed with Williamsburg gastroculture. The burger with caramelized onion is the trademark dish, but the place's main virtue is the two-course set lunch that costs ₽350 including a drink. It's a convenient pit stop before getting the Aeroexpress to Sheremetyevo airport.

Fresh VEGETARIAN $
(Свежий; Map p74; ☎965-278 90 89; http://freshrestaurant.ru; ul Bolshaya Dmitrovka 11; mains ₽450; ⊙11am-11pm; ; Ⓜ Teatralnaya) Fresh out of Canada, this is the kind of vegetarian restaurant that people pour into not for lifestyle reasons, but because the modern, postethnic food and the escapist ambience are actually great. Definitely go for the smoothies. Vegans and rawists will not feel neglected.

★**Delicatessen** INTERNATIONAL $$
(Деликатесы; Map p74; www.newdeli.ru; Savodvaya-Karetnaya ul 20; mains ₽450-700; ⊙noon-midnight Tue-Sat; ; Ⓜ Tsvetnoy Bulvar) The affable (and chatty) owners of this place travel the world and experiment with the menu a lot, turning burgers, pizzas and pasta into artfully constructed objects of modern culinary art. The other source of joy is a cabinet filled with bottles of ripening fruity liquors, which may destroy your budget if consumed uncontrollably (a pointless warning, we know).

Lavka-Lavka INTERNATIONAL $$
(Лавка-Лавка; Map p74; ☎495-724 3532; http://lavkalavka.com; ul Petrovka 21, str 2; ₽400-600; ⊙6pm-midnight Mon-Fri, 11am-midnight Sat & Sun; ; Ⓜ Teatralnaya) Welcome to the Russian Portlandia – all the food here is organic and hails from little farms where you may rest assured all the lambs and chickens lived a very happy life before being served to you on a plate. Irony aside, this a great place to sample local food cooked in a funky improvisational style.

Each item on the menu is attributed to an individual farmer. Geography spans from central Russia to Sakhalin. Of special note are the ales and different kinds of *kvas* (fermented rye bread drink) produced on farms near Moscow. The restaurant comes with a great (if expensive) shop selling farm produce.

★**Brasserie Most** FRENCH $$$
(Map p74; ☎495-660 0706; http://brasseriemost.ru; ul Kuznetsky most 6/3; mains ₽620-2200; ⊙8am-midnight Mon-Fri, 9am-midnight Sat & Sun; Ⓜ Teatralnaya) Moscow's most venerated and erudite restaurateur Aleksander Rappoport shares his love for regional French cuisine in this classy and expensive place on Kuznetsky most. The menu is a grand gastrotour taking in seemingly every major area of France from Bretagne to Alsace. Authenticity is religion. If they say bouillabaisse, be sure it will taste exactly like Marseille's best.

Meshchansky & Basmanny

Avocado VEGETARIAN $
(Map p74; www.avocadocafe.ru; Chistoprudny bul 12/2; mains ₽290-420; ⊙10am-11pm; ; Ⓜ Chistye Prudy) With a slightly austere interior, Avocado has a diverse menu drawing on cuisines from around the world. Meatless versions of soups and salads, pasta and *pelmeni* (Russian-style ravioli) are all featured. Vegans and rawists will find specially dedicated sections on the menu.

★**Kitayskaya Gramota** CHINESE $$
(Китайская грамота; Map p74; ☎495-625 4757; ul Sretenka 1; mains ₽300-900; ⊙noon-midnight) Never mind the dubious humour in dressing waitresses as Mao's soldiers, this is the place to try outstanding Cantonese fare in an atmosphere echoing that of the opium wars decadence. A true culinary magician, the Chinese chef turns any ingredient – from

hog paw to octopus to simple milk – into mouth-watering delicacies.

The cheapish, but sumptuous 'fried milk' dessert is to die for.

Madam Galife GEORGIAN $$

(Map p74; www.madamgalife.ru; pr Mira 26/1; mains ₽370-800; ⏲noon-5am; 📶; Ⓜ Prospekt Mira) A brainchild of famous Georgian film director Rezo Gabriadze, this is much more than just another Caucasian restaurant. It faces the charming Aptekarsky Ogorod gardens for starters, and the interior design – mixing naive art with antiques brought from Georgia – is superb. Food is a mixture of Georgian and European. To avoid disapointment, stick to the former.

Also adding to the awesome atmosphere is the live music – mostly piano and some other jazzy ensembles – that plays every night.

Odessa-Mama UKRAINIAN $$

(Map p74; ☎8-964-647 1110; www.cafeodessa.ru; per Krivokolenny 10, str 5; mains ₽380-540; ⏲noon-midnight; Ⓜ Chistye Prudy) Come here to celebrate Odessa, affectionately called 'mama' by the residents of this port city. What mama cooks is a wild fusion of Jewish, Ukrainian and Balkan foods, with a strong emphasis on Black Sea fish. It's like island-hopping – from *forshmak* (Jewish herring pâté) to Ukrainian borsch and eventually to fried Odessa gobies.

If seafood is not your thing, try Ukrainian *varenyky* dumplings or Greek meatballs. Also worth checking out – for cultural as much as gastronomical reasons – are *makarony po-flotski* (navy-style pasta), a classic Soviet staple, filling locals with nostalgia for the good old times.

Presnya District

Cafe Receptor FUSION $

(Кафе Рецептор; Map p80; www.cafereceptor.ru; Bolshaya Nikitskaya ul 22/2; mains ₽200-400; ⏲noon-midnight; 🚭📶📝👪; Ⓜ Okhotny Ryad) Colourful graffiti, amateur artwork and old photographs adorn the walls of this quirky basement cafe. It creates an arty setting for healthy, veg-heavy meals, fresh juices and fancy teas. There's also free-flowing wine, house cocktails and occasional live music. There is another outlet near **Patriarch's Ponds** (Map p80; Bolshoy Kozikhinsky per 10; Ⓜ Tverskaya).

★ **As Eat Is** INTERNATIONAL $$

(Как Есть; Map p80; ☎495-699 5313; www.aseatis.ru; Tryokhprudny per 11/13; mains ₽500-900; ⏲noon-11pm; 🚭📝📋; Ⓜ Mayakovskaya) We love the understated, eclectic interior, with its mismatched textures, appealingly packed bookshelves and vintage detailing. Even more, we love the contemporary seasonal fare, which is delightful to look at and divine to eat. It's the kind of food that would normally cost big bucks, but prices are reasonable. Extra love for the bilingual pun of a name.

★ **Khachapuri** GEORGIAN $$

(Map p80; ☎8-985-764 3118; http://hacha.ru; Bolshoy Gnezdnikovsky per 10; khachapuri ₽200-350, mains ₽400-600; 🚭❄📶📋; Ⓜ Pushkinskaya) Unassuming, affordable and appetising, this urban cafe exemplifies what people love about Georgian culture: the warm hospitality and the freshly baked *khachapuri* (cheese bread). Aside from seven types of delicious *khachapuri*, there's also an array of soups, shashlyki (kebabs), *khinkali* (dumplings) and other Georgian favourites.

★ **Favorite** AMERICAN $$

(Map p80; ☎495-691 1850; www.favorite-pub.ru; ul Spiridonovka 24; mains ₽500-800; ⏲8am-last guest; 🚭❄📋; Ⓜ Mayakovskaya) Moscow's Favorite Pub is this cool and casual Brooklyn-style hang-out, serving tasty gourmet burgers and grilled steaks. There's micro-brewed beer on tap (Brickstone Beer, made in Moscow) and a football game on the TV.

★ **Cafe Pushkin** RUSSIAN $$$

(Кафе Пушкинъ; Map p80; ☎495-739 0033; www.cafe-pushkin.ru; Tverskoy bul 26a; business lunch ₽750, mains ₽1000-2200; ⏲24hr; 🚭❄📶📋; Ⓜ Pushkinskaya) The tsarina of *haute-russe* dining, with an exquisite blend of Russian and French cuisines – service and food are done to perfection. The lovely 19th-century building has a different atmosphere on each floor, including a richly decorated library and a pleasant rooftop cafe.

Arbat & Khamovniki

★ **Varenichnaya No 1** RUSSIAN $

(Map p84; www.varenichnaya.ru; ul Arbat 29; mains ₽200-400; ⏲10am-midnight; 🚭📝📋👪; Ⓜ Arbatskaya) Retro Soviet is all the rage in Moscow, but this old-style Varenichnaya does it right, with books lining the walls, old movies on the B&W TV, and Cold War–era prices. The menu features tasty, filling *vareniki* and *pelmeni* (different kinds of dumplings), with sweet and savoury fillings. Bonus: an excellent house-made pickled-veggie plate to make you pucker.

★Elardzhi GEORGIAN $$
(Эларджи; Map p84; 495-627 7897; www.ginzaproject.ru; Gagarinsky per 15a; mains ₽600-800; ; Kropotkinskaya) Moscow's Georgian restaurants all serve very tasty food, but this one is also tasteful. You'll be charmed from the moment you enter the courtyard, where live rabbits and lambs greet all comers. Sink into a sofa in the romantic dining room or on the light-filled porch; then feast on delicacies, such as the namesake dish, *elarji* (cornmeal with Sulguni cheese).

★Zhurfak Cafe RUSSIAN $$
(Кафе Журфак; Map p84; 985-212 5050; www.jurfak-cafe.ru; Bolshoy Afanasyevsky per 3; mains ₽500-800; 9.30am-11pm; ; Kropotkinskaya) One of our favourite secret spots, this smart cafe is named for the MGU Journalism Faculty, which is located nearby. In summer, there's a shady outside eating area. Otherwise, descend into the comfy basement quarters for lively conversation, traditional food, jazz music (Wednesday and Friday) and a hint of Soviet nostalgia.

Cafe Schisliva RUSSIAN $$
(Кафе Щислива; Map p84; ul Volkhonka 9; mains ₽400-600; 8am-midnight Mon-Fri, 10am-midnight Sat & Sun; ; Kropotkinskaya) With a prime location in the midst of the art museums along ul Volkhonka, this small cafe strikes the right balance between trendy and traditional, serving up classic Russian soups, salads and mains, and presenting them in artful and appetising ways. Highlights include hearty breakfast, fresh fruit drinks and an excellent 'business lunch'.

Zamoskvorechie & Taganka

★Mizandari GEORGIAN $
(Map p90; 8-903-263 9990; nab Bolotnaya 5, str 1; mains ₽300-400; 11am-11pm; Kropotkinskaya) Georgian restaurants in Moscow tend to be either expensive or tacky. This small family-run place is neither. Come with friends and order a selection of appetizers, such as *pkhali* and *lobio* (both made of walnut paste), *khachapuri* (cheese pastry) and *kharcho* (spicy lamb soup). Bless you if can still accomodate a main course after all that!

A bottle of Kindzmarauli red wine might help to increase your consumption capacity.

Ochen Domashneye Kafe RUSSIAN $
(Очень домашнее кафе; Map p90; 495-951 1734; www.dom-cafe.ru; ul Pyatnitskaya 9/28, str 1; ₽380-550; 8am-11pm Mon-Fri, 11am-11pm Sat & Sun; Novokuznetskaya) The name, which translates as 'a very homey cafe', is also its motto. This is as close as it gets to the kind of food Russians eat at home, which inevitably means *borsch* or mushroom soup for starters, and all kinds of *kotlety* meatballs (meat, chicken or fish) as the main course.

Portions are fairly small, and appetizers go for about the same price as main courses, which may bring the cost of an entire meal close to ₽1000 per person.

★Produkty ITALIAN $$
(Продукты; Map p90; 8-903-789 3474; https://facebook.com/productscafe; Bersenevsky per 5, Bldg 1; meals ₽600-1000; noon-midnight Sun-Thu, to 6am Fri & Sat; ; Kropotkinskaya) The success of this Red October highlight is determined by the cool, post-industrial decor, simple Italian food and the proximity to the premises of several editorial offices, including the embattled Dozhd TV. It's not really visible from the street – enter the courtyard on the left of the Burger Brothers window.

★Darbazi GEORGIAN $$
(Map p90; 495-915 3632; www.darbazirest.ru/; ul Nikoloyamskaya 16; ₽390-860; noon-midnight; ; Taganskaya) The vast majority of Georgian restaurants focus on the most popular, tried-and-true fare, such as shashlyk and *khinkali*. This classy place goes far beyond these, listing less well-known delicacies with almost encyclopedic meticulousness. Our favourite is *chakapuli* (lamb cooked in white wine with tarragon) and *Megreli kharcho* (duck in walnut sauce).

Definitely go for one of the desserts, such as *pelamushi* (red grape mousse).

Chugunny most BISTRO $$
(Чугунный мост; Map p90; 495-959 4418; https://facebook.com/chugunniimost; ul Pyatnitskaya 6; mains ₽360-550; 9am-midnight; Tretyakovskaya) This place illustrates the direction in which the entire Moscow restaurant scene seems to be heading – a bistro-cum-bar that would not be out of place somewhere like Prenzlauerberg,

Berlin. The subdued, wood-dominated decor is almost therapeutic and the inventive post-ethnic food makes you want to live or work in the vicinity, just so it can be your local.

The ₽390 set-lunch deal is about the best value for money in town. It's a good breakfast choice too.

Drinking & Nightlife

Back in the day, the local pub was the *ryumochnaya*, which comes from the word *ryumka*, or 'shot'. This was a grim place, serving up 100mL, but nothing else. Moscow's drinking possibilities have expanded exponentially (although there are still a few old-school *ryumochnye* around). Now, drinkers can choose from wine bars, whisky bars, cocktail bars, sports bars, microbreweries and more.

Pedestrian streets such as ul Arbat and Kamergersky per are hot spots for strollers and drinkers. Red October in Zamoskvorechie is now packed with diverse drinking establishments, while Gorky Park has plenty of summer spots.

Kitay Gorod

Cafe Tantsy BAR

(Кафе Танцы; Map p70; Nikolskaya ul 11; noon-midnight Sun-Thu, to 6am Fri & Sat; ; M Ploshchad Revolyutsii) Truly, a hole in the wall. Moscow does not have enough of these cozy cafes, where the cramped quarters and rough-around-the-edges decor are a part of the attraction. High stools, exposed brick and hipster clientele create an atmosphere of convivial bohemia. It's a popular spot for a mid-afternoon tipple or a late-night top-off.

Incidentally, *tantsy* means 'dance', but there is no room for that. They must be speaking metaphorically.

Tverskoy District

3205 CAFE

(Map p74; 905-703 3205; www.veranda3205.ru; ul Karetny Ryad 3; 11am-3am; M Pushkinskaya) The biggest drinking/eating establishment in Hermitage Gardens, this verandah positioned at the back of the main building looks a bit like a greenhouse. In summer, tables (and patrons) spill out into the park, making it one of the city's best places for outdoor drinking. With its long bar and joyful atmosphere, the place also heaves in winter.

Enthusiast BAR

(Энтузиаст; Map p74; per Stoleshnikov, str 5; noon-11pm; M Teatralnaya) Scooter enthusiast, that is. But you don't have to be one in order to enjoy this superbly laidback bar hidden at the far end of a fancifully shaped courtyard and disguised as a spare-parts shop. On a warm day, grab a beer or cider, settle into a beach chair and let harmony descend on you.

Meshchansky & Basmanny

★ Sisters Cafe CAFE

(Map p74; 495-623 0932; www.facebook.com/sistacafe; ul Pokrovka 6; noon-11pm; ; M Kitay-Gorod) This cosy and quiet cafe-cum-bar has a distinct feminine touch about it – as if Chekhov's sisters have finally made their way to Moscow and started a new

FACE CONTROL

'Face control' is the common practice of denying entry to clubs and bars based on a person's appearance. It's not unusual for nightlife hot spots to try to create an illusion of exclusivity, but some Moscow clubs take the practice to a new level.

A few tips for avoiding rejection:

- Dress up: skirts and heels for women, dress pants and leather shoes for men.
- Arrive in a small group, preferably with more men than women.
- Speak English. Foreigners are not as special as they used to be, but they're still sort of special.
- Smile. Show the bouncer that you are going to enhance the atmosphere inside.
- Come early for dinner. Once you're in, you're in.
- Most importantly, don't take it personally if you are refused entry. There are plenty of equally cool but more casual nightclubs that extend a warm welcome to most international travellers.

life here. Cheapish smoothies, lemonades and teas are on offer, but the wine and cocktail lists are equally impressive. If you're hungry, it serves lovingly prepared Italian standards.

OMG! Coffee CAFE
(Map p74; ☎495-722 6954; www.omgcoffee.net/; ul Staray Basmannaya 6, str 3; ⊙8.30am-11pm Mon-Fri, 11am-11pm Sat & Sun; Ⓜ Krasnye Vorota) The more Russia falls out with the US, the more Brooklyn-esque the Moscow cafe scene becomes. This smallish local is very scientific (or in its own words – psychotic) about coffee, which it buys from trusted roasting specialists and brews using seven different methods. It also serves delightful gourmet burgers and sandwiches.

Chaynaya Vysota TEAROOM
(Чайная высота; Map p74; http://cha108.ru/; ul Pokrovka 27, str 1; 📶; Ⓜ Chistye Prudy) Tearoom? Gelateria? This place looks more like an academic library of tea and ice cream, an impression enhanced by the fact that it shares premises with a bookshop. The tea menu is an endless list of pu'ers and oolongs, while ice-cream flavours represent everything that grows in the former USSR – from gooseberry or fir-needle juice to chestnuts and Crimean rose petals.

Solyanka CAFE, CLUB
(Map p74; http://s-11.ru; ul Solyanka 11; cover Fri & Sat ₽500; ⊙11am-6am; 📶) Solyanka No 11 is a historic 18th-century merchant's mansion that has been revamped into an edgy, arty club. Wide-plank-wood floors, exposed brick walls, leather furniture and funky light fixtures transform the space. By day it's an excellent restaurant, serving contemporary, creative Russian and European food.

On Thursday, Friday and Saturday nights, the big bar room gets cleared of tables and the DJ spins hip-hop, techno and rave. The music usually starts at 11pm (and so does the face control).

Presnya District

Time-Out Bar COCKTAIL BAR
(Map p80; www.timeoutbar.ru; 12th fl, Bolshaya Sadovaya ul 5; ⊙noon-2am Sun-Thu, to 6am Fri & Sat; Ⓜ Mayakovskaya) On the upper floors of the throwback Pekin Hotel, this trendy bar is nothing but 'now'. That includes the bartenders sporting plaid and their delicious concoctions, especially created for different times of day. The decor is pretty impressive – particularly the spectacular city skyline. Perfect place for sundowners (or sun-ups, if you last that long).

Noor BAR
(Map p80; ☎499-130 6030; www.noorbar.com; ul Tverskaya 23; ⊙3pm-3am Mon-Wed, noon-6am Thu-Sun; Ⓜ Pushkinskaya) There is little to say about this misleadingly unassuming bar, apart from the fact that everything in it is close to perfection. It has it all – prime location, convivial atmosphere, eclectic DJ music, friendly bartenders and superb drinks. Though declared 'the best' by various magazines on several occasions, it doesn't feel like it cares.

Art Lebedev Cafe Studio CAFE
(Кафе Студия Артемия Лебедева; Map p80; lik.artlebedev.ru; Bolshaya Nikitskaya ul 35b; 📶; Ⓜ Arbatskaya) Owned by design guru Artemy Lebedev, this tiny space invites an attractive arty crowd to sip fancy coffee drinks and exotic teas. Regulars love the house-made *kasha* (porridge) for breakfast and the shady terrace in summer months. Don't miss the shop downstairs.

Bar Klava BAR
(Бар Клава; Map p80; www.bar-klava.com; Malaya Bronnaya ul 26; ⊙noon-6am; 📶; Ⓜ Mayakovskaya) The chic interior and intimate atmosphere make for a sophisticated little bar, which manages to be trendy but not pretentious. The menu features a full page of whiskeys and some enticing house cocktails. It's an expensive place to drink, if that's your activity for the evening, but a perfectly pleasant place to pop in for a sip before or after your night out.

Jagger NIGHTCLUB, BAR
(Map p64; www.ginza.ru; Rochdelskaya ul 15, bldg 30; ⊙noon-midnight Mon-Wed, noon-6am Thu-Sat, 2pm-midnight Sun; Ⓜ Ulitsa 1905 Goda) Tucked into the courtyard in the Tryokhgornaya Manufacturing complex, Jagger is a super hot bar with a super cool vibe. Excellent cocktails, sharp clientele and laidback atmosphere are characteristic of a new Moscow nightlife that is cosmopolitan and cultured, not over-the-top outrageous. Still, you have to know where to look for this place. And you have to look good.

Enter from ul 1905 goda and head to the inner courtyard.

Arbat

Gavroche Wine Bar WINE BAR

(Винный бар Гаврош; Map p84; www.thewinebar.ru; ul Timura Frunze 11; ⏲9am-midnight Sun-Wed, to 2am Thu-Sat; 📶; Ⓜ Park Kultury) First came the beer bars, and then the cocktail lounges. It only stands to reason that wine bars would be next. This one is stylish but not pretentious, with exposed-brick walls, and wines listed on a blackboard behind the bar. You'll find dozens of vintages from around the world, with a menu of Med-style small plates to complement them.

Zhiguli Beer Hall BREWERY

(Пивной зал Жигули; Map p84; www.zhiguli.net; ul Novy Arbat 11; ½L beer ₽210-350; ⏲10am-2am Sun-Thu, to 4am Fri & Sat; 📶; Ⓜ Arbatskaya) It's hard to classify this old-style *stolovaya* (cafeteria) that happens to brew great beer. The place harks back to the Soviet years, when a popular *pivnoy* bar by the same name was a Novy Arbat institution. The minimalist decor and cafeteria-style service recalls the heyday, although this place has been updated with big-screen TVs and a separate table-service dining room.

Zamoskvorechie & Taganka

Le Boule BAR

(Map p64; ☎8-926-376 9366; Gorky Park; ⏲noon-midnight; 📶; Ⓜ Oktyabrskaya) The goatee and mustache factor is high in this hipster-ridden verandah bar that comes with a dozen *petanque* lanes. Grab a pitcher of sangria or a pint of cider and have a go at what is arguably the most alcohol-compatible sport. Live bands often play on the verandah in the early evening.

Bar Strelka CAFE, CLUB

(Map p90; barstrelka.com; bldg 5a, Bersenevskaya nab 14/5; ⏲9am-midnight Mon-Thu, to 3am Fri & Sat, from noon Sat & Sun; 📶; Ⓜ Kropotkinskaya) Located just below the Patriarshy most, the bar-restaurant at the Strelka Institute is the ideal starting point for an evening in the Red October complex. The rooftop terrace has unbeatable Moscow River views, but the interior is equally cool in a shabby-

GAY & LESBIAN MOSCOW

Although homosexuality is legal, this is a socially conservative country where open displays may attract unwanted attention. Watchdog groups have reported an increase in violence since legislation banning 'gay propaganda' was enacted in 2011. There have also been reports of police harassment around gay clubs and cruising areas in Moscow. Exercise extra caution around LGBT-specific venues (or avoid them) and you are unlikely to experience any problems.

That said, Moscow is the most cosmopolitan of Russian cities, and the active gay and lesbian scene reflects this attitude. Newspapers such as the *Moscow Times* feature articles about gay and lesbian issues, as well as listings of gay and lesbian clubs.

Gay & Lesbian Venues

12 Volts (12 Вольт; Map p74; www.12voltclub.ru; bldg 2, Tverskaya ul 12; ⏲6pm-6am; Ⓜ Mayakovskaya) The founders of Moscow's lesbian movement opened this cafe-cum-social club, hidden away in a courtyard off Tverskaya ul. Buzz for admission. Once you're in, you'll find both gays and lesbians socialising together in a cosy environment, enjoying great drink specials and listening to pop music.

Secret (Map p74; www.secret-club.ru; Nizhny Susalny per 7, Bldg 8; Ⓜ Kurskaya) The 'sliding scale' cover charge and cheap drinks attract a young, student crowd to this gay nightclub. The earlier you arrive, the cheaper the admission, but if you're a male aged 18 to 22, it's free any time. Two dance floors, plus live music or drag shows on weekends.

Moscow Pride

Moscow Pride takes place in May or June, but in recent years city officials have refused to grant permission to assemble (despite fines from the European Court of Human Rights in 2010). Activists have been violently attacked by extremists when they attempt to carry out their event as planned. **Gay Russia** (www.gayrussia.eu) is an advocacy group that has been involved with the organisation of Moscow Pride and other campaigns.

chic sort of way. The bar menu is excellent and there is usually somebody tinkling the ivories.

Lebedinoe Ozero BAR
(Лебединое озеро; Map p64; ☎495-782 5813; http://s-11.ru/lebedinoe-ozero; Gorky Park; ⏲noon-5am Apr-Oct; Ⓜ Frunzenskaya) The name means 'Swan Lake' and, yes, it overlooks a little pond where resident swans float contentedly. Aside from the idyllic setting at the southern end of Gorky Park, this place is a happening summertime haunt thanks to lounge chairs in the sun, (expensive) fruity cocktails and a small swimming pool for cooling dips or late-night aquatic dancing.

There is face control, which gets stricter in the bar-hopping rush hour around midnight.

Rolling Stone CLUB
(Map p90; Bolotnaya nab 3; ⏲10pm-7am Thu-Sat; Ⓜ Kropotkinskaya) Plastered with covers of the namesake magazine and lit by naked bulbs, this place has the feel of an upscale dive bar. What makes it upscale is its location in the ultratrendy Red October complex, and the clientele – they might be dressed in casual gear but they still have to look impeccable to get past the face control. The music spans all genres and there is a small dance floor if you are so inclined.

Gipsy CLUB, CAFE
(Map p90; www.bargipsy.ru; Bolotnaya nab 3/4; ⏲6pm-1am Sun-Thu, 2pm-6am Fri & Sat) Euphoria reins in this post-modern, nomad camp of a bar that has a strategic rooftop position on Red October. The decor is bright-coloured kitsch, which among other oddities means fake palm trees and toilet doors covered with artificial fur. The DJ and live-music repertoire are aptly eclectic.

You don't have to be rich to pass the face control, but some natural coolness does help.

☆ Entertainment

The classical performing arts are one of Moscow's biggest attractions. Highly acclaimed, professional artists stage productions in elegant theatres around the city, most of which have been recently revamped and look marvellous. To find out what's on, check out the weekly 'Calendar Picks' in the *Moscow Times*.

Nowadays, most theatres sell tickets online. Or, you can do it the old-fashioned way and buy tickets directly from the theatre box office or from a *teatralnaya kassa* (theatre kiosk), several of which are scattered about the city. Many theatres are closed between late June and early September.

Classical Music

Moscow International House of Music CLASSICAL MUSIC
(Map p90; ☎495-730 1011; www.mmdm.ru; Kosmodamianskaya nab 52/8; tickets ₽200-2000; Ⓜ Paveletskaya) This graceful, modern, glass building has three halls, including Svetlanov Hall, which holds the largest organ in Russia. Needless to say, organ concerts held here are impressive. This is the usual venue for performances by the **National Philharmonic of Russia** (☎495-730 3778; www.nfor.ru), a privately financed, highly lauded, classical-music organisation. Founded in 1991, the symphony is directed and conducted by the esteemed Vladimir Spivakov.

Tchaikovsky Concert Hall CLASSICAL MUSIC
(Концертный зал имени Чайковского; Map p80; ☎495-232 0400; www.meloman.ru; Triumfalnaya pl 4/31; tickets ₽300-3000; ⏲closed Jul-Aug; Ⓜ Mayakovskaya) Home to the famous Moscow State Philharmonic (Moskovskaya Filharmonia), the capital's oldest symphony orchestra, Tchaikovsky Concert Hall was established in 1921. It's a huge auditorium, with seating for 1600 people. This is where you can expect to hear the Russian classics such as Stravinsky, Rachmaninov and Shostakovich, as well as other European favourites. Look out for special children's concerts.

Moscow Tchaikovsky Conservatory CLASSICAL MUSIC
(Московская консерватория имени Чайковского; Map p80; ☎box office 495-629 9401; www.mosconsv.ru; Bolshaya Nikitskaya ul 13; Ⓜ Okhotny Ryad) The country's largest music school, named for Tchaikovsky of course, has two venues, both of which host concerts, recitals and competitions. It's best known for the prestigious International Tchaikovsky Competition (www.tchaikovsky-competition.net), which takes place every four years, awarding titles of top pianist, singer, cellist and violinist.

Opera & Ballet

★ **Bolshoi Theatre** BALLET, OPERA
(Большой театр; Map p74; www.bolshoi.ru; Teatralnaya pl 1; tickets ₽200-4000; Ⓜ Teatralnaya) An evening at the Bolshoi is still one of Moscow's most romantic and entertaining options for a night on the town. The

TICKETS FOR THE BOLSHOI

Although it's not entirely impossible to get a ticket a from the box office a few days in advance, don't bet on it – they sell like hotcakes. You may have better luck in summer, when visiting troupes often perform. At the height of the season (October to December) your chances are, frankly, minimal. Tickets can be purchased from the theatre's website (www.bolshoi.ru/en/timetable). There are many other websites offering Bolshoi tickets, but usually with a high mark-up.

Unlike other theatres around Moscow, it is not possible to buy tickets to the Bolshoi at the *teatralnaya kassa* (theatre kiosk). What *is* possible is to buy tickets from a scalper. Scalpers are easy to find (they will find you); the trick is negotiating a price that is not several times the ticket's face value. Expect to pay upwards of ₽3000. Most importantly, make sure you examine the ticket and the date of the show (even the year) before money changes hands.

A limited number of reduced-price student tickets (₽20) go on sale at the box office one hour before the performance. Go to window number four and bring your student ID.

glittering six-tier auditorium has an electric atmosphere, evoking over 235 years of premier music and dance. Both the ballet and opera companies perform a range of Russian and foreign works here. After the collapse of the Soviet Union, the Bolshoi was marred by politics, scandal and frequent turnover. Yet the show must go on – and it will.

Stanislavsky & Nemirovich-Danchenko Musical Theatre OPERA, BALLET

(Музыкальный театр Станиславского и Немирович-Данченко; Map p74; ☎495-629 2835; www.stanislavskymusic.ru; ul Bolshaya Dmitrovka 17; ⏰box office 11.30am-7pm; Ⓜ Chekhovskaya) This historic company was founded when two legends of the Moscow theatre scene – Konstantin Stanislavsky and Vladimir Nemirovich-Danchenko – joined forces in 1941. Their newly created theatre became a workshop for applying the innovative dramatic methods of the Moscow Art Theatre to opera and ballet.

Kremlin Ballet BALLET

(Кремлевский балет; Map p70; ☎495-628 5232; www.kremlinpalace.org; ul Vozdvizhenka 1; ⏰box office noon-8pm; Ⓜ Aleksandrovsky Sad) The Bolshoi Theatre doesn't have a monopoly on ballet in Moscow. Leading dancers also appear with the Kremlin Ballet, which performs in the Kremlin Palace. The Bolshoi is magical, but seeing a show inside the Kremlin is something special too. The repertoire is unapologetically classical. The box office is near the entrance to the metro station.

Novaya Opera OPERA

(Новая опера; Map p74; ☎495-694 0868; www.novayaopera.ru; ul Karetny Ryad 3; ⏰box office noon-7.30pm; Ⓜ Tsvetnoy Bulvar) This theatre company was founded in 1991 by then-mayor Luzhkov and artistic director Evgeny Kolobov. Maestro Kolobov stated, 'we do not pretend to be innovators in this beautiful and complicated genre of opera'. As such, the 'New Opera' stages the old classics, and does it well. The gorgeous, modern opera house is set amid the Hermitage Gardens.

Folk Music

While opera and ballet dominate the playbills at the top Moscow venues, there are also a few elaborate folk shows, with Cossack dancing, gypsy music and traditional costumes.

Russian Ball at Yar FOLK SHOW

(Яр; Map p64; ☎495-960 2004; www.sovietsky.ru; Leningradsky pr 32/2, Sovietsky Hotel; tickets ₽1000, dinner ₽800-1200; Ⓜ Dinamo) Everything about Yar is over the top, from the vast, gilded interior to the traditional Russian menu to the Moulin Rouge–style dancing girls. The thematic show is infamous for its elaborate costumes. The old-fashioned Russian food is pretty elaborate, too. Buy tickets in advance. Walk 1km southeast from Dinamo metro station.

Theatre

Moscow has around 40 professional and numerous amateur theatres, with a wide range of plays – contemporary and classic, Russian and foreign – staged each year. Most performances are in Russian.

Moscow Art Theatre (MKhT) THEATRE

(Московский художественный театр (МХАТ); Map p74; http://art.theatre.ru; Kamergersky per 3; ⌚ box office noon-7pm; Ⓜ Teatralnaya) Often called the most influential theatre in Europe, this is where method acting was founded over 100 years ago, by Stanislavsky and Nemirovich-Danchenko. Besides the theatre itself and an acting studio-school, a small museum about the theatre's history is also on-site.

Maly Theatre THEATRE
(Малый театр; Map p74; ☎ 495-624 4046; www.maly.ru; Teatralnaya pl 1/6; ⌚ box office 11am-8pm; Ⓜ Teatralnaya) 'Maly' means small, meaning smaller than the Bolshoi across the street. Actually, these names date back to the time when there were only two theatres in town: the opera theatre was always called the 'Bolshoi', while the drama theatre was the 'Maly'. Founded in 1824, it mainly features performances of 19th-century works by Ostrovsky and his fellow classic playwrights.

Moscow English Theatre THEATRE
(MET; Map p80; ☎ 495-690 4658; www.moscowenglishtheatre.com; Bol Nikitskaya ul 19/13; Ⓜ Arbatskaya) Recognising the capital's rich theatrical tradition, in 2013 visiting English actor Jonathan Bex founded the Moscow English Theatre (MET), which performs contemporary American and British plays for English-speaking audiences. The company's original production – the comedy *Educating Rita* by Willy Russell – sold out five straight seasons. The MET continues to expand its repertoire, which now includes drama and mystery.

The MET performs on the Small Stage at the Mayakovsky Theatre, though plans are afoot to move to a newly built 300-seat theatre in the future.

Circus

The circus has long been a favourite form of entertainment for Russians young and old. There are two highly lauded, permanent circuses in Moscow, putting on glittering shows for Muscovites of all ages. The shows performed by both companies feature acrobatics and animals, as well as dance, cabaret and clowns. The displays of daring-do are truly amazing, especially the aerial arts. The animals are not apparently mistreated – though their very involvement in the show might make you cringe.

Nikulin Circus on Tsvetnoy Bulvar CIRCUS
(Цирк Никулина на Цветном бульваре; Map p74; ☎ 495-625 8970; www.circusnikulin.ru; Tsvetnoy bul 13; tickets ₽400-2500; ⌚ box office 11am-2pm & 3-7pm; Ⓜ Tsvetnoy Bulvar) Founded in 1880, this circus is now named after beloved actor and clown Yury Nikulin (1921–97), who performed at the studio here for many years. Nikulin's shows centre on a given theme, which serves to add some cohesion to the productions. There are lots of trapeze artists, tightrope walkers and performing animals.

STANISLAVSKY'S METHODS

In 1898, over an 18-hour restaurant lunch, actor-director Konstantin Stanislavsky and playwright-director Vladimir Nemirovich-Danchenko founded the Moscow Art Theatre as the forum for method acting. The theatre is known by its Russian initials, MKhT, short for Moskovsky Khudozhestvenny Teatr (Московский Художественный театр).

More than just providing another stage, the Art Theatre adopted a 'realist' approach, which stressed truthful portrayal of characters and society, teamwork by the cast (not relying on stars) and respect for the writer. 'We declared war on all the conventionalities of the theatre...in the acting, the properties, the scenery, or the interpretation of the play', Stanislavsky later wrote.

This treatment of *The Seagull* rescued playwright Anton Chekhov from despair after the play had flopped in St Petersburg. *Uncle Vanya, Three Sisters* and *The Cherry Orchard* all premiered in the MKhT. Gorky's *The Lower Depths* was another success. In short, the theatre revolutionised Russian drama.

The influence of method acting in Western theatre has been enormous. In the USA, Stanislavsky's theories are, and have been, the primary source of study for many actors, including such greats as Stella Adler, Marlon Brando, Sanford Meisner, Lee Strasberg, Harold Clurman and Gregory Peck.

MKhT, now technically called the Chekhov Moscow Art Theatre, still stages regular performances of Chekhov's work, among other plays.

Bolshoi Circus on Vernadskogo CIRCUS
(Map p64; ☎495-930 0300; www.bolshoicircus.ru; pr Vernadskogo 7; tickets ₽600-3000; ⊙shows 7pm Wed-Fri, 1pm & 5pm Sat & Sun; ; Ⓜ Universitet) This huge circus holds 3400 spectators, but the steep pitch means that everyone has a view of the action. The company includes hundreds of performers – mostly acrobats, but some animals too (bears, sea lions, monkeys). It is a great spectacle that is certain to entertain and amaze.

Live Music

Masterskaya LIVE MUSIC
(Мастерская; Map p74; www.mstrsk.ru; Teatralny proyezd 3, str 3; ⊙noon-6am; ; Ⓜ Lubyanka) All the best places in Moscow are tucked into far corners of courtyards, and they often have unmarked doors. Such is the case with this super-funky music venue. The eclectic, arty interior makes a cool place to chill out during the day. Evening hours give way to a diverse array of live-music acts or the occasional dance or theatre performance.

Sixteen Tons LIVE MUSIC
(Шестнадцать тонн; Map p80; ☎495-253 1550; www.16tons.ru; ul Presnensky val 6; cover ₽600-1200; ⊙11am-6am, concerts 8pm Sun-Wed, 9pm Thu-Sat, midnight Fri & Sat; ; Ⓜ Ulitsa 1905 Goda) Downstairs, the brassy English pub-restaurant has an excellent house-brewed bitter. Upstairs, the club gets some of the best Russian bands that play in Moscow, hosting such names as Mara and Theodor Bastard, among others. Show times are subject to change so check the website for details.

Art Garbage LIVE MUSIC
(Map p74; www.art-garbage.ru; Starosadsky per 5; ⊙noon-6am; ; Ⓜ Kitay-Gorod) Enter this funky club-cafe through the courtyard littered with sculpture. Inside, the walls are crammed with paintings of all genres, and there are DJs spinning or live music playing every night. The restaurant is relatively minimalist in terms of decor, but the menu is creative. Is it art or is it garbage? We'll let you decide.

Rhythm Blues Cafe LIVE MUSIC
(Блюз Кафе Ритм; Map p84; ☎499-697 6008; www.rhythm-blues-cafe.ru; Starovagankovsky per; ⊙shows 9pm; Ⓜ Aleksandrovsky Sad) If your dog got run over by a pick-up truck, you might find some comfort at the Rhythm Blues Cafe, with down-and-out live music every night, plus cold beer and a whole menu of salty cured meats. Great fun and a

Metro Tour
Underground Art

START KOMSOMOLSKAYA PL
END PLOSHCHAD REVOLYUTSII
LENGTH 18KM; ONE TO TWO HOURS

Every day, nine million people ride the Moscow metro – more than in New York and London combined. The metro marries function and form: many stations are marble-faced, frescoed, gilded works of art. This tour is an overview of Moscow's most impressive metro stations.

Start at ❶ **Komsomolskaya**, where the red line (Sokolnicheskaya liniya) intersects with the Ring line (Koltsevaya liniya). Both stations are named for the youth workers who helped with early construction. In the red-line station, look for the Komsomol emblem at the top of the limestone pillars and the majolica-tile panel showing volunteers hard at work.

From Komsomolskaya, proceed anticlockwise around the Ring line, getting off at each stop along the way.

Originally named for the nearby MGU Botanical Garden, ❷ **Prospekt Mira** station features elegant, white-porcelain depictions of figures planting trees, bringing in the harvest and living in harmony.

❸ **Novoslobodskaya** station is enveloped by the art nouveau artistry of 32 stained-glass panels. Six windows depict the so-called intellectual professions: architect, geographer, agronomist, engineer, artist and musician. At one end of the central hall is the mosaic Peace in the Whole World. The pair of white doves was a later addition, replacing a portrait of Stalin.

At ❹ **Belorusskaya** station, the ceiling mosaics celebrate the culture, economy and history of Russia's neighbour. The 12 ceiling panels illustrate different aspects of their culture, while the floor pattern reproduces traditional Belarusian ornamentation.

Switch here to the green Zamoskvoretskaya line (where the Belarusian theme continues) and travel south.

❺ **Mayakovskaya** station is the metro's pièce de résistance. The grand-prize winner at the 1938 World's Fair in New York has an art deco central hall of pink

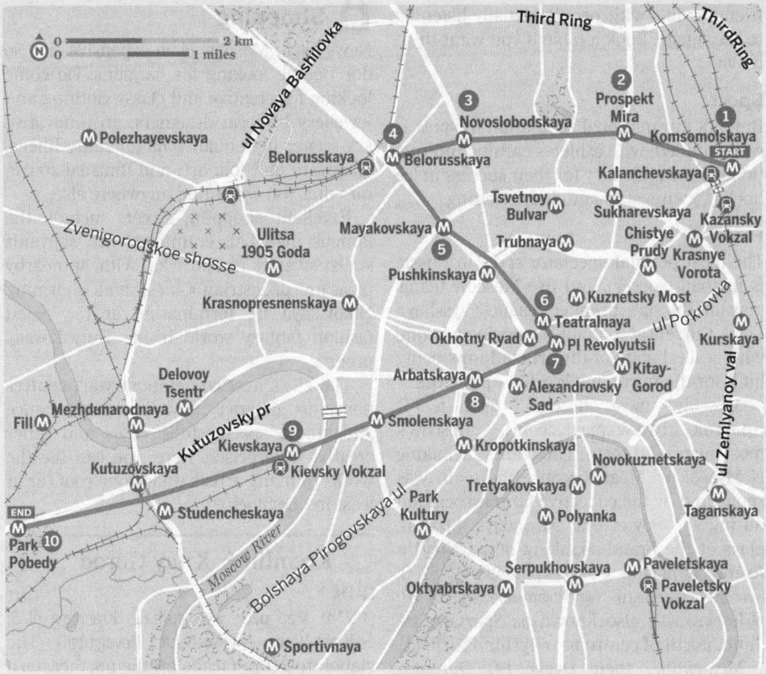

rhodonite, with slender, steel columns. The upward-looking mosaics on the ceiling depict 24 Hours in the Land of the Soviets. This is one of the deepest stations (33m) and so it served as an air-raid shelter during WWII.

The decor at 6 **Teatralnaya** station follows a theatrical theme. The porcelain figures represent seven of the Soviet republics by wearing national dress and playing musical instruments from their homeland.

Change here to Ploshchad Revolyutsii station on the dark-blue line (Arbatsko-Pokrovskaya liniya).

The dramatic 7 **Ploshchad Revolyutsii** station is an underground sculpture gallery. The life-sized bronze statues represent the crucial roles during the revolution and in the 'new world' that comes after. Heading up the escalators, the themes are: revolution, industry, agriculture, hunting, education, sport and child rearing. Touch the nose of the border guard's dog for good luck on exams. Take the dark-blue line heading west.

The shallow 8 **Arbatskaya** station was damaged by a German bomb in 1941. The station was closed and a parallel line was built much deeper. Service was restored on this shallow line the following decade, which explains the existence of two Arbatskaya stations (and two Smolenskaya stations, for that matter) on two different lines.

At 250m, Arbatskaya is one of the longest stations. A braided moulding emphasises the arched ceiling, while red marble and detailed ornamentation give the station a baroque atmosphere.

At 9 **Kievskaya** station, the elegant white-marble hall is adorned with a Kyivan-style ornamental frieze, while the frescoed panels depict farmers in folk costume, giant vegetables and aspects of an idyllic Ukrainian existence. The fresco at the end of the hall celebrates 300 years of Russian-Ukrainian cooperation (without a hint of irony).

The newer 10 **Park Pobedy** station opened after the complex at Poklonnaya Gora, which commemorated the 50th anniversary of the victory in the Great Patriotic War. It is the deepest Moscow metro station and has the longest escalators in the world. The enamel panels at either end of the hall depict the 1812 and 1945 victories.

From here you can return to the centre by retracing your ride on the dark-blue line.

friendly vibe, with people actually listening to the music. Book a table if you want to sit down.

Sport

Russia's international reputation in sport is well founded, with athletes earning international fame and glory for their success in ice hockey, gymnastics and figure skating.

Football

The most popular spectator sport in Russia is football (soccer), and five Moscow teams play in Russia's premier league (Vysshaya Liga). Currently, football is enjoying a boom, with several state-of-the-art stadiums being built for the upcoming World Cup in 2018.

Moscow's most successful team is **FC Spartak** (www.spartak.com), Moscow's most successful team. The team's nickname is Myaso, or 'Meat', because the team was sponsored by the collective farm association during the Soviet era. Nowadays, Spartak plays at the brand spanking new **Otkrytie Arena** (Стадион Спартак; ☎495-411 5200; www.otkritiearena.ru; Volokolamskoe shosse 67; Ⓜ Tushinskaya), also known as Spartak Stadium, north of centre near Tyshino Airfield.

Meanwhile, their rivals, **FC Dynamo** (www.fcdynamo.ru) are looking forward to the new ultramodern VTB Arena – a 45,000-seat stadium complete with its own shopping and entertainment complex – expected to open in 2016.

Other Moscow teams in the league are two-time winner **FC Lokomotiv** (www.fclm.ru), three-time winner **Central Sports Club of the Army** (CSKA; www.pfc-cska.com) and **FC Moskva** (www.fcmoscow.ru).

Ice Hockey

Moscow's main entrant in the Continental Hockey League (KHL) is **HC CSKA** (www.cska-hockey.ru), or the Red Army team. HC CSKA has won more Soviet championships and European cups than any other team in history. They play at the **CSKA Arena** (Арена и Стадион ЦСКА; Map p64; ☎495-225 2600; Leningradsky pr 39a; Ⓜ Aeroport).

Basketball

Men's basketball has dropped in popularity since its days of Olympic glory in the 1980s. But Moscow's top basketball team, **CSKA** (www.cskabasket.com), still does well in European league play. They play at the CSKA Arena, but they'll move to VTB Arena when it's complete.

Shopping

News flash: Moscow is an expensive city. So don't come looking for bargains. Do come looking for creative and classy clothing and jewellery by local designers; an innovative art scene; high-quality handicrafts, linens, glassware and folk art; and unusual souvenirs that you won't find anywhere else.

Excellent shopping streets include the famous ul Arbat, crammed with souvenir stalls; swanky ul Petrovka, with its nearby pleasant pedestrian lanes; and charming Nikolskaya ul, terminating at the gated fashion fantasy world inside Tretyakovsky proezd.

The city's new contemporary-art centres house art galleries, as well as performance and studio space, clubs, cafes and other creative enterprises. Here, you can see the works of many artists under one roof (or at least in one block).

Kremlin & Kitay Gorod

GUM MALL

(ГУМ; Map p70; www.gum.ru; Krasnaya pl 3; ⏲10am-10pm; Ⓜ Ploshchad Revolyutsii) The elaborate 240m facade on the northeastern side of Red Square, GUM is a bright, bustling shopping mall with hundreds of fancy stores and restaurants. With a skylight roof and three-level arcades, the spectacular interior was a revolutionary design when it was built in the 1890s, replacing the Upper Trading Rows that previously occupied this site.

Pronounced *goom*, the initials GUM originally stood for the Russian words for 'State Department Store'. When it was privatised in 2005, the name was officially changed to 'Main Department Store'. Fortunately, the words for 'state' and 'main' both start with a Russian 'G'.

Tverskoy District

★**Yekaterina** CLOTHING, ACCESSORIES

(Екатерина; Map p74; www.mexa-ekaterina.ru; ul Bolshaya Dmitrovka 11; Ⓜ Teatralnaya) One of Russia's oldest furriers, this place has been manufacturing *shapky* (fur hats) and *shuby* (fur coats) since 1912. While Yekaterina has always maintained a reputation for high-quality furs and leather, its designs are constantly changing and updating to stay on top of fashion trends.

Yeliseev Grocery FOOD & DRINK
(Елисеевский магазин; Map p74; Tverskaya ul 14; 8am-9pm Mon-Sat, 10am-6pm Sun; M Pushkinskaya) Peek in here for a glimpse of prerevolutionary grandeur, as the store is set in the former mansion of the successful merchant Yeliseev. It now houses an upscale market selling caviar and other delicacies. It's a great place to shop for souvenirs for your foodie friends back home.

Flakon SHOPPING CENTRE
(Map p64; www.flacon.ru; ul Bolshaya Novodmitrovskaya 36; variable; M Dmitrovskaya) Like the Bolsheviks a hundred years ago, Moscow hipsters are capturing one factory after another and redeveloping them, according to their hipster tastes. Flakon is arguably the most visually attractive of all the redeveloped industrial areas around town, looking a bit like the far end of Portobello Rd, especially during the weekends. Once a glassware plant, it is now home to dozens of funky shops and other businesses. Shopping for designer clothes and unusual souvenirs is the main reason for coming here. The main shopping area covers two floors of the factory's central building.

Depst DESIGNER GOODS
(Map p74; www.depst.ru; Tsvetnoy bul 15 (inside Tsvetnoy shopping mall); 10am-10pm) This is the ultimate place to shop for Russian designer items – from clothes to furniture, and jewellery to cutlery. The shop occupies pretty much the entire underground floor of Tsvetnoy shopping centre, which has a few other trappings, including a nice food court on the top floor.

Podarki vMeste s Vorovski SOUVENIRS
(Подарки вМесте с Воровски; Map p74; www.m-rosemarie.ru; Kuznetsky most 21/5; 10am-9pm; M Lubyanka) This sweet little boutique houses a cooperative of four designer gift producers. The rather cramped space is filled with hundreds of useful and useless (but pretty) items, including Galereyka's felt slippers and hats (some shaped as Soviet tanks) and Ptitsa Sinitsa's stylish ceramics with East European folklore motives.

Basmanny

Odensya Dlya Schastya CLOTHING
(Оденься для счастья; Map p74; ul Pokrovka 31; 11am-9pm; M Kurskaya) This sweet boutique – encouraging shoppers to 'dress for happiness' – carries unique clothing by a few distinctive designers, including Moscow native Oleg Biryukov. The designer's eponymous label features refined styles with long, flowing lines and subdued, solid colours. The tastefulness and elegance exemplify the new direction of Russian fashion.

Ochevidnoyeneveroyatnoye SOUVENIRS
(Очевидноеневероятное; Map p74; www.orz-design.ru/; 4-y Syromyatnichesky per 1, str 6, entrance 13; 11am-9pm) True to its name, which translates as 'Evidentlyimprobable', this is the place to shop for surreal gifts and souvenirs – from a lamp shaped as an oil rig to a toilet-paper roll that allows the owner to learn a new Russian word before using each sheet. The Soviet theme is well-represented in notebooks and passport covers.

Prosto Tak SOUVENIRS
(Просто Так; Map p74; www.buro-nahodok.ru; Maly Gnezdnikovsky per 12/27; 11am-9pm; M Pushkinskaya) For quirky, clever souvenirs, stop by this network of artists' cooperatives. Each outlet has a different name, but the goods are more or less the same: uniquely Russian gifts such as artist-designed *tapki* (slippers) and hand-woven linens. Most intriguingly, artist Yury Movchan has invented a line of funky, functional fixtures (lights, clocks etc) made from old appliances and other industrial discards.

Khokhlovka Original CLOTHING
(Map p74; http://xoxloveka.ru/; per Khokhlovsky 7; noon-10pm; M Kitay-Gorod) This is about the most clandestine fashion store we've ever reviewed. To get in, enter a graffiti-covered courtyard, then look for a small gap between two single-storey buildings on your left – the door is inside the tiny passage. The small showroom displays clothes and accessories produced by dozens of young (but often stellar) Russian designers.

The design may often seem controversial, but you may rest assured you'll never see anyone wearing the same item back home.

Tricotage Club CLOTHING, ACCESSORIES
(Трикотаж-клуб; Map p74; www.sviterok.ru; ul Pokrovka 4; 10am-10pm Mon-Fri, 11am-10pm Sat & Sun; M Kitay-Gorod) Hand-knit sweaters, socks and mittens in all shapes and sizes. But that's not all. You'll find a fun selection of toys and homemade souvenirs, as well as sleek and sexy styles of men's and women's clothing. This is not your grandmother's knitwear.

DON'T MISS

IZMAYLOVSKY MARKET

Never mind the kitschy faux 'tsar's palace' it surrounds, **Izmaylovsky Market** (www.kremlin-izmailovo.com; Izmaylovskoye shosse 73; 10am-8pm; M Partizanskaya) is the ultimate place to shop for *matryoshka* dolls, military uniforms, icons, Soviet badges and some real antiques. Huge and diverse, it is almost a theme park, which includes shops, cafes and a couple of not-terribly-exciting museums.

Serious antiquarians occupy the 2nd floor of wooden trade row surrounding the palace, but for really good stuff you need to come here in the most ungodly hours on Saturday morning and compete with pros from Moscow galleries. Keep in mind that Russia bans the export of any item older than 100 years.

Presnya District

Bolshe ART
(Больше; Map p80; www.bolshe-chem.ru; Malaya Bronnaya ul 28/2; 11am-9pm Mon-Fri, noon-9pm Sat & Sun; M Mayakovskaya) This outlet of the clever artists' cooperative that has shops scattered around Moscow, features handmade, original and totally impractical stuff – great gifts or fun souvenirs.

Dom Knigi BOOKSTORE
(Дом Книги; Map p80; www.mdk-arbat.ru; ul Novy Arbat 8; 9am-11pm Mon-Fri, 10am-11pm Sat & Sun; M Arbatskaya) Among the largest bookstores in Moscow, Dom Knigi has a selection of foreign-language books to rival any other shop in the city, not to mention travel guidebooks, maps, and reference and souvenir books. This huge, crowded place holds regularly scheduled readings, children's programs and other bibliophilic activities.

Arbat & Khamovniki

Association of Artists of the Decorative Arts (AHDI) SOUVENIRS
(Ассоциация художников декоративно-прикладного искусства; Map p84; www.ahdi.ru; ul Arbat 21; 11am-8pm; M Arbatskaya) Look for the ceramic plaque and the small sign indicating the entrance to this 'exposition hall', which is actually a cluster of small shops, each one showcasing arts and crafts by local artists. In addition to paintings and pottery, the most intriguing items are the gorgeous knit sweaters, woolly coats and embroidered dresses – all handmade and unique.

Russian Embroidery & Lace SOUVENIRS
(Русская вышивка и кружево; Map p84; www.yp.ru/vishivka; ul Arbat 31; 11am-8pm Mon-Sat, to 5pm Sun; M Smolenskaya) Considering the lack of flashy signs and kitsch, it would be easy to miss this plain storefront on the Arbat. But inside there are treasures galore, from elegant tablecloths and napkins to delicate handmade sweaters and embroidered shirts.

Artefact Gallery Centre ART
(Map p84; ul Prechistenka 30; 10am-6pm, individual gallery hours variable; M Kropotkinskaya) Near the Russian Academy of Art, the Artefact Gallery Centre is a sort of art mall, housing a few dozen galleries under one roof. Look for paintings, sculptures, dolls, pottery and other kinds of art that people actually buy, as opposed to the more avant-garde exhibits at other art centres.

Zamoskvorechie & Taganka

Central House of Artists (TsDKh) ART, SOUVENIRS
(Центральный дом художника; Map p90; www.cha.ru; admission ₽200; 11am-7pm Tue-Sun; M Park Kultury) Sometimes called by its initials (ЦДХ), this huge building attached to the New Tretyakov contains studios and galleries, as well as exhibition space for rotating collections. This is a great place to browse if you're in the market to acquire a painting or print from Moscow's red-hot contemporary-art scene.

Bookhunter BOOKSTORE
(Map p90; www.bookhunter.ru; ul Tatarskaya Bolshaya 7; 9am-7pm; M Novokuznetskaya) Inside a business centre, this small shop is stuffed with fiction and nonfiction books in English (not to mention German, French and Spanish). You'll find all sorts of art, academic and other reference books (including a good selection of travel guides), as well as Russian and foreign literature.

Information

DANGERS & ANNOYANCES

Although street crime is on the rise, Moscow is a mostly safe city with few dangerous areas.

- As in any big city, be on your guard against pickpockets and muggers, especially around train stations and in crowded metro cars.
- Always be cautious about taking taxis late at night, especially near bars and clubs that are in isolated areas. Never get into a car that already has two or more people in it.
- Always carry a photocopy of your passport, visa and registration stamp. If stopped by a member of the police force, do not hand over your passport. It is perfectly acceptable to show a photocopy instead.
- Your biggest threat in Moscow is xenophobic or overly friendly drunks.

EMERGENCY

Ambulance (☎03)
Fire (☎01)
Police (☎02)
Universal Emergency Number (☎112) Currently functional from mobile phones, this universal number will eventually replace the separate numbers for ambulance, fire and police.

INTERNET ACCESS

- Almost all hotels and hostels offer wi-fi, as do many bars, restaurants and cafes. It isn't always free, but it is ubiquitous.
- Also popular is shared work space, which offers a comfortable work space, functional wi-fi, and sometimes drinks and snacks, for a per-minute or per-hour fee.
- Most hostels and hotels offer internet access for guests who are not travelling with their own computers. Internet cafes are a thing of the past.

Ziferblat (Циферблат; www.ziferblat.net; per min ₽2) Tverskaya (Map p74; Tverskaya ul 12c1; ⏲11am-midnight; Ⓜ Pushkinskaya); Pokrovka (Map p74; ul Pokrovka 12 c 1; ⏲11am-midnight Sun-Thu, 11am-7pm Fri-Sat; Ⓜ Chistye Prudy).

MEDIA

Moscow Times (www.themoscowtimes.com) This first-rate daily is the undisputed king of the hill for locally published English-language news, covering Russian and international issues, as well as sport and entertainment. The Friday edition is a great source for information about what's happening at the weekend.

MEDICAL SERVICES

Hospitals

The American Medical Center and the European Medical Center both accept health insurance from major international providers.

American Medical Centre (Map p74; ☎495-933 7700; www.amcenter.ru; Grokholsky per 1; ⏲24hr; Ⓜ Pr Mira) Offers 24-hour emergency service, consultations and a full range of medical specialists, including paediatricians and dentists. There is also an on-site pharmacy with English-speaking staff.

Botkin Hospital (Map p64; ☎495-945 0045; www.mosgorzdrav.ru; 2-y Botkinsky proezd 5; ⏲24hr; Ⓜ Begovaya) The best Russian facility. From Begovaya metro station, walk 1km northeast on Khoroshevskoe sh and Begovoy pr. Turn left on Begovaya ul and continue to 2-y Botkinsky proezd.

European Medical Centre (Map p80; ☎495-933 6655; www.emcmos.ru; Spirodonevsky per 5; ⏲24hr; Ⓜ Mayakovskaya) Includes medical and dental facilities, which are open around the clock for emergencies. The staff speak 10 languages.

Pharmacies

A chain of pharmacies called **36.6** (Аптека 36.6; ☎495-797 6366; www.366.ru) has many branches all around the city:

36.6 Arbat (Map p84; ul Novy Arbat 15; ⏲9am-10pm; Ⓜ Arbatskaya)

36.6 Pokrovka (Map p74; ul Pokrovka 1/13; ⏲9am-9pm; Ⓜ Kitay-Gorod)

36.6 Tverskaya (Map p80; Tverskaya ul 25/9; ⏲24hr; Ⓜ Mayakovskaya)

36.6 Zamoskvorechie (Map p90; Klimentovsky per 12; ⏲8am-10pm; Ⓜ Tretyakovskaya)

MONEY

- Banks, exchange counters and ATMs are ubiquitous in Moscow, but currencies other than US dollars and euros are difficult to exchange and yield bad rates.
- Credit cards, especially Visa and MasterCard, are widely accepted in hotels, restaurants and shops. US travellers who do not have a 'chip-and-pin' card may have some difficulty in local shops.
- Many ATMS offer the option to withdraw roubles or euros.

POST

Service has improved dramatically in recent years, but the usual warnings about delays and disappearances of incoming mail apply. Note that mail to Europe and the USA can take two to six weeks to arrive.

Central Telegraph (Map p80; Tverskaya ul 7; ⏲post 8am-10pm, telephone 24hr; Ⓜ Okhotny Ryad)

Main Post Office (Map p74; Myasnitskaya ul 26; ⏲24hr; Ⓜ Chistye Prudy)

TELEPHONE

- There are now three area codes operating within Moscow. The most common code is ☎495, while some numbers – especially on the outskirts – use ☎498 or ☎499.

➡ For all calls within Moscow (from landline or mobile phone), you must dial 8 then the 10-digit number including the area code.

USEFUL WEBSITES

A number of publications also offer electronic versions of their newspapers/magazines.

Art Guide (www.artguide.ru) Listings for exhibits, auctions and other arty events, as well as museum listings.

Moscow Expat (www.expat.ru) Run by and for English-speaking expats living in Russia. Provides useful information about real estate, restaurants, children in Moscow, social groups and more.

Moscow is my Oyster (www.moscow-ismyoyster.tumblr.com) A fun blog about eating, drinking, shopping and people-watching in Moscow.

ℹ Getting There & Away

AIR

International flights from Moscow's airports incur a departure tax, which is included in the price of the airline ticket.

Airports

Moscow has three main airports servicing international and domestic flights.

Domodedovo (Домодедово; www.domodedovo.ru) Domodedovo, located about 48km south of the city, has undergone extensive upgrades since 2003, and has become the city's largest and most efficient international airport. The Aeroexpress train leaves Paveletsky vokzal every half-hour between 6am and midnight for the 45-minute trip to Domodedovo.

Sheremetyevo (Шереметьево, SVO; ☎495-578 6565; www.svo.aero) Sheremetyevo international airport is 30km northwest of the city centre. The Aeroexpress train makes the 35-minute trip between Sheremetyevo (located next to Terminal E) and Belorussky vokzal every half-hour from 5.30am to 12.30am.

Vnukovo (Внуково; www.vnukovo.ru) About 30km southwest of the city centre, Vnukovo serves most flights to/from the Caucasus, Moldova and Kaliningrad, as well as domestic flights and a smattering of flights to Europe. The Aeroexpress train makes the 35-minute run from Kievsky vokzal to Vnukovo airport every hour from 6am to 11pm.

Tickets

You can buy domestic airline tickets from most travel agents, and at Aeroflot and Transaero offices all over town. Convenient ticket offices:

Aeroflot (www.aeroflot.ru) Moscow to Havana, twice weekly.

Transaero (☎495-788 8080; www.transaero.ru/en)

BOAT

Moscow is a popular start or end point for cruises that ply the Volga River.

BUS

Buses run to a number of towns and cities within 700km of Moscow. Bus fares are similar to *kupeyny* (2nd-class) train fares. In general, bus is not a recommended way to travel, mainly due to the terrible traffic heading out of town. If at all possible, get out of town by train.

Otherwise, the long-distance **Shchyolkovsky Bus Station** (Щёлковский автовокзал; www.

DOMESTIC FLIGHTS FROM MOSCOW

Destination	Duration	Flights per day	Fare (R)
Arkhangelsk	1hr 50min	4-5	4900-6800
Astrakhan	2hr 15min	4-5	4800-6800
Irkutsk	5½hr	9-10	13,000-17,000
Kaliningrad	2hr	10-12	3800-7000
Krasnodar	2hr	14-16	4300-5000
Murmansk	2½hr	4-5	6200-8200
Novosibirsk	4hr	13-15	7100-7800
Rostov-on-Don	1hr 45min	13-17	3700-4700
Samara	1hr 45min	12-14	4800-5400
Sochi	2hr 15min	20-24	5400-7000
Ufa	2hr	12-14	4500-5500
Vladivostok	8½hr	3-4	16,200-17,800
Volgograd	1hr 45min	12-15	5300-5700
Yekaterinburg	2½hr	18-20	5500-6500

busmow.ru; M Shchyolkovskaya) is 8km east of the city centre. Buses also depart from outside the various train stations, offering alternative transport to the destinations served by the train. These buses do not generally run according to a particular schedule, but rather leave when the bus is full. Likewise, they cannot be booked in advance.

CAR & MOTORCYCLE

Ten major highways, numbered M1 to M10 (but not in any logical order), fan out from Moscow to all points of the compass. Most are in fairly good condition, at least near the city:

M1 The main road to/from Poland via Brest, Minsk and Smolensk.

M2 Heads southwest towards Oryol and Ukraine.

M7 Heads east to Vladimir and Nizhny Novgorod.

M8 Heads northeast to Yaroslavl, via Sergiev Posad.

M10 The road to St Petersburg; dual carriageway as far as Tver.

Hire

There's little reason for travellers to rent a car to get around Moscow, as public transport is quite adequate. However, you might want to consider car rental for trips out of the city. Be aware that driving in Russia is an unfiltered Russian experience, mainly due to poor signage and ridiculous traffic.

Avis (Авис-Москва; www.avis.com) Leningradsky vokzal (Map p74; ☎495-988 6216; Komsomolskaya pl 3; ⏲10am-8pm; M Komsomolskaya); Zamoskvorechie (Map p64; ☎495-988 6216; 4-y Dobryninsky per 8; ⏲9am-9pm; M Oktyabrskaya)

Europcar (Map p64; ☎495-926 6373; www.europcar.ru; 4-y Dobryninsky per 8; ⏲9am-6pm; M Oktyabrskaya) From Oktyabrskaya metro station, walk two blocks south on Mytnaya ul and turn left on 4-y Dobryninsky per. Hire cars are prohibited from leaving Moscow Oblast.

Hertz (Map p64; ☎495-232 0889; www.hertz.ru; 1-ya Brestskaya ul 34; ⏲9am-9pm; M Belorusskaya)

Thrifty (☎495-788-6888; www.thrifty.ru) Outer North (Yaroslavskoe sh 31; ⏲9am-6pm; M Babushinskaya); Outer South (Profsoyuznaya ul 65; ⏲9am-9pm; M Kaluzhskaya) Mileage limited to 200km per day.

Petrol

Moscow has no shortage of petrol stations selling all grades of fuel. Most are open 24 hours and can be found on the major roads in and out of town.

TRAIN

Moscow has rail links to most parts of Russia, most former Soviet states, many Eastern and Western European countries, as well as China and Mongolia.

Stations

Moscow has nine main stations. Multiple stations may service the same destination, so be sure to confirm the arrival/departure station.

Belorussky Vokzal (Belarus Station; Tverskaya Zastava pl; M Belorusskaya) This station serves trains to/from Smolensk, Kaliningrad, Belarus, Lithuania, Poland and Germany; some trains to/from the Czech Republic; and suburban trains to/from the west, including Mozhaysk, Borodino and Zvenigorod. Belorussky is also the starting point for the Aeroexpress train to Sheremetyevo.

Kazansky Vokzal (Kazan Station; Komsomolskaya pl; M Komsomolskaya) This station serves trains to/from Kazan, Izhevsk, Ufa, Ryazan, Ulyanovsk, Samara, Novorossiysk and Central Asia; some trains to/from Vladimir, Nizhny Novgorod, the Ural Mountains, Siberia, Saratov, Rostov-on-Don; and suburban trains to/from the southeast, including Bykovo airport, Kolomna, Gzhel and Ryazan.

Kievsky Vokzal (Kyiv Station; Kievskaya pl; M Kievskaya) This station serves Bryansk, Kyiv, western Ukraine, Moldova, Slovakia, Hungary, Austria, Prague, Romania, Bulgaria, Croatia, Serbia, Greece and Venice; suburban trains to/from the southwest, including Peredelkino and Kaluga. Kievsky Vokzal is also the starting point for the Aeroexpress train to Vnukovo airport.

Kursky Vokzal (Kursk Station; pl Kurskogo vokzala; M Kurskaya) This train station serves Oryol, Kursk, Krasnodar, Adler, the Caucasus, eastern Ukraine, Crimea, Georgia and Azerbaijan. It also has some trains to/from Rostov-on-Don, Vladimir, Nizhny Novgorod and Perm; and suburban trains to/from the east and south, including Petushki, Podolsk, Chekhov, Serpukhov and Tula.

Leningradsky Vokzal (Leningrad Station; Komsomolskaya pl; M Komsomolskaya) This train station serves Tver, Novgorod, Pskov, St Petersburg, Vyborg, Murmansk, Estonia and Helsinki; and suburban trains to/from the northwest, including Klin and Tver. Note that sometimes this station is referred to on timetables and tickets by its former name, Oktyabrsky.

Paveletsky Vokzal (Pavelets Station; Paveletskaya pl; M Paveletskaya) This train station serves Yelets, Lipetsk, Voronezh, Tambov, Volgograd and Astrakhan; some trains to/from Saratov; and suburban trains to/from the southeast, including Leninskaya and Domodedovo airport.

Rizhsky Vokzal (Rīga Station; Rizhskaya pl; M Rizhskaya) This train station serves Latvia, with suburban trains to/from the northwest, including Istra and Novoierusalimskaya.

Yaroslavsky Vokzal (Yaroslavl Station; Komsomolskaya pl; M Komsomolskaya) This train station serves Yaroslavl, Arkhangelsk, Vorkuta, the Russian Far East, Mongolia, China and North Korea; some trains to/from Vladimir, Nizhny Novgorod, Kostroma, Vologda, Perm, the Ural Mountains and Siberia; and suburban trains to/from the northeast, including Abramtsevo, Khotkovo, Sergiev Posad and Alexandrov.

TRAIN TRAVEL

Sample Moscow–St Petersburg Trains

NAME & NO	DEPARTURE	DURATION	FARE
Krasnaya Strela (2)	11.55pm	8hr	1st-/2nd-class ₽5800/3600
Ekspress (4)	11.30pm	9hr	1st-/2nd-class ₽5500/3400
Tversk (20)	12:56am	8hr	1st-/2nd-class ₽6000/4000
Grand Express (54)	11.40pm	9hr	1st-/2nd-class ₽7600/3600
Sapsan (752)	6.45am	4hr	₽11,800
Sapsan (758)	1.30pm	4½hr	₽3400
Sapsan (762)	4.30pm	4hr	₽3200
Sapsan (764)	7.25pm	4hr	₽3200

Sample International Trains

DESTINATION	TRAIN	DEPARTURE	STATION	DURATION	FARE (₽)
Almaty	Kazakhstan (007)	10.55pm (even dates)	Paveletsky	3 days & 6hr	11,900
Kyiv	Stolichny Express (001)	10.54pm (odd dates)	Kievsky	9½hr	****
Minsk	Slavyansky Express (007)	11:03pm	Belorussky	8hr	4100
Rīga	Latvia Express (001)	7pm	Rizhsky	15½hr	6455
Tallinn	Tallinn Express (034)	6.05pm	Leningradsky	15hr	4700
Vilnius	Lietuva (005)	6.55pm	Belorussky	14hr	7620

Sample Domestic Trains

DESTINATION	TRAIN	DEPARTURE	STATION	DURATION	FARE (KUPE)
Irkutsk	Rossiya (002)	1.50pm	Yaroslavsky	3 days & 2hr	₽15,380
Kazan	Premium (002)	10.08pm	Kazanksky	11½hr	₽3045
Murmansk	Arktika (016)	12.43am	Leningradsky	35hr	₽8146
Nizhny Novgorod	Lastochka (732)	11am	Kursky	4hr	₽460 (seat)
Pskov	Pskov (010)	6.30pm	Leningradsky	13hr	₽3800
Samara	Zhiguli (010)	8.08pm	Kazansky	13hr	₽3162
Tver	Sapsan (754)	7am	Leningradsky	1hr	₽1436 (seat)
Vladimir	Lastochka (732)	11am	Kursky	1hr 45min	₽430
Yaroslavl	Belmorie (016)	10.05am	Yaroslavsky	4hr	₽1600
Yekaterinburg	Ural (016)	4.50pm	Kazansky	25hr	₽4900

Suburban Trains

When taking trains from Moscow, note the difference between long-distance and 'suburban' trains. Long-distance trains run to places at least three or four hours out of Moscow, with limited stops and a range of accommodation classes. Suburban trains, known as *prigorodnye poezdy* or *elektrichki*, run to stops within 100km or 200km of Moscow. These slow trains stop almost everywhere, and have a single class of hard bench seats. You simply buy your ticket before the train leaves, and there's no capacity limit – so you may have to stand part of the way.

Most Moscow stations have a separate ticket hall for suburban trains, usually called the *Prigorodny Zal* (Пригородный зал) and often tucked away beside or behind the station building. These trains are usually listed on separate timetables and may depart from a separate group of platforms.

Tickets

For long-distance trains it's best to buy your tickets in advance, especially in summer. Buying train tickets is no longer the hassle it used to be. The easiest way is to purchase them online (as long as you have access to a printer). Try **Tutu.ru** (www.tutu.ru) or the official site of the **Russian Railways** (www.rzd.ru). The former is easier to use, but the latter has an English version.

If you prefer to buy your tickets from a human, most hotels offer this service. You can also go to the train station, where queues are no longer the nightmare they used to be. Be sure to bring your passport.

Getting Around

The central area around the Kremlin, Kitay Gorod and the Bolshoi Theatre is best seen on foot. Otherwise, the fastest, cheapest and easiest way to get around is almost always on the metro.

TO/FROM THE AIRPORTS

All three airports are accessible by the convenient **Aeroexpress train** (☎8-800-700 3377; www.aeroexpress.ru; ₽340-400; ⏲6am-midnight) from the city centre (book online to get the lower price). If you wish to take a taxi, book an official airport taxi through the dispatcher counter at the airport (₽2000 to ₽2500).

Domodedovo The Aeroexpress train leaves Paveletsky vokzal every half-hour between 6am and midnight for the 45-minute trip to Domodedovo.

Sheremetyevo The Aeroexpress train makes the 35-minute trip between Sheremetyevo (located next to Terminal E) and Belorussky vokzal every half-hour from 5.30am to 12.30am.

Vnukovo The Aeroexpress train makes the 35-minute run from Kievsky vokzal to Vnukovo airport every hour from 6am to 11pm.

BOAT

Capital Shipping Co (p96) ferries ply the Moscow River from May to September (every 20 minutes); board at any dock along the route. This is more of a tour than a form of transportation, unless you buy the full-day pass, which allows you to get on and off at will.

BUS, TROLLEYBUS & TRAM

Buses, trolleybuses and trams might be necessary for reaching some sights away from the city centre. They can also be useful for a few cross-town or radial routes that the metro misses. Tickets (₽40) are usually sold on the vehicle by a conductor or by the driver.

METRO

The **Moscow metro** (www.mosmetro.ru) is by far the easiest, quickest and cheapest way of getting around Moscow. Plus, many of the elegant stations are marble-faced, frescoed, gilded works of art. The 150-plus stations are marked outside by large 'M' signs.

Reliability The trains are generally reliable: you will rarely wait on a platform for more than three minutes. Nonetheless, they do get packed, especially during the city's rush hour.

Tickets Magnetic tickets (₽40) are sold at ticket booths. Queues can be long, so it's useful (and slightly cheaper) to buy a multiple-ride ticket (11 rides for ₽320 or 20 rides for ₽520). The ticket is actually a contactless smart card, which you must tap on the reader before going through the turnstile.

Maps & Signage Stations have maps of the system at the entrance and signs on each platform showing the destinations. The maps are generally in Cyrillic and Latin script, although the signs are usually only in Cyrillic. The carriages also have maps inside that show the stops for that line in both Roman and Cyrillic letters.

Transfers Interchange stations are linked by underground passages, indicated by *perekhod* signs, usually blue with a stick figure running up the stairs. Be aware that when two or more lines meet, the intersecting stations often (but not always) have different names.

TAXI

The safest and most reliable way to get a taxi is to order an official taxi by phone or book it online. Normally, the dispatcher will ring you back within a few minutes to provide a description and licence number of the car. Most companies will send a car within 60 minutes of your call. Some reliable companies offer online scheduling.

Central Taxi Reservation Office (Центральное бюро заказов такси; ☎495-627 0000; www.6270000.ru; 30min for ₽400)

Detskoe Taxi (Детское Такси; ☎495-765 1180; www.detskoetaxi.ru; 8km for ₽500) 'Children's Taxi' has smoke-free cars and car seats for your children.

New Yellow Taxi (Новое жёлтое такси; ☎495-940 8888; www.nyt.ru; per km ₽30, min ₽400)

Taxi Bistro (Такси Бистро; ☎495-685 1300; www.taxopark.ru; per 20min ₽320-420)

Unofficial Taxis

Almost any car in Moscow could be a taxi if the price is right, so if you're stuck, get on the street and stick your arm out.

- Many private cars cruise around as unofficial taxis, and other drivers will often take you if they're going in roughly the same direction.
- Expect to pay ₽200 to ₽400 for a ride around the city centre.
- Don't hesitate to wave on a car if you don't like the look of its occupants. As a general rule, it's best to avoid riding in cars that already have a passenger. Be particularly careful taking a taxi that is waiting outside a nightclub or bar.

AROUND MOSCOW

As you leave Moscow, the fast-paced modern capital fades from view and the slower-paced, old-fashioned countryside unfolds around you. The subtly changing landscape of the Moscow region (Подмосковье) is crossed by winding rivers and dotted with peasant villages – the classic provincial Russia immortalised by artists and writers over the centuries.

Most of these destinations are accessible from Moscow by *elektrichka,* or suburban train. Renting a car for a day allows much more flexibility once you arrive at your destination. That said, with patience or endurance (or both), all of these places are accessible on foot or by local bus.

Country Estates

Moscow's elite have long escaped the heat and hustle of city life by retreating to the surrounding regions. The quintessential aristocratic getaway is Prince Yusupov's palatial estate at Arkhangelskoe. On a more modest scale, Tchaikovsky, Chekhov and Pasternak all sought inspiration in the countryside around Moscow, not to mention the countless painters and sculptors who retreated to the artists colony at Abramtsevo. Even Lenin maintained a country estate on the outskirts of Moscow. These properties are now all house-museums to inspire the rest of us.

Abramtsevo Абрамцево

Railway tycoon and art patron Savva Mamontov built this lovely estate 45km north of Moscow. Here, he hosted a whole slew of painters and musicians, including Ilya Repin, landscape artist Isaak Levitan, portraitist Valentin Serov and ceramicist Mikhail Vrubel, as well as opera singer Fyodor Chaliapin. Today the **Abramtsevo Estate Museum-Preserve** (Музей-заповедник Абрамцево; ☎495-993 0033; www.abramtsevo.net; Museynaya ul 1, Abramtsevo; grounds ₽55, all exhibits ₽295; ⏲10am-6pm Wed-Sun Apr-Sep, 10am-4pm Wed-Sun Oct-Mar) is a delightful retreat from Moscow or addition to a trip to Sergiev Posad. Several rooms of the **Manor House** (Усадебный дом; adult/child ₽250/150) have been preserved intact, complete with artwork by various resident artists, and other buildings on the grounds are also open. The prettiest building is the **Saviour Church 'Not Made by Hand'** (Храм Спаса Нерукотворного).

Suburban trains run every half-hour from Yaroslavsky station (₽245, two hours). Most – but not all – trains to Sergiev Posad or Alexandrov stop at Abramtsevo. There are also regular buses between Abramtsevo and Sergiev Posad (20 minutes). From the train platform, follow the foot trail through the woods, straight across the fire road, through a residential community and down a rough set of stairs. Before reaching the highway, turn left to cross the bridge and continue up into the parking area. The 1km walk is not well signposted.

Arkhangelskoe Архангельское

In the 1780s the wealthy Prince Nikolai Yusupov purchased this grand palace on the outskirts of Moscow and turned it into the spectacular **Arkhangelskoe Estate** (Музей-усадьба Архангельское ; www.arkhangelskoe.su; admission ₽150, all exhibits ₽400; ⏲grounds 10am-8pm Wed-Sun, exhibits 10.30am-4.30pm Wed-Fri, 10am-6pm Sat-Sun). Now his palace displays the paintings, furniture, sculptures, glass, tapestries and porcelain that Yusupov accumulated over the years. In summer, the

Around Moscow

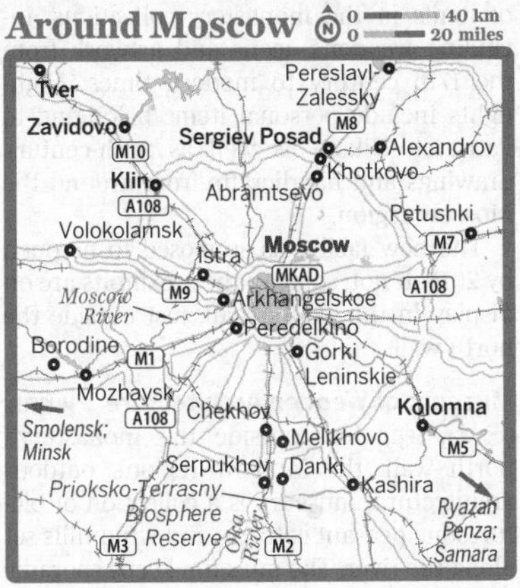

estate is the exquisite setting for the popular **Usadba Jazz Festival** (www.usadba-jazz.ru) in June. From Tushinskaya metro, take bus 541 or 549 or *marshrutka* (fixed route minibus) 151 to Arkhangelskoe (30 minutes).

Peredelkino Переделкино

Boris Pasternak – poet, author of *Doctor Zhivago* and winner of the 1958 Nobel Prize for literature – lived for a long time on Moscow's southwestern outskirts, just 5km beyond the city's outer ring road, where there is now the **Pasternak House-Museum** (Дом-Музей Бориса Пастернака; www.pasternakmuseum.ru; ul Pavlenko 3; admission ₽150; ⏲10am-4:30pm Tue-Sun). Run by his descendents, it's an authentic glimpse into the life of the writer.

Frequent suburban trains go from Moscow's Kievsky vokzal to Peredelkino (₽30, 30 minutes) on the line to Kaluga-II station. From Peredelkino station, follow the path west along the train tracks past the cemetery (where Pasternak is buried) and over the bridge. After about 400m, ul Pavlenko is on the right-hand side.

Gorki Leninskie Горки Ленинские

In Lenin's later years, he and his family spent time at the 1830s Murozov manor house, set on lovely wooded grounds 32km southeast of the capital. Designed by Fyodor Shekhtel, it now houses a **Lenin Museum** (Музей-Заповедник "Горки Ленинские"; www.mgorki.info; all exhibits ₽400; ⏲10am-7pm Sun & Tue-Fri, 10am-9pm Sat May-Sep, 10am-4pm Wed-Sun Oct-Apr), where you can see a re-creation of Lenin's Kremlin office, as well as his vintage Rolls-Royce – one of only 15 such automobiles in the world.

Bus 439 (₽60, 30 minutes) leaves every 90 minutes for the estate from the Domodedovskaya metro station in Moscow. By car, follow the M4 highway (Kashirskoe sh) to 11km beyond MKAD, then turn left to Gorki Leninskie.

Klin Клин

From 1885, Pyotr Tchaikovsky spent his summers in Klin, 75km northwest of Moscow. In a charming house on the edge of town, he wrote the *Nutcracker* and *Sleeping Beauty,* as well as his famous *Pathétique* Symphony No 6. After he died in 1893, the estate was converted into the **Tchaikovsky House-Museum** (Дом-Музей Чайковского; www.tchaikovsky-house-museum.ru; ul Chaykovskogo 48; admission ₽300, audio guide ₽150; ⏲10am-5pm Fri-Tue). It's a beautiful house, maintained just as when Tchaikovsky lived here. You can peruse photographs and personal effects, but only special guests are allowed to play his grand piano. Occasional concerts are held in the concert hall.

Suburban trains from Moscow's Leningradsky vokzal run to Klin (₽175 to ₽200, 1½ to two hours) throughout the day. Most of these continue to Tver (₽133 to ₽145, one to 1½ hours). From the station, take *marshrutka* 5 to Tchaikovsky's estate.

Melikhovo Мелихово

'My estate's not much,' wrote playwright Anton Chekhov of his home at Melikhovo, south of Moscow, 'but the surroundings are magnificent'. Here, Chekhov lived from 1892 until 1899 and wrote some of his most celebrated plays, including *The Seagull* and *Uncle Vanya*. Today the estate houses the **Chekhov Museum** (Музей-заповедник Чехова ; www.chekhovmuseum.com; exhibits each ₽60-120, all ₽290; ⏲10am-4pm Tue-Sun), dedicated to the playwright and his work. Theatre buffs should visit in May, when the museum hosts Melikhovo Spring, a week-long theatre festival.

Suburban trains (₽140 to ₽190, 1½ hours) run frequently from Moscow's Kursky vokzal to the town of Chekhov, 12km west of Melikhovo. Bus 25 makes the 20-minute journey between Chekhov and Melikhovo, with departures just about every hour.

DON'T MISS

LIVING HISTORY

The first Sunday in September, the Borodino Museum Complex hosts a re-enactment of the historic Battle of Borodino, complete with Russian and French participants, uniforms and weapons.

Istra Истра

In the 17th century, Nikon – the patriarch whose reforms drove the Old Believers from the Orthodox Church – decided to show one and all that Russia deserved to be the centre of the Christian world. He did this by building a little Holy City right at home, complete with its own Church of the Holy Sepulchre.

Sights & Activities

New Jerusalem Monastery MONASTERY
(Новоиерусалимский монастырь; www.n-jerusalem.ru; grounds admission free, museums each ₽50-200; 10am-5pm Tue-Sun year-round, to 6pm Jun-Aug) This grandiose complex was founded in 1656 near the picturesque Istra River (renamed the 'Jordan' by Patriarch Nikon). Unlike other Moscow monasteries, this one had no military use.

The centrepiece is the **Cathedral of the Resurrection** (Воскресенский собор), modelled after Jerusalem's Church of the Holy Sepulchre. After years as a museum, the monastery is now in Orthodox hands and renovation of the buildings is ongoing (expected completion in 2016). Like its prototype, it's really several churches under one roof, including the detached Assumption Church (Успенская церковь) in the northern part of the cathedral. Here, pilgrims come to kiss the relics of the holy martyr Tatyana, the monastery's patron saint.

The unusual underground **Church of SS Konstantin & Yelena** (Константино – Еленинская церковь) has only its belfry peeping up above the ground. Patriarch Nikon was buried in the cathedral, beneath the Church of John the Baptist (церковь Иоанна Предтечи).

New Jerusalem Museum MUSEUM
(Музей Новый Иерусалим; www.museum-new-jerusalem.ru; 10am-5pm Tue-Sun year-round, to 6pm Jun-Aug) The 'new' New Jersalem Museum is a modern, state-of-the-art museum, located across the river from the monastery. Exhibits draw on the hundreds of thousands of items in the monastery collections, including weapons, icons and artwork from the 17th century to modern times. Highlights include personal items belonging to Patriarch Nikon, as well as 20th-century drawings and handicrafts from around the Moscow region.

The new facility is supposed to be open by 2015. If not, some of these exhibits are on display in the exhibit hall, just outside the north wall.

Museum of Wooden Architecture MUSEUM
(May-Sep) Just outside the monastery's north wall, the Moscow region's outdoor architectural museum is a collection of picturesque peasant cottages and windmills set along the river. The museum keeps sporadic hours but the views of the river and meadows are lovely.

Getting There & Around

Suburban trains run from Moscow's Rizhsky vokzal to Istra (₽130, 1½ hours, hourly), from where buses run to the Muzey stop by the monastery. A 20-minute walk from the Istra train station is a pleasant alternative.

Borodino Бородино

Borodino battlefield is the site of turning-point battles in the Napoleonic War of 1812. Two hundred years later, the rural site presents a vivid history lesson. Start at the Borodino Museum, which provides a useful overview, then spend the rest of the day exploring the 100-sq-km preserve. If you have your own car, you can see monuments marking the sites of the most ferocious fighting, as well as the headquarters of both French and Russian armies. If you come by train, you'll probably be limited to the many monuments along the road between the train station and the museum.

The rolling hills around Borodino and Semyonovskoe are largely undeveloped, due to their historic status. Facilities are extremely limited; be sure to bring a picnic lunch.

Sights & Activities

Borodino Museum MUSEUM
(Музей-панорама "Бородинская битва"; www.borodino.ru; ₽50; 10am-5pm Tue-Sun Apr-Oct, 9am-3.30pm Tue-Sun Nov-Mar) This museum is an excellent place to start when you arrive in Borodino. You can study an interactive diorama of the Battle of Borodino before set-

ting out to see the site in person. Otherwise, the main exhibits feature original objects from the battle, including uniforms, weapons, documents and personal items. The displays, created by soldiers and their contemporaries, demonstrate the perception of the war and the battle at the time. There is also an exhibit dedicated to the WWII battle at this site.

Borodino Field HISTORICAL SITE
(Бородинское поле; www.borodino.ru) The entire battlefield – more than 100 sq km – is now part of the **Borodino Field Museum-Preserve**, basically vast fields dotted with dozens of memorials to specific divisions and generals (most erected at the centenary of the battle in 1912). The hilltop monument about 400m in front of the museum is **Bagration's tomb** (Могила Багратиона), the grave of Prince Bagration, a heroic Georgian infantry general who was mortally wounded in battle.

The **front line** was roughly along the 4km road from Borodino village to the train station: you'll see many monuments close to the road.

Further south, a concentration of monuments around **Semyonovskoe** marks the battle's most frenzied fighting. Here, Bagration's heroic Second Army, opposing far more numerous French forces, was virtually obliterated. Apparently, Russian commander Mikhail Kutuzov deliberately sacrificed Bagration's army to save his larger First Army, opposing lighter French forces in the northern part of the battlefield. **Kutuzov's headquarters** are marked by an obelisk in the village of Gorky. Another obelisk near Shevardino to the southwest, paid for in 1912 with French donations, marks **Napoleon's camp**.

The battle scene was re-created during WWII, when the Red Army confronted the Nazis on this very site. Memorials to this battle also dot the fields, and **WWII trenches** surround the monument to Bagration. Near the train station are two WWII mass graves.

BATTLE OF BORODINO

In 1812 Napoleon invaded Russia, lured by the prospect of taking Moscow. For three months the Russians retreated, until on 26 August the two armies met in a bloody battle of attrition at the village of Borodino. In 15 hours more than one-third of each army was killed – over 100,000 soldiers in all. Europe would not again experience fighting as devastating as this until WWI. The French seemed to be the winners, as the Russians withdrew and abandoned Moscow. But Borodino was, in fact, the beginning of the end for Napoleon, who was soon in full, disastrous retreat.

Saviour Borodino Monastery MUSEUM
(Спасо-Бородинский монастырь; www.borodino.ru; per exhibit ₽30; ⏲10am-5pm Wed-Sun) This monastery was built by widows of the Battle of Borodino. There are several exhibits on the grounds related to the events at Borodino. Leo Tolstoy stayed here when he was writing about the events that transpired nearby for his novel *War and Peace*. Nowadays, the building where he stayed contains an exhibit dedicated to the historical and fictional characters that populate his pages.

ℹ Getting There & Around

Suburban trains leave from Moscow's Belorussky vokzal to Borodino (₽228, two hours) at 7.56am and 8:43am (with additional trains on weekends). They return at 2:20pm and 4:02pm.

Since the area is rural, visiting by car is more convenient and probably more rewarding. If driving from Moscow, stay on the M1 highway (Minskoe sh) until the Mozhaysk turn-off, 95km beyond the Moscow outer ring road. It's 5km north to Mozhaysk, then 13km west to Borodino village.

Golden Ring

Includes ➡

Best Places to Eat

- Chaynaya (p135)
- Gostevaya Izba (p149)
- Dudki Bar (p144)
- Podbelka (p144)
- Salmon & Coffee (p130)

Best Places to Stay

- Surikov Guest House (p134)
- Yablonevy Sad (p139)
- Godzillas Suzdal (p134)
- Romanov Les (p137)
- Volzhskaya Zhemchuzhina (p143)

Why Go?

The Golden Ring (Золотое кольцо) is textbook Russia: onion-shaped domes, kremlins and gingerbread cottages with cherry orchards. It is a string of the country's oldest towns that formed the core of eastern Kyivan Rus. Too engrossed in fratricide, they failed to register the rise of Moscow, which elbowed them out of active politics. Largely untouched by Soviet industrialisation, they now attract flocks of Russian tourists in search of the lost idyll. The travel boom has led to the proliferation of new hotels and guesthouses, while competition keeps prices at bay.

When travelling here, brace for a flow of images that are quite literally iconic. Themselves architectural icons, local churches contain Russia's oldest religious art. There is more – picturesque country roads are inviting for a bicycle adventure, while steam baths will clear your mind after mead-drinking sessions. Moose milk may also help, but science is silent on that.

When to Go

Vladimir

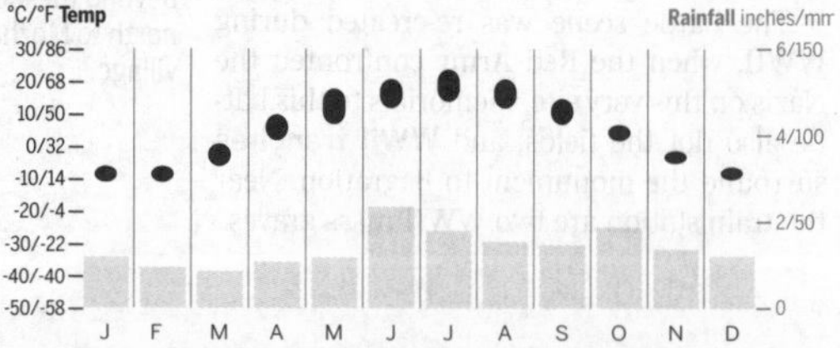

Late Jan The air is crisp, the snow is fluffy and a hot *banya* is readily available.

Jun Fields are covered in wild flowers – Russian nature never looks more beautiful.

Aug Thousands flock into forests to pick mushrooms and wild berries.

Vladimir Владимир

4922 / POP 340,000 / MOSCOW

Vladimir may look like another Soviet Gotham City, until you pass the medieval Golden Gate and stop by the cluster of exquisite churches and cathedrals, some of the oldest in Russia. Hiding behind them is an abrupt bluff with spectacular views of the Oka Valley. Prince Andrei Bogolyubsky chose Vladimir as his capital in 1157 after a stint in the Holy Land where he befriended European crusader kings, such as Friedrich Barbarossa. They sent him their best

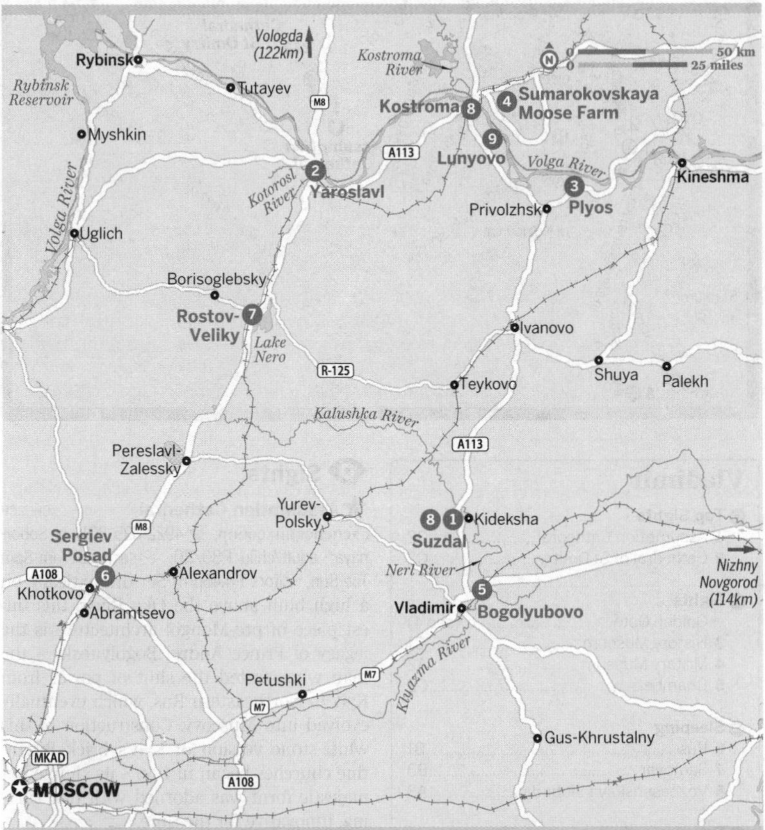

Golden Ring Highlights

1. Criss-cross beautiful **Suzdal** (p131) by bicycle or on foot, listening to the music of church bells and nightingales.
2. Count church domes on a stroll in Yaroslavl, then try downing as many beers at **Dudki Bar** (p144).
3. Ponder the landscape artist's career in **Plyos** (p136).
4. Sample moose milk at **Sumarokovskaya Moose Farm** (p140).
5. Admire the stunning simplicity of Bogolyubovo's **Church of the Intercession on the Nerl** (p131).
6. See the universe reflected in Christ's eyes at Sergiev Posad's **Trinity Cathedral** (p149).
7. Take a dip in Lake Nero and watch the sun set under the pink walls of **Rostov-Veliky's kremlin** (p145).
8. Steam off church fatigue at **Helio Spa** (p134) in Suzdal or **Azimut** (p139) in Kostroma.
9. Log your Golden Ring memories in your log house at **Romanov Les** (p137) in Lunyovo.

Vladimir

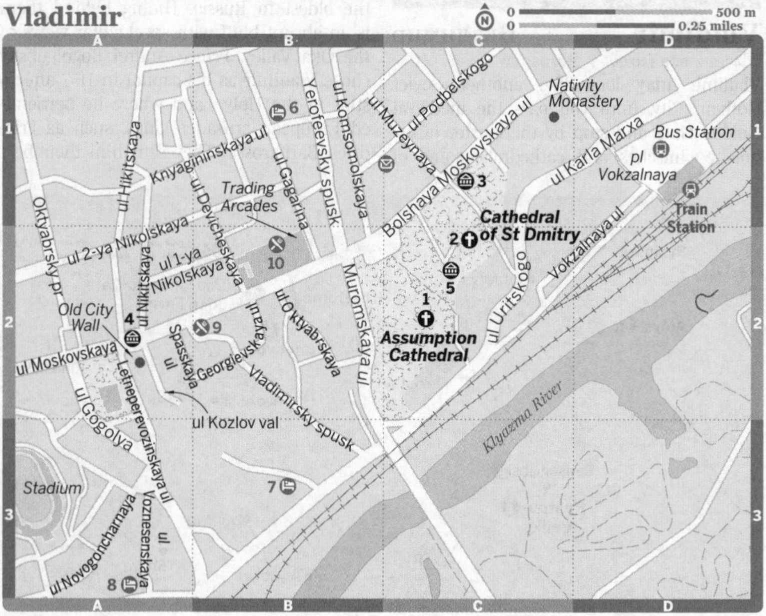

Vladimir

Top Sights

- 1 Assumption Cathedral C2
- 2 Cathedral of St Dmitry C2

Sights

- Golden Gate .... (see 4)
- 3 History Museum C1
- 4 Military Museum A2
- 5 Chambers C2

Sleeping

- 6 Rus B1
- 7 Samovar B3
- 8 Voznesenskaya Sloboda A3

Eating

- 9 Piteyny Dom Kuptsa Andreyeva B2
- 10 Salmon & Coffee B2

architects, who designed the town's landmarks, fusing Western and Kyivan traditions. Vladimir flourished for less than a century under Andrei's successor Vsevolod III, until a series of devastating Tatar-Mongol raids led to its decline and dependence on Moscow. The last, a 1408 siege, is vividly if gruesomely reenacted in Andrei Tarkovsky's film *Andrei Rublyov.*

Sights

★ Assumption Cathedral CHURCH

(Успенский собор; ☎4922-325 201; pl Sobornaya; adult/child ₽80/30; ⏲services 7am-8pm Tue-Sun, visitors 1-4.45pm) Set dramatically on a high bluff above the Oka River, this finest piece of pre-Mongol architecture is the legacy of Prince Andrei Bogolyubsky – the man who started the shift of power from Kyiv to Northeastern Rus, which eventually evolved into Muscovy. Construction of this white-stone version of Kyiv's brick Byzantine churches began in 1158 – its simple but majestic form was adorned with fine carving, innovative for the time.

Inside the working church, a few restored 12th-century murals of peacocks and prophets can be deciphered about halfway up the inner wall of the outer north aisle; this was originally an outside wall. The real treasures, though, are the Last Judgment frescoes by Andrei Rublyov and Daniil Chyorny, painted in 1408 in the central nave and inner south aisle, under the choir gallery towards the west end.

Comply with the standard church dress code (no shorts for men; covered head, long skirts for women) at all times and be especially mindful of people's sensitivities outside the designated 'tourist time'.

★Cathedral of St Dmitry CHURCH

(Дмитриевский собор; Bolshaya Moskovskaya ul 60; adult/child ₽50/30; ⌚10am-5pm Wed-Mon summer, to 4pm winter) Never before or after this beauty was built between 1193 and 1197 have Russian stone carvers achieved such artistic heights. The attraction here is the cathedral's exterior walls, covered in an amazing profusion of images. The top centre of the north, south and west walls all show King David bewitching the birds and beasts with music.

Vladimir Prince Vsevolod III (Vsevolod the Big Nest) had this church built as part of his palace. He appears at the top left of the north wall, with a baby son on his knee and other sons kneeling on each side. Above the right-hand window of the south wall, Alexander the Great ascends into heaven, a symbol of princely might; on the west wall appear the labours of Hercules.

Chambers MUSEUM

(Палаты; Bolshaya Moskovskaya ul 58; adult/child ₽180/100; ⌚10am-5pm Tue-Sun) The grand 18th-century court building between the two cathedrals is known as Palaty – the Chambers. It contains a children's museum, art gallery and historical exhibition. The former is a welcome diversion for little ones, who may well be suffering from old-church fatigue. The art gallery features art since the 18th century, with wonderful depictions of the Golden Ring towns.

History Museum MUSEUM

(Исторический музей; ☎4922-322 284; Bolshaya Moskovskaya ul 64; adult/child ₽50/30; ⌚10am-5pm Wed-Mon) This museum displays many remains and reproductions of the ornamentation from Vladimir's two cathedrals. It is part of an extensive exhibition that covers the history of Vladimir from Kyivan princes to the 1917 revolution. Reminiscent of Moscow's History Museum, the red-brick edifice was purpose-built in 1902.

Golden Gate HISTORIC BUILDING

(Золотые ворота; www.vladmuseum.ru; Zolotye Vorota; adult/child ₽50/30; ⌚10am-6pm Fri-Wed) Vladimir's Golden Gate, part defensive tower, part triumphal arch, was modelled on a very similar structure in Kyiv. Originally built by Andrei Bogolyubsky to guard the western entrance to his city, it was later restored under Catherine the Great. You can climb the narrow stone staircase to check out the **Military Museum** (☎4922-322 559; adult/child ₽40/20; ⌚10am-6pm Fri-Wed) inside. It's a small exhibit, the centrepiece of which is a diorama of old Vladimir being ravaged by nomadic raiders in 1238 and 1293.

THE FULL RING

There is undoubtedly an obsession with rings in Moscow – hence all the four ring roads inside the city and more outside. When Soviet tourism officials were devising a new brand for attractions accessible from the capital, they drew a loop beginning and ending in Moscow and called it the Golden Ring, reminding us that it is a circuit route. For no good reason, we personally prefer doing it in an anticlockwise direction.

It is best done with your own vehicle, hired in Moscow. But if you are using public transport, take a Sapsan train to Vladimir in the morning, spend the day checking its attractions, then take a bus to Suzdal, 36km away.

A scenic road continues from Suzdal to Ivanovo (79km), where you can change for a bus to Plyos. The bus travels along M7 for another 51km until Privolzhsk. Plyos is 20km away from it.

From Privolzhsk, the road goes along the Volga all the way to Yaroslavl, passing Kostroma. The 280km Yaroslavl–Moscow section of M8 road is a fairly modern highway, with Rostov, Pereslavl-Zalessky and Sergiev Posad breaking it into four more or less equal sections. Fast trains between Yaroslavl and Moscow stop at Rostov, from where you can choose to continue by bus to Pereslavl-Zalessky.

Whichever way you do the circuit, try to avoid leaving or arriving in Moscow by bus – you are likely to lose many hours in traffic. If you are going by car, leave in the morning and come back in the evening on a weekday. By all means, avoid weekends.

Finally, if you plan to travel the Golden Ring during winter holidays (New Year's Eve to 10 January) or May holidays (1 to 9 May), book your hotel at least a month in advance – hotels will be packed.

🛏 Sleeping

Given the proximity of the much more idyllic Suzdal, there is no big reason to overnight in Vladimir, unless you need to catch an early morning train to Moscow or Nizhny Novgorod. As with everywhere along the Golden Ring, the hotel is scene is rapidly changing, with newer places offering better standards than old ones.

Samovar HOSTEL $

(Самовар; ☑ 8-900 586 0151; www.samovarhostel.ru; ul Kozlov tupik 3; dm from ₽400, d ₽1400; 🛜🌐) For starters, it does have a real samovar, inviting for a tea party (not in the Boston sense, though). More importantly, it's a brand new purpose-built hostel with English-speaking personnel, many amenities and great atmosphere. The surroundings are admittedly slightly dingy, but the stairs leading to the garden by Assumption Cathedral are right in front of the entrance.

Rus HOTEL $$

(Русь; ☑ 4922-322 736; www.rushotel33.ru; ul Gagarina 14; s/d incl breakfast from ₽2900/3400; ❄🛜) Occupying an old mansion-house in a quieter street not far from the main drag, this new hotel offers nice and comfortable, if slightly faceless rooms. Reception staff are superfriendly.

★ Voznesenskaya Sloboda HOTEL $$$

(Вознесенская слобода; ☑ 4922-325 494; www.vsloboda.ru; ul Voznesenskaya 14b; d incl breakfast ₽4800; ❄🛜) Perched on a bluff with tremendous views of the valley, this hotel might have the most scenic location in the whole of the Golden Ring area. Outside is a quiet neighbourhood of old wooden cottages and villas dominated by the elegant Ascension church. The interior of the new building is tastefully designed to resemble art nouveau style c 1900.

The popular restaurant Krucha is on the premises.

🍴 Eating & Drinking

The main drag Bolshaya Moskovskaya ul is lined with cafes. You will not stay hunrgy, but you'll be pressed to find any outstanding culinary delights in Vladimir.

★ Salmon & Coffee INTERNATIONAL $$

(Лосось и кофе; www.losos-coffee.ru; Bolshaya Moskovskaya ul 19a; mains ₽300-600; 🛜📶) Salmon is yet to be found in the Oka, while coffee is not exactly what medieval princes had for breakfast. But instead of hinting at the city's past, this DJ cafe serving Asian as well as European dishes is here to give a cosmopolitan touch to the ancient town.

Lots of dark wood, dim lights and magenta-coloured metal railings create a cool, intriguing atmosphere.

Piteyny Dom Kuptsa Andreyeva RUSSIAN $$

(☑ 4922-232 6545; www.andreevbeer.com/dom; Bolshaya Moskovskaya ul 16; mains ₽250-400; ⏱ 11am-midnight; 🛜📶) Merchant Andreyev's Liquor House, as the name translates, makes a half-hearted attempt to pass itself off as an old world Russian *kabak* (pub), but its main virtue is a dozen home-brewed beers on tap and hearty Russian meals, including all the classics, from *shchi* (cabbage soup) to bliny.

ℹ Information

Post & Telephone Office (Почтамт и переговорный пункт; ul Podbelskogo; ⏱ 8am-10pm)

ℹ Getting There & Away

Vladimir is on the main Trans-Siberian line between Moscow and Nizhny Novgorod and on a major highway leading to Kazan.

BUS

Bus is a poor option for Moscow or Nizhny Novgorod – train is much faster and more reliable. Conveniently for those heading to Suzdal, the bus station is right in front of the train station.

Murom ₽340, two hours, hourly

Pereslavl-Zalessky four hours, four weekly

Suzdal ₽65, one hour, half-hourly

Yaroslavl ₽560, five hours, two daily

TAXI

Taxi drivers charge ₽700 for a one-way trip to Suzdal.

TRAIN

There are frequent services from Moscow, with the old-school Lastochka (₽300, three daily) and the modern Sapsan (₽900, two daily) being the fastest – they cover the distance in 1¾ hours. Both of these continue to Nizhny Novgorod (two hours; Lastochka ₽300, Sapsan ₽1050). All long-distance trains heading towards Tatarstan and Siberia also call at Vladimir.

ℹ Getting Around

Trolleybus 5 from the train and bus stations runs up Bolshaya Moskovskaya ul.

DON'T MISS

THE CHURCH OF PERFECTION

Tourists and pilgrims all flock to Bogolyubovo, just 12km northeast of Vladimir – the reason being a small 12th-century church standing amid a flower-covered floodplain.

The **Church of the Intercession on the Nerl** (Церковь Покрова на Нерли; ⏲10am-6pm Tue-Sun) is the golden standard of Russian architecture. Apart from ideal proportions, its beauty lies in a brilliantly chosen waterside location (floods aside) and the sparing use of delicate carving.

Legend has it that Prince Andrei Bogolyubsky had the church built in memory of his favourite son, Izyaslav, who was killed in battle against the Bulgars. As with the Cathedral of St Dmitry in Vladimir, King David sits at the top of three facades, the birds and beasts entranced by his music. The interior has more carvings, including 20 pairs of lions. If the church is closed (from October to April the opening hours are more sporadic), try asking at the house behind.

To reach this famous church, get bus 152 from the Golden Gate or Sobornaya pl in Vladimir and get off by the hard-to-miss **Bogolyubsky Monastery**, which contains remnants of Prince Andrei's palace. Walk down Vokzalnaya ul, immediately east of the monastery. At the end of the street, cross the railroad tracks and follow the cobblestone path across the field. You can catch a ride in the horse-drawn carriage for ₽250 per person, two people minimum.

Suzdal Суздаль

☎49231 / POP 12,000 / ⏲MOSCOW

The Golden Ring comes with a diamond and that's Suzdal. If you have only one place to visit near Moscow, come here – even though everyone else will do the same. In 1864 local merchants failed to coerce the government into building the Trans-Siberian Railway through their town. Instead it went through Vladimir, 35km away. As a result Suzdal was bypassed not only by trains, but by the 20th century altogether. This is why the place remains largely the same as ages ago – its cute wooden cottages mingling with golden cupolas that reflect in the river, which meanders sleepily through gentle hills and flower-filled meadows.

As it happens, Suzdal served as a royal capital when Moscow was a mere cluster of cowsheds. It transformed into a major monastic centre in the times of Ivan the Terrible and an important commercial hub later on. But nowadays, it seems perfectly content in its retirement from both business and politics.

Sights

★Kremlin FORTRESS

(Кремль; exhibits each ₽30-70, joint ticket adult/child ₽250/100; ⏲10am-6pm Wed-Mon) This kremlin is the grandfather of the one in Moscow. In the 12th century it was the base of prince Yury Dolgoruky, who ruled the vast northeastern part of Kyivan Rus and, among many other things, founded an outpost, which is now the Russian capital. The 1.4km-long earth rampart of Suzdal's kremlin encloses a few streets of houses and a handful of churches, as well as the main cathedral group on Kremlyovskaya ul.

The **Nativity of the Virgin Cathedral** (Церковь Казанской иконы Божьей Матери; Kremlyovskaya ul), its blue domes spangled with gold, was founded in the 1220s. Only its richly carved lower section is original white stone, though, the rest being 16th-century brick. The inside is sumptuous, with 13th- and 17th-century frescoes and 13th-century damascene (gold on copper) west and south doors.

Within the Kremlin, the **Archbishop's Chambers** (Архиерейские палаты; Kremlyovskaya ul; admission ₽70; ⏲10am-5pm Wed-Mon) houses the **Suzdal History Exhibition** (☎49231-21 624; admission ₽70; ⏲10am-5pm Wed-Mon), which includes the original 13th-century door from the cathedral, photos of its interior and a visit to the 18th-century **Cross Hall** (Крестовая палата), which was used for receptions. The tent-roofed 1635 kremlin **bell tower** (Звонница) on the east side of the yard contains additional exhibits.

★Saviour Monastery of St Euthymius MONASTERY

(Спасо-Евфимиев мужской монастырь; ☎49231-20 746; grounds & individual exhibitions

Suzdal

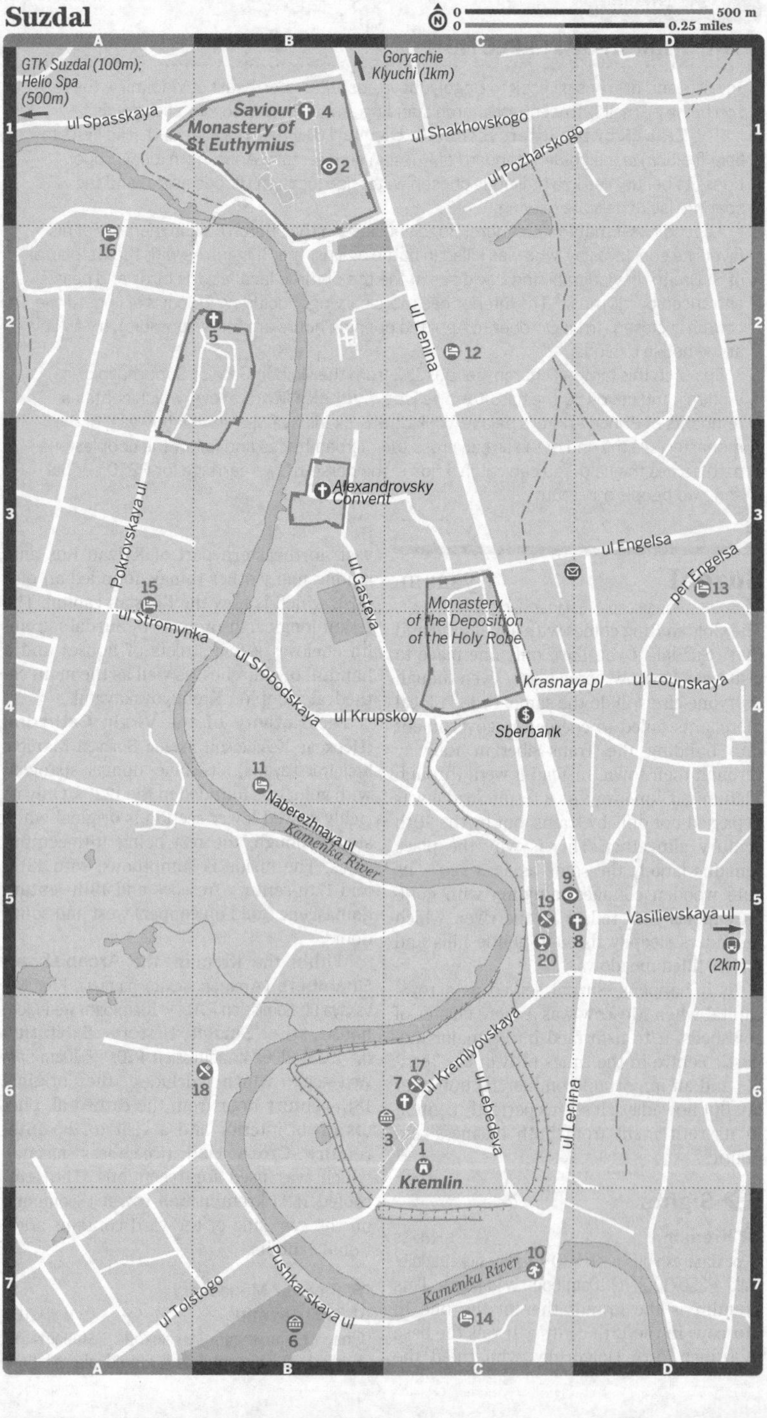
0 500 m
0 0.25 miles
A
B
C
D
1
2
3
4
5
6
7
GTK Suzdal (100m);
Helio Spa
(500m)
Goryachie
Klyuchi (1km)
ul Spasskaya
Saviour
Monastery of
St Euthymius
4
2
ul Shakhovskogo
ul Pozharskogo
16
5
ul Lenina
12
Alexandrovsky
Convent
Pokrovskaya ul
ul Engelsa
per Engelsa
13
15
ul Gasteva
Monastery
of the Deposition
of the Holy Robe
ul Stromynka
ul Slobodskaya
Krasnaya pl
ul Lounskaya
ul Krupskoy
Sberbank
11
Naberezhnaya ul
Kamenka River
9
19
8
20
Vasilievskaya ul
(2km)
17
7
ul Kremlyovskaya
18
3
ul Lebedeva
ul Lenina
1
Kremlin
10
Kamenka River
ul Tolstogo
Pushkarskaya ul
14
6

Suzdal

each adult/student ₽70/30, all-inclusive ticket adult/student ₽350/150; ⌚10am-6pm Tue-Sun) Founded in the 14th century to protect the town's northern entrance, Suzdal's biggest monastery grew mighty in the 16th and 17th centuries after Vasily III, Ivan the Terrible and the noble Pozharsky family funded impressive new stone buildings, and big land and property acquisitions. It was girded with its great brick walls and towers in the 17th century.

Right at the entrance, the **Annunciation Gate-Church** (Благовещенская надвратная церковь) houses an interesting exhibit on Dmitry Pozharsky (1578–1642), leader of the Russian army that drove the Polish invaders from Moscow in 1612.

A tall 16th- to 17th-century cathedral **bell tower** (Звонница) stands before the seven-domed **Cathedral of the Transfiguration of the Saviour** (Спасо-Преображенский собор). Every hour on the hour from 11am to 5pm a short concert of chimes is given on the bell tower's bells. The cathedral was built in the 1590s in 12th- to 13th-century Vladimir-Suzdal style. Inside, restoration has uncovered some bright 1689 frescoes by the school of Gury Nikitin from Kostroma. The tomb of Prince Dmitry Pozharsky is by the cathedral's east wall.

The 1525 **Assumption Refectory Church** (Успенская церковь), facing the bell tower, adjoins the old **Father Superior's chambers** (Палаты отца-игумена), which house a display of Russian icons and the excellent naïve art exhibition showcasing works by local Soviet-era amateur painters.

The old **Monastery Dungeon** (Монастырская тюрьма), set up in 1764 for religious dissidents, is at the north end of the complex. It now houses a fascinating exhibit on the monastery's prison history, including displays of some of the better-known prisoners who stayed here. The Bolsheviks used the monastery as a concentration camp after the 1917 revolution. During WWII, German and Italian officers captured in the battle of Stalingrad were kept here.

The combined **Hospital Chambers & St Nicholas Church** (Больничные кельи и Никольская церковь; ul Lebedeva) feature a rich collection of church gold treasures.

Torgovaya Ploshchad SQUARE

Suzdal's Torgovaya pl (Market Sq) is dominated by the pillared **Trading Arcades** (Торговые ряды; 1806–11) along its western side. There are four churches in the immediate vicinity, including the **Resurrection Church** (Воскресенская церковь; Torgovaya pl; admission ₽50). Make the precarious climb to the top of the bell tower and be rewarded with wonderful views of Suzdal's gold-domed skyline. The five-domed 1707 **Emperor Constantine Church** (Царево-Константиновская церковь) in the square's northeastern corner is a working church with an ornate interior.

Intercession Convent CONVENT

(Покровский монастырь; Pokrovskaya ul) FREE It's one of the classic Suzdal pictures – the whitewashed beauty surrounded by green meadows on the banks of the lazily meandering river. Inside it's all flowers. The nuns, who live in wooden cottages left over from a rustic hotel that existed on the premises, seem to be quite obsessed with floriculture. This convent was founded in 1364, originally as a place of exile for the unwanted wives of tsars.

Museum of Wooden Architecture & Peasant Life MUSEUM
(Музей деревянного зодчества и крестьянского быта; www.vladmuseum.ru; ul Pushkarskaya; adult/student ₽200/80; ⌚9am-7pm Thu-Tue May-Oct, to 4pm Nov-Apr) This open-air museum, illustrating old peasant life in this region of Russia, is a short walk across the river, south of the Kremlin. Besides log houses, windmills, a barn, and lots of tools and handicrafts, its highlights are the 1756 **Transfiguration Church** (Преображенская церковь) and the simpler 1776 **Resurrection Church** (Воскресенская церковь).

Activities

The rolling hills and attractive countryside around Suzdal are ideal for cycling, with bicycles available for rent at many hotels.

Helio Spa BANYA
(Горячие ключи; ☎49231-24 000; www.parilka.com; ul Korovniki 14; ⌚11am-1am) Rural Suzdal is a great place to cleanse body and soul in a Russian *banya*. Beautiful, lakeside *bani* are available for rental at Helio Park Hotel (former Goryachie Klyuchi) starting at ₽1200 per hour for up to four people. Each is an individually designed wooden cottage with different types of steam and comfort zones.

Boat Cruise BOAT TRIPS
(₽250) Four times a day, a small tented boat takes tourists on a 40-minute cruise up and down the Kamenka River, leaving from the bridge by the kremlin. It's a good chance to watch and take pictures of Suzdal's many monasteries and churches from a different perspective.

Sleeping

Suzdal is experiencing a tourist boom, which means there is plenty of choice in the mid-range and high-end bracket – from quaint two- or three-room guest houses to vast holiday resorts. You may save up to ₽1000 per night if you avoid visiting Suzdal during weekends or holidays.

★ **Godzillas Suzdal** HOSTEL $
(☎in Moscow 495-699 4223; www.godzillashostel.com; Naberezhnaya ul 32; dm incl breakfast from ₽700; 📶) An affiliate of the namesake hostel in Moscow, this big log-cabin facility overlooking the river opened just a few years ago, but has already undergone a thorough renovation. Each dorm room has its own bathroom and balcony. Guests can also enjoy the blooming garden and Russian *banya*, as well as the chill-out lounge and the bar in the basement.

★ **Surikov Guest House** GUESTHOUSE $$
(Гостевой дом Суриковых; ☎49231-21 568; www.surikovs.ru; ul Krasnoarmeyskaya 53; incl breakfast, weekdays d/tr/q ₽2000/2500/3000, weekends d/tr/q ₽2500/3000/3500; 📶) Drifting into the boutique hotel category, this guest house is positioned at a picturesque bend of the Kamenka River under the walls of St Euthymius monastery. It has modestly sized, but comfortable rooms equipped with antique-style furniture made by the owner, and a Russian restaurant catering for guests only on the 1st floor. Visitors rave about this place.

Pushkarskaya Sloboda RESORT $$
(Пушкарская слобода; ☎49231-23 303; www.sloboda-gk.ru; ul Lenina 45; incl breakfast, hotel d ₽2900, village d from ₽4300; ❄🏊👨‍👩‍👧) This holiday village has everything you might want from your Disney vacation including accommodation in the log-cabin 'Russian inn' or the reproduction 19th-century 'Gunner's Village'. It also has three restaurants, ranging from the rustic country tavern to a formal dining room; a spa-centre with a pool; and every service you might dream up. It's attractive, family friendly and good value.

Stromynka 2 HOTEL $$
(Стромынка 2; ☎49231-25 155; www.stromynka2.ru; ul Stromynka 2; s/d from ₽2600/3000; 📶) A cross between a Russian gingerbread cottage and a Swiss chalet, this medium-sized hotel prides itself in having used only natural materials in the construction. Large and airy rooms are well equipped, smell like untreated wood and offer nice views of the Kamenka River valley. Bikes are available for hire.

Petrov Dom GUESTHOUSE $$
(Петров дом; ☎49231-23 326, 8-919-025 8884, 8-910-188 3108; www.petrovdom.ru; per Engelsa 18; r weekdays/weekends/holidays ₽1500/2000/, holidays ₽2500; 📶👨‍👩‍👧🚭) Vlad and Lena of-

fer three nicely furnished and strictly non-smoking rooms in their wooden dacha-style house with a lovely garden on a quiet street (not to be confused with ul Engelsa). This is a great option for travellers with children, with a sumptuous breakfast included. Self-caterers are welcome to use the kitchen and garden grill.

It's not signposted; look out for a house with a geometrically perfect triangular roof and a sun symbol on the gates.

Nikolayevsky Posad RESORT $$$

(Николаевский посад; ☎49231-23 585; www.nposad.ru; ul Lenina 138; incl breakfast, dm ₽1050, weekdays s/d/tr from ₽3650/4300/4950, weekends & holidays s/d/tr from ₽4750/5600/6950;) This large, manicured resort is located right by St Euthymius Monastery. It has modern and comfortable, if slightly faceless rooms as well as four- to eight-bed dorms in two-storey buildings styled as merchants' mansion houses. There is a nice restaurant, a 'hangover' cafe on-site and a 25m pool (in case the hangover lingers). Bicycles are available for rent.

Although created by Russians, Nikolayevsky Posad has been recently taken over by the Best Western chain.

Eating & Drinking

Large hotels also have restaurants.

★Chaynaya RUSSIAN $

(Чайная; www.restoran-suzdal.ru/chaynaya; ul Kremlyovskaya 10g; mains ₽120-350; ⏰10am-9pm;) It is hidden inside a kitschy crafts market, but the place is a gem. Russian standards – bliny, *shchi* (cabbage soup), mushroom dishes and pickles – are prominently represented, but it is all the unusual (and rather experimental) items on the menu that make the place so special. Red buckwheat pancakes anyone? Pickled apple stuffed with herring?

Or the ultimate treat – fried, salted cucumber with pickled ashberry served on a toast with sour cream and horseradish paste? If you are in a group, definitely order a samovar of tea, which will be served with cream sugar and *baranki* (doughnut-shaped cookies).

Kvasnaya Izba RUSSIAN $

(☎8-915 779 0577; www.kvasnaya-izba.ru; ul Pushkarskaya 51; mains ₽200-400; ⏰10am-9pm;) It is slightly out of the way, but it's worth an extra walk if you'd like to sample all kinds of *kvas* – Russia's traditional drink made of fermented rye bread. Flavours on offer include apple, thyme and blackcurrant. You may have it as a refreshment, but it goes equally well with the hearty Russian meals here.

Kvas is so synonymous with the traditional lifestyle in Russia that there is even an ironic term – 'kvas patriot'.

Salmon & Coffee INTERNATIONAL $$

(Лосось и кофе; www.losos-coffee.ru; Trading Arcades, ul Lenina 63a; mains ₽340-590; ⏰10am-11pm;) Like its sister in Vladimir, Suzdal's S&C is about the best place for an unhurried lunch or a cup of coffee. It is, however, much quainter, with lots of whitewashed wood interior aged to evoke the 'Cherry Orchard' dacha ambience. Despite the name, salmon is not really prominent on the menu, which includes inventive fusion European dishes and sushi.

Graf Suvorov & Mead-Tasting Hall RUSSIAN

(Граф Суворов и зал дегустаций; Trading Arcades, ul Lenina 63a; tasting menu ₽130-350) This place has vaulted ceilings and kitschy wall paintings depicting Russian military hero Count Suvorov's exploits in the Alps. It serves standard Russian food and a few dozen varieties of locally produced *medovukha*, a mildly alcoholic honey ale that was drunk by princes of old. Go for tasting sets, which include 10 samples each. Apart from the regular one, there are separate sets of berry- and herb-flavoured *medovukha*.

Information

Post & Telephone Office (Почтамт и переговорный пункт; Krasnaya pl; ⏰8am-8pm) Open 24 hours for phone calls.

Sberbank (Сбербанк; ul Lenina 73a; ⏰8am-4.30pm Mon-Fri) Exchange office and ATM.

Getting There & Away

The bus station is 2km east of the centre on Vasilievskaya ul. Some long-distance buses pass the central square on the way.

A train/bus combination via Vladimir is by far the best way of getting from Moscow. Buses run every 45 minutes to/from Vladimir (₽115, one hour).

There are two daily transit buses to Kostroma (₽415, 4½ hours). For Plyos, change at Ivanovo (₽130, every two hours, two hours), which has hourly direct services to Plyos (₽140, two hours).

Plyos Плёс

49339 / POP 3000 / MOSCOW

A tranquil town of wooden houses and hilly streets winding down to the Volga waterfront, Plyos is halfway between Ivanovo and Kostroma. Though fortified from the 15th century, Plyos' renown stems from its role as a late-19th-century artists retreat. Isaak Levitan, Russia's most celebrated landscape artist, found inspiration here in the summers of 1888 to 1890. The playwright Anton Chekhov commented that Plyos 'put a smile in Levitan's paintings'. But he made the artist cross by depicting Levitan's love life in Plyos in the rather sexist short story 'The Grasshopper'.

Sights

Town Centre NEIGHBOURHOOD

The oldest part of town is along the river, as evidenced by the ramparts of the old fort, which dates from 1410. The hill is topped by the simple 1699 **Assumption Cathedral** (Успенский собор), one of Levitan's favourite painting subjects. From the cathedral the road winds down to the main square. The town's oldest street is supershort **ul Kalashnaya**. It has been converted into a flea market and descends to the embankment.

Levitan House Museum MUSEUM

(Дом-музей Левитана; www.plyos.org; ul Lunacharskogo 4; adult/student ₽90/40; 10am-5pm Tue-Sun) Works by the master and his disciples are displayed against the background of the Volga. The artist moved to this dacha from a poor potter's hut when money from sold paintings started trickling in. Walk down ul Kalashnaya, turn right and follow the embankment.

Landscape Museum ART GALLERY

(Музей пейзажа; adult/student ₽60/30; 10am-2pm & 3-5pm Tue-Sun) See how the same landscapes inspire contemporary artists in this museum at the far end of the embankment. Nearby, a bronze Chekhovian lady examines the environs through the empty frame of an easel. Head down ul Kalashnaya, turn right and follow the embankment.

Sleeping & Eating

Russian Prime Minister Dmitry Medvedev has made Plyos his favourite holiday spot, which – given the size of his entourage – resulted in the proliferation of VIP holiday homes and inflated prices for other accommodation. Check www.plyos.info for homestay options, which will come much cheaper than proper hotels.

Volga-Volga GUESTHOUSE $$$

(Волга-Волга; 8-910-999 8822; www.volga-ples.ru; ul Spusk Gory Svobody 12b; s/d incl breakfast from ₽3700/4900) A large wooden edifice designed to resemble a traditional Russian gingerbread cottage, perched on the slope of a deep ravine leading to the Volga, has rustic-styled rooms and a relaxed dacha atmosphere.

Chastny Visit GUESTHOUSE $$$

(Частный визит; 8-920-343 2998, 8-901-191 9819; www.pless.ru; ul Gornaya Sloboda 7; garden house with outside bath half-pension ₽7500, r half-pension ₽13,500) Occupying a prime spot on the edge of a spectacular Volga-facing bluff, this sweet wooden cottage filled with antiques is run by a French-Russian family. Prices, however, completely damage the idyll. There is an expensive restaurant on the premises.

Dacha RUSSIAN

(49339-432 07; ul Sovetskaya 39; ₽200-400) The only restaurant that stays open when cruise ships are gone, Dacha is a large tourist-oriented affair that serves well-cooked traditional Russian food. It is positioned in a prime spot on the embankment. Service is patchy.

Getting There & Away

Plyos is a 20km detour from Privolzhsk on the main Golden Ring route. Travelling to/from Suzdal by bus, change at Ivanovo (₽140, hourly, two hours).

Heading from Plyos to Kostroma, take a taxi or Ivanovo bus to Privolzhsk, where you can catch one of the hourly transit buses plying the route between Ivanovo and Kostroma.

Kostroma Кострома

4942 / POP 274,500 / MOSCOW

The Volga flows lazily past the mansions of tsarist-era merchants in this modest-sized city, which played a crucial role in the advent of the Romanov dynasty and hasn't achieved any prominence ever since, shunning the calls of modernity for the sake of peace and quiet. Founded by Yury Dolgoruky in 1152, Kostroma developed as a market town on the river, its former commercial glory evidenced by the enormous trading arcade on the equally huge main square. One day is probably enough to explore Kostroma museums, visit St Ipaty Monastery and down a few beers at Dudki Bar. You'll need another day if you fancy a trip to the moose farm.

Sights

★Monastery of St Ipaty MONASTERY
(Ипатьевский монастырь; ☎4942-312 589; entry free, exhibitions adults/students ₽130/50; ⏰9am-5pm) There is a bizarre similarity in the names of the Romanov dynasty's start and end points. The last tsar's family was executed in engineer Ipatyev's house in Yekaterinburg, while St Ipaty Monastery in Kostroma – standing at the confluence of the Volga and the smaller Kostroma River – is where a large delegation of citizens came in 1613 to insist that the young Mikhail Romanov accept the Russian throne, thus ending the Time of Troubles and Polish intervention.

The 18-year-old tsar-to-be had spent 13 years in exile, his family being chief rivals of Tsar Boris Godunov. Interestingly, the monastery is believed to have been founded by an ancient ancestor of the latter, the semilegendary Tatar Prince Chet who saw a vision of St Ipaty on the spot and decided to convert.

In 1590 the Godunovs built the monastery's **Trinity Cathedral** (Троицкий собор), which contains more than 80 old frescoes by a school of 17th-century Kostroma painters, headed by Gury Nikitin, as well as some 20th-century additions. The fresco in the southern part of the sanctuary depicts Chet's baptism by St Ipaty.

In the Romanov era, all successive tsars came here to visit the monastery's red **Romanov Chambers**, opposite the cathedral, which contain a dull historic exhibition. Much more exciting is the **Refectory**, which displays church treasures and old icons. Footage of Tsar Nicholas II and his family visiting Kostroma in 1913 for the 300-year jubilee of the Romanov House is shown nonstop on a large screen at the entrance. The 400-year jubilee in 2013 turned out to be a fairly low-key event.

The monastery is 2.5km west of the town centre. Take bus 14 from the central Susaninskaya pl and get off once you cross the river.

Museum of Wooden Architecture MUSEUM
(Музей деревянного зодчества; ☎4942 373 872; admission ₽70; ⏰dawn-dusk May-Oct) Essentially a park on the bank of the Volga, the museum is a large collection of northern-style wooden buildings, including peasant houses, windmills and churches (one built without nails). Some of the buildings house small exhibits and the grounds are pleasant for strolling, listening to the chirping of resident frogs and admiring the handiwork of the artists. The museum is nearly indistinguishable from the surrounding neighbourhood, which consists of storybook houses, blossoming gardens and pretty churches.

★Susaninskaya Ploshchad SQUARE
(Сусанинская площадь) Picturesque Susaninskaya pl was built as an ensemble under Catherine the Great's patronage after a fire in 1773. It was nicely revamped on the occasion of the Romanov dynasty's 400-year anniversary in 2013. Its centrepiece is the immense **Trading Arcade** which used to house hundreds of shops selling goods shipped up and down the Volga. These days one can only imagine how this capitalist anthill might have looked like in its heyday around 1880.

The opposite side of the square is graced by an imposing 19th-century **Fire Tower**, which houses a history exhibition, and a former **Guardhouse** (Здание бывшей

WORTH A TRIP

LOG INN

Overdosed on onion domes? It's time to go rural. Golden Ring towns are surrounded by deep forests, but few travellers – apart from those infected by the Russian mushroom-picking craze – actually venture outside town walls. In the village of Lunyovo, some 20km from Kostroma off the road leading to Plyos, **Romanov Les** (☎Kostroma 8-903-634 5222, Moscow 8-495-724 5969; www.romanovles.ru; ul Podlipayeva, Lunyovo; incl breakfast, s/d weekdays from ₽3900/4700, weekends from ₽5100/5900, cottages for 6 ₽18,000) resort provides a perfect tree-hugging experience. Accommodation is in large, fully-equipped log houses. There are two nice restaurants and a spa with a pool (though annoyingly even guests have to pay ₽200 to visit) on the vast wooded premises. The Volga is about 500m away, accessed via the nearby Soviet-style Lunyovo Resort. Reception can arrange transfer from Kostroma.

Kostroma

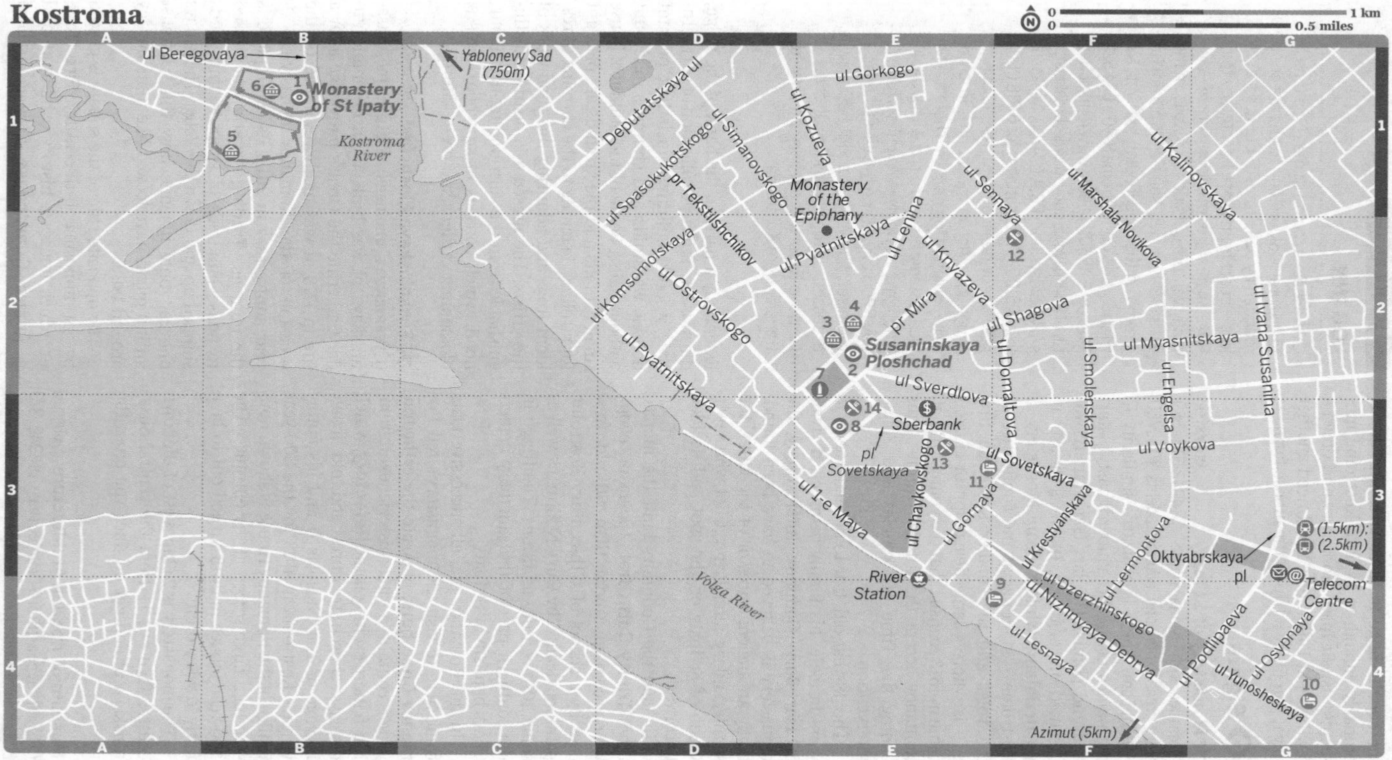
0 — 1 km
0 — 0.5 miles
ul Beregovaya
Monastery of St Ipaty
Kostroma River
Yablonevy Sad (750m)
Deputatskaya ul
ul Gorkogo
ul Spasokukotskogo
ul Simanovskogo
ul Kozueva
Monastery of the Epiphany
pr Tekstilshchikov
ul Komsomolskaya
ul Ostrovskogo
ul Pyatnitskaya
ul Lenina
ul Knyazeva
ul Sennaya
ul Marshala Novikova
ul Kalinovskaya
pr Mira
ul Shagova
Susaninskaya Ploshchad
ul Sverdlova
ul Domaltova
ul Smolenskaya
ul Myasnitskaya
ul Engelsa
ul Ivana Susanina
ul Voykova
Sberbank
pl Sovetskaya
ul Chaykovskogo
ul Sovetskaya
ul Gornaya
ul Krestyanskaya
ul Lermontova
Oktyabrskaya pl
(1.5km); (2.5km)
Telecom Centre
ul 1-e Maya
River Station
Volga River
ul Dzerzhinskogo
ul Nizhnyaya Debrya
ul Lesnaya
ul Podlipaeva
ul Osypnaya
ul Yunosheskaya
Azimut (5km)
1 2 3 4 5 6 7 8 9 10 11 12 13 14
A B C D E F G

Kostroma

Top Sights

1 Monastery of St Ipaty B1
2 Susaninskaya Ploshchad E2

Sights

3 Fire Tower E2
4 Guardhouse E2
5 Museum of Wooden Architecture B1
6 Refectory B1
Romanov Chambers .... (see 6)
7 Susanin Monument E2
8 Trading Arcade E3
Trinity Cathedral .... (see 6)

Sleeping

9 Hostel Academy F4
10 Hotel Snegurochka G4
11 Old Street E3

Eating

12 Dudki Bar F2
13 Horns & Hoofs E3
14 Slaviansky E3

гауптвахты). All the buildings in the square were freshly revamped on the occasion of the 400th anniversary of the Romanov dynasty.

The **monument**, standing in a small park between the arcades, celebrates local hero Ivan Susanin. Susanin guided a Polish detachment hunting for Mikhail Romanov into a swamp and subsequently to their deaths. He didn't survive either. His deed was lionized by Mikhail Glinka in the opera *A Life for the Tsar*.

Activities

Azimut BANYA

(4942-390 505, 8-800-200 0048; ul Magistralnaya 40; 2hr banya rent for up to 6 people ₽3000, treatments per person ₽900-1400) Right by the turn towards the centre on the main Yaroslavl road, this countryside hotel is famous for its *banya* complex, which offers a dozen treatments, from traditional to slightly left field. Most involve quick shifts between boiling-hot and ice-cold tubs, and a steam master beating the hell out of you with birch-tree twigs.

Sleeping

Whichever hotel you go to, it makes sense asking bus drivers to drop you off at Oktyabrskaya pl once you cross the Volga. You'll save yourself the trek back into town from the bus station.

Hostel Academy HOSTEL $

(Хостел Академия; 4942-496 165; www.achostel.com; ul Lesnaya 11a; incl breakfast, dm from ₽500, d ₽1500;) Equipped with dorms sleeping four and six, this friendly hostel occupies the ground floor of a new and centrally located residential compound on the Volga embankment. A washing machine and fans are available for visitors. It also rents bicycles (great way of getting to Ipatyevsky Monastery) at ₽700 per day.

Resident woodcarving artists are promising to turn the hostel into an art object – results are yet to be seen.

★ **Yablonevy Sad** GUESTHOUSE $$

(Apple Orchard; Яблоневый сад; 8-953-656 7513; ul Osoviakhima 6a; r ₽2500) We'd call it a boutique *izba* (log house). The stylishly designed wooden cottage built around a tiled hearth has smallish ergonomic rooms with large beds and lots of tiny artful details that make them feel like a fairy-tale forest refuge. A sumptuous Russian breakfast (think porridge and *oladyi* – thick pancakes with apples) is included.

The house is located away from the centre, near St Ipaty Monastery. There is a small antiques exhibition in the adjacent heritage house.

Hotel Snegurochka HOTEL $$

(Snow Maiden; 4942 423 201; www.hotel-snegurochka.ru; ul Lagernaya 38/13; s/d incl breakfast ₽2300/3200;) Snow Maiden is in the name because Kostroma unilaterally declared itself the birthplace of Father Frost's companion. Expectedly, cool blue colours prevail in the modern, fully equipped rooms and you may find a Christmas tree or a pair of felt winter boots in your room, even at the height of summer.

Old Street HOTEL $$$

(4942-496 999; www.oldstreethotel.ru; ul Sovietskaya 10; incl breakfast, s/d from ₽2500/2900, s/d with terrace from ₽4500;) A heritage house in the main street has been transformed into a rather plush little hotel to the delight of Kostroma regulars who rave about it on booking sites. We counted seven pillows sitting on top of king-sized beds and found a few comfy armchairs (purple- or magenta-coloured) as well as a working station in the rooms. Suites come with roof terraces.

WORTH A TRIP

HORNYCULTURE

Many dumbfoundingly bold experiments were set in the Soviet era. One of them was an attempt to domesticate moose for dairy farming. Moose milk is much more nutritious than cows' milk and is said to be good for ulcer treatment.

Some 25km from Kostroma, the **Sumarokovskaya Moose Farm** (4942-359 433, 8-903-895 4078; www.moosefarm.newmail.ru) was created in 1963. It is essentially a science institute dedicated to one branchy-horned and clumsy-legged research object. But although local scientists insist that moose don't need domestication since they 'just love living with humans', moose farming never took off for a multitude of practical reasons. These days the focus has shifted to breeding moose for areas where this iconic taiga animal is becoming extinct. But the farm is still supplying milk to **Susaninsky Sanatorium** (4942-660 384; www.sansusanin.ru; p/o Borovikovo; r ₽1500-2650), where it is used for medical treatments.

The farm is best visited in the first weeks of May when you get a chance to see newly born calves, or in September when they are taken out of quarantine enclosures and you are allowed to pet them and feed them carrots. Milk is available at all times.

The moose farm makes for a pleasant half-day countryside trip if you have a car. From the centre of Kostroma, go along Kineshemskoye sh, past the bus station, to Poddubnoye. Turn left to Ikonnikovo and continue till Gridino where you'll find a signposted turn. A taxi from Kostroma with one-hour wait will cost around ₽800.

It's tougher by public transport. Take a Gushchino- or Sintsovo-bound bus (20 minutes, six daily) to the Spas stop in Gridino. From there, it is a 6km trek to the farm. In winter, the whole moose population is moved to temporary enclosures in nearby locations, so you need to inquire. Heavy snow often renders the access road impassable.

Eating & Drinking

To stock up on fresh garden produce and Caucasian *lavash* (flat bread), head to the **food market** inside the trading arcade.

Horns & Hoofs EUROPEAN $

(Рога и копыта; ul Sovetskaya 2; mains ₽200-350; 9am-midnight;) This frivolously decorated restaurant is inspired by the fictional adventures of 1920s literary character Ostap Bender, a charming crook who travels down the Volga in pursuit of a treasure. Wrought-iron furniture, black-and-white photos and waiters dressed as old-world chauffeurs set the atmosphere. The menu has a good selection of soups, salads and main dishes, as well as pastries and coffee drinks.

After a meal here, you might be inspired to read *The Twelve Chairs* by Ilya Ilf and Evgeny Petrov – Ostap's literary parents. Some Russians know it nearly by heart.

Dudki Bar GASTROPUB $$

(Дудки бар; 4942-300 003; pr Mira 18; meals ₽200-450;) It's a sheer delight to find such a hip and self-ironic bar at the end of the universe, which Kostroma sometimes seems to be. Smaller than its Yaroslavl sister, this place is ruled by local hipsters, with just a few tracksuit-clad thugs looking envious and ripe for personal gentrification. Food is European and East Asian, with a tad of Indian spice. Look for the unassuming cottage at the end of pr Mira.

Slaviansky RUSSIAN $$

(Славянский; 4942-315 460; ul Molochnaya Gora 1; meals ₽250-500) Here is a great place for locally produced beer and various vodka-based liquors, with flavours ranging from cranberry to horseradish. That's if you can get a table, for this popular restaurant is fully booked more often than not. Sumptuous meat dishes are broadly based on traditional Russian recipes, but – another downside – service can be atrociously slow.

Information

Post & Telephone Office (Почтамт и переговорный пункт; cnr ul Sovetskaya & ul Podlipaeva; 9am-9pm)

Telecom Centre (4942-621 162; cnr ul Sovetskaya & ul Podlipaeva; per hour ₽60; 8am-8pm) To access the internet, buy a card at window number five and stick it in the slot at the computer of your choice.

Getting There & Away

The bus station is 4.5km east of Susaninskaya pl on Kineshemskoye sh, the continuation of ul Sovetskaya. There are hourly services to Yaroslavl (₽240, two hours, hourly). Heading to Plyos, take one of the hourly Ivanovo buses and change at Privolzhsk. For Suzdal, change in Ivanovo (₽300, three hours, hourly).

There are also direct services to Moscow (₽1000, eight hours, 10 daily) and Nizhny Novgorod (₽1100, 9½ hours, two to three daily).

There are four daily suburban trains to and from Yaroslavl (₽220, 2½ hours, six daily) and at least three long-distance trains to/from Yaroslavsky vokzal in Moscow (₽1300 to ₽2300, 6½ hours). The train station is 3.5km east of Susaninskaya pl.

Getting Around

Buses 1, 2, 9, 14K, 19 and others run between the bus station and Susaninskaya pl, along the full length of ul Sovetskaya. Trolleybus 2 runs between the train station and Susaninskaya pl. For St Ipaty Monastery and nearby hotels take bus 14 from the centre and get off once you cross the bridge.

Yaroslavl Ярославль

4852 / POP 604,000 / MOSCOW

Embraced by two rivers, the mighty Volga and the smaller Kotorosl, Yaroslavl's centre is dotted with onion domes like no other place in Russia. It indeed boasts a record-breaking 15-dome church. This religious zeal dates back to the times of Kyivan Rus, when the town was founded by Prince Yaroslav of Kyiv to guard his realm's north-eastern flank.

The place was then known as Bear's Corner. According to the legend, Prince Yaroslav forced local Finno-Ugric people into Christendom by axing their totem bear, which now appears on the city's coat of arms.

However, most churches and houses gracing the quaint city centre are products of 17th- to 19th-century merchants competing to outdo each other in beautifying their city. Much of that beauty remains unscathed by Soviet development.

Sights

You'll find most sights either very close to or right on the city's main attraction: the riverside promenade that runs along the Volga and the Kotorosl.

★Monastery of the Transfiguration of the Saviour MONASTERY

(Спасо-Преображенский монастырь; 4852-303 869; www.yarmp.yar.ru; Bogoyavlenskaya pl 25; grounds ₽25, exhibits ₽30-60 each; exhibits 10am-5pm Tue-Sun year-round, grounds 8am-8pm daily Oct-May) Founded in the 12th century, the Monastery of the Transfiguration of the Saviour was one of Russia's richest and best-fortified monasteries by the 16th century. The oldest surviving structures, dating from 1516, are the **Holy Gate** near the **main entrance** (Главный вход) by the river and the **Cathedral of the Transfiguration** (Преображенский собор и звонница; admission ₽60; Thu-Mon).

Other buildings house exhibitions on history, ethnography, icons and the **Treasures of Yaroslavl Exhibition** (adults/students ₽150/60), featuring works of gold, silver and precious gems.

★Music & Time MUSEUM

(Музыка и время; 4852-328 637; Volzhskaya nab 33a; adult/student/child ₽180/100/70, joint ticket for all exhibits adult/student/child ₽300/100/100; 10am-7pm) Every object has a voice in this little house containing ex-conjuror John Mostoslavsky's impressive collection of clocks, musical instruments, bells and old vinyl records. Guides, including the owner himself, turn each tour into a bit of a concert. There are also exhibitions of porcelain and wrought-iron objects on the premises. English-language guides are available most days. It's great for children.

Church of Elijah the Prophet CHURCH

(Церковь Ильи Пророка; Sovetskaya pl; adult/student ₽80/40; 9.30am-7pm) The exquisite church that dominates Sovetskaya pl was built by prominent 17th-century fur dealers. It has some of the Golden Ring's brightest frescoes, done by the ubiquitous Gury Nikitin of Kostroma and his school, and detailed exterior tiles. The church is closed during wet spells.

John the Baptist Church at Tolchkovo CHURCH

(Церковь Иоанна Крестителя в Толчково; 2-ya Zakotoroslnaya nab 69; adult/student ₽60/30; 10am-4.30pm Wed-Sun) It's a shame that dingy industrial surroundings discourage most people from visiting Yaroslavl's most unique church. Protected by Unesco, the red-brick 17th-century structure boasts a staggering 15 green-coloured cupolas and some of the most extensive series of frescoes in the Orthodox world – a whole Biblical encyclopedia authored by local artists Dmitry Plekhanov and Fyodor Ignatyev. The

Yaroslavl

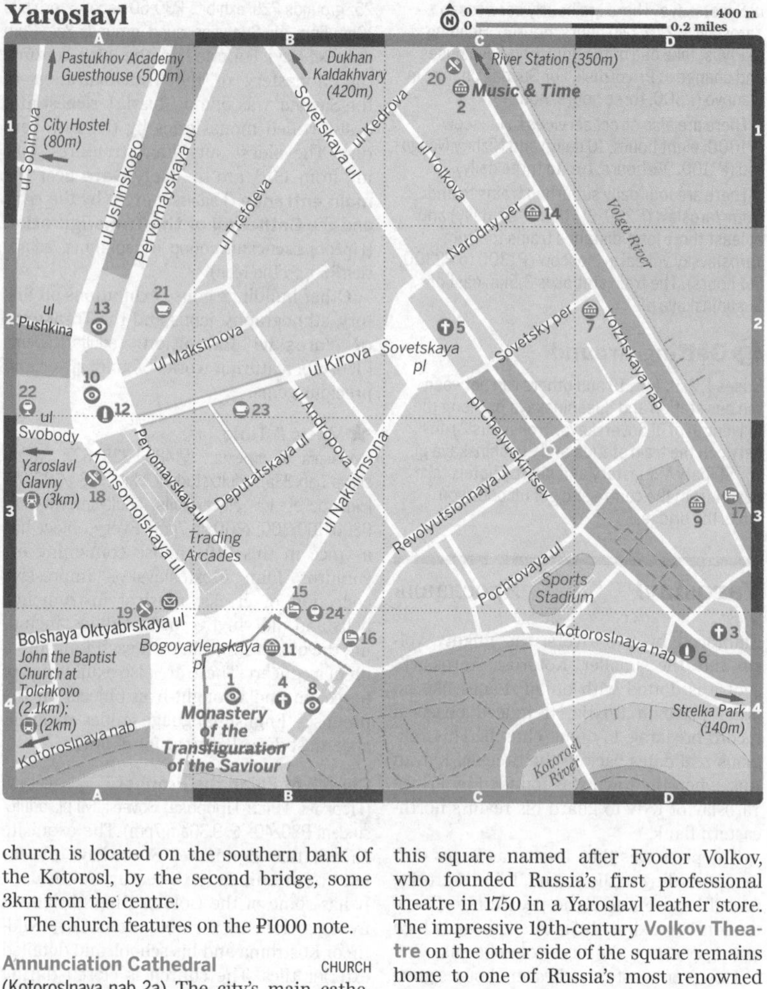

church is located on the southern bank of the Kotorosl, by the second bridge, some 3km from the centre.

The church features on the ₽1000 note.

Annunciation Cathedral CHURCH
(Kotoroslnaya nab 2a) The city's main cathedral originally dated from 1215, but was blown up by the Bolsheviks in 1937. What you see now is a modern replica erected for the city's millennium celebrations in 2010. In front of it, a stone-slab **monument** marks the spot where Yaroslav founded the city in 1010. The new **Strelka Park** stretches right onto the tip of land between the Volga and the Kotorosl Rivers where the **Yaroslavl Millennium Monument** was opened in 2010.

Ploshchad Volkova SQUARE
The massive 17th-century gate-shaped **Vlasyevskaya Watchtower** combined with the **Church of the Sign** loom over this square named after Fyodor Volkov, who founded Russia's first professional theatre in 1750 in a Yaroslavl leather store. The impressive 19th-century **Volkov Theatre** on the other side of the square remains home to one of Russia's most renowned troupes.

Old Art Exhibition ART GALLERY
(Volzhskaya nab 1; adult/student ₽80/40; ⏲10am-5pm Sat-Thu) The 17th-century chambers of the former metropolitan showcase icons and other religious art from the 13th to 19th centuries.

Yaroslavl Art Museum ART GALLERY
(Ярославский художественный музей; ☎4852-303 504; www.artmuseum.yar.ru; Volzhskaya nab 23; adult/student ₽160/60; ⏲10am-5pm Tue-Sun) The restored former governor's mansion now showcases 18th- to 20th-century Russian art with a large hall dedicated to impressionist Konstantin Korovin.

Yaroslavl

History of Yaroslavl Museum MUSEUM
(Музей Истории Ярославля; ☎4852-304 175; Volzhskaya nab 17; admission ₽55; ⊙10am-6pm Wed-Mon) This museum is in a lovely 19th-century merchant's house. A monument to victims of war and repression in the 20th century is in the peaceful garden.

Activities

River Station BOAT TRIPS
(Речной вокзал) Summer services from the city's riverine gateway include a range of slow boats to local destinations. The best trip is to **Tolga** (one hour, four daily), where you'll find a convent with lovely buildings from the 17th century.

Sleeping

City Hostel HOSTEL $
(☎4852-304 192, 8-910-973 5263; ul Sverdlova 18; dm from ₽450, s/q ₽1500/3000) Modern and arguably stylish (light-coloured wooden surfaces abound), this hostel boasts a quiet, but central location. Managers are nice, but hardly speak any English. Doubles are available, but two of them are right by the entrance, which means serious noise pollution. You can use the washing machine free of charge.

★ **Alyosha Popovich Dvor** HOTEL $$
(Алеша Попович Двор; ☎4852-643 101; www.ap-dvor.ru; ul Pervomayskaya 55; s/d from ₽2600/3400;) Themed on Russian fairy tales and slightly kitschy in the post-Soviet theme park way, Alyosha occupies what looks like an old Russian *terem* (a wooden palace), but in reality – a functional, ergonomic recreational anthill with small, but comfortable rooms (complete with bathtubs) and a few restaurants in the premises.

Attic-style rooms on the 3rd floor go cheaper than conventional ones on the 2nd. Buffet breakfast is so-so.

★ **Volzhskaya Zhemchuzhina** HOTEL $$
(Волжская жемчужина; ☎4852 731 273; www.riverhotel-vp.ru; Volzhskaya nab; s/d from ₽2500/3700;) The floating 'Volga Pearl' is a converted river station – dozens of such floating hubs lined the Volga when boat travel was still in vogue. Polished maple furniture and plenty of natural light ensure that the place doesn't feel too cramped. Double rooms have access to a shared balcony.

Pastukhov Academy Guesthouse HOTEL $$
(☎4852-370 379; www.gapm.ru; ul Respublikanskaya 42; s/d from ₽2500/2700, without bathroom ₽2000/2200;) This small hotel occupies a former dormitory in a grand neoclassical 19th-century building that's part of a management school. Rooms are modern, though sound protection is a problem. Cheaper ones come in a block of two with a tiny shared hallway through which you access your own private bathroom.

★ **Ioann Vasilyevich** HOTEL $$$
(Иоанн Васильевич; ☎4852 670 760; www.ivyar.ru; Revolyutsionnaya ul 34; r from ₽4200;) If you don't mind a Soviet spy, a tsar or an alien staring at you from the wall when you wake, here is your chance to immerse yourself in Russian cinema. Each large comfortable

room in this new hotel is themed on a popular film, with colour schemes, furniture and fixtures selected accordingly.

Eating

Bars and pubs will often be just as good for lunch or dinner as restaurants.

★MeatMe TURKISH $
(ul Komsomoskaya 4; mains ₽200-250; ⏲10am-11pm) Meataholics are welcome to gorge on excellent Turkish kebabs and doners in this smartly designed little shop located on one of the busiest streets in the city. The owners made sure their food not only tastes, but also looks good served on cute metal trays. A kebab boutique, meataphorically speaking.

★Podbelka RUSSIAN $
(Подбелка; ul Bolshaya Oktyabrskaya 28; mains ₽120-200; ⏲24hr) Podbelka is how Yaroslavl's first Soviet *pelmennaya* (dumpling cafeteria), which occupied these premises in the 1920s, was colloquially known to the townsfolk. In its post-Soviet, or rather posthistorical reincarnarion it is a hip eatery serving traditional *pelmeni* (Russian-style ravioli stuffed with meat) along with many of its foreign siblings, such as Georgian *khinkali* (dumplings).

In a separate room is a little bar with cheap (₽80 to ₽100) beer on tap. Kudos to the owners for not turning their place into even remotely authentic Soviet *pelmennaya* – they were quite dreadful, frankly. That said, the smallish 200g portions do remind you of the bread-queue era.

Sobranie RUSSIAN $$
(Собрание; ☎4852-303 132; Volzhskaya nab 33; mains ₽250-500; 📶) On the grounds of the museum complex Music & Time (p141), this traditional Russian restaurant is decorated with stained glass, artwork and antiques that look like they might be part of the collection. This quaint place caters to hungry tourists in search of traditional Russian cuisine. Much of the cooking is done in the old-fashioned stone oven.

Dukhan Kaldakhvary CAUCASIAN $$
(Духан Калдахвары; Sovetskaya ul 21; mains ₽200-400) This Caucasian eatery offers an unusual mixture of Armenian, Abkhazian and Mengrel (West Georgian) dishes. Regional nuances aside, a straightforward mutton shashlyk will easily make your day. Entrance is from a small lane at the back of the building.

Drinking

★Dudki Bar GASTROPUB
(☎4852-330 933; ul Sobinova 33) One of the most happening places in town, this Kostroma import is heaving during weekends, and most other days too. Brass instruments (the word 'pipe' is in the bar's name) and pictures of dogs portrayed as aristocratic ancestors adorn the walls. There is a large bar on the 2nd floor and a more intimate one downstairs.

European and Asian (including some Indian) food is superb by local standards, but getting a table without reservation can be problematic.

Pivovar BEER HALL
(Пивовар; ☎4852 640 431; www.yarpivovar.ru; Revolyutsionny proezd 4) In a spacious and noisy premises, waiters dressed as members of a Bavarian um-pah-pah band run up and down the stairs bringing 1L beer mugs and meaty Czech dishes to tipsy customers. Cheap home-brewed Pivovar beer is available as well as dozens of imported brands. Chinese, Slovenian or name-the-country beer festivals take place regularly.

Anti-Cafe Samoye Vremya ANTI-CAFE
(Самое время; 2nd fl, ul Trefoleva 22; 1st hour ₽120, subsequent hours ₽90; ⏲10am-midnight) A part of the nationwide trend, Samoye Vremya charges for time you spend on the premises and provides coffee and great homemade cookies for free. You can lounge on a couch surfing the internet, play Xbox on a large screen in a dedicated room or make friends with young Russians who come along to play table games and chat.

La Gavroche CAFE
(ul Kirova 5; 📶) This friendly cafe on the main pedestrian drag is good for breakfasts, a cup of macchiato and catching up on your Facebook news.

Information

Post & Telephone Office (Почтамт и переговорный пункт; Komsomolskaya ul 22; ⏲8am-8pm Mon-Sat, to 6pm Sun)

Getting There & Away

BUS

The **bus station** (Moskovsky pr) is 2km south of the Kotorosl River. There are hourly services to/from Moscow (₽700, six hours). Most of these stop at Rostov-Veliky (₽180), Pereslavl-Zalessky (₽360, three hours) and Sergiev Posad.

Buses depart almost hourly to Kostroma (₽190, two hours) and Uglich (₽300, 3½ hours). There are also three buses daily for Suzdal (₽510, 4½ hours).

Some buses bound for Moscow and Uglich either depart from or stop at the main train station on the way.

TRAIN

The main **train station** (ul Svobody) is Yaroslavl Glavny, 3km west of the centre. Numerous trains bound for northern Russia and Siberia call at Yaroslavl, but they are slower and more expensive than the direct high-speed service (₽900, 3½ hours, three daily), which call at Rostov-Veliky.

There are four daily suburban trains to/from Kostroma (₽220, 2½ hours, six daily). Transit northbound trains continue to Vologda (₽400 to ₽800, four hours, 10 daily) and Arkhangelsk (₽2800, 16 hours, four daily). Eastbound trains go to Perm (₽4200, 20 hours) and beyond the Urals.

Getting Around

From Yaroslavl Glavny train station, trolleybus 1 runs along ul Svobody to pl Volkova and onto Krasnaya pl. From the bus station trolleybus 5 or 9 goes to Bogoyavlenskaya pl.

Rostov-Veliky
Ростов-Великий

48536 / POP 33,200 / MOSCOW

Coloured in the same delicate shade of pink as the sunsets they have been watching for hundreds of years, the impregnable walls and perfectly proportioned towers of Rostov's kremlin rise magnificently above the shimmering Lake Nero. Frowning upon Moscow for its relatively young age, Rostov (first chronicled in 862) was the original capital of Kyivan princes who moved into Finno-Ugric lands, which would become known as Muscovy and Russia.

Today, it is a sleepy village-like town that wakes you up with the sound of cockerels and gets eerily quiet when darkness falls. However, it feels considerably more neglected than other Golden Ring towns and good restaurants are hard to come by.

Considering the proximity of Yaroslavl, it's probably not worth spending a night here.

Sights

Kremlin FORTRESS

(www.rostmuseum.ru; grounds ₽50, joint ticket to exhibitions adult/student ₽450/550, individual exhibitions ₽40-80; 10am-5pm) Rostov's main attraction is unashamedly photogenic. Though founded in the 12th century, nearly all the buildings here date to the 1670s and 1680s.

With its five magnificent domes, the **Assumption Cathedral** (Успенский собор) dominates the kremlin, although it is just outside the latter's north wall. Outside service hours, you can get inside the cathedral through the door in the church shop on ul Karla Marksa.

The cathedral was here a century before the kremlin, while the belfry was added in the 1680s. Each of 15 bells in the **belfry** (Звонница; admission ₽100) has its own name; the largest, weighing 32 tonnes, is called Sysoy.

The west gate (the main entrance) and the north gate are straddled by the **Gate-Church of St John the Divine** (Надвратная церковь Иоанна Богослова) and the **Gate-Church of the Resurrection** (Надвратная церковь Воскресения), both of which are richly decorated with 17th-century frescoes. Enter these churches from the **monastery walls** (admission ₽45), which you can access from the stairs next to the north gate.

The metropolitan's private chapel, the **Church of the Saviour-over-the-Galleries** (Церковь Спаса-на-Сенях), contained within the **metropolitan's house** (Покои митрополита), has the most beautiful interior of all, covered in colourful frescoes. Other rooms in the house are filled with exhibits: the **White Chamber** (Белая палата) displays religious antiquities, while the **Red Chamber** (Красная палата) shows off *finift* (luminous enamelled miniatures), a Rostov artistic speciality.

Monastery of Saviour & St Jacob MONASTERY

(ul Engelsa 44; 10am-5pm) The restored monastery is the fairy-tale apparition you'll see as you approach Rostov by road or rail. Take bus 1 or 2 or walk alongside Lake Nero 2km west from the kremlin. English-language excursions may be available for ₽300 from the excursion bureau next to the gates. For a donation of ₽20 you can climb the wall on its lake-view side.

Activities

Boat Trips BOAT TRIPS

(adult/student ₽150/100; May-Sep) For a different perspective of Rostov, take a

WORTH A TRIP

NORTHERN VOLGA CIRCUIT

If you are in for a melancholic trip of markedly less touristy and slightly desolate northern Russian towns and villages, here is a circuit route, starting in Yaroslavl. It is totally doable by local buses, but much better in a rented car – roads are almost empty and the scenery is captivating.

From Yaroslavl, a regional road goes northeast along the Volga River to **Tutayev** (also known by its old name, Romanov-Borisoglebsk), 39km away. It is slightly drab on the west bank of the Volga, but the view of its eastern bank, reached by ferry, is jaw-droppingly idyllic, with quaint churches and wooden houses scattered around green hills.

From Tutayev, it is 51km to **Rybinsk**. This busy city has a well-preserved historic centre and a beautiful Volga embankment graced by the towering edifice of the New Bread Exchange, built in the Russian revivalist style in 1912. It now houses an interesting regional museum. There are several hotels in Rybinsk, the best value for money being **Vikonda** (Виконда; ☎4855-238 808; http://rybinsk.vikonda.ru; ul Babushkina 29; r ₽2400), even though it is located in a shopping mall away from the centre. **Soupberry** (ul Stoyalaya 16; mains ₽200-500; ⏰10am-11pm) is a great, centrally located gastropub.

After Rybinsk, the route turns sharply southwest towards **Myshkin**, 47km away. The best part of the trip is a ferry, which you (and your vehicle) will take at the very end. Largely comprised of wooden cottages, Myshkin has for years been exploiting its name, which contains the Russian word for 'mouse'. You can indeed find the **Museum of Mice** here, although the eclectic collection of the **History Museum**, across the road, is considerably more interesting.

Myshkin is 54km northeast of **Uglich** (oo-gleech) – the scene of Russia's best-known unsolved crime that changed the country's history. It was here, in 1591, that the son of Ivan the Terrible, Dmitry (later to be impersonated by the string of False Dmitrys in the Time of Troubles), died in rather suspicious circumstances – officially he threw himself on a sword in a bout of epilepsy. It is, however, widely believed that he was killed on the orders of his foster father Boris Godunov.

Within the waterside **kremlin**, the 15th-century Prince's Chambers house a historical exhibit that tells the sordid tale of Dmitry. The star-spangled **Church of St Dmitry on the Blood** (Tserkov Dmitria-na-krovi) was built in the 1690s on the spot where the body was found. The 300kg bell was banished for many years to the Siberian town of Tobolsk (this after Godunov ordered it to be publicly flogged and have its tongue ripped out); it has since returned to its rightful location in Uglich. You can splash out on an overnight stay at the opulent (New Russian way) **Volzhskaya Riviera** (Волжская Ривьера; ☎48532 91 900; www.volga-hotel.ru; Uspenskaya pl 8; incl breakfast, r ₽3150-3890, river view s/d from ₽3680/4410; ⊖❄@☜≋).

Going east from Uglich, after 70km you'll reach **Borisoglebsky**, home of the astounding fortress of Rostov-Borisoglebsky monastery, built in 1363. Rostov-Veliky, on the Moscow-Yaroslavl highway, is another 22km from here.

40-minute cruise of Lake Nero. Boats leave from a pier near the west gate of the kremlin and pass both monasteries as well as an island in the middle of the lake.

Dom Remyosel CRAFTS
(☎48536-67 223; www.domremesel.com; Tolstovskaya nab 16; ⏰10am-7pm) Apart from being a great shop, the 'House of Crafts' invites visitors to try their hand in making dolls, clay whistles, bark shoes, Easter eggs and other traditional souvenirs. Classes cost ₽55 to ₽350.

Sleeping

Russkoye Podvorye HOTEL $
(Русское подворье; ☎48536-64 255; ul Marshala Alexeyeva 9; s without bath weekdays/weekends/holidays ₽800/1000/1200, d weekdays/weekends/holidays ₽1700/2200/2500; ⊖❄) This newish hotel occupies the arcaded house of 18th-century merchant Ivan Khlebnikov. Inside, however, it is all quite modern, with spirit-lifting floral ornaments in the rooms and comfy beds. Breakfasts are served in perhaps the best restaurant in

town. You can splash out an extra ₽2000 on a suite with a spa bath.

Dom na Pogrebakh HISTORIC HOTEL $
(Дом на погребах; ☎48536-61 244; www.domnapogrebah.ru; r without/with bath from ₽1000/2500) Right inside the kremlin near the east gate, this place has clean, wood-panelled rooms with heavy doors and colourful tapestries. The location within the building varies, but if you can snag a room with a view of the west gate it is charming indeed. Service is Soviet-style.

Eating

All the hotels have cafes on-site, but overall Rostov's restaurant scene is stuck in the early 1990s and decent restaurants are few and far between.

Cafe Alaverdy GEORGIAN $
(Кафе Алаверди; per Sovetsky 1; mains ₽200-400) This is a simple Georgian eatery that makes *khachapuri* (Georgian bread) cheese pies and *khinkali* (dumplings) as they do it back home. If you are not bothered about the looks of the place – totally faceless, but clean – you can have a jolly good meal here.

Russkoye Podvorye RUSSIAN $$
(Русское подворье; ul Marshala Alexeyeva 9; mains ₽200-400) What claims to be a 'medieval Russian' menu is essentially a fresh and intelligent take on Russian cuisine as it was before mayo and potatoes. Mushrooms, turnips and more unusual ingredients feature in inventive dishes. There is also a good selection of porridges, which used to be the main staple in the old times.

Getting There & Away

The train and and the bus station are in the same place, 2km north of the Kremlin.

BUS

The most convenient option to/from Yaroslavl is by bus, either transit or direct (₽200, 1½ hours, every 90 minutes). Transit buses also pass through on the way to Moscow (₽600, four to five hours, every 90 minutes); most of them go via Pereslavl-Zalessky and Sergiev Posad. One lone bus goes to Uglich (₽200, three hours).

TRAIN

The best option from Moscow is the fast Moscow-Yaroslavl train (₽840, three hours, three daily). There are also five slow *elektrichki* (suburban trains) daily plying the route between Yaroslavl and Alexandrov, where you can change for Moscow trains.

Pereslavl-Zalessky
Переславль - Залесский

☎48535 / POP 42,700 / ⏲MOSCOW

Another ancient lakeside town, Pereslavl is a popular dacha getaway for Muscovites. Its attractions are scattered around a large and not always interesting area, which makes it hard to explore without a car or a bicycle. But you'll easily find a few quiet and pretty spots once you escape from the main drag.

The town's main claim to fame is as the birthplace of Alexander Nevsky. Its earthen walls and the little Cathedral of the Transfiguration are as old as the town itself. Pereslavl is also famous as the unlikely cradle of Russian naval might thanks to a holidaying teenager who went on to become Peter the Great.

Sights

Town Centre

Kremlin HISTORIC SITE
The walls of Yury Dolgoruky's kremlin are now a grassy ring around the centre of town. The 1152 **Cathedral of the Transfiguration of the Saviour** (Преображенский собор; Krasnaya pl; adult/child ₽50/30; ⏲Wed-Sun 10am-5pm), one of the oldest buildings in Russia, is inside this green ring. A bust of Alexander Nevsky stands out in front, while three additional churches across the grassy square make for a picturesque corner. These include the tent-roofed **Church of Peter the Metropolitan** (Церковь митрополита Петра; ul Sadovaya 5), built in 1585 and renovated in 1957, and the 18th-century twin churches fronting the road.

Trubezh River PROMENADE
The Trubezh River, winding 2km from the kremlin to the lake, is fringed by trees and narrow lanes. You can follow the northern riverbank most of the way to the lake by a combination of paths and streets. The **Forty Martyrs' Church** (Сорокосвятская церковь; Levaya nab 165) sits picturesquely on the south side of the river mouth.

Botik Area

The main sights are located on the southern bank of Lake Pleshcheyevo. From the main road, turn to ul Podgornaya under Goritsky Monastery.

Goritsky Monastery
MONASTERY

(Горицкий монастырь; grounds ₽20, exhibits adult/student ₽120/80 each; ⊙10am-6pm May-Oct, 9am-5pm Nov-Apr) This large monastery standing at the turn to Botik Museum (2.5km south of the centre) was founded in the 14th century, though the oldest buildings today are the 17th-century gates, gate-church and belfry. The centrepiece is the **Assumption Cathedral** (Uspensky sobor; admission ₽80), with its beautiful carved iconostasis. The other buildings hold art and history exhibits.

Botik Museum
MUSEUM

(Ботик Петра; grounds ₽20, exhibitions adult/student ₽150/100; ⊙10am-5pm Tue-Sun) Lake Pleshcheyevo is the place where Peter the Great developed his obsession with the sea. As a young man, he studied navigation and built a 'toy flotilla' of more than 100 little ships by age 20. You can explore some of this history at the Botik Museum, situated in Veskovo 4km along the road past the Goritsky Monastery.

Its highlight is the sailboat Fortuna, one of only two of Peter the Great's boats to survive fire and neglect. It occupies a whole building in the premises. There is also an interesting history exhibition in another building known as White Palace.

Kukushka.ru
MUSEUM

(☑48535-49 479; www.kukushka.ru; adult/child ₽150/50, handcart adult/child ₽150/50; ⊙Wed-Sun 10am-6pm) A further 12km along the road passing Botik Museum is the turn-off to this unique railway museum. The collection of locomotives occupies the tracks and depot that were used up until the middle of the 20th century. Don't miss the opportunity to ride on the **handcart**. Visitors are ferried from the parking lot 1km away from the museum in vintage WWII-era cars.

Sleeping

Albitsky Sad Motel
HOTEL $$

(Альбицкий сад; ☑48535-31 430; www.albitski-isad.ru; ul Kardovskogo 21; d weekdays/weekends from ₽2000/2500; ⊙❋) On the main road just south of the centre, 'Albitsky Garden' resembles an old manor house, its yellow exterior adorned with white trim. The motel offers 16 tastefully decorated rooms, as well as an inviting restaurant. The location on the main road is a bit annoying, but a flower-filled garden at the back serves as a consolation.

Art Hotel
APARTMENTS $$$

(Арт-Отель; ☑48535-98 130; www.arthotel.ucoz.ru; Bol Protechnaya 45; 1-/2-bedroom apt ₽5000/₽7000) Sure, it's pricey. But for your money, you get a fully equipped, artistically designed apartment set amid flowering gardens, with an art gallery and a *banya* on site. The two apartments (sleeping two to six people each) are lovingly decorated in a funky, contemporary style featuring original artwork by the owners. Bol Protechnaya runs parallel to the main road, on the eastern side.

Eating

Prosto Cafe&Bar
INTERNATIONAL $$

(Просто кафе; ☑48535 31 633; www.prosto-bar.com; ul Rostovskaya 27; mains ₽250-450; ⊙9am-2am) Resembling an outsize dolls house (we like the bar covered in a patchwork of varicoloured little doors), this place strives to satisfy all tastes: the menu contains Mexican and Asian dishes as well as grilled meat and Italian pasta. At night, it becomes more of a drinking and dancing venue, with DJs taking the floor.

ℹ Getting There & Around

Pereslavl-Zalessky is not on the train line, but buses travel frequently to Moscow (₽400, 2½ hours, eight daily). Many, but not all, of these stop at Sergiev Posad (₽200, one hour, at least three daily). Others travel to Yaroslavl (₽200, three hours, hourly) via Rostov-Veliky (₽100, 1½ hours).

Bus 1 runs up and down the main street from just south of the bus station (Автовокзал); heading out from the centre you can catch it just north of the river. Taxis wait at Narodnaya pl.

Sergiev Posad
Сергиев Посад

☑496 / POP 112,700 / ⊙ MOSCOW

Blue and golden cupolas offset by snow-white walls – this colour scheme lies at the heart of the Russian perception of divinity, and Sergiev Posad's monastery is a textbook example. It doesn't get any holier than here in Russia, for the place was founded in 1340 by the country's most revered saint, St Sergius of Radonezh. Since the 14th century, pilgrims have been journeying to this place to pay homage to him.

Although the Bolsheviks closed the monastery, it was reopened following WWII as a museum, residence of the patriarch and a working monastery. The patriarch and the church's administrative centre moved to the Danilovsky Monastery in Moscow in 1988, but the Trinity Monastery of St Sergius remains one of the most important spiritual sites in Russia.

Sergiev Posad is an easy day trip from Moscow and that's how most people visit it. If you plan to move further to Pereslavl-Zalessky, consider doing it on the same day: clogged with pilgrims and traffic, the town is not a great place to overnight.

Pr Krasnoy Armii is the main street, running north to south through the town centre. The train and bus stations are on opposite corners of a wide square to the east of pr Krasnoy Armii. The monastery is about 400m north of there.

Sights

Trinity Monastery of St Sergius MONASTERY
(Troitse-Sergieva Lavra; ☎496-544 5356; www.stsl.ru; ⏰5am-9pm) FREE In 1340, St Sergius of Radonezh founded this monastery, which soon became the spiritual centre of Russian Orthodoxy. St Sergei was credited with providing mystic support to Prince Dmitry Donskoy in his improbable victory over the Tatars in the battle of Kulikovo Pole in 1380. Soon after his death at the age of 78, Sergius was named Russia's patron saint.

Spruced up on the occasion of St Sergius' 700-year anniversary in 2014, the monastery is an active religious centre with a visible population of monks in residence. This mystical place is a window into the age-old belief system that has provided Russia with centuries of spiritual sustenance.

Built in the 1420s, the squat, dark **Trinity Cathedral** (Троицкий собор) is the heart of the Trinity Monastery. The tomb of St Sergius stands in the southeastern corner, where a memorial service for him goes on all day, every day. The icon-festooned interior, lit by oil lamps, is largely the work of the great medieval painter Andrei Rublyov and his students.

The star-spangled **Cathedral of the Assumption** (Успенский собор) was modelled on the cathedral of the same name in the Moscow Kremlin. It was finished in 1585 with money left by Ivan the Terrible in a fit of remorse for killing his son. Outside the west door is the **grave of Boris Godunov**, the only tsar not buried in the Moscow Kremlin or St Petersburg's SS Peter & Paul Cathedral in the fortress of the same name. Another notable grave is that of St Innokenty, known as the apostle of America. He founded the Russian Orthodox community in Alaska.

Nearby, the resplendent **Chapel-at-the-Well** (Накладезная часовня) was built over a spring that is said to have appeared during the Polish siege. The five-tier baroque bell tower took 30 years to build in the 18th century, and once had 42 bells, the largest of which weighed 65 tonnes.

The **Vestry** (⏰10am-5.30pm Wed-Sun), behind the Trinity Cathedral, displays the monastery's extraordinarily rich treasury, bulging with 600 years of donations by the rich and powerful – tapestries, jewel-encrusted vestments, solid-gold chalices and more. It was closed for reconstruction at the time of research. The timeframe for reopening wasn't clear.

The huge block with the 'wallpaper' paint job is the **Refectory Church of St Sergei** (Трапезная церковь преподобного Сергия), so called because it was once a dining hall for pilgrims. Now it's the Assumption Cathedral's winter counterpart, holding morning services in cold weather. It is closed outside services, except for guided tours. The green building next door is the metropolitan's residence.

Toy Museum MUSEUM
(Музей игрушек; www.museumot.ru; pr Krasnoy Armii 123; adult/student ₽150/70; ⏰11am-5pm Wed-Sun) Houses toys from throughout history and around the world. The museum has a particularly good collection of nesting dolls, as Sergiev Posad was the centre of *matryoshka* (nesting doll) production before the revolution.

Sleeping & Eating

Old Lavra Hotel HOTEL $$
(Старая гостиница Лавры; ☎496-549 9000; pr Krasnoy Armii 133; s/d weekdays ₽2500/2800, weekends ₽2700/3000) Revived in its original capacity, this massive monastery hotel has no trappings that might distract its supposedly puritan guests from prayer and contemplation – not even TV! But despite their blandness, rooms are modern and very clean. A vast restaurant is on the premises. Expectedly, alcohol is strictly banned in the whole complex.

Gostevaya Izba RUSSIAN $$
(Гостевая Изба; Aptekarsky per; mains ₽300-500; ⏰11am-11pm) Right by the monastery walls, this restaurant makes a rather scientific effort to re-create the kind of food

metropolitans of the past would gorge on outside fasting periods, although – to the delight of vegetarians – the menu has a considerable fasting section, too. Products come from monastery farms – some located nearby, some as far as the White Sea.

Art Cafe San Marino ITALIAN $$
(pr Krasnoy Armii 138/2; mains ₽250-400; ⏲11am-midnight) Looking utterly unorthodox in such close proximity to the holy site, this little cellar cafe is filled with art and books. Salads and pastas with a few vegetarian options dominate the menu. Live jazz concerts happen regularly. A singing canary bird will keep you awake at other times.

Information

Post & Telephone Office (Почтамт и переговорный пункт; pr Krasnoy Armii 127a) Outside the southeastern wall of the monastery.

Getting There & Away

Considering horrendous traffic jams on the approaches to Moscow, train is a much better way of getting to Sergiev Posad from the capital.

BUS

Bus 388 to Sergiev Posad from Moscow's VDNKh metro station departs hourly from 7am to 10pm (₽145). Transit buses for Kostroma (₽700), Yaroslavl (₽500) or Rybinsk pass almost hourly; all these will take you to Pereslavl-Zalessky (₽150) and Rostov-Veliky (₽320) if you can get a ticket.

TRAIN

The fastest transport option is the express commuter train that departs from Moscow's Yaroslavsky vokzal (₽160, one hour, six daily). A couple of long-distance trains call at Sergiev Posad daily on the way to Yaroslavl (₽1200, three hours). There are no direct trains to Rostov.

St Petersburg

Includes ➡

Best Places to Eat

- Teplo (p197)
- Yat (p195)
- Duo Gastrobar (p195)
- Dom Beat (p196)
- Koryushka (p199)

Best Places to Stay

- Soul Kitchen Hostel (p192)
- Baby Lemonade Hostel (p189)
- Andrey & Sasha's Homestay (p193)
- Rossi Hotel (p191)
- Rachmaninov Antique Hotel (p189)

Why Go?

Beautiful, complex and imperious, with a hedonistic, creative temperament, St Petersburg (Санкт-Петербург) is the ultimate Russian diva. From her early days as an uninhabited swamp, the 300-year-old city has been nurtured by a succession of rulers, enduring practically everything that history and nature's harsh elements could throw at her. Constantly in need of repair but with a carefree party attitude, Piter (as she's affectionately known by locals) still seduces all who gaze upon her grand facades, glittering spires and gilded domes. Such an environment has inspired many of Russia's greatest artists, including Pushkin, Gogol, Dostoevsky, Rachmaninov, Tchaikovsky and Shostakovich.

The long summer days of the White Nights season are particularly special – the fountains flow, parks and gardens burst into colour and locals hit the streets to party. With a little preparation, though, the icy depths of winter have their own magic, and are the perfect time for warming body and soul in all those museums and palaces.

When to Go

St Petersburg

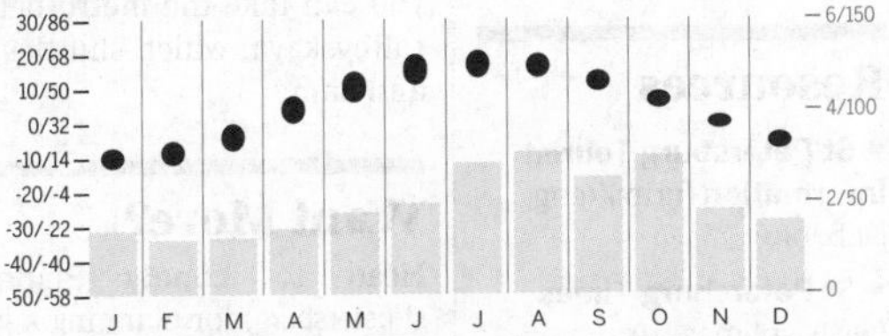

Mid-May–mid-Jul Visit during the White Nights, when the sun never truly sets.

May & Sep A great time to visit St Petersburg, avoiding the crowds of the peak months.

Nov–Jan Freezing, dark and blanketed in snow, winter in St Petersburg is magical.

NEED TO KNOW

While the majority of St Petersburg's museums close on a Monday, always check your Lonely Planet guide before you head off somewhere. Many museums also open at lunchtime Wednesday until late.

Fast Facts

- **Telephone area code** ☎812
- **Population** 4.8 million
- **Number of metro stations** 67
- **Name changes** 3
- **Number of bridges** 342
- **St Petersburg Time** Moscow (GMT/USC +3 hours)

Don't Drink the Water

Tiny traces of *Giardia lamblia,* a nasty parasite that causes stomach cramps, nausea, bloated stomach, diarrhoea and frequent gas, have been found in St Petersburg's water. There's no preventative drug so it's best to only drink bottled water during your stay.

Resources

- **St Petersburg Tourist Information** (http://eng.ispb.info)
- **St Petersburg Times** (www.sptimes.ru)
- **In Your Pocket** (www.inyourpocket.com/russia/st-petersburg)
- **Way to Russia** (www.waytorussia.net)

Arriving in St Petersburg

Most people arrive at St Petersburg's Pulkovo Airport (p207), a brand new terminal from where an official taxi costs between ₽800 and ₽1000 to the city centre. Those on a budget can take a bus (₽25) to the nearby Moskovskaya metro station and then connect from there to elsewhere in the city (₽28). Arrivals from Helsinki by train will come into Finland Station, next to Ploshchad Lenina metro, while those coming by train from Moscow will arrive at Moscow Station next to Ploshchad Vosstaniya metro. Boats arrive at one of five ports scattered around the city.

GUIDED TOURS

Those arriving on a cruise ship or by ferry at any of St Petersburg's various ports are able to profit from 72-hour visa-free entry into Russia. The only conditions are that you also leave the city by boat and that you book a guided tour from a licensed operator. These include:

DenRus (www.denrus.ru)

Peter's Walking Tours (p187)

Red October (www.redoctober.ru)

These operators are used to working with cruise-ship and ferry passengers, and tend to offer a far higher standard of tour than the mass-market ones the cruise ships promote. It's important to know that you are still able to use the visa-free entry if you do not book the tour sold by the cruise ship, as long as you privately arrange a tour with one of these companies.

Bridges Up!

From April to November, all bridges across the Neva River rise at around 1.30am nightly to let ships pass through the city and on to the rest of the world, or into Russia's deep interior. Don't find yourself on the wrong side of the river when the bridges go up, or you'll have to wait until they go back down again at around 5am. Alternatively you can take the metro between Sportivnaya and Admiralteyskaya, which shuttles back and forth between 1am and 3am.

Want More?

Head to **Lonely Planet** (www.lonelyplanet.com/russia/st-petersburg) for planning advice, author recommendations, traveller reviews and insider tips.

History

Peter's Window on the West

The area around the mouth of the Neva River may have been a swamp but it's been long fought over. Alexander of Novgorod defeated the Swedes here in 1240 – earning the title Nevsky (of the Neva), and becoming one of Russia's most revered national heroes. Sweden retook control of the region in the 17th century, but it was Peter the Great's desire to crush this rival and make Russia a European power that led to the founding of St Petersburg. At the start of the Great Northern War (1700–21), he captured the Swedish outposts on the Neva, and in 1703 he began the construction of his city with the Peter & Paul Fortress.

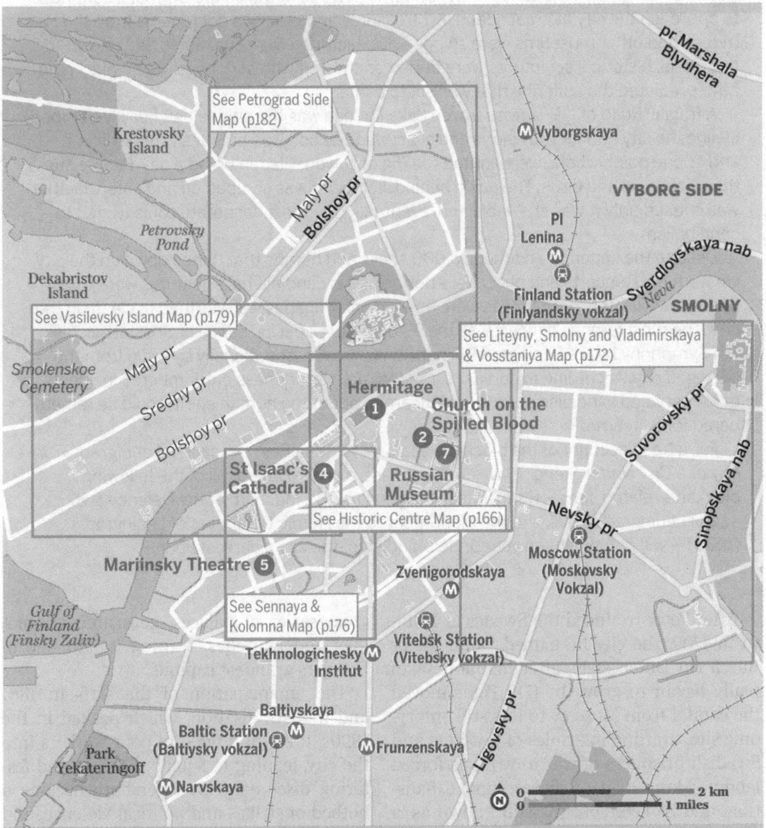

St Petersburg Highlights

1. Spend a day (or more!) in the **Hermitage** (p160), one of the world's most unrivalled art collections.
2. Witness the amazing kaleidoscope of colours that is the **Church on the Spilled Blood** (p164).
3. Revel with locals during the ethereal endless daylight of the **White Nights** (p188).
4. Climb the enormous dome of **St Isaac's Cathedral** (p176) for the best view over the imperial city.
5. Have the ultimate Russian experience by taking in a ballet at the **Mariinsky Theatre** (p202) or the brand new **Mariinsky II** (p203).
6. Head out of town to **Tsarskoe Selo** (p215), Catherine the Great's incredible summer palace, and see the magnificent Amber Room.
7. Take in the excellent collection of art, from icons to the avant-garde, at the **Russian Museum** (p164).

THE LENINGRAD BLOCKADE

The defining event of the 20th century for St Petersburg was the Nazi blockade of the city during WWII. Around a million people died from shelling, starvation and disease in what's often called the '900 Days' (actually 872). By comparison, the USA and UK suffered about 700,000 dead between them in total for the whole of WWII.

The Nazi plan, as indicated in a secret directive, was to 'wipe the city of Petersburg from the face of the earth'. After the Germans launched their surprise attack on the Soviet Union on 22 June 1941, many residents fled Leningrad as the Germans continued to approach the city at great speed. Art treasures and precious documents from the Hermitage and other museums were shipped out; factories were evacuated and relocated to Siberia; historical sculptures were buried or covered with sandbags. Yet no one could have predicted the suffering that was yet to come.

A fragile 'Road of Life' across frozen Lake Ladoga was the only (albeit heavily bombed) lifeline the city had for provisions and evacuations. Food was practically nonexistent, and at one point rations were limited to 175g of sawdust-laden bread a day. People ate their pets, rats and birds. The paste behind wallpaper was scraped off and eaten, leather was cooked until it was chewable and, eventually, the most desperate souls turned to cannibalism.

Despite the suffering and the 150,000 shells and bombs that rained down on the city, life went on. Concerts and plays were performed in candlelit halls, lectures were given, poetry was written, orphanages were opened and brigades were formed to clean up the city. The most famous concert was the 9 August 1942 performance of Shostakovich's 7th Symphony by the Leningrad Philharmonic, broadcast nationally by radio from the besieged city. According to survivors, random acts of kindness outnumbered incidents of robbery and vandalism, and lessons learned about the human spirit would be remembered for a lifetime.

For a fresh account of the blockade years, read Anna Reid's excellent *Leningrad, Tragedy of a City Under Siege, 1941–44*. Otherwise, a visit to one or all of the following blockade-related sites – Rumyantsev Mansion (p178), Museum of the Defence & Blockade of Leningrad (p171), and the Monument to the Heroic Defenders of Leningrad (p185) – will greatly enrich your understanding of the city's darkest hour.

After Peter trounced the Swedes at Poltava in 1709, the city he named Sankt Pieter Burch (in Dutch style, after his namesake) really began to grow. In 1712 Peter moved the capital from Moscow to this still embryonic site, drafting in armies of peasants and Swedish prisoners of war to work as forced labour. Many died of disease and exhaustion, and St Petersburg is still known as 'a city built upon bones' to many Russians. Architects and artisans came to St Petersburg from all over Europe though, and by Peter's death in 1725 the city had a population of 40,000 and some 90% of Russia's foreign trade passed through it.

Peter's immediate successors moved the capital back to Moscow but Empress Anna Ioannovna (r 1730–40) returned it to St Petersburg. Between 1741 and 1825, during the reigns of Empress Elizabeth, Catherine the Great and Alexander I, it became a cosmopolitan city with an imperial court of famed splendour. These monarchs commissioned great series of palaces, government buildings and churches, turning it into one of Europe's grandest capitals.

The emancipation of the serfs in 1861 and industrialisation, which peaked in the 1890s, brought a flood of poor workers into the city, leading to squalor, disease and festering discontent. St Petersburg became a hotbed of strikes and political violence, and was the hub of the 1905 revolution, sparked by 'Bloody Sunday' on 9 January 1905, when a strikers' march to petition the tsar in the Winter Palace was fired on by troops. In 1914, in a wave of patriotism at the start of WWI, the city's name was changed to the Russian-style Petrograd.

Revolution

In 1917 the workers' protests turned into a general strike and troops mutinied, forcing the end of the monarchy in March and the establishment of a provisional government. Seven months later, Lenin's Bolshevik Party staged an audacious coup and the Soviet government came into being. Fearing a German attack on Petrograd, the new government moved the capital back to Moscow in March 1918.

Renamed Leningrad after Lenin's death in 1924, the city became a hub of Stalin's 1930s industrialisation program. By 1939 its population had grown to 3.1 million and it accounted for 11% of Soviet industrial output. Stalin feared the city as a rival power base, however, and the 1934 assassination of the local communist chief Sergei Kirov at the Smolny Institute was the start of his 1930s Communist Party purge.

When Germany attacked the USSR in June 1941, its armies took only two and a half months to reach Leningrad. As the birthplace of Bolshevism, Hitler swore to wipe the city from the face of the earth. His troops besieged the city from 8 September 1941 until 27 January 1944 – Leningrad survived and, after the war, was proclaimed a 'hero city'. It took until 1960 for the city's population to exceed pre-WWII levels.

During the 1960s and '70s, Leningrad developed a reputation as a dissident's city with an artistic underground spearheaded by the poet Joseph Brodsky and, later, rock groups such as Akvarium. In 1989 Anatoly Sobchak, a reform-minded candidate, was elected mayor. Two years later, as the USSR crumbled, the city's citizens voted to bring back the name of St Petersburg (though the region around the city remains known as Leningradskaya Oblast).

St Petersburg Again

In the anarchic post-Soviet years of the early 1990s, it often seemed like the local 'Mafia' were more in charge than the city's elected officials, who proved to be equally corrupt. Romanov ghosts returned to the city on 17 July 1998, when the remains of Tsar Nicholas II and some of his family were buried in the crypt at the SS Peter & Paul Cathedral within the fortress of the same name.

Five years later enormous sums were budgeted to spruce up the city for its tercentenary celebrations. Local boy made good Vladimir Putin didn't waste the opportunity to return to his birthplace and show it off to visiting heads of state and other dignitaries. The city still enjoys a prominent status in modern Russia today and is a favourite spot for summits and other governmental meetings.

Sights

While St Petersburg is a huge and sprawling city spread over many different islands, its main sights are fairly well centred in the Historic Centre, the area broadly surrounding the main avenue, Nevsky pr. Other rich

ST PETERSBURG IN...

Two Days

On day one wander down **Nevsky pr** (p164), dropping in to the Church on the **Spilled Blood** (p164) and the **Kazan Cathedral** (p165), **Palace Square** (p160) and **St Isaac's Cathedral** (p176). Then visit the **Yusupov Palace** (p175) and the **Nikolsky Cathedral** (p177). In the evening spend some time checking out St Petersburg's drinking scene on Dumskaya ul or ul Zhukovskogo. Devote day two to the wondrous **Hermitage** (p160) and its extraordinary collection, including the modern painting in the **General Staff Building** (p164) on the other side of Palace Sq. When you leave, relax by taking a sightseeing cruise around the canals. Spend the evening seeing a ballet or opera at the traditional **Mariinsky Theatre** (p202) or the brand new **Mariinsky II** (p203).

Four Days

On day three start at the **Peter & Paul Fortress** (p181) to see where the city began, and wander past the **Mosque** (p181) and take in the Style Modern architecture of Kamennoostrovsky pr. Wander across the bridge to Vasilevsky Island and see the **Strelka** (p180), the fascinating **Kunstkamera** (p178) and then either the **Menshikov Palace** (p180), for history fans, or the **Erarta Museum of Contemporary Art** (p179), for art fans. Spend day four outside the city to get a taste of tsarist splendour. Start at Tsarskoe Selo for a visit to the extraordinary **Catherine Palace** (p215), and then continue to nearby Pavlovsk for a walk in the gorgeous gardens. When you get back to the city in the afternoon, choose between the superb **Russian Museum** (p164) or the **Alexander Nevsky Monastery** (p174).

The Hermitage

A HALF-DAY TOUR

Successfully navigating the State Hermitage Museum, with its four vast interconnecting buildings and around 360 rooms, is an art form in itself. Our half-day tour of the highlights can be done in four hours, or easily extended to a full day.

Once past ticket control start by ascending the grand **Jordan Staircase** (1) to Neva Enfilade and Great Enfilade for the impressive staterooms, including the former throne room St George's Hall and the 1812 War Gallery (Room 197), and the Romanovs' private apartments. Admire the newly restored **Great Church** (2) then make your way back to the Neva side of the building via the Western Gallery (Room 262) to find the splendid **Pavilion Hall** (3) with its view onto the Hanging Garden and the gilded Peacock Clock, always a crowd pleaser.

Make your way along the series of smaller galleries in the Large Hermitage hung with Italian Renaissance art, including masterpieces by **Da Vinci** (4) and **Caravaggio** (5). The Loggia of Raphael (Room 227) is also impressive. Linger a while in the galleries containing Spanish art before taking in the Dutch collection, the highlight of which is the hoard of **Rembrandt** (6) canvases in Room 254.

Descend the Council Staircase (Room 206), noting the giant malachite vase, to the ground floor where the fantastic Egyptian collection awaits in Room 100 as well as the galleries of Greek and Roman Antiquities. If you have extra time, it's well worth booking tours to see the two special exhibitions in the **Gold Rooms** (7) of the Treasure Gallery.

TOP TIPS

» **Queues** Reserve tickets online to skip the long lines.

» **Dining** Bring a sandwich and a bottle of water with you: the cafe is dire.

» **Footwear** Wear comfortable shoes.

» **Cloakroom** Bear in mind the only one is before ticket control, so you can't go back and pick up a sweater.

KEVEN OSBORNE / FOX FOTOS / GETTY IMAGES ©

Jordan Staircase
Originally designed by Rastrelli, in the 18th century this incredible white marble construction was known as the Ambassadorial Staircase because it was the way into the palace for official receptions.

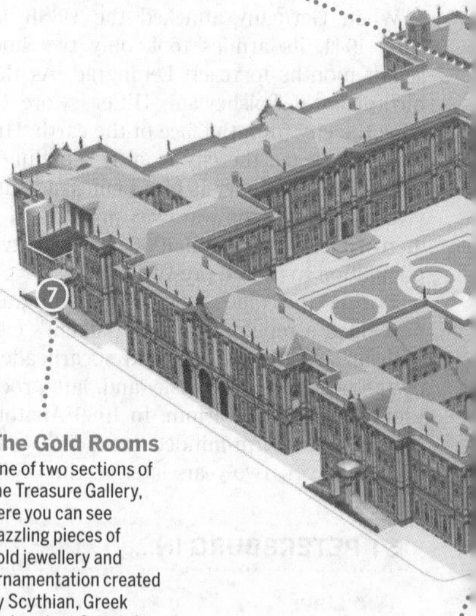

The Gold Rooms
One of two sections of the Treasure Gallery, here you can see dazzling pieces of gold jewellery and ornamentation created by Scythian, Greek and ancient Oriental craftsmen.

IMAGE SOURCE / GETTY IMAGES ©

Great Church
This stunningly ornate church was the Romanovs' private place of worship and the venue for the marriage of the last tsar, Nicholas II, to Alexandra Feodorovna in 1895.

MONDADORI PORTFOLIO / GETTY IMAGES ©

Rembrandt
A moving portrait of contrition and forgiveness, *Return of the Prodigal Son* (Room 254) depicts the biblical scene of a wayward son returning to his father.

SUPERSTOCK / GETTY IMAGES ©

Da Vinci
Along with the *Benois Madonna*, also here, *Madonna and Child (Madonna Litta;* Room 214) is one of just a handful of paintings known to be the work of Leonardo da Vinci.

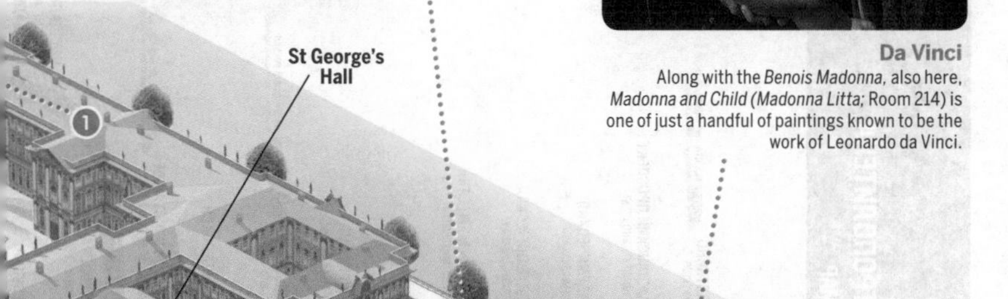

Pavilion Hall
Apart from the Peacock Clock, the Pavilion Hall also contains beautifully detailed mosaic tables made by Italian and Russian craftsmen in the mid-19th century.

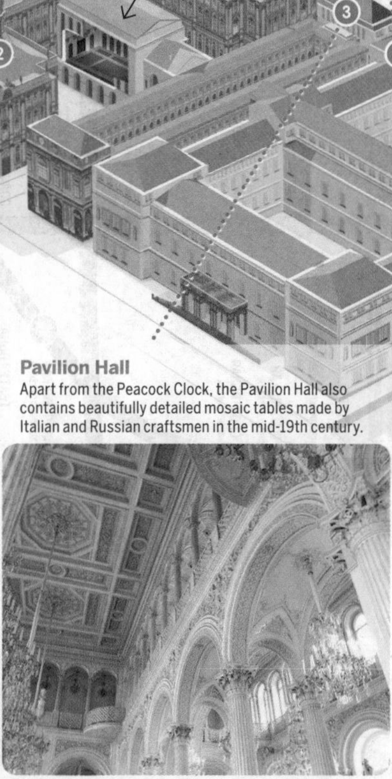

LOUI JONES / GETTY IMAGES ©

Caravaggio
The Lute Player (Room 237) is the Hermitage's only Caravaggio, and a work that the master of light and shade described as the best piece he'd ever painted.

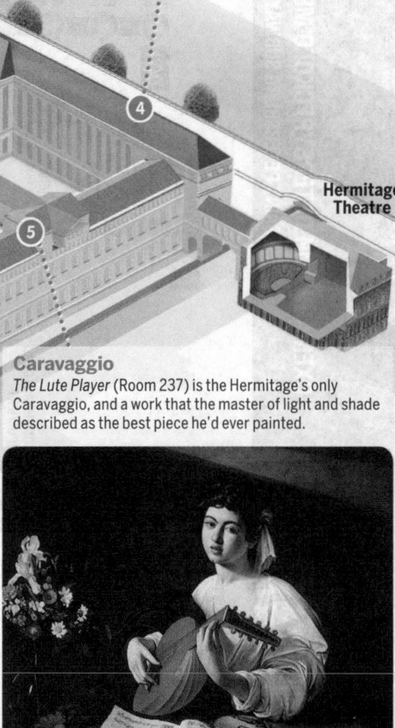

ANATOLY SAPRONENKOV / GETTY IMAGES ©

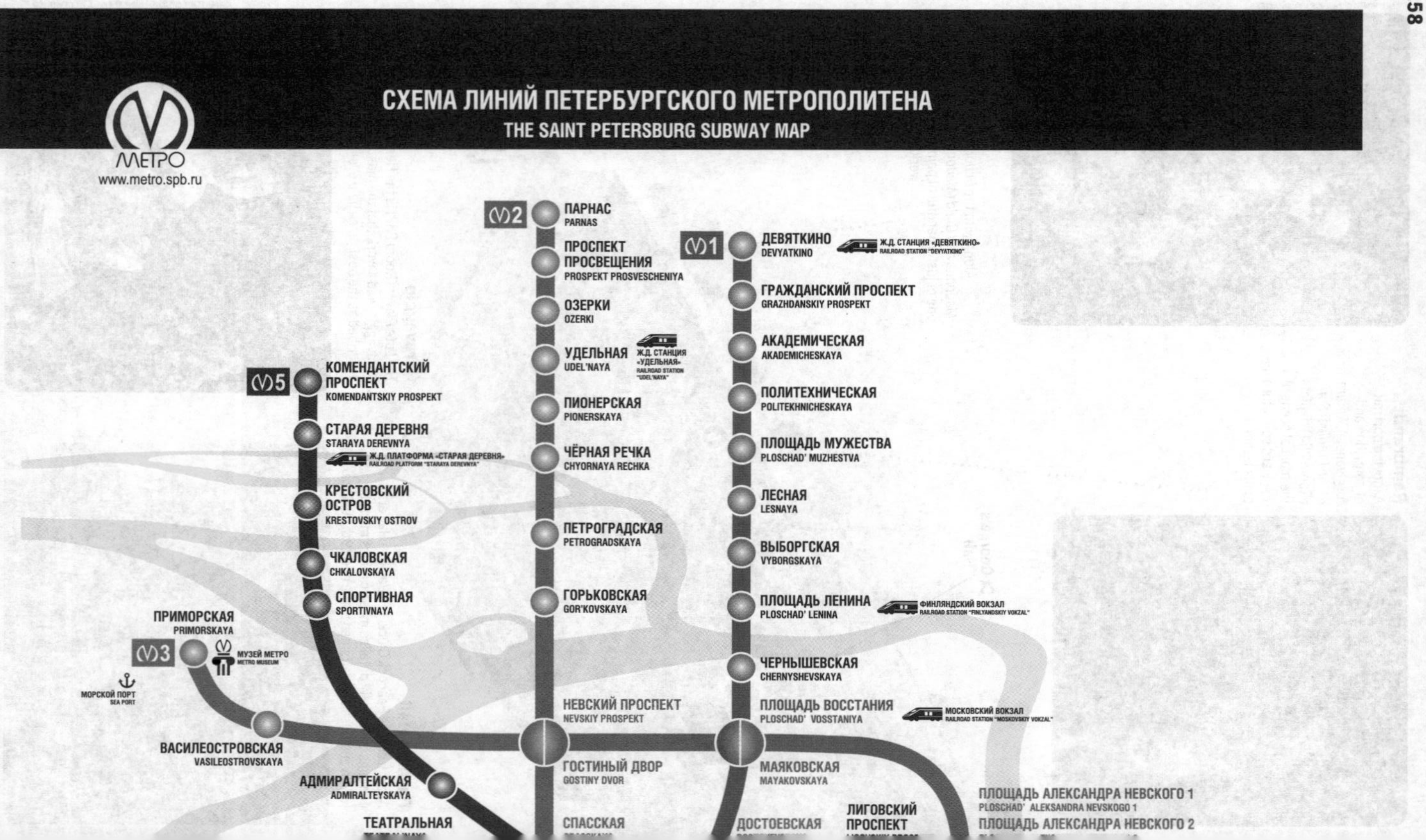
СХЕМА ЛИНИЙ ПЕТЕРБУРГСКОГО МЕТРОПОЛИТЕНА
THE SAINT PETERSBURG SUBWAY MAP
МЕТРО
www.metro.spb.ru
2
ПАРНАС
PARNAS
ПРОСПЕКТ ПРОСВЕЩЕНИЯ
PROSPEKT PROSVESCHENIYA
ОЗЕРКИ
OZERKI
УДЕЛЬНАЯ
UDEL'NAYA
Ж.Д. СТАНЦИЯ «УДЕЛЬНАЯ»
RAILROAD STATION "UDEL'NAYA"
ПИОНЕРСКАЯ
PIONERSKAYA
ЧЁРНАЯ РЕЧКА
CHYORNAYA RECHKA
ПЕТРОГРАДСКАЯ
PETROGRADSKAYA
ГОРЬКОВСКАЯ
GOR'KOVSKAYA
НЕВСКИЙ ПРОСПЕКТ
NEVSKIY PROSPEKT
ГОСТИНЫЙ ДВОР
GOSTINY DVOR
СПАССКАЯ
1
ДЕВЯТКИНО
DEVYATKINO
Ж.Д. СТАНЦИЯ «ДЕВЯТКИНО»
RAILROAD STATION "DEVYATKINO"
ГРАЖДАНСКИЙ ПРОСПЕКТ
GRAZHDANSKIY PROSPEKT
АКАДЕМИЧЕСКАЯ
AKADEMICHESKAYA
ПОЛИТЕХНИЧЕСКАЯ
POLITEKHNICHESKAYA
ПЛОЩАДЬ МУЖЕСТВА
PLOSCHAD' MUZHESTVA
ЛЕСНАЯ
LESNAYA
ВЫБОРГСКАЯ
VYBORGSKAYA
ПЛОЩАДЬ ЛЕНИНА
PLOSCHAD' LENINA
ФИНЛЯНДСКИЙ ВОКЗАЛ
RAILROAD STATION "FINLYANDSKIY VOKZAL"
ЧЕРНЫШЕВСКАЯ
CHERNYSHEVSKAYA
ПЛОЩАДЬ ВОССТАНИЯ
PLOSCHAD' VOSSTANIYA
МОСКОВСКИЙ ВОКЗАЛ
RAILROAD STATION "MOSKOVSKIY VOKZAL"
МАЯКОВСКАЯ
MAYAKOVSKAYA
ДОСТОЕВСКАЯ
ЛИГОВСКИЙ ПРОСПЕКТ
ПЛОЩАДЬ АЛЕКСАНДРА НЕВСКОГО 1
PLOSCHAD' ALEKSANDRA NEVSKOGO 1
ПЛОЩАДЬ АЛЕКСАНДРА НЕВСКОГО 2
5
КОМЕНДАНТСКИЙ ПРОСПЕКТ
KOMENDANTSKIY PROSPEKT
СТАРАЯ ДЕРЕВНЯ
STARAYA DEREVNYA
Ж.Д. ПЛАТФОРМА «СТАРАЯ ДЕРЕВНЯ»
RAILROAD PLATFORM "STARAYA DEREVNYA"
КРЕСТОВСКИЙ ОСТРОВ
KRESTOVSKIY OSTROV
ЧКАЛОВСКАЯ
CHKALOVSKAYA
СПОРТИВНАЯ
SPORTIVNAYA
АДМИРАЛТЕЙСКАЯ
ADMIRALTEYSKAYA
ТЕАТРАЛЬНАЯ
3
ПРИМОРСКАЯ
PRIMORSKAYA
МУЗЕЙ МЕТРО
METRO MUSEUM
МОРСКОЙ ПОРТ
SEA PORT
ВАСИЛЕОСТРОВСКАЯ
VASILEOSTROVSKAYA

4
САДОВАЯ
SADOVAYA
СЕННАЯ ПЛОЩАДЬ
SENNAYA PLOSCHAD'
ВЛАДИМИРСКАЯ
VLADIMIRSKAYA
ПУШКИНСКАЯ
PUSHKINSKAYA
ВИТЕБСКИЙ ВОКЗАЛ
RAILROAD STATION "VITEBSKIY VOKZAL"
ЗВЕНИГОРОДСКАЯ
ZVENIGORODSKAYA
ТЕХНОЛОГИЧЕСКИЙ ИНСТИТУТ 1
TEKHNOLOGICHESKIY INSTITUT 1
ТЕХНОЛОГИЧЕСКИЙ ИНСТИТУТ 2
TEKHNOLOGICHESKIY INSTITUT 2
НОВОЧЕРКАССКАЯ
NOVOCHERKASSKAYA
ЛАДОЖСКАЯ
LADOZHSKAYA
ЛАДОЖСКИЙ ВОКЗАЛ
RAILROAD STATION "LADOZHSKIY VOKZAL"
ПРОСПЕКТ БОЛЬШЕВИКОВ
PROSPEKT BOL'SHEVIKOV
УЛИЦА ДЫБЕНКО
ULITSA DYBENKO
4
ОБВОДНЫЙ КАНАЛ
OBVODNY KANAL
АВТОВОКЗАЛ
BUS STATION
БАЛТИЙСКИЙ ВОКЗАЛ
RAILROAD STATION "BALTIYSKIY VOKZAL"
БАЛТИЙСКАЯ
BALTIYSKAYA
НАРВСКАЯ
NARVSKAYA
КИРОВСКИЙ ЗАВОД
KIROVSKIY ZAVOD
АВТОВО
AVTOVO
ЛЕНИНСКИЙ ПРОСПЕКТ
LENINSKIY PROSPEKT
1
ПРОСПЕКТ ВЕТЕРАНОВ
PROSPEKT VETERANOV
ФРУНЗЕНСКАЯ
FRUNZENSKAYA
МОСКОВСКИЕ ВОРОТА
MOSKOVSKIYE VOROTA
ЭЛЕКТРОСИЛА
ELEKTROSILA
ПАРК ПОБЕДЫ
PARK POBEDY
МОСКОВСКАЯ
MOSKOVSKAYA
АВТОБУС В АЭРОПОРТ
BUS TO AIRPORT
ЗВЁЗДНАЯ
ZVYOZDNAYA
2
КУПЧИНО
KUPCHINO
Ж.Д. СТАНЦИЯ «КУПЧИНО»
RAILROAD STATION "KUPCHINO"
ВОЛКОВСКАЯ
VOLKOVSKAYA
БУХАРЕСТСКАЯ
BUKHARESTSKAYA
МЕЖДУНАРОДНАЯ
MEZHDUNARODNAYA
ПРОСПЕКТ СЛАВЫ
PROSPEKT SLAVY
ДУНАЙСКАЯ
DUNAYSKAYA
5
ШУШАРЫ
SHUSHARY
ЕЛИЗАРОВСКАЯ
YELIZAROVSKAYA
ЛОМОНОСОВСКАЯ
LOMONOSOVSKAYA
ПРОЛЕТАРСКАЯ
PROLETARSKAYA
РЕЧНОЙ ПОРТ
RIVER PORT
ОБУХОВО
OBUKHOVO
Ж.Д. СТАНЦИЯ «ОБУХОВО»
RAILROAD STATION "OBUKHOVO"
3
РЫБАЦКОЕ
RYBATSKOYE
Ж.Д. СТАНЦИЯ «РЫБАЦКОЕ»
RAILROAD STATION "RYBATSKOYE"
УСЛОВНЫЕ ОБОЗНАЧЕНИЯ
MAP SYMBOLS
1 2 3 4 5
ЛИНИИ МЕТРОПОЛИТЕНА
SUBWAY LINES
СТАНЦИИ ПЕРЕСАДОК
CHANGE FOR ANOTHER LINE
СТАНЦИЯ СТРОИТСЯ ИЛИ ПРОЕКТИРУЕТСЯ
THE STATION IS UNDER CONSTRUCTION
ЖЕЛЕЗНОДОРОЖНЫЕ ВОКЗАЛЫ, СТАНЦИИ, ПЛАТФОРМЫ
RAILROAD STATIONS
АВТОВОКЗАЛ
BUS STATION
АВТОБУС В АЭРОПОРТ
BUS TO AIRPORT
МУЗЕЙ МЕТРО
METRO MUSEUM
ПОРТЫ
SEA AND RIVER PORTS

pockets of sights include those on Vasilyevsky Island and the Petrograd Side, just across the Neva River from the Historic Centre; and those further down Nevsky pr in the areas around Smolny and pl Vosstaniya.

Historic Centre

★State Hermitage Museum MUSEUM

(Государственный Эрмитаж; Map p166; www.hermitagemuseum.org; Dvortsovaya pl 2; adult/student ₽400/free, 1st Thu of month free, camera ₽200; ⏲10.30am-6pm Tue & Thu-Sun, to 9pm Wed; Ⓜ Admiralteyskaya) Mainly set in the magnificent Winter Palace and adjoining buildings, the Hermitage fully lives up to its sterling reputation. You can be absorbed by its treasures for days and come out wanting more.

The enormous collection (over three million items, only a fraction of which are on display in around 360 rooms) almost amounts to a comprehensive history of Western European art. Viewing it demands a little planning, so choose the areas you'd like to concentrate on before you arrive.

Catherine the Great, one of the greatest art collectors of all time, began the collection. Nicholas I also enriched it and opened the galleries to the public in 1852.

It was the post-revolutionary period that saw the collection increase threefold, as many valuable private collections were seized by the state, including those of the Stroganovs, Sheremetyevs and Yusupovs. In 1948 it incorporated the renowned collections of post-Impressionist and Impressionist paintings of Moscow industrialists Sergei Shchukin and Ivan Morozov.

The State Hermitage consists of five linked buildings along riverside Dvortsovaya nab. From west to east they are:

➡ Winter Palace

This stunning mint-green, white and gold profusion of columns, windows and recesses, with its roof topped by rows of classical statues, was commissioned from Bartolomeo Rastrelli in 1754 by Empress Elizabeth. Catherine the Great and her successors had most of the interior remodelled in a classical style by 1837. It remained an imperial home until 1917, though the last two tsars spent more time in other palaces.

➡ Small Hermitage

The classical Small Hermitage was built for Catherine the Great as a retreat that would also house the art collection started by Peter the Great, which she expanded.

➡ Old Hermitage

At the river end of the Little Hermitage is the Old Hermitage, which also dates from the time of Catherine the Great.

➡ New Hermitage

Facing Millionnaya ul on the south end of the Old Hermitage, the New Hermitage was built for Nicholas II, to hold the still-growing art collection. The Old and New Hermitages are sometimes grouped together and labelled the Large Hermitage.

➡ State Hermitage Theatre

Built in the 1780s by the classicist Giacomo Quarenghi, who thought it one of his finest works. Concerts and ballets are still performed here. In the same building but accessed from the Neva Embankment are the remains of the Winter Palace of Peter I.

➡ Other branches

As much as you see in the museum, there's about 20 times more in its vaults, part of which you can visit at the Hermitage Storage Facility. Other branches of the museum include the east wing of the General Staff Building (home to the Hermitage's amazing collection of Impressionist and post-Impressionist works), the Menshikov Palace on Vasilyevsky Island, and the Imperial Porcelain factory in the south of the city.

Palace Square SQUARE

(Дворцовая площадь; Map p166; Ⓜ Admiralteyskaya) This vast expanse is simply one of the most striking squares in the world, still redolent of imperial grandeur almost a century after the end of the Romanov dynasty. For the most amazing first impression, walk from Nevsky pr, up Bolshaya Morskaya ul and under the triumphal arch.

In the centre of the square, the 47.5m **Alexander Column** was designed in 1834 by Montferrand. Named after Alexander I, it commemorates the 1812 victory over Napoleon.

On windy days, contemplate that the pillar is held on its pedestal by gravity alone!

The square's northern end is capped by the **Winter Palace** (Zimny Dvorets), a rococo profusion of columns, windows and recesses, topped by rows of larger-than-life statues. A residence of tsars from 1762 to 1917, it's now the largest part of the Hermitage.

Curving an incredible 580m around the south side of the square is the Carlo Rossi-designed General Staff Building completed in 1829. The east wing (p164) now houses a branch of the Hermitage while the west wing is the headquarters of the Western Military District. The two great blocks are joined by a triumphal arch over Bolshaya Morskaya ul, topped by the *Chariot of Glory* by sculptors Stepan Pimenov and Vasily Demuth-Malinovsky, another monument to the Napoleonic Wars.

VISITING THE HERMITAGE

The main entrance to the Hermitage is through the courtyard of the Winter Palace from Dvortsovaya pl (Palace Sq). The ticket counters are just inside, flanking a useful information booth where you can pick up free colour maps of the museum in most major European languages. Groups enter from the embankment side of the Winter Palace.

Queues for tickets, particularly from May to September, can be horrendous. The museum can also be very busy on the first Thursday of the month, when admission is free for everyone. Apart from getting in line an hour or so before the museum opens or going late in the day when the queues are likely to be shorter, there are a few strategies you can use. The best is to book your ticket online through the **Hermitage** website (www.hermitagemuseum.org): US$17.95 gets you entry to the main Hermitage buildings, plus use of camera or camcorder; US$25.95 buys you the two-day ticket to all of the Hermitage's collections in the city (except the storage facility). You'll be issued with a voucher that allows you to jump the queue and go straight to the ticket booth.

Joining a tour is another way to avoid queuing. These whiz round the main sections in about 1½ hours but at least they provide an introduction to the place in English. It's easy to 'lose' the group and stay on until closing time. To book a tour, call the museum's **excursions office** (☎812-571 8446; ⏲11am-1pm & 2-4pm); the staff will tell you when they are running tours in English, German or French and when to turn up.

Also contact the excursions office if you plan to visit the **Gold and Diamond Rooms** (rooms 41 to 45), special collections in the Treasure Gallery. English tours of both rooms cost an extra ₽300 each and places are limited, so book early if you're interested. The focus is a hoard of fabulously worked Scythian and Greek gold and silver from the Caucasus, Crimea and Ukraine, dating from the 7th to 2nd centuries BC.

There is a special entrance for people with disability from Dvortsovaya pl (the museum also has a few wheelchairs) – call in advance if you need this. The rest of the museum is wheelchair accessible, including lifts for getting between the floors.

Highlights of the Hermitage

It would take days to fully do justice to the Hermitage's huge collection. If your time is limited, head straight to the following rooms:

Room 100 Ancient Egypt.

Jordan Staircase Directly ahead when you pass through the main entrance inside the Winter Palace.

Rooms 143–146 Hidden treasures revealed: French late-19th-century and early-20th-century paintings taken from private collections in Germany in 1945.

Rooms 175–98 Imperial staterooms and apartments including the Malachite Hall, Nicholas Hall, Armorial Hall and Hall of St George.

Room 204 The Pavilion Hall.

Rooms 207–238 Italian art, 13th to 18th centuries.

Rooms 239–40 Spanish art, 16th to 18th centuries.

Rooms 245–47 Flemish art, 17th century.

Rooms 249–254 Dutch art, 17th century.

Room 271 Grand Church, the imperial family's cathedral.

Room 298–301 English art.

Greater St Petersburg

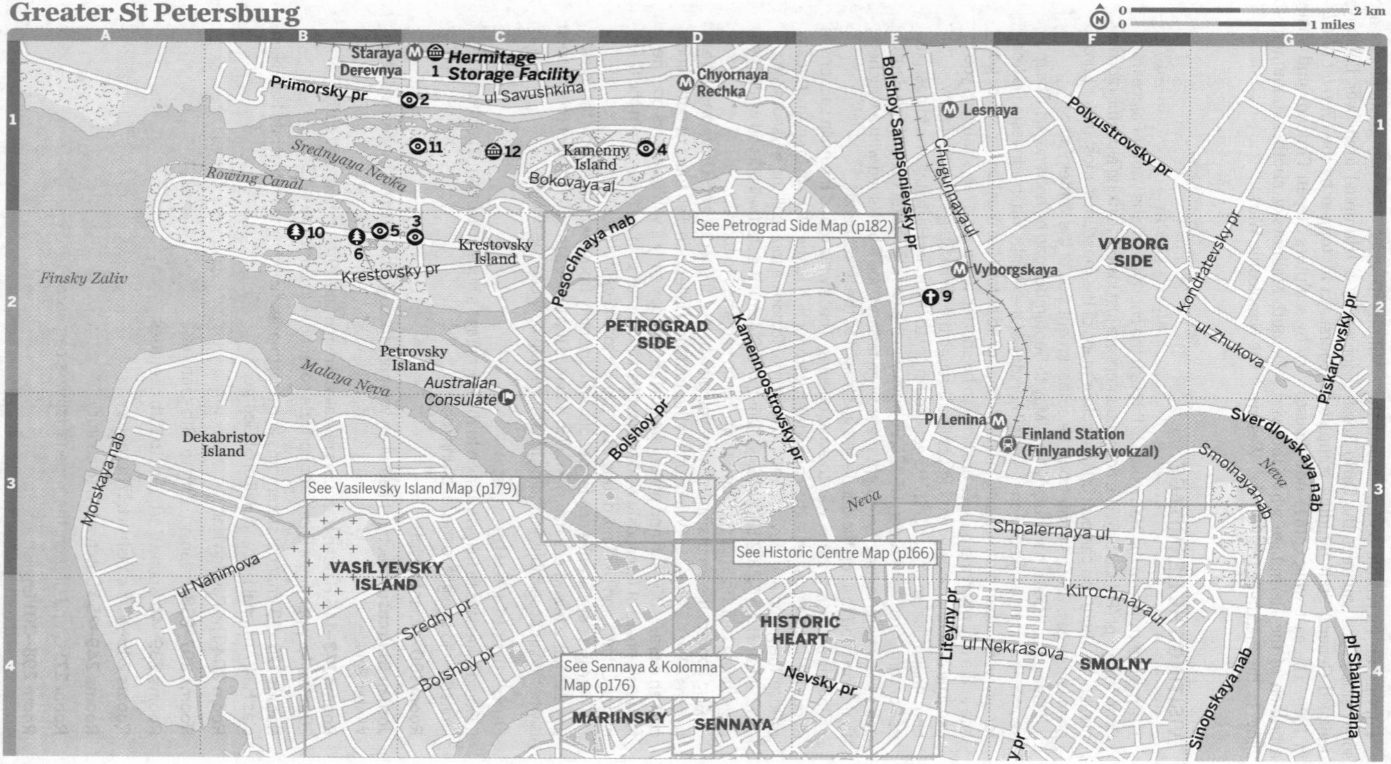

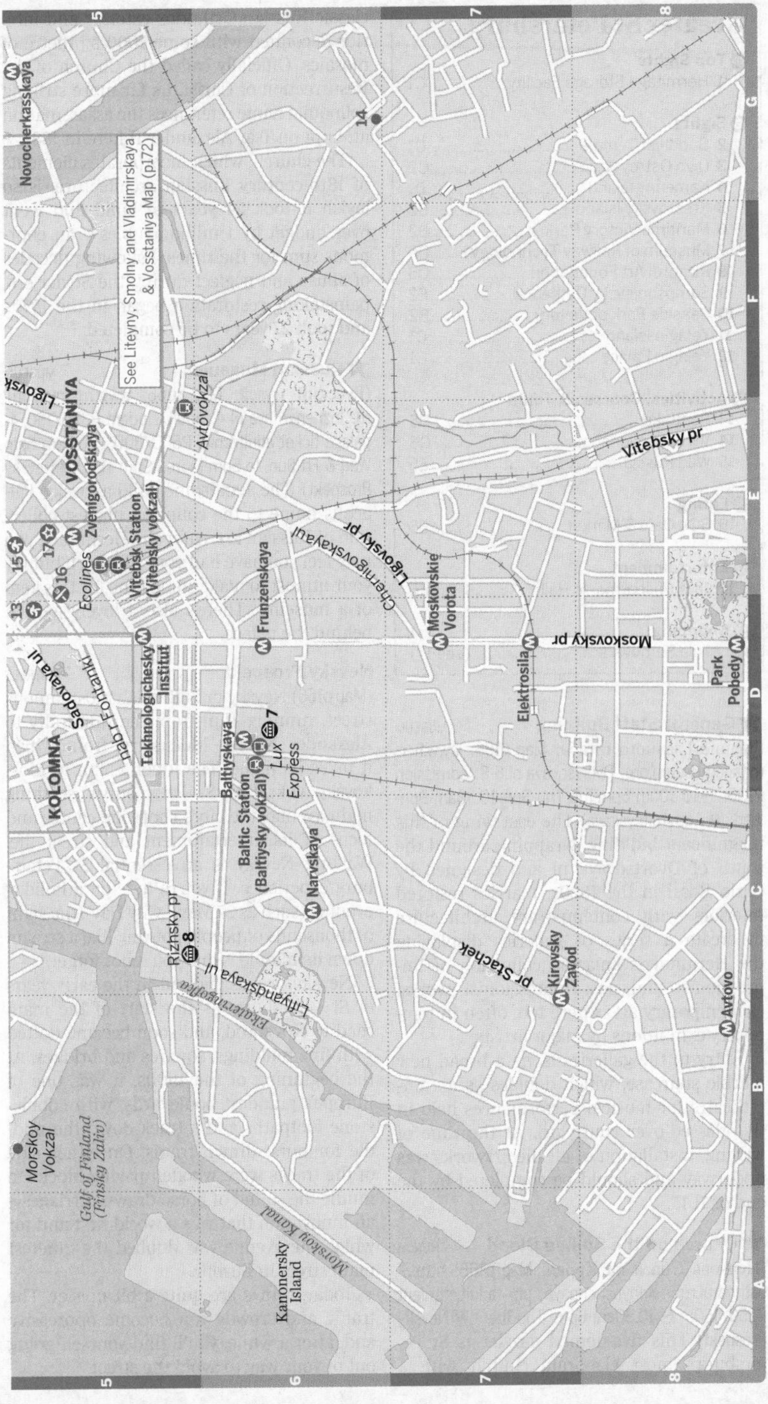
Novocherkasskaya
See Liteyny, Smolny and Vladimirskaya & Vosstaniya Map (p172)
14
Ligovsk
VOSSTANIYA
Vosstaniya
Zvenigorodskaya
Avtovokzal
Vitebsk Station (Vitebsky vokzal)
Ecolines
13
15
16
17
Zvenigorodskaya
Vitebsky pr
Ligovsky pr
Cherrnigovskaya ul
Frunzenskaya
Moskovskie Vorota
Moskovsky pr
Tekhnologichesky Institut
Sadovaya ul
nab r Fontanki
KOLOMNA
Elektrosila
Park Pobedy
Baltiyskaya
Baltic Station (Baltiysky vokzal)
Lux Express
7
Narvskaya
Rizhsky pr
8
Liflyandskaya ul
Ekateringofka
pr Stachek
Kirovsky Zavod
Avtovo
Morskoy Vokzal
Gulf of Finland (Finsky Zaliv)
Morskoy Kanal
Kanonersky Island
A
B
C
D
E
F
G
5
6
7
8

Greater St Petersburg

Top Sights

1 Hermitage Storage Facility ... C1

Sights

2 Buddhist Temple ... C1
3 Divo Ostrov ... C2
4 Kamenny Island ... D1
5 Krestovsky Island ... B2
6 Maritime Victory Park ... B2
7 Museum of Railway Technology ... D6
8 Rizzordi Art Foundation ... C5
9 Sampsonievsky Cathedral ... E2
10 Seaside Park of Victory ... B2
11 Yelagin Island ... C1
12 Yelagin Palace ... C1

Activities, Courses & Tours

13 Rentbike ... D5
14 VB Excursions ... G6
15 Wild Russia ... E5

Eating

16 BGL Cafe & Market ... E5

Entertainment

17 Jazz Philharmonic Hall ... E5

Shopping

Tula Samovars ... (see 17)

★ General Staff Building — MUSEUM

(Здание Главного штаба; Map p166; www.hermitagemuseum.org; Dvortsovaya pl 6-8; admission ₽100; 10.30am-6pm Tue, Thu-Sun, 10.30am-9pm Wed; M Admiralteyskaya) The east wing of this magnificent building, wrapping around the south of Dvortsovaya pl and designed by Carlo Rossi in the 1820s, marries restored interiors with contemporary architecture to create a series of galleries displaying the Hermitage's amazing collection of Impressionist and post-Impressionist works. Contemporary art is here too, often in temporary exhibitions by major artists.

Entry to the galleries is via a broad new marble staircase, which doubles as an ampitheatre for musical performances held in the glassed-over courtyard. At the time of writing, installation of all the artworks was underway and should be completed by the end of 2015.

★ Church on the Spilled Blood — CHURCH

(Церковь Спаса на Крови; Map p166; http://cathedral.ru; Konyushennaya pl; adult/student ₽250/150; 10.30am-6pm Thu-Tue; M Nevsky Prospekt) This five-domed dazzler is St Petersburg's most elaborate church with a classic Russian Orthodox exterior and interior decorated with some 7000 sq metre of mosaics. Officially called the Church of the Resurrection of Christ, its far more striking colloquial name references the assassination attempt on Tsar Alexander II here in 1881.

The church, which incorporates elements of 18th-century Russian architecture, is so lavish it took 24 years to build and went over budget by 1 million rubles – an enormous sum for the times. Following decades of abuse and neglect during the Soviet era, painstaking restoration began in the 1970s and took 27 years to be completed.

★ Russian Museum — MUSEUM

(Русский музей; Map p166; www.rusmuseum.ru; Inzhenernaya ul 4; adult/student ₽350/150, 4-palace ticket adult/child ₽600/300; 10am-6pm Wed & Fri-Sun, to 5pm Mon, 1-9pm Thu; M Nevsky Prospekt) The handsome Mikhailovsky Palace is home to the country's biggest collection of Russian art. After the Hermitage you may feel you have had your fill of art, but try your utmost to make some time for this gem of a museum. There's also a lovely garden behind the palace.

Nevsky Prospekt — STREET

(Map p166) Nevsky pr is Russia's most famous street, running 4km from the Admiralty to Alexander Nevsky Monastery, from which it takes its name. The inner 2.5km to Moskovsky vokzal is St Petersburg's seething main avenue, the city's shopping centre and focus of its entertainment and street life. Walking Nevsky is an essential St Petersburg experience. If you're here on a holiday evening (such as 27 May – City Day), the sight of thousands of people pouring like a stream down its middle is one you'll not forget.

Nevsky pr was laid out in the early years of St Petersburg, as the start of the main road to Novgorod, and soon became dotted with fine buildings, squares and bridges. At the beginning of the 1900s, it was one of Europe's grandest boulevards, with cobblestone footpaths and a track down the middle for horse-drawn trams. On either side of the tracks were wooden paving blocks to muffle the sound of horse-drawn carriages – an innovation that was a world first and for which the avenue was dubbed the quietest main street in Europe.

Today, things are quite a bit noisier. The traffic and crowds can become oppressive and, after a while, you'll find yourself going out of your way to avoid the street.

Stroganov Palace MUSEUM

(Строгановский дворец; Map p166; www.rusmuseum.ru; Nevsky pr 17; adult/student ₽300/150; ⌚10am-6pm Wed & Fri-Mon, 1-9pm Thu; Ⓜ Nevsky Prospekt) One of the city's loveliest baroque exteriors, the salmon-pink Stroganov Palace was designed by court favourite Bartolomeo Rastrelli in 1753 for one of the city's leading aristocratic families. The building has been superbly restored by the Russian Museum, and you can visit the impressive state rooms upstairs, where the Arabesque Dining Room, the Mineralogical Study and the Rastrelli Hall, with its vast frieze ceiling, are the obvious highlights.

Famously, the Stroganov's chef created here a beef dish served in a sour cream and mushroom sauce that became known to the world as 'beef stroganoff'.

Kazan Cathedral CHURCH

(Казанский собор; Map p166; http://kazansky-spb.ru; Kazanskaya pl 2; ⌚8.30am-7.30pm; Ⓜ Nevsky Prospekt) FREE This neoclassical cathedral, partly modelled on St Peter's in Rome, was commissioned by Tsar Paul shortly before he was murdered in a coup. Its 111m-long colonnaded arms reach out towards Nevsky pr, encircling a garden studded with statues.

Inside, the cathedral is dark and traditionally orthodox, with a daunting 80m-high dome. There is usually a queue of believers waiting to kiss the icon of Our Lady of Kazan, a copy of one of Russia's most important icons.

Look for the victorious Napoleonic War field marshal Mikhail Kutuzov (whose remains are buried inside the cathedral) and his friend and aide Mikhail Barclay de Tolly.

The cathedral's design reflects Paul's eccentric desire to unite Catholicism and Orthodoxy in a kind of 'super-Christianity' as well as his fascination with the Knights of Malta, of which he was a member.

Marble Palace PALACE

(Мраморный дворец; Map p166; www.rusmuseum.ru; Millionnaya ul 5; adult/student ₽350/150; ⌚10am-6pm Mon, Wed & Fri-Sun, 1-9pm Thu;

HIGHLIGHTS OF THE RUSSIAN MUSEUM

Mikhailovsky Palace, 2nd floor

Room 11 The White Hall, the most ornate in the palace, with period furniture by Rossi, is where Strauss and Berlioz performed concerts.

Room 14 Karl Bryullov's massive *Last Day of Pompeii* (1827–33), which was, in its time, the most famous Russian painting ever; there were queues for months to see it. Ivan Aivazovsky's Crimea seascapes also stand out, most frighteningly *The Wave*.

Room 15 Features a huge number of studies for Alexander Ivanov's most famous work, *The Appearance of Christ to the People*, which hangs in Moscow's Tretyakov Gallery.

Mikhailovsky Palace, 1st floor

Rooms 23–38 The Wanderers (Peredvizhniki) and associated artists, including Nikolai Ghe's fearsome *Peter I Interrogating Tsarevitch Alexey in Peterhof* (room 26); KA Savitsky's *To War* (room 31); and Vasily Polenov, including his *Christ and the Adulteress* (room 32).

Rooms 33–34 & 54 Works by Ilya Repin (1844–1930), probably Russia's best-loved artist; room 33 has portraits *Barge Haulers on the Volga* (an incomparable indictment of Russian 'social justice') and *Zaporozhye Cossacks Writing a Mocking Letter to the Turkish Sultan*.

Benois Building, 2nd & 1st floors

Room 71 Boris Kustodiev's smug *Merchant's Wife at Tea*.

Room 72 Nathan Altman's world-famous cubist *Portrait of Anna Akhmatova*.

Room 75–76 Works by suprematist Kasimir Malevich, including his *Red Square (Painterly Realism of a Peasant Woman in Two Dimensions)* and *Black Square*.

Rooms 77–78 Constructivist works by Alexander Lebedev and Alexander Rodchenko.

Rooms 79 Kuzma Petrov-Vodkin's *Portrait of Akhmatova* and *Mother of God*.

Historic Centre

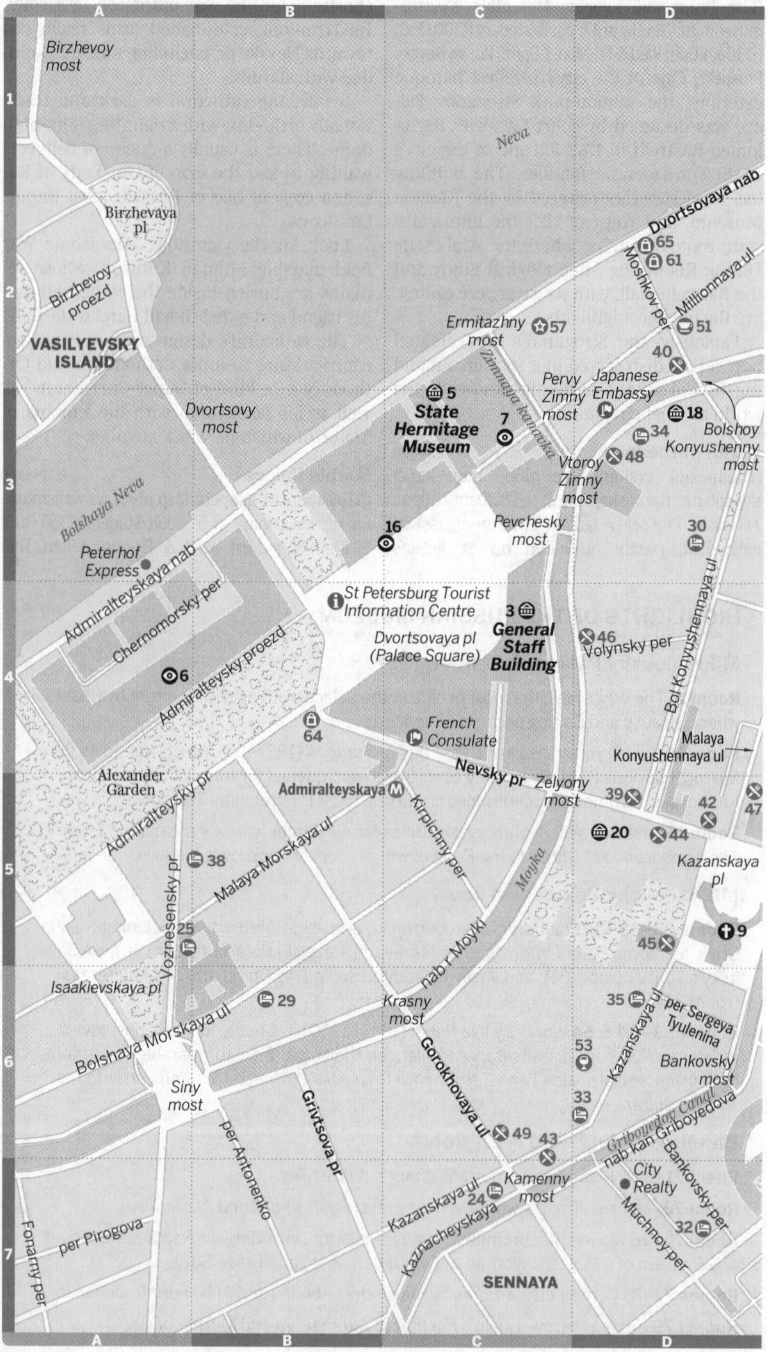

A
B
C
D
1
2
3
4
5
6
7
Birzhevoy most
Neva
Dvortsovaya nab
Birzhevaya pl
Birzhevoy proezd
VASILYEVSKY ISLAND
65
61
Moshkov per
Millionnaya ul
Ermitazhny most
57
51
40
Zimnaya kanavka
Pervy Zimny most
Japanese Embassy
5
State Hermitage Museum
Dvortsovy most
7
18
Bolshoy Konyushenny most
34
48
Vtoroy Zimny most
Bolshaya Neva
16
Pevchesky most
30
Peterhof Express
Admiralteyskaya nab
Chernomorsky per
St Petersburg Tourist Information Centre
3
General Staff Building
46
Volynsky per
Dvortsovaya pl (Palace Square)
Admiralteysky proezd
6
Bol Konyushennaya ul
64
French Consulate
Malaya Konyushennaya ul
Alexander Garden
Nevsky pr
Zelyony most
Admiralteyskaya
39
42
47
Admiralteysky pr
Kirpichny per
20
44
Malaya Morskaya ul
38
Moyka
Kazanskaya pl
Voznesensky pr
25
nab r Moyki
9
45
Isaakievskaya pl
29
Krasny most
35
per Sergeya Tyulenina
Kazanskaya ul
53
Bankovsky most
Bolshaya Morskaya ul
Gorokhovaya ul
Siny most
Grivtsova pr
33
per Antonenko
49
43
Griboyedov Canal
nab kan Griboyedova
City Realty
Bankovsky per
Kamenny most
Kazanskaya ul
24
Kaznacheyskaya
Muchnoy per
32
Fonarny per
per Pirogova
SENNAYA

ST PETERSBURG

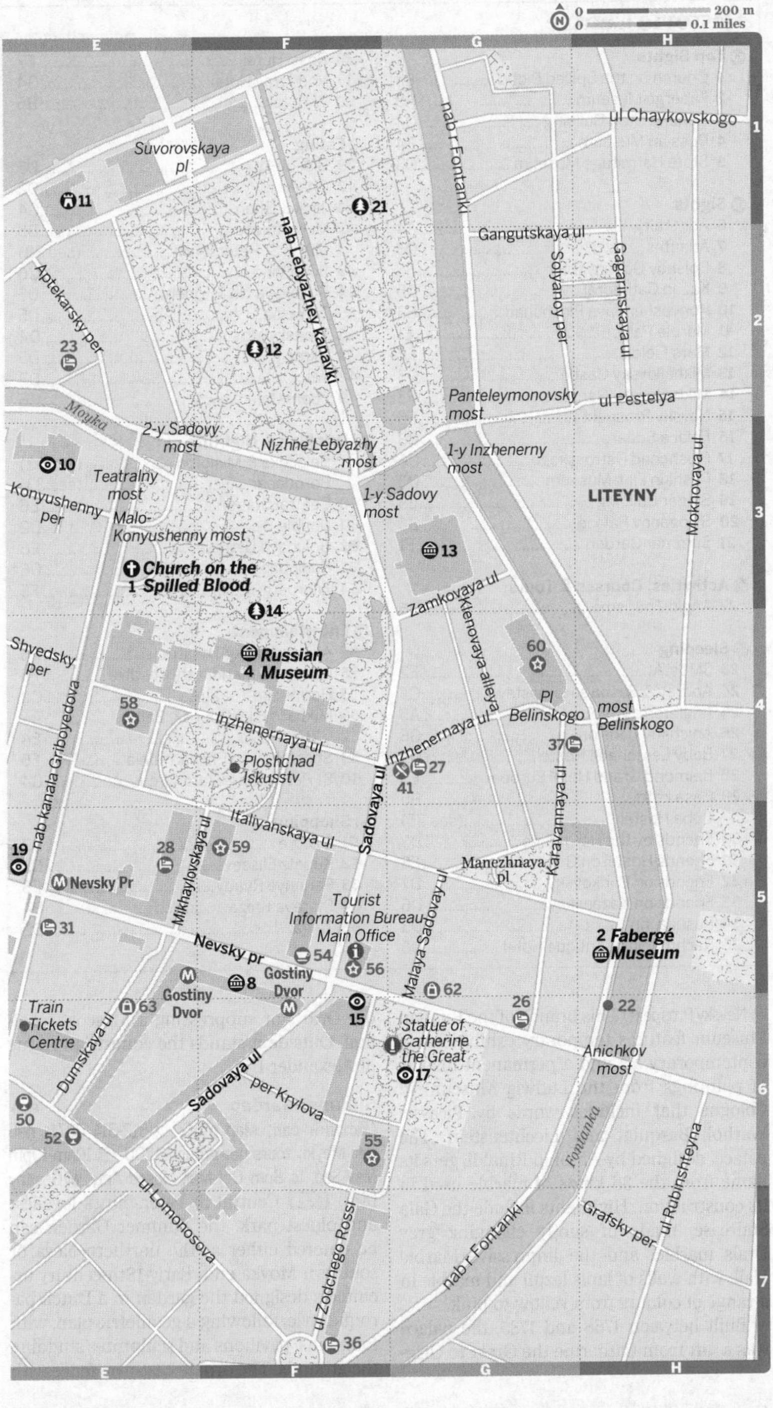
0 200 m
0 0.1 miles
Suvorovskaya pl
11
21
nab r Fontanki
ul Chaykovskogo
Gangutskaya ul
Solyanoy per
Gagarinskaya ul
nab Lebyazhey kanavki
Aptekarsky per
23
12
Moyka
Panteleymonovsky most
ul Pestelya
2-y Sadovy most
Nizhne Lebyazhy most
1-y Inzhenerny most
10
Teatralny most
Konyushenny per
Malo-Konyushenny most
1-y Sadovy most
LITEYNY
Mokhovaya ul
13
Church on the Spilled Blood
1
Zamkovaya ul
14
Klenovaya alleya
Shvedsky per
Russian Museum
4
60
Pl Belinskogo
most Belinskogo
nab kanala Griboyedova
58
Inzhenernaya ul
37
Ploshchad Iskusstv
Sadovaya ul
27
41
Italiyanskaya ul
Karavannaya ul
19
28
59
Mikhaylovskaya ul
Manezhnaya pl
Nevsky Pr
Malaya Sadovaya ul
Tourist Information Bureau Main Office
31
2 Fabergé Museum
Nevsky pr
54
56
Gostiny Dvor
8
62
Train Tickets Centre
63
15
26
22
Dumskaya ul
Statue of Catherine the Great
17
Anichkov most
Sadovaya ul
per Krylova
50
52
55
Fontanka
ul Rubinshteyna
ul Lomonosova
nab r Fontanki
Grafsky per
ul Zodchego Rossi
36
E
F
G
H
1
2
3
4
5
6
7

Historic Centre

Top Sights
1 Church on the Spilled Blood ... E3
2 Fabergé Museum ... H5
3 General Staff Building ... C4
4 Russian Museum ... F4
5 State Hermitage Museum ... C3

Sights
6 Admiralty ... A4
7 Atlantes ... C3
8 Bolshoy Gostiny Dvor ... F5
9 Kazan Cathedral ... D5
10 Konyushennaya Ploshchad ... E3
11 Marble Palace ... E1
12 Mars Field ... F2
13 Mikhailovsky Castle ... G3
14 Mikhailovsky Gardens ... F3
15 Nevsky Prospekt ... F6
16 Palace Square ... C3
17 Ploshchad Ostrovskogo ... G6
18 Pushkin Flat-Museum ... D3
19 Singer Building ... E5
20 Stroganov Palace ... D5
21 Summer Garden ... F1

Activities, Courses & Tours
22 Anglo Tourismo ... H6

Sleeping
23 3MostA ... E2
24 Andrey & Sasha's Homestay ... C7
25 Angleterre Hotel ... A5
26 Anichkov Pension ... G6
27 Baby Lemonade Hostel ... G4
28 Belmond Grand Hotel Europe ... E5
29 Casa Leto ... B6
Cuba Hostel ... (see 35)
30 Friends by the Hermitage ... D3
31 Friends Hostel on Griboedov ... E5
32 Friends on Bankovsky ... D7
33 Friends on Kazanskaya ... D6
34 Pushka Inn ... D3
35 Rachmaninov Antique Hotel ... D6
36 Rossi Hotel ... F7
37 Vodogray Hotel ... G4
38 W Hotel ... B5

Eating
39 Biblioteka ... D5
40 Chaiki ... D2
41 Jack & Chan ... G4
42 Marketplace ... D5
MiX in St Petersburg ... (see 38)
43 Soup Vino ... C6
44 Stolovaya No 1 Kopeika ... D5
45 Terrassa ... D5
46 Troitsky Most ... D4
47 Ukrop ... D5
48 Yat ... D3
49 Zoom Café ... C6

Drinking & Nightlife
Belochka & Mielofon ... (see 32)
Borodabar ... (see 33)
50 Central Station ... E6
51 Double B ... D2
52 Golubaya Ustritsa ... E6
53 Radiobaby ... D6
54 Ziferberg ... F5

Entertainment
55 Alexandrinsky Theatre ... F6
56 Demmeni Marionette Theatre ... F5
57 Hermitage Theatre ... C2
58 Mikhailovsky Opera & Ballet Theatre ... E4
59 Shostakovich Philharmonia ... F5
60 St Petersburg State Circus ... G4

Shopping
61 8 Store ... D2
62 Kupetz Eliseevs ... G5
63 Perinnye Ryady ... E6
64 Staraya Kniga ... B4
65 Taiga ... D2

M Nevsky Prospekt) This branch of the Russian Museum features temporary exhibitions of contemporary art and a permanent display of paintings from the Ludwig Museum in Cologne that includes works by Picasso, Warhol, Basquiat and Liechtenstein. The palace, designed by Antonio Rinaldi, gets its name from the 36 kinds of marble used in its construction. Highlights include the Gala Staircase, made of subtly changing grey Urals marble; and the impressive Marble Hall, with walls of lapis lazuli and marble in a range of colours from yellow to pink.

Built between 1768 and 1785, the palace was a gift from Catherine the Great to Grigory Orlov for suppressing a Moscow rebellion. Outside it stands the equestrian statue of Alexander III.

Summer Garden PARK

(Летний сад; Map p166; 812-314 0374; nab reki Moyki; tours per group ₽1200; 10am-10pm May-Sep, to 8pm Oct-Mar, closed Apr; M Gostiny Dvor) FREE Central St Petersburg's loveliest and oldest park, the Summer Garden can be entered either at the northern Neva or southern Moyka end. Early-18th-century architects designed the garden in a Dutch baroque style, following a geometric plan, with fountains, pavilions and sculptures studding the grounds. The ornate cast-iron fence with the granite posts was a later addition, built between 1771 and 1784.

The gardens functioned as a private retreat for Peter the Great (his modest **Summer Palace**, currently closed for renovations, is here) before becoming a strolling place for St Petersburg's 19th-century leisured classes. Only in the 20th century were commoners admitted.

There's a small museum in the garden, devoted to the few archaeological finds discovered during the garden's recent restoration.

★Fabergé Museum MUSEUM

(Map p166; ☎812-333 2655; www.fsv.ru/en/collection; nab reki Fontanki 21; tour ₽300; ⏲11am-7pm; Ⓜ Gostiny Dvor) Book by email at least five days in advance for one of the hour-long tours of the magnificently restored Shuvalovsky Palace, home to the largest collection of pieces manufactured by the jeweller Peter Carl Fabergé (including nine imperial Easter eggs) and fellow master craftsmen and women of pre-revolutionary Russia.

Mikhailovsky Castle MUSEUM

(Михайловский замок; Map p166; www.rusmuseum.ru; Sadovaya ul 2; adult/student ₽300/150; ⏲10am-6pm Wed & Fri-Sun, 10am-5pm Mon, 1-9pm Thu; Ⓜ Gostiny Dvor) A branch of the Russian Museum, the castle is worth visiting for its temporary exhibits, permanent display of art by foreigners working in Russia in the 18th and early 19th centuries as well as a few finely restored state rooms, including the lavish burgundy throne room of Tsar Paul I's wife Maria Fyodorovna.

Rastrelli's original fairy-tale wooden palace for Empress Elizabeth was knocked down in the 1790s to make way for this bulky edifice, a bizarre take on a medieval castle, quite unlike any other building in the city.

The son of Catherine the Great, Tsar Paul I, was born in the wooden palace and he wanted his own residence on the same spot. He specified a defensive moat as he (quite rightly) feared assassination. But this erratic, cruel tsar only got 40 days in his new abode before he was suffocated in his bedroom in 1801.

In 1823 the palace became a military engineering school (hence its Soviet-era name, Engineer's Castle, or Inzhenerny Zamok), whose most famous pupil was Fyodor Dostoevsky.

Admiralty ARCHITECTURE

(Адмиралтейство; Map p166; Admiralteysky proezd 1; Ⓜ Admiralteyskaya) The gilded spire of the Admiralty is a prime St Petersburg

THE BRIDGES OF ST PETERSBURG

Some 342 bridges span St Petersburg's network of canals and waterways. With the exception of the new Big Obukhovsky, all the *mosty* (bridges) across the Neva are drawbridges. From mid April to late November they are raised every evening at designated times to let the ships pass, an impressive spectacle that is well worth seeing. Some of the most charming bridges, though, are the smaller structures that span the canals around the city. Here are a few of our favourites:

Anichkov most Features rearing horses at all four corners, symbolising humanity's struggle with, and taming of, nature.

Bankovsky most Suspended by cables emerging from the mouths of golden-winged griffins. The name comes from the Assignment Bank (now a university), which stands on one side of the bridge.

Most Lomonosova Four Doric towers contain the mechanism that pulls up the moveable central section, allowing tall boats to pass along the Fontanka underneath.

Lviny most (Bridge of Four Lions) Another suspension bridge, this one is supported by two pairs of regal lions.

Panteleymonovsky most At the confluence of the Moyka and the Fontanka, this beauty features lamp posts bedecked with the double-headed eagle and railings adorned with the coat of arms.

1-y Inzhenerny most (First Engineer Bridge) While there is no shortage of adornment on the cast-iron bridge leading to Mikhailovsky Castle, the highlight is the Chizhik-Pyzhik, the statue of the little bird that hovers over the Moyka.

landmark, visible from Gorokhovaya ul, Voznesensky pr and Nevsky pr, as all of these roads radiate outwards from this central point. From 1711 to 1917, this spot was the headquarters of the Russian navy; now it houses the country's largest military naval college and is closed to the public.

Ploshchad Ostrovskogo SQUARE
(Площадь Островского; Map p166; Ⓜ Gostiny Dvor) Created by Carlo Rossi in the 1820s and 1830s, this square is named for Alexander Ostrovsky (1823–86), a celebrated 19th-century playwright. An enormous **statue of Catherine the Great** (1873) stands amid the chess, backgammon and mah-jong players who crowd the benches here. At the Empress' heels are renowned statesmen of the 19th century, including her lovers Orlov, Potemkin and Suvorov.

Pushkin Flat-Museum MUSEUM
(Музей-квартира А.С. Пушкина; Map p166; ☎812-314 0006; www.museumpushkin.ru; nab reki Moyki 12; adult/student ₽250/100; ⏲10.30am-5pm Wed-Sun; Ⓜ Admiralteyskaya) Alexander Pushkin, Russia's national poet, had his last home here on one of the prettiest curves of the Moyka River. He only lived here four months, and died here after his duel in 1837. The little house is now the Pushkin Flat-Museum, which has been reconstructed to look exactly as it did in the poet's last days. You can only visit on a tour (run hourly on the hour), and these are given in Russian only.

Mars Field PARK
(Марсово поле; Map p166; nab Lebyazhey kanavki; Ⓜ Nevsky Prospekt) Named after the Roman god of war and once the scene of 19th-century military parades, the grassy Mars Field is a popular spot for strollers, even though in the early 20th century it was used as a burial ground for victims and heroes of the revolution. At its centre, an **eternal flame** has been burning since 1957 in memory of the victims of all wars and revolutions in St Petersburg.

Liteyny & Smolny

This area includes sights east of the Fontanka Canal and north of Nevsky pr. It also includes Smolny, a governmental region and one of the less-touristed areas of the city, running east from Liteyny pr towards Smolny Cathedral.

Smolny Cathedral CHURCH
(Смольный собор; Map p172; ☎812-577 1421; pl Rastrelli 3/1; adult/student/child ₽150/90/50, bell tower ₽100, general ticket ₽200; ⏲10.30am-6pm Thu-Tue; Ⓜ Chernyshevskaya) If baroque is your thing, then look no further than the sky-blue Smolny Cathedral, an unrivalled masterpiece of the genre that ranks among Bartolomeo Rastrelli's most amazing creations. The cathedral is the centrepiece of a convent mostly built to Rastrelli's designs between 1748 and 1757. His inspiration was to combine baroque details with the forest of towers and onion domes typical of an old Russian monastery. There's special genius in the proportions of the cathedral (it gives the impression of soaring upwards), to which the convent buildings are a perfect foil.

In stark contrast, the interior is a disappointingly austere plain white as Rastrelli fell from favour before he was able to begin work on it. Today the cathedral is no longer a working church, but serves instead as a concert hall and exhibition space. If you're lucky there may well be rehearsals for concerts going on while you visit, to which you're welcome to listen, otherwise it's not really worth paying to enter the cathedral itself.

However, it's definitely worth paying to climb the 277 steps to one (or both) of the two 63m-high bell towers for stupendous views over the city.

Anna Akhmatova Museum at the Fountain House MUSEUM
(Музей Анны Ахматовой в Фонтанном Доме; Map p172; www.akhmatova.spb.ru; Liteyny pr 51; adult/child ₽80/40; ⏲10.30am-6.30pm Tue & Thu-Sun, noon-8pm Wed; Ⓜ Mayakovskaya) Housed in the south wing of the Sheremetyev Palace, this touching and fascinating literary museum celebrates the life and work of Anna Akhmatova, St Petersburg's most famous 20th-century poet. Akhmatova lived here from 1924 until 1952, as this was the apartment of her common-law husband Nikolai Punin. The apartment is on the 2nd floor and is filled with mementos of the poet and correspondence with other writers.

A visit to this peaceful and contemplative place is also an interesting chance to see the interior of an (albeit atypical) apartment from the early to mid-20th century, even if relatively few pieces of original furniture have survived. Particularly moving is the study where, in her own words, Akhmatova 'quite unexpectedly' started her masterpiece

Poem Without a Hero in 1940, and her living room where the poet had a famous all-night conversation with British diplomat Isaiah Berlin during the height of Stalinism, an event that has become legendary in Russian literary history. There are information panels in English in each room, as well as a ₽200 audio guide available in English.

Admission also includes the Josef Brodsky American Study. Brodsky did not live here, but his connection with Akhmatova was strong. For lack of a better location, his office has been re-created here, complete with furniture and other artifacts from his adopted home in Massachusetts. Funds are currently being collected to open a Josef Brodsky Museum at the poet's former home a few blocks away on Liteyny pr.

When coming to the museum, be sure to enter from Liteyny pr, rather than from the Fontanka River, where the main palace entrance is, as it's not possible to reach the museum from there.

Museum of Decorative & Applied Arts — MUSEUM

(Музей декоративного и прикладного искусства; Map p172; www.spbghpa.ru; Solyanoy per 15; adult/student ₽100/50 excursion in Russian ₽200; ⌚11am-5pm Tue-Sat; Ⓜ Chernyshevskaya) Also known as the **Stieglitz Museum**, this fascinating establishment is as beautiful as you would expect a decorative-arts museum to be. An array of gorgeous objects is on display, from medieval furniture to 18th-century Russian tiled stoves and contemporary works by the students of the Applied Arts School, also housed here. This museum is less visited than some of its counterparts in the city, but the quiet atmosphere only adds to its appeal.

Sheremetyev Palace — MUSEUM

(Шереметьевский дворец; Map p172; ☎812-272 4441; www.theatremuseum.ru; nab reki Fontanki 34; admission ₽300; ⌚11am-7pm Thu-Mon, 1-9pm Wed; Ⓜ Gostiny Dvor) Splendid wrought-iron gates facing the Fontanka River guard the entrance to the Sheremetyev Palace (built 1750–55), now a branch of the **State Museum of Theatre & Music**, which has a collection of musical instruments from the 19th and 20th centuries. The Sheremetyev family was famous for the concerts and theatre performances they hosted at their palace, which was a centre of musical life in the imperial capital.

Museum of the Defence & Blockade of Leningrad — MUSEUM

(Музей обороны и блокады Ленинграда; Map p172; www.blokadamus.ru; Solyarnoy per 9; adult/student ₽300/150; ⌚10am-5pm Thu-Mon, 12.30-9pm Wed; Ⓜ Chernyshevskaya) The grim but engrossing displays here contain donations from survivors, propaganda posters from the blockade period and many photos depicting life and death during the siege. An audio guide in English should be made available by the time you read this, which will compensate for the lack of English signage elsewhere in the museum.

This museum opened just three months after the blockade was lifted in January 1944 and boasted 37,000 exhibits, including real tanks and aeroplanes. But three years later, during Stalin's repression of the city, the museum was shut, its director shot, and most of the exhibits destroyed or redistributed. Not until 1985's *glasnost* (openness) was an attempt made once again to gather documents to reopen the museum; this happened in 1989.

Cathedral of the Transfiguration of Our Saviour — CATHEDRAL

(Спасо-преображенский собор; Map p172; Preobrazhenskaya pl; ⌚8am-8pm; Ⓜ Chernyshevskaya) The interior of this marvellous 1743 cathedral, which has been beautifully restored and repainted both outside and in, is one of the most gilded in the city. The grand gates bear the imperial double-headed eagle in vast golden busts, reflecting the fact that the cathedral was built on the site where the Preobrazhensky Guards (the monarch's personal protection unit) had their headquarters. Architect Vasily Stasov rebuilt the cathedral from 1827 to 1829 in the neoclassical style. It is dedicated to the victory over the Turks in 1828–29; note the captured Turkish guns in the gate surrounding the cathedral.

Tauride Palace & Gardens — PARK

(Таврический дворец и сад; Map p172; ⌚8am-10pm May-Jul, to 8pm Aug-Mar; Ⓜ Chernyshevskaya) Catherine the Great had this baroque palace built in 1783 for Grigory Potemkin, a famed general and her companion for many years of her life. Today it is home to the Commonwealth of Independent States and is closed to the public. The gardens, on the other hand, are open to all; once the romping grounds of the tsarina, they became a park for the people under the

Liteyny, Smolny and Vladimirskaya & Vosstaniya

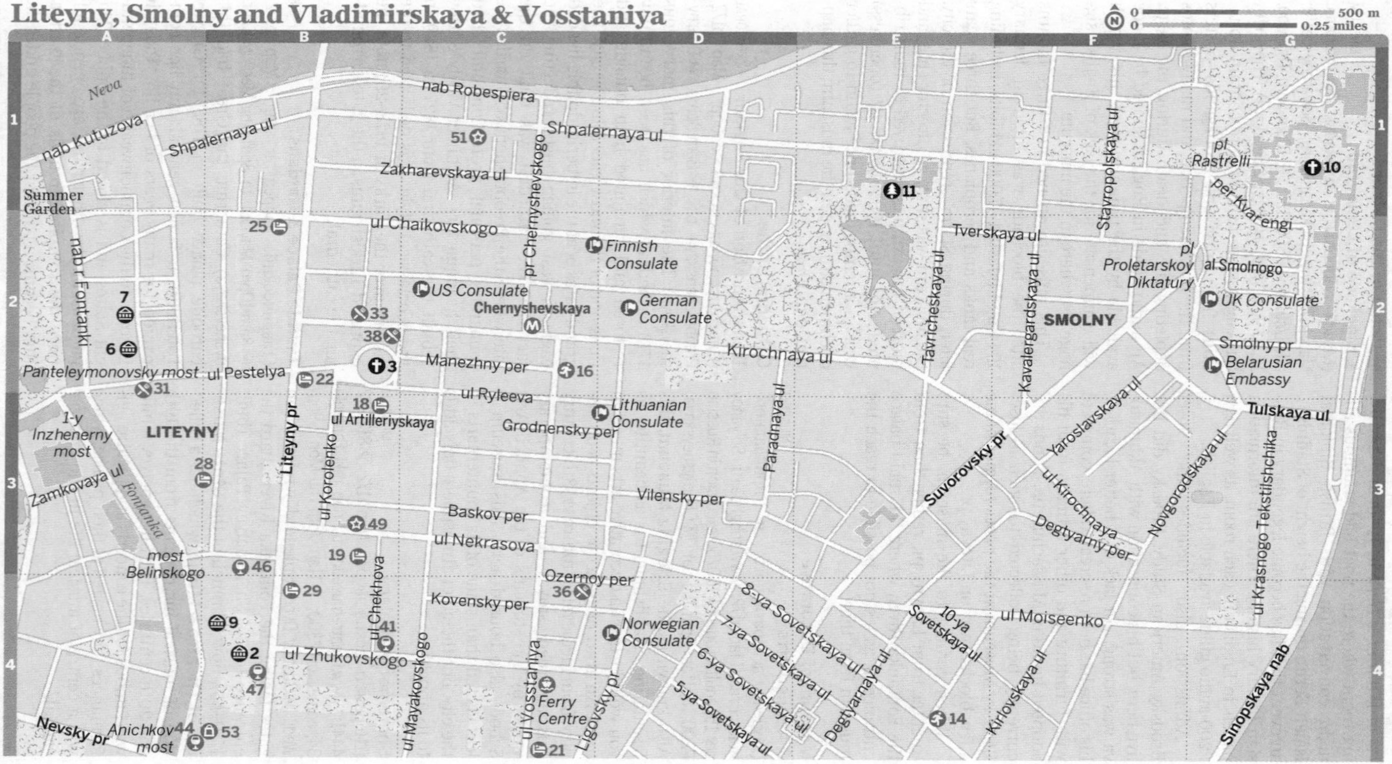

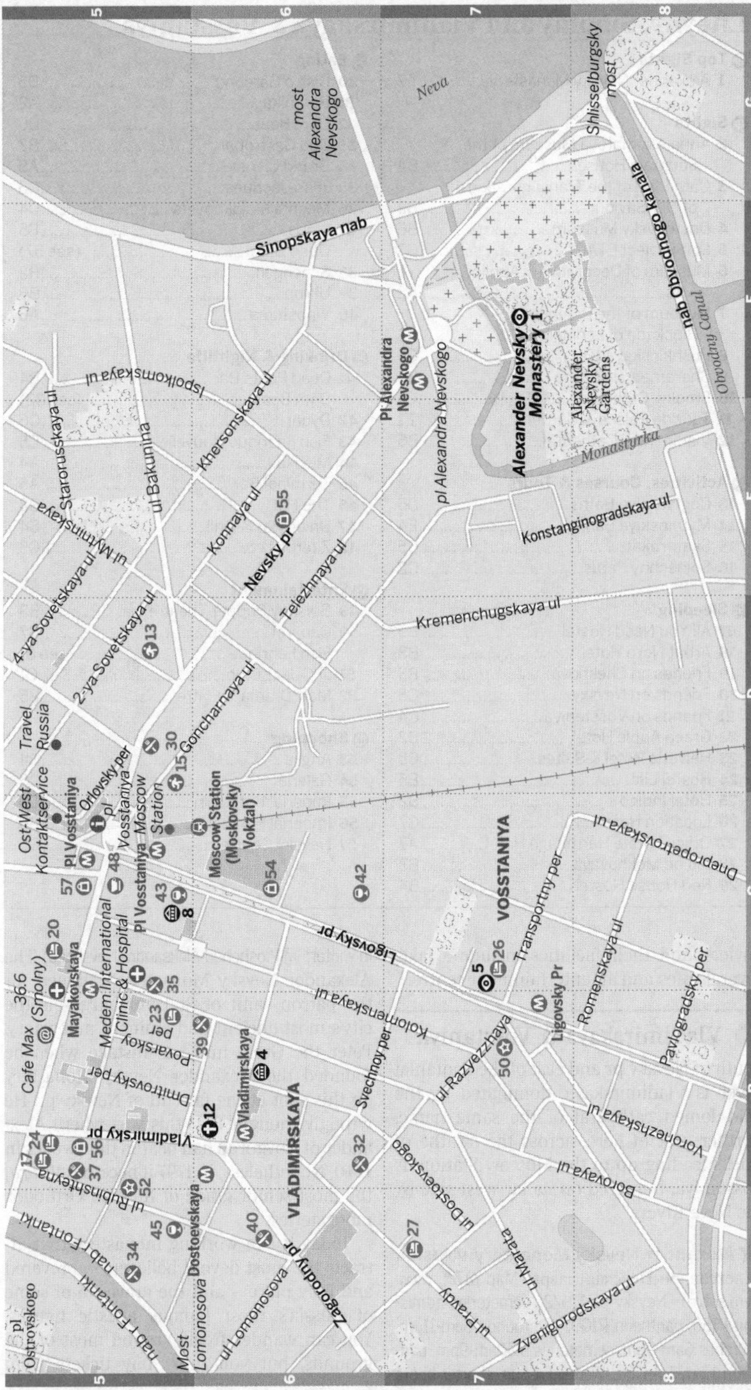
Neva
most Alexandra Nevskogo
Shlisselburgsky most
Sinopskaya nab
nab Obvodnogo kanala
Obvodny Canal
Monastyrka
Alexander Nevsky Monastery 1
Alexander Nevsky Gardens
Pl Alexandra Nevskogo
pl Alexandra Nevskogo
Ispolkomskaya ul
Kharsonskaya ul
Starorusskaya ul
ul Bakunina
ul Mytninskaya
Konnaya ul
Nevsky pr
55
Telezhnaya ul
Konstanginogradskaya ul
Kremenchugskaya ul
4-ya Sovetskaya ul
2-ya Sovetskaya ul
13
Travel Russia
Goncharnaya ul
30
15
Ost-West Kontaktservice
Orlovsky per
Pl Vosstaniya
pl Vosstaniya
Vosstaniya Moscow Station
Moscow Station (Moskovsky Vokzal)
Pl Vosstaniya
57
48
43
8
54
42
VOSSTANIYA
Dnepropetrovskaya ul
Transportny per
Ligovsky pr
Cafe Max (Smolny)
36.6
20
Mayakovskaya
Medem International Clinic & Hospital
35
23
Povarskoy per
39
Dmitrovsky per
Vladimirskaya
4
Kolomenskaya ul
Svechnoy per
5
26
Ligovsky Pr
Romenskaya ul
Pavlogradsky per
ul Razyezzhaya
50
Voronezhskaya ul
Vladimirsky pr
12
17
24
56
37
ul Rubinshteyna
52
VLADIMIRSKAYA
32
ul Dostoevskogo
Borovaya ul
45
Dostoevskaya
40
27
nab r Fontanki
34
Zagorodny pr
ul Marata
ul Pravdy
Zvenigorodskaya ul
pl Ostrovskogo
Most Lomonosova
ul Lomonosova
A
B
C
D
E
F
G
5
6
7
8

Liteyny, Smolny and Vladimirskaya & Vosstaniya

Top Sights

1 Alexander Nevsky Monastery F7

Sights

2 Anna Akhmatova Museum at the Fountain House B4
3 Cathedral of the Transfiguration of Our Saviour B2
4 Dostoevsky Museum B6
5 Loft Project ETAGI C7
6 Museum of Decorative & Applied Arts A2
7 Museum of the Defence & Blockade of Leningrad A2
8 Pushkinskaya 10 .... C5
9 Sheremetyev Palace B4
10 Smolny Cathedral G1
11 Tauride Palace & Gardens E1
12 Vladimirsky Cathedral B6

Activities, Courses & Tours

13 Degtyarniye Baths D5
14 Mytninskiye Bani E4
15 Skatprokat D5
16 Solnechny Parus C2

Sleeping

17 All You Need Hostel B5
18 Arbat Nord Hotel B3
19 Friends on Chekhova B3
20 Friends on Nevsky C5
21 Friends on Vosstaniya C4
22 Green Apple Hotel B2
23 Helvetia Hotel & Suites B5
24 Hostel Life B5
25 Hotel Indigo B2
26 Location Hostel C7
27 Official State Hermitage Hotel A7
28 Pio on Mokhovaya B3
29 Red House Hostel B4

Eating

30 Bistro Garçon D5
31 Botanika A2
32 Dom Beat B6
33 Duo Gastrobar B2
34 Grand Cru A5
35 Jean-Jacques C5
36 Mechta Molokhovets C4
37 Mops B5
Obed Bufet .... (see 57)
38 Schengen B2
39 Ukrop B6
40 Vinostudia A6

Drinking & Nightlife

41 Dead Poets Bar B4
Dom Beat .... (see 32)
42 Dyuni C6
43 Fish Fabrique Nouvelle C5
44 Mishka A4
45 Terminal Bar A5
46 The Hat B3
47 Union Bar & Grill B4
48 Ziferblat C5

Entertainment

49 Bolshoy Puppet Theatre B3
50 Cabaret B7
Fish Fabrique .... (see 8)
51 JFC Jazz Club C1
52 Maly Drama Theatre B5

Shopping

53 Anglia B4
54 Galeria C6
55 Imperial Porcelain E6
56 Imperial Porcelain B5
57 Nevsky Centre C5

Soviets, and their facilities include a lake, several cafes and an entertainment centre.

Vladimirskaya & Vosstaniya

South of Nevsky pr and east of the Fontanka River is Vladimirskaya, dominated by the gold-domed cathedral of the same name. Further east of here, across the swathe of tracks leading up to the Moscow Station, is Vosstaniya, bordered on its far west side by the Neva River.

★ **Alexander Nevsky Monastery** MONASTERY
(Александро-Невская лавра; Map p172; www.lavra.spb.ru; Nevsky pr 179/2; cemeteries admission ₽150, pantheon ₽100; grounds 6am-11pm, churches 6am-9pm, cemeteries 9.30am-9pm, pantheon 11am-5pm Tue, Wed & Fri-Sun, shorter hours in winter; M Ploshchad Aleksandra Nevskogo) The Alexander Nevsky Monastery – named for the patron saint of St Petersburg – is the city's most ancient and eminent monastery. Peter the Great made a mistake when he founded the Alexander Nevsky Monastery on this spot at the far end of Nevsky pr. He wrongly thought that this was where Alexander of Novgorod had beaten the Swedes in 1240. Nonetheless, in 1797 it became a *lavra*, the most senior grade of Russian Orthodox monasteries.

Today it is a working monastery that attracts the most devout believers – a revered and holy place – and the gravesite of some of Russia's most famous artistic figures. You can wander freely around most of the grounds, but you must buy tickets from the kiosk on your right after entering the main gates to enter the most important two graveyards.

Dostoevsky Museum MUSEUM

(Литературно-мемориальный музей Ф.М. Достоевского; Map p172; www.md.spb.ru; Kuznechny per 5/2; adult/student ₽160/80, audio tour ₽200; 11am-6pm Tue-Sun, 1-8pm Wed; M Vladimirskaya) Fyodor Dostoevsky lived in flats all over the city, mostly in Sennaya, but his final residence is this 'memorial flat' where he lived from 1878 until he died in 1881. The apartment remains as it was when the Dostoevsky family lived here, including the study where he wrote *The Brothers Karamazov,* and the office of Anna Grigorievna, his wife, who recopied, edited and sold all of his books.

Two rooms of the museum are devoted to his novels; literature fans will want to pay close attention to the map of Dostoevsky's Petersburg, which details the locations of characters and events in his various works. A rather gloomy sculpted likeness of the man himself (as if there's any other kind) is just outside the nearby Vladimirskaya metro station.

Vladimirsky Cathedral CHURCH

(Владимирский собор; Map p172; Vladimirsky pr 20; admission free; 8am-6pm, services 6pm daily; M Vladimirskaya) This fantastic, five-domed cathedral, ascribed to Domenico Trezzini, is the namesake of this neighbourhood. Incorporating both baroque and neoclassical elements, the cathedral was built in the 1760s, with Giacomo Quarenghi's neoclassical bell tower added later in the century. Over the centuries the congregation has included Dostoevsky, who lived around the corner. The cathedral was closed in 1932 and the Soviets turned it into an underwear factory, but in 1990 it was reconsecrated and has resumed its originally intended function.

Loft Project ETAGI CULTURAL CENTRE

(Лофт проект ЭТАЖИ; Map p172; www.loftprojectetagi.ru; Ligovsky pr 74; noon-10pm; M Ligovsky Prospekt) This fantastic conversion of the former Smolninsky Bread Factory has plenty to keep you interested, including many of the original factory fittings seamlessly merged with the thoroughly contemporary design. There are several galleries and exhibition spaces, lots of shops, a hostel, a bar and a cafe with a great summer terrace all spread out over five floors.

While it's true that ETAGI has become much more of a commercial than an artistic venture in recent years, it's still a good place to take the pulse of St Petersburg's contemporary-art scene and a good environment to meet a young and creative crowd. In summer months the roof of the building is open (₽250), with comfortable furniture to lounge on while overlooking the city. Enter through the doors to one side of the main gate and you'll find ETAGI in the courtyard.

Pushkinskaya 10 ART GALLERY

(Арт-Центр Пушкинская 10; Map p172; www.p-10.ru; Ligovsky pr 53; 4-8pm Wed-Sun; M Ploshchad Vosstaniya) This now legendary locale is a former apartment block – affectionately called by its street address despite the fact that the public entrance is actually on Ligovsky pr – that contains studio and gallery space, as well as music clubs Fish Fabrique (p202) and **Fabrique Nouvelle** (Map p172; www.fishfabrique.spb.ru; Ligovsky pr 53; 3pm-late; M Ploshchad Vosstaniya), plus an assortment of other shops and galleries. It offers a unique opportunity to hang out with local musicians and artists, who are always eager to talk about their work.

Sennaya & Kolomna

This area, south and west of St Isaac's Cathedral, contains some interesting sights but is also fine just for casual wandering, particularly around the meandering Griboyedova Canal, which flows close to Sennaya pl, the Mariinsky Theatre and through Kolomna.

★ **Yusupov Palace** PALACE

(Юсуповский дворец; Map p176; 812-314 9892; www.yusupov-palace.ru; nab reki Moyki 94; adult/student/child incl audioguide ₽500/380/280, Rasputin tour adult/student ₽300/180; 11am-5pm; M Sadovaya) This spectacular palace on the Moyka River has some of best 19th-century interiors in the city, in addition to a fascinating and gruesome history. The palace's last owner was the eccentric Prince Felix Yusupov, a high-society darling and at one time the richest man in Russia. Most notoriously, the palace is the place where Grigory Rasputin was murdered in 1916, and the basement where this now infamous plot unravelled can be visited as part of a guided tour.

★ **Mariinsky Theatre** THEATRE

(Мариинский театр; Map p176; 812-326 4141; www.mariinsky.ru; Teatralnaya pl; box office 11am-7pm; M Sadovaya) The Mariinsky Theatre

Sennaya & Kolomna

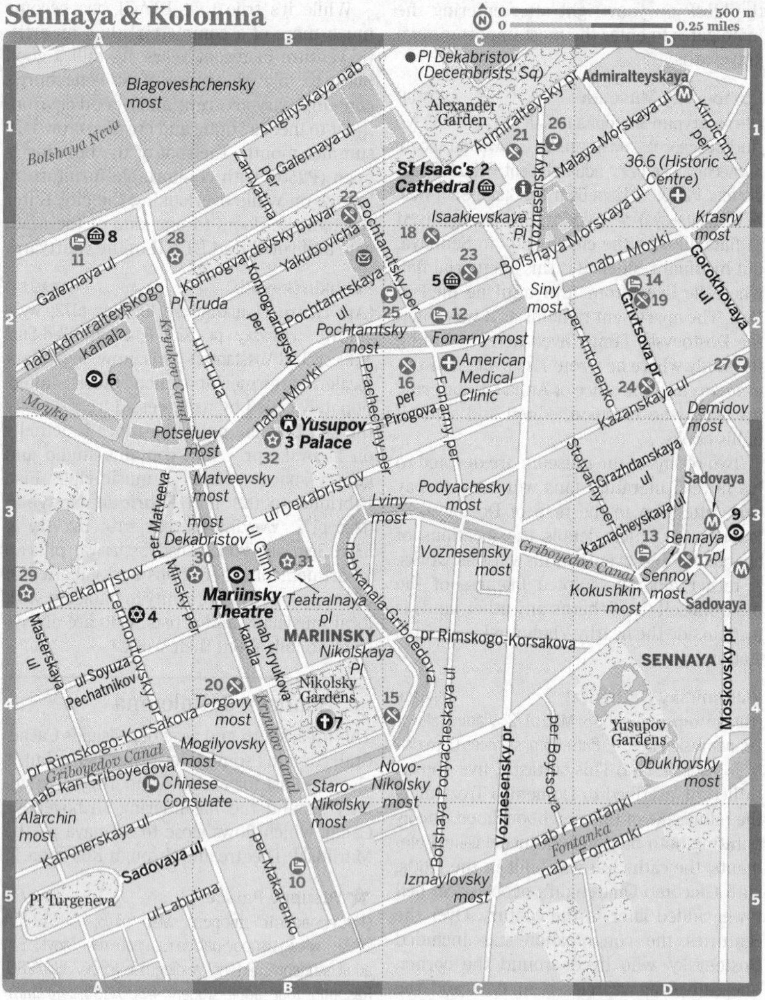

has played a pivotal role in Russian ballet ever since it was built in 1859 and remains one of Russia's most loved and respected cultural institutions. Its pretty green-and-white main building on aptly named Teatralnaya pl (Theatre Sq) is a must for any visitor wanting to see one of the world's great ballet and opera stages, while its brand-new second stage, the Mariinsky II, is a state-of-the-art opera house for the 21st century.

★St Isaac's Cathedral MUSEUM

(Isaakievsky Sobor; Map p176; www.cathedral.ru; Isaakievskaya pl; cathedral adult/student ₽250/150, colonnade ₽150; ⏲10.30am-6pm Thu-Tue, cathedral closed Wed, colonade 1st & 3rd Wed; Ⓜ Admiralteyskaya) The golden dome of St Isaac's Cathedral dominates the St Petersburg skyline. Its obscenely lavish interior is open as a museum, although services are held in the cathedral on major religious holidays. Most people bypass the museum to climb the 262 steps to the *kolonnada* (colonnade) around the drum of the dome, providing superb city views.

French designer Auguste Montferrand began designing the cathedral in 1818, despite the fact that he was no architect. The

Sennaya & Kolomna

cathedral took so long to build (until 1858) that Nicholas I was able to insist on an even more grandiose structure than Montferrand had originally planned. More than 100kg of gold leaf was used to cover the 21.8m-high dome alone. Since 1990, after a 62-year gap, services have been held here on major religious holidays even though St Isaac's is officially classed as a museum.

Nikolsky Cathedral CHURCH

(Никольский собор; Map p176; Nikolskaya pl 1/3; 9am-7pm; M Sadovaya) FREE Surrounded on two sides by canals, this ice-blue cathedral is one of the most picture-perfect in the city, beloved by locals for its baroque spires and golden domes. It was one of the few churches that continued to work during the Soviet era, when organised religion was effectively banned. Nicknamed the Sailor's Church (Nicholas is the patron saint of sailors), it contains many 18th-century icons and a fine carved wooden iconostasis, though visitors are limited to only a small area of the church's interior.

A graceful bell tower overlooks the Griboyedov Canal, which is crossed by Staro-Nikolsky most. From this bridge, you can see seven other bridges, more than from any other spot in the city.

Nabokov Museum MUSEUM

(Музей Набокова; Map p176; www.nabokovmuseum.org; Bolshaya Morskaya ul 47; 11am-6pm Tue-Fri, noon-5pm Sat & Sun; M Admiralteyskaya) FREE This 19th-century town house was the suitably grand childhood home of Vladimir Nabokov, infamous author of *Lolita* and arguably the most versatile of 20th-century Russian writers. Here Nabokov lived with his wealthy family from his birth in 1899 until the revolution in 1917, when they left the country. Nabokov artefacts on display include family photographs, first editions of his books and parts of his extensive butterfly collection, as well as rooms given over to temporary exhibits.

Sennaya Ploshchad SQUARE

(Сенная площадь; Map p176; M Sennaya Ploshchad) Immortalised by Dostoevsky, who lived all over the neighbourhood and set *Crime and Punishment* here, St Petersburg's Haymarket was once the city's filthy underbelly. Indeed, until a much-needed facelift just over a decade ago, the square was overloaded with makeshift kiosks and market stalls, which made it a magnet for the homeless, beggars, pickpockets and drunks. Despite the square's big clean-up in 2003, Sennaya pl retains a fundamental insalubriousness. Be on your guard walking around here at night.

The peripatetic Dostoevsky, who occupied some 20 residences in his 28-year stay in the city, once spent a couple of days in debtors' prison in what is now called the Senior Officers' Barracks, just across the square from the Sennaya pl metro station.

Alyona Ivanovna, the elderly moneylender murdered in *Crime and Punishment*, lived a few blocks west of here, at nab kanala Griboyedova 104. Her flat would have been No 74, in the courtyard on the 3rd floor.

Rumyantsev Mansion MUSEUM
(Особняк Румянцева; Map p176; www.spbmuseum.ru; Angliyskaya nab 44; adult/student ₽150/80; 11am-6pm Thu-Tue; Ⓜ Admiralteyskaya) History buffs should not miss this oft-overlooked but superb local museum. Part of the State Museum of the History of St Petersburg, the mansion contains an exhibition of 20th-century history, including displays devoted to the 1921 New Economic Policy (NEP), the industrialisation and development of the 1930s, and the Siege of Leningrad during WWII. Exhibitions are unusual in that they depict everyday life in the city during these historic periods. Each room has an explanatory panel in English.

Grand Choral Synagogue SYNAGOGUE
(Большая хоральная синагога; Map p176; 812-714 4332; http://eng.jewishpetersburg.ru; Lermontovsky pr 2; 8am-8pm Sun-Fri, services 10am Sat; Ⓜ Sadovaya) FREE Designed by Vasily Stasov, the striking Grand Choral Synagogue opened in 1893 to provide a central place of worship for St Petersburg's growing Jewish community. Its lavishness (particularly notable in the 47m-high cupola and the decorative wedding chapel) indicates the pivotal role that Jews played in imperial St Petersburg. The synagogue was fully revamped in 2003. Visitors are welcome except on the Sabbath and other holy days. Men and married women should cover their heads upon entering.

New Holland HISTORIC BUILDING
(Новая Голландия; Map p176; www.newholland-sp.ru; cnr nab kanala Kryukova & Bolshaya Morskaya ul; Ⓜ Sadovaya) This triangular island has been closed to the public for the majority of the last three centuries, and its structures appear to be little more than ruins at present. Its fortunes are slowly changing, however, and it has been taken over by the city authorities who are slowly transforming the island into an arts and entertainment centre. While the island remains closed at the time of writing, parts of it have been open over recent summers, so may be possible to visit during your stay.

Vasilyevsky Island

The most convenient metro station for this area is Vasileostrovskaya, but for sights around the Strelka you'd do just as well to walk over the Neva from the Hermitage or catch one of the numerous buses that run there from Nevsky pr.

★ **Kunstkamera** MUSEUM
(Кунсткамера; Map p179; www.kunstkamera.ru; Tamozhenny per; adult/child ₽250/50; 11am-7pm Tue-Sun; Ⓜ Admiralteyskaya) Also known as the Museum of Ethnology and Anthropology, the Kunstkamera was the city's first museum and was founded in 1714 by Peter himself. It is famous largely for its ghoulish collection of monstrosities, preserved 'freaks', two-headed mutant foetuses, deformed animals and odd body parts, all collected by Peter with the aim of educating the notoriously superstitious Russian people. While most rush to see these sad specimens, there are also very interesting exhibitions on native peoples from around the world.

Peter's aim in setting up the museum was to demonstrate that the malformations were not the result of the evil eye or sorcery, but rather caused by 'internal damage as well as fear and the beliefs of the mother during pregnancy' – a marginally more enlightened view. This fascinating place is an essential St Petersburg sight, although not one for the faint-hearted. Think twice about bringing young children here and definitely give Kunstkamera a wide berth if you are pregnant yourself. Indeed, where else can you see specimens with such charming names as 'double-faced monster with brain hernia'?

Yet the famous babies in bottles make up just a small part of the enormous collection that also encompasses some wonderfully kitsch dioramas exhibiting rare objects and cultural practices from all over the world, and you can easily spend an hour or two picking through these. The 3rd floor of the museum is given over to an exhibition about polymath Mikhail Lomonosov, with a re-creation of his study-laboratory. The top floors of the museum are only open as part of a guided **tour** (in English, for up to 4 people ₽2700, call in advance to book), and include the great Gottorp Globe, a rotating globe and planetarium all in one.

Vasilevsky Island

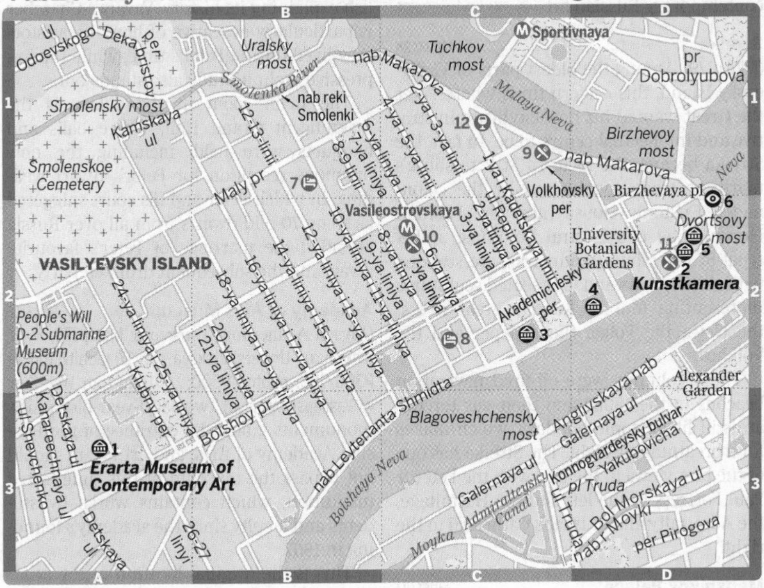

Vasilevsky Island

Top Sights
- 1 Erarta Museum of Contemporary Art A3
- 2 Kunstkamera D2

Sights
- 3 Academy of Arts Museum C2
- 4 Menshikov Palace D2
- 5 Museum of Zoology D2
- 6 Strelka D2

Sleeping
- 7 NasHotel B1
- 8 Sokos Hotel Vasilyevsky C2

Eating
- 9 Buter Brodsky C1
- 10 Marketplace C2
- 11 Restoran D2

Drinking & Nightlife
- Buter Brodsky ..... (see 9)
- 12 Helsinki Bar C1

★ **Erarta Museum of Contemporary Art** MUSEUM
(Музей современного искусства Эрарта; Map p179; www.erarta.com; 29-ya Liniya 2; adult/under 21/family ₽400/200/650; ⊙10am-10pm Wed-Mon; 📶; Ⓜ Vasileostrovskaya then bus 6 or 7, or trolleybus 10 or 11 from the opposite side of the road) This fantastic contemporary-art museum has made this far-flung and otherwise totally dead area of Vasilyevsky Island a destination in itself. The museum divides neatly into two parts, spread over five floors. On the left-hand side is the permanent collection of some 2000 works of Russian art produced between the 1950s and the present day, while on the right-hand side the same number of floors house temporary exhibits and commercial galleries, where the work on display is also on sale.

Your ticket includes entrance to the entire permanent collection and the first three floors of the temporary exhibits, but those on the 4th and 5th floors are an extra ₽150 each. The permanent collection is an excellent survey of the past half-century of Russian art, and is particularly strong on late Soviet underground art. One nice curatorial touch is the frequent inclusion of objects depicted in paintings in real life – a bowl of apples will sit, for example, in front of a painting entitled *Apple Picking*. It's all terribly sleek, beautifully presented and the best place in St Petersburg to get a feel for contemporary Russian art.

Strelka
LANDMARK

(Map p179) Among the oldest parts of Vasilyevsky Island, this eastern tip is where Peter the Great wanted his new city's administrative and intellectual centre to be. In fact, the Strelka became the focus of St Petersburg's maritime trade, symbolised by the colonnaded Customs House (now the Pushkin House). The two Rostral Columns, archetypal St Petersburg landmarks, are studded with ships' prows and four seated sculptures representing four of Russia's great rivers: the Neva, the Volga, the Dnieper and the Volkhov.

These columns were oil-fired navigation beacons in the 1800s and their gas torches are still lit on some holidays, which makes for a breathtaking sight. The Strelka has one of the best views in the city, with the Peter & Paul Fortress to the left and the Hermitage, the Admiralty and St Isaac's Cathedral to the right.

Menshikov Palace
MUSEUM

(Государственный Эрмитаж-Дворец Меншикова; Map p179; www.hermitagemuseum.org; Universitetskaya nab 15; admission ₽100; ⌚10.30am-6pm Tue-Sat, to 5pm Sun; Ⓜ Vasileostrovskaya) The first stone building in the city, the Menshikov Palace was built to the grandiose tastes of Prince Alexander Menshikov, Peter the Great's closest friend and the first governor of St Petersburg. It is now a branch of the Hermitage and while only a relatively small part of the palace is open to visitors, it's well worth coming here to see the impressively restored interiors.

Menshikov was of humble origins (he is said to have sold pies on the streets of Moscow as a child), but his talent for both organisation and intrigue made him the second-most important person in the Russian Empire by the time of Peter's death in 1725. His palace, built mainly between 1710 and 1714, was the city's smartest residence at the time (compare it to Peter the Great's tiny Summer Palace across the river). Peter used the palace for official functions and its interiors are some of the oldest and best preserved in the city.

The 1st floor displays some stunning Dutch tile work, intended to fortify the rooms against humidity to help ease Menshikov's tuberculosis. Original furniture and the personal effects of Menshikov are on display, and each room has a fact sheet in English explaining its history. Vavara's Chamber is particularly evocative of how the aristocracy lived during Peter's time, while the impressive Walnut Study also stands out.

The main room in the palace is the magnificent Grand Hall, where balls and banquets were held, including the now infamous reception for Peter's dwarf wedding, in which Peter and his court sniggered as some 70-odd dwarfs from all over Russia attended the marriage of Peter's favourite dwarf and the subsequent drunken party.

Academy of Arts Museum
MUSEUM

(Музей Академии Художеств; Map p179; www.nimrah.ru; Universitetskaya nab 17; adult/student ₽300/150, photos ₽500; ⌚11am-7pm Wed-Sun; Ⓜ Vasileostrovskaya) Two 3500-year-old sphinx monuments guard the entrance of the Russian Academy of Arts, and art lovers should not bypass the museum of this time-tested institution, which contains works by students and faculty since the academy's founding in 1857.

This is the original location of the academy, where boys would live from the age of five until they graduated at age 15. It was an experiment to create a new species of human: the artist. For the most part, it worked; many great Russian artists were trained here, including Ilya Repin, Karl Bryullov and Anton Losenko. But the curriculum was designed with the idea that the artist must serve the state, and this conservatism led to a reaction against it. In 1863, some 14 students left to found a new movement known as the Peredvizhniki Wanderers, which went on to revolutionise Russian art.

Nonetheless, the Academy of Arts has many achievements to show off, including numerous studies, drawings and paintings by academy members. On the 3rd floor you can examine the models for the original versions of Smolny Cathedral, St Isaac's Cathedral and the Alexander Nevsky Monastery. When you enter through the main door take the flight of stairs on your left up to the 2nd floor, where you can buy tickets.

Museum of Zoology
MUSEUM

(Зоологический музей; Map p179; www.zin.ru; Universitetskaya nab 1; adult/student ₽200/70, Thu free; ⌚11am-6pm Wed-Mon; Ⓜ Admiralteyskaya) One of the biggest and best of its kind in the world, the Museum of Zoology was founded in 1832 and has some amazing exhibits, including a vast blue whale skeleton that greets you in the first hall. The highlight is unquestionably the 44,000-year-old woolly mammoth thawed out of the Siberian ice in 1902, although there are a further three mammoths, including a baby one – all incredible finds.

On top of the extraordinarily comprehensive collection of beasts from around the globe, upstairs you'll also find thousands of categorised insects, as well as a **live-insect zoo** (adult/student ₽100/50), a favourite with kids.

👁 Petrograd Side

The Petrograd Side is a cluster of delta islands between the Malaya Neva and Bolshaya Nevka channels, including little Zayachy Island, where Peter the Great first broke ground for the city.

★ Peter & Paul Fortress FORTRESS

(Петропавловская крепость; Map p182; www.spbmuseum.ru; grounds free, exhibitions adult ₽60-150, student ₽40-80; ⊙ grounds 8.30am-8pm, exhibitions 11am-6pm Mon, Thu-Sun, 10am-5pm Tue; Ⓜ Gorkovskaya) Housing a cathedral where the Romanovs are buried, a former prison and various exhibitions, this large defensive fortress on Zayachy Island is the kernel from which St Petersburg grew into the city it is today. History buffs will love it and everyone will swoon at the panoramic views from atop the fortress walls, at the foot of which lies a sandy riverside beach, a prime spot for sunbathing.

Individual tickets are needed for each of fortress's attractions; the best deal is the combination ticket for the Peter and Paul Cathedral and the Trubetskoy Bastion (adult/child ₽350/180). The main entrance is across the Ioannovsky Bridge at the island's northeast end; there's also access via the Kronwerk Bridge, which is within walking distance of Sportivnaya metro station.

Mosque MOSQUE

(Соборная мечеть; Map p182; ☑ 812-233 9819; http://dum-spb.ru/kontakty; Kronverksky pr 7; ⊙ 7am-9pm; Ⓜ Gorkovskaya) This beautiful working mosque (built 1910–14) was modelled on Samarkand's Gur-e Amir Mausoleum. Its fluted azure dome and minarets are stunning and surprisingly prominent in the city's skyline. Outside of prayer times, if you are respectfully dressed (women should wear a head covering, men long trousers),

you can walk through the gate at the northeast side and ask the guard for entry – the interior is equally lovely.

Museum of Political History MUSEUM

(Музей политической истории России; Map p182; ☑ 812-313 6163; www.polithistory.ru; ul Kuybysheva 4; adult/student ₽150/60; ⊙ 10am-6pm Fri-Tue, to 8pm Wed; Ⓜ Gorkovskaya) The elegant Style Moderne Kshesinskaya Palace (1904) is a highly appropriate location for this excellent museum – one of the city's best – covering Russian politics in scrupulous detail up to contemporary times.

The palace, previously the home of Mathilda Kshesinskaya, famous ballet dancer and one-time lover of Nicholas II in his pre-tsar days, was briefly the headquarters of the Bolsheviks, and Lenin often gave speeches from the balcony.

Artillery Museum MUSEUM

(Музей Артиллерии; Map p182; ☑ 812-610 3301; www.artillery-museum.ru; Alexandrovsky Park 7; adult/student ₽300/150; ⊙ 11am-6pm Wed-Sun; ♿; Ⓜ Gorkovskaya) Housed in the fort's original arsenal, across the moat from the Peter & Paul Fortress, this fire-powered museum chronicles Russia's military history, with examples of weapons dating all the way back to the Stone Age. The centrepiece is Lenin's armoured car, which he rode in triumph from the Finland Station (Finlyandsky vokzal).

Kirov Museum MUSEUM

(Музей Кирова; Map p182; www.kirovmuseum.ru; Kamennoostrovsky pr 26/28; admission ₽120; ⊙ 11am-6pm Thu-Tue; Ⓜ Petrogradskaya) Leningrad party boss Sergei Kirov was one of the most powerful men in Russia in the early 1930s. His decidedly unproletarian apartment is now a fascinating museum showing how the Bolshevik elite really lived: take a quick journey back to the days of Soviet glory, including choice examples of 1920s technology, such as the first-ever Soviet-produced typewriter and a conspicuously noncommunist GE fridge, complete with plastic food inside.

Botanical Gardens GARDENS

(Ботанический сад; Map p182; ☑ 812-372 5464; http://botsad-spb.com; ul Professora Popova 2; adult/child ₽220/110; ⊙ grounds 10am-6pm Tue-Sun May-Sep, greenhouse 11am-4pm Tue-Sun year round; Ⓜ Petrogradskaya) On eastern Aptekarsky (Apothecary) Island, this was once a garden of medicinal plants – founded by Peter

Petrograd Side

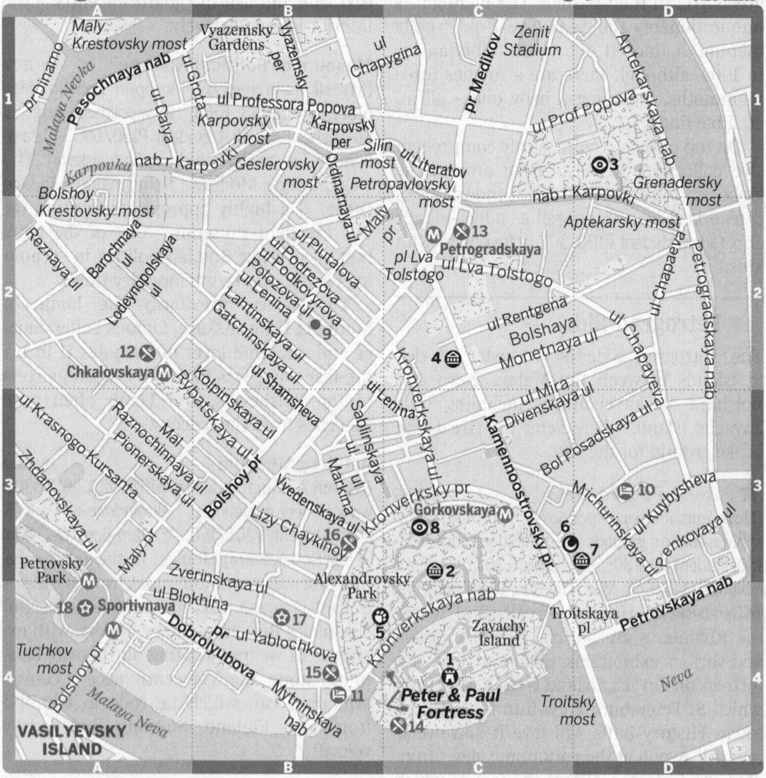

Petrograd Side

Top Sights

1 Peter & Paul Fortress C4

Sights

2 Artillery Museum C3
3 Botanical Gardens D1
4 Kirov Museum C2
5 Leningradsky Zoo B4
6 Mosque C3
7 Museum of Political History D3
8 Planetarium C3

Activities, Courses & Tours

9 Liberty B2

Sleeping

10 Hotel Aurora D3
11 Tradition Hotel B4

Eating

12 Blizkie Druzya A2
13 Chekhov C2
14 Koryushka C4
15 Le Menu B4
16 Mesto B3

Entertainment

17 Kamchatka B4
18 Petrovsky Stadium A4

the Great himself in 1714 – that gave the island its name. Today the botanical gardens contain 26 greenhouses on a 22-hectare site. It is a lovely place to stroll and a fascinating place to visit – and not just for botanists.

Kirovsky Islands

This is the collective name for the three outer delta islands of Petrograd Side – Kamenny, Yelagin and Krestovsky. Once marshy jungles, the islands were granted to 18th- and 19th-century court favourites and developed into bucolic playgrounds. Still mostly parkland, they remain huge leafy venues for picnics, river sports and White Nights cavorting.

Kamenny Island ISLAND
(Map p162; Ⓜ Chyornaya Rechka) Century-old dachas (country cottages) and mansions, inhabited by very wealthy locals, line the wooded lanes that twist their way around Kamenny (Stone) Island. The island is punctuated by a series of canals, lakes and ponds, and is pleasant for strolling at any time of year. At its east end, the **Church of St John the Baptist** (built 1776–81) has been charmingly restored.

Yelagin Island ISLAND
(Map p162; http://elaginpark.org; admission Mon-Fri free, Sat, Sun & public holidays adult/student ₽70/30; ⏲6am-11pm; 👪; Ⓜ Krestovsky Ostrov) This island is one giant park, free of traffic, and is a serene place to wander. It was attractively landscaped by the architect Carlo Rossi, and its centrepiece, also by Rossi, is the beautiful restored **Yelagin Palace** (Map p162; http://elaginpark.org; Yelagin ostrov 1; adult/child ₽150/75; ⏲10am-6pm; Ⓜ Krestovsky Ostrov), which Alexander I commissioned for his mother, Empress Maria. The gorgeous interiors, with detailed murals and incredible inlaid-wood floors, are furnished with antiques.

Krestovsky Island ISLAND
(Map p162; 👪; Ⓜ Krestovsky Ostrov) The biggest of the three northern islands, Krestovsky consists mostly of the vast **Maritime Victory Park** (Приморский парк Победы; Map p162; www.primparkpobedy.ru; Krestovsky pr; Ⓜ Krestovsky Ostrov), dotted with sports fields; at the far western end the giant **Zenit Stadium**, under construction for years, is scheduled to be ready in time for the 2018 FIFA World Cup.

At the main entrance opposite the metro station you can rent bikes and in-line skates. Also here is Divo Ostrov (p188) is a Disney-style amusement park with exciting fairground rides that kids will adore.

Vyborg Side

Attractions on the north bank of the Neva are few and far between – several of those that do exist, though, are worth seeing.

★ **Hermitage Storage Facility** MUSEUM
(Реставрационно-хранительский центр Старая деревня; Map p162; ☎812-340 1026; www.hermitagemuseum.org; Zausadebnaya ul 37A; tours ₽200; ⏲tours 11am, 1pm, 1.30pm & 3.30pm Wed-Sun; 👪; Ⓜ Staraya Derevnya) Guided tours of the Hermitage's state-of-the-art restoration and storage facility are highly recommended. This is not a formal exhibition as such, but the guides are knowledgable and the examples chosen for display (paintings, furniture and carriages) are wonderful.

The storage facility is directly behind the big shopping centre opposite the metro station – look for the enormous golden-yellow glass facility decorated with shapes inspired by petroglyphs.

The highlight is undoubtedly the gorgeous wool and silk embroidered Turkish ceremonial tent, presented to Catherine the Great by the Sultan Selim III in 1793. Beside it stands an equally impressive modern diplomatic gift: a massive wood carving of the mythical garuda bird, given by Indonesia to the city for its 300th anniversary.

Other notable displays are of ancient Russian icons and frescoes; selections from the collection of 3500 canvases by Russian

HISTORIC RAILWAY STATIONS

As the birthplace of Russia's railway system, it's not surprising that St Petersburg has some grand stations. The oldest and most elegant is the Vitebsk Station (p208), originally built in 1837 for the tsar's private train line to Tsarskoe Selo. The current building dates from 1904 and is partly graced with gorgeous Style Moderne interiors.

While you're at the Moscow Station (p207), look up at the expansive ceiling mural in the main entrance hall. There's also a striking giant bust of Peter the Great in the hall leading to the platforms.

The Finland Station (p207), rebuilt after WWII, is famous as the place where, in April 1917, Lenin arrived from exile and gave his legendary speech atop an armoured car. When the progress of the revolution began to look iffy, it was from here that Lenin hightailed it to Finland, only to return again in October to seize power. Lenin's statue, pointing across the Neva towards the old KGB headquarters, stands outside the station.

WORTH A TRIP

STREET ART MUSEUM

A 2011 graffiti party in an abandoned workshop of laminated-plastics factory Slopast sparked the grand idea of creating a **Street Art Museum** (812-448 1593; www.streetartmuseum.ru; shosse Revolutsii 84, Okhta; M Ploshchad Lenina, then bus 137 or 530). Workers at the factory in the industrial zone of Okhta, a 20-minute bus ride east of Ploshchad Lenina, were the first, fortunate audience for what is shaping up to be one of Russia's contemporary-art highlights.

Covering 11 hectares and with 150,000 to 200,000 sq metre of walls, Slopast is practically the perfect, postindustrial canvas for street artists. The factory has a busy production schedule but on a far smaller footprint of its site than during Soviet times. But it's not just the abandoned parts of the complex that are the set of a spray-canned artistic facelift. Some of the workshops are already decorated with epic works by the likes of top Russian streets artists Timothy Radya, Kirill Kto and Nikita Nomerz as well as Spanish artist Escif. Before he died in 2013, Pasha 183, frequently referred to as Russia's Banksy because of his anonymity, also contributed *Walls Don't Sleep*, a beautiful monochrome mural based on an image of Soviet factory workers.

Public tours of the complex started in mid 2014. The aim is that by 2016 the complex will have some 70 works of varying formats, the former boilerhouse will become an exhibition space, and the resin factory will be a concert venue and a skateboard park.

artists down the ages; eight giant vertically hanging tapestries that can be moved simultaneously to a musical accompaniment; a hall of imperial carriages; and a depository stacked with all kinds of furniture – a veritable imperial IKEA!

Sampsonievsky Cathedral CHURCH
(Сампсониевский собор; Map p162; www.cathedral.ru; Bolshoy Sampsonievsky pr 41; 10am-6pm Thu-Tue; M Vyborgskaya) FREE This light-blue baroque cathedral dates from 1740, and having been repainted and restored to its original glory both inside and out, glistens like a pearl amid a gritty industrial area. Its most interesting feature is the calendar of saints, two enormous panels on either side of the nave, each representing six months of the year, where every day is decorated with a mini-icon of its saint(s).

The enormous silver chandelier above the altar is also something to behold, as is the stunning baroque, green-and-golden iconostasis. Don't miss the frieze of a young Peter the Great, on the wall behind you when you face the main iconostasis.

This is also believed to be the church where Catherine the Great married her one-eyed lover Grigory Potemkin in a secret ceremony in 1774.

Buddhist Temple TEMPLE
(Буддистский Храм; Map p162; 812-239 0341; www.dazan.spb.ru; Primorsky pr 91; 10am-7pm Thu-Tue; M Staraya Derevnya) Another in the city's collection of grand religious buildings is this beautiful functioning *datsan* (temple) where respectful visitors are welcome. The main prayer hall has lovely mosaic decoration and there's a cheap and cheerful **cafe** in the basement. The temple was built between 1909 and 1915 at the instigation of Pyotr Badmaev, a Buddhist physician to Tsar Nicholas II.

Southern St Petersburg

Stalin tried to relocate the city centre to the south, and you can see some of the grand Soviet master plan along Moskovsky pr and south of the Narva Gate along pr Stachek leading to the Kirovsky Zavod heavy engineering plant. Elsewhere, dotted around southern St Petersburg, there are a few other worthwhile attractions.

Museum of Railway Technology MUSEUM
(Музей железнодорожной техники; Map p162; nab kanala Obvodnogo 118; adult/child ₽100/50; 10am-5pm Wed-Sun Apr-Oct, 11am-4pm Nov-Mar; ; M Baltiyskaya) Trainspotters should hasten to view the impressive collection of decommissioned locomotives and carriages at the Museum of Railway Technology. Some 75 nicely painted and buffed engines and carriages dating back to the late 19th century are on display, as well as a mobile intercontinental nuclear missile launcher that looks like the unlikely secret weapon of a 1960s Bond villain.

Monument to the Heroic Defenders of Leningrad MONUMENT
(Монумент героическим защитникам Ленинграда; www.spbmuseum.ru; pl Pobedy; adult/student ₽120/70; ⏲10am-6pm Thu-Mon, until 5pm Tue; Ⓜ Moskovskaya) On the way to or from the airport you won't miss the awe-inspiring Monument to the Heroic Defenders of Leningrad. Centred on a 48m-high obelisk, the monument is a sculptural ensemble of bronze statues symbolising the heavy plight of defence and eventual victory.

Chesme Church CHURCH
(Чесменская церковь; http://chesma.spb.ru; ul Lensoveta 12; admission free; ⏲10am-7pm; Ⓜ Moskovskaya) East off Moskovsky pr is the striking red-and-white 18th-century Gothic Chesma Church, built from 1774 to 1780 in honour of Russia's victory over the Turks at the Battle of Çesme (1770). Its relatively remote location is due to the fact that Catherine the Great was on this spot when news arrived of the victory, so that's where she ordered the church to be built.

Activities

St Petersburg offers plenty of ways to relax and enjoy yourself without spending days in museums. As with everywhere else in Russia, locals love to sweat it out in the *banya* (bathhouse) and there are plenty of great places for you to join them.

Cycling is a growing pastime in the city, as well as an increasingly popular mode of transport. Pancake-flat St Petersburg is a great city to explore by bike and you'll avoid the major traffic-choked roads. There's even a useful new bicycle-sharing scheme called **Velobike** (www.velobike-spb.ru) which allows you to register (₽100 per day or ₽250 per week) and then use bikes for up to 30 minutes for free.

Bathhouses & Spas

Mytninskiye Bani BANYA
(Мытнинские бани; Map p172; www.mybanya.spb.ru; Mytninskaya ul 17-19; per hr ₽100-200; ⏲8am-10pm Fri-Tue; Ⓜ Ploshchad Vosstaniya) Unique in the city, Mytninskiye Bani is heated by a wood furnace, just like the log-cabin bathhouses that are still found in the Russian countryside. It's actually the oldest communal *banya* in the city, and in addition to a *parilka* (steam room) and plunge pool, the private 'lux' *banya* includes a swanky lounge area with leather furniture and a pool table.

Degtyarniye Baths BANYA
(Дегтярные бани; Map p172; www.d1a.ru; Degtyarnaya ul 1a; per hr ₽400-1425; ⏲8.30am-10pm; Ⓜ Ploshchad Vosstaniya) These modern baths are divided up into mixed, men's and women's sections, or you can book private unisex *banyas* of varying degrees of luxury. Book ahead, though, as they are often full. English is spoken and the website has a helpful English-language guide to how to take a *banya* for novices.

Cycling

Skatprokat CYCLING
(Map p172; ☎812-717 6838; www.skatprokat.ru; Goncharnaya ul 7; per day from ₽400; ⏲11am-8pm; Ⓜ Ploshchad Vosstaniya) This outfit offers rental bicycles that include brand-new mountain bikes by the Russian company Stark. You'll need to leave either ₽2000 and your passport, or ₽7000 as a deposit per bike. If you are in town for a while, this place also sells secondhand bikes and does repairs. It also offers excellent Saturday- and Sunday-morning bike tours of the city

Rentbike CYCLING
(Map p162; ☎812-981 0155; www.rentbike.org; ul Yefimova 4a; per day from ₽400; ⏲24hr; Ⓜ Sennaya Ploshchad) This centrally located company rents out well-maintained bikes at good rates. It will also deliver to your hotel for free if you're staying in the city centre. You'll need to leave a passport or ID card with them with a deposit of ₽2000 per bike.

The place is a little tricky to find, off ul Yefimova and through two car parks; see the website for details.

Tours

In a city as large and foreign as St Petersburg, a lot of travellers prefer (at least initially) to be shown around on a walking tour to kick things off. There are several excellent ones on offer, as well as bike tours and a hop-on, hop-off bus that can take you around the main sights of the centre. Viewing St Petersburg from a boat is an idyllic way to tour the city, and during the main tourist season (May to October) there are plenty of boats offering to help you do this. They are typically found at the Anichkov most landing on the Fontanka River, just off Nevsky pr; on the Neva outside the Hermitage and the Admiralty; beside the Kazansky most over the Griboyedova Canal; and along the Moyka River at Nevsky pr.

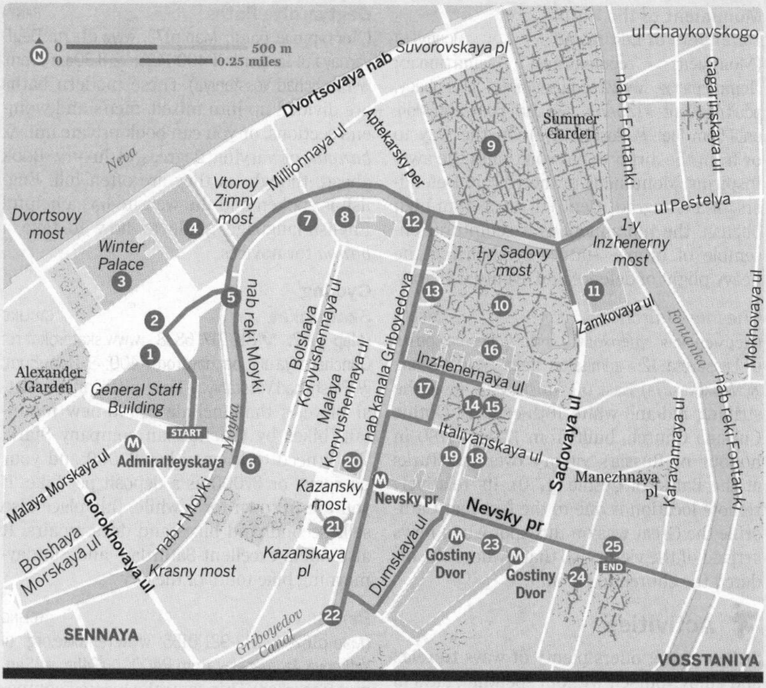

Walking Tour Historic Heart

START DVORTSOVAYA PL (NEVSKY PR)
FINISH KUPETZ ELISEEVS (GOSTINY DVOR)
LENGTH 2KM; TWO HOURS

Approach 1 **Dvortsovaya pl** (Palace Sq) from Bolshaya Morskaya ul. Turning the corner from Nevsky pr, behold the 2 **Alexander Column**, framed under the triumphal arch. Ahead is the 3 **Hermitage** (p212); don't miss the colossal 4 **Atlantes** holding aloft the portico fronting the Large Hermitage.

At the 5 **Moyka River** look northwest for a wonderful view of the Neva; to the south is the lavish 6 **Stroganov Palace** (p165). Head north along nab reki Moyki to No 12, final residence of Russia's most celebrated poet and now the 7 **Pushkin Flat-Museum** (p170).

8 **Konyushennaya pl** is dominated by 18th-century court stables currently being restored. Formerly the imperial guard parade grounds, 9 **Mars Field** (p170) became a burial ground for revolution and civil-war victims. South is the canal-side 10 **Mikhailovsky Gardens** (p188) and the unusual 11 **Mikhailovsky Castle** (p169).

Near the intersection of the Moyka and Kanal Griboyedova, 12 **Teatralny most** gives a spectacular perspective on the 13 **Church on the Spilled Blood** (p164).

Centred on a 14 **Pushkin statue**, pretty 15 **pl Iskusstv** (Arts Sq) is ringed by cultural institutions, including the 16 **Russian Museum** (p164), 17 **Mikhailovsky Theatre** (p203) and 18 **Shostakovich Philharmonia** (p203), as well as the historic 19 **Grand Hotel Europe** (p191).

The Style Moderne 20 **Singer Building**, on the corner of Nevsky and the canal, provides a contrast to formidable 21 **Kazan Cathedral** (p165) opposite. Behind it, 22 **Bankovsky most** is the city's most picturesque bridge.

Crowds pour out of the metro at 23 **Gostiny Dvor**. The National Library of Russia, Alexandrinsky Theatre and Anichkov Palace surround 24 **pl Ostrovskogo** (p170) (Ostrovsky Sq). Finish at one of the cafes in the grand food hall 25 **Kupetz Eliseevs**.

WORTH A TRIP

RIZZORDI ART FOUNDATION

If you've visited the galleries of Ligovsky pr and Vosstaniya, and you're still looking for some more contemporary art, head out to the **Rizzordi Art Foundation** (Map p162; ☎812-643 0483; www.rizzordi.org; 4th floor, Kurlyandskaya ul 49; ⊙noon-8pm during exhibits; Ⓜ Baltiyskaya) FREE, the most exciting contemporary-art venue in the city. Opened in summer 2011, this impressive factory conversion is worth seeing in itself – it's a huge space taking up the top two floors of a disused 19th-century brewery. Very interesting temporary exhibits from local up-and-coming artists are showcased here. Half the adventure is just getting to the site (not to mention the incredible postindustrial wasteland you have to travel through). It's a 30-minute walk from Baltiyskaya metro, or you can take bus 49 from Sennaya pl towards Dvinskaya ul and get off at Kurlyandskaya ul, the second stop after you cross the Fontanka River.

★Peter's Walking Tours WALKING TOURS
(☎812-943 1229; www.peterswalk.com; scheduled tours per person ₽750 per person; ⊙scheduled tours Apr-Oct) Established in 1996, Peter Kozyrev's innovative and passionately led tours are highly recommended as a way to see the city with knowledgable locals. The daily Original Peterswalk is one of the favourites and leaves daily from Hostel Life (p192) at 10.30am from mid April to late October.

The choice of tours available is enormous and include a Friday-night pub crawl, a Rasputin Walk and a WWII and the Siege of Leningrad tour.

★Sputnik Tours WALKING TOURS
(www.sputnik8.com) This online tour agency is one with a difference: it acts as a marketplace for locals wanting to give their own unique tours of their own city. Browse, select a tour, register and pay a deposit and then you get given the contact number of the guide. A superb way to meet locals you'd never meet otherwise.

Anglo Tourismo BOAT, WALKING
(Map p166; ☎921-989 4722; www.anglotourismo.com; 27 nab reki Fontanki; 1hr tour adult/student ₽650/550; Ⓜ Gostiny Dvor) There's a huge number of companies offering cruises all over the Historic Centre, all with similar prices and itineraries. However, Anglo Tourismo is the only operator to run tours with commentary in English. Between May and September the schedule runs every 1½ hours between 11am and 6.30pm. From 1 June to 31 August there are also additional night cruises.

The company also runs free daily walking tours starting at 10.30am and lasting three hours.

VB Excursions WALKING TOURS
(Map p162; ☎812-380 4596; www.vb-excursions.com) Offers excellent walking tours with clued-up students on themes including Dostoevsky and Revolutionary St Petersburg. Its 'Back in the USSR' tour (₽2300 per person) includes a visit to a typical Soviet apartment for tea and bliny.

Liberty TOURS
(Map p182; ☎812-232 8163; www.libertytour.ru; ul Polozova 12, Office 1; Ⓜ Petrogradskaya) Specialising in wheelchair-accessible tours in and around St Petersburg, this unique-in-Russia company has specially fitted vans. It can also advise on and book hotels with rooms for the disabled.

Festivals & Events

Whether through the carnival atmosphere of White Nights or merrymaking during the freezing, dark winter days, Petersburgers love to celebrate festivals or special events.

April

Mariinsky Ballet Festival BALLET
(www.mariinsky.ru) The city's principal dance theatre hosts this week-long international ballet festival, where the cream of Russian ballet dancers showcase their talents.

Easter CHRISTIAN
(Paskha) Head to Kazan Cathedral to see Russia's most important religious festival in full Russian Orthodox style: the church (as well as many others around the city) is packed out.

May

Victory Day CELEBRATION
On 9 May, St Petersburg celebrates not only the end of WWII in 1945 but also the breaking of the Nazi blockade. The highlight is a

victory parade on Nevsky pr, culminating in soldiers marching on Dvortsovaya pl and fireworks over the Neva in the evening.

City Day ANNIVERSARY
Mass celebrations are held throughout the city centre on 27 May, the city's official birthday, known as *den goroda* (city day). Brass bands, folk dancing and mass drunkenness are the salient features of this perennial favourite.

June & July

Stars of the White Nights Festival MUSIC
(www.mariinsky.ru) Held at the Mariinsky, the Conservatoire and the Hermitage Theatre, this festival from late May until July has become a huge draw and now lasts far longer than the White Nights (officially the last 10 days of June) after which it is named. You'll see ballet, opera and classical music concerts premiered and reprised.

Festival of Festivals FILM
(www.filmfest.ru) This annual international film festival held in late June is a noncompetitive showcase of the best Russian and world cinema.

September & October

Early Music Festival MUSIC
(www.earlymusic.ru) Held from mid-September until early October, this ground-breaking musical festival includes performances of forgotten masterpieces from the Middle Ages, the Renaissance and the baroque era. Musicians come from around the world to perform here.

December

Arts Square Winter Festival MUSIC
(www.artsquarewinterfest.ru) A musical highlight of the year, this festival held from late December to early January at the Philharmonia takes different themes each year. Both classical and contemporary opera and orchestral works are staged.

Sleeping

There has been a revolution in hotel accommodation in St Petersburg over the past decade and a large expansion of modern, professionally run establishments. That said, most hotels are still fairly expensive, with a real lack of good, midrange places in the city centre. They do exist, however, but tend to get booked up well in advance (particularly during the summer months), so book ahead if you want to be in the Historic Centre.

ST PETERSBURG FOR CHILDREN

There's heaps to do with kids in St Petersburg – there are even museums your kids will like. Older children will appreciate the Kunstkamera (p178), an all-time favourite for its display of mutant babies in jars, while all age groups will like the Museum of Zoology (p180) for its stuffed animals and live insect zoo. The Artillery Museum (p181) makes for great fun climbing on its impressive collection of tanks.

Other big hitters for children include **Leningradsky Zoo** (Ленинградский зоопарк; Map p182; www.spbzoo.ru; Alexandrovsky Park 1; adult/child ₽400/150; ⏲10am-6pm; 👪; Ⓜ Gorkovskaya), which is worth visiting for its range of species, including a large number of polar bears. There's also a **Planetarium** (Планетарий; Map p182; ☎812-233 2653; www.planetary-spb.ru; Alexandrovsky Park 4; adult/child ₽350/150; ⏲10.30am-6pm; Ⓜ Gorkovskaya) here, which might interest older children.

The city's parks are charming, and many have kids' playgrounds with swings, roundabouts and climbing frames: check out the Tauride Gardens (p171) and the **Mikhailovsky Gardens** (Map p166; ⏲10am-10pm May-Sep, 10am-8pm Oct-Mar, closed Apr; Ⓜ Nevsky Prospekt) FREE. For more high-tech amusements there's always the **Divo Ostrov** (Map p162; www.divo-ostrov.ru; rides ₽50-300; ⏲noon-7pm; 👪; Ⓜ Krestovsky Ostrov) FREE amusement park on Krestovsky Island (p183). And if you need the little darlings to burn off even more energy, check out some of the city's boat, bicycle and in-line skate hiring opportunities.

Theatres in town catering to kids include a couple offering puppet shows and, of course, the circus. Several restaurants also have childrens' play sections; there are particularly good ones at Botanika (p195), Yat (p195), Stroganoff Steak House (p198) and Teplo (p197).

Rates quoted here are for the high season (generally from mid-May to the end of August). Rates drop substantially during the November to March low season.

At the budget end of the spectrum (under ₽3000), more Western-style hostels have continued to open up – which is great news for cash-strapped travellers since St Petersburg remains a pricey city in which to bed down. If cost is an issue, consider homestays and apartment rentals: the latter can work out as the best deal for groups of travellers or families.

ACCOMMODATION AGENCIES

The following recommended agencies can help you with short-term accommodation in St Petersburg:

Bed & Breakfast (www.bednbreak fast.sp.ru)

City Realty (www.cityrealtyrussia.com)

HOFA (www.hofa.ru)

Intro by Irina (www.introbyirina.com)

Travel Russia (www.travelrussia.su)

Historic Centre

★Baby Lemonade Hostel HOSTEL $

(Map p166; ☎812-570 7943; www.facebook.com/pages/Baby-Lemonade-Hostel; Inzhhernernaya ul 7; dm/d with shared bathroom, incl breakfast from ₽790/2590, d with bathroom from ₽3250; @☎; Ⓜ Gostiny Dvor) The owner of Baby Lemonade is crazy about the 1960s and it shows in the pop-art, psychedelic design of this friendly, fun hostel with two pleasant, large dorms and a great kitchen and living room. However, it's worth splashing out for the boutique-hotel-worthy private rooms that are in a separate flat with great rooftop views.

★Friends Hostel on Griboedov HOSTEL $

(Map p166; ☎812-571 0151; www.friendsplace.ru; nab kanala Griboyedova 20; dm/d ₽500/2500; @☎; Ⓜ Nevsky Prospekt) In a quiet courtyard near Kazan Cathedral, this is our favourite out of the many branches of this truly friendly, very colourful hostel chain. The dorms and rooms are spotless, have lockers and share good bathrooms and a kitchen. Perks include free international calls, English-speaking staff and organised daily events such as pub crawls and historical walks.

The following are the other locations: **Friends on Bankovsky** (Map p166; ☎812-310 4950; www.friendsplace.ru/druzya-na-bankovskom; Bankovsky per 3; dm/r with shared bathroom ₽800/2500; @☎; Ⓜ Sennaya Pl), **Friends on Nevsky** (Map p172; ☎812-272 7178; www.friendsplace.ru/druzya-na-nevskom; Nevsky pr 106; dm/r with shared bathroom ₽800/2500; @☎; Ⓜ Mayakovskaya), **Friends on Chekhova** (Map p172; ☎812-272 7178; www.friendsplace.ru/druzya-na-chehova/; ul Chekhova 11; r with shared bathroom from ₽2500; @☎; Ⓜ Mayakovskaya), **Friends on Vosstaniya** (Map p172; ☎812-401 6155; www.en.friendsplace.ru/friends-on-vosstaniya; ul Vosstaniya 11; dm/r with shared bathroom ₽800/2700; @☎; Ⓜ Ploshchad Vosstaniya), **Friends on Kazanskaya** (Map p166; ☎812-331 7799; www.friendsplace.ru/druzya-na-kazanskaya; Kazanskaya ul 11; r with shared bathroom ₽2600; @☎; Ⓜ Nevsky Prospekt) and **Friends by the Hermitage** (Map p166; ☎921-429 2640; www.friendsplace.ru/friends-by-the-hermitage; ul Bolshaya Konyushennaya 11; dm/r with shared bathroom ₽800/3000; @☎; Ⓜ Admiralteyskaya). There are also several Friends apartments.

Cuba Hostel HOSTEL $

(Map p166; ☎812-921 7115; www.cubahostel.ru; Kazanskaya ul 5; dm/tw from ₽500/1350; @☎; Ⓜ Nevsky Prospekt) One of the first contemporary-styled hostels in town is still a great place to stay. Rainbow-coloured paint covers the walls in dorm rooms that are equipped with metal bunk beds and private lockers. Bathrooms are cramped, but very clean. Staff members are young, speak English and are eager to please.

★Rachmaninov Antique Hotel BOUTIQUE HOTEL $$

(Map p166; ☎812-327 7466; www.hotelrachmaninov.com; Kazanskaya ul 5; s/d incl breakfast from ₽6300/7100; @☎; Ⓜ Nevsky Prospekt) The long-established Rachmaninov still feels like a secret place for those in the know. Perfectly located and run by friendly staff, it's pleasantly old world with hardwood floors and attractive Russian furnishings, particularly in the breakfast salon which has a grand piano.

Each bedroom door has been individually painted by a local artist, turning the hallways into an interesting gallery.

Casa Leto BOUTIQUE HOTEL $$

(Map p166; ☎812-314 6622; http://casaleto.com; Bolshaya Morskaya ul 34; r incl breakfast from

WORTH A TRIP

REPINO РЕПИНО

Come summer, St Petersburgers stream out of the city to relax on the beaches to the north between Sestroretsk and Zelenogorsk on the Gulf of Finland. Between these two towns you'll find the village of Repino, 45km from St Petersburg. From 1918 to the end of WWII, this area was part of Finland and the village was known as Kuokkala. In 1948, back in Russian hands, the village was renamed in honour of its most famous resident, Ilya Repin.

The artist's charming house and small estate, **Penates** (adult/student ₽300/100; ⏲museum 10.30am-6pm Wed-Sun, grounds to 8pm), is now a museum and park, and it's a pleasant day trip any time of year. You can also visit the nearby beach and even stay in one of the area's many resort-style hotels and sanatoriums in the summer.

Repin bought land here in 1899, named the estate after a Roman household god and designed the light-flooded house in an arts-and-crafts style. The artist produced many of his later works here and several of his paintings still hang on the walls. The furnishings have been left just as they were during Repin's residence, which was up to his death in 1930. His grave, marked by a simple Russian Orthodox wooden cross, is in the park, along with a couple of wooden follies also designed by Repin.

Next to Penates there are a couple of decent cafes for lunch. The nearest, also called **Penates** (mains ₽200-450; ⏲11am-5pm), serves a range of Russian dishes including salads, soups and various shashlyks. A little further down the road towards the heart of Repino village is the far more upmarket **Skazka** (mains ₽500-1000; ⏲11am-11pm), which offers a very meaty menu and even has rabbits in hutches scattered about the premises (though they are apparently decorative and not for eating).

The easiest way to get to Repino is to take the frequent *marshrutky* 400 (fixed-route minibus, ₽85, one hour) that leave from just outside Finlyandsky vokzal, or bus 211 (₽60, one hour) from beside Chyornya Rechka metro station. Be sure to tell the driver that you want to get out at Penates.

₽7900; ❄@📶; Ⓜ Admiralteyskaya) A dramatically lit stone stairwell sets the scene for this discreet and stylish boutique hotel with five guest rooms named after famous St Petersburg architects. With king-size beds, heated floors, soft pastel shades and plenty of antiques, the spacious, high-ceilinged quarters are deserving of such namesakes.

Pushka Inn BOUTIQUE HOTEL **$$**
(Map p166; ☎812-312 0913; www.pushkainn.ru; nab reki Moyki 14; s/d incl breakfast from ₽6000/11,500; ❄📶👪; Ⓜ Admiralteyskaya) On a particularly picturesque stretch of the Moyka River, this charming inn is housed in an historic 18th-century building. The rooms are decorated in dusky pinks and caramel tones, with wide floorboards and – if you're willing to pay more – lovely views of the Moyka.

Multibedroom family-style apartments are also available from ₽17,000.

3MostA BOUTIQUE HOTEL **$$**
(Map p166; ☎812-332 3470; www.3mosta.com; nab reki Moyki 3a; s/d from ₽4500/8000; ❄📶; Ⓜ Nevsky Prospekt) Near three bridges over the Moyka River, this 26-room property is surprisingly uncramped given its wonderful location. Even the standard rooms are of a good size with tasteful furniture, minibars and TVs. Some rooms have great views across to the Church on the Spilled Blood, and all guests have access to the roof for the panoramic experience.

Anichkov Pension HOTEL **$$**
(Map p166; ☎812-314 7059; www.anichkov.com; apt 4 Nevsky pr 64; s/d incl breakfast ₽5240/6460; ❄📶; Ⓜ Gostiny Dvor) On the 3rd floor of a handsome apartment building with an antique lift, this self-styled pension has just six rooms. The standard rooms are fine, but the suites are well worth paying a little more for. The delightful breakfast room offers balcony views of the bridge from which the pension takes its name. Look for the entrance on Karavannaya ul.

Vodogray Hotel HOTEL **$$**
(Map p166; ☎812-570 1717; www.vodogray-hotel.ru; Karavannaya ul 2; s/d with breakfast from ₽4000/6000; 📶; Ⓜ Gostiny Dvor) Its Ukranian country-cottage style, all pretty patchwork

quilts, pillows and dried flowers, puts this well-located minihotel in a grade of its own. Breakfast is served in the even more stylised Ukranian restaurant on the ground floor.

★ Rossi Hotel BOUTIQUE HOTEL $$$

(Map p166; ☎812-635 6333; www.rossihotels.com; nab reki Fontanki 55; s/d/ste incl breakfast from ₽12,000/12,900/18,000; ❄@📶; Ⓜ Gostiny Dvor) Occupying a beautifully restored building on one of St Petersburg's prettiest squares, the Rossi's 53 rooms are all designed differently, but their brightness and moulded ceilings are uniform. Antique beds, super-sleek bathrooms, exposed-brick walls and lots of cool designer touches create a great blend of old and new.

The best rooms have superb views over the Fontanka River. A new spa with sauna and plunge pool adds to overall cachet.

★ W Hotel LUXURY HOTEL $$$

(Map p166; ☎812-610 6161; www.wstpetersburg.com; Voznesensky pr 6; r from ₽18,630; ❄@📶🏊; Ⓜ Admiralteyskaya) If you're familiar with the W brand, then little at its St Petersburg outpost will disappoint. Rooms in several different categories are spacious and luxurious, with contemporary styling. The lobby is also a very inviting space.

The rooftop MiXup Bar (p200) offers superb views, there's good food at the Alain Ducasse restaurant MiX (p195), and there's a beautiful spa with sauna, Jacuzzi, treatment rooms and plunge pool.

Belmond Grand Hotel Europe LUXURY HOTEL $$$

(Map p166; ☎812-329 6000; www.grandhoteleurope.com; Mikhailovskaya ul 1/7; r/ste from ₽18,000/41,890; ❄@📶🏊; Ⓜ Nevsky Prospekt) Since 1830, when Carlo Rossi united three adjacent buildings with the grandiose facade we see today, little has been allowed to change in this heritage building. No two rooms are the same at this iconic hotel, but most are spacious and elegant in design.

Regular guests quite rightly swear by the terrace rooms that afford spectacular views across the city's rooftops.

Angleterre Hotel LUXURY HOTEL $$$

(Map p166; ☎812-494 5666; www.angleterrehotel.com; Malaya Morskaya ul 24; r/ste from ₽12,000/47,000; ❄@📶🏊; Ⓜ Admiralteyskaya) With supremely comfortable king-sized beds, huge bathrooms and a confidently understated style, the Angleterre's best rooms provide breathtaking views of St Isaac's Cathedral. More pluses are a great fitness centre, a small pool, a cinema showing original-language movies, and an excellent Italian restaurant, Borsalino.

Liteyny & Smolny

Red House Hostel HOSTEL $

(Map p172; ☎812-380 7527, 8-921-443 8424; www.redhousehostel.com; Liteyny pr 46, Smolny; dm/d incl breakfast from ₽550/1990; 🚭📶; Ⓜ Mayakovskaya) With its very desirable central location and unusually interesting building, the Red House Hostel is a great choice. There's a Jimi Hendrix theme, and while the dorms are somewhat cramped, there's a very friendly atmosphere, good communal areas and even a double room available. Other services include a washing machine (₽100) and bike hire.

Green Apple Hotel HOTEL $$

(Map p172; ☎812-272 1023; www.greenapplehotel.ru; ul Korolenko 14, Smolny; s/d/tr incl breakfast from ₽2700/3200/3700; 🚭❄📶; Ⓜ Chernyshevskaya) This stylish, thoroughly modern 15-room hotel in the backstreets of Liteyny has the feel of an adult youth hostel. Some of the best-value rooms are the so-called *ekonom* (economy) ones, which sleep up to three people (the third bed is on a mezzanine). They're a great bargain, as the location is good, and there's also a communal kitchen you can use.

Arbat Nord Hotel BOUTIQUE HOTEL $$

(Map p172; ☎812-703 1899; www.arbat-nord.ru; Artilleriyskaya ul 4, Smolny; s/d incl breakfast ₽3900/4600; ❄@📶; Ⓜ Chernyshevskaya) Facing an unsightly Soviet-era hotel across the street, the sleek, modern Arbat Nord seems to be showing its neighbour how to run a good establishment. The modern rooms are decorated in gold and green hues, and even though the furniture is fairly cheap, there's plenty of space. Efficient English-speaking staff are on hand and the welcome is warm.

Pio on Mokhovaya B&B $$

(Map p172; ☎812-273 3585; www.hotelpio.ru; Mokhovaya ul 39, Smolny; s/d/tr/q incl breakfast ₽4200/5000/6000/6800; 🚭📶👪; Ⓜ Chernyshevskaya) This lovely lodging is the second Pio property in St Petersburg. It's very spacious, stylish and comfortable, as well as being child friendly, with family groups warmly welcomed and provided for. It's in a quiet, residential neighbourhood a short walk from the Historic Centre. There is also a Finnish sauna on-site. Call 10 on the interphone to be buzzed in.

Hotel Indigo HOTEL $$

(Map p172; ☎812-454 5577; www.indigospb.com; ul Chaykovskogo 17, Smolny; r from ₽6300; ; Ⓜ Chernyshevskaya) A total overhaul of the original building, a prerevolutionary hotel in its day, has paved the way for the brand new Hotel Indigo, a sleek and stylish hotel with an excellent management team. The incredible atrium makes even the interior-facing rooms light-filled, and touches such as rain showers and free minibars in rooms are also very welcome.

Super city views, a gym, sauna and small pool complete this excellent and much-needed midrange deal.

Vladimirskaya & Vosstaniya

Location Hostel HOSTEL $

(Map p172; ☎812-329 1274; www.hostel74.ru; Ligovsky pr 74, Vosstaniya; dm/r from ₽700/1500, design rooms ₽6000; ; Ⓜ Ligovsky Prospekt) Come and stay in St Petersburg's coolest art gallery and cultural space – the 3rd floor of Loft Project ETAGI is given over to this superfriendly hostel. Some of the dorms here are enormous (one has 20 beds in it!) but the facilities are spotless, and include washing machines and a small kitchen.

As well as the dorms there are three 'design rooms' that are boutique hotel quality at budget price.

All You Need Hostel HOSTEL $

(Map p172; ☎8-921-950 0574; www.youneedhostel.com; ul Rubinshteyna 6, Vosstaniya; dm from ₽650; ; Ⓜ Mayakovskaya) With one of the best locations in town, this friendly and stylish hostel is basically one large apartment with three dorm bedrooms sleeping six to 12. Each room has lockers and wooden bunks, while the kitchen and sitting room are spacious, the latter having a balcony overlooking buzzing ul Rubinshteyna. Be prepared for chalk stains from the walls!

Hostel Life HOSTEL $

(Map p172; ☎812-318 1808; www.hostel-life.ru; Nevsky pr 47, Vosstaniya; dm from ₽950, tw/tr ₽3325/3515; ; Ⓜ Mayakovskaya) From the moment you arrive you're made to feel at home – slippers are provided – and the premises are spacious and bright. The 15 rooms range from doubles to dorms sleeping eight and Room 7 has an amazing corner window on Nevsky pr – surely the best view available for this low price!

There's a big kitchen, clean bathrooms, free laundry and professional English-speaking staff – all in all, a great option.

Helvetia Hotel & Suites HOTEL $$

(Map p172; ☎812-326 5353; www.helvetiahotel.ru; ul Marata 11, Vosstaniya; r incl breakfast from ₽6650; ; Ⓜ Mayakovskaya) Pass through the wrought-iron gates into a wonderfully private and professionally run oasis of calm and class. The rooms may be a little less atmospheric than the early 19th-century exterior might suggest, but they make up for it in comfort, each having a bathtub, safe and minibar. The buffet breakfast is excellent and there are two on-site restaurants.

Official State Hermitage Hotel LUXURY HOTEL $$$

(Map p172; ☎812-777 9810; www.thehermitagehotel.ru; ul Pravdy 10, Vosstaniya; r from ₽9410; ; Ⓜ Zvenigorodskaya/Vladimirskaya) Despite its rather odd location, which is central but rather incongruously run-down for a hotel with such lofty aspirations, the 126-room Official State Hermitage Hotel is a dazzling affair with enough Italian marble and chandeliers to keep even the fussiest of Romanovs happy. Rooms are spacious and old-world elegant without being too chintzy, and Hermès goodies stuff the bathrooms.

The Hermitage connection is fairly weak: there's a free shuttle bus to the museum every two hours, and guests staying for more than three nights get free entry as well.

Sennaya & Kolomna

★ **Soul Kitchen Hostel** HOSTEL $

(Map p176; ☎8-965-816 3470; www.soulkitchenhostel.com; apt 9, nab reki Moyki 62/2, Sennaya; dm/d from ₽900/3600; ; Ⓜ Admiralteyskaya) Soul Kitchen blends boho hipness and boutique-hotel comfort, scoring perfect 10s in many key categories: private rooms (chic), dorm beds (double-wide with privacy-protecting curtains), common areas (vast), kitchen (vast *and* beautiful) and bathrooms (downright inviting). There is also bike hire, table football, free Macs to use, free international phone calls and stunning Moyka views from a communal balcony.

★ **Hello Hostel** HOSTEL $

(Map p176; ☎812-643 2556; www.hellohostel.ru; Angliyskaya nab 50, Kolomna; dm incl breakfast ₽600-1000, d without bathroom ₽2500-3000;

⊘📶; Ⓜ Admiralteyskaya) This eclectic, arty hostel has a party vibe thanks to its popular lobby bar, and nice touches such as film screenings on its impressive central staircase. The big dorm rooms have extra-tall wooden bunk beds, some with curtains for privacy, and incredible (if semidecayed) ceiling mouldings. There are also four good-value private doubles.

The hostel occupies a gorgeous historic building on the Neva embankment, and still has the atmosphere of the communal flat it was under the Soviets. Welcome extras include free washing machine use, bike hire (₽600 per 24 hours) and superb Neva views.

★ Andrey & Sasha's Homestay APARTMENT $$
(Map p166; ☎8-921-409 6701, 812-315 3330; asamatuga@mail.ru; nab kanala Griboyedova 51, Sennaya; s/d ₽2600/4000; Ⓜ Sadovaya) Energetic Italophiles Andrey and Sasha extend the warmest of welcomes to travellers lucky enough to rent out one of their three apartments (by the room or in their entirety). All are centrally located and eclectically decorated with lots of designer touches and an eye for beautiful furniture, tilework and mirrors. Bathrooms are shared, as are kitchen facilities.

Socialising is definitely encouraged, and your hosts will likely invite you to join them sipping wine by the fire or drinking coffee on the rooftop. Staying here is a great way to get to know the city through bohemian locals.

Hotel Gogol HOTEL $$
(Map p176; ☎812-571 1841; www.gogolhotel.com; nab kanala Griboyedova 69, Sennaya; s/d from ₽3600/4500; ⊘❄📶; Ⓜ Sadovaya) There's great value to be had at this centrally located hotel, a conversion of the house where the great writer Nikolai Gogol himself apparently once lived. The rooms are cosy and enjoy inoffensive decoration, with views over the canal or a quiet residential courtyard. Reception is on the 2nd floor, and there's a basement restaurant.

Hotel Domina Prestige HOTEL $$$
(Map p176; ☎812-385 9900; www.dominarussia.com; nab Reki Moyki 99, Sennaya; r from ₽7590; ⊘❄📶; Ⓜ Admiralteyskaya) This excellent new property makes an immediate impression as its traditional Moyka embankment exterior gives way to a bright, modern and colourful atrium. Some of the decor is undoubtedly rather Russian in taste, but it's still stylish and fun. Rooms are comfortable and spacious, with extras such as coffee facilities and great bathrooms. There's also a sauna, gym and restaurant.

★ Alexander House BOUTIQUE HOTEL $$$
(Map p176; ☎812-334 3540; www.a-house.ru; nab kanala Kryukova 27, Kolomna; s/d incl breakfast from ₽10,625/11,475; ⊘❄📶; Ⓜ Sadovaya) Owners Alexander and Natalya have converted this historic building opposite the Nikolsky Cathedral, styling each of the 14 spacious rooms after their favourite international cities. While these can vary in success and taste, when they get it right, the effect is great. Lovely common areas include a fireplace-warmed lounge and a vine-laden courtyard containing a guests-only restaurant. Book in advance.

Vasilyevsky Island

NasHotel HOTEL $$
(Map p179; ☎812-323 2231; www.nashotel.ru; 11-ya liniya 50; s/d from ₽5800/6400; ❄📶; Ⓜ Vasileostrovskaya) Despite being half a decade old, this spotless place still looks like it has just opened. The very tall, beautifully remodelled building on this quiet side street has a striking exterior and its rooms are blazes of colours, complete with modern furnishings and great views from the higher floors.

Garish touches include some truly dreadful room art and a preponderance of plants throughout, but these gripes aside, this is generally a smart and stylish modern hotel.

Sokos Hotel Vasilyevsky HOTEL $$$
(Map p179; ☎812-335 2290; www.sokoshotels.com; 8-ya liniya 11-13; r from ₽8500; ⊘❄📶; Ⓜ Vasileostrovskaya) This surprisingly enormous hotel has more than 200 rooms, although you hardly notice it from the street. It's a sleek, well-designed place aimed at business travellers and the upper end of the holiday market. The rooms are spacious, with nice design touches, while the large Repin Lounge downstairs takes care of all food and drink needs.

Petrograd & Vyborg Side

Hotel Aurora HOTEL $
(Map p182; ☎812-233 3641; www.hotel-aurora.ru; Malaya Posadskaya ul 15; s/d incl breakfast with shared bathroom ₽2100/2800, with private bathroom ₽2450/3150; 📶; Ⓜ Gorkovskaya) Not far from the Peter & Paul Fortress, this spunky

minihotel offers affordable, friendly accommodation. The four spacious rooms sport quaintly charming, Soviet-style decor, with parquet floors, rickety beds and monochrome linens. Nonetheless, sparkling clean bathrooms and a kitchen make this an excellent deal.

Tradition Hotel HOTEL $$$
(Map p182; 812-405 8855; www.tradition-hotel.ru; pr Dobrolyubova 2; s/d incl breakfast ₽11,220/12,710; Sportivnaya) This charming small hotel is a consistent traveller favourite due to its smiling, helpful staff who really go out of their way for guests. Its rooms are comfortable and well appointed with good-size bathrooms and a vaguely antique style.

Eating

It may have taken two decades since the end of communism, but finally Petersburg has become a place where good food is prized and defined not by its high price tag but rather by the talents of the chef. You certainly have to pay for quality in most cases, and it's worth planning where you'd like to eat rather than leaving it to the last moment and choosing the nearest place, as the good places are rarely the most obvious.

Many places have bargain business-lunch deals for around ₽150 to ₽250 and offer 15% discounts to diners eating before 4pm, making lunch the most economical time to eat out.

Historic Centre

★ **Marketplace** RUSSIAN, INTERNATIONAL $
(Map p166; http://market-place.me; Nevsky pr 24; mains ₽200-300; 9am-6am; Nevsky Prospekt) The most central branch of this minichain that brings a high-class polish to the self-serve canteen concept with many dishes cooked freshly on the spot to order. The hip design of the multilevel space is very appealing, making this a great spot to linger, especially if you indulge in one of the desserts or cocktails served on the 1st floor.

Stolovaya No 1 Kopeika RUSSIAN $
(Столовая No.1 Копейка; Map p166; Nevsky pr 25; mains ₽25-50, set lunch ₽99; 24hr; Nevsky Prospekt) We doubt there are cheaper places to eat this well on Nevsky – no wonder the lines are long at this self-serve canteen in a cheerfully decorated basement. It's standard Russian dishes but all are freshly prepared and available around the clock.

Troitsky Most VEGETARIAN $
(Map p166; www.t-most.ru; nab reki Moyki 27; mains ₽200-300; 9am-11pm; Admiralteyskaya) This is the most central branch of the excellent vegie-cafe chain. It serves up the same excellent fare, including great vegetarian lasagne, in a cosy interior.

★ **Jack & Chan** INTERNATIONAL $
(Map p166; http://jack-and-chan.com; Inzhenernaya ul 7; mains ₽350; 10am-midnight; Gostiny Dvor) The restaurant name, a punning reference to Jackie Chan in Russian, neatly sums up the burger-meets-Asian menu at this fine and stylish casual diner. Try the sweet-and-sour fish and the prawn-and-avocado salad with glass noodles.

Zoom Cafe EUROPEAN $
(Map p166; www.cafezoom.ru; Gorokhovaya ul 22; mains ₽300-450; 9am-midnight Mon-Sat, from 11am Sat, from 1pm Sun; Nevsky Prospekt) A perennially popular cafe (expect to wait for a table at peak times) with a funky feel and an interesting menu, ranging from Japanese-style chicken in teriyaki sauce to potato pancakes with salmon and cream cheese. Well-stocked bookshelves, a range of board games and adorable cuddly toys encourage lingering.

Soup Vino MEDITERRANEAN $
(Map p166; 812-312 7690; www.supvino.ru; Kazanskaya ul 24; mains ₽310-410; noon-11pm; Nevsky Prospekt) This tiny place is a foodie dream. Fresh daily specials such as artichoke salad and gazpacho complement a large range of freshly made soups. There are also several pasta dishes and delicious panini that can be taken away or enjoyed in the cute, wood-heavy premises.

Chaiki ITALIAN $
(Чайки; Map p166; www.chaykibar.ru; nab reki Moyki 19; mains ₽350; noon-midnight; Admiralteyskaya) Whitewashed brick walls and a lime-green bike (seemingly a currently obligatory piece of decor for all local hipster joints!) set the tone for this relaxed basement cafe-bar which does excellent pizza and decent salads. Wash the food down with locally made sweet cherry or ginger cider.

Ukrop VEGAN $
(Map p166; www.cafe-ukrop.ru; Malaya Konyushennaya ul 14; mains ₽200-300; 9am-11pm; Nevsky Prospekt) Proving vegie, vegan and raw food can be inventive and tasty as well as wholesome, Ukrop (meaning 'dill') also

makes an effort with its bright and whimsical craft design, which includes swing seats and lots of natural materials.

There's also a branch on **ul Marata** (Укроп; Map p172; ul Marata 23; 9am-11pm; ; Mayakovskaya).

Biblioteka INTERNATIONAL $
(Map p166; www.ilovenevsky.ru; Nevsky pr 20; mains ₽250-450; cafe/restaurant 8am-1am, bar 5pm-5am; ; Nevsky Prospekt) You could spend the better part of a day here. On the ground floor is a waiter-service cafe where it's difficult to avoid being tempted by the cake and dessert display by the door; next up is a more formal restaurant; and on the top floor there's a multiroomed lounge bar with live music and DJs late into the night.

★ **Yat** RUSSIAN $$
(Ять; Map p166; 812-957 0023; http://eatinyat.com; nab reki Moyki 16; mains ₽500; 11am-11pm; ; Admiralteyskaya) Perfectly placed for eating near to the Hermitage, this country-cottage-style restaurant has a very appealing menu of traditional dishes, which are presented with aplomb. The *shchi* soup is excellent and it offers a tempting range of flavoured vodkas. There's also a fab kids area with pet rabbits for them to feed.

Hand-painted crockery items are available for sale and make excellent souvenirs.

Terrassa EUROPEAN $$
(Map p166; 812-937 6837; www.terrassa.ru; Kazanskaya ul 3a; mains ₽600-1000; 11am-1am, from noon Sat & Sun; ; Nevsky Prospekt) Sleek and buzzing, Terrassa is centred on its namesake terrace, which boasts unbelievable views (open only in warmer months). Inside you can watch the chefs, busy in the open kitchen, preparing fresh fusion cuisine that exhibits influences from Italy, Asia and beyond.

You'll usually need reservations to sit on the terrace, but you can just drop by and hope to get lucky.

MiX in St Petersburg INTERNATIONAL $$$
(Map p166; 812-610 6166; www.wstpetersburg.com; Voznesensky pr 6; mains ₽1000-2200; noon-3pm & 7pm-midnight; ; Admiralteyskaya) French cookery star Alain Ducasse is the man behind this slick and creative kitchen attached to the W Hotel. Sublime yet simple dishes tend to be French in essence with an international or Russian edge. A nice touch is the vegetarian set meal, a great deal at ₽700/1100 for two/three courses. Service and atmosphere are both top-notch.

Sinhoto ASIAN $$$
(Map p176; www.fourseasons.com/stpetersburg/dining/restaurants/sintoho; Four Seasons Hotel Lion Palace, Admiralteysky pr; mains ₽1000; 4-11pm; ; Admiralteyskaya) Classic dishes, with creative twists, from Singapore, Hong Kong and Tokyo (hence the SinHoTo name) are served in the Four Season's luxurious and contemporary styled restaurant. A Singaporean chef is in charge ensuring the chicken rice is excellent at least (we also liked the dumplings).

If this doesn't appeal, the hotel has a lovely winter garden for meals and afternoon tea and the gentleman's-club-like Xander bar, with a double-sided central fireplace – the perfect place to hole up on a wintery night.

Liteyny & Smolny

★ **Duo Gastrobar** FUSION $
(Map p172; 812-994 5443; www.duobar.ru; ul Kirochnaya 8a; mains ₽200-500; 1pm-midnight, to 2am Fri & Sat; ; Chernyshevskaya) This light-bathed place, done out in wood and gorgeous glass lampshades, has really helped put this otherwise quiet area on the culinary map. Its short fusion menu excels, featuring such unlikely delights as passionfruit and gorgonzola mousse and salmon with quinoa and marscarpone. There are also more conventional choices such as risottos, pastas and salads.

Obed Bufet CAFETERIA $
(Обед Буфет; Map p172; 5th fl, Nevsky Centre, Nevsky pr 114; mains ₽100-200; 10am-11pm; ; Mayakovskaya) Just what St Petersburg needs: a well-run, central and inviting cafeteria run by the city's most successful restaurant group. Here you'll find an extraordinary range of salads, soups, sandwiches, pizzas and meat dishes. There's even a 50% discount until noon and after 9pm, making this a superb deal (come at 9pm for the latter though, otherwise there will be no food left).

Botanika VEGETARIAN $
(Ботаника; Map p172; www.cafebotanika.ru; ul Pestelya 7; mains ₽200-500; 11am-midnight; ; Chernyshevskaya) Enjoying perhaps the friendliest and most laid-back atmosphere of any restaurant in St Petersburg, this vegetarian charmer wins on all counts. The menu takes in Russian, Indian, Italian

and Japanese dishes, all of which are very well realised, service is friendly, there's no loud TV on, English is spoken and there's even a playroom and menu for the kids.

Schengen INTERNATIONAL $$
(Шенген; Map p172; ☑812-922 1197; ul Kirochnaya 5; mains ₽400-850; ⊙11am-midnight; 🕾 📵; Ⓜ Chernyshevskaya) A breath of fresh air just off Liteyny pr, Schengen represents local aspirations to the wider world. The menu is truly international, has a Mac & Cheese section, chili con carne, Thai green curry and Norwegian trout fillet on it, and is served up in a cool and relaxing two-room space where efficient staff glide from table to table.

Food is of very high quality and there's a 20% discount until 3.30pm on weekdays.

★ Mechta Molokhovets RUSSIAN $$$
(Мечта Молоховец; Map p172; ☑812-929 2247; www.molokhovets.ru; ul Radishcheva 10; mains ₽1450-1800; ⊙noon-11pm Mon-Fri, 2-11pm Sat & Sun; ❄🕾📵; Ⓜ Ploshchad Vosstaniya) Inspired by the cookbook of Elena Molokhovets, the Russian Mrs Beeton, the menu at 'Molokhovets' Dream' covers all the classics from borsch to beef stroganoff, as well as less frequently seen dishes such as goose breast in forest berry sauce and veal cutlets in mushroom ragu. Whatever you have here, you can be sure it's the definitive version.

✕ Vladimirskaya & Vosstaniya

BGL Cafe & Market BAGELS $
(Map p162; nab reki Fontanki 96; bagels ₽50-250; ⊙11am-11pm; ➿🕾📵👶) Finally, somewhere decent to enjoy freshly filled bagels! This cool little cafe is popular with a young and worldly crowd, and has a great location overlooking the Fontanka River. Good lunch deals (until 4pm) make this a great lunch stop, with good coffee and cake on offer too. Bagels to go are also available, as are unfilled ones for sale.

★ Vinostudia ITALIAN $$
(Map p172; ☑812-380 7838; www.vinostudia. com; ul Rubenshteina 38; mains ₽350-700; 🕾📵📵) Another superb addition to ul Rubenshteina's impressive eating options, Vinostudia is a serious and passionately run enoteca. All wine is available by the glass (₽130 to ₽350) and the staff are knowledgable and friendly. There's a good Italian-leaning menu, with dishes such as grilled tiger shrimp, calamari and duck breast rounding out more traditional fare.

Its brick walls mean that it can be rather loud come weekend evenings, when the place is busy and reservations are a good idea. The whitewashed walls, large glass wine cooler and industrial touches all add to the atmosphere.

★ Dom Beat INTERNATIONAL $$
(Дом Быта; Map p172; www.dombeat.ru; ul Razyezzhaya 12; mains ₽300-500; 🕾📵📵; Ⓜ Ligovsky Prospekt) As if naming St Petersburg's coolest bar, lounge and restaurant after a Soviet all-purpose store and then dressing the model-gorgeous staff in tailored pastiches of factory uniforms wasn't a solid enough start, the sleek, retro-humorous interior, sumptuous menu and great atmosphere add up to make this one of the best eating choices in town.

As well as great breakfasts (served until 7pm), there's a wide choice of dishes ranging from top-notch Asian cuisine (Thai red curry, chicken tikka masala) to modern takes on Russian meals and international bar food. Portions aren't huge, though, but dishes are affordable enough to order a couple if you're hungry.

Bistro Garçon FRENCH $$
(Map p172; www.garcon.ru; Nevsky pr 95; mains ₽450-850; ⊙10am-midnight; 🕾📵; Ⓜ Ploshchad Vosstaniya) This gorgeous little bistro is smart and unpretentious, with low lighting, upscale but still charming decor, and professional staff. Prices are reasonable given the excellent standard of the cooking and service. While this is the main restaurant of the group in town, you can find its bakeries and patisseries, which serve up excellent sandwiches and cakes, all over St Petersburg.

Mops THAI $$
(Map p172; www.mopscafe.ru; ul Rubinshteyna 12; mains ₽500-1000; ⊙2pm-1am Sun-Wed, to 3am Thu-Sat; 🕾📵📵; Ⓜ Mayakovskaya) The first and only dedicated Thai restaurant in the city is a visual treat: the elegant street-level dining room is all white painted floorboards and linen tablecloths and embellished with gorgeous Thai furniture, while inside the feel is dark and moody. Whichever vibe you want to go with, it makes for a stylish place to eat out.

The enormous pictorial menu offers a mouth-watering selection of Thai classics. There's a 20% discount between 2pm and 5pm during the week, which makes it very reasonable.

Jean-Jacques FRENCH $$

(Жан-Жак; Map p172; www.jan-jak.com; ul Marata 10; mains ₽300-600; 24hr; ; Mayakovskaya) This is the most conveniently located of the several St Petersburg branches of this smart French bistro. With a pleasant terrace outside and a burgundy and hunter green interior that could be that of your favourite Parisian cafe, this restaurant has a typically delicious brasserie menu, from *magret de canard* to boeuf Bourguignon.

★**Grand Cru** FINE DINING $$$

(Великий Крю; Map p172; www.grandcru.ru; nab reki Fontanki 52; mains ₽800-2000; noon-11pm;) This wine emporium may function as a shop, but its excellent gastronomic restaurant is no afterthought; it's a beautifully decorated space with moody red lighting, timber floors and big windows. The menu is ambitious and expensive, with dishes such as rabbit with millet risotto and beetroot mousse presented on slabs of black slate and paired with a wine.

Sennaya & Kolomna

Testo ITALIAN $

(Тесто; Map p176; www.testogastronomica.ru; per Grivtsova 5/29; mains ₽250-500; 11am-11pm; ; Sennaya Ploshchad) This pleasant little place is good value and yet takes Italian cookery very seriously. Choose from a wide range of homemade pastas and top them with your favourite sauce, whether tomato-based bolognese or a rich, creamy salmon sauce. A few options for soup, salad and pizza round out the menu, but the pasta is the main focus.

★**Teplo** MODERN EUROPEAN $$

(Map p176; 812-570 1974; www.v-teple.ru; Bolshaya Morskaya ul 45; mains ₽250-650; 9am-midnight; ; Admiralteyskaya) This much-feted, eclectic and original restaurant has got it all just right. The venue itself is a lot of fun to nose around, with multiple small rooms, nooks and crannies. Service is friendly and fast (when it's not too busy) and the peppy, inventive Italian-leaning menu has something for everyone. Reservations are usually needed, so call ahead.

The restaurant is full of unexpected props, from table football to a child's play room. Dishes come from all over the world and there's plenty of vegetarian choice, as well as breakfasts served daily from 9am to noon.

★**Khochu Kharcho** GEORGIAN $$

(Хочу харчо; Map p176; Sadovaya ul 39/41; mains ₽500-1200; 24hr; ; Sennaya Ploshchad) This sparkling, friendly and capacious offering right on the Haymarket effortlessly outshines the generally dire offerings to be found elsewhere in this area. A delicious fully photographic menu of comfort food awaits, focused on Mingrelian (West Georgian) cooking, meaning that you can expect calorific *khachapuri* (cheese-stuffed bread), *khinkali* (dumplings), and of course the eponymous *kharcho*, a beef, rice, tomato and walnut soup.

This is the best thing that has happened Sennaya pl for years.

Romeo's Bar & Kitchen ITALIAN $$

(Map p176; www.romeosbarandkitchen.ru; Pr Rimskogo-Korsakova 43; mains ₽400-1000; 9am-midnight; ; Sadovaya) This stylish Italian-run restaurant on one side of the charming Kryukov Canal offers a full menu of traditional Italian cooking, from its large fish selection to main courses such as osso busco with mashed potatoes and calf's liver with spinach. Ask for its pizza menu (₽300 to ₽500), as it's separate from the main one. Breakfast is served daily until noon.

Oh! Mumbai INDIAN $$

(Map p176; Per Grivtsova 2; mains ₽350-670; noon-11pm; ; Admiralteyskaya) Incense infused but pleasantly bright and popular with a young crowd who come here as much to drink as to eat, Oh! Mumbai provides a modern take on Indian food in a city with plenty of old-school, somewhat cliché-ridden establishments from the subcontinent. The menu includes curries, tandoors and a delicious selection of vegetarian options.

Service is very polite and staff speak English.

Entrée FRENCH $$

(Map p176; Nikolskaya pl 5; sandwiches ₽240-500, mains ₽450-650; noon-midnight Mon-Fri, 11am-midnight Sat & Sun; ; Sadovaya) Charming Entrée comes in two parts: the cafe-cum-deli to the right has a chessboard floor, rustic decor, delicious cakes and sandwiches and, for some reason, Michael Douglas' signature scrawled on the wall. To the right is a far more formal restaurant with a classic but clever French menu and a huge wine list.

Service could be a little friendlier, but otherwise this place is a great find in an otherwise rather desolate stretch of the city centre. Breakfast (blink and you miss it!) is served from 11am to 1pm at weekends.

Stroganoff Steak House STEAKHOUSE **$$**
(Map p176; 812-314 5514; www.stroganoffsteakhouse.ru; Konnogvardeysky bul 4; mains ₽400-3000; ; Admiralteyskaya) Beef lovers can indulge their habit at this 12,000-sq-metre restaurant, the city's biggest. Thanks to clever design, though, it doesn't feel overwhelmingly large or impersonal, with the huge space divided into six stylish yet informal dining spaces. The steaks menu is impressive and there's a large list of side orders, salads and other main courses to choose from as well.

There's a fun children's playroom here, making it good for young families.

Idiot VEGETARIAN **$$**
(Map p176; nab reki Moyki 82; mains ₽300-1000, brunch ₽410; 11am-1am; ; Sennaya Ploshchad) Something of an expat favourite, the Idiot is a charming place and has been providing brunch for travellers for years now. Insidiously vegetarian (you may not even notice that there's no meat on the menu, as there's plenty of fish), the friendly basement location is all about atmosphere, relaxation and fun (encouraged by the complimentary vodka coming with each meal).

The cosy subterranean space, the antique furnishings and crowded bookshelves make it an extremely pleasant place to come to eat or drink.

Mansarda INTERNATIONAL **$$$**
(Мансарда; Map p176; 946 4303; www.ginza.ru; ul Pochtamskaya 3; mains ₽500-1400; noon-midnight; ; Admiralteyskaya) It's all about glass at the rooftop restaurant of the Gazprom building. This impressive place definitely has the best views in town and you can almost touch the dome of St Isaac's Cathedral from the best tables (book in advance). Yet despite the fixation, the food is no afterthought, with a delicious range of international cooking and a superb winelist on offer.

To get here, enter the Gazprom building and take the dedicated lift to the top floor.

Vasilyevsky Island

Marketplace CANTEEN **$**
(Map p179; www.market-place.me; 7-ya liniya 34/2; mains ₽100; 8.30am-11pm; ; Vasileostrovskaya) This chain of cafeteria-style restaurants has a popular outlet on Vasilyevsky Island's main commercial strip. With appealing, light-bathed dining areas, a large choice of excellent-value salads, soups, meat dishes and desserts and with friendly service to boot, this spotless place is a lifeline for students and anyone after a low-cost lunch. There's also a cafe downstairs.

★**Restoran** RUSSIAN **$$**
(Ресторанъ; Map p179; www.elbagroup.ru/restoran; Tamozhenny per 2; mains ₽500-1000; noon-11pm; ; Admiralteyskaya) After 15 years on the scene, this excellent place is still going strong. Stylish and airily bright, Restoran is somehow formal and relaxed at the same time. The menu manages to combine the best of *haute russe* cuisine with enough modern flare to keep things interesting: try duck baked with apples or whole baked sterlet in white wine and herbs.

In winters fire roar, while in the summer the thick stone walls make for an oasis from the heat. Do not miss the superb Napoleon dessert, or the interesting selection of quality Russian wines.

Buter Brodsky MODERN EUROPEAN **$$**
(Бутер Бродский; Map p179; www.bbbar.su; nab Makarova 16; mains ₽450-750; ; Vasileostrovskaya) Just when you thought you'd go through life without visiting a Josef Brodsky theme restaurant, along comes Buter Brodsky (the name is a pun on the Russian word for sandwich, *buterbrod*), a super stylish, if unlikely, addition to Vasilyevsky Island's eating scene. The menu runs from *smørrebrød* (open sandwiches) to various set meals of salads and soups.

But it's the decor that is particularly cool: Brodksy's (literally) chiseled features stare down on you from where they've been hammered into the cracked old walls, while elements of the historic building have been preserved and gorgeously integrated into the design. Shabby chic has never looked so good, and with *smørrebrød* at just ₽250, you can be sure of a great value lunch as well.

Petrograd Side

Blizkie Druzya BAKERY, CAFE $
(Близкие друзья; Map p182; ul Bolshoy Zelenina 16; mains ₽200; 9am-11pm; ; M Chkalovskaya) Meaning 'Best Friends', this is the most comfy of several pleasant cafes and bars opening up along this street. It's perfect for a light meal of soup or a quiche. The bakery offers savoury and sweet creations, including pastel-coloured meringue and macaroons.

Le Menu VEGETARIAN $
(Map p182; http://le-menu.ru; Kronverksky pr 79; mains ₽300; 9am-11pm; ; M Gorkovskaya) This smart cafe is brought to you by the passionate vegetarians who run vegie-chain Troitsky Most. In fact there's near-identical fare here, the only difference is the more sophisticated setting – all wooden floorboards and chandeliers for those who appreciate meatless meals in style. Fish is also on the menu.

★**Mesto** INTERNATIONAL $$
(Map p182; 812-405 8799; Kronverksky pr 59; mains ₽400-600; 11am-midnight; ; M Gorkovskaya) Art deco fittings, a beautiful glass and marble counter and upholstered benches you could almost fall asleep on are a good start. The menu is eccentric but interesting: Anglophile shepherd's pie, chateaubriand and beef Wellington are supplemented by creative dishes such as green gazpacho and pumpkin and prawn soup. Portions are not huge but very tasty.

Mesto's tagline – 'we have a small menu and fresh produce' – certainly rings true. Live piano playing Friday and Saturday from 7pm.

★**Chekhov** RUSSIAN $$
(Чехов; Map p182; 812-234 4511; http://restaurant-chekhov.ru; Petropavlovskaya ul 4; mains ₽590-1110; noon-11pm; ; M Petrogradskaya) Despite a totally nondescript appearance from the street, this restaurant's charming interior perfectly recalls that of a 19th-century dacha and makes for a wonderful setting for a delicious meal. The menu (not to mention the staff's attire) is very traditional and features lovingly prepared Russian classics such as 'fresh beef…stroganoff style'.

★**Koryushka** RUSSIAN, GEORGIAN $$
(Корюшка; Map p182; 812-917 9010; http://ginzaproject.ru/SPB/Restaurants/Korushka/About; Petropavlovskaya krepost 3, Zayachy Island; mains ₽500; noon-midnight; ; M Gorkovksaya) Lightly battered and fried smelt (*koryushka*) is a St Petersburg speciality every April, but you can eat the small fish year-round at this relaxed, sophisticated restaurant beside the Peter & Paul Fortress. There's plenty of other very appealing Georgian dishes on the menu to supplement the stunning views across the Neva.

Drinking & Nightlife

A city of midnight hedonists, St Petersburg has plenty of bars, pubs and cafes where you can enjoy a cold beer, a hot coffee or a strong cocktail at almost any time of day. Coffee culture is flourishing with numerous chains, although the most atmospheric places remain the quirky, independent cafes.

You can drink almost everywhere; even in smart restaurants you're generally welcome to come in and order just a beer, while the city's best cocktail bars are superb. The undoubted centre of the drinking scene is Dumskaya ul and ul Lomonosova, home to dozens of bars and clubs and a sea of drunken students after midnight at the weekends. The more underground drinking scene can be found in the bars and music venues around ul Zhukovskogo near Ploshchad Vosstaniya.

Historic Centre

★**Borodabar** COCKTAIL BAR
(Map p166; Kazanskaya ul 11; 6pm-6am; ; M Nevsky Prospekt) Boroda means beard in Russian, and sure enough you'll see plenty of facial hair and tattoos in this hipster cocktail hang-out. Never mind, as the mixologists really know their stuff – we can particularly recommend their smoked old fashioned, which is infused with tobacco smoke, and their colourful (and potent) range of shots.

★**Radiobaby** BAR, CLUB
(Map p166; www.radiobaby.com; Kazanskaya ul 7; 6pm-6am; M Nevsky Prospekt) Go through the arch at Kazanskaya 5 (not 7 – that's just the street address), turn left through a second arch and you'll find this supercool barnlike bar on your right. It's divided into several different rooms, there's a 'no techno, no house' music policy, table football, a relaxed crowd and an atmosphere of eternal hedonism. After 10pm each night, the place becomes more a club than a bar.

GAY & LESBIAN ST PETERSBURG

There's a small but vibrant gay scene in St Petersburg. The main gay clubs are the large and mainstream **Central Station** (Map p166; www.centralstation.ru; ul Lomonosova 1/28; cover after midnight ₽100-300; ⌚6pm-6am; Ⓜ Nevsky Prospekt) and the more alternative **Golubaya Ustritsa** (Map p166; www.boyster.ru; ul Lomonosova 1; ⌚7pm-6am; Ⓜ Nevsky Prospekt), a self-styled 'trash bar' that guarantees a raucous and cheap night out for anyone. Another option is the long-running Soviet-style club **Cabaret** (Кабаре; Map p172; www.cabarespb.ru; Razyezzhaya ul 43; cover ₽200-500; ⌚11pm-6am Thu-Sat; Ⓜ Ligovsky Prospekt), where the 2.30am drag show at weekends is very popular.

Further information can be found on the useful local website **Excess** (www.xs.gay.ru/english).

★Ziferberg ANTI-CAFE

(Map p166; http://ziferburg.ziferblat.net; 3rd fl, Passage, Nevsky pr 48; 1st/subsequent hr per min charge ₽2/1, max charge ₽360; ⌚11am-midnight Sun-Thu, to 7am Fri & Sat; 📶; Ⓜ Gostiny Dvor) Occupying much of the 3rd-floor gallery of Passage is this anti-cafe with a range of quirky, boho-hipster decorated spaces, some intimate, others very social. There's an excellent range of activities to enjoy with your coffee or tea, from boardgames and movies to concerts by classical music students, particularly on the weekends.

Double B CAFE

(Дабл би; Map p166; http://vk.com/doublebspb; Millionnaya ul 18; ⌚9am-10pm Mon-Fri, 11am-10pm Sat & Sun; 📶; Ⓜ Admiralteyskaya) The young baristas are friendly and take their coffee brewing seriously at this serene hipster hangout, with specially roasted beans from Ethiopia, Costa Rica and Kenya and methods including Aeropress and drip. They also do various artisan teas, too.

Belochka & Mielofon BAR

(Map p166; Bankovsky per 3; ⌚6pm-6am; Ⓜ Sennaya Pl) Cool, friendly and relaxed, this basement bar is a little tricky to find: walk past Friends Hostel into the courtyard behind it, take the first right and listen for music to work out the door. There are two low-slung rooms, one with a bar, busy dance floor and DJ, the second with the ubiquitous table football and plenty of comfy sofas.

MiXup Bar BAR

(Map p176; www.wstpetersburg.com; W Hotel, Voznesensky pr 6; ⌚1pm-midnight Sun-Thu, to 2am Fri & Sat; 📶; Ⓜ Admiralteyskaya) The W's superb cocktail bar offers fantastic city views from its Antonio Citterio–designed lounge area to be enjoyed over top-notch libations. One floor up is the MiXup Terrace (May to September), an outdoor space with seating in cosy cabanas and views straight onto St Isaac's Cathedral.

Liteyny & Smolny

★Union Bar & Grill BAR

(Map p172; Liteyny pr 55; ⌚6pm-4am Sun-Thu, to 6am Fri & Sat; 📶; Ⓜ Mayakovskaya) The Union is a glamorous and fun place, characterised by one enormous long wooden bar, low lighting and a New York feel. It's all rather adult, with a serious cocktail list and designer beers on tap. It's crazy at the weekends, but quiet during the week, and always draws a cool 20- and 30-something crowd.

There's a full food menu and the beard and tattoo levels often reach Williamsburg/Shoreditch levels, quite a feat for fusty old St Petersburg.

★The Hat JAZZ CLUB

(Map p172; ul Belinskogo 9; ⌚7pm-5am; Ⓜ Gostiny Dvor) The wonderfully retro-feeling Hat is a serious spot for jazz and whiskey lovers, who come for the nightly live music and the cool cat crowd that makes this wonderfully designed bar feel like it's been transported out of 1950s Greenwich Village. A very welcome change of gear for St Petersburg's drinking options, but it can be extremely full at weekends.

Mishka BAR

(Мишка; Map p172; www.miskhabar.ru; nab reki Fontanky 40; ⌚6pm-2am Mon-Thu, 2pm-6am Fri-Sun; 📶; Ⓜ Gostiny Dvor) Hipster ground zero in St Petersburg is this two-room basement place that is massively popular with a cool student crowd. The front room is hectic, smoky and becomes a dancefloor later in the evening, while the quiet, nonsmoky back-room is a chill out area. DJs spin nightly and there's a big cocktail list.

Dead Poets Bar COCKTAIL BAR

(Map p172; ul Zhukovskogo 12; 2pm-2am; ; Mayakovskaya) This very cool place is an adult's cocktail bar, with a sophisticated drinks menu and an almost unbelievable range of spirits stacked along the long bar and served up by a committed staff of mixologists. It's more of a quiet place, with low lighting, a jazz soundtrack and plenty of space to sit down.

Vladimirskaya & Vosstaniya

★**Dom Beat** COCKTAIL BAR

(Дом Быта; Map p172; www.dombeat.ru; ul Razyezzhaya 12; noon-6am; ; Ligovsky Prospekt) The big draws at this place are the superb cocktails and wide drinks menu. Funky '70s interior, a cool crowd and tables cleared for dancing later in the evening make it a great spot.

Ziferblat ANTI-CAFE

(Циферблат; Map p172; 8-960-285 6946; www.ziferblat.net; 2nd fl, Nevsky pr 81; per min ₽2; 11am-midnight Mon-Thu, to 7am Fri & Sat, to midnight Sun; ; Ploshchad Vosstaniya) A charming multiroom 'free space' that has started a worldwide trend, Ziferblat is the original anti-cafe in St Petersburg. Coffee, tea, soft drinks and biscuits are included as you while away your time playing computer games, reading, watching movies and just hanging out with the arty young locals who frequent its cosy rooms.

Dyuni BAR

(Дюны; Map p172; Ligovsky pr 50; 4pm-midnight, to 6am Fri & Sat; ; Ploshchad Vosstaniya) FREE What looks like a small suburban house sits rather incongruously here amid repurposed warehouses in this vast courtyard. There's a cosy indoor bar and a sand-covered outside area with table football and ping pong, which keeps the cool kids happy all night in the summer months. To find it, simply continue in a straight line from the courtyard entrance.

Terminal Bar BAR

(Map p172; ul Rubinshteyna 13a; 4pm-last customer; ; Dostoevskaya) A slice of New York bohemia on one of the city's most happening streets, Terminal is great for a relaxed drink with friends, who can spread out along the length of the enormous bar, while great music (and live piano from anyone who can play) fills the long, arched room under the grey vaulted ceilings. One of our favourites.

Sennaya & Kolomna

★**Mayakovsky** COCKTAIL BAR

(Map p176; www.mayakovskybar.su; Pochtamtsky per 5; noon-last customer Mon-Fri, from 4pm Sat; Admiralteyskaya) Despite its over-abundance of disco balls, Mayakovsky lives up to its self-given description of 'intelligent bar'. There's a very adult cocktail menu (try a superb Karamazov: Martini Rosso, Becherovka, Bacardi, lemon and cinnamon), red velvet bar stools, a jazz soundtrack and a dark and moodily lit lounge where you can also eat from an impressive international menu.

Stirka 40 BAR

(Стирка; Map p176; Kazanskaya ul 26; 11am-midnight Sun-Thu, to 4am Fri & Sat; ; Sennaya Ploshchad) This friendly joint, whose name means 'washing', has three washing machines, so you can drop off a load and have a few beers while you wait. A novel idea, though one few people seem to take advantage of. Its small and unassuming layout makes it a great place for a quiet drink with a cool young crowd.

Vasilyevsky Island

Helsinki Bar BAR

(Map p179; www.helsinkibar.ru; Kadetskaya liniya 31; noon-2am, to 6am Sat & Sun; ; Vasileostrovskaya) A slice of neighbouring Finland in the heart of St Petersburg, Helsinki is hands down the coolest place to drink on the island. The vibe is retro, with vinyl-spinning DJs, '70s Finnish ads on the walls, vintage furniture and Finnish home cooking. This is a great late-night option if you're staying locally and don't want to worry about the bridges.

Buter Brodsky BAR

(Map p179; www.bbbar.su; nab Makarova 16; noon-midnight; ; Vasileostrovskaya) This super funky and beautifully designed bar, a homage to local poet Josef Brodsky, is easily the coolest spot to drink on the island. As well as offering a full cocktail menu, wine list and selection of nonalcoholic drinks, there is also its range of home-made spirits and tinctures.

✪ Entertainment

St Petersburg offers world-class classical music, ballet and opera performances, often at a fraction of the price you'd pay at home, even when there are hefty mark-ups on tickets for foreigners. As well as high culture, there's plenty of fun to be had clubbing, listening to live music, and at the cinema and circus.

Tickets

There are ticket-booking kiosks and offices all over the city, or you can book tickets directly on the websites of most of the main theatres.

Live Music

St Petersburg has long been the centre of Russian rock music, sprouting such influential Soviet bands as Akvarium and Kino from its legendary underground, and is still home to numerous famous groups today. Its live-music scene remains exciting and vibrant, with a large selection of venues, both mainstream and – particularly – underground, to choose from.

Fish Fabrique LIVE MUSIC
(Map p172; www.fishfabrique.spb.ru; Ligovsky pr 53; ⏲3pm-6am, concerts from 8pm Thu-Sun, & sometimes on other days; 📶; Ⓜ Ploshchad Vosstaniya) There are St Petersburg institutions and then there's Fish Fabrique, the museum of local boho life that has been going for two decades. Here, in the dark underbelly of Pushkinskaya 10, artists, musicians and counter culturalists of all ages meet to drink beer and listen to music.

Nowadays, the newer Fabrique Nouvelle in the same courtyard hosts concerts nightly, while the old Fish Fabrique has them just at weekends, but whichever one you're in, you're sure to rub shoulders with an interesting crowd.

Kamchatka CLUB
(Map p182; www.clubkamchatka.ru; ul Blokhina 15; cover ₽200-300; Ⓜ Sportivnaya) A shrine to Viktor Tsoy, the late Soviet-era rocker who worked as caretaker of this former boilerhouse bunker with band mates from Kino. Music lovers flock here to light candles and watch a new generation thrash out their stuff. The line-up is varied and it's worth dropping by if only for a quick drink in this highly atmospheric place – find it tucked in a courtyard off the street.

JFC Jazz Club JAZZ
(Map p172; ☎812-272 9850; www.jfc-club.spb.ru; Shpalernaya ul 33; cover ₽100-500; ⏲7-11pm; Ⓜ Chernyshevskaya) Very small and very New York, this cool club is the best place in the city to hear modern, innovative jazz music, as well as blues, bluegrass and various other styles (see the website for a list of what's on). The space is tiny, so book a table online if you want to sit down.

Jazz Philharmonic Hall JAZZ
(Map p162; www.jazz-hall.spb.ru; Zagorodny pr 27; cover ₽500-1500; ⏲concerts 7pm Wed-Sun, Ellington Hall concerts 8pm Tue, Fri & Sat; Ⓜ Vladimirskaya) Founded by legendary jazz violinist and composer David Goloshchokin, this venue represents the more traditional side of jazz. Two resident bands perform straight jazz and Dixieland in the big hall, which seats up to 200 people. The smaller Ellington Hall is used for occasional acoustic performances. Foreign guests also appear doing mainstream and modern jazz; check the website for details.

Classical Music, Opera & Ballet

Mariinsky Theatre OPERA, BALLET
(Мариинский театр; Map p176; ☎812-326 4141; www.mariinsky.ru; Teatralnaya pl 1; ₽1000-6000; Ⓜ Sadovaya) Petersburg's most spectacular venue for ballet and opera, the Mariinsky Theatre is an attraction in its own right. Tickets can be bought online or in person, but they should be bought in advance during the summer months. The magnificent interior is the epitome of imperial grandeur, and any evening here will be an impressive experience.

Known as the Kirov Ballet during the Soviet era, the Mariinsky has an illustrious history, with troupe members including such ballet greats as Nijinsky, Nureyev, Pavlova and Baryshnikov. In recent years the company has been invigorated by the current Artistic and General Director Valery Gergiev, who has worked hard to make the company solvent while overseeing the construction of the impressive and much-needed second theatre, the Mariinsky II, across the Kryukov Canal from the company's green-and-white wedding cake of a building. It is rumoured that the Mariinsky Theatre will close at some point in the near future for a full (and, again, much needed) renovation, so visit the Mariinsky's faded grandeur while you can.

Mariinsky II THEATRE
(Мариинский II; Map p176; ☎326 4141; www.mariinsky.ru; ul Dekabristov 34; tickets ₽300-6000; ⊙ticket office 11am-7pm; Ⓜ Sadovaya) Finally opening its doors in 2013 after more than a decade of construction, legal wrangles, scandal and rumour, the Mariinsky II is a showpiece for Petersburg's most famous ballet and opera company. It is one of the most technically advanced music venues in the world, with superb sightlines and acoustics from all of its 2000-seats.

There's no denying that the modern-yet-not-modern-enough-to-be-interesting exterior is no great addition to St Petersburg's magnificent wealth of buildings. Inside, it's a different story though. The interior is a beautifully crafted mixture of back-lit onyx, multi-level public areas between which staircases, lifts and escalators weave, limestone walls, marble floors and Swarovski chandeliers. The simple yet superbly designed auditorium boasts plenty of leg room, three stages that can be combined to form one and an orchestra pit that can hold no fewer than 120 musicians. Serious music fans should come here to see a state-of-the-art opera and ballet venue, while anyone curious to see the results of a decade of building work will also not leave disappointed. As well as the main auditorium, there are also several smaller venues within the venue (Prokofiev Hall, Stravinsky Foyer, Shchedrin Hall, Mussorgsky Hall), all of which host regular concerts that can be a cheaper alternative to seeing a performance in the main hall.

Mariinsky Concert Hall CLASSICAL MUSIC
(Мариинский концертный зал; Map p176; www.mariinsky.ru; ul Dekabristov 37; tickets ₽600-1500; ⊙ticket office 11am-8pm; Ⓜ Sadovaya) Opened in 2007, this concert hall is a magnificent multifaceted creation. It manages to preserve the historic brick facade of the set-and-scenery warehouse that previously stood on this spot, while the modern main entrance, facing ul Dekabristov, is all tinted glass and angular lines, hardly hinting at the beautiful old building behind.

Shostakovich Philharmonia CLASSICAL MUSIC
(Map p166; www.philharmonia.spb.ru; Ⓜ Nevsky Prospekt) Under the artistic direction of world-famous conductor Yury Temirkanov, the Philharmonia represents the finest in orchestral music. The **Bolshoy Zal** (Big Hall) on pl Iskusstv is the venue for a full program of symphonic performances, while the nearby **Maly Zal** (Small Hall) hosts smaller ensembles. Both venues are used for numerous music festivals, including the superb **Early Music Festival** (www.earlymusic.ru).

Rimsky-Korsakov Conservatory MUSIC SCHOOL
(Консерватория имени Н. А. Римского-Корсакова; Map p176; ☎812-312 2519; www.conservatory.ru; Teatralnaya pl 3; tickets ₽200-2000; Ⓜ Sadovaya) This illustrious music school was the first public music school in Russia. The Bolshoy Zal on the 3rd floor is an excellent place to see performances by up-and-coming musicians throughout the academic year, while the Maly Zal often hosts free concerts from present students and alumni; check when you're in town for what's on.

Mikhailovsky Opera & Ballet Theatre OPERA, BALLET
(Map p166; ☎812-595 4305; www.mikhailovsky.ru; pl Iskusstv 1; Ⓜ Nevsky Prospekt) While not quite as grand as the Mariinsky, this illustrious stage still delivers the Russian ballet or operatic experience, complete with multi-tiered theatre, frescoed ceiling and elaborate concerts. Pl Iskusstv (Arts Sq) is a lovely setting for this respected venue, which is home to the State Academic Opera & Ballet Company.

Hermitage Theatre BALLET
(Map p166; www.hermitageballet.com; Dvortsovaya nab 34; online tickets $160; Ⓜ Admiralteyskaya) This intimate neoclassical theatre, designed by Giacomo Quarenghi and once the private theatre of the imperial family, stands on the site of the original Winter Palace of Peter I. Book early if you'd like to see a ballet (usually classics such as *Swan Lake* and *Giselle*) in this intimate space. Access to the theatre is via an entrance to the Large Hermitage on Dvortsovaya nab.

Yusupov Palace Theatre THEATRE
(Театр Юсуповского дворца; Map p176; ☎812-314 9883; www.yusupov-palace.ru; nab reki Moyki 94; tickets ₽500-3000; Ⓜ Sadovaya) Housed inside the outrageously ornate Yusupov Palace, this elaborate yet intimate venue was the home entertainment centre for one of the city's foremost aristocratic families. While you can visit the theatre when you tour the palace, seeing a performance here is a treat, as you can imagine yourself the personal guest of the notorious Prince Felix himself.

Circus & Puppets

Contact the theatres to check on performance times.

St Petersburg State Circus CIRCUS

(Map p166; ☎812-570 5390; www.circus.spb.ru; nab reki Fontanki 3; Ⓜ Gostiny Dvor) While Russia's oldest permanent circus complex (built in 1877) undergoes renovation of its roof for a couple of years, the shows will happen in a big top elsewhere in the city – check the website for details. Circus troupes and artists from other cities and countries perform shows here, too.

Bolshoy Puppet Theatre PUPPET THEATRE

(Большой театр кукол; Map p172; www.puppets.ru; ul Nekrasova 10; tickets ₽250-600; Ⓜ Chernyshevskaya) This 'big' puppet theatre is indeed the biggest in the city, and has been active since 1931. The repertoire includes a wide range of shows for children and for adults.

Demmeni Marionette Theatre PUPPET THEATRE

(Map p166; ☎812-571 2156; www.demmeni.ru; Nevsky pr 52; Ⓜ Gostiny Dvor) Since 1917, this venue under the arches on central Nevsky is the city's oldest professional puppet theatre. Mainly for children, the shows are well produced and professionally performed.

Sports

Petrovsky Stadium SPORTS

(Спортивный комплекс Петровский; Map p182; www.petrovsky.spb.ru; Petrovsky ostrov 2; Ⓜ Sportivnaya) Until the new stadium on Krestovsky Island is finally finished, this is the home ground of Zenit, St Petersburg's top football team. Games are well worth attending.

Theatre & Dance Shows

Drama is taken seriously in St Petersburg and there are dozens of theatrical performances each night, all in Russian. Even if you don't speak the language, some theatres are visual treats in themselves. There are also cabaret and dance shows that require little in the way of language skills for appreciation.

Feel Yourself Russian Folkshow DANCE

(Map p176; ☎812-312 5500; www.folkshow.ru; ul Truda 4, Nikolayevsky Palace; ticket incl drinks & snacks ₽2900; ⏲ box office 11am-9pm, shows 7pm & in high season 9pm; Ⓜ Admiralteyskaya) Terrible title, but not a bad show of traditional Russian folk dancing and music. The two-hour performance features four different folk groups, complete with accordion, balalaika and Cossack dancers. It's worth attending to get a look inside the spectacular Nikolayevsky Palace, if nothing else.

Maly Drama Theatre THEATRE

(Малый драматический театр; Map p172; www.mdt-dodin.ru; ul Rubinshteyna 18; Ⓜ Vladimirskaya) Also called the Theatre of Europe, the Maly is St Petersburg's most internationally celebrated theatre. Its director Lev Dodin is famed for his long version of Fyodor Dostoevsky's *The Devils,* as well as Anton Chekhov's *Play Without a Name,* which both toured the world to great acclaim. It's also one of the few theatres that does performances with subtitles.

Alexandrinsky Theatre THEATRE

(Map p166; ☎812-710 4103; www.alexandrinsky.ru; pl Ostrovskogo 2; Ⓜ Gostiny Dvor) This magnificent venue is just one part of an immaculate architectural ensemble designed by Carlo Rossi. The theatre's interior oozes 19th-century elegance and style, and it's worth taking a peek even if you don't see a production here.

This is where Anton Chekhov premiered *The Seagull* in 1896; the play was so badly received on opening that the playwright fled to wander anonymously among the crowds on Nevsky pr. Chekov is now a beloved part of the theatre's huge repertoire, ranging from Russian folk tales to Shakespearean tragedies.

Shopping

St Petersburg's shopping scene is rather uneven. There are certainly a few charming, stand-out independent stores selling antiques, art and unique fashion, but the city is increasingly dominated by big shopping centres, which boast most of the best contemporary fashion and design boutiques.

★ Udelnaya Fair FLEA MARKET

(Удельная ярмарка; Skobolvesky pr, Vyborg Side; ⏲ 8am-5pm Sat & Sun; Ⓜ Udelnaya) This treasure trove of Soviet ephemera, pre-revolutionary antiques, WWII artefacts and bonkers kitsch from all eras is truly worth travelling for. Exit the metro station to the right and follow the crowds across the train tracks. Continue beyond the large permanent market, which is of very little interest, until you come to a huge area of independent stalls, all varying in quality and content.

The sheer size of the place means you'll really have to comb it to find the gems.

★Taiga FASHION

(Тайга; Map p166; http://space-taiga.org; Dvortsovaya nab 20; ⌚1-9pm; 📶; Ⓜ Admiralteyskaya) Like several other of Piter's trendy hangouts, Taiga keeps a low profile despite its prime location close by the Hermitage. The warren of small rooms in the ancient building are worth exploring to find cool businesses ranging from a barber to guitar workshop. **8 Store** (Map p166; http://8-store.ru; Dvortsovaya nab 20; ⌚1pm-9pm; Ⓜ Admiralteyskaya) is one of the best, a stylish boutique stacked with clothes and accessories by local designers.

Perinnye Ryady ARTS & CRAFTS

(Периные ряды, арт-центр; Map p166; ☎812-440 2028; www.artcenter.su; Dumskaya ul 4; ⌚10am-8pm; Ⓜ Nevsky Prospekt) Scores of arts-and-craft stores can be found in this arcade in the midst of Dumskaya ul, amongst them Collection, with a wide range of painted works, several by members of the Union of Artists of Russia; and Pionersky Magazin, specialising in Soviet-era memorabilia, where you're guaranteed to find a bust of Lenin and colourful propaganda and art posters.

There's also a small exhibition space here (adult/student ₽300/200).

Staraya Kniga BOOKSHOP

(Старая книга; Map p166; Nevsky pr 3; ⌚10am-7pm; Ⓜ Admiralteyskaya) This long-established antique bookseller is a fascinating place to rummage around. The stock ranges from fancy, mint-edition books to secondhand, well-worn Soviet editions, maps and art (in the section next to the art supplies shop). It's a great place to look for an unusual, unique souvenir. Find it in the courtyard off the main road.

Galeria SHOPPING CENTRE

(Галерия; Map p172; www.galeria.spb.ru; Ligovsky pr 30a; ⌚10am-11pm; Ⓜ Ploshchad Vosstaniya) This extraordinary place has rather changed everything for shopping in St Petersburg – there are probably as many shops here as elsewhere in the entire city centre. Spread over five floors, with around 300 shops (including H&M, Gap, Marks & Spencer and Zara), this really is a one-stop shop for pretty much all your shopping needs.

Imperial Porcelain HOMEWARES

(Императорский Фарфор; Map p172; www.ipm.ru; Vladimirsky pr 7; ⌚10am-8pm; Ⓜ Vladimirskaya) This is the convenient city centre location of the famous porcelain factory that once made tea sets for the Romanovs. If you're determined to get a bargain, head out to the **factory outlet** (Императорский Фарфор; www.ipm.ru; pr Obukhovsky Oborony 151; ⌚10am-8pm; Ⓜ Lomonosovskaya) where prices are far cheaper. There's a **second city-centre branch** (Map p172; Nevsky pr 160; ⌚10am-9pm; Ⓜ Ploshchad Vosstaniya) on the other side of pl Vosstaniya.

Anglia BOOKSHOP

(Map p172; nab reki Fontanki 30; ⌚10am-8pm Mon-Fri, from 11am Sat, noon-7pm Sun; Ⓜ Gostiny Dvor) The city's only dedicated English-language bookshop has a large selection of contemporary literature, classics, dictionaries, history and travel writing. It also hosts small art and photography displays, organises book readings and generally is a cornerstone of expat life in St Petersburg.

Tula Samovars SOUVENEIRS

(Тульские самовары; Map p162; www.samovary.ru; per Dzhambula 11; Ⓜ Zvenigorodskaya) Nearly all samovars (metal containers holding boiling water) in Russia are made in the town of Tula, south of Moscow, but this beautiful showroom is the place in St Petersburg to buy a truly unique souvenir of your visit. The samovars range from small, simple designs to enormous and elaborate ones with precious stones and other embellishments.

Nevsky Centre SHOPPING CENTRE

(Невский Центр; Map p172; www.nevskycentre.ru; Nevsky pr 112; ⌚10am-11pm; Ⓜ Ploshchad Vosstaniya) Nevsky Centre is a smart and central multifloor shopping centre. It houses some 70 shops over seven floors, including the city's largest department store, Stockmann, which includes the excellent basement Stockmann supermarket. Elsewhere there's a food court and lots of independent fashion and furnishing stores.

ℹ Information

DANGERS & ANNOYANCES

Crime & Violence

Watch out for pickpockets, particularly along Nevsky pr. St Petersburg is notorious for its incidence of race-related violent attacks. Precautions for non-Caucasians to take include not wandering around alone late at night and sticking to busy main roads in the suburbs at any time of day.

STREET NAMES

Be aware that St Petersburg has two streets called Bolshoy pr: one on Petrograd Side and one on Vasilyevsky Island. The two sides of some streets on Vasilyevsky Island are known as lines *(linii)*, and are effectively different streets, thus the opposite sides of one street have different names. For example 4-ya liniya (4th line) and 5-ya liniya (5th line) are the east and west sides of the same street – but are referred to as individuals. This is due to the fact that the original plan for Vasilyevsky Island foresaw canals being built down the middle of these wide streets to please the boat-mad tsar. Following Peter's death, however, the plans were dropped, leaving locals with this strange phenomenon.

Environmental Hazards

It's not just the ice on the streets that you have to look out for in winter – every year in early spring and during winter thaws, several people die when hit by child-sized, sword-shaped icicles falling from rooftops and balconies. Keep your eyes peeled to make sure one of these monsters is not dangling above your head.

From May to September mosquitoes are a nightmare. The plug-ins that slowly heat repellent-saturated cardboard pads are available everywhere in the city and are very effective. Alternatively bring repellent or cover up.

Tiny traces of *Giardia lamblia*, a nasty parasite that causes stomach cramps and diarrhoea, have been found in St Petersburg's water. There's no preventative drug so the best advice is not to drink straight from the tap. To be absolutely safe, drink only bottled water. However, brushing your teeth, bathing, showering and shaving with tap water will cause no problems.

EMERGENCY

Most emergency numbers have operators who speak Russian only. For serious matters, contact your embassy or consulate as well.

Ambulance (☎03)

Fire department (☎01)

Gas leak (☎04)

Police (☎02)

INTERNET ACCESS

Wireless access is ubiquitous across the city's hotels and restaurants. In nearly all cases it's free, but you'll have to ask for the password. If you don't have a smartphone or a laptop, your best bet is an internet cafe.

Cafe Max (Map p172; www.cafemax.ru; Nevsky pr 90/92; per hr ₽120; ⌚24hr; Ⓜ Mayakovskaya) A big fancy place with 150 computers, a game zone and a comfy cafe and beer bar. It's located on the 2nd floor.

MEDIA

There is a decent amount of English-language media in St Petersburg, although publications aren't regular: The *St Petersburg Times*, despite constantly slimming down and having gone from twice weekly to once weekly, remains the most useful source of news and listings in town. Russian speakers have the choice of *Afisha* and *Time Out St Petersburg*, both similar publications with excellent listings.

MEDICAL SERVICES

Clinics

The American Medical Clinic and Medem International Clinic are open 24 hours and have English-speaking staff.

American Medical Clinic (Map p176; ☎812-740 2090; www.amclinic.ru; nab reki Moyki 78; ⌚24hr; Ⓜ Admiralteyskaya)

Medem International Clinic & Hospital (Map p172; ☎812-336 3333; www.medem.ru; ul Marata 6; ⌚24hr; Ⓜ Mayakovskaya)

Pharmacies

Look for the sign *apteka*, or the usual green cross, to find a pharmacy. All 36.6 pharmacies are open 24 hours. The two most central branches are:

36.6 (Historic Centre) (Map p176; Gorokhovaya ul 16; ⌚24hr; Ⓜ Sadovaya)

36.6 (Smolny) (Map p172; Nevsky pr 98; ⌚24hr; Ⓜ Mayakovskaya)

MONEY

ATMs and currency exchange offices (обмен валют) can be found all over the city. If you need to change money at odd times, there are lots of 24-hour exchange offices on Nevsky pr and in big hotels.

POST

Post office branches are scattered throughout St Petersburg and they vary in services, usually in proportion to size.

Main post office (Map p176; Pochtamtskaya ul 9; ⌚24hr; Ⓜ Admiralteyskaya)

TOILETS

Portakabin-type toilets (around ₽25) outside metros and the major sights are common. Shopping centres, hotels and chain cafes are the best places to look for a clean, odour-free bathroom.

TOURIST INFORMATION

The English-speaking staff at the **Tourist Information Bureau Main Office** (Map p166; ☎812-310 2822; http://eng.ispb.info; Sadovaya ul 14/52; ⏰10am-7pm Mon-Fri, noon-6pm Sat; Ⓜ Gostiny Dvor) do their best to help with advice and information. There are also kiosks outside the **Hermitage** (Map p166; Dvortsovaya pl 12; ⏰10am-7pm; Ⓜ Admiralteyskaya), on **pl Vosstaniya** (Map p172; pl Vosstaniya; ⏰10am-7pm; Ⓜ Ploshchad Vosstaniya) and **Isaakievskaya pl** (Map p176; Isaakievskaya pl), and at the airport.

TRAVEL AGENCIES

A number of agencies have English-speaking staff.

City Realty (Map p166; ☎812-570 6342; www.cityrealtyrussia.com; Muchnoy per 2; ⏰9am-7pm Mon-Fri, to 5pm Sat; Ⓜ Nevsky Prospekt)

Ost-West Kontaktservice (Map p172; www.ostwest.com; Ligovsky pr 10; ⏰9am-6pm Mon-Sat; Ⓜ Ploshchad Vosstaniya)

Travel Russia (Map p172; www.travelrussia.su; Office 408, 4th fl, Senator Business Centre, 2-ya Sovetskaya ul 7; ⏰9am-8pm Mon-Fri, to 5pm Sat; Ⓜ Ploshchad Vosstaniya)

ℹ Getting There & Away

AIR

St Petersburg now has a state-of-the-art airport at Pulkovo, following the closure of its two Soviet-era terminals and the opening of the new **Pulkovo Airport** (LED; www.pulkovoairport.ru) nearby.

St Petersburg has direct air links with all major European capitals and many larger Russian cities.

BOAT

Between early April and late September, international passenger ferries connect Stockholm, Helsinki and Tallinn with the **Morskoy vokzal** (Морской вокзал; Map p162; pl Morskoy Slavy 1). It's a long way from the metro, so either take bus 7 or trolleybus 10 from outside the Hermitage.

In summer, regular river cruises depart from the **River Passenger Terminal** (☎812-262 0239, 812-262 6321; Obukhovskoy Oborony pr 195; Ⓜ Proletarskaya) and float along the Neva to inland Russia, including cruises to Valaam, Kizhi and Moscow. Tours can be booked through most travel agents, or through the **Ferry Centre** (Паромный центр; Map p172; ☎812-327 3377; www.paromy.ru; ul Vosstaniya 19; Ⓜ Ploshchad Vosstaniya).

Cruise ships dock at one of five ferry terminals around the city.

BUS

St Petersburg's main bus station, **Avtovokzal** (Автобусный вокзал; Map p162; ☎812-766 5777; www.avokzal.ru; nab Obvodnogo kanala 36; Ⓜ Obvodny Kanal) has both international and European Russia services. The website has current timetables and routes. The single cheapest way to get to Helsinki is to take a *marshrutka* (fixed-route minibus) from pl Vosstaniya (₽600); they leave all day when full from the corner of Nevsky pr and Ligovsky pr, opposite the metro station.

Other international buses are offered by a number of companies.

Ecolines (Map p162; ☎812-325 2152; www.ecolines.ru; Podezdny per 3; Ⓜ Pushkinskaya) Daily overnight bus from Vitebsk Station to Riga (₽1320, nine hours). Other buses run to Minsk, Kiev and Odessa.

Lux Express (Map p162; ☎812-441 3757; www.luxexpress.eu; Mitrofanievskoye sh 2, Admiral Business Centre; ⏰9am-9pm; Ⓜ Baltiyskaya) Runs five daily buses from the Baltic Station to Tallinn (₽1850, seven hours); daily buses go from the Baltic Station to Riga (₽1095, 11 hours).

CAR & MOTORCYCLE

Take it slowly; not only are there numerous speed traps, but also the state of some roads can easily lead you to the repair shop in no time.

Avis (☎812-600 1213; www.avisrussia.ru; pl Alexandra Nevskogo 2; Ⓜ Ploshchad Alexandra Nevskogo)

Europcar (☎812-385 5284; www.europcar.ru; Pulkovo Airport; Ⓜ Kirovsky Zavod)

Hertz (☎812-454 7099; www.hertz.ru; Pulkovo Airport)

TRAIN

There are several major long-distance train stations in St Petersburg, which also run suburban services. Tickets can be purchased at the train stations where self-service ticket machines in English mean you no longer have to wait for hours in line, as well as from the **Central Train Ticket Office** (Кассы ЖД; Map p166; nab kanala Griboyedova 24; ⏰8am-8pm Mon-Sat, to 4pm Sun; Ⓜ Gostiny Dvor), and from many travel agencies around town.

Finland Station (Финляндский вокзал; Map p162; www.finlyandsky.dzvr.ru; pl Lenina 6; Ⓜ Ploshchad Lenina) Has services to Helsinki and Vyborg.

Ladozhsky Station (Ладожский вокзал; www.lvspb.ru; Zanevsky pr 73; Ⓜ Ladoszhskaya) To/from Helsinki, the Leningrad Oblast, the far north of Russia and towards the Urals.

Moscow Station (Московский вокзал; Map p172; www.moskovsky-vokzal.ru; Nevsky pr 85;

ℹ MOVING ON?

For tips, recommendations and reviews, head to shop.lonelyplanet.com to purchase a downloadable PDF of the Finland chapter from Lonely Planet's *Scandinavia* guide.

Ⓜ Ploshchad Vosstaniya) Trains to Moscow, Siberia, Crimea and the Caucasus.

Vitebsk Station (Витебский вокзал; Map p162; Zagorodny pr 52; Ⓜ Pushkinskaya) Trains to Riga, Vilnius, Kaliningrad, Kyiv, Minsk, Berlin, Prague and Budapest. Local trains also leave here throughout the day to Detskoe Selo, the station for Tsarskoe Selo.

Baltic Station (Балтийский вокзал; Map p162; Obvodny Kanal 120; Ⓜ Baltiyskaya)

Moscow

All trains to Moscow from St Petersburg depart from the Moscow Station (p207). Take your pick from the overnight sleeper trains or the super-fast Sapsan day trains. All train tickets can be bought online at www.rzd.ru, or from the machines at any station in St Petersburg.

There are about 10 overnight trains travelling between St Petersburg and Moscow. Most depart between 10pm and 1am, arriving in the capital the following morning between 6am and 8am. On the more comfortable *firmeny* trains, a 1st-class *lyuks* ticket (two-person cabin) runs from ₽5000 to ₽6000, while a 2nd-class *kupe* (four-person cabin) is ₽2000 to ₽3500. You will often have to pay extra for bed linen, although with some tickets bed linen and breakfast is included.

The Sapsan high-speed trains travel at speeds of 200km/h to reach Moscow in four to 4½ hours. There are six to eight daily departures. Comfortable 2nd-class seats are ₽2560 to ₽3800, while super-spacious 1st-class seats run from ₽5000 to ₽6000.

Elsewhere in Russia

St Petersburg has excellent connections to the rest of European Russia, with daily trains to Murmansk, Petrozavodsk, Kaliningrad, Nizhny Novgorod, Novgorod, Pskov and Yekaterinburg. Less frequent services connect the city to Arkhangelsk and Kazan. Southern Russia and Siberia are generally reached via Moscow, although there are some direct trains to the Black Sea coast from St Petersburg. However, be aware that these don't go via Moscow and cut through Belarus, necessitating a transit visa for Belarus and a double entry visa.

Finland & Other International Destinations

From Helsinki there are four daily Allegro express trains that take you from the Finnish capital to St Petersburg in an impressive 3½ hours; see www.vr.fi for prices and timetables. Services in both directions stop at Vyborg.

St Petersburg is well connected by train to lots of cities throughout Eastern Europe, including Berlin, Budapest, Kaliningrad, Kyiv, Prague and Warsaw, but all trains pass through Belarus, for which you're required to hold a transit visa. The train to Smolensk in Russia also passes through Belarus. Border guards have been known to force people off trains and back to where they came from if they don't have a visa.

ℹ Getting Around

St Petersburg can be a frustrating place to get around for visitors: the metro, while an excellent system, actually has relatively few stations in the centre of the city, and distances from stations to nearby sights can be long. Many visitors find buses and *marshrutky* a little daunting. All the signage is in Russian only and you need to know where you're going, so many people just walk: bring comfortable shoes.

TO/FROM THE AIRPORT

From Pulkovo Airport, taking a taxi to the city centre has never been easier or safer. Leave the terminal building and outside you'll find an

TRAINS FROM ST PETERSBURG TO MOSCOW

NAME & NO	DEPARTURE	DURATION	FARE *(KUPE)*
1 Krasnaya Strela	11.55pm	8hr	₽2900
3 Ekspress	11.59pm	8hr	₽2500
53 Grand Express	11.40pm	9hr	₽5000-6200
752 Sapsan	6.45am	4hr	₽2612
754 Sapsan	1.30pm	4½hr	₽2354
161A Sapsan	3.15pm	4hr	₽2870
165A Sapsan	7.45pm	4hr	₽2870

official taxi dispatcher who will ask you for your destination's address, write you a price on a slip of official paper that you can then give to your driver, and who will indicate which taxi to go to. Prices vary, but expect between ₽800 to ₽1000 to the centre, depending on where exactly you're headed. Drivers usually won't speak much English, but just hand over the money on arrival – you don't need to tip.

For those on a budget, *marshrutka* K39 shuttles you from outside the terminal building to the nearest metro station, Moskovskaya (₽36, every five minutes, from 7am to 11.30pm). The bus terminates at the Moskovskaya metro station, so you don't need to worry about where to get off, and you can connect to the rest of the city from there. There's also bus 39 (₽25, every 15 minutes, from 5.30am to 1.30am) that runs the same route over longer hours, but trundles along somewhat more slowly.

BUS, MARSHRUTKA, TROLLEYBUS & TRAM

Tickets (₽23 to ₽30 depending on the service) are bought inside the vehicle. Bus stops are marked by roadside 'A' signs (for *avtobus*), trolleybus stops by 'm' (representing a handwritten Russian 'T'), tram stops by a 'T', all usually indicating the line numbers too. Stops may also have roadside signs with little pictures of a bus, trolleybus or tram. *Marshrutky* stop anywhere you hail them (except on Nevsky pr, where they're banned from operating). Most transport runs from 6am to 1am.

Useful routes across the city:

Hermitage to Vasilyevsky Island Bus 7; trolleybus 10.

Kirovsky Islands Bus 10 from the corner of Bolshaya Morskaya ul and Nevsky pr.

Ligovsky pr to Petrograd Side *Marshrutka* K76, via Troitsky most and Peter & Paul Fortress.

Nevsky pr From Admiralty to Moskovsky vokzal, buses 7 and 22; trolleybuses 1, 5, 7, 10 and 22. Trolleybuses 1 and 22 continue to pl Alexandra Nevskogo. Trolleybuses 5 and 7 continue to Smolny.

Vitebsky vokzal to Vasilyevsky Island *Marshrutka* K124, via Sennaya pl and Mariinsky Theatre.

METRO

The **St Petersburg metro** (www.metro.spb.ru; ⌚6am-12.45am) is a very efficient five-lined system. The network of some 67 stations is best used for travelling long distances, especially connecting the suburbs to the city centre.

Zhetony (tokens, ₽28), valid for one ride, can be bought from the booths in the stations. You're supposed to buy an extra ticket if you're carrying a large amount of luggage. If you are staying more than a day or two, however, it's worth buying a smart card (₽55), which is good for loading multiple journeys over a fixed time period. The more trips you buy, the more you save, though note, you can't share a card with a friend.

TAXI

Nearly all official taxis are unmetered (though there are plans to introduce these), so if you flag one down you'll have to go through a similar process of negotiation to that involved in catching a car, only the driver will want more money for being 'official'.

The best way to get a taxi is to order one through a company, as prices will be a lot lower than those charged if you flag a driver down on the street. Operators will usually not speak English, so unless you speak Russian you might want your hotel reception to call for you.

Peterburgskoye Taxi (☎068, 812-324 7777; www.taxi068.spb.ru)

Taxi-4 (☎812-633 3333; www.taxi-4.ru)

Taxi Blues (☎812-321 8888; www.taxiblues.ru)

Taxi Million (☎812-600 0000; www.6-000-000.ru) Has operators and drivers who speak English.

> ### ℹ RAISING THE BRIDGES
>
> From the end of April to November, all major bridges rise at the following times nightly to let seagoing ships through. The schedule (which changes every year by five minutes here or there) governs the lives of the city's motorists and nighthawks trying to get from one area to another.
>
> **Birzhevoy most** 2am to 4.55am
>
> **Blagoveshchensky most** 1.25am to 2.45am and 3.10am to 5am
>
> **Bolsheokhtinsky most** 2am to 5am
>
> **Dvortsovy most** 1.25am to 2.50am and 3.10am to 4.55am
>
> **Liteyny most** 1.40am to 4.45am
>
> **Most Alexandra Nevskogo** 2.20am to 5.10am
>
> **Troitsky most** 1.35am to 4.50am
>
> **Tuchkov most** 2am to 2.55am and 3.35am to 4.55am

AROUND ST PETERSBURG

There are several grand imperial palaces and estates surrounding St Petersburg. Peterhof and the palace-park ensembles at Tsarskoe Selo and Pavlovsk are the best and a visit to

Around St Petersburg

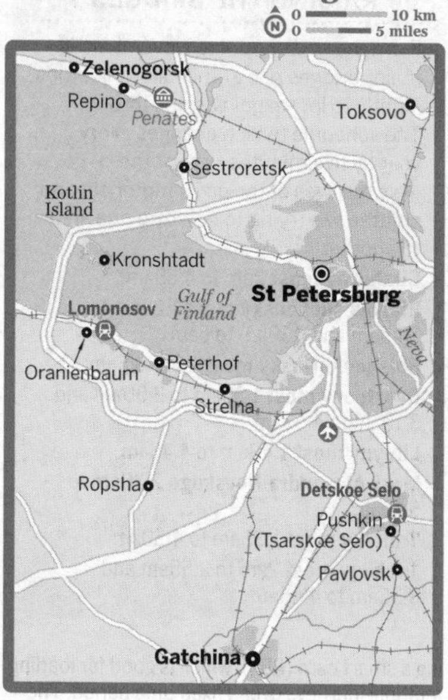

St Petersburg is not complete without a trip to at least one of them. Be warned that at the height of summer the endless tourist crowds can be frustrating. Moreover, while Peterhof is the most impressive palace, it's overpriced for foreigners. Tsarskoe Selo is the best value-for-money day trip.

If your time is short, or you wish to avoid the long queues, book yourself on a guided tour of either palace with a travel agency, and make sure that they prebook your entry ticket. **Peter's Walking Tours** (☎812-943 1229; www.peterswalk.com) in St Petersburg can do this for you.

If you have more time, there are several other options, including the charming old Finnish town of Vyborg, the sleepy village of Staraya Ladoga and the monastery town of Tikhvin.

Peterhof Петергоф

Hugging the Gulf of Finland, 29km west of St Petersburg, **Peterhof** (Петергоф; www.peterhofmuseum.ru; ul Razvodnaya 2), the 'Russian Versailles', is a far cry from the original cabin Peter the Great had built here to oversee construction of the Kronshtadt naval base. Peter liked the place so much he built a villa, Monplaisir, here and then a whole series of palaces and ornate gardens. Peterhof was renamed Petrodvorets (Peter's Palace) in 1944 but has since reverted to its original name. The palace and buildings are surrounded by leafy gardens and a spectacular ensemble of gravity-powered fountains.

What you see today is largely a reconstruction since Peterhof was a major casualty of WWII. Apart from the damage done by the Germans, the palace suffered the worst under Soviet bombing raids in December 1941 and January 1942 because Stalin was determined to thwart Hitler's plan of hosting a New Year's victory celebration here.

Sights

★Lower Park PARK

(Нижний парк; adult/student ₽500/250, free Nov-Apr; ⏲9am-8pm) Peterhof's masterpiece is the **Grand Cascade** (ul Razvodnaya 2; ⏲10am-6pm Mon-Fri, to 8.30pm Sat, to 7pm Sun, May–early Oct), a symphony of more than 140 fountains and canals engineered partly by Peter himself. To see the fountains you have to pay to enter the **Lower Park** and although they work only from May to early October, the gilded ensemble looks marvellous at any time of the year.

The central statue of Samson tearing open a lion's jaws celebrates – as do so many things in St Petersburg – Peter's victory over the Swedes. If you're interested in knowing how the fountains work, pay a visit to the Grotto beneath the Grand Cascade, where you can also see some trick fountains.

★Grand Palace PALACE

(Большой дворец; adult/student ₽550/300, audioguide ₽500; ⏲10.30am-6pm Tue-Sun, closed last Tue of month) The Grand Palace is an imposing building, although with just 30-something rooms, it is not nearly as large as your typical tsarist palace. From the start of June to the end of September it is open to foreign tourists only between 10.30am and noon, and again from 2.30pm until 4.15pm, due to guided tours being only in Russian at other times (it is quite possible to leave your group, however).

While Peter's palace was relatively modest, Rastrelli grossly enlarged the building for Empress Elizabeth. Later, Catherine the Great toned things down a little with a redecoration, although that's not really apparent from the glittering halls and art-filled galleries that are here today. All the paintings, furniture and chandeliers are original,

Peterhof

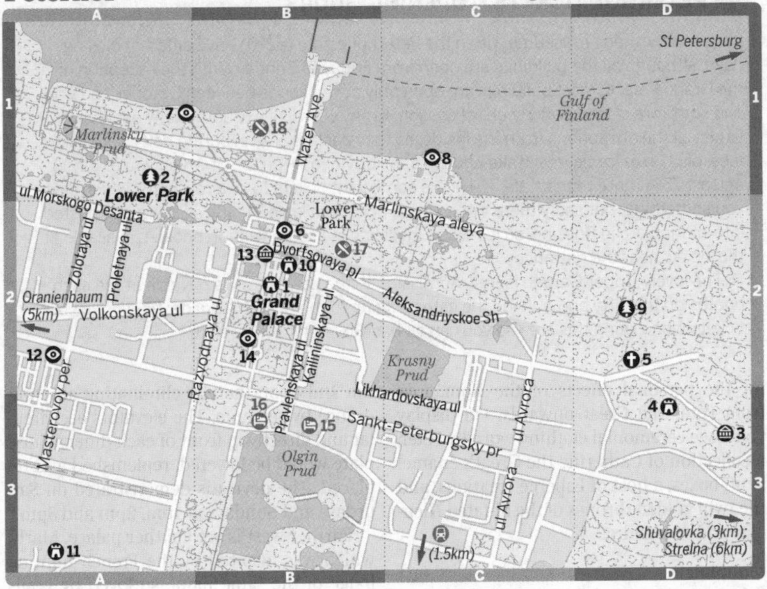

Peterhof

Top Sights

1 Grand Palace B2
2 Lower Park A1

Sights

3 Cottage D3
4 Farmer's Palace D3
5 Gothic Chapel D2
6 Grand Cascade B2
7 Hermitage A1
8 Monplaisir C1
9 Park Alexandria D2
10 Peterhof B2
11 Petrodvorets A3
12 Raketa Petrodvorets Watch Factory A2
13 Special Treasury B2
14 Upper Garden B2

Sleeping

15 New Peterhof Hotel B3
16 Samson Hotel B3

Eating

17 Grand Orangerie B2
18 Shtandart Restaurant B1

as everything was removed from the premises before the Germans arrived in WWII. The **Chesme Hall** is full of huge paintings of Russia's destruction of the Turkish fleet at Çesme in 1770. Other highlights include the exquisite **East and West Chinese Cabinets**, Picture Hall and **Peter's study**. The **Throne Room** is the biggest in the palace, and the centrepiece is Peter's red velvet throne, while the **Picture Hall** lives up to its name, with hundreds of portraits crowding its walls.

After WWII, Peterhof was largely left in ruins. Hitler had intended to throw a party here when his plans to occupy the Astoria Hotel were thwarted. He drew up pompous invitations, which obviously incensed his Soviet foes. Stalin's response was to preempt any such celebration by bombing the estate himself, in the winter of 1941–42, so it is ironic but true that most of the damage at Peterhof occurred at the hands of the Soviets. What you see today is largely a reconstruction; the main palace was completely gutted and only a few of its walls were left standing.

Special Treasury MUSEUM
(Музей Особая кладовая; adult/student ₽500/250; ⊙10.30am-6pm) This small museum within the main palace is a repository

PETERHOF TICKETS & OPENING HOURS

Inexplicably, many museums within the Peterhof estate (p210) have different closing days, although all the buildings are open from Friday to Sunday. With the exception of the Grand Palace, most buildings are open only at weekends between October and April, and some are closed entirely out of season. In any case, it's extraordinarily expensive to see all the attractions from the inside, as they each charge separate hefty admission fees, plus an extra ticket to take photographs or videos – on top of which you're paying at least 75% more than locals. There are some joint tickets to several sights, which save you something, but sadly there's no general ticket available. Nearly all tours and posted information are in Russian, so it's worth investing in an information booklet, available at the kiosks near the entrances.

The lovely Upper Garden is free. Admission to the Lower Park is payable at the cash booths on the jetty and outside the gates leading to the Grand Cascade; hold on to your ticket when exiting this area so you can go back in later if you need to.

for the personal effects of the Romanovs from Peter the Great onwards. On display you'll see ceremonial clothing worn by Peter, a collection of Catherine the Great's enamel snuff boxes, a host of Fabergé creations, and the twin golden thrones of the ill-fated Nicholas and Alexandra.

Monplaisir VILLA

(Монплезир; adult/student ₽400/200; 10.30am-6pm late May–early Oct) This humble, sea-facing, wood-panelled villa was always Peter the Great's favourite retreat and it's easy to see why. It is snug, elegant and peaceful, even when there's a crowd – which there used to be all the time, what with Peter's mandatory partying ('misbehaving' guests were required to gulp down huge quantities of wine).

Also in this complex is an annex called the Catherine Building, which was built by Rastrelli between 1747 and 1755. Its name derives from the fact that Catherine the Great was living here when her husband Peter III was overthrown, paving the way for her ascension to the throne. The interior contains the bedroom and study of Alexander I, as well as the huge Yellow Hall. On the right side is the magnificent Bath Building, built by Quarenghi in 1800, which is nothing special inside. Look out for some more trick fountains in the garden in front of the buildings.

Hermitage VILLA

(Эрмитаж; adult/student ₽250/150; 10.30am-6pm Wed-Mon May-Oct) Along the shore to the west, the 1725 Hermitage is a two-storey yellow-and-white box featuring the ultimate in private dining: special elevators hoist a fully laid table into the imperial presence on the 2nd floor, thereby eliminating any hindrance by servants. The elevators are circular and directly in front of each diner, whose plate would be lowered, replenished and replaced. The device is demonstrated on Saturdays and Sundays at 1pm, 2pm and 3pm.

Further west is yet another palace, Marly, which was inspired by the French hunting lodge of the same name so loved by Louis XIV.

Park Alexandria PARK

(Парк Александрия; adult/student ₽200/100; 9am-10pm) Even on summer weekends, the rambling and overgrown Park Alexandria is peaceful and practically empty. Built for Tsar Nicholas I (and named for his tsarina), these grounds offer a sweet retreat from the crowds. Originally named for Alexander Nevsky, the **Gothic chapel** (adult/student ₽250/150; 10.30am-6pm Tue-Sun) was completed in 1834 as the private chapel of Nicholas I. Nearby is the **cottage** (Коттедж; adult/student ₽400/200; 10.30am-6pm Tue-Sun) that was built around the same time as his summer residence.

Also part of this ensemble is the beautifully restored **Farmer's Palace** (Фермерский дворец; adult/student ₽500/250; 10.30am-6pm Tue-Sun), built here in 1831 as a pavilion in the park and designed to inspire pastoral fantasies of rural life for the royal family; it became the home of the teenage *tsarevitch* Alexander (later Alexander II), who loved it throughout his life.

Peterhof Town TOWN

The centre of Peterhof Town has plenty of sights. In front of the Grand Palace is the beautiful **Upper Garden** (dawn-dusk) FREE, which backs onto the Grand Palace.

Wander down Pravlenskaya ul and you'll find yourself in the middle of town. It's well worth wandering past the handsome St Peter and Paul Cathedral and continuing around the edge of Olga's Pond (Olgin Prud) to the Tsaritsyn & Olgin Pavilions, two buildings that sit on two islands in the middle of the pond. Nicholas I had these elaborate pavilions built for his wife (Alexandra Fyodorovna) and daughter (Olga Nikolayevna) respectively. Only recently restored and reopened, they boast unique Mediterranean architectural styles reminiscent of Pompeii.

Further down Sankt-Peterburgsky pr is the **Raketa Petrodvorets Watch Factory** (☑8-921-632 0313; www.raketa.com; Sankt-Peterburgsky pr 60; ⊗9am-4pm Mon-Fri) FREE, one of the town's biggest employers, which has an on-site shop selling very cool watches. It's best to visit in the morning if you'd like to see the whole production process.

🛏 Sleeping & Eating

Samson Hotel
HOTEL **$$**

(☑812-334 7155; www.samsonhotel.ru; Sankt-Peterburgsky pr 44; s/d from ₽2350/3000; ❋🛜) This hotel and restaurant complex is bang opposite the Upper Garden should you wish to beat the tour groups into the palace in the morning. The rooms are spacious and blandly modern. There's a large cellar-like restaurant serving Russian and European cuisine.

New Peterhof Hotel
HOTEL **$$**

(☑812-319 1090; www.new-peterhof.com; Sankt Peterburgsky pr 34; s/d from ₽3800/4400; 🐾) This impressive new hotel complex has 150 rooms in a most unusually designed building kitty corner to Peterhof's Upper Garden. Rooms are modern and sleek with all the amenities you'd expect, plus a pool and sauna that are free for guests to use in the mornings. There's decent food to be had at the two on-site restaurants as well.

Shtandart Restaurant
RUSSIAN **$$**

(Ресторан Штандарт; www.restaurantshtandart. spb.ru; Lower Park; mains ₽500-800; ⊗11am-8pm; 🐾) This large and upmarket restaurant overlooks the Gulf of Finland, just west of the boat dock, with plenty of seating both inside and out. It has a large and meaty menu full of filling but interesting Russian classics.

Grand Orangerie
RUSSIAN **$$**

(Lower Park; set menus ₽450-800; ⊗11am-8pm; 🐾) This cafe in the charming orangery is

an elegant choice for lunch. It gets busy at lunchtime, so you may have to queue for a spot. The menu is packed with Russian classics and there's also a good cake selection.

❶ Getting There & Away

It's easy and cheap to reach Peterhof by bus or *marshrutka*. *Marshrutka* 300, 424 and 424A (₽55) leave from outside the Avtovo metro station, while *marshrutka* 103 leaves from outside Leninsky Prospekt station. All pass through the town of Peterhof, immediately outside the palace. Tell the driver you want to go '*v dvaryéts*' ('to the palace') and you'll be let off near the main entrance to the Upper Garden, on Sankt-Peterburgsky pr.

There's also a reasonably frequent suburban train (₽67, 30 minutes) from Baltiysky vokzal to Novy Petrodvorets, from where you can walk (around 20 minutes) or take any bus except 357 to the fifth stop, which will take another 10 minutes.

From May to September, the **Peterhof Express** (Map p166; adult single/return ₽650/1100, student single/return ₽450/800; ⊗10am-6pm) departs from the jetty in front of the Admiralty every 30 minutes. It's an expensive but highly enjoyable way to get to Peterhof, and you arrive right in front of the palace. The last hydrofoil leaves Peterhof at 7pm, and the trip takes 30 minutes.

Oranienbaum Ораниенбаум

While Peter was building Monplaisir, his right-hand man, Alexander Menshikov, began his own palace, Oranienbaum (Orange Tree), 5km down the coast from Peterhof. This grand enterprise eventually bankrupted Menshikov. Following Peter's death and Menshikov's exile, the estate served briefly as a hospital and then passed to Tsar Peter III, who didn't much like ruling Russia and spent a lot of time here before he was dispatched in a coup led by his wife Catherine (later the Great).

Spared Nazi occupation and, after WWII, ruined by Soviet neglect, Oranienbaum and the surrounding town were renamed after the scientist-poet Mikhail Lomonosov. The palatial estate is once again known as Oranienbaum (though the town remains Lomonosov) and it doubles as a museum and **public park** (Музей-заповедник Ораниенбаум; www.peterhofmuseum.ru; adult/student ₽200/100 May-Oct, free Nov-Apr; ⊗9am-8pm), with gorgeous landscaped gardens and an ornamental lake. Generally bypassed by tour groups, it's a pleasant setting for a picnic or a tranquil walk away from the crowds.

Menshikov's impressive **Great Palace** (Большой дворец; adult/student ₽400/200; ⌚10.30am-6pm Wed-Mon) underwent a full restoration and reopened its state rooms in 2014. Most of the interiors are restorations of the 19th-century ones, so reflect the taste of the various Romanovs who used the palace, rather than Menshikov himself, of whom there is no trace. There are impressive ceiling mouldings in the Concert Hall, while the ground floor is given over to an exhibit about the long restoration project. Overall the palace is more impressive from the outside.

One of the ground's buildings open for inspection is the **Palace of Peter III** (Дворец Петра III; adult/student ₽250/150; ⌚10.30am-6pm May-Oct, to 5pm Sat & Sun Nov-Apr), a boxy miniature palace, with rich, uncomfortable-looking interiors and some Chinese-style lacquer-on-wood paintings. It was restored in the late 1950s and early '60s, but is in dire need of attention again: its salmon-pink walls are flaking and chipped. It is approached through the **Gate of Honour**, all that remains of a toy fortress where Peter amused himself drilling his soldiers.

Worth a peek also is Catherine's over-the-top **Chinese Palace** (Китайский дворец; adult/student ₽400/200; ⌚10.30am-6pm Tue-Sun), designed by Antonio Rinaldi. Rococo on the inside and baroque on the outside, the private retreat features painted ceilings and fine inlaid-wood floors and walls.

Opposite the palace entrance there's a reasonably good restaurant, **Okhota** (Охота; Dvortsovy pr 65a; mains ₽500-1000; ⌚noon-midnight; 📋), that's big on taxidermy for its hunting-themed decor. A better and cheaper option is the **Mimino** (Мимино; mains ₽200-400; ⌚11am-2am) Georgian restaurant near the train station: walk past the church and turn left after the orange building.

ℹ Getting There & Away

The train from St Petersburg's Baltiysky vokzal to Peterhof continues to Oranienbaum (₽67, one hour). Get off at Lomonosov Station, an hour from St Petersburg. From the station, walk diagonally across the little park in front, keep going up to the main road, turn right, pass the unmissable Archangel Michael Cathedral and you'll reach the park entrance on your left. Alternatively you can take *marshrutka* 300, 424 or 424A to Lomonosov (₽55) from outside metro Avtovo. Once in Lomonosov town, the bus eventually comes down a hill with the Archangel Michael Cathedral at the bottom. Get off here and follow the park perimeter to the left until you reach the entrance.

Strelna & Around
Стрельна и Окрестности Стрельны

Six kilometres east of Peterhof is the town of Strelna, where you'll find two more palaces originally built for Peter. The butterscotch-painted Konstantinovsky Palace was chosen by Vladimir Putin as his St Petersburg residence, underwent total renovation and reopened as the **Palace of Congress** (Дворец Конгрессов; www.konstantinpalace.ru; Beryozovaya al 3; admission ₽350; ⌚10am-5pm Thu-Tue). It's best to call ahead to book a tour, or book one online, as the palace is often used for official functions and therefore closed. Not a must-see sight, the palace nonetheless provides a fascinating glimpse of how a modern-day Russian leader likes to entertain his guests. There's a small collection of medals from the Hermitage's collection here and some reconstructed rooms from the time of Grand Duke Konstantin Konstantinovich, the palace's last imperial owner, and something of a poet and musician.

Opposite the entrance to the palace and scoring high on the modern kitsch factor is **Lindstrem's Dacha** (www.dachalindstrema.ru; ul Glinka 7; ⌚10am-6pm), once the home of the grand duke's doctor Peter I von Lindstrem. Restored for the 2005 G8 summit, also hosted at the Konstantinovsky Palace, the modest-sized building was used by Putin to entertain his opposite numbers and their wives. One can only wonder what they thought of the garish *nouveau-russe* interior, which has since been supplemented by a small shrine to all things Putin, including a chance to have a three-minute audience with a life-sized hologram of the man himself.

A short walk to the west of the Palace of Congress lies the compact and infinitely more charming **Peter I's Palace at Strelna** (Дворец Петра I; adult/student ₽200/100; ⌚10.30am-5pm Tue-Sun). This is one of the first palaces that Peter the Great built out this way while supervising his far grander enterprise down the road. It has some well-furnished interiors with interesting exhibits, most notably a combined travelling chest and camp bed belonging to Alexander III.

All those visiting VIPs need somewhere to stay, so next to the Palace of Congress is the luxurious **Baltic Star Hotel** (☑812-438 5700; www.balticstar-hotel.ru; Beriozovaya al 3; r from ₽5800, ste ₽9000; ◉❄@☎☀). It's a fancy enough place, but there's really no compelling reason to stay this far out of St Petersburg.

ℹ Getting There & Away

Trains and buses serving Peterhof pass through Strelna.

Pushkin (Tsarskoe Selo)
Пушкин (Царское Село)

The grand imperial estate of **Tsarskoe Selo** (☑812-465 2281; http://eng.tzar.ru; Sadovaya ul 7, Tsar's Village) in the town of Pushkin, 25km south of St Petersburg, is often combined on a day trip with the palace and sprawling park at Pavlovsk, 4km further south. It's a great combination, but start out early as there's lots to see: Pushkin can easily be a full-day trip in itself.

The railway that connects Pushkin and Pavlovsk with St Petersburg was Russia's first, opened in 1837 to carry the imperial family between here and the then capital. The town changed its name to Pushkin in 1937 after Russia's favourite poet, who studied here and whose school and dacha you can also visit. While the palace and park complex's name has reverted to Tsarskoe Selo (The Tsar's Village), the town remains proudly named for the national bard.

◉ Sights

★**Catherine Palace** PALACE
(Екатерининский дворец; http://eng.tzar.ru; adult/student ₽400/200, audioguide ₽150; ◷10am-6pm Wed-Sun, to 9pm Mon) The centrepiece of Tsarskoe Selo, created under Empresses Elizabeth and Catherine the Great between 1744 and 1796, is the vast baroque Catherine Palace, designed by Rastrelli and named after Peter the Great's second wife. The palace can only be visited by individuals between noon and 2pm, and 4pm and 5pm, otherwise it's reserved for pre-booked tour groups, such is its rightful popularity. The audioguide is well worth taking, as it gives detailed explanation of what you'll see in each room.

As at the Winter Palace, Catherine the Great had many of Rastrelli's original interiors remodelled in classical style. Most of the gaudy exterior and 20-odd rooms of the palace have been beautifully restored – compare them to the photographs of the devastation left by the Germans.

The interiors are superb, with highlights including the Great Hall, the Arabesque Hall, the baroque Cavalier's Dining Room, the White State Dining Room, the Crimson and Green Pilaster Rooms, the Portrait Hall and of course the world-famous Amber Room. The panels used in the latter were a gift given to Peter the Great, but not put to any use until 1743 when Elizabeth decided to use them decoratively, after which they were ingeniously incorporated into the walls here. What you see is a reconstruction of the original that disappeared during WWII and is believed to have been destroyed.

THE MYSTERY OF THE AMBER ROOM

The original Amber Room was created from exquisitely engraved amber panels given to Peter the Great by King Friedrich Wilhelm I of Prussia in 1716. Rastrelli later combined the panels with gilded woodcarvings, mirrors, agate and jasper mosaics to decorate one of the rooms of the Catherine Palace. Plundered by the Nazis during WWII, the room's decorative panels were last exhibited in Königsberg's castle in 1941. Four years later, with the castle in ruins, the Amber Room was presumed destroyed. Or was it?

In 2004, as Putin and then German Chancellor Gerhardt Schröder presided over the opening of the new US$18 million Amber Room, restored largely with German funds, rumours about the original panels continued to swirl. There are those who believe that parts, if not all, of the original Amber Room remain hidden away (see www.amberroom.org). The mystery gained traction in February 2008 as attention focused on the possible contents of an artificial cavern discovered near the village of Deutschneudorf on Germany's border with the Czech Republic. Nothing conclusive has yet been unearthed here, though, so the mystery continues.

Pushkin

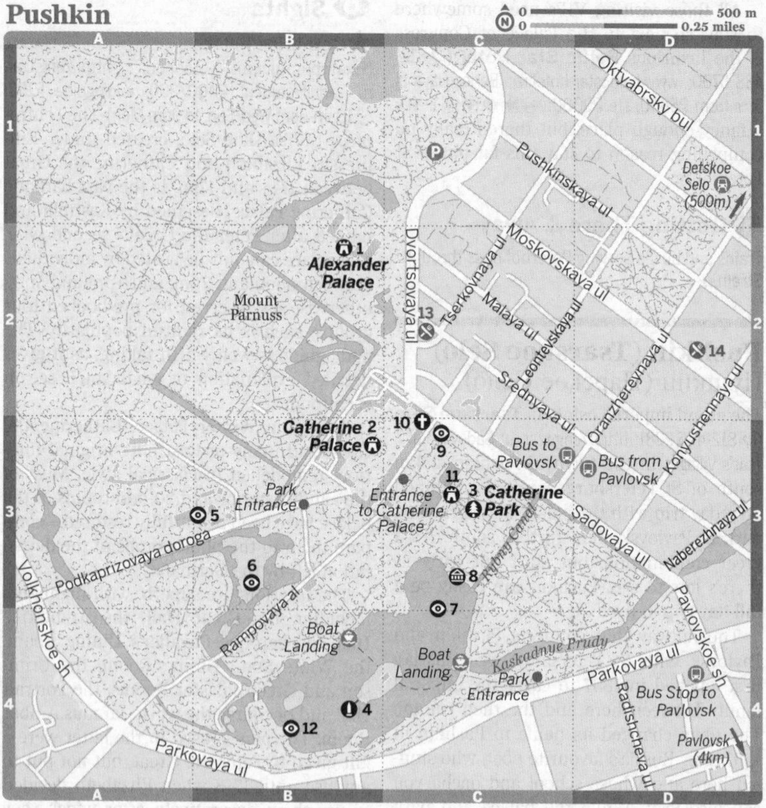

Pushkin

Top Sights

1	Alexander Palace	B2
2	Catherine Palace	B3
3	Catherine Park	C3

Sights

4	Chesme Column	B4
5	Chinese Pavilion	B3
6	Concert Hall	B3
7	Great Pond	C3
8	Grotto Pavilion	C3
9	Main Entrance to Catherine Park	C3
10	Palace Chapel	C3
11	Tsarskoe Selo	C3
12	Turkish Bath	B4

Eating

	19th Century Restaurant	(see 13)
13	Daniel	C2
14	White Rabbit	D2

★Catherine Park

PARK

(Екатерининский парк; adult/student May-Sep ₽120/60, Oct-Apr free; ⌚9am-6pm) Around the Catherine Palace extends the lovely Catherine Park. The **main entrance** is on Sadovaya ul, next to the **Palace Chapel**. The park extends around the ornamental Great Pond and contains an array of interesting buildings, follies and pavilions.

Near the Catherine Palace, the Cameron Gallery normally has rotating exhibitions, but was closed for renovations at the time of writing. Between the gallery and the palace, notice the south-pointing ramp that Cameron added for the ageing empress to walk down into the park.

The park's outer section focuses on the **Great Pond**. In summer you can take a ferry to the little island to visit the **Chesme**

Column (adult/child ₽250/150; ⏰11am-6pm May-Sep). Beside the pond, the blue baroque **Grotto Pavilion** (⏰10am-5pm Fri-Wed) FREE houses temporary exhibitions in summer. A walk around the Great Pond will reveal other buildings that the royals built over the years, including the very incongruous-looking **Turkish Bath** with its minaret-style tower, the wonderful Marble Bridge, the **Chinese Pavilion** and a **Concert Hall** isolated on an island, where concerts take place every Saturday at 5pm (tickets ₽400).

★ **Alexander Palace** PALACE
(Александровский дворец; Dvortsovaya ul 2; adult/student/under 18yr ₽300/150/free, audio-guide ₽100; ⏰10am-5pm Wed-Mon, closed last Wed of month) The classical Alexander Palace, built by Quarenghi between 1792 and 1796 for the future Alexander I, is surrounded by the charming Alexander Park. Nicholas II, the last Russian tsar, was its main tenant and he made it his residence for much of his reign. Nicholas and his wife Alexandra cared for their haemophiliac son and heir to the Romanov throne, Alexei, within this sad palace's walls, as his empire and dynasty slowly collapsed.

Only three rooms are open to visitors, but they're impressive, with a huge tiger-skin carpet and an extremely ropey portrait of a young Queen Victoria to boot. It's a poignant and forgotten place that doesn't get many tourists; it's a welcome contrast to the Catherine Palace.

Eating

White Rabbit INTERNATIONAL $$
(ul Moskovskaya 22; mains ₽500-1000; ⏰11am-11pm; 📶📋) In the centre of town, this pub-like place has good-quality food and attentive service. There's an international menu with plenty of choice and a local atmosphere worth leaving the palace for.

19th Century Restaurant RUSSIAN $$
(Ресторан 19-й век; www.restaurantpushkin.ru; Srednyaya ul 2; mains ₽400-750; 📶) Admire the owner's impressive collection of miniature bottles of alcohol at the entrance, before choosing one of four differently decorated dining rooms in which to eat a traditional Russian meal.

Daniel INTERNATIONAL $$$
(Даниель; www.apriorico.com; Srednyaya ul 2/3; mains ₽750-1500; ⏰11am-11pm; 📶) Daniel offers a blow-out gastronomic feast within stumbling distance of the Catherine Palace. Swedish chef Eric Viedgård conjures culinary magic with his seasonally changing menu in an elegant contemporary space with heritage touches.

Getting There & Away

From Moskovskaya metro station, take the exit marked 'Buses for the airport', and then pick up *marshrutka* 286, 299, 342 or K545 towards Pushkin (₽35). These buses all continue to Pavlovsk (₽40). Look for Пушкин or Дворец on the buses.

Suburban trains run from Vitebsky vokzal in St Petersburg, but they're infrequent except for weekends. For Pushkin, get off at Detskoe Selo (Детское село, ₽55, 30 minutes) and for Pavlovsk (₽60, 40 minutes) at Pavlovsk Station (Павловск). From Detskoe Selo station *marshrutky* (₽20) frequently run the 500m or so to Tsarskoe Selo.

Pavlovsk Павловск

Between 1781 and 1786, on orders from Catherine the Great, architect Charles Cameron designed the Great Palace in Pavlovsk. The palace was designated for Catherine's son Paul (hence the name, Pavlovsk), and it was Paul's second wife, Maria Fyodorovna, who orchestrated the design of the interiors. It served as a royal residence until 1917. Ironically, the original palace burnt down two weeks after WWII when a careless Soviet soldier's cigarette set off German mines (the Soviets blamed the Germans). As at Tsarskoe Selo, its restoration is remarkable.

Sights

Pavlovsk Great Palace PALACE
(Большой павловский дворец; www.pavlovskmuseum.ru; adult/child ₽450/250; ⏰10am-6pm, closed Fri mid-Sep & mid-May) The finest rooms in Pavlovsk's Great Palace are on the middle floor of the central block. Cameron designed the round Italian Hall beneath the dome and the Grecian Hall to its west, though the lovely green fluted columns were added by his assistant Vincenzo Brenna. Flanking these are two private suites designed mainly by Brenna – Paul's along the north side of the block and Maria Fyodorovna's on the south.

The Hall of War of the insane, military-obsessed Paul contrasts with Maria's Hall of Peace, decorated with musical instruments and flowers. On the middle floor of the south block are Paul's Throne Room and the Hall of the Maltese Knights of St John, of whom he was the Grand Master.

Pavlovsk Park PARK
(Павловский парк; adult/child ₽150/80; ⏲10am-6pm, closed Fri mid-Sep–mid-May) You'll have to pay to enter the serene Pavlovsk Great Park just to access the palace, so it's worth exploring and seeing what you come across while you're here. Filled with rivers and ponds, tree-lined avenues, classical statues and hidden temples, it's a delightful place to get lost. Highlights include the Rose Pavilion and the Private Garden, with its beautifully arranged flowerbeds and impressive sculpture of the Three Graces.

Bike hire (₽250 per hour) is available in several locations around the park and is a great way to explore, as distances are great.

Eating

Podvorye RUSSIAN $$$
(☎812-465 1399; www.podvorye.ru; Filtrovskoye sh 16; mains ₽600-1500; ⏲noon-11pm) A short walk northeast of Pavlovsk train station, you'll find this traditional Russian log house on steroids. Huge portions of delicious Russian food are dished up, with a side order of live Russian music and dancing.

Getting There & Away

Trains and *marshrutky* running from St Petersburg to Pushkin continue to Pavlovsk. *Marshrutky* (₽20) frequently shuttle between Pushkin and Pavlovsk; catch one from Pavolovskoe sh near the southeast corner of Catherine Park, and get off either at Pavlovsk station (for entry to the park) or in front of Pavlovsk's palace.

Gatchina Гатчина

☎81371

Far less touristy than the other country palaces close to St Petersburg, Gatchina, 45km southwest of the city, can make for a very pleasant half-day trip. Gatchina is a busy and bustling town that just happens to also host a tsarist palace and park. You can buy a ₽250 ticket that covers entry to the palace and all three pavillions in the grounds.

Sights

While the Great Palace and the park are the obvious draws, there are a couple of interesting churches in the town centre. The baroque **Pavlovsk Cathedral** (Павловский собор; ul Sobornaya), at the end of the pedestrianised shopping street off the central pr 25 Oktyabrya, has a grandly restored interior with a soaring central dome. A short walk west is the **Pokrovsky Cathedral** (Покровский собор; Krasnaya ul), a red-brick building with bright-blue domes.

Gatchina Great Palace PALACE
(Большой гатчинский дворец; www.gatchinapalace.ru/en; adult/student ₽200/100, photos ₽100, audioguide ₽200; ⏲10am-6pm Tue-Sun, closed 1st Tue of month) Shaped in a graceful curve around a central turret, the Gatchina Great Palace certainly lives up to its name – its enormous (if surprisingly plain) facade is quite a sight to behold, overlooking a vast parade ground and backing onto the huge landscaped grounds. Built by Rinaldi between 1766 and 1781 in an early classicism style for Catherine the Great's favourite Grigory Orlov, the palace curiously combines motifs of a medieval fortress with elements commonly seen in Russian imperial residences.

It's hard to call it beautiful, but there's no doubt that it's extremely impressive. After Orlov's death in 1783, Catherine the Great bought the palace from his heirs and gifted it to her son Paul, who redesigned the exterior between 1792 and 1798.

Inside, the 10 State Rooms on the 2nd floor are impressive, including Paul I's Throne Room, hung with huge tapestries, and his wife Maria Fyodorovna's Throne Room, the walls of which are covered in paintings. Most impressive of all is the White Hall, a Rinaldi creation from the 1770s that was redone by Brenna in the 1790s. On the balcony is an impressive collection of sundials.

Gatchina Park PARK
(Гатчинский парк; ⏲dawn-dusk) FREE Gatchina Park is more overgrown and romantic than the other palaces' parklands. The park has many winding paths through birch groves and across bridges to islands in the large White Lake. Look out for the frankly bizarre **Birch House** (Березовый домик; adult/student ₽50/20; ⏲10am-6pm Tue-Sun May–mid-Sep), which was a present from Maria Fyodorovna to Paul I. With a rough facade made of birch logs, the interior is actually very refined, with a beautiful hardwood floor made from timber from around the world.

Paul I later built a neoclassical 'mask' to hide the Birch House's facade from the view of casual strollers.

Down on the lake, the **Venus Pavilion** (Павильон Венеры; adult/student ₽50/20; ⏲10am-6pm Tue-Sun May–mid-Sep) is a beautiful spot jutting out into the water with an elaborately painted interior. Continue around the lake to find the best picnicking spots – it's even possible to swim in a second lake (see where the locals go) if the weather is good.

It's also possible to visit Paul I's **private garden** (Собственный садик; adult/student ₽50/20; ⏲10am-6pm Tue-Sun May–mid-Sep), adjacent to the palace, laid out in the late 18th century by Vincenzo Brenna for the private use of the royal family. It's a charming place to stroll, full of sculptures, flowers and neatly trimmed hedges.

Eating

There is a cafe in the Grand Palace and a couple of simple cafes in the grounds, but as the place was made for picnicking, your best bet is to bring your own lunch. However, if you haven't done so, there are a couple of decent options in the town spread out along pedestrianised ul Sobornaya.

Kafe Piramida RUSSIAN $

(Кафе Пирамида; ul Sobornaya 3a; mains ₽180-300; ⏲10am-11pm) Serving a wide range of traditional Russian dishes as well as delicious cakes and coffees, this cosy place is near the Pavlovsk Cathedral. It's poorly signposted, but is above a far better advertised Finnish Burger place.

Slavyansky Dvor RUSSIAN $

(Славянский двор; ul Dostoevskogo 2; mains ₽200-500; ⏲11am-midnight) Housed in a restored historic building near the Pokrovsky Cathedral, this traditional Russian place inside a hotel complex of the same name (meaning 'Slavic Yard') will prepare you a filling meal at any time of day.

Getting There & Away

The quickest way to get to Gatchina is by bus. Bus K18, K18A and 431 (₽70, 45 minutes) run this route from outside Moskovskaya metro station and stop right by the park. Bus 100 (₽70, one hour) also runs regularly from Moskovskaya; buses wait outside the massive House of Soviets and stop just short of Gatchina Park. Tell the driver you want to go to the palace ('*v dvaryéts*') – the bus turns off before you get to the park.

There are trains to Gatchina Baltiysky (₽84, one hour) from Baltiysky vokzal every one to two hours. The train station is directly in front of the palace.

Kronshtadt Кронштадт

☎812 / POP 43,000

Within a year of founding St Petersburg, Peter – desirous of protecting his new Baltic toehold – started work on the fortress of Kronshtadt on Kotlin Island, 29km out in the Gulf of Finland. It's been a pivotal Soviet and Russian naval base ever since, and was closed to foreigners until 1996.

In 1921 the hungry and poor Red Army sailors stationed here organised an ill-fated mutiny against the Bolsheviks. They set up a Provisional Revolutionary Committee and drafted a resolution demanding, among other things, an end to Lenin's harsh War Communism. On 16 March 1921 the mutineers were defeated when 50,000 troops crossed the ice from Petrograd and massacred nearly the entire naval force. The sailors' stand wasn't entirely in vain as afterwards Lenin did scrap War Communism.

Sights & Activities

Kronshtadt's key sight is the unusual and beautiful **Naval Cathedral** (Морской собор; Yakornaya pl; ⏲9am-6.30pm) FREE. Built between 1903 and 1913 to honour Russian naval muscle, this neo-Byzantine wonder stands on Yakornaya pl (Anchor Sq), where you'll also find an eternal flame for all of Kronshtadt's sailors, and the florid art-nouveau monument of Admiral Makarov. The cathedral underwent a thorough renovation for its recent centennial celebrations and is now looking breathtaking both inside and out. Its 75m-high cupola is the highest point in town, and its enormous interior makes its use in the Soviet Union as a cinema rather logical.

In the harbourside Petrovsky Park, 700m southwest of the cathedral, there's a statue of Peter the Great. You can also glimpse Russian warships and even some submarines: be careful about taking photographs, though, as these are militarily sensitive subjects and a quick snap could land you a long chat with a police officer. From the Middle Harbour you can take two-hour cruises on the **Reeperbahn** (☎821-382 0888; Middle Harbour; adult/student ₽650/400; ⏲departures 1.30pm, 3.30pm & 5.30pm May-Sep) to several forts around the island, including Fort Konstantin, where the boat stops for you to explore on foot.

Eating

For eating in Kronshtadt, try **Cafe Kashtan** (Кафе Каштан; pr Lenina 25; mains ₽300-500;

⏲11am-11pm), just off the town's main shopping street, pr Lenina on ul Andreevskaya. It's friendly and has a large selection of Russian dishes, as well as good coffee and cake.

Getting There & Away

Catch bus 101 to Kronshtadt from Staraya Derevnya metro station (₽25, 40 minutes). Upon exiting the metro, turn hard left and then walk past the *marshrutky* and trams until you come to a second bus park where the 101 bus begins and ends its route. Alternatively take *marshrutka* 405 from Chyornaya Rechka station (₽60, 40 minutes); exit the station to your left and cross the street to find the stop. The buses back to St Petersburg depart from outside the large 'Dom Byta' on the corner of ul Grazhdanskaya and pr Lenina. From there it's about a 1km walk southeast to the Naval Cathedral.

With the completion of St Petersburg's ring road, it's now possible to reach Kronshtadt from Oranienbaum, meaning it's perfectly feasible to combine a trip here with a visit to one of the Tsarist palaces.

Leningrad Region

Several places in the Leningrad region (Ленинградская область) can be seen in a day trip from St Petersburg. For more about the region, see http://eng.lenobl.ru.

Vyborg Выборг

☎81378 / POP 80,000 / ⏲MOSCOW

This appealing Gulf of Finland provincial town is dominated by a medieval castle and peppered with beautiful Finnish art-nouveau buildings and romantic cobblestone streets. An important port and rail junction, Vyborg (*vih*-bork) is 174km northwest of St Petersburg and just 30km from the Finnish border. It has just about enough to do to justify staying over, but is also an easy day trip from St Petersburg.

The border has jumped back and forth around Vyborg for most of its history. Peter the Great captured it from the Swedes in 1710. A century later it fell within autonomous Finland, and after the revolution Vyborg remained part of independent Finland. Since then the Finns have called it Viipuri. Stalin took Vyborg in 1939, lost it to the Finns during WWII, and on getting it back at the end of the war deported all the Finns. Today the Finns are back by the coachloads for sightseeing and carousing on the weekends.

Sights

With the exception of Park Monrepo, all Vyborg's main sights are neatly arranged around a compact peninsula, making it an ideal town to explore on foot.

★Vyborg Castle HISTORIC BUILDING
(Выборгский замок; Zamkovy Island; grounds admission ₽10, museum ₽60, tower ₽40, exhibits ₽30; ⏲museum 11am-7pm Tue-Sun, tower 10am-8pm daily) Rising stoutly from an islet in Vyborg Bay, this castle was built by the Swedes in 1293 when they first captured Karelia from Novgorod. Most of it now consists of 16th-century alterations. The castle contains a couple of exhibition halls, including a mildly diverting small museum on local history, but the main attraction is climbing the many steps of whitewashed St Olaf's Tower for commanding views over the town.

An interesting website with history of the castle and other fortifications across northern Russia is www.nortfort.ru.

Park Monrepo PARK
(Парк Монрепо; www.parkmonrepos.org; adult/student ₽50/25; ⏲10am-8pm May-Oct, to 6pm Nov-Apr) A lovely place to escape the world for a few hours, if not most of the day, is this 180-hectare park facing on to tranquil Zashchitnaya Bay. It's laid out in a classical style, with various pavilions, curved bridges, arbours and sculptures. Bus 1 or 6 (₽20, 15 minutes) will get you here from outside the train and bus stations.

★Hermitage Vyborg MUSEUM
(Эрмитаж Выборг; ul Ladanova 1; adult/student ₽250/150; ⏲10am-6pm) Housed in a wing of a striking building designed by Finnish architect Uno Ulberg in 1930, this small museum hosts themed exhibitions, curated from the Hermitage's massive collection, that change every six months. The functional white building, which sits in the middle of an old defensive bastion, is shared with Vyborg's arts school, which also has a **gallery** FREE with regularly changing exhibitions.

Lenin & Esplanade Parks PARK
Explore these two central and adjacent leafy parks, separated by Leningradsky pr, to find intriguing statutes and carved trees. At the southern end of Lenin Park is the **Alvar Aalto Library**, designed by the famous Finnish architect in 1935 and, in the Esplanade Park, the Lutheran **SS Peter & Paul Cathedral** (Собор святых апостолов Петра и Павла).

Vyborg

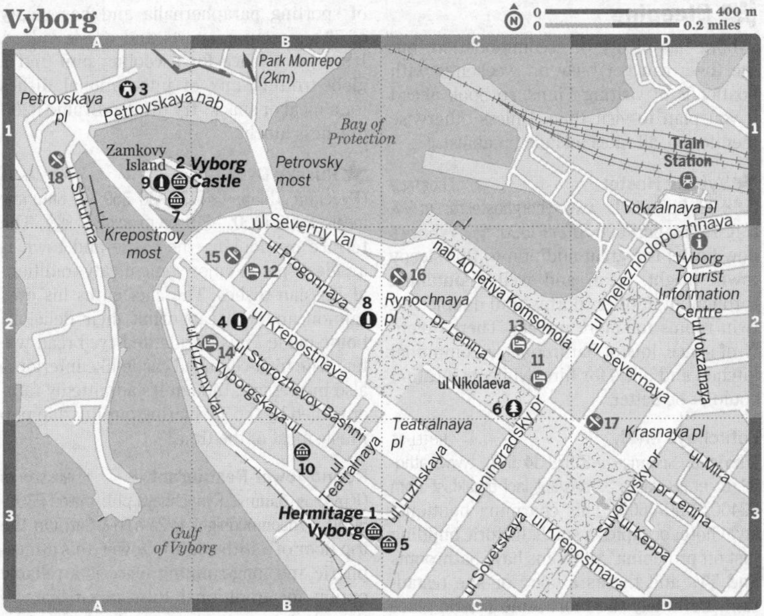

Vyborg

Top Sights
1 Hermitage Vyborg B3
2 Vyborg Castle A1

Sights
3 Anninskie Fortifications A1
4 Clock Tower B2
5 Hermitage Vyborg Gallery C3
6 Lenin & Esplanade Parks C2
7 Museum A1
8 Round Tower B2
9 St Olaf's Tower A1
10 Town Hall B3

Sleeping
11 Apart-Hotel Ullberg C2
12 Atlantik B2
13 Letuchaya Mysh C2
14 Vyborg Hostel B2

Eating
15 Café Respect B2
16 Central Market C2
17 Champion D3
Round Tower Restaurant .... (see 8)
18 Russky Dvor A1

Anninskie Fortifications FORTRESS
(Аннинские укрепления; Ostrovnaya ul) At the southern end of Tverdysh Island is this double line of fortifications built between 1730 and 1750, as protection against the Swedes, and named after Empress Anna Ioanovna. Nearby, on a hill just above the restaurant Russky Dvor, a handsome statue of **Peter the Great** surveys the town, erected on the bicentenary of the city's capture by Russia.

Swedish Relics HISTORIC SITE
As well as the castle, other relics of Vyborg's Swedish times are found in the squat **Round Tower** (pl Rynochnaya), which now houses a restaurant; the remains of the 15th-century **Town Hall** (Башня Ратуши; ul Vyborgskaya 15), with its distinctive white tower crowned with what resembles a giant metallic wizard's hat; and the **Clock Tower** (Часовая башня; ul Krepostnaya 5), dating to 1490 – if the caretaker is around to let you in, it's worth climbing for the views of town.

Festivals & Events

In July the town hosts the ambitious five-day **Vyborg Intelligent Performance** (www.vkontakte.ru/vbgpromenade) arts festival, which includes live music, theatre and lectures.

Sleeping

Vyborg has plenty of accommodation, but the town can get busy on weekends with boatloads of visiting Finns, so book ahead if you plan to visit then. Unless otherwise mentioned, all rates include breakfast.

★ Vyborg Hostel HOSTEL **$**
(☎8-921-950 0201; www.vyborghostel.ru; ul Vyborgskaya 4; dm ₽600-700, r ₽1500;) Vyborg's new hostel is a great addition to this sleepy town. Bright, clean and well maintained throughout, it offers dorms, and double and twin rooms for more privacy. There's plenty of space, lots of bathrooms, a communal kitchen and bikes for hire, while its location couldn't be better.

Letuchaya Mysh HOTEL **$$**
(Летучая мышь; ☎81378-34 537; www.bathotel.ru; ul Nikolaeva 3; s/d/apt incl breakfast from ₽2400/2700/4600) This charming boutique-style hotel occupies a small, historic building just off pr Lenina. All rooms have bathrooms and TVs and there's a good on-site restaurant. Definitely the most atmospheric place to stay in Vyborg, even if it is overshadowed by a large Soviet block of flats.

Apart-Hotel Ullberg APARTMENTS **$$**
(☎81378-55 417; www.hotel-apart.ru; Leningradsky pr 10; apt incl breakfast ₽3100-3600;) This well-located guesthouse overlooks Park Lenina from inside a handsome 1915 building. It has five brightly decorated, comfy rooms, all of which have minikitchens.

Atlantik HOTEL **$$**
(☎81378-24 776; www.hotelatlantik.ru; ul Podgornaya 9; s/d incl breakfast ₽2400/2900;) This small hotel, close to the castle, offers comfortable if unexciting accommodation in a quiet street in the old town. It offers a variety of rooms and has a restaurant opening onto a quiet courtyard.

Eating & Drinking

Cafe Respect CAFE **$**
(Кафе Респект; ☎81378-34 007; ul Podgornaya 10; mains ₽200-400; ⏲11am-11pm Thu-Sat, from noon Sun-Wed) This cosy place with only a few tables and an old European feel is found on a charming old street in the middle of the old town. It only has a Russian menu but has the usual range of dishes such as salads and soups.

Champion PUB FOOD **$**
(Чемпион; pr Lenina 10; mains ₽200-400; ⏲11am-2am;) This modern pub is full of sporting paraphernalia and has plenty of TVs screening sports and music videos. It's a good place for a cooling pint and a globe-trotting mix of international dishes for a meal or snack. Try the good-value ₽200 business lunch.

★ Russky Dvor RUSSIAN **$$**
(Русский Двор; ☎81378-36 369; ul Shturma; meals ₽300-1000; ⏲noon-midnight;) The terrace overlooking the castle and town is an ideal spot to enjoy some meaty traditional Russian dishes. The chef cures his own salmon and you can drink their delicious home-made *kvas* (fermented rye-bread water). The high-ceilinged castle-like interior is also impressive, though it's admittedly rather ruined by the TV blaring out Russian pop music most of the time.

Round Tower Restaurant RUSSIAN **$$**
(Круглая башня; Rynochnaya pl 1; mains ₽300-6000; ⏲noon-midnight, to 2am Fri & Sat) On the top floor of a 16th-century tower, this atmospheric and long-running place is a reliable option for traditional Russian cuisine, although it can sometimes be booked out by tour groups.

Central Market MARKET **$$**
(Центральный рынок; Rynochnaya pl; ⏲8am-6pm) Pull together supplies for a picnic from the Central Market just north of the Round Tower.

Information

Vyborg Tourist Information Centre (☎8-905-210 5555; www.vyborg-info.ru; Vokzalnaya ul 13; ⏲9am-5pm) Welcoming English-speaking staff can provide you with a town map and lots of other info and assistance.

Getting There & Away

The bus and train stations are opposite each other on Vokzalnaya pl.

BOAT

Saimaa Travel (www.saimaatravel.fi) arranges visa-free cruises (one/two days from €65/108 per person) from Lappeenranta in Finland to Vyborg.

BUS

Services to/from St Petersburg (₽230, to/from either metro station Devyatkino or Parnas) run every 20 minutes from 6.30am to 8pm. Theoretically, travel time is two hours, but the poor road conditions and traffic can double this, so the train remains the best option.

TRAIN

Elektrichki (suburban trains; ₽243, 2½ hours, hourly) leave from St Petersburg's Finlyandsky vokzal. Of these, there are also a handful of express services (1½ hours, four daily) for the same price, or the far more expensive Helsinki-bound trains, which stop in Vyborg (₽2016, one hour).

Staraya Ladoga Старая Ладога

☎81363 / POP 3000 / ⏱MOSCOW

Although you'd hardly guess it now, this tranquil village, 125km east of St Petersburg on the winding banks of the Volkhov River, lays claim to being Russia's first capital. The idea of this place being a 'capital' of anywhere is quite extraordinary, though, and today you'll find an ancient fortress, several churches and some prettily painted wooden cottages. It makes for a pleasant escape from St Petersburg, particularly in summer when a swim in the river adds to the charm.

The town was known simply as Ladoga until 1704, when Peter the Great founded Novaya (New) Ladoga to the north as a transfer point for the materials arriving to build St Petersburg. Protected as a national reserve, the town's basic layout has remained virtually unchanged since the 12th century, give or take a few ugly Soviet blocks.

Sights

Everything of interest lies along the main road that runs parallel to the river.

Staraya Ladoga Fortress HISTORIC SITE
(Староладожская крепость; grounds admission ₽20; ⏱9am-5pm Mon, to 6pm Tue-Sun) FREE Towards the southern end of the village, and with an excellent view along the river, the 7m-thick walls and stout towers of this fortress are slowly being rebuilt. Inside the grounds you'll find the small stone **St George's Church** (adult/student ₽50/40), only open May to October in order to protect the remains of the delicate 12th-century frescoes still visible on its walls, and the cute wooden **Church of Dimitry Solun**.

The Vorotnaya Tower houses the good **Historical-Architectural & Archaeological Museum** (adult/student ₽30/20), which displays an interesting retrospective of the area's history, including a scale model of how the fortress once looked, items found on archaeological digs and English explanations.

Visiting this soulful old place and wandering around its crumbling ramparts is a unique experience and you might feel you're in a Tarkovsky film.

Nikolsky Monastery MONASTERY
(Никольский монастырь; ⏱9am-7pm) This attractive walled complex dates to the 12th century and is still in the process of being rebuilt following its decommissioning during the Soviet years. The main church and bell tower now look quite handsome. Nearby is a pontoon from which you can swim in the river.

Church of John the Baptist CHURCH
(Церковь Рождества Иоанна Предтечи; ⏱9am-7pm) Marking the north end of the village, this blue onion-domed church dates from 1695 and is pretty as a picture with a colourful iconostasis and frescoes.

Sleeping & Eating

Mini-Hotel Ladya MINIHOTEL $$
(Гостиница Ладья; ☎81363-49 555; Sovetskaya 3; r from ₽2000-2200; 📶) While not looking promising from the outside, this five-room hotel, which shares the premises of the

RUSSIA'S ANCIENT CAPITAL

Just as the origins of Rus are continually debated, so is Staraya Ladoga's status as 'Russia's first capital'. Nevertheless, its age (historians have given 753 as the village's birth date) and significance remain uncontested.

When the Scandinavian Viking Rurik, along with his relatives Truvor and Sineus, swept into ancient Russia in 862, he built a wooden fortress on the Volkhov River and made this his base. Rurik is depicted in a colourful mosaic on the side of the village school. Locals also claim that one of the **tumuli** (Урочище Сопки) at the north end of the village is the grave of Oleg, Rurik's successor.

Archaeological expeditions continue to uncover a wealth of information about the town's past. In 1997 a second 9th-century fortress was discovered 2km outside the village. Evidence of Byzantine influences in the frescoes of the village's 12th-century churches point to the town as a cultural as well as historical and commercial crossroads.

WORTH A TRIP

KONEVETS ISLAND ОСТРОВ КОНЕВЕЦ

Around 100km north of St Petersburg, and 6km off the western shore of Lake Ladoga, this peaceful island with clean beaches and lots of forests to wander through is home to the beautiful sky-blue domed **Konevets Monastery** (www.konevps.ru), founded in 1393 by Arseny Konevetsky. Part of Finland between world wars, in Soviet times the island became an off-limits military base. The monastery reopened in the early 1990s and has since undergone massive restoration with Finnish funding.

From May to late October, tours (including transport and some meals) are organised by the monastery's St Petersburg **office** (812-571 8079; Zagorodny pr 7, St Petersburg; 1-/2-day tours ₽1990/3850; M Vladimirskaya). One-day tours make for a very long day, while two-day tours include accommodation in simple guesthouses for pilgrims (₽1000 per night if you are not on a tour, also arranged via the monastery office).

It's possible to do the trip by public transport, but far more complicated, and you'll need to overnight on the island anyway. Take an *elektrichka* (suburban train) from St Petersburg's Finlyandsky vokzal to Otradnoye, then a bus to Vladimirovka. Here, hire a boat to sail the 5km to the island, a total trip of around seven hours.

The monastery's website has a good map of the island. **Wandering Camera** (www.enlight.ru/camera/290/index_e.html) offers a visual preview.

local clinic, has pleasant, contemporary-styled rooms and even a sauna. Only tea and coffee are served, so you'll have to make your own breakfast arrangements.

Knyaz Rurik RUSSIAN **$$**
(Князь Рюрик; ul Shishkanya 10; meals ₽300-500; 9am-9pm, to 11pm Fri & Sat) Rurik's family tree is painted across the brick wall of this small, nicely designed restaurant, which screens videos of the village's sights and displays ye olde local shields as further decoration. Portions of soup, salad and shashlyk are small but tasty.

Getting There & Away

Elektrichki to Volkhov (the Volkhovstroy I station) depart from both St Petersburg's Moskovsky and Ladozhsky stations (₽500, 2½ hours, 20 daily). From Volkhov, the 23 bus (₽30, 20 minutes, hourly) heads towards Novaya Ladoga from the main bus stop outside the station and passes through Staraya Ladoga. Get off when you see the fortress.

Buses to and from Tikhvin also pass near the Yuzhkovo turn-off to the village, so you can combine a visit to both destinations. When you get off at Yuzhkovo, take a taxi (there are usually a couple hanging around to meet buses) to Staraya Ladoga (₽200).

Tikhvin Тихвин

81367 / POP 58,500 / MOSCOW

The highlight of this small, quiet town on the banks of the Tikhvinka River is a beautiful monastery established in 1560 by decree of Ivan the Terrible. There's been a community here since the 14th century and for thousands of years before that the area formed part of the hereditary lands of the Finnic Veps (also known as Vepsians). Tikhvin is also the birthplace of Nikolai Rimsky-Korsakov, whose music was inspired by the local nature, folk tunes and religious ringing of bells.

Some 200km east of St Petersburg, it's possible to see Tikhvin in a long day trip, but should you decide to linger there are a couple of accommodation options. The town is on the rail route to Vologda and Arkhangelsk, so you could break your journey to or from either of those destinations here.

The town is easy to get around by foot; buy a map at the train-station booking kiosk when you arrive. The region's website is www.tikhvin.org.

Sights

Tikhvin Monastery of the Mother of God MONASTERY
(Тихвинский Богородичный Успенский мужской монастырь; www.tihvinskii-monastyr.ru; ul Tikhvinskaya 1; 8am-8pm) FREE Rising like a fairy tale across the Tabory pond, this complex is about a 1km walk from the train station straight along Sovetskaya ul. At its heart is the onion-domed **Assumption Cathedral**, established in 1510, and painted inside and partially outside with detailed frescoes. A famous icon of Mary and Jesus

said to have been painted by the apostle Luke draws awed pilgrims from across Russia, particularly on 9 July, when a procession celebrates the return of the icon to Tikhvin.

The complex's nunnery, crowned by a five-spired belfry, is where Ivan the Terrible sent his fourth wife to be confined. Within the walls you'll also find the **Tikhvin Historical Memorial & Architectural Museum** (adult/concession ₽100/80; ⊙10am-5pm Tue-Sun), which has interesting displays on the monastery's history and examples of its religious art dating back to the 16th century. Expect to be followed around suspiciously.

Rimsky-Korsakov House-Museum MUSEUM
(Государственный Дом-музей Римского-Корсакова; ☑81369-51 509; ul Rimskogo-Korsakova 12; adult/child ₽90/50; ⊙10am-5.30pm Tue-Sun) This early-19th-century wooden house was Rimsky-Korsakov's childhood home until the age of 12. It became a museum in 1944, the centenary of his birth, and the rooms have been reconstructed to look as they would have done when his family was living there. The charming guides, who may even let you look around when it's officially closed on Monday, will point out all the original features, including a Becker grand piano on which concerts are sometimes given. Call for details.

There's a stone bust of the composer on a plinth in the small park next to the house. Opposite is the tiny **Church of All Saints Polkovaya** (Церковь Всех Святых "Полковая"), which also sometimes hosts concerts.

Transfiguration Cathedral CHURCH
(Спасо-Преображенский собор; pl Svobody) This attractive cathedral frames one side of Tikhvin's central square, where Lenin's statue still stands.

🛏 Sleeping & Eating

Podvorye HOTEL **$$**
(Подворье; ☑81367-51 330; www.podworie.ru; ul Novgorodskaya 35; d incl breakfast from ₽2400; 🛜) The interior of this small hotel emulates a log house, with spacious clean rooms that are thickly carpeted. Its adjoining restaurant is the place in town for a meal with a menu of mainly Russian dishes (₽200 to ₽500). It also offers a business-lunch deal for ₽250, not listed on the English menu.

Verizhitsa HOTEL **$$$**
(Верижица; ☑81367-71 374; www.verizhitsa.ru; s/d ₽5000/6000) This appealing complex of wooden log cabins (each of which accommodates up to six people) has a leafy forest setting 5km east of Tikhvin. The cabins are comfortable and there's a restaurant (daily lunch deal ₽300) and traditional-style *banya* (extra fee). A taxi from Tikhvin costs around ₽200.

Chainaya CAFE **$**
(Чайная; meals ₽190; ⊙11am-6pm) In the monastery grounds, you'll find this simple canteen, serving delicious bliny, homemade *pelmeni* (Russian-style ravioli stuffed with meat) and *kvas*. In summer you can enjoy your refreshments on an outdoor terrace.

ℹ Getting There & Away

Tikhvin's bus and train stations are opposite each other on Vokzalny per. Trains here leave from St Petersburg's Ladozhsky vokzal (*platskart/kupe* ₽580/1160, 4½ to five hours, three daily). There are five buses a day to both St Petersburg's bus station and to Devyatkino metro station (₽330, four to five hours, 10 daily), with the last departure at 5pm (or 6.35pm Friday to Sunday). To travel to Staraya Ladoga, there are no direct buses, so instead buy a ticket to Yuzhkovo and then take any St Petersburg-bound bus and get off at the Yuzhkovo turn-off, where the bus pauses for a 10-minute toilet break anyway. From here a taxi to Staraya Lagdoa is ₽200.

Western European Russia

Best Places to Eat

- Pyotr Petrovich (p231)
- 17 Bar (p239)
- Mamonts (p247)
- Tirol (p244)
- Nice People (p254)

Best Places to Stay

- Armenia (p230)
- Retrotur (p238)
- Hotel 903 (p259)
- Hotel Staraya Russa (p256)
- Izborsk Park (p261)

Why Go?

This ancient, Arcadian region showcases Mother Russia at her most fertile: Tolstoy, Turgenev, Dostoevsky's *The Brothers Karamazov* and nothing less than the modern country itself were all born here. It's a lofty legacy and nowhere does Western European Russia (Западно – Европейская Россия) let you forget it. The imposing kremlins, soaring cathedrals and cultural treasures of cities such as Veliky Novgorod, Pskov and Smolensk bear stunning testament to golden eras. Budding writers flock to the area's wealth of literary estates – Staraya Russa, Spasskoe-Lutovinovo, Yasnaya Polyana and Pushkin's ancestral home, Mikhailovskoe – with high hopes there's something in the water; and character-filled smaller towns such as Yelets and Oryol are photogenic throwbacks to prerevolutionary Russia. Even the tiny, far-flung village of Stary Izborsk – a stone's throw from the Estonian border – claims a distinguished heritage: it's home to the oldest stone fortress in Russia.

When to Go

Smolensk

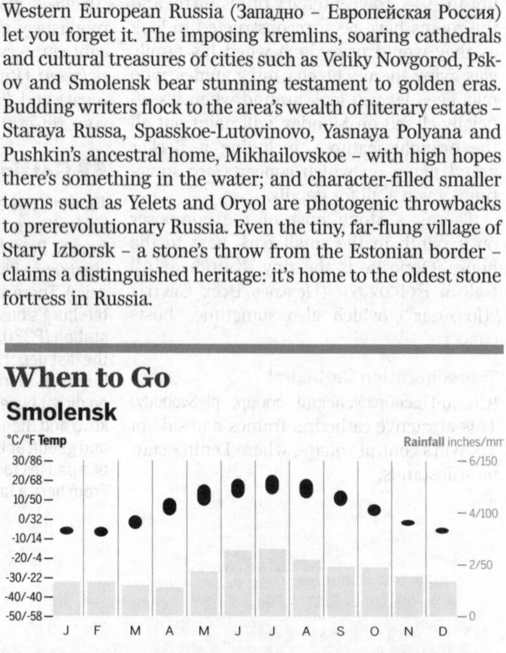

Apr Catch the Alexander Nevsky Festival in Veliky Novgorod.

End May–early Jun The Glinka Festival of classical music is held in Smolensk.

Nov–Mar Witness magnificent European bison in the wild at Orlovskoye Polesye National Park.

SOUTH OF MOSCOW

Tula Тула

☎4872 / POP 501,000 / ⏲MOSCOW

A town centre graced by a picturesque kremlin, a fascinating industrial history reflected in several museums, and several great restaurants: there's much to recommend in Tula. The key attraction, though, is Yasnaya Polyana, Leo Tolstoy's country estate, just south of the city.

Sights

★Tula Kremlin HISTORICAL BUILDING

(Тульский кремль; ul Mendeleevskaya 10; admission ₽100; ⏲9am-5pm Tue-Sun) The five burnished onion domes of the 18th-century **Assumption Cathedral** (Успенский собор)

Western European Russia Highlights

1. Return to rural 19th-century Russia at **Yasnaya Polyana** (p231), the leafy estate and final resting place of Leo Tolstoy.
2. Light a candle in the spooky underground tombs of **Pechory Monastery** (p262), where solemn monks show you their dead.
3. Explore a magnificent kremlin, ancient churches and monasteries in tourist-friendly **Veliky Novgorod** (p249).
4. Go on a museum crawl in the hilly Hero City of **Smolensk** (p240).
5. Acquaint yourself with Russia's literary talent in the house-museums of Oryol, including **Spasskoe-Lutovinovo** (p239), Turgenev's lovely country estate.
6. Admire the beautifully decorated churches of **Yelets** (p232).

Tula

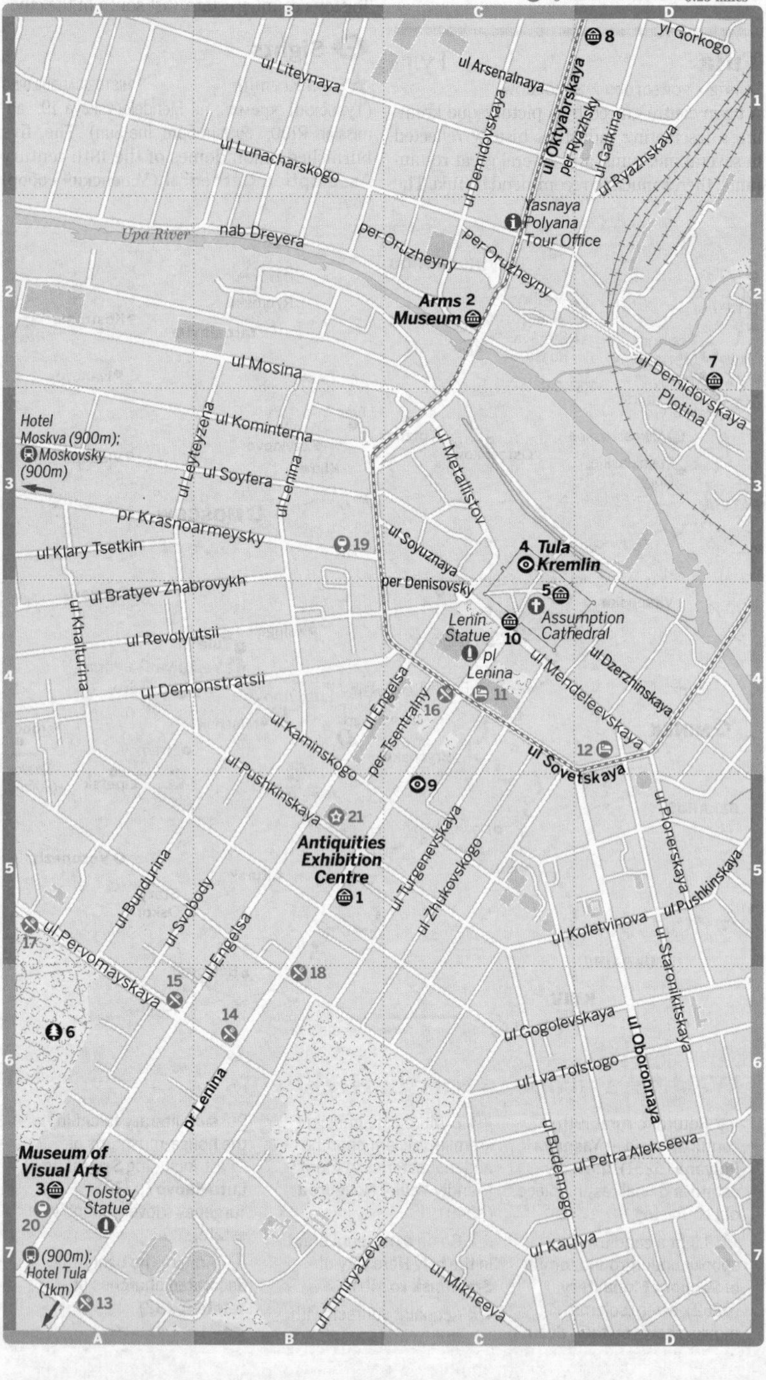

0.5 km
0.25 miles
ul Liteynaya
ul Arsenalnaya
ul Oktyabrskaya
per Ryazhsky
ul Galkina
yl Gorkogo
ul Ryazhskaya
ul Demidovskaya
ul Lunacharskogo
Yasnaya Polyana Tour Office
Upa River
nab Dreyera
per Oruzheyny
per Oruzheyny
Arms Museum 2
ul Mosina
ul Demidovskaya Plotina
7
8
Hotel Moskva (900m); Moskovsky (900m)
ul Leyteyzena
ul Kominterna
ul Soyfera
ul Lenina
ul Metallistov
pr Krasnoarmeysky
ul Soyuznaya
ul Klary Tsetkin
19
4 Tula Kremlin
5
ul Bratyev Zhabrovykh
per Denisovsky
Assumption Cathedral
Lenin Statue
10
ul Khalturina
ul Revolyutsii
pl Lenina
ul Dzerzhinskaya
ul Demonstratsii
16
11
ul Mendeleevskaya
ul Engelsa
per Tsentralny
ul Kaminskogo
12
ul Sovetskaya
9
ul Pushkinskaya
21
Antiquities Exhibition Centre
1
ul Turgenevskaya
ul Zhukovskogo
ul Pionerskaya
ul Pushkinskaya
ul Bundurina
ul Svobody
ul Engelsa
ul Koletvinova
17
ul Pervomayskaya
18
15
14
ul Staronikitskaya
6
ul Gogolevskaya
ul Oboronnaya
ul Lva Tolstogo
pr Lenina
ul Budennogo
ul Petra Alekseeva
Museum of Visual Arts
3
Tolstoy Statue
20
(900m); Hotel Tula (1km)
ul Kaulya
13
ul Timiryazeva
ul Mikheeva

Tula

Top Sights

1	Antiquities Exhibition Centre	B5
2	Arms Museum	C2
3	Museum of Visual Arts	A7
4	Tula Kremlin	C3

Sights

5	Arms Museum - Tula Kremlin	C4
6	Central Park	A6
7	Metal Working Museum	D2
8	Pryanik Museum	D1
9	Tula Necropolis	C5
10	Tula Samovar Museum	C4

Sleeping

11	Armenia	C4
12	Profit	D4

Eating

13	Biblioteka	A7
14	Frau Marta	B6
15	Lisya Nora	A6
16	Podkre Pizza	C4
17	Pyotr Petrovich	A5
18	Skovoroda	B6

Drinking & Nightlife

19	Beerlin	B3
20	Premier	A7

Entertainment

21	Drama Theatre	B5

rising over the ramparts of this restored stone fortress, first constructed out of wood in the early 16th century, are a visual delight. The kremlin's grounds are entered through the green-domed Odoyevskikh Vorog Tower. Climb up to the ramparts (admission ₽120) to view the insides of some of the other eight towers punctuating the walls.

The complex stands in stark contrast to the brutal architecture of the old Soviet city, where a giant **Lenin statue** frames the approach across pl Lenina.

★ Arms Museum — MUSEUM

(Музей Оружия; www.arms-museum.tula.ru; ul Oktyabrskaya 2; admission ₽300; ⏲10am-6pm Sun-Thu, to 8pm Fri & Sat, closed last Mon of the month) Tula has been a weapons manufacturing centre for centuries, a legacy celebrated at this fantastically kitted-out new building that houses an impressive collection of metal weaponry and armoury dating back to medieval times. It's impossible not to appreciate the delicate skill and artistry applied to some of the weapons. The museum also has a branch within the **Tula kremlin**; one ticket gives access to both.

The Oktyabrskaya museum has a miniature shooting range on-site and also offers weapon decorating classes with a master gunsmith; see the website for booking information.

Tula Samovar Museum — MUSEUM

(Музей Тульские самовары; www.samovar.museum-tula.ru; ul Mendeleevskaya 8; admission ₽100; ⏲10am-6pm Tue-Sun) 'To take one's own samovar to Tula' is a Russian idiom coined by Anton Chekhov, denoting a pointless activity. Local production of this essential part of the Russian tea-making tradition was started in the late 18th century. This small museum showcases that history with a collection of samovars, including one that belonged to Stalin and a cute collection of mini samovars. You can buy samovars at this small museum, although there's more choice in the kiosk in Tula's train station.

★ Antiquities Exhibition Centre — MUSEUM

(Музейно-выставочный центр Тульские древности; ☎4872-361 663; pr Lenina 47; admission ₽40; ⏲10am-5pm, closed last Wed of month) Stone Age and Bronze Age finds from the Tula area are displayed in this wonderful interactive museum, including arrowheads, fish hooks and jewellery. English tours (₽1000 per group) tell the stories behind the collections. Have a go at pottery and blacksmithery, or sip tea and nibble gingerbread in the reconstruction of a 19th-century wooden Tula home.

The centre also arranges trips to **Kulikovo Pole**, about 130km southeast of Tula, where in 1380 the Grand Prince of Moscow's army took on the Golden Horde and won. The large nature reserve is home to three **museums** (www.kulpole.ru; ⏲10am-7pm May-Sep, to 5pm Oct, to 4pm Wed-Mon Nov-Apr) and hosts a reenactment of the battle every September.

Tula Necropolis — HISTORICAL SITE

(Тульский некрополь; pr Lenina 31; museum admission ₽40; ⏲museum 9am-6pm Mon-Fri) Photography buffs will love this huge, gorgeously creepy graveyard, with hundreds of telegenic tombstones slowly being devoured by forest. There's a small museum attached, but the most fun comes from poking around in the wonderfully peaceful grounds, which are free to enter.

The graveyard was set up in the 1700s for plague victims. There are also statues and sarcophagi honouring old Tula's wealthy elite, fallen Soviet soldiers and local heroes.

Central Park PARK

(Центральный парк Белоусова; ul Engelsa 66) Approach this large, pleasant park from pr Lenina to see the absolutely huge **Tolstoy statue** – local wags have it that the writer was on his way to the vodka factory that was once housed in the brick building opposite. **Bicycles and rollerblades** (rollerblades/bikes per hour from ₽80/100, open noon to 9pm, last rental 7.30pm) can be rented in the park.

★Museum of Visual Arts MUSEUM

(Музей изобразительных искусств; ul Engelsa 66; admission ₽150; ⌚10am-6pm Tue-Sun) This exceptional gallery charts a course from gilded icons and late-15th-century European paintings through to fascinating pieces of socialist realism from the 20th century, including animated porcelain figurines of heroic workers and explorers. The exquisite collection includes works by Russian artists such as Ivanov, Shishkin and Repin, as well as furniture and classical marble statues.

Metal-Working Museum MUSEUM

(Выставочный зал Тульский металл; ul Demidovskaya Plotina 13; admission ₽60; ⌚10am-6pm Tue-Sun) Tula's long history as a centre of metalwork and gun manufacture is told through displays at this small museum.

Pryanik Museum MUSEUM

(Музей Тульский пряник; www.oldtula.ru; ul Oktyabrskaya 45b; admission ₽50; ⌚9am-5pm Tue-Sat) Tula is renowned Russia-wide for its *pryaniki* (inscribed ginger cakes). The sweet-toothed can find out all about them at this one-room museum in a bakery that has been churning them out in all shapes and sizes – check out the monster 16kg loaf! – since 1881. It's more of a prelude to shopping and eating at the attached **shop and cafe** (8am to 8pm) than a hugely educational experience.

Sleeping

Most places include breakfast in their rates.

★Armenia HOTEL $$

(Армения; ☎4872-250 600; www.ind-garnik.ru; ul Sovetskaya 47; s/d ₽3400/3900; ❄📶🏊) Part of a swish business and entertainment complex, this appealing hotel offers kremlin views and spacious, well-furnished rooms. There's also a sauna and pool (free to guests from 7am to 11am), a restaurant serving Armenian and Russian dishes and a billiards club.

Hotel Moskva HOTEL $$

(Гостиница Москва; ☎4872-208 952; ul Puteyskaya 3; s unrenovated/renovated ₽780/1860, d ₽3150; 📶) The convenient location opposite the train station makes up for the shabbiness of the cheapest rooms here. Nevertheless they come with attached bathrooms and are fine for one night. Renovated singles and the doubles have passable furnishings, far better bathrooms and a lick of paint.

Hotel Tula HOTEL $$

(Гостиница Тула; ☎4872-351 960; www.hoteltula.ru; pr Lenina 96; s/d/tr without bathroom ₽1100/1800/2700, s/d ₽2200/2600; ❄@) Next to the bus station and across from the impressive WWII monument in Pobedy pl, this Soviet relic offers small, well-worn and oft-smoky rooms. The renovated rooms are larger and far more tolerable. From the train station, take trolleybus 5.

Profit MINIHOTEL $$

(Профит; ☎4872-252 020; www.profit.megatula.ru; ul Sovetskaya 59; s/d from ₽3000/3500; ❄@📶) This minihotel on the 4th and 5th floors of a business centre has sparse but decent rooms that you'll probably spend very little time in, given its proximity to the kremlin and other local attractions.

Eating

Frau Marta GERMAN $

(Фрау Марта; ul Pervomayskaya 8; mains ₽200-500; ⌚noon-midnight) A belt-loosening range of sausage dishes, sauerkraut and potato-everything is served by costumed waitresses to a soundtrack of jaunty German tunes.

Podkre Pizza PIZZA $

(Подкре Пицца; ul Sovetskaya 60/12; meals ₽200-400; ⌚10am-10pm) Popular self-serve pizza-and-pasta place with views of the main square and the kremlin walls.

★ **Pyotr Petrovich** RUSSIAN $$

(Пётр Петрович; ☎4872-717 400; ul Pervomayskaya 13; mains ₽270-600; ⏰noon-1am Sun-Thu, to 2am Fri & Sat; 📶) Sitting pretty in an exquisitely restored mansion near the entrance to Central Park, this merry brasserie should not be missed by anyone with taste buds. With its own brewery on-site, dozens of sinful dishes, including homemade sausages (and ubiquitous lashings of cream sauce), famous desserts and a lively atmosphere, it's rightfully popular and gets predictably crowded.

Lisya Nora RUSSIAN $$

(Лисья Нора; ul Pervomayskaya 12; mains ₽290-800; ⏰noon-midnight) This woodsy little den comes across all hunters' lodge, with onion-bunch decor and taxidermied talking points hanging on the walls. A popular hang-out, its menu is all about meat, sizzling plates of which are chomped down with homemade bread and domestic liqueurs with 'medicinal' properties. There's a 20% discount on meals ordered between noon and 4pm.

Biblioteka FRENCH $$

(Библиотека; ☎4872-305 076; pr Lenina 91; meals ₽350-650; ⏰noon-midnight; 📶) The svelte cutlery, rows of Russian novels, piles of magazines and clubby atmosphere lend an air of sophistication to this star performer. A perfect French onion soup, tender lamb in flaky pastry and delectable desserts are among the many appealing dishes on the Russian-only menu. From noon to 5pm, there's a 20% discount.

Skovoroda UKRAINIAN $$

(Сковорода; ☎4872-364 707; pr Lenina 57; meals ₽400-600; ⏰noon-midnight; 📶📋) Locals swear by this convivial place, claiming it has the best borsch this side of the Ukrainian border. It also does chicken Kiev and *vareniki* (dumplings). Those with more adventurous tastes can try the *salo* (creamy squares of cured pig fat) tasting plate or sample dishes with calf brains and chicken intestines as ingredients.

Drinking & Nightlife

Premier NIGHTCLUB

(Премьер; ☎4872-357 606; ul Engelsa 66) This busy complex is the social hub of Tula, with a cinema, several bars, a nightclub and a patio restaurant. While the club gets going late on weekends, the patio is a nice place for a drink on summer afternoons.

Beerlin BAR

(pr Krasnoarmeysky 4; ⏰11am-11pm Sun-Thu, to 1am Fri & Sat; 📶) Work your way through the many fine cask-pumped ales (five/10 tasters for ₽320/560) from around Europe at this spacious bar and restaurant. With its wood-panelled walls, bar and furniture, it does a fine impersonation of a traditional English country pub.

☆ Entertainment

Drama Theatre THEATRE

(Тульский академический театр драмы; ☎4872-367 332; pr Lenina 34a; tickets from ₽100) The drama, dance and opera held here are well produced.

Getting There & Away

BUS

From the **bus station** (pr Lenina), services run to Moscow (₽368, three hours, four daily), Oryol (₽230, four hours, seven daily), Voronezh (₽550, eight hours, two daily) and Yelets (₽315, four hours, five daily).

Private minibuses (₽320, three hours) connect regularly with various metro stations in Moscow, departing from the train and bus stations.

TRAIN

Both *elektrichki* (suburban trains) and regular trains run to Moscow (*platskart/kupe* ₽750/1300, three hours, 25 daily) from the **Moskovsky train station** (ul Puteyskaya). Other services include Oryol (₽1050/1680, 2½ hours, 25 daily) and Yelets (₽843/1492, 5½ hours, six daily).

Getting Around

Many buses and *marshrutky* (fixed-route minibuses; ₽12) run from the train station along pr Krasnoarmeysky to Lenina pl and then up pr Lenina. For the bus station and Hotel Tula, take trolleybus 5 from outside the train station.

Yasnaya Polyana
Ясная Поляна

Located 14km south of central Tula, **Yasnaya Polyana** (☎4872-393 599; www.ypmuseum.ru; grounds ₽50, Tolstoy & Kuzminsky House ₽200; ⏰9am-5pm Tue-Sun) is billed as a 'typical Russian estate' of the late 19th century, which it is save for one important fact: this is where Leo Tolstoy, author of *War* *and Peace* and *Anna Karenina,* was born, lived most of his life and is buried. Beyond the addition of a few helpful signs, little has changed since that time.

A long birch-lined avenue leads from the entrance to the modest, whitewashed **Tolstoy House**, where the great writer lived and worked. The rooms have been kept as they were at the time of his death in 1910, with portraits, books, furniture and some of Tolstoy's clothes laid out. Nearby, the **Kuzminsky House** has an imaginatively designed exhibition covering Tolstoy's inspirations from 1851 to 1869 when he finished *War and Peace*. Deep into the forest is **Tolstoy's grave**, unmarked – as per his request – except for bouquets left by admirers.

Horse riding (one hour ₽400, 10-minute wagon ride ₽150) is available on the estate grounds. Russian-language courses are also available; see the website for details. For an English-language guided trip of the estate and surrounds, contact **Yasnaya Polyana Tour Office** (☎4872-393 599; tour@tolstoy.ru; ul Oktyabrskaya 14; ⊙10am-6pm Mon-Fri) in Tula.

From where the bus from Tula stops on the main road, heading in the opposite direction to Yasnaya Polyana, it's a pleasant country walk for 3.5km to the historic train station and museum at **Kozlova Zaseka** (Козлова Засека; admission ₽50; ⊙9.30am-4pm Tue-Sun). Tolstoy used this station many times and set off for his final journey from here.

Located 1.5km from the estate, the cosy **Yasnaya Polyana Hotel** (☎48751-76 146; hotel@tgk.tolstoy.ru; s/d ₽2000/3000, breakfast not included) offers comfortable rooms in peaceful wooded surrounds. Opposite the entrance gate to the estate is **Cafe Preshpekt** (Кафе Прешпект; meals ₽200-350; ⊙8am-8pm), a simple cafe featuring hearty home-cooked Russian fare. House specialities are said to be prepared according to recipes by Leo's wife, Sofia Andreevna.

From Tula, take *marshrutka* 114, 117 or 280 (₽20, 20 minutes) from anywhere along pr Lenina; tell the driver to let you off at Yasnaya Polyana – it's a 1km walk from the main road to the estate. Trolleybuses 6 and 7 also depart from Tula. If you walk to Kozlova Zaseka, you can also use bus 218 or 30 to get back to Tula.

Yelets Елец

☎47467 / POP 108,400 / ⊙MOSCOW

On the tranquil Sosna River, sleepy Yelets stands out as one of the early Rus settlements to have retained some of its traditional character. The town centre is a visual delight, littered with large and small churches in various stages of disrepair and lined

TOLSTOY TITBITS

Everyone knows *War and Peace* (though far fewer have actually read it), and *Anna Karenina* is considered by many to be the greatest novel ever written. But what do you know about the man behind these great works, Count Lev Nikolayevich Tolstoy? Arm yourself with these fascinating facts before you set out to his estate, Yasnaya Polyana.

➡ When Tolstoy was a boy, he and his brother would test their mental fortitude by trying not to think of a polar bear. It's harder than it sounds...

➡ He was a university dropout, described by his teachers as 'unable and unwilling' to learn.

➡ Tolstoy underwent a profound moral and spiritual crisis after the success of *Anna Karenina.* Feeling he didn't deserve his wealth, he gave up copyright of his earlier books, worked the land with peasants and took up bootmaking.

➡ His book *The Kingdom of God is Within You* dealt in depth with the theory of nonviolent protest. It inspired Mahatma Gandhi and Martin Luther King Jr. Tolstoy and Gandhi enjoyed a regular correspondence; Tolstoy's last-ever letter was to the future Indian leader.

➡ Aged 82, Tolstoy snuck out of Yasnaya Polyana – and away from his displeased wife – to embark on a spiritual pilgrimage. It was not to be: he died shortly afterwards of pneumonia at Astapavo Station, in the town now called Lev Tolstoy, 200km southwest of Tula. The station's clock is permanently set to 6.05pm, the time when the great writer breathed his last.

with pastel-coloured buildings and wooden cottages.

Founded in 1146 as a fortification against the Turkic invaders from the east, Yelets became a punching bag for the Mongol Tatars, who devastated it half a dozen times during the Middle Ages. The town became famous for its intricate lacemaking from the 18th century.

Yelets' centre is laid out in a grid, with ul Kommunarov connecting Hotel Yelets in the east with Ascension Cathedral in the west. Further west (downhill) lies the Sosna River. The train station and long-distance bus stop are about 3km southeast of the centre. Ul Mira, the main shopping street, runs into pl Lenina. The **Knizhni Klub** (ul Mira 92; ⌚9am-6pm) bookstore sells maps.

Sights

★ Ascension Cathedral CHURCH
(Вознесенский собор; ul Pushkinskaya; ⌚services 8-11am & 5-7pm daily) Designed by Konstantin Ton (1794–1881), the genius behind Moscow's Cathedral of Christ the Saviour, the Kremlin Armoury and the Grand Kremlin Palace, this beautiful cathedral lords over Yelets from the foot of ul Kommunarov. Beneath the cathedral's gleaming golden dome, the eye-popping, multicoloured interior glitters with gilt-framed iconography stacked high on each wall.

At 74m in height (including the golden cross), this is one of the tallest cathedrals in Russia. Its looming glory is visible from almost anywhere in Yelets, but you can catch the best view from the bridge crossing the Sosna, just east of town.

Great Count's Church CHURCH
(Великокняжеская церковь; ul Sovetskaya; ⌚9am-5pm) Built during the early 1900s, this inventive piece of religious architecture has distinctly modernist, art nouveau flair, with an exotically tiled interior of metallic hues. The cross on the top is made of crystal.

Znamensky Monastery MONASTERY
(Знаменский монастырь; ul Slobodskaya 5; ⌚6am-10pm) There are fine views across town from this restored early-19th-century hilltop monastery. The white steeple and gold-domed church are easily recognisable from afar, and the interior is decorated with some seriously fabulous frescoes. The grounds are well tended with flower beds, a small aviary with peacocks, and an attractive wooden chapel. Look for the natural spring (beside a blue ablutions hall) at the bottom of the hill near the steps.

Regional Museum MUSEUM
(Городской краеведческий музей; ul Lenina 99; admission ₽100; ⌚9.30am-4.30pm Tue-Sat) Housed in a sweet pink-and-white 19th-century building, this surprisingly diverse museum is worth a couple hours of exploration. Among the miscellany, you'll find a model of ancient Yelets, a room dedicated to the Mongol cavalry that ran roughshod over Yelets in the 13th century, a beautiful collection of local lace, paintings by local 19th-century artist Meshchkov and information on Yelets' devastating WWII experience.

Khrennikov Museum MUSEUM
(Дом-музей Хренникова; ul Mayakovskogo 16; admission ₽50; ⌚9.30am-4.30pm Wed-Sat) Successful Soviet composer Tikhon Khrennikov grew up and first studied music in this rust-red wooden house. Original furniture, photos and artefacts are on display. The documentation is also interesting as a history of Soviet aesthetics.

Ivan Bunin Museum MUSEUM
(Дом-музей Бунина; ul Maksima Gorkogo 16; admission ₽45; ⌚9am-5pm Tue-Sat) The writer, poet and 1933 Nobel laureate Ivan Bunin (1870–1953) spent some of his childhood in Yelets, studying at the town's gymnasium. This small museum chronicles his life and works. Check out the wall map that has pins marking the places he visited – Mogadishu, Sri Lanka and Spain, to name a few.

House Museum of Yelets Lace MUSEUM
(Дом-музей Елецкого кружева; ☎47467-27 506; www.elez-mezenat.ru; ul Oktyabrskaya 108; admission ₽60; ⌚by appointment) This quaint, bright-blue building contains an exquisite collection of Yelets lacework displayed in elegant surrounds. The 2nd floor has a collection of paintings by local artists. It's best to phone or email ahead for an appointment, though it may be open if you just pop by.

City Park PARK
(Городской парк; ul Kommunarov) The park has a summertime **Ferris wheel** (₽50), a concert stage, amusement rides and a statue of Ivan Bunin. Next to the main entrance is the antique red-brick fire station; ask the firefighters if you can climb the **observation tower** for a bird's-eye view of the town's gilded cupolas.

Vvedenskaya Church CHURCH
(Введенская церковь, Vvedensky spusk) This jewel box of a church stands near a cluster of photogenic late-17th- and early-18th-century wooden houses. Follow the road to the bottom of the hill and check out a riverside **beach** popular with sunbathing locals.

Sleeping

Bazilik HOTEL $$
(Базилик; 8-919-167 8110; www.gostinica-elets.ru; ul Mira 88/17; s/d/tr ₽1500/2500/3000;) A new – and much-needed – face on the Yelets accommodation scene, the Bazilik is a nifty little number, with small but serviceable rooms, delicious breakfasts and a stellar location just 400m from the town centre (pl Lenina). Free slippers are a nice touch, as is the wacky wallpaper.

Hotel Yelets HOTEL $$
(Гостиница Елец; 47467-22 235; www.intourist-elets.ru; ul Kommunarov 14; s/d unrenovated ₽1000/1600, renovated ₽2100/3300) This nine-storey monstrosity is unmissable: it's the colour of a smurf and looms over the cityscape. It offers well-worn unrenovated rooms or better renovated ones; both have nice views of the cupolas. The lobby cafe operates around the clock.

Eating

Jem Cafe CAFE $
(Кафе Джем; ul Sverdlova 17; mains ₽50-300; 9am-midnight;) The Jem is a snuggly little joint near the city centre with a summer terrace and flash service. There's nothing unexpected on the menu (bliny, pasta, sandwiches, risotto) but it's all done well, as are the strong coffees (₽50 to ₽150).

Milano Pizzeria WESTERN $
(Милано Пиццерия; ul Mira; dishes ₽50-120; 10am-10pm) Local takeaway with surprisingly good pizza slices, salads and *shawarma* (grilled meat and salad wrapped in flat bread).

Stary Gorod RUSSIAN $$
(Старый Город; ul Mira 100; meals ₽200-460; 11am-4pm & 5pm-1am) The faux Greek statues, low lighting and heavy drapes signal this as Yelets' fanciest restaurant. There are plenty of Russian meals to choose from. Prices drop for its set business lunches (₽180) from noon to 3pm.

Getting There & Away

BUS

There are two long-distance bus stops in Yelets: Avtostantsiya-1 is near the train station on the main highway (this is where buses from Voronezh arrive and depart), while Avtostantsiya-2 is 2.5km west of City Park off ul Kommunarov. Bus services include Moscow (₽700, 7½ hours, daily), Oryol (₽320, five hours, three daily), Voronezh (₽220, three hours, five daily) and Tula (₽315, four hours, five daily).

TRAIN

Trains travel from Yelets to Moscow (*platskart/kupe* ₽865/1444, eight hours, 11 daily) and Tula (₽734/1195, 5½ hours, three daily). To get from the train station to the town centre, walk to the west end of the platform and cross the tracks to the bus stop.

Voronezh Воронеж

4732 / POP 1,014,610 / MOSCOW

A stop in this industry-focused metropolis can be useful to break up the long journey between Moscow and destinations in Ukraine or the Caucasus. There are some grand buildings worth a gander around pl Lenina and along pr Revolyutsii towards the impressive Annunciation Cathedral.

Following the development of a navy shipyard (the first in Russia) by Peter the Great in the late 1600s, Voronezh became the largest city in southern Russia and a major hub for agriculture and manufacturing. Between 1928 and 1934, it was the capital of the Central Black Earth Oblast, a huge expanse of Western Russia noted for its good soil. Destroyed in WWII, the city is now back on track, with a renovated city centre and new developments sprouting every year.

Sights

Annunciation Cathedral CHURCH
(Благовещенский кафедральный собор; Pervomaisky sad; 7am-7pm) Russia's third-largest working church, this handsome 97m-high structure was built in Russo-Byzantine style in the late 19th century. Outside stands a statue of the early-18th-century cleric St Mitrofan surrounded by four angels. By contrast, the metal fence ringing the complex is decorated with Soviet-era symbols.

IN Kramskoy Regional Fine Arts Museum MUSEUM
(Воронежский областной художественный музей им. И.Н. Крамского; www.kramskoi.vzh.

WORTH A TRIP

KURSK КУРСК

The biggest tank battle of WWII took place near Kursk in July and August of 1943. The deadly clash proved a major turning point in the conflict, with the defeat of the Nazis – still reeling from the horrors of Stalingrad – signalling the beginning of the end for Hitler, who never launched another major attack on the Eastern Front.

Unsurprisingly, Kursk itself was thoroughly trashed, with little architecture left standing. The town today honours its history with museums and monuments that will be of interest to history buffs. **Victory Memorial** (Мемориал Победы; Pobedy pr), Kursk's massive 'Arc de Triomphe', dominates the northern entrance to the city – the monument is flanked by tanks and heavy artillery from WWII, plus an eternal flame and a memorial to those who died on the submarine *Kursk* in 2000. The **Regional Museum** (Курский областной краеведческий музей; ☎4712-702 128; www.kursk-museum.ru; ul Lunacharskovo 6; admission ₽40; ⏲10am-5.30pm Sat-Thu) has loads of displays and information on Kursk's part in the war, while the **Young Defenders of the Motherland Museum** (Военно-исторический музей-Юные защитники Родины; ul Sumskaya 6; admission ₽15; ⏲10.30am-5pm Sat-Thu) tells the tragic stories of the children and teenagers who fought against fascism.

There are frequent trains to Kursk from Moscow (*platskart/kupe* ₽1454/2732, 7½ hours), St Petersburg (₽1525/2928) and all over the region, including Oryol (₽758/1212, two hours) and Tula (₽673/1300, four hours).

ru; pr Revolyutsii 18; admission ₽100; ⏲10am-6pm Wed, Thu, Sat & Sun, from 11am Fri) Reached through a passage leading into a courtyard, this excellent regional arts museum offers up a solid collection of Russian painting and sculpture, Greek and Roman sculpture and an Egyptian sarcophagus. Exhibitions of modern local artists are held behind the main building.

St Alexey of Akatov Women's Monastery CONVENT
(Алексеево-Акатов женский монастырь; ul Osvobozhdeniya Truda 1) This restored nunnery, founded in 1674, is near the river on lovely grounds, which include a tiny graveyard surrounded by colourful, lopsided cottages. The interior of the church is covered entirely with frescoes. If you're lucky, you'll catch the nuns' choir in action.

Resurrection Church CHURCH
(Свято-Воскресенский храм; ul Ordzhonikidze 15) This attractive large green-domed church, a short walk east of pl Lenina, boasts a colourful fresco-covered interior that hosts regular choral services.

Regional Museum MUSEUM
(Краеведческий музей; ul Plekhanovskaya 29; admission ₽140; ⏲11am-6pm Wed, noon-8pm Thu, 10am-6pm Fri-Sun) Displays permanent exhibits on Peter the Great and the history of the region from the pre–Bronze Age to the Soviet era.

Oceanarium AQUARIUM
(Воронежский океанариум; www.cityparkgrad.ru/entertainment/oceanarium; Citypark Grad Shopping Centre, Voronezh-Moscow Hwy; adult/child from ₽450/200; ⏲2-9pm Mon, 10am-9pm Tue-Sun) That one of Europe's largest aquariums can be found in a shopping centre in a landlocked town synonymous with Black Earth may seem a little odd, but you'll find the huge collection of marine life even more astounding. There are over 200 fish species, including tiger sharks (feeding shows Tuesday to Sunday), piranhas, seals and a very creepy giant Japanese spider crab. Buses run regularly from Voronezh: see the website for details.

Street Statues MONUMENT
The streets of Voronezh are scattered with a miscellany of amusing bronze statues. Among others, there's the lucky kitten (touch its left paw and make a wish!), a 'therapeutic' chair said to imbue the sitter with positive energy, and a cute balalaika and accordion sitting casually near the more formal bust of a local composer.

Sleeping

★Roof Hostel HOSTEL $
(Хостел Крыша; ☎4732-606 885; www.roofhostel.ru/en; ul Revolyutsii 1905 goda 31a; dm ₽500-700, d ₽1500;) With sociable, English-speaking staff, bright, clean rooms, a well-equipped kitchen and within walking

distance of the best of Voronezh, this sparkling new hostel is a joy. Fun extras include board-game nights, bike rental (24 hours ₽600) and free slippers.

Petrovsky Passazh Hotel HOTEL $$$
(Отель Петровский Пассаж; ☎4732-556 070; www.petrohotel.ru; ul 20-ti Letiya VLKSM 54a; s/d from ₽3900/5600; ❄📶) The owner here is a hunter – which accounts for the stuffed bear and wild cat in the corridors. Spacious rooms are cabled for broadband internet and offer modern furnishings and big flatscreen TVs. Staff speak English. It's on the 2nd floor above a shopping centre.

Art Hotel HOTEL $$$
(☎4732-399 299; www.arthotelv.ru; ul Dzerzhinskogo 5b; s/d from ₽4900/5900; 📶) Offers pleasant, modern rooms, helpful English-speaking staff and a classy Italian restaurant, Portofino. If you're feeling flush, there are also a couple of sauna suites (₽8600) with spas and bidets.

Eating & Drinking

★ **CoVok Sovetskoe Cafe** RUSSIAN $
(ul Kukolkina 29; mains ₽140-390; ⊙noon-midnight Sun-Thu, until 2am Fri & Sat) This nostalgia cafe recalls the days of the USSR, not with kitsch propaganda posters but with cosy nooks, black-and-white TVs flickering on the walls and a witty menu highlighting the best of erstwhile republics such as Georgia (dumplings), Belorussia (potato pancakes), Uzbekistan (pilaf) and Ukraine (brisket, borsch). There's also an entire section devoted to *salo* (pig fat): what's not to love?

Marusya Cafe CAFE $
(Benefit Plaza Congress Hotel, ul Vladimira Nevskogo 29; mains ₽150-430; ⊙noon-midnight Sun-Thu, to 2am Fri & Sat) For somewhere that looks so hip, this friendly place dishes up fairly non-inventive fare. But it all tastes good (especially the addictive fried cheese sticks) and there are plenty of other reasons – art exhibitions, DJ play-offs, speed-dating events – to spend a few hours here.

Bar Duck BAR
(ul Plekhanovskaya 23; ⊙6pm-6am) Find this quirky little basement bar, with walls plastered with scrapbook cuttings (and a clientele just plastered), a few blocks northwest of pl Lenina.

Entertainment

Opera & Ballet Theatre THEATRE
(☎4732-553 927; http://theatre.vzh.ru; pl Lenina 7) Quality productions are mounted at this handsome classical-style theatre.

BARak O'mama LIVE MUSIC
(www.barakomama.ru; pr Revolyutsii 35; ⊙noon-midnight Thu-Sun, to 3am Fri & Sat) Live music most nights from 9pm at this centrally located cafe-bar with an unforgettable name.

Getting There & Away

AIR

The **airport** (www.voronezhavia.ru) is 10km north of the centre along Zadonskoe sh, with several flights daily to Moscow's Domodedovo Airport (₽3900, one hour).

BUS

The **bus station** (Moskovsky pr 17) is 3km northwest of pl Lenina, with daily services to Moscow (₽800, 12 hours), Saratov (₽910, 12 hours) and Volgograd (₽960, 13 hours). Six services a day run to Yelets (₽220, three hours).

TRAIN

The main train station is **Voronezh 1** (pl Chernyakhovskogo), around 1.5km north of pl Lenina, with services to Moscow (*platskart/kupe* ₽1194/2493, 10½ hours, 10 daily), St Petersburg (₽2283/3326, 24 hours, two daily) and Yelets (₽788/1036, 5½ hours, four daily).

Getting Around

From Voronezh 1 train station there are many buses, *marshrutky* and trams; to reach the city centre, look for those going to pl Lenina (Площадь Ленина). Some long-distance trains stop at Pridacha (Придача) a few kilometres outside the city. If you arrive there, follow the crowd 300m out of the station, where you'll find a car park full of *marshrutky* to whisk you into town.

To reach the city centre from the bus station, exit the station and catch bus 5a (₽12), which runs along ul Plekhanovskaya.

Oryol Орёл

☎4862 / POP 318,136 / ⊙MOSCOW

With its attractive mix of grand old buildings, riverside parks, footbridges and red-and-yellow trams, Oryol (arr-*yol*) harks back to prerevolutionary Russia. Ivan Turgenev is one of 12 local writers whose work is remembered at several small house-museums, and the town is the ideal base

Oryol

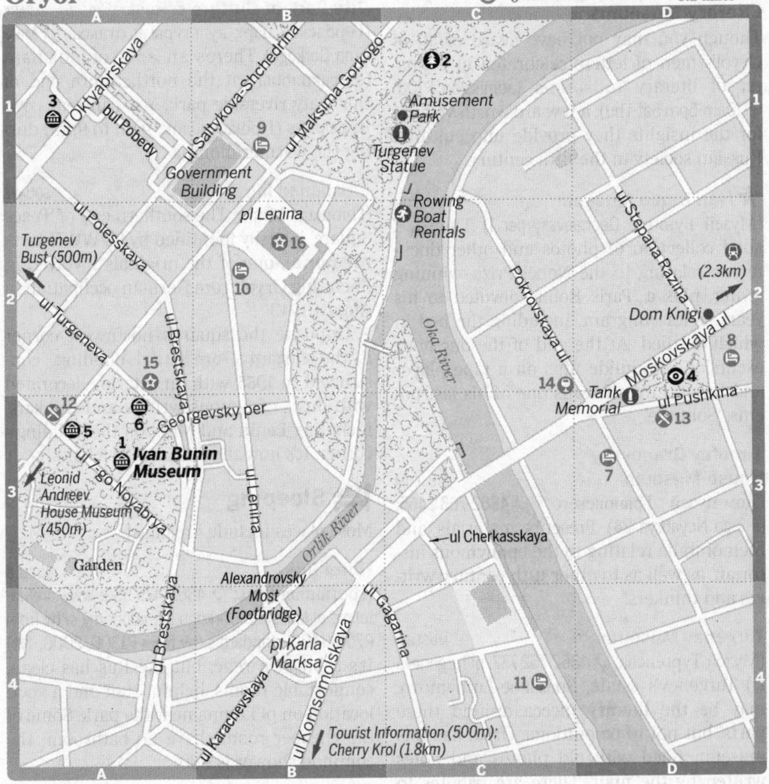

Oryol

Top Sights
1 Ivan Bunin Museum A3

Sights
2 City Park of Culture & Rest C1
3 Nikolai Leskov House Museum A1
4 Ploshchad Mira D2
5 Timofey Granovsky House-Museum ... A3
6 Turgenev Museum A3

Sleeping
7 Atlantida D3
8 Hotel Oryol D2
9 Hotel Rus B1
10 Hotel Salyut B2
11 Retrotur C4

Eating
12 17 Bar A3
3 Etazh .... (see 13)
13 Labirint D3

Drinking & Nightlife
14 Pint House C2

Entertainment
15 Teatr Russky Stil A2
16 Turgenev Theatre B2

for visiting Turgenev's beautiful estate, Spasskoe-Lutovinovo. It's also the gateway to the Orlovskoye Polesye National Park, home to almost 300 European bison.

A fortress is thought to have stood on the bluff overlooking the confluence of the Oka and Orlik Rivers since at least the 12th century. Legend has it that an eagle (*oryol* in Russian) alighted on the fortress, giving the settlement its name. The city reached its peak during the 19th century, when a surprising number of gentry (19,000 out of a population of 32,000) lived here.

Sights

Literary Museums

Though you may not have heard of all of Oryol's men of letters celebrated in a cluster of literary **museums** (admission ₽100; ⌚10am-5pm Sat-Thu), a few are worth visiting for the insights they provide into cultured Russian society in the 19th century.

★Ivan Bunin Museum MUSEUM
(Музей Бунина; Georgievsky per 1) There's a good collection of photos and other documents relating to the Nobel Prize–winning writer, plus a 'Paris Room' devoted to his years as an emigrant, including the bed in which he died. At the end of the one-hour excursion, the guide flips on a tape player and Bunin himself reads one of his last poems, 'Solitude'.

Timofey Granovsky House-Museum MUSEUM
(Дом-музей Грановского; ☎4862-763 465; ul 7-go Noyabrya 24) Presents materials and memorabilia relating to the eponymous historian, as well as to other 19th-century writers and thinkers.

Turgenev Museum MUSEUM
(Музей Тургенева; ☎4862-762 737; ul Turgeneva 11) Turgenev's estate, Spasskoe-Lutovinovo, may be the literary mecca around these parts, but not to be outdone, Oryol has this museum filled with old photos and notes written by the man. There are tributes to Turgenev throughout town, including a **statue** of him overlooking the Oka on Turgenevsky spusk, the sloping street off pl Lenina, and a **bust** in the public garden.

Leonid Andreev House Museum MUSEUM
(Дом-музей Леонида Андреева; ul 2-a Pushkarnaya 41) Inside this cottage, the birthplace of writer and dramatist Leonid Andreev, there is a beautiful piano and examples of Andreev's art and photography: he was an early Russian exponent of colour photography and his compositions are remarkable.

Nikolai Leskov House Museum MUSEUM
(Дом-музей Лескова; ☎4862-763 304; ul Oktyabrskaya 9; 📶) Author and journalist Nikolai Leskov (1831–95), who wrote the book on which the opera *Lady Macbeth of Mtsensk* is based, is remembered at this turquoise-and-cream wooden house. His death mask is in one corner; in another you'll find incredible miniature silhouette cut-outs of rural scenes.

Other Sights & Activities

City Park of Culture & Rest PARK
(Городской парк культуры и отдыха; ul Maksima Gorkogo) There's an **amusement park** (аттракционы) at the northeastern end of this leafy riverside park. You can rent **rowing boats** (Прокат лодок; 9am to 9pm) during the warmer months.

Ploshchad Mira SQUARE
(Площадь Мира) The southern end of 'Peace Square' is easily identified by its WWII **tank memorial**, one of the originals involved in liberating Oryol from German occupation in August 1943.

Opposite the square's northwest corner is the elegant **Dom Knigi** building, constructed in 1955 with an exterior decorated with busts of famous writers and thinkers, including Lenin and Marx on the building's corner. It's now the entrance to a bank.

Sleeping

Most places include breakfast.

Hotel Rus HOTEL $
(Гостиница Русь; ☎4862-475 550; www.orelhotel.ru; ul Maksima Gorkogo 37; economy s/tw from ₽700/1400, standard s/tw from ₽1300/2000; 📶) It's a bit of a relic, but the Rus has clean, comfortable rooms, helpful staff and a good location on pl Lenina near the park. Some of the cheaper rooms have no bathroom; the common shower is ₽60.

★Retrotur HOTEL $$
(Гостиница Ретро-Тур; ☎4862-050 249; www.retrotur-orel.ru; ul Levyy Bereg Reki Oki 15; s/d from ₽2000/2500; ❄📶) Sitting pretty on the banks of the Oka River, this hotel is within walking distance of the centre but offers respite from the hubbub in calm, forested surrounds. Rooms may enjoy loads of natural lighting and lovely polished timber floors. A good **restaurant** (set meals ₽170) is attached.

Hotel Oryol HOTEL $$
(Гостиница Орёл; ☎4862-550 525; www.orelhotel.ru; pl Mira 4; s/d from ₽2000/2700, lyux from ₽6000; ❄📶) A touch of grandeur remains in the distinguished exterior, public areas and *lyux* rooms of this historic hotel. It's not quite as gilded in the more affordable rooms, but they are airy and comfortable.

Atlantida HOTEL $$
(Атлантида; ☎4862-558333; www.atlantida-hotel.ru; ul Fomina 4a; s/d ₽3300/3700; 📶🏊) Over-

SPASSKOE-LUTOVINOVO СПАССКОЕ-ЛУТОВИНОВО

Surrounded by beautiful countryside, **Spasskoe-Lutovinovo** (www.spasskoye-lutovino-vo.ru; guided tour ₽150, grounds only ₽50; ⊙9am-5pm), 65km north of Oryol, is the family estate of Ivan Turgenev (1818–83), where the 19th-century novelist completed his most famous book, *Fathers and Sons*.

The estate was originally given to the Turgenev family by Ivan the Terrible. Though he spent much of his life in Moscow, St Petersburg, Germany and France, Turgenev thought of Spasskoe-Lutovinovo as his home and returned here many times. He was also exiled here in 1852–53 as a result of his work *A Sportsman's Sketches,* which displeased the tsar. To learn more about the writer, see www.turgenev.org.ru.

The main house contains some original furniture, books and Turgenev's personal effects. There's an icon hanging in Turgenev's study that was given to the family by Ivan the Terrible, and the chessboard is set ready to play (Turgenev was a masterful player).

Also on the grounds is the restored family church, which holds regular services. The big oak tree planted as a sapling by Turgenev and the writer's 'exile house' are a short walk from the main house.

Take a *marshrutka* from Oryol to Mtsensk (₽72, one hour, every 30 minutes from 6am to 9pm), then switch at Mtsensk's bus station to a Spasskoe-Lutovinovo bus (₽25, 30 minutes, hourly), or take a taxi (around ₽170).

look the nouveau-riche decorative touches, but ignore the insanely OTT jungle-waterfall pool at your peril. Delusions of grandeur aside, this midsized hotel, restaurant, sauna and business complex is a decent option, and its ye olde restaurant-bar (theme: cashed-up woodsman) is lots of fun.

Hotel Salyut HOTEL **$$**
(Гостиница Салют; ☑4862-435 040; www.salut.orel.ru; ul Lenina 36; s/d from ₽1450/2100) These typical Soviet digs are very central, and some rooms have the added bonus of flashy pink or lime-green wallpaper.

🍴 Eating & Drinking

★17 Bar WESTERN **$$**
(☑4862-487 307; ul Maksima Gorkogo; mains ₽130-520; ⊙noon-midnight Sun-Thu, to 2am Fri & Sat; 🛜) With a dapper wooden interior, nouveau-cool deer antlers on the wall and an arty clientele/staff, this new bar is a little slice of hipster heaven. To a backdrop of indie tunes, it dishes up 'American' sandwiches, great pastas and fine steaks, plus a big range of alcoholic drinks, including cider and mead.

3 Etazh WESTERN **$$**
(3 Этаж; www.3etaj.com; 3rd fl, ul Pushkina 6; pizzas ₽160-470; ⊙noon-1am Sun-Thu, to 2am Fri & Sat; 🛜) Excellent thin-crust pizzas, topped waffles and filling sandwiches are just the start of the great things about this whimsical cafe. Vegetarians will find some solace

here, with actual meals designed just for them.

Labirint EUROPEAN **$$**
(Лабиринт; ☑4862-426 532; www.labirintclub.ru; ul Pushkina 6; meals ₽280-590; ⊙noon-1am Sun-Thu, to 2am Fri & Sat; 🛜📶) This appealing, upmarket cafe-lounge serves up excellent salads, pastas and meat dishes such as shashlyk (kebabs) and pork fillets, plus some vego options, including a no-meat version of steak tartare.

Pint House PUB
(Pokrovskaya ul 3; ⊙noon-2am; 🛜) When the weekend comes, this is Oryol's premier party place, with quaffing crowds going bonkers to live bands. The rest of the time, it is a fairly distinguished watering hole, with gentlemen's lounge–style booths and classy beers on the menu. There's a fine pub-grub menu and a ₽195 business-lunch deal from noon to 4pm.

Cherry Krol ANTI-CAFE
(Антикафе Вишнёвый Кроль; Komsomolskiy per 26a; per min ₽1 (minimum stay 20min); ⊙6-11pm Tue-Sun; 🛜) Though it's not open during the day, it's worth the trip out to this anti-cafe for the free wi-fi, hot drinks and general sociability.

⭐ Entertainment

Given Oryol's literary heritage, it's no surprise to find a number of quality theatres in town.

OFF THE BEATEN TRACK

ORLOVSKOYE POLESYE NATIONAL PARK

Orlovskoye Polesye National Park (www.orlpolesie.ru), 85km northwest of Oryol, is a placid slice of taiga, with over 360 sq km of thick forest, lakes and wildflower-dotted grasslands. It's a fantastic spot for fishing, camping and walking, but this is more than your average nature getaway. The park is home to almost 300 European bison, which roam free under a special protection and breeding program. The well-managed park runs **bison tours** (₽2000 per group, winter only), where visitors can observe the grand beasts feeding and at play. The park also houses an open-air zoo (adult/child ₽180/90), a sacred spring and an ostrich farm. Outdoorsy types can trek along signposted ecotrails or take a load off on a rented bike, boat or horse. The website has full details of activities and accommodation options.

Get there via *elektrichki* from Oryol (₽320, three hours, four daily) to Bryansk; alight at Khotynets and take a bus to Zhudre village (30 minutes, three daily). Oryol's tourism centre (www.tourism-orel.ru) also runs various daily tours to the park out of Oryol.

Turgenev Theatre THEATRE
(Орловский государственный академический театр имени И.С. Тургенева; ☎4862-761 639; pl Lenina) Hosts plays and concerts in a clever modernist building – the facade mimics the effect of a stage with the curtains drawn.

Teatr Russky Stil THEATRE
(Муниципальный театр Русский стиль; ☎4862-762 024; ul Turgeneva 18) A fun, small-scale, occasionally experimental theatre that presents mostly comedies.

Information

Tourist Information (www.tourism-orel.ru; ul Komsomolskaya 63; ⏲9am-6pm Mon-Fri) Handy website (in English) with lots of info on Oryol as a literary city, plus links to various tour operators. It can also help arrange Oka River and Orlovskoye Polesye tours.

Getting There & Away

BUS

The **bus station** (Avtovokzalnaya ul) is 4km to the south, with services to Moscow (₽800, seven hours, five daily), Smolensk (₽720, nine hours, daily), Tula (₽230, four hours, three daily), Voronezh (₽340, seven hours, two daily) and Yelets (₽320, five hours, daily).

TRAIN

The **train station** (pl Privokzalnaya) is around 2.5km north from central pl Mira. Trains run to Moscow (*platskart/kupe* ₽1501/2282, five hours, 20 daily), St Petersburg (₽1705/2578, 11 hours, daily), Voronezh (₽1000/1409, 7½ hours, two daily) and Tula (₽1094/1380, 2½ hours, 18 daily).

Getting Around

From the train station, trams 1 and 4 and trolleybus 3 (all ₽9) stop at ul Karla Marksa, on the southeastern end of the Alexandrovsky bridge leading to ul Lenina, before continuing on to the bus station. Trolleybuses 4 and 6, which run along ul Turgeneva, also provide convenient access to the bus station. Trolleybus 5 to the train station runs along ul Maksima Gorkogo.

Taxis to the train or bus station from pl Lenina charge about ₽120.

NORTH & WEST OF MOSCOW

The western route out of Moscow, towards Belarus, takes you through to Smolensk, a Hero City home to many fine museums. To the north, ancient settlements such as Veliky Novogord, the birthplace of Russia, offer fascinating glimpses into Russia's distant past.

Smolensk Смоленск

☎4812 / POP 326,861 / ⏲MOSCOW

Set on the upper Dnepr River, this handsome city offers 16th-century fortress walls and towers to explore, onion-dome churches and well-landscaped parks. The highlight is the magnificent Assumption Cathedral, but art and music are also well represented in the home town of composer Mikhail Glinka and 19th-century arts patron Princess Maria Tenisheva, whose estate of Flyonovo makes for an interesting side trip.

History

Smolensk was first mentioned in 863 as the capital of the Slavic Krivichi tribe. The town's auspicious setting gave it early control over trade routes between Moscow and the west, and between the Baltic and Black Seas. By the late 1100s, Smolensk was one of the strongest principalities in Eastern Europe.

As Muscovy and Lithuania vied for power in the 13th century, Smolensk was caught in the middle and was successively invaded from both sides. The battle between Russia and Napoleon's army outside Smolensk in 1812 (later immortalised in Tolstoy's *War and Peace*) is commemorated by a couple of monuments in town. Composer Mikhail Glinka, regarded as the founder of Russian classical music, grew up near Smolensk and performed frequently in the Nobles' Hall, facing what is now the Glinka Garden.

Almost 95% of Smolensk was destroyed in WWII, but was quickly rebuilt, often along original plans. It was later awarded the rare status of Hero City (город-герой).

⊙ Sights

Information on many of Smolensk's galleries and museums can be found at www.smolensk-museum.ru.

★ **Assumption Cathedral** CHURCH
(Успенский кафедральный собор; ul Sobornaya Gora 5; ⊙7am-8pm) Dominating the skyline is this huge green-and-white working cathedral topped by five silver domes. A church has stood here since 1101; this one was built in the late 17th and early 18th centuries. Its spectacular gilded and icon-encrusted interior so impressed Napoleon that, according to legend, he set a guard to stop his own men from vandalising the cathedral.

Immediately on your left as you enter, look for a small framed icon of the Virgin, richly encrusted with pearls drawn from the Dnepr around Smolensk. Further on, a cluster of candles marks a supposedly wonder-working icon of the Virgin. This is a 16th-century copy of the original, said to be by St Luke, which had been on this site since 1103 and was stolen in 1923.

Trinity Monastery MONASTERY
(Свято-Троицкий женский монастырь; ul Bolshaya Sovetskaya 9) Much restoration work has been done on this charming, pink-walled female monastery, which also runs a small girls' orphanage. Donations are welcome.

Museum of Russian Vodka MUSEUM
(Музей Русской водки; ☑4812-381 382; ul Studencheskaya 4; admission ₽50; ⊙9am-5pm Tue-Sat) A one-room exhibition provides a brief overview of the drink's colourful history. Guided tours (in Russian) end at the makeshift bar, where you can purchase some noteworthy Smolenskiy brands.

In the World of Fairytales Museum MUSEUM
(Музей В мире сказки; ☑4812-382 226; ul Lenina 15; adult/child ₽50/40; ⊙10am-6pm Sun-Thu, to 5pm Fri; ⊞) One for the kids, where they've smashed the boring don't-touch rules. It's a wonderful, creative space full of activities and interactive exhibits based around Russian fairy tales. Even Baba Yaga is there: yikes!

★ **Smolensk Flax Museum** MUSEUM
(Музей Смоленский лён; Nicholas Tower, ul Marshala Zhukova 6; admission ₽50; ⊙10am-6pm Tue-Sun, to 5pm Fri) Flax production developed from the Middle Ages as one of Smolensk's main industries, as the moderate climate sustained soil ideal for growing the plant. Exhibits and hands-on demonstrations will give you an idea of how the process works and of the lovely products that can be made from the resulting cloth.

History Museum MUSEUM
(Исторический музей; ☑4812-383 862; ul Lenina 8; history gallery ₽50, all galleries ₽150; ⊙10am-6pm Tue-Thu, Sat & Sun, to 5pm Fri) This gorgeous mustard-coloured building is home to a range of different galleries, covering natural and local history.

Konenkov Sculpture Museum MUSEUM
(Музей скульптуры Коненкова; ☑4812-382 029; ul Mayakovskogo 7; admission ₽50; ⊙10am-6pm Tue-Thu, Sat & Sun, to 5pm Fri) Contains playful woodworks by Smolensk Oblast native Sergei Konenkov, otherwise known as the 'Russian Rodin'. The museum also has works from other noted Smolensk artists.

Glinka Garden PARK
(Городской сад Глинки) At the east end of this shady garden with fountains, an 1885 statue of the composer Glinka is surrounded by a fence with excerpts from his opera *A Life for the Tsar* wrought into the iron. Opposite is the concert hall (p245) in which he performed. The north side of the garden is bordered by the expansive pl Lenina, where

Smolensk

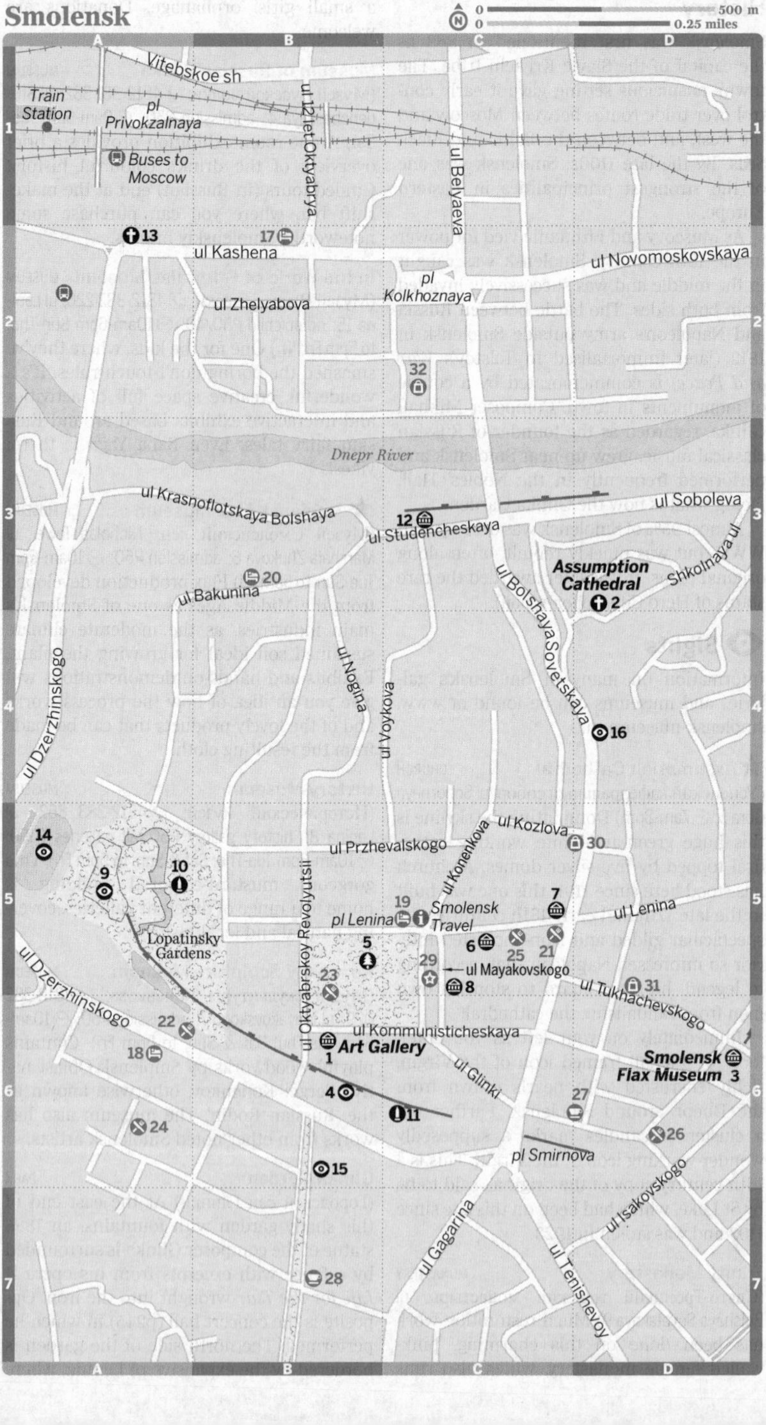
0 500 m
0 0.25 miles
A
B
C
D
1
2
3
4
5
6
7
Vitebskoe sh
Train Station
pl Privokzalnaya
Buses to Moscow
ul 12 let Oktyabrya
ul Belyaeva
13
17
ul Kashena
ul Novomoskovskaya
pl Kolkhoznaya
ul Zhelyabova
32
Dnepr River
ul Krasnoflotskaya Bolshaya
ul Soboleva
12
ul Studencheskaya
Shkolnaya ul
Assumption Cathedral
2
ul Bolshaya Sovetskaya
20
ul Bakunina
ul Nogina
ul Voykova
ul Dzerzhinskogo
16
14
ul Kozlova
ul Konenkova
30
ul Przhevalskogo
9
10
19
Smolensk Travel
7
pl Lenina
ul Lenina
6
25
21
Lopatinsky Gardens
5
29
ul Mayakovskogo
8
31
23
ul Tukhachevskogo
ul Dzerzhinskogo
22
ul Kommunisticheskaya
Art Gallery
1
18
ul Oktyabrskoy Revolyutsii
ul Glinki
Smolensk Flax Museum
3
4
11
27
24
26
pl Smirnova
15
ul Isakovskogo
ul Gagarina
ul Tenishevoy
28

Smolensk

a statue of Vladimir Ilyich himself stands in front of the palatial city hall, once the House of Soviets.

★ Art Gallery ART GALLERY
(Художественная галерея; ☎4812-381 591; ul Kommunisticheskaya 4; admission ₽100; ⏲10am-6pm Tue, Wed, Sat & Sun, 11am-7pm Thu, 10am-5pm Fri) This splendid collection includes pieces by luminaries such as Valentin Serov, Ilya Repin and Vasily Tropinin, as well as a good sampling of socialist realism, 14th- to 18th-century icons and European old masters. You'll also find portraits of Princess Maria Tenisheva, who created the Teremok estate at Flyonovo.

Fortress Walls & Around HISTORICAL SITE
(Крепостные стены и вокруг) Making a circuit of the restored city walls, long sections of which boast fine towers reminiscent of the Moscow Kremlin, is a pleasant way to pass a warm summer evening, with parks, various monuments and churches to be encountered along the way. Originally built between 1596 and 1602, the impressive 6.5km-long, 5.5m-thick, 15m-high walls had 38 towers, with 17 still standing.

Overlooking the **Spartak Stadium** (Стадион Спартак), just outside the line of the walls on the west side of the park, the **Korolevsky Bastion** (Королевский бастион) is a high earth rampart built by the Poles who captured Smolensk in 1611. It saw heavy fighting in 1654 and 1812.

Backing onto a longish southwest stretch of the walls, the Lopatinsky Gardens have a 26m-high cast-iron **monument to the 1812 defenders** (Памятник защитникам Смоленска 1812 г). At the foot of the walls southeast of Glinka Garden you'll find an **eternal flame memorial** (Мемориал Вечный огонь), plus another **monument to the heroes of 1812** (Памятник героям 1812 г). The nearby, witch-hatted **Thunder Tower** (Громовая башня) offers city views from its fourth tier; a small **museum** (admission ₽50, 10am to 6pm Tuesday to Sunday) on the 3rd floor covers the kremlin's history.

Peter & Paul Church CHURCH
(Церковь Петра и Павла; ul Kashena 20) With obvious Byzantine influences, this red-brick 12th-century chapel is the oldest in the city and a local icon.

Festivals & Events

Glinka Festival MUSIC
A showcase of Russian classical music that runs between the last week of May and the first week of June.

Shooting Stars Fireworks Festival FIREWORKS
Smolensk's skies erupt every September with artfully choreographed fireworks set to classical and live music.

Sleeping

Felix Hostel HOSTEL $

(Феликс Хостел; 8-904-360 0032; www.felix-hotel.ru; Dzerzhinskogo ul 19; dm/d ₽500/1000;) Moments from some of the city's top attractions and across from Lopatinsky Gardens, Smolensk's only hostel is a great find. It's nothing flash, but it's clean and cheerful with solid bunks and a good communal kitchen.

★**Usadba** MINIHOTEL $$

(Усадьба; 4812-385 931; www.smolhotel.ru; ul Bakunina 2b; s/d from ₽2700/3300;) In a quiet residential area that's still close to the city centre, this cute, 12-room minihotel offers comfortable rooms with good facilities. There's an attached cafe where breakfast and other meals are served, DVD library and a small traditional wooden sauna (₽800 per hour before 4pm, ₽1100 per hour after 4pm).

Derzhava Hotel HOTEL $$

(Гостиница Держава; 4812-022 779; www.derzhava-smolensk.ru; ul Kashena 5a; d/ste from ₽1700/2300;) These are some of the cheapest rooms in Smolensk, and while they're certainly – ahem – interesting (mismatched *everything*), this place is an OK option close to the bus or train stations. Escape the eye-crossing decor in the sauna or Turkish bath (no such respite in the over-the-top restaurant).

Smolenskhotel HOTEL $$$

(Гостиница "Смоленскотель"; 4812-383 604; www.smolensk-hotel.ru; ul Lenina 2/1; s/d/studio ₽3200/4200/6990;) Set on the edge of Glinka Garden, this centrally located five-storey hotel has clean, bright rooms and polite, efficient service. Discounts are available for longer stays and groups.

Eating & Drinking

Domino EUROPEAN $

(Домино; www.pizzadomino.ru; ul Dzerzhinskogo 16; pizza from ₽80, meals ₽70-200; 24hr) Kitsch! Glorious kitsch! Even if peasant-on-acid decor isn't your thing, you'll still enjoy the fast-food offerings from this chain. The front and side patios that open in summer are good for a drink. There are seven Dominos across town, including a **branch** (10am-10pm) at Bolshaya Sovetskaya 18.

Russky Dvor RUSSIAN $

(Русский Двор; www.pizzadomino.ru/Russkiy_Dvor; Glinka Garden; meals ₽80-180; 10am-11pm, to midnight Sat;) This place looks like a cross between St Basil's Cathedral and McDonald's. It's fast food, but the quality is surprisingly high, which may explain the long queues at lunchtime.

Samovar RUSSIAN $

(Самовар; ul Lenina 14; meals ₽120-300; 10am-9pm) This appealing self-serve restaurant specialises in traditional savoury and sweet pies.

★**Tirol** RUSSIAN $$

(Тироль; 4812-385 851; ul Marshala Zhukova 9; mains ₽400-750; noon-1am;) You won't want to leave this charming, snug little den, done up like a babushka's house with old-style wallpaper, figurine lamps and knick-knacks galore. There's a hearty, soul-warming menu to match, featuring some of the chubbiest sausages you'll ever have the pleasure of biting into.

Smolenskaya Krepost RUSSIAN $$

(Смоленская Крепость; 4812-327 690; ul Studencheskaya 4; meals ₽500-760) Set in the old castle walls, this charming restaurant has plenty of character – from the stained-glass windows to the tiny fireplace and exposed-brick walls – with lovely views of the Dnepr from its balcony. The menu features well-prepared traditional Russian dishes.

Saint Jacques FRENCH $$

(Сен-Жак; 4812-242 444; www.san-jak.ru; Churilovskiy per 19; mains ₽450-1200; 11am-late) This posh new place adds a bit of ooh-la-la to the Smolensk dining scene. The St Petersburg chef doffs his beret to Paris with upmarket quiches, pasta with foie gras and meaty mains such as suckling pig in Parisienne sauce. This being Russia, there is also pizza on the menu.

Vanil CAFE

(Ваниль; ul Oktyabrskaya Revolyutsii 7; 9am-11pm;) Chirpy little cafe with good coffee, ridiculously delicious cheesecake, pastries and brightly coloured macaroons.

Dvoinoe Solntse TEAHOUSE

(Двойное Солнце; 4812-630 220; www.doublesun.ru; ul Barklaya-de-Tolli 7; 1pm-1am) Taking a stab at re-creating a traditional Japanese teahouse, this place has floor seating, screens and low tables. Sushi is also available. Inexplicably, so are Indian curries and Mexican tortillas.

WORTH A TRIP

FLYONOVO ФЛЁНОВО

In the late 19th and early 20th centuries, illustrious artists and musicians, including Stravinsky, Chaliapin, Vrubel and Serov, visited Flyonovo, the pretty riverside estate of art lover Princess Maria Tenisheva, near Talashkino, 18km southeast of Smolensk. The visitors joined in applied-art workshops, which the princess organised for her peasants, and helped in building projects.

The most striking result is the almost psychedelic decoration on the exterior of the brick **Holy Spirit Church** (Церковь Святого Духа), particularly the mural of Christ over the entrance designed by well-known landscape painter Rerikh. The ornately decorative wooden house **Teremok** (Изба Теремок; admission ₽50; ⏲10am-5pm Tue-Sun, closed last Thu of month), covered with peasant-style carving, is now a folk-art museum, while the interior of another large but simpler **wooden building** (admission ₽50) resembles a school room. A smaller building sells crafts still produced here.

Take *marshrutka* 104 from Smolensk's bus station to Talashkino (₽28, 20 minutes), from where it's a pleasant 2km walk to the estate. You can hop on the same *marshrutka* at pl Smirnova. The 130 often goes direct from Smolensk: ask at the station.

☆ Entertainment

Glinka Concert Hall CLASSICAL MUSIC
(Концертный зал им. М. И. Глинки Смоленской государственной филармонии; ☎4812-32 984; www.smolensk-filarmonia.ru; ul Glinki 3; tickets from ₽100; ⏲box office noon-7pm) Attending a concert is the best way to get a look at the reconstructed hall where Glinka once entertained Russian nobility and launched the history of secular art music in Russia.

Shopping

Smolenskaya Izba SOUVENIRS
(Художественная мастерская гончарного искусства-Смоленская Изба; ☎4812-407 404; www.km67.ru; ul Tukhachevskogo 5; ⏲10am-7pm Wed-Sun) Not only does this great little place sell souvenirs and crafts the likes of which you won't find elsewhere, but it allows visitors to have a go at creating their own. Pottery, painting and doll-making workshops for groups and individuals (from ₽1500) are loads of fun: book before showing up.

Dom Knigi BOOKSTORE
(Дом Книги; ul Bolshaya Sovetskaya 12/1; ⏲10am-7pm Mon-Sat, 11am-6pm Sun) Sells Russian-language maps out of a beautiful blue baroque building.

Zadneprovsky Market MARKET
(Заднепровский рынок; pl Kolkhoznaya) Pick up fresh food and ogle the bustle at Smolensk's main market.

Information

Smolensk Travel (☎4812-404 375; www.smolensk-travel.ru; Smolenskhotel, ul Lenina 2/1; ⏲10am-7pm Mon-Fri, 11am-4pm Sat) Can assist in buying transport tickets and booking hotels. Also arranges tours of the city and region.

Getting There & Away

BUS

Buses for Moscow (₽600, 5½ hours, 14 daily) leave from outside the main train station and less often from the **bus station** (Автовокзал; ul Dzerzhinskogo). Other services include Oryol (₽720, nine hours, two daily), Pskov (₽840, eight hours, two daily) and St Petersburg (₽1150, 15 hours, daily).

TRAIN

From the **train station** (ul 12 let Oktyabrya) there are around 18 daily connections with Moscow (*platskart/kupe* ₽913/1856, 5½ hours); trains to St Petersburg (₽1580/2311, 17 hours) leave on odd days. International services run to Minsk, Warsaw, Prague and Vienna.

Getting Around

From the train and bus stations, you can take the bus, tram (₽14) or *marshrutka* 41 to the centre of town. Taxis to the centre cost around ₽120.

Tver Тверь

☎4822 / POP 408,852 / ⏲MOSCOW

On the Volga, 150km northwest of Moscow, the charming town of Tver dates back to the 12th century. After a fire levelled most of the town in 1763, the architect Pyotr Nikitin

Tver

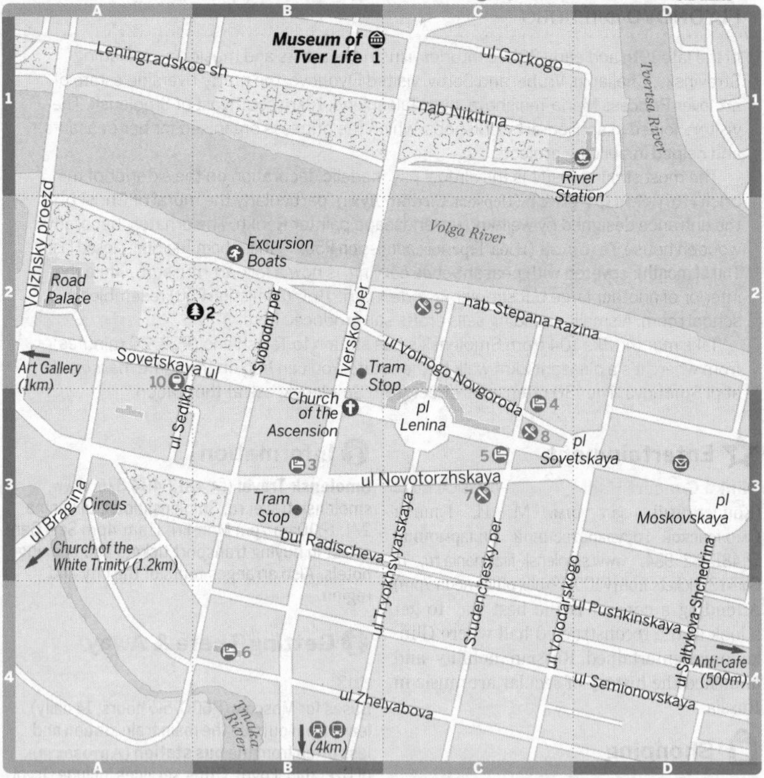

replanned Tver's centre on a three-ray system and built his patron, Catherine the Great, a 'road palace' to rest in on journeys between the then-Russian capital of St Petersburg and Moscow.

Picturesque town houses and churches from the 18th and 19th centuries still line the main streets and riverbank, but the Soviet period was unkind to Tver. Not only was the town renamed Kalinin (after local Mikhail Kalinin, Stalin's puppet president during WWII), the authorities tore down the Cathedral of the Transfiguration of our Saviour in 1935 (one had stood on the same spot since the late 13th century) and converted the mosque into a cafe. The latter has since been returned to the Muslim community.

There are English signboards around the city centre explaining the history of various key locations. It's a good place to break a journey between Moscow and St Petersburg, and is also an access point for historic Torzhok and Lake Seliger.

Sights & Activities

★Museum of Tver Life MUSEUM

(Музей тверского быта; ☎4822-528 404; ul Gorkogo 19/14; admission per gallery ₽80; ⌚11am-5pm Wed-Sun) This museum is split across two adjacent houses: one is set up to display the life of wealthy merchants; the other has more general exhibits, including a reconstruction of a wooden dwelling typical of country folk, plus beautiful examples of embroidery and traditional costumes.

Art Gallery ART GALLERY

(Тверская областная картинная галерея; ☎4822-342-561; www.gallery.tver.ru; ul Dmitry Donskoy 37; admission ₽100; ⌚11am-5pm Tue-Sun) The gallery is usually housed in Catherine the Great's 1775 Road Palace (which is being very slowly restored), but for now

Tver

you'll find the collection in a less-imposing business centre just out of the town centre. There's a bit of everything here, from folk art to furniture, and 14th-century icons to some impressive Soviet-era paintings.

City Garden PARK
(Городской сад; Sovetskaya ul) On the grounds of what once was Tver's kremlin, this park has a funfair with a Ferris wheel and cafes, and often hosts live concerts on summer weekends. Part of the park lies on the north bank of the Volga, where a promenade provides lovely views of the old houses to the south. In summer, **excursion boats** (Экскурсионный причал; 45-minute trip from ₽250, operate 11am to 9pm) sail from the jetty.

Church of the White Trinity CHURCH
(Церковь Белая Троица; pl Troitskaya) Amid a quaint neighbourhood of old wooden houses with carved eaves and window frames, west of the market on ul Bragina, you'll find Tver's oldest building, a stately stone church dating from 1564 that miraculously escaped the usual fate during the Soviet years.

Sleeping

★**Hostel Kalinin** HOSTEL $
(Хостел Калинин; ☎4822-609 060; www.kalininhostel.ru; ul Volnogo Novgoroda 19; dm from ₽600, d ₽1800; 📶) You can practically smell the fresh (and incredibly bright) paint at this riverside beauty, where everything is new, comfortable and remarkably clean. Rainbow-hued rooms come with lockers, and the designer kitchen and common room must be seen to be believed. The staff – on duty 24/7 – are as sparkling as the interior.

Gubernator Hotel HOTEL $$
(Отель Губернаторъ; ☎4822-579 909; www.gubernatorhotel.ru; ul Novotorzhskaya 15; s/d ₽3400/3600; 📶) This mega-central hotel is housed in a pure-white 18th-century building. The interior is equally attractive, with spacious, squeaky-clean rooms. There's no lift, but there are loads of little bonuses such as complimentary bathrobes, toothbrushes and slippers.

Hotel Seliger HOTEL $$
(Гостиница Селигер; ☎4822-320 753; www.seligerhotel.ru; Sovetskaya ul 38; s/d from ₽2800/3000) The Seliger offers a wide range of pleasant, reasonably priced rooms in a central location. The complex has a sauna, fitness club and billiards hall, as well as the popular Zebra club-restaurant next door.

Hotel Volga HOTEL $$
(Гостиница Волга; ☎4822-348 123; www.volga-tver.ru; ul Zhelyabova 1; s/d from ₽2800/3000; 📶) Overlooking the Tmaka River, this revamped hotel has sharp-looking rooms, friendly service and free wi-fi. The inexpensive 24-hour self-serve bistro comes in handy for midnight munchies. The sauna is ₽500 per hour.

Eating & Drinking

Pedestrianised ul Tryokhsvyatskaya is a pleasant place to stroll, shop and stop for a bite to eat, with several options.

Matryoshka Pelmeni Bar RUSSIAN $
(Пельмень-бар Матрёшка; nab Stepana Razina 5; meals ₽100-350; ⌚11am-midnight; 📋) Super-colourful decor inspired by the traditional nesting dolls sets the scene for this '*pelmeni* bar' offering no fewer than 16 types of the dumplings, plus plenty of other dishes.

★**Mamonts** WESTERN $$
(Мамонтс; ☎4822-415 107; www.mamonts-bar.ru; ul Novotorzhskaya 18; mains from ₽300-650; ⌚noon-2am) With an oddly elegant, prehistoric-hipster ambience, meaty menu and dim little seating caves, Mamonts brings caveman cool to the Tver dining scene. Troglodytes, however, need not apply: offerings such as duck with raspberry sauce and caramelised apple, and the divine rabbit with bacon in cream sauce, are made for a modern palate.

WORTH A TRIP

TORZHOK ТОРЖОК

Hugging the Tvertsa River, the church spire and domed skyline of Torzhok seems straight out of a Russian fairy tale. An easy day trip from Tver, or a pit stop en route to Ostashkov, Torzhok was once on the main road from St Petersburg to Moscow. Pushkin passed through several times on his travels. His visits are commemorated in the **AS Pushkin Museum** (Музей Пушкина; ul Dzerzhinskogo 71; admission ₽70; 9am-5.30pm Wed-Fri, 11am-5pm Sat & Sun); it's in a grey painted wooden building on the right as you enter town on the bus from Tver. Among the exhibits are doodles by Pushkin that evoke scenes along this major highway in the 19th century.

The highlight of Torzhok's many religious buildings is the **Borisoglebsky Monastery** (Борисоглебский мужской монастырь; ul Staritskaya 7; museum ₽30, grounds admission free; 8am-8pm), one of the oldest such complexes in Russia and only partly restored. Nearby, the operational, whitewashed and blue-domed **Archangel Michael Church** (Михайло-Архангельский храм) has a beautifully decorated interior. Nearby is the worthwhile **All-Russian Museum of History and Ethnography** (Всероссийский историко-этнографический музей ; www.viemusei.ru; ul Bakunina 6; admission ₽200; 10am-6pm Wed-Sun), which covers the history of the region and includes frescoes, religious relics and archaeological finds from the Upper Volga region.

Torzhok is also famous for its stunning gold-wire embroidery, found in artwork, insignia and royal clothing. There are exquisite displays at the **Goldwork Embroidery Museum and Factory** (Музей фабрикиТоржокские золотошвеи ; www.zolotoshveya.com; Kalinin sh 12; adult/child ₽50/15; 9am-5pm Mon-Sat, to 3pm Sun); the attached shop sells superb crafts and clothing.

Buses (₽150, 1¾ hours, three to four per hour) and trains (₽132, 1½ hours, four daily) connect Torzhok with Tver, as well as with Ostashkov.

Manilov RUSSIAN $$
(Манилов; www.manilovkafe.ru; Sovetskaya ul 17; meals ₽200-600) Step into a 19th-century-style parlour at this sweet restaurant with its entrance on Studenchesky per; even the flat-screen TV on the wall screens period dramas. Dig into traditional favourites such as borsch and beef stroganoff, mop it up with homemade bread and sample the horseradish-flavoured spirit. Different menu items are discounted daily by 20%.

Anti-cafe ANTI-CAFE
(Smolensky per 15/33; 1st hour ₽2 per min, then ₽1 per min; noon-11pm Mon-Fri, to 2am Sat & Sun) This fun hang-out follows the anti-cafe script to the letter: you pay for your time, not your coffee (or anything else). The chummy crew here are big into board games, craft workshops and lots of chinwagging. BYO food is allowed, though free nibblies are available.

Citybar BAR
(Sovetskaya ul 14; 8am-late) With eight rooms and a summer terrace, this joint does it all: cocktails, karaoke, DJ nights, live bands, shisha, dance-offs, you name it. Pizzas (₽260 to ₽340) and pastas (₽260 to ₽380) are available.

Getting There & Around

The train station is 4km south of the centre on ul Kominterna, with the bus station 400m to its east. Cruise ships and other long-distance riverboats dock at the river station (Речной вокзал) on the north shore of the Volga.

Elektrichki (₽342, three hours) stopping at Tver leave roughly every hour between 6.50am and 10pm from Moscow's Oktyabrskaya vokzal. Long-distance trains between Moscow and St Petersburg and between Moscow and Pskov also pause at Tver.

There are also buses (₽300, three hours) to/from Moscow's Yaroslavsky and Leningradsky stations.

Trams and *marshrutky* 2, 5, 6 and 11 run from the bus and train stations up Chaykovskogo and Tverskoy pr to the town centre.

Ostashkov & Lake Seliger
Осташков и Озеро Селигер

48235 / POP 23,708 / MOSCOW

Ostashkov, 199km west of Tver, is the main base for exploring the lakes, waterways and islands around Lake Seliger. The resort town, sitting on a peninsula at the southern end of the lake, is a jumble of tumbledown wooden cottages, decaying Soviet-era apartment blocks and artfully crumbling churches, some of which are under repair.

Sights & Activities

Some have compared Lake Seliger to Lake Baikal for its beauty and diversity of nature – it's not nearly as impressive, but is still a lovely spot, best appreciated on a **boat excursion** (☎48235-51 568; www.seligerkruiz.ru; Leninsky pr 41; 2/4hr cruises from ₽400/500; ⏲Jun-Sep).

Alternatively, relax by wandering along the town's promenades, lounging on the beaches, swimming in Seliger's clear, clean waters and climbing the bell tower of the handsome Trinity Cathedral, now the **regional museum** (ul Volodarskogo 19; admission ₽50; ⏲11am-5pm Wed-Sun), for a brilliant view of the surroundings.

Sleeping & Eating

It's possible to camp at the tip of the isthmus that juts out north of Ostashkov's monastery. Most hotels include breakfast in their rates.

★**Orlovskaya Dom 1** GUESTHOUSE **$$**
(Орловская Дом 1; ☎8-910-830 0515; www.orlovskaja.ru; per Chaikin Bereg; r from ₽2000) You couldn't wish for a better location, on the edge of the lake with the cupolas of the Trinity Cathedral right behind. Spotless rooms sport Juliet balconies. There's a cafe, table tennis and sauna, and boats and pedal boats for rent.

Ashkhen HOTEL **$$**
(Ашхен; ☎48235-53 994; www.ashkhen.ru; ul Zagorodnaya 26; s/d/lyux from ₽1000/2000/5000) It doesn't have the lakefront location of other offerings, but what you spend in leg power, you save in your pocket. Rooms are the usual shiny-bedspread affair, but they're clean and liveable. There's a fantastic Caucasian restaurant (meals ₽150 to ₽500) attached. It's 500m from the train station.

Epos HOTEL **$$**
(Эпос; ☎48235-51 499; www.seliger-hotelepos.ru; Leninsky pr 136; s/d from ₽1800/2100) The Epos offers clean, modern and spacious rooms, and the lake is a mere stroll away. The restaurant (meals ₽600) serves decent renditions of the usual Russian dishes.

SDL Hotel HOTEL **$$**
(СДЛ Отель; ☎48235-54 983; www.sdl-tour.ru; ul Volodarskogo 187b; r from ₽2500; 📶) Handy for the train and bus stations at the southern end of town, this modern high-rise block harbours good rooms and a cafe. It's part of a group that also has a luxurious resort made up of wooden chalets (from ₽4500) 7km south of Ostashkov, facing the small Lake Sig.

Getting There & Away

Buses (₽437, four hours, at least four daily) and minibuses (₽250, three hours, at least three daily) connect Ostashkov with Tver; the buses run via Torzhok (₽295, 2½ hours), from where there's one daily *elektrichka*. Minibuses also head to and from Moscow (₽660, six hours, at least three daily). In summer, there's one direct train from Moscow each week (Thursday, *platskart/kupe* ₽1061/1849, 12½ hours), and one to Moscow (11 hours) on Sunday evenings.

Veliky Novgorod
Великий Новгород

☎8162 / POP 219,925 / ⏲MOSCOW

Veliky Novgorod (usually shortened to Novgorod) is a proud and beautiful city, billed as the 'Birthplace of Russia'. It was here, in 862, that Prince Rurik proclaimed the modern Russian state – the Rurik dynasty went on to rule Russia for more than 750 years. The ancient settlement was a major centre for trade, literacy, democracy and the spread of Orthodoxy; its glorious Cathedral of St Sophia is the oldest church in Russia. Straddling the Volkhov River, this attractive, tourist-friendly destination is a popular weekend getaway for St Petersburg residents – to avoid the crowds, come during the week. Novgorod is also a good base for visiting Staraya Russa, Dostoevsky's home town.

History

Much of Novgorod's early history is known through Norse sagas, as this was the first permanent settlement of the Varangian Norsemen who established the embryonic Russian state. By the 12th century the city was Russia's biggest: an independent quasi-democracy whose princes were hired and fired by an assembly of citizens, and whose strong, spare style of church architecture, icon painting and down-to-earth *byliny* (epic folk songs) would become distinct idioms.

Spared from the Mongol Tatars, who got bogged down in the surrounding swamps, Novgorod suffered most at the hands of other Russians: Ivan III of Moscow

Veliky Novgorod

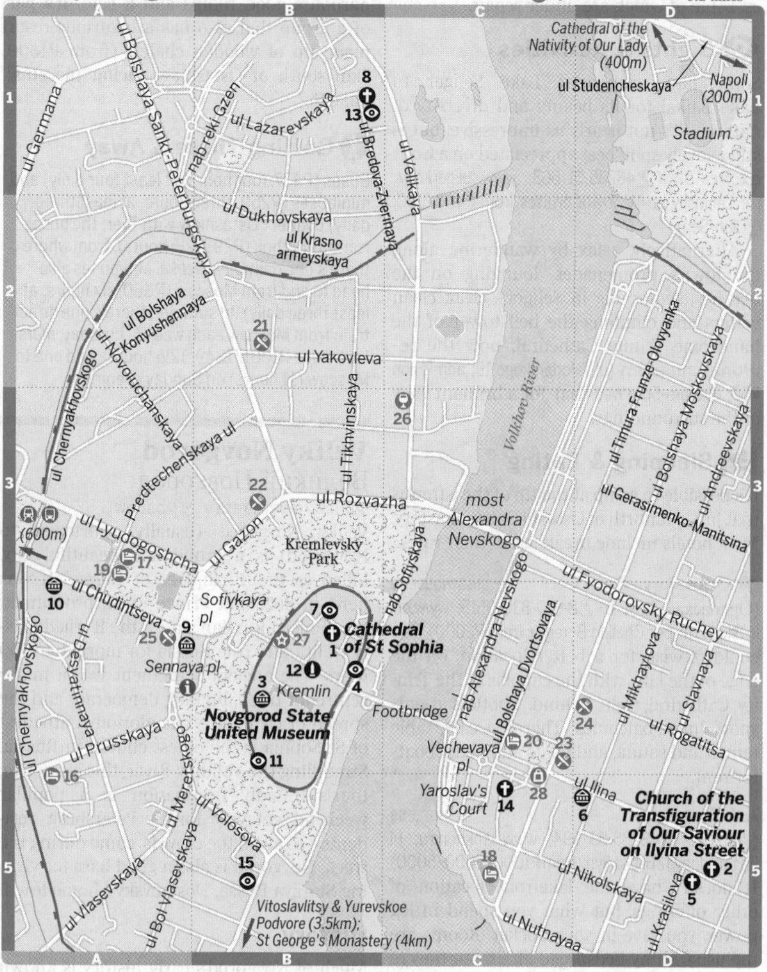

attacked and annexed it in 1477, and Ivan the Terrible's stormtroopers razed the city and slaughtered 60,000 people in a savage pogrom. The founding of St Petersburg finished it off as a trading centre.

Sights

There are scores of old churches and monasteries around town. The helpful tourist office can provide details of which ones are open either as museums or for services.

Kremlin

On the west bank of the Volkhov River, and surrounded by a pleasant wooded park, the **kremlin** (6am-midnight) **FREE** is one of Russia's oldest. Originally called the Detinets (and still often referred to as such), the fortification dates back to the 9th century, though it was later rebuilt with brick in the 14th century. The complex is worth seeing with a guide; arrange one through the tourist office. From May to October, **boat tours** (₽300) run hourly from the Kremlin's pier and Yaroslav's Court towards Lake Ilmen: contact the tourist office to book.

Veliky Novgorod

★**Cathedral of St Sophia** CHURCH

(Софийский собор; www.saintsofianovg.ortox.ru; 8am-8pm, services 10am-noon daily & 6-8pm Wed-Sun) This is the oldest church in Russia (finished in 1050) and one of the country's oldest stone buildings. It's the kremlin's focal point and you couldn't miss it if you tried – its golden dome positively *glows*. St Sophia houses many icons dating from the 14th century, but none are as important as that of Novgorod's patron saint, Our Lady of the Sign, which, the story goes, miraculously saved the city from destruction in 1170 after being struck by an arrow.

The cathedral's domes were probably added during the 14th century – they are perhaps the first example of this most Russian of architectural details. The west doors, dating from the 12th century, have tiny cast-bronze biblical scenes and portraits of the artists.

Belfry NOTABLE BUILDING

(Звонница Софийского собора; adult/child ₽100/50; 10am-1pm & 2-6pm Thu-Tue Apr-Oct) The Belfry, with its enormous steel bells, also has an observation platform.

★**Novgorod State United Museum** MUSEUM

(Новгородский государственный объединенный музей-заповедник; www.novgorodmuseum.ru; adult/student ₽150/100; 10am-6pm Wed-Mon, closed last Thu of the month) This must-see museum houses three strikingly comprehensive exhibitions covering the history of Veliky Novgorod, Russian woodcarving and Russian icons. The latter contains one of the world's largest collections of icons, with around 260 pieces placed in chronological order, allowing you to appreciate the progression of skills and techniques through the centuries.

Downstairs in the history section (minimal English signage), birch-bark manuscripts are displayed, some of them 800 years old. The letters, documents and drawings by people of all ages and social classes indicate that literacy was widespread in medieval Novgorod.

The woodcarving exhibits include everything from the mundane (kitchen utensils and furniture) to more elaborate religious objects. In a separate exhibition are glittering pieces from Novgorod's **gold treasury** (adult/student ₽100/80), some dating back to the 6th century AD.

Millennium of Russia Monument MONUMENT

(Памятник Тысячелетию России) This gargantuan 16m-high, 100-tonne sculpture was unveiled in 1862 on the 1000th anniversary of the Varangian Prince Rurik's arrival, a moment heralded as the start of Russian history. It depicts 127 figures captured in heavy bronze, including rulers, statesmen, artists, scholars and a few fortunate hangers-on.

The women at the top are Mother Russia and the Russian Orthodox Church. Around

WORTH A TRIP

ST GEORGE'S MONASTERY & VITOSLAVLITSY

Set amid peaceful marsh and lakelands a 15-minute bus ride south of the Veliky Novgorod town centre, these two sights make for a relaxing excursion. Founded in 1030 by Yaroslav the Wise, the picturesque **St George's Monastery** (Свято-Юрьев мужской монастырь; www.georg.orthodoxy.ru; ⌚10am-8pm) functions as a theological school. It features the heavily reconstructed Cathedral of St George and a clutch of 19th-century add-ons.

About 600m up the road is **Vitoslavlitsy** (Витославлицы; www.novgorodmuseum.ru/vitoslavlicy; adult/student ₽150/100; ⌚10am-8pm May-Sep, to 5pm Oct-Mar), an evocative open-air museum of 22 beautiful wooden peasant houses and churches. Some of the structures date back to the 16th century, the highlight being the soaring **Church of the Nativity of Our Lady** (1531). What makes these buildings all the more remarkable is that they were all constructed without nails. Bring a picnic; otherwise, there's a cafe on the grounds, plus a good souvenir shop and craft sellers.

Opposite Vitoslavlitsy is the rustic, charming 16-room hotel **Yurevskoe Podvore** (Юрьевское Подворье; ☎8162-946 060; www.tk-podvorie.ru; Yurevskoe sh 6a; d incl breakfast from ₽3200; 📶). The attached restaurant prepares traditional Russian food (meals ₽500 to ₽1000).

Buses 7 and 7A (₽16) from opposite the Novgorod tourist office run here. The bus route goes in a loop; it first stops at the monastery and then outside the museum before returning to town.

the middle, clockwise from the south, are Rurik, Prince Vladimir of Kyiv (who introduced Christianity), tsars Mikhail Romanov, Peter the Great and Ivan III, and Dmitry Donskoy trampling a Mongol Tatar. In the bottom band on the east side are nobles and rulers, including Catherine the Great with an armload of laurels for all her lovers. Alexander Nevsky and other military heroes are on the north side, and literary and artistic figures are on the west.

Kokui Tower NOTABLE BUILDING
(Башня Кокуй; adult/student ₽100/80; ⌚noon-2.30pm & 3.30-8pm Tue, Wed & Fri-Sun Apr-Oct) The 41m-tall Kokui Tower provides panoramic views across the kremlin complex.

Chamber of Facets HISTORICAL BUILDING
(Грановитая палата; adult/student ₽100/80) Part of a palace built in 1433, the Gothic chamber once housed Novgorod's Supreme Court and was the scene of many ceremonies and soirées, not all of them pleasant – Ivan the Terrible reputedly slaughtered tablefuls of noble guests right here, (wrongly) believing they were plotting against him. These days, you'll find religious artefacts, some fine ancient craftwork and frescoes. The gorgeous interior, recently renovated, is worth the admission price alone.

Yaroslav's Court Ярославово Дворище
Across a footbridge from the kremlin are the remnants of an 18th-century market arcade. Beyond that is the market gatehouse, an array of churches sponsored by 13th-to-16th-century merchant guilds, and a 'road palace' built in the 18th century as a rest stop for Catherine the Great.

Several of the buildings are open as museums, the best being the 12th-century **St Nicholas Cathedral** (Собор Святого Николая; adult/student ₽100/60; ⌚10am-noon & 1-6pm Wed-Sun, closed last Fri of month), all that remains of an ancient palace complex from which Yaroslav's Court gets its name. Inside are displays of pieces of ornate decorative tiles from churches in the region and intriguing fragments from the church's original frescoes.

Other Sights

★**Church of the Transfiguration of Our Saviour on Ilyina Street** CHURCH
(Церковь Преображения Господня Спасителя на улице Ильина; ul Ilina; adult/student ₽100/60; ⌚10am-5pm Wed-Sun, closed last Thu of month) This compact church is famous for housing the only surviving frescoes by legendary Byzantine painter Theophanes the Greek (they came close to extinction when the church served as a Nazi machine-gun nest). Restoration has exposed as much of the frescoes as possible, though they are still faint.

A small exhibit upstairs includes reproductions with explanations in Russian.

Cathedral of Our Lady of the Sign CHURCH
(Знаменский собор; adult/student ₽70/40; ⏲10am-5pm Thu-Mon, closed first Thu of the month) While the outside of this 17th-century Moscow-style complex has seen better days, the interior is festooned with frescoes done by masters from Kostroma in the Golden Ring. The cathedral occasionally hosts choral concerts.

Centre of Musical Antiquities MUSEUM
(Центр музыкальных древностей; www.centrpovetkina.ru; ul Ilina 9b; admission ₽180; ⏲2-6pm Sun-Fri) This small but lovingly maintained museum houses a wonderful collection of traditional folk music instruments specific to the Novgorod region and around. The centre hosts occasional concerts and workshops – see website for updates.

Theatre of Time HISTORICAL SITE
(Троицкий Раскоп; Troitsky ul 9; adult/student ₽60/40, guided tours ₽150/100; ⏲9.30am-7pm Jun-Sep, guided tours 6pm Mon-Sat, 5.30pm Sun) Opposite the Trinity Church (Троицкая церковь), the Troitsky Excavation archaeological dig has uncovered much about Novgorod's past, all the way back to the 10th century. The viewing area, overlooking what are believed to be remains of a 14th-century nobleman's home, includes some English signboards. It's best to join a **guided tour** – the tourist office can assist with an English interpreter.

Fine Arts Museum MUSEUM
(Музей изобразительных искусств; www.artmus.natm.ru; pl Pobedy-Sofiyskaya 2; adult/student ₽140/60; ⏲10am-6pm Tue-Sun, closed 3rd Wed of month) A strong but unspectacular provincial collection of paintings by 18th- and 19th-century Russian artists. The 3rd floor features Novgorod artists.

Hall of Military Glory MUSEUM
(Зал воинской славы; ul Chudintseva 11/62; adult/student ₽60/40; ⏲10am-1pm & 2-5pm Tue-Sat) Novgorod boasts status as a City of Military Glory and now has the museum to prove it. Wax statues and bas reliefs tell the stories of the city's heroism from ancient Rus to modern times.

Novgorod Regional Folk Arts Centre ARTS CENTRE
(Новгородский областной Дом народного творчества; ☎8162-739 626; www.dnt-folk.ru; ul Bredova-Zverinaya 14; ⏲9am-5.30pm) The folk arts centre is on the grounds of the former 15th-century Zverin Monastery (Зверин-Покровский монастырь). The craft shop sells exquisitely woven dresses, dolls and hats. Ask the local tourist office to call in advance if you'd like to participate in two-hour workshops (from ₽700 for less than six people) on producing Russian crafts, including amulet making, birch-bark crafts and textiles.

Also on the monastery grounds is the tiny **Church of St Simeon** (Церковь Симеона Богоприимца; adult/student ₽80/60; ⏲10am-5pm Sat-Wed, closed 1st Sat of month), which contains very colourful frescoes that form a religious calendar.

Cathedral of the Nativity of Our Lady CHURCH
(Собор Рождества Богородицы Антониева монастыря; ul Studencheskaya; admission ₽60; ⏲10am-5pm Tue-Sun, closed 1st Wed of month) Legend has it that St Anthony took just three days to sail down Europe's rivers from Italy to Novgorod on a rock in 1106. You can view the supposed boulder – which apparently has healing properties – at the entrance to this church on the grounds of the Antoniev Monastery.

Festivals & Events

See www.visitnovgorod.ru for a full list of annual events.

Alexander Nevsky Festival HISTORICAL
Held during the second weekend in April, this festival honours Novgorod's best-known prince. Members of historical clubs dress up as knights, engage in mock battle and storm the kremlin walls.

Sadko Festival CULTURAL
Held over the first weekend of June, this celebration includes traditional folk art, dancing, singing and a craft fair.

City Day CULTURAL
Concerts, processions and fairs attend the city's birthday during the second weekend in June.

Kupala CULTURAL
Held on the banks of Lake Ilmen in early July, this traditional St John's Day celebration combines old pagan rites with Orthodox rituals. Events include music, dance, food and swimming in the lake.

Sleeping

The pickings are pretty slim for such a popular destination. The tourist office can recommend homestays (around ₽1000 per person for a room). Most places include breakfast in their rates.

Hostel Cruise Bolshaya Yel HOSTEL $

(Хостел Круиз-Большая Ель; ☎8-905-239 8485; ul Prusskaya 11; dm ₽600, d with bathroom from ₽2400; 📶) If you're looking for bells and whistles, keep moving. But for decent, clean budget accommodation with an ace location a brief stroll from the kremlin, you could do far worse than spend some time at the Cruise. Free wi-fi.

★ **Hotel Volkhov** HOTEL $$

(Гостиница Волхов; ☎8162-225 500; www.hotel-volkhov.ru; ul Predtechenskaya 24; s/d from ₽2150/3100; @📶) This centrally located, modern hotel runs like a well-oiled machine, with nicely furnished rooms, pleasant English-speaking staff, laundry service and free wi-fi. A sauna (extra fee) is available to guests. The included breakfasts (choice of Continental, Russian or 'American') are actually very good.

Hotel Rossiya HOTEL $$

(Гостиница Россия; ☎8162-634 185; www.novgorod.amaks-hotels.ru; nab Aleksandra Nevskogo 19/1; s/d from ₽2100/2400; 📶) Though it's a bit of a relic, the location right on the river is delightful and some rooms have nice views of the kremlin. There's also a billiards hall and bike rental (₽150 per hour).

Hotel Akron HOTEL $$

(Гостиница Акрон; ☎8162-736 906; www.hotel-acron.ru; ul Predtechenskaya 24; s/d without breakfast ₽1540/2100, with breakfast ₽1760/2540; 📶) There's no lift here, but it can't hurt to walk when the prices are this fair. Rooms have modern bathrooms, cable TV and a minifridge. Friendly service comes free.

Hotel Voyage HOTEL $$

(Вояж; ☎8162-664 166; www.hotel-voyage.ru; ul Dvortsovaya 1; r incl breakfast from ₽2000; 📶) Beside Yaroslav's Court, this small hotel offers serviceable rooms. The standard rooms are sparse, but move up a notch and you may share your space with tiger-print bedspreads and kaleidoscopic wallpaper. It also has a sauna (from ₽500).

Eating & Drinking

During summer, several open-air cafes facing the kremlin's west side make pleasant spots for a drink.

Kolobok CAFETERIA $

(Колобок; ul Bolshaya Moskovskaya 28; piroshki & pastries from ₽20; ⏲8am-2pm & 2.30-8pm) A Novgorodian institution, this Soviet throwback is no retro homage – this is the real deal, with a communal coffee tank (for the sweet-toothed only), trillion-kilojoule salads and cheap, super-fresh pastries right from the oven. The daily onslaught of students and locals gives some clue as to this place's popularity.

★ **Nice People** INTERNATIONAL $$

(Хорошие люди; ☎8162-730 879; www.gonicepeople.ru; ul Meretskova-Volosova 1/1; meals ₽380-620; ⏲8am-midnight; 📶📋) By far the most appealing choice in Novgorod, this cafe-bar lives up to its name – you'll get a warm welcome from English-speaking staff, and the clientele is pretty easygoing, too. The menu includes speciality DIY salads, with a huge range of ingredients from which to choose. Other tasty treats and daily specials are written on the walls.

Dom Berga RUSSIAN $$

(Дом Берга; ☎8162-948 838; ul Bolshaya Moskovskaya 24; cafe/restaurant meals from ₽80/460; ⏲cafe 9am-9pm, restaurant noon-midnight) Enjoy expertly prepared Russian dishes in this 19th-century former merchant's home near Yaroslav's Court – there's a choice between a simple cafe and fancier restaurant. Be sure to try the honey mead.

Derzhavny RUSSIAN $$

(Державный; ☎8162-773 023; ul Gazon 5/2; meals ₽180-500; ⏲noon-11.30pm Mon-Thu & Sun, to 2am Fri & Sat) Nudgng the kremlin complex, this cavernous place is suitably ye-olde Novgorod, with faux-frescoes on the ceiling and artefacts on the walls. The menu is heavy on hearty Russian cuisine and includes plenty of beautifully prepared game meats. It takes the slow-cooking concept very literally: be prepared to wait for your order.

Cafe Asia INTERNATIONAL $$

(Кафе Азия; ☎8162-772 227; ul Yakovleva 22/1; meals from ₽230-800; ⏲noon-midnight) Japanese, Uzbek and Russian cuisine, together at last! If miso soup, chicken pilaf and Russian salad combos float your boat, this place –

with a decor that's part Russian-staid, part bellydancer-a-go-go – is for you. It all comes together nicely somehow, and Asia is a popular hang-out. Business lunches (noon to 4pm weekdays) are ₽170.

Napoli ITALIAN $$

(Наполи; ☎8162-636 307; www.napoli-restaurant.ru; ul Studencheskaya 21/43; mains ₽350-1100; ⏰noon-midnight; 📶) Novgorod's best Italian kitchen bakes its pizzas in a brick oven and serves tasty delicacies such as beef carpaccio and a divine chilli seafood dish. Sorry kids, no shorts. Buses 4 and 20 will get you there.

Greensleeves Irish Pub PUB

(ul Velikaya 5/12; ⏰noon-1am Mon-Fri, to 2am Sat & Sun) An Irish bar in the birthplace of Russia may seem like a bizarre concept, but they've definitely got the *craic* down pat here. It's a tiny place, which adds to the atmosphere on crowded nights (there are many). There are loads of beers on tap and the obligatory whiskies if you're sick of vodka and cognac.

☆ Entertainment

Concert Hall CLASSICAL MUSIC

(Концертный зал Новгородской филармои; ☎8162-772 777; www.filarmon.natm.ru; Kremlin 8; tickets from ₽200) Novgorod's Philharmonic Concert Hall often hosts live classical and popular music concerts; check the website for the schedule and ticket prices.

Shopping

Souvenir shops abound, with a prominent row of vendors near the tourist office selling woven birch boxes, miniature wooden churches, *matryoshka* dolls and lacquer boxes.

Na Torgu SOUVENIRS

(На Торгу; ☎8162-664 472; ul Ilina 2; ⏰10am-8pm) Has one of Novgorod's best selections of local arts and crafts souvenirs. It has a cracking art gallery upstairs.

ℹ Information

Free wi-fi abounds in Novgorod – visit the tourist office for a full list of hotspots.

Tourist Office (Туристский информационный центр-Красная Изба; ☎8162-773 074; www.visitnovgorod.ru; Sennaya pl 5; ⏰9.30am-6pm) Friendly staff hand out Russian- and English-language maps and provide comprehensive local advice. City tours – on foot or bicycle – and more excursions tailored to specific interests can be arranged; services are available in English, French or German. It even has a **24-hour tourist helpline** (☎8162-998 686).

ℹ Getting There & Away

The train station (Новгород-на-Волхове on RZD timetables) and bus station (Автовокзал) are next to each other on Oktyabryaskaya ul, 1.5km northwest of the kremlin.

Elektrichki run to St Petersburg's Moscow Station (₽400, three hours, two daily). There's also a handy overnight train to Moscow (*platskart/kupe* ₽1250/2400, eight hours) leaving at 9.20pm.

Bus services include St Petersburg (₽330, four hours, 13 daily), Pskov (₽470, 4½ hours, 8am and 4pm) and Staraya Russa (₽194, two hours, 14 daily).

ℹ Getting Around

Buses 1A, 4, 8, 20 and 35 leave from the stand opposite the bus and train stations for the town centre.

Staraya Russa Старая Русса

☎81652 / POP 31,809 / ⏰MOSCOW

Set along the tranquil Polist River, Staraya Russa retains the idyllic charm of the 19th century, when Dostoevsky wrote much of *The Brothers Karamazov* here. The town is the setting for the novel – visit the streets and churches the characters frequented.

The town, 100km southeast of Novgorod, can easily be visited for the day. From the bus station (next to the train station), you can either catch a taxi (₽70) to Dostoevsky's old home or take a 40-minute walk. Head under the road bridge, cross the tracks, then continue along ul Karla Libknekhta until you hit the river. Cross it, turn right and follow the riverside path south to the museum.

Sights

★Dostoevsky House Museum MUSEUM

(Дом-музей Ф. М. Достоевского; ☎81652-21 477; ul Dostoevskogo 42; adult/student ₽70/40; ⏰10am-5.30pm Tue-Sun) The author's family lived on the 1st floor of this riverside dacha (summer country house), which contains many original pieces. Dostoevsky's bookcase is still stocked, and his desk has copies from his mazelike drafts – you can see his doodles on the pages. An English-language handout available at the ticket office details the collection.

Dostoevsky Cultural Centre ARTS CENTRE
(Научно-культурный центр Достоевского; ☎81652-37 285; ul Dostoevskogo 8; adult/student ₽100/60; ⏲10am-6pm Tue-Fri & Sun) This handsome little neoclassical building hosts temporary Dostoevsky-centric exhibitions; you can also arrange Russian-language tours of the town (₽500, two hours). From here, it's just a short stroll to the gorgeously restored 17th-century **Resurrection Cathedral** (Воскресенский собор) and bell tower.

Church of the Holy Martyr Mina CHURCH
(Церковь святого великомученика Мины; ul Georgievskaya 44) If you like your churches photogenically abandoned and seasoned with a dash of the fantastic, this one's for you. Legend has it that in the 17th century, Swedish invaders sought refuge in the church after a long day of looting and pillaging, only to be struck blind upon crossing the threshold. They were sent back to Sweden as proof of the miracles of Russian Orthodoxy.

Regional Museum MUSEUM
(Старорусский краеведческий музей; pl Timura Frunze; adult/student ₽100/60; ⏲10am-6pm Wed-Mon) This museum, offering the usual historical displays and religious relics, is housed in an attractive whitewashed 12th-century monastery; you can also see fragments from the church's original frescoes.

A neighbouring building houses the small **Kartinnaya Gallery** (Картинная Галерея; pl Timura Frunze; adult/student ₽70/40; ⏲10am-6pm Wed-Fri & Mon, to 5pm Sat & Sun), which has a noteworthy selection of paintings (and a few sculptures) of artists who spent time in Staraya Russa.

Sleeping & Eating

★**Hotel Staraya Russa** SANATORIUM $$
(Отель Старая Русса; ☎81652-57 888; www.russa.amaks-kurort.ru; ul Mineralnaya 62; s/d from ₽2350/2750) A throwback to the town's heyday as a popular spa destination, this huge complex offers treatments, therapies and procedures for whatever ails you. Even if you're feeling tip-top, there are loads of indulgent options, including massages and saunas. It's also great fun for kids. The restaurant caters to just about every possible dietary whim.

Hotel Polist HOTEL $$
(Гостиница Полисть; ☎81652-37 547; www.polist-tour.ru; ul Engelsa 20; s/d from ₽1400/1800;) This well-maintained hotel is a solid option. It also houses a decent restaurant that passes for fancy around these parts.

Apelsin CAFE $
(Блинная Апельсин; ul Karla Marksa 10; meals ₽250; ⏲10am-10pm) Cute little creperie dishing up all manner of bliny and other light meals. Set breakfasts from ₽50.

Kafe Sadko RUSSIAN $
(Кафе Садко; ul Lenina 7; meals ₽100-350; ⏲9am-9pm) Small portions of standard canteen Russian fare are served at this basic cafe facing the central square.

Okami INTERNATIONAL $$
(Кафе-бар Оками; ul Karla Libknekhta 10; meals ₽370-620; ⏲noon-11pm;) Offers a typical new-Russian menu that mixes pizza and sushi. The set meals of the latter are a reasonable deal – just don't expect anything too authentic.

Getting There & Away

There are regular buses to and from Novgorod (₽210, two hours, 14 daily). Going back to Novgorod, tickets tend to sell out fast, so best to buy your return ticket when you arrive. There are at least six daily buses to and from St Petersburg (₽580, 5½ hours).

The train station, next to the bus station (Автостанция), is on the route between Pskov (*platskart/kupe* ₽1090/1500, 3½ hours, two daily) and Moscow (₽1720/2570, 8½ hours, two daily); services are at inconvenient hours. There are no direct trains to or from St Petersburg.

Pskov Псков

☎8112 / POP 206,730 / ⏲MOSCOW

Only 30km from the Estonia border, church-studded Pskov is dominated by its mighty riverside kremlin, an enormous bulwark that has faced up to its fair share of invading armies down the centuries. Leafy lanes and parks wriggle their way round the attractive old quarter on the east bank, past weathered churches, city-wall ruins and handsome 19th-century brick residences.

Day trips include the old fortress and beautiful countryside at Stary Izborsk, the technicolor church and spooky cave necropolis at Pechory, and Mikhailovskoe, the family estate and last resting place of Alexander Pushkin in Pushkinskie Gory.

Pskov

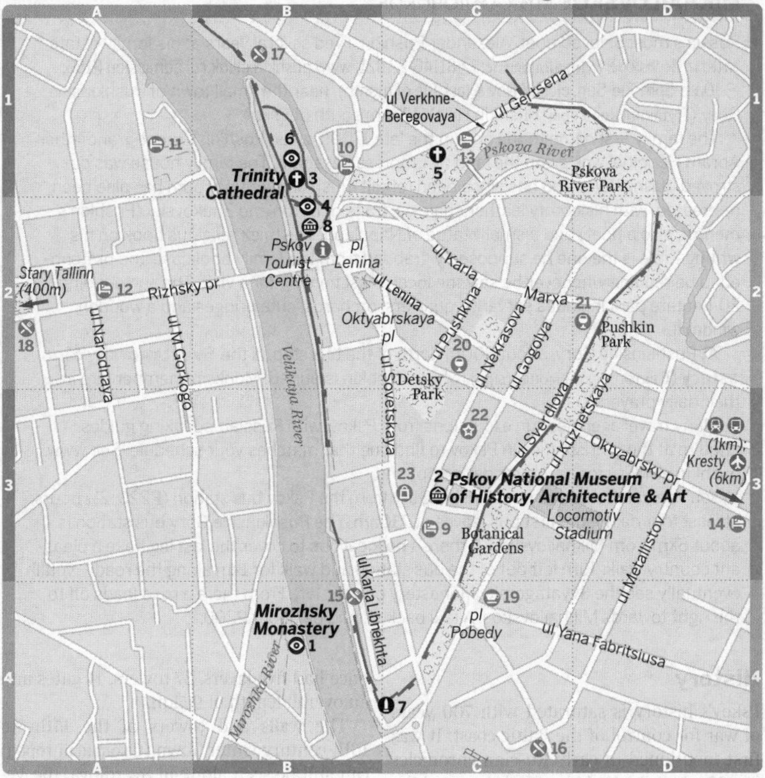

Pskov

Top Sights

1 Mirozhsky Monastery B4
2 Pskov National Museum of History, Architecture & Art C3
3 Trinity Cathedral B1

Sights

4 Dovmont Town B2
5 Epiphany Church of Zapskovie C1
6 Kremlin B1
7 Pokrovskaya Bashnya C4
8 Writ Chamber B2

Sleeping

9 Dvor Podznoeva C3
10 Golden Embankment Hotel B1
11 Hotel 903 .... A1
12 Hotel Rizhskaya A2
13 Old Estate Hotel & Spa C1
14 Red October Hostel D3

Eating

Dvor Podznoeva .... (see 9)
15 Frigate B4
16 Grafin C4
17 Pozharka Tavern B1
18 Stary Tallinn A2
Trapeznie Palat .... (see 9)

Drinking & Nightlife

19 Chocolate Cafe C4
20 Old School Bar C2
Pivnoi Dom .... (see 10)
21 TIR D2

Entertainment

22 Pskov Region Philharmonia C3

Shopping

23 Menshikovikh C3

WORTH A TRIP

MIKHAILOVSKOE МИХАЙЛОВСКОЕ

Russia's most beloved poet, Alexander Pushkin, lived several years at his family estate **Mikhailovskoe** (Михайловское; ☎81146-22 321; www.pushkin.ellink.ru; admission ₽156; ⏰10am-5pm Tue-Sun, closed Nov & last Tue of month), near the small town of Pushkinskie Gory (Пушкинские Горы; Pushkin Hills), 120km south of Pskov.

The family first came to the area in the late 1700s, when Pushkin's great-grandfather Abram Hannibal was given the land by Empress Elizabeth. The family house was destroyed during WWII and has since been rebuilt. Pushkin's writing room has also been re-created, with his comfy leather chair, portraits of Byron and Zhukovsky (Pushkin's mentor, also a poet) and a small statue of Napoleon. The thick religious book on his writing table is the one he supposedly grabbed from the family bookcase and pretended to be reading whenever he saw the local priest coming for a visit. The surrounding 20-hectare park includes servants' quarters, orchards, cute bridges and a wooden windmill.

At Pushkinskie Gory, about 800m north of the bus stop, is the **Svyatogorsky Monastery** (Святогорский монастырь), where Pushkin is buried. Monks remember him in their daily prayers.

Many travel agencies run excursions from Pskov, with Russian-speaking guides. Enquire at the tourist office in Pskov to find one that matches your schedule. See www.pushkin.ellink.ru for accommodation options.

You can catch a bus to Pushkinskie Gory from the Pskov bus station (₽220, 2½ hours, at least four daily); the first bus leaves at 7.10am. The Pushkinskie Gory bus station is about 6km from Mikhailovskoe. If there's no local bus to cover the last leg, take a pleasant country walk. Turn left out of the bus station and walk for 1km along the road – you'll eventually see the Svyatagorsky Monastery on your left. From there a road leads off to the right towards Mikhailovskoe. A taxi back should be about ₽200.

History

Pskov's history is saturated with 700 years of war for control of the Baltic coast. It was first mentioned in early Russian chronicles in 903 when Prince Igor of Kyiv married the future saint Olga of Pskov. Teutonic Knights captured the town in 1240, but Alexander Nevsky routed them two years later in a famous battle on the ice of Lake Peipsi.

In the 14th century, like Veliky Novgorod, Pskov was its own sovereign republic and a member of the Hanseatic League. The Poles laid siege in the 16th century and the Swedes did likewise in the following century. Peter the Great used Pskov as a base for his drive to the sea, Nicholas II abdicated at its train station and the Red Army fought its first serious battle against Nazi troops outside the city.

Sights

Kremlin HISTORICAL SITE

(Псковский Кремль (Кром); ⏰6am-10pm) Rising up from a high narrow cape on the banks of the Velikaya River, the mighty kremlin (also known as the Krom) is the most complete portion of a fortress that once had five layers, 37 towers, 14 gates and an overall length of 9.5km.

The walls and towers of the 15th- to 16th-century Outer Town (Окольный город) can still be seen along ul Sverdlova, the Velikaya River embankment and across the tributary Pskova River. The largest tower – a whopping 90m in diameter and 50m tall – is the **Pokrovskaya Bashnya** (Покровская башня) beside Pyatidesyatiletiya Oktyabrya most.

★**Trinity Cathedral** CHURCH

(Троицкий собор; Kremlin; ⏰11am-5pm) This blindingly white 72m-high structure can be seen from miles away on a clear day. Consecrated in 1699, it's the fourth version of a church to have stood on this spot since the early 11th century, when a wooden one was commissioned by Princess Olga, an early convert to the Orthodox faith. The interior contains a large collection of bejewelled icons of the Madonna.

Writ Chamber MUSEUM

(Приказные Палаты; www.museums.pskov.ru; Kremlin; adult/student ₽150/100; ⏰11am-6pm Tue-Sun, closed last Tue of the month) This

17th-century stone building once held the administrative chambers of Pskov. Today it houses a small museum that gives some insight into the workings and officialdom of the old city; there's also a decent souvenir shop on the premises and an information centre. Outside, you'll find preserved foundations of a dozen 12th- to 15th-century churches that once made up the independent city of **Dovmont Town** (Довмонтов город; Kremlin).

★Pskov National Museum of History, Architecture & Art MUSEUM
(Псковский государственный объединённый историко-архитектурный и художественный музей-заповедник; ☎8112-663 311; www.museums.pskov.ru; ul Nekrasova 7; Pogankin Chambers ₽250, art & history galleries ₽100; ⊙11am-6pm Tue-Sun, closed last Tue of the month) As you can guess from its title, this museum, spread over several buildings, includes history and art exhibitions. The architecture bit comes from the museum's key block – the **Pogankin Chambers** (Поганкины палаты) – the fortress-like house and treasury of a 17th-century merchant. Art from local churches, many of which have closed, has been collected here. The museum offers a rare chance to thoroughly examine one particular style of iconography at close range.

The maze of galleries in the chambers holds 14th- to 18th-century pottery, weaving and weaponry, including the original 15th-century sword of one of Pskov's princes. Equally impressive is the huge collection of silver artefacts, including beautifully crafted baroque-style bible covers. The largest, a 25kg beast, was originally housed at Pskov's Trinity Cathedral.

The 2nd floor houses the war collection, with photos and artefacts from WWII and more recent conflicts. The picture gallery has works spanning the 18th to 20th centuries, including paintings by Nikitin, Tropinin and Zhukovsky, plus representations from the Russian avant-garde, including a couple of Petrov-Vodkins.

★Mirozhsky Monastery MONASTERY
(Мирожский монастырь; ☎8112-576 403; www.mirozhsky-monastery.ru; Mirozhskaya nab 2; grounds admission free, cathedral adult/student ₽350/250; ⊙11am-6pm Tue-Sun, closed last Tue of the month) The attraction here is the Unesco-listed **Cathedral of the Transfiguration of the Saviour** (Спасо-Преображенский Собор Мирожского монастыря), with its 12th-century frescoes that are considered one of the most complete representations of the biblical narrative to have survived the Mongols. The frescoes have been partially restored after centuries of damage – 80% of what you see today is original. The artists are unknown but were almost certainly from Greece, as the Byzantine style of the frescoes suggests.

The cathedral was based on a 12th-century Greek model, formed around a symmetrical cross – you can still see traces of the original structure along exterior walls. The church closes often due to inclement weather – too hot, too cold or too wet – so it's best to call in advance.

The monastery is also a working iconography school; ask to see any current activity. Get there on bus 2 from the vicinity of Hotel Rizhskaya.

Epiphany Church of Zapskovie CHURCH
(Церковь Богоявления с Запсковья; ul Gertsena 7) This attractive, working church overlooking the Pskova tributary was built in 1494 and includes a separately standing five-column belfry – its open gables and large pillars are distinctive of the Pskovian style. Around the church is a lovely stretch of park.

Sleeping

Many places include breakfast in their rates.

Red October Hostel HOSTEL $
(Хостел Красный Октябрь; ☎8-951-751 0807; hostelpskov@gmail.com; Oktyabrsky pr 31; dm/s from ₽350/900; 📶) With cheerful dorms and a location near the bus and train stations, this hostel is a good – if one of Pskov's only – budget option. There's a good kitchen and plenty of cafes nearby. Bus 17 will take you to and from the town centre. There's no signage: if you get lost, just give them a call.

★Hotel 903 HOTEL $$
(Гостиница 903; ☎8112-560 660; www.pskov903.ru; ul Maxima Gorkogo 2B; d/tw from ₽2700/2900; 📶) This sparkling new hotel has exceptional river and kremlin views, comfortable beds and lots of nice little extras, including free hot drinks all day and good hairdryers in the bathrooms. All rooms have balconies and some have lovely exposed timber ceilings. Top-notch staff and a cute restaurant round out the deal.

Golden Embankment Hotel MINIHOTEL $$
(Отель Золотая Набережная; ☎8112-627 877; www.zn-hotel.ru; Sovetskaya nab 2;

s/d ₽2600/2800; 📶) With a prime position in the shadow of the kremlin, this intimate hotel in the unmissable peach building offers top-notch views, pleasant, reasonably priced rooms and a friendly welcome.

Hotel Rizhskaya HOTEL $$
(Гостиница Рижская; ☎8112-562 223; www.rijskaya.ru; Rizhsky pr 25; s/tw without breakfast ₽1600/2900; 📶) Overlooking a grassy square, this old Intourist offers modern, renovated rooms. Some of the friendly staff speak English. Buffet breakfast ₽290 extra.

Dvor Podznoeva HOTEL $$
(Двор Подзноева; ☎8112-797 000; www.dvorpodznoeva.ru; ul Nekrasova 1; d & tw from ₽3500; 📶) Next to the flash dining complex of the same name, this hotel in a 19th-century-style building has smallish but nicely decorated rooms. Most have twin beds.

Old Estate Hotel & Spa HOTEL $$$
(☎8112-794 545; www.oldestatehotel.com; ul Verkhne-Beregovaya 4; s/d from ₽5000/5500; 📶🏊) Pskov's most upmarket option stands in a leafy street near the Epiphany Church. Service here matches the prices. Guests can use the spa with sauna, Jacuzzi and splash pool for free between 7am and 10am (₽500 afterwards).

Eating

Pozharka Tavern RUSSIAN $
(Таверна Пожарка; ul Nabat 2A; mains ₽160-420; ⏰11am-2am Mon-Fri, from noon Sat & Sun) This popular hang-out by the kremlin draws the crowds for all the right reasons: a lovely summer terrace with brilliant river views, warm-n-woodsy interior and a carnivore-pleasing menu that stars grilled meat and various treats prepared in Pozharka's own smokehouse. Beer brewed at next door's Beer Bar 903 is available on tap.

Stary Tallinn RUSSIAN, ESTONIAN $$
(Старый Таллинн; ☎8112-724 158; www.caferp.ru; Rizhsky pr 54; mains ₽275-500; ⏰noon-1am; 📶) Tucked away in a housing-block basement, this reasonably sophisticated option complements its Russian menu with dishes popular in neighbouring Estonia, such as *kilkis* (small fish), herring and rabbit.

Frigate SEAFOOD $$
(Фрегат; ul Karla Libnekhta 9; mains ₽200-700; ⏰noon-11pm Sun-Thu, to 2am Fri & Sat) This waterfront restaurant – complete with portholes – specialises in creative fish dishes and equally mouth-watering views of Mirozhsky Monastery. There's live music and discounted menu items on weekends.

Grafin INTERNATIONAL $$
(Графин; ☎8112-665 016; www.steakpskov.ru; ul Sovetskaya 83; mains ₽250-460, steaks ₽320-680; ⏰11am-2am Mon-Fri, from noon Sat & Sun) Grafin bills itself as a steakhouse, and while it does a mean mignon, there's plenty more than beef on the menu. Classics such as pork, lamb and chicken get a good workout, as do specialities such as rabbit and liver.

★ **Dvor Podznoeva** RUSSIAN $$$
(Двор Подзноева; www.dvorpodznoeva.ru; ul Nekrasova 1; meals ₽1000-1200; 📶) There's something for everyone at this imaginatively designed complex: a bakery cafe, well-stocked wine-and-cheese cellar, and a relaxed beer restaurant with outdoor tables. Best is **Trapeznie Palat** (Трапезные Палаты; ☎8112-797 111; ul Nekrasova 1), which re-creates the colourful interior of a 17th-century merchant's home and serves traditional local dishes. Soak them up with vodkas flavoured with ginger, horseradish, juniper and cedar.

Drinking & Nightlife

Chocolate Cafe CAFE
(Кафе Шоколад; www.caferp.ru; ul Yana Fabritsiusa 2/17; ⏰11am-11pm) Stylish little cafe specialising in coffee, tea and light meals. There's also a kids' menu.

Pivnoi Dom BAR
(Пивной Дом; www.zn-hotel.ru; Sovetskaya nab 1/2; ⏰8am-2am) A cooling beer or beverage on the terrace at this joint facing the kremlin is perfect on a sunny day. It also does wonderfully fattening, German-style snacks.

Old School Bar NIGHTCLUB
(3rd fl, Oktyabrskaya pr 20; ⏰4pm-2am Sun-Thu, to 5am Fri & Sat) Join the hip Pskovians here for late-night boogieing to thumping DJs, or just soak up the scene on gigantic sofas.

TIR NIGHTCLUB
(www.tirclub.ru; ul Sverdlova 52; ⏰noon-late, from 4pm Sat & Sun; 📶) This arty, two-level hang-out is the hub of Pskov's underground music scene, staging local and national bands and DJs. Nibbles available throughout the day.

Entertainment

Pskov Region Philharmonia CLASSICAL MUSIC
(Псковская областная филармония; ☎8112-668 920; www.philpskov.ru; ul Nekrasova 24; tickets

from ₽150) Home of the city's classical orchestra; see website for concert details.

Shopping

Menshikovikh SOUVENIRS
(Палаты Меншиковых; ☎8112-661 575; ul Sovetskaya 50; ⌚9am-9pm) There's a huge range of local artsy-crafty gifts at this multihalled store. A naive-art gallery is attached.

Information

Pskov Tourist Centre (Туристский информационный центр Красная Изба; ☎8112-722 532; www.tourism.pskov.ru; pl Lenina 3; ⌚10am-8pm) English-speaking assistants can provide maps, advice and information on tours to Stary Izborsk or Mikhailovskoe.

Getting There & Away

The train and bus stations are next to each other on ul Vokzalnaya.

AIR

Pskovavia (www.pskovavia.ru) has irregular passenger flights between Moscow's Domodedovo Airport and Pskov's Kresty Airport, 6km southeast of the city centre; check website for details.

BUS

Bus connections from Pskov include St Petersburg (₽480, five hours, hourly), Novgorod (₽543, 4½ hours, two daily), Pechory (₽150, one hour, 10 daily), Smolensk (₽780, eight to 10 hours, two daily) and Stary Izborsk (₽72, 45 minutes, six to 10 daily).

Buses also run to Tallinn (₽1000, six hours, daily at 8.20am) and Tartu (₽600, three hours, two daily). Both pass through Izborsk and Pechory – you could pick up the bus in either place rather than backtracking to Pskov. Other Russian and international services can be found on www.tourism.pskov.ru.

TRAIN

Pskov is connected by train to Moscow (*platskart/kupe* ₽1910/3827, 13 hours), St Petersburg (₽850/2172, five hours, two to three daily), Rīga (₽2312/3444, 10 hours, daily) and Vilnius (₽2588/4077, nine hours).

Getting Around

Buses 11 and 17 run from the train station down Oktyabrsky pr and through the centre (₽16). Bus 2 or 17 takes you to Hotel Rizhskaya from the station (taxis charge about ₽120). Bus 2 also runs past Mirozhsky Monastery.

Stary Izborsk Старый Изборск

☎81148 / POP 789 / ⌚MOSCOW

Meaning 'old Izborsk', this sleepy village is indeed ancient – it celebrated its 1150th anniversary in 2012. The ruins of its ancient stone fortress are among the oldest in Russia, and from its ridge location it overlooks a beautiful slice of countryside.

Sights & Activities

The surrounding countryside, threaded with trails, is ideal for gentle hiking or exploring on **horseback** (☎8-964-316 6393, per hr ₽600). **Bicycles** (per hr ₽150) are available to rent from the Izborsk Hotel. There's also a traditional **banya** (2hr ₽1800) at Izborsk Park.

Fortress FORTRESS
(Крепость; admission ₽20; ⌚9am-6pm) Inside is the small 14th-century **Church of St Nicholas** and a **stone tower** (Башня Луковка; admission ₽40) with a viewing platform at the top. A path behind the fortress leads to the tranquil **Gorodishchenskoye Lake**. The locals toting water bottles are coming from the **Slovenian Springs** (Словенские ключи) – legend has it that the water will bring love, happiness, health and good luck.

Izborsk Museum MUSEUM
(Музей Изборск; www.museum-izborsk.ru; ul Pechorskaya 39; admission ₽50; ⌚9am-6pm May-Sep, to 5pm Oct-Apr) This museum houses a one-room display of local archaeological finds and explanations, in Russian, of the town's rich history. Various cultural and sightseeing tours are run from here. The museum website has information on village festivals.

Sleeping & Eating

★**Izborsk Park** GUESTHOUSE $
(Изборск-Парк; ☎81148-23 327; www.izborsk-park.ru; ul Pechorskaya 43; d from ₽990, meals ₽90-300; ⌚cafe 10am-8pm) Join the chickens, geese and one lazy cat at this idyllic spot overlooking the fortress walls. It's country living, Russian-style, at its finest: rooms are basic but cosy, the air smells of wood fires, and the grounds themselves are ridiculously Arcadian. The attached cafe serves up wholesome, hearty food such as soup and cabbage rolls.

Izborsk Hotel HOTEL $$
(Гостиничный комплекс Изборск; ☎8112-607 031, 8-921-703 7031; www.izborsk-hotel.ru; ul Pechorskaya 13; s/d incl breakfast from ₽2300/2500;) This pretty complex ticks all the twee boxes: it's romantic, quaint and revels in retro. The attached craft shop sells enchanting gifts, and the restaurant cooks with locally sourced ingredients. You'll find it at the entrance to the village from the main road.

Gostevoy Dom GUESTHOUSE $$
(Гостевой Дом; ☎81148-96 612; www.museum-izborsk.ru; d without/with bathroom ₽1500/2000, ste with bathroom ₽3500) This bucolic guesthouse overlooks the valley from beneath the back of the fortress; it's attached to the Izborsk Museum. The two-room *lyux* suite has a broad private balcony. Guests can use the communal kitchen.

Blinnaya RUSSIAN $
(Блинная; bliny from ₽60; 9am-6pm) Beyond the kremlin walls, near the Church of St Sergius, is this sweet little cafe boasting 'Izborskian' bliny. The outside area is ideal for an afternoon beer.

Getting There & Away

Stary Izborsk is 32km from Pskov, on the road to Estonia. There are bus connections with Pskov (₽72, 45 minutes, six daily) and Pechory (₽48, 20 minutes, seven daily). Several of the buses from Pskov to Pechory stop in Stary Izborsk, so it's easy to combine a trip to both places.

Pechory Печоры

☎81148 / POP 11,195 / MOSCOW

This tiny town, just 2.5km from the Estonian border, is home to the photogenic **Pechory Monastery** (Свято-Успенский Псково-Печерский монастырь) and its eerie burial caves. Founded in 1473, the monastery sits in a ravine full of hermits' grottoes. With all the high ground outside, it's an improbable stronghold, but several tsars fortified it and depended on it. A path descends under the 1564 **St Nicholas Church** (Никольская церковь) into a Disneyesque palette of colours and architectural styles, where several dozen monks still live and study.

Taking photos of the buildings is acceptable if you make a contribution at the front gate, but photographing the monks is taboo. Women must wear skirts and cover their heads and shoulders (shawls and skirts to be worn over trousers are available to borrow at the entrance). Men should wear long pants.

The central yellow church comprises two buildings. At ground level is the original **Assumption Cathedral** (Успенский собор), built into the caves. Upstairs is the 18th-century baroque **Intercession Church** (Покровская церковь). Below the belfry on the left is the entrance to the **caves** (near caves 10am-5pm, far caves 10am-5pm Tue-Thu, Sat & Sun), where some 10,000 bodies – monks, benefactors and others – are bricked up in vaults.

You can wander the monastery grounds and visit most of the churches on your own. To visit the caves you'll probably have to join a tour to lead you through the dark, spooky, near-freezing sand tunnels. Everyone carries a candle, which in places you can thrust through holes in the tunnel walls to see the wooden coffins lying lopsided on top of each other. It's sometimes possible to tag onto a group that is entering, which won't cost you anything. Bring a strong torch.

There's a booth outside the monastery gates housing an **excursion office** (☎8-911-3794 815; www.pechori.ru; 10am-5pm). It can arrange tours in English; for prices, contact the office with a date and group size. Tours in Russian are ₽600 for up to five people.

If you need a place to stay, the charming **Hotel Pechory Park** (Гостиница Печоры-Парк; ☎81148-23 327; www.pechorypark.ru; ul Gagarin 2B; d/q ₽1895/3400) is 500m from the monastery. The simpler **Hotel Planeta** (Гостиница Планета; ☎81148-24 516; www.hotelpechory.ru; ul Mira 10; s/d ₽1000/2000;) is next to the bus station. Both have eateries, or try the **Old Tower Cafe** (Кафе Старая Башня; Oktyabrskaya pl 7; meals ₽120-250; 9am-10pm;).

You can get to Tallinn (₽960, five hours) and Tartu (₽680, three hours) on buses originating in Pskov. Hourly buses shuttle between Pskov and Pechory (₽150, one hour) between 8am and 11pm. At least six buses a day make a stop in Stary Izborsk (₽48, 20 minutes). See www.pechori.ru for updated timetable links.

Kaliningrad Region

Best Places to Eat

- Fish Club (p271)
- Zarya (p270)
- Korvet (p274)
- Prichal (p270)

Best Places to Stay

- Skipper Hotel (p269)
- Dom Skazochnika (p274)
- Galera (p275)
- Hotel Paraiso (p270)
- Koshkin Dom (p276)

Why Go?

On paper, the Kaliningrad Region seems ripe for an identity crisis. Its eponymous capital was the medieval seat of Prussia and an important port that was fought over for centuries. Today, less than 500,000 people visit each year. Until the 1940s, the province was almost entirely German; bratwurst made way for borsch as Stalin repopulated the region with Russians and Ukrainians. And though it's geographically separated from Russia by Lithuania and Poland, the exclave is intimately attached to the motherland.

Yet for all of its chaotic history and cultural foibles – or perhaps because of them – 'Little Russia' is a fascinating place to visit. The city of Kaliningrad teems with interesting sights and surprisingly sophisticated accommodation and dining options; seaside towns Svetlogorsk and Zelenogradsk dish up old-world charm by the spadeful; sparkling Yantarny is the world's amber capital; and the dunes, pine forests and tranquil villages of Kurshskaya Kosa National Park make for a serene sojourn.

When to Go

Kaliningrad

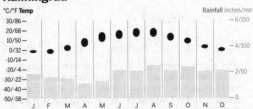

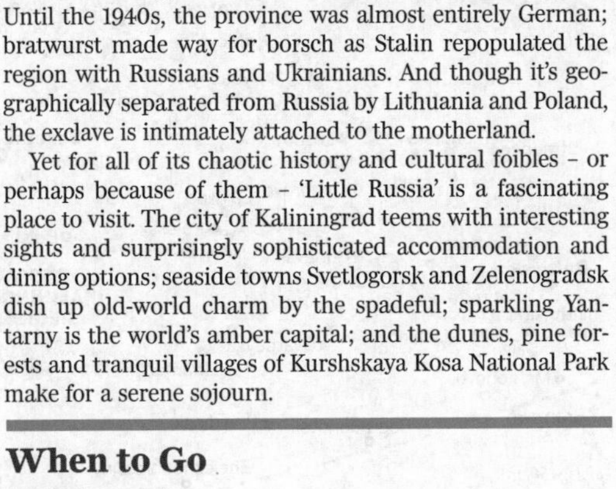

Jul Russian Navy Day in Baltiysk, HQ of the Baltic fleet.

Aug Yantarny celebrates Amberfest.

Sep Kaliningrad's Baltic Season performing arts festival kicks off.

History

The region has been famous since Roman times for its amber deposits. Ruled by Teutonic Knights since the 13th century, the area became the Duchy of Prussia, Europe's first Protestant state, in 1525 with Königsberg as its capital. The city had been founded in 1255 and joined the Hanseatic League in 1340. From 1457 to 1618 Königsberg was the residence of the grand masters of the Teutonic order and their successors, the dukes of Prussia. Prussia's first king, Frederick I, was crowned in 1701 in the city's castle. Königsberg's liberal atmosphere attracted scholars, artists and entrepreneurs from across Europe, and for the next couple of centuries the city flourished – in 1697 Peter the Great visited as part of his Grand Embassy and the 18th-century philosopher Immanuel Kant lived there all his life.

For four years of the Seven Years' War (1756–63), East Prussia – as the Duchy became known as in the early 18th century – became part of the Russian Empire and, later, during the Napoleonic Wars, Russia and Prussia were allies. After WWI, East Prussia was separated from the rest of Germany when Poland regained statehood. The three-month campaign by which the Red Army took East Prussia in 1945 was one of the fiercest battles of WWII; there were massive casualties on both sides and Königsberg was left in ruins.

In 1946 the region was renamed Kaliningrad in honour of Mikhail Kalinin, one of Stalin's more-vicious henchmen, and the capital was rebuilt in grand Soviet concrete style, albeit tempered by parks, ponds, waterways and Kaliningrad Lagoon. The surviving German population was relocated to far-flung corners of the Soviet Union, deported or killed. The Russian Baltic fleet was

Kaliningrad Region Highlights

1. Pay your respects at philosopher Immanuel Kant's grave, then attend an organ concert in **Kaliningrad Cathedral** (p265).
2. Explore Russia's maritime history on former expedition vessels and a submarine at Kaliningrad's **Museum of the World Ocean** (p265).
3. Soak up the beauty of **Kurshskaya Kosa National Park** (p276), where the forest dances and the dunes roll on as far as the eye can see.
4. Splash in the Baltic at **Yantarny** (p275), then visit the amber mine.
5. Stroll the shady lanes of **Svetlogorsk** (p273), discovering old German villas and the sculptures of Herman Brachert.
6. Explore ruined castles and saddle up at the Georgenburg Stud Farm in **Chernyakhovsk** (p272).

headquartered in Baltiysk, and the region was closed to foreigners for over 40 years.

Like much of Russia, Kaliningrad struggled through extreme economic difficulties in the early 1990s. The discovery of oil off the coast and the granting of special economic zone status has helped it turn the corner. One of the venues for the 2018 FIFA World Cup, the region remains of key strategic importance to Russia, particularly in light of recent EU expansion east.

THE AMBER COAST

You can hardly move in Kaliningrad without someone trying to sell you souvenirs made of amber – the hard resin of coniferous trees that grew in the region approximately 45 to 50 million years ago. Ninety per cent of the world's amber hails from the region, its colour varying through more than 200 different shades, from milky white to a deep orange. The region's sanatoriums even offer 'amber therapy', said to combat fatigue and other health disorders. Although a tiny percentage is collected by hand from the beach, the main opencast mine is at Yantarny (p275), where more than 700 tonnes of amber are dug up annually.

Kaliningrad Калининград

☎4012 / POP 431,900 / ⌚MOSCOW -1HR

While Königsberg revelled in regal architecture and a cosmopolitan European culture, Kaliningrad carries more than a whiff of its days as an outpost of the USSR. But despite vast swathes of brutal Stalin-stamped buildings and unmistakably Soviet monuments, the city is a pleasant one, softened by leafy parks, revitalised historical enclaves, exceptional museums, charming neighbourhoods and its trademark city gates. Kaliningrad is easy to navigate: public transport abounds, as do welcoming locals all too willing to lend visitors a hand.

After Kaliningrad Cathedral, the most visible remains of Königsberg are its redbrick fortification walls, bastions and gates, built in stages between the 17th and 19th centuries. The remains of the city's castle were destroyed and replaced by the hideous Dom Sovetov (Дом Советов; House of Soviets) in the 1960s. During the eyesore's construction it was discovered that the land below was hollow, housing a (now-flooded) four-level underground passage connecting to the cathedral. The decaying, half-finished building has never been used.

Sights

Kaliningrad Cathedral CHURCH

(Кафедральный собор Кёнигсберга; ☎4012-631 705; www.sobor-kaliningrad.ru; Kant Island; adult/student ₽150/130, photos ₽50, concerts ₽250-300; ⌚10am-5pm) Photos displayed inside this Unesco World Heritage Site attest to how dilapidated the cathedral was until the early 1990s – the original dates back to 1333. The lofty interior is dominated by an ornate organ used for regular **concerts**. Upstairs, the carved-wood **Wallenrodt Library** has interesting displays of old Königsberg. The top floor is devoted to Immanuel Kant; the exhibition includes his death mask. Kant's **tomb** (могила Канта) is on the building's outer north side.

★**Kant Island & Riverside** NEIGHBOURHOOD

This once densely populated island – now a parkland dotted with sculptures – is dominated by the Kaliningrad Cathedral. A few nearby buildings – the **former Stock Exchange** (Биржа; Leninsky pr 83) from the 1870s and the neotraditional row of shops, restaurants and hotels known as **Fish Village** – hint at what this area looked like pre-WWII. Get a bird's-eye view from the 31m-high **lighthouse viewing tower** (admission ₽50; ⌚10am-10pm).

Friedland Gate MUSEUM

(Ворота Фридланд; www.fvmuseum.ru; pr Kalinina 6; adult/child ₽20/10, multimedia show ₽30; ⌚10am-7pm May-Aug, to 6pm Sep-Apr, closed 1st Fri of month) The best way to see what pre-WWII Königsberg looked like is to attend the 40-minute **multimedia show** screened in the halls of this museum occupying one of the 13 original city gates. The evocative show is made up of projections of photos taken in the city between 1908 and 1913, and grainy footage shot around the castle in 1937.

★**Museum of the World Ocean** MUSEUM

(Музей Мирового Океана; www.world-ocean.ru/en; nab Petra Velikogo 1; adult/student ₽300/200, individual vessels adult/student ₽100/80; ⌚10am-6pm Wed-Sun) Strung along the banks of the Pregolya River are the several ships, a sub, maritime machinery and exhibition halls

Kaliningrad

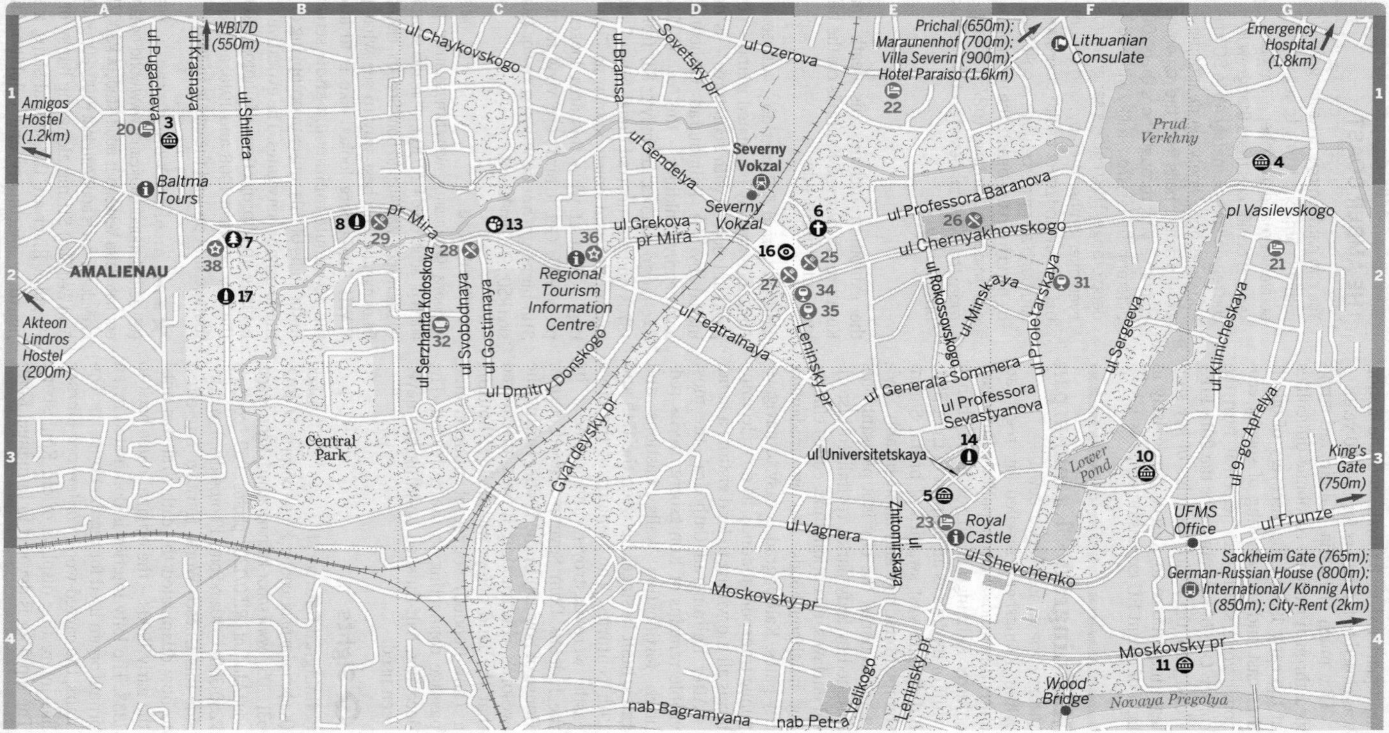

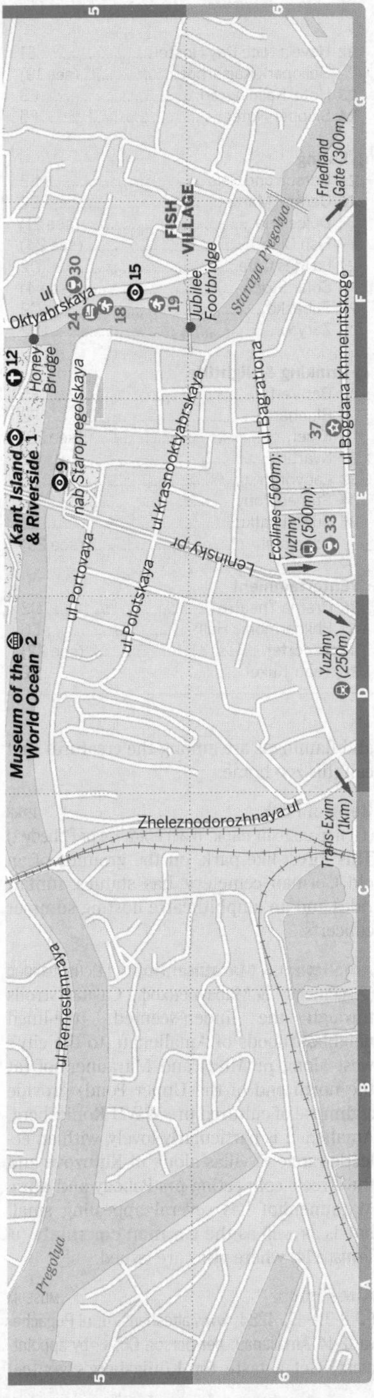

that make up this excellent museum. The highlight is the handsome former scientific expedition vessel *Vityaz,* moored alongside the *Viktor Patsaev,* with its exhibits relating to space research; visits to this are by guided tour (included in admission price, every 45 minutes). The pre-atomic B-413 submarine gives a taste of what life was like for its former 300 inhabitants.

A restored storehouse has interesting displays on the sea-connected history of Kaliningrad, as well as the remains of a 19th-century wooden fishing boat. There's also a pavilion with a sperm whale skeleton, and halls with small aquariums and general information about the ocean.

Kaliningrad Art Gallery ART GALLERY

(Калининградская художественная галерея; www.kaliningradartmuseum.ru; Moskovsky pr 60-62; adult/student ₽100/80; ⏲10am-6pm Tue & Wed, Fri-Sun, to 9pm Thu) View modern and contemporary works by local artists, including some striking pieces from the Soviet decades. The gallery shop sells art books and local creations.

Bunker Museum MUSEUM

(Музей Блиндаж; ul Universitetskaya 3; adult/student ₽100/70; ⏲10am-6pm Tue-Sun) The city's last German commander, Otto van Lasch, capitulated to the Soviets from this buried command post in 1945. It now houses informative presentations about East Prussia during WWII.

History & Arts Museum MUSEUM

(Историко-Художественный музей; ☎4012-453 844; www.westrussia.org; ul Klinicheskaya 21; adult/student ₽80/70; ⏲10am-6pm Tue-Sun) Housed in a reconstructed 1912 concert hall on the banks of the pretty Lower Pond (Нижний пруд), this museum mainly focuses on events since Russia's takeover of the region, though Kaliningrad's German past does get a look-in.

King's Gate MUSEUM

(Королевские ворота; ul Frunze 112; adult/student ₽60/30; ⏲11am-7pm Wed-Sun) Focusing on Peter the Great's Grand Embassy to the city in 1697, this revamped gate also has good models of old Königsberg and exhibits on the personalities who shaped the region's history. A little south of here, where Moskovsky pr meets Litovsky val, is the twin-towered **Sackheim Gate** (Закхаймские ворота).

Kaliningrad

Top Sights
1 Kant Island & Riverside E5
2 Museum of the World Ocean D5

Sights
3 Altes Haus A1
4 Amber Museum G1
Baron Munchausen Monument .... (see 17)
5 Bunker Museum E3
6 Cathedral of Christ the Saviour E2
7 Central Park B2
8 Cosmonaut Monument B2
9 Former Stock Exchange E5
10 History & Arts Museum F3
11 Kaliningrad Art Gallery F4
12 Kaliningrad Cathedral F5
13 Kaliningradsky Zoopark C2
14 Kant Statue E3
15 Lighthouse Viewing Tower F5
16 Ploshchad Pobedy D2
17 Vladimir Vysotsky Monument B2
Woody Allen Monument .... (see 29)

Activities, Courses & Tours
18 Boat Tours F5
19 Helio Spa F5

Sleeping
20 Chaika A1
21 Dona Hotel G2
22 Have a Nice Day Hostel E1
Heliopark Kaiserhof .... (see 19)
23 Hotel Kaliningrad E3
24 Skipper Hotel F5

Eating
25 Borsch and Salo E2
26 Central Market E2
Dolce Vita .... (see 21)
Fish Club .... (see 24)
27 La Plas Cafe D2
Solar Stone .... (see 4)
28 Tabasko C2
29 Zarya B2

Drinking & Nightlife
30 Bar Verf F5
31 Blueberry F2
Kmel .... (see 25)
32 Kvartira C2
33 Labyrinth E6
34 Stoned Pony E2
35 Suhomyatku E2
Universal .... (see 29)

Entertainment
36 Drama Theatre C2
37 Philharmonic Hall E6
Reporter .... (see 22)
38 Teatr Kukol B2

Amber Museum MUSEUM
(Музей Янтаря; www.ambermuseum.ru; pl Marshala Vasilevskogo 1; adult/student ₽190/130; 10am-6pm Tue-Sun) Housed in the Dohna Tower (Башня Дона), this museum features over 6000 amber exhibits, including marvellous artworks, a whopping 4.28kg nugget and ancient specimens with prehistoric insects and plants fossilised within the resin. You can buy amber jewellery in the museum or from the vendors outside. Adjacent to the museum, **Rossgarten Gate** (Росгартенские Ворота) houses the Solar Stone (p271) restaurant.

Ploshchad Pobedy SQUARE
(Площадь победы) The city's centre has come a long way since 1934, when it was known as Adolf-Hitler Platz. Today it's surrounded by shopping malls and the gold-domed **Cathedral of Christ the Saviour** (Кафедральный Собор Христа Спасителя; pl Pobedy), built in 2006 in the Russo-Byzantine style.

Kaliningradsky Zoopark ZOO
(Калининградский Зоопарк; www.kldzoo.ru; pr Mira 26; weekend/weekday ₽150/100; 9am-8pm May-Sep, until 5pm Oct-Apr) Bears, hippos, seals and flamingos are among the creatures that call this zoo home.

Central Park PARK
(Центральный парк; main entrance pr Pobedy 1) This forest-like park, on the grounds of an old German cemetery, has statues, funfair rides and an amphitheatre hosting summer concerts.

Amalienau & Maraunenhof NEIGHBOURHOOD
(Амалиенау & Мараунехоф) Casual strolls through the linden-scented, tree-lined neighbourhoods of Amalienau (to the city's west along pr Mira) and Maraunenhof (at the north end of the Upper Pond) provide a glimpse of cultured pre-WWII Königsberg. Amalienau is particularly lovely, with an eclectic range of villas along ul Kutuzova and the streets connecting prs Pobedy and Mira. Maraunenhof has several appealing small hotels as well as the **German consulate** (ul Telmana 14) where visas are issued.

Altes Haus MUSEUM
(8-911-451 4284; www.alteshaus.ru; ul Pugacheva 12-14, Amalienau; per person €5; by appointment) Get a taste for Königsberg's genteel

past at this new museum, where you're free to touch lovely period pieces, sit on the gorgeous antique furniture and generally carry on – politely – as if you owned the joint.

Activities

Boat Tours BOAT TRIPS
(per person ₽250; ⊙May-Sep) Small passenger boats leave from the promenade beside Fish Village to sail around Kant Island and down the Pregolya River (45 minutes).

Helio Spa SAUNA, SPA
(☎4012-592 200; www.heliopark.ru; ul Oktyabrskaya 6a; admission from ₽1000, price varies by the day; ⊙7am-10pm) Five different saunas, a medium-sized swimming pool, spa and a swim-up bar make up this swish spa complex attached to the Heliopark Kaiserhof hotel (p270).

Festivals & Events

For a small city, Kaliningrad has a wealth of festivals livening up the calendar. See www.visit-kaliningrad.ru/en/events for the full rundown.

First Summer Music Festival MUSIC
Local and international musicians rocking out reggae, punk and ska style. Held at the start of June.

Kaliningrad City Jazz Festival MUSIC
(www.jazzfestival.ru) Open-air jazzfest held in Central Park over the first weekend in August.

Baltic Season ARTS
(www.baltseasons.ru) Celebrating the best in modern Russian theatre, dance and music from September to December in the Drama Theatre.

Sleeping

Kaliningrad is well served with midrange and top-end hotels, and is experiencing a hostel mini-boom. Many rates include breakfast.

Amigos Hostel HOSTEL $
(Амигос Хостел; ☎8-911-485 2157; www.amigoshostel.ru; ul Yablonevaya Alleya 34; dm ₽500-550, d ₽1200;) One of Kaliningrad's first hostels, Amigos has a new home in a charming house in a lovely part of town. Rooms are airy and bright, the kitchen and common areas are super clean and there are loads of public transport options on the doorstep. It also rents bicycles (₽250 per hour) and roller skates (₽70 per hour).

Akteon Lindros Hostel HOSTEL $
(Хостел Актеон Линдрос; ☎8-900-568 3333; ul Engelsa 14; dm/d from ₽500/1190;) Quiet and clean, this new hostel offers standard-issue bunks, a good kitchen and happy-to-help staff. It's well serviced by public transport: buses 5, 9, 12, 14 and 35 will get you there from the city centre.

Have a Nice Day Hostel HOSTEL $
(☎8-900-351 4621; www.likehostels.ru/kaliningrad; ul Ozerova 20; d from ₽530;) It's not the most schmick of places, but the fun staff will go out of their way to make sure you do as the name says. Brightly coloured decor does much to make up for the ramshackle surrounds.

★**Skipper Hotel** HOTEL $$
(Гостиница Шкипер; ☎4012-307 237; www.skipperhotel.ru; ul Oktyabrskaya 4a; r from ₽2800;) Location, ahoy! In a quaint period building with a superb riverside position in Fish Village, the Skipper is within stumbling

KALININGRAD'S MOTLEY CREW OF STATUES

Kaliningrad is littered with all manner of amusing, eclectic statues and monuments, celebrating everything from cosmonauts to well-endowed bulls. Königsberg's most famous son, **Immanuel Kant** (ul A Nevskogo, Kant State University), stands in front of the university named after him, tucked off Leninsky pr. Up in pl Pobedy, a statue of two **Fighting Bulls** – cast as nature intended them – often falls victim to jocular students and strategically placed dabs of bright paint.

Along pr Mira, the **Cosmonaut Monument** (Памятник Землякам Космонавтам; pr Mira) is a gem of Soviet iconography, honouring the four Kaliningrad-born cosmonauts, including Alexey Leonov, the first man to conduct a space walk. In the lobby of the nearby Scala cinema is a witty monument to **Woody Allen** (born Allen Konigsberg) – a pair of the film director's trademark glasses jut from the wall. In Central Park, you'll find legendary tall-tale teller and supposed Kaliningrad visitor **Baron Munchausen**, and **Vladimir Vysotsky**, a massively popular singer from the 1960s and '70s.

distance of many of Kaliningrad's main attractions, cafes and bars. Rooms are clean, with a vague nautical theme, and have great views of the bustling surrounds.

Hotel Paraiso MINIHOTEL **$$**
(Гостиница Параисо; ☎4012-216 969; www.hotelparaiso.ru; ul Turgeneva 32a; s/d from ₽1700/2000; @ 📶) This inviting minihotel comes over all country lodge, with ivy creeping over its old German-stye walls and a delightful garden. Rooms are simple and comfortable, there's a small sauna and the attached restaurant serves wholesome Russian and German meals.

Dona Hotel HOTEL **$$**
(Отель Дона; ☎4012-351 650; www.hoteldona.ru; pl Marshala Vasilevskogo 2; s/d from ₽2700/3200; ❄ @ 📶) This modern, mirrored manse is hard to miss, and you'll be glad you didn't. The Dona has a fantastic location in a pretty part of town, English-speaking staff, good buffet breakfasts and the wonderful Dolce Vita restaurant. See-through glass doors to the rooms' toilets are an interesting design touch.

Villa Severin GUESTHOUSE **$$**
(Вилла Северин; ☎4012-365 373; www.villa-severin.ru; ul Leningradskaya 9a; s/d from ₽1600/2200; ❄ @ 📶) This villa looks like a doll's house, with an adorable garden and lovely setting by Upper Pond (Prud Verkhny) to match. There are 10 comfortably furnished rooms, including one simple student room (₽1000 without breakfast). It also has a small sauna and cafe.

Hotel Kaliningrad HOTEL **$$**
(Гостиница Калининград; ☎4012-536 021; www.hotel.kaliningrad.ru; Leninsky pr 81; s/d from ₽1950/2250; ❄ @ 📶) An easy stroll to Kaliningrad's main attractions, this hulking hotel offers nondescript refurbished rooms, many with views of the cathedral. The substantial breakfast buffet costs ₽270.

Chaika HOTEL **$$$**
(Чайка; ☎4012-352 211; www.hotelchaika.ru; ul Pugacheva 13; s/d from ₽3500/4450; ❄ @ 📶) On a leafy street near the picturesque Amalienau area, 'Seagull' is a delightful 28-room property decorated with classy heritage touches. It also has a restaurant, comfy lounge and fitness room.

Heliopark Kaiserhof HOTEL **$$$**
(☎4012-592 222; www.heliopark.ru; ul Oktyabrskaya 6a; s/d from ₽4500/4950; ❄ @ 📶 🏊) Part of the Fish Village development, this nicely designed and furnished hotel has light-filled rooms and a full-service spa and sauna. Rates are almost halved Friday to Sunday.

Eating

Head to the lively **central market** (Центральный рынок; ul Chernyakhovskogo; ⏰8am-6pm) for self-catering and engrossing people-watching.

Tabasko INTERNATIONAL **$**
(Табаско; pr Mira 19; pizzas ₽140-630, sushi ₽35-100; ⏰11am-11.30pm Sun-Thu, to 1.30am Fri & Sat) That time-honoured Russian classic – pizza and sushi – gets a good workout at this popular joint, with a massive range of both on offer.

Zarya RUSSIAN, EUROPEAN **$$**
(Заря; ☎4012-300 388; pr Mira 43; meals ₽200-540; ⏰10am-3am; 📶) This fashionable brassiere in the Scala cinema lobby is beautifully decorated and has an attractive outdoor area. A popular hang-out for pre- and post-movie nibbles, it whips up everything from steak and seafood to the inutterably sinful deep-fried Camembert.

Prichal RUSSIAN, EUROPEAN **$$**
(Причал; ☎4012-936 666; ul Verkhneozyornaya 2a; meals ₽480-780; ⏰noon-1am Sun-Thu, to 2am Fri & Sat) Set in a lush garden overlooking the north end of Upper Pond, alfresco dining at Prichal is a summer must-do. The menu includes juicy shashlyk (kebabs), seafood and soup in a bowl made of bread. There's also a children's menu and playground.

THE BIG GUNS OF BALTIYSK

The formerly off-limits port town of Baltiysk (Балтийск) hosts Kaliningrad's annual **Russian Navy Day** every July (last Sunday), a triumphant display of the country's firepower, might and skill. Even if battleships aren't your bag, the large-scale historical reenactments and grand parades are spine-tingling. Baltiysk, Russia's westernmost town and headquarters of the Baltic fleet, is easily reached from the capital: buses (₽90, 1½ hours) shuttle between the two every few minutes until 10pm.

Borsch and Salo UKRAINIAN $$
(Борщ и Сало; pl Pobedy 10; meals ₽300-500; ⌚noon-midnight Sun-Thu, to 2am Fri & Sat; 📶) Decked out like a Ukrainian village hut, this cosy cafe has all the flavoursome, fattening treats you'd expect from its name. It also has a huge variety of flavoured brandies; if you're nice, they might even give you one on the house.

Solar Stone SEAFOOD $$
(Солнечный камень; Rossgarten Gate; mains ₽280-2000; ⌚noon-2am) Housed in the Rossgarten Gate, this period-themed place specialises in upmarket seafood, though it does have other options on the menu.

La Plas Cafe RUSSIAN, EUROPEAN $$
(pl Pobedy 1; meals ₽290-470; ⌚24hr) Offering big windows with views onto pl Pobedy and a tasty miscellany of food, this happening place almost certainly has whatever you're hankering for.

★**Fish Club** SEAFOOD $$$
(Рыбный клуб; ul Oktyabrskaya 4a; meals ₽500-1500; ⌚noon-midnight) For a seafood splurge with a view, this classy waterfront restaurant cannot be beaten. Everything on the menu is fresh and elegantly prepared and the service is the best in the city. If you're not supping in the sunshine, ask for a table near the aquarium.

Dolce Vita EUROPEAN, RUSSIAN $$$
(☎4012-351 612; www.dolcevita-kaliningrad.ru; pl Marshala Vasilevskogo 2; mains ₽420-1450; ⌚noon-midnight; 📶✍) Many of Dolce Vita's inventive dishes appear overly fussy on the menu, but the competent chef makes them work. There's an excellent selection for vegetarians, superb seafood and divine pastas.

Drinking & Nightlife

Kaliningrad is home to a surprising number of anti-cafes, social hang-outs where you pay for your time, but nothing else. Sweet snacks, hot drinks and wi-fi – not to mention a good amount of chat and games – are on offer at **Blueberry** (Черника; ul Proletarskaya 82-84; per min ₽1.50; ⌚noon-midnight Mon-Thu, to 2am Fri, 2pm-4am Sat, 2pm-midnight Sun), **Labyrinth** (Лабиринт; ul Orekhovaya 7-19; per min ₽1.50; ⌚11am-1pm Sun-Thu, to 6am Fri & Sat; 📶) and **Suhomyatku** (Сухомятка; Leninsky pr 5; per min ₽1.50; ⌚11am-midnight Mon-Thu, to 3am Fri, to 4am Sat, noon-midnight Sun). For full listings, see www.anticafe.com.ru/city/kaliningrad.

LOCAL KNOWLEDGE

KVARTIRA

Kvartira (Apartment; ☎4012-216 736; ul Serzhanta Koloskova 13; 📶) Hiding on the ground floor of an apartment block, Kvartira is unquestionably one of Kaliningrad's coolest hang-outs. Lined with a fascinating range of pop-culture books, CDs, records and DVDs, all for sale or rent (as is everything else, including the stylish furniture), Kvartira – which means 'apartment' – also serves drinks and snacks, but there's no menu. Movies are screened for free on several nights, while on others there may be a party or an art event. Whatever's happening, you're sure to make friends with locals. It's best to visit in the early evening, but opening hours are erratic, so call before setting off.

Stoned Pony NIGHTCLUB
(ul Chernyakhovskogo 2a; ⌚11am-2am Mon-Thu, to 6am Fri & Sat, to midnight Sun) This fun indie club attracts a young and open-minded crowd; talented mixologists add fuel to the frivolities.

WB17D BAR
(ul Yanalova 17d; ⌚6pm-6am) The 'WB' in the name stands for 'whisky bar', and there certainly is a huge range of it at this super-slick nightspot. Frock up and bring all the attitude you can muster; there are no wallflowers here.

Kmel MICROBREWERY
(Clover City Centre, pl Pobedy 10; ⌚noon-2am) Four types of beer are brewed at this appealing multilevel gastropub. An interesting menu (₽350 to ₽600) includes unusual dishes such as reindeer and wild boar.

Bar Verf WINE BAR
(ul Oktyabrskaya 4a, Fish Village; ⌚11am-midnight; 📶) This relaxed wine bar has outdoor tables overlooking the cathedral. It screens movies and provides coloured pencils and paper for doodling.

Universal NIGHTCLUB
(☎4012-921 005; pr Mira 43; admission from ₽500) Kaliningrad's classiest club hosts DJs and fashion shows. It shares a location with Scala cinema.

WORTH A TRIP

CHERNYAKHOVSK ЧЕРНЯХОВСК

Founded by Teutonic Knights in 1336, the former Prussian city of Insterburg was thoroughly trashed during WWII. Once Kaliningrad's second-largest city, all that remains of its former grandeur are two ruined castles, **Georgenburg** (Замок Георгенбург; ul Tsentralnaya; tour ₽200; ⏲10am-5pm) and **Insterburg** (Замок Инстербург; ul Zamkovaya 1; admission by donation; ⏲10am-5pm). The estate of the former now nudges the **Georgenburg Stud Farm** (☎40141-22 929; www.georgenburg.com; ul Tsentralnaya 18) and its attached **hotel** (☎40141-22 929; www.georgenburg.com; ul Tsentralnaya 18; s/d from ₽2000/2650); the latter houses a studio-gallery and cultural centre. If horses aren't your thing, you can stay at the cute **Pivnoy Dvor** (Пивной Двор; ☎40141-34 627; www.pivdhotel.ru; ul Suvorova 14; d ₽1300; wi-fi), which you'll find opposite the Orthodox **St Michael's Cathedral** (Св Михайловский собор; ul Suvorova), one of the town's last remaining examples of pre-WWII architecture. The pretty **Akvatoria** (Акватория; ul Lenina 11a; meals ₽240-520; ⏲noon-midnight Sun-Thu, to 2am Fri & Sat) cafe is a relaxing spot for lunch or dinner.

The train and bus stations are opposite each other at the southern end of ul Lenina. *Elektrichka* (₽150, 1¾ hours, one to two daily) make the journey to/from Kaliningrad; services to/from Moscow and St Petersburg also pause here. Buses and minibuses (₽119, 1¾ hours, every 30 minutes) to and from Kaliningrad are more frequent. Bus 5 (₽10) will take you into town from the stations.

Amsterdam NIGHTCLUB
(www.amsterdam-club.ru; 38/11 Litovsky val; admission ₽1000; ⏲9am-6am Fri & Sat) This large alternative and gay-friendly club is in an old brick building 200m down an unnamed side street off Litovsky val.

☆ Entertainment

Reporter LIVE MUSIC
(Клуб Репортёр; ☎4012-571 601; www.reporter-club.ru; ul Ozerova 18; ⏲11am-1am) Eclectic live gigs and jams kick off at this industrial-cool club most nights at 9pm. It also does set lunches for ₽150.

Philharmonic Hall CLASSICAL MUSIC
(Филармония; ☎4012-643 451; www.kenigfil.ru; ul Bogdana Khmelnitskogo 61a; tickets from ₽200) This beautifully restored neo-Gothic church has excellent acoustics, perfect for organ concerts, chamber-music recitals and the occasional symphony orchestra.

Drama Theatre THEATRE
(Театр драмы и комедии; ☎4012-212 422; www.dramteatr39.ru; pr Mira 4; tickets from ₽200) Several plays staged here are included in the annual **Baltic Season** (www.baltseasons.ru) program.

Teatr Kukol PUPPET THEATRE
(☎4012-214 335; www.teatrkukol39.ru; pr Pobedy 1; admission ₽150) Performances are on Saturdays and Sundays at noon in the 19th-century Lutheran Queen Luisa Church.

ℹ Information

Most hotels and hostels have free wi-fi; see www.visit-kaliningrad.ru/en/info/477 for a full list of internet cafes.

Baltma Tours (☎4012-931 931; www.baltma.ru; 4th fl, pr Mira 94) The multilingual staff can arrange visas, accommodation, city tours and local excursions.

Emergency Hospital (Городская больница скорой медицинской помощи; ☎4012-466 989; ul A Nevskogo 90; ⏲24hr)

Konigsberg.ru (www.konigsberg.ru) Loads of info on visas, hotels and what's happening in Kaliningrad.

Regional Tourism Information Centre (☎4012-555 200; www.visit-kaliningrad.ru; pr Mira 4; ⏲9am-8pm Mon-Fri, 11am-6pm Sat May-Sep, 9am-7pm Mon-Fri, 11am-4pm Sat Oct-Apr) Helpful, English-speaking staff and lots of information on the region.

Royal Castle (☎4012-350 782; www.kaliningradinfo.ru; Hotel Kaliningrad, Leninsky pr 81; ⏲8am-8pm Mon-Fri, 9am-4pm Sat) Access the internet and book tours to Kurshskaya Kosa (Curonian Spit) and elsewhere.

UFMS Office (УФМС Офис; ☎4012-563 809; www.fms39.ru; room 9, ul Frunze 6) For visa queries.

ℹ Getting There & Away

AIR

Khrabrovo airport (☎4012-610 620; www.kgd.aero) is 24km north of the city. There are daily flights to Moscow, St Petersburg and Rīga; see the website for other connections.

BOAT

Trans-Exim (☎ 4012-660 470; www.transexim.ru; ul Suvorova 45) has weekly car ferries between Baltiysk and Ust-Luga, 150km west of St Petersburg. See the website for the latest prices and schedules.

BUS

Mainly local buses depart from the **Yuzhny bus station** (ul Zheleznodorozhnaya 7), as well as international bus services run by **Ecolines** (☎ 4012-758 733; www.ecolines.net) to Warsaw and several German cities. **Könnig Avto** (☎ 4012-999 199; www.kenigavto.ru) international services leave from the **international bus station** (Moskovsky pr 184); there's a Könnig Avto booking office at Yuzhny vokzal.

Buses 118 and 125 to Svetlogorsk (₽69, one hour) and the 140, 114 and 141 to Zelenogradsk (₽60, 45 minutes) leave from both the Yuzhny bus station and next to the **Severny vokzal** (Северный вокзал; North Station; pl Pobedy) on Sovetsky pr. Services run about every 30 minutes or so until about 8pm.

Bus Departures

DESTINATION	PRICE (₽)	DURATION (HR)	FREQUENCY
Gdansk	500	4½	3 daily
Klaipėda	500	4	3 daily
Rīga	820	9	3 daily
Stuttgart	4620	24	1 weekly
Tallinn	1340	14	2 daily
Vilnius	850	6	2 daily
Warsaw	1000	9	1 daily

TRAIN

All long-distance and most local trains go from **Yuzhny vokzal** (Южный вокзал; South Station; pl Kalinina), some passing through, but not always stopping, at Severny vokzal (p273).

Local train services (ie those between Kaliningrad and Svetlogorsk) run on local time, but those beyond the region to Moscow, St Petersburg and abroad have their arrival and departure times listed in Moscow time; if a Moscow-bound train is scheduled to depart at 10am it will leave at 9am Kaliningrad time.

Train Departures

DESTINATION	PRICE (₽)	DURATION (HR)	FREQUENCY
Moscow	*platskart/kupe* from 2000/3995	20	1-2 daily
St Petersburg	*platskart/kupe* from 2097/4242	25	1 daily
Svetlogorsk	*obshchiy* 52	1	at least 6 daily
Vilnius	*platskart/kupe* from 2122/3900	6	2-3 daily
Zelenogradsk	*obshchiy* 40	30min	at least 4 daily

Getting Around

Trams, trolleybuses (both ₽10), buses (₽12) and minibuses (₽12 to ₽17) will get you most places. For the airport, take bus 144 from the Yuzhny bus station (₽30, 30 minutes). A taxi to/from the airport is ₽500 with **Taxi Kaliningrad** (☎ 4012-585 858; www.taxi-kaliningrad.ru).

Car rental is available from **City-Rent** (☎ 4012-509 191; www.city-rent39.com; Moskovsky pr 182a), which also has a branch at the airport. Rates start at ₽1200 per day.

Svetlogorsk Светлогорск

☎ 40153 / POP 10,772 / ⏲ MOSCOW -1HR

Once called Rauschen, Svetlogorsk is a pleasant, slow-placed spa town, 35km northwest of Kaliningrad. The narrow beach backed by steep sandy slopes is nothing to speak of, but the pretty old German houses, revamped sanatoriums, top-class hotels and dappled forest setting make it worth a visit. Fairly untouched by WWII, Svetlogorsk has benefited from being declared a federal health resort, with good infrastructure and facilities.

The main street, ul Oktyabrskaya, is lined with handsome buildings.

Sights

Herman Brachert House-Museum MUSEUM
(Дом-музей Германа Брахерта; www.brachert.ru; ul Tokareva 7; admission ₽100; ⏲ 10am-5pm Mon-Thu, to 4pm Sat & Sun) This museum features the work of Herman Brachert (1890–1972), the sculptor whose work can be spotted all around Svetlogorsk; his bronze **Nymph statue** resides in a mosaic-decorated shell on the promenade. His small former home is decorated with more of his pieces and other works by contemporary sculptors. Head around 2km west along the main road from Svetlogorsk II station to reach the suburb of Otradnoe.

Water Tower NOTABLE BUILDING
(ul Oktyabrskaya) The beautiful 25m-high Jugendstil (art nouveau) water tower on the main street is the symbol of Svetlogorsk. Take a peep inside the sanatorium beneath it to see the colourful murals.

Mousetrap Museum MUSEUM
(Музей Мышеловка; myshelovka_museum@mail.ru; Staraya pl 2; adult/child ₽100/50; ⏲11am-7pm Tue-Sun) Mouse toys, mouse artworks, mice in literature: if there's a mouse in any medium, you'll find it here. It's an interactive, touchy-feely collection and great fun for the kids.

Organ Hall NOTABLE BUILDING
(Зал Органной музики; www.organhall.ru; ul Kurortnaya 3; tickets ₽300) The quaint, half-timbered Organ Hall holds concerts throughout the week.

Sundial MONUMENT
(ul Morskaya) On the promenade, this impressive sundial is decorated with an eye-catching mosaic of the zodiac.

Sleeping

Most rates include breakfast and are for the July/August season; prices can drop by a third or more at other times.

★**Dom Skazochnika** GUESTHOUSE $$
(Дом Сказочника; ☎40153-22 396; www.hoffmann-house.ru; Skazochnika Gofmana per 2; s/d from ₽2200/2800, breakfast ₽150) The name means 'House of the Storyteller', and what a fairy-tale place this is. Named in honour of fantasist Ernst Hoffman, this enchanting guesthouse has a babes-in-the-woods setting, an art gallery and a delightful miniature sculpture garden. Rooms are comfortable with high ceilings, service is superb and the attached restaurant is wonderful.

Rauschen Hotel HOTEL $$
(Гостиница Раушен; ☎40153-21 564; www.rauschenhotel.ru; ul Lenina 48a; s/d from R 2200/2800; Wi-Fi) This well-priced option has comfortable beds, a good breakfast buffet and on-site sauna and masseur (one hour ₽2000). It's about 500m from the seaside.

Stary Doktor HOTEL $$
(☎40153-21 362; www.alterdoktor.ru; ul Gagarina 12; d from ₽3000, attic with shared bathroom ₽2000) Set in an imposing old mansion, this place oozes ye olde charm. Rooms are simple and cosy.

Yantarny Bereg SANATORIUM $$
(Янтарный берег; ☎40153-21 604; www.yantar-bereg.ru; pr Kaliningradsky 79; economy/standard r from ₽1870/2400) If you'd like to sample a sanatorium, this large, busy and professionally run place is a fine option. You'll need to speak Russian and be prepared for a holiday-camp-meets-hospital atmosphere.

Hotel Georgensvaldye HOTEL $$
(Георгенсвальде; ☎40153-21 526; www.walde.ru; ul Tokareva 6; s/d ₽2700/3400) In Otradnoe, opposite the Herman Brachert House-Museum, this elegant place is ideal for those seeking peace and quiet.

Lumier Art Hotel HOTEL $$$
(Люмьер Арт-отель; ☎40153-507 750; www.hotellumier.ru; per Lermontovsky 2a; standard/theme r from ₽4500/5600; A/C Wi-Fi) This playful boutique hotel has silver-screen-inspired themed rooms ranging from *Little Red Riding Hood* to *Gone With the Wind*. Even the standard rooms come with cable TV and DVD players. Some have balconies.

Royal Falke Resort & Spa HOTEL $$$
(☎40153-21 600; www.falke-hotel.ru; ul Lenina 1b; s/d from ₽4400/5200; A/C @ Wi-Fi Pool) This luxurious hotel is a good choice for pampering. Its indoor pool, surrounded by landscaping and murals, is big enough for a decent swim. Families with small children are exceptionally well taken care of here, with everything from babysitters to bottle warmers available.

Grand Palace HOTEL $$$
(☎40153-33 232; www.grandhotel.ru; per Beregovoy 2; s/d from ₽4000/7500; A/C @ Wi-Fi Pool) Overpriced glitz pad, but what a location! There are sea views from the pricier rooms, indoor and outdoor pools and a private strip of beach.

Eating & Drinking

Most hotels also have restaurants. Open-air eating and drinking options sprout like daisies during high season.

Kafe Blinnaya CAFE $
(Кафе Блинная; Oktyabrskaya ul 22; bliny from ₽30; ⏲9am-7pm) This simple cafe with street-side seating is cheap, crowded and has loads of scrumptious pancakes and salads on the menu.

★**Korvet** INTERNATIONAL $$
(Корвет; ul Oktyabrskaya 36; meals ₽280-600; ⏲11am-midnight, to late Fri & Sat) Specialising in pizza, this cafe based in the 1901 Kurhaus

is a relaxing place for a meal or coffee break. On Friday and Saturday nights it morphs into partytown, with DJs keeping things going into the early hours.

Vika
RUSSIAN $$

(Вика; Tsentralnaya pl; meals ₽400-700; ⊙noon-midnight) In the town square, this upmarket cafe has a good selection of the usual Russian offerings, local fish dishes and outdoor seating in summer.

ℹ Information

Svetlogorsk Tourist Information Centre
(☑40153-22 098; www.svetlogorsk-tourism. ru; ul Karl Marksa 7a; ⊙10am-7pm Mon-Sat, to 4pm Sun) Helpful staff assist with hotel bookings, tours, car rental etc. There's also internet access (₽35 per hour), a good gift shop and a small museum about the resort's history.

ℹ Getting There & Away

From Kaliningrad take a train (₽52, one hour, at least six daily) or bus (₽69, one hour, every 30 minutes). Buses arrive and depart from in front of the Svetlogorsk II train station. The bus stop for Yantarny is on pr Kaliningradsky, facing Lake Tikhoe.

Svetlogorsk is spread out but easy to navigate on foot or by bicycle: rent a bike from the stall along ul Oktyabrskaya for ₽50 per hour. There's another bike-rental stall on ul Lenina, opposite a small shopping centre.

Yantarny Янтарный

☑401532 / POP 5524 / ⊙ MOSCOW -1HR

Formerly Palmniken, this peaceful resort, 42km northwest of Kaliningrad and 24km southwest of Svetlogorsk, is where 90% of the world's amber is sourced. Visit the amber mine and Yantarny's long, wide sandy beach – the best in Kaliningrad.

⊙ Sights & Activities

Amber Mine
MINE

(Калининградский янтарный комбинат; ☑40153-37 444; www.ambercombine.ru; ul Balebina 1; admission ₽140; ⊙9am-5pm) About 90% of the world's amber is found in Kaliningrad, and this fascinating mine is where it gets processed. There's an observation deck over the quarry, amber-hunting opportunities and the astonishing Amber Pyramid, a huge structure made of 800kg of amber. Tickets can be bought on-site. For more detailed tours with an interpreter, contact the mine or email info@visit-kaliningrad.ru.

Park Becker
PARK

Enjoy a picnic in this park stretched along the headland above the beach in the centre of town.

Diving
DIVING

(☑8-909-775 3222; www.demersus.ru; ul Ozernaya 1) Yantarny is famed for its beach, but its lake – a 26m-deep former amber quarry – attracts divers from around the world. Visibility is up to 10m and you might just find some leftover nuggets down there.

✯✯ Festivals & Events

Amberfest
CULTURAL

(www.amberfest.ru) Celebrate the solar stone each August with amber-centric events and live music on the beach.

🛏 Sleeping & Eating

★ Galera
BUNGALOWS $$

(Галера; ☑8-921-614 7441; www.a-kovalsky.ru; ul Sovetskaya 1; bungalow from ₽3000) These mega-modern beach bungalows offer stunning sea views from huge glass doors and balconies. They have self-contained kitchens, or you can eat at the attached restaurant (11am to 11pm Sunday to Thursday, to 4am Friday and Saturday) that's shaped like a huge ship.

Hotel Becker
HOTEL $$

(Отель Беккер; ☑4012-565 195; www.hotel-becker.ru; ul Sovetskaya 72; s/d incl breakfast from ₽2900/3900; 🐾) The Becker, a quick stroll to the beach, has pleasantly furnished rooms; some have balconies. The attached Kafe Becker (meals ₽300 to ₽500) has a terrace overlooking the seaside.

Schloss Hotel
HOTEL $$$

(☑4012-555 040; www.schloss-hotel.ru; ul Sovetskaya 70; s/d from ₽6800/8000; ❋🐾🐾) This new decadent hotel offers elegance to the max. Its renovated, snow-white mansion was once the hunting lodge of Prussian King George Friedrich and today houses luxurious rooms – some with plunge baths and balconies – a sophisticated spa, upmarket bar and restaurant and summer terrace with sea views.

ℹ Getting There & Away

Bus 120 runs to Yantarny from Kaliningrad (₽75, 1½ hours, hourly). Buses 282 and 286 run to Yantarny from Svetlogorsk (₽54, 45 minutes, eight daily).

Zelenogradsk Зеленоградск

☎40150 / POP 13,026 / ⊙ MOSCOW -1HR

The long beach that gave Zelenogradsk (formerly Kranz) the status of royal bathing resort for the Kingdom of Prussia is still the town's prime attraction. It's a low-key place with a nostalgic atmosphere: crumbling Soviet eyesores, lovely German buildings and modern villas stand side by side. Renovation of the promenade has been going on for years, but it's still possible to enjoy a seaside perambulation. The town also appears to be populated by crazy cat people, with a guesthouse and **museum** (www.murarium.ru; ul Saratovskaya 2a; admission ₽100; ⊙noon-7pm Tue-Sun) devoted to its feline friends.

Zelenogradsk is the gateway to Kurshskaya Kosa (Curonian Spit) National Park.

Sleeping & Eating

High season is in July and August and most rates include breakfast.

★Koshkin Dom GUESTHOUSE $$

(Кошкин Дом; ☎40150-775 859; www.koshkin-dom.ru; ul Gagarina 1a; s/d from ₽2400/3000;) Zelenogradsk's famous 'Cat House' is a welcoming, homey spot metres from the beach. In addition to the cornucopia of cat figurines and artworks, there's also a sauna, a tiny swimming pool, barbecue area and a billiards room. Bike rental is ₽50 per hour.

Hotel Sambia HOTEL $$

(Отель Самбия; ☎40150-36 221; www.sambia-hotel.ru; ul Volodarskogo 20; s/d from ₽2600/3500;) The biggest hotel in Zelenogradsk and one of the best, this fun, family-friendly complex has two restaurants, an 'English Room' for posh tea drinking and a water park. Some rooms have balconies with sea views.

Loger Haus GUESTHOUSE $$

(Гостевой дом; ☎40150-32 306; www.logerhaus.ru; ul Zheleznodorozhnaya 1; s/d from ₽2900/3600;) This guesthouse features classy decor and fine furniture in even the cheapest rooms; you'll never forget the gilt frames around the TVs. Attached is a fancy restaurant serving Russian and European dishes (₽600 to ₽800). It's steps away from the bus and train stations.

Villa Lana GUESTHOUSE $$$

(Вилла Лана; ☎40150-33 410; www.villa-lana.ru; ul Gagarina 3a; s/d/apt ₽5000/5500/6000;) This professionally run guesthouse just 50m from the beach offers spacious, nicely decorated rooms, plus a separate self-catering apartment sleeping four. Helpful staff speak six languages and can help arrange tours.

Captain Flint STEAKHOUSE $

(Капитан Флинт; ☎40150-32 459; Kurortniy per 1; mains ₽195-320; ⊙noon-2am) This popular eatery dishes up mounds of grilled meat in an unmistakable building decorated in all manners mariner. There are business lunches (₽180) every day from noon to 4pm and occasional live music.

Getting There & Away

Frequent buses run from both of Kaliningrad's stations (₽50, 45 minutes, every 30 minutes). There are also regular trains to and from Kaliningrad (₽48, 30 minutes) and Svetlogorsk (₽31, 40 minutes).

Kurshskaya Kosa Куршская Коса

☎40150 / ⊙ MOSCOW -1HR

Tall, windswept dunes, pristine beaches and dense pine forests teeming with wildlife lie along the 98km-long Curonian Spit (Kurshskaya Kosa), a Unesco World Heritage Site that divides the tranquil Curonian Lagoon from the Baltic Sea. The 50km of the spit within Russian territory (the rest is in Lithuania) constitutes **Kurshskaya Kosa National Park** (Национальный парк Куршская коса; www.park-kosa.ru; admission per person/car ₽40/300). The park is home to the highest drifting dunes in Europe, with some reaching a lofty 60m. Mellow fishing and holiday villages dot the east coast. From south to north they are **Lesnoy** (Лесной; formerly Sarkau), **Rybachy** (Рыбачий; formerly Rossitten) and **Morskoe** (Морское; formerly Pilkoppen).

Sights

Epha's Height VIEWPOINT

(Высота Эфа; km42) Near Morskoe village, this photogenic 2.8km hiking trail has boardwalks stretching from one side of the spit to the other, climaxing at the 40m-high **Big Dune Ridge** (Коса Большая Дюна). Along the way you'll see Europe's highest drifting dune, the 62m-high **Orekhovoy Dune** (also called Petsh Dune).

Dancing Forest FOREST
(Танцующий лес; km37) One of the park's most remarkable sights is this aptly named forest, where the pines have been sculpted into twisting shapes by the elements – they do indeed appear to be frozen mid-boogie.

National Park Museum MUSEUM
(Национальный парк-музей; ☎40150-45 247; km14; admission ₽50; ⏲9.30am-5pm Tue-Sun May-Sep, 10am-4.30pm Tue-Sun Oct-Apr) This museum offers loads of information about the park's habitat and history. The complex is also home to more than 100 carved-wood mythological characters at the **Museum of Russian Superstitions** (Музей Русских Суеверий; www.dom-domovogo.ru; km14; ⏲11am-5pm, closed Mon & Thu). Prearrange an excursion to the **Fringilla Ornithological Station** (Орнитологическая станция Фрингилла; km23; tour ₽80; ⏲9am-6pm Apr-Oct), a bird-ringing centre where enormous funnelled nets can trap an average of 1000 birds a day; the birds are then tagged, studied and released.

Sleeping & Eating

Many places include breakfast in their rates. High season is July and August.

Dune CAMPGROUND $
(Турбаза Дюны ; ☎8-905 241 1001; km16; unpowered cabins per person ₽450-600) These cosy cabins and scenic campsites are a pleasant stroll from the beach. There's no power, but there is an authentic *banya* (hot bath; ₽900 per hour), social barbecue area, cafe and bracing sea breezes. It's between Lesnoy and Rybachy villages.

Kurshskaya Kosa HOTEL $$
(Куршская Коса; ☎40150-45 242; www.kosa-hotel.ru; Tsentralnaya ul 17, Lesnoy; d ₽3420-4560; @) Cheery, modern and steps from the beach, this solid option has a restaurant, internet access, cash machine and rents bicycles (₽100 per hour). It's also known as the Fligerhouse (Флигерхаус).

Traktir HOTEL $$
(Трактир; ☎40150-41 290; www.traktir-morskoe.ru; ul Lesnaya 8, Rybachy; r ₽1700-3500) At the entrance to Rybachy village, this log-cabin-style hotel has small but serviceable rooms. Crowds often descend on the adjoining restaurant (mains ₽260 to ₽540, 10am to midnight) – a hit with locals since President Putin dropped by for a meal. Solid home-cooked meals are served on rustic pottery.

Altrimo HOTEL $$
(Гостиничный комплекс Альтримо; ☎8-909-790 5588; www.altrimo.ru; ul Porganichnaya 11, Rybachy; r/ste from ₽3600/5600; ❄ 📶) Kurshskaya Kosa's most upmarket option has a top location next to the lagoon. Facilities include a pleasant open-air restaurant and a giant replica fishing boat that's part sauna, part playground. Jet skis, kayaks and other watercraft are available for rent.

Rossiten GUESTHOUSE $$
(Росситен; ☎40150-41 391; ul Pobedy 24, Rybach; s/d ₽2300/2650) This no-frills inn, at the heart of Rybach village, offers simple accommodation and a passable cafe.

Getting There & Away

Buses from Kaliningrad head up the spit en route to Morskoe (₽130, two hours, four daily). All stop in Zelenogradsk, Lesnoy and Rybachy on the way there and back; Kaliningrad's tourism information centre has the current timetable.

Alternatively, rent a car (from around ₽1500) or arrange a tour (around ₽700) in either Kaliningrad or Zelenogradsk.

Northern European Russia

Includes ➡

Best Churches

- ➡ St Sofia's Cathedral (p309)
- ➡ Kirillov-Belozersky Monastery (p312)
- ➡ Church of the Entry into Jerusalem (p315)
- ➡ Solovetsky Transfiguration Monastery (p289)
- ➡ Transfiguration Monastery (p287)

Best Northern Fun

- ➡ Teriberka (p308)
- ➡ Bolshoy Zayatsky Island (p290)
- ➡ Snow Village (p298)
- ➡ Husky Park Lesnaya Elan (p301)
- ➡ Arctic Circle PADI Dive Center (p299)

Why Go?

Cold hands, warm heart? The idiom has never rung more true than in this land of polar winters and cliché-busting Russian hospitality, where those braving daunting long hauls and off-radar destinations are rewarded with a hearty reception by curious locals.

The realm that spawned the epic poetry of the *Kalevala* is home to a profound historical and scenic landscape that includes the iconic wooden architecture of Kizhi Island, the far-flung Solovetsky Islands' imposing monastery/erstwhile Gulag camp, and the vast wilderness of the Kola Peninsula and the Barents Sea's frigid shore. The far north is also one of the best places to witness the eerily beautiful Northern Lights.

Whether you're here for the region's short summer – perfect for fishing for prize salmon and frolicking beneath the midnight sun – or taking to the snow on husky sleds or skis, you will find Northern European Russia beguiling.

When to Go

Murmansk

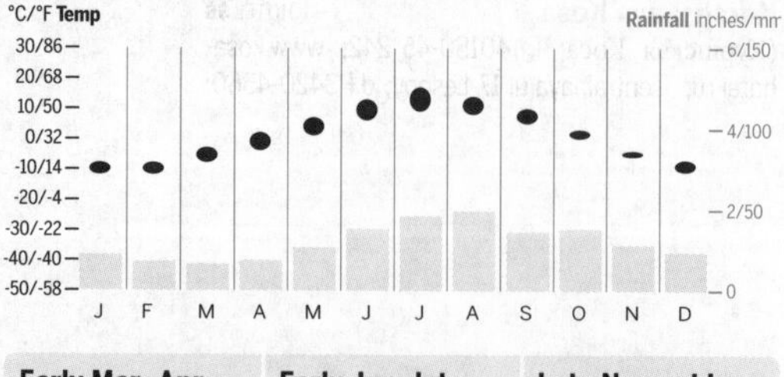

Early Mar–Apr Days are long and there's plenty of snow for husky sledding and skiing.

Early Jun–late Jul The fleeting summer is ideal for island access and fun in the midnight sun.

Late Nov–mid-Jan Scan the perpetually sunless skies for the gasp-inducing aurora borealis.

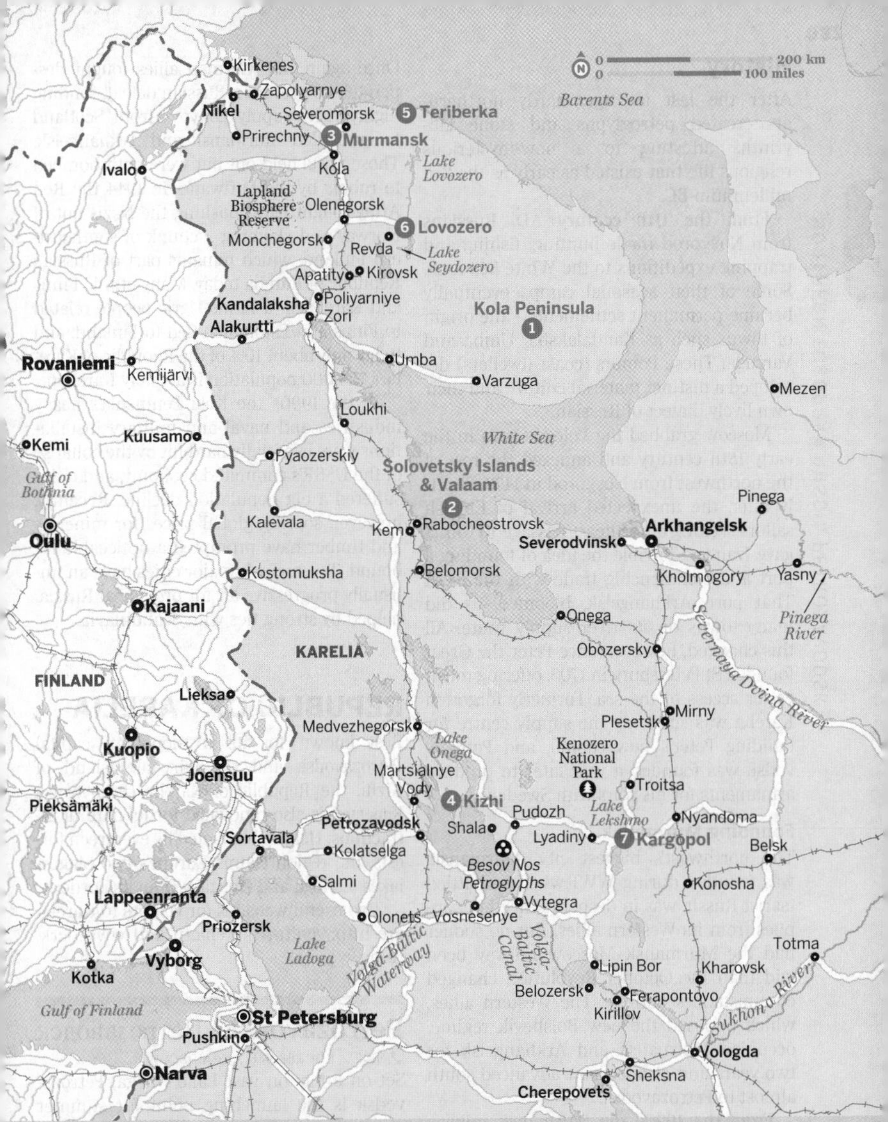

Northern European Russia Highlights

1. Hunt for the aurora borealis, hike into the wilderness or go skiing on the **Kola Peninsula** (p297).
2. Go monastery hopping at the ever-evocative **Solovetsky Islands** (p288) and the sylvan retreat of **Valaam** (p286).
3. Swim with the human walruses then board a nuclear icebreaker in **Murmansk** (p302), the world's biggest Arctic city.
4. Marvel at the glorious ancient wooden architecture of **Kizhi** (p284), including the iconic multidomed Transfiguration Church.
5. Explore the stunning coast of the frigid Barents Sea near the post-apocalyptic village of **Teriberka** (p316).
6. Delve into the culture of the Sami, buy traditional handicrafts and go husky sledding at **Lovozero** (p301).
7. Go church gazing and try your hand at traditional folk art in the tranquil town of **Kargopol** (p315).

History

After the last ice age, hardy northerners created petroglyphs and stone labyrinths attesting to a now-mysterious religious life that existed as early as the 3rd millennium BC.

From the 11th century AD, Russians from Novgorod made hunting, fishing and trapping expeditions to the White Sea area. Some of their seasonal camps eventually became permanent settlements – the origin of towns such as Kandalaksha, Umba and Varzuga. These Pomors (coast dwellers) developed a distinct material culture and their own lively dialect of Russian.

Moscow grabbed the Vologda area in the early 15th century and annexed the rest of the northwest from Novgorod in 1478. Shortly after, the unexpected arrival of English sailors seeking a northeast passage to China gave Ivan the Terrible the idea of founding a port and commencing trade with the west. That port, Arkhangelsk, bloomed, as did many towns on its river supply route. All this changed, however, once Peter the Great founded St Petersburg in 1703, offering much easier access to the sea. Formerly forgotten Karelia was suddenly the supply centre for building Peter's new capital, and Petrozavodsk was founded a year later to produce armaments for his wars with Sweden.

Founding Murmansk

The northwest's biggest city, Murmansk, was founded during WWI when embattled tsarist Russia was in desperate need of supplies from its Western allies. But no sooner had the Murmansk–Moscow railway been laid than the October Revolution changed circumstances entirely. The Western allies, which opposed the new Bolshevik regime, occupied Murmansk and Arkhangelsk for two years and at one point advanced south almost to Petrozavodsk.

From the 1920s the Murmansk railway helped Soviet governments unlock the Kola Peninsula's vast mineral resources, bringing new towns such as Monchegorsk and Kirovsk into existence. Gulag prisoners were part of the force that built the region's new factories and the White Sea–Baltic Canal.

WWII & After

Stalin invaded Finland in 1939–40. Having been independent from Russia only since 1917, Finland allied with Germany to counterattack along the entire Soviet–Finnish border, eventually occupying Petrozavodsk. Once again, anti-German allies fought desperately to prevent a Russian defeat, sending highly risky supply convoys from Scotland to embattled Murmansk and Arkhangelsk. Those ports held out but were both bombed to rubble by the Luftwaffe. In 1944 the Red Army fought back, pushing the Nazis out of Norway and claiming a chunk of southeastern Finland, which remains part of Russia's Republic of Karelia today. Many ethnic Finns and Karelians (a Finno-Ugric people related to Finns and Estonians) fled to Finland, and today only about 10% of the Republic of Karelia's 720,000 population is actually Karelian.

In the 1990s the Kola Peninsula's heavy industries and naval and military installations were especially hard hit by the collapse of the USSR's command economy, and cities suffered a big population decline. Recently, however, soaring global prices for minerals and timber have prompted a noticeable rebound. The region's major cities have an unusually progressive air for provincial Russia, helped by strong ties with Scandinavia.

REPUBLIC OF KARELIA

Best known for its cosmopolitan capital Petrozavodsk and the fairy-tale island of Kizhi, the Republic of Karelia (Республика Карелия) is also renowned for its natural attractions. Heavily blanketed by evergreen forests, the region claims Europe's two biggest lakes, Ladoga and Onega, within its borders.

Two useful websites for visitors to Karelia are http://culture.karelia.ru and www.ticrk.ru/en.

Petrozavodsk Петрозаводск

☎8142 / POP 268,946 / ⏰MOSCOW

Set on a bay on vast Lake Onega, Petrozavodsk is the launching point for summer visits to two of the region's biggest attractions: Kizhi Island and Valaam Monastery. The name ('Peter's factory') refers to a munitions plant founded here by Peter the Great in 1703, superseded 70 years later by the Alexandrovskiy Ironworks (still standing). But Petrozavodsk is by no means the gritty, industrial city its name would suggest. Its neoclassical facades, a large student population and connections with Finland all make for a distinctly European atmosphere, and the appealing lakefront promenade is just made for strolling.

Sights & Activities

Ploshchad Lenina SQUARE
(Площадь Ленина) The circular pl Lenina is the original heart of neoclassical Petrozavodsk, skirted by matching semicircular buildings built in 1784. In its centre is a 1933 **statue of Lenin**, who seems to be striking a 'My Heart Will Go On' pose (cue the musical stylings of Celine Dion). Steps pass an **eternal flame** into the pretty riverside park, from where a bridge crosses to the grand facade of the former Alexandrovskiy Ironworks, now part of the vast **Onezhskiy Tractor Factory**.

Museum of Regional Studies MUSEUM
(Карельский государственный краеведческий музей; pl Lenina 1; admission ₽200; ⏲10am-5.30pm Tue-Sun; 🚌17) Besides exhibitions on trade between Russia's north and the Byzantine world, the history of the city and regional trades, this excellent museum (with English captioning) introduces you to the mysteries of ancient stone labyrinths and the *Kalevala,* Finland's national epic, which was pieced together in the 19th century from northern Karelian song-poems.

Lakeside Promenade PARK
On a fine summer's day, scores of strolling families, rollerbladers and cyclists take to the Lake Onega promenade – an appealing park area scattered liberally with summer cafes serving shashlyk kebabs and beer, and a host of contemporary sculptures by homegrown and international talent. The most striking of them are the silver **Fishermen** throwing in a net and the elk-like **Sleeping Beauty**, symbolising unity between Karelian woman and nature.

★ **Fine Arts Museum** ART GALLERY
(Музей изобразительных искусств; pr Marksa 8; admission ₽300; ⏲10am-6pm Tue-Sun) Besides the permanent exhibitions that feature medieval icons, folk art such as embroidery, weaving and birch-bark creations, there's a collection of 18th-century Russian Masters that includes the dark and creepy *Christ in Gethsemane* by Ilya Repin, and interesting temporary exhibitions.

Statue of Yury Andropov MONUMENT
(Памятник Юрию Андропову; ul Andropova) Unveiled to protests and arrests in 2005, a youthful statue of Yury Andropov commemorates the USSR's 1982–84 supremo and chief of Petrozavodsk's Komsomol (Communist Party youth wing) some 50 years earlier. Andropov was a long-term KGB director and some believe that had he not died, he would have implemented necessary reforms without breaking up the Soviet Union, unlike Gorbachev.

Puppet House MUSEUM
(Дом Кукол; http://kukla.karelia.ru; nab La Rochelle 13; admission ₽100; ⏲noon-5pm Mon-Sat; 🚌21) A remarkable and somewhat creepy collection of handmade creations by one of Russia's foremost puppet mistresses. Storybook heroes, mythological creatures and folk-tale evildoers are recreated here and each doll is unique.

Statue of Peter the Great MONUMENT
(Памятник Петру I; pr Karla Marksa) Close to the hydrofoil terminal is a jaunty statue of Peter the Great pointing to the spot where Petrozavodsk would be founded.

Tours

Intourist-Petrozavodsk TOUR COMPANY
(Интурист-Петрозаводск; ☎8142-592 900; http://intourist.onego.ru/eng/index.html; Hotel Severnaya, pr Lenina 21; 🚌17, 1) Multilingual agency that can help arrange fishing, skiing and adventure tours around Karelia.

RussiaDiscovery North-West ADVENTURE TOURS
(☎921-458 6465; www.russiadiscovery.ru) Specialist in active Karelia adventures such as quad-bike tours and snowmobile tours. Based in Moscow.

Nordic Travel TOUR COMPANY
(☎8142-762 330; www.nordictravel.ru; ul Engelsa 10; 🚌17) Tours of Karelia, the Russian Arctic and Solovetsky Islands.

Festivals & Events

Hyperborea Festival WINTER
Chase the winter blues away at this festival celebrating all things snow and ice. Held lakeside in January/February.

Sleeping

★ **Mini-Hotel Ilma** HOTEL **$$**
(Гостиница Илма; ☎8-911-661 4516; ul Volodarskogo 10; s/d from ₽1500/2000; 📶; 🚌20) Well located minihotel with brand-new furniture in its spacious en suites, a fresh colour scheme, friendly staff and a small guest kitchen.

★ **Hotel Onego** HOTEL **$$**
(Отель Онего; ☎8142-796 130; www.karelia.onego.ru; ul Rigachina 3a; s/d from ₽750/1500; 🚌19,

Petrozavodsk

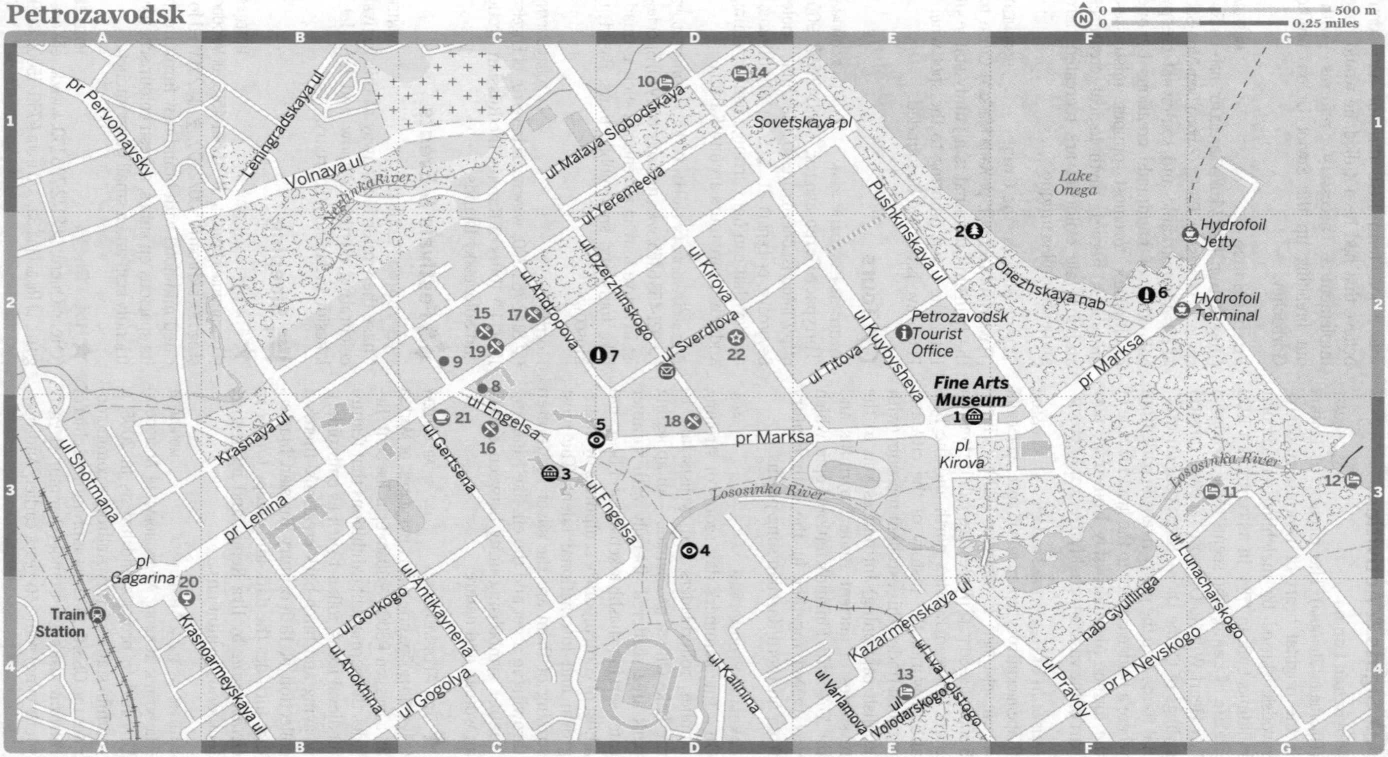

0 500 m
0 0.25 miles
Lake Onega
Hydrofoil Jetty
Hydrofoil Terminal
Petrozavodsk Tourist Office
Fine Arts Museum
pl Kirova
Sovetskaya pl
Pushkinskaya ul
Onezhskaya nab
pr Marksa
ul Kuybysheva
ul Titova
ul Kirova
ul Sverdlova
ul Dzerzhinskogo
ul Andropova
ul Yeremeeva
ul Malaya Slobodskaya
Volnaya ul
Neglinka River
Leningradskaya ul
pr Pervomaysky
ul Engelsa
ul Gertsena
Krasnaya ul
pr Lenina
ul Shotmana
pl Gagarina
Train Station
Krasnoarmeyskaya ul
ul Gorkogo
ul Antikaynena
ul Anokhina
ul Gogolya
ul Kalinina
Lososinka River
ul Varlamova
ul Volodarskogo
ul Lva Tolstogo
Kazarmenskaya ul
ul Pravdy
pr A Nevskogo
nab Gyullinga
ul Lunacharskogo

Petrozavodsk

25) Get your lake legs on at this 'floating' accommodation alternative. Budget rooms are basic affairs, but it's cheap, cheerful and comes with views that leave the landlubbers for dead. Ideally located for early morning staggers to the hydrofoil terminal.

13 Chairs HOTEL **$$**
(Бутик-отель 13 Стульев; ☎8-921-220 4444; http://13hotel.ru; nab Neglinskaya 13; s/d/ste from ₽2900/3400/5400;) The rooms at this brand-new boutiquey hotel are designed to imitate a romantic 19th-century fantasy without actually investing in period furniture. Extra (anachronistic) pampering comes in the form of a pool, sauna and spa.

Hotel Karelia HOTEL **$$$**
(Отель Карелия; ☎8142-733 333; www.karelia-hotel.ru; nab Gyullinga 2; s/d/apt/ste from ₽3960/4960/6960/11,960; ; 19, 25) This bustling multistorey tower feels a little like an upmarket clinic, with a health-spa complex offering various massages, baths and beauty treatments. Many rooms have good lake views. Staff are multilingual and can assist with jaunts to Kizhi and beyond.

Onego Palace HOTEL **$$$**
(Гостиничный комплекс Онего Палас; ☎8142-790 790; www.onegopalace.com; ul Kuybysheva 26; s/d/lyux/ste from ₽4250/5300/8800/20,000; ; 101) This monolith looks a bit like a UFO looming over the lake from which it takes its name. Thankfully its interior is a lot less gauche, with classically styled rooms and three upmarket restaurants, including a summer shashlyk terrace. Athletic types will appreciate the gym and saunas; for everyone else, there's a 24-hour lobby bar.

Eating

Deja Vu FUSION **$**
(Дежавю; pr Lenina 20; mains from ₽150; 9am-2am; 17) Small but inexpensive salads, soups and light mains served in an upbeat, youthful atmosphere where the déjà vu in question is the Eiffel Tower, a giant photo of which is echoed in ironwork motifs above the bar.

La Parisienne FUSION **$**
(Парижанка; http://parizhanka-cafe.ru; pr Marksa 22; mains from ₽180; 8am-midnight; ; 17) This local chain's nine (!) locations in Petrozavodsk are constantly packed, thanks to hip decor and an eclectic menu – where else can you scoff sushi and sip cranberry lemonade while humming along to Edith Piaf?

Sigma SUPERMARKET **$**
(Сигма; ul Lenina 18; 8am-10pm; 17) Enormous, well-stocked supermarket. There's a very good food court in the shopping centre above, too.

★ **Karelskaya Gornitsa** KARELIAN **$$**
(Карельская Горница; www.gornica.ru; ul Engelsa 13a; mains ₽320-850; noon-midnight; 17) Claiming to be the first Karelian restaurant in the world, this ye-olde hotspot boasts efficient costumed waiters and excellent, hearty fare, including rabbit borsch and rich, gamey and fishy mains, washed down with its own *medovukha* (honey mead).

Dobra Khata UKRAINIAN $$

(Добра Хата; ul Engelsa 13; mains from ₽240; ⊙noon-midnight) The rustic Ukrainian theme is worked to the max here – expect a cheery stove, woven tablecloths, sunflowers, clay jugs and nostalgic sepia prints of Ukrainian peasantry. Maidens in traditional costume serve you all the favourites: *draniki* (potato fritters), *vareniki* (filled dumplings), borsch, grilled meats and tankards of *kvas* (fermented rye bread water).

Kavkaz STEAKHOUSE $$

(Кавказ; ul Andropova 16; mains from ₽240; ⊙11am-11pm;) Kavkaz serves sizzling shashlyk and grilled meats to the carnivorously inclined.

Drinking & Nightlife

Fusion BAR

(Krasnoarmeyskaya ul 33; ⊙8.30am-2am) This super-sleek Russo-Japanese-style hang-out by the train station dishes up lethal cocktails every bit as delicious as the authentic sushi snacks (from ₽70). Popular with the young trendies.

Kaffee Haus CAFE

(Кофейный Дом; pr Lenina 23; ⊙9am-1am; ; 17) Widely acclaimed for Petrozavodsk's best coffee and cakes.

Entertainment

FM-Art Kafe LIVE MUSIC

(Арт-кафе FM; www.artcafefm.ru; ul Kirova 12; admission free; ⊙from 6pm daily; 12) This large student-oriented basement beneath the Philharmonia offers entertainment as varied as the clientele, with revolving theme evenings ranging from jazz to folk to indie.

Information

Petrozavodsk Tourist Office (Информационный туристский центр РК; 8142-764 835; www.ticrk.ru; ul Titova 3; ⊙9am-5pm Mon-Sat; 29) Very obliging English-speaking staff offer loads of information and advice.

Post Office (Почта; ul Dzerzhinskogo 5; ⊙8am-8pm Mon-Fri, 9am-6pm Sat) Main post office.

Getting There & Away

For updated transport timetables, both urban and intercity, consult http://ptz-trans.ru.

BOAT

In summer, hydrofoils usually operate up to five times daily to Kizhi (₽2500 return).

BUS

From the **bus station** (Автостанция; ul Chapaeva 3) there are regular departures for Helsinki, Finland (₽1750, 13 hours, 5am), St Petersburg (₽800, 8½ hours, four to five daily), Sortavala (₽570, four to seven hours, seven to eight daily) and Vologda (₽1010, 12½ hours, 7.10am Tuesday, Thursday, Friday and Sunday). There's a handy bus schedule and price list in English pinned to the bus station wall.

TRAIN

From the train station, there are departures for Moscow (₽530, 12¾ to 16¼ hours, four to eight daily), with the ideal overnight choice being train 17, which departs at 8.20pm and arrives at 9.05am. The best timed of five services to St Petersburg is train 11, departing at 10.40pm (arriving at 6.24am). Between six and seven services run daily to/from Murmansk (₽1900, 18¾ to 24 hours), the swiftest being train 16. Train 294 (departing at 9.32pm) is the best bet for Kem (₽1103, 8½ hours), arriving at 6.05am.

Getting Around

2GIS (2ГИС; www.2gis.ru) provides up-to-date transport route info online and via its handy app. Trolleybuses and buses (₽19) trundle up and down pr Lenina. From the train station, trolleybus 1 is the most useful, going straight through the heart of the city and down as far as the lake.

Around Petrozavodsk

Stretching north and west of Petrozavodsk, Karelia is Russia's Land O' The Lakes, dotted with villages and with ample opportunities for fishing and hiking. Wild camping is permitted almost anywhere unless there are signs with the words 'Не разбивать палатку'. Signs saying 'Не разжигать костры' mean 'no campfires'. Lakes and rivers offer canoeing opportunities and some outfits offer rafting, albeit without many rapids. Culturally, the most rewarding day-trip destination from Petrozavodsk is Kizhi, a wonder of wooden architecture.

Kizhi Кижи

This enchanting green sliver is by far the most visited of Lake Onega's 1600-plus islands, thanks to the iconic Transfiguration Church. Bubbling magnificently with 30 miniature domes, this is Russia's most instantly recognisable wooden landmark. The **Kizhi Museum Reserve** (Музей-заповедник 'Кижи'; http://kizhi.karelia.ru; admission ₽625, audio guide ₽150; ⊙8am-8pm Jun-Aug, 9am-4pm Sep–mid-Oct & 15-31 May, 10am-3pm mid-Oct–

mid-May) is home to dozens more 18th- and 19th-century log buildings, some furnished in period style, which were moved here from Karelian villages during Soviet times.

Kizhi is truly one of Russia's unmissable attractions. Visitors typically get four hours on the island, more than enough time to visit the main reserve and stroll up to the lived-in Yamka village. Guided excursions are on offer but much of what you'll see is self-explanatory and placards are in English. Stay on the marked paths – a decline in the island's poisonous-snake population has led to a proliferation of ticks that potentially carry encephalitis.

Hydrofoils dock at a landing flanked by souvenir kiosks. From the ticket office, visitors head south into the main reserve.

Sights

Main Reserve Area

An obvious coastal path loops around the main attractions, followed anticlockwise by most visitors, starting with the unmissable **Kizhi Enclosure** (Корпус музея 'Кижи'). It contains a striking pair of churches, their cupolas covered with wooden 'scales', a modest graveyard and an 1862 wooden **bell tower**. Kizhi's world-famous 1714 **Transfiguration Church** features a chorus of wooden domes, gables and ingenious decorations to keep water off the walls. Entry isn't allowed as it's undergoing extensive renovation. However, the lovely nine-domed **Church of the Intercession** (1764) next door hosts a rich collection of 16th- to 18th-century icons and a splendid iconostasis.

Directly south of the Kizhi Enclosure, the 1876 **Oshevnev House** is typical of larger historical Karelian rural homes where house and stable-barn were combined into one unit. Notice the 'bed cupboard' and the dried herbs hanging from the ceiling (Old Believers considered tea drinking a sin).

Further south is a **black banya**, a tiny wooden bathhouse hut so known because there was no chimney to allow the escape of smoke from the heater fires.

Outside the furnished 1880 **Elizarov House**, a craftsman carves little human and animal figures, while within the **Chapel of the Archangel Michael**, note the 'sky' – the wooden icons that make up the ceiling. A merry ringing of church bells usually accompanies your visit.

Just south of **Schepin House** is a working **smithy**, while in the southernmost **Sergiev House** an exhibition compares the coexisting worlds of male and female peasants in the late 19th century. Women were in charge of cooking, embroidery, sewing, and child rearing, while men worked in the fields and fished. No surprises there.

Further north, the little 14th-century **Church of the Resurrection of Lazarus** from Murom monastery is the oldest structure on Kizhi – some claim it to be the oldest wooden building in Russia.

An interesting **carpentry exhibit** en route to **Yakovlev House** gives a great visual explanation of how wooden buildings were made without nails. The house itself is the most affluent of the lot, with lace tablecloths and a group of weavers who burst into Old Russian song as you walk in.

From here you could return to the dock past a carved wooden **cross**, a once common roadside waymarker in rural Karelia. Alternatively, stroll on to Yamka.

Yamka & Around

Extravagantly bearded Old Believers, genuinely lived-in (and well-labelled) historic houses and a pretty east-coast setting make the village of **Yamka** well worth the 15-minute walk up the coast. The reserve's seasonal staff sleep communally here in the 1905 **Pertyakov House**, with a traditional-style outdoor *banya* hut at the waterside. Two doors south, outside the **Moshikova House**, is a curious blue-eyed pagan **totem** that's somewhat reminiscent of an Easter Island *moai*.

Walking west across the island towards Vasilyevo village takes you via the hilltop 17th-century **Veronica's Veil Chapel**, from where there are wonderful panoramas right across Kizhi. An alternative path from here leads back to the hydrofoil landing.

Getting There & Away

From the end of May until late August, hydrofoils (return ₽2500) make the 1¼-hour trip from Petrozavodsk between one and five times daily, according to demand and weather. In summer there are scheduled departures at 10.30am, 11.30am and 12.15pm, returning at 3.45pm, 4.45pm and 5.30pm, with extra departures depending on demand. Check the **Tourholding Karelia** (http://tourholding.ru/ru/trans_facil/sailings) website for up-to-date timetables. Double-check a day ahead at the Petrozavodsk hydrofoil terminal (Водный вокзал). Sporadic boats run in early May and from September to mid-October.

In winter, some tour agencies can arrange visits to Kizhi by snowmobile or hovercraft.

Northern Lake Ladoga

The top attraction in Europe's largest lake is the monastery island of Valaam. Coming from Petrozavodsk, it's most conveniently reached via Sortavala, though there's an alternative hydrofoil connection from the historic castle town of Priozersk (formerly Käkisalmi) in Leningradsky Oblast, as well as pricey cruises from St Petersburg.

Sortavala Сортавала

81430 / POP 19,034 / MOSCOW

Founded by the Swedes in 1632, sleepy Sortavala became better known as Serdobol during its first Russian phase (1721 to 1812), when its quarries provided much of the stone for St Petersburg's great palaces. It was part of Finland until WWII, when, after severe bombing, its population evacuated and the area was forced into the USSR.

Sortavala is primarily a launching point for reaching Valaam, but it's well worth peeking into the **Kronid Gogolev Museum** (Музей Кронида Гоголева; www.artgogolev.ru; ul Komsomolskaya 6; admission ₽100; 10am-8pm) near the dock. The unique woodcarving style of local artist Gogolev has resulted in wooden tableaux that portray entertaining rural scenes, with peasants making merry, getting into fights and seducing village maidens. A couple of blocks away sits the *kantele*-plucking **statue of Petri Shemeikka** (pl Vainamoinen), one of the last great rune singers connected with the *Kalevala* epic poem that's central to the spiritual history of Finnish and Russian Karelia.

If staying overnight, central Sortavala options include portside **Hotel Kaunis** (81430-24 910; hotelkaunis@onego.ru; ul Lenina 3; s/d ₽2900/3900;), with spacious rooms, powerful showers, English-speaking staff and on-site cafe; fully equipped two–four-person **Uyutnyy Dom Apartments** (921-224 8489; nikitkaonego@yandex.ru; Kirova 18; apt ₽1000-2000;), ideal for self-caterers; and compact ensuite rooms inside a five-storey grey apartment building that hides **Hotel Scandinavia** (921-623 9636, 81430-25 223; scandi.sort@mail.ru; ul Sadovaya 28; s/d ₽1300/2300;). Basic eateries along main ul Karelskaya are unlikely to win culinary prizes, with the exception of **Boulevard** (Бульвар; ul Karelskaya 35; mains ₽200-360; 10am-2am), its nicely presented dishes including *ukha* (hearty fish soup) with vodka, Janssen's temptation, and chicken stuffed with mushrooms, served by prompt and congenial waiters.

Sberbank (Сбербанк; ul Komsomolskaya 8) has a 24-hour ATM.

From Sortavala's **bus station** (9am-6pm), daily buses and scheduled *marshrutky* (fixed route minibuses) run to Petrozavodsk (₽570, four to seven hours, up to six daily). There are also daily departures to St Petersburg at 2.15pm (₽650, 5¾ hours) and at an ungodly 2.30am Friday to Monday.

Train 350 from St Petersburg (₽929, 5½ hours) arrives in Sortavala on Friday at 8.21pm and departs the town on Sunday at 8.26am.

Valaam Валаам

81430 / POP 200 / MOSCOW

This beautiful, mostly forested archipelago consists of around 50 isles tightly clustered around a 27.8-sq-km main island, where the **Transfiguration Monastery** (Валаамский Спасо-Преображенский монастырь) is the main drawcard. If you're overwhelmed by the stampede of pilgrims, explore a dozen other smaller churches, chapels and sketes on pretty headlands, quiet inland bays or bridged islets.

Mystics like to claim that Valaam was visited by St Andrew within a generation of Christ's crucifixion. True or not, a monastery was founded here around the late 14th century. Its dual role as fortress against Swedish invaders failed in 1611 when the Swedes destroyed it completely. Rebuilt in the 18th century with money from Peter the Great, the monastery burned down again in 1754. In the 19th century Valaam pioneered the idea of sketes, sort of halfway houses between hermitages and monasteries, where novice monks could retreat and learn from more experienced peers.

When the Soviet Union took northern Lake Ladoga from Finland in WWII, many of the monks and much of the monastery's treasure were moved to a site near Karvio, Finland, where the Uusi Valamo (New Valaam) monastery remains active. Today there's a renewed community of about 200 monks, the Transfiguration Monastery is beautifully restored and several outlying sketes have been rebuilt.

Most boats and hydrofoils from Sortavala arrive at the Monasterskaya landing, close to the main Transfiguration Monastery. Numerous souvenir stands at both ports sell useful, if flawed, maps of the archipelago.

Valaam is a big island. As such, it's crying out for a bicycle-rental place, as travellers not attached to a tour group are faced with very long walks, or else they're reliant on taxis that occasionally loiter by the dock.

Sights

Map guides show various other interesting walks and attractions, but be aware that not all marked routes actually connect as shown.

Transfiguration Monastery MONASTERY
(Спасо-Преображенский монастырь) FREE To the left, souvenir stalls line the short road that leads, via short-cut steps, up to Valaam's main attraction. The monastery is radiant in gleaming white and sky-blue, topped with red crosses. With a sturdy spire and five domes, it appears more Catholic than Orthodox at first glance, an impression instantly dispelled upon entering the candlelit semi-gloom. A stairway, splendidly muralled with saints, leads to an upper chapel that's a soaring masterpiece of gilt, icons and awe.

Nikonovskaya Area HISTORICAL BUILDINGS
One of the few parts of the island that's easily accessible on foot from the monastery is the forested Nikonovskaya area, dotted with chapels and sketes.

Amid trees directly above the Nikonovskaya jetty, the modest red-brick **Resurrection Church** isn't a real attraction but sporadic minibuses (₽70) shuttle visitors to the main monastery from here. If none materialise, the 6km walk is blissfully peaceful. Alternatively, walk 1km west along the main track then, just beyond the pretty wooden **Gethsemane Skete**, take the forest footpath to the left, then soon after turn left again. This path winds round past the **Ascension Chapel**, with lovely views down to a wood-lined bay, then curves down and back around past the **Konevsky Skete** to the Valaam monastery farm complex. From here you can return to Gethsemane Skete, or walk 2km back to the main track near Tikhvin Bridge and hope for a passing vehicle to pick you up (not assured).

Nikolski Skete MONASTERY
(Никольский скит) For a great picnic site, stroll about 20 minutes north of the Transfiguration Monastery to the quaint, heptagonal bell tower of Nikolski Skete.

Sleeping & Eating

In summer, booking ahead is virtually essential.

Inside the monastery, there's a tiny **bakery** window hidden deep within the northwest corner of the cloister and monks sell locally smoked trout nearby.

Hotel Igumenskaya MONASTERY ROOMS $$
(Гостиница Игуменская; ☎8-921-629 3311; http://vp.valaam.ru/hotels_valaam/3241; s/d ₽2700/3000) Wood-panelled rooms inside the monastery with simple beds come complete with an icon in a corner niche. From the top of the main approach stairway, enter the first lilac-scented courtyard of the main monastery, turn right and press the buzzer at the third door. There's no sign. Not the best ratio of guest numbers per shared bathroom.

V Starom Sadu CAFE $
(В старом саду; mains from ₽200; ⏰noon-7pm) Basic summer cafe inside the monastery orchard, sometimes serving shashlyk and local *pryaniki* (gingerbread).

Getting There & Away

From June till early September it's usually possible to reach the island daily from Sortavala, though not 100% guaranteed. Scheduled hydrofoils typically sail at 9.30am and 11am (₽1600 return, 45 minutes), but they are reserved for tour groups, so solo travellers will only get a seat if there's space. In peak season, private speedboat captains round up solo travellers and charge the same as hydrofoils for the journey to/from Valaam. Double-check the return times from the island. Booking a tour with one of the many Petrozavodsk agencies is a safer bet.

In February and March a hovercraft runs from Sortavala, ice conditions allowing. With a minimum of seven passengers, tickets cost around ₽2000 per person; book through Intourist (p281) in Petrozavodsk.

Overnight river cruises run regularly in summer from St Petersburg.

WHITE SEA БЕЛОЕ МОРЕ

Kem & Rabocheostrovsk
Кемь и Рабочеостровск

☎81458 / POP 12,454 / ⏰MOSCOW

If you're heading for the Solovetsky Islands, the most reliable boat connection is from tiny Rabocheostrovsk, 12km northeast of the logging town of Kem and easily reachable by bus 1 (₽45, 20 minutes, every 20 to 40 minutes from around 6.30am to 8.30pm) from Kem's railway station. A taxi to Rabocheostrovsk costs around ₽400 and Kem's

Sberbank (Кемовский сбербанк; pl Kirova 3) is your last chance to withdraw cash, as there are no ATMs on the Solovetsky Islands.

Boats to the Solovetsky Islands depart from behind Rabocheostrovsk's **Turkomplex Prichal** (Рабочеостровской Туркомплекс Причал; ☎81458-56 060; www.prichalrk.ru/eng; Naberezhnaya 1; s/d/tr from ₽1200/2200/3300), whose reception desk sells the tickets (and reserves them for guests if notified). Popular with tour groups, the Prichal has fairly bright, well-maintained, pine-furnished rooms in eight chalet-style blocks. The friendly on-site cafe serves light meals (mains ₽200).

From Petrozavodsk there are six to seven trains daily to Kem (₽736, eight to 11 hours); daily train 294 that runs via St Petersburg gets in at 6.05am, in time for you to catch one of the morning boats. Of the eight daily trains from Murmansk (₽1305, 11 to 13½ hours), the most convenient is the overnight train 115 that gets into Kem at 6.22am.

If you catch the 4pm boat from the islands, you can make the night trains heading both north and south: the 21 to St Petersburg via Petrozavodsk leaves at 8.49pm (₽1645), and there are two trains departing for Murmansk after 9pm.

Solovetsky Islands

Соловецкие Острова

☎8183590 / POP 950 / ⊙MOSCOW

Alternatively called Solovki, these distant, lake-dappled White Sea islands are home to one of Russia's best-known monasteries. Transformed by Stalin into one of the USSR's most notorious prison camps, Solovki was described in Solzhenitsyn's *Gulag Archipelago* as being so remote that a 'scream from here would never be heard'.

Visiting the islands is an adventure. The brief summer is pretty much your only window of opportunity as the autumn brings storms and soup-thick fog, and during the long winter Solovki are swept clean by howling blizzards. Solovki warrant several days' exploration to properly absorb the history and the silence of the forests, bays and outer islands. Bring mosquito repellent, warm clothes and plenty of patience.

The archipelago has six main islands and more than 500 lakes. By far the largest island, **Bolshoy Solovetsky** (24km by 16km) is home to the main monastery, which dominates the rural idyll of **Solovetsky Village**, the islands' main settlement.

History

Many millennia ago, the ancestors of the present-day Sami adorned these islands with stone 'labyrinths' and burial mounds, possibly considering Solovki a gateway to the spiritual world. Permanent occupation began in 1429 when monks from Kirillo-Belozersky Monastery founded a wooden hermitage at Savvatevo. Bequests and royal patronage meant the monastery rapidly grew into a rich landholder, and in the 1570s the complex became enclosed within vast fortress walls, useful as a defence against Swedish incursions. Ironically, greater damage was self-inflicted when, from 1668, the monastery endured an eight-year siege for opposing the ecclesiastical reforms of Patriarch Nikon – doubly ironic as Nikon had

PRISONERS OF THE MOTHERLAND

Billed 'the mother of the gulag' by Aleksandr Solzhenitsyn, Solovki was home to one of the USSR's first labour camps. Established in 1923, it was given the name SLON (Solovetsky Lager Osobogo Naznachenia; Solovetsky Special Purpose Camp). In Russian, 'slon' means 'elephant', and upon receiving their sentences, Solovki-bound prisoners grimly joked that they were 'off to see the elephant'.

Back-breaking logging duty, coupled with inadequate tools and clothing, very little sleep and starvation rations, was enough to reduce most prisoners to shells within weeks. Escape from the islands was very difficult, as prisoners had to break out in groups, navigate their way across the sea and then avoid all settlements en route to the Finnish border. In the gulag's history, only three escape attempts were successful.

This wasn't the first time the monastery was used for less-than-pious purposes – 'undesirables' had been shipped off to the White Sea outpost since the reign of Ivan the Terrible. Prisoners of note included Count Pyotr Tolstoy – forebear of novelist and anarcho-pacifist Leo Tolstoy – and Cossack leader Petro Kalnyshevsky, who was incarcerated here for 25 years and died on the island in 1803…aged 111!

been a young monk here (on Anzer Island) – before being betrayed by one of its own.

In a bizarre sideshow to the Crimean War, two British frigates sailed by and bombarded the kremlin with nearly 2000 cannonballs. Given that Russia lost that war, punching a hole in one of the ships and not losing a single man put Solovki back into the minds of Russia's faithful. Donations rolled in and monks arrived to repopulate the monastery, which remained vibrant until the Soviet government closed it in 1920.

Three years later the islands were declared a work camp for 'enemies of the people'. At first, the prisoners were permitted to work fairly freely, keeping up the monastery's botanical garden and libraries. But it wasn't long until the camp was repurposed, turning into one of the USSR's most severe and dreaded Gulag camps. Over 350,000 prisoners from all over the Soviet Union and beyond passed through Solovki, and for 20,000 or so the islands became their grave. The prison was closed in 1939 and replaced by a naval training base.

Restoration work on the badly damaged monastery began in the 1960s. Monks started returning in the late 1980s and the islands acquired Unesco World Heritage listing in 1992. Today the monastic community is flourishing but reconstruction remains a long-term task.

Sights & Activities

Bolshoi Solovetsky Island

★Solovetsky Transfiguration Monastery MONASTERY
(Спасо-Преображенский Соловецкий монастырь; www.solovky.ru; admission ₽200; grounds 8am-10pm, museums 10am-6pm)
This imposing, stone-walled monastery is the heart and soul of the Solovetsky Islands. Founded in 1429, it has played various roles throughout its existence: a hermit's retreat, a vibrant religious community, a rebel enclave that held out against the Patriarch of the Russian Orthodox Church, a fortress victorious against British warships, a gulag for the Soviet Union's damned and a museum. Revived post-*perestroika*, it flourishes once more as a spiritual institution.

The kremlin yard is contained within massive boulder-chunk walls with six sturdy fortress towers topped with conical wood-shingle roofs. These, along with a quivering flurry of church towers and domes, reflect magnificently in Svyatoe Lake. The centrepiece is the 1566 **Transfiguration Cathedral** (Спасо-Преображенский собор), with its blend of Pomorsky architecture, powerful foundations and whitewashed walls, clusters of domes covered in a dense carpet of wooden scales and a dazzling six-level iconostasis upstairs.

Upstairs is the vast dining room, connected to the rest of the complex by covered walkways. Next to it is the **Assumption Church** (Успенская церковь), a cavernous former refectory with sparse photo-history boards focusing especially on the 1992 return of the relics of monastery founders Sts Zosima, Savvaty and Herman.

The **sacristy** (ризница) upstairs was used to house the monastery's treasures, but many artefacts were carted off by the Bolsheviks and destroyed.

The tiny but magnificently mural-covered 1601 **Annunciation Church** (Благовещенская церковь) is entered through an unmarked door, one floor above the main gate.

The **prison** has been in use since the 16th century, first to house those who'd committed crimes against the faith and later to punish those who'd erred against the state. The harshest punishments (leg irons, dreadful food) was reserved for the 'secret' prisoners who arrived with nothing but accompanying papers stating the conditions in which they should be kept.

The monastery complex was heated using three powerful stoves and a series of heating vents that ran through the walls, with underfloor heating used to dry the grain before it was ground into flour. The **17th-century water mill**, in turn, was powered by a network of canals that the industrious monks dug to connect the island's 500-something lakes.

VISITING THE MONASTERY

Entry to the kremlin yard at Solovetsky Transfiguration Monastery, and to some churches within, is free. However, exhibition halls and linking corridors require a 'Riznitsa' (ризница) ticket, purchased inside the sacristy upstairs. Access to the towers and the prison is limited to those on guided tours. Dress code is typical for active monasteries – headscarves for women, trousers for men; no shorts or short skirts allowed.

Solovetsky Forced Labour Camps & Prison 1920-1939 MUSEUM
(Соловецкие лагеря и тюрьма особого назначения (1920–1939); ul Zaozyorskaya 7; adult/student ₽200/150; ⏲10am-7.30pm) Inside former gulag barracks, this excellent exposition (in Russian) takes you through the different stages of the Solovetsky gulag – from punishing 'counter-revoluntionary elements' and providing a slave labour force to build the infamous Belomorsky Canal, to the summary mass executions during the Great Terror of 1937-38.

Bold displays are interspersed with gulag prisoner testimonies and a short black-and-white film at the end merges truth and propaganda – real inmates are the ones not looking at the camera.

A tour by the knowledgeable local archivist (₽400) makes the visit particularly worthwhile; book at the tourist office.

Gora Sekirnaya HISTORICAL SITE
(Секирная гора) Literally translated as Hatchet Mountain, this infamous 71m-high hill was the site of tortures described in Aleksandr Solzhenitsyn's *Gulag Archipelago*. The unassuming hilltop **Ascension Church** (1857–62) that doubles as a lighthouse was used for solitary confinement. With the cold, starvation and ill-treatment came the added terror of visiting Cheka officials who liked to shoot inmates for fun.

At the foot of the stairs leading up to the church, a 1992 cross commemorates all who died on Solovki.

The site is about 10km from the village, 7km beyond the botanical garden towards Savvatyevsky minor monastery. Tours cost about ₽380.

Labyrinth HISTORICAL SITE
(Лабиринт) If you don't have time to visit the mysterious concentric swirls of stones that cover Bolshoi Zayatsky Island, this accessible, reconstructed example is just five minutes' walk south of the Solovki Hotel. Take the right woodland path where the track splits in three and the labyrinth is near the shore.

Botanical Garden GARDENS
(Ботанический сад; admission ₽180; ⏲9am-7.30pm) Around 3km northwest of the village, the botanical garden enjoys a special microclimate – monks have grown vegetables and hothouse fruits here for centuries. For views, climb nearby Alexander Hill, topped by the miniature **Alexander Nevsky Chapel** (1854).

Cape Beluzhy WILDLIFE
(Мыс Белужий) In early summer, white beluga whales breed off Cape Beluzhy (west coast) and raise their young here. Whale-watching tours (₽600 per person, minimum 15 people) involve a 6km walk along the cape to the observation points.

Other Solovetsky Islands

Bolshoy Zayatsky Island ISLAND
(Большой Заяцкий остров; tours ₽550) This small, wind-whipped island is famous for its 13 stone labyrinths, including the largest one in northern Russia. A circular boardwalk loops around the island from the dockside wooden church, passing by numerous stone burial mounds and two forlorn crosses. Bolshoy Zayatsky Island was used for female solitary confinement during gulag years, but not a trace remains.

Anzer Island HISTORICAL SITE
(Остров Анзер) The second-largest island in the archipelago, Anzer Island has its share of stone labyrinths and burial mounds, as well as a scattering of monastic sketes, the oldest dating back to the 17th century. One

MYSTERIES IN STONE

Dating back around 4000 years, concentric swirls of shrub-covered stones known as **labyrinths** occur widely in northern Scandinavia, the Kola Peninsula and the outer Solovetsky Islands. Each has a single entrance/exit and a cairn at its heart. Their purpose is still unknown, but since no human remains have been found in the few labyrinths excavated, it is assumed that they were used for religious ceremonies.

Human and animal remains have been found, however, underneath the **stone mounds** that dot the outer Solovetsky Islands. Given that the remains are relatively few in number, it is believed that only the most unquiet of souls were given a burial on remote islands.

Stones played an important spiritual role in the lives of the Sami ancestors. Anthropomorphic rocks and mounds of rocks scattered around the Kola Peninsula, known as **seids**, are believed to have been worshipped as deities.

of these was used a typhoid hospital in the 1920s, and hundreds of prisoners died here.

Full-day visits to Anzer cost ₽1300 per person.

Tours

Tourist Office TOUR COMPANY
(Соловецкий центр гостеприимства) Offers a whole slew of excursions. Thematic tours within the monastery (in English from ₽380) can be far more insightful than wandering around alone. Minibus trips to rural sites save exhausting pedal power and avert the risks of getting lost in the forest. Tour pricing assumes a minimum of 10 (sometimes 15) people, but individuals can add their names to a sign-up list. Based in the main village on Bolshoi Solovetsky Island.

Sleeping

With the exception of Hotel Priyut and Solovetskaya Sloboda, accommodation options operate from early June to early September. Basic camping on private land is possible – contact the tourist office for details.

Peterburgskaya Hostel HOSTEL $
(Петербургская Гостиница; ☎8183590-375; dm/s/d/tr ₽450/1100/1600/2250) Once a 19th-century inn, the Peterburgskaya Hostel is located in a large wooden building beside the monastery walls and its range of spartan rooms caters primarily to groups. The overall vibe is one of function over form.

★**Hotel Priyut** HOTEL $$
(Гостиница Приют; ☎8183590-297; shelter@atnet.ru; ul Primorskaya 11; s/d from ₽2050/2700) Charming, family-run Priyut comprises two homely converted houses. The cheaper Yellow House (shared bathrooms) is adorably kitted out with dried flowers and endearing bric-a-brac, while the Green House's downstairs rooms have private facilities. Upstairs rooms enjoy fabulous monastery views, and there's a guest *banya*. The delightful **cafe** (breakfast/dinner ₽300/410) opens only for resident groups.

Hotel Solo HOTEL $$
(Гостиница Соло; ☎8183590-246; solo-vky@yandex.ru; ul Kovalyova 8; s/d/tr from ₽3100/3200/4200, s/d without bathroom ₽1600/2500; 📶) Compact, wood-panelled, mosquito-net-equipped rooms, most with equally compact bathrooms. Cheapies share clean facilities. 'Extras' cost extra, be they a kettle (₽100 a day) or wi-fi (₽200 an hour!).

Solovetskaya Sloboda HOTEL $$
(Гостиница Соловецкая слобода; ☎8183590-288; www.solsloboda.ru; ul Zaozyornaya 17a; d/q/lyux/apt ₽3700/4000/5000/8000; 📶) Centrally located brick hotel, its modern rooms ideal for couples, groups and families. There's functioning wi-fi – a rare beast on the island – and a restaurant serving a mix of European and Russian cuisine.

Solovki Hotel HOTEL $$$
(Гостиница Соловки-Отель; ☎8183590-331; www.solovki-tour.ru; ul Zaozyornaya 26; s/d/lyux from ₽5000/5400/8700) With three double-storey log houses, a fine restaurant and a woodsy setting, this is the island's poshest hotel. Standard rooms are cosy, though more expensive ones have twee pseudo-antique painted headboards and share a sitting room with a giant bearskin. Rates include breakfast.

Eating

Locals are very proud of Solovetskaya herring, which you can sample from July onwards in pies and in salted, fried and raw forms.

Hotel Solo Cafe RUSSIAN $
(ul Kovalyova 8; mains from ₽160; ⏲9am-10pm) Open to nonguests, this friendly cafe serves inexpensive, tasty dishes – from filled bliny and grilled fish to hearty *solyanka* (a soup made from pickled vegetables and potato).

Solovetsky Raipo SUPERMARKET $
(Соловецкое Райпо; ul Zaozyornaya; ⏲9am-9pm) Marked simply 'Produkty' (Продукты), this is the island's best-stocked grocery.

★**Izba** RUSSIAN $$
(Изба; ul Zaozyornaya 26; mains ₽350-560; ⏲8am-10pm) Don't let Izba's cutesy log-cabin-with-folky-embroidered-curtains interior fool you – Solovki Hotel's restaurant serves the most sophisticated fare on the island, from cod poached in milk and expertly grilled meats to handmade fish *pelmeni* (Russian-style ravioli) and Solovki's very own herring. Help it down with a 'morozhka-ice' – one of its signature 'northern' cocktails made with lingonberry alcohol (₽240). Wonderful service, too.

Information

Bring plenty of cash with you as there are no ATMs on the island and cards are not readily accepted.

Tourist Office (Соловецкий центр гостеприимства; ☎8183590-321; www.solovky.ru; Peterburgskaya Hostel; ⊙9am-7pm mid-May–mid-Oct) Information and a wide range of tours. Some English spoken. The website is a comprehensive and regularly updated source of info on the islands.

Getting There & Away

AIR

Planes are unable to land in fog or strong winds. As weather here can change incredibly rapidly, departures from Solovki can be confirmed only an hour before – ie once the incoming plane has actually left Arkhangelsk.

Nordavia (Нордавиа; ☎800-200 0055; www.nordavia.ru/eng) Flights to Solovki from Arkhangelsk (one way/return ₽4495/8890, 50 minutes) between April and late October. Flights depart at 1.30pm on Tuesday and Sunday, with the return flight at 3pm. In July and August there are additional flights on alternate Saturdays and in August on Wednesdays as well.

BOAT

From early June to late August, two daily passenger ferries run from Rabocheostrovsk to Solovki, as well as daily hydrofoil services to Solovki from Belomorsk. Ice usually prevents sailings in May but sporadic ferry services might continue as late as October. Ferries moor at Prichal Tamarin (Причал Тамарин), a jetty northwest of the village.

Metel-4 (Метель-4; ☎81458-56 060; www.prichalrk.ru; adult/child ₽1000/500) Departs Rabocheostrovsk for Solovki (two to three hours) at 12.30pm, leaving Solovki at 4pm.

Sapphire (Сапфир; ☎81437-54 200; www.belomorye.com) Departs Belomorsk at 10.30am Monday to Friday and at 8.30am on Saturday and Sunday (four hours). Return services run at 8.30pm on weekdays and 6.30pm on weekends.

Vasily Kosyakov (Василий Косяков; ☎81458-56 060; www.prichalrk.ru; adult/child ₽1000/500) Departs Rabocheostrovsk for Solovki (two to three hours) at 8am, leaving Solovki at 6pm.

Getting Around

Veloprokat (Велопрокат; per hr/day from ₽80/400; ⊙mid-Jun–mid-Sep) Rents everything from single-gear Soviet sturdies to mountain bikes – the latter are best for tackling the unpaved, bumpy roads. A deposit in the form of a valuable (driver's licence, watch, mobile phone) is required.

Arkhangelsk Архангельск

☎8182 / POP 350,985 / ⊙MOSCOW

In the 17th century Arkhangelsk was immensely important as Russia's only seaport and in 1693 Peter the Great began shipbuilding operations here, launching the Russian navy's tiny first ship, the *Svyatoy Pavel*, the following year. Though the founding of St Petersburg in 1703 pushed Arkhangelsk out of the limelight, it later became a centre for Arctic exploration, a core of the huge northern lumber industry and a crucial supply point during the 20th-century world wars.

Only a few historical timber houses remain from the city's heyday, but there's a cosmopolitan charm to the city's parks and waterfront promenade, and Arkhangelsk's lively jazz scene and smattering of good restaurants make it a great stopover en route to two of the region's big attractions: the Solovetsky Islands and the beautifully preserved wooden architecture of Malye Karely.

Arkhangelsk was also the dystopian setting for much of Robert Harris' dark novel *Archangel*, and fans of the book may find themselves feeling decidedly jumpy at the sight of Stalinlike shadows in the nearby forest.

Sights

★Northern Naval Museum MUSEUM

(Северный Военно-морской музей; www.sevmormuseum.ru; nab Severnoy Dviny 80; admission ₽100; ⊙11am-7pm Tue-Sun; 🚌1, 54) Beautifully presented nautical exhibits cluster around the striking centrepiece – the prow of a ship – in the light-filled main hall of Arkhangelsk's most modern museum. Lose yourself amid fishing and whaling tools, maps of northern seas and fine models of icebreakers, and then head upstairs to check out the miraculous rescue of the passengers of naval ship *Cheliuskinets*, who lived for three weeks on ice when their ship was crushed. Our kingdom for English captioning, though.

Gostiny Dvor HISTORICAL BUILDING

(Гостиный Двор; nab Severnoy Dviny 85/86; per exhibition ₽80; ⊙10am-9pm Tue-Sun; 🚌1, 4) In the 17th and 18th centuries, Arkhangelsk's heart and soul was this merchants' yard, a grand, turreted brick trading centre built between 1668 and 1684. The huge, fortress-like complex has been largely restored and its exhibition rooms host anything from contemporary photography and landscape paintings by regional talent to literary displays honouring Tove Jansson, the creator of the Moomins.

★ **Regional Studies Museum** MUSEUM
(Архангельский областной краеведческий музей; pl Lenina 2; adult/child ₽160/80; ⏲10am-6pm Tue-Sun; 🚌1, 54) The history section charts the development of the harsh north, from its settlement by dispossessed and exiled peasantry in the 1930s, to the Gulag camps, to the suffering of the 'second St Petersburg' during WWII, with the second-highest number of civilian casualties in Russia. Downstairs, the extensive nature section shows off the taxidermied wildlife of the land shaped by retreating ice.

Fine Arts Museum ART GALLERY
(Музей изобразительных искусств; pl Lenina 2; admission ₽200; ⏲10am-5pm Wed-Mon; 🚌1, 54) Arkhangelsk's most compelling art gallery has regularly changing exhibitions that range from modern reflections on Soviet propaganda to nude studies. Upstairs are impressive icons, bone carvings and decorative art displays.

Prospekt Chumbarova-Luchinskogo STREET
(Проспект Чумбарова-Лучинского; pr Chumbarova-Luchinskogo) Arkhangelsk's appealing pedestrian street is lined with a few surviving traditional timber houses that are in the process of being restored, as well as a score of whimsical statues that passers-by rub for good luck.

Naberezhnaya Severnoy Dviny PARK
(Набережная Северной Двины) Given the first hint of warm summer weather, Arkhangelskians emerge to stroll this broad promenade and loiter in any of its many seasonal beer-and-shashlyk tents.

★ **EK Plotnikova House-Museum** ART GALLERY
(Усадебный Дом Е. К. Плотниковой; Pomorskaya ul 1; adult/student ₽150/80; ⏲10am-5pm Wed-Mon; 🚌1, 11) This historical building houses an impressive collection of Russian art from the 18th to the 20th centuries and charts the switch to 'critical realism' in the late 19th century, when peasants and other 'common people' became the subjects of paintings. Highlights include wintry landscapes, *Fugitives in Siberia* and *A Grey Beard but a Lusty Heart*.

AA Borisov Museum MUSEUM
(Музей А. А. Борисова; Pomorskaya ul 3; admission ₽100; ⏲10am-5pm Wed-Mon; 🚌1, 11) Artwork by AA Borisov, dedicated to the Arctic scenery of Novaya Zemlya and settlement of the north.

War Victory Monument 1941-1945 MONUMENT
(Монумент Победы в войне 1941-1945; pl Mira; 🚌1, 10) Memorial consisting of an eternal flame flanked by grim-faced statues of servicemen, honouring the fallen of the Great Patriotic War.

Peter I Statue MONUMENT
(Памятник Петру Первому; nab Severnoi Dviny) This windswept take on Peter the Great and the unexotic River Terminal building both feature on Russia's ₽500 banknotes.

Tours

Kompaniya Solovki TOUR COMPANY
(Компания Соловки; ☎8182-655 008; www.solovkibp.ru; 5th fl, Troitsky pr 37; ⏲10am-6pm Mon-Fri; 🚌1, 11) Good range of tour options to the Solovetsky Islands, Kargopol and around, White Sea regional tours and more.

Pomor Tur TOUR COMPANY
(Помор Тур; ☎8182-203 320; www.pomor-tur.ru; ul Voskresenskaya 99; ⏲10am-7pm Mon-Fri; 🚌1, 10) City and regional excursions, including themed tours to the Solovetsky Islands and one-week paddle-steamer cruises along the Dvina to Kotlas/Veliky Ustyug.

Festivals & Events

Adventure Race 80 dg SAILING REGATTA
(www.rusarc.com) Since 2009 Arkhangelsk has been both a stopover and the finishing point of adventurous annual regattas organised by Rusarc. In 2013 almost a dozen countries took part in the challenging race from Arkhangelsk to Franz Josef Land. Check the website for future Arctic sailing challenges.

Sleeping

Hostel Lomonosov HOSTEL $
(Хостел Ломоносов; ☎8-952-254 4445; www.hostellomonosov.com; pr Lomonosova 84; dm ₽400-480; 📶; 🚌53) One of only two hostels in town, Lomonosov has by far the best location. The dorms are sparsely furnished but clean, and enthusiastic staff offer discounts for students: ask when booking.

Arkhangelsk

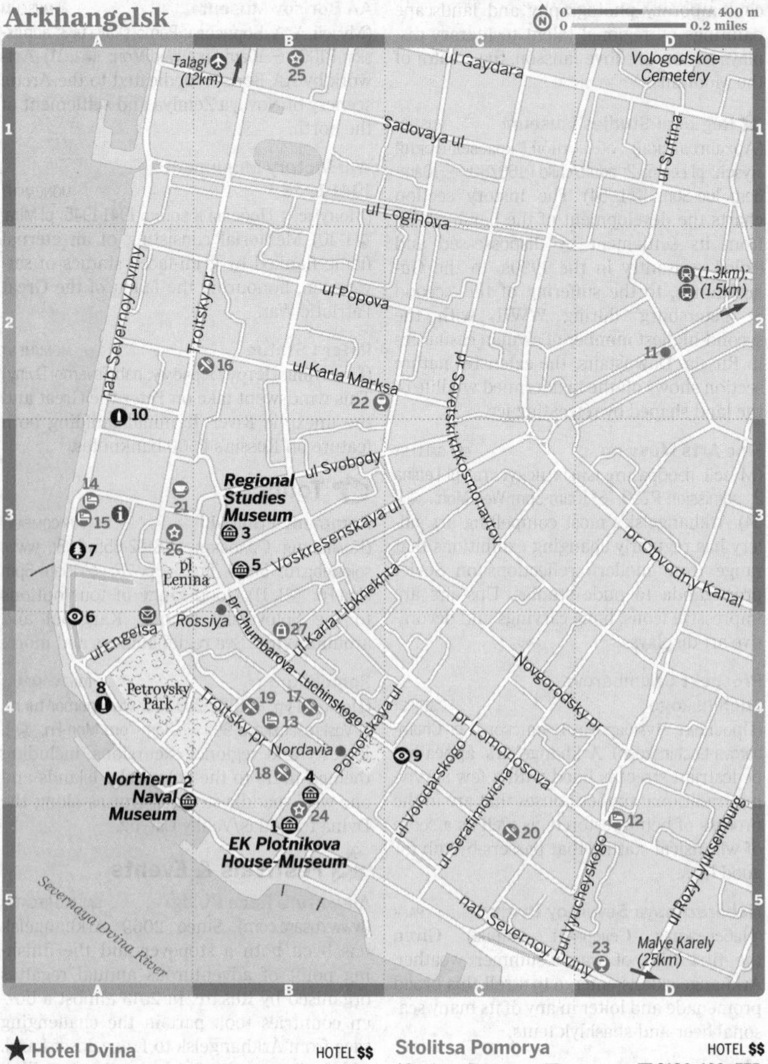

★ Hotel Dvina HOTEL **$$**

(Гостиница Двина; ☎8182-288 888; www.hoteldvina.ru; Troitsky pr 52; s/d/ste from ₽2900/3400/8000; 📶; 🚌1, 11) This 13-storey pink Soviet beauty is a super-central, international-standard hotel that's been tastefully refurbished with quality linens, tiled bathrooms, gym and a delightful restaurant with an extensive Russian/European menu. Ask for mosquito netting for your window if it's missing. Very helpful desk staff speak English.

Stolitsa Pomorya HOTEL **$$**

(Отель Столица Поморья; ☎8182-423 575; http://hotelarh.ru; nab Severnoy Dviny 88; s/d/ste from ₽2800/3400/5000; 📶; 🚌1, 54) Appealing business hotel with a cracking location overlooking the Dvina. The compact, modern rooms are particularly well geared towards solo travellers and perks include an on-site *banya* and massage centre.

Pur Navolok Hotel HOTEL **$$$**

(Отель Пур-Наволок; ☎8182-217 200; www.purnavolok.ru; nab Severnoy Dviny 88; s/d/ste from ₽4200/5100/9600; 📶; 🚌1, 54) Though the exterior resembles an air traffic control tower,

Arkhangelsk

Top Sights

1	EK Plotnikova House-Museum	B5
2	Northern Naval Museum	A4
3	Regional Studies Museum	B3

Sights

4	AA Borisov Museum	B4
5	Fine Arts Museum	B3
6	Gostiny Dvor	A4
7	Naberezhnaya Severnoy Dviny	A3
8	Peter I Statue	A4
9	Prospekt Chumbarova-Luchinskogo	C4
10	War Victory Monument 1941-1945	A2

Activities, Courses & Tours

	Kompaniya Solovki	(see 4)
11	Pomor Tur	D2

Sleeping

12	Hostel Lomonosov	D5
13	Hotel Dvina	B4
14	Pur Navolok Hotel	A3
15	Stolitsa Pomorya	A3

Eating

16	Bratya Grill	B2
17	El Fuego	B4
18	Restoran Pomorsky	B4
19	Sigma	B4
20	Treskoed	C5

Drinking & Nightlife

21	Blin-House	A3
22	Historic Route 66	B2
23	Lock Stock	D5

Entertainment

24	Arkhangelsk Jazz	B5
25	Koleso	B1
26	Philharmonia	A3

Shopping

27	Dom Knigi	B4

the professionally run Pur Navolok offers bright, international-style rooms (some with beach views) accessed by glass elevator and there's a sauna/plunge pool/hammam complex to ward off the northern chill. Rates include extensive buffet breakfasts and the panorama bar is a fun place to hang out.

Eating

Bratya Grill RUSSIAN $

(Братья Гриль; Troitsky pr 104; mains ₽250-330; 9am-midnight Mon-Fri, 24hr (but closed 8am-9am) Sat & Sun; 1, 54) As befitting the name, buzzy 'Brothers Grill' specialises in grilled meats, though there are salads and cakes for noncarnivorous customers. The young staff are attentive, the drinks are unusual (cucumber lemonade, y'all?) and the wallpaper looks like something out of a demented fairy tale.

Sigma SUPERMARKET $

(Сигма; Troitsky pr 52; 9am-10pm) Large, well-stocked supermarket.

★ **Treskoed** SEAFOOD $$

(Трескоед; pr Chumbarova-Luchinskogo 8; mains ₽230-400; noon-11pm; 1, 11) Appropriately named 'Cod-eater', this folksy 'restaurant museum' specialises in Neptune's subjects. While you're waiting for your baked 'tsar-style' cod, cod and salmon *pelmeni*, *ukha* or pikefish cutlets, you can learn about the Pomorsky region's fishing trade from the surrounding displays, as well as what a *grabilka*, an *endova* and a *bezmen* are for. We'll be testing you!

Restoran Pomorsky RUSSIAN $$

(Ресторан Поморский; Troitsky pr; mains ₽250-900; noon-midnight) Set in log-cabin-effect alcoves, this local favourite serves imaginatively named dishes such as Bride of Three Bridegrooms (salmon caviar bliny) and the Herder Bag (pork stuffed with cheese). The affordable business lunch (₽230) is filling, but not a thrill for the senses. It's hidden on the rear of the 3rd floor of the office building above Polina Cafe.

El Fuego STEAKHOUSE $$$

(pr Chumbarova-Luchinskogo 39; steak ₽580-3900; noon-2am; 1, 11) Top-notch dining for the discerning carnivore. Extremely knowledgeable waitstaff, an exemplary steak menu that ranges from tender veal to Kobe ribeye, and chefs of international calibre make for a special night out. Its grill-scented, dark surrounds feel especially cosy during winter.

Drinking

Blin-House CAFE

(Блин Хаус; Troitsky pr 94; ; 1, 6, 10) Branches of this appealing chain pepper the city. Great for tea, coffee, milkshakes, imaginative cocktails, sweet and savoury bliny, burgers, sausage-and-chips combos and stomach-warming mulled wine.

Lock Stock PUB
(www.lockstockpub.ru; nab Severnoy Dviny 30; 11am-1am; 1, 4, 11) Hugely popular Anglo pub with authentic local-boozer decor and a hugely comprehensive list of ales, stouts and beers from England, Scotland and elsewhere.

Historic Route 66 BAR
(pr Lomonosova 177; noon-2am; 1, 6, 10) American-style diner/bar with orange leather seats, a surprisingly good selection of English beers as well as its palatable own brew and live bands on weekends.

Entertainment

★Koleso LIVE MUSIC
(Колесо; 8182-209 799; www.arkoleso.ru; ul Gaydara 4/1; 5pm-late; 1, 6) The 'Wheel', an Arkhangelsk institution, hosts rock, thrash metal, folk, rockabilly and country gigs from local and visiting acts on weekends and some weeknights. Check the regularly updated website to see what's on while you're in town.

Arkhangelsk Jazz LIVE MUSIC
(Архангельск Джаз; www.arkhangelsk-jazz.com; Pomorskaya ul 3; admission from ₽200; from 8pm; 1, 54) This rickety-looking historic building plays host to the city's most exciting jazz and blues events. An international jazz festival takes place here in May and live gigs take place on weekends.

Philharmonia CLASSICAL MUSIC
(Поморская филармония; 8182-215 669; www.pomorfil.ru; pl Lenina 1; ticket office noon-7pm Mon-Sat; 1, 54) The Philharmonia hosts orchestral concerts and operas, while its **Kamerny Zal** (ul Karla Marksa 3) stages organ and chamber music in the 1768 Lutheran church of St Catherine.

Shopping

Dom Knigi BOOKSTORE
(Дом Книги; pl Lenina 3; 10am-8pm Mon-Fri, to 6pm Sat & Sun) Stocks good city and regional maps plus a few guidebooks.

Information

Post Office (Почта; Voskresenskaya ul 5; 8am-9pm Mon-Fri, 9am-6pm Sat & Sun) Main post office.

Tourist Office (Туристический информационный центр; 8182-214 082; www.pomorland.info; ul Svobody 8; 9am-1pm & 2-5pm Mon-Thu, to 4pm Fri; 1, 54) Enthusiastic, well-informed, English-speaking staff are an inspiring source of information for the city and the whole of the Arkhangelsk region. Extensive website.

Getting There & Away

AIR

Arkhangelsk's main airport, **Talagi** (Талаги; www.arhaero.ru), is 12km northeast of the centre. Most flights are operated by **Nordavia** (Нордавиа; www.nordavia.ru/eng) and **Rossiya** (Россия ; www.rossiya-airlines.ru/en). Destinations include Moscow (1¾ hours, up to four daily), Murmansk (two hours, five weekly), Solovetsky Islands (50 minutes, Tuesday, Wednesday, Saturday and Sunday in summer), St Petersburg (1½ hours, up to five daily) and Tromsø, Norway (five hours, Monday and Friday).

Weather permitting, further Solovetsky Islands flights leave in small planes from **Vaskovo airport** (Аэропорт Васьково; 8182-462 166), 20km southwest of the city centre.

BUS

From the **bus station** (Автовокзал; ul 23-y Gvardeyskoy Divizii 13) services run to Veliky Ustyug (₽1310, 11½ hours, 8am daily) and Kargopol (₽890, 13 hours, 8.15am Wednesday, Saturday and Sunday).

TRAIN

Two or three daily trains run to Moscow's Yaroslavsky station (₽1864, 20 to 23 hours) via Vologda (₽1157, 11 to 14 hours) and Yaroslavl (₽1397, 15½ to 18 hours). Daily train 009 for St Petersburg (₽1981, 24½ hours) departs at 8.43pm. Train 671 heads south every other day at 9.49pm to Nyandoma (₽871, 9¼ hours) via Kem (₽1094, 15½ hours), with one carriage detaching en route and continuing to Murmansk (₽1716, 30 hours) – this train arrives in Nyandoma at 7.06am, ideal for reaching Kargopol.

Getting Around

The **2GIS** (2ГИС; www.2gis.ru) app offers complete coverage of all the city transport routes.

Appearing as MR Vokzal (МР Вокзал) on destination boards, the River Terminal is a major hub for city buses and *marshrutky*. From here the rare bus 110 runs to Vaskovo airport and frequent route 12 runs every few minutes to Talagi airport via pl Lenina and northern Troitsky pr.

Handy buses 4, 41 and 54 run down ul Voskresenkaya from the railway station and then turn east along Troitsky pr at pl Lenina. Bus 11 makes a loop around the city centre from MR Vokzal, and buses that run up and down Troitsky pr include 1, 4, 12 and 44.

Malye Karely

Малые Корелы

Set in pretty rolling dales 25km southeast of Arkhangelsk's centre, the delightful open-air **Malye Karely Wooden Architecture Museum** (Музей деревянного зодчества и Народного Искусства Малые Корелы; www.korely.ru; admission ₽150; 10am-5pm Jul-May, to 9pm Jun; 104, 108) is Arkhangelsk's foremost attraction. It features dozens of 16th- to 19th-century wooden buildings – churches, windmills, peasant houses and barns – relocated here from rural villages during the 1970s, and its authentic surrounds have been used as a film set on local and international productions. The museum is divided into four sectors, with buildings grouped according to their geographical origin. Allow at least two hours for sightseeing.

You enter the **Kargolopsko-Onezhsky sector** past a series of boxy windmills, inside the largest of which you can admire the complete interior workings. Cut across to the impressive 1669 **Ascension Church** (Вознесенская церковь) with its top-knot of wooden domes and forest-scented, icon-plastered interior. The 19th-century **Tretyakov House** displays curious furnishings of the era, while the quaint little **Miracle Worker's Chapel** (Часовня Макария Унженского; Chasovnya Makariya Unzhenskogo) has retained intact its eight-panelled octagonal ceiling icons ('skies').

To reach the other sectors, take the path heading north from the **bell tower** by the Ascension Church, descend the steep steps, cross the river and walk up another flight of stairs; you'll have to return the same way.

The villagelike **Dvinskoy sector** consists of a smattering of wealthy peasant houses. Notice the curious **Rusinova house**, former home of Old Believers, with a tiny chapel hidden in a back room. Unlike other Russian peasants, each family member had his or her own eating utensils – if a guest used some, they were then thrown out. The sector's centrepiece is the splendid 1672 **St George's Church** (Георгиевская церковь), displaying a small but valuable selection of remarkable wayside crosses, including one gigantic example that virtually fills the nave.

In both **Pinezhsky sector** and **Mezensky sector**, check out the *chyornye izby* (black cottages), so called because their lack of a chimney resulted in smoke-stained walls. Mezensky sector's 19th-century **Elkino House** has an exhibition on Pomor fishing and boat building and there's a great view over the river below.

Just 200m from the museum entrance is the holiday-hotel complex **Turisticheskaya Derevnya Malye Karely** (Туристическая деревня Малые Карелы; 8182-462 472; www.karely.ru; d/apt/ste from ₽4900/6200/8500; ; 104, 108), which consists of modern timber cottages and apartments. The excellent restaurant has an olde-Russia theme, serving anything from grilled meats and poached fish to *vareniki*.

Every 20 to 30 minutes, little bus 104 from Troitsky pr in central Arkhangelsk runs all the way to Malye Karely (₽45, 45 minutes), while bus 108 runs directly from the railway station. Both terminate opposite the hotel complex.

KOLA PENINSULA

КОЛЬСКИЙ ПОЛУОСТРОВ

The Kola Peninsula is a 100,000-sq-km knob of tundra, bogs and low mountains between the White and Barents Seas. Lying almost entirely north of the Arctic Circle, its mesmerising expanses of wilderness are fabulous places to be dazzled by the aurora borealis or midnight sun.

Central Kola

Mineral strata beneath the Khibiny and Lovozero mountains contain a treasure trove of exotic minerals that get the world's geologists and rock collectors salivating. Apatity has secret museums, Lovozero is the heart of Russia's Sami community and Kirovsk is the gateway to pristine wilderness and has the region's best skiing. Wilderness lovers will find Central Kola particularly rewarding, with husky and reindeer sledding on the menu, while those with an interest in indigenous cultures should know that new Sami-related attractions have also been making an appearance.

Apatity — Апатиты

81555 / POP 58,681 / MOSCOW

Central Kola's second-biggest town, Apatity is an *akademgorodok*, a town of chemists responsible for processing the raw product from Kirovsk's apatite mines (hence the name) and home to nine research institutes. Several of

ADVANCE PLANNING

If you wish to properly explore the Kola Peninsula, its remote towns and attractions are not places to turn up on spec. *We cannot stress this enough:* call ahead and book tours well in advance, lest you turn up at closed doors.

those have 'museums' – by appointment, more specialist visitors can arrange a guided visit to a second **Mineralogy Museum** (Минералогический музей; ☎81555-79 739; ul Fersmana 14; ⊙9am-5pm Mon-Fri by arrangement) FREE on the top floor of the Kola Scientific Centre. Friendly academics speak English and can show off more than 900 types of minerals and ores, many of them rare and unique. The museum is an easy stroll downhill from pl Lenina on Apatity's main drag, ul Lenina.

Experienced tour firm **South Kola** (Южная Кола; ☎81555-74 178; www.kolak-lub.com/southkola; room 114, Hotel Ametist; ⊙10am-6pm Mon-Fri, 11am-5pm Sat) can show you around the **North-Russian Exploration Museum** (Музей истории изучения и освоения Европейского севера России; Akademgorodok 40a; admission ₽60; ⊙2-5pm Mon-Fri), which showcases the history of the region as well as Sami culture. Run by the super-enthusiastic Sergei Burenin and wife Viktoria, South Kola also offers tailor-made mineral-collecting, snowmobile and fishing tours on and around Kola's White Sea coast, and cruises to the Solovetsky Islands. Its office is within Apatity's conveniently central Soviet monstrosity Hotel Ametist. Across the street, **Hotel Apatity** (Гостиница Апатиты; ☎953-750-8472; http://apatity.su; ul Lenina 2a; d/tr ₽1500/2000; 📶) trumps all local competition with its cosy, carpeted rooms, functioning wi-fi and self-catering kitchen. Nearby, **Dzhaga** (Джага; ul Fersmana 18; pizza from ₽300; ⊙11am-9pm; 📶) serves arguably the best pizza in Arctic Russia.

From Apatity's pl Lenina, buses run to Murmansk (₽472, 4½ hours, four daily), Kirovsk (₽50, 25 minutes, three to six daily) and Monchegorsk (₽169, 1½ hours, four to six daily).

Kirovsk Кировск

☎81531 / POP 28,074 / ⊙MOSCOW

Kirovsk is a miners' town that owes its existence to the world's purest deposits of apatite, as testified by the giant lump of the stuff on a pedestal along main ul Lenina and a cute *gornyachok* (little miner) sculpture nearby. There's a grim beauty to the industrial detritus of Kirovsk, founded in 1929, with gaping shells of abandoned Soviet buildings and open-pit mines set against the backdrop of Lake Veliky Vudyavr and the surrounding snow-covered mountains.

With its own microclimate, Kirovsk really comes into its own in the long winter, with a surprisingly good skiing scene that lasts until mid-May and local daredevils freeriding off-piste even after the ski lifts shut down for the season. In winter, ice skaters and *morzhi* (hardy Russians who swim year-round, cutting swimming holes in lakes in winter) take to the frozen lakes and sculptors take up chisels at the Snow Village. In the brief warmer months, Kirovsk's cluster of hotels, located within walking distance of the central clock tower ('Big Ben'), makes a good springboard for rambles in the surrounding wilderness.

You can find a super-detailed online map of Kirovsk at www.kartami.ru/kirovskmurmanskoy.

Sights

★Snow Village THEME PARK
(Снежная Деревня; adult/child from ₽400/200; ⊙4-9pm Mon-Fri, 11am-9pm Sat & Sun Dec-Mar; 👪) Every November, ice sculptors from all over the region make their way to Kirovsk to chisel into existence the snowy halls and tunnels of the Snow Village, wowing visitors with ice sculptures and annually changing themed displays carved into walls – from snowy pharaohs in chariots to fairy-tale creatures.

For extra thrills, ride a giant banana attached to a snowmobile or marry your sweetie in the Ice Chapel. The Snow Villlage is located just beyond the botanical gardens.

Polar-Alpine Botanical Gardens GARDENS
(Полярно-альпийский ботанический сад; ☎81531-51 436; www.pabgi.ru; ⊙9am-4pm Tue-Sat Jun-Sep by arrangement) Russia's vast, northernmost botanical gardens and its special hothouses nurturing tropical plants can be accessed by tour only (book in advance) at 9.30am, 11am, 1.30pm and 3pm (2pm on Saturdays), while the 2km summer-only eco-trail climbs to the alpine tundra. Take buses 1, 12, 16 or 105 (₽19) towards Kukisvumchorr ('25km'), north of Lake Bolshoy Vudyavr, alight by the turn-off on the left before reaching '25km' and walk for 1.5km.

WORTH A TRIP

KOLA'S WHITE SEA COAST

With rafting, amethyst hunting, salmon fishing and petroglyph gawking among its offerings, the Kola Peninsula's unspoilt southern shore is one of the region's offbeat delights. The **Varzuga River** is famous in angling circles for its first-class fly fishing, with the prized Atlantic salmon found in remarkable abundance. Keen (and cashed-up) anglers can contact the UK-based **Roxtons** (www.roxtons.com) for information on all-inclusive six-day Varzuga packages. Just over 140km to the northeast, river camps near the coast's biggest town, **Umba**, also offer good, and far cheaper, spots to cast a line. South Kola (p298) specialises in the Umba region.

Northwest of Umba, the cryptic petroglyphs (2nd to 3rd millennium BC) of **Lake Kanozero** have intrigued and bewildered experts since their discovery in 1997. Rafting tours stop at the island site. Between Umba and Varzuga, a gravel road takes rock spotters to the **Tersky Coast**, where amethyst stones litter the coastline. Contact Kola Travel (p300) for details on mineralogical and rafting expeditions. East of Tersky coast is a patch of genuine desert where humans rarely set foot; wild horses can be spotted near there. For wildlife spotting beneath the waves, team up with the **Arctic Circle PADI Dive Center** (☎8-925-381 2243; www.pkrug.ru) to go ice diving, snorkelling with beluga whales and more.

Activities

A modern cable car ski lift was being built at research. When completed, it will connect the slopes of Bolshoy Vudyavr with the Old Ski Station. Think twice before joining local freeriders off-piste, as every year the mountains claim their due through avalanches.

Bolshoy Vudyavr Ski Station SKIING
(Горнолыжный комплекс 'Большой Вудъявр'; ☎800-200 2000; www.bigwood.ru; 📶) The best of Kirovsk's three ski stations, boasting modern lifts (two hour/day pass ₽400/1100), downhill runs suitable for all abilities and lit-up slopes during the winter. Ski and snowboard rental is ₽140/700 per hour/day; bring ID to hire the equipment. It's just across the mountain east of Kirovsk, but 12km away by road (around ₽500 by taxi).

Khibiny Mountains HIKING
(Хибины) Divided by deep valleys, the bald, barren Khibiny range throws down the gauntlet to experienced hikers. Challenges include anything from strenuous day hikes to multiday wilderness expeditions. Note that though the mountains only rise to 1200m above sea level, weather can be extreme and fast changing, so go with knowledgeable locals.

Old Ski Station SKIING
Immediately above town, a day on the slopes here is cheaper than elsewhere, but you'll have to brave the scary Soviet chairlift until the new cable car is completed.

Sleeping & Eating

Hotel prices rise around 30% in ski season (December to May).

Hotel Gornitsa HOTEL $$
(Гостиница Горница; ☎81531-59 111; www.gornitsahotel.com; ul Dzerzhinskogo 19; s/d/tr/q ₽1700/2800/3900/4900; 📶) This unpretentious, family-style 17-room hotel is in fantastic nick, with breakfast included in the price of the en suite rooms. Winter visitors will appreciate the underfloor heating in bathrooms, and the presence of the sauna (from ₽600 per hour).

Hotel Severnaya HOTEL $$$
(Гостиница Северная; ☎81531-33 100; www.bigwood.ru; pr Lenina 11; s/d/ste from ₽3000/4000/6000; 📶) This forest-green, outwardly classy, neoclassical-styled hotel has 61 good-sized rooms, some of which have massive bathtubs. It's central, modern and the staff are obliging. Ski storage and transport to Bolshoy Vudyavr ski station available on request.

Hotel Ekkos HOTEL $$$
(Гостиница Эккос; ☎81531-32 716; pr Lenina 12b; s/d/apt ₽3200/4400/7200; 📶) This memorable 'castle' behind the Kirov statue may look a bit ramshackle from the outside, but the renovated rooms and four-person apartments tell a different story. Breakfast is available on request and there's a communal kitchen for self-caterers.

NORTHERN LIGHTS

Between October and March, the Kola Peninsula is one of the best places on earth to witness the aurora borealis, the natural phenomenon that has been wowing both locals and travellers alike since time immemorial. Spirals, waves and ripples of green (and sometimes yellow, white, red, blue or purple), caused by the collisions between electrically charged particles from the sun entering the earth's atmosphere, move across the dark sky.

The Northern Lights are the subject of many Sami legends, and the Kola Sami gather to watch the spectacle unfold above Lake Lovozero, one of the better places for viewing due to relative lack of light pollution. Murmansk-based tour companies (p303) organise ventures into the tundra in search of the Northern Lights, but bear in mind that your quarry is unpredictable and not visible on a daily basis. Success depends on the weather, so you'll need plenty of time and a bit of luck.

Cafe Schokolad CAFE $
(Кафе Шоколад; ul Olimpiyskaya 17; mains from ₽150; ⏲11am-9pm) Cosy branch of the popular cafe chain inside the Olimp shopping centre. Come here for hot chocolate, sweet and savoury bliny, fried-egg-and-bacon brunches and strong coffee.

Fusion RUSSIAN, JAPANESE $$
(mains ₽210-480; ⏲11am-midnight; 📶) This entertainment complex houses a casual, luridly painted cafe downstairs and Kirovsk's smartest restaurant upstairs. The menu at both runs the gamut from schnitzel and *pelmeni* to pizza, kimchi soup and decent sushi rolls. Your typical Russian restaurant, then.

Information

Tourist Office (Туристический информационный центр; ☎81531-55 711; www.kirovsk.ru/tourism; pr Lenina 7; ⏲9am-1pm & 2-5pm Mon-Fri) Maps and info on the area.

Getting There & Away

Frequent *marshrutky* and local buses to Apatity (₽50, 30 minutes) pick up along the main ul Lenina.

A **ticket office** (Билетная касса; ☎81531-94 160; ul Yubileynaya 13; ⏲8.30am-7pm Mon-Fri, to 4pm Sat) sells tickets for buses to Murmansk (₽554, 5½ hours, four daily) via Monchegorsk (₽209, 1½ hours), leaving from next to the Kaskad shopping centre, across the street. It also sells train tickets ex Apatity.

Monchegorsk Мончегорск

☎81536 / POP 44,007 / ⏲MOSCOW

Though 'Moncha' means 'beautiful' in Sami, and though its mountain-fringed setting on the vast Bolshaya Imandra Lake is undeniably idyllic, visitors to Monchegorsk may be put off by the noxious emissions belched out by nearby factories. Still, the town makes for a convenient stopover if you're looking to explore the Lovozero area and delve into Sami culture.

Monchegorsk-based **Kola Travel** (☎81536-71 313; www.kolatravel.com; pr Metallurgov 17/52), an experienced, multilingual Russo-Dutch firm, offers an inspiring selection of Kola adventures, including hiking, rock hunting, snowmobile safaris and traditional hut stays, as well as expeditions to Franz Josef Land and really good day-trip options.

The **Geological Museum** (Музей цветного камня им.В.Н. Дава; pr Metallurgov 46; admission ₽50; ⏲noon-6pm Tue-Sun) offers an in-depth introduction to the minerals on which Monchegorsk and its nearby towns have been built. The smooth spheres of jasper, may just, erm, rock your world.

The only decent place to stay, and one of the most comfortable hotels in central Kola, is the modern, business-style **Laplandia Hotel** (Гостиница Лапландия; ☎81536-74 551; www.laplandia.ru; pr Metallurgov 32; d/ste from ₽2600/7150; 📶), which comes complete with friendly, helpful receptionists and comfortable en suites. Next door, at Murmansk export **Kruzhka** (www.krugka.ru; pr Metallurgov 34a; mains ₽280-405; ⏲11am-midnight; 📶), you can chow down on surprisingly good sushi rolls, pasta, pizza, shashlyk, ribs, wings and salads in a plasticky enchanted-forest setting.

From the bus station, one block off pr Metallurgov, there are departures for Murmansk (₽345, 2¾ hours, up to 10 daily) via Olenegorsk railway station (₽86, 40 minutes), and Kirovsk (₽209, 1¾ hours, four daily) via Apatity (₽169, 1¼ hours, four to six daily).

Lovozero Ловозеро

81538 / POP 2871 / MOSCOW

Under Stalin the once-nomadic Sami people were brutally suppressed and forced into *kolkhozy* (collective farms). Today, of Russia's roughly 1600 Sami, close to 900 now live in the administrative village of Lovozero (Luyavvr), where the excellent **Sami History & Culture Museum** (Музей истории, культуры и быта кольских саамов; ul Sovetskaya 28; admission/guided tour ₽25/100; 9am-1pm & 2-5pm Tue-Sat) delves into their troubled history and their way of life, which continues to be threatened. It also celebrates the heroic efforts to keep Sami culture alive, and the revival of the Sami language and of traditional Sami crafts. Here you can both admire and purchase knives in carved reindeer-antler sheaths, bone jewellery and wooden vessels inlaid with bone by **Nikolai Anisimov** (Николай Анисимов; 8-921-513 7746) and **Vladimir Chuprov** (Владимир Чупров; 8-921-289 8989), leatherwork and beadwork by **Maria Kalmykova** (Мария Калмыкова; 8-921-664 0519) and **Maria Khvashchenok** (Мария Хващенок; 8-921-175 3649) and other beautiful, delicate creations by local Sami masters. The museum staff have their contact details if you want something made on demand. Traditional costume, hunting tools and photos of ancient stone labyrinths, rock carvings and Sami fighters during WWII also feature prominently in the museum.

A pair of buildings in the city centre resemble oversized *chumy* (tepee-shaped tents). One of these is the **Sami Cultural Centre** (Ловозёрский районный национальный культурный центр; ul Sovetskaya 8), which hosts occasional exhibitions.

Fourteen kilometres east of Lovozero is **Husky Park Lesnaya Elan** (Хаски-Парк Лесная Елань; 8152-688 836, 921-734 0533; http://vk.com/huskypark; Km 14; dog-sled ride adult/child ₽400/150;), with dog and reindeer sledding in winter and husky encounters in summer. Further west towards Olenegorsk, the main road branches into two – take the Murmansk road for **Sami Village 'Sam-Siyt'** (Саамская Деревня; 921-169 6299, 911-306 0675; http://lovozero1.ru), where you can go reindeer sledding and snowmobiling in winter, learn about Sami traditions and lunch on traditional Sami

THE PLIGHT OF RUSSIA'S SAMI

The Kola Peninsula's indigenous people, the Sami, have been residents in this harsh land for millennia. The Sami haven't had it easy, with their semi-nomadic hunter-turned-reindeer-herdsman lifestyle under threat from everyone else who came to the Kola Peninsula after them. Exploitation by traders and settlers and forced Christianisation in the 19th century, the forced collectivisation of their reindeer in the 1920s, repression of their culture under the Soviets, and the continuous infringement of Sami land rights by mining, timber, mineral development, commercial fishing and tourism companies have all taken their toll.

While Russia's 1600-or-so Sami have set up the Association of the Kola Sami to protect and promote Sami interests, the association has no legal power under Russian law. Another problem is the lack of enforcement of existing laws, under which 'in historically established areas of habitation, Sami enjoy the rights for traditional use of nature and [traditional] activities'. In practise, they have been repeatedly forced off land to be used for mineral exploitation and had their fishing rights curtailed to make room for commercial-fishing tourism catering to foreigners. On top of that, high unemployment and alcoholism affect many members of the small community of Lovozero.

It's not all doom and gloom, though. The Sami language (Southern Sami), repressed in Soviet times, now flourishes in both written and spoken form. Credit goes to dedicated members of the community, such as writer and linguist Aleksandra Antonova who put together the first Russian-Sami dictionary in 1982, collected oral Sami folk tales and had them compiled into storybooks. Sami *duodji* (traditional crafts such as knife making, leatherwork, bone carving and beadwork) has taken off, with Russian Sami masters exchanging ideas with their visiting Scandinavian brethren, the interaction between all Sami groups once again reestablished.

cuisine year-round. Both can be booked through Kola Travel (p300).

Twenty-or-so kilometres east of Lovozero, and then 8km south, is unpretty Revda, gateway to a spectacular, rugged eight-hour hike over the Lovozyorskiye Tundry Mountains to pristine **Lake Seydozero** – holy to the Sami – where you can camp in blissful wilderness.

The only place to stay in Lovozero is the mediocre **Hotel Nadezhda** (Гостиница Надежда; ☎81538-40 309, 921-1503 124; ul Danilova 21/22; r from ₽1000), a converted apartment with room for up to six guests and shared facilities. For groceries, there's a small **produkty** (Продукты; ul Sovetskaya 9; ⏲7am-midnight).

Lovozero is reached on an 80km road that branches off the Murmansk-bound M-18 dual carriageway at the transport hub of Olenegorsk. Olenegorsk is connected to Murmansk by frequent trains and buses. If you're reliant on public transport, buses run from Olenegorsk to Revda (₽156, 45 minutes) at 10.30am, 6.05pm (except Sunday) and 8pm, returning at 5.55am (except Sunday), 8.35am, and 5pm. From Revda there are buses to Lovozero (₽55, 30 minutes) at 8.15am, 1.20pm, 4.40pm and 7.55pm on weekdays, and 8.30am, 2.20pm and 7.55pm on weekends. Returning to Revda, buses depart at 9.10am, 2.05pm, 5.25pm and 8.40pm on weekdays and at 9.25am, 3.30pm and 8.45pm on weekends. Revda is also the closest place to Lovozero to fill up on petrol.

Murmansk Мурманск

☎8152 / POP 302,468 / ⏲MOSCOW

The world's biggest Arctic city is a mere baby by Russian standards: Murmansk will celebrate its 100th birthday in 2016. This bustling, rapidly modernising place gets much of its wealth from the cornucopia of minerals found beneath the ground of the Kola Peninsula, the controversial exploitation of natural resources in the Arctic and close ties with its Scandinavian neighbours.

Murmansk's raison d'être is its port, kept ice-free by comparatively warm Gulf Stream waters. Founded in 1916 as Romanov-na-Murmanye, the city developed almost overnight during WWI, and was occupied until 1920 by pro-White allies fighting the Bolsheviks. Renamed Murmansk, the 'hero city' was bombed to bits in WWII.

A traveller's first glimpse of stolid Soviet-era architecture and the gritty port may not be the stuff of dreams, but beyond that, impressions get better and better. This lively city is surrounded by incomparable (and, in some cases, post-apocalyptic) Arctic scenery and is a playground for outdoor adventurers during the months of the midnight sun (late May to late July). During the winter darkness (late November to mid-January) the Northern Lights over the snow-covered landscape are an eerie, magical sight. Russian emigre Ernest Beaux claimed that the inspiration behind his creation of the distinctive bouquet of Chanel No 5 was the fresh polar air of this region where he fought in 1920.

Murmansk came to global attention in September 2013 when Russian forces seized the Greenpeace ship *Arctic Sunrise* that was protesting against oil drilling in the Arctic, and charged its crew with piracy. In the two months that the 'Arctic 30' were kept in a Murmansk jail, the resulting media circus greatly boosted the city's businesses.

Sights

★Nuclear Icebreaker Lenin BOAT

(Атомный ледокол Ленин; ☎8152-553 512; Portovy pr 25; adult/child ₽150/50; ⏲tours noon Wed-Fri, noon, 1pm & 2pm Sat & Sun; 🚌1, 4) Murmansk is a centre for nuclear icebreakers that carve their way to the North Pole (p307), but even in port you can give in to your wildest seafaring/Arctic explorer/Cold War spy fantasies aboard the 1957 NS *Lenin,* the world's first nuclear-powered icebreaker. Tours take in the canteen, the nuclear reactor (powered by uranium 235), the map room and the captain's bridge. By the end of 2014 there should also be interactive displays on Arctic exploration – a joint effort with the Norwegian consulate. Call ahead for tours in English.

★Alyosha MONUMENT

(Алёша; 🚌4, 10) One of Murmansk's most memorable sights is a gigantic concrete soldier nicknamed Alyosha, erected to commemorate the Arctic fighters who perished in the Great Patriotic War (WWII). From his hilltop perch, Alyosha's stony visage stares across the Kola Inlet at the snow-speckled Arctic moors beyond. To the south the port spreads out in all its magnificent industrial dreariness. The statue is a 20-minute ramble past Lake Semyonovskoye through the hilly park from one of the Ozero bus stops.

★**Regional Studies Museum** MUSEUM
(Мурманский областной краеведческий музей; www.mokm51.ru; pr Lenina 90; adult/student ₽100/20; ⏲11am-6pm Sat-Wed; 🚌3, 6, 18) Comprehensive exhibits at Murmansk's oldest museum include one on Sami culture and handicrafts, a vast natural-history section with all manner of taxidermied beasts and 'Wait For Me' – an exhibition on the fierce defence of the north during the Great Patriotic War. Delve also into the history of Arctic exploration, contemplate the mysterious ancient stone labyrinths and get nostalgic over prehistoric radios and Zenit cameras in the 'Made in the USSR' section.

Oceanarium ZOO
(Океанариум; www.okeanarium51.ru; adult/under 14 ₽450/350; ⏲shows 11am, 3pm & 5pm Wed-Sun; 👪; 🚌10) On the northern shore of Lake Semyonovskoe, this little bubble-domed building is home to six trained Arctic seals showing off their stuff. Beside it is a sweet funfair with merry-go-rounds and bouncy castles.

Church of the Saviour on the Waters CHURCH
(Храм Спас на Водах; ul Chelyuskintsev; ⏲11am-7pm; 🚌4, 10) This gold-domed church, built in 2002 from public donations, is part of a memorial complex dedicated to the memory of Murmansk's seamen who perished in peacetime. Just below is the **lighthouse monument**, and next to it is part of the ill-fated submarine *Kursk*, whose entire 118-man crew perished in 2000 during naval exercises in the Barents Sea. When it sank, following an on-board explosion, the Russian government refused foreign assistance in the rescue operation until it was too late.

British Naval Cemetery HISTORICAL SITE
(ul Rogozerskaya; 🚌10) In 1919 the British navy assisted the White Russians against the Reds – Winston Churchill, war secretary at the time, wanted to see if the Bolsheviks could be crushed before they could really get going. A number of British sailors found eternal rest in Russian soil, in a small graveyard that's remarkably well tended, even in winter. To find it, walk past the Statoil gas station on your left, and take a sharp right after 100m towards some rusty-looking sheds.

Museum of the Northern Fleet MUSEUM
(Военно-морской музей Северного флота; www.severnyflot.ru; ul Tortseva 15; admission ₽150; ⏲9am-1pm & 2-5pm Thu-Mon; 🚌10) The mass of exhibits inside this turquoise, crumbling, anchor-flanked building covers everything from the founding of Russia's first navy in Arkhangelsk, to 17th- and 18th-century Arctic exploration, to Murmansk convoys of WWII – a joint effort with British servicemen. The most recent exhibition is a showstopping collection of landscape photos of the icy Franz Josef Land. Alight from bus 10 at the penultimate stop, Nakhimova (Нахимова), walk on for 300m then turn left and it's 80m up ul Tortseva.

Fine Arts Museum MUSEUM
(Мурманский областной художественный музей; www.artmmuseum.ru; ul Kominterna 13; admission per exhibit ₽60-200; ⏲11am-7pm Wed-Sun; 🚌1, 2, 4, 5) The 1927 Fine Arts Museum hosts temporary exhibitions that range from female nude photography and Kanozero petroglyphs to severe Arctic landscape painting.

Tours

All Murmansk tour companies can arrange aurora borealis trips.

Arctic Land TOUR COMPANY
(Арктическая Земля; ☎8152-688 836; www.arcticland.ru; office 206, Hotel Moryak, ul Knipovicha 23; 🚌6, 18) Tours to Husky Park Lesnaya Elan in both summer and winter and fishing trips in summer.

Nord Extreme Tour TOUR COMPANY
(Норд Экстрим Тур; ☎8152-701 498; www.nordextrme.ru; ul Yegorova 14; 🚌3, 18) Kola Peninsula tours for active travellers, with fishing, diving, overland 4WD and snowmobile ventures and more.

Festivals & Events

Festival of the North SPORTS
(Праздник Севера) The annual 10-day Festival of the North in late March to early April includes a 'Polar Olympics', with participation from resident Scandinavians, reindeer-sled races, ski marathons, ice hockey and snowmobile contests. Many events are held at Dolina Uyuta (Cosy Valley), 25 minutes south of the train station by bus 1.

Murmansk Mile SPORTS
(Мурманская Миля) Taking place on the third weekend in June, this fun festival centres around the main bridge across the Kola Bay, with a mini-marathon, swimming race across the bay, wheelchair event, volleyball, sailing and much more.

Murmansk

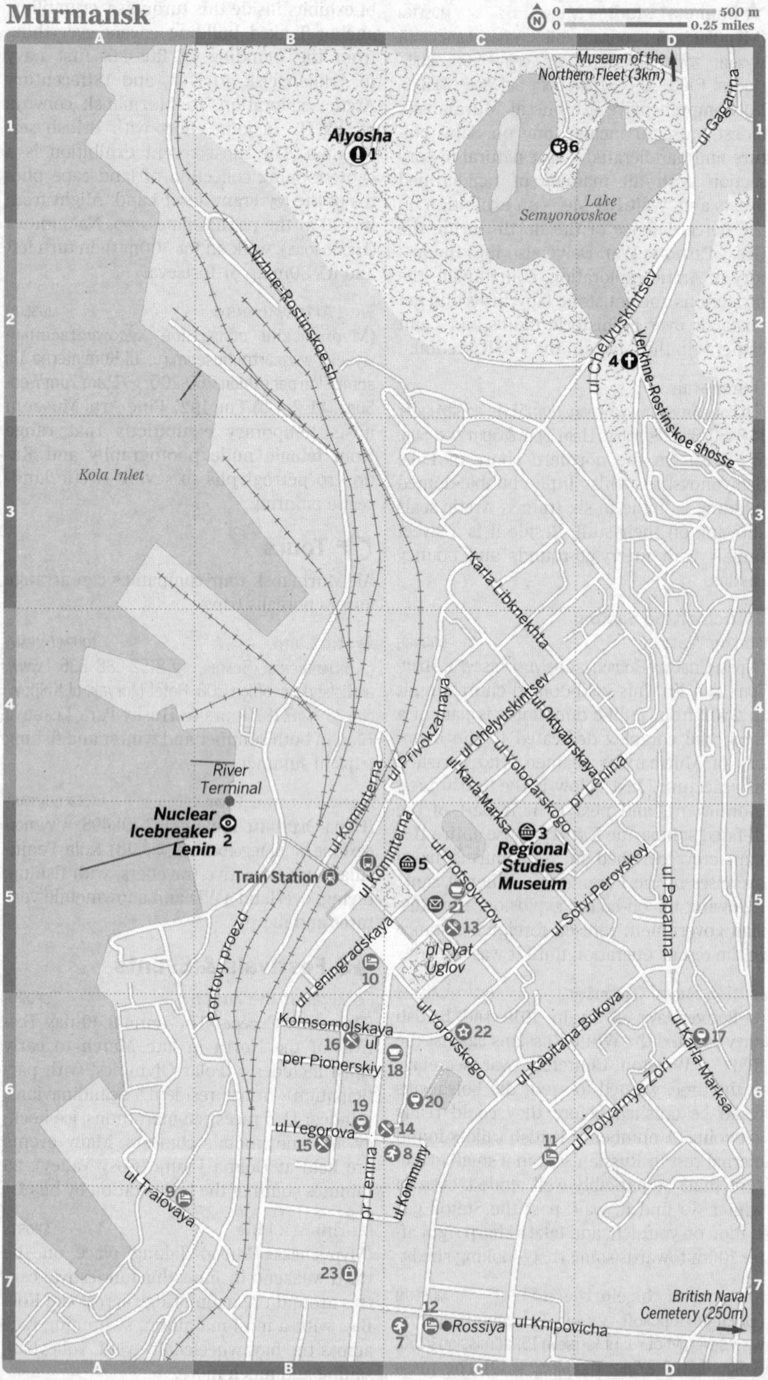
0 500 m
0 0.25 miles
A
B
C
D
1
2
3
4
5
6
7
Museum of the Northern Fleet (3km)
Alyosha
1
6
Lake Semyonovskoe
ul Gagarina
Nizhne-Rostinskoe sh
ul Chelyuskintsev
Verkhne-Rostinskoe shosse
4
Kola Inlet
Karla Libknekhta
ul Privokzalnaya
ul Chelyuskintsev
ul Oktyabrskaya
ul Volodarskogo
ul Karla Marksa
pr Lenina
River Terminal
Nuclear Icebreaker Lenin
2
ul Kominterna
ul Kominterna
3
Regional Studies Museum
Train Station
5
ul Profsoyuzov
21
13
ul Sofyi Perovskoy
ul Papanina
Portovy proezd
ul Leningradskaya
10
pl Pyat Uglov
ul Vorovskogo
22
ul Kapitana Bukova
17
ul Karla Marksa
Komsomolskaya ul
16
per Pionerskiy
18
ul Polyarnye Zori
20
19
ul Yegorova
14
15
8
11
ul Kommuny
pr Lenina
9
ul Tralovaya
23
12
Rossiya
ul Knipovicha
7
British Naval Cemetery (250m)

Murmansk

Sleeping

Most prices rise 30% during the trade exhibitions of May, June and mid-November.

The Murmansk CouchSurfing community (www.couchsurfing.org) is a very active one. Besides providing free hospitality, English-speaking Murmansk members are fantastic sources of information about the city and the region.

Hostel Prichal HOSTEL $
(Хостел Причал; www.prichalhotel.ru; ul Tralovaya 6a; dm/s from ₽600/1000; 📶; 🚌2, 4) Basic, clean cheapie with beds rather than bunks. No kitchen, though, and the shower lacks power.

★ **Mini-Hotel S-Terminal** MINIHOTEL $$
(Мини-отель S-Terminal; ☎8152-250 794; www.s-terminal.com/hostel.html; ul Kapitana Orlikovoy 2; s/d/tr/f ₽1600/2200/3000/4800; 📶; 🚌6, 10, 18) Run by an absolute darling of a proprietress, this is the closest Murmansk comes to having a bona fide hostel. The rooms are spacious and cosy, nothing is too much trouble and, in the morning, your hostess will stuff you full of porridge and hard-boiled eggs.

Mini Hotel Dis MINIHOTEL $$
(Мини-отель Дис; ☎8152-259 397; www.dis51.ru; pr Lenina 11a; s/d/ste from ₽1700/2200/6800; 📶; 🚌6, 10, 18) The mirrored ceilings in this minihotel give an illusion of height, but if you're over 165cm, you won't be fooled. Even the cheapest rooms are en suite but share a toilet, while in a suite you can bubble in your own spa. The staff are friendly and wonderfully accommodating. Breakfast included in the price for suite and 'standard' customers.

Mini Hotel Rooms & Breakfast MINIHOTEL $$
(Мини-отель Rooms & Breakfast; ☎8152-426 666; www.vk.com/hotel_murmansk; ul Polyarniye Zory 38; s/d from ₽2500/3000; 📶; 🚌10) The compact lodgings at this central minihotel are just about big enough to swing a cat. Rooms are all spotless, en suite, high-tech and an anonymous beige. Free tea and coffee around the clock and a light breakfast is thrown in. The colour scheme in the lounge/dining room is not something you wish to see if you're hungover.

Mini-Hotel Polar Circle MINIHOTEL $$
(Мини-отель Полярный Круг; ☎8152-251 521; www.murmansk-hotel.ru; pr Kolsky 39; s/d/lyux from ₽1950/2500/4300; 🚌2, 5, 6, 18) Hidden in an apartment building, this new minihotel consists of just a few spotless, compact rooms with supremely comfortable mattresses, a well-equipped guest kitchen and a good ratio of guests per shared bathroom.

Park Inn Hotel Polyarnye Zori HOTEL $$$
(Парк Инн Полярные Зори; ☎8152-289 505; www.parkinn.ru/hotel-murmansk/; ul Knipovicha 17; s/d/ste from ₽4600/7200/9700; 📶; 🚌3, 10, 18) An understandable favourite for Scandinavian and Russian businessmen,

TOP SECRET TOWNS

During the Cold War, the Murmansk area housed the world's greatest concentration of military and naval forces. Despite drastic scale backs, the Kola Peninsula is still home to plenty of closed military zones known as ZATOs (Zakrytiye Administrativo-Territorialnye Obrazovania; Closed Administrative-Territorial Formations):

Severomorsk is headquarters of the Northern Fleet.

Shchyukozero, 8km beyond, was the scene of a potentially catastrophic near miss in 1984 when a fire swept through silos bristling with nuclear-tipped missiles.

Polyarny and **Gadzhievo** are nuclear-submarine bases, with more than 50 decommissioned reactor compartments stored at nearby Sayda-Guba.

Vidyaevo and **Zaozersk** nuclear-submarine bases are west of the Kola Inlet. Vidyaevo was the home port of the ill-fated *Kursk*.

Ostrovnoy, on the Kola Peninsula's remote eastern coast, is a former submarine base that's now a dumping and recycling centre for dismantled submarines and radioactive waste.

Access to these 'closed areas' is strictly limited to Russians who either work there or are registered there, so your curiosity about Russia's secrets must remain unsated.

this spotless business hotel has efficient, English-speaking staff, two bars, a restaurant, a nightclub that stages free blues gigs on Thursdays (not in summer), a sauna for business room/suite dwellers and big buffet breakfasts. Rooms come with the perks you expect from Park Inn, with flat-screen cable TV and underfloor heating in the bathrooms.

Hotel Meridian HOTEL $$$

(Отель Меридиан; ☎8152-288 650; www.meridian-hotel.ru; ul Vorovskogo 5/23; s/d/ste from ₽3500/4900/₽7400; 📶; 🚌3, 6, 18) This centrally located business hotel is tidy and the location is super-convenient, but beds are narrow and furnishings rather lacklustre given the price. There's in-house bowling, free breakfast, the boisterous M-Club on-site and scary-looking security guys in the lobby at night.

Eating

Murmansk has a surprisingly diverse eating scene, not to mention the world's northernmost McDonald's (with a commemorative plaque).

★**Traktir Zhily-Bily** RUSSIAN $

(Трактир Жили-Были; ul Samoylovoy 5; mains ₽200-350; ⏲11am-11.30pm; 📝; 🚌3, 18) The owners have opted for a rustic Russian folk-tale theme and have run with it a few miles. Quaff *kvas* and gobble down hearty Russian dishes such as giblets with buckwheat, pike cutlets, grilled meats and soups under the watchful eye of Baba-Yaga and three-headed Zmei Gorynich while sitting in what looks like the back end of a wagon.

Northern Bakeries BAKERY $

(ul Samoylovoy 6; ⏲9am-8pm; 🚌18) For self-catering or a cupcake fetish, there's this tempting European-style bakery.

Evroros SUPERMARKET $

(Европос; pr Lenina 71; ⏲7am-midnight; 🚌18) Murmansk's best supermarket chain with huge variety and premade food. Another handy branch at ul Knipovicha 37.

★**Leto** CAFE $$

(Лето; pr Lenina 61; mains ₽360-800; ⏲noon-11pm; 🚌6, 18) Don't let yourself be blinded by the in-your-face lime-green and neon-orange decor – this cafe serves some of the most imaginative food in town. Feast on crab cutlets with ginger rice, roast leg of lamb and the best take on *golubtsy* (meat-filled cabbage rolls) we have ever tasted. Nice selection of cocktails, wines and hot drinks (including sea buckthorn tea), too.

Terrasa FUSION $$

(Терраса; www.krugka.ru/terrasa; pr Lenina 69; mains ₽289-760; ⏲noon-midnight; 🚌3, 18) Festooned with hams and with greenery growing out of every available crevice, this hip lounge bar with open kitchen complements its imaginative dishes (tagliatelle with crab sauce, venison with chocolate) with an extensive list of cocktails. Located on the 3rd floor of the shopping centre. Party on at the Terrasa DJ Bar upstairs.

Steak House Torro STEAKHOUSE $$$
(Стейк Хаус Торро; pr Lenina 80; mains from ₽650; noon-midnight; 3, 18) This elegant restaurant is a favourite with visiting businessmen and anyone with a carnivorous inclination. A special occasion treat if you've got roubles to chargrill, with the meat expertly prepared. The service is attentive and (mostly) prompt.

Fresh SUSHI $$$
(Фреш; ul Samoylovoy 6; sushi sets from ₽480; noon-midnight; 6, 18) Murmansk is in the grip of sushi mania, with anything even notionally aquatic being wrapped in seaweed to sate demand. Fresh, thankfully, lives up to its name, delivering top-quality rolls, sushi sets and noodle dishes in hip surrounds.

Drinking & Nightlife

★Cafe-Cafe CAFE
(pr Lenina 65; 11am-11pm) A Venetian plague doctor's mask and some creepy laughing heads on the brick wall preside over this relaxed, hip cafe. Come here for the delicious pizzas, fresh salads, exotica such as crab spring rolls, strong coffee and good beer. Happy-hour food discounts between 1pm and 3pm.

Fusion BAR
(www.krugka.ru/fusion/; pr Lenina 72; 10am-midnight; 18) The beaded curtain, water features and young, trendy clientele make you feel as if you're in an MTV video. Order from the looooooong list of cocktails, or grab a delicious salad and kick back to the sounds of a lounge version of 'I'm Every Woman'.

Bulldog PUB
(Бульдог; ul Karla Marksa 38; noon-2am; 10, 18) Atmospheric English-style pub, with dark wood furniture and a good selection of imported beers.

Pinta Pub PUB
(Паб Пинта; ul Yegorova 13a; noon-midnight Sun-Thu, to 5am Fri & Sat; 18) With its Germanic facade, Scottish decor and merry-old-England bathroom tiles, geography mightn't be the Pinta's strongest point, but who cares when it has its own on-site microbrewery? Regular live gigs on weekends by everyone from rock bands to jazz troupes.

Yunost CAFE
(Юность; pr Lenina 86; 10am-midnight) A local institution, Yunost has been enriching Murmansk's dentists for over 50 years. Come for tea, coffee and delectable-looking cakes (from ₽60), or grab a cheap lunch at the canteen-style dining room.

M-Club NIGHTCLUB
(М-Клуб; ul Vorovskogo 5; 18) This entertainment complex inside Hotel Meridian consists of a bar, billiards, bowling and large dance floor with music themes changing nightly.

☆ Entertainment

Philharmonia CLASSICAL MUSIC
(Филармония; www.murmansound.ru; ul Sofyi Perovskoy 3; most shows 7pm Sep-Jun; 18) To

CRUISES TO THE NORTH POLE

It should come as no surprise that the Russians were the inventors – and perfectors – of the ice-faring vessel. The northern Pomors constructed the first ice-clearing ships (called *kochy*) in the 11th century, built with ice-resistant hardwood and used for the exploration of Arctic waters. The boats' round shape propelled them onto the ice when squeezed by floes.

Fast forward 900 years, and the development of nuclear icebreakers has literally cleared the way for northern-bound cargo ships, scientific voyages and tourist expeditions with a force hitherto thought impossible with diesel-powered predecessors. Today's vessels – mammoth double-hulled constructs comprising steel bows and two onboard reactors – power their way through ice up to 3m thick at speeds reaching 10 knots. Nuclear icebreakers are stationed at Murmansk's Atomflot base at Kola Bay.

In summer, when on a break from their official duties, NS *Lenin* and other icebreakers take tourists on two-week visits to dramatic Franz Josef Land and on through the ice to the North Pole (though NS *Lenin* may discontinue cruising as of 2015). Packages start at around US$25,000. Don't expect to arrange things at the last minute. Berths are sold way ahead through (often foreign) adventure-tour operators, including **Nordic Travel** (www.nordictravel.ru), **Quark Expeditions** (www.quarkexpeditions.com) and **Poseidon** (www.northpolevoyages.com).

DON'T MISS

TERIBERKA

Hemmed in between the Barents Sea and snow-covered hills around it, the dying-out Sami village of **Teriberka** is one of the most picturesque spots in Arctic Russia. With its skeletons of old fishing ships on the shore, cute wooden cabins, empty shells of Soviet-era housing and a colourful seafront graveyard, this spot is easily accessed from Murmansk by car or by daily bus through spectacular Arctic scenery.

From the paved main road heading east of Murmansk, a good, signposted gravel road branches off north after about 100km and runs through the vast tundra. It's a beautiful 60km drive that passes pristine, ice-covered lakes and a sinister Grim Reaper/skier figure wearing a gas mask. If you don't have your own wheels, you can catch the daily bus from Murmansk at 5.40pm, returning the following morning at 7am, and take advantage of the 24-hour summer light. Explore the hills and the coastline, dip your toes in the frigid waters, have a BBQ or simply enjoy the solitude and your proximity to the world's northernmost ocean.

Note that some of the wilderness near Teriberka falls under ZATOs (Zakrytiye Administrativo-Territorialnye Obrazovania; Closed Administrative-Territorial Formations; see p306).

attend opera, folk music or classical concerts, buy tickets in advance from the on-site ticket office.

Shopping

Bookvoyed BOOKSTORE
(Буквоед; pr Lenina 62; 10am-8pm; 18) Well-stocked bookstore with the best selection of regional maps.

Information

Main Post Office (Почта; pr Lenina 82a; 9am-2pm & 3-7pm)

Murman (www.murman.ru) News, weather, flights and other useful service listings.

Murmanout (http://murmanout.ru/places) Wide-ranging listings with customer comments. See http://murmanout.ru/events for what's-on information.

Murmansk Tourism Portal (www.murmantourism.ru) Info on active tourism in the area.

Getting There & Away

AIR

Some of the airlines using **Murmansk Airport** (Аэропорт Мурманск; www.airport-murmansk.ru) include **Nordavia** (Нордавиа; www.nordavia.ru/eng), **Rossiya** (Россия ; www.rossiya-airlines.com/en) and **Sky Express** (www.skyexpress.ru). Destinations include Moscow (2½ hours, six daily), St Petersburg (two hours, four to five daily), Arkhangelsk (1¾ hours, daily except Tuesday and Saturday) and Tromsø, Norway (two hours, Monday and Friday).

BUS

From Murmansk's **bus station** (Автовокзал; 8152-454 884; www.murmanbus.ru; ul Kominterna 16), buses run to Kirovsk (₽554, 5½ hours, four daily) via Olenegorsk (₽262, three hours), Monchegorsk (₽345, 3½ hours) and Apatity (₽472, five hours). A daily bus runs to Teriberka (₽331, 4¼ hours) at 5.40pm.

Finland

On Monday, Wednesday and Friday a bus runs to Rovaniemi (₽3400, 12 hours) via Ivalo (₽2150, 6½ hours) from the bus station.

Norway

Two daily minibuses run to Kirkenes (₽1000/1200 to Kirkenes town/airport, 4½ to six hours), managed by **Pasvikturist** (+47-7899 5080; www.pasvikturist.no; Dr Wesselsgate 9, Kirkenes; 8.30am-4pm Mon-Fri). Sputnik minibus leaves the Park Inn Hotel Polyarnye Zori (p305) at 7am (noon on Sunday), while Gulliverus runs daily at 7am from Hotel Meridian (p306).

Returning from Kirkenes, Gulliverus departs daily at 3pm from Europris Hotel, while Sputnik departs from Rica Arctic Hotel at 2pm (weekdays), 3pm (Saturday) and 4pm (Sunday).

TRAIN

From the **train station** (Железнодорожный вокзал; ul Kominterna 14) at least three daily trains run to both St Petersburg (₽2410, 26¼ to 27 hours) and Moscow Oktyabrskaya (₽3048, 35¼ to 39 hours). All go via Apatity (₽741, 3½ to 4½ hours) and Petrozavodsk (₽1900, 19 to 24 hours). Daily train 15 bound for Moscow departs at 7.35pm and is ideally timed for Kem (₽1979), arriving at 6.22am.

Getting Around

Murmansk airport is 27km southwest of the city at Murmashi, and can be reached by bus/

marshrutka 106 (40 minutes), which departs from directly opposite the bus station every 30 minutes or so between 5.20am and 11.30pm. Frequent trolleybus 6 covers the vast length of Kolsky pr, crosses the city centre on pr Lenina then swings left on ul Karla Libknekhta. Bus 18 follows almost the same route. Pr Kirova is covered by trolleybuses 2 and 4, while useful bus 10 follows Kolsky pr, bypasses the centre on ul Polyarnye Zori and ul Papanina and rejoins the main drag near Lake Semyonovskoe.

Murmansk is a good place to rent a car if you want to explore the Kola Peninsula solo. Professional agency **Rent a Car** (☎921-285 7478, 8152-253 804; www.rentacar51.ru; office 24, pr Lenina 24) has a good selection of vehicles for hire (per day from ₽1400) and can deliver to your hotel at extra cost.

VOLOGDA & AROUND
ВОЛОГДА И ВОКРУГ

The vast, seemingly endless region of Vologda (Вологодская область) is given character by a scattering of ancient monasteries, the tattered charm of once-grand towns…and the Russian Santa Claus. Some highlights, such as Kargopol, are places that time forgot once railways supplanted river transport. Others, such as friendly little Totma, are only now starting to realise their tourism potential, while Veliky Ustyug has become a wintertime theme park in itself.

Vologda — Вологда

☎8172 / POP 306,487 / ⏲MOSCOW

Having taken Moscow's side against all comers seemingly from its inception, Vologda was rewarded by Ivan the Terrible, who considered the quaint city perhaps worthy of his presence there – Vologdians remain steadfast in their belief that the city was a contender for Russian capital.

Until the 17th century, Vologda was an important centre of industry, commerce and arts, with Vologda lace becoming renowned as a luxury item. However, with the development of St Petersburg, Vologda was pushed into the background. At the start of the 20th century, political undesirables such as Josef Stalin and religious philosopher Nikolai Berdyaev were exiled here. Nonetheless, for just a few months in 1918, Vologda became the diplomatic capital of Russia, and today this laid-back, church-studded city is a great base for exploring the region.

For background information on the city's connection to lace, visit www.artrusse.ca/lace.htm.

Sights & Activities

★St Sofia's Cathedral — CHURCH

(Софийский собор; adult/child ₽150/70; ⏲10am-6pm Wed-Sun, service 9am Wed-Sun; 🚌7) Powerful five-domed St Sofia's Cathedral has a soaring interior smothered with beautiful 1680s frescoes. The astonishingly tall iconostasis is filled with darkly brooding saintly portraiture.

The massive stone cathedral was erected in just two years (1568–70) on the direct orders of Ivan the Terrible.

Ivan's ruthlessness at Novgorod (where he sacked his own city and fried citizens alive in large pans made especially for the occasion) was known and feared throughout Russia. So the Vologda workers jumped to it. But haste, of course, makes waste. Local legend has it that Ivan, upon walking into St Sofia's for the first time, was struck on the head by a tile that had been grouted to the ceiling without due care. Ivan stormed out, never to return, and the cathedral was consecrated only after the Terrible One's death.

★Kremlin — HISTORICAL SITE

(Вологодский Кремль; Kremlyovskaya pl; ⏲10am-5pm Wed-Sun; 🚌7) FREE Vologda's multi-domed, attractive kremlin is the city's historical centrepiece, a 17th-century fortified enclosure built as a church administrative centre to accompany St Sofia's Cathedral next door. Peeking into the various museums that surround the crumbling courtyard makes for a good introduction to Vologda's city history, natural history of the region and folk art.

The natural-history section at the **Regional Studies Museum** (Вологодский областной краеведческий музей; www.vologdamuseum.ru; adult/child ₽80/40; ⏲10am-5pm Wed-Sun) has clearly benefited from the untimely demise of numerous regional species of wildlife, such as the dramatically posed stuffed lynx, wolves, foxes and a tiny cub-under-glass mournfully watching his bear family from across the room. The history exhibition tells the story of the city from its very conception, while the star of the rich prehistory exhibition is a 3500-year-old lady skeleton clasping at her modesty.

On the eastern side of the main courtyard, Muppet-style wooden dolls, lacquered wood items and embroidery briefly grab

Vologda

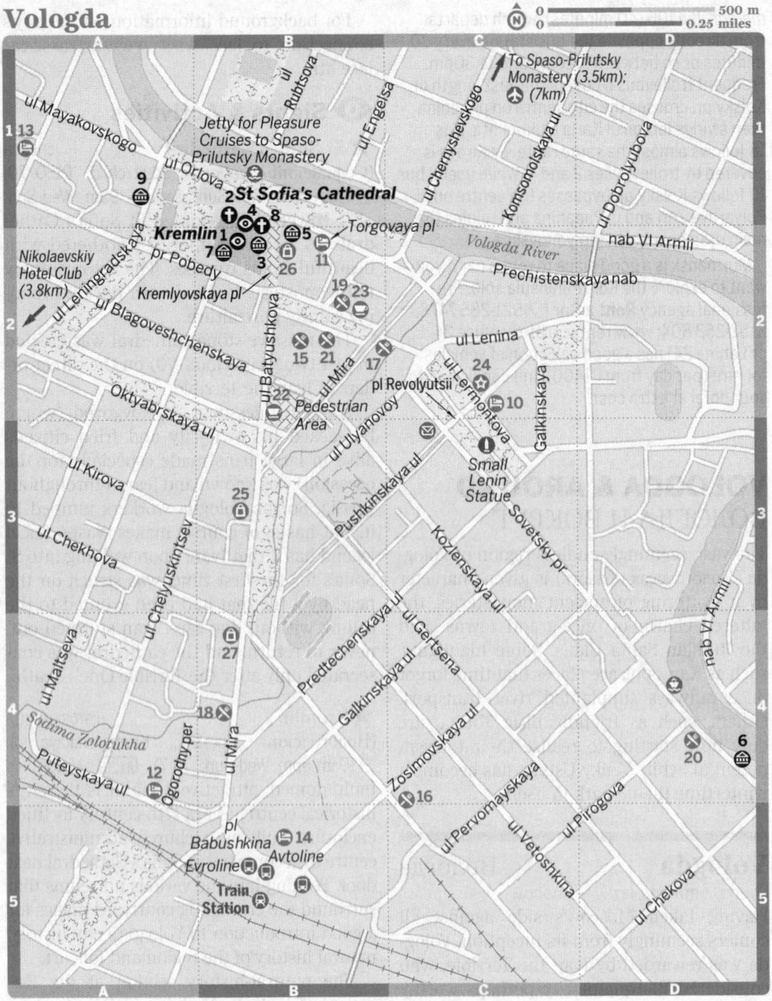

your attention before the **Art Department** (Художественный отдел Кремля; adult/child ₽80/40; ⏲10am-5pm Wed-Sun) gets down to business with some truly first-class icons and the remarkable abstract wood carvings of local artist Victor Shumilov.

Bell Tower HISTORICAL BUILDING

(Колокольня; adult/child ₽150/70; ⏲10am-4.30pm Wed-Sun; 🚌7) Climbing the 288 steps of St Sofia's Cathedral's separate 78.5m-high, gold-topped bell tower offers breathtaking views down upon the cathedral's grand onion domes. Mind your own dome on the way up: the ceilings were clearly built with gnomes in mind.

Lace Museum MUSEUM

(Музей Кружева; www.vologdamuseum.ru; Kremlyovskaya pl 12; adult/child ₽100/50; ⏲10am-5pm Wed-Sun; 🚌7) The sparklingly modern Lace Museum, across the square from the kremlin, patches together some great examples of this archetypal Vologda craft, with fun communist-era examples incorporating tractors, hammer-and-sickle symbols and an intricate piece celebrating Russia's exploration of the cosmos.

Vologda

Top Sights
1 Kremlin ... B2
2 St Sofia's Cathedral ... B1

Sights
3 Art Department ... B2
4 Bell Tower ... B1
5 Lace Museum ... B2
6 Peter the Great House ... D4
7 Regional Studies Museum ... B2
8 Resurrection Cathedral ... B1
9 World of Forgotten Things ... A1

Sleeping
10 Hotel Angliter ... C2
11 Hotel Palisad ... B2
12 Hotel Sputnik ... A4
13 Istoriya ... A1
14 Resting Rooms ... B5

Eating
15 Central Market ... B2
16 Gud'OK ... C4
17 Kamenny Most ... B2
18 Oasis Supermarket ... B4
19 Ogorod ... B2
20 Puzatiy Patsyuk ... D4
21 Sem Vecherov ... B2

Drinking & Nightlife
22 Arbat ... B2
DJ Cafe MC2 ... (see 18)
23 Parizhanka ... B2

Entertainment
24 Philharmonia ... C2

Shopping
25 Dom Knigi ... B3
26 Dom Suvenirov ... B2
27 Vologdskie Suveniry ... B4

Spaso-Prilutsky Monastery MONASTERY
(Спасо-Прилуцкий монастырь; ul Monastyrskaya 12; 8am-6pm; 2, 28) FREE Painted in circus-tent stripes, the powerful fortress towers of this active 14th-century monastery are photogenically reflected in the river, best viewed from the nearby railway bridge. Visitors may explore the western half of the compound, including a partial rampart walk and the five-domed 16th-century **Transfiguration Cathedral** (Спасо-Преображенский собор).

The site is 4km north of town. Alight at Priluki (Прилуки) stop or join one of the **pleasure cruises** from the kremlin pier (₽700 return, noon, 3pm and 6pm).

Resurrection Cathedral CHURCH
(Воскресенский собор; Kremlevskaya pl 3; adult/child ₽80/40; 9am-5pm Tue-Sun; 7) Just outside the kremlin enclosure, the amply domed 1776 Resurrection Cathedral adds photogenic foreground to kremlin views. It also houses an **art gallery** of regularly changing exhibits.

World of Forgotten Things MUSEUM
(Мир Забытых Вещей; www.vologdamuseum.ru; ul Leningradskaya 6; adult/child ₽60/30; 10am-5pm Wed-Sun; 7) One of several enchanting old wooden buildings at the eastern end of ul Leningradskaya, this little museum evokes the life of a 19th-century, 17-child middle-class family. Amid portraits of bewigged children and army officers is a very whimsical gramophone that still plays and the beautiful landscape photography on the 1st floor is a definite highlight.

Peter the Great House MUSEUM
(Петровский Домик; Sovetsky pr 47; adult/child ₽60/30; 10am-1pm & 2-5pm Tue-Sat; 1) Vologda's oldest museum (1885) is a compact late-17th-century stone house that belonged to the Gutman traders who hosted Tsar Peter I during his March 1724 visit to Vologda. Exhibits include a copy of Rastrelli's death mask of Peter the Great and the tsar's red tunic, underlining his remarkable height (204cm).

Sleeping

Resting Rooms HOSTEL $
(Комнаты отдыха; komnaty otdykha; 8-921-233 8323; pl Babushkina 6a; 6/12/24hr from ₽300/400/600) Neat, clean shared rooms in the courtyard building across the street from the railway station. There are two twins and a triple, all of which can be rented as solo digs if you value your privacy.

Hotel Palisad HOTEL $$
(Гостиница Палисадъ; 8172-722 761; www.palisad-vologda.ru; Torgovaya pl 17; s/d/ste ₽2600/3000/4100; ; 13) Sweet little hotel right near the river, with compact, modern rooms, decked out in neutral tones, attentive personnel and a generous buffet breakfast featuring local produce. Promixity to the kremlin is either a boon or a bane, depending on how much you enjoy the sound of church bells.

WORTH A TRIP

KIRILLOV-BELOZERSKY MONASTERY

Founded in 1397 by a monk from Moscow, **Kirillov-Belozersky Monastery** (Кирилло-Белозерский монастырь; www.kirmuseum.ru/en; combined ticket ₽400) grew from a cave in the ground to magnificent grounds comprising 12 churches, mighty three-storey fortress walls and the glorious centrepiece, the Assumption Cathedral.

The prosperity of the monastery was made possible by wealthy patrons, including the Romanovs and Ivan the Terrible. Ivan had a personal room within the monastery and planned to take his own vows here. Things did not go quite as planned, however, with the tsar becoming disenchanted with what he saw as the 'lecherous' goings-on within the cloister. A prolific and polemic letter writer, Ivan penned a no-holds-barred epistle to the abbot of the time, blasting the lack of asceticism within its walls: 'Today in your cloister Sheremetyev sits in his cell like a tsar; Khabarov and other monks come to him and drink and eat as though they were laymen, and Sheremetyev – whether from weddings or births, I don't know – sends sweets and cakes, and other spiced delicacies around to all the cells, and behind the monastery is a courtyard, and in it are supplies for a year.'

Entry to the grounds is free, but if you wish to see the icons and other treasures displayed in the churches and exhibition rooms, pay individual entry fees or buy a combined ticket.

Buses connect Kirillov and Vologda (₽275, 2¾ hours, up to six daily).

Hotel Sputnik HOTEL $$
(Гостиница Спутник; ☎8172-777 975; www.sputnic-hotel.ru; Puteyskaya ul 14; s ₽1500-2350, d ₽2200-2650, s/d without bathroom from ₽700/980; 📶) The exterior may be institutional Soviet, but inside it's one pleasant surprise after another and the rooms are great value for money. Even the cheapest rooms are spacious, bright and come equipped with sinks and armchairs, the shared facilities are spotless and the reception staff are friendly and helpful. We're still in Russia, right?

Nikolaevskiy Hotel Club HOTEL $$
(Николаевский Клуб; ☎8172-512 299; www.hotel.nikolaevskiy.ru; ul Kostromskaya 14; s/lyux ₽2700/4000; 📶; 🚌1) Utterly neutral rooms are instantly forgettable, solo travellers are well catered for, the service is impeccable and the restaurant is quite grand. However, charging ₽3000 per hour to use the sauna/gym/pool may be pushing the friendship. Buffet breakfast is included. It's 4km out of the centre – alight at Kostromskaya (Костромская) stop, then walk eight minutes west.

Istoriya HOTEL $$
(История; ☎8172-723 200; www.history-hotel.ru; ul Vorovskogo 28; s/d/lyux from ₽2450/2850/3750; 📶; 🚌7) Cute little hotel a couple of blocks from the kremlin, with classic decor in its several buildings and on-site restaurant (full board available). Pros? Secure parking, reliable wi-fi, spotless rooms, use of sauna and a little plunge pool. Cons? Thin walls, so you may feel as if you're in bed with your neighbours, and the less-than-exciting breakfast.

★ **Hotel Angliter** BOUTIQUE HOTEL $$$
(Отель Англитеръ; ☎8172-762 436; www.angliter.ru; ul Lermontova 23; s/d/apt/lyux from ₽3500/5700/7300/5800; 📶; 🚌1, 6) With tirelessly helpful, multilingual staff and a supercentral location, this very comfortable boutique hotel is still Vologda's top choice, though we're not crazy about the over-abundance of crystal lamps, marble toilets and pseudo-antique walnut-inlay furniture. Breakfast is included.

Eating

★ **Gud'OK** RUSSIAN, ITALIAN $
(Гуд'ОК; ul Chekhova 51; mains ₽250-350; ⏰noon-2am) Gud'OK tries to ooze urban sophistication, with its wall-length prints of night-time Manhattan and red leather seats, but doesn't quite make it. The food, on the other hand, is lovingly prepared and its chicken cutlets with buckwheat, beef ragout with Guinness and tiramisu are very 'gud' rather than OK. The prompt service is a boon for nearby railway-station departures.

Ogorod RUSSIAN $
(Огород; pr Pobedy 10; mains ₽90-190; ⏰8.30am-11pm; 🥗; 🚌7) Grab a tray and make your way around this plant-strewn cafeteria, picking up your salads, soups and hearty mains as you go along. There's an appealing summer terrace in the warmer months.

Central Market MARKET $
(Центральный рынок; ul Batyushkova 3a; ⏰7.15am-7pm Tue-Sun, to 4pm Mon; 🚌7, 28) In-

door/outdoor market selling all manner of fresh produce.

Oasis Supermarket SUPERMARKET $
(Oasis Mall, ul Mira; ⌚9am-10pm; 🚌1) Large and well stocked.

Puzatiy Patsyuk UKRAINIAN $$
(Пузатый Пацюк; Sovetsky pr 80; mains ₽340-800; ⌚9am-4am; 🍴; 🚌1, 2) This rustic-effect nostalgia restaurant serves top-notch food such as duck in a wonderfully tart apple-and-cowberry sauce *(kachka s yablykami)*, *draniki* and goose with a honey crust. The menu (in Ukrainian with Russian translations) is a well-crafted take on a tsarist-era police report, but the ambience is lacking unless you're here on a weekend when there's live entertainment.

Sem Vecherov RUSSIAN $$
(Семь Вечеров; www.sem-vecherov.ru; pr Pobedy 13; mains ₽260-420; ⌚noon-midnight; 📶🍴; 🚌7, 28) Good things come in sevens here: seven chef's specials, seven (mostly) vegetarian (постные) dishes, seven types of filled bliny…you get the picture. Downstairs is the cheery cafe section, and upstairs middle-aged couples boogie on down to live pop in the evenings. Don't miss the pikefish cutlets or the porcini mushroom soup served in a bread bowl.

Kamenny Most RUSSIAN, ITALIAN $$
(Каменный Мост; ul Chelyuskintsev 47; mains ₽300-650; ⌚9am-midnight Mon-Thu & Sun, to 2am Fri & Sat; 🚌7, 28) The menu at this classy split-level restaurant flits between classic Russian (golubtsy, grilled carp, clay pot dishes), Italian (tagliatelle with scallops) and barely imaginable (liver with banana sauce). Service is attentive and the comprehensive wine list and buzzing ambience help make this one of central Vologda's top nosh spots.

Drinking & Nightlife

Arbat CAFE, BAR
(Арбать; cnr ul Mira & ul Batyushkova; ⌚11am-1am Mon-Thu & Sun, to 4am Fri & Sat; 📶; 🚌7, 28) A chatty veranda hang-out by day that serves a mix of European dishes and sushi, this cafe transforms into a pop-walloping bar once the sun goes down, with the local trendies taking to the dance floor.

Parizhanka CAFE
(Парижанка; pr Pobedy 8; ⌚24hr; 📶; 🚌7) This 'Parisian' cafe is a favourite with locals for its decent coffee and delectable cakes (skip the pasta, though). Open (mostly) around the clock.

DJ Cafe MC2 NIGHTCLUB
(ul Mira 82; ⌚8pm-6am Fri & Sat; 📶; 🚌1, 13) Local hipsters make their way to the 5th floor of Oasis shopping centre on weekend nights to hear the resident DJs and guest talent from across Russia who specialise in deep house. If you don't feel like hitting the dance floor, the sofas are comfy, the sushi is good enough and the original cocktails pack a punch.

Entertainment

Philharmonia CLASSICAL MUSIC
(Филармония; ☎8172-757 513; www.volfilarmonia.ru; ul Lermontova 21) As well as its vibrant program of mostly classical music (October to May), the Philharmonia also organises a two-week 'Summer at the Kremlin' festival of open-air concerts (June to July).

Shopping

Dom Knigi BOOKSTORE
(Дом Книги; ul Mira 38; ⌚10am-7pm Mon-Fri, to 6pm Sat & Sun) Dom Knigi sells some regional and detailed city maps, including a useful double street map (₽150) that also covers Veliky Ustyug.

Dom Suvenirov SOUVENIRS
(Дом Сувениров; Kremlyovskaya pl 8; ⌚10am-7pm Mon-Sat) Well-stocked gift shop selling locally produced, high-quality linen clothing, nesting dolls, clay whistles, lace parasols and so much more.

Vologdskie Suveniry SOUVENIRS
(Вологодские Сувениры; cnr ul Mira & ul Chekhova; ⌚10am-7pm Mon-Fri, to 5pm Sat & Sun) Vologodskie Suveniry sells classic *kruzhevo* (Vologda lace), colourful lacquerware, painted wooden trays and delicately carved birchwood items.

Information

Main Post Office (Почта; Sovetsky pr 4; ⌚8am-8pm Mon-Fri, 9am-6pm Sat & Sun)

Vologda Oblast (www.vologda-oblast.ru/en/) Government-run website, with lots of information on the region.

Getting There & Away

BUS

From the bus station (Автовокзал) at pl Babushkina 10, next to the train station, there are regular buses to Petrozavodsk (₽1010, 12½

WORTH A TRIP

VELIKY USTYUG ВЕЛИКИЙ УСТЮГ

This laid-back, church-studded, historical town, founded in 1147 and once a key trading port, was a forgotten backwater till 1998 when then-Moscow mayor Yury Luzhkov proclaimed it to be the official home of Ded Moroz, Russia's version of Santa Claus.

Fast forward to the present day. Veliky Ustyug is overflowing with Ded Moroz–related 'attractions', from the **Grandfather Frost Post Office** (Почта Деда Мороза; per Oktyabrsky 1a; ⏲8am-8pm Mon-Fri, 10am-6pm Sat, 10am-5pm Sun), overflowing with sacks of letters from greedy children, to a Grandfather Frost fashion boutique (!). The tip of this hilarious iceberg of kitsch is **Grandfather Frost's Estate** (Вотчина Деда Мороза; www.dom-dm.ru/en; adult/child ₽675/165; ⏲10am-5pm), an expensive-yet-low-budget theme park of sorts, where visitors have to run the gauntlet of determinedly cheerful storybook characters and talking animals along the **Tropa Skazok** (Fairy Tale Path), answering riddles and participating in games. The centrepiece of the forested 'estate' is the vast, wooden **Dom Deda Moroza** (Grandfather Frost's House) – the climax involves meeting the fat, bewhiskered man himself, who proceeds to hand out presents to kiddies and beardy smooches to ladies. The entire proceedings take place in Russian. The set-up is more tolerable in winter, with festive-looking reindeer wandering around the snow-covered forest. The estate is reachable by taxi (₽200) and you can catch bus 122 back into town at 1.50pm (₽45).

Places to bed down include the professional **Hotel Veliky Ustyug** (Гостиница Великий Устюг; ☎81738-26 766; www.hotelvu.ru; ul Krasnoarmeyskaya 15; s/d/lyux from ₽1200/2400/4000; 📶), with smart rooms and a summer terrace serving shashlyk and beer, and friendly **Hotel Dvina** (Гостиница Двина; ☎81738-20 348; www.hotel-dvina.ru; ul Krasnaya 104; s/d from ₽1300/1500; 📶), with decent-sized, cream-coloured rooms and breakfast served at the cafe next door. The best place to chow down is the atmospheric vaulted cellar **Pogrebok** (Погребок; Sovetsky pr 121a; mains ₽190-600; ⏲noon-midnight), which serves imaginative mains such as chicken cutlets with apple and lamb with baked aubergine, washed down with locally brewed beer or *kvas*.

From the bus station, 2.5km north of the centre, there are regular departures for Vologda (₽702, 10 hours) via Totma (₽380, 4¾ hours). A faster way of reaching both is getting your hotel to book you a seat on the daily Evroline (p314) and Avtoline (p314) *marshrutky* that pick you up from the bus stop at ul Kuznetsova 18. Bus 1 (₽20) connects the bus station to ul Krasnaya, the main drag.

hours, 8.10am Monday, Wednesday, Thursday and Saturday), Totma (₽480, four to 4½ hours, up to nine daily), Veliky Ustyug (₽850, seven hours, two to three daily) and Yaroslavl (₽510, 4¾ hours, 2.20pm daily).

Evroline (Евролайн; ☎921-682 8885, 8172-732 116) and **Avtoline** (Автолайн; ☎931-506 0607) *marshrutky* run twice daily to Veliky Ustyug (4½ hours) via Totma (2½ hours) and are much faster than buses, but you need a Russian speaker to make a reservation for you.

TRAIN

Around seven daily services run to Moscow (eight to nine hours), of which trains 315 and 317 (₽1562), leaving on alternate days at 9.53pm, are the best-timed overnighters. Day train 375, departing at 7.01am, is much cheaper (₽590) and handy for reaching Yaroslavl (₽411, four hours).

In summer three to four trains run overnight to St Petersburg (₽1736, 11½ to 12½ hours).

There are five daily trains to Arkhangelsk, the most convenient overnighter being train 16 (₽1358) leaving at 7.07pm. Train 374 to Murmansk (₽2332, 37 hours) leaves at 2.40pm on alternate days and arrives at an ungodly 3.40am. Arkhangelsk- and Murmansk-bound trains stop at Nyandoma (for Kargopol).

ℹ Getting Around

The handy **2GIS** (2ГИС; www.2gis.ru) app has up-to-date transport info. From the train station, trolleybuses 1 and 4 run up ul Mira; bus 35 takes ul Mira and then heads west along ul Gertsena.

Totma Тотьма

☎81739 / POP 9860 / ⏲MOSCOW

Totma was founded prior to 1137 (about a decade before the first mention of Moscow) and makes an intriguing short stop along the Vologda–Veliky Ustyug route. Though landlocked, this soporific, church-heavy town with unpaved streets and wooden 'lace' framing the windows of its fading historic buildings revels in a rich marine heritage, an anomaly explained in two attractive museums.

From the bus station the town centre is four blocks south down ul Belousovskaya. Turn right halfway along ul Kirova to reach the Seafarers' Museum.

Sights

Seafarers' Museum MUSEUM
(Музей Мореходов; ul Kirova; admission ₽100; ⏲10am-5pm Tue-Sun) Located within the stop-you-in-your-tracks-striking **Church of the Entry into Jerusalem** (Церковь Входа Господня в Иерусалим; ul Kirova), this museum highlights Totma's unlikely contributions to marine exploration (one-fifth of all Russian mid-18th-century expeditions originated here) and the discovery of strategic islands off Alaska. The church itself was built from donations from returning Totma-based seamen and is constructed to give the odd sensation of being at sea.

Kuskov Museum MUSEUM
(Дом-музей Кускова; Chkalovskiy per 10; admission ₽100; ⏲10am-5pm Tue-Sun) Beyond the beautifully proportioned **Church of the Nativity of Christ** (Церковь Рождества Христова) and just off ul Lenina, this small log house is the birthplace of Ivan Kuskov (1765–1823), a wooden-legged explorer of Alaska, who went on to found Fort Ross, California. Fort Ross remained a thriving Russian settlement until sold in 1841 and the museum explores Kuskov's vagabond life.

Saviour-Sumorin Monastery MONASTERY
(Спасо-Суморин монастырь) Enough to give a taste of its former grandeur, the evocative remains of this monastery are bleakly derelict, in sharp contrast to the beautifully tended football field next to it. Its neoclassical **Ascension Cathedral** (Вознесенский собор) has a fine columned portico and seems to be partially restored. To get here, start at the Seafarers' Museum then curve west along unpaved ul Babushkina for 15 minutes.

Sleeping & Eating

Hotel Varnitsy HOTEL $$
(Отель Варницы; ☎81739-24 288; Severny per 1; s/d/lyux from ₽1700/2000/4500) The pine-furnished modern rooms with private bathrooms of Totma's most upmarket option are on the 3rd floor of the building beside the bus station – perfectly located for an early departure (which may be the case if you can't slumber through the pounding beats from the restaurant's summer terrace below).

Hotel Rassvet HOTEL $$
(Гостиница Рассвет; ☎81739-23 154; ul Kirova 12; s/d from ₽1500/2000) Right beside the Church of the Entry into Jerusalem, this pink, two-storey hotel is rather institutional looking, but even the cheapest of the cosy, compact rooms have taps and water heaters – more upmarket digs have their own showers. Toilets are shared but very clean and the service is friendly and helpful.

Pechki-Lavochki RUSSIAN $
(Печки-Лавочки; per Severny; mains ₽120-400; ⏲11am-midnight) The decor at Totma's best restaurant is rustic folklore, complete with embroidered tablecloths, national dress and a random stuffed seagull. The menu runs the gamut from *solyanka* and salads to shashlyk and bliny, served to an accompaniment of pounding techno by glacially slow service.

Getting There & Away

Buses to Vologda (₽480, 4½ hours) leave up to nine times daily between 6am and 3.30pm. There's usually a mid-morning and a late-evening bus to Veliky Ustyug (₽480, 4¾ hours).

Considerably faster Evroline (p314) and Avtoline (p314) *marshrutky* to both Veliky Ustyug and Vologda pick up passengers from cafe Aurora, 3km out of town. Get a Russian speaker to call ahead and book your spot.

Kargopol Каргополь

☎81841 / POP 10,103 / ⏲MOSCOW

Gently attractive Kargopol was one of Russia's richest cities in the 16th and 17th centuries, when it commanded the Onega River route to the White Sea, then Muscovy's only coastline. Once Russia had gained access to the Baltic, Kargopol lost its raison d'être and faded into obscurity, hardly helped by a devastating 1765 fire. Today, languor envelops this out-of-the-way historical town, known for its naive-style painted clay figurines (*Kargopolskiye igrushki*), and there seem to be more churches than people.

Pr Oktyabrsky and parallel ul Lenina run southwest past the hotels, pl Lenina and grassy Sobornaya Pl, the town's main square.

UNDER CHURCH 'SKIES'

The so-called 'sky' (небо) is a unique feature of 16th- and 17th-century wooden churches in the Russian north. The church ceiling is not painted. Instead it's panelled, made up of individual wooden trapeze-shaped icons, each depicting a saint or an angel, with a circular image of Christ in the centre. The design draws its inspiration from the painted cupolas of Byzantine churches and the dominant blue colour creates an illusion of height.

Sights

★Nativity Cathedral CHURCH

(Христорождественский собор; Sobornaya Pl; admission ₽100; ⏲10am-1pm & 2-5pm Tue-Sun) The five-domed, 1562 star of Sobornaya Pl sports intriguing timber-encased corner buttresses and houses a splendid iconostasis on the 1st floor (only open in summer). On a pillar, the superb Starshni Sud (Judgement Day) icon is a who's who of saints on what looks like a heavenly snakes-and-ladders board.

On the ground floor, 19th-century wooden 'skies' from the region's churches depict Adam and Eve hiding their shame, Isaac about to be killed and other biblical scenes.

Bell Tower HISTORICAL BUILDING

(Колокольня; Sobornaya Pl; admission ₽80; ⏲10am-1pm & 2-5pm Tue-Sun) Sweeping views from this sturdy 1778 bell tower justify the somewhat claustrophobic climb from the main grassy square. Enter through a hobbit-sized door. Sometimes the caretaker only turns up around noon to set off the merry ringing of bells.

John the Baptist Church CHURCH

(Церковь Иоанна Предтечи; Sobornaya Pl) This 1751 church on the grassy main square has an impressively Gothic bulk with unusual octagonal windows and distinctive double domes on long cylindrical towers.

Vvedenskaya Church CHURCH

(Введенская Церковь; Sobornaya Pl; admission ₽80; ⏲10am-1pm & 2-5pm Tue-Sun) Historically important, the 1809 Vvedenskaya Church stored the hidden chattels of the Russian royals during Napoleon's 1812 attack on Moscow. Now the upstairs interior hosts changing exhibitions of local artwork.

Annunciation Church CHURCH

(Благовещенская церковь; Krasnoarmeyskaya pl) The disused 1692 Annunciation Church catches your eye with some unusually intricate window mouldings.

Rozhdenstva Bogooroditsy Church CHURCH

(Церковь Рождества Богородицы; ul Lenina) The active 1680 Rozhdenstva Bogoroditsy Church is elegant despite the discordant red-green metallic gleam of its multiple domes. A stylistic effect? No, it's just rust.

Museum Administration Building CULTURAL HERITAGE

(www.kargopolmuseum.narod.ru; pr Oktyabrskaya 50; folklore events admission ₽60-120; ⏲folklore events 9pm Fri-Sun mid-Jun–Aug) Low-key musical, dance and **folklore events** are held outside on most summer weekend evenings.

Bereginya MUSEUM

(Берегиня; Oktyabrsky pr 72; admission ₽60; ⏲9am-noon & 1-5.15pm Mon-Fri, 10am-noon & 2-4pm Sat & Sun) Bereginya displays and sells a range of folk crafts and organises all manner of masterclasses – from making clay toys to traditional weaving.

Tours

Lache Turbureau TOUR COMPANY

(Турбюро Лаче; ☎81841-22 056; www.lachetur.ru; ul Akulova 23; ⏲9am-6pm Mon-Sat) This accommodating tour agency organises rural accommodation and tours of the surrounding countryside – from day trips to historic wooden churches to multiday tours of Kenozero National Park in summer and winter. Also rents bicycles, canoes and rafts. Some English and French spoken. It's also possible to book train tickets here.

Sleeping & Eating

Hotel Kargopolochka HOTEL $

(Гостиница Каргополочка; ☎81841-21 264; ul Lenina 83; s/d/tr/q without bathroom ₽780/1020/1300/1750, s/d with bathroom ₽800/1600) The landing may look like something out of *The Green Mile* and the decor may be firmly Soviet, but the basic rooms are comfortable enough (the priciest have own toilets). Shared shower downstairs is ₽50 extra. Check-out time is 24 hours after your arrival time and the on-site cafe serves decent breakfasts, salads and mains.

Hotel Kargopol HOTEL $$
(Гостиница Каргополь; ☎81841-21 165; ul Lenina 60; s/d/ste ₽2600/3300/5200; 📶) Kargopol's best hotel, with modern rooms, all with fridge and good bathrooms (with underfloor heating in the suites). Staff range from very obliging to those who look at you as if you're responsible for all the misery in their life. The basement restaurant is Kargopol's best, with bargain 'business lunches' (soup ₽45, mains ₽95) and wild game dishes (₽250 to ₽950).

Tsentralny Magazin SUPERMARKET $
(Центральный магазин; ul Lenina 57; ⏲24hr) Well-stocked grocery store.

ℹ Information

Map-guide pamphlets sold at the hotels (₽80) are in Russian but have photos. Hotel Kargopolochka sells maps of the region.

Kargopol Town (www.kargopol.ru) Useful English-language website about the town.

Sberbank (Сбербанк; ul Pobedy 12) Kargopol's only ATM.

ℹ Getting There & Away

BUS

Virtually all visitors arrive by train at Nyandoma, 80km east of Kargopol on the Vologda–Arkhangelsk line. Buses to Kargopol (₽168, 1½ hours) run from the car park in front of the railway station at 2.30pm and 1.30am daily, and at 7.30pm on Friday and Sunday, returning from Kargopol at noon and 9.30pm daily, and 4pm on Friday and Sunday. Shared taxis (₽400 to ₽500 per person, one hour) await each train.

TRAIN

Arriving at 10.03am on train 316 or 318 from Moscow, you could see all of Kargopol's sights in a day, then continue to Arkhangelsk on train 16 at 12.08am (every other day) or on daily train 371 at 1.36am. Southbound from Arkhangelsk, slow train 671 runs conveniently overnight, departing at 9.49pm and arriving at 7.06am. There are two or three departures for Vologda daily after midnight and at least three daily afternoon/evening arrivals from Vologda.

Around Kargopol

Kargopol district is known for its wealth of historic wooden churches, with specialised tours running from Kargopol.

The most impressive ensemble of 17th- and 18th-century wooden churches used to be beside the Pudozh road in the archetypal log-cottage village of **Lyadiny** (aka Gavrilovskaya), 35km west of Kargopol, but it perished in a fire of divine origin in 2012 when the bell tower was struck by lightning.

Kenozero National Park
Кенозерский национальный парк

The southern gateway to this delightful patchwork of forests, lakes and historic wooden churches is the quaint village of **Lekshmozero** (aka Morschihinskaya), which sits idyllically on the shores of large Lake Lekshmo. From where the bus terminates, walk back 30m to a *zhurval* (shadoof-style lever-well) and turn left along ul Zapadnaya to find the picturesquely crumbling lakeside **church**. A footpath along the shore brings you round to a striking yellow building that's both a hotel (single/double ₽750/880) and a helpful **national park visitor centre** (Визит-центр Кенозерского национального парка; ☎921-477 9075; www.kenozero.ru; ⏲9am-9pm Jun-Aug) that can arrange accommodation and tours of the area. Nearby, the **Fisherman's Hut Hotel**, managed by the visitor centre, offers woodsy double rooms for ₽1250 and a *banya* for guest use. There are no eateries in the village, but no less than four small grocery stores.

Lekshmozero is also the launching point for the popular **Ecological Route**, a one-day open-boat trip to a reconstructed traditional mill via a series of lakes and tiny linking canals – be prepared to get wet feet! Your best bet is to book through an agency: Lache Turbureau (p316) can help.

Buses from Kargopol to Lekshmozero (₽150, 1¾ hours) depart at 6.15am and 5.15pm on Tuesday and Friday, returning roughly two hours later. In spring the unpaved road is impassable by bus.

Volga Region

Includes ➡

Best Places to Eat

- Kafe-Bar Sasha (p338)
- Priyut Kholostyaka (p331)
- Staraya Kvartira (p337)
- Restoratsia Pyatkin (p324)
- Sharlay (p348)

Best Natural Settings

- Volga Delta (p348)
- Kalmykia (p349)
- Samara Bend (p339)
- Shiryaevo (p339)

Why Go?

The Volga (Волга), one of Europe's great rivers, winds for some 3530km through Russia's heartland and has been a part of the continent's longest 'highway' since time immemorial. The stretch of the Volga between Nizhny Novgorod and the Caspian Sea forms a rich and fascinating cultural region with over a dozen different ethnic groups, most notably the Volga Tatars. Travelling along or alongside the river you encounter spectacular hilltop kremlins in Nizhny Novgorod, Kazan and Astrakhan, bombastic architecture in Volgograd, numerous lively provincial capitals and picturesque stretches such as the Samara Bend. This natural beauty culminates in the magnificent Volga Delta south of Astrakhan, a vast region of reeds and waterways. West of the Volga River, Kalmykia takes in a windswept area of steppe that is home to the Buddhist Kalmyks, who originate from western Mongolia.

When to Go

Astrakhan

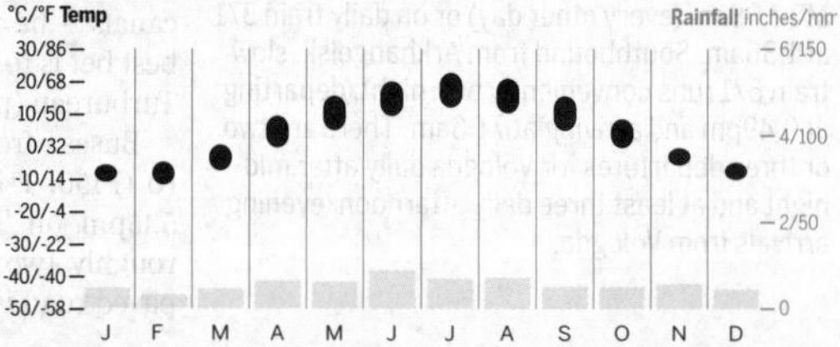

Feb Much of the Volga River is frozen over and draped in a winter landscape.

Late Apr–late May Spring sun warms the air and accommodation is plentiful.

Late Jul–Sep Navigation season is in full swing and lotus flowers bloom in the delta.

History

Since ancient times, the Volga has supported agricultural settlements and served as a main link in transcontinental commerce. More than 1000 years ago, the Vikings plied its waters, establishing a trade route between Baghdad and the Baltic.

Medieval Volga

In the Middle Ages, the Lower Volga was dominated by the Khazars, a Turkic tribe whose leaders converted to Judaism. The Khazar capital stood at Itil (present-day Astrakhan). The Middle Volga was the domain of another Turkic tribe, the Bulgars. Descendants of the Huns and distant relatives of the Balkan Bulgarians, they migrated eastwards, mixed with local Finno-Ugric

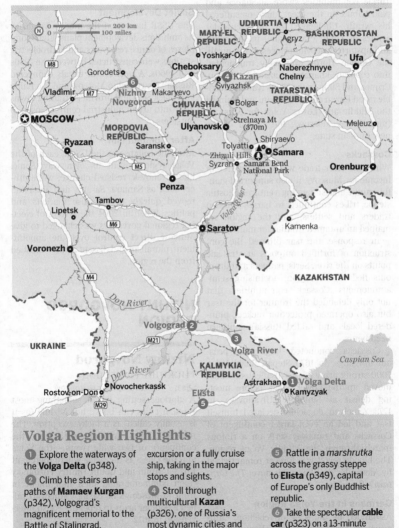

Volga Region Highlights

1. Explore the waterways of the **Volga Delta** (p348).
2. Climb the stairs and paths of **Mamaev Kurgan** (p342), Volgograd's magnificent memorial to the Battle of Stalingrad.
3. Sail the **Volga River** (p339) on a short excursion or a fully cruise ship, taking in the major stops and sights.
4. Stroll through multicultural **Kazan** (p326), one of Russia's most dynamic cities and home to a picturesque kremlin.
5. Rattle in a *marshrutka* across the grassy steppe to **Elista** (p349), capital of Europe's only Buddhist republic.
6. Take the spectacular **cable car** (p323) on a 13-minute ride across the Volga River in Nizhny Novgorod.

tribes and adopted Islam in the 10th century. The river was also a vital conduit in the lucrative fur trade for Novgorod's merchants.

The Golden Horde

In the 13th century, the entire Volga region was conquered by the heirs of Chinggis (Genghis) Khaan, the Mongol-led Golden Horde, who made Saray (near present-day Volgograd and Astrakhan) their capital. For the next 200 years, the Volga's Slavic and Turkic communities swore allegiance and paid tribute to the great khan, or suffered his wrath. Challenged by the marauder armies of Timur (Tamerlane) in the south and upstart Muscovite princes in the north, the Golden Horde eventually fragmented into separate khanates: Kazan, Astrakhan, Crimea and Sibir. In the 1550s Ivan the Terrible razed Kazan and Astrakhan, and claimed the Middle and Lower Volga for Muscovy (modern-day Moscow), the capital of the new Russian state.

Cossacks

While the river trade was a rich source of income for Muscovy, it also supported gainful bandit and smuggling ventures. Hostile steppe tribes continued to harass Russian traders and settlers, and the region remained an untamed frontier for many years.

In response, the tsar ordered the construction of fortified outposts at strategic points on the river. Serfs, paupers and dropouts fled to the region, organising semiautonomous Cossack communities that not only defended the frontier for the tsar but also operated protection rackets, plundered locals and raided Russia's southern neighbours.

Cossacks conducted large-scale peasant uprisings. In 1670 Stepan Razin led a 7000-strong army of the disaffected, which moved up the Lower Volga before meeting defeat at Simbirsk (Ulyanovsk). In 1773 Yemelyan Pugachev declared himself tsar and led an even larger contingent of Cossacks and runaway serfs on a riotous march through the Middle Volga region. The bloody revolt was forever romanticised by Alexander Pushkin in his novel *The Captain's Daughter*.

Germans in the Volga Region

Astounded by the scale of rebellion, Catherine the Great sought to bolster the economic development of the region by inviting Germany's peasants to settle there from 1763, especially around Saratov. By the end of the 19th century, the population of ethnic Germans had reached more than 1.5 million.

In the 1920s a German autonomous republic was established along the Lower Volga, but it was dissolved amid persecutions during WWII and German inhabitants were forced into exile. After Stalin's death, nearly a million survivors were liberated from Siberian labour camps, but were not allowed to return to their old villages.

Soviet Development

The USSR harnessed the mighty Volga for its ambitious development plans. Eight complexes of dams, reservoirs and hydroelectric stations were constructed between the 1930s and 1960s. A network of canals connected Russia's heartland to Moscow and the Baltic and Black Seas and provincial trading towns grew into urban industrial centres closed to outsiders.

After Communism

After the collapse of the USSR, each of the Volga regions went its own way. Some, like Ulyanovsk, resisted change, while others such as Samara, Saratov and Tatarstan moved quickly to liberalise markets and politics. When in 2004 the system of electing regional governors was changed to give Moscow direct control over the appointment, pluralism and dissent all but vanished from the region.

NIZHNY NOVGOROD REGION

Nizhny Novgorod
Нижний Новгород

☎831 / POP 1.25 MILLION / ⏲ MOSCOW

A glorious setting is not something most Russian cities can boast, but Nizhny (as it is usually called) is a lucky exception. The mighty clifftop kremlin overlooking the confluence of two wide rivers – the Volga and the Oka – is the place where merchant Kuzma Minin and Count Dmitry Pozharsky (men commemorated in a monument in front of Moscow's St Basil's Cathedral) rallied a popular army to repel the Polish intervention in 1612.

Nizhny has been a major trading centre since its foundation in 1221. In the 19th century, when the lower bank of the Oka housed

NIZHNY NOVGOROD'S STATE MUSEUMS

Nizhny Novgorod has an excellent ensemble of museums inside and around the kremlin.

Nizhegorodsky State Art Museum (Нижегородский государственный художественный музей; www.ngiamz.ru; admission ₽100; 11am-6pm Wed-Mon) The former governor's house inside the kremlin is now the Nizhegorodsky State Art Museum. Exhibits range from 14th-century icons to 20th-century paintings by artists such as Nikolai Rerikh and Vasily Surikov.

The museum begins (on the left after you enter) with 14th-century icons. The entire collection is chronological, so you can see by room 6 how rudimentary landscape perspectives creep into 17th-century icons. After the icons comes the large collection of mostly oil-on-canvas paintings by Russian masters, culminating in Soviet art. The English descriptions are excellent.

National Centre of Contemporary Art (Государственный центр coвepeмeннoгo исткуства; www.ncca.ru; admission ₽100; noon-8pm Tue-Sun) Situated in the former arsenal on the right after you enter the main gate of the kremlin, this top-ranking gallery has changing exhibitions of international and Russian contemporary artists. From early 2015 the complete arsenal will have been restored and the centre will also have a concert venue, expanded exhibition space and a restaurant.

Western European Art Collection (Собрание Западноевропейское искусство; www.ngiamz.ru; Verkhne-Volzhskaya nab 3; admission ₽120; 11am-6pm Wed & Fri-Mon, noon-8pm Thu) This fine gallery is just a short walk from the kremlin along Verkhne-Volzhskaya nab, an attractive street lined with restored 19th-century buildings. Inside the art gallery you will find a collection of mostly anonymous or lesser-known European painters who, despite their modest credentials, produced some remarkable works.

Rukavishnikov Mansion (Усадьба Рукавишникова; www.ngiamz.ru; Verkhne-Volzhskaya nab 7; Russian/foreigner ₽80/200, tours ₽200/300; 10am-5pm Tue-Thu, noon-7pm Fri-Sun) This exhibition space is located inside a 19th-century mansion once belonging to the Rukavishnikov merchant family. You can wander through the rooms on your own or join one of the hourly 40-minute excursions in Russian and English. Furniture and the illustrious interior of the unusual mansion are the threads running through the tours or a visit, and these are complemented by changing exhibitions – often with a focus on household furnishing and objects.

the country's main fair – *yarmarka* – it was said that 'St Petersburg is Russia's head; Moscow its heart; and Nizhny Novgorod its wallet'. During Soviet times the city was named Gorky, after the writer Maxim Gorky, born here in 1868. Closed to foreigners by the Soviets, Gorky was chosen as a place of exile for the dissident physicist Andrei Sakharov.

Nizhny is often called Russia's 'third capital', but it is the fifth-largest Russian city and markedly quieter than Moscow and St Petersburg, with a laid-back ambience characteristic of the Volga cities downstream.

Sights

★Kremlin HISTORICAL SITE

(Нижегородский Кремль; www.ngiamz.ru) FREE Built upon remnants of an earlier settlement, Nizhny Novgorod's magnificent kremlin dates back to 1500–15 when the Italian architect Pyotr Fryazin began work on its 13 towers and 12m-high walls. Inside, most of the buildings are government offices. The small 17th-century **Cathedral of the Archangel Michael** (Собор Михаила Архангела) is a functioning church. Behind it, an eternal flame burns near a striking **Monument to Heroes of WWII**.

Dmitry Tower MUSEUM

(Дмитриевская башня; museum ₽60, kremlin wall walk incl other towers Russian/foreigner ₽180/240; 10am-5pm Tue-Sun, kremlin wall walk May-Oct) The Dmitry Tower, the main entrance to the kremlin, has changing exhibitions on local history. This is a good place to start a 1.2km walk around the kremlin walls.

Nizhny Novgorod

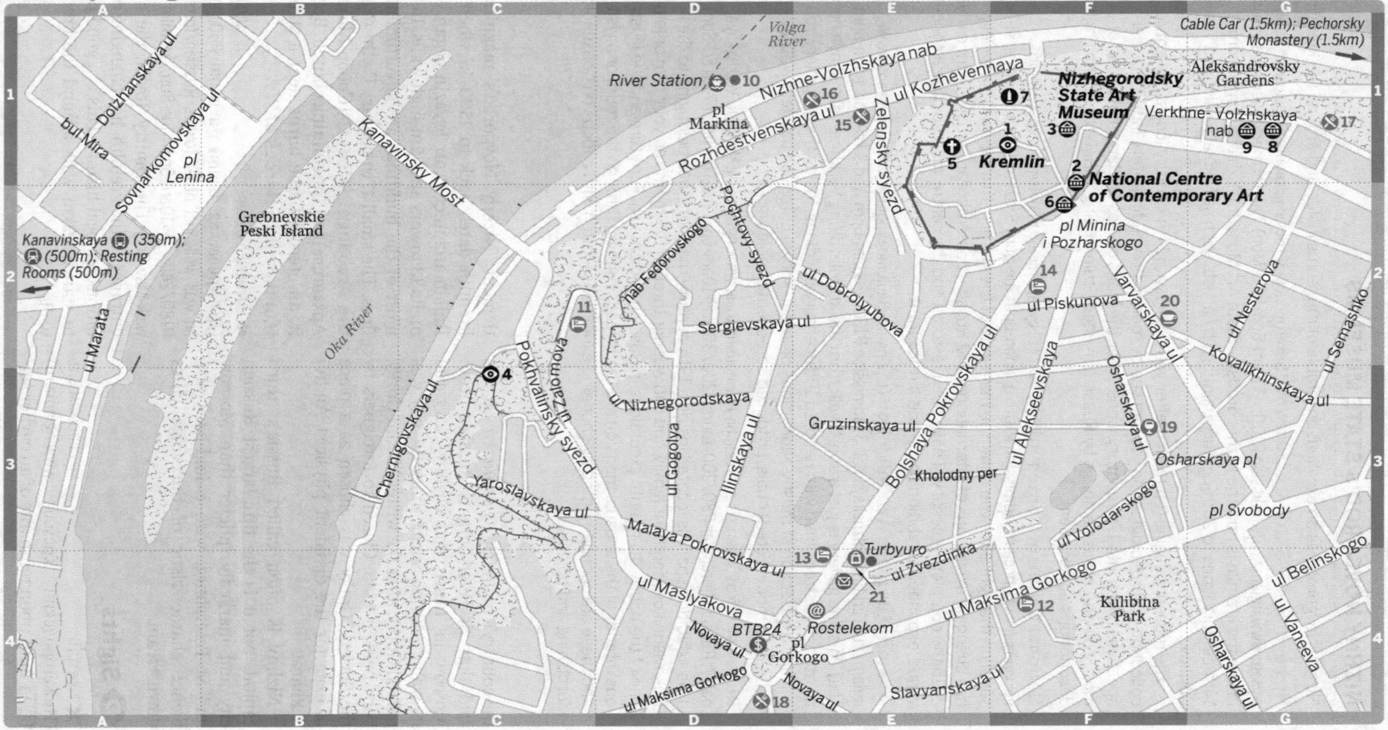
0 1 km
0 0.5 miles
A B C D E F G
1 2 3 4
Cable Car (1.5km); Pechorsky Monastery (1.5km)
Aleksandrovsky Gardens
Volga River
River Station
10
Nizhne-Volzhskaya nab
ul Kozhevennaya
Nizhegorodsky State Art Museum
7
1
3
5
Kremlin
2
National Centre of Contemporary Art
6
Verkhne- Volzhskaya nab
9
8
17
16
15
pl Markina
Rozhdestvenskaya ul
Zelensky syezd
pl Minina i Pozharskogo
14
Dolzhanskaya ul
bul Mira
Sovnarkomovskaya ul
pl Lenina
Kanavinsky Most
Grebnevskie Peski Island
Kanavinskaya (350m); (500m); Resting Rooms (500m)
Pochtovy syezd
nab Fedorovskogo
ul Dobrolyubova
ul Piskunova
20
Varvarskaya ul
ul Nesterova
ul Semashko
11
Sergievskaya ul
Oka River
ul Marata
4
Pokhvalinsky syezd
ul Zalomova
ul Nizhegorodskaya
Kovalikhinskaya ul
Gruzinskaya ul
Bolshaya Pokrovskaya ul
ul Alekseevskaya
Osharskaya ul
19
Chernigovskaya ul
Ilinskaya ul
ul Gogolya
Kholodny per
Osharskaya pl
Yaroslavskaya ul
pl Svobody
ul Volodarskogo
Malaya Pokrovskaya ul
13
Turbyuro
ul Zvezdinka
21
ul Maslyakova
ul Maksima Gorkogo
12
Kulibina Park
ul Belinskogo
ul Vaneeva
Osharskaya ul
Rostelekom
BTB24
pl Gorkogo
Novaya ul
ul Maksima Gorkogo
Novaya ul
18
Slavyanskaya ul

Nizhny Novgorod

Top Sights

1 Kremlin F1
2 National Centre of Contemporary Art F1
3 Nizhegorodsky State Art Museum F1

Sights

4 Annunciation Monastery C3
5 Cathedral of the Archangel Michael E1
6 Dmitry Tower F2
7 Monument to Heroes of WWII F1
8 Rukavishnikov Mansion G1
9 Western European Art Collection G1

Activities, Courses & Tours

10 Vodokhod Tour Office D1

Sleeping

11 AZIMUT Hotel Nizhny Novgorod C2
12 Ibis Hotel F4
13 Jouk-Jacques E4
14 Smile F2

Eating

15 Bezukhov E1
Biblioteka .... (see 21)
16 Restoratsia Pyatkin E1
17 Tiffani G1
18 Vesyolaya Kuma D4

Drinking & Nightlife

19 Art-Cafe Bufet F3
20 Tsiferblat F2

Shopping

21 Dirizhabl E4

★ **Cable Car** CABLE CAR

(Kazanskaya naberezhe; one way ₽75; 6.45am-10pm Mon-Sat, from 9am Sun, closed 11am-1pm Mon & Thu) Connecting Nizhny Novgorod with the unattractive settlement of Bor across the Volga, this cable car offers a spectacular 13-minute ride. In winter there are views of dot-sized figures fishing on Volga ice below, and in summer there's swamp, lush greens and gentle blues. Take any bus to Sennaya bus station and walk back for a few minutes towards the mosque. The ride peaks at over 80m and is a nerve-shattering 3.6km long.

Pechorsky Monastery MONASTERY

(Privolzhskaya sloboda 108) This 17th-century monastery, overlooking the Volga, is perfect for a tranquil stroll in small but picturesque grounds. Take any *marshrutka* or bus from pl Minina i Pozharskogo to pl Sennaya.

➡ **Museum of the Nizhny Novgorod Diocese** MUSEUM

(Церковно-археологический музей Нижегородской епархии; admission ₽100; 9am-5pm) Located inside the Pechorsky Monastery, this small museum has a moving exhibition on Bolshevik repressions against the church and a floor with changing exhibitions on religious themes.

Annunciation Monastery MONASTERY

(Благовещенский монастырь; ul Garshina; 7am-8pm) FREE Set at the foot of attractive parkland, the 13th-century Annunciation Monastery, above Chernigovskaya ul, is one of Nizhny Novgorod's oldest buildings. Most of the churches themselves are from the 17th century and are well worth visiting for their interiors.

Museum of Volga People's Architecture & Culture MUSEUM

(Музей архитектуры и быта народов Нижегородского Поволжья; 831-422 4054; Gorbatovskaya ul 41; admission ₽60; 10am-5pm Tue-Sun) The open-air Museum of Volga People's Architecture & Culture has a pleasant woodland setting and a collection of traditional wooden buildings from Russian and Mordva (a Finno-Ugric people) villages. The museum is located in the remote Shchelokovsky Khutor Park, which is the final stop of bus 28 (30 minutes, every hour), passing ul Belinskogo in the centre. *Marshrutka* 62 also stops close.

Sakharov Museum MUSEUM

(Музей Сахарова; pr Gagarina 214; admission ₽70; 9am-5pm Sat-Thu) The Sakharov Museum is in the flat where dissident scientist Andrei Sakharov spent six years in exile. The Nobel laureate was held incommunicado until 1986 when a KGB officer came to install a telephone – when it rang, Mikhail Gorbachev was calling to inform Sakharov of his release. The phone is a highlight of the exhibition. To get there, take bus 1 from pl Minina i Pozharskogo or *marshrutka* 3 or 19 from pl Gorkogo to the Muzey Akademika Sakharova stop.

Tours

Team Gorky TOUR COMPANY

(831-278 9404; www.teamgorky.ru; ul 40 let Oktyabrya 1a; 8.30am-7.30pm Mon-Fri) Gorky takes visitors on summer canoe and rafting tours, and on winter ski treks in the Nizhny Novgorod region and beyond. Weekend cross-country ski tours cost ₽7300. Be flexible about dates as individuals join groups.

Vodokhod Tour Office TOUR COMPANY
(Водоходъ; ☎831-461 8030; www.vftour.ru; ⊙10am-9pm Mon-Fri, to 7pm Sat & Sun) Inside the river station building and the cash office on the embankment, this office sells mostly weekend day trips, departing early morning, to the ancient Makaryev Monastery (₽1500), in the village of Makaryevo, 60km to the east. Book ahead. Food and an excursion are included.

Sleeping

★Smile HOSTEL $
(☎831-216 0222; www.smilehostel.net; Bolshaya Pokrovskaya ul 4; dm/d ₽590/1690; ⊜@☜) Bright, friendly and efficient, this centrally located hostel has two doubles with twin beds that can be booked as a single, as well as five-, six- and eight-bed dorms. There's free tea and coffee, separate male and female bathroom facilities and a nice communal area.

Resting Rooms HOSTEL $
(Комнаты отдыха; ☎831-248 2107; train station; 12/24hr from ₽400/690, registration ₽300) Located in a separate building on your right as you exit the train station.

AZIMUT Hotel Nizhny Novgorod HOTEL $$
(☎831-461 9242; www.azimut-nn.ru; ul Zalomova 2; with breakfast s ₽3500, d ₽3700-5000, ste ₽7400; ⊜☜) This concrete eyesore has good refurbished rooms, some with fabulous river views. Steps just to the left as you exit lead directly to the Rozhdestvenskaya bus stop, where bus 45 picks up for pl Minina i Pozharskogo and buses 43, 26 and 5 go to the train station. Pl Gorkogo is 1km by foot.

Ibis Hotel HOTEL $$
(Ибис Отель; ☎831-233 1100; www.ibishotel.com; ul Maksima Gorkogo 115; r from ₽3100; ⊜@☜) Nizhny's Ibis offers a high standard of rooms and comforts, with the advantage that it's large enough to cope with busy periods.

★Jouk-Jacques BOUTIQUE HOTEL $$$
(Жук-Жак; ☎831-433 0462; www.jak-hotel.ru; Bolshaya Pokrovskaya ul 57; with breakfast s ₽3750-6825, d/ste ₽6825/9375; ❄☜) This cosy boutique hotel is one of the best in town. Rooms are modern and decorated in soft tones, some facing the yard. The cheapest are a bit cramped but they're neat, and breakfasts are superb.

Eating & Drinking

Biblioteka ITALIAN $
(Библиотека; Bolshaya Pokrovskaya ul 46; mains ₽250; ⊙11am-10pm; ⊜✎▤) Upstairs from the Dirizhabl bookshop with generic but tasty Italian dishes in an informal, quirky atmosphere.

★Restoratsia Pyatkin RUSSIAN $$
(Ресторация Пяткин; ☎831-430 9183; Rozhdestvenskaya ul 23; mains ₽400; ⊙noon-midnight; 👪) Pyatkin makes you feel like a merchant back in his mansion after a great trading day at the fair. The menu is full of Volga fish specialities; it brews the unusual apple *kvas* (fermented rye bread water) for ₽65 and has a children's menu.

Bezukhov RUSSIAN, INTERNATIONAL $$
(Безухов; www.bezuhov.ru; Rozhdestvenskaya ul 6; mains ₽400; ⊙24hr; ☜✎▤) This literary cafe with antique furnishings, stucco ceiling and the feel of a living room is part of a Nizhny Novgorod project called 'Eda i Kultura' (Food and Culture), which brings food and culture together into a delicious whole. The menu is overflowing with salads, pastas and fish, poultry and red-meat dishes, and augmented by good breakfasts.

Vesyolaya Kuma UKRAINIAN $$
(ul Kostina 3; mains ₽400; ⊙noon-midnight Sun-Wed, to 2am Thu-Sat; ⊜▤) Set among a row of lesser restaurants, the 'Happy Godmother' merrily serves hearty borsch and other Ukrainian fare.

Tiffani INTERNATIONAL $$
(Тиффани; ☎831-419 4101; Verkhne-Volzhskaya nab 8; mains ₽600; ⊙11am-2am; ☜✎▤) This upmarket all-rounder is a restaurant during the day and evening, a cafe at any time and has well-known DJs some nights. The views across the Volga to the forest are spectacular.

★Art-Cafe Bufet BAR
(Арт-Кафе Буфет; Osharskaya ul 14; ⊙noon-2am; ☜) Descending the steps of this excellent art bar is to step into a bohemian world of monkey-motif wallpaper. The ambience is relaxed and alternative, and it stages lots of events as part of the Eda i Kultura movement.

Tsiferblat ANTI-CAFE

(Циферблат; http://nino.ziferblat.net; Kovalikhinskaya ul 4a; 1st 30min ₽60, ₽1 per min subsequently; ⌚11am-midnight Sun-Thu, to 2am Fri & Sat; 📶) This anti-cafe, located upstairs in the building with the 'Photohouse' sign, has cosy rooms for reading, playing the piano, balalaika and guitar, indulging in a board game or simply enjoying the coffee and tea.

Shopping

Dirizhabl BOOKSTORE

(Bolshaya Pokrovskaya ul 46; ⌚10am-9pm Mon-Sat, 11am-8pm Sun) A good selection of maps and local guidebooks, and some books in foreign languages.

Information

BTB24 (БТБ24; pl Maksima Gorkogo 4/2) ATM, accepts major cards.

Central Post Office (Центральный почтамт; pl Gorkogo; ⌚8am-8pm Mon-Fri, 10am-5pm Sat & Sun) Has a railway and airline booking office.

Rostelekom (pl Gorkogo; per 30min ₽50; ⌚9am-9pm)

Getting There & Away

AIR

The **Nizhny Novgorod International Airport** (www.nnov-airport.ru/eng) is 15km southwest of the city centre. **S7** (www.s7.ru) flies at least daily to/from Moscow and **Lufthansa** (www.lufthansa.com) flies directly to/from Frankfurt six times a week. Airline tickets are available at agencies around the city, including **Turbyuro** (Турбюро; ☎381-437 0101; www.tourburo.nnov.ru; ul Zvezdinka 10b; ⌚8am-8pm Mon-Sat).

BOAT

The **river station** (Речной вокзал; Nizhne-Volzhskaya nab) is below the kremlin. All services on the Volga are cruise, day-excursion or tourist boats. Unfortunately, there are no short-hop ferries between major towns. Hydrofoils to Gorodets leave from their own pier at the river station.

BUS

Buses to Vladimir (₽540, four hours, eight daily), Kostroma (₽900, nine hours, daily) and Gorodets (₽170, two hours, about every half-hour) depart from the small **Kanavinskaya bus station** (Автостанция Канавинская; ☎831-246 2021; www.nnov.org/transport/busm/kanavinskaya; ul Sovetskaya 20a). Private operators run minibuses to Moscow (₽700, six hours, at least six daily), which depart across the road from the train station; others leave from the bus station.

TRAIN

Nizhny Novgorod train station is still sometimes known as Gorky-Moskovsky vokzal, so 'Gorky' appears on some timetables. It's on the western bank of the Oka River, at pl Revolyutsii. The service centre at the train station is helpful for buying rail tickets and also has internet.

Westbound

The high-speed *Sapsan/Lastochka* runs to Moscow's Kursky vokzal (seat ₽1325, four hours, two daily). More than a dozen other trains also serve Moscow (₽1100, seven hours) via Vladimir (₽700, three hours). The *Volga* (059) runs to/from St Petersburg (₽2800, 14½ hours, daily).

Eastbound

Trans-Siberian flagships run to Perm (₽2495, 14½ hours, daily) and beyond, but lesser trains do the trip for ₽1650 – for Kazan (₽1717, nine hours, daily) the No 41 is a top-flight (and only) choice. Other trains go to Yekaterinburg (₽3227, 21 hours, five to eight daily) and beyond.

Getting Around

The three major hubs for public transport are the train station (Московский вокзал), pl Minina i

NICK CAVE & THE VOLGA

The connection between rock musician Nick Cave, the Seekers – a popular Australian folk band of the 1960s – and the Volga River would seem tenuous, but one of the most popular songs by the Seekers, and a classic cover that any Nick Cave fan will know, is the mournful 'The Carnival Is Over'. In fact, this classic dirge is a Volga folk song about the ataman Stepan Razin, who threw a kidnapped Persian princess overboard from a pirated ship on the Volga to prevent his men from dallying with her (probably not the best solution for such circumstances, but anyway). Songwriter Tom Springfield (brother of 1960s singer Dusty, for trivia freaks) wrote the English lyrics to the Seekers' version, and this obscure Volga song popular in the late 19th century acquired a double-bass backing and a slightly de-Russified folk edge, eventually landing high among the top-50 best-selling records of all time. You can check out the three versions on YouTube.

A VOLGA ENCOUNTER

The first traveller to write a Volga diary was Ahmed ibn-Fadlan, a secretary of the Baghdadi embassy who arrived in Great Bulgar in 922 to convert the local khan and his people to Islam. His travelogue is one of very few preserved written documents describing the ancient people who populated the area and travelled up and down the Volga. One of his most striking stories describes an encounter with Scandinavian travellers, whom ibn-Fadlan describes as 'people with most perfect bodies', but also as 'the dirtiest of Allah's creatures'.

Pozharskogo (пл Минина и Пожарского) near the kremlin, and pl Gorkogo (пл Горького) south of this. Buses and *marshrutky* from the train station serve the latter two, and you can change for one or the other at the stop on the city side of the bridge, Kanavinsky most. At pl Minina i Pozharskogo, transport heading back to the train station picks up from the kremlin side of the road.

The city's metro has a useful link between pl Gorkogo and the train station.

Gorodets Городец

This neat little town, famous for its distinct style of folk art, appeals to day trippers arriving in hydrofoils or by bus from Nizhny Novgorod. At the time of the schism in the Russian Orthodox Church (1660), Gorodets became home to a population of Old Believers seeking religious sanctuary. They became skilful craftsmen, artists and wealthy tradesmen.

In a largely illiterate society, Gorodets' oil-on-wood paintings played the role of glossy magazines about lifestyle and current events. Today you can buy pictures (from ₽200) or a whole piece of furniture, painted in Gorodets style. The town's other speciality is *pryaniki* – hard honey-rich cakes sold in most shops.

Sights

Countess Panina's House MUSEUM
(Дом графини Паниной; ul Rublyova 16; admission ₽40; ⏲10am-5pm Tue-Fri, to 4pm Sat & Sun) This museum recreates the atmosphere of the 19th century. The countess Panina was the last of the residents in the mansion, where the mainstay is a large collection of irons and historic clothing.

Museum of Samovars MUSEUM
(Музей самоваров в Городце; nab Revolyutsii 11; admission ₽50; ⏲9am-5pm Tue-Fri, 10am-4pm Sat & Sun) All types of the quintessential Russian tea-making equipment are on display here.

Gorodets Regional Museum MUSEUM
(Городецкий краеведческий музей; ul Lenina 11; admission ₽50; ⏲9am-5pm Tue-Fri, 10am-4pm Sat & Sun) Exhibits on the history of Gorodets and the region include the Virgin of Feodorovo icon – a curious three-dimensional depiction of Jesus creating a holographic effect.

Children's Museum MUSEUM
(Детский музей на Купеческой; ul Lenina 12; admission ₽40; ⏲10am-5pm Tue-Fri, to 4pm Sat & Sun) This replica of a 19th-century schoolroom offers classes in the making of Gorodets-style animal-shaped clay penny whistles.

Getting There & Away

Several hydrofoils leave daily for Gorodets from Nizhny Novgorod's river station (₽200, one hour) in season. Vodokhod Tour Office (p324) in Nizhny Novgorod runs excursions for around ₽700. Buses run from Nizhny Novgorod's bus station (₽170, two hours, about half-hourly).

REPUBLIC OF TATARSTAN

Kazan Казань

☎843 / POP 1.45 MILLION / ⏲MOSCOW

Kazan (meaning a cooking pot in Tatar) is the Istanbul of the Volga, a place where Europe and Asia curiously inspect each other from the tops of church belfries and minarets. It is about 150 years older than Moscow and the capital of the Tatarstan Republic (Республика Татарстан) – the land of the Volga Tatars, a Turkic people commonly associated with Chinggis Khaan's hordes.

Tatar autonomy is strong here and is not just about bilingual street signs. Moscow has pumped vast sums into the republic to persuade it to remain a loyal part of Russia. It also ensures that Tatarstan benefits greatly from the vast oil reserves in this booming republic.

Although Tatar nationalism is strong, it is not radical, and the local version of Sunni Islam is very moderate. Slavic Russians make up about half of the population, and this cultural conflux of Slavic and Tatar cultures makes Kazan an all-the-more-interesting city.

History

Kazan was founded as a northeastern outpost of Volga Bulgaria around AD 1000. After the Tatar Mongols flattened Great Bulgar, it became the capital of the region and was incorporated into the Golden Horde. The independent Kazan khanate was created in 1438. It was ravaged in 1552 by Ivan the Terrible's troops and Tatar allies, and the collapse also cleared the way for Slavic Russians to move into the Urals region around Perm.

Tsar Ivan was quick to build a new – Russian – city on the ruins. Architects responsible for St Basil's Cathedral in Moscow (which honours the seizure of Kazan) were employed to plan the kremlin. Tatars were banished from the northern side of the Bulak Canal (about 500m east of the Volga shoreline) until the enlightened age of Catherine the Great, which is why the main Tatar quarter is southeast of the canal.

Kazan grew into one of Russia's economic and cultural capitals, with the country's third university opening here in 1804. Its alumni include Leo Tolstoy and Vladimir Ulyanov (ie Lenin), who stirred up political trouble and was expelled.

◉ Sights

★ Kremlin HISTORICAL SITE

(Казанский Кремль; ⊘ 8am-10pm, to 8pm in winter) **FREE** Kazan's striking kremlin is home to government offices, pleasant parks, museums, the enormous Kul Sharif Mosque and other religious buildings. Among the highlights are the Hermitage Kazan gallery and the Tatarstan Museum of Natural History. Some of the white limestone kremlin walls date from the 16th and 17th centuries.

➡ Musa Dzhalil Monument MONUMENT

(Памятник Мусе Джалилю; kremlin) This striking bronze figure of a man tearing barbed wire is at the entrance to the kremlin and was erected to honour the Tatar poet who was executed by the Nazis in Berlin's Moabit Prison in 1944, leaving a notebook full of poems to a Belgian friend.

➡ ★ Hermitage Kazan MUSEUM

(Эрмитаж-Казань; kremlin; admission ₽150; ⊘ 10am-5.30pm Tue-Thu, Sat & Sun, noon-8.30pm Fri) Located inside the former cadet school building, the Hermitage Kazan has top-flight rotating exhibitions, many of them from the collection of St Petersburg's Hermitage.

➡ ★ Tatarstan Museum of Natural History MUSEUM

(Музей естественной истории Татарстана; kremlin; admission ₽150; ⊘ 10am-6pm Tue-Thu, Sat & Sun, noon-9pm Fri) About a dozen rooms here tell the story of the planets, geology and minerals, and the development of life forms on Earth. The most interesting sections are on dinosaurs and the rise of mammals.

VOLGA REGION KAZAN

THE TRUE STORY OF THE DEFIANT PRINCESS

When Ivan the Terrible seized Kazan, a local tale goes, he planned to marry Syuyumbike, the beautiful niece of the deposed khan. Nobody wants an ugly, paranoid dictator as a husband, so out of sheer desperation she agreed to marry him only if he built a tower higher than anything either of them had ever seen. Once the construction was complete, she ascended the tower and threw herself off in front of the bewildered Ivan.

A neat little tale, but residents of the small town of Kasimov, hidden in the forests of the Ryazan region on the banks of the Oka, have a different story. In medieval times, Kasimov was a Tatar stronghold and a major rival of Kazan. Therefore its khan, Shakh-Ali, was all too keen to accept Tsar Ivan's invitation to join the expedition against Kazan, especially since he was promised Syuyumbike as a trophy. When he met the captured princess, Shakh-Ali disliked her from first sight, but he eventually succumbed to Ivan's dynastic manipulations and married her. The newlyweds went to Kasimov and avoided each other for the rest of their long lives, with Syuyumbike transforming from a tiny Eastern beauty into a bulky matriarch keen on political intrigue.

Kazan

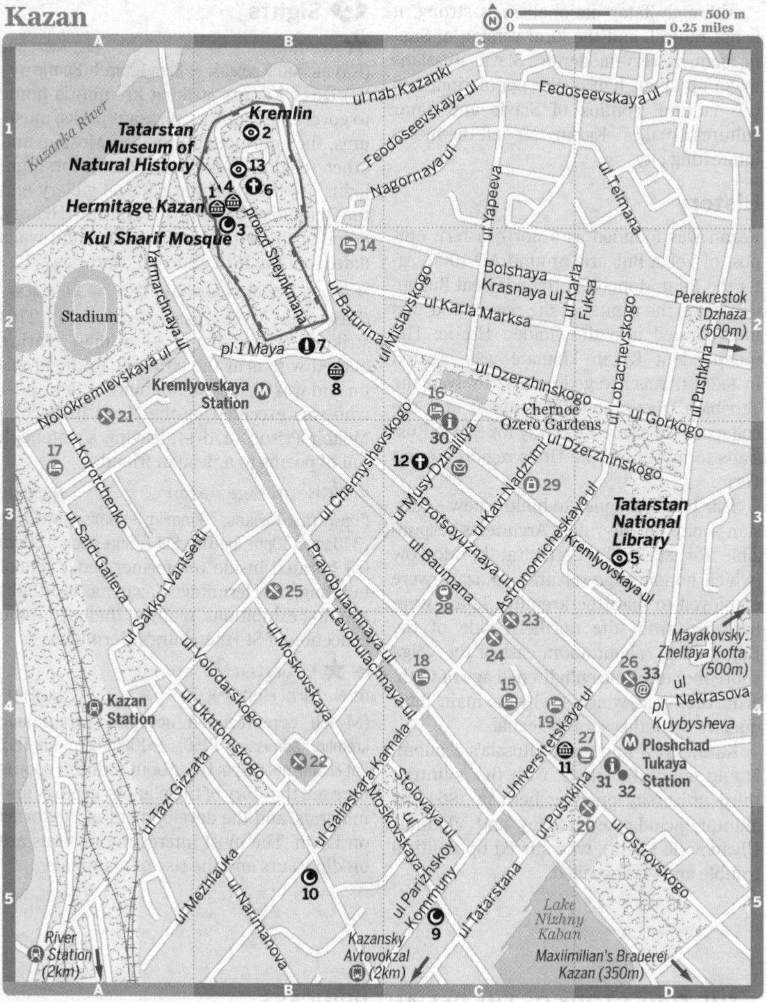

➡ ★ **Kul Sharif Mosque** MOSQUE

(Мечеть Кул Шариф; kremlin; museum admission ₽100; ⌚noon-9pm Fri, 10am-6pm Sat-Thu) The Kul Sharif Mosque was completed in 2005 and is named after the imam who died defending the city against the troops of Ivan the Terrible in 1552. The museum inside tells the story of Islam, especially on the Volga, and includes manuscripts, some pieces of furniture and women's costumes.

➡ **Annunciation Cathedral** CHURCH

(Благовещенский собор; kremlin) The attractive Annunciation Cathedral, built on the foundations of a razed eight-minaret mosque, was designed by Postnik Yakovlev, who was also responsible for St Basil's Cathedral in Moscow.

➡ **Syuyumbike Tower** HISTORICAL BUILDING

(Башня Сююмбике; kremlin) The 59m-high leaning Syuyumbike Tower is the subject of the most romantic of Kazan's legends (p327).

National Museum of the Republic of Tatarstan MUSEUM

(Национальный музей Республики Татарстан; Kremlyovskaya ul 2; admission ₽150; ⌚10am-6pm Tue-Sun) Opposite the

Kazan

Top Sights

1	Hermitage Kazan	B1
2	Kremlin	B1
3	Kul Sharif Mosque	B1
4	Tatarstan Museum of Natural History	B1
5	Tatarstan National Library	D3

Sights

6	Annunciation Cathedral	B1
7	Musa Dzhalil Monument	B2
8	National Museum of the Republic of Tatarstan	B2
9	Nurullah Mosque	C5
10	Soltanov Mosque	B5
11	Soviet Lifestyle Museum	C4
12	SS Peter & Paul Cathedral	C3
13	Syuyumbike Tower	B1

Sleeping

14	Hostel Kremlin	B2
15	Hotel Art	C4
16	Hotel Giuseppe	C2
17	Hotel Volga	A3
18	Ibis Hotel	C4
19	Shalyapin Palace Hotel	C4

Eating

20	Art Café	D5
21	Bahetle	A2
22	Central Market	B4
23	Dom Tatarskoy Kulinarii	C4
	Giuseppe	(see 16)
24	Kazan Askhane-Chai Yorty	C4
25	Priyut Kholostyaka	B3
26	Stolle	D4

Drinking & Nightlife

27	Capital Coffee House	D4
28	Cuba Libre	C3

Shopping

29	Dom Knigi	C3

Information

30	Kazan Tourist Information Centre	C3
31	Kazan Tourist Office branch	D4

Transport

32	Aviakassa	D4
33	Tattelekom	D4

kremlin's main entrance, the National Museum occupies an ornate 1770 building and has a worthwhile archaeology collection as well as jewellery, weapons and exhibits on the history of the Tatar people and its literary figures.

Tatarstan National Library LIBRARY
(Национальная библиотека Республики Татарстан; ☎843-238 79100; Kremlyovskaya ul 33; tours in English/Russian ₽200/100; ⏰9am-6pm) This small but extraordinary library dates from 1919, when several mid-19th-century houses were united and restyled to give each room its own art nouveau theme. Call ahead for English tours, or just drop by for one in Russian.

Soviet Lifestyle Museum MUSEUM
(Музей социалистического быта; www.muzeisb.ru; Universitetskaya ul 6; admission ₽160; ⏰11am-7pm) Kazan's most unusual museum, packed with Soviet knick-knacks, is proof that Russia's socialist epoch fostered a lively contemporary cultural scene – especially music – in the 1970s and 1980s.

SS Peter & Paul Cathedral CHURCH
(Петропавловский собор; ul Musy Dzhalilya 21) This is Kazan's most attractive Orthodox church, built between 1723 and 1726 to commemorate Peter the Great's visit in 1722.

Soltanov Mosque MOSQUE
(Мечеть Солтанов; ul Gabdully Tukaya 14) The Soltanov mosque, dating from 1867, is located near the central market in the Tatar quarter of town. The colourful interior has a rustic feel. Remove your shoes and make a donation.

Nurullah Mosque MOSQUE
(Мечеть Нурулла; ul Moskovskaya 74) The Nurullah mosque, one of the most historic of the 41 surviving mosques in Kazan, has been rebuilt several times since 1849. A shop sells Islamic paraphernalia. Remove your shoes and donate during the visit.

Festivals & Events

Sabantuy CULTURAL
(koresh) Joking competitions and serious sport events – horse races and wrestling matches – feature prominently during Sabantuy, the main Tatar holiday celebrated all over Tatarstan and beyond on the third Saturday of June. The winner of the wrestling competition is named Batyr and has to lift an overweight ram onto his shoulders for the cheering crowd.

Sleeping

★**Hostel Kremlin** HOSTEL $
(Хостел Кремлин; ☎8-905 311 4488; www.hostelkremlin.com; Bolshaya Krasnaya ul 8; dm

WORTH A TRIP

BOLGAR – BACK TO THE ROOTS

It might be the smallest town in Tatarstan, but Bolgar (Болгар) shares its name on equal terms with the country of Bulgaria. The word 'Volga' is most likely a Slavic corruption of the same name. Bolgar is the descendant of Great Bulgar, the capital of one of the most powerful states of early medieval Eastern Europe. Ruins of that city, on the outskirts of the modern town, have been turned into an open-air museum, which has become a major place of pilgrimage for Tatars in search of their roots.

The Bulgars were a Turkic tribe based south of the Don when they came under pressure from the Khazars and had to migrate. One branch headed west and occupied the eastern Balkans, but it was soon assimilated by local Slavs, leaving no trace but the name. The eastern branch settled on the Volga and mixed with local Finno-Ugric tribes. Sunni Islam became the official religion in 921.

Sights

Bolgar State Historical-Architectural Museum Reserve (Болгарский Государственный историко-архитектурный музей-заповедник; ul Nazarovykh 67; admission ₽430 incl all museums; ⌚8am-5pm) This sprawling museum reserve is located 1km east of the town, with a boat landing directly in front of the large Museum of Bolgar Civilisation (Музей Болгарской цивилизации), an enormous neo-Bolgar building that houses the site's main exhibits on Bolgar's history. Ruins and other museums are scattered around a vast expanse of grassland on top of a high cliff above the Volga. The reserve is dominated by a minaret, and the Russian 18th-century Assumption Church, which today houses one of the museums.

Sleeping

Hotel Regina (Отель Регина; ☎84347-310 44; www.hotelregina.ru; ul Gorkogo 30; s/d ₽1400/1700) Ask for a quiet room, as kids and loud groups can be a problem.

Getting There & Away

Hydrofoils leave Kazan early morning (usually 9am) and return from Bolgar late afternoon, usually at 3pm or 4pm, giving you about three hours to look around. Check exact times, as they tend to change from one navigation season to the next (roughly from May to October). They dock at the quay directly in front of the Museum of Bolgar Civilisation. Expect to pay ₽360 return.

Kazan Tourist Information Centre (p332) runs 11-hour boat excursions to Bolgar (twice weekly in the season, ₽2000 including lunch).

Buses depart Kazan's Yuzhny Avtovokzal bus station year-round at 10am and 5.45pm daily, and return from Bolgar at 2pm and 10pm (₽310, four hours). Some Saturdays, Kazan Tourist Information Centre runs day excursions by bus (₽2000, 11 hours) with lunch.

If you speak Russian, call ☎8-937-287 1895 for a collective taxi. Expect to pay from ₽350 per person each way for four people, or from ₽2400 return if alone.

₽600-700, tw ₽1500; ⊜@🛜) Clean, centrally located and well-run hostel with four- to eight-bed dorms and twins.

★**Hotel Volga** HOTEL $$
(☎843-231 6349; www.volga-hotel.ru; ul Said-Galieva 1; with breakfast s ₽1500-2500, d ₽1700-5800; ⊜❄@🛜) The furbishing can be a little tired in some of the rooms and breakfast is a meagre affair, but the Volga is clean, welcoming and convenient to Kazan-1 (Kazan Pass) train station and the kremlin.

Ibis Hotel HOTEL $$
(Ибис Отель; ☎843-567 5800; www.ibishotel.com; Pravobulachnaya ul 43/1; r from ₽2200; ⊜❄🛜) This centrally located chain hotel offers excellent value.

★**Hotel Giuseppe** HOTEL $$$
(Гостиница Джузеппе; ☎843-292 6934; www.giuseppe.ru; Kremlyovskaya ul 15/25; with breakfast s ₽2900-5300, d ₽3900-7000, ste ₽6600-14,000; ❄🛜) Run by a family with Italian ancestry, Hotel Guissepe has spacious, comfortable

rooms, with corridors decorated tastefully to give the atmosphere of a Venetian villa.

Shalyapin Palace Hotel
HOTEL $$$

(☑843-238 2800; www.shalyapin-hotel.ru; Universitetskaya ul 7/80; with breakfast s ₽4400-5700, d ₽5900-7200, ste ₽7500-32,000; ⊛❋☎☒) Named after Russia's greatest opera singer, whose statue greets you at the door, this large hotel has rooms decorated in a classical style, a fitness centre, sauna and 25m pool. Wi-fi is free in the lobby but costs ₽5 per megabyte in the rooms.

Hotel Art
HOTEL $$$

(☑843-567 3003; www.hotelart-kazan.ru; ul Ostrovkogo 33; with breakfast s ₽3500-6000, d ₽4000-5500, ste ₽6000-7100; ⊛☎☞) This central design hotel is close to the lively ul Baumana pedestrian zone. Sleek with modern rooms. Good rates apply for kids.

✕ Eating

★ Stolle
CAFE, BAKERY $

(Штолле; www.stolle.ru; Profsoyuznaya ul 23/12; pastries 250g ₽110-190; ⊗9am-9pm; ⊛☎) Part of a chain across Russia, Stolle specialises in savoury and sweet *pierogi* and delicious German-style leavened pastry filled with fruits, served in a rustic and relaxed setting.

Central Market
MARKET $

(Центральный рынок; ul Martyna Mezhlauka; ⊗8.30am-5.30pm Tue-Sun) The colourful, sprawling central market is good for stocking up on snacks or just for browsing.

Bahetle
SUPERMARKET $

(Бахетле; ul Moskovskaya 2; ⊗9am-10pm) The Bahetle supermarket, on the 1st floor of the TsUM Shopping Mall (ЦУМ), sells anything you might need for the day or on the road.

Kazan Askhane-Chai Yorty
TATAR $

(Дом чая, кафе 'Казанская ашхане'; ul Baumana 64; mains ₽80, pastry ₽40; ⊗9am-8pm Mon-Fri, to 7pm Sat, to 6pm Sun) This cheap eatery serves hearty Tatar food. Go for pastry – *echpohmak* with meat, *bekken* with cabbage, *kystyby* with mashed potatoes or *gubadiya* with sweet rice and raisins.

★ Perekrestok Dzhaza
INTERNATIONAL, RUSSIAN $$

(Перекресток Джаза; ☑843-264 2550; www.tatinter.ru/perekrestok-dzhaza; ul Karla Marksa 55; mains ₽600; ⊗restaurant 11am-midnight Sun-Thu, to 2am Fri & Sat, cafe 8am-11pm daily; ☎) The downstairs restaurant and attractively styled upstairs cafe take a creative approach, especially to Russian favourites such as veal salad with a tasty chilli edge. The summer veranda is pleasant. Take trolleybus 2 from pl Tukaya to the corner of ul Gogolya and ul Karla Marksa.

★ Art Cafe
CAFE $$

(Арт-кафе; ul Ostrovkogo 38; mains ₽450; ⊗8am-midnight Mon-Thu & Sun, to 6am Fri & Sat; ☎☐) At first glance Art Cafe appears deceptively formal but in spirit it's a relaxed and quite informal hang-out both night and day. Expect Russian and international favourites.

Priyut Kholostyaka
INTERNATIONAL $$

(Приют холостяка; ☑843-292 0771; www.prihol.ru; ul Chernyshevskogo 27a; mains ₽500; ⊗11am-midnight Mon-Fri, to 2am Sat & Sun; ☎) 'Bachelor's Shelter' is a spotlessly white oasis of style with surrealist glass painting and coat hangers shaped like wild garlic flowers. International food, including the inevitable sushi, is on the menu, and it serves the best latte this side of the Volga.

Giuseppe
ITALIAN $$

(Джузеппе; ☑843-292 6934; www.giuseppe.ru; Kremlyovskaya ul 15; mains ₽550; ⊗10am-1am; ☎☐) One of Kazan's longest-running Italian restaurants is also one of the best, and close to the kremlin if you feel like a formal meal between sights or in the evening. Dress quite well for this.

Dom Tatarskoy Kulinarii
TATAR $$$

(Дом татарской кулинарии; ☑843-292 7070; ul Baumana 31/12; mains ₽1000; ⊗lunch & dinner) Prices are hefty for many of the mains, but here you can find horsemeat with stewed vegetables as well as a few cheaper dishes such as the *manti* (steamed dumplings).

🍷 Drinking & Nightlife

Capital Coffee House
CAFE

(Кофейня Капитал; ul Pushkina 5; breakfast ₽200; ⊗8am-midnight Mon-Thu, to 2am Fri, 11am-midnight Sat & Sun; ☎) Apart from making good coffee and serving decent international food, these people promise to fix any cocktail according to your recipe. It has a slightly retro feel. The nonsmoking area gets a bit smoky at times.

Maximilian's Brauerei Kazan
BREWERY

(☑843-526 5566; http://maximilians.ru/kazan/en; ul Spartakovskaya 6; ₽50 surcharge for music, or ₽150-200 after 7pm; ⊗11am-2am Sun-Thu, to 5am Fri & Sat; ☎) The food is filling if unspectacular,

KAZAN'S BUS STATIONS

Kazan has two bus stations, each serving different destinations.

Kazansky Avtovokzal (Казанский автовокзал; www.avtovokzal-kzn.ru; Devyataeva 15) The Kazansky Avtovokzal, also known locally as the 'Stolichny Avtovokzal', is located near the river station and has online timetables. Most long-distance destinations depart from here, including those for Ulyanovsk (₽502, four hours, 12 daily) and Samara (₽750, nine hours, three daily).

Yuzhny Avtovokzal (Южный автовокзал; ☎843-261 5636; Orenburgsky trakt 207) Yuzhny Avtovokzal is located up to an hour away (allowing for traffic jams) from pl Tukaya by bus 37. This station serves Bolgar.

and the best thing by far about this chain microbrewery is its dance floor and the live bands playing most nights. It's a 500m walk from pl Tukaya. Teatr Kukol is the closest stop.

Cuba Libre BAR
(Куба Либре; ☎843-253 5532; ul Baumana 58; ⏲noon-2am; 📶) A convivial drinking den where you can chat to friendly bartenders and other visitors while sipping Kazan's best mojitos. Wild Latin dancing may erupt at any moment.

Mayakovsky.Zheltaya Kofta NIGHTCLUB
(Ресторан-клуб Маяковский.Желтая кофта; www.zheltaya-kofta.ru; ul Mayakovskogo 24a; cover ₽100-1000, free without band) It can be Tatar rap or punk bands singing covers of Soviet soundtrack faves, or something even more experimental in this club with a youthful crowd and decor inspired by artist Kasimir Malevich. Take tram 9 from pl Tukaya towards KGSA and ask for ul Mayakovskaya.

Shopping

Dom Knigi BOOKSTORE
(Дом книги; Kremlyovskaya ul 25; ⏲9.30am-7.30pm) Come here for maps and books in Russian.

Information

Kazan Tourist Information Centre
(Казанский туристско-информационный центр; ☎843-292 3010; www.gokazan.com; Kremlyovskaya ul 15/25; ⏲9.30am-6.30pm Mon-Fri, to 3.30pm Sat) Staff in this city-affiliated tourist office are knowledgeable and keep an excellent sheet map of town (also available in many hotels). It's also useful for booking excursions in advance. A second office is located inside Hotel Tatarstan (Hotel Tatarstan, ul Pushkina 4; ⏲9am-6pm Mon-Fri, to 8pm Sat, to 4pm Sun), and a third at the airport, which is open from 8am to midnight daily.

Main Post & Telephone Office (Почта и телеграф; Kremlyovskaya ul 8; internet per hr ₽35; ⏲8am-10pm Mon-Fri, 9am-6pm Sat & Sun)

Tattelekom (Таттелеком; ul Pushkina 15; internet per hr ₽48; ⏲9am-7.45pm Mon-Fri, to 5.45pm Sat, 10am-5.45pm Sun)

Getting There & Away

The **Aviakassa** (☎843-238 1555; Hotel Tatarstan, ul Pushkina 4) booth inside Hotel Tatarstan is convenient for both air and railway tickets.

AIR

Kazan International Airport (☎843-267 8807; www.kazan.aero), located 30km south of the city, has good connections with the rest of Russia, including Astrakhan, Perm, Novosibirsk, Moscow and St Petersburg. There are also useful connections with Barcelona in Spain and Istanbul in Turkey.

BOAT

Boats for Sviyazhsk and Bolgar leave from the river station at the end of ul Tatarstan. It's best to buy tickets from the river station well in advance. Boats depart Kazan at 8.45am for Sviyazhsk and leave Sviyazhsk at 4.30pm (₽100, two hours, daily); excursion boats to Sviyazhsk, with a Russian-speaking guide, leave Kazan at 9am (₽400, Saturday and Sunday).

TRAIN

Kazan has two train stations. The old station is on ul Said-Galieva in the centre and variously known as Kazan-1, Stary Vokzal or Kazan-Pass (passenger). The historic building is now a waiting room. Long-distance tickets are sold in the building alongside the large suburban station. Queues are shorter at ticket counters on the 2nd floor, where the service centre is also located. Kazan-2 (also known as Vosstanie-Pass on timetables) is located north of the centre and easily reached by metro. Many of the Siberian trains go through this station but there's little infrastructure for travellers, so check your ticket carefully.

Heading west, frequent trains connect Kazan with Moscow (₽1457, 12 hours). Heading east, the No 16 to Yekaterinburg (₽2312, 13½ hours) is the best service but its departure time (5am) is less convenient than several others.

Getting Around

Aeroexpress (free call 800 700 33 77; standard/business class ₽200/400; to airport 8am-12.45am, from airport 7am-12.15am) train service connects the airport and Kazan-1 (20 minutes) every two hours. Bus 97 (every half-hour 5am to 11pm, last bus from airport 9.45pm) connects the airport with Kazan's centre, passing metro Prospekt Pobedy. Stations Kremlyovskaya and Ploshchad Tukaya are located at either end of ul Baumana. This line runs north to Severniy Vokzal (Kazan-2). Tram 2 and bus 53 link Kazan-1 train station with the bus and river stations. Tram 2 and bus 54 go from the river station via the bus station to pl Tukaya.

Sviyazhsk Свияжск

A favourite escape for Kazan's artists, this island has some of the oldest architecture in the region and a fascinating history.

When Ivan the Terrible decided to end the Kazan khanate, he first ordered a base be built for the coming onslaught on top of Mt Kruglaya at the mouth of the Sviyaga River. A wooden kremlin was also built 700km upstream in the town of Myshkin near Yaroslavl. When finished, the builders marked each log, disassembled the fortress and sent it floating down the river to Sviyazhsk, where it was reassembled. Immediately after the Tatar defeat, Ivan's favourite architect, Postnik Yakovlev (co-creator of Moscow's St Basil's Cathedral and Kazan's Annunciation Cathedral), embarked on the construction of churches and monasteries here.

The Bolsheviks destroyed about half of Sviyazhsk's churches – wooden crosses now mark their locations – but several highlights were spared. These include the **Assumption Monastery**, where the St Nicolas Church is used for exhibitions of local artists, and **John the Baptist Monastery**, where the wooden Trinity Church looks like a modern dacha (summer country house) and is the only edifice inside the monastery from the original Myshkin-built fortress (though it doesn't look anything like the original, having been rebuilt in 2002).

In the navigation season boats depart Kazan at 8.45am for Sviyazhsk, and leave Sviyazhsk at 4.30pm (₽100, two hours, daily); excursion boats leave Kazan at 9am (₽370, Saturday and Sunday).

The train station in Sviyazhsk is so far away from the island that a bus excursion is best outside the navigation season.

ULYANOVSK & SAMARA REGIONS

Ulyanovsk Ульяновск

8422 / POP 614,000 / MOSCOW

The view of the Volga from the Venets promenade is arresting, but turn around and what you'll see is uninspiring. Welcome to the communist Bethlehem, the birthplace of Lenin.

Founded as Simbirsk in the 17th century, the city was dubbed the Nobles' Nest as many young aristocrats spent summers here dreaming of great endeavours while lounging between noon-time breakfast and late-afternoon nap, their lifestyle epitomised by Simbirsk native Ivan Goncharov in his novel *Oblomov*.

Today it's a greyish city with mediocre sights dedicated to Lenin, but much more interesting museums celebrating the historic town of old Simbirsk. The list of all 13 is available at www.ulzapovednik.ru.

Sights

★Goncharov Museum MUSEUM
(Музей Гончарова; ul Lenina 134; admission all exhibition sections ₽125; 10am-6pm Tue-Sun) The writer Ivan Goncharov grew up in this three-storey house, which today is one of Ulyanovsk's most important museums. It tells the story of the house itself (dating from the late 18th century, with lots of 19th-century period-piece rooms), the writer and his era.

★Museum Estate of Simbirsk Urban Life in the Late 19th and Early 20th Centuries MUSEUM
(Музей-усадьба городского быта Симбирск конца XIX-начала XX вв; www.ulzapovednik.ru; ul Lenina 90; museum Russian/foreigner ₽50/100, yard ₽50; 9am-5pm Tue-Sun) Among the museums dedicated to the historic quarter of town known as old Simbirsk, this is easily the most interesting. It consists of a main museum building with period furnishings and pictures of old Simbirsk, and a large yard with a series of small wooden buildings such as a kitchen and bathhouse. Lenin lived in the main building for one year in 1876–77.

Museum of Fire Fighting in Simbirsk-Ulyanovsk MUSEUM
(Музей 'Пожарная охрана Симбирска-Ульяновска'; www.ulzapovednik.ru; ul Lenina 43; admission ₽50; 9am-5pm Tue-Sun) This excellent museum traces the history of

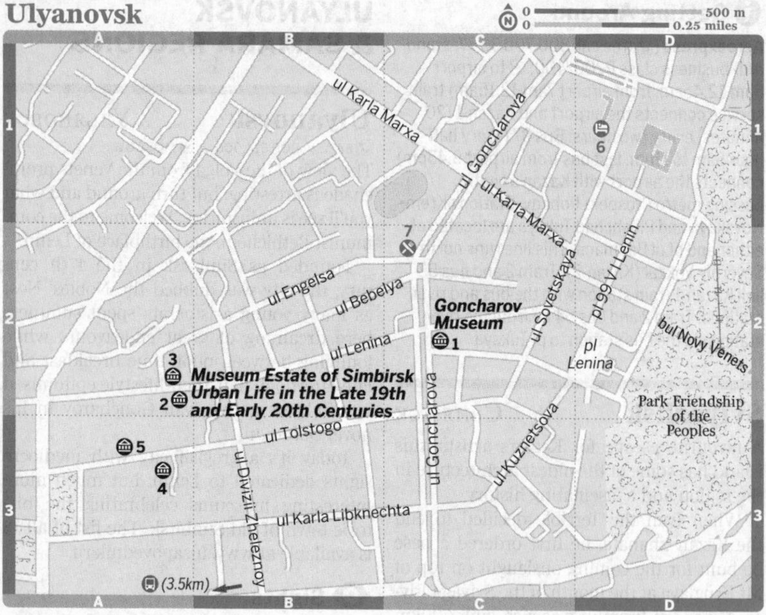

Ulyanovsk

Top Sights

1 Goncharov Museum C2
2 Museum Estate of Simbirsk Urban Life in the Late 19th and Early 20th Centuries A2

Sights

3 Museum of Fire Fighting in Simbirsk-Ulyanovsk A2
4 Museum of Ulyanovsk Architecture A3
5 Museum of Ulyanovsk Architecture A3

Sleeping

6 Hotel Venets D1

Eating

7 Papa Giovanni Trattoria C2

fire-fighting in Simbirsk and modern Ulyanovsk. The town's most serious fire was in 1864, ushering in the era of brick-and-concrete construction. Highlights are a fire-fighting motorcycle from the 1980s and a truck from 1938.

Museum of Ulyanovsk Architecture MUSEUM
(Музей Градостроительство и архитектура Симбирска-Ульяновска; ul Tolstogo 24a & 43; admission each bldg ₽50; ⏲9am-5pm Tue-Sun) Spread over two houses, this museum contains a wooden model of the 17th-century kremlin at **Ulitsa Tolstogo 24a** (ul Tolstogo branch), the house that focuses on the 17th to 20th centuries. The branch at ul Tolstogo 43 is a brick building opposite the local FSB (former KGB) headquarters and has a full-size replica of a Simbirsk wooden fortress watchtower and specifically covers the late 19th and early 20th centuries.

Sleeping & Eating

Hotel Venets HOTEL $$
(Гостиница Венец; ☎8422-441 870; www.venets-hotel.ru; ul Sovetskaya 15; with breakfast s ₽2500-3500, d ₽2800-4000, ste ₽4000-6900; 📶) This formidable piece of Soviet hotel architecture in a towering block is clean, central to the best sights, has stunning views, lots of cheaper rooms but mediocre breakfasts.

Papa Giovanni Trattoria ITALIAN $$
(ul Goncharova 15; pizza/soup/mains ₽350/200/450; ⏲10am-midnight) Good Italian soups, pizzas, pastas and mains served in a cosy cellar.

Getting There & Around

The **long-distance bus station** (http://avtovokzal73.ru) is 4km from the centre, served by tram 2 and *marshrutky* 4 and 96 from Hotel Venets. Several buses run to Kazan (₽550, five hours), Samara (₽500, five hours) and Syzran (₽275, three hours, hourly).

Ulyanovsk-Tsentralnaya train station is 4.5km from the centre and is served by *marshrutka* 94 or tram 4. Trains run to Kazan (₽759, six hours, two daily), Moscow (₽2312, 15 hours, three daily), Ufa (*platskart*/seat ₽1205/667 14 hours, two daily) and Volgograd (₽1456, 19 hours, two daily) via Saratov (₽1038, 11 hours). Buses are a better option to Samara.

From the train and bus stations, **taxis** (☎8422-494 949, 8422-555 000) to the centre costs about ₽300, or ₽200 if you call ahead.

Samara Самара

☎846 / POP 1.16 MILLION / ⏰MOSCOW +1HR

'Oh, Samara, the little town, I am so restless – give me some rest.' The quintessential drinking song is now only partly true: this city of over a million is little no more, and in recent years has focused on drawing visitors to the city. Not without justification, for Samara is a pleasant place to visit. On a summer day, the riverbanks are packed with bathing beauties, in-line skaters and beer drinkers. It has a couple of interesting museums and a small but lively arts scene. Samara also serves as the base for excursions into the nearby Zhiguli Hills.

Samara grew up where the Volga meets the Samara River, at a sharp bend across from the Zhiguli Hills. Founded as a border fortress in 1568, it saw the local governor drowned by Stepan Razin's Cossacks in 1670 and another governor flee Yemelyan Pugachev's peasant army in 1774. The Russian Civil War began in Samara, when a unit of Czechoslovakian prisoners of war commandeered their train and seized control of the city, turning it into a stronghold for the emerging White Army. During WWII a bunker was built here for Stalin but he never used it. In the post-WWII period Samara remained a closed city due to its strategic industries.

Sights

As well as visiting the key sights, take the time to stroll along the banks of the Volga River, which is flanked by lush parks and sandy beaches.

★Samara Art Museum — ART GALLERY

(Художественный музей; www.artmus.ru; ul Kuybysheva 92; admission Russian/foreigner ₽70/110; ⏰10am-6pm Thu-Mon, to 8pm Wed) Easily the most important cultural attraction in the city, the Samara Art Museum exhibits mainly Russian art, including works by those artists who came to the region to paint. Look for *Boyarishina*, given by Vasily Surikov to a local doctor who treated him when he fell ill. The museum also holds an impressive collection of early Kazimir Malevich works.

★Zhiguli Brewery — BREWERY

(Жигулёвское пиво; ☎8462-642 116; www.samarabeer.ru; Volzhsky pr 4) This unlikely highlight of Samara is best enjoyed on a warm day. Here you can take your plastic bottle out of the rucksack and fill it up at the kiosk that sells the amber gold from the tap. Rows of stalls sell smoked and salted fish, all which can be enjoyed on the Volga bank, followed by a stroll along the embankment into the centre. Most *marshrutky* going east from Leningradskaya ul along ul Kuybysheva stop here. Check and ask the driver to stop at Pivzavod.

Gallereya Viktoria — ART GALLERY

(Галерея Виктория; ☎846-277 8912; www.gallery-victoria.ru; ul Nekrasovskaya 2; ⏰11am-7pm) **FREE** This private gallery is excellent for viewing (and purchasing) works by the best of the Volga region artists in regular exhibitions. Check the website for openings and downtime.

Stalin's Bunker — HISTORICAL BUILDING

(Бункер Сталина; ☎846-333 3571; ul Frunze 167; ⏰prebook group tours) Stalin's Bunker, built nine storeys below the Academy of Culture and Art, was never used by Stalin, who stayed in Moscow during WWII. It's almost impossible to get in without booking a group tour with a tour company. Samara Intour (p336) can organise one – this costs ₽2400 plus ₽1500 for the guide (per individual or group) and is best shared with travel companions.

Alabin Museum — MUSEUM

(Музей Алабина; www.alabin.ru; Leninskaya ul 142; Russian/foreigner ₽90/100; ⏰10am-6pm Wed-Sun, to 8pm Tue) Come here for exhibits on regional palaeontology and archaeology, including dinosaur fossils found in the Zhiguli Hills.

Samara

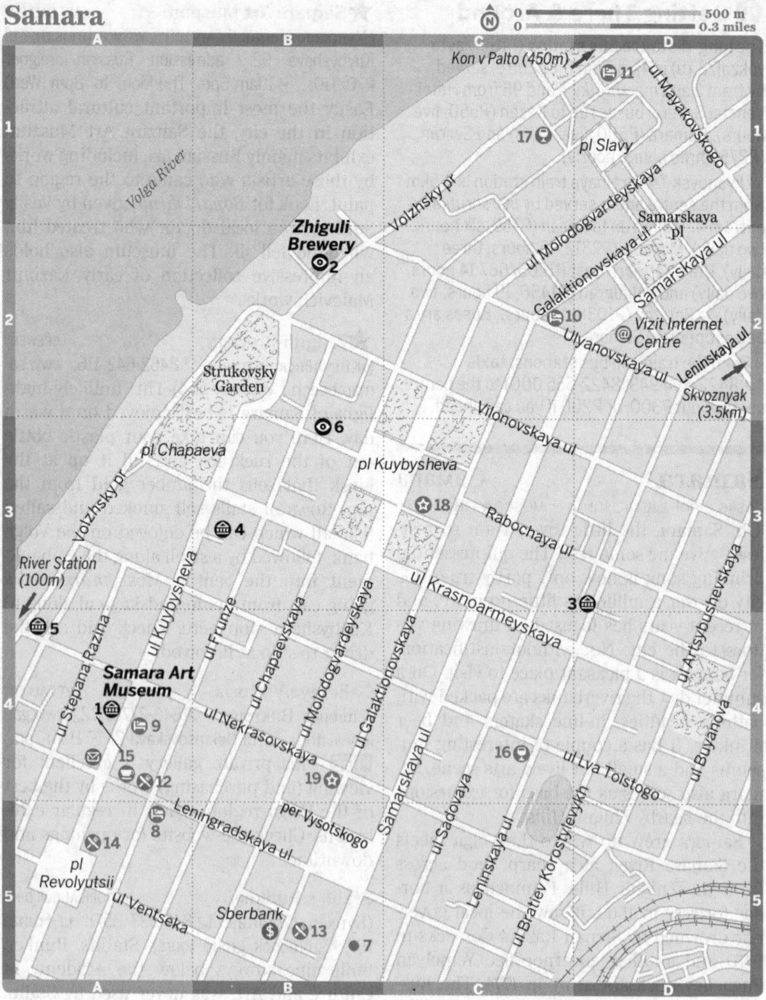

Children's Art Gallery ART GALLERY
(Детская художественная галерея; http://chgal.ssu.samara.ru; ul Kuybysheva 139; adult/child ₽100/70; ⌚9am-5pm; 👪) Housed in the landmark Engineer Klodt's House (Дом инженера Клодта), which resembles a fairy-tale castle and contains a collection of children's art and art for children, who can pick up a brush here.

☞ Tours

Samara Intour TOUR COMPANY
(Самара Интур; ☎846-279 2040; www.samaraintour.ru; Samarskaya ul 51/53; ⌚9am-7pm Mon-Fri, 10am-5pm Sat) This highly professional travel agency has some staff who speak English and German. It can organise an individual tour into the bunker built for Stalin (p335), and often runs excursions into the attractive Samara Bend region around Shiryaevo.

Typically excursions include rafting, horse riding and cycling, but these change according to what the local operators are offering, so ask in the lead up to the season (ie May for the summer). It also books flights and train tickets.

Samara

Sleeping

Volga Hotel HOTEL $$

(Гостиница Волга; 846-242 1196; Volzhsky pr 29; with breakfast s ₽2600-3000, d ₽3000-3800, ste ₽4200-4500;) Located at the northern end of the embankment, the Volga has a mixed bag of recently renovated rooms and others that received their makeover some time ago. It staidly retains its Soviet style.

Azimut Hotel HOTEL $$

(Гостиница Азимут; 846-277 8080; www.azimuthotels.ru; ul Frunze 91/37;) This excellent hotel is centrally located but closed until early 2015 due to restorations. Go to the website for the latest information on opening and prices. Generally, prices start from about ₽2500.

Bristol-Zhiguli Hotel HOTEL $$$

(Гостиница Бристоль-Жигули; 846-331 6555; www.bristol-zhiguly.ru; ul Kuybysheva 111; with breakfast s ₽2700-4700, d ₽4400-11,000, apt ₽6800;) The most expensive room in this hotel inside an ornate 19th-century building is the one where opera singer Fyodor Chaliapin once stayed, using the balcony as a stage to sing for a crowd of adoring fans. Cheaper rooms without bathrooms are available from ₽550.

Hotel Europe HOTEL $$$

(Гостиница Европа; 846-270 8740; www.hoteleurope.ru; ul Galaktionovskaya 171; with breakfast s ₽3300-3900, d ₽4290-5700, apt ₽7670-12,900;) Housed in a lovely 1902 mansion, this hotel has 20 guest rooms and a highly respected restaurant. The decor is comfortable and modern.

Eating

Zhili-Byli RUSSIAN $

(Жили-были; 846-704 132; ul Kuybysheva 81; mains ₽250; 11am-midnight) This is a good-value chain restaurant with rustic decor.

Troitsky Market MARKET $

(Троицкий рынок; ul Galaktionovskaya; 7am-7pm Mon-Sat, 10am-6pm Sun) Stalls full of fresh fruit and vegies, and lots of fresh and smoked fish, as well as breads, meats and cheeses.

★ **Kipyatok** RUSSIAN $$

(Кипяток; 846-333 2720; Leningradskaya ul 40; mains ₽300; 11am-midnight;) This funky restaurant re-creates the golden age of the Russian culinary arts in the early 20th century. Creative dishes are complemented by homemade *kvas* and freshly produced cranberry *mors* (fruit drink).

★ **Staraya Kvartira** RUSSIAN $$

(Старая квартира; www.oldflat.ru; Samarskaya ul 51/53; mains ₽500; noon-midnight;) The 'Old Flat' is a rabbit warren of rooms accessed via the souvenir shop (downstairs from Samara Intour). The food is excellent, especially the lamb casserole *(razboynichye zharkoye)* with eggplant, garlic and peppers.

Drinking & Nightlife

★ **Budilnik** ANTI-CAFE

(Будильник; Leningradskaya ul 36; 1st hr ₽120 then ₽60 per hr; 11am-1am;) The only drawback of anti-cafes is that most are 'dry' areas – in this case, tea and coffee are tippled with biscuits. The cosy 'Alarm Clock' definitely makes up for this with something that will warm the soul of every guitarist longing to pick up an axe on the road – a

WORTH A TRIP

TOLYATTI – HOME OF THE LADA

Welcome to Lada-land, the place where one of the world's most ridiculed vehicles is produced. The city is a particularly depressing Soviet urban sprawl, where the quality of the roads matches that of Lada cars. That said, it is strategically placed by the giant Kuybyshev reservoir dam, with the Zhiguli Hills starting right across the water.

Sights & Activities

Technical Museum (Yuzhnoye sh 137; admission ₽100; ⏲9am-5pm) Situated in the New Town (Novy Gorod) and opposite the VAZ plant that makes Ladas, this museum has a vast collection of mostly military hardware, including a nuclear submarine.

Spin Sport (Спин-Спорт; ☎8482-489 120; www.spin-sport.ru; Komsomolskoye sh 28; mountain-bike hire 1hr ₽500; ⏲8am-11pm) With its 20km of bicycle lanes in a forested area and a swimming pool for chilling out after the exercise, the Spin Sport park is a good place to knead your muscles and relax.

Sleeping & Eating

Zhiguli Star (Звезда Жигулей; ☎8482-223 311; www.lada-gam.ru; ul Mira 77; with breakfast s ₽2640-3700, d ₽2900-6050; ⊜📶) This comfortable business hotel in the central district is your best option if you're staying overnight. The restaurant (mains ₽270) is open for breakfast, lunch and dinner.

Getting There & Around

Buses go to/from Samara (₽190, two hours, hourly), Ulyanovsk (₽317, four hours, at least hourly) and Kazan (₽650, 6½ hours, three daily).

Tolyatti has three districts. Expect to pay about ₽250 for trips between these, less for just one district.

Expect to pay ₽110 to ₽150 for a **taxi** (☎8482-70 000) from the bus station to the Zhiguli Star hotel if you call ahead.

Gibson electric guitar and amp. On Fridays local musos usually jam from 7pm.

★ **Kafe-Bar Sasha** BAR
(Кафе-бар Саша; ☎846-333 5535; ul Leninskaya 116; ⏲11am-midnight Mon-Thu, to 4am Fri & Sat, noon-11pm Sun; 📶) This sleek bar and cafe in a large historic building attracts a mixed crowd and has a slightly arty edge, with live music each Friday, often featuring jazz. The food (mains ₽300) is international and well prepared, and the garlic bread, made from sticks of rye bread, goes down well with a beer or wine.

Kon v Palto BAR
(Конь в пальто; Volzhsky pr 19; ⏲noon-11pm Mon-Thu, to 4am Fri, 6pm-3am Sat, 3-11pm Sun) This excellent grill restaurant (mains ₽800, soups ₽200) is locally famous for its Whisky Bar upstairs, dance space and outdoor 'Art Terrace' on warm Volga nights.

Skvoznyak BAR, NIGHTCLUB
(Сквозняк; www.skvoznyak.ru; ul Novo-Sadovaya 106g; cover charge ₽200; ⏲from 7pm Fri & Sat) With its wood-design bar section and DJs, Skvoznyak is a long-time favourite among locals. Trams (5, 15, 20 and 22) going north along ul Galaktionovskaya then pr Lenina take you there. Ask the conductress for the entertainment centre Zvezda – it's opposite.

☆ Entertainment

Opera & Ballet Theatre THEATRE
(Театр оперы и балета; ☎846-332 2509; www.opera-samara.net; pl Kuybysheva 1; ⏲ticket office 10am-7pm) The main venue for ballet, classical concerts and opera.

Podval LIVE MUSIC
(Подваль; ul Nekrasovskaya 63; admission about ₽150; ⏲7pm-3am Wed-Sun) The 'Basement' has live rock, metal, gothic and other acts for a youngish crowd.

ℹ Information

Post Office (Почтамт; ul Kuybysheva 82; ⏲9am-7pm Mon-Fri, to 5pm Sat & Sun)

Sberbank (ul Galaktionovskaya; ⏲9am-7pm Mon, Tue, Thu & Fri, 10am-7pm Wed, 9am-5pm Sat)

Vizit Internet Centre (Визит интернет центр; Samarskaya ul 199; per MB ₽4; ⏲9am-5pm Mon-Fri, to 3pm Sat) A crowded basement place with plenty of computers.

Getting There & Away

Air and rail tickets are available at Samara Intour (p336). It charges a ₽300 commission on train fares.

AIR

Samara has regular connections with Frankfurt am Main (Germany). Domestic connections include Moscow, Perm, St Petersburg, Ufa and Yekaterinburg.

BOAT

The river station (Речной вокзал) is at the west end of the embankment, in front of Hotel Rossiya. Long-distance cruises operate to various destinations along the Volga. Several cruise agencies have kiosks here. **Infoflot** (☎846-276 7491; www.infoflot.com; river station) sells return cruises to Kazan (from ₽7300, three days), Ulyanovsk via Shirayevo (from ₽6500, three days), and Volgograd (from ₽11,300, five days). Book several months in advance for the cheapest berths. There are also boats to closer destinations, including Shiryaevo (about ₽90, 2½ hours, two daily).

BUS

The central bus station is 6km southeast of the centre. It has connections to Kazan (₽750, nine hours, three daily), Syzran (₽318, three hours, six daily), Tolyatti (₽200, two hours, hourly) and Ulyanovsk (₽500, five hours, hourly).

TRAIN

Samara's flagship *Zhiguli* train is fastest to Moscow (*kupe* ₽4679, 14 hours) but the most expensive. Other connections are to Saratov (₽1061, nine hours) and Volgograd (₽1580, 17 hours). For Kazan, bus is better, and for Astrakhan book via Volgograd as direct trains pass through Kazakhstan.

Getting Around

Most bus and *marshrutky* routes run straight as a nail in the central part of town, so it's easiest just to walk to the major street to grab one (eg ul Kuybysheva to go east to pl Slavy, or ul Samarskaya for pl Samarskaya).

TO/FROM THE BUS & TRAIN STATIONS

Trolleybuses 2, 4, 12 and 17 run between the train and bus stations. For pl Revolyutsii or ul Kuybysheva, take tram 5 or 16 from the train station. From the bus station to the centre take *marshrutka* 1 or 14 to the train station and change.

Haggle **taxis** (☎846-302 0202) down to ₽350 or less from the bus station to the centre. The price is about ₽150 from the train station to most central areas.

Samara Bend
Самарская Лука

Samara sits on the left bank of the Volga, while the right bank is dominated by the rocky Zhiguli Hills. The river loops around the hills, creating a peninsula encompassing 32,000 hectares of national forest reserve. The **Samara Bend National Park** (Samarskaya Luka in Russian) is a prime area for hikes along rocky ledges and grand Volga vistas. The peaks – the highest being Strelnaya Mountain at 370m – are in the northwest corner of the reserve. These hills were the hideout of peasant rebel Stepan Razin in the 17th century.

The easiest way to reach the reserve in summer is to take a boat to any of the villages on the right bank, such as Shiryaevo. If you want to explore the area by public transport or bicycle, local hubs Tolyatti and Syzran come into the equation. Together with Samara, they form an almost equilateral triangle and often have better connections with adjacent regions than the provincial capital.

Every year, thousands of locals raft *zhigulyovskaya krugosvetka,* which translates as 'Zhiguli round-the-world trip'. The 10-day rafting route follows the loop in the river, then cuts back up north through a channel on the west side of the park. Samara Intour (p336) sometimes organises these trips; ask ahead.

Shiryaevo Ширяево

In the 1870s Ilya Repin spent two years in this village just north of Samara on the west bank of the Volga. Here he completed sketches for his famous painting *Barge Haulers on the Volga,* which is now in St Petersburg's Russian Museum. Today, this pleasant village welcomes art lovers and day trippers.

Sights

Repin Museum MUSEUM

(ul Sovetskaya 14; admission ₽60; ⏲11am-4pm Tue-Sun) The Repin Museum has a nice selection of Volga River paintings, including some Ilya Repin reproductions. The appeal lies less in seeing the art, however, than in experiencing this quintessential Volga village.

❶ Getting There & Away

Regular boat from Samara (about ₽90, 2½ hours, two daily) is the best way to reach Shiryaevo. You can also reach it by bus from Tolyatti (₽150, 2¾ hours, daily).

SARATOV & VOLGOGRAD REGIONS САРАТОВСКАЯ И ВОЛГОГРАДСКАЯ ОБЛАСТИ

Saratov Саратов

☑ 8452 / POP 838,000 / ⊘ MOSCOW

Saratov lacks major tourist attractions, but it's a laid-back place and has a bit of a seaside resort atmosphere. The former name of ul Kirova is Nemetskaya (German), a sure sign that Saratov was once at the heart of the Volga German region. Wartime deportations spared few Volga Germans and only a handful returned here from exile, but their presence can be felt in the city's distinctly Central European ambience.

Across the Volga river in Engels, once known as Pokrovsk when it was the capial of the Autonomous Socialist Soviet Republic of the Volga Germans, is an outstanding collection of paintings (p342) by the Volga German Yakov Veber.

The first man in space, cosmonaut Yury Gagarin, lived in Saratov and studied at the local university, which now bears his name.

❂ Sights

Sokolovaya Gora PARK
(Соколовая гора) The strategic Sokolovaya Gora, overlooking the city and the river bending around it, is a popular getaway for Saratovians. The main attraction here is the **Victory Park**, its lanes packed with military hardware. The main park lane eventually leads you into the **Ethnic Village**, with houses representing numerous ethnic groups that inhabit Saratov Oblast. To get to Sokolovaya Gora, take *marshrutka* 72 from the train station or 72k from ul Radishcheva.

Gagarin Museum MUSEUM
(Музей Гагарина; ☑ 8542-237 666; ul Sakko i Vanzetti 15; ⊘9am-4pm Mon-Fri, 8am-3pm Sat)

FREE This is an interesting museum telling the life of the world's first man in space through photos and personal objects. Yury Gagarin not only lived and studied in Saratov, but also landed (crashed?) his Vostok 1 capsule nearby after his much-lauded flight. The landing site, 40km out of town near the village of Kvasnikovka, is marked by a commemorative monument.

Radishchev Museum ART GALLERY
(Радищевский музей; http://radmuseumart.ru; ul Pervomayskaya 75; Russian/foreigner ₽50/200; ⊘10am-6pm Tue, Wed & Fri-Sun, noon-8pm Thu) This is the main branch of the city's Fine Arts Museum. It contains a good selection from the 18th to the 20th centuries.

🛏 Sleeping

★ **Pioner Lyux Bohemia** HOTEL $$
(Отель Пионер-Люх Богемия; ☑ 8452-454 501; www.bohemiahotel.ru; pr Kirova 15/1; with breakfast s ₽2000-2500, d ₽3900-6700, apt ₽5900; ⊛@🎅) This hotel offers excellent value. Rooms are decorated in postmodern tones and spread over several floors (reception is on the 6th floor), right in a courtyard alongside Cafe V and the Pioner Cinema complex. It provides free transfer from arrival points.

Hotel Volga HOTEL $$
(☑ 8452-263 645; www.astoria.saratov.ru; pr Kirova 34; with breakfast s ₽2750, d ₽3500-4800, ste ₽5300; ⊛🎅) Statues of black knights and naked runners observe you from the roof as you enter this art nouveau masterpiece. Staff are helpful, rooms are rudimentary and poor value for money, but those without bathrooms (from ₽1500) are a low-budget alternative. The central location is its saving grace.

🍴 Eating & Drinking

House of Culinary Zhulien RUSSIAN $
(Дом кулинарии Жюльен; http://gulien.ru; pr Kirova 42; meals ₽300; ⊘9am-9pm; ⊛) This cafeteria with loud colours sells inexpensive and decent ready-made dishes mostly by weight. **Bakery Confectionist Zhulien** (Булочная Кондитерская Жульен; http://gulien. ru; pr Kirova 54; pastries ₽35; ⊘8am-9pm; ⊛) sells Russian pastries that you can eat at stand-up tables on the premises.

Pivnoy Zavod MICROBREWERY $
(Пивной завод; pr Kirova 5; mains ₽200; ⊘11am-11pm; 🎅🍺) Beer brewed on the premises, sausages and other hearty fare are on the

food and drinks menu here. Servings are not large, though – the Caucasian lamb sausage is quite decent. It also has fresh *mors*.

Buratino
RUSSIAN $$

(Буратино; ☑ 8542-277 479; pr Kirova 10; mains ₽350; ⊙ 11am-midnight; ⊕ 🖼 🍴) This is a quintessential Saratovian cafe-restaurant themed on 'Red Count' Alexey Tolstoy's version of *Pinocchio*. Beneath it, there is a basement cafe called Grass, decorated in green and with rural motifs.

★ KGBar
BAR

(КГБар; http://kgb-live.com/place/kgbar; ul Moskovskaya 57; ⊙ 11am-11pm Mon-Thu & Sun, to 2am Fri, to 5am Sat) This hip downstairs bar is one of Saratov's most popular nightspots and serves salads, soups and a selection of international mains (₽250).

Kafe i Shokolad
CAFE

(Кафе и Шоколад; www.coffeechoco.ru; Volzhskaya ul 23; ⊙ 9am-11pm; 🕿) Samara has lots of branches of Kafe i Shokolad (Cafe and Chocolate), which serve four of five mains (₽375) such as chicken salad or pasta along with delicious desserts and crêpes (₽160 to ₽215). This branch has an art edge and a slight hint of Gaudi, with a colourful tiled staircase. The works of local artists hang on the walls and can be purchased.

☆ Entertainment

Schnittke Philharmonic Theatre
THEATRE

(Саратовская Областная Филармония им. А. Шнитке; ☑ 8452-224 872; www.sarphil.com; Sobornaya pl 9) This hall remains true to the ideology of polystylism fostered by homegrown composer Alfred Schnittke, so jazz is as much at home here as classical music.

Sobinov Conservatory
CLASSICAL MUSIC

(Саратовская государственная консерватория имени Л. В. Собинова; ☑ 8452-230 652; www.sarcons.ru; pr Kirova 1) One of the best conservatories in Russia, holding frequent performances by resident and visiting musicians in an architectural highlight of Saratov.

🛍 Shopping

Dom Knigi
BOOKSTORE

(Дом Книги; ul Volskaya 81; ⊙ 9am-10pm Mon-Fri, to 9pm Sat & Sun) This bookstore has good city maps and lots of reference books in Russian.

ⓘ Information

Cyber Kafe Smile (pr Kirova 10; per hr ₽50; ⊙ 24hr) In the courtyard.

ⓘ Getting There & Away

BOAT
Inside the river station at the eastern end of ul Moskovskaya, **Volga-Heritage** (☑ 8452-280 874; www.rech-vokzal.ru; nab Kosmonavtov 7a) sells cruises in the navigation season to destinations along the Volga, such as Astrakhan (return from ₽9800, five days) and Samara (return from ₽5000, three days). They can tell you which boats have the best facilities and food. Saratov-Moscow one way costs from ₽21,000 (eight days) and St Petersburg from ₽25,000 one way (20 days).

BUS
Eurolines (www.eurolines.de) runs weekly buses from Germany to the region (from around €175, two days). Check the website for current destinations.

TRAIN
The **train station** (Privokzalnaya pl) is at the western end of ul Moskovskaya. The No 17 (₽2019, 16 hours, daily) is the best (but most expensive) of the frequent trains to Moscow. Others go to Samara (₽982, 9½ hours) and Volgograd (*platskart* ₽1061, eight hours).

ⓘ Getting Around

Trolleybus 1 connects the train and river stations, following ul Moskovskaya (get off at ul Maksima Gorkogo and walk south four blocks for pr Kirova). Bus 11 runs along ul Moskovskaya to the river station. Trolleybus 15 connects the train station with the market in the town centre (Krytiy Rynok). *Marshrutka* 79 does this route, too. For a taxi call ☎ 8452-777 777.

Volgograd
Волгоград

☑ 8442 / POP 1.02 MILLION / ⊙ MOSCOW

Volgograd is a grandiose city in all senses. It was founded in 1589 as Tsaritsyn, but it made history during a 36-year period when it appeared on maps as Stalingrad. In 1942 the city became the scene of an epic battle that changed the course of WWII. The number of soldiers and citizens who died in this battle is almost twice the current population of the city. Volgograd had to be rebuilt from scratch, which explains the Stalinesque grandeur of public buildings and broad avenues, all of which is Soviet baroque at its most eloquent or hideous, depending on your architectural taste.

WORTH A TRIP

ENGELS

Engels (Энгельс; formerly Pokrovsk) is situated across the Volga River from Saratov and became the capital of the Autonomous Socialist Soviet Republic of the Volga Germans from 1924, which survived until the republic was dissolved in 1941 and the Volga Germans were deported. It's a mostly unattractive, Soviet-style place but worth visiting for its regional museum, feeling of 'otherness' and views of the Volga as you cross the almost-3km-long bridge.

The highlight of the **Engels Regional Museum** (Энгельсский краеведческий музей; ☎8453-567 073; http://ekmuzeum.ru; ul Maksima Gorkogo 4; admission ₽40; ⏲10am-5pm Tue & Thu-Sun, to 9pm Wed) is not its military hardware, which hammers home the point about what WWII was about (ie defeating Germany), but a truly magnificent collection of some 40 works by the Volga German realist artist Yakov Veber (1870–1958), whose style is reminiscent of Ilya Repin. Veber was arrested in 1937 on the dubious – if not spurious – grounds of 'anti-Soviet activities' and spent 19 years in Kazakhstan before being rehabilitated and allowed to return to Engels.

Take any bus from ul Moskovskaya to the Torgoby Tsentr Lazurny in Engels. The museum is almost directly across the road.

In the far corner of this sprawling city, you can marvel at a feat of Soviet engineering – the first lock of the Volga-Don Canal. Nearby is the partially restored town square of Tsaritsyn's German district.

In late 2013 Volgograd was the target of several suicide bombings, including one that caused massive damage to the main train station and killed 17 people. Despite the bombings, Volgograd remains a safe city for travellers.

Sights & Activities

Mamaev Kurgan MONUMENT
(Мамаев курган) Known as Hill 102 during the Battle of Stalingrad, Mamaev Kurgan was the site of four months of fierce fighting and is now a memorial to all who died in this bloody-but-victorious fight. The complex's centrepiece is an extraordinarily evocative 72m-high statue of Mother Russia wielding a sword that extends another 11m above her head. To get here take the high-speed tram to the Mamaev Kurgan stop, 3.5km north of the centre.

The *kurgan* (mound) is covered in statues, memorials and ruined fortifications, and more recently has received an attractive church. The Pantheon is inscribed with the names of 7200 soldiers – over one million Russian soldiers died here in battle in WWII.

Panorama Museum of the Battle of Stalingrad MUSEUM
(Музей-панорама Сталинградская битва; ☎8442-236 723; http://stalingrad-battle.ru; ul Imena Marshala Chuykova 47, cnr ul 13-ya Gvardeyskoy Divizii; admission ₽150; ⏲10am-6pm Tue-Sun) This museum, part of the Battle of Stalingrad museum complex, has dozens of exhibits on the Battle of Stalingrad and the soldiers who fought. The model of the ruined city (post-battle) is a moving display of the human capacity for both destruction and rebuilding, and a highlight is the vivid 360-degree Battle of Stalingrad Panorama. It's two blocks east of the pl Lenina high-speed tram stop, or a 20-minute stroll through the river park from alleya Geroyev.

Museum Reserve Old Sarepta MUSEUM
(Музей-заповедник Старая Сарепта; http://altsarepta.ru; ul Vinogradnaya 6; Russian/foreigner ₽110/150, tours per person ₽400 (minimum of 3 people); ⏲9am-5.30pm Tue-Sun) An hour by *marshrutka* from the centre, what is now known as the Krasnoarmeysk district was once the German colony of Sarepta. Today the entire quarter is a museum reserve set around a beautiful square and Lutheran church, dating from the late 18th century. To get here, take *marshrutka* 15a, 91a, 93a, 93c, 93 or 55a from pr Lenina and ask the driver to stop at Vinogradnaya.

The original settlers of old Sarepta were German Catholic missionaries from Moravia (in the Czech Republic) who arrived here in 1765 with the aim of proselytising the Kalmyks. Failing that, they became the mustard tycoons of Russia. The museums – one an historic pharmacy, the other telling about the history and lifestyle of the colony – are interesting but a tour in Russian, English or German is useful, also taking you into the otherwise closed church. Buy tickets for the two museums from the white building alongside the church.

Volga-Don Canal CANAL

(Волго-Донской судоходный канал имени В. И. Ленина (Волго-Донской канал)) Built in 1952, the Volga-Don Canal is the grandiose gateway of an aquatic avenue that now connects the White and the Black Seas via the Volga and Don Rivers. The huge Stalinesque neoclassical arch marks the first lock in the Volga-Don Canal. Take *marshrutka* 15a, 91a, 93a, 93c, 93 or 55a from ul Lenina to the first stop after crossing the canal.

One million people, including 236,000 Axis prisoners of war and Russian Gulag inmates, took part in the construction of the canal, and even a planet is named after it.

Museum of the Volga-Don Canal MUSEUM

(Музей Волго-Донского канала; ul Fadeyeva 35a; admission ₽50; ⌚10am-noon & 1-4.30pm Tue, Wed & Fri) Alongside the canal, this small museum tells the story of the canal and gives insight into water transport in Europe.

Sleeping

★Stary Stalingrad MINIHOTEL $$

(Отель Старый Сталинград; ☎8442-385 501; http://hotelstalingrad.pro34.ru; pl Pavshikh Bortsov 2; with breakfast s/d/ste ₽2800/3500/4500; ☏) Behind the Univermag shops and part of the same building, this modern minihotel has nicely furnished rooms with an individual touch. It's especially worth trying if the larger hotels are full.

Hotel Volgograd HOTEL $$

(Гостиница Волгоград; ☎8442-551 955; www.hotelvolgograd.ru; ul Mira 12; with breakfast s ₽2600, d ₽2800-6500, ste ₽5000-16,000; ⊜❄☏) South across pl Pavshikh Bortsov, this hotel has professional staff and clean and comfortable rooms in one of the few buildings remaining from Tsaritsyn times – although it was considerably altered after the war.

Hotel Finanz-Yug HOTEL $$

(Отель Финанс-Юг; ☎8442-742 174; http://hotelfinansyug.ru; ul Kommunisticheskaya 40; with breakfast s ₽2400-2700, d ₽2300-2400, ste ₽3800-6000; ⊜☏) Occupying floors seven, eight and nine in the modern office tower of Sberbank, Hotel Finanz-Yug offers modern rooms, with breakfast served in the canteen on the 2nd floor. Take the metro to pl Lenina and walk one block northwest.

Hotel Intourist HOTEL $$$

(☎8442-302 301; ul Mira 14; with breakfast s ₽3150-4200, d ₽6000, ste ₽7400-11,000; ⊜❄☏) This is a vintage Soviet-era gem with the high level of service matching the bright, welcoming lobby. Rooms are well lit and tasteful.

VOLGOGRAD RIVER STATION & TOURS

Once one of the grandest on the river, Volgograd's river station (речной вокзал; Rechnoy vokzal) is today among the tackiest, mostly given over to average bars, clubs and restaurants.

Only Body (☎8442-900 572; www.onlybody.pro34.ru; 2nd fl, Rechnoy vokzal; ⌚by appointment only) Only Body offers 30-minute face (₽600) and one-hour body (₽1400) massages. It also does waxing and has a solarium. Book ahead.

Kruiz (Круиз; ☎8442-381 081; www.kruiztur.ru; 1st fl, Rechnoy vokzal) This tour agency offers many different segments of the Volga, including to/from Moscow (₽22,210 to ₽57,310, eight days), St Petersburg (₽27,500 to ₽51,700, 12 days), Astrakhan (return ₽7700 to ₽14,500, four days) and Kazan (₽17,800 to ₽35,000, seven days).

Gostinitsa Rechnoy Vokzal (Гостиница речной вокзал; ☎8442-900 896; 4th fl, Rechnoy vokzal) Upstairs via a separate staircase, this hotel is currently undergoing long-term renovations.

Coffee House (Кофе Хаус; 2nd fl, Rechnoy vokzal; sushi & Japanese menu ₽250, mains ₽300; ⌚24hr) Amid the tacky restaurants and dubious bars inside the river station, Coffee House stands out for its well-prepared food and strong wine selection, dignified wooden decor and especially for the glorious views of the Volga through the large windows.

Eating

Shokoladnitsa CAFE $
(Шоколадница; cnr alleya Geroyev & Sovetskaya ul; dishes ₽150-300; 10am-midnight;) Although its speciality is hot chocolate, this cafe is also good for a bagel, wraps, sandwiches and especially soups and light dishes. Wi-fi is fast, staff are friendly and in summer it has a marquee.

Grand Cafe RUSSIAN $
(Гранд Кафе; ul Mira 12; meals ₽400, pizza & pasta ₽250; 8am-6am;) Situated on the ground floor of Hotel Volgograd, this is the city's most popular spot to sip a cappuccino and scope out the scene. Part of the premises is a pizzeria open from noon to 1am daily.

Rimini ITALIAN $
(Римини; www.trattoria-rimini.ru; ul Gagarina 9; pizza ₽200-300, meat mains ₽350; 11am-midnight;) This large, bustling Italian place has neorustic decor and a large menu offering straight-up-and-down Italian pizza, pasta and meat dishes complemented by salads. Ul Gagarina is about five blocks north along pr Lenina.

Central Market MARKET $
(Центральный рынок; 7am-7pm Tue-Sat, to 5pm Sun & Mon) This market, between Sovetskaya ul and pr Lenina, stocks everything from Astrakhan watermelons to Volga fish.

★ **Na Allee** GEORGIAN $$
(На Аллее; 8442-381 974; alleya Geroyev 3; mains ₽300; 9am-11pm) This excellent Georgian restaurant has a family atmosphere and serves homemade wine from Georgia. It does a tasty lamb *ketsi* with vegetables (baked in an earthenware dish).

★ **Kayfe** CAFE, RUSSIAN $$
(Кайфе; pr Lenina 23a; mains ₽300; 9am-6am;) A cosy cafe that offers everything you might want, be it a large meal or a light snack, tea, coffee or one of the many alcoholic beverages on the menu. It's good for breakfast, lunch and especially a predawn chill-out.

Bochka GERMAN $$
(Бочка; 8442-919 319; http://bochka.gidm.ru; Sovetskaya ul 16; mains ₽350, day menu ₽200; 11am-midnight;) Basement beer cellar and restaurant that draws a business-lunch crowd, but it's more fun in the evening, when live music is staged.

Drinking & Nightlife

Klub Amsterdam NIGHTCLUB
(Клуб Амстердам; Komsomolskaya ul 3; admission ₽100-200; from 10pm Wed-Sun) This centrally located club gets a student crowd.

Information

Post Office (Главпочтамт; pl Pavshikh Bortsov; per MB ₽6; 9am-5pm Mon-Fri) Post office with internet access.

Sberbank (ul Gogolya; 9.30am-7.30pm Mon-Fri, 9am-5pm Sat) Alongside the post office.

Getting There & Away

Tickets can be bought at **TAVS Volga** (ТАВС Волга; 8442-380 010; alleya Geroyev 5; 8am-7pm) – especially useful for picking up bus tickets to Elista.

AIR

Volgograd has good air connections with Moscow and St Petersburg and occasional connections with Perm and Samara.

BUS

For frequent buses to Elista (₽500, five hours), Astrakhan (₽855, 10 hours) and Rostov-on-Don (₽800, nine hours) head to the Central Bus Station (Центральный автовокзал), a 750m walk across the tracks or through the underpass from the train station. Frequent buses leave from the train-station square to Moscow (₽1500, 14 hours). Booths and offices there sell tickets.

TRAIN

Train connections from Volgograd include Astrakhan (₽982, eight to 11 hours, two daily), Moscow (train 1, ₽1824, 19 hours, almost daily), Rostov-on-Don (₽1050, 12½ hours, at least daily), Saratov (₽1061, 7½ hours, frequent) and St Petersburg (₽2678, 36 hours, at least daily) – train 79 is the best for St Petersburg.

There are cheaper but slower train connections to Moscow and St Petersburg.

Getting Around

The city centre is accessible on foot. Kiosks sell city maps of the centre for ₽100. To get to Mamaev Kurgan or the Panorama Museum of the Battle of Stalingrad, take the *skorostnoy tramvay* (high-speed tram), which is a single metro line that runs along or under pr Lenina. To get to Krasnoarmeysk take *marshrutka* 15a, 91a, 93a, 93c, 93 or 55a from pr Lenina on the city side of the road (ie not the Volga side). To get to the airport, catch *marshrutka* 6 (₽20, every 30 minutes) from the stop on pr Lenina on the Volga side of the road, or at the train station.

ASTRAKHAN REGION

Astrakhan Астрахань

8512 / POP 520,500 / MOSCOW

With its East-meets-West feel, Astrakhan is an unusual provincial capital where a pretty river promenade and city parks are offset by architectural heritage in a shocking state of decay. Once upon a time, its streets saw German pastors mingling with Indian tea traders and Kazakh herdsmen. These days you can still feel an abrupt change as the striking kremlin, stone mansions and churches of the European and Christian centre give way to Tatar and Persian *sloboda* (suburbs) with their wooden cottages, mosques and quaint courtyards where garlands of drying vobla fish flutter in the breeze.

Built in 1558 after Ivan the Terrible defeated the local Tatar khanate, Astrakhan is the successor of two imperial capitals in the area: Saray of the Golden Horde and Itil of the earlier Khazar kaganate, which adopted Judaism as its official religion. Both cities prospered thanks to their location on the Silk Route and by the sea.

Today, however, Astrakhan is first and foremost a jumping-off point for the Volga Delta, where the intricate wetlands are home to hundreds of bird and fish species and the scene of sharp tourist growth.

Sights

★Kremlin HISTORICAL SITE

(Астраханский кремль; http://astrakhan-musei.ru; 7am-7pm;) FREE The kremlin on top of Zayachy Hill is a peaceful green haven in what can be a hot, dusty city. Its walls and gate towers were built in the 16th century using bricks from the ruins of the Golden Horde's capital Saray, located near the present-day village of Selitrennoye north of Astrakhan. Today the kremlin encompasses several museums and two churches.

➡ ★Assumption Cathedral CHURCH

(Успенский собор; http://astrakhan-musei.ru; kremlin; 7am-7pm) Dating from 1698–1720, the Assumption Cathedral dominates the kremlin grounds and is decorated inside with attractive frescoes.

➡ Artillery Yard MUSEUM

(Артиллерийский двор; http://astrakhan-musei.ru; kremlin; admission ₽135; 7am-7pm) The artillery yard and museum has an interesting collection of historic weapons and a mock *izba* (Russian cottage).

➡ Torture Tower MUSEUM

(Пыточная башня; http://astrakhan-musei.ru; kremlin; admission ₽50; 10am-6pm Tue-Sun May-Oct) Tells the story of physical torture from the 16th to the 18th century.

➡ Guardhouse MUSEUM

(Гауптвахта; http://astrakhan-musei.ru; kremlin; admission ₽50; 10am-6pm Tue-Sun) Located inside the guardhouse from 1807, this museum gives quite a good insight into the everyday life of soldiers in 19th-century Astrakhan.

➡ Red Gates HISTORICAL BUILDING

(Красные ворота; kremlin; admission ₽50; 10am-6pm Tue-Sun May-Oct) Covers the history of Astrakhan as a southern outpost of the Russian Empire from the 16th to the 19th century.

➡ Trinity Cathedral CHURCH

(Троицкий собор; http://astrakhan-musei.ru; kremlin) Closed for restoration at the time of research.

Dogadin Art Gallery ART GALLERY

(Художественная галерея Догадина; 8512-511 121; http://agkg.narod.ru; ul Sverdlova 81; admission ₽80, guided tour ₽500; 10am-6pm Tue, Wed & Fri-Sun, 1-9pm Thu) The Dogadin Art Gallery is especially strong on works of Astrakhan-born Boris Kustodiev, who painted lushly coloured semi-folkloric scenes of merchant life. Guided tours are in English. Call ahead.

Kryusha Quarter NEIGHBOURHOOD

(Крюша) The Kryusha area of former Tatar and Persian suburbs south of the May 1st Canal is still predominantly Muslim, which is reflected in the proliferation of mosques. It's quaint in a run-down sort of way, best avoided in the evening and a quarter where stray dogs roam along dirt roads.

Velimir Khlebnikov Museum MUSEUM

(Дом-музей Велимира Хлебникова; 8512-516 496; http://agkg.ru; ul Sverdlova 53; Russian/foreigner ₽40/120, bilingual tours ₽500; 10am-6pm Tue-Sun) Come here for a small collection of portraits, drawings and personal objects from this futurist poet.

Local Studies Museum MUSEUM

(Краеведческий музей; ul Sovetskaya 15; admission ₽40; 10am-5pm Fri-Wed, to 9pm Thu) The Local Studies Museum contains some interesting treasures excavated from the region,

Astrakhan

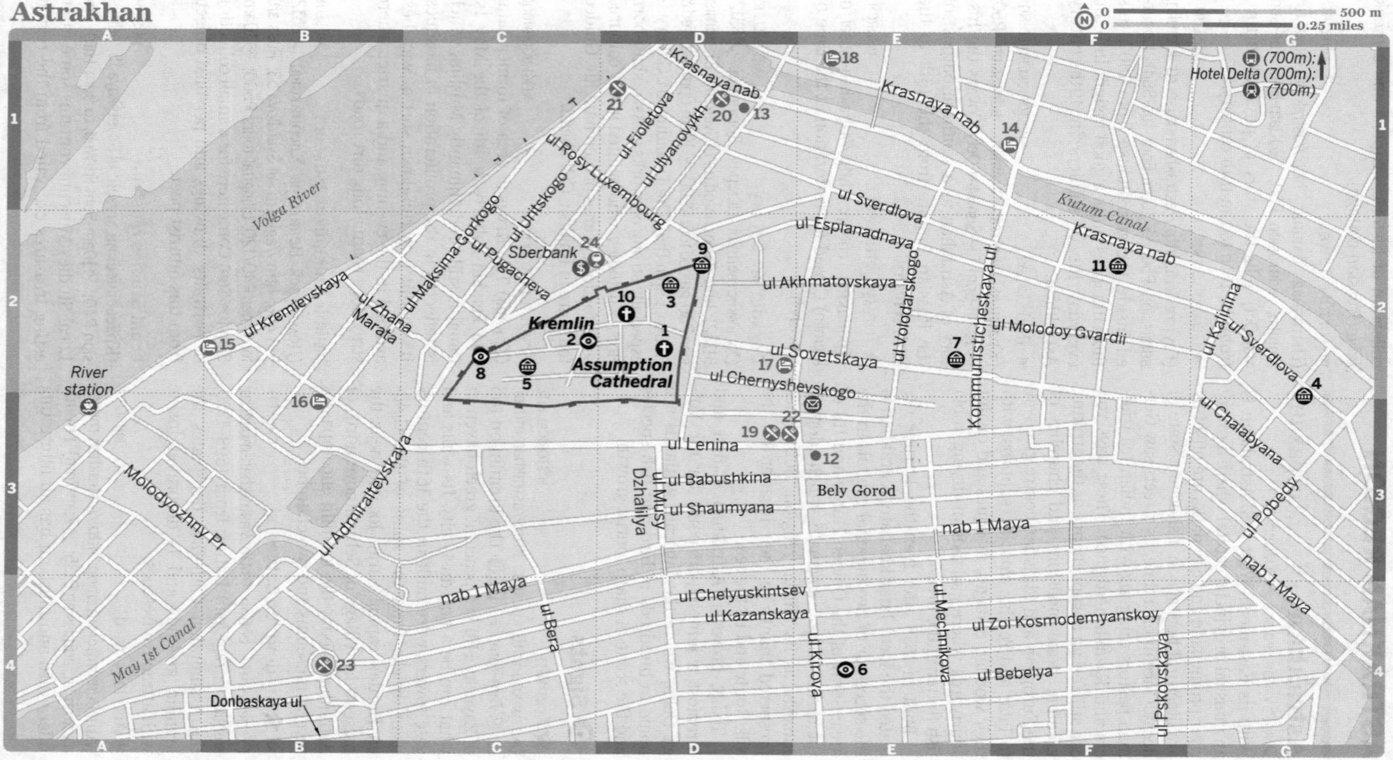
0 500 m
0 0.25 miles
A B C D E F G
1 2 3 4
(700m);
Hotel Delta (700m);
(700m)
Krasnaya nab
Kutum Canal
Volga River
ul Sverdlova
ul Esplanadnaya
ul Akhmatovskaya
ul Molodoy Gvardii
ul Sovetskaya
ul Chernyshevskogo
ul Volodarskogo
Kommunisticheskaya ul
ul Kalinina
ul Chalabyana
ul Pobedy
nab 1 Maya
ul Fioletova
ul Ulyanovykh
ul Rosy Luxembourg
ul Uritskogo
ul Maksima Gorkogo
ul Pugacheva
Sberbank
ul Kremlevskaya
ul Zhana Marata
River station
Kremlin
Assumption Cathedral
ul Lenina
ul Babushkina
ul Shaumyana
ul Musy Dzhalilya
Bely Gorod
Molodyozhny Pr
ul Admiralteyskaya
May 1st Canal
ul Bera
ul Chelyuskintsev
ul Kazanskaya
ul Kirova
ul Mechnikova
ul Zoi Kosmodemyanskoy
ul Bebelya
ul Pskovskaya
Donbaskaya ul
1 2 3 4 5 6 7 8 9 10 11 12 13 14 15 16 17 18 19 20 21 22 23 24

Astrakhan

Top Sights

Sights

Activities, Courses & Tours

Sleeping

Eating

Drinking & Nightlife

as well as exhibits on nature (including Volga fish) and local life. Temporary exhibitions fill one section.

Tours

Procosta TOUR COMPANY
(☎8512-999 812; www.procosta.ru; ul Admiraleyskaya 43; ⊙9am-6pm) Organises tours into the Volga Delta to its own tourist base (twin cottage ₽2000). A day excursion with boat and ranger from Astrakhan costs from ₽3800 per person, while a transfer each way costs ₽4000, which can be shared.

Cezar TOUR COMPANY
(Цезарь; ☎8512-392 954; www.zesar.ru; office 306, ul Lenina 20; ⊙9am-6.30pm Mon-Fri, 10am-4pm Sat) Cezar has highly professional staff who are very experienced in dealing with foreigners. It can organise day trips and lodge stays anywhere in the Volga Delta, as well as an excursion to Baskunchak Salt Lake and Bogdo Mountain (₽1700, including one meal and all costs; border permit required), sacred to Buddhists.

Astrintur TOUR COMPANY
(Астринтур; ☎8512-392 406/984; www.astrintour.ru; ul Lenina 20; ⊙9am-6pm Mon-Fri, 10am-3pm Sat) This agency is reliable and handles hotel bookings, individual tours and boat trips to the delta.

Sleeping

★**Hotel Azimut** HOTEL $$
(Гостиница Азимут; ☎8512-326 839; www.azimuthotels.ru; ul Kremlevskaya 4; with breakfast s ₽2700-3600, d ₽3700-4000, ste ₽4400-7100; ⊖@📶) This excellent business and tourist hotel not only has the best river views in town, it offers some of the best value, with comfortable, refurbished rooms, good breakfasts and efficient staff. Take *marshrutka* 1 from the train station to pl Lenina and walk towards the river for a few minutes.

Hotel 7 Nebo HOTEL $$
(Отель 7 Небо; ☎8512-640 810; www.7nebo-hotel.ru; Krasnaya nab 27; with breakfast s ₽2900-3500, d ₽3200-4000, ste ₽6000; 📶) This hotel, upstairs in a modern office building, offers good value for clean, parquet-floored rooms in tasteful colours. From the train station, take *marshrutka* 13 and ask for Krasnaya naberezhnye.

Hotel Delta HOTEL $$
(Гостиница Дельта; ☎8512-253 821; www.astdayspa.ru; pl Vokzalnaya 1; with breakfast s ₽1500-1800, d ₽2000-3000; ⊖📶) This well-run hotel is behind the enormous Yarmark (Ярмарка) shopping centre, opposite the train station. It also has a public sauna and spa treatments. Rooms can be rented from ₽500 for two hours' rest.

Lotus Hotel MINIHOTEL $$$
(Лотус Отель; ☎8512-262 200; http://hotel-lotus.ru; ul Maksima Gorkogo; with breakfast s ₽2900-4300, d ₽4400-5000; 📶🏊) This is a top-quality minihotel with a small pool for sauna-goers. Rooms are modern and spacious.

Victoria Palace HOTEL $$$
(Гостиница Виктория Палас; ☎8512-394 801; www.victoriapalas.ru; Krasnaya nab; with breakfast s ₽2800-5300, d ₽5000-6100, ste ₽7200-20,000; ❄@📶🏊) A shiny business hotel with 36 rooms and the usual 'business' facilities such as a bar, disco and sauna. It's located conveniently close to the major sights.

Novomoskovskaya HOTEL $$$
(☎8512-271 527; www.nvmsk.com; ul Sovetskaya 4/ul Kirova 18; with breakfast s ₽4000-7500, d ₽5000-8500;) A newcomer on the scene, opening in 2014, this hotel has marble-tiled bathrooms with bathtubs in spacious rooms cosily decorated in soft browns. Some rooms have views across the tranquil Bratsky Gardens.

Eating & Drinking

★ **Sharlay** CAFE $
(Кафе Шарлай; ul Kirova 26; meals ₽250; 9am-10pm Mon-Fri, from 11am Sat & Sun;) This canteen-style place is the eatery of choice for local office workers, and for good reason: the food is well prepared, the atmosphere is convivial and you feel far from the bustle of the busy street outside. Order at the counter and place the number on your table.

Tatar-Bazar MARKET $
(Татар-базар; pl Svobody 12 & 15; 7am-5pm) For famous Astrakhan watermelons and other fruit, try this market in Kryusha. *Marshrutky* 1, 52 and many others run out here from pl Oktyabrskaya.

Beer Academy PUB FOOD $$
(Академия Пива; ☎8512-444940; www.academy-piva.ru; ul Lenina 7; mains ₽400; 11am-midnight;) Among the pubs in Astrakhan, this one generally serves the best food, with an extensive menu that spans Russian Volga classics such as fish, pub classics like sausages, and steak. It also has a great selection of draught beers.

Cafe Izba RUSSIAN $$
(Кафе Изба; ul Krasnaya nab; mains ₽300, business lunch ₽200; noon-midnight;) Decorated in the style of a Russian cottage, Izba is one of Astrakhan's best traditonal restaurants, serving well-prepared classic cuisine popular with local office workers.

Krem Cafe CAFE $$
(Крем Кафе; ☎8512-440 400; ul Uritskogo 5; mains ₽200-400, salads ₽250; 11am-11pm Sun-Thu, to midnight Fri & Sat;) This cafe does good salads, sushi and meats, with great views of the river promenade. Staff are young and friendly.

Perfect BAR
(6th fl, Primium Kholl Bldg, ul Admiralteyskaya 15; 10am-midnight;) Perched high above the street, with the best views of the kremlin in town, Perfect is a sleek bar with DJs and dance space, a good wine list, inexpensive Baltika 7 if you're just making ends meet, and a range of reasonable salads, soups and mains.

Information

Post Office (Почта; cnr ul Kirova & ul Chernyshevskogo; per MB ₽3.15; 8am-10pm Mon-Fri, 9am-6pm Sat & Sun) Post office with internet access.

Sberbank (ul Admiralteyskaya 21; 10am-7pm Mon-Wed & Fri, to 6pm Thu, to 5pm Sat, 9am-1pm Sun)

Getting There & Away

AIR

S7, Aeroflot and Moskovya fly to Moscow (two to three times daily).

BOAT

Astrakhan is the end point – more rarely the starting point – for cruises on the Volga. There are no regular passenger boats to the other Caspian Sea ports. Cruise ships dock at the eternally uncompleted **river station** (Речной вокзал; ul Kremlevskaya 1).

BUS

The bus station has regular services to Elista (₽550, six hours) and Volgograd (₽855, 10 hours).

TRAIN

Book via Volgograd (₽982, eight to 11 hours, two daily) to Moscow (₽2806, at least 30 hours) to avoid passing through Kazakhstan. There are also services to Baku in Azerbaijan (₽2406, 24 hours) and east to Atyrau in Kazakhstan (*kupe* ₽995, 13 hours).

Getting Around

Marshrutka 5 runs from the airport (located about 10km south of the centre in the Sovetsky Rayon) to pl Lenina, passing the train and bus stations and pl Oktyabrskaya. Allow at least 30 minutes for the journey from the centre. *Marshrutka* 1 goes from the train station to pl Oktyabrskaya and pl Lenina.

Volga Delta Дельта Волги

The Volga Delta is the natural highlight of any trip to the region and, if you are travelling from north to south, you are likely to feel a sense of enormous achievement in reaching the point where this magnificent river flows into the Caspian Sea in Central Asia.

About 70km south of Astrakhan, the river bursts like a firecracker into thousands

ORGANISING TRIPS TO THE DELTA

Permits & Excursions

The delta region is a border zone. Regardless of whether you go down to the delta on a day trip or overnight, copies of your passport main page, visa and migration card need to be presented to the tour agency or place of stay a few days, or up to 10 days, in advance. If on a day trip, you need nothing more. If you're staying overnight, the place of stay will register you (which is your permit).

Cezar (p347) in Astrakhan and Procosta (p347) in Moscow, St Petersburg and Astrakhan are two very experienced tour agencies in the region. Procosta takes you to its own base, which is a couple of kilometres by boat from the Caspian Sea and the nearest road, with cottages set entirely on stilts. The cottages, linked by a boardwalk, sleep two to four people. Cezar can organise virtually any *turbaza* (holiday camp) or hotel on the delta. Rybnoye Mesto in Stanya (Станья), situated about 80km south of Astrakhan and a couple of kilometres from the last settlement of any size, Kamyzyak (Камызяк), is the springboard to the Procosta *turbaza* and other tourist bases in this part of the delta. Typically, a package consists of accommodation, an excursion for a couple of hours with a ranger and full board.

Tourist Bases & Hotels

Rybnoye Mesto (☎8-927-070 7007; http://vipvolga.ru; ul Rybatskaya 25, Stanya; per person with full board from ₽2500) Unless you speak Russian, Rybnoye Mesto is best booked through agencies in Astrakhan – it's a small hub for boat hire and transfers in this part of the delta.

Zolotoy Lotos (Золотой Лотос; ☎8-927-282 3002; www.astradelta.ru; near Karalat; per person per day from ₽3000, day excursion to Caspian Sea ₽5000) A good floating hotel that offers various excursions. It has one building on land and another on the water.

of streams, creating a unique ecosystem teeming with wildlife. The three symbols of the delta are the Caspian lotus flower (abundant), the sturgeon (critically threatened) and the Caspian flamingo – a semi-legendary bird that the average ranger will have seen once in his or her life, if at all.

The most biologically diverse area is covered by the **Astrakhan Biosphere Reserve**, which you can visit on excursions organised by Astrakhan travel agencies. The rest of the delta is dotted with floating and land-based lodges that mostly specialise in fishing and hunting. These days operators are used to the occasional foreigner drifting down here for the simple pleasure of experiencing this beautiful wetland area and travelling by boat into the *raskaty* (channels) to watch the birdlife. Although there are many tourist bases along the broader northern arms of the delta, the experience will be richer if you organise a stay deeper in the delta. In addition to the visiting hunters and anglers, local rangers and others from the nearby villages provide a rudimentary infrastructure and protect the park and border zone. Needless to say, even the dirt roads peter out into *raskaty* quickly here, making boat the best means of transport.

The best time to visit is between late July and late September when lotus flowers blossom and there are not as many mosquitoes as in May and June. April and October are major fishing seasons.

REPUBLIC OF KALMYKIA
РЕСПУБЛИКА КАЛМЫКИЯ

Elista — Элиста

☎84722 / POP 103,700 / ⌚MOSCOW

Prayer drums, red-robed monks, boiled guts and butter tea for lunch… Wait, it's still Europe! Elista is the capital of Kalmykia (Калмыкия), the continent's only Buddhist region and a fragment of Mongolia thrown onto the shores of the Caspian Sea. Much of the republic consists of sparsely populated steppe occasionally punctuated by straight or squiggly lines of wooden electricity poles running to the horizon. With its colourful, Tibetan-style *khuruls* (temples), the otherwise-very-drab Elista is a good starting point for further exploration of this region.

History

Kalmyks are nomads (nowadays at heart rather than in practice) and their history is that of migration – forced and voluntary. They descend from the Oirats, the western branch of Mongolians who embraced Buddhism in the early 17th century and soon after resolved to look for pastures green in the west.

In the last massive nomadic migration in the history of Eurasia, the Oirats traversed thousands of kilometres and ended up on the banks of the Volga, which at that time marked the border of the emerging Russian empire. Moscow welcomed the newcomers, allowing them to retain their way of life in return for guarding the border. However, in the 18th century, the Oirats came under pressure from Russian and German settlers encroaching on their lands. One winter's night in 1771 they made their second escape – back to Mongolia. But the ice on the Volga was not strong enough for those on the western bank to cross the river, so 20,000 out of 160,000 families stayed. The flight turned into a disaster, with two-thirds of the people killed by enemies on the way.

Those who remained on the Volga lived quietly and not entirely unhappily until the 1920s when the Bolsheviks destroyed all *khuruls*, arrested most monks and expropriated the cattle. No surprise that during the short-lived German occupation in 1942 some Kalmyks joined Hitler's army. At the same time, thousands of others fought on the Soviet side.

Stalin's reprisal was terrible. On 28 December 1943 all Kalmyks, including party members and policemen, were put in unheated cattle cars and sent to Siberia. When in 1957 Nikita Khrushchev allowed them to return, less than half the prewar population of 93,000 could make it home. The others perished in Gulag camps.

In 1993 the Kalmyks elected their first president – 31-year-old multimillionaire Kirsan Ilyumzhinov – who presided over the republic until 2010 and left his footprint through his two chief fascinations: chess and a predilection for the fictional trickster Ostap Bender. This conflux of chess, fiction and the reality of Kalmyk history lends the steppe republic a rather bizarre edge. The 14th Dalai Lama has visited several times despite Moscow's reluctance to spoil relations with China. Boring it is not.

Ul Lenina is Elista's main axis. The long, narrow stretch of green south of it is alleya Geroyev, which is flanked on the eastern side by the nameless main square where government buildings are located. The website www.rus-trip.ru/content/view/163/2 has a map of the city.

Sights

National Museum of the Republic of Kalmykia MUSEUM

(Национальный музей Республики Калмыкия им. Н. Н. Пальмова; http://museum.kalm.ru; ul Dzhangara 9; Russian/foreigner ₽60/80, deportation exhibition extra ₽100, museum tour Russian/foreigner extra ₽100/120; 9am-6pm Tue-Fri, 10am-4pm Sat & Sun) The modern building of the National Museum offers a perfect space for gaining an insight into the Kalmyk people and the republic, with eight rooms covering their history, ecology and culture. One room deals with the deportations during WWII. The exhibition is in Russian, so it's worth paying extra for an English (or Russian) tour for greater insight. Take *marshrutka* 5 and ask the driver to stop at the museum.

Golden Abode of Buddha Shakyamuni BUDDHIST TEMPLE

(Gol-Syume Burkh Bagshin Altn Syume; 84722-40 109; www.buddhisminkalmykia.ru; ul Klykova; grounds & temple 8am-8pm daily, library & museum 10am-6pm Tue-Sun, daily prayer 9-10.30am, prayer for the deceased 2-4pm Fri) The Golden Abode of Buddha Shakyamuni, also called the New Khurul, was built in 2005 in the Tibetan style. The prayer hall sports an 11m-high statue of Buddha and the monk's robe of the 14th Dalai Lama. Downstairs a small museum depicts the history of Kalmyk Buddhism. Take *marshrutka* 9 or any other going east along ul Lenina.

Geden Sheddup Goichorling BUDDHIST TEMPLE

(Syakyusn-syume; 84722-40 109) Geden Sheddup Goichorling is the oldest *khurul* in Kalmykia and consists of a lavishly decorated large temple from 1996, a small temple behind it containing the throne of the Dalai Lama, and a brick cottage for monks, surrounded by the steppe. To get there, take *marshrutka* 15 at the corner of ul Pushkina and ul Gorkogo. Once out of town, ask to stop by the *stary khurul*.

The figure of Buddha Shakyamuni is at the centre of the altar, and the frescoes on the walls depict his 12 deeds and tell about his life. The temple is usually closed, but you can get inside by asking at the monks' cottage or by calling ahead to arrange a time.

Chess City NEIGHBOURHOOD

A literary fantasy taken from the pages of the book *The Twelve Chairs*, and brainchild of former president Kirsan Ilyumzhinov, Chess City was built for the 1998 Chess Olympics and has an air of surreal suburban bliss. It's clustered on the edge of the steppe as a large ensemble of cottages around the glass Chess Palace. *Marshrutka* 7 takes you there from Hotel Elista.

From Chess City, take *marshrutka* 7 back one stop or walk back about 500m to the roundabout, where you will find the Ostap Bender monument, complete with all the tale's 12 chairs (which you can sit on).

Return Memorial MONUMENT

(www.enstudio.com) Located 500m along ul Khrushcheva from the roundabout, in the direction away from the centre, the Return Memorial by sculptor Ernst Neizvestny is a striking monument to the Kalmyk deportation.

Alleya Geroyev PARK

This pleasant park stretching along a narrow ravine is the city's main promenade and has Elista's largest concentration of sculptures and Buddhist architecture. Enter by crossing ul Lenina from Hotel Elista and walk east towards the main square, taking in the different monuments along the way.

Tours

Kalmykia Tour TOUR COMPANY

(961-548 5420; www.kalmykiatour.com) Few tour companies are used to handling foreigners, but Kalmykia Tour can organise accommodation (from ₽1500) and arrival transfer (₽450) if you need it.

Pegas Touristik TOUR COMPANY

(8-960-899 1705; destino-tur@yandex.ru; ul Neyman 1; 10am-7pm Mon-Fri, 11am-4pm Sat) Pegas can stitch together a sightseeing package with an English- or German-speaking guide and arrange accommodation. Expect to pay around ₽4000 for two people, excluding hotel costs and transport to/from Elista.

Sleeping

Bely Lotos HOTEL $$

(Белый Лотос; 84722-34 416; www.hotel-elista.ru; ul Khoninova 7; with breakfast s/d ₽2000/3000, ste ₽5200-7500;) Tucked away on a quiet street near alleya Geroyev at the Gostinitsa stop, the 'White Lotus' is professionally run, friendly and the best hotel in the city. The 14th Dalai Lama stayed here when in town.

Hotel Elista HOTEL $$$

(Korpus 1 84722-25 540; www.hotelelista.ru; Korpus 1: ul Lenina 241, Korpus 2: ul Lenina 237; with breakfast s ₽1500-3300, d ₽4500-5200;) This Soviet relic occupies two Stalinesque buildings (Korpus 1 and Korpus 2), which almost behave as separate hotels. Korpus 1 has the better facilities by far, with a 24-hour supermarket and a coffee bar. Avoid dumpy Korpus 2. Take any *marshrutka* going to the Gostinitsa (Гостиница) stop.

Eating & Drinking

Elista is the place to try Kalmyk food and the delicious pastries. The main staples include meat-filled *berg* (or *berigi*) dumplings, *doutour* (a mixture of intestines, kidneys and liver in a broth), *hasn makhn* (sliced beef with flat pasta) and *dzhomba* (butter tea).

Choko Time CAFE, INTERNATIONAL $

(ul Neyman 10; mains ₽260, pizza ₽230; noon-midnight) This cafe and restaurant almost seems to have a foot in the door of every cuisine, with sushi, Mexican, Italian and pan-European dishes in a relaxed but stylish ambience.

Gurman KALMYK, INTERNATIONAL $$

(84722-50 707; Kalmyk dishes ₽180-230, mains/steaks ₽350/450; noon-2am) Gurman is a grill restaurant located inside the modern entertainment complex (bowling, cinema, billiards, you name it). It's arguably the best midrange place in town and offers Kalmyk

THE DZHANGARIADA FESTIVAL

The Kalmyk equivalent of the Mongolian Naadam, Dzhangariada (late August or September) is an annual celebration of the Kalmyk epic *Dzhangar* – a 12-song story about life in the blessed land called Bumba. Held on open steppe just outside Elista (the location changes every year), it includes wrestling and archery contests and performances by *dzhangarchi* (traditional singers). Book accommodation early for the festival. Buses run out to the festival location from the city. Your hotel can help you.

dishes along with Russian and international cuisine ranging from steaks to sushi.

Praha PUB

(ul Nomto Ochirova 5; ⏲noon-2am) This pub has a laid-back beer-hall feel and slightly off-beat edge.

Cafe-Bar Alyans BAR

(Кафе-Бар Альянс; ul Nomto Ochirova 5a; ⏲noon-2am) Set among a constellation of eating and drinking places along ul Nomto Ochirova – many of them popular with a very young crowd – Alyans caters to a more mixed crowd. The food (mains ₽250 to ₽450) is decent, but its chilled-out mood, small dance floor and nightly DJ are its main attractions.

Information

Internet Kafe Online (ul Lenina 247; per hr ₽40; ⏲9am-9pm)

Sberbank (ul Suseyeva 13; ⏲9am-7pm Mon-Sat) A central branch with ATMs and currency exchange. Other ATMs are scattered around town and inside Hotel Elista.

Getting There & Away

AIR

Three flights to Moscow – on Sunday, Tuesday and Thursday – are all that keep Elista airport busy. Airline tickets are available at **Elya** (☎84722-41 297; ul Lenina 247/2; one way ₽4650-7750).

BUS

The bus station is on the outskirts of town. Elista is approximately the same distance from Volgograd, Astrakhan, Mineralnye Vody (Caucasus) and Stavropol (Caucasus). A trip to any of these takes about five hours and costs around ₽550. Currently there are no train services to Kalmykia.

Getting Around

Marshrutky are the only mode of public transport. Their main hub is in front of Hotel Elista (appearing as Гостиница on signs), from where you can get to any part of town. *Marshrutky* 2, 6, 9 and 17 go to the bus station, *marshrutka* 7 to Chess City.

Russian Caucasus

Includes ➡

Best Places to Eat

- Khachapuri (p365)
- Cafe 2200 (p371)
- Restoran Zamok (p378)
- Restaurant Sosruko (p384)

Best Places to Stay

- Grand Hotel & Spa Rodina (p364)
- Grand Hotel Polyana (p370)
- Hotel Zamok (p377)
- Tarelka (p381)

Why Go?

For most Russians, the word Caucasus (Кавказ) summons up images of fiery mountain folk, the high-tempo *lezginka* dance and the troubled history of volatile regions such as Chechnya. But there's more to this ethnically rich region than the stereotypes and the horror stories. Come to also experience relaxing spa towns, breathtaking scenery and world-class ski resorts near Sochi, host city for the 2014 Winter Olympics.

On top of that, there's superb trekking and horse riding amid soaring peaks, as well as the chance to climb Mt Elbrus, Europe's highest mountain. Black Sea resort towns offer coastal intrigue – sun and sea, festive nightlife – while the Caucasus also boasts its own regional cuisine.

This may not be the easiest area to travel in, with taxis and infrequent buses the only way to reach some destinations, but for anyone looking to get off the tourist trail, the Caucasus offers wide-open spaces, bustling markets and rugged mountain roads with stunning views around every corner.

When to Go

Sochi

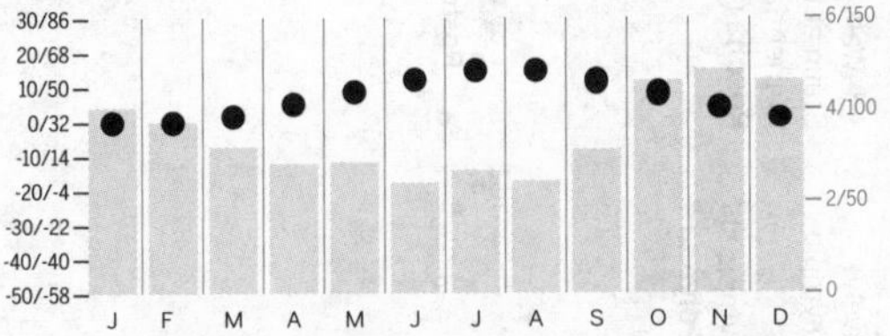

Jan Ski season kicks off at resorts in Krasnaya Polyana and Mt Elbrus.

May Enjoy sunny days and lower prices at Black Sea resorts and spa towns.

Jun-Sep Best time for climbing and hiking in the mountains. Peak season on the Black Sea.

Russian Caucasus Highlights

1. Stroll along the lively promenade of post-Olympic **Sochi** (p361).
2. Check out the Olympic ski slopes at **Krasnaya Polyana**'s resorts (p369).
3. Walk in the footsteps of Stalin at the Soviet dictator's former dacha, **Zelenaya Roscha** (p367).
4. Take a journey to the dramatic snow-capped peaks and glaciers of **Dombay** (p378).
5. Admire the breathtaking views from Europe's highest peak, **Mt Elbrus** (p384).
6. Drink the carbonic Narzan spring waters in the relaxing spa town of **Kislovodsk** (p376).
7. Immerse yourself in Cossack history in **Starocherkassk** (p358).

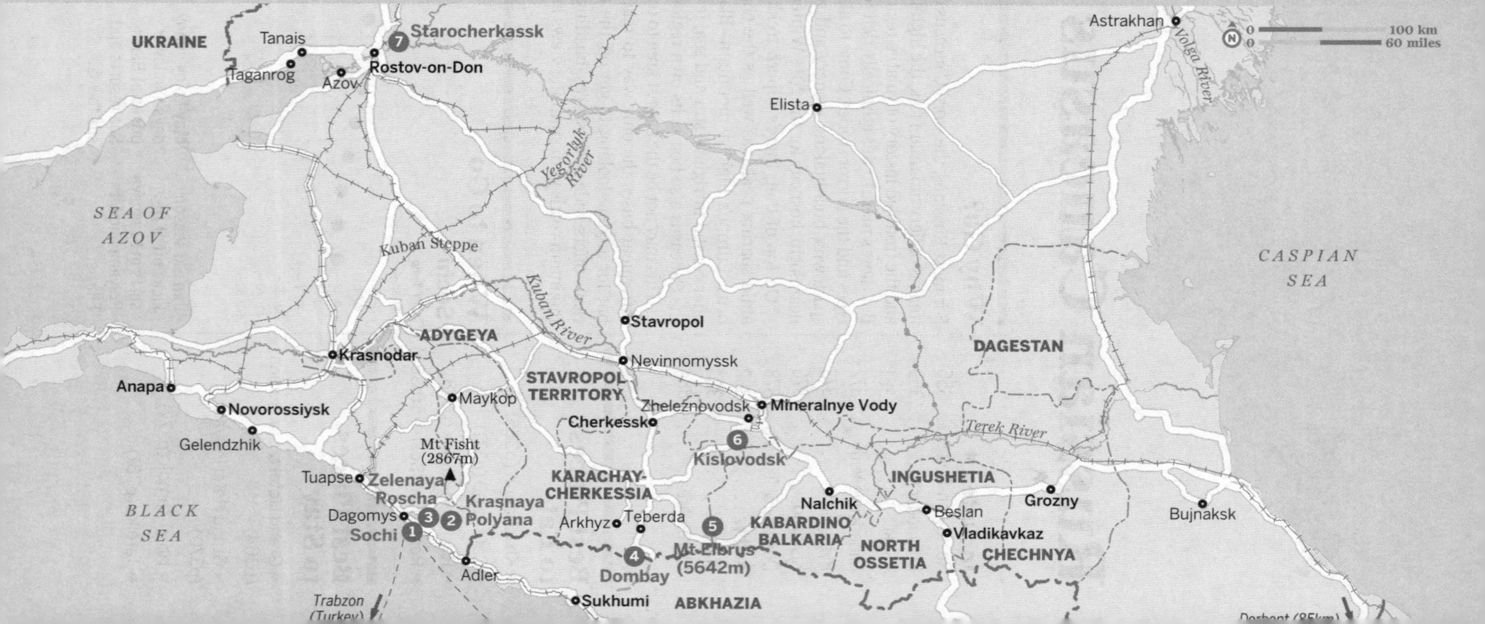

History

The Caucasus has stood at the crossroads of Asian and European cultures since the Bronze Age. The result is an extraordinary mix of races with three main linguistic groups: Caucasian, Indo-European and Turkic. The Caucasus has suffered many invasions and occupations, having been squeezed between rival Roman, Byzantine, Persian, Arab, Ottoman and Russian empires.

Life Before the Russians

Earliest human traces in the Russian Caucasus date from Neolithic times, when farming was replacing hunting and gathering. The first communities evolved in Dagestan's valleys around the same time as agriculture developed in West Asia and China, establishing this region as an early cradle of civilisation.

The first dominant state was created by the Alans, ancestors of modern Ossetians. It blossomed during the 10th century AD and, at its peak, ruled most of the Northern Caucasus. The Alans were Christians, probably having been introduced to the religion by the Georgians. The Alan state was conquered by the Mongol Tatar invasions of the early 13th century and any remnants destroyed by the army of Timur (Tamerlane) in 1395.

The Russians Arrive

Escaping Russian serfs and adventurers had already settled in the lower Terek River region when Russian military power arrived here in the late 1500s. In 1696 Peter the Great captured the Turkish stronghold of Azov and expanded imperial influence southward.

Later, Catherine the Great began the subjugation of the Caucasus in earnest, assisted by the area's Cossacks. The campaign picked up steam in the early 1800s as the Caucasus became a strategically important region in the so-called 'Great Game' being played out between Russia and Great Britain.

In 1816 General Yermelov, a veteran of the Napoleonic Wars, began a ruthless campaign to pacify the mountain peoples. The predominantly Muslim populace resented this intrusion by European and Christian Russians, and bitter guerrilla-type warfare ensued, led by the Cherkess (Circassians) in the north and the legendary Dagestani leader Imam Shamil further south. Shamil united Dagestani and Chechen tribes for a 30-year fight against the Russians that ended with Shamil's surrender in 1859.

The Soviet Era

During the October Revolution, many tribes united to form the Mountain Republic. Independence lasted until 1921 when Soviet forces overran the Caucasus. Soviet policy was to divide and rule by creating small autonomous regions, often combining two totally different nationalities. The Muslim-dominated portion of the Caucasus was split into five autonomous regions: Dagestan, Adygeya, Chechnya, Kabardino-Balkaria and Karachay-Cherkessia.

In 1944 Stalin ordered the mass deportation of Balkar, Chechen, Ingush and Karachay peoples to Central Asia and Siberia, on the pretext of potential collaboration with German forces. Khrushchev allowed the exiled groups to return in 1957 but without compensation or repossession of their property. The Soviet regime smothered any potential conflict caused by this injustice, but the situation changed quickly after the collapse of the USSR in 1991.

Post-Soviet Era

The sudden split of the Soviet Union triggered a spark in ethnic hostilities, as long-suppressed grudges and rivalries bubbled to the surface of the newly independent Russia. Chechnya witnessed two devastating wars from 1994-96 and 1999-2000, as federal troops battled a mixture of secular separatists and Islamist fighters, with multiple atrocities committed by both sides. The violence frequently spilled over into other North Caucasus republics, including the tragic Beslan school siege in North Ossetia in 2004, Russia's worst-ever terrorist atrocity. In 2005 separatist Chechen guerrillas, led by the late warlord Shamil Basayev, launched multiple attacks on police and military posts in Kabardino-Balkaria's capital, Nalchik.

The violence in the North Caucasus was becoming increasingly jihadist in nature. In October 2007 veteran Chechen militant Doku Umarov was named emir of the 'Caucasus Emirate', a purported Islamic state that would span much of the region. Using the North Caucasus as their base, Umarov's followers launched a series of bloody attacks on Moscow and other cities in the Russian heartland. In 2011, in what appeared to signal a new phase in militant tactics, three tourists from Moscow were killed en route from the Mineralnye Vody airport to a ski resort in the Mt Elbrus area.

THE CIRCASSIAN MASSACRE

Sadly, one of the great tragedies of the 19th century is all but forgotten today and remains unacknowledged by the Russian government. Russian tsars dating back to Peter the Great had long eyed the Caucasus and the strategic access to the Black Sea as keys to imperial expansion. The bloody conquest of the Caucasus kicked off in earnest in 1816, with Russian general Alexey Yermolov using a campaign of terror to pacify the mountain peoples.

Despite fierce resistance, the Circassians eventually surrendered in 1864. What happened next was the complete ethnic cleansing of all Muslim peoples from the Black Sea coast and surrounding areas. The Circassians were given a choice: leave the mountains and move to the far-off plains, or leave the country. According to 19th-century Russian historian Adolf Berzhe, some 400,000 Circassians were killed, nearly 500,000 forced to flee to Turkey and only 80,000 permitted to settle elsewhere in Russia. Along with those who fled earlier, however, the total estimated number of expelled or slaughtered is believed to be far higher. Today's descendants of the Circassians can be found in Turkey, Kosovo, Syria, Jordan and Israel – though you will find no trace of them in the resort towns along the Black Sea, their former ancestral homeland. See Oliver Bullough's excellent book, *Let Our Fame Be Great*, for more details.

Today, although the North Caucasus remains a volatile, frequently violent region, there are indications that the security situation is improving. Terrorist attacks are on the decline, and Umarov is widely believed to have been killed during a clash with Russian security forces in late 2013 or early 2014, although details remain hazy. One obvious indication of growing stability in the North Caucasus was Russia's ability to hold the 2014 Winter Olympics in Sochi, just a few hours from Chechnya. Despite fears the Games would be targeted by militant fighters, the Olympics passed peacefully.

KUBAN STEPPE

From Rostov-on-Don, the overland routes to the Northern Caucasus and the Black Sea coast cross the Kuban Steppe (Кубанская Степь), named after its river flowing from Elbrus into the Sea of Azov. The region is an important agricultural centre and is often referred to as the bread basket of Russia. It's also the traditional home of the Cossacks, the proud horsemen who helped protect Russia's tsarist-era borders.

Rostov-on-Don
Ростов -на -Дону

863 / POP 1.1 MILLION / MOSCOW

Rostov-on-Don (simply 'Rostov' to locals) is the gateway to the Northern Caucasus region. It's southern Russia's largest and most cosmopolitan city, as well as an important industrial centre. Flowing through the city is the Don River, celebrated in Mikhail Sholokhov's novels of the Russian Civil War, *And Quiet Flows the Don* and *The Don Flows Home to the Sea*. There is no particular reason to linger here for more than a day or two, but the city makes a pleasant stopover on the way to Sochi and the Black Sea coast. If possible, take a boat ride along the Don.

Rostov is mostly on the northern bank of the Don. The main east-west axis is Bolshaya Sadovaya ul; the bus and train stations are at its western end. Parallel to it runs park-lined, pedestrianised Pushkinskaya ul.

Sights & Activities

Civil War Monument MONUMENT

(pl Sovetov) This colossal monument commemorates the Red Army soldiers who took part in the 1917–23 Russian Civil War. The square was home to the Alexandro-Nevsky Cathedral until 1930, when it was destroyed by Soviet authorities. There is a miniature of the cathedral to the right of the monument. Opposite Bolshaya Sadovaya ul 71.

Riverside Area PROMENADE

Along the Don it's a pure carnival atmosphere by night, with sizzling shashlyk kebab stands, outdoor discos, karaoke and cranking music. There's also a statue of *And Quiet Flows the Don* author Mikhail Sholokhov that depicts the writer gazing thoughtfully at the river that helped make his name.

Gorky Park PARK
(Парк Горького; Bolshaya Sadovaya ul 55;) Leafy Gorky Park is home to open-air cafes and a cheap and cheerful funfair. There's also an impressive Soviet-era monument to the 1917 Bolshevik Revolution to one side of the rickety-looking Ferris wheel. The park is popular with chess-playing locals and lazy cats from spring onwards.

Pushkinskaya Ulitsa PROMENADE
(ул Пушкинская) This idyllic promenade is blissfully free of traffic and sprinkled with fountains, sculptures, cafes and restaurants, with outdoor seating and music-playing buskers during the summer.

Nativity of the Virgin Cathedral CHURCH
(Ростовский Кафедральный Собор Рождества Пресвятой Богородицы; ul Stanislavskogo 58; 8am-7pm) The lavish, neo-Byzantine Nativity of the Virgin Cathedral, built in 1856, overlooks the central market.

Regional Museum MUSEUM
(Ростовский областной музей краеведения; www.rostovmuseum.ru; Bolshaya Sadovaya ul 79; adult/child ₽130/50; 10am-5.30pm Tue-Sun) From the 3rd century BC until the 4th century AD, Greek trading colonies flourished at the mouth of the Don. Rostov's Regional Museum has exhibits from this era, as well as pieces covering the last 1600 years. A large display on the 2nd floor is devoted to the Don Cossacks. There is also, somewhat incongruously, a brand new planetarium.

River Cruise BOAT TRIPS
(party boats admission ₽150-230) For an entertaining slice of local life, head to the river embankment and board a cruise boat for a one-hour disco-infused trip along the Don. These kick off mid-morning and run until 1am, getting more raucous as the day progresses. Prices vary – they're highest on weekend evenings.

Sleeping

Airport Hotel HOTEL $
(Гостиница 'Аэропорт'; 8-863-276 7894; pr Sholokhova 270/1; s/d from ₽800/1300;) At the airport, you'll find this friendly, functional, budget-friendly hotel. It's an easy 20-minute bus ride into the centre. A taxi costs around ₽350.

Park City Rose HOTEL $$
(Гостиница Парк Сити; 8-863-288 8222; www.hotelparkciti.ru; Shaumyana ul 90; s/d incl breakfast from ₽2500/₽3000;) Park City Rose offers a friendly and professional service and spacious, tasteful rooms. It has free wi-fi and good breakfasts and is conveniently located for the main sights and parks.

Marins Park Hotel HOTEL $$$
(Маринс Парк Отель; 8-863-290 7666; www.rostovhotel.ru; Budyonovsky pr 59; s/d incl breakfast from ₽3150/4150;) This centrally located business hotel has bright and attractive rooms, as well as free wi-fi. Friendly English-speaking staff are happy to offer advice on city sights.

Don Plaza HOTEL $$$
(8-863-263 9052; www.don-plaza.ru; Bolshaya Sadovaya ul 115; s/d incl breakfast from ₽4700/5700;) This massive, remodelled, Soviet-style high-rise has modern rooms that boast good views from upper floors and decent amenities (including free wi-fi). Prices have dropped slightly in recent years, but it remains one of the pricier options in town. It does, however, serve tasty breakfasts that will fill you up for the rest of the day.

Eating & Drinking

Smetana RUSSIAN, UKRAINIAN $
(Сметана; Bolshaya Sadovaya ul 80; mains ₽130-200; 10am-midnight Mon-Fri, from noon Sat & Sun;) Bright and friendly Smetana serves traditional Russian and Ukrainian food – mainly *pelmeni* (ravioli) and *vareniki* (dumplings) – in a tasteful setting that is big on Warhol-esque displays of canned food.

Beliy Slon VEGETARIAN $
(Белый Слон; ul Pushkinskaya 135/33; mains ₽90-130; 10am-9pm;) A real godsend for vegetarians in the shashlyk-fixated Caucasus region. This friendly basement cafe offers a wide range of tasty and good-value dishes, from stinging-nettle soup to meat-free versions of traditional Russian cuisine. Free wi-fi and tasty desserts, as well.

Zolotoy Kolos CAFE $
(Золотой колос; Bolshaya Sadovaya ul 43; pizza ₽110-150; 8am-10pm) Popular with families, this cafe stretches across two halls. Its outdoor tables are ideal for enjoying pizza, soups, ice cream, desserts and cold beer in the warmer months. It's next to Gorky Park.

Pasha UZBEK, CAUCASIAN $$
(Паша; ul Beregovaya 29; mains ₽450-800; noon-midnight Mon-Fri, to 2am Sat & Sun;) Right on the Don embankment, this atmospheric restaurant's speciality is

meat-based dishes from Uzbekistan and the Caucasus region.

Ryba SEAFOOD $$
(Рыба; ul Beregovaya 23; mains ₽400-800; ⊙noon-midnight Mon-Fri, to 2am Sat & Sun; ❄📶) This spacious seafood restaurant is opposite the bank of the Don. It serves a decent *ukha* fish soup, as well as more expensive sturgeon and caviar-based dishes.

Information

Post & Telegraph Office (ul Lermontovskaya 116; ⊙8am-6pm)

Getting There & Away

AIR

Both Aeroflot and Transaero run Moscow–Rostov–Moscow flights, with one-way tickets at around ₽4500. Aeroflot also flies to St Petersburg (from ₽5000) and other Russian and international destinations. Austrian Airlines flies daily to Vienna (return €720).

BOAT

Don Tour (☎8-863-279 7366; www.dontour.ru; Beregovaya ul 23) runs *teplokhody* (passenger boats) to Starocherkassk at 9am on Saturday and Sunday from May to October, returning to Rostov at 5pm (return including food ₽550). It also runs boats to the former fortress town of Azov on summer weekends, departing at 9am and returning 5pm (from ₽600).

BUS

Private bus companies parked in front of the **bus station** (pr Siversa 1) run express trips to Moscow (₽1400, 17½ hours, three daily), Pyatigorsk (₽750, 9½ hours, twice daily) and Volgograd (₽660, 9¼ hours, 9.20am daily). Public buses also serve those destinations plus Anapa (₽530, 10 hours, daily), Astrakhan (₽950, 14 hours, two daily) and Krasnodar (₽320, 5½ hours, three daily).

TRAIN

Numerous trains pass through Rostov's **main train station** (pl Privokzalnaya), chugging north to Moscow (*platskart/kupe* from ₽1900/2900, 17½ to 25 hours) and south to Sochi (*platskart/kupe* from ₽1200/1900, nine to 15 hours) via Krasnodar.

The **local train station** (pr Siversa) is 200m south of the main train station. *Elektrichki* (suburban trains) trundle to Krasnodar (₽340, 3¾ hours, two daily).

Getting Around

Buses 7 and 1 and *marshrutka* 7A shuttle between the airport and the train station via Bolshaya Sadovaya ul (25 minutes).

Around Rostov

To see the various sights around Rostov more efficiently, you might consider a tour. Typical tours include Starocherkassk and the ancient Greek trading colony of Tanais, which has an archaeology museum and excavation; the 'new' Don Cossack capital of Novocherkassk, with its well-regarded Don Cossack museum; and Taganrog, birthplace of Anton Chekhov. Hotels in Rostov can arrange tour guides.

Starocherkassk Старочеркасск

☎863 / POP 5500 / ⊙MOSCOW

Founded in 1593, flood-prone Starocherkassk was the Don Cossack capital until the early 18th century. Once a fortified town of 20,000, it's now a farming village with a main street restored to near-19th-century appearance.

Allegedly, Peter the Great met a drunken Cossack here sitting on a barrel, wearing only a rifle. This image of a soldier who'd sooner lose his clothes than his gun so impressed the tsar that he commissioned the scene as the Don Cossack army seal.

There are several tourist attractions here, but the real appeal is the town's mellow, old-Russia feel. The village hosts boisterous Cossack fairs, with much singing, dancing, horse riding and merrymaking, on the last Sunday of the month from May to September. There are also annual Maslenitsa celebrations here, with pancakes and traditional games galore, when village residents prepare for the Great Lent fast and greet the coming spring.

Sights & Activities

Ataman Palace MUSEUM
(Атаманский дворец; ul Pochtovaya 7; admission ₽120; ⊙9am-5pm daily) Once the living quarters of the Cossack chiefs, the Ataman Palace is home to an exhibition that traces the development of Don Cossack culture from the 16th century to the present day. Exhibits include an impressive 400-year-old sundial and antique Cossack weapons.

Adjacent to the palace is the 1761 **Church of Our Lady of the Don**, which was the private church of the Cossack chiefs. Within is a magnificent golden iconostasis with rows of saints.

Fortified House of Kondraty Bulavin MUSEUM

(Дом атамана Кондратия Булавина; ul Sovetskaya; admission ₽75; ⏲10am-5pm Tue-Sun) Near the western end of ul Sovetskaya stands the fortified house of Kondraty Bulavin, the Cossack rebel leader during the Peasant War (1707–09). Bulavin lived and died in this solid stone house with 1m-thick walls, iron doors and an elevated basement to stave off flooding.

'We shall die as one rather than remain silent before the wicked deeds of evil men,' Bulavin declared at the height of his uprising. But his rebellion was unsuccessful – a series of military failures turned his followers against him, and he was found dead in unclear circumstances in 1708.

Resurrection Cathedral CHURCH

(Воскресенский собор; ul Sovetskaya) In a square at the eastern end of ul Sovetskaya, the Resurrection Cathderal contains a soaring golden iconostasis, a baroque chandelier and an unusual floor of metal tiles. Peter the Great took a special interest in the church, and even helped lay the altar brickwork when he visited in 1709. The adjacent bell tower provides a bird's-eye panorama.

The cathedral's actual bells are, however, currently in use at the nearby monastery.

Eating

Cafe Starocherkassk CAFE $

(Кафе Старочеркасск; ul Begovaya 8; mains ₽200-400; ⏲10am-10pm) This cosy cafe is set in attractive grounds and serves some fine fish soups, as well as local bottled beers. If you feel like staying the night, it also has comfortable rooms for rent (single/double ₽800/1100).

Getting There & Away

Boat tours provide a good-value and fun way to visit Starocherkassk if you come on a weekend. These typically run on Saturday and Sunday, from May to early October, setting off from Rostov at 9am and returning at 5pm (from ₽550). Otherwise, it's *marshrutka* 151 (₽40, 50 minutes, six to 12 daily) from pl Karla Marksa in Rostov. The last return service is 8pm.

Krasnodar Краснодар

☎861 / POP 650,000 / ⏲MOSCOW

When Catherine the Great travelled south to tour the lands conquered from the Turks, her lover Potemkin had cheerful facades erected along her route. These hid the mud-splattered hovels that made up the newly founded city bearing her name, Yekaterinodar ('Catherine's Gift').

It's been a long time since Krasnodar has needed those facades. Today, its lively centre boasts clean and pleasant streets lined with countless cafes and restaurants. Externally renovated, tsarist-era buildings give parts of the city an elegant, European-style appearance that have earned it the sobriquet 'Little Paris'. There isn't a great deal to see in the city, but it's a pleasant place to relax for a day or two.

The road from Rostov-on-Don feeds into the northern end of Krasnaya ul, Krasnodar's 2km-long leafy colonnade of a main street. Train and bus stations are to the southeast, just north of the Kuban River, which snakes around the city's southern and western flanks.

'CAUCASIAN MALE, HEIGHT...'

Ever wondered why white people are referred to as Caucasian? Well, in 1795 the German ethnologist Johann Blumenbach visited the Caucasus and was impressed by the health and physique of the mountain people. Despite them not being quite white, he used the term 'Caucasian' as one of his five great divisions of mankind. In bartending, a Caucasian is a mixed drink also referred to as a White Russian.

Sights

Statue of Catherine the Great MONUMENT

(cnr Postovaya ul & Krasnaya ul) At the foot of Krasnaya ul, an elaborate statue of Catherine the Great, with lute-strumming Cossacks and Potemkin at her heels, roosts in an attractive park. There are fine old buildings in the side streets east of here, plus the converted mosque at ul Pushkina 61 and the restored neo-Renaissance facade of ul Kommunarov 8.

★ **Museum of Military Hardware** MUSEUM

(Музей военной техники; ul Krasina 2; ⏲24hr) FREE Located by the river in Victory Park (Парк Победы), this open-air museum's display of WWII tanks and rocket launchers conjures up images of Soviet-era military parades. Kids love to clamber all over the tanks.

The walk to the museum takes you past a host of funfair rides and cheap and cheerful cafes.

Dog Capital Scultpure MONUMENT
(ul Mira 35) This unusual sculpture, on the corner of central ul Krasnaya, features two elegantly dressed dogs out for a stroll. It was inspired by a quip by famed Soviet-era poet Vladimir Mayakovsky, who dubbed Krasnodar a 'canine capital' due to the number of dogs in the city.

Unveiled in 2007, residents of Krasnodar believe if you rub the dogs' noses you will be lucky in love, while if you rub their paws, you will be fortunate with your travel plans.

Regional Museum MUSEUM
(Краснодарский государственный историко-археологический музей; Gimnazicheskaya ul 67; admission per exhibition ₽30-60; ⏲10am-6pm Tue-Sun) Archaeological finds and an exhibit on the history of the Kuban Cossacks headline the Regional Museum.

Sleeping

Resting Rooms HOSTEL $
(komnaty otdykha; ☎861-214 7344; dm/d ₽650/2600) At the train station, the immaculate resting rooms are a fine option if your stay is short.

Hotel Platan HOTEL $$
(Гостиница Платан; ☎861-268 3007; www.platanhotel.ru/platan; ul Postovaya 41; s & d from ₽3900; ❄📶) This pleasant business hotel has functional, if unimaginative rooms. The hotel is well located in a quiet area near the centre. It's also close to the Catherine the Great monument.

Hotel Intourist HOTEL $$$
(Гостиница Интурист; ☎861-255 8897; www.int-krd.ru; Krasnaya ul 109; s/d from ₽4000/4500; ❄@📶) This refurbished Soviet-era high-rise has bright, comfortable rooms with oversized windows and sleek bathrooms, and boasts an overall business-class feel despite dashes of colour. Friendly reception staff speak English and can arrange airport transfers, airline ticketing and excursions.

Eating & Drinking

Krasnaya ul boasts many indoor and outdoor eateries. Self-caterers should head to the central **Sennoy Bazaar** (ul Budyonnogo; ⏲7am-6pm) market or the **Kooperativny Market** (cnr ul Golgolya & Krasnoarmeyskaya ul; ⏲7am-6pm) for rows of fresh fruit, pickled vegetables and dairy products.

Khlebnie Istorii CAFE $
(Хлебные истории; Krasnaya ul 68; pastries ₽35-55; ⏲8am-10pm; 🚭📶) This bright and friendly cafe serves a satisfying selection of pastries, cakes and freshly squeezed juices, as well as the usual tea and coffee. A great place to spend a few hours if you are waiting for an onwards train. Free wi-fi.

Lyubo-Dorogo RUSSIAN, EUROPEAN $
(Любо-дорого; Krasnaya ul 33; mains ₽200-400; ⏲10am-11pm) This good-value restaurant serves a wide range of tasty European and Russian dishes. A central location and outdoor covered seating makes it perfect for a spot of people-watching in the summer months.

Mirage RUSSIAN $
(Мираж; cnr Kubana nab & ul Gogolya; shashlyk per 100g ₽100-180) This pleasant cafe, down by the river, has tasty shashlyk and salads. You can also just drain a few beers and watch the Kuban River pass patiently by.

Information

There are currency changers and ticketing agents in the main hotels, and ATMs along Krasnaya ul.

Main Post Office (Rashpilevskaya ul 58)

Getting There & Away

Krasnodar's airport is 15km east of town. Aeroflot flies daily to Adler (from ₽2400), Moscow (from ₽4400), St Petersburg, Kaliningrad and other destinations. Take trolleybus 7 or bus 1 to the airport from the train station (around 50 minutes) or a taxi (₽700, 30 minutes).

The **bus station** (pl Privokzalnaya) has services to Anapa (₽260, 3½ hours, frequent), Novorossiysk (₽195, three hours, frequent) and Rostov-on-Don (from ₽360, four to six hours, six daily).

From the **train station** (pl Privokzalnaya), *elektrichki* serve Mineralnye Vody (₽510, six hours, Monday, Thursday and Saturday), Novorossiysk (₽200, 3½ hours, four daily) and Rostov-on-Don (₽325, 3¾ hours, three daily), with passenger trains to Moscow (*platskart/kupe* from ₽2200/4500, 22 to 31 hours, frequent) and Sochi (*platskart/kupe* from ₽1100/1600, 5½ to seven hours, frequent).

A combined daily train, ferry, bus service (₽880, 12 hours) takes passengers to Russia's newly annexed Crimea territory during the summer months. As of research time, tickets were only available at Russian Railways ticket offices, not online.

BLACK SEA COAST

A narrow coastal strip edges the Black Sea from where rolling hills ascend fairly rapidly into mountains in the southeast and low uplands in the northwest. This is the Black Sea coast (Побережье Чёрного моря), Russia's sole seaside playground until the Kremlin's 2014 annexation of Crimea. A long summer from June to October gives rise to pleasant weather, plenty of sunshine and a warm sea. Several resort towns dot the sometimes-rugged coast, the best known being Sochi, host city for the 2014 Winter Olympics.

Besides the mostly pebbly beaches in Sochi and nearby Adler, the region offers terrific walking in the Greater Caucasus foothills. Another highlight is Krasnaya Polyana, a once-sleepy mountain village that was transformed at great expense into the venue for Olympic ski and snowboard events. A new high-speed railway line, built especially for the Olympics, whisks passengers along the Black Sea coastline to Krasnaya Polyana from Sochi's main train station.

Sochi Сочи

8622 / POP 343,000 / MOSCOW

The gateway to the optimistically named 'Russian Riviera', Sochi is a Black Sea resort that received massive investment and media attention as host city for the 2014 Winter Olympics. However, what was billed as 'Sochi' for the Games actually embraced both the neighbouring resort of Adler – home to the Olympic ice-skating arena – and Krasnaya Polyana, a mountain village that hosted skiing and snowboarding events. No actual Olympic events were held in the city of Sochi.

Sochi's lively, pedestrian-only sea embankment is packed with restaurants, cafes and bars, some of which are ideally placed for watching the sun drop slowly behind the Black Sea horizon. In the summer, coastline nightclubs pump out disco hits from dusk till dawn. However, while the sea is warm and the climate subtropical (among Russia's warmest destinations in winter), the beaches are disappointingly rocky and grey, although imported sand is used on some beaches in the summer months. Away from the embankment, magnolia- and cypress-filled parks provide a fine setting for relaxing strolls, while just outside of town you'll find memorable hikes amid waterfalls and sublime views in the Agura Valley. A little further north lie the towering peaks of Krasnaya Polyana.

The high season is early May to late September, with the big crowds arriving in July and August, driving up the already exorbitant prices.

Kurortny pr runs the length of Sochi a few blocks from the sea. The train and bus stations are centrally located a few blocks north of Kurortny pr.

History

Sochi began life as a holiday resort in the final decades of the 19th century, when wealthy Russians came here to enjoy the sun and take spa treatments. Its development accelerated under Soviet authorities in the 1920s, when the city's malaria-infested swamps were dried out and a nature reserve was established.

It was during Josef Stalin's reign that Sochi first flourished, however. Throughout the 1930s, a series of sanatoriums were constructed on the Black Sea coast to provide heavily subsidised holidays to Soviet workers. A typical Russian holiday would once have been a month at the sanatorium in Sochi related to one's profession, such as the **Metallurg** (8-8622-672 554; www.metallurg-sochi.ru; Kurortny pr 92; per person per night from ₽2300;) for metal workers (still open for business in today's capitalist Russia). Sochi's reputation as a resort grew further when Stalin elected to have his very own dacha (p367) built in the verdant hills around the city in 1937.

Post-Stalin, Sochi continued to vie with Crimea as the Soviet Union's number-one holiday resort. The city's distinctive train station and port were constructed in the 1960s, and Sochi served as the backdrop to the immensely popular Soviet comedy, Бриллиантовая рука (Diamond Arm).

With the split-up of the Soviet Union and the opening of Russia's borders, Sochi lost much of its appeal, as Russian holidaymakers opted en masse for package holidays on the beaches of Turkey and other previously forbidden shores. Sochi continued to attract crowds, but it was a resort on the decline.

The city received a massive boost, however, in 2007, when it was chosen by the International Olympic Committee as host for the 2014 Winter Olympics. It was a decision that left many Russians scratching their heads in puzzlement. After all, Sochi was not only better known for palm trees than snow, but

Sochi

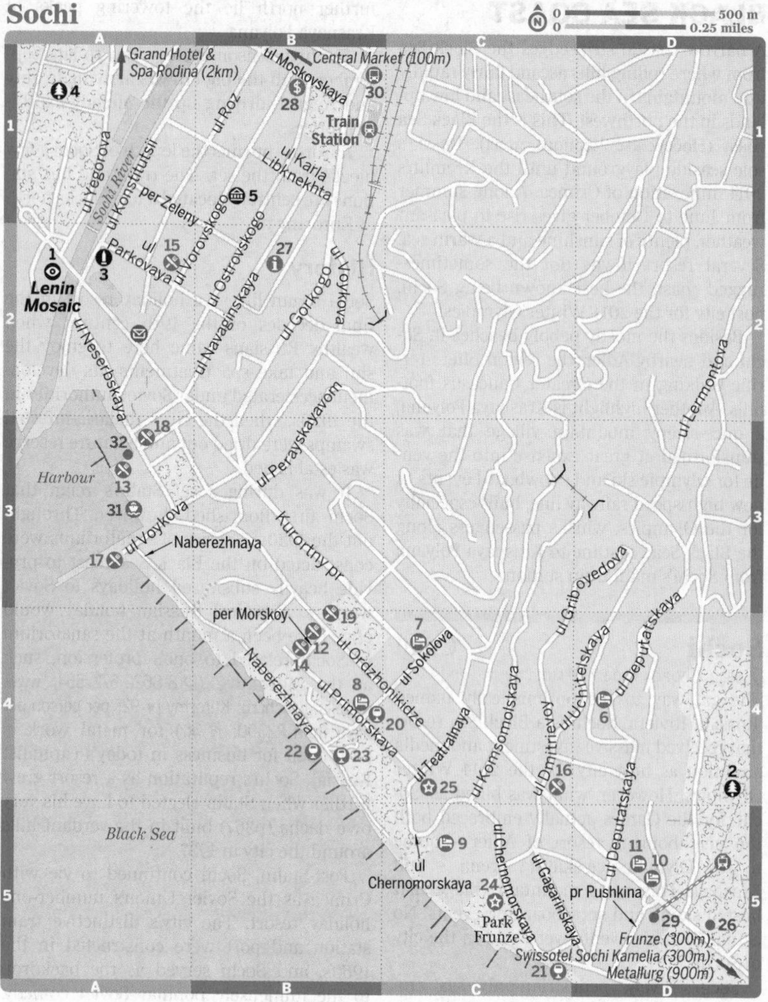

it was also within striking distance of the separatist insurgency that had devastated nearby Chechnya. Its creaking infrastructure was also far from Olympic standard.

Eager to prove to the world that Russia is a modern, powerful country that has shaken off its Soviet past, spending soared from an initial estimate of $12 billion to a reported $51 billion – making the Games by far the most expensive Olympics in history. Along with the building of stadiums and new hotels, dozens of infrastructure projects were undertaken, including new roads, power stations, sewage systems, an upgraded airport and a high-speed rail to connect Krasnaya Polyana with Sochi and Adler.

Post-Olympics, it remains to be seen if Sochi will be able to meet the expectations of the Russian authorities, who have spoken of their desire to see the city transform into 'an international-level mega-resort'.

Sights & Activities

No more than 10m wide in most areas, Sochi's narrow and stony beaches are dressed up with artificial trees, sunbathing loungers, awnings and private changing pavilions. The main beaches are along Naberezhnaya

Sochi

Top Sights
1 Lenin Mosaic A2

Sights
2 Arboretum D4
3 Memorial to Victims of Political Repression A2
4 Park Rivera A1
5 Town History Museum B1

Activities, Courses & Tours
Reinfo .... (see 7)

Sleeping
6 Hostel Lermontov D4
7 Hotel Magnolia C4
8 Hotel Primorskaya B4
9 Hotel Zhemchuzhina C5
10 Sochi Breeze Spa Hotel D5
11 Villa Anna D5

Eating
12 Beliye Nochi B4
13 Brigantina A3
14 Dom 1934 .... B4
15 Khachapuri A2
16 Perekrestok C4
17 Prichal No 1 .... A3
18 Stary Bazar A3
19 Yakamoz B4

Drinking & Nightlife
20 Cabaret Mayak B4
21 Sanremo C5
22 Sea Zone B4
23 Stargorod B4

Entertainment
24 Summer Theatre C5
25 Winter Theatre C4

Information
26 Arboretum Ticket Office D5
27 TAVS B2
28 Yug Bank B1

Transport
29 Arboretum Cable Car D5
30 Bus Station B1
31 Sea Terminal A3
32 Silver Line Shipping Company A3

and in front of Park Rivera. More private and secluded beaches, including some nude beaches, extend north for around 160km. To access these beaches, simply hop on the Krasnaya Polyana–bound high-speed train from Sochi's main railway station. Get off at the Matsesta, Khosta or Izvestiya stations and wander up the coastline.

The snow-capped mountains behind Sochi can be appreciated only from a sea cruise, which may carry the bonus of seeing dolphins. One- to two-hour cruises aboard a variety of vessels (yachts, passenger boats, catamarans, speedboats) leave throughout the day from the **sea terminal** (Морской вокзал; cruise per person ₽350-600).

Arboretum PARK
(Дендрарий; ☎8622-975 117; Kurortny pr; adult/child ₽250/120, cable car ₽500/260; ⏰park 8am-8pm, cable car 9am-8pm Tue-Sun, 11am-8pm Mon) Sochi's lovely arboretum, with more than 1500 species of trees and shrubs, including numerous species of palm, makes for a relaxing wander. For a scenic overview, take the **cable car** (Канатная Дорога Дендрарий) to the top and walk back down.

Town History Museum MUSEUM
(Музей истории города-курорта Сочи; ☎8622-642 326; ul Vorovskogo 54; adult/child ₽100/50; ⏰9am-7.30pm) The Town History Museum delves into Sochi's maritime roots, with the usual sprint through history from Stone Age relics to WWII memorabilia. What shines is the space display, with the Soyuz 9 capsule that returned to Earth in June 1970 after 18 days in orbit. On board were a local lad, engineer Sevastyanov, and his pilot, Nikoliev.

Park Rivera PARK
(Парк Ривьера; Kurortny pr; ⏰10am-1am) Inside the small but lively Park Rivera are several **funfairs** (rides ₽100 to ₽250) and an **oceanarium** (admission ₽200). Some of the palm trees here were planted by Soviet and Russian cosmonauts.

★ **Lenin Mosaic** MURAL
(Мозаика Ленина; Kurortny pr) Try the 8m-high Lenin Mosaic, opposite Park Rivera, for a backdrop with a difference for your holiday photos. It was unveiled in 1980 to mark the 110th anniversary of the birth of the father of the Bolshevik Revolution.

Memorial to Victims of Political Repression MONUMENT
(Памятники жертвам политических репрессий; ul Parkovka 42) This modest memorial lists the dozens of Sochi residents who perished in Stalin-era purges.

WORTH A TRIP

VORONTSOVSKAYA CAVE

A popular and worthwhile excursion is to **Vorontsovskaya Cave** (Воронцовская Пещера; admission ₽350; ⏲11am-6pm Tue & Sat winter, daily summer), inland from Matsesta. It has about 500m of illuminated passages with stalactites and the like. It gets cold inside, so dress accordingly. The scenic drive from Sochi takes about one hour; a round-trip taxi should cost about ₽3000 or you could join an organised tour (per person ₽400).

Tours

Pavement sellers and most hotels sell Sochi city tours (from ₽300, two hours) and excursions to Mt Bolshoy Akhun and Agura Waterfalls (₽350, half day), Krasnaya Polyana (₽500, full day) and Vorontsovskaya Cave (₽400, half day). Prices are per person, excluding admission.

Masterskaya Priklucheny ADVENTURE TOURS
(☎8-928-292 0596; www.extreme-sochi.ru; Matsesta) Specialises in canyoning, rock climbing, rafting, caving, backcountry skiing and one- to 10-day trekking trips.

Reinfo ADVENTURE TOURS
(Реинфо; ☎8-8622-622 042; www.reinfo-sochi.ru; 3rd fl, Hotel Magnolia, Kurortny pr) Well established tour operator with a range of programmes: heliskiing and white-water rafting in Krasnaya Polyana; sailing in Sochi; and hiking to Mt Fisht, Vorontsovskaya Cave and lesser-known places.

Festivals & Events

Beer Festival BEER FESTIVAL
The holiday season starts in late May with a weekend beer festival on Naberezhnaya.

Kinotavr Film Festival CINEMA FESTIVAL
(www.kinotavr.ru) The week-long Kinotavr Film Festival in June attracts many big Russian film stars and the occasional foreign actor. Screenings outside the Winter Theatre are free, whereas you have to pay for screenings inside the theatre.

Sleeping

Accommodation prices in Sochi rocketed before and during the Olympics. They remain high, although there are signs of a return to relatively cheaper days. Still, budget travellers will find better deals in nearby Adler. Rates increase by about 25% between May and August.

Those looking for complete immersion in Russian culture might consider staying for a week or more in a sanatorium.

Hostel Lermontov HOSTEL $
(Хостел Лермонтов; www.hostel-lermontov.ru/; ul Lermontova 3; dm ₽800; 📶) A haven for budget travellers in Sochi, the recently opened Hostel Lermontov offers beds in four- and six-person dorms. No frills, as you would expect, but the friendly owners and staff do their best to ensure a comfortable stay for guests. Not too far from the centre and the beach, to the north of Hotel Zhemchuzhina.

Hotel Primorskaya HOTEL $$
(Гостиница Приморская; ☎8-8622-620 113; www.hotelprimorskaya.ru; ul Sokolova 1; r incl breakfast from ₽2100; ❄📶) This striking yellow-and-white architectural jewel dates from the 1930s. Endless corridors link the 382 rooms, all wrapped around an interior courtyard. The cheapest rooms are basic but clean and good value for pricey Sochi. Hot water supplies are erratic in the summer months, though.

The stylish indoor-outdoor restaurant has free wi-fi.

Sochi Breeze Spa Hotel HOTEL $$
(Сочи Бриз Спа Отель; ☎8-8622-663 800; www.sochibreeze.ru; Kurortny pr 72; s/d from ₽3500/3900; 🚭❄📶🏊) This pleasant and decent-value (for Sochi, at least) hotel has its own swimming pool and is well located for both the beach and the Arboretum.

★**Grand Hotel & Spa Rodina** HOTEL $$$
(Гранд Отель и СПА Родина; ☎8-8622-539 000; www.grandhotelrodina.ru; ul Vinogradnaya 33; r from ₽15,000; ❄📶🏊) This sprawling former sanatorium just north of Park Rivera is Sochi's crème de la crème in terms of luxury living. Caviar and champagne breakfasts, sprawling gardens with a private beach and just 60 luxurious rooms with terraces make this one of the region's very top accommodation options.

Also features six eating options, from a rooftop terrace with views of the Black Sea coast to the Black Magnolia evening restaurant, with its well-stocked wine cellar.

Grand Hotel Polyana SAS Lazurnaya HOTEL $$$
(Гранд Отель Поляна САС Лазурная; ☎7095-255 3800; www.radisson.ru/hotel-sochi; Kurortny

pr 103; r with breakfast from ₽8800;) This 25-storey four-star hotel is set in copious grounds with a private beach, a children's playroom and both Russian and Turkish baths. All 300 rooms have sea views, internet connections and satellite TV. Pricier rooms have bigger bathrooms, spas and balconies. The location, about 6km south of the centre, is a drawback.

Swissotel Sochi Kamelia HOTEL $$$
(Swissotel Сочи Камелия; 8-8622-296 8801; www.swissotel.com/hotels/sochi-kamelia; Kurortny pr 89; s/d from ₽9000/14,000;) Another luxury hotel built with the Winter Olympics in mind, Swissotel Sochi Kamelia is tucked away from the centre of town, heading southeast along Kurortny pr. Located in a park overlooking the Black Sea, the rooms are spacious and tastefully fitted out, some with excellent sea views.

Villa Anna HOTEL $$$
(Вилла Анна; 8-8622-250 5181; www.villaanna.ru; Kurortny pr 72/7; s & d from ₽4500;) Designed in the style of a 'Scottish castle in the 16th century', Villa Anna offers large, bright, well-furnished rooms. Also has its own *banya*, which is perfect for unwinding at the end of the day. Right next to the Arboretum.

Hotel Magnolia HOTEL $$$
(Гостиница Магнолия; 8-8622-620 166; www.sochi-magnolia.ru; Kurortny pr 50; s/d ₽5000/5400;) Named after the flowering trees fronting this 126-room complex, Magnolia has bright, renovated rooms with balconies, minifridges and modern bathrooms. Also has a well-equipped gym.

Hotel Zhemchuzhina HOTEL $$$
(Гостиница Жемчужина; 8-8622-661 188; www.zhem.ru; ul Chernomorskaya 3; s/d incl breakfast from ₽4400/5000;) This colossal concrete landmark has been popular with tour operators since the Soviet period. Some of its spacious and recently renovated rooms have great sea views. Free fast wi-fi and good breakfasts.

Eating

Open-air restaurants line the seaside path, Naberezhnaya. You'll also find a few options sprinkled near the beach south of Park Rivera and along per Riversky, the shaded walkway along the Sochi River's west side. For self-catering, visit the colourful **Central Market** (Центральный рынок; ul Moskovskaya; 6am-6pm) or the large **Perekrestok** (cnr ul Uchitelskaya & Kurortny pr; 24hr) supermarket in the centre of town.

★ **Khachapuri** CAUCASIAN $
(Хачапури; ul Vorovskogo 33; mains ₽150-300; 9am-10pm) This tiny, friendly cafe is reassuringly popular with the locals, who flock here for takeaway and lunch at one of its four tables. Khachapuri is the cafe's name and tasty, filling *khachapuri* (Georgian cheese bread) is its thing. Try the *khachapuri* stuffed with stewed kidney beans and herbs for a rare treat.

Beliye Nochi CAUCASIAN, EUROPEAN $$
(Белые Ночи; ul Ordzhonikidze 9; mains ₽300-450; 10am-11pm;) A long-time Sochi favourite, Beliye Nochi does some of the finest *lobio* (a stewed and flavoured Georgian kidney bean dish) in town. Just around the corner from the Marins Park Hotel.

Brigantina RUSSIAN, FRENCH $$
(Бригантина; ul Neserbskaya 3; mains ₽450-1000; 8am-11pm) This pleasant French-owned restaurant enjoys a breezy location overlooking the harbour, with outdoor tables and a big menu of seafood and grilled meats. Mussels (served a variety of ways) and bouillabaisse (fish stew) are among the highlights.

Stary Bazar CAUCASIAN, EUROPEAN $$
(Старый Базар; ul Neserbskaya 4; mains ₽300-700; 11am-midnight) Set in lush, verdant territory overlooking the harbour, Stary Bazar is another established Sochi restaurant that continues to pack them in. And for good reason – the menu here ranges from rich and satisfying Georgian food to a variety of fish dishes and shashlyk. Look out for the *Wizard of Oz*–type tin man and woman outside.

Dom 1934 EUROPEAN, RUSSIAN $$
(Дом 1934; per Morskoy 2; mains ₽300-950; 10am-midnight;) Designed to look like a series of cosy living rooms, Dom 1934 takes its name from the year this former residential building was constructed. Good fish and pasta dishes. It's right opposite the Marins Park Hotel.

Prichal No 1 SEAFOOD $$
(Причал No 1; ul Voykova 1; mains ₽700-1300; noon-midnight;) Near the sea terminal, Prichal No 1 serves up seafood delights such as Kamchatka crab, oysters and warming fish soups. Seafront outdoor seating in the warmer months provides a great opportunity for dolphin spotting.

Yakamoz TURKISH $$

(Якамоз; Park Kultury; mains ₽400; ⏲9am-midnight; 📶) In a shaded park setting, you can enjoy kebabs, salads, pizzas and strong Turkish coffee amid gurgling fountains (and pumping disco by night). Find it just off ul Ordzhonikidze.

Drinking & Nightlife

Stargorod BREWERY

(Старгород; ☎8622-951 111; Naberezhnaya; ⏲11am-1am; 📶) Below the Winter Theatre, this three-storey brewery-restaurant offers great views of the Black Sea alongside its own beers and a grilled meat-based menu (meals ₽300 - ₽750). The fried and flavoured dark bread makes a great snack. Cheesy Europop is the order of the day (and night).

Sanremo LOUNGE BAR

(Сан-Ремо; Naberezhnaya; ⏲noon-3am daily; 📶) 'Seafood, music, sunset' is the logo of this chilled lounge bar on the seafront. The seafood (mains from ₽500) ranges from grilled salmon to sturgeon, while the music is jazzy pop. Serves local and international wines (from ₽1200 a bottle). Paddle in the small pool here as you watch the sun go down.

Cabaret Mayak GAY BAR

(Кабаре Маяк; ul Sokolova 1; free entry weekdays, men/women ₽300/500 weekends; ⏲6pm-7am Mon-Fri, 10pm-4am Sat & Sun) Perhaps Russia's most famous gay club. Cabaret Mayak may have received massive media attention during the 2014 Sochi Olympics, but it doesn't exactly scream about its presence: ring the bell above the small sign to be let in. Inside, drag queens and other performers strut their stuff on the small stage. Gets very busy on Saturdays.

Sea Zone BAR

(Naberezhnaya; ⏲10am-2am; 📶) With comfy sofas and friendly service, Sea Zone is another popular place to relax with a drink and savour the sunset.

Entertainment

Try the English-language www.sochicity-guide.com website for club and bar listings. The Russian-language www.afisha.ru/sochi is far more extensive, however.

Winter Theatre THEATRE

(Зимний театр; Zimny Teatr; ☎8-8622-629 616; pl Teatralnaya; ⏲booking office 10am-7pm) Built in a majestic imperial style, this massive, colonnaded building would add grace to any world capital. Opera, ballet and drama are presented here.

Summer Theatre THEATRE

(Летний театр; Letny Teatr; Park Frunze) True to its name, this architecturally striking, neo-classical theatre stages open-air concerts and drama performances during the summer.

Information

Post Office (cnr ul Vorovskogo & Kurortny pr)

TAVS (ТАВС; ☎8-8622-641 101; www.so-chitavs.ru; ul Navaginskaya 16; ⏲8am-8pm) Efficient air and train ticketing agency.

Getting There & Away

AIR

Sochi's **airport** (http://sochi-airport.com) is at Adler, which is 25km away. Both Aeroflot and S7 airlines fly daily to Moscow (from ₽5100). In summer there are flights to most other major Russian cities.

BOAT

The **sea terminal** (Ul Voykova 1) has various information kiosks with posted departures.

Trabzon (Turkey)

From May to October, catamarans depart Sochi on Thursday and Sunday at noon (₽4200, five to six hours). Returning to Sochi, they depart Trabzon on Tuesday and Friday at the same time. Purchase tickets from ticket office 7 at the sea terminal. The **Erke** (☎8-8622-260 9702), a slower car ferry (from ₽4000, 12 hours), makes the journey to Trabzon on Monday or Tuesday and back on Tuesday or Wednesday. Call in advance for details. Tickets from ticket office 5 at the sea terminal.

Batumi (Georgia)

Restrictions on foreign travellers entering Georgia from Russia have been lifted, and catamarans from the **Silver Line Shipping Company** (☎8-918-409 1296; ul Neserbskaya 5; ⏲9am-5pm daily) sail weekly for Batumi (₽4000, 5½ hours, 2pm Friday). They set off on the return journey at noon on Sunday.

BUS

From the **bus station** (Автовокзал; ul Gorkogo 56a), there are daily services to Kislovodsk (₽710, 18 hours, 12.20pm). This service also calls at Krasnodar and Pyatigorsk.

TRAIN

Sochi's revamped-for-the-Olympics **train station** (ul Gorkogo) has services to Adler (fast/slow ₽42/30, 22/35 minutes, frequent), Kislovodsk (*platskart/kupe* from ₽1100/2030, 15 hours, 7.44pm daily), Krasnodar (*platskart/kupe* ₽730/1200, around six hours, over 12 daily), Krasnaya Polyana ₽112, 1¼ hours, five daily), Moscow (*platskart/kupe* from ₽2300/4500, 24 to 37 hours, at least six daily), Rostov-on-Don (*platskart/kupe* from ₽1135/1800, eight to 15 hours, frequent) and St Petersburg (*platskart/kupe* from ₽3300/6000, 40 hours, 12.17pm and 6.03pm daily).

Train 644 to Kislovodsk goes via Mineralnye Vody and Pyatigorsk. All Moscow-bound trains go via Krasnodar. The regular *elektrichki* stop frequently at beaches and coastal towns along their route, the fast *(skory)* ones less so.

ℹ Getting Around

From the bus station take *marshrutka* or bus 105 (₽85, 40 minutes, every 20 minutes) to the airport in Adler. There are also frequent trains to the airport (₽56, 43 minutes). A taxi costs about ₽800.

Around Sochi

The main 2014 Winter Olympic sites, Krasnaya Polyana and Adler, are part of Greater Sochi.

Zelenaya Roscha Зелёная Роща

⭐ **Stalin's Dacha** MUSEUM
(Дача Сталина; Kurortny pr 120; tours ₽300; ⊙9am-6pm) Stalin's dacha, Zelenaya Roscha, dates from 1937. It is an amazing place, built to accommodate a small, private man who caused death and misery to millions of Russians. Tours are in Russian but the patriotic guides (ours was ex-KGB) speak some English. From Sochi take any Adler-bound bus and get off at the Zelenaya Roscha stop. Alternatively, take a taxi from Sochi (₽400). It's a fair walk uphill to the dacha, so be prepared.

Visitors can see Stalin's private rooms (some original furniture remains), the movie theatre where he checked every film before public release, and his billiards room. Stalin was a lousy player – he played only those he could beat or who were wily enough to lose. The Stalin portraits on the walls were added after his death, although the mirrors are mostly originals.

The depth of the water in Stalin's swimming pool (just 1.5m) and the height of the stair treads, sofas, chairs, tables, bed and even billiards table were fixed to accommodate his small stature (165cm). Security was extremely tight: a guard every 15m around the dacha, a secret lift and tunnel down to the sea, and buildings painted green to camouflage them within the forest.

There is also a waxwork figure of Stalin smoking his favourite pipe. Visitors have been known to swear they can smell pipe tobacco while in its presence.

Agura Valley Агурское Ущелье

There's scenic, easy-to-access hiking in this valley beneath **Mt Bolshoy Akhun** (662m), about 7km east of Sochi's centre. From the entrance of **Sochi National Park** (www.sochinp.ru; admission ₽120), located east of Matsesta, a well-marked trail follows the Agura River past three waterfalls.

From Sochi, bus 124 or 125 turns east off pr Kurortny about 750m south of Zelenaya Roscha and drops passengers off at the Sputnik skyscraper. From here the entrance is a 1km walk; follow the road along Agura River until you get to Salkhino restaurant and the entrance beyond. Alternatively, walk from Zelenaya Roscha (about 30 minutes).

After one hour the trail forks. The right (southeast) fork leads up to Mt Bolshoy Akhun, topped by a **lookout tower** (⊙10am-6pm Oct-Apr, to 9pm May-Sep). The tower gives commanding views of Sochi, Adler and Mt Fisht. Locals say you can see the Turkish coastline from here on a clear day.

The left fork leads to the precipitous **Orlinye Skaly** (Eagle Cliffs), with good views of the waterfalls, Mt Bolshoy Akhun and snow-capped peaks in Abkhazia. The rotten-egg smell here is from the mineral water that flows from a nearby spring. Also sharing the view is a golden statue of Prometheus waving his broken chains. In Greek mythology Prometheus stole fire from the gods to give to humankind. As a punishment, Zeus had him chained to a Caucasian mountain thought to be Mt Fisht.

Pick up an Agura Valley trail map (₽40) at the park entrance. You can do these walks in reverse (ie starting in Matsesta or Mt Bolshoy Akhun) and pay your entrance fee at the park entrance upon concluding your hike.

Near the park entrance, **Salkhino** (Салхино; ☑8-8622-389 111; mains ₽350-650) restaurant prepares popular *khashlama* (Caucasian-spiced lamb stew), among many other dishes. There are Kuban dry reds on the wine list, along with Georgian and French vintages. In favourable weather sit outdoors in a hut. Reservations recommended.

Mt Bolshoy Akhun is also serviced by an 11km road, which makes it a popular organised tour from Sochi. A 5½-hour excursion costs ₽350 and includes a stop at the Agura waterfalls.

Mt Fisht Гора Фишт

This 2687m mountain, one of the highest around Sochi, makes a splendid three- to four-day trek. The walk usually starts in Solokhay, about 25km inland from Dagomys. From here, a rough road leads another 20km to the trailhead – you can hike it or hire an expensive 4WD.

From the trailhead it's 14km to stunning alpine Khmelnovskogo Lake, where you can camp in view of the surreal lunar landscape and spires of Mt Fisht.

You'll need to go with a guide from a company such as Reinfo (p364) in Sochi or Masterskaya Priklucheny (p364) in Matsesta. Tours start from ₽8300 per person, including food, camping gear, national park permits and transport to Solokhay.

Adler Адлер

☑ 8622 / POP 71,000 / ⊙ MOSCOW

Despite a grand overhaul of its transport infrastructure for the 2014 Winter Olympics, the Black Sea resort of Adler lacks the nouveau riche affluence and attitude of Sochi, which is 30km to the north. Traditionally a popular destination for lower-income Russian holidaymakers, prices for lodging and food are slightly lower here.

Like other nearby resort towns, the main action is along the promenade (nonsmoking since the Olympics), where you'll find a wide variety of cafes, a funfair and souvenir stalls. If you're lucky, you'll spot dolphins frolicking in the Black Sea.

⊙ Sights

Sochi Park THEME PARK

(Сочи Парк; www.sochipark.ru/en/article/about-park; Olimpisky pr 21; adult/child ₽1500/free; ⊙10am-7pm Wed-Sun) Billed as Russia's Disneyland, this sprawling funfair is located in the former Olympic Park. Rides are based around traditional Russian fairy tales. It also hosted its first Formula One motor race in 2014. Take *marshrutka* 124 from Sochi's train station, or a train to the Olimpisky Park station.

Silver Lenin MONUMENT

(ul Lenina 3) Fans of Soviet kitsch will enjoy Adler's silver-painted Lenin statue. Come out of the central market, turn left and Lenin is waiting for you on the right, some 100m down – what else? – ul Lenina.

🛏 Sleeping

There are private rooms galore in Adler, starting from around ₽700. Talk to babushkas in the train station, or just stroll the streets knocking on doors that say 'сдаёться' (rooms for rent).

There are a number of options near the seaside promenade, a short walk from the bus station.

Fregat-1 HOTEL $$

(Фрегат-1; ☑ 8-8622-407 000; www.fregat-adler.ru; ul Karla Marksa 1; s/d ₽1800/2500; ❄ 🛜) Relatively low prices, both during high and low season, combined with an excellent seafront location and huge, comfortable rooms, make Fregat-1 a great deal. Seaside restaurants are just outside the entrance.

Chernomor HOTEL $$

(Черномор; ☑ 8-8622-404 582; www.hotel-chernomor.ru; ul Prosveshcheniya 25a; rear-facing/seafront r ₽3500/4000; ❄🛜) A good-value seafront option, the modern, four-storey Chernomor has clean and spacious rooms with wooden floors and big windows. The best have seafront balconies hanging over Naberezhnaya.

Hotel Prichal HOTEL $$

(Гостиница Причал; ☑ 8-8622-209 6973; www.hotel-prichal.ru/; ul Prosveshcheniya 7; d rear/seafront from ₽3600/5800; ➖❄🛜) A pebble's throw away from the Black Sea, Hotel Prichal's bright and airy rooms are perfect for waking up to the sound of gently (or otherwise) breaking waves. Good breakfasts and friendly service complement the overall sense of positivity.

Radisson Blu Resort HOTEL $$$

(☑ 8-8622-296 8100; www.radissonblu.com/resort-congress-sochi; ul Golubaya 1a; s/d ₽4700/5200; ➖❄@🛜🏊) One of a number of new hotels built for the 2014 Winter Olympics, Radisson Blu Resort sits a short distance from the former Olympic Park on the Adler coastline. Rooms are spacious and boast good views of either the Caucasus mountains or the Black Sea. Some good bargains to be had off-season.

🍴 Eating

Dozens of cafes, bars and restaurants line the lively promenade.

Cafe Radost RUSSIAN $

(Кафе Радость; ul Karla Marksa 2; shashlyk per 100g ₽140-230; ⊙10am-2am) In addition to pork, lamb and salmon shashlyk, there's cold Russian and imported beer on hand and a festive open-air atmosphere.

Cafe Fregat RUSSIAN, INTERNATIONAL $
(Кафе фрегат; ul Karla Marksa; mains ₽250-500; ⏲10am-midnight) An open-air spot with tables surrounding a gurgling fountain and live music most nights. Big menu of Western and Russian standards.

Royal Fish SEAFOOD $$
(☎8-928-458 9988; http://royalfish-sochi.ru/index-en.html; Bestuzhava per; mains ₽400-900; ⏲10am-1am;) Tucked away in the far-left corner of Adler's promenade, Royal Fish is a classy seafood restaurant. A good wine list and carefully prepared dishes mean this is a great place to linger over your meal. The salmon with cream sauce and red caviar (₽490) is recommended.

Mayak EUROPEAN, RUSSIAN $$
(Маяк; ul Prosveshcheniya 35; mains ₽250-750; ⏲10am-11pm Mon-Fri, to 1am Sat & Sun) Mayak serves a good mixture of seafood, pizza and traditional Russian dishes in an attractive courtyard sheltered by palm trees. Located in the far-right corner of the promenade.

Getting There & Away

The **bus station** (ul Lenina) is near the central market, a 1km walk to the hotel- and restaurant-lined seaside promenade. Pick up frequent buses and *marshrutky* to Sochi (₽45, 40 minutes) here or opposite the revamped **train station** (ul Lenina), which is an inconvenient 3km north of the bus station.

All long-distance trains to Sochi continue to and terminate in Adler. The express train to Krasnaya Polyana also stops here (₽42, 22 minutes). A taxi from the airport or bus station to the seaside area should cost around ₽300.

Krasnaya Polyana Красная Поляна

☎8622 / POP 4000 / ELEV 550M / ⏲MOSCOW

A scenic road passing through a deep, narrow canyon leads up from Adler to Krasnaya Polyana (Red Valley), Russia's newly built ski mecca that hosted the 2014 Winter Olympics ski events. The scenery here is simply spectacular, with snow-capped mountains looming above three world-class ski resorts containing kilometres of high-quality pistes. A new high-speed train service from Sochi via Adler makes getting to the area easier than ever.

The undoubted jewel in the Olympic crown here is the Roza Khutor Alpine Resort, which hosted downhill skiing events at the Winter Games and today offers world-class skiing and snowboarding. Popular with day trippers from Sochi, it's the best place to stay if you just want to check out the spectacular scenery.

The Gornaya Karusel resort staged the ski-jumping events, while Gazprom's elaborate Grand Hotel Polyana complex sits on Psekhako Ridge. It's popular with a wealthier, older crowd.

As for Krasnaya Polyana itself, this sleepy mountain village has retained a certain tranquillity, despite the arrival of new hotels and restaurants backed by cash-seeking developers.

Krasnaya Polyana is approximately 40km east of Adler along the Mzymta River.

Sights & Activities

Heliskiing in the winter and rafting, horse riding and 4WD tours in the summer are the main outdoor activities in Krasnaya Polyana. Activities can be organised by all of the big hotels in Roza Khutor and Gornaya Karusel, as well as through the **Sphere** (☎8-8622-646 305; www.csochi.com; ul Navaginskaya 11; ⏲9am-6pm) travel agency in Sochi.

Skiing

Roza Khutor SKIING
(Роза Хутор; ☎8-8622-419 222; www.rozaski.com; Alpika; all day ski passes from ₽1600, all-inclusive ski lift & cable car pass (no skiing) ₽600; ⏲9am-4pm) This world-class ski complex was the largest venue for the Sochi Winter Olympics. It consists of a staggering 18 modern lifts and almost 80km of piste catering for all levels of proficiency. Skis, snowboards and other equipment can be hired from the office next to the entrance to the lifts.

Ski lessons are available for all ages from five upwards. If you aren't planning on skiing or snowboarding, it's still worth taking a cable car to the top of the Rosa Pik plateau (2320m) to enjoy the stunning views of nearby snow-capped mountains. Even if you're not a skier or a snowboarder, it's possible to spend at least half a day here simply enjoying the magnificent views and hanging out in the complex's pleasant cafes.

Grand Hotel Polyana SKIING
(Гранд Отель Поляна; ☎8-8622-595 595; www.grandhotelpolyana.ru/mountain_tourist_centre; ul Achipsinskaya 16, Esto-Sadok; lift ticket weekdays/

weekends from ₽1200/1350; ⏲9am-11pm) Gazprom's plush resort has six lifts and 15km of trails that cover a range of difficulty levels. Although it's primarily a downhill mountain, some Olympic Nordic events were held atop its broad, gently sloping ridge. Five runs are floodlit for night skiing (from 5pm to 11pm). Offers excellent opportunities for hiking in the surrounding countryside in the summer months. Also has two good 5km cycle paths with great views. Bicycles are available for rent from ₽250 per hour. The turn-off to the Grand Hotel is just east of Gornaya Karusel.

Gornaya Karusel SKIING

(Горная карусель; ☎8-8622-241 4444; www.eng.gornaya-karusel.ru; Esto-Sadok; all-day ski pass ₽1200, cable car pass (without skiing) from ₽400, 2hr ski & snowboard lessons from ₽3500; ⏲9am-6pm) The Gornaya Karusel ski resort was constructed for the 2014 Winter Olympics. Today it boasts 12 modern lifts, plus 30km of high-quality piste amid the rugged terrain of the Aibga mountain. There are some memorable views of neighbouring mountains and countryside from three transfer levels at 960m, 1450m and 2200m above sea level.

Ski and snowboard equipment is available to hire from a well-stocked, on-site rental shop. Refuel in one of the complex's pleasant cafes. In summer the resort offers hiking around the stunning glaciers, lakes and rivers that wind down to the nearby Black Sea.

Banya

After a day spent skiing or hiking in the mountains, the warm Russian *banya* makes a great spot to recover.

British Banya BANYA

(British-баня; ☎8-918-607 6611; www.britishbanya.com; per Kosmolsky; per person 3hr from ₽5000 (20% discount after midnight); ⏲9am-last visitor) In Krasnaya Polyana village, British Banya has a beautiful setting against a mountainous backdrop with a round dipping pool and two saunas – all beautifully designed in natural wood and stone. Massages and other treatments are available, plus good teas on hand.

Banya Land BANYA

(Баня-Land; ☎8-8622-437 044; www.banya-land.ru; ul Zapovdnaya 94; per person per hr ₽1600) Also in Krasnaya Polyana village, Banya Land is a big complex with five artfully designed spas, including a Russian-style sauna with mosaic tiles, Native American–style sweat lodge and Japanese *o-furo* (traditional wooden tub). Many treatments are available.

Sleeping

The majority of top-end hotels are clustered around the Roza Khutor and Gornaya Karusel ski resorts. Some cheaper options can be found in Krasnaya Polyana village. See http://en.rosaski.com/hotels/for a full list of Roza Khutor accommodation options.

Utomlyonnye Solntsem HOTEL $$

(Утомленные солнцем; ☎8-8622-437 419; ul Michurina 5; d from ₽2000; 📶) Named after the Oscar-winning film by director Nikita Mikhalkov (*Burnt by the Sun* in English), this budget (by local standards, anyway) hotel has clean but basic rooms in Krasnaya Polyana village. Opposite the massive Peak Hotel. Closed off-season.

Hotel Tatyana HOTEL $$

(Гостиница Татьяна; ☎8-8622-439 111; www.tatyana-alpik.ru; Esto-Sadok; r winter/summer incl breakfast from ₽3000/3800; ❄📶) On the Krasnaya Polyana road, opposite the mammoth Marriott, Hotel Tatyana offers bright, airy rooms and a warming open fire in the lobby. Also has a good *banya* for rent (₽2800 per hour, maximum six people).

Valset Apartments APARTMENT $$$

(Апарт-отель Valset; ☎Moscow 007-495-937 5545; www.heliopark.ru/node/219?id=32; Roza Khutor; apt from ₽5000; 🚭❄📶) These stylish apartments at the heart of the Roza Khutor resort are a good alternative to expensive hotel rooms. A range of options are available, from cosy studios to two-bedroom apartments. All have pleasant views of the mountains. Free wi-fi.

Grand Hotel Polyana HOTEL $$$

(Гранд Отель Поляна; ☎8-8622-595 595; www.grandhotelpolyana.ru; ul Achipsinskaya 16, Esto-Sadok; r with breakfast & dinner low/high season from ₽10,300/13,000; 🚭❄📶🏊👪) Offering Krasnaya Polyana's finest accommodation, the Grand Hotel is Gazprom's crown jewel. The sprawling 400-room resort has spacious, handsomely designed rooms (gold-framed oil paintings on the wall, luxury linens, Bulgari bath products), plus indoor and outdoor pools, tennis courts, spa centre, saunas, restaurants and its own ski slopes right on the grounds. Also offers villas for rent.

Heliopark Freestyle Hotel HOTEL $$$

(☎8-8622-431 331; www.heliopark.ru/node/218?id=31; Naberezhnaya Polyanka 4; s/d from ₽4100/5200; 🚭❄📶) This stylish three-star hotel is popular with well-to-do Russian snowboarders. Friendly service and sleek, tasteful rooms, some with excellent views of the nearby mountains. It's the first hotel on the left in the Roza Khutor resort as you walk along the embankment from the train station.

Peak Hotel HOTEL $$$

(Пик Отель; 8-8622-595 999; www.peakhotel.ru; ul Zaschitnikov Kavkaza 77; r with breakfast low/high season from ₽5500/7000;) Apart from high-class accommodation, this top-end hotel in Krasnaya Polyana village has excellent amenities, including a top-notch restaurant, fitness centre, indoor pool and sauna and free transfers to the slopes, which are 4km away. After skiing, the stylish 24-hour lobby bar with open fire is a fine place to recharge. Some good special offers off-season include three nights for the price of two.

Marriott HOTEL $$$

(Сочи Марриотт Красная Поляна; 8-8622-354 392; www.marriott.com; Vremena Goda 1; s/d from ₽5000/5800;) This colossal top-end hotel at the foot of the Gornaya Karusel ski lifts might belong to a major European chain, but its imposing facade is best described as nouveau-Soviet. Inside, however, things are much better, with spacious, comfortable rooms that boast memorable views. Also has spa facilities. Check the website for some bargain deals off-season.

Eating

Aside from a decent selection of restaurants and cafes in and around the resorts, all the major hotels also have their own in-house restaurants.

Perekrostok SUPERMARKET $

(Перекрёсток; Naberezhnaya Vremena Goda, Gorky Gorod Mall; 24hr) Self-caterers will find everything they need on the 1st floor of this chain supermarket in Gornaya Karusel.

★**Cafe 2200** RUSSIAN, EUROPEAN $$

(Кафе 2200; Gornaya Karusel plateau; mains ₽650-1300; 10am-6pm) Sup a warming soup as you watch the snow fall on the ski slopes outside. Located at 2200m above sea level (hence the name), this classy two-floor restaurant has an open fire, great views and serves a surprisingly wide mixture of European and Russian food. Also has a good wine list.

Nebesa CAFE $$

(Небеса; Roza Pik plateau; mains ₽400-1100; 10am-5pm) Located at 2320m above sea level, Nebesa is the perfect place to kick back after skiing and snowboarding. Designed to resemble a well-equipped ski lodge, floor-length windows mean it's ideal for watching the action unfold outside. The menu includes good fish soup, as well as pasta and meat-based dishes. The Black Sea is visible from here on a clear day.

Chyo? Kharcho! CAUCASIAN $$

(Чё? Харчо!; ul Olimpiskaya 37; mains ₽450-900) This popular restaurant serves generous portions of Caucasian dishes, including *kharcho,* the spicy Georgian soup that inspired its unusual name ('Huh? Kharcho!' in English). Also offers pizza among all the *khachapuri* and shashlyk. Indoor and outdoor seating and live music in the evenings. Find it right next to the Roza Khutor ski lifts.

Modus ITALIAN $$

(Модус; Naberezhnaya Panorama 3; pizzas ₽400-900; 10am-11pm Mon-Fri, to midnight Sat & Sun) This spacious and well-designed pizzeria has comfortable sofas and friendly service. It's in the Roza Khutor resort, on the left side of the river.

Trikoni RUSSIAN, EUROPEAN $$

(Трикони; Krasnaya Polyana; mains ₽350-800; 11am-11pm;) Opposite Peak Hotel on the main road, Trikoni has a diverse menu of Russian and Italian fare (pasta, lasagne, risotto) and local hits such as trout stuffed with vegetables. The all-wood interior conjures classic ski country and there's a deck with mountain views.

Moscow CAFE $$

(Москва; Naberezhnaya Vremena Goda 3; mains ₽400-700; 6am-10pm ski season, 10am-10pm off-season) This stylish cafe is just a snowball's throw away from the Gornaya Karusel ski lifts. Opens early to cater to hungry skiers and snowboarders during the high season. Breakfasts from ₽300 and buffet dinners from ₽500. Service can be hit-or-miss, however.

Drinking

Krasnaya Polyana Tasting Complex WINE BAR

(Дегустационный комплекс 'Красная Поляна'; Naberezhnaya Panorama 2; 10am-9pm) This popular tasting complex in the Roza Khutor resort serves up local liqueurs, balsams and wines infused with mountain herbs, fruit and honey from Krasnaya Polyana and nearby Abkhazia.

Cosmos Night Bar NIGHTCLUB
(Ночной клуб Космос; Naberezhnaya Panorama 4; entry ₽500; ⏲9pm-4am Mon-Fri, to 3am Sat & Sun) This Roza Khutor nightclub is big on 1980s disco and cheesy Russian pop.

Shopping

Souvenir stalls and shops in all three Krasnaya Polyana ski resorts sell rather large hairy Caucasian hats called *papakha*, tacky souvenirs, homemade wine, pickles and honey.

Information

There are ATMs at all top-end hotels and at the Grand Hotel and Alpika base stations. Ski-hire shops abound at both ski areas and in Krasnaya Polyana village.

Emergency Services (☎8-8622-430 422)

Tourist Information Office (Gornaya Karusel 5; ⏲9am-6pm ski season, 10am-5pm off-season) The helpful staff in this tourist information office, to the right of the Gornaya Karusel ski lifts, speak English and German. They can organise hiking and other activities in the summer months.

Getting There & Away

Getting to Kransnaya Polyana has never been easier thanks to the region's new high-speed link, built specially for the Olympics. Comfortable trains make the 1¼-hour journey to and from Sochi five times a day (₽112).

From the Sochi bus station, take bus or *marshrutka* 105, which goes to Krasnaya Polyana and continues to Alpika (₽85, 1¾ hours, 20 daily). In summer the first one leaves at 6am and the last returns around 7.30pm. These also pass the airport in Adler.

Getting Around

The Roza Khutora ski resort is across the bridge and along the embankment as you exit the Krasnaya Polyana train station. To get to Gornaya Karusel's ski resort, take bus 105 or 135 from the train station, or a taxi for ₽200. Get off at the Gornaya Karusel stop, opposite the massive Marriott hotel. It's also possible to walk here from the station, but dangerous roads built with no apparent concern for pedestrians make this risky. To reach the Grand Hotel Polyana ski resort, take a taxi from the station (₽400) – if you are staying, hotel staff can arrange a transfer from Sochi or Adler.

MINERAL WATER SPAS

The central Caucasus rises from the steppe in an eerie landscape studded with dead volcanoes and spouting mineral springs. The curative powers of the springs have attracted unhealthy, hypochondriac or just holiday-minded Russians since the late 18th century.

Today the healthy outnumber the ailing in the spas, sanatoriums and hotels scattered across the region known as Kavkazskie Mineralnye Vody (Caucasian Mineral Waters; Кавказские Минеральные Воды). The parks and elegant spa buildings recall the 19th century, when fashionable society trekked from Moscow and St Petersburg to see, be seen and look for a spouse.

Many of the 130-plus springs have, however, fizzled out from lack of maintenance. Those that remain feed fountains in drinking galleries and provide the elixir for sanatorium treatments of muscles, bone, heart, circulation, nervous systems, joints and skin problems.

Pyatigorsk and Kislovodsk are the main resorts here. The main transport hub, Mineralnye Vody, lacks mineral spas of its own despite the name.

Mineralnye Vody
Минеральные Воды

☎86531 / POP 75,000 / ELEV 316M / ⏲MOSCOW

'Minvody' is the main air-transport hub not only for Mineral Waters but also for skiing and hiking around Mt Elbrus and Dombay.

There's little to divert you in Minvody. If you arrive late and need a bed, the **train station resting rooms** (komnaty otdikha; r 12hr from ₽700) offer reasonably clean, affordable accommodation.

Getting There & Away

During ski season, unscheduled *marshrutky* await planes arriving at Minvody airport and shuttle groups of people straight to the Dombay and Elbrus ski areas (per person ₽550).

AIR

Minvody's airport is 2km west of the centre on the M29 highway. Flights to Moscow are frequent and start at ₽4500. Try S7 or Ural Airlines.

BUS

The bus station is on the M29 highway, about 1.5km east of the airport.

Elista ₽630, eight hours, twice daily
Krasnodar ₽580, 7½ hours, 11 daily
Moscow ₽1450, 22 hours, one daily

Nalchik ₽230, two hours, eight daily
Rostov-on-Don ₽630, 9½ hours, two daily
Stavropol ₽290, 3¼ hours, frequent
Teberda ₽315, six hours, daily at 2.45pm
Vladikavkaz ₽290, four hours, eight daily

The buses to Rostov-on-Don and Moscow come from Pyatigorsk and may be full.

Bus 223 to Pyatigorsk (₽55, 45 minutes) departs every 30 minutes from ul XXII Partsezda near the train station. For Kislovodsk you're much better off on an *elektrichka*.

TAXI

Sample taxi prices from the bus station are Pyatigorsk ₽650, Kislovodsk ₽1200, Nalchik ₽2000, Terskol/Elbrus ₽3500 and Dombay ₽4000. Taxis at the airport typically ask 25% extra.

TRAIN

Minvody is on the main train line and thus well connected to points north and south. The centrally located **train station** (ul XXII Partsezda) picks up all trains heading to/from Pyatigorsk, Kislovodsk, Nalchik and Vladikavkaz.

Elektrichki service Kislovodsk (₽115, 1¾ hours) via Pyatigorsk (₽65, 50 minutes) roughly every 30 minutes until 10pm. There are also *elektrichki* to Krasnodar (₽540, six hours, three weekly), Nalchik (₽250, three hours, 9.45am and 5.50pm daily) and Vladikavkaz (₽275, 4½ hours, daily).

Getting Around

Marshrutky 9, 10 and 11 link the airport and train station, passing by the bus station. A taxi between the airport and train station costs around ₽300.

Pyatigorsk Пятигорск

8793 / POP 141,000 / ELEV 510M / MOSCOW

Pyatigorsk – the name being a Russification of Mt Beshtau (Five Peaks) – began life as Fort Konstantinovskaya in 1780. It quickly developed into a fashionable resort as it attracted Russian society to its spas and stately buildings. Today it is the most urbanised and least touristy of the spa towns. If you are pressed for time, however, you would be advised to skip the city and head on to the much more attractive Kislovodsk instead.

Pyatigorsk sprawls south and west from Mt Mashuk (993m). Tree-lined pr Kirova is the main street, running west from the Academic Gallery at the foot of Mt Mashuk through the town centre to the train station. To the northwest looms Mt Beshtau (1400m).

Sights & Activities

★ **Mt Mashuk** MOUNTAIN

There are various sites spread along the base of Mt Mashuk, some of which require long walks or a taxi to reach. Closer to the city centre, a **cable car** (bul Gagarina; one way adult/child ₽150/75; 10am-5.30pm) whisks you to the top of Mt Mashuk for a great panorama. The best views of Mt Elbrus are early in the morning.

If you're hoofing it, Mt Mashuk is about a 45-minute climb from the cable-car station.

Lermontov Museum MUSEUM

(Музей-заповедник Лермонтова; ul Karla Marksa 15; adult/child ₽120/60; 10am-5pm Wed-Sun) Many Pyatigorsk attractions revolve around larger-than-life writer, poet, painter, cavalry soldier, society beau and duellist Mikhail Lermontov. Chief among them is this museum. Three cottages contain some original furniture, copies of Lermontov's poems, sketches and 19th-century trinkets. Lermontov lived here during his final months.

Lermontov Duel Site HISTORICAL SITE

(bul Gagarina) In a clearing on the forested western flank of Mt Mashuk is a

A HERO OF OUR TIME

The Mineral Waters area is haunted by the Romantic writer Mikhail Lermontov, whose tale 'Princess Mary' from his novel *A Hero of Our Time* is set here. In an uncanny echo of the novel's plot, Lermontov was killed in a duel at Pyatigorsk in 1841.

Lermontov was banished twice from his native St Petersburg to serve in the army in Pyatigorsk – first, after blaming the tsarist authorities for the death in a duel of another 'troublesome' writer, Pushkin; and second, for himself duelling. Lermontov was challenged once again in Pyatigorsk for jesting about the clothes of one Major Martynov. Lermontov, firing first, aimed into the air but was in return shot through the heart. Many saw his death, like Pushkin's, as orchestrated by the authorities.

Many places in Kislovodsk and Pyatigorsk are linked to the man and his fiction, and a visit to the superb Lermontov Museum (p373) in Pyatigorsk is essential.

Pyatigorsk

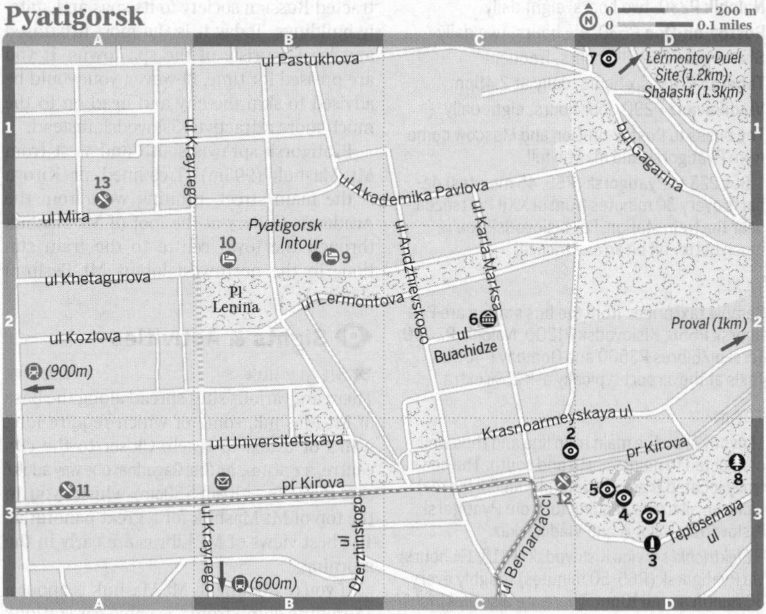

monument marking the Lermontov duel site. The actual duel site is unknown but is thought to be near the needle-point obelisk that even today is bedecked with flowers. To get here ride *marshrutka* 113a or bus 16 from the Upper Market to the 'Mesto Duely' (Duel Site) stop (five minutes). From there walk around 500m to a fork in the road, bear left and continue for around the same distance.

Lermontov Gallery NOTABLE BUILDING
(Лермонтовская галерея; ☎8-8793-58 350; pr Kirova) The striking light-blue and beautifully proportioned Lermontov Gallery, built in 1901 in cast iron with stained-glass windows, is now a concert hall. Closed for repairs at the time of writing, the gallery was due to reopen in October 2014. Behind are the **Lermontov & Yerrmelov Baths** (Лермонтовские бани и Ермоловские бани), built in 1831 and 1810, respectively. The latter is now a treatment centre.

Drinking Gallery NOTABLE BUILDING
(Питьевая Галерея; pr Kirova; ⏲7-10am, 11am-3pm & 4-7pm) Opposite Lermontov Gallery is a modern drinking gallery, where you can sample the local mineral water (cups are ₽4 if you need one).

Park Tsvetnik PARK
(Парк Цветник) The hill rising up behind the Lermontov Gallery is Park Tsvetnik, which forms a 1km-long arc around the eastern end of pr Kirova. Walk around the right side of the Lermontov Gallery and ascend to the park via **Diana's Grotto** (Грот Дианы), a favourite picnic spot in Pyatigorsk. At the top of the hill a network of paths leads to a much-photographed bronze **eagle sculpture** (Скульптура Орла).

Proval HOT SPRINGS
(Провал; bul Gagarina; ⏲9am-5pm) FREE On the south slope of Mt Mashuk, the Proval natural spring lies hidden inside a cavern. There is a religious icon on the wall inside. Outside, a bronze statue of Ostap Bender, the fictional fraudster who ran a ticket scam here in the popular Soviet-era film and novel *The Twelve Chairs*, greets guests.

Tours

Full-day group excursions to Dombay (₽900, Wednesday, Saturday and Sunday) and Arkhyz (₽800, Sunday) are hawked from in front of the university on pr Kirova. These tours involve about eight hours of drive time and just four hours on the ground at your destination. More worthwhile are the short-

Pyatigorsk

Sights

1 Diana's Grotto ... D3
2 Drinking Gallery ... C3
3 Eagle Sculpture ... D3
4 Lermontov & Yerrmelov Baths ... D3
5 Lermontov Gallery ... D3
6 Lermontov Museum ... C2
7 Mt Mashuk Cable Car ... D1
8 Park Tsvetnik ... D3

Sleeping

9 Hotel Intourist ... B2
10 Hotel Pyatigorsk ... B2
Resort Bureau ... (see 4)

Eating

11 Art Café Nostalgia ... A3
12 Cafe Fontan ... C3
13 Upper Market ... A1

er afternoon trips to Ring Rock (p376) near Kislovodsk (₽400, Wednesday and Saturday). Trips to Elbrus start at ₽1000.

Sleeping

Accommodation is a real problem in Pyatigorsk, where hotels are either overpriced or – unusual these days – unwilling or unable to accept foreigners.

Resort Bureau APARTMENT $
(Курортное бюро; ☎8-8793-393 900, after hours 8-905-443 8519; Yermelov Baths, pr Kirova 21; r/apt from ₽700/1400; ⏰9am-3pm Mon-Sat summer) This private accommodation agency can set you up in private apartments.

Hotel Intourist HOTEL $$
(Гостиница Интурист; ☎8-8793-392 222; www.pyatigorskintour.ru; pl Lenina 13; standard s/d ₽2200/2500, renovated from ₽3500/3700; ❄📶) Pyatigorsk's biggest hotel, the partially refurbished Intourist, is conveniently located for Mt Mashuk. The grim 'standard class' rooms are vastly overpriced, however. The renovated rooms are much more pleasant, but also expensive. All rooms have balconies and access to free wi-fi.

Hotel Pyatigorsk HOTEL $$
(Гостиница Пятигорск; ☎8-8793-477 000; www.hotel-pyatigorsk.ru; ul Kraynego 43/1; s/d without bathroom from ₽1300/2200, with bathroom from ₽2000/3100; 📶) It's not going to win any awards, but it's perfectly located in the centre. The cheapest rooms are basic but clean. Superior-class rooms are much nicer but wildly overpriced. Friendly service and free wi-fi in the lobby.

Eating

Upper Market MARKET $
(Верхний рынок; Verkhny Rynok; ul Levanevskogo; ⏰7am-4pm) Here you can gorge on shashlyk and filling *Balkarsky khichiny* (Balkar-style stuffed flatbread) for under ₽100.

Art Cafe Nostalgia RUSSIAN $$
(Арт Кафе Ностальжи; ☎8-8793-357 051; pr Kirova 56; mains ₽300-700; 📝) On restaurant-lined pr Kirova, Nostalgia has a relaxing outdoor terrace where you can dine on *pelmeni*, *pirozhki* (pies), trout, salmon and lots of other choices, including vegetarian options. Slow service.

Cafe Fontan CAFE $$
(Кафе Фонтан; pr Kirova 27; mains ₽300-600; ⏰10am-midnight) A short walk from Park Tsevnik, the lively Cafe Fontan serves a cheap and cheerful selection of Russian and European dishes, including shashlyk. Outdoor seating in summer.

Shalashi CAUCASIAN $$
(Шалаши; Lermontov Duel Site; mains ₽350-850; ⏰11am-1am) This peaceful Caucasian restaurant, hidden in the forest 50m from the Lermontov duel site, has outdoor seating in round twig huts. The house speciality is Azeri *sadzh* (a sizzling meat dish served in a cast-iron pan with potatoes and onions). Also serves local Stavropol and imported Azeri wine (around ₽100 to ₽150 a glass).

Getting There & Away

Pyatigorsk's long-distance bus station is south of the centre, along pr Kalinina. There are numerous buses to Nalchik (₽140, 1½ hours). The daily bus to Teberda (near Dombay) departs at 3.35pm (₽360, four hours).

A better way to Dombay is to buy a one-way trip on a regularly scheduled tour bus (one way from ₽800).

The Pyatigorsk **train station** (Oktyabrskaya ul) has frequent *elektrichki* to both Kislovodsk (₽62, one hour) and Mineralnye Vody (₽53, 50 minutes).

Getting Around

Trams 3 and 5 connect the train station with the town centre through pr Kirova. A taxi to Mineralnye Vody airport costs around ₽700.

Kislovodsk Кисловодск

☎87937 (5-DIGIT NOS), 8793 (6-DIGIT NOS) / POP 133,000 / ELEV 822M / ⏲ MOSCOW

This pleasant spa town, which was entirely closed to cars until the early 1990s, has been a popular destination for Russian holiday-makers since the early 19th century, when the Romantic writer Mikhail Lermontov spent time in its verdant parks and rugged countryside.

The name means 'Sour Waters', but Kislovodsk has a decidedly sweet vibe. Despite the many tourists and the time-worn sanatoriums scattered about, Kislovodsk remains relaxing to the core. The landscape is green, the many gardens well manicured and the air, at nearly 1km above sea level, is crisp.

Pedestrianised Kurortny bul, running north-south from the post office to the Narzan Gallery, is Kislovodsk's main drag and spiritual nerve centre. The train station is just east of Kurortny bul up a smaller pedestrianised street, cobblestoned ul Karla Marksa. Kurortny Park spreads southeast from Narzan Gallery.

Sights & Activities

Dozens of pleasant, relaxing walking trails have been carved out of the lush, hilly landscape for the benefit of sanatorium-goers. Pick up a map of trails from kiosks behind the colonnade in Kurortny Park.

Kurortny Park — NATURE RESERVE

(Курортный парк) Many of Kislovodsk's walking trails intersperse the hills, ponds and forests of this huge park, which is among the largest in Europe. The park ascends southeast from a plaza behind the semicircular **colonnade** in the town centre to the peak of Mt Maloe Sedlo (Little Saddle; 1376m).

The walking trails materialise south of the park's plaza. It's a two- to three-hour hike from the colonnade to the top of the so-called Olympic Complex (1200m), where the cable car terminates. On the way you'll pass various cafes, statues and other points of interest, including the luscious **Valley of Roses** (Dolina Roz). At 1065m you reach the **Krasnoe Solnyshko Hill** (Red Sun Hill) where, on a clear day, there are great panoramas of the yawning valleys and green plateaus of the pretty surrounding countryside.

From the top there are good views of Mt Maloe Sedlo to the west and, on clear mornings, Mt Elbrus to the south. It's another 45-minute walk to Mt Maloe Sedlo. Trails also lead to Mt Maly Dzhinal (1484m) and Mt Bolshoe Sedlo (1409m); Kislovodsk maps show all the walks, most of which are numbered and signed.

For a speedier ascent, make your way to Ordzhonikidze Sanatorium, then walk 500m to the cable car. *Marshrutka* 21 runs to Ordzhonikidze Sanatorium every 20 minutes from Snizhenka Cafe, across from the main post office.

★Narzan Gallery — HOT SPRINGS

(Нарзанная Галерея; cup of water ₽5; ⏲7-9am, 11am-2pm & 4-7pm) This graceful and well preserved 1850s building recalls the spa town of Bath, England. Inside, the rich, carbonic Narzan Spring bubbles up inside a glass dome and spits out nearly undrinkable water – both hot and cold – into more than a dozen fountains. Never mind the foul taste; if you come here you're obliged to have a cup, so drink up! Bottling the water is, however, forbidden. Narzan means 'Drink of Brave Warriors' in Turkish.

Ring Rock — MOUNTAIN

(Гора-Кольцо) This curious natural circle in a limestone cliff is on the outskirts of Mirny village, some 5km from Kislovodsk. It's an intriguing sight, despite the abundance of graffiti. Below the rock, locals hawk handmade woolly socks and souvenirs. Come here with an excursion from Kislovodsk or take a taxi here and back from the city centre (around ₽800).

★Narzan Baths — NOTABLE BUILDING

(Нарзанные ванны; Kurortny bul 4) The eerie-looking Narzan Baths date from 1901 and could easily double as the setting for a horror film. Unfortunately, the baths have been closed for years. Fortunately, workers hammering away inside the building assured us they are due to be reopened 'soon'.

Fortress Museum — MUSEUM

(Кисловодский историко-краеведческий музей "Крепость"; pr Mira 11; adult/child ₽75/30; ⏲10am-6pm) To secure Russia's new southern frontier, Catherine the Great built a line of forts along the Caucasus mountain range. Kislovodsk was one of them, and the Fortress Museum is within the remaining walls of that 1803 fort. The museum traces the city's history. Notable Russian writers such as Alexander Pushkin, Leo Tolstoy and Mikhail Lermontov were visitors to

Kislovodsk, and the late dissident writer Alexandr Solzhenitsyn was born here.

Chaliapin Dacha Literary Museum MUSEUM
(Музей 'Дача Шаляпина'; ul Shalyapina; adult/child ₽50/20; ⌚8.30am-6pm) Fyodor Chaliapin, the legendary Russian opera singer, lived in a palatial wood and stained-glass villa near the train station in 1917, which is now this museum. There are lots of photos of him in various roles, plaster ceilings bursting with cherubs and fruit designs, and a lovely glaze-tiled chimney.

Lermontov Statue MONUMENT
(Kurortny bul) On the east edge of Kurortny bul's plaza, up some steps, is a Lermontov statue. Caged in a grotto below is an effigy of the demon from Lermontov's famous poem, 'The Demon', believed to be his troubled alter ego.

Tours

Excursion bureaus clustered around the south end of Kurortny bul sell trips to Dombay (₽700, 6.30am Tuesday, Friday, Saturday and Sunday) and Arkhyz (₽650, Monday), as well as a trip to Ring Rock and the local Honey Waterfalls (₽350, 12.30pm daily). Also see the travel agency **Vershina** (Вершина; ☎7-928-304 5400; Tsandera 4; ⌚9am-6pm daily) for more trips.

Sleeping

Pansionat Beshpagir GUESTHOUSE $
(Пансионат Бешпагир; ☎8-928-376 2443; www.beshpagir.ru; ul K Tsetkin 47; s/d without bathroom ₽500/1000, with bathroom from ₽1600/1800; wi-fi) Family-run Pansionat Beshpagir is a three-storey guesthouse that provides excellent value for its simple but clean rooms. A mere ₽400 extra nets you full board, or you could self-cater in the common kitchen. Rooms are bright with painted wood panelling and well-maintained bathrooms. In a quiet neighbourhood some way from the centre, it is best to take a taxi here from Kurortny bul (₽150).

★ **Hotel Zamok** HOTEL $$
(Гостиница Замок; ☎8-87937-34 606; www.kmv-zamok.ru; Alikonovka Gorge; d from ₽3500) Some 7km west of Kislovodsk in the Alikonovka Gorge, this pseudo-medieval hotel and restaurant complex has 12 double rooms. The standards are modern and comfortable, but nothing out of the ordinary. However, the more expensive options (from ₽5500) are located in the upper section of the castle and boast beautiful beds and furniture, as well as working open fires. A taxi from Kislovodsk costs around ₽400.

Grand Hotel HOTEL $$
(Гранд Отель; ☎8-87937-33 119; www.grandhotel-kmv.ru; Kurortny bul 14; s/d incl breakfast from ₽2400/3200; air-con, wi-fi, pool) This classy, perfectly located place has a grand entrance staircase, friendly service and large, well-furnished rooms, complete with spacious bathrooms. Fast, free wi-fi, but only in common areas.

Pan Inter HOTEL $$
(Гостиниица Пан Интер; ☎8-87937-28 877; www.hotel-paninter.ru; Kurortny bul 2; s/d incl breakfast from ₽2500/3500; wi-fi) Well-located Pan Inter has small but spotless, well-equipped rooms with a subdued colour scheme and shimmery fabrics. There's a small desk, stocked minibar and modern bathroom. Good free wi-fi throughout.

Park Hotel HOTEL $$
(Парк Отель; ☎8-87937-33 314; www.parchotel.ru; Pervomaiskaya 2; s/d ₽2000/2900) Right behind the main tourist stretch, Park Hotel is something of a mixed bag. Its cheapest singles are cramped, yet liveable. The economy doubles are somewhat better, while the more expensive variants are comfortable and spacious.

Eating

Mimino GEORGIAN $
(Мимино; Kurortny bul 6; mains ₽200-500) This lively spot has an outdoor terrace that always draws a crowd. Start with piping-hot *khachapuri* and Georgian-style *solyanka* (a spicy soup) before moving onto sizzling kebabs.

Kazan House RUSSIAN $
(Казанский дом; ul Kirova 50; shashlyk per 100g ₽60-130) Quieter and cheaper than similar places on the main tourist stretch. The *lulya* (minced-meat sausage cooked on an open flame) kebabs are encouragingly popular with locals. To get there, head north along Kurortny bul to ul Kirova, turn right and follow this road another 400m as it veers to the left.

Cafe Gurma CAFE $
(Кафе Гурма; ul Karla Marksa 1; mains ₽200-500; ⌚10am-9pm) This pleasant cafe is just off the main Kurortny bul and serves a mixture

of European and Russian food, including piping-hot lasagne.

★ **Restoran Zamok** GEORGIAN $$

(Ресторан Замок; ☎8-87937-34 609; mains ₽300-750) This modern castle, 7km west of Kislovodsk in the Alikonovka Gorge, trades on a legend about a boy who leapt from the edge of a nearby cliff out of love for a local girl. The girl was supposed to leap too, but thought better of it. The setting is pseudo-medieval and the tasty Georgian dishes are beautifully prepared. A taxi there and back, with around an hour and a half's waiting time, should cost about ₽1000.

The on-site Hotel Zamok (p377) has good rooms.

Kavkazskaya Plenitsa RUSSIAN, CAUCASIAN $$

(Кавказская пленница; Kurortny bul 4; mains canteen ₽200-350, restaurant ₽300-850) Named after a famous Soviet-era film, the 1st floor is a cheap canteen that serves filling soups and meat-based dishes. Upstairs is a much grander affair, with well-prepared and tasty Georgian food, including several varieties of *khachapuri*.

Getting There & Away

BUS

The **bus station** (ul Promyshlennaya 4) is terribly located, 6km north of the centre (a throwback from the days when vehicles were banned from Kislovodsk).

Arkhyz ₽345, five hours, two daily

Cherkessk ₽175, two hours, six daily

Krasnodar ₽800, 8½ hours, daily

Nalchik ₽195, two hours, two daily

Stavropol ₽335, five hours, 10 daily

Vladikavkaz ₽405, 5½ hours, three daily

Frequent *marshrutky* and shared taxis leave from the train station for Pyatigorsk (₽90, one hour) all day until late evening.

The easiest way to Dombay is on a regularly scheduled tour bus (from ₽700). Alternatively, head to Cherkessk and transfer there.

TRAIN

Trains depart from Kislovodsk's attractive **train station** (Vokzalnaya ul).

Mineralnye Vody ₽75, 1¾ hours, half-hourly (*elektrichka*)

Moscow *platskart/kupe* from ₽2500/₽4500, 25 to 36 hours, three daily (3C express at 7.39pm)

Pyatigorsk ₽55, one hour, half-hourly (*elektrichka*)

Rostov-on-Don ₽465, eight hours, two daily (*elektrichka*)

Sochi *platskart/kupe* ₽1103/2030, 14½ hours, daily at 4.40pm

St Petersburg *platskart/kupe* ₽3555/6830, 50 hours, daily

Passenger trains also pass through Pyatigorsk on their way to Sochi and St Petersburg.

CENTRAL CAUCASUS

Most visitors to the Russian Caucasus have their sights set firmly on the awesome Greater Caucasus mountains, in the central Caucasus (Центральный Кавказ), Europe's highest peaks by a considerable margin. There are 200 peaks over 4000m, 30 over 4500m and seven over 5000m, including the granddaddy, Mt Elbrus (5642m). Mont Blanc, the highest in Western Europe at 4807m, is exceeded by 15 Caucasus peaks.

But the statistics speak nothing of the savage beauty of these mountains, where smooth green foothills morph with brutal assertiveness into a virtually impenetrable wall of rock spires, glaciers and daunting cliffs rising hundreds of metres into the air.

The Greater Caucasus mountains are an adventure lover's playground. The two places most visited by foreigners for wonderful skiing, hiking and climbing are Dombay and Elbrus.

Dombay & Teberda
Домбай и Теберда

☎87872 / POP 600 / ELEV 1600M / ⌚ MOSCOW

Even those well travelled in the world's most stunning wilderness areas can only gape in awe when they first set eyes on Dombay. Wedged into a box canyon at the confluence of three raging mountain rivers, the town is surrounded by a soaring crown of jagged, Matterhornlike peaks of rock and ice, festooned with glaciers and gushing waterfalls.

There's only one snag – the town itself, dishevelled and dominated by several brash concrete hotels, is an eyesore. A spate of Olympic-related construction – Dombay was a backup venue for the 2014 Winter Olympics in Sochi – has done little to improve the town's appearance. Fortunately, it takes only a brisk walk to be far removed from the town proper.

Dombay and its surrounding mountains lie within the **Teberdinsky State Natural**

Central Caucasus

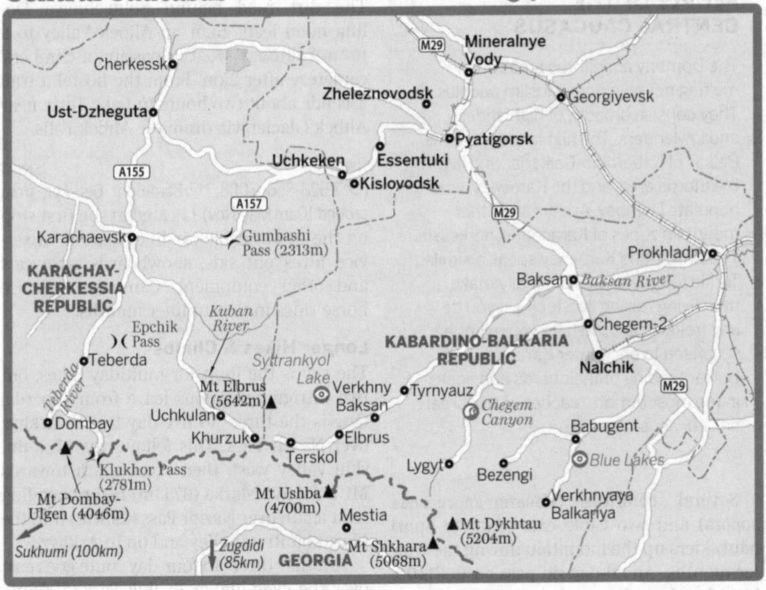

Biosphere Reserve. Most locals belong to the mountain-dwelling Karachay ethnic minority.

Three *ushchelie* (deep valleys) watered by glacier-fed torrents – Alibek from the west, Amanauz from the south and Dombay-Ulgen from the east – meet here to flow north, eventually as the Teberda River. Straddling both sides of the Amanauz River is the village of Dombay. From here two cable cars and several chairlifts ascend the Mussa-Achitara (Horse Thief) Ridge to the east.

The winding ul Karachaevskaya goes right through the village, past the cable cars and most hotels. The tatty residential zone lies to the south of the village.

You'll find good hikes and horse riding in Teberda, 20km north of Dombay. There's a good map (in Russian) of the village, including all hotels, restaurants and cafes at www.dombaj.ru/map_Dombay.php.

Sights & Activities

The main activities are skiing in winter and hiking in summer.

Teberdinsky State Natural Biosphere Reserve NATURE RESERVE
(Тебердинский государственный биосферный заповедник; admission ₽60; 9am-1pm & 2-6pm) This park, near the reserve office in Teberda, has a small museum with stuffed animals and info on wildlife and geology. It also has stiflingly small enclosures with deer, foxes, wolves and other local fauna.

Hiking & Skiing

Many routes require a border permit and additionally may require a nature reserve pass (currently ₽75, payable at the guard post at the entry to the hike). No guide is needed for Amanauz Valley or Alibek Falls. Other hikes, including Lake Turie, require mountaineering experience or a guide, as they may involve crossing glaciers and torrential rivers. There's also a bear population.

★ **Mussa-Achitara Ridge** HIKING, SKIING
(Хребет Мусса-Ачитара) The 3012m-high Mussa-Achitara Ridge provides magnificent skiing, similar to the European Alps, from November until late May. Trails drop an eye-popping 1400 vertical metres from the top to the valley floor. There is bowl skiing up above the treeline as well as some mogul and glade runs for experts, and plenty of intermediate terrain. Plenty of backcountry terrain exists for freeriders, but take a local guide and beware of avalanches.

PEOPLE OF THE CENTRAL CAUCASUS

The Dombay and Elbrus areas are a melting pot of various Muslim peoples. They consist, broadly, of highlanders and lowlanders. The highlanders are the Balkar of Kabardino-Balkaria, who live in the Elbrus area, and the Karachay, who populate Dombay, Arkhyz and other mountain zones of Karachay-Cherkessia. The Balkar and Karachay speak a similar Turkic tongue and traditionally make their living raising livestock – if you do any trekking around here you might be surprised to encounter Karachay and Balkar tending to their herds and flocks in the most remote reaches of the Greater Caucasus.

Several chairlifts (Канатно-кресельная дорога) and two cable cars (8am to 5pm) haul skiers up the mountain during the winter months. An all-day ski pass costs ₽1400. Most hotels and several shops around town hire out skis and snowboards. The cable car remains open for sightseeing in the summer months. A round trip to the top of the ridge costs ₽800, where some truly memorable views of snow-capped mountains await.

Chuchkhur Waterfalls HIKING

(Чучхурский водопад) It's a scenic, relatively easy walk from the start of chairlift 1 to two fine waterfalls on the Chuchkhur River. First, follow the vehicle track and then branch across the **Russkaya Polyana** clearing and continue to the first set of waterfalls, the most impressive of which is 12m high. It takes about two hours (6km) to get here. Twenty minutes downstream from these falls, a 2km path forks south up Severny (North) Ptysh Valley to another waterfall.

Amanauz Valley HIKING

South of town, a short (45-minute, 3km) but tricky walk follows the Amanauz River to **Chyortova Melnitsa** (Devil's Mill), with good views of the **Amanauz Glacier**. Head south out of town past the Dombay housing area and pick up the trail along the river. After negotiating a slippery stream crossing (icy through June) the path dissipates. Head uphill through the woods until the trail materialises again and follow it to the viewpoint.

Alibek Valley HIKING

The dirt road behind Solnechnaya Dolina hotel leads 6km up Alibek Valley to a **mountaineers' hostel**, passing a climbers' cemetery after 2km. From the hostel a trail ascends about two hours to Lake Turie near Alibek Glacier, via dramatic Alibek Falls.

Iolam SKIING

(☎7-928-656 3088; ⏰8am-6pm Dec-Apr, from around 10am May-Nov) Located at the first stop on the newer cable-car line, this rental service hires out skis, snowboards, snowcats and other equipment. Can also organise horse rides in the summer months.

Longer Hikes & Climbs

The sky is the limit for multiday hikes, but two intriguing options leave from Teberda. One is the three- to five-day trip to Arkhyz over Nazgir Pass. This follows the Mukhinskie Valley west, then veers south towards Mt Bolshaya Marka (3753m) before heading west again over Nazgir Pass (2981m) into the Marukha River valley and on to Arkhyz.

Another three- to four-day route goes east over the even-higher Epchik Pass (3006m). The route then continues to Lozhny Pass before dropping into the village of Uchkulan, just 30km due west of Mt Elbrus. A couple of kilometres east of Uchkulan is Khurzuk. Hard-core mountaineers can use Khurzuk as a base for ascents up the western flank of Mt Elbrus.

Peaks that serious climbers can tackle from Dombay include Sofrudzhu (3780m), Dombay-Ulgen (4046m), Sulakhat (3409m) and Semyonovbashi (3602m) above Alibek Valley. Check www.dombai.info for more information on these and other technical climbs.

One recommended guide who leads hikes in the area is **Rassul** (☎8-928-925 6038).

Lakes

There are several pretty lakes in the area that make for a fine swim on a warm summer day. **Ozero Karakel** is located 800m south of Teberdinsky State Natural Biosphere Reserve in Teberda. **Ozero Tumanlykel** is 7km northeast of Dombay, best reached by taxi (around ₽400).

Horse Riding

Oleg HORSE RIDING

(☎7-928-032 9960, 7-928-388 8872) Friendly horse-trekking guide Oleg operates out of stables located inside the Teberdinsky State Natural Biosphere Reserve in Teberda. He leads full-day rides taking in stunning alpine scenery. You can also do a four-day return ride over Epchik Pass to Uchkulan, one of the highest horse treks in the world. It costs a bargain ₽3000 per day for a group of up to five people (food, guide and tents included).

Oleg can arrange the necessary border permits, though you'll need to contact him at least a week in advance.

Sleeping

Rates double or triple in the ski season. It's also possible to rent private rooms or flats from the women who gather near the cable cars every morning.

Snezhnaya Koroleva HOTEL $
(Снежная Королева; ☎8-87872-58 370, 8-928-906 5958; www.dombai.org/snezhnaya-koroleva; ul Karachaevskaya 39; s/d from ₽1000/1500;) These comfortable and good-value rooms have ample space to accommodate both you and your ski equipment. There's also a sauna and pool. The hotel is 300m from the northern entrance to the village. Look for the model penguins outside.

Solnechnaya Dolina HOTEL $
(Гостиница Солнечная Долина; ☎7-8622-330 943; www.dolina-dombai.ru; ul Karachaevskaya 119; d from ₽900;) Built in 1936 as the first hotel in Dombay, the old wing of this picturesque place is made entirely of wood without nails in the manner of north Russian buildings. Many rooms have balconies though some lack views, and the cheapest quarters have vintage wallpaper and aged bathrooms. To find it, walk across the bridge behind the Grand Hotel, cross the field and follow the road uphill for around 800m.

Hotel Snezhny Bars HOTEL $$
(Отель Снежный Барс; ☎8-87872-58 813, 8-928-923 1734; www.snezhny-bars-hotel.ru; Rodnikovy 1; s/d ₽2700/3000;) Snezhny Bars has nicely appointed rooms with redwood furniture, comfy queen-sized beds and balconies with views. Upper-price rooms add even more space to the equation. Follow ul Karachaevskaya after the cable-car station near Grand Hotel and take the third turning on the right.

Grand Hotel HOTEL $$
(Гранд Отель; ☎7-928-923 8888; www.dombayinfo.ru/hotels/complex/hotel_grandotel; ul Karachaevskaya 62; d from ₽3000;) A newish option in the centre of town, Grand Hotel has modern rooms with redwood furniture, attractive bedspreads and efficient service. Many rooms lack views owing to new buildings surrounding the hotel. There's a pool, billiards and *banya* (₽1500 per hour). It's so close to the new cable-car station that from some upper rooms you can almost reach out and touch skiers as they ascend the ridge.

★ **Tarelka** MINIHOTEL $$$
(Тарелка; www.dombai.aelita.su/ufo-hotel; Mussa-Achitara Ridge; entire minihotel for ₽9400) Possibly the most unusual accommodation option in Russia, this Soviet-era minihotel is designed to resemble a flying saucer that has landed in the heights of the Dombay mountains. Located on the edge of the Mussa-Achitara Ridge, at an altitude of 2250m, it sleeps a maximum of six people in three separate cabins. It's not possible to book individual rooms, however, only the entire hotel. It's warm and cosy inside, with shared shower, toilet and a small kitchen space.

Open only between October and April, it's very popular with skiers and snowboarders, so book well in advance.

Eating

U Zuli RUSSIAN $$
(У Зули; ul Karachaevskaya 78; mains ₽300-650; 10am-midnight) Popular U Zuli draws in Karachay regulars to feast on *zharkoye* (meat, potatoes and spices served in a sizzling cast-iron pan), buttery *khichiny* and other regional specialities in a rustic wood-panelled dining room (with animal skins on the wall). Costumed servers add verve to the place.

Cafe Kristall RUSSIAN $$
(Кафе Кристалл; ul Karachaevskaya 103; meals ₽250-700; 9am-midnight) This place specialises in Karachay cuisine, including *sokhta* (a mammoth, sausagelike creation stuffed with minced liver and rice) and *dzhyorme* (smaller Karachay sausage). Specify weight (in grams) to avoid a hefty meal (and bill). Seating is outside on a porch along the river or in the small dining room with refectory tables.

Cafe Alibek CAUCASIAN $$
(Кафе Алибек; ul Karachaevskaya 140; mains ₽300-600; 9am-11pm Dec-Apr, 10am-10pm May-Nov) Enjoy the views of the nearby mountains at this friendly cafe with a stuffed bear in the courtyard. The tasty Caucasian dishes come in generous portions.

ⓘ BORDER PERMITS

Unfortunately, if you show up to Dombay without a proper *propusk* (permit), you won't be able to do any hiking – or see much beyond the village – which is of course the highlight of visiting this region. Foreigners require border permits for anywhere other than the village environs and Mussa-Achitara Ridge. Permit processing through the **border control office** (⊘ 9am-5pm Mon-Fri) in Teberda is generally painless and swift, but has been known in some cases to take up to one month. Plan well in advance and contact a local travel agent such as Dombay Tourist (see below) several months before your visit to be on the safe side.

🛍 Shopping

Market stalls around the village and chairlift stations sell shawls, felt Georgian-style hats, woolly rugs and bags of tasty 'mountain tea'.

ⓘ Information

Dombai Info (www.dombai.info) Infrequently updated website, but with some nonperishable information and photographs.

Dombay Tourist (☑ 8-905-422 2383; www.dt-tour.ru) Can organise day and multiday excursions, including hikes, 4WD tours and horse riding, plus transfers. Can arrange border permits, but contact it well in advance. On the 2nd floor of the new cable-car base station.

Rescue Service (Спасательная Служба; Spasatelnaya sluzhba; ☑ 8-87872-58 138; ⊘ 24hr) Emergency help, plus guiding and/or advice on more technical hikes and climbs. On the main floor of the new cable-car base station.

Sberbank (Сбербанк; ul Karachaevskaya 105; ⊘ 9am-4pm Mon-Fri) Currency exchange and ATM.

Teberdinsky State Natural Biosphere Reserve Office (☑ 8-87872-51 261; Teberda; ⊘ 9am-5pm Mon-Fri) The nature reserve office issues reserve passes and can arrange guides for hikes originating in Teberda. It's just off the main road on the north edge of Teberda.

ⓘ Getting There & Away

All buses originate at the Ekspres grocery (Экспрес) in the residential area southwest of town. Buses also pick up passengers outside the Grand Hotel. The latest schedule is displayed in the window of the grocery, or ask the friendly staff.

Marshrutky and buses serve Cherkessk (₽225, 3½ hours, daily at 8am and 11am), Karachaevsk (₽120, two hours, four daily), Uchkeken (₽325, four hours, two daily), Rostov-on-Don (₽750, nine hours, daily at 5.20pm). All buses pass through Teberda (₽45, 25 minutes).

For Arkhyz, the fastest route is to take the daily bus to Zelenchuk (₽180, 2½ hours, 9am), where you catch an onward *marshrutka* or a taxi (from ₽600) to Arkhyz.

Additional daily *marshrutky* from Teberda head to Mineralnye Vody via Pyatigorsk (₽300, six hours) and Krasnodar (₽600, 7½ hours). In ski season, frequent *marshrutky* shuttle people straight to Minvody airport (per person ₽700).

An easier but more expensive method of arriving is on a tour bus from Pyatigorsk (from ₽700) or Kislovodsk (from ₽700). Unlike public transport, these excursions take you over the 2313m Gumbashi Pass, with sublime views of Mt Elbrus lording it above the whole mountain chain.

Arkhyz Архыз

☑ 87878 / POP 2000 / ELEV 1450M / ⊘ MOSCOW

Famed throughout Russia for its mineral water, Arkhyz has seen intense development in recent years as part of the Kremlin's ambitious bid to boost tourism in the North Caucasus, including the construction of a new cable-car ski lift and a new road into the village.

An all-day ski pass here costs ₽900, with some 10km of ski trails of varying difficulties. Ski lifts whisk skiers up to an altitude of 2200m, where stunning views of the Caucasus mountains await. Cable-car passes for nonskiers cost ₽300.

Talk to guides in Dombay or Pyatigorsk about the many treks around here, including some easy-to-access day hiking around Lunaya Polyana. As in Dombay you'll need a border permit. Apply through travel agencies in Dombay or Pyatigorsk, or through Arkhyz's border control office, 2km south of town.

Both rafting (30-minute trip per person from ₽500) and horse riding (from ₽450 per hour) can be easily arranged through your guesthouse.

🛌 Sleeping

Ogonyok Turbaza LODGE $
(Орлиное гнездо; ☑ 8-928-279 3140; www.arkhyz.net/gostinitci_arhiza/turbaza_orlinoe_gnezdo.html; cabins from ₽1300; 🛜) An alternative to hotels, these rustic cabins boast great views of the surrounding mountains. The

cheaper options lack charm, however. The cabins are next to the Arkhyz mineral water bottling plant in the centre of the village.

Romantik HOTEL $$

(Романтик; 8-909-493 2079; www.hotelromantik.ru; s/d ₽2400/4000;) Close to the ski lifts, this newish hotel has bright and comfortable rooms, as well as friendly staff. Popular with well-off tourists from Moscow and other major cities. Good breakfasts, but wi-fi was unreliable when we visited.

Pansionat Energetik HOTEL $$

(Пансионат Энергетик; 8-928-393 8777; www.arkhyz.com; ul Beregovaya 2; r from ₽2100;) This four-storey hotel is in the centre of the village and has decent alpine-style rooms overlooking the rushing Bolshoy Zelenchuk river. Guides here can also organise hikes into the nearby mountains. Bicycles are available for rent (₽300).

Eating

There are a number of small cafes around the ski lifts, with more in the centre of the village. The Romantik hotel also has a good on-site restaurant that serves Russian and Caucasian dishes.

Getting There & Away

Buses for Arkhyz leave Kislovodsk daily at 7.55am (₽350, 4½ hours). Heading back, the bus leaves Arkhyz at 11am. There are also several daily *marshrutky* to and from Cherkessk and Karachaevsk. For Dombay, catch the 11am *marshrutka* to Teberda (₽235) and transfer there.

Nalchik Нальчик

86622 / POP 283,000 / ELEV 445M / MOSCOW

The pleasant capital of Kabardino-Balkaria Republic straddles the rise of the steppes to the foothills of the Caucasus. Apart from a worthwhile museum and side trips to Chegem Valley and some medieval villages, visitors come to Nalchik to reach Mt Elbrus.

Security remains tenuous in Nalchik. In 2005 dozens of people were killed in fighting after Islamic militants took several government buildings. Recent years have seen a number of smaller-scale attacks. Russian security forces continue to carry out regular operations in the city and its outskirts, while billboards plead with locals not to 'become pawns in the hands of terrorists'.

Two parallel streets, pr Lenina and pr Shogentsukova, run southwest through the centre from the train station on Osetinskaya ul.

Sights & Activities

Dolinsk Park PARK

(Парк Долинск) Lush Dolinsk Park is one of Nalchik's highlights. Stroll the long promenade down to the **chairlift** (round-trip ₽180, 9am to 6pm), which ascends over a lake to the Restaurant Sosruko (p384). Climb the staircase inside Sosruko's 'head' for great views of the city and the mountains in the distance. The park also has small green lakes with paddle boats, an amusement park and the scenic Nalchik River, where locals take a dip to cool off on hot days. To get there, walk or jump on *marshrutka* 1 heading west along pr Shogentsukova.

★ Aushiger Hot Spring HOT SPRINGS

(Аушигер Горячий источник; Aushiger Village; admission ₽50; 7am-9pm) This open-air swimming pool near Nalchik is filled with water from a nearby hot spring. Locals swear by its medicinal properties. Regardless, it's a memorable experience. Lunch at one of the small cafes inside the complex. There are also two small hotels (doubles from ₽2000), should you wish to prolong your stay. *Marshrutky* leave for here from central Nalchik, or take a taxi (₽500).

Tours

Caucasus Explorer TOUR COMPANY

(8-499-653 9019; www.caucasus-explorer.com) This travel agency specialises in trips around the Kabardino-Balkaria Republic, as well as across the entire Caucasus region (including Chechnya, Dagestan and Ingushetia). It can also tailor trips to individual needs. The friendly guides and staff speak English.

Sleeping

Trek HOTEL $$

(8-86622-720 576; www.trek.web-box.ru; Dolinsk Park, Gorodskoy Park; s/d ₽2000/3000;) Near the chairlift in Dolinsk Park, Trek has spacious and attractive rooms with queen-size beds, sparkling modern bathrooms and oversized windows to take in the surrounding greenery.

Hotel Rossiya HOTEL $$

(Гостиница Россия; 8-86622-775 378; www.hotelrussia07.ru; pr Lenina 32; s/d ₽1500/2500;) Right in the middle of town, the five-storey Rossiya has small but nicely renovated rooms with parquet floors and big windows.

Eating

Nalchik is a good place to sample spicy Kabardian national dishes such as *zharuma* (fiery sausage stuffed with minced lamb, onion and spices).

Central Market MARKET $
(Центральный рынок; ul Pacheva) Browsing the aisles of fruit and fresh-baked flatbread (₽15) to the ubiquitous strains of *lezginka* dance music in the central market is a Nalchik highlight.

Arabic Home MIDDLE EASTERN $$
(Ресторан Арабик Хоум; ul Lenina 52; mains ₽200-600; noon-1am) If you can't face another *khachapuri,* head to stylish Arabic Home, located next to the Rossiya hotel. Relax on a comfy sofa or take a window seat with a view of central Nalchik as you enjoy freshly made hummus and tasty falafel.

★ **Restaurant Sosruko** KABARDIAN $$
(Ресторан Сосруко; 8-86622-720 070; off Profsoyuznaya ul; mains ₽250-850; 10am-late) This architecturally unusual restaurant, at the terminus of the chairlift in Dolinsk Park, comprises the head of local hero Sosruko with an outstretched arm and hand holding a flame. It's *the* place to try Kabardian national cuisine, including the Sosruko special, a concoction of minced meat, mushrooms and herbs in a pastry pear.

Shopping

Dom Knigy BOOKSTORE
(Дом Книги; pr Lenina 10; 9am-9pm) This store has a superb selection of Caucasus maps.

Getting There & Away

Buses from long-distance **bus station No 1** (ul Gagarina 124) serve Pyatigorsk (₽140, 1¾ hours, 12 daily), Kislovodsk (₽185, 2½ hours, three daily) and Terskol (₽194, three hours, one daily). Another option to Terskol is to take a *marshrutka* to Tyrnyauz (₽140, two hours) and transfer to a Terskol-bound *marshrutka* or taxi there.

For Mineralnye Vody, hope for an open seat on the passing Vladikavkaz–Mineralnye Vody bus (₽170, two hours, eight daily) or take a taxi (₽2000).

From the **train station** (ul Osetinskaya) there are two daily *elektrichki* to Mineralnye Vody (₽154, three hours, 7.06am and 11.26am). Train 061C to Moscow (*platskart/kupe* from ₽2450/4900, 36 hours, 4.20pm) passes through Rostov-on-Don (*platskart/kupe* from ₽1350/2510, 12½ hours).

Elbrus Area Приэльбрусье

86638 / ELEV (TERSKOL) 2085M / MOSCOW

Mt Elbrus rises imperiously on a northern spur of the Caucasus ridge at the end of the Baksan Valley. Surrounding it, and flanking the valley, are mountains that are lower in height but equally awe-inspiring.

Most foreign visitors come for the challenge of climbing Europe's highest peak, but there are dozens of fantastic, less-strenuous hikes in the area, and there's year-round skiing. Day trippers can ride the chairlifts and cable cars for views of Elbrus and nearby mountains. Mt Elbrus and its surrounding peaks and towns all lie within the vast **Prielbruse National Park**.

Three villages lining the Baksan Valley make up the area known in Russian as Prielbruse (Around Elbrus). Driving in, the first town you'll hit is the bustling ski village of Cheget Polyana, at the base of Mt Cheget. Next is Terskol, the ramshackle administrative hub. About 3km beyond Terskol the valley ends at Azau, base for the Mt Elbrus cable car and ski area. Mt Elbrus can't be seen from either of these villages – to catch a glimpse, walk up a mountain or jump on any ski lift in Azau or Cheget. If you are wondering what caused all the crooked trees here, the answer is avalanches, which hit the area with varying ferocity every few years or so.

Maps of the Elbrus area are available from stalls at the base of the Cheget and Azau ski lifts.

Sights & Activities

★ **Mt Elbrus** MOUNTAIN
Mt Elbrus, enigmatically unusual with two peaks – the western at 5642m and eastern at 5621m – bulges nearly 1000m above anything else in the vicinity. This volcanic cone has upper slopes reputedly coated in ice up to 200m thick; numerous glaciers grind down its flanks and several rivers start here. The name 'Elbrus', meaning 'Two Heads', comes from Persian. In Balkar it's 'Mingi-Tau' (meaning 'thousands', ie very big mountain).

The first (unconfirmed) climb of Mt Elbrus was in 1829 by a Russian expedition with Killar, a lone Circassian hunter hired as a guide, apparently reaching the peak on his own. The lower eastern peak was officially climbed on 31 July 1868 and the western peak on 28 July 1874, both by British expeditions. For propaganda purposes in Soviet times, there were mass ascents involving hundreds of climbers. A telephone cable was even taken to the top so Comrade Stalin could share the news.

The Climb

The climb on Elbrus is not technically difficult, but it's harder than, say, Mt Kilimanjaro, with which it is often compared. Climbing experience on ice is advisable, and a good degree of fitness is paramount.

The climb itself takes just one long day, but most climbers require at least seven days of training and altitude acclimatisation before attempting the summit. Climbers typically spend a few days in Terskol or Azau before taking the lifts up to spend a few nights in and hike around the Barrels (p386), a series of cylindrical lodges at 3800m. Slightly further up from the Barrels is the LeapRus 3912 (p386) hotel, a new accommodation option that sleeps up to 40 people.

The actual climb starts around 4am from one of two points: the Diesel Hut (p386) (also called Priyut 11) at 4130m, from where it's a 10- to 12-hour hike to the summit; or the **Pastukhov Rocks** at 4700m, from where it's a seven- to eight-hour hike. Both are accessible by snowcat from the Barrels. Most people start from Pastukhov Rocks.

One mistake you don't want to make is to take this mountain lightly. As on any 5500m-plus peak, clear weather can quickly turn into thick fog. On average, about 10 people perish on Mt Elbrus each year. Do the sensible thing and take a guide.

Ascents above 3700m require a permit. These are free, for the time being, but must be applied for in advance from the **Elbrus Area National Park Office** (☎8-8663-878 141; parkelbrus@yandex.ru; ul Lesnaya 2, Elbrus; ⌚9am-6pm) - email the office. Tour operators or local guides can also arrange these for you.

See the Elbrus Club (p388) website (Russian only) for some useful information on the climb.

Skiing

The piste skiing on Elbrus is generally easier than on nearby Cheget, with terrain to suit all levels. The skiing beneath the lower cable-car station is good for beginners. The upper cable-car (Mir) station services a few steep and challenging runs for experts.

All-year skiing is possible from the uppermost chairlift, which terminates at 3800m. From here snowcats bring advanced skiers a couple of hundred metres further up to the Diesel Hut, from where there are opportunities for off-piste skiing. These run regularly in the peak ski season (per person ₽1000), but must be arranged in advance at other times. Call **Akhmad** (☎8-928-7093 438) to book snowcats. He also has 10-person snowcats for hire from ₽10,000.

An all-day ski pass costs ₽1300 and allows you to ride the cable cars and chairlift but not the gondola, which is run by a separate company. Multiday passes give you access to Elbrus and Cheget (but not both on the same day). Gear can be hired at any hotel or at numerous ski shops in Azau or Cheget Polyana.

Cable Cars & Chairlift

A **gondola** (₽450, 9am to 3.30pm) runs parallel to the **cable car** (all-day pass, including chairlift, no skiing ₽800, 9am to 3.30pm). The gondola terminates at the cable-car mid-station (2870m). For now only the old cable car goes from the mid-station to the upper Mir station; both stations have small cafes.

A **chairlift** continues to 3800m. Both cable cars and the chairlift run year-round except at times of maintenance during late autumn and spring.

Tour buses start arriving at 10am from June to August, and the queues at the cable-car base station and mid-station can be brutal – waits of up to two hours are common at weekends. If it looks bad, consider just taking the gondola up to the mid-station, which affords exceptional views of Elbrus' twin peaks and, to the southwest, Mt Cheget and Mt Azaubashi.

Mt Cheget — MOUNTAIN

Expert skiers relish the moguls, steeps and glades offered by this ski area on the south side of the Baksan Valley. The piste occupies the lower reaches of 3769m Mt Cheget (Mt Donguz-Orunbashi). Two delightfully anachronistic single **chairlifts** (per lift ₽350, 9am to 4pm) haul skiers up to 3040m. There are a couple of T-bars on the back (north) side of the mountain. A day ski pass in season costs ₽1100.

Riding the chairlift up, the raw majesty of the surrounding mountains is quickly revealed. To the west are the smooth, milky-white twin humps of Mt Elbrus, to the east the jagged peaks and near-vertical sides of 4454m Mt Donguzorun (Mt Donguzorun-Chegetkarabashi), with a distinctive glacier shaped like the numeral seven plastered to its side.

Hiking

A couple of easy, two- to three-hour walks start on the dirt road behind (north of) the white obelisk in Terskol village. The dirt road's right fork leads up the Terskol Valley to a dramatic view of Mt Elbrus behind the hanging **Terskol Glacier**, dripping over a cliff edge. The left fork follows a 4WD track to an observatory, with wonderful views across the Baksan Valley to Mt Cheget, Mt Donguzorun and Mt Kogutanbashi (3819m).

From the top of Cheget's lower chairlift, it's an easy one-hour walk around the side of the mountain to **Donguzorunkel Lake**.

These routes did not require permits when we visited, but guides told us the situation is changeable at short notice. Check locally on the latest requirements before you set out, just to be safe.

Walks towards the Georgian border will require a border permit. It's easiest to arrange permits in advance through a tour operator. Contact them at least a month before you plan to visit.

Vladimir Vysotsky Alpine Museum MUSEUM
(Альпинистско-охотничий музей В.С. Высоцкого; ☎8-928-724 0008; Tegenek village; adult/child ₽50/free; ⏲10am-6pm daily) This small but interesting museum is named after the Soviet-era singer-songwriter and actor Vladimir Vysotsky, who was a great fan of the Elbrus region. The museum's exhibits aren't exclusively devoted to Vysotsky, however, and also include a number of fascinating photographs of Soviet ascents of Elbrus, as well as some sad stuffed animals. To get here, follow the road from the turn-off to Cheget for 3km or so until you see the Vysotsky bust.

Tours

Rather than being just folk in offices selling tickets, recommended agencies are either active tour leaders or providers of specialist services for climbers, skiers and hikers. Most also offer 'light' packages for do-it-yourselfers, which include accommodation and logistical support, but no active tour guiding. English-, German- and French-speaking guides are usually readily available. They can also help with visa and border-permit logistics.

Go-Elbrus ADVENTURE TOURS
(☎86638-78 171; www.go-elbrus.com) The German-Balkar couple in charge here are accomplished free skiers and mountaineers. Highly recommended for backcountry skiing trips, ski touring, ice climbing, Elbrus climbs and more creative ascents.

Adventure Alternative ADVENTURE TOURS
(☎in UK 44-28708 31258; www.adventurealternative.com) This UK company organises Mt Elbrus climbs.

Pilgrim Tours ADVENTURE TOURS
(Pilgrim-Tours-Бюро путешествий; ☎495-660 3501; www.pilgrim-tours.com; Ostozhenka 41, Moscow) Pilgrim is a large and efficient Moscow-based company that leads Elbrus climbs.

Viktor Yanchenko ADVENTURE TOURS
(☎8-928-225 4623; yanki-viktor@rambler.ru) Contact Viktor for an English-speaking climbing and skiing guide.

Wild Russia ADVENTURE TOURS
(☎812-703 3215; www.wildrussia.spb.ru; Fontanka nab 59, St Petersburg) This St Petersburg agency specialises in Mt Elbrus climbs and adventure tours throughout Russia.

Sleeping & Eating

Expect to pay double to triple June rates during the peak ski season (late December to early May).

In the winter especially, you'll find eating options aplenty on the ski slopes – everything from bundled-up babushkas hawking shashlyk, *khichiny* and *schorpa* (Balkar soup) to the fire-warmed restaurants at the cable-car stations on Elbrus.

Accommodation on Mt Elbrus itself is in the **Barrels** (dm ₽800), a series of cylindrical huts about 200m beyond the chairlift, and at the **LeapRus 3912** (www.caucasus.ru/en/placement/item/1?; dm in high season ₽3500; 📶) hotel, a new, sleek, sci-fi-inspired option with wi-fi, a cafe and panoramic views of the mountainside. There is more space for tired climbers at the **Diesel Hut** (dm ₽800) at

CHECHNYA, DAGESTAN & INGUSHETIA

Why does Lonely Planet not recommend travel to these areas?

While the security situation in all three republics appears to be improving, they are still far from safe areas for tourists. Every month brings reports of shoot-outs between security forces and militants in both Dagestan and Ingushetia, where poverty and corruption have created a fertile recruiting ground for Islamic extremists. In nearby Chechnya, which witnessed two horrific separatist wars in the 1990s and early 2000s, a former rebel fighter called Ramzan Kadyrov has brought about an uneasy peace for his Kremlin masters. Both Kadyrov and his feared personal army have been accused of torture and murder, as well as other human rights violations. Russian laws are largely irrelevant, especially when it comes to gun possession, but elements of Islamic law are very much in force. Alcohol and gambling are banned and women who leave their head uncovered or wear jeans in public are asking for grave trouble. A few who defied the rules have been killed in recent years.

Further information

Russian journalist Anna Politkovskaya's book *A Dirty War,* and *Chienne de Guerre* by another fearless female war reporter, Anne Niva, are both available in English and are worth reading, as is *Conversation with a Barbarian* by Paul Klebnikov. Politkovskaya and Klebnikov top the list of journalists killed in Russia in recent years.

Human Rights Watch (www.hrw.org) Remains a vocal defender of people's right to live without fear in the Caucasus.

Institute of War and Peace Reporting (http://iwpr.net/programme/caucasus) London-based institute with a network of stringers in the Caucasus who provide an unbiased and detailed look at recent developments in the region.

4200m. Spaces are limited so book through a tour operator.

Cheget Polyana Поляна Чегет

With a clutch of private hotels, slope-side cafes, market stalls and even a legitimate après-ski bar, Cheget Polyana ski area is a more attractive proposition than Terskol, especially during the ski season.

Nakra HOTEL $$
(Накра; ☎8-86638-716 39; www.nakrahotel.ru; d from ₽2100;) This stylish four-floor hotel has big, bright rooms and plenty of storage space for ski and snowboard equipment. Also has a good cafe and a small swimming pool. Friendly staff can provide tips on hiking. Free transport from Minvody.

Pansionat Cheget HOTEL $$
(Пансионат Чегет; ☎8-86638-71 339; www.hotelcheget.ru; s/d from ₽1900/2100;) This huge, eight-storey, ex-Soviet concrete block is time-worn but clean and has a certain Soviet-era charm. There are good views from the upper-floor balconies. The cheap canteen is open to all, as are the ski shop, bank and other services.

Cafe Ai RUSSIAN, CAUCASIAN $
(Кафе Ай; Mt Cheget; mains ₽250-650; 8am-3pm) This friendly cafe at the first chairlift stop on Mt Cheget serves tasty Russian and Caucasian dishes, as well as homemade wine (₽100 a glass) and souvenir T-shirts. Look out for notices advertising guide services on the wall as you come in.

Captain Pete's RUSSIAN $
(mains ₽250-600;) The balcony in view of the ski mountain and Mt Donguzorun is a prime place to sink suds après-ski. Aside from standard Caucasian food, there are European specialities such as schnitzel and baked salmon on the (English) menu.

Terskol Терскол

Terskol has a good selection of accommodation and its central location allows for relatively easy exploration of both Cheget and Azau.

Povorot HOTEL $$
(Поворот; ☎86638-71 499; www.povorot.ru; s/d incl breakfast & dinner from ₽2900/3500;) This well-run hotel is popular with those who come to climb Mt Elbrus or hike in the area.

Nicely furnished rooms have beautiful views of the surrounding countryside and there are loads of amenities – sauna, pool and billiards. The hotel can also arrange permits, provide guides and airport transfers and more.

Hotel Elbrusiya HOTEL $$
(Отель Эльбрусия; ☎86638-711 77; www.elbrus07.ru; s/d ₽1600/2200;) Almost the last building on the left as you leave Terskol, friendly Hotel Elbrusiya has spacious though basic rooms. Some nice views, only slightly spoiled by the crumbling Soviet-era tower block at the back of the hotel. Fast, free wi-fi. Staff can arrange guides and transfers.

Kupol Cafe RUSSIAN $
(Кафе Купол; mains ₽250-650; ⏲8am-11pm Nov-Apr, 10am-10pm Map-Oct;) Popular with climbers, this cafe is housed in a cupola-shaped building and is decorated with photos from both Elbrus and Everest expeditions. Serves simple, but tasty Russian and Caucasian dishes with a smile. It's next to Hotel Elbrusiya.

Azau Азау

While not as pleasant as Cheget Polyana, Azau is a better choice for intermediate skiers who want to be closer to Elbrus' gentler groomed slopes. Elbrus climbers also usually end up here for a night or two before moving up to the Barrels.

Shakherezada Hotel HOTEL $$
(Гостиница Шахерезада; ☎71 327, 8-928-937 2815; www.shaherezada-km.ru; d incl breakfast & dinner from ₽2000;) Big comfortable beds and Eastern-style furnishings make this recently renovated hotel one of Azau's top choices.

Shopping

Seven Summits OUTDOOR GEAR
(Семь Вершин; ⏲10am-6pm daily) Just after the turn-off to Cheget Polyana on the way to Terskol, this well-stocked shop sells all manner of mountaineering and hiking gear.

Information

For visa and border permit support, go through one of the tour companies.

Elbrus (www.elbrus.net) Website with maps and practical information.

Elbrus Club (www.elbrusclub.ru) A good Russian-language-only website with info on the Elbrus climb from those who have reached the summit (or are planning to).

Pansionat Cheget (⏲9am-4.30pm Tue-Sat) Sberbank currency exchange booth and 24-hour ATM in Cheget Polyana.

Post & Telephone Office (Terskol)

Rescue Service (☎8-86638-71 489; Terskol; ⏲24hr) Check in here before setting out for hikes. Look for the letters 'МЧС' on a fence near the Bayramuk cafe on the east edge of Terskol.

Getting There & Away

There's a bus and two *marshrutky* daily to Nalchik (₽1180, three hours). Alternatively, take a taxi (₽800) or bus (₽64, one hour, five daily) to Tyrnyauz and then a frequent *marshrutka* to Nalchik. Taxis to and from Minvody cost around ₽3500.

Arrange with tour operators running out of Kislovodsk and Pyatigorsk to use their excursions as a means of getting to and from Elbrus. Buses leave from the main road near the post office in Terskol. They do not pass through Cheget Polyana proper.

Getting Around

A taxi costs ₽200 from Terskol to Azau or Cheget. In ski season plenty of *marshrutky* and free shuttles operate between Cheget and Azau. Otherwise, walk or hitch a ride.

The Urals

Includes ➜

Best Places to Eat

- ➜ Grill Taverna Montenegro (p395)
- ➜ Vkus Stranstvy (p395)
- ➜ Rosy Jane (p401)
- ➜ Nigora (p401)

Best Places to Stay

- ➜ Hotel Tsentralny (p400)
- ➜ Red Star Hostel (p400)
- ➜ Ecopark Zyuratkul (p407)

Why Go?

Marking the border between Europe and Asia, the Ural Mountains (Урал) stretch from the Kara Sea in the north to Kazakhstan in the south. Modest in scale in the south, they nevertheless proved to be rich in resources, and when Russia stumbled onto this Aladdin's cave full of lustrous treasures many centuries ago, the mineral riches filled the coffers and allowed Russia to expand into Siberia beyond.

Today Yekaterinburg, the largest of the Ural Mountains towns, is a bustling centre with interesting sights; it also offers a base for exploring less-visited towns. West of Yekaterinburg, the city of Perm – better known in Soviet times for its Gulag camps and industries – has some strong cultural attractions. Kungur has a spectacular ice cave, and the Urals countryside offers opportunities for hiking, cycling, rafting or horse-riding expeditions.

When to Go

Yekaterinburg

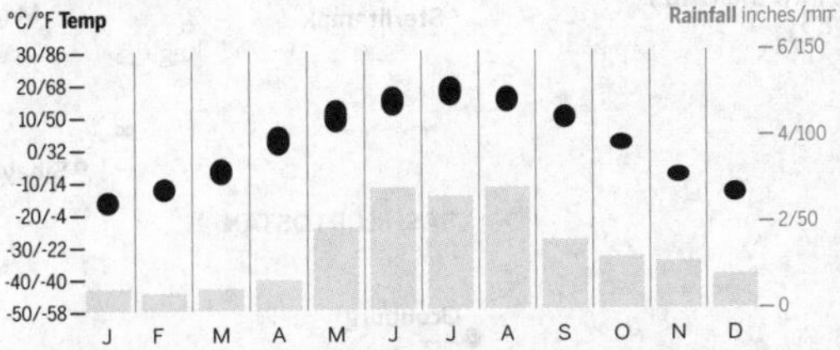

Dec–Feb Best for winter sports and culture.

Late Apr–May Fewer travellers in spring means little advance booking is needed.

Jun & Jul Street life, summer festivals and hiking can be enjoyed.

The Urals Highlights

1. Experience ice and a moment of pitch darkness in Kungur's **ice cave** (p396).
2. Hike into the **Zyuratkul** mountain range or stroll the shoreline of Lake Zyuratkul. (p407)
3. Visit **Perm-36** (p394), the former labour camp and today a haunting Gulag memorial.
4. Make sense of the modern at **PERMM** (p392), the museum of contemporary art in Perm.
5. Trace the historical contours of the murder of Russia's last tsar and his family by visiting Yekaterinburg's **Church upon the Blood** (p397) and **Ganina Yama** (p403).
6. Take an excursion to the top of Nevyansk's **leaning tower** (p403) for spectacular views.
7. Get away from it all on a rafting, horse-riding or hiking trip into the **Urals** (p392).

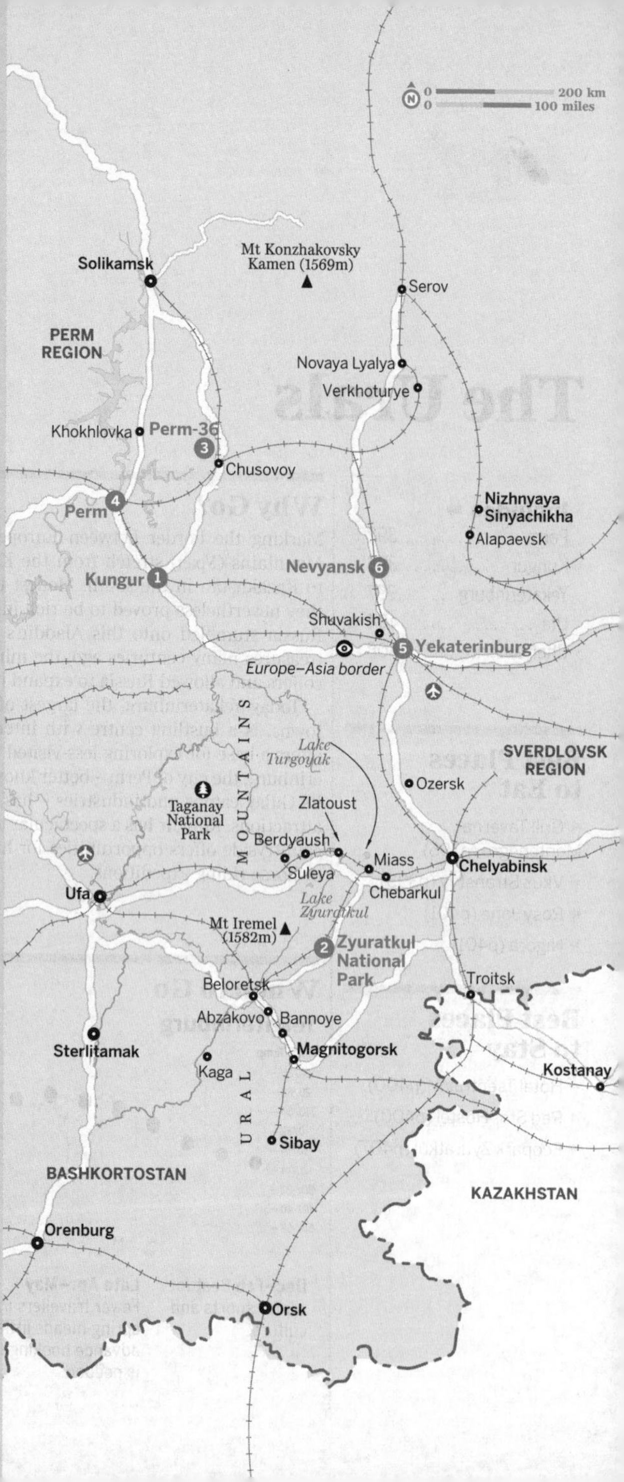

History

The Ural Mountains, running north to south and stretching from the Arctic ice to the Central Asian steppe, are one of the world's oldest mountain chains, the geological consequence of a colossal continental collision that occurred over 300 million years ago. Today the range marks the borderline of these once separate landmasses – Europe and Asia.

Before the arrival of Slavs, the region was populated by Uralic tribes, whose contemporary descendants include the Khanty and Mansi peoples of Western Siberia as well as the Finns and Hungarians of central Europe.

Slavic Expansion

In the 16th century, the rising Muscovite principality won a series of strategic battles against its tribal foes that finally opened the way for eastward expansion. Russian settlement of the Ural Mountains was led by monks, merchants and Cossacks.

Russia gained control over the lands between Moscow and the Ural Mountains through the work of St Stephan, the bishop of Perm, who built a string of monasteries and converted the native tribes. Seeking to exploit the natural wealth of the taiga (northern pine), pioneering merchants followed the clergy. They set up markets next to the monasteries, erecting great churches with their profits from the fur trade. Industrial families such as the Demidovs and Stroganovs began establishing factories in the region.

Industrial Expansion

The discovery of mineral wealth in the Ural Mountains during the reign of Peter the Great led to the first large-scale Russian settlements. Yekaterinburg, founded in 1723 and named for the Empress Catherine I (Yekaterina), wife of Peter the Great, emerged as the region's economic centre. Rich deposits of coal, iron ore and precious stones gave rise to a mining industry, including science and engineering institutes. By the early 19th century the region's metals industry supplied nearly all the iron produced in Russia and exported to European markets. The Statue of Liberty in New York and the roof on London's Houses of Parliament were made from copper and iron from the Ural Mountains.

In 1917 the Russian Empire was consumed by the outbreak of revolution and civil war. Red revolutionaries and White loyalists fought back-and-forth battles across the Ural Mountains. Yekaterinburg became the site of one of history's most notorious political murders when Tsar Nicholas, Tsaritsa Alexandra and their children were shot in the middle of the night and disposed of in an abandoned mine.

The region figured prominently in the Soviet Union's successful industrialisation drive in the 1930s. Some of the world's largest steelworks and industrial complexes were built there, including Uralmash in Sverdlovsk (modern-day Yekaterinburg), and in Magnitogorsk in Chelyabinsk.

During WWII more than 700 factories were relocated to the region, beyond the reach of the advancing Nazis. The Ural Mountains became a centre of Soviet weapons manufacturing: Kalashnikov rifles from Izhevsk, T-34 tanks from Nizhny Tagil and the quaintly named 'Katyusha' (Katya) rockets from Chelyabinsk. During the Cold War, secret cities, identified only by number, were constructed in the region to house the military nuclear and biochemical industries.

The Urals after Communism

In the late Soviet period, a Urals-bred construction engineer turned anticommunist crusader was instrumental in toppling the Soviet system. Boris Yeltsin had gained a reputation as the energetic and populist-leaning communist governor of Sverdlovsk when the reform-minded Mikhail Gorbachev first introduced him to the national political stage, a move that Gorbachev would soon regret.

In his political fights against the old Soviet order and the neocommunists of the post-Soviet transition, the region provided Yeltsin with strong support. Despite the hardships that radical economic reform inflicted on the heavily subsidised industrial sector, the region remained a strong power base for Yeltsin.

As elsewhere in Russia, the postcommunist transition in the Ural Mountains did not go according to the early optimistic plans. The region suffered the severe collapse of its manufacturing and agricultural sectors. Public employees went without wages. Rocket scientists became taxi drivers. Mafia turf wars were waged over the right to 'protect' the nascent private-business sector.

Today the region has recovered to become an economic powerhouse in Russia, and the main town of Yekaterinburg is the most economically dynamic and politically liberal town in the Urals.

PERM TERRITORY

Perm Пермь

☎342 / POP 991,000 / ⏲ MOSCOW +2HR

The word 'Perm' once meant a mysterious Finno-Ugric land encompassing most of the northwestern Ural Mountains that was slowly colonised by Russians since the early medieval ages. But the city is relatively new, founded by the lieutenants of Peter I in 1723.

It is believed that Chekhov used Perm as the inspiration for the town his Three Sisters were so desperate to leave, and Boris Pasternak sent his Doctor Zhivago to a city clearly resembling Perm.

Today the city has some interesting museums and cultural attractions, and is also the base from which to visit one of the best wooden architecture museums in Russia, located in Khokhlovka; the famous ice cave in Kungur; and a grim reminder of Soviet-era political persecution – the Perm-36 labour camp.

Sights

A green line runs through the centre connecting the major sights, with descriptions at each location in Russian and English. Permturist has a free, multilingual *Green Line* booklet for self-guided city walks. This is complemented by a red line, focusing on local love stories.

★Museum of Contemporary Art PERMM ART GALLERY
(Музей современного искусства PERMM; ☎342-254-35-73; www.permm.ru; ul Monastyrskaya 2; admission ₽100; ⏲noon-9pm Tue-Sun) The brainchild and legacy of its former curator Marat Guelman, who was sacked amid fallout over an exhibition satirising the Sochi Winter Olympics of 2014, the Museum of Contemporary Art is housed inside the former river station hall on the banks of the Kama River and has changing exhibitions. Trolleybus 1 and bus 3 take you there.

★Perm State Art Gallery ART GALLERY
(Пермская государственная художественная галерея; ☎342-212 9524; www.sculpture.permonline.ru; Komsomolsky pr 4; admission ₽120; ⏲11am-6pm Tue-Sun) Housed in the grand Cathedral of Christ Transfiguration on the banks of the Kama, the Perm State Art Gallery is renowned for its collection of Permian wooden sculpture. Take trolleybus 1 to the stop Galereya or tram 3, 4, 7, 12 or 13 to the stop Tsum.

The brightly coloured figures are a product of an uneasy compromise between Christian missionaries and the native Finno-Ugric population. The Finno-Ugric population closely identified the Christian saints these sculptures depict with their ancient gods and treated them as such by smearing their lips with the blood of sacrificed animals.

★Perm Regional Museum MUSEUM
(Пермский краевой музей; ul Monastyrskaya 11; admission ₽120; ⏲10am-7pm Tue, Wed & Fri-Sun, noon-9pm Thu) Located inside the imposing Meshkov House, the regional museum only gets really interesting when you see the small collection of intricate metal castings of the 'Perm animal style' used in the shamanistic practices of ancient Finno-Ugric Permians.

Museum of Perm Prehistory MUSEUM
(Музей пермских древностей; www.museumperm.ru; Sibirskaya ul 15; admission ₽120; ⏲10am-7pm Fri-Sun & Tue-Wed, noon-9pm Thu) The archaeological collection sometimes has objects in the 'Perm animal style' of metal casting, supplementing those in the Perm Regional Museum.

Sergei Diaghilev Museum MUSEUM
(Музей Дягилева; ☎342-212 0610; Sibirskaya ul 33; admission by donation; ⏲9am-6pm Mon-Fri, call ahead 31 May-1 Sep) The Sergei Diaghilev Museum is a small, lovingly curated school museum dedicated to the impresario (1872–1929) who turned Russian ballet into a world-famous brand. Children speaking foreign languages, including English, serve as guides on interesting general tours as well as themed ones, such as the history of the house.

Tours

Krasnov ADVENTURE TOURS
(Краснов; ☎342-238 3520; www.uraltourism.ru; ul Borchaninova 4; ⏲10am-6.30pm Mon-Fri, 11am-5pm Sat) Offers active and adventure tourism such as rafting or cross-country skiing in the Urals, beginner Russian courses, river cruises and many more activities. The Russian version of the website has a wider and sometimes less expensive choice.

Permturist ADVENTURE TOURS
(Пермтурист; ☎excursions 342-218 6999; www.hotel-ural.com/tourist; office 219, ul Lenina 58; ⏲10am-7pm Mon-Fri, Sat by arrangement) Located inside the Hotel Ural, Permturist organises excursions in Russian and English such as to the Kungur ice cave (from ₽7000, plus admission), as well as city tours in Perm and

Perm

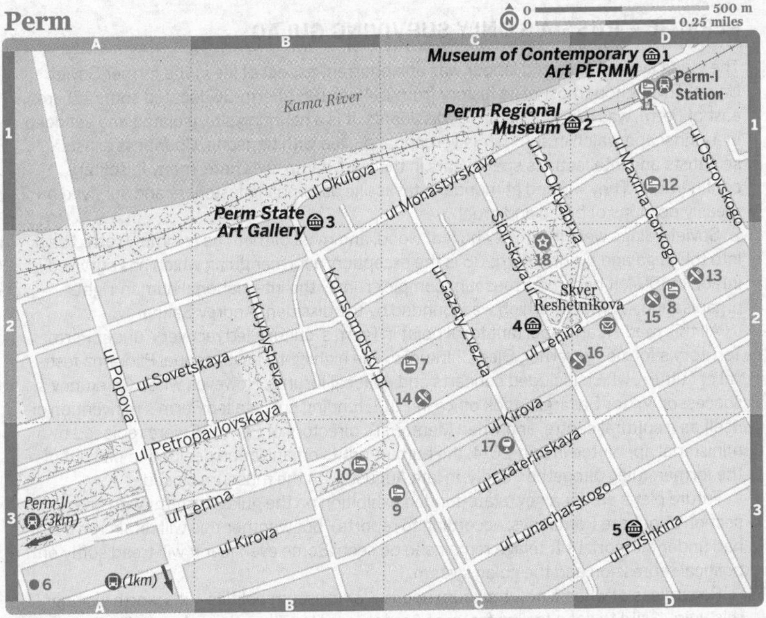

Perm

Top Sights

1 Museum of Contemporary Art PERMM D1
2 Perm Regional Museum D1
3 Perm State Art Gallery B1

Sights

4 Museum of Perm Prehistory C2
5 Sergei Diaghilev Museum D3

Activities, Courses & Tours

6 Krasnov A3
Permturist .... (see 10)

Sleeping

7 Hotel Astor C2
8 Hotel Edem D2
9 Hotel Prikamye C3
10 Hotel Ural B3
11 Resting Rooms D1
12 Travel Otel D1

Eating

13 Grill Taverna Montenegro D2
14 Pasternak C2
15 Sakartvelo D2
16 Vkus Stranstvy D2

Drinking & Nightlife

17 Kama C3

Entertainment

18 Tchaikovsky Theatre of Opera & Ballet C2

Transport

Aviakassa .... (see 10)
Railways Booking Office .... (see 10)

Kama river cruises. It can also help with information about, and whether, tours are running to the Perm-*36* former gulag. The office stocks the *Green Line* booklet outlining the sights around town.

Festivals & Events

Kamwa Festival CULTURAL
(www.kamwa.ru) The annual 'ethno-futuristic' Kamwa Festival held in summer in Perm and Khokhlovka, and brings together ancient ethno-Ugric traditions and modern art, music and fashion. Dates vary considerably each year – see the website.

White Nights CULTURAL
(www.permfest.com) The White Nights festival runs through most of June, presenting a month of contemporary music, street art, theatre, readings and interesting side-festival events.

PERM-36 – RUSSIA'S ONLY SURVIVING GULAG

The gulag system of forced labour was an abhorrent aspect of life in the former Soviet Union. Throughout most of its history from 1946 to 1987, Perm-36, located some 125km east of Perm, was a labour camp for dissidents. It is a haunting site, isolated and set deep in a landscape which in summer is verdant and filled with birdsong. Countless artists, scientists and intellectuals spent years in the cold, damp cells here, many in solitary confinement. They worked at mundane tasks like assembling fasteners and survived on measly portions of bread and gruel.

Soviet gulags were invariably built of wood, and most of them have simply rotted back into the taiga and tundra. Perm-36 is the exception: a former gulag which has survived intact. In 1994, it became a museum complex run by the international human-rights organisation, Memorial, which was founded by the dissident Andrey Sakharov.

All this made it an important focal point in Perm's 'culture-led recovery' under Perm Territory's former governor, Oleg Chirkunov. The highlight was its annual Pilorama festival of culture, which included concerts and political forums. However, when Chirkunov's successor, Viktor Basargin, took office in 2012, funding cuts stalled Perm's reinvention of itself as a cultural centre, and when Memorial's directors of Perm-36 were replaced by a ministerial appointee in mid-2014, the human-rights organisation decided to pull out of the former gulag altogether. Sadly, in late August 2014 the museum closed.

Future plans are for a new state-funded exhibition on the gulag system (with one section about the Romanovs, according to reports), but whether this will retain the bite it had under Memorial's tutelage remains to be seen. Some even fear it will tread softly on political repression and the gulag system.

Regardless of when a new museum opens – or museum politics – it's worth visiting this unique site to get a feeling for what a gulag was like. The gulag is located in the village of Kuchino, about 25km from the town of Chusovoy, which itself is 100km from Perm. To reach it, take a bus bound for Chusovoy or Lysva, get off at Tyomnaya (₽200, two hours) station, walk back to the main road and backtrack to the Kuchino turn-off (also leading to Makhnutino), then walk another 2.5km to the village. Permturist in Perm can help with the latest information on the gulag and available tours.

🛏 Sleeping

Resting Rooms
RESTING ROOMS $

(Комнаты отдыха; ☑342-230 21 76; Main Station, 3rd fl; 12/24hr from ₽440/660; 🌐) Usually no need to book ahead.

★ Hotel Edem
HOTEL $$

(☑342-255 3787; ul Maxima Gorkogo 21b; r ₽2200-2800; 🛜) The five large rooms with double beds in this excellent minihotel are named by their colour scheme – the 'Pink Room', and so on. As with some minihotels, service is friendly but patchy; here you get a kettle, coffee, plates and cutlery, as well as a fridge in some to make good use of the 24-hour supermarket across the road.

Travel Otel
MINIHOTEL $$

(☑342-222 1818; hotel.travel@bk.ru; ul Maxima Gorkogo14b; s incl breakfast ₽4100-5200, d per person incl breakfast ₽2900-3700; 🌐🛜) This quiet, modern minihotel has 10 large and stylish doubles which are excellent value, as well as five higher category singles.

Hotel Ural
HOTEL $$

(Гостиница Урал; ☑342-218 6262; www.hotel-ural.com; ul Lenina 58; s incl breakfast ₽3100-3900, d incl breakfast ₽4000-4800, ste incl breakfast ₽5500-12,000; 🌐@🛜) This one-time Soviet monolith rising up in the heart of the city has adapted to the age and boasts a shimmering, high-tech lobby and modern, reasonably sized rooms.

Hotel Astor
HOTEL $$

(Гостиница Астор; ☑342-212 2212; www.astorhotel.ru; ul Petropavlovskaya 40; s incl breakfast ₽3800-4300, d incl breakfast ₽4600-5600; 🌐❄🛜) 🐾 Spotless white dominates this hotel's colour scheme. It's a favourite among business travellers, and rooms are low allergy.

Hotel Prikamye
HOTEL $$

(Гостиница Прикамье; ☑342-219 8353; www.prikamie-hotel.ru; Komsomolsky pr 27; s incl breakfast ₽3200-4500, d incl breakfast ₽3700-5200, ste incl breakfast ₽5500; 🛜) Nicely spruced-up rooms in this former Soviet eyesore make

Prikamye a very decent option. Deals are better if you book well ahead on the web.

Eating

★ Vus Stranstvy CAFETERIA $
(Вкус странствий; Sibirskaya ul 8; meals ₽300; 11am-9pm Mon-Sat;) With the feel of a mid-priced restaurant, the cheerful 'Taste for Travel' neo-*stolovaya* (canteen) serves some of the best cafeteria food in the Ural Mountains.

Sakartvelo GEORGIAN $$
(Сакартвело; 342-254 3045; http://sakartvelo-perm.ru; ul Lenina 24; mains ₽350; 11am-midnight Sun-Fri, to 2am Sat;) This excellent Georgian restaurant makes good use of chilli in its dishes, including the excellent Tbilisi salad, a borsch with a chilli edge, and a good variety of shashlyk (meat kebab), served in a lavish but homely interior.

Pasternak RUSSIAN $$
(Пастернак; 342-235 1716; ul Lenina 37; Pasternak: mains ₽450; 9am-2am Mon-Fri, 11am-2am Sat & Sun;) This restaurant for the well heeled and the literary inclined is actually two in one. Pasternak downstairs has a lounge-like, post-modernist cafe feel, while Zhivago upstairs is a fully fledged upmarket restaurant.

★ Grill Taverna Montenegro BALKAN $$$
(Гриль-Таверна Монтенегро; ul Maxima Gorkogo 28; meals ₽1000; noon-midnight Mon-Sat, to midnight Sun;) The trompe l'œil village fresco downstairs, upstairs pseudo-portico and outdoor terrace lend nice touches to this excellent restaurant. The Kalmyk lamb kebab is superbly grilled.

Drinking & Nightlife

Kama BREWERY
(Кама; www.pivzavodkama.ru; Sibirskaya ul 25; mains ₽400; noon-2am;) This microbrewery does several tasty varieties of own-brew. The food, including its vegetarian borsch, is reasonably priced by Russian microbrewery standards. Sometimes good bands perform live here; other times it's a guitar soloist with canned backing.

Entertainment

Tchaikovsky Theatre of Opera & Ballet THEATRE
(Театр оперы и балета Чайковского; ticket office 342-212 3087; www.arabesque.permonline.ru/; ul Petropavlovskaya 25; ticket office 10am-2pm & 3-7pm) One of Russia's top ballet schools. Prices are from about ₽100 to ₽1000, depending on seat, venue and performance.

Information

Main Post Office (ul Lenina 29; per hr ₽42; 8am-10pm Mon-Fri, 9am-6pm Sat & Sun) Also offers internet access.

Getting There & Away

Inside the Hotel Ural you will find a **railways booking office** (342-233 0203; 8am-7pm Mon-Fri, to 6pm Sat & Sun) and an **Aviakassa** (ticket office 342-233 2509; 8.30am-8pm Mon-Fri, 10am-5pm Sat & Sun).

AIR

Several airlines fly to Moscow (from ₽7000, two hours, frequent).

BOAT

The river station (Речной вокзал) is at the eastern end of ul Monastyrskaya, in front of Perm-I station. Boats do short tours of the Kama in the navigation season. Permturist (p392) offers a wide range of boats and tours at competitive prices, such as one-way from St Petersburg from €503 and Perm–Astrakhan return from €370. Krasnov (p392) also sells tours but the prices it gives are higher.

BUS

From the **bus station** (Автовокзал; http://avperm.ru; ul Revolyutsii 68) numerous buses go to Kungur (₽208, 1¼ hours); there are frequent buses to Khokhlovka (₽90, 1½ hours) and two daily buses to Ufa (₽1100, 11½ hours). Buses to Kazan depart every two days, with some additional services Friday and Saturday (₽1370, 12 hours).

TRAIN

Perm-II, the city's major train station, 3km southwest of the centre, is on the trans-Siberian route. Many trains travel the route to/from Moscow, including all of the Trans-Siberian *firmeny* (premium, long-distance) trains. If you're on a tighter budget, many cheaper trains do the route from ₽2190. Heading east, the next major stop on the Trans-Siberian route is Yekaterinburg (*platskart/kupe* ₽1000/1444, six hours). For Kazan (₽1800, 19 hours) the most direct route is with an inconvenient change in Izhevsk. Bus can be better. Note that some trains depart from the *gorny trakt* (mountain track) on the north side of Perm-II, as opposed to the *glavny trakt* (main track).

Getting Around

Bus 42 and *marshrutka* (fixed-route minibus) 1t go between the bus station and the airport. Trolleybus 5 connects Perm-II station with Hotel Ural, tram 7 connects Perm-II with the corner of ul Lenina and ul Maksima Gorkogo via ul

Petropavlovskaya, and tram 11 connects ul Maxima Gorkogo with the central market (about 400m from the bus station) via ul Petropavlovskaya and ul Borchaninova.

Around Perm

Khokhlovka Хохловка

Architecture-Ethnography Museum MUSEUM
(☑ 342-299 7181; www.museum.perm.ru; admission ₽120; ☉ 10am-6pm, closed last Mon in month) This museum is located near Khokhlovka, about 45km north of Perm. Its impressive collection of wooden buildings includes two churches dating from the turn of the 18th century. Most of the structures are from the 19th or early 20th centuries, including an old firehouse, a salt-production facility and a Khanty *izba* (traditional wooden cottage). A few buses a day serve Khokhlovka from Perm (₽90, 1½ hours), the best ones departing Perm at 9.55am and returning from Khokhlovka at 4.30pm.

Kungur Кунгур
☑ 34271 / POP 66,000 / ☉ MOSCOW +2HR
Kungur's rundown appearance belies a skyline graced by a multitude of pretty church cupolas, including the 18th-century Tikhvinskaya Church in the centre and the Transfiguration Church on the other bank of the Sylva. The frozen magic of its ice cave, however, is the main attraction, drawing a stream of curious visitors.

◎ Sights

Kungur Ice Cave CAVE
(guided tour ₽500-600; ☉ 10am-4pm, laser show 11am, 1pm & 3pm) The Kungur Ice Cave is about 5km out of town. The network of caves stretches for more than 5km, although only about 1.5km are open to explore. The ancient Finno-Ugric inhabitants of the Perm region believed the cave to be the home of a fiery underground creature, and the grottoes are adorned with unique ice formations, frozen waterfalls and underground lakes. You can enter only on guided tours which depart every two hours. Bring warm clothes for the first grottoes.

The cost of the excursion includes admission to a small museum on the site with displays of rocks and fossils.

Regional Museum MUSEUM
(ul Gogolya 36; admission ₽70; ☉ 10am-5pm Wed-Sun) Founded in 1663 on the banks of the meandering river, Kungur was a copper-smelting centre during the 17th and 18th centuries, which is a key focus of the Regional Museum.

🛏 Sleeping & Eating

Stalagmit Tourist Complex HOTEL $
(☑ 34271-62 602; http://hotel.kungurcave.ru; Kunger Cave; s incl breakfast ₽800-2000, d incl breakfast ₽1400-3000; ❀🛜🖭) This popular complex is close to the cave entrance and offers excellent rooms with their own bathroom (the cheaper ones don't have fridges and TV). Take bus 9 from the train station to the last stop.

The beautiful countryside surrounding Kungur is great for outdoor sports, and bicycles as well as rafts, canoes and cross-country skis can be hired inexpensively at Stalagmit.

Hotel Iren HOTEL $
(☑ 34271-32 270; ul Lenina 30; without bathroom s/d ₽800/1300, with bathroom s incl breakfast ₽1300-1800, d incl breakfast ₽2200-2500; ❀🛜) In the centre of town, Hotel Iren is good value, but it doesn't have a lift. Even the rooms without bathrooms are pleasant enough, and the shared toilets and showers are very clean.

Tri Medvedya RUSSIAN $
(ul Vorovskaya 5; mains ₽175; ☉ noon-2am Sun-Thu, to 3am Sat & Sun; 🛜) Across the bridge in the centre of town, the riverside cafe-disco Tri Medvedya has very decent food. Helpful staff can order a taxi for you back to the bus and train stations.

ℹ Getting There & Around

Bus is the best option from Perm, however, with departures every one to two hours; the most convenient leaves Perm at 8.25am or 9.25am and returns from Kungur at 6.40pm or 7.55pm (₽181, 2½ hours). Buses to Ufa (₽740, one daily) depart at 10am.

Located on the Trans-Siberian route, Kungur is served from Perm by frequent intercity trains (₽670, 1½ hours), suburban trains (₽138, 2¼ hours, four daily) and trains to/from Yekaterinburg (₽463 to ₽1258, four hours).

In Kungur, the bus and train stations are located alongside each other. Bus 9 (every one to two hours) plies the route between Hotel Iren, the train and bus stations, and the Stalagmit complex.

SVERDLOVSK REGION

Yekaterinburg

Екатеринбург

☎343 / POP 1.35 MILLION / ⏱MOSCOW +2HR

Gem rush; miners' mythology; the execution of the Romanovs; the rise of Russia's first president, Boris Yeltsin; and legendary gangster feuds of the 1990s – Yekaterinburg is not only Russia's fourth-largest city, it is like a piece of conceptual art with a fascinating historical subtext.

Bustling but less than startling on the outside, the political capital of the Ural Mountains is overflowing with history and culture, while its economic growth is manifested in a thriving restaurant scene and, as in many other regional capitals, in atrociously trafficked avenues.

With one of the best international airports in Russia and a couple of agencies experienced in dealing with foreign travellers, Yekaterinburg is a good base camp for exploring the Ural Mountains.

History

Yekaterinburg was founded as a factory-fort in 1723 as part of Peter the Great's push to exploit the Ural region's mineral riches. The city was named after two Catherines: Peter's wife (later Empress Catherine I), and the Russian patron saint of mining.

The city is notorious, however, for being the place where the Bolsheviks murdered Tsar Nicholas II and his family in July 1918. Six years later, the town was renamed Sverdlovsk, after Yakov Sverdlov, a leading Bolshevik who was Vladimir Lenin's right-hand man until his death in the flu epidemic of 1919. The region still bears Sverdlov's name.

WWII turned Sverdlovsk into a major industrial centre, as hundreds of factories were transferred here from vulnerable areas west of the Ural Mountains. The city was closed to foreigners until 1990 because of its many defence plants.

During the late 1970s a civil-engineering graduate of the local university, Boris Yeltsin, began to make his political mark, rising to become regional Communist Party boss before being promoted to Moscow in 1985. Several years later he was standing on a tank in Moscow as the leading figure in defending the country against a putsch by old-guard communists. He became the Russian Federation's first president in June 1991.

That year Yekaterinburg took back its original name. After suffering economic depression and Mafia lawlessness in the early 1990s, the city has boomed in recent years. Yekaterinburg is one of the very few cities in Russia governed by a mayor, Yevgeny Roizman, not from a party loyal to the Kremlin.

Sights

Each summer from May after the snow has cleared, Yekaterinburg paints a red line on the footpath to guide visitors past major sights. It's marked on the tourist office (p402) city map.

★**Romanov Death Site** CHURCH
(Место убийства Романовых; ul Karla Libknekhta & ul Tolmachyova 34; ⏱dawn-dusk) The massive Byzantine-style **Church upon the Blood** (Храм на Крови; ☎343-371 6168; ul Tolmachyova 34) dominates this site where Tsar Nicholas II, his wife and children were murdered by Bolsheviks on the night of 16 July 1918. Nearby, the pretty wooden **Chapel of the Revered Martyr Grand Princess Yelizaveta Fyodorovna** (⏱10am-6pm Mon-Fri) honours the imperial family's great-aunt and faithful friend.

The executions took place in the basement of a local engineer's house, known as Dom Ipatyeva (named for its owner, Nikolay Ipatyev). During the Soviet period, the building housed a local museum of atheism, but it was demolished in 1977 by then governor Boris Yeltsin, who feared it would attract monarchist sympathisers, and for many years the site was a vacant block marked by a small cross and the wooden chapel to Grand Princess Yelizaveta Fyodorovna. Yelizaveta Fyodorovna was a pious nun who met an even worse end than the other Romanovs when she was thrown down a mineshaft, poisoned with gas and buried.

Rastorguev-Kharitonov Mansion HISTORIC BUILDING
(Усадьба Расторгуев-Харитонова; ul Karla Libknekhta 44) Situated across the road from the site where the Romanov family were executed, this mansion dates from the late 18th and early 19th centuries and has a pretty park behind it.

Ascension Church CHURCH
(Вознесенская церковь; ul Klary Tsetkin 11; ⏱dawn-dusk) The restored late-18th-century Ascension Church is the oldest in Yekaterinburg and rises up moodily alongside parkland perfect for a stroll.

Yekaterinburg

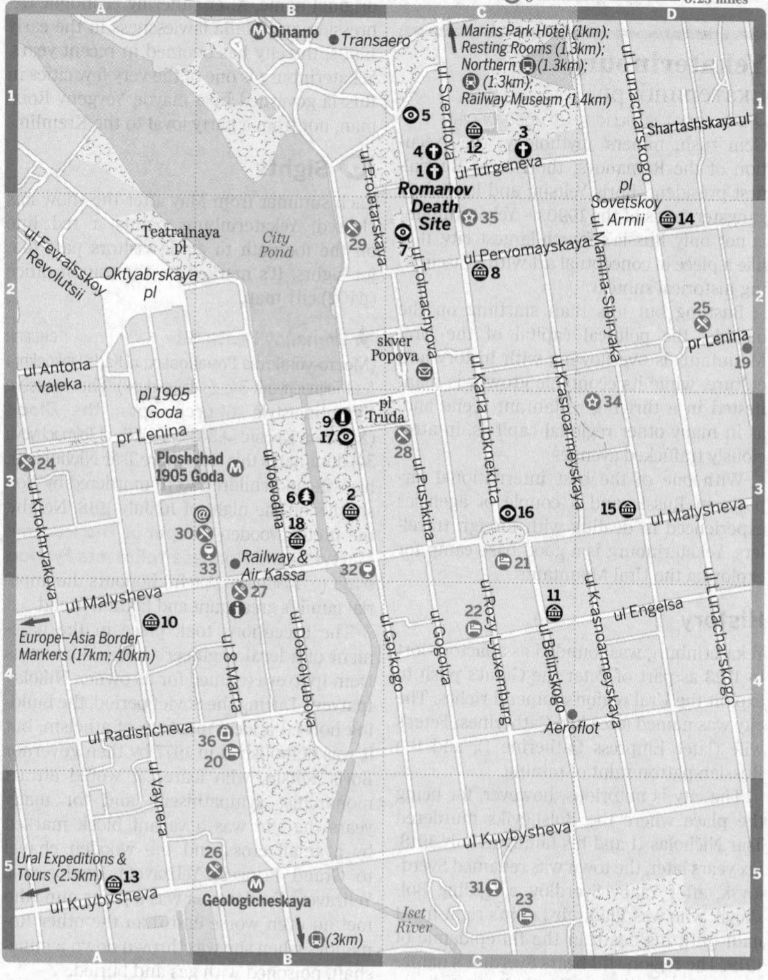

Istorichesky Skver PARK

The prettiest and most lively part of Yekaterinburg in summer is the landscaped parkland alongside the City Pond (Gorodskoy prud), where pr Lenina crosses a small dam. This was where Yekaterinburg began back in 1723.

The **Monument to the Founders of Yekaterinburg** (Памятник основателям Екатеринбурга) standing on one side of the square depicts founders Vasily Tatishchev and George Wilhelm de Gennin. The old **water tower** (Водонапорная башня) here is one of the city's oldest structures.

Yekaterinburg Museum of Fine Arts ART GALLERY

(Екатеринбургский музей изобразительных искусств; ☎343-371 0626; www.emii.ru; ul Voevodina 5; admission ₽150; ⊙11am-7pm Tue & Fri-Sun, to 8pm Wed & Thu) The star exhibit of the Museum of Fine Arts is its elaborate Kasli Iron Pavilion, which won prizes in the 1900 Paris Expo. The museum has a good collection of icons, paintings and decorative art, whereas the **Vaynera branch** (☎343-371 0626; www.emii.ru; ul Vaynera 11; admission ₽150; ⊙11am-7pm Tue & Fri-Sun, to 8pm Wed & Thu) has a small collection of 20th-century Rus-

Yekaterinburg

Top Sights

1 Romanov Death Site ... C1

Sights

2 Architecture and Design History Museum ... B3
3 Ascension Church ... C1
4 Chapel of the Revered Martyr Grand Princess Yelizaveta Fyodorovna ... C1
5 Church upon the Blood ... C1
6 Istorichesky Skver ... B3
7 Literary Quarter ... C2
8 Metenkov House-Museum of Photography ... C2
9 Monument to the Founders of Yekaterinburg ... B3
10 Museum of Fine Arts - Vaynera Branch ... A4
11 Nevyansk Icon Museum ... C4
12 Rastorguev- Kharitonov mansion ... C1
13 Ural Geological Museum ... A5
14 Urals Military History Museum ... D2
15 Urals Mineralogical Museum ... D3
16 Vysotsky Viewing Platform ... C3
17 Water Tower ... B3
18 Yekaterinburg Museum of Fine Arts ... B3

Activities, Courses & Tours

19 Ekaterinburg Guide Centre ... D2

Sleeping

20 Hotel Chekhov ... B4
21 Hotel Tsentralny ... C3
22 Novotel Yekaterinburg Centre ... C4
23 Red Star Hostel ... C5

Eating

24 Dacha ... A3
25 Khmeli Suneli ... D2
26 Nigora ... B5
27 Pozharka ... B4
28 Rosy Jane ... C3
29 Stolle ... B2
30 Thank God It's Friday ... B3
Vertikal ... (see 16)

Drinking & Nightlife

31 Ben Hall ... C5
32 Dr Scotch ... B3
33 New Bar ... B3

Entertainment

34 Opera & Ballet Theatre ... D3
35 Philharmonic ... C2

Shopping

36 Grinvich ... B4

sian avant-garde works and mostly low-key changing exhibitions.

Vysotsky Viewing Platform NOTABLE BUILDING
(ul Malysheva 51; viewing platform ₽250-300, museum free; ⏲viewing platform 1-11pm, museum 10am-7pm Wed-Sat, 11am-6pm Sun) Take the lift up 54 floors and 180m to the viewing platform for one of Russia's best urban panoramas. Children under 15 must be accompanied by an adult. The name of the tower is a pun on the Russian word for 'high' and the name of the singer Vladimir Vysotsky. A small museum is dedicated to 'Russia's raspy Dylan' here, with his original Mercedes.

Architecture & Design History Museum INDUSTRIAL MUSEUM
(Музей истории архитектуры и дизайна; ☎343-371 3369; ul Gorkogo 4a; ⏲11am-6pm Tue-Sat) Situated on Istorichesky skver (Historical Sq), this museum is where the first ironworks was established in Yekaterinburg in 1723. Today the 19th-century factory and mint building here house machinery and industrial technology used in the mining industry from the 18th and 19th centuries to WWII. Note that the museum was closed for restoration during our visit, but is expected to reopen in 2015.

Literary Quarter NEIGHBOURHOOD
(www.ompu.ur.ru) Located north of skver Popova, the Literary Quarter features restored wooden houses, some of them now museums about celebrated local writers such as Dmitry Mamina-Sibiryak and Pavel Bazhov; a full list of museums is on the website.

Urals Mineralogical Museum MUSEUM
(Уральский минералогический музей; ☎343-219 0388; ul Krasnoarmeyskaya 1a; admission ₽100; ⏲11am-7pm Mon-Fri, to 5pm Sat & Sun) A private collection offering a stunning introduction to the region's semiprecious stones, located in the Bolshoy Ural Hotel.

Ural Geological Museum MUSEUM
(Уральский геологический музей; ☎343-257 4938; http://ugm.ursmu.ru; ul Khokhryakova 85; admission ₽120; ⏲11am-5.30pm Tue-Sat) Over 500 minerals from the Ural Mountains region and a collection of meteorites. It's inside the Urals State Mining University.

Military Technology Museum MUSEUM
(Музей военной техники «Боевая слава Урала»; www.ugmk.com/ru/value/mvt; ul Lenina 1, in Verkhnyaya Pyshma; admission exhibition hall ₽100, outdoor exhibition free) This vast indoor and open-air collection of tanks and armoured vehicles is the best of the bunch of military museums in and around Yekaterinburg, located on the northern outskirts in Verkhnyaya Pyshma. Take bus 111 or *marshrutky* 111 or 111a from stop 'Kinotsentr Zarya' (at 'Uralmash' metro station) to 'Zavodskaya'.

Urals Military History Museum MUSEUM
(Военно-исторический музей Урала; ☎343-350 1742; http://ugvim.ru; ul Pervomayskaya 27; admission ₽50; ⊙9am-4pm Thu-Sun, to 8pm Wed) Worthwhile for buffs, this military museum has two halls, one dedicated to the Urals Volunteer Tank Corp. In the yard is a collection of tanks and planes.

Metenkov House-Museum of Photography MUSEUM
(Музей Фотографии; ☎343-371 0637; ul Karla Libknekhta 36; admission ₽150; ⊙10am-6pm Mon-Fri, from 11am Sat & Sun) Features several evocative photos of old Yekaterinburg and changing exhibitions.

Nevyansk Icon Museum MUSEUM
(Музей Невянская икона; ☎343-220 6650; ul Engelsa 15; ⊙noon-8pm Wed-Sun) FREE Excellent icons from the 17th to the 20th centuries, from the local Nevyansk school.

Railway Museum MUSEUM
(Железнодорожный музей; ul Chelyuskintsev; ☎343-358 4222; ul Chelyuskintsev; admission ₽100; ⊙10am-6pm Tue-Sat) Railway buffs will enjoy the good collection here, housed in and around the old train station, dating from 1881. Exhibits highlight the history of the railroad in the Urals, including a re-creation of the office of the Soviet-era railway director.

Tours

Ekaterinburg Guide Centre ADVENTURE TOURS
(Екатеринбургский центр гидов; ☎343-384 0048; www.ekaterinburgguide.com; office 12, pr Lenina 52/1) Organises English-language tours of the city and trips into the countryside, including Nevyansk, Tobolsk and Nizhnyaya Sinyachikha, as well as winter activities and summer hiking and rafting expeditions. Day trips cost anything between ₽1500 and ₽8800, depending on destination and numbers. It also books hotel and hostel accommodation, often at discount rates.

The centre can also take you to the historic but hard-to-reach Verkhoturye. If taking the seven-hour tour to Nevyansk and the nearby old potters' village of Tavolgi, ask to stop on the way at the village of Kunary, where a local blacksmith has turned his wooden *izba* into a masterpiece of naive art.

Yekaterinburg For You TOUR GUIDE
(☎8-912-280 0870; www.yekaterinburg4u.ru) Experienced guide and journalist Luba Suslyakova offers a range of city and regional tours, including Nevyansk and the pottery town of Tavolgi, winter dog sledding, and the eclectic Mafia Tour, which takes visitors into the graveyards where Yekaterinburg's rival 'Uralmash' and 'Central' gangsters of the 1990s rest in peace.

Ural Expeditions & Tours ADVENTURE TOURS
(☎343-382 5366; http://welcome-ural.ru; office 4, ul Baumana 6; ⊙11am-5pm Mon-Fri) This group of geologists who graduated from the Sverdlovsk Mining Institute leads trekking, rafting and horse-riding trips to all parts of the Ural Mountains, including Taganay and Zyuratkul National Parks. English-speaking guides.

Sleeping

Contact Ekaterinburg Guide Centre for accommodation in its centrally located hostel rooms upstairs from the office, and other budget alternatives.

★**Red Star Hostel** HOSTEL $
(☎343-383 5684; www.redstarhostel.ru; ul Narodnoy Voli 69, off ul Rozy Lyuksemburg; 6-12-bed dm ₽550-650, d ₽1600) This excellent hostel opened in 2014 and has quickly established itself as a comfortable, very professionally run place, with 44 beds divided among male, female and mixed dorms, and a double with a large bed. The six-bed male dorm has no windows but good ceiling ventilation. It can process visa registration. Take trolleybus 1 or 9 from the train station to stop Kuybsheva.

Resting Rooms RESTING ROOMS $
(Комнаты отдыха; ☎343-358 5783; 4th fl; 12/24hr from ₽750/1200;) Book ahead as these fill fast.

★**Hotel Tsentralny** HOTEL $$
(Отель Центральный; ☎343-350 0505; www.hotelcentr.ru; ul Malysheva 74; s incl breakfast ₽3600-4680, d incl breakfast ₽4650-6120;) This historical hotel is housed in a grand art nouveau building in the heart of town, with excellent business-class and standard rooms.

Eating and nightlife are never far away from here. Trolleybuses 1 and 9 are among the many going there from the train station.

★**Hotel Chekhov** HOTEL **$$**
(Гостиница Чехов; ☑ 343-282 9737; http://chek-hov-hotel.ru; ul 8 Marta 32; s incl breakfast ₽4500-5500, d incl breakfast ₽5000-6000; 🛜) Hotel Chekhov is a newcomer to Yekaterinburg's hotel scene and offers modern, stylishly furnished rooms which make good use of exposed brick in a historic building . Take bus 23 from the train station to TRTs Grinvich.

Marins Park Hotel HOTEL **$$**
(Маринс Парк Отель; ☑ 343-228 0000; www.sv-hotel.ru; ul Chelyuskintsev 106; s incl breakfast ₽2320-3200, d incl breakfast ₽3120-4000; ❄🛜) Formerly known as the Sverdlovsk, Marins Park is quite successfully reinventing itself as a modern congress hotel; all rooms are small, and renovation in the cheaper ones is simply a coat of pastel paint, but others are modern and it has two enormous advantages: it's right across the road from the train station, and it does your laundry same-day for free.

HHotel Apartments APARTMENT **$$**
(HHotel Апартаменты; ☑ 343-219 5488; www.hhotel.ru; apt from ₽2300) Very centrally located apartments in new buildings for short stays of a couple of days or more.

Novotel Yekaterinburg Centre HOTEL **$$$**
(☑ 343-253 5383; http://novotel-ekaterinburg.ru; ul Engelsa 7; s incl breakfast ₽5900-7700, d incl breakfast ₽6900-8100, ste incl breakfast ₽9000; ⊖❄🛜) This excellent four-star chain hotel in the centre has variable rates and good deals online. The easiest way from the station is trolleybus 1 or 9 to ul Rozy Lyuksemburg stop.

✖ **Eating**

Ul 8 Marta between pr Lenina and ul Malysheva has lots of eating and drinking options, and ul Vaynera has a moderate choice of eateries.

★**Nigora** UZBEK **$**
(Нигора; ☑ 343-295 1417; http://nigora.ru; ul Kuybysheva 55; mains ₽200; ⏱noon-midnight) Yekaterinburg has several of these inexpensive Uzbek restaurants, all with young staff attired in Uzbek caps serving delicious Uzbek specialties. *Manty* (steamed, palm-sized dumplings), soups, sausages and shashlyk feature on the menu, including a very worthy lamb shashlyk.

Stolle CAFE, RUSSIAN **$**
(Штолле, Shtolle; ul Maxima Gorkogo 7a; pirogi from ₽100; ⏱10am-10pm Sun-Thu, to midnight Fri & Sat; ⊖🛜🍴) Stolle specialises in sweet and savoury Russian *pirozhki* (pies), which you can buy by weight at the counter to take away or enjoy here in a relaxed atmosphere to the gentle twinkling of jazz music.

Khmeli Suneli GEORGIAN **$$**
(Хмели Сунели; ☑ 343-350 6318; www.hmeli.ru; pr Lenina 69/10; mains ₽450; ⏱10am-midnight Mon-Thu, to 2am Fri, noon-2am Sat, noon-midnight Sun; ⊖🛜📱) This large Georgian restaurant has a relaxed feel and is currently the best of its ilk in Yekaterinburg, serving a large range of soups, salads, fish and red-meat dishes and delicious shashlyk.

Thank God It's Friday INTERNATIONAL, BAR **$$**
(ul 8 Marta 8; burgers ₽325-535, steaks ₽650-1000; ⏱9am-2am Mon-Wed, to 4am Thu, to 8am Fri & Sat, 11am-2am Sun; ⊖🛜📱) 'TGIF' is loud and boisterous, has staff who introduce themselves by name before they take your order, and kitsch decoration many will know from other branches. The food's capably prepared but it's the atmosphere that draws people here for drinks and meals.

Pozharka PUB FOOD **$$**
(ul Malysheva 44; mains ₽450; ⏱noon-midnight Sun-Thu, to 2am Fri & Sat) Pozharka is popular for its range of 15 beers and vast menu of pub food, including seafood, red meats and poultry and lots of sausage dishes.

★**Rosy Jane** PUB **$$$**
(pr Lenina 34; mains ₽600-1500; ⏱6am-4am; 🛜) This English-style pub aims at the New Russian drinking and eating crowd, who grace the bar and perch at polished wood tables noshing on steak and other very well-prepared Russian and international dishes. Steaks are top of the range.

Dacha INTERNATIONAL, RUSSIAN **$$$**
(Дача; ☑ 343-379 3569; pr Lenina 20a, enter from ul Khokhryakova; business lunches ₽300, mains ₽500-800; ⏱noon-midnight) Each room in this elegant restaurant is decorated like a Russian country house, from the casual garden to the more formal dining room.

Vertikal INTERNATIONAL **$$$**
(Вертикаль; ☑ 343-200 5151; www.vertical51.ru; ul Malysheva 51, fl 51; mains ₽850-2100; ⏱noon-midnight Sun-Thu, to 2am Fri & Sat) Located on the 51st floor of the Vysotsky tower, Vertikal offers a formal, upmarket

experience of pan-European dishes and some steaks, and its trump card: sensational views over town. Reserve ahead.

Drinking

★New Bar BAR
(ul 8 Marta 8; ⏲10am-2am Mon-Thu & Sun, to 6am Fri & Sat; 📶) Relaxed art-scene cafe and bar on the top floor of Mytny Dvor mall.

Dr Scotch PUB
(ul Malysheva 56a; ⏲noon-2am) Doc Scotch is one of the liveliest pubs in town and has the advantage of being very central. Expect lots of wood in the interior and even more beer.

Ben Hall PUB
(☎343-251 6368; ul Narodnoy Voli 65; mains ₽450; ⏲noon-2am Sun-Thu, to 4am Fri & Sat) This popular pub hosts local rock bands at weekends, its owner being a well-known musician. Trams 15 and 27 from Operny Teatr or along pr Lenina to Tsirk (Цирк) drop you close by.

Entertainment

Philharmonic CLASSICAL MUSIC
(Филармония; ☎tickets 343-371 4682; http://filarmonia.e-burg.ru; ul Karla Libknekhta 38; tickets from ₽100) Yekaterinburg's top venue for the classical performing arts often hosts visiting directors and soloists, as well as the regular performances of the acclaimed Ural Mountains academic orchestra.

Opera & Ballet Theatre OPERA, BALLET
(Театр оперы и балета; ☎343-350 8101; www.uralopera.ru; pr Lenina 45a; tickets from ₽100) This ornate baroque theatre is a lovely place to see the Russian classics of a high standard.

Shopping

Grinvich SHOPPING MALL
(www.grinvich.com/; ul 8 Marta 46; ⏲10am-10pm) This enormous shopping complex near the ul Vaynera pedestrian zone is an oasis away from the traffic.

Information

Main Post Office (Почтамт; pr Lenina 39; per MB ₽2.50; ⏲8am-10pm Mon-Fri, 9am-6pm Sat & Sun) With internet.

Tourist Information Service (TIS; ☎343-222 2445; http://its.ekburg.ru; ul 8 Marta 21; ⏲10am-7pm Mon-Fri) Helpful official city tourist office, with free maps of town showing the Red Line walking trail to major sights.

Tourist Information Service (☎343-222 2445; http://its.ekburg.ru; Koltsovo Airport, International terminal, fl 2; ⏲10am-7pm Mon-Fri) Airport branch of the city tourist office.

Traveller's Coffee (ul 8 Marta 8; ⏲8am-midnight; 📶) Free internet with an order.

Getting There & Away

AIR

The main airport is **Koltsovo** (☎343-226 8582; www.koltsovo.ru), 15km southeast of the city centre. Frequent services include Moscow, Novosibirsk, Krasnoyarsk, Irkutsk, Khabarovsk, Ufa, St Petersburg, Samara, Vladivostok and a host of Black Sea hubs. International services include Frankfurt am Main (Germany), Beijing (China), Prague (Czech Republic) and Astana (Kazakhstan). **Transaero** (Трансаэро; ☎343-287 0873; http://transaero.ru; ul Nikolaya Nikonova 6; ⏲9am-8pm) and **Aeroflot** (☎343-356 5570; www.aeroflot.ru; ⏲9am-6pm Mon-Fri) have offices here.

BUS

The **main bus station** (Южный автовокзал, Yuzhny avtovokzal; ☎343-257 1260; ul 8 Marta 145) is 3km south of the city centre, but most buses pass the northern bus station (Северный автовокзал; Severny avtovokzal), conveniently located by the train station. Here you can catch frequent buses to Chelyabinsk (₽561, four hours) and Alapaevsk (₽297, three hours, five daily). There is also a bus station at Koltsovo airport serving destinations in the Sverdlovsk region and Chelyabinsk (₽561, 3½ hours, frequent). Touts sell tickets in minibuses to Chelyabinsk (₽700, 2½ hours, about every hour) at the main bus station.

TRAIN

Yekaterinburg – sometimes still called 'Sverdlovsk' on timetables – is a major rail junction with connections to all stops on the trans-Siberian route. All trains to Moscow stop at either Perm (₽1000, 5½ hours) or Kazan (₽1580, 14½ hours). Frequent trains to/from Moscow include the *Ural* (₽3777, 26 hours, every couple of days) via Kazan. Heading east, the next major stops are Omsk (₽1580, 14 hours) and Novosibirsk (₽2434, 22 hours). You can buy tickets at outlets throughout the city, including the convenient **Railway & Air Kassa** (ЖД и Авиа кассы; ☎343-371 0400; www.bilet-vsegda.ru; ul Malysheva 31d; ⏲24hr).

Getting Around

Bus 1 links the Sverdlovsk-Passazhirskaya train station and Koltsovo airport (one hour) from 6.30am to 11.30pm. *Marshrutka* 26 goes from the airport to metro pl 1905 Goda. *Marshrutka* 39 goes to metro Geologicheskaya.

Many trolleybuses such as 1, 3 and 9 and *marshrutky* (pay on board) run along ul Sverdlova/

STRADDLING THE CONTINENTS

The Ural Mountains have numerous monuments marking the border between Europe and Asia. Interestingly, the border was thought to be the Don River by the Ancient Greeks, but Yekaterinburg's founder Vasily Tatishchev drew it at the Ural Mountains in the mid-18th century, based on ideas of the day.

One of the more historic monuments is located 40km west of Yekaterinburg near Pervouralsk. It was erected in 1837 to commemorate a visit by Tsar Alexander II, who drank wine there and inadvertently began a favourite pastime of locals – drinking a glass in Europe and another glass in Asia (as if you needed an excuse!). To reach the monument, take a taxi (about ₽1000 return if you order in advance) to Pervouralsk. Expect to pay another ₽200 per hour for the driver to wait. Very frequent bus 150 leaves from the Severny bus station to Pervouralsk (₽87; platform 9).

The city has erected a new border marker, more conveniently located just 17km out of Yekaterinburg and looking a little like a mini Eiffel Tower. This one is more kitsch, but a taxi will take you out there for about ₽600 return, with an hour at the monument.

Expect to pay ₽3600 to ₽4000 as an individual (less in groups) with reliable outfits like Ekaterinburg Guide Centre (p400) or Luba Suslyakova (p400).

ul Karla Libknekhta between the train station and pr Lenina. Marshrutka 55 connects the train station with pl 1905 Goda, continuing along ul 8 Marta to the Grinvich shopping centre. Bus 24 runs along ul 8 Marta to the Northern Bus Station alongside the train station. Trams 13, 15 and 18 cover long stretches of pr Lenina.

A single metro line runs between the north-eastern suburbs and the city centre, with stops at the train station (Uralskaya), pl 1905 Goda and ul Kuybysheva near the synagogue (Geologicheskaya).

Around Yekaterinburg

Ganina Yama — Ганина Яма

Monastery of the Holy Martyrs CHRISTIAN
(☎343-217 9146) After the Romanov family was shot in the cellar of Dom Ipatyeva, their bodies were discarded in the depths of the forests of Ganina Yama, 16km northeast of Yekaterinburg. In their honour, the Orthodox Church has built the exquisite Monastery of the Holy Martyrs at this pilgrimage site. Expect to pay around ₽3600 to ₽4200 as an individual (less in groups) on tours conducted by Ekaterinburg Guide Centre or Luba Syuslakova.

The nearest train station to Ganina Yama is Shuvakish, served by *elektrichka* (suburban train; ₽46, 30 minutes, every one to two hours) from the central station. Buses from the Northern Bus Station (Severny) run out here at 3.30pm Saturday and 10am Sunday (platform 11), returning at 8pm Saturday and 11.30am Sunday.

Nevyansk & Around — Невьянск

The small town of Nevyansk is in the heart of the former patrimony of the Demidovs, a family of industrialists who effectively controlled much of the Ural Mountains and who received Peter I's blessing to develop the region. At their most decadent stage, they bought the Italian feudal title of Count San-Donato.

Nevyansk History & Architecture Museum MUSEUM
(☎excursion booking 343-562 2056; http://museum-nev.ru; pl Revolyutsii 2; museum ₽70, Nevyansk tower excursion per group of 1-5 people ₽1500; ⊙admission museum 9am-6pm Tue & Thu-Sun, to 8pm Wed, excursions 9am-7pm Apr-Sep) The main highlight in Nevyansk is the Nevyansk Leaning Tower, an impressive structure flanked by an equally impressive Saviour-Transfiguration Cathedral. The worthwhile excursions (in Russian) into the tower are the only way to climb up for the fantastic views unless you can latch onto a group.

Byngi HOMESTAY $$
(☎8-922 158 2183, in Germany Oct-Mar +49 (0)421-40 89 66 60; www.semken.eu; ul Frunse 25, in Byngi; s/d €48/63, with full board €70/107; ⊙May-Sep) Seven kilometres from Nevyansk, the lovely Byngi is the perfect place to experience Russian life in an Old Believers' village. Here an entrepreneurial German and his Russian wife have converted an *izba* into a guesthouse in the main building and erected four summer yurts in the yard. Excursions are available, and on a visit you will be very

much integrated eclectically into local life in and around the village. Elektrichka (₽115, 1½–2½ hours, 9 daily) serve Nevyansk.

ℹ Getting There & Away

Elektrichka (₽115, 2½ hours, nine daily) – some of them express trains (1½ hours) – run to Nevyansk, most bound for Nizhny Tagil.

Nizhnyaya Sinyachikha & Around
Нижняя Синячиха

Architecture Museum MUSEUM
(☑ 343-467 5118; admission ₽100/160; ⊙ 10am-5pm) The pretty village of Nizhnyaya Sinyachikha, about 150km northeast of Yekaterinburg and 12km north of the town of Alapaevsk, is home to an excellent open-air Architecture Museum. Here you find 15 traditional Siberian log buildings, featuring displays of period furniture, tools and domestic articles. Five buses a day go to Alapaevsk (₽297, three hours) from Yekaterinburg (Yuzhny Avtovokzal). A taxi (☑ 343-463 0703; one way from Alpaevsk ₽250-300) can take you to the museum.

While in town, visit the stone cathedral, which houses a good collection of regional folk art. This impressive ensemble of art and architecture was gathered from around the Ural Mountains and recompiled by the single-handed efforts of Ivan Samoylov, an enthusiastic local historian.

REPUBLIC OF BASHKORTOSTAN & CHELYABINSK REGION

Ufa Уфа

☑ 347 / POP 1.03 MILLION / ⊙ MOSCOW +2HR
Ufa is the capital of the autonomous Republic of Bashkortostan (Республика Башкортостан), home of the Bashkirs, a Muslim Turkic people who dominated most of the southern Ural Mountains before Russian colonisation. Although they're only a third of the republic's population, you can hear their lispy language spoken on the streets of Ufa, in rural areas and on the radio. Substantial hydrocarbon reserves have turned Bashkortostan into something of an oil khanate.

Although Ufa has no major sights, you can spend a pleasant day walking through the streets where wooden cottages are reflected in glass office blocks.

Ufa's main thoroughfare is ul Lenina. Pick up the *Ufa City Transport Map* (Схема городского транспорта Уфы; ₽43) from the **Belaya Reka Dom Knigi** (ul Lenina 24; ⊙ 9.30am-9pm Mon-Fri, 10am-8pm Sat & Sun) bookshop. The map has all routes (with a few inaccuracies) and stops, and doubles as a useful street map.

Note that ul Zaki Balidi is sometimes called by its old name, ul Frunze.

⊙ Sights & Activities

Trading Arcade HISTORIC BUILDING
(Гостинный Двор; ul Lenina) The focus of appealing ul Lenina is the 19th-century Trading Arcade, set back from the street. Behind the renovated facade is a luxuriously marble-lined shopping mall full of boutiques and cafes. Take any *marshrutka* (fixed route minibus) going to the stop Gostiny Dvor (Гостиний двор).

Nesterov Art Gallery ART GALLERY
(Картинная Галерея Нестерова; ☑ 347-322 9780; ul Gogolya 27; admission ₽70; ⊙ 10am-6pm Tue-Sat) This small but interesting gallery contains a fabulous collection of artwork by Ufa native Mikhail Nesterov and 50 paintings by Ukrainian futurist David Burlyuk, which he left in a Bashkir village when escaping from the Red Army during the Civil War. It's located two blocks west of ul Lenina, on the corner of ul Pushkina.

Bashkortostan National Museum MUSEUM
(Национальный музей Башкортостана; http://museumrb.ru; ul Sovetskaya 14; admission ₽150; ⊙ 11am-6pm Tue-Fri & Sun, 1-9pm Sat, closed Mon) Housed in a renovated art nouveau building behind the government office, the National Museum has two rooms downstairs dedicated to the natural environment and rooms upstairs on culture. The exhibits on Bashkir history and current events are the most interesting; all descriptions are in Russian only. Walk a few minutes south along ul Lenina from the Trading Arcade to ul Pushkina.

Tengri ADVENTURE TOURS
(Тенгри; ☑ 347-251 7215, 347-279 6009; www.tengri.ru; 2nd fl, Gostinny Dvor; ⊙ 9am-8pm Mon-Fri, 11am-4pm Sat) Offers a wide range of inexpensive adventure trips in the southern Urals.

🛏 Sleeping & Eating

Hostel Afrika HOSTEL $
(Хостел Африка; ☑ 347-266 2099; www.ufahostel.ru; ul Karla Marksa 69; 4-10 bed dm ₽500-750, tw ₽2500; ❀ ☎) This hostel run by a Russian couple is used to putting up foreigners.

WORTH A TRIP

EASTERN BASHKORTOSTAN

The highly industrial city of Magnitogorsk is of limited interest to travellers, but once you leave it you enter eastern Bashkortostan and the southern Ural Mountains, a region where picture-perfect birch groves and large blue lakes fill depressions between gentle grass-covered hills and the mountain ranges. The region is a favourite locally for rafting, horse riding and skiing.

Sanatorium Yubileyny (☎hotel 351-925 5550, in Magnitogorsk 351-926 6782; www.bannoe.mmk.ru; incl full board s ₽1850-2300, d ₽2350; ⊖📶) Located in Lake Bannoye (Yakhty-Kul in Bashkir), 43km from Magnitogorsk, this health resort is one of several good options in the village and around the lake.

Abzakovo Bungalo Club (☎347-927 3916; www.bungalo.net.ru; Proezd Gorny 8; s/d incl breakfast from ₽2000/2500; ⊖) This popular resort has skiing in winter months and is located 20km along the road towards Ufa from Lake Bannoyeis Prices are for the summer season and can double in winter. Abzakovo (also called Novoabzakovo, is not to be confused with the small village of Abzakovo even further down the road).

Beloretsk (Белорецк), 30km from Novoabzakovo along the road to Ufa, is an access point for several interesting country lodges specialising in horse-riding and rafting trips.

Turbaza Malinovka (☎8-906-370 7150, 347-9224 6306; www.go-ural.com/malinovka; s/d from ₽800/1600) Located 10km away from Beloretsk (₽400 by taxi; call ☎34792-56 677) under the Malinovaya (Raspberry) mountain, this place has several log houses sleeping up to about 17 people, plus a two-to-four-person dacha. Use of the sauna costs from ₽700 per hour. A range of tours is offered, including two-hour horse rides for ₽800 per person, but if you contact them directly they can stitch together a package for you.

Transport

Magnitogorsk–Ufa Daily train service (*kupe* – 2nd class – from ₽700, 9½ hours)

Magnitogorsk–Chelyabinsk Buses every 30 minutes (₽600, five hours, every hour)

Magnitogorsk–Bannoye *Marshrutky* (fixed-route minibuses) from train station (₽40, 40 minutes, frequent)

Magnitogorsk–Beloretsk Hourly buses (₽90, 1½ hours, two hourly), via Novoabzakovo station

Ufa–Beloretsk The nightly Ufa–Sibay train calls at Beloretsk at 6.10am local time (₽620, six hours)

Rooms are bright and there's a communal kitchen. It doesn't do registrations. Bus 74 runs here to the stop Park im. Yakutova (Парк им. Якутова) from the train station.

Resting Rooms RESTING ROOMS $
(Комнаты отдыха; ☎347-229 1756; 2nd fl.; from 24hr ₽750; ⊖) No reduced price for 12-hour stays.

Hotel Azimut HOTEL $$
(☎347-235 9000; http://azimuthotels.com; pr Oktyabya 81; s/d incl breakfast from ₽3300/4100; ⊖❄@📶) Located 5km from the central area, Azimut is a comfortable, contemporary hotel with good connections to the centre and train station. Breakfast is available from ₽400. Two excellent places are very close by: the restaurant Burzhuika (p406) and the live-music pub Rock's Cafe (p406). Take buses or *marshrutka* 226, 249 or 290 from the centre or 74 from the train station to stop 'Gossovet' (Госсовет).

Hotel Agidel HOTEL $$
(Гостиница Агидель; ☎347-272 5680; www.agidelhotel.ru; ul Lenina 14; s incl breakfast ₽3400, d incl breakfast ₽4000-8000; ⊖❄📶) Rooms are comfortable, tastefully furnished and fully renovated in this centrally located hotel almost opposite Gostinny Dvor.

Pyshka CAFETERIA, TATAR $
(Пышка; ul Revolyutsionnaya 32; meal ₽200; ⏲9am-9pm Mon-Sat, to 8pm Sun) This branch of the Pyshka chain serves classic Bashkir dishes such as *belish* (meat pie) and *tukmas* (chicken broth). Also try one of the pastries from the bakery section. Take any bus or *marshrutka* from the centre to the stop TK Tsentralny (ТК Центральный).

WORTH A TRIP

LAKE TURGOYAK

Although it's not as isolated or as beautiful as other lakes in the region such as Lake Zyuratkul, **Lake Turgoyak** (http://turgoyak.com), near the factory town of Miass, is surrounded by mountains and provides a tranquil getaway for the locals of Chelyabinsk.

Golden Beach (☎3513-298 091; www.goldenbeach.ru; weekday/weekend s ₽4800/5800, d ₽5300/6300;) This is one of the prime resorts on the lake and has several large log-house buildings with joyfully polychromic rooms, each with an individual design. A Chinese medicine centre is on the premises. Cheaper deals are available with early booking or in low-demand periods.

Golden Beach can organise boat trips to St Vera's Island, the location of an ancient site abandoned about 9000 years ago and later used by Old Believers in the 19th century. Excursions last two hours, including the 30-minute-each-way trip, and take in monoliths and small caves.

Taxi Miass (☎3513-284 949) Takes you from Miass to Golden Beach hotel for about ₽250 to ₽400 (no other transport goes there). Miass can be reached by distance trains and regular *elektrichka* (₽198, two hours) from Chelyabinsk.

Burzhuika INTERNATIONAL, RUSSIAN $$
(Буржуйка; ☎347-257 2585; www.burzhuynka.com; pr Oktyabrya 79/1; soups ₽250, mains ₽480, salads from ₽290; noon-late;) Ufa's hippest location for dinner, drink or a hookah is located outside the centre on pl Lenina, near the Hotel Azimut. The food is excellent and served in well-sized portions. Take buses or *marshrutka* 226, 249 or 290 from the centre or 74 from the train station to stop 'Gossovet' (Госсовет).

Shinok Solokha UKRAINIAN $$
(Шинок солоха; ☎347-272 5333; Kommunisticheskaya ul 47; mains ₽300; noon-11pm;) A homely Ukrainian cottage restaurant. One in a row of themed restaurants, including a decent Czech beer pub.

Drinking & Entertainment

Coffee-Time CAFE
(Кофе-Тайм; ☎347-220 435; ul Oktyabrskoy Revolyutsii 3; coffee from ₽90; 24hr;) One of Ufa's most popular spots for a coffee break, with jazz music, B&W photos and fashionable young folk.

Rock's Cafe LIVE MUSIC
(☎347- 292 7927; pr Oktyabrya 79/1, set back from street; free except for larger acts; 7pm-2am Sun-Thu, to 6pm Fri & Sat) FREE Not to be missed for live gigs, Rock's lives up to its name with local and national acts, ranging from the Monday acoustic night to punk and metal.

Bashkir Opera & Ballet Theatre THEATRE
(Башкирский театр оперы и балета; ☎tickets 347-272 7712; www.bashopera.ru; ul Lenina 5/1; performances ₽150-400; ticket office 9am-9.30pm) The theatre where Rudolf Nureyev took his first steps.

Lights of Ufa LIVE MUSIC
(Огни Уфы; ☎347-290 8690; http://ogni-ufa.ru; ul 50 let Oktyabrya 19; noon-2am, microbrewery closed Sun) Concert hall, disco, sports bar and microbrewery in one. From ul Lenina, take any bus north to 'Dom Pechati'. See website for concert prices.

Information

Post Office (Почтамт; ul Lenina 28; per hour ₽39; 8am-10pm Mon-Fri, 9am-6pm Sat & Sun, internet 8am-5pm Mon-Thu, to 4pm Fri) Internet left from the entrance.

Getting There & Away

The train station is 2km north of the centre at the end of ul Karla Marksa. There are daily trains to Moscow (₽2237, 27 hours) some via Samara (₽1043-1645, 8½ hours). Trains also go to Ulyanovsk (₽1157, 14 hours) in the west and Chelyabinsk (₽997, 9½ hours) in the east. There is an overnight service to Magnitogorsk (₽1332, nine hours). Air and train tickets are available from **Sputnik Yulgash** (Спутник Юлгаш; ☎347-273 8666; www.sputnik-ufa.ru; ul Tsyurupy 93; 9am-8pm Mon-Fri, 11am-5pm Sat), including a daily flight to Kazan.

Getting Around

The handy if convoluted bus 101 route snakes between the train station (climb the high steps outside to the top) and the airport, via Yuzhny Vokzal bus station and Gostinny Dvor on ul Lenina.

Ufa to Chelyabinsk

It might hearten (or annoy) Australian travellers, but the area west of Chelyabinsk is called Sinegorye (Blue Mountains). Unlike its down-under namesake, it is conifer not eucalyptus forest that makes the low, gently sloped ranges of the southern Ural Mountains look like frozen blue waves. Also blue are the large placid lakes between the mountains, of which the most lauded are Lakes Turgoyak and Zyuratkul. The lakes and two national parks are accessed from stations along the Ufa–Chelyabinsk railway.

Zyuratkul National Park Национальный парк Зюраткуль

Zyuratkul National Park NATURE RESERVE
(☎Satka headquarters 35161-42 901; park levy per day ₽40) This very remote and quietly beautiful part of the Ural Mountains is a great place for hiking, climbing the Zyuratkul range, swimming in a lake, going to a *banya* (hot bath) and sleeping in a log house. If you stay on the lake, you may wake up and feel rather like Henry Thoreau at Walden Pond.

The **national park** is dominated by several forest-covered ranges and Lake Zyuratkul, which translates from Bashkir as 'heart lake'. This is best observed from the Zyuratkul range nearby – an easy four-hour hike along a boardwalk through the forest and then along the mostly well-marked mountain path, though the *kurum* (path of loose rocks) at the top can be challenging in wet weather. Access is through the wooden arch on the main road, 100m before the lake and about a 10-minute walk back from Ecopark Zyuratkul.

Sleeping

Zyuratkul National Park Guesthouses CAMPGROUND $
(☎Satka headquarters 35161-42 901; www.zuratkul.ru; cottages from ₽500-600) Zyuratkul National Park guesthouses are a 10-minute walk along the main road curving around the lake shore from the settlement around Ecopark Zyuratkul. Staff can also organise overnight guided expeditions into the park.

Ecopark Zyuratkul HOTEL, RESORT $$
(☎8-902-894 9269, 8-922-716 1944; Lake Zyuratkul; r without bathroom ₽2800, cottages sleeping 4/5/7 ₽12,000/15,000/21,000) This resort consists of cottages and a simple hotel. Stays of less than two nights cost about 20% more. You'll find yourself in a realm of manicured lawns, asphalt paths, tennis courts, large modern cottages and a restaurant, but it is

GETTING TO ZYURATKUL

Getting to Zyuratkul National Park takes a little planning. Coming from Chelyabinsk, catch the bus to Satka and then a taxi to Zyuratkul. Travelling from west to east, get off the train at Berdyaush, take a taxi to Zyuratkul and then a taxi either back to Satka for the Chelyabinsk bus or to Berdyaush for the train.

Trains to Berdyaush

The main way from Ufa or Chelyabinsk into Zyuratkul National Park is by long-distance train to Berdyaush (Ufa ₽911, 5½ hours; from Chelyabinsk, seat ₽376, 3¾ hours). The town of Suleya (west of Berdyaush) is also an option.

Marshrutky Between Berdyaush & Satka

Amost hourly minibuses daily leave Berdyaush from the bus station (near the train station) and leave Satka from the main bus station.

Buses Between Satka & Chelyabinsk

At least four buses go daily to/from Chelyabinsk Severny bus station (₽365, four hours).

Taxis to Lake Zyuratkul

There are no *marshrutky* (fixed route minibuses) or buses to the lake, so you need to take a taxi – the best springboard is Berdyaush, but Satka (off the main line) is also good. Taxis from either cost roughly ₽900-1000 and take about an hour.

Satka taxi companies (☎8-904-803 1010, 8-922-236 8878) Book an hour or more ahead for taxis to the lake.

Ecopark Zyuratkul (p407) This tourist base can book taxis for you (one-way ₽1000 all up).

a well-run and friendly resort that offers a wide range of activities, including expeditions into the wilderness.

Taganay National Park Национальный парк Таганай

Dramatically set in a lake-filled valley, the otherwise gloomy town of Zlatoust serves as the gateway to one of the most popular national parks and hiking, mountain biking and rafting getaways in the Ural Mountains. Taganay National Park is a narrow 52km-long band containing a wide variety of landscapes, from flower-filled meadows to mountain tundra, as well as some of the southern Ural Mountains' notable ridges (Small, Middle and Big Taganay, and Itsyl).

Sleeping

Taganai Travel Turbaza LODGE $
(☎8-951 468 5475, 8-902 895 4989; Pushkinsky Poselok, Zlatoust; 4-/6-bed cottages ₽4000/₽6000) Located at the park's entrance, with spartan cottages and *banya* on the premises.

Hotel Bellmont HOTEL $$
(☎3513-655 700; www.bellmont.ru; ul Taganayskaya 194a, Zlatoust; s ₽1600-2990, d ₽2990-5200, ste ₽5200;) A good business-class option in Zlatoust with sauna and beauty treatments.

Information

Taganay Park Headquarters (☎3513-637 688; np-taganay@taganay.org; ul Shishkina 3a) The headquarters is located on the other side of Zlatoust from the national park and reached by *marshrutka* 33. The park administration can organise a stay at one of the *kordony* (forest lodges) inside the national park and at Taganai Travel's turbaza (p408).

Getting There & Around

Zlatoust is served by distance trains from Ufa on the Ufa–Chelyabinsk route (₽975, 6½ hours) and *elektrichka* or long-distance train from Chelyabinsk (from ₽304, three hours, frequent).

The park entrance is located on the outskirts of Zlatoust, reached from the train station by *marshrutka* 33. From its final stop, take the road leading towards the forest to a signposted turn.

Chelyabinsk Челябинск

☎351 / POP 1.13 MILLION / ⏲ MOSCOW +2HR

Industrial, earthy, like many Russian cities in shocking disrepair beyond the main squares and streets, and lacking high-profile sights, Chelyabinsk would at first glance seem to be a place best visited as a springboard rather than as a destination in itself. If you are doing the lakes and cities of the region, however, take the time to stay in this oft-overlooked and underrated city to get a taste of everyday Ural Mountains life.

Sights

Ulitsa Kirova STREET
Chelyabinsk's highlight is strolling down pedestrianised ul Kirova, paved with cobblestones. Life-sized bronze statues of local personages dot the street – look out for an Asian lad with a camel. The animal is the heraldic symbol of the Chelyabinsk region, signifying its importance as a fortress on the border with Asia.

Local Studies Museum MUSEUM
(ul Truda 100; admission Russian/foreigner ₽160/300; ⏲10am-7pm) At the northern end of ul Kirova, the modern Local Studies Museum uses natural light well to create an attractive exhibition space. Floor 1 has an unspectacular display on 20th-century history and a few household items, but the sections upstairs on the region's prehistory and fauna and flora are very worthwhile. Some explanations are in English.

Fine Arts Gallery ART GALLERY
(☎351-2630 934; ul Truda 92; admission Russian/foreigner ₽200/300; ⏲11am-7pm Tue-Sun) Containing a small and moderately interesting collection of European and Russian paintings and earthenware.

Sleeping

Yuzhny Ural HOTEL $
(☎351-247 4510; www.hotel74.ru; pr Lenina 52; s/d incl breakfast without bathroom ₽850/1600, r incl breakfast with bathroom ₽3500 ;) The higher-priced rooms in this hotel are shoddy and poor value for money, but the rooms without bathrooms – though in even worse shape – are a safe, cheap option in town. Take any transport going to pl Revolyutsii.

★**Congress Hotel Malakhit** HOTEL $$
(☎351-245 0575; www.hotel74.ru; ul Truda 153; s incl breakfast ₽3000-3900, d incl breakfast ₽4400-4800;) This hotel has reinvented itself as a spa hotel with sauna, small sauna pool and treatments. Rooms are modern and clean, at rates often considerably less than its formal prices. Malakhit houses

Mirage, a lively disco and karaoke bar. It's a 10-minute walk down ul Kirova from pl Revolyutsii or take bus 18 from the train station to stop Operny Teatr.

Wall Street MINIHOTEL $$
(351-263 7454; www.wall-street74.ru; ul Kirova 82; r incl breakfast ₽3500;) This excellent minihotel has large, well-styled rooms, right among the sights and restaurants. It's a 10-minute walk down ul Kirova from pl Revolyutsii or take bus 18 from the train station to stop 'Operny Teatr'.

★Parkcity HOTEL $$$
(351-731 2222; www.parkcityhotel.ru; ul Lesoparkovaya 6; s incl breakfast ₽4400-5300, d incl breakfast ₽5300-6200, ste incl breakfast ₽7000-9000;) This hotel has friendly, efficient staff and, as well as the usual business facilities, bicycles for hire. Mini-standard rooms for singles cost ₽2600, and other discounts are available. *Marshrutky* 3 and 86 run here from pl Revolyutsy.

Eating

★Uralskiye Pelmeni RUSSIAN $
(351-265 9591; pr Lenina 66a; pelmeni ₽220, 3-course meals ₽900; noon-2am) When Russians first crossed the Urals, they were a tribe of porridge-eaters, but through the encounter with Asian tribes they found something that changed their cuisine forever – *pelmeni* (Russian-style ravioli). This two-storey restaurant-cum-disco (often heaving with golden oldies) is all about *pelmeni*.

Meet.Point INTERNATIONAL, SUSHI $$
(ul Kirova 141; mains ₽350; 10am-6am;) As well as a small selection of Russian and international mains, this cafe, bar, restaurant and – later in the evening – dance space serves sushi, pizza and fish. It has a children's play area.

Bon Bon FRENCH $$
(ul Tsvillinga 31; mains ₽260-530; 9am-11pm;) Excellent cafe and restaurant with a summer outdoor deck. Serves wine but not beer.

Drinking & Nightlife

Nu i Che Art Pub BAR, DISCO
(Ну и Чё Art Pub; www.monopoly74.ru; ul Truda 105; admission free; 24hr) Part of the larger 'Monopoly' complex (it includes the restaurant and live venue Lunny Svet at ul Kirova 82), Art Pub is the pub-disco arm attracting a good mix from young to late 30s.

Information

PKD Internet (per 20min ₽15)

Getting There & Away

Sputnik (pr Lenina 61b; 9am-7pm Mon-Fri, 10am-4pm Sat & Sun) sells rail and air tickets.

Buses depart from the Severny Bus Station to Yekaterinburg (₽561, four hours) and Magnitogorsk (₽600, five hours, every hour). Touts sell tickets in minibuses to Yekaterinburg (₽700, 2½ hours, about every hour) in front of the Severny Bus Station.

Trains go daily to Moscow (₽4326, 35 hours), via Ufa (₽1122, 9½ hours) and Samara (₽1824, 19 hours). Trains 146 and 39 run on odd and even days respectively via Yekaterinburg to St Petersburg (*kupe* ₽5790, two days). Heading east, most trains cut through Kazakhstan (separate visa required). There are one to three daily trains to the capital, Astana (*kupe* ₽3423, 22 hours).

Several fast trains run daily to Yekaterinburg (₽843, five hours).

Getting Around

The train station is on ul Svobody, 2.5km south of the centre. Bus 18 and tram 3 connect the train station with pl Revolyutsii in the centre and run north along ul Tsvillinga to Operny Teatr, near the bottom of ul Kirova. Trams 7 and 8 go to pl Revolyutsii from the train station.

For a taxi call 737 3737. Bus 1 runs to the airport from the train station.

Western Siberia

Includes ➡

Best Places to Eat

- Slavyansky Bazar (p428)
- Yermolaev (p413)
- Chaynaya Sinyukha (p441)
- La Maison (p423)

Best Places to Stay

- Vsyo Prosto! (p413)
- Hotel Yamskaya (p417)
- Avenue Hotel (p422)
- Gogol Hotel (p427)

Why Go?

Heading east from the Ural Mountains, the influence and reach of Moscow noticeably begins to wane as one enters Western Siberia (Западная Сибирь). Unforgiving winters and a history of gulags give the region a bad rap. The reality is much different. Western Siberia is surprisingly friendly, with plenty to offer the passing traveller. Expect contrasts and extremes, from mountain-ringed lakes to underground cafes, from urban chaos to remote areas where an encounter with a fellow traveller is a real event. It's not the easiest place in which to travel. Visitors need a willingness to rough it, and it helps to be able to speak at least rudimentary Russian. But those who make the effort will be rewarded with an insight into the Siberian way of life and – perhaps more importantly – receive a dose of the locals' legendary hospitality.

When to Go

Novosibirsk

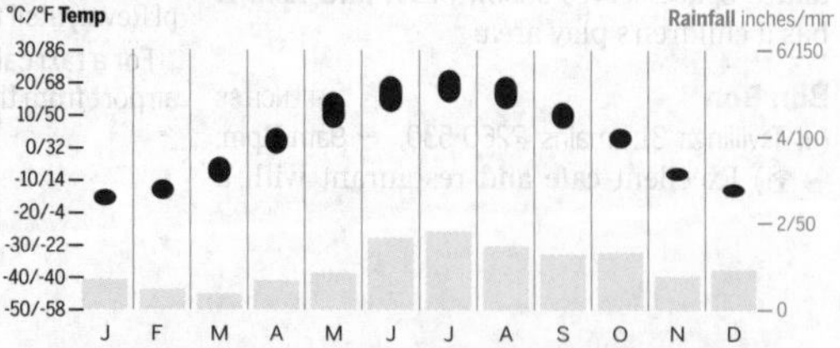

May Grand WWII Victory Day celebrations in Novosibirsk, wildflowers blooming in Altai.

Jul–Sep Bustling street scene in cities, trekking season in Altai.

Dec–Jan Tramp through Tomsk's winter wonderland and greet the New Year, Russian style.

History

Siberia's early Altai people were conceivably progenitors of the Inuit-Arctic cultures and of the Mongol-Turkic groups, which expanded in westbound waves with Attila, Chinggis (Genghis) Khaan and Timur (Tamerlane). The name Siberia comes from Sibir, a Turkic khanate and successor-state to the Golden Horde that ruled the region following Timur's 1395 invasion.

From 1563, Sibir started raiding what were then Russia's easternmost flanks. A Volga brigand called Yermak Timofeevich was sent to counterattack. Though he had only 840 Cossack fighters, the prospect of battle seemed better than the tsar's death sentence that hung over him. With the unfair advantage of firearms, the tiny Cossack force managed to conquer Tyumen in 1580, turning Yermak into a Russian hero. Two years later Yermak occupied Sibir's capital

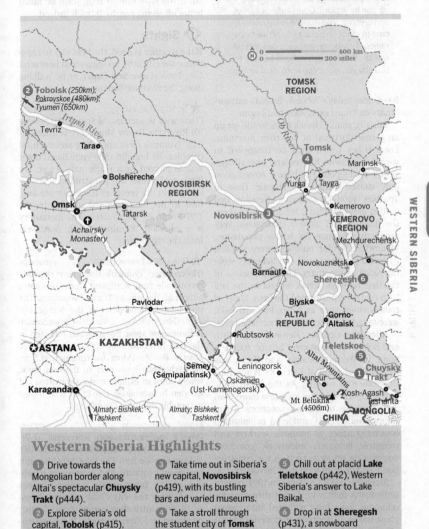

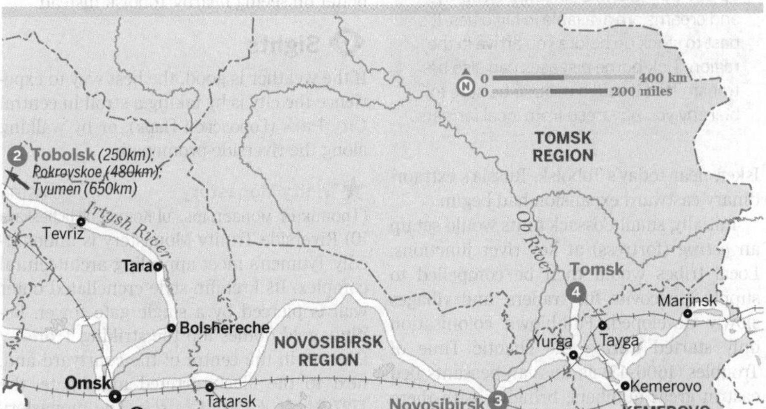

Western Siberia Highlights

1 Drive towards the Mongolian border along Altai's spectacular **Chuysky Trakt** (p444).

2 Explore Siberia's old capital, **Tobolsk** (p415), with its glorious kremlin and Old Town.

3 Take time out in Siberia's new capital, **Novosibirsk** (p419), with its bustling bars and varied museums.

4 Take a stroll through the student city of **Tomsk** (p425) and its picturesque wooden homes.

5 Chill out at placid **Lake Teletskoe** (p442), Western Siberia's answer to Lake Baikal.

6 Drop in at **Sheregesh** (p431), a snowboard mecca with a blistering party scene.

TICK WARNING

The encephalitis and Lyme disease threat is often underestimated in Siberia (both Western and Eastern). The ticks *(kleshchi)* that spread these nasty diseases are alarmingly plentiful from late April to September. The threat is worst in the taiga (mountain pine), especially in Altai, but ticks have even been found in city parks. Don't panic, but do cover up and be vigilant. Good antitick sprays and creams are available in big cities. It's best to stock up before you arrive in the region. Tick-borne diseases can also be transmitted through milk, so be sure to boil any you buy fresh from local farmers.

Isker, near today's Tobolsk. Russia's extraordinary eastward expansion had begun.

Initially, small Cossack units would set up an *ostrog* (fortress) at key river junctions. Local tribes would then be compelled to supply Muscovite fur traders, and villages slowly developed. Full-blown colonisation only started during the chaotic Time of Troubles (1606–13) as Russian peasants fled east in great numbers, bringing with them the diseases and alcohol that would subsequently decimate the native population. Meanwhile, settler numbers were swollen by exiled prisoners, and Old Believers seeking religious sanctuary. The construction of the first railways across Siberia in the late 19th century transformed the area. Many of today's cities, such as Novosibirsk in 1893, were founded as the rail lines stretched east.

After the October Revolution of 1917, anti-Bolshevik resistance briefly found a home in Western Siberia, and Omsk was the centre of Admiral Kolchak's White Russia from 1918 to 1919. As the USSR grew into a superpower, the area saw more than its fair share of Stalin's notorious Gulag camps. Nonetheless, unforced colonisation continued apace as patriotic workers and volunteer labourers undertook grandiose engineering projects, such as the construction virtually from scratch of Novokuznetsk.

Since the USSR's collapse in 1991, certain settlements built with Soviet disregard for economic logic have withered into virtual ghost towns. In contrast, discoveries of vast oil and gas deposits have led to booms in now-flashy remote cities like Tyumen.

Tyumen Тюмень

3452 / POP 507,000 / MOSCOW +2HR

Founded in 1586, Tyumen was the first Russian settlement in Siberia. These days the city is the youthful, business-oriented capital of a vast, oil-rich *oblast* (region) stretching all the way to the Yamal and Gydansk peninsulas on the Arctic Kara Sea. There's enough here to keep you (mildly) entertained for a day or so, but if you have limited time you'd be much better off seeing nearby Tobolsk instead.

Sights

If the weather is good, the best way to experience the city is by taking a stroll in central **City Park** (Городской Парк), or by walking along the riverside promenade.

★Trinity Monastery MONASTERY

(Троицкий монастырь; ul Kommunisticheskaya 10) Riverside Trinity Monastery is undoubtedly Tyumen's most appealing architectural complex. Its kremlin-style crenellated outer wall is pierced by a single gate tower. Behind, gold domes top the striking **Troitsky Church** in the centre of the courtyard and, next to the black-turreted main gate, the 1727 **Peter & Paul Church**. The monastery is a pleasant 30-minute walk northwest from the city centre.

★Riverside Promenade PROMENADE

(Набережная) Tyumen's sleek new riverside promenade runs northwest from the centre almost all the way to Trinity Monastery. The promenade offers views of the **Voznesensko Georgievskiy Church** (Вознесенско-Георгиевский храм; Beregovaya ul) reflected in the Tura River from the opposite (east) bank. **Lovers Bridge** (Мост влюблённых; ul Kommunisticheskaya) leads over to the east bank, where you can explore curiously twisted old wooden houses along tree-lined **Bergovaya ul** (notably numbers 73 and 53).

Fine Arts Museum MUSEUM

(Музей изобразительного искусства; ul Ordzhonikidze 47; admission per exhibition ₽100-150; 10am-6pm Tue-Sun) The Fine Arts Museum has several rotating and permanent exhibits ranging from ornate window frames saved from the city's old wooden houses to tiny, intricately carved bone figures produced by Siberian artists. It gets expensive if you want to see all of the exhibits, however.

House-Museum of 19th-& 20th-Century History MUSEUM
(Музей истории дома XIX-XX вв; ul Respubliki 18; admission ₽160; ⌚10am-6pm Wed-Sun) This museum contains artifacts from Tyumen's past and is housed in the city's finest carved cottage.

Znamensky Cathedral CHURCH
(Знаменский собор; ul Semakova 13) With its voluptuously curved baroque towers, the 1786 Znamensky Cathedral is the most memorable of a dozen 'old' churches that have recently come back to life following years of neglect.

Archangel Mikhail Church CHURCH
(Храм Михаила Архангела; ul Turgeneva) The attractive Archangel Mikhail Church sits at the top of a hill just off ul Lenina. Follow **ul Turgeneva** southwest behind the church to a network of back streets full of old wooden houses.

Sleeping

★**Vsyo Prosto!** HOSTEL $
(Всё Просто!; ☎3452-441 072; www.hostelvse-prosto.ru; ul Pervomayskaya 40/1; dm ₽590-750, s/d ₽990/1490; @📶) This marvelous hostel just a seven-minute walk from the train station is the obvious choice for budget and even midrange travellers. There's just one double room, but even the dorm-averse will do well sleeping in the spacious dorms and hanging out in the equally spacious kitchen.

Hotel Vostok HOTEL $$
(Гостиница Восток; ☎3452-686 111; www.vostok-tmn.ru; ul Respubliki 159; s/d from ₽2500/3200; ⊖@📶) This former Soviet monstrosity has seen a massive facelift (inside, at least) and now boasts modern rooms, albeit still with Soviet dimensions (ie small). It's two easy bus stops from the centre along ul Respubliki.

Business Hotel Eurasia HOTEL $$$
(Бизнес-отель Евразия; ☎3452-222 000; www.eurasiahotel.ru; ul Sovetskaya 20; s/d incl breakfast from ₽4900/6900; ⊖❄@📶) While not overloaded with character, it covers business travellers' needs with well-appointed rooms, a decent restaurant and a fitness centre. But the best part is that everything in the minibar is free of charge!

Eating & Drinking

★**Yermolaev** RUSSIAN $$
(Ермолаев; ul Lenina 37; mains ₽250-550; ⌚noon-1am; 📶) This spacious place is a bit like a Soviet-themed beerhall. There are eight types of mostly unfiltered homebrew (from ₽135) and an extensive picture menu that includes traditional Russian fare, Bavarian sausages and Siberian specialties such as *stroganina* (raw frozen fish).

Schaste GEORGIAN $$
(Счастье; Kalinka Trade Centre, ul Respubliki 65; mains ₽300-700; ⌚11.45am-1am; 📶) This eatery serves Georgian specialties such as fried *suluguni* (Georgian cheese), *kharcho* (beef stew) and *khinkali* (dumplings) in a fishbowl-like main dining hall with 270-degree views of the city centre.

Malina Bar CAFE $$
(Малина Бар; ul Pervomayskaya 18; meals ₽400-800; ⌚24hr; ⊖📶) Stylish Malina Bar has a huge menu of Russian and European food, sushi, filling breakfasts, fast wi-fi and cozy seating in grand leather couches. Upstairs is sister Italian restaurant–steak house **Berlusconi** (ul Pervomayskaya 18; mains ₽300-1200; ⌚11am-3am).

In Da USA AMERICAN $$
(Ин Да Юса; ul Chelyuskintsev 10; mains ₽300-500; ⌚noon-2am Sun-Thu, to 6am Fri & Sat; 📶) In Da USA is, naturally, festooned with Americana and serves Tyumen's best burgers along with Tex-Mex and a host of bar appetizers. It

CORPSE OF HONOUR

Vladimir Lenin himself paid a visit to Tyumen – in 1941. Yes, he was already dead. The Soviets evacuated his body (just the body – his brain remained in Moscow) to Tyumen to keep it safe from the invading Germans. The body was kept under a veil of secrecy in the **Selskhoz Academy** (Сельсхоз Академия; ul Respubliki 7), an attractive early-20th-century brick building that still stands today, before being shipped back to Moscow in 1945. Throughout it all, the citizens of Tyumen remained blissfully unaware of the presence of a distinguished guest in their midst. Indeed, until after the war, few Russians had any idea the corpse had ever been transferred out of its mausoleum on Red Square!

Tyumen

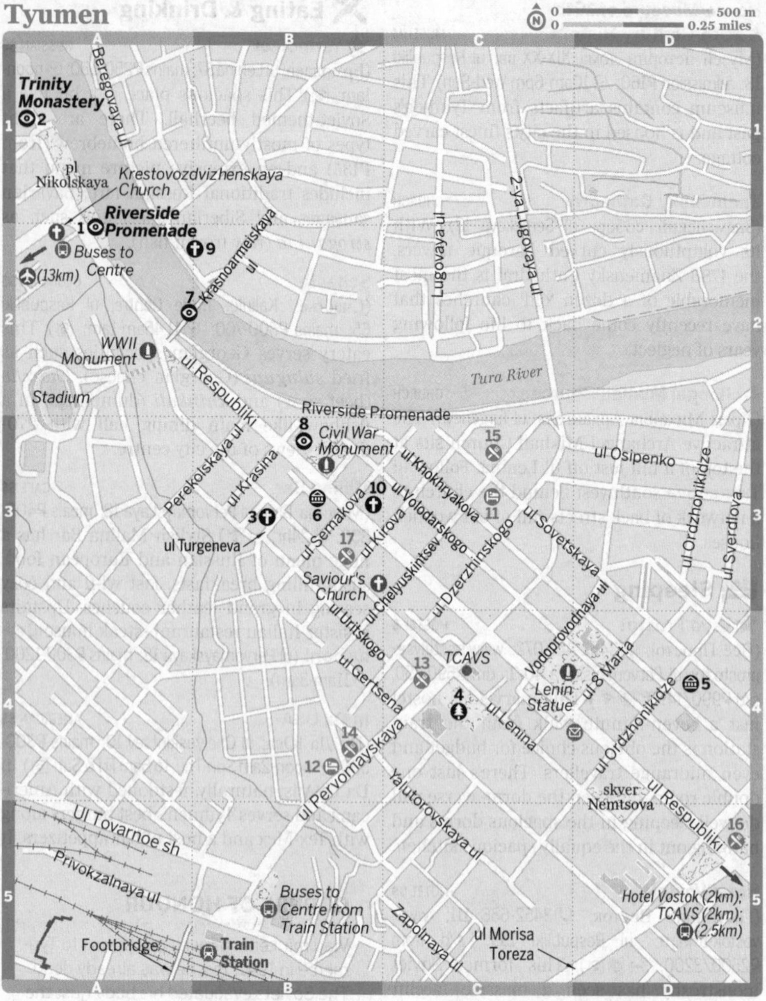

becomes a club famous for table-top dancing at weekends.

Don Julio MEXICAN $$
(Дон Хулио; ul Pervomaiskaya 38a; mains ₽300-500; ⏰ noon-2am Mon-Fri, to 4am Fri & Sat; 📶) This Mexican food (mains ₽300 to ₽500) is reasonably good (this isn't Cancun, after all), and on weekend nights DJs and live music take over.

ℹ Information

City maps and bus-route plans are sold at newspaper kiosks in the train station and throughout the city.

Main Post Office (Почтамт; ul Respubliki 56; ⏰ 8am-10pm Mon-Fri, 9am-6pm Sat & Sun)

ℹ Getting There & Away

Air and rail tickets are sold by **TCAVS** (ul Lenina 61, also on **ul Respubliki** ul Respubliki 156; ⏰ 8am-8pm).

AIR

S7 and Aeroflot are among airlines with daily flights to Moscow (three hours), while regional carrier **Yamal Airlines** (http://yamal.aero) serves Novosibirsk (two hours, three weekly) and arctic hubs Novy Urengoy (daily) and Salekhard (daily) among many other destinations in Tyumen

Tyumen

Top Sights

1	Riverside Promenade	A2
2	Trinity Monastery	A1

Sights

3	Archangel Mikhail Church	B3
4	City Park	C4
5	Fine Arts Museum	D4
6	House-Museum of 19th- & 20th-Century History	B3
7	Lovers Bridge	A2
8	Selskhoz Academy	B3
9	Voznesensko Georgievskiy Church	B2
10	Znamensky Cathedral	B3

Sleeping

11	Business Hotel Eurasia	C3
12	Vsyo Prosto!	B4

Eating

13	Berlusconi	C4
14	Don Julio	B4
15	In Da USA	C3
	Malina Bar	(see 13)
16	Schaste	D5
17	Yermolaev	B3

Oblast and beyond. Note that foreigners usually need a special permit to visit most Arctic Circle destinations. A second regional carrier, **UTAir** (www.utair.ru), serves Khanty-Mansiysk among other remote destinations in Tyumen Oblast.

BUS

From the **bus station** (ul Permyakova), 3km east of the centre, buses to Tobolsk (₽550, four hours, seven daily) travel via Rasputin's home town of Pokrovskoe (₽200, 1½ hours).

TRAIN

Several day and overnight trains go to Omsk (*platskart/kupe* ₽880/1824, 8½ hours, 10.19pm) and points east along the Trans-Siberian mainline, and dozens of westbound trains serve Yekaterinburg and beyond.

There are many daily trains to Tobolsk (*platskart* ₽550 to ₽800, 3½ hours), plus a rather ill-timed nightly *elektrichka* (suburban train; ₽254, four hours, 11.54pm). If you're looking to explore the arctic, trains continue beyond Tobolsk all the way to Novy Urgenoy (at least twice daily). Other useful trains serve Barnaul (₽2200/4500, 29 hours, daily at 6.36am) and Tomsk (₽3500/6200, 23 hours, even-numbered days at 9.17am).

Getting Around

Tyumen's Roshchino Airport is 13km west of the centre. Catch *marshrutka* 35 or bus 141 anywhere along ul Respubliki (30 minutes). Taxis from the city centre cost ₽250 if ordered by phone through your hotel.

From the train station, bus 27 serves Hotel Vostok and passes near the bus station; hop off at the Krosno stop, and cross ul Respubliki. Taxis around town cost ₽150.

Tobolsk — Тобольск

3456 / POP 101,000 / MOSCOW +2HR

Once Siberia's capital, Tobolsk is one of the region's most historic cities, sporting a magnificent kremlin and a charmingly decrepit old town. Tobolsk is off the Trans-Siberian main line but is easily reached from Tyumen.

The centre of the Russian colonisation of Siberia, Tobolsk was founded in 1587. Its strategic importance started to wane in the 1760s, when the new Great Siberian Trakt (post road) took a more southerly route. However, until the early 20th century it remained significant as a centre for both learning and exile. Involuntary guests included Fyodor Dostoevsky en route to exile in Omsk, and deposed Tsar Nicholas II and his family, who spent several months here in 1917 before being taken to Yekaterinburg and executed.

Buses from the inconvenient train station (some 10km north) give visitors a dismal first impression. Concrete drabness reaches a glum centre around Hotel Slavyanskaya, but don't be put off. Tobolsk's glories begin 3km further south around the splendid kremlin. Immediately beyond and below the kremlin, the old town sinks into the Irtysh's boggy floodplain.

Sights

★Kremlin HISTORIC BUILDING

(grounds 8am-8pm) The centrepiece of the tower-studded 18th-century kremlin is the glorious 1686 **St Sofia Cathedral** (Софийский собор; Krasnaya pl 2). Less eye-catching from the outside, but with splendid arched ceiling murals, is the 1746 **Intercession Cathedral** (Покровский собор).

Between the two is a 1799 **bell tower**, built for the Uglich bell, which famously signalled a revolt against Tsar Boris Godunov. The revolt failed; in a mad fury, Godunov ordered the bell to be publicly flogged, detongued and banished to Tobolsk for its treacherous tolling. A tatty copy of the bell is displayed in the Deputy's Palace Museum.

Built in 1855, the Kremlin prison is now the **Castle Prison Museum**

Tobolsk

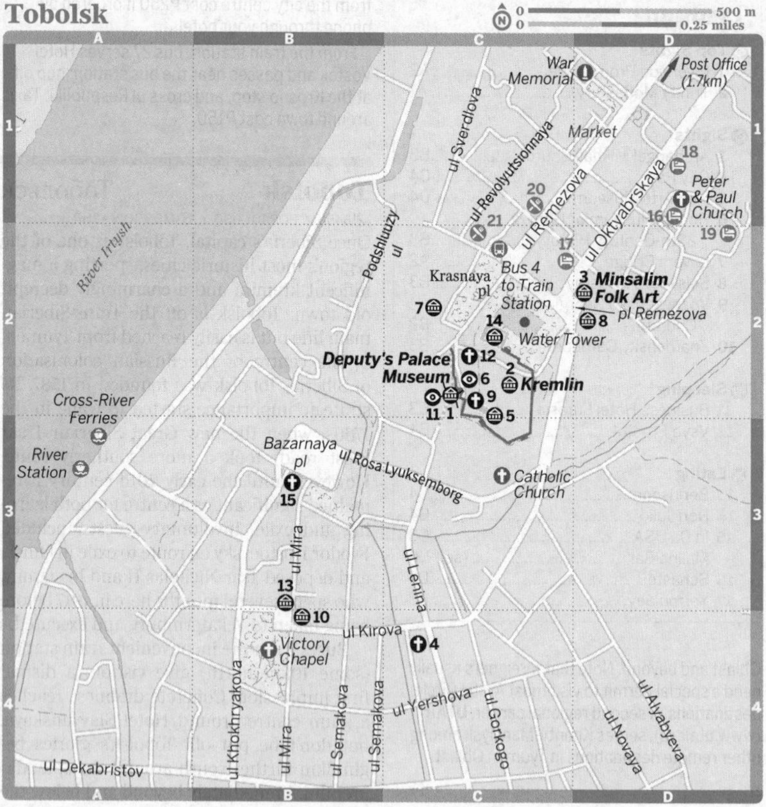

(Тюремный замок; Krasnaya pl 1; admission ₽300; ⏲10am-6pm Tue-Sun), where you can get a sense of the grim life behind bars in both Tsarist and Soviet times. The elegant **Arkhiereysky Mansion** (Архиерейский Дом) was closed for renovations when we visited and will eventually be reopened as an Orthodox history museum; the intriguing **Trading Arches** (Гостиный двор) were being converted into yet another museum.

Wooden stairs lead beneath the kremlin's **Pryamskoy Vzvoz** (Прямской Взвоз) (gatehouse) to the wonderfully dilapidated old town full of weather-beaten churches and angled wooden homes sinking between muddy lanes.

★ Deputy's Palace Museum MUSEUM
(Дворец наместника; www.tiamz.ru; Krasnaya pl 1; admission ₽300; ⏲10am-6pm Tue-Sun) Tobolsk's best museum occupies a beautiful 18th-century former administration building on the southwestern edge of the kremlin. The Romanovs called in here during their brief stint in Tobolsk in 1917, and a section of this remarkably modern museum is devoted to their time in Tobolsk. Tactile multimedia exhibits profile the characters who shaped Siberia before the Bolshevik revolution, and hometown heroes such Dmitri Mendeleev, who created the first periodic table. There's an impressive collection of local art up on the 3rd floor.

Most exhibits have English placards. The space-age multimedia displays are in Russian only but are fun to play with regardless. Visitors really emerge from here with a sense of Tobolsk's importance in the 18th and 19th centuries, when it was the capital of all Siberia.

★ Minsalim Folk Art ART GALLERY
(Мастерская Минсалим; www.minsalim.ru; ul Oktyabrskaya 2; ⏲9am-6pm) **FREE** Minsalim is a master bone-carver who turns mammoth tusks and antler fragments into detailed fig-

Tobolsk

Top Sights

1	Deputy's Palace Museum	C2
2	Kremlin	C2
3	Minsalim Folk Art	D2

Sights

4	Archangel Mikhail Church	C4
5	Arkhiereysky Mansion	C2
6	Bell Tower	C2
7	Castle Prison Museum	C2
8	Gubernsky Museum	D2
9	Intercession Cathedral	C2
10	Kornilov Mansion	B4
11	Pryamskoy Vzvoz	C2
12	St Sofia Cathedral	C2
13	Tobolsk Rayon Administration Building	B3
14	Trading Arches	C2
15	Zachary & Elisabeth Church	B3

Sleeping

16	Hotel Georgievskaya	D1
17	Hotel Sibir	C2
18	Hotel Tobol	D1
19	Hotel Yamskaya	D2

Eating

20	Kofeynya u Ershova	C1
21	Ladeyny	C2

urines related to myths and legends of the local brand of shamanism. With a long mustache and flowing mane, eccentric Minsalim is something of a shaman himself, and will gladly lead you on a tour of his workshop behind the gallery. His son and some members of staff speak English.

Gubernsky Museum MUSEUM
(Губернский музей; ul Oktyabrskaya 1; admission ₽200; ⊙10am-6pm Tue-Sun) Built in 1887 for the 300th anniversary of the founding of Tobolsk, the Gubernsky Museum has displays on the history of Tobolsk, a mammoth skeleton and a display of bone carvings.

Kornilov Mansion MUSEUM
(Дом Корнилова; ul Mira 9) The grand Kornilov mansion, named after a 19th-century statesman and philanthropist, is closed while being converted into a museum dedicated to the Romanovs, but is still worth a look for its lavish exterior.

Tobolsk Rayon Administration Building HISTORIC BUILDING
(ul Mira 10) Less eye-catching than the Kornilov Mansion opposite, the Tobolsk Rayon Administration Building was the home-in-exile of the last tsar, before his fateful journey to execution in Yekaterinburg. It's now a museum of legal studies (admission free).

Archangel Mikhail Church CHURCH
(Церковь Архангела Михаила; ul Lenina 24) The attractive Archangel Mikhail Church has a colourfully restored interior. The character of Tatiana Larina in Pushkin's epic *Eugene Onegin* is said to have been modelled on Natalya Fonvizina, a Decembrist wife who prayed here.

Zachary & Elisabeth Church CHURCH
(Церковь Захария и Елизаветы; Bazarnaya pl 8) The 1759 Zachary & Elisabeth Church, with its soaring black-tipped spires, is extremely photogenic.

Sleeping & Eating

While Tobolsk has seen a modest tourist boom in recent years, there is still no restaurant scene to speak of.

Resting Rooms HOSTEL $
(komnaty otdykha; ☎3456-62 522; train station; dm 12/24hr from ₽500/600, s/d from 1200/1800) Clean and friendly. The location is utterly impractical for visiting the city, but ideal if you're arriving late or waiting for an early-morning connection.

★ **Hotel Yamskaya** HOTEL $$
(Гостиница Ямская; ☎3456-226 177; yamskaya-tobolsk@mail.ru; ul Bolshaya Sibirskaya 40; s/d/tw incl breakfast ₽2100/2600/3000;) With cosy rooms, friendly service, a perfect location near the Kremlin and a warm and inviting overall atmosphere, this 12-room hotel borders on boutique. The prices are extremely reasonable for what you get.

Hotel Sibir HOTEL $$
(Гостиница Сибирь; ☎3456-222 390; pl Remezova 1; s/d incl breakfast from ₽2200/3900;) Sibir's rooms are comfortable, spacious and festooned with classy old photos, giving it a historical vibe. It's the closest to the kremlin of all Tobolsk's hotels. The breakfast is tasty and filling and the 24-hour restaurant (meals ₽150 to ₽600, beer from ₽100, no English menu) does a mean *pokhlebnaya ribnaya* (fish soup; ₽170).

Hotel Georgievskaya HOTEL $$
(Гостиница Георгиевская; ☎3456-220 909; www.hotel-georgievskaya.ru; ul Lenekaya 35; s ₽2380-2960, d ₽3330-4040;) Right behind a Dostoyevsky statue, this large hotel

has spacious rooms that are a tad overdone with velvet curtains, satin bedspreads and the like. The bathrooms are quite nice and there's a sumptuous restaurant.

Hotel Tobol HOTEL $$
(Гостиница Тобол; ☎3456-246 614; ul Oktyabrskaya 20; s/d/tw incl breakfast from ₽2200/2800/3300; 📶) The Tobol is a renovated Soviet hotel, which means rooms on the small side and generic furniture, but at least it's clean, well located and relatively affordable. There's a bowling alley and a disco on the ground level if you get bored.

Ladeyny RUSSIAN $
(Ладейный; ul Revolutsionnaya 2; mains ₽200-400; ⌚11am-2am; 📶📋) This place is a revolution as far as Tobolsk is concerned, an extra-large Siberian *izba* (wood house) that specializes in Siberian fish and homemade *pelmeni* (ravioli) and *varenyky* (dumplings). Nights sometimes bring live music. The English menu is extremely rare for these parts.

Kofeynya u Ershova CAFE $
(Кофейня у Ершова; ul Remezova 7; mains ₽120-300; ⌚10am-11pm) An easy stop near the Kremlin for relatively quick and cheap Russian eats – think lunch standards such as *bishteks* (Russian-style hamburger), *solyanka* (pickled vegetables and potato soup) and stuffed bliny (pancackes).

Information

Post Office (Почта; Komsomolsky pr 42; ⌚8am-6pm)

Getting There & Away

The best way to Tyumen is on the daily 8.40am *elektrichka* (₽254, four hours).

There are many day and overnight options to Yekaterinberg (*platskart/kupe* ₽1200/2300, 10 hours) and points west via Tyumen (*platskart* ₽550-800, 3½ hours). The 125 train trundles to Novosibirsk on odd-numbered days at 9.21am (₽1400/3750, 24 hours) via Omsk, while the 115 is a late-night option to Omsk on odd-numbered days (₽2200/4500, 13¼ hours, 1.26am).

Buses are another option to Tyumen (₽550, four hours) via Pokrovskoe (₽300, 2½ hours), Rasputin's home village. Eight buses per day to various destinations pass through nearby Abalak, site of an interesting monastery.

In the warm months ferries cruise the Irtysh north to Salekhard (1st/2nd/3rd-class ₽3000/1200/900, five days, about six monthly) via Khanty-Mansiysk (two days), and south to Omsk (₽2200/1000/850, three days, about three monthly).

Getting Around

Bus 4 and *marshrutka* 20 link the train station, new town and kremlin. Taxis from/to the station cost around ₽250.

Omsk Омск

☎3812 / POP 1.145 MILLION / ⌚MOSCOW +3HR

With its modest sights hidden behind busy roads, this big industrial city is not worth a special detour. You may find it a convenient stopover to break up long journeys.

If you're looking to kill some time, the **Fine Arts Museum** (Музей изобразительных искусств; ul Lenina 23; admission ₽100; ⌚10am-6pm Tue-Sun) displays a lot of fussy decorative arts. The rectilinear 1862 building, a historical curiosity in itself, was built as the Siberian governor's mansion and hosted passing tsars. In 1918–19, however, the building was home to Admiral Kolchak's counter-revolutionary government.

Cross the the bridge at ul Lenina and continue north and you'll pass several parks and more notable buildings, including the ornate **Drama Theatre** (Омский театр драмы; www.omskdrama.ru; ul Lenina 8a); a 1905 building housing another branch of the **Fine Arts Museum** (ul Lenina 3); and the massive, turquoise-and-gold-domed **Assumption Cathedral** (Успенский собор; Sobornaya pl), rebuilt after the collapse of the USSR. Check out the great catalog in the Ibis Sibir hotel for more walking tours and sightseeing ideas.

Sleeping & Eating

Resting Rooms HOSTEL $
(komnaty otdykha; ☎3812-442 347; train station; 12/24hr from ₽700/1200) Spacious and with ensuites, these are some of the best train-station rooms we've seen in Siberia.

Hotel Turist HOTEL $$
(Отель Турист; ☎3812-316 414; www.tourist-omsk.ru; ul Broz Tito 2; s/d incl breakfast from ₽3000/3600; ⊖@📶) A fairly central renovated Soviet high-rise with bright rooms and fine views of the river from upper floors. Discount of 25% on weekends, 40% discount if you check in after 10pm, and the minibar is free of charge.

Ibis Sibir HOTEL $$$
(☎3812-311 551; www.ibishotel.com; ul Lenina 22; s/d incl breakfast from ₽4000/4600; ⊖❄@📶)

Bright and cheery, the always-reliable Ibis shuns Soviet dimensions and is by far the nicest hotel in Omsk. Beds are lavish, the breakfast excellent and there's a catalog in English outlining sightseeing opportunities in and around Omsk. No minibar.

★**Gollandskaya Chashka** INTERNATIONAL $$
(Голландская Чашка; www.hollcup.ru; 3rd fl, Pyat Zvyozd shopping mall, ul Karla Libknekhta; mains ₽250-450; ⏰10am-midnight; 📶📄) Excellent northern European and Russian comfort food, elaborate salads, mulled wine, inviting decor, reasonable prices, fine city views – there's plenty to like about Chashka. Follow pr Marksa over the bridge and take the second left.

Kolchak ITALIAN $$
(Ресторан-клуб Колчакъ; ul Broz Tito 2; mains ₽300-500; 📶) Conveniently located near the River Station, Kolchok combines an Irish pub and an Italian restaurant under one roof. There's an excellent beer selection including Leffe on tap, and a business lunch of Russian faves.

ℹ Information

K2 Adventures (☎3812-693-075; www.adventuretravel.ru) Igor Fedyaev is the guru of adventure travel in Western Siberia. English-speaking, affable and responsive, he specializes in mountaineering expeditions in Altai and elsewhere, but can arrange just about any tour you want around Omsk or elsewhere in the region.

Post Office (Почтамт; ul Gertsena 1; ⏰8am-10pm Mon-Fri, 9am-6pm Sat & Sun)

ℹ Getting There & Away

Omsk is on the Trans-Siberian main line, which means numerous connections both east towards Novosibirsk (*platskart/kupe* from ₽1300/3000, about 8½ hours) and west towards Yekaterinburg. Destinations off the main line served from Omsk include Abakan (₽2500/5000, 30 hours, daily), Barnaul (₽1515/2995, 16 hours, one or two daily), Tomsk (₽2400/4250, 14 hours, even-numbered days) and Tobolsk (₽2200/4500, 12 hours, odd-numbered days at 8.30pm, even-numbered days at 10.16am).

An *elektrichka* serves Novosibirsk Tuesdays, Thursdays and Sundays at 2.55pm (1st/2nd/3rd-class ₽1600/1250/840, 6¾ hours).

Various pleasure cruises depart from a jetty near the Yubileyny Bridge at ul Lenina, notably for Achairsky Monastery (₽400 return, 4½ hours return, five times daily mid-May to early September).

In the warm months ferries cruise the Irtysh River to Salekhard on the Arctic Circle (1st/2nd/3rd class ₽4500/2000/1500, eight days) via Tobolsk (₽2200/1000/850, three days) and Khanty-Mansiysk (₽2800/1500/1200, five days), departing roughly three times monthly.

ℹ Getting Around

The main streets, Ul Lenina and pr Marksa, run parallel to each other through the centre of town and cross the Om River just north of central pl Lenina. From the train station, trolleybus 4 and bus 69 are among many options that go to the centre along pr Marksa.

Novosibirsk Новосибирск

☎383 / POP 1.5 MILLION / ⏰ MOSCOW +3HR

Once crusty and impersonal, Russia's third-largest city has embraced its status as capital of Siberia and opened its doors to the world. A slew of quirky museums and monuments, a relaxed big-city vibe, a pulsating nightlife and a wealth of great accommodation at both the high and low ends make Novosibirsk a logical and worthwhile Trans-Siberian pitstop. You can also jump off from here to architecturally splendid Tomsk, some 4½ hours away by bus.

Novosibirsk grew up in the 1890s around the Ob River bridge built for the Trans-Siberian Railway, and the city is festooned with original examples of the wood-lace architecture that prevailed at the time before the Soviets took over and started chucking concrete everywhere. Named Novo-Nikolaevsk until 1925 for the last tsar, it grew rapidly into Siberia's biggest metropolis, a key industrial and transport centre exploiting coalfields to the east and mineral deposits in the Urals.

Despite its daunting scale, Novosibirsk has a manageable centre focused on pl Lenina. The city's main axis, Krasny pr, runs through this square linking most points of interest.

👁 Sights

★**NK Rerikh Museum** MUSEUM
(Музей Н.К. Рериха; www.sibro.ru; ul Kommunisticheskaya 38; admission ₽100, free every 2nd Sat; ⏰10am-6pm) This museum is dedicated to the works and life of the painter Nikolai Rerikh (Nicholas Roerich), beloved in these parts because of his life-long passion for Altai. While the many paintings on display are reproductions, they provide a thorough synopsis of his life's work, and you can buy affordable prints in the excellent gift shop.

Rerikh was also a writer, philosopher, scientist, archaeologist, statesman – and traveller. An epic five-year expedition around Central Asia (including Altai) and the Himalayas in the 1920s provided fodder for many of his paintings and philosophies. That journey is explored in depth here, making the museum an inspiring spot for modern vagabonds. Incredibly, the expedition traversed 35 mountain passes of more than 14,000 feet! There is a 15-minute movie in English on the artist's life, and rooms dedicated to the works of his wife and two sons – talented artists, writers and thinkers in their

Novosibirsk

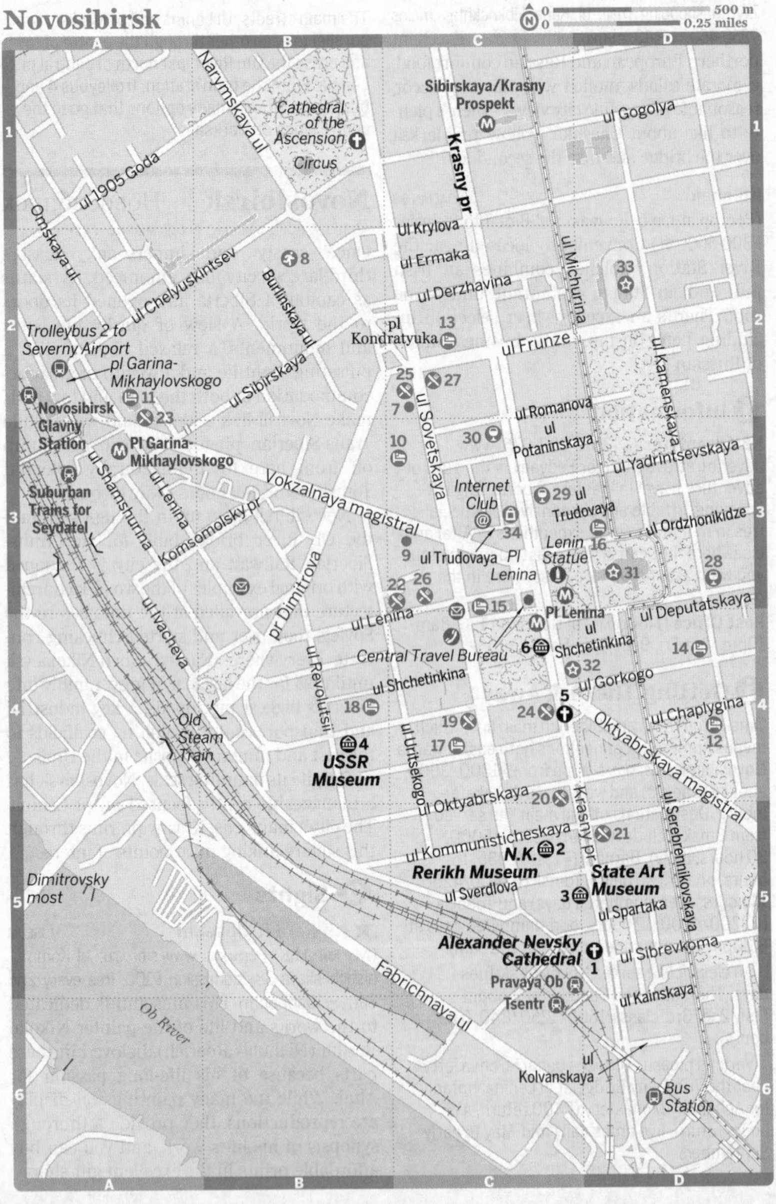

own right. The second Saturday of every month sees free classical concerts at 3pm.

★State Art Museum MUSEUM
(Художественный музей; Krasny pr 5; admission ₽100; ⏲11am-7pm Tue-Fri, 1-7pm Sat & Sun) The highlight is the museum's collection of 65 original paintings by Nikolai Rerikh on the 2nd floor, mostly mountainscapes from the celebrated drifter's time in the Himalayas. The 2nd floor also has a room of 17th-century European (mostly Dutch) masters, a collection of icons and several rooms dedicated to 18th- to 19th-century Russian art. The 3rd floor has some wonderful pieces from the Soviet era.

★USSR Museum MUSEUM
(Музей СССР; ul Gorkogo 16; admission ₽150; ⏲noon-6pm Tue-Sat) While the collection of '70s Soviet bric-a-brac in this basement museum isn't particularly original, you get free reign over the place, which means photo ops galore. Dress yourself up (don't worry, it's allowed!) as a Soviet apparatchik, country *dyevushka* (girl) or Great Patriotic War soldier and snap away. We killed an afternoon here taking goofy selfies.

★Alexander Nevsky Cathedral CHURCH
(Собор Александра Невского; Krasny pr 1a) The 1898 Alexander Nevsky Cathedral is a red-brick Byzantine-style building with gilded domes and colourful murals.

Regional Museum MUSEUM
(Краеведческий музей; Krasny pr 23; admission ₽250; ⏲10am-5.30pm Tue-Sun) In an elegant mansion, the Regional Museum was closed for renovations when we last visited. It has Altai shaman coats, cutaway pioneer houses and some splendid religious artefacts.

Chapel of St Nicholas CHURCH
(Часовня Святителя Николая; Krasny pr) The pretty little Chapel of St Nicholas was said to mark the geographical centre of Russia when it was built in 1915. Demolished in the 1930s, it was rebuilt in 1993 for Novosibirsk's centenary. Today it is an oasis of calm in the bustling city centre.

Sleeping

The best Novosibirsk hostels book out fast, especially from May to October, so booking ahead isn't a bad idea, and can usually be done informally by email. At the top end, a new **Marriott** (ul Ordzhonikidze) was going up opposite the Drama Theatre.

Zokol Hostel HOSTEL $
(☎383-223 3611; www.zokolhostel.ru; ul Shchetinkina 34; dm ₽500-650, d ₽1600-1800; ⊖📶) With down-to-earth English-speaking staff, a superb sightseeing map and an ideal location within walking distance of the train station, the Zokol is the most user-friendly of Novosibirsk's many hostels. It's an

Novosibirsk

Top Sights
1 Alexander Nevsky Cathedral ... D5
2 N.K. Rerikh Museum ... C5
3 State Art Museum ... C5
4 USSR Museum ... B4

Sights
5 Chapel of St Nicholas ... C4
6 Regional Museum ... C4

Activities, Courses & Tours
7 Altair-Tur ... C2
8 Sibir Altai ... B2
9 Tour Academy ... C3

Sleeping
10 Avenue Hotel ... C3
11 Congress-Hotel Novosibirsk ... A2
12 DoubleTree by Hilton ... D4
13 FunKey ... C2
14 Hostel Dostoevsky ... D4
15 Hotel Tsentralnaya ... C3
16 Marriott Hotel (under construction) ... D3
17 Provence Hostel ... C4
18 Zokol Hostel ... B4

Eating
19 La Maison ... C4
20 Nikolaevskaya Pelmennaya ... C4
21 People's Bar & Grill ... D5
22 Shashlikoff ... C3
23 Shashlikoff ... A2
24 Shashlikoff ... C4
25 Tiflis ... C2
26 Universam Avangard ... C3
27 Vilka-Lozhka ... C2

Drinking & Nightlife
28 Brodyachaya Sobaka ... D3
Friends Cocktail Bar ... (see 21)
29 Lebowsky ... C3
30 Rock City ... C3
Truba ... (see 27)

Entertainment
31 Opera & Ballet Theatre ... D3
32 Philharmonia ... C4
33 Spartak Stadium ... D2

Shopping
34 Book Look ... C3

NOVOSIBIRSK'S WOOD HOUSES

While it can't quite match the wood-lace architecture of nearby Tomsk, Novosibirsk has some fine Tsar-era houses hidden among the hulking Soviet structures of the centre. Photogenic streets include **ul Kommunisticheskaya** (Check out Nos 3, 13, 19, 21, 23, 25 and 36), **ul Oktyabrskaya** (Nos 5, 9, 15 and 47), **ul Chaplygina** (Nos 25, 27 and 29) and **ul Gorkogo** (Nos 18, 20, 40, 81 and the brick No 26a).

intimate basement space with 19 beds in mostly windowless triples and quads, plus two cosy kitchen/common areas. The ₽100 breakfast is a bargain.

Provence Hostel
HOSTEL $

(Хостел Прованс; www.provence-hostel.ru; ul Chaplygina 45; dm ₽650-700, d ₽2200; @ 🛜) Occupying the 3rd floor of an attractive century-old brick building, 42-bed Provence is the biggest hostel in Novosibirsk and one of the best. The location is absolutely prime, the beds lovely, the English-speaking staff capable, the ambience bright and cheery. The kitchen/common area could be larger.

FunKey
HOSTEL $

(☑383-263 6503; www.funhostel.ru; ul Frunze 5/2; dm ₽600-700, d ₽1600; 🟢🛜) Funkey indeed. It backs up its quirky name with one of Siberia's most creative hostel spaces. Bright paint and murals enliven walls, extra-tall bunk beds penetrate soaring ceilings and guests kick back in a delightfully wide-open kitchen/common area. Not as English-savvy or informative as some other hostels.

Hostel Dostoevsky
HOSTEL $

(☑8-983-510 7583; www.hosteldostoevsky.com; ul Gorkogo 85, 3rd fl; ⏱dm ₽450-650; 🟢🛜) Climb the dodgy stairs to the oasis that is the Dostoevsky, Novosibirsk's original hostel, newly relocated to the city centre. It's an arty, bustling space with predominantly large (8- to 12-bed) dorms and an airy, open common area.

★ Avenue Hotel
MINIHOTEL $$

(Авеню Отель; ☑383-227 0534; www.avenu.vipngs.ru; ul Sovetskaya 57; s incl breakfast ₽2400-3400, d ₽2800-3800; 🛜) The five rooms in the main wing of this quiet minihotel are huge and exceptionally well-appointed – a welcome change from the standard renovated Soviet fare. And staff are friendly to boot! Cheaper rooms are in a neighboring annexe. Both buildings are in a quiet residential courtyard behind ul Sovetskaya 55.

Hotel Tsentralnaya
HOTEL $$

(Гостиница Центральная; ☑383-222 7294; www.hotel-l.ru; ul Lenina 3; s/tw/tr from ₽1500/1800/1800; 🛜) The cheapest private rooms in the centre are the simple 'economy' rooms, with shared bathrooms, found here. With peeling wallpaper and saggy beds, they retain every morsel of their Soviet, um, charm. That said, they are clean and the location can't be beat.

DoubleTree by Hilton
HOTEL $$$

(☑383-223 0100; www.novosibirsk.doubletreebyhilton.com; ul Kamenskaya 7/1; s/d incl breakfast weekday from ₽7000/8100, weekend from ₽4000/5100; 🟢❄@🛜🏊) Has all the amenities you would expect, highlighted by luscious beds, mood lighting, ginormous plasma TVs, rain showers and (separate) extra-long bathtubs. The weekend rates are ripe for occasional splurgers, although we'd like to see a bit more space in the standard rooms.

Congress-Hotel Novosibirsk
HOTEL $$$

(Конгресс-Гостиница Новосибирск; ☑383-364 0101; www.hotel-novosibirsk.ru; Vokzalnaya magistral 1; s/d incl breakfast from ₽4300/4600; 🟢❄@🛜) Boasting awesome views of the city centre from its upper floors, this formerly glum Soviet-era tower has been transformed into a plush modern hotel with fantastic service. It's possible to get two nights for the price of one if you arrive after midnight for the first night, and weekend rates are at least 30% less.

✘ Eating

★ Vilka-Lozhka
CAFE $

(ul Frunze 2; meals ₽100-180; ⏱9am-10pm; 🛜) This upmarket *stolovaya* (canteen) is popular for a reason – hip and cool with groovy tunes and piping-hot Russian staples like *bliny* (pancakes) and borsht at dirt-cheap prices. It even has beer on tap (from ₽80).

Nikolaevskaya Pelmennaya
RUSSIAN $

(Николаевская Пельменная; Krasny pr 13; mains ₽130-180; ⏱10am-10.30pm) Cheap and simple *pelmeni* with meat and fish fillings in an equally modest cafe located beneath a sex shop.

Universam Avangard SUPERMARKET $
(Универсам Авангард; ul Lenina 10; 24hr) Centrally located and well stocked – a godsend for self-caterers.

Shashlikoff RUSSIAN $$
(Шашлыкофф; ul Lenina 12; mains ₽200-300; 9am-1am;) This popular chain is fantastic value. Its signature shashlyk (meat kebabs) come in meat and fish varieties, accompanied by a full complement of Russian soups and salads and washed down with home-brewed beer (from ₽85). Additional branches opposite the **train station** (Vokzalnaya magistral 1;) and on **Krasny pr** (Krasny pr 17;).

Tiflis GEORGIAN $$
(Тифлис; www.tiflisnsk.ru; ul Sovetskaya 65; mains ₽350-600; 11am-11pm;) This atmospheric tavern-cavern offers the most authentic Georgian cuisine in town. The filling and delicious *khachapuri po-adzharski* (Georgian cheese bread with a raw egg swimming in the middle) is well worth a try.

★ **La Maison** EUROPEAN $$$
(ul Sovetskaya 25; mains ₽600-1500; noon-midnight;) In a beautiful former theatre dating to 1908, this is Novosibirsk's most sumptuous restaurant. The French- and Russian-leaning menu features quail, rabbit, rack of lamb and octopus along with upmarket versions of *solyanka* and other Russian country faves. Extensive wine list and rich desserts such as mille feuille.

Drinking & Nightlife

★ **Friends Cocktail Bar** BAR
(Krasny pr 22; 6pm-6am) With bearded bartenders whipping up some of Siberia's best (and strongest) cocktails and a convivial crowd, this is unquestionably Novosibirsk's best spot to warm up for a night out. Indeed you may elect to not go anywhere else. Reliably action-packed on weekdays as well as weekends, and you can eat at equally trendy **People's Bar & Grill** (Krasny pr 22; mains ₽350-800; 24hr) in the same building.

Truba BAR
(Труба; http://jazzclubtruba.ru in Russian; ul Frunze 2; 7pm til late;) It bills itself as a jazz bar but the line-up runs the gamut from jazz and blues to trash rock and grunge. Whatever is playing, this underground institution is well worth checking out. On Wednesdays beer and wine are ₽50.

Lebowsky CLUB
(Krasny pr 42a; admission ₽500; 10pm-6am Thu-Sat, 6-11pm Sun) Novosibirsk's best club at the time of writing, Lebowski is a fairly intimate affair that often draws top Moscow DJs.

Rock City CLUB
(Рок Сити; 383-227 0108; www.rockcity.ru; Krasny pr 37; admission ₽150-350) Everything from Latin dancing to DJs to heavy-rock concerts. Thursday is ladies' night and Tuesdays feature two-for-one cocktails.

Entertainment

★ **Opera & Ballet Theatre** THEATRE
(Театр оперы и балета; 383-347 8484; www.opera-novosibirsk.ru; Krasny pr 36; admission ₽200-4000; Oct-Jun, most shows at 6.30pm) For classical culture don't miss an evening at this gigantic silver-domed theatre. Built in 1945, it's the largest theatre in Russia – bigger even than Moscow's Bolshoi. The grand interior alone makes performances here one of the city's highlights. Ticket prices depend on seats and performances.

Brodyachaya Sobaka LIVE MUSIC
(Бродячая Собака; http://sabaka.su in Russian; Kamenskaya ul 32; noon-midnight, to 6am Fri & Sat;) Weekends usually see live music performing at this grungy cabaret bar, while weekdays bring all manner of performing arts – check the website for the schedule.

Philharmonia CLASSICAL MUSIC
(Филармония; www.philharmonia-nsk.ru; Krasny pr 32; tickets ₽200-1500; Oct-Jun, most shows 7pm) Classical music concerts.

Spartak Stadium SPORTS
(Стадион Спартак; 383-224 0488; http://fc-sibir.ru; ul Frunze 15) This 12,500-capacity venue is the home of local football team Sibir. Games are usually played on Saturday or Sunday, and tickets cost from ₽200 to ₽700.

Shopping

Book Look BOOKSTORE
(2nd fl, Pyramid Shopping Centre, Krasny pr 29/1; 9am-9pm) Has the best selection of maps in town, including maps of all Western Siberia *oblasti* (regions).

Information

Internet Club (ul Trudovaya 1; per hr ₽50; 24hr)
Main Post Office (Главпочтамт; ul Sovetskaya 33; 8am-10pm Mon-Fri, 9am-6pm Sat & Sun)

ℹ Getting There & Away

The well-located **Central Travel Bureau** (Центральное Бюро путешествий; Krasny pr 25; ⊙9am-8pm) is one of dozens of places to buy rail and air tickets, and also sells bus tickets (commission ₽100 to ₽200).

AIR

Novosibirsk's **Tolmachyovo Airport** (http://en.tolmachevo.ru), 30km west of the city, is well connected to Moscow (four hours) and various other domestic destinations. International destinations served by direct flights from Novosibirsk include Beijing, Prague and several cities in Central Asia, plus seasonal flights to Bangkok.

BUS

From the **bus station** (Автовокзал; Krasny pr 4) buses depart every hour or so to Barnaul (₽450, four hours) and Tomsk (₽544, 4½ hours). For roughly double the price, shared taxis shave an hour or more off those times but can take a while to fill up.

TRAIN

The city's huge main train station, **Novosibirsk Glavny** (ul Shamshurina 43), sits right on the Trans-Siberian main line and there are plentiful trains west to Moscow (48 to 55 hours) via Omsk, Tyumen and Yekaterinburg, and east to Irkutsk and beyond via Krasnoyarsk. The destinations listed below are off the Trans-Siberian main line. For Tobolsk you might be better off transferring in Tyumen. For Tomsk the bus is a better option.

ℹ Getting Around

From the bus station, bus 111z (111з) goes to Tolmachyovo airport every 30 minutes from 6am to 12.30am, stopping by the train station on the way. Allow an hour to get there (more during Novosibirsk's infamous rush hour). A **taxi** (☎383-212 212) to the airport ordered by phone costs ₽350 (30 minutes, or one hour during rush hour).

The metro has a major north–south line running beneath Krasny pr and across the river to ul Studencheskaya and pl Karla Marksa. For the main train station you'll need metro stop Ploshchad Garina-Mikhaylovskogo, which is on a second three-stop line that intersects with the major line at Sibirskaya/Krasny Prospekt.

Generally, buses are handier than the metro within the centre. Buses 8, 21 and 37 link the train station with the river station via pl Lenina, Krasny pr and the bus station.

TRAINS FROM NOVOSIBIRSK

DESTINATION	MAIN TRAINS SERVING DESTINATION & FREQUENCY	PRICE PLATSKART/KUPE	DURATION (HR)
Abakan	68 (daily, 6.01am)	₽1750/3490	23
Almaty	301 (odd-numbered days, 4.48pm)	₽3569/5120	41
Barnaul	601 (daily, 8.03pm), 391 (odd-numbered days, 8.12am)	₽750/1350	5
Biysk	601 (daily, 8.03pm)	₽700/1770	9½
Novokuznetsk	105 (even-numbered days, 9.20pm), 118 (odd-numbered days, 8.45pm)	₽1200/1936	8
Severobaikalsk	92 (even-numbered days, 6.04pm)	₽3090/6350	40
Tashkent	369 (7 per month, 1.51pm)	₽8270/10,310	63
Tobolsk	116 (odd-numbered days, 1.04am)	₽3300/6400	21¾
Tomsk	38 (odd-numbered days, 3.36am), 392 (odd-numbered days, 12.37am)	from ₽838/1555	5½

ELEKTRICHKI (SUBURBAN TRAINS) FROM NOVOSIBIRSK

DESTINATION	SCHEDULE	PRICE	DURATION (HR)
Novokuznetsk	daily except Wed, 2.40pm	1st-/2nd-class ₽940 /721	6
Omsk	Mon, Wed, Fri, 2.55pm	1st-/2nd-/3rd class ₽1600/1250/840	6¾

Tomsk Томск

☎3822 / POP 524,000 / ⏲ MOSCOW +3HR

One of Siberia's oldest cities, Tomsk was founded in 1604 and was a major trade outpost before the founding of Novosibirsk (then Novo-Nikolaevsk) and the subsequent relocation of the trans-Siberian railway line. It's a university city where around one in every five residents is a student – hence the youthful, intellectual atmosphere.

Magnificent in snow, but pleasant at any time of the year, Tomsk also boasts endless examples of fine wooden buildings and an animated cafe and art scene. The city has enjoyed the reputation as the 'cultural capital of Siberia' since the 1960s, when artists, writers, and theatre and film directors were invited to take up residence here.

Sights

★Resurrection Hill HISTORICAL AREA

This was the location of Tomsk's original fortress, and the replica of its central wooden *spasskaya bashnya* (savior's tower) that stands on it today was built in 2004 for the city's 400th-anniversary celebrations. Next to the tower, the **History of Tomsk Museum** (Исторический музей Томска; admission ₽125; ⏲10am-7pm Tue-Sun) has spouted its own wooden observation tower (admission ₽43); try to spot the seven historic churches from the top. The museum's moderately interesting collection of old artefacts and clothing is well presented, with placards in English.

For ₽100 you can rent historical costumes for silly photo ops. The stone just outside the museum entrance marks the founding of the city. Also up on Resurrection Hill is a pretty **Catholic Church** (ul Bakunina 4) dating to 1883.

★Oppression Museum MUSEUM

(Мемориальный музей 'Следственная тюрьма НКВД'; pr Lenina 44; admission ₽50, camera ₽100, tours in Russian/English ₽200/400; ⏲10am-6pm) The gloomy basement of this former NKVD (proto-KGB) building is now a memorable Oppression Museum. Tours are recommended, but should be ordered in advance. Look out for the stunning Gulag map, the system of Soviet labour camps depicted as an uncountable mass of red dots across the territory of the former USSR.

Prisoners who passed through here included gulag chronicler Eufrosinia Kersnovskaya and the family of the purged Kazakh writer Akhmet Baytursinuli. Outside the museum are two monuments to victims of Stalinist repression – the larger to local victims, the second to Poles slaughtered by Uncle Joe and his cronies.

★Ploshchad Lenina HISTORIC SITE

Central pl Lenina isn't really a square so much as a jumbled collection of beautifully restored historic buildings interspersed with banal Soviet concrete lumps. The frustrated **Lenin statue** (pl Lenina), now relegated to a traffic circle, points at the ugly concrete of the **Drama Theatre** (Драматический театр; ☎3822-512 223; www.dramatomsk.ru; pl Lenina 4; ⏲Oct-Jun), apparently demanding 'build more like that one'. Fortunately, nobody's listening. Topped with a golden angel, in a second circle beside Lenin, is the **Iverskaya Chapel** (Иверская часовня; ⏲10am-6pm); its celebrated icon is dubbed 'Tomsk's Spiritual Gateway'.

The drama theatre is flanked by the splendid 1784 **Epiphany Cathedral** (Богоявленский собор; pl Lenina 7), the former **trading arches** (Гостиный Двор), and the elegant 1802 Hotel Magistrat.

Tomsk Art Museum ART MUSEUM

(Художественный музей; www.artmuseum.tomsk.ru; per Nakhanovicha 3; admission per exhibit ₽100; ⏲10am-6pm Tue-Sun) Well worth popping into for its wide range of permanent and temporary exhibits. The highlight is the collection of 19th- and early 20th-century Russian art, and there's a small exhibit of 12th- to 13th-century religious icons.

University HISTORIC BUILDING

(Томский Государственный Университет) The classically colonnaded main buildings of the university lie in resplendently leafy grounds, giving Tomsk the sobriquet 'Oxford of Siberia'. There's not much open to the public, but there's nothing to stop you taking a walk around the grounds.

Regional Museum MUSEUM
(Краеведческий музей; pr Lenina 75; admission ₽200; ⏲10am-6pm Tue-Sun) Housed in the splendid Atashev Palace, this modest museum has a 2500-year-old bear amulet and an interesting exhibit on the Great Tea Trail. But it's the building, commissioned in 1842 by the gold-mining entrepreneur Ivan Atashev, that's the main attraction. It was once used as a church, hence the incongruous steeple tower and wonderful organ hall.

Voznesenskaya Church CHURCH
(Вознесенская церковь; ul Oktyabrsky Vzvoz 10) This Gothic edifice with five gold-tipped black spires has great potential as a Dracula movie set. A truly massive bell hangs in its lurid-pink belfry.

WWII Memorial MONUMENT
A Tomsk landmark, this moving mother-and-son monument is at the very southern end of pr Lenina. The beautiful birch tree park (Лагерный сад) here is a local favourite for strolls, not least for its fine views across the Tom River.

☞ Tours

Tomskturist WALKING TOURS
(Томсктурист; ☎3822-528 179; www.tomskturist.ru; pr Lenina 59; ⏲9am-7pm Mon-Fri, 11am-4pm Sat) Tomskturist can arrange two-hour walking tours of the city, with English-, French- and German-speaking guides, although the price (₽4500) makes this more of a group option. Can also help sort out Altai border-zone permits, arrange regional excursions and sell plane and train tickets. Darya speaks English.

Sleeping

Lucomoria Hostel HOSTEL $
(☎3822-504 218; www.lucomoria.ru; ul Sovetskaya 75; 🚭@📶) An excellent all-around hostel within walking distance of the centre, with comfortable beds, a nice kitchen, double rooms with queen beds, and a six-bed women's dorm. Door code: 19.

Dom Okhotnika Hostel HOSTEL
(Хостел Дом Охотника; ☎3812-258 646; www-hunter-hostel.ru; ul Gagarina 42; dm ₽400-600, d ₽1200; 🚭📶) Rich with potential because of its location in the lovely 19th-century 'Hunter's House', the spartan interior unfortunately lacks the charm of the glorious exterior. Still, the location is the best of Tomsk's hostels and the private rooms are fantastic value. However, the large dorm rooms are geared more towards locals than tourists. No English spoken.

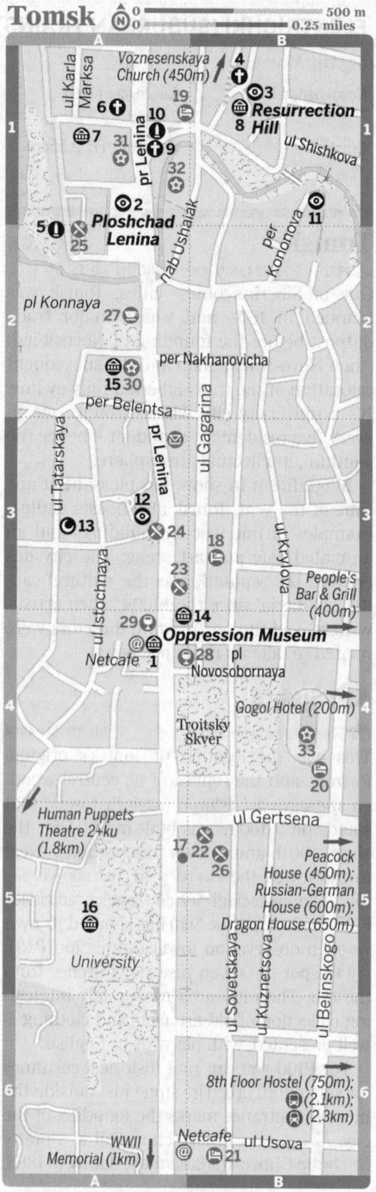

Tomsk

Top Sights
1 Oppression Museum ... A4
2 Ploshchad Lenina ... A1
3 Resurrection Hill ... B1

Sights
4 Catholic Church ... B1
5 Chekhov Statue ... A2
6 Epiphany Cathedral ... A1
7 Former Trading Arches ... A1
8 History of Tomsk Museum ... B1
9 Iverskaya Chapel ... A1
10 Lenin Statue ... A1
11 per Kononova 2 ... B1
12 Prospekt Lenina 56 ... A3
13 Red Mosque ... A3
14 Regional Museum ... A4
15 Tomsk Art Museum ... A2
16 University ... A5

Activities, Courses & Tours
17 Tomskturist ... A5

Sleeping
18 Dom Okhotnika Hostel ... B3
19 Hotel Magistrat ... A1
20 Hotel Sputnik ... B4
21 Lucomoria Hostel ... B6

Eating
22 Obzhorni Ryad ... B5
23 Pelmeni Project ... A3
24 People's Bar & Grill ... A3
25 Slavyansky Bazar ... A2
26 Vechny Zov ... B5

Drinking & Nightlife
27 Bulanzhe ... A2
28 Sibirsky Pub ... A4
29 Underground Jazz Café ... A4

Entertainment
30 Aelita Theatre ... A2
31 Drama Theatre ... A1
Organ Hall ... (see 14)
32 Philharmonia ... A1
Tom Tomsk FC ... (see 33)
33 Trud Stadium ... B4

8th Floor Hostel HOSTEL $
(☎3822-565 522; www.8hostel.com; ul Dzherzhinskogo 56; dm ₽450-550, d ₽1200; ⊜@☎) This 20-bed hostel is – wouldn't you know it – on the 8th floor of a Soviet high-rise. It checks out nicely on all fronts, especially the cocoon-like bunk beds, but finding it is tricky. It's in the 10-storey building behind ul Kirova 39; take the southernmost entrance and dial 55.

Hotel Sputnik HOTEL $$
(Гостиница Спутник; ☎3812-526 660; www.sputnik.tomskturist.ru; ul Belinskogo 15; s/d incl breakfast from ₽3500/4200, without bathroom incl breakfast ₽1050/2300; ⊜@☎) The winner of Tomsk's first hotel competition in the 1990s, the Sputnik remains one of the few decent places to stay at the midrange, especially after a recent makeover. The rooms, however, retain their small Soviet dimensions and narrow beds. The breakfast is hardly worth getting up for.

★ **Gogol Hotel** HOTEL $$$
(☎3822-909 709; http://gogolhotel.ru; s/d incl breakfast ₽3900/4500, ste ₽5900-8000; ⊜❄☎) Bordering on boutique, this classy 19-room property has quickly become Tomsk's most sought-after address. Rooms are spacious with muted gray tones and walls emblazoned with photos of old Tomsk. You can swim in the king-sized beds and the breakfast is fantastic.

CHEKHOV ON TOMSK – 'BORING CITY, DULL PEOPLE'

Not everyone falls in love with Tomsk. Playwright Anton Chekhov – who visited the city on his way to Russia's Far East – certainly didn't. 'Tomsk isn't worth a damn,' he wrote in his diary. 'A boring city...with dull people.' He also described it as 'a drunken city' where there were 'no beautiful women at all'. He also complained that a waitress had wiped a spoon 'against her backside' before handing it to him. But then, as legend has it, he did almost drown while crossing the Tom River, so maybe he was feeling grumpy. The city had its revenge though. In 2004, on Tomsk's 400th anniversary, a caricature of the famous writer was unveiled, in the form of a bronze **statue** entitled 'Anton Pavlovich [the writer's patronymic] through the eyes of a drunk lying in a ditch'. The statue is on the riverbank opposite Slavyansky Bazar restaurant. Rubbing its well-polished nose is said to bring good luck.

WOODEN ARCHITECTURE

Much of Tomsk's appeal lies in its well-preserved late-19th- and early-20th-century 'wooden-lace' architecture – carved windows and tracery on old log and timber houses. There are a few streets to hone in on if touring the city on foot.

Ul Tatarskaya has perhaps the richest concentration of such houses. It's reached via the steps beside a lovely old house at **prospekt Lenina 56** (пр Ленина 56). The best examples are on the block north of ul Trifonova, where you'll also find the modest **Red Mosque** (Красная Мечеть; ul Tatarskaya 22), which dates from 1904. It was used as a vodka factory by the atheist Soviets, but was reopened to worshippers in 1997. Over on the east side of pr Lenina, **ul Gagarina** is similarly endowed with graceful heritage houses.

A few blocks east of ul Belinskogo, near the corner of ul Krasnoarmeyskaya and ul Gertsena, look out for the spired, bright-turquoise 1904 **Russian-German House** (Российско-Немецкий Дом; ul Krasnoarmeyskaya 71); the late-19th-century **Dragon House** (Дом Дракона; ul Krasnoarmeyskaya 68) which is home to a clinic; and the early-20th-century, fan-gabled **Peacock House** (Дом Павлина; ul Krasnoarmeyskaya 67a). **Ul Dzerzhinskogo**, one block east of ul Krasnoarmeyskaya, is worth a wander for wood houses as well as the colourful outdoor **Dzherzhinskogo Market** (Дзержинского рынка; ul Dzherzhinskogo), which sprawls for a full block south of ul Kartashova, providing photo ops as well as fuel in the form of local fruits and nuts.

Other streets worth strolling are **per Kononova** (look for **No 2**, where the doomed communist mastermind Sergei Kirov lodged in 1905); and nearby **ul Shishkova**.

Hotel Magistrat HOTEL $$$
(Гостиница Магистрат; ☎3822-511 111; www.magistrathotel.com; pl Lenina 15; d/tw incl breakfast from ₽5800/6600; ❄📶) Behind the palatial 1802 facade, the rooms and restaurant are done up in the ultra-luxurious style that Russians seem to love but foreigners find overdone. You can't beat the location, however. No lift.

Eating

Obzhorni Ryad RUSSIAN $
(Обжорный ряд; ul Gertsena 1; mains ₽100-200; ⏲11am-11pm; 📶) For penny-pinchers in search of good-value Russian fare, look no further than this *stolovaya,* the name of which translates as Guzzler's Row.

Pelmeni Project RUSSIAN $
(pr Lenina 81; mains ₽150-250; ⏲24hr; 📶🗐) Besides the best *pelmeni* in town, this buzzing, centrally located eatery serves Russian staples, burgers and even some Italian fare. The outdoor terrace is ripe for people-watching in the warm months.

★ **Bulanzhe** CAFE
(Буланже; pr Lenina 80; mains ₽200-350; ⏲10am-11pm; 📶) Fantastic cafe – bright and cheery with an exciting menu of international food, fresh salads, great coffee and a wide tea selection. The Belgian waffles are highly recommended. It's a place to chat and chew rather than work on a laptop.

People's Bar & Grill INTERNATIONAL $$
(pr Lenina 54; mains ₽250-450; ⏲noon-2am; 📶🗐) This trendy bar and grill embraces pop culture with movie-star photos, music videos and Hollywood-inspired dishes – Big Lebowski (beef steak with with potatoes) and Pulp Fishion (salmon steak). Another branch just off **pr Frunze** (ul Krasnoarmeyskaya 31; mains ₽250-450; ⏲noon-2am; 📶🗐).

Vechny Zov RUSSIAN $$
(Вечный Зов; ul Sovetskaya 47; mains ₽200-800; ⏲noon-2am; 📶🗐) Named after a popular Soviet TV serial, this the place to sample Siberian specialties like *stroganina, muksun* (an Ob River whitefish) and bear meat. Try the four-meat (bear, deer, pork, beef) *pelmeni.* It boasts a mock Siberian ranch outside and a cosy antique-filled home feel inside.

★ **Slavyansky Bazar** RUSSIAN $$$
(Славянский Базар; ☎3812-515 553; pl Lenina 10; mains ₽500-1200; ⏲noon-midnight; 📶🗐) On the bank of the Tom River, Slavyansky Bazar is Tomsk's fanciest restaurant, housed in a 19th-century building. Penny-pinchers can order from the *pelmeni/varenyky* menu or stop in for the business lunch. Chekhov ate at an earlier incarnation of the present-day establishment in 1890. The food was one of the few things he liked about the city.

Drinking & Nightlife

★ **Underground Jazz Cafe** BAR
(www.jazzcafe.tomsk.ru; pr Lenina 46; cover charge weekends ₽250 to ₽400; ⏲ noon-midnight Sun-Thu, to 2am Fri & Sat; 📶) A hip and literally underground basement with live jazz, including frequent US guests, most weekends. Also has an extensive drinks and food menu. We liked the vegetarian borsch and the screenings of old black-and-white films.

Sibirsky Pub PUB
(Сибирский Паб; pl Novosobornaya 2; Guinness per pint ₽340; ⏲ 1pm-1am; 📶) Siberia's first British pub was founded over a century ago by a certain Mr Crawley, an Anglo-Egyptian albino who'd got stuck in Tomsk after touring with a circus freak show. Today's pub is no relation. Bands play live at weekends).

Entertainment

★ **Tom Tomsk FC** SPORTS
(Томь Томск ФК; tickets from ₽300) **Trud Stadium** (ul Belinskogo 15/1) is the home of Siberia's top football club. Since 2004 Tom Tomsk has spent most years in the Russian Premier League, making it Europe's most easterly top-flight football club. Unfortunately the team was relegated to the second flight in 2014. At the stadium there's a shop selling Tomsk scarves and T-shirts. It's open 11am to 7pm Monday to Friday, and on weekends on home match days.

Human Puppets Theatre 2+ku PUPPET THEATRE
(Театр живых кукол 2+ку; www.2ky.tomsk.ru; Yuzhny per 29; admission ₽200-500) Housed in a quaint log cabin near the WWII memorial (take ul Savinikh all the way down until you can't go any further), this one-man, homey 'robotic puppet' theatre is a real experience, and one you don't need to understand Russian to appreciate.

Aelita Theatre THEATRE
(Театр Аэлита; ☎3822-514 436; www.aelita.tom.ru in Russian; pr Lenina 78) Eclectic offerings from rock concerts to Indian dance to experimental plays.

Philharmonia CONCERT HALL
(Филармония; ☎3822-515 956; http://bkz.tomsk.ru; pl Lenina 1) Classical music and great big-band jazz. Hosts the Tomsk International Jazz Festival in the first week in June.

Organ Hall CLASSICAL MUSIC
(pr Lenina 75; tickets ₽200-500) Beautiful organ concerts are held several times a month upstairs in the Atashev Palace. The acoustics are brilliant.

Information

Afisha (www.afisha.westsib.ru) Has concert and cinema details.

Main Post Office (Почтамт; pr Lenina 95; ⏲ 8am-10pm Mon-Fri, 9am-6pm Sat & Sun) Stamps, but no postcards of Tomsk (find postcards in most museums).

Netcafe (Неткафе; pr Lenina 44; per hour ₽47; ⏲ 9am-11pm) Another branch (pr Lenina 41; per hr ₽47; ⏲ 9am-11pm) south of the University.

Sent to Siberia (http://senttosiberia.wordpress.com) A now-departed American Fulbright scholar's humorous and affectionate account of life in Tomsk.

Getting There & Away

AIR

Bogashevo Airport, 22km southeast of Tomsk, has several daily flights to Moscow plus some regional services on **Tomskavia** (Томскавиа; ☎3822-412 466; www.tomskavia.ru; ul Yelizarovkh). The choice is much wider from Novosibirsk.

BUS

For Novosibirsk, buses (₽544, 4½ hours, every hour) depart from the central **bus station** (Автовокзал; ☎3822-540 730), which is right next to the main train station. Buses also serve Abakan (₽1750, 17 hours, four weekly), Barnaul (₽850, nine hours, two daily), Gorno-Altaisk (₽1750, 15 hours, 6.45pm), Krasnoyarsk (₽690, 12 hours, 8.05pm) and Novokuznetsk (₽825, seven hours, two daily).

TRAIN

From Tomsk I (main) train station, there's a train on even-numbered days to Barnaul (*platskart/kupe* ₽1100/2000, 15½ hours, 9.20pm) via Novosibirsk. There are trains on odd-numbered days to Novokuznetsk (₽1100/1530, 12½ hours, 7.33pm) and Moscow (₽7350/11,060, 56 hours), and a train every 4th day to Vladivostok.

For more frequent connections east (towards Irkutsk) and west (towards Novosibirsk), take an *elektrichka* to Taiga (₽112, two hours, 9.06am and 4.15pm) or a bus to Yurga (₽210, two hours, four daily); most main-line Trans-Siberian trains stop at both stations. *Elektrichki* from Taiga to Tomsk depart at 7.07am and 4.15pm.

Getting Around

The bus station and Tomsk 1 (main) train station sit together about 2km southeast of the centre. Good maps are available in the train station and at street kiosks.

Buses 4, 12 and 12a run from pl Lenina to the train station via pr Lenina and pr Kirova. Hop on and off trolleybuses 1 and 3, or bus 17, which all go along pr Lenina.

Tomsk's antiquated and atmospheric trams are a great way to take a cheap (₽15) city tour. Tram 2 runs the length of ul Sovetskaya before connecting with the train station via pr Kirova. Tram 1 trundles all the way to the city's northern outskirts via ul Sovetskaya and ul Bolshaya Podgornaya.

Novokuznetsk Новокузнецк

☎3843 / POP 563,000 / ⏰MOSCOW +3HR

Novokuznetsk, the largest city in the industrial Kemerovo region, boasts a well-laid-out centre and some remarkable Soviet-era monuments. However, if you come here chances are you're heading somewhere else: the city makes a convenient stopover point between Abakan and Biysk when overlanding between Tuva and Altai, and is also the jumping-off point to snowboarder haven Sheregesh.

Founded on the right bank of the Tom River in 1618, the frequently enlarged Kuznetsk Fortress became one of the most important guardians of imperial Russia's southeastern frontier. The city's left (west) bank, named Stalinsk until 1961, was constructed almost from scratch by Soviet 'shockworkers' (superproductive workers) in the 1930s and is now the city centre. Novokuznetsk's metal plants, which supply 70% of Russia's train tracks, are mainly responsible for Novokuznetsk being one of the five most polluted cities in Russia, according to government figures.

Sights & Activities

Kuznetsk Fortress HISTORIC SITE
(Кузнецкая крепость; http://kuzn-krepost.ru; Krepostnoy proezd 1; admission ₽15 plus ₽30-50 per museum; ⏰museums 9.30am-5.30pm Mon-Fri, 10am-5pm Sat & Sun) The restored stone ramparts of the Kuznetsk Fortress are massive and topped with cannons but represent only 20% of their 1810 extent. Kids ride ponies around the attractive grounds and there are a couple of modest museums that you can pop into – the archaeology museum, which contains mammoth tusks and old stone tools, is probably the most interesting.

The fortress is in the old part of town on the right (east) bank of the Tom River. To get here take frequent bus 5 from outside the bus station and get off at the first stop over the bridge (15 minutes). It's a 15-minute walk up the hill to the fortress via the beautiful 1792 **Transfiguration Cathedral** (Преображенский собор; ul Vodopadnaya 18).

Park Gagarina PARK
(pr Metallurgov) If you only have a couple of hours to kill, take a strolll though this oasis of green just north of the train station. It contains a bust of a jolly-looking Yuri Gagarin, a mothballed **planetarium** and the constructionist (and now empty) **Kommunar Theatre** (Кинотеатр Коммунар; pr Metalurgov 18), which once housed Siberia's first audio cinema. Just north of the theatre, two splendidly reverential statues of Soviet-era metalworkers guard pleasant **Mettalurgists' Garden** (Park Gagarina).

Statue of Vladimir Mayakovsky MONUMENT
(cnr ul Ordzhonikidze & pr Metallurgov) Although the doomed writer never actually visited Novokuznetsk, he was so moved by the Soviet project to build a new city that he penned a poem starting with the lines, famous all over Russia, '*Ya znau budet gorod, ya znau sadu svest*' ('I know there will be a city, I know the gardens will bloom'). The statue is opposite pr Metallurgov 39.

Former Soviet Builders Club HISTORIC BUILDING
(ul Ordzhonikidzye 23) Guarded by two more statues of Soviet workers, wielding a hammer and a plasterer's board, the one-time cement-workers' club is now used as a cultural centre. Take the first left after the Mayakovsky statue.

Lenin & Gorky Statue MONUMENT
An apparently coal-caked Lenin and Maxim Gorky (founder of socialist realism) discuss – or plot? – something or other, next to the main post office at pr Metallurgov 21.

Sleeping & Eating

Resting rooms HOSTEL $
(komnaty otdykha; ☎3843-743 131; 12/24hr from ₽1000/1500; 📶) The sparkling ensuite resting rooms in Novokuznetsk's flashy new train station are a logical place to lay your head if laying over in Novokuznetsk.

Hotel Novokuznetsk HOTEL $$
(Гостиница Новокузнецк; ☎8800-700 1485; www.novokuznetskaya.com; ul Kirova 53; s/d from

₽2200/2600; @ wifi) This renovated Soviet-built hotel smack-dab in the middle of the city has a wide variety of decent if unimaginative rooms at good prices.

Pechki-Lavochki RUSSIAN $
(Печки-Лавочки; ul Kirova 21a; mains ₽200-400; ⏰11am-midnight) Traditional Russian food served in a rustic setting by waitresses dressed as peasants. The chain is named after a 1972 Soviet road film. It's on the city's main intersection (ul Kirova and pr Metallurgov), with sushi and pizza restaurants at the same address.

Mariya-Ra SUPERMARKET
(pr Metallurgov 2; ⏰24hr) Easy snacks for self-caterers just opposite the train station.

Orientation

Pr Metallurgov stretches north from the train station to the main drag, ul Kirova. The Tom River is a couple of kilometres east along ul Kirova. Maps are available in a kiosk inside the train station.

Information

Main Post Office (pr Metallurgov 21; ⏰8am-10pm Mon-Fri, 9am-6pm Sat & Sun)

Getting There & Away

There are a few flights a day from Novokuznetsk's Spichenkovo Airport to Moscow (four hours). To get to the airport, take bus or *marshrutka* 160 from the train station.

The *elektrichka* to Novosibirsk leaves at 7.05am every day except Wednesday (1st-/2nd-class ₽940/721, six hours). There are one or two slower regular trains to Novosibirsk per day as well, including an overnight option on odd-numbered days. Trains run daily to Abakan (*platskart/kupe* ₽900/1700, nine hours, 9.20pm), and on even-numbered days to Tomsk (₽1050/2010, 12 hours, 5.24pm). There's a snail-slow *elektrichka* to Tashtagol (jumping-off point to Sheregesh) on odd-numbered days at 5.10am (from ₽136, five hours); the bus is a much better option.

From the **bus station** (Автовокзал; ☎3843-745 472), right next to the train station, there are hourly buses to Tashtagol (₽379, 3½ hours). Shared taxis are an option to Tashtagol in the ski season (about ₽700, two hours). Buses also serve Barnaul (₽791, seven hours, three daily), Biysk (₽484, 5¼ hours, five daily), Krasnoyarsk (₽1425, 14½ hours, 6.40pm), Novosibirsk (₽725, eight hours, four daily), and Tomsk (₽825, seven hours, two daily).

Sheregesh Шерегеш

☎3843 / POP 9600 / ⏰MOSCOW +3HR

Isolated and tiny Sheregesh is a mining village that has become the focus of a booming snowboarding and skiing scene in recent years. Those who make it here are rewarded with some of the most prolific snowfall in Russia, uncrowded slopes and a raucous aprés-ski scene that would put many European resorts to shame. If you arrive out of season, Sheregesh is also a fine place to relax and/or go hiking in the taiga and around the mountain. The journey here is an added bonus, winding through tiny villages and deserted country roads in view of the Gorniya Shoriya mountains.

Activities

In the off-season, you can hike up the ski mountain or any of the other peaks around Sheregesh, or rent good-quality **mountain bikes** from Ays Club (per hour/half-day ₽200/400) to explore Sheregesh village or seek out more rugged terrain in the hills (ask the knowledgable folks at Ays).

Sheregesh Ski Resort SKIING
(www.sheregesh.ru in Russian; Gondolas per ride ₽200, chairlifts per ride ₽100-150; ⏰9.30am-5pm) The ski resort sprawls over Zelyonaya (Green) Mountain (1257m), which is reputed to get Russia's finest powder. The mountain is well-served by three gondolas and several chairlifts. The slopes close around late April, but a few lifts stay open in the off-season to bring tourists up the mountain for spectacular views of the village and the surrounding taiga. Ski and snowboard rental is widely available at the base of the mountain from ₽200 per hour including boots.

The lifts are run by several different operators, which means you pay by the ride instead of by the day, but it ends up being fantastic value no matter how many runs you take.

Off-piste *rattrak* (snowcat) skiing is another option, and continues into July (although you'll be hard-pressed to find equipment for rent after April). Snowcats gather skiers near the top of the main gondola and proceed up to the unusual 'Verbluda (camel) Rocks'. Three hours of riding costs ₽500 per person – a real bargain.

Snowmobiles also make the trip to Verbluda Rocks (₽800 for the half-hour round-trip journey). With the wind in your face as you speed through the snow, it's hard not to feel a little like James Bond. Hold on tight! The trip lasts about half an hour, with time for photos and clambering about on the rocks.

Sleeping

The vast majority of hotels are based around the mountain. Prices listed are for ski-season weekdays; rates rise substantially on weekends in the ski season, and drop in the off-season.

★ Ays Club HOSTEL $
(Айс Клуб; ☎8-923-625 1516; www.ays-club.ru; dm ₽450-600, d from ₽2900;) One of the first hotels you'll come across as you approach the mountain, hip and funky Ays is a self-contained party zone – a hostel, a pumping basement nightclub ('Bunker'), a cafe and an Irish pub rolled into one. The cheap dorms make it an obvious choice for young snowboarders on a budget, while the stylish, spacious private rooms will appeal to midrange travellers. It's also one of the few places open year-round.

Ays Laska HOSTEL $
(Айс Ласка; ☎8-960-904 8474; www.ays-club.ru; dm ₽450-600, s/d from ₽1200/2900;) A couple of hundred metres up the road from Ays Club, Ays Laska is similarly fun and funky, if slightly more subdued than its sister property. Perks include great linens, ping-pong, minibars, flat-screen TVs with Playstation and an affordable *stolovaya* (mains ₽150 to ₽250) on premises.

Resting rooms HOSTEL $
(komnaty otdykha; Tashtagol Bus Station; s/d ₽950/1600) If you get stuck in Tashtagol the ensuite resting rooms above the bus station are an option.

Olga HOTEL $$
(Ольга; ☎3843-975 975; www.olgahotel.ru; d/tr/ste from ₽3300/4000/6500) One of the biggest hotels in the area, Olga's economy rooms are decent but uninspiring. Its suites are, however, superb, but pricey. It offers a range of activities throughout the year, from excursions to paintball. Next door, an ice rink is attached to its Beer Gesh restaurant. Olga's nearby sister hotel, **Berloga** (Берлога; ☎3843-203 040; www.berlogahotel.ru; d/tr/q from ₽3000/4000/5000;), is another option. Both are a five-minute walk to the lifts.

Eating & Drinking

There are several eateries at the top and the base of the mountain for lunch, plus plenty of shashlyk and other open-air snacks available. Breakfast and dinner are typically taken in your hotel. While you are in Sheregesh, be sure to try the local wild leek. Local women sell it by the roadside for around ₽25 a bag. Known as *kabla* locally and *cheremsha* in Russian, its distinctive garlicky taste is one you won't forget in a hurry!

Yurta CENTRAL ASIAN $$
(mains ₽200-500) Hearty Central Asian fare served in an oversized heated yurt at the main base area.

Mariya-Ra SUPERMARKET
(ul Yubileynaya 2; ⏰8am-10pm) Very well-stocked self-catering option opposite the bus station in the centre of town.

★ Grelka BAR
(mains ₽300-400; ⏰noon-11pm) Right at the main base area, Grelka is *the* aprés-ski place. Convivial atmosphere, pub grub and competent bartenders serving a wide range of local and imported beers. When it warms up the party moves out to the patio – it's a party you don't want to miss. Grelka is also the brains behind Sheregesh's infamous 'Bikini Ride', an annual event held during 'Grelka Fest' that owns the world record for most people in swimwear on the slopes at one time (women *and* men).

Clever PUB
(Ays Laska Hotel; Guiness pint ₽320) This cleverly named Irish pub is a fine place for a pint of Guiness or a round of aprés-ski shooters.

Orientation

Ul Gagarina runs from the ski slope down to the village, where it intersects with the main street, ul Dzherzhinskogo, which runs through the centre of town.

Information

There are plenty of ATMs both in the town and at the base of the slopes, including in most hotels.

Getting There & Around

Bus 101 connects Sheregesh with the village of Tashtagol every 30 minutes from 6.45am to 11.30pm (₽27, 30 minutes). A taxi from Sheregesh to Tashtagol should cost ₽400. There are hourly buses until 7pm from Tashtagol to Novokuznetsk (₽379, 3½ hours).

In the ski season, Ays-Club and a few other resorts run fun buses directly from Novosibirsk to their respective properties on the slopes – contact Ays-Club for details.

There is no public transport to Altai. A taxi to Gorno-Altaisk (3½ hours) or Artybash (three hours) from Sheregesh will set you back about ₽6000; from Tashtagol it will cost about ₽5000. The road to Altai is unsealed but passable year-round.

Sheregesh's main bus stop is in the middle of town at the corner of ul Yubileynaya and ul Dzerzhinskogo. A taxi from the main bus stop to the slopes costs a flat ₽150.

ALTAI

Greater Altai (Алтай), bordering on Kazakhstan, China and Mongolia, consists of the Altai Territory and the Altai Republic. The Altai Territory, while pleasant enough, is most noteworthy as a gateway to the wonders of the unforgettable Altai Republic. This sprawling and sparsely populated region is home to snow-capped mountains – including Siberia's highest peak (Mt Belukha, 4506m) – and over 7000 lakes. The Altai Republic has long been regarded as an area of spiritual and occult significance, and Russian philosopher and painter Nikolai Rerikh (Nicholas Roerich) visited the region in the early 20th century in an attempt to locate the entrance to Shambala, the mythical enlightened land of Tibetan Buddhism. He failed, but you might not…

Gorno-Altaisk, the capital of the Altai Republic, is the logical jumping-off point to most of Altai's attractions. Be sure to get your visa registered here before heading onwards (see p439). Also note that if you plan to do any trekking in the high peaks of southern Altai you'll need a border permit. If you are heading to Ust-Koksa or beyond (including Tyungur), you will also need a border permit (see boxed text, p438). If you are heading to Mongolia you will not need a permit as long as you don't venture off the M52 highway (aka the Chuysky Trakt).

Prices remain low across Altai, one of Russia's poorest regions. For maps, try the Dom Knigi shops in any big city, which sporadically stock 1:200,000 Altai sheets.

Altai Culture

Asiatic ethnic-Altai people constitute around 30% of the Altai Republic's 200,000-strong population, and a vastly lower proportion in the heavily Russianised Altai Territory. Despite strong animist undercurrents, most Altai are nominally Christian and villages aren't visually distinct, though some rural Altai homes still incorporate an *ail* (yurt-like traditional dwellings). In the Altai language, hello is *yakhshler,* thank you (very much) is *(dyan) biyan/biyan bolzyn* and beautiful is *charash*. Altai tea is served milky: add a bran-rich flour called *talkan* and it becomes a sort of porridge.

Some of the Altai Republic's 5% ethnic Kazakhs are still nomadic herders living in traditional felt yurts, notably around Kosh-Agach. Most Kazakhs are Muslims who are keen on *kumiss* (fermented mare's milk) but don't generally drink vodka and, consequently, Kazakh settlements have lower rates of violence than Altai ones.

Barnaul — Барнаул

☎3852 / POP 575,000 / ⌚MOSCOW +3HR

The capital of the Altai Territory, Barnaul is a fairly prosperous industrial city and has been so almost since its foundation in 1730 as Ust-Barnaulskaya. It offers just enough cafes and museums to keep you amused between transport connections. The main drag is pr Lenina, which runs 8km northwest from the river station.

Sights

★Altai Arts, Literature & Culture Museum — MUSEUM
(Музей истории, литературы, искусства и культуры Алтая; http://gmilika22.ru; ul Tolstogo 2; admission ₽30; ⌚10am-5.40pm Tue-Sat) The impressively eclectic – not to mention good-value – Altai Arts, Literature & Culture Museum occupies a restored, furnished 1850s mansion. There are some fine icons, Rerikh sketches and an impressive WWII room.

★War History Museum — MUSEUM
(Музей истории войны; Komsomolsky pr 73b; admission ₽50; ⌚9.30am-5.30pm Tue-Sat) In an old brick house, the War History Museum is simple and all in Russian but the moving understatement of its Afghanistan and Chechnya memorials is particularly affecting.

★Pokrovsky Church — CHURCH
(Покровский собор; ul Nikitina 135-7) This bulbous-domed brick building is the most appealing of the city's many churches and has a fine, gilded interior.

Altai Republic

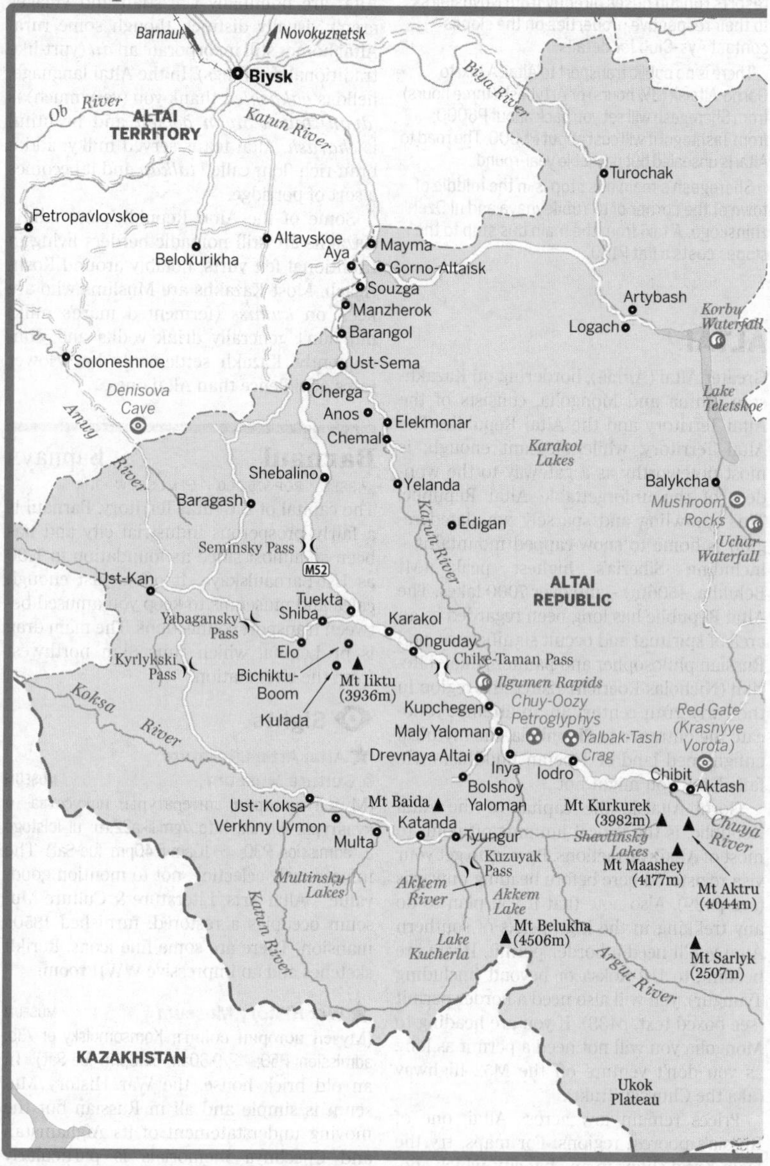

Wooden-Lace Houses NOTABLE BUILDING

Rapacious redevelopment has destroyed much of Barnaul's older architecture. Nonetheless, centuries-old remnants are dotted between the shopping malls. A few splendid examples include those at **ulitsa Korolenko 96**, **ulitsa Pushkina 80** and **ulitsa Polzunova 31** and **48**.

FSB Headquarters NOTABLE BUILDING

(Штаб ФСБ; pr Lenina 30) The city's Federal Security Services (FSB) headquarters is worth a

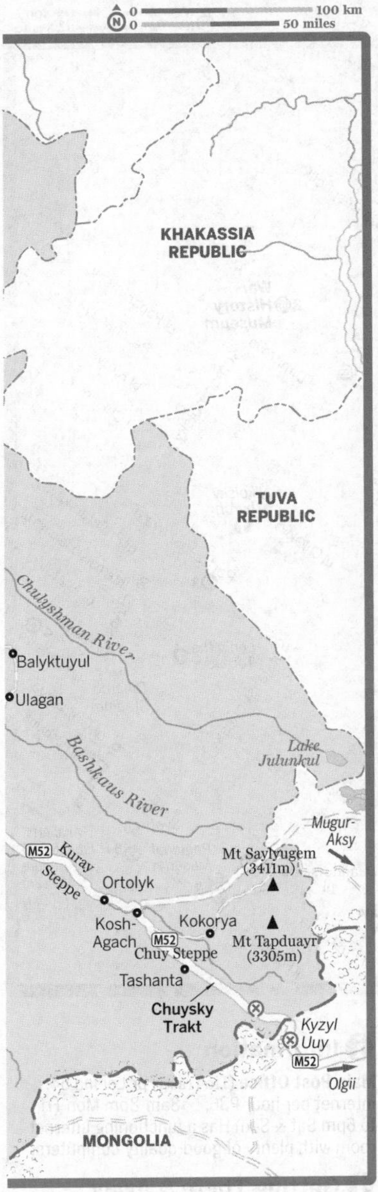

peek. The bearded dude in the courtyard is Felix Dzerzhinsky, Cheka (KGB and FSB forerunner) founder. A much larger monument to Iron Felix was torn down in Moscow as the USSR imploded, and he is a very uncommon face indeed in modern Russia.

Sleeping

★Hostel Arbuz HOSTEL $

(Хостел Арбуз; ☎3852-778 956; www.hostelarbuz.com; ul Severo-Zapadnaya 48d; dm ₽400-550, d ₽1200; @📶) Although some rooms are windowless, the cafe and overall vibe is bright and optimistic. And how can you not like the watermelon theme? Take any bus northwest along ul Lenina, hop off at No 134 (two stops beyond the railroad tracks), walk three minutes west and look for it in the courtyard.

Hotel Altai HOTEL $

(Гостиница Алтай; ☎3852-639 247; hotelaltay@bk.ru; pr Lenina 24; d/q ₽2400/3120, s/tw without bathroom ₽750/1200; 📶) In an early 1940s building, this good budget choice has certain elements of faded grandeur. It has big, exceptionally clean double rooms and friendly receptionists overly fond of late-night soaps. Nearby is an odd statue of Lenin apparently posing as a bullfighter.

Resting Rooms HOSTEL $

(komnaty otdykha; dm in d/q ₽1000/1200) A decent option at the train station with clean, shared hot showers.

Hotel Barnaul HOTEL $$

(Гостиница Барнаул; ☎3853-201 600; www.barnaulhotel.ru; pl Pobedy 3; s incl breakfast from ₽2200, tw from ₽2700; ❄@📶) This thoroughly renovated 12-storey block near the train station is exactly what you would expect from a former Soviet hulk – clean and efficient, but with small beds and bathrooms. The kicker is that if you check in after midnight, the next night is free.

Hotel Sibir HOTEL $$$

(Гостиница Сибирь; ☎3852-624 200; www.siberia-hotel.ru; Sotsialistichesky pr 116; s/d/ste from ₽5000/5400/8500; ❄@📶) This posh business hotel is built almost to international standards. Clean, quiet and comfortable.

Eating & Drinking

★Pozharka INTERNATIONAL $$

(Пожарка; Prospekt Shopping Centre, pr Lenina 39; mains ₽200-350; ⏲10am-2am) The firehouse theme extends to the presence of a shiny red firetruck at this buzzing upstairs eatery with great views of central Nikolsky Church. Staff fire up everything from pan pizza to sizzling dishes to *langosh* (Hungarian cheese pastries) and don't skimp on portions. Another floor up is boisterous nightclub Kefir, which gets going on weekends.

Barnaul

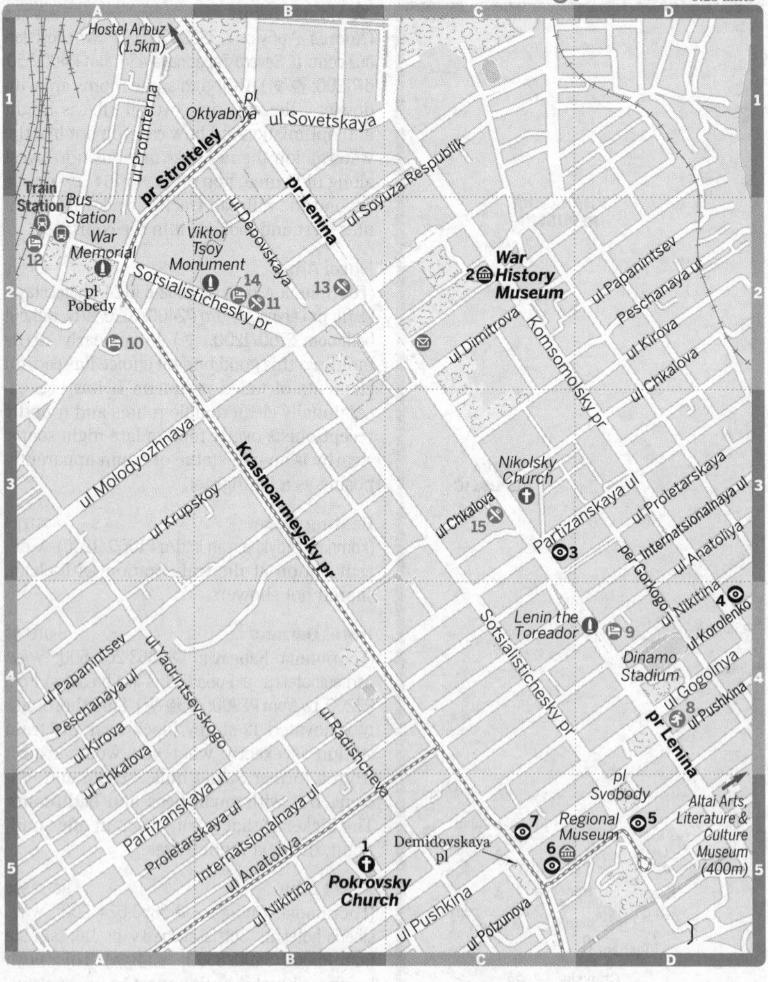

Krem Coffee Hall CAFE $$

(Крем Кофе Холл; Sotsialistichesky pr 116; mains ₽250-350, sandwiches ₽100-150; 24hr;) This urbane cafe adjacent to the Hotel Sibir is the logical stop for a caffeinated, wi-fi-enabled morning or afternoon in range of the train station. With a huge cocktail list, it doubles as a trendy bar by night.

Carte Blanche CAFE $$

(ul Molodyozhnaya 26; mains ₽350-1000; noon-1am;) Water pipes, cocktails, creative salads and grilled meat make this swanky bar-cum-restaurant popular with a young and lively crowd. Live music at weekends.

Information

Main Post Office (Почтамт; pr Lenina 54; internet per hour ₽36; 8am-8pm Mon-Fri, to 6pm Sat & Sun) Has a functioning internet room with plenty of good-quality computers.

Getting There & Away

Moscow (4½ hours, three daily) is the only destination served from Barnaul's airport.

There's a train to Tomsk (*platskart/kupe* ₽1100/2000, 12 hours, 6.12pm) via Novosibirsk (₽750/1350, six hours) on odd-numbered days. There's one or two trains every night to Omsk (₽1520/3000, 16 hours), some of which contin-

Barnaul

Top Sights

Sights

Activities, Courses & Tours

Sleeping

Eating

Information

ue to Moscow. There's a train every fourth day to Novokuznetsk but the bus is much more convenient. Transfer in Novosibirsk for Krasnoyarsk and points east on the Trans Siberian main line.

Elektrichki to Biysk depart daily at 9am and 6.22pm (1st-/2nd-class ₽259/197, three hours).

Shared taxis can get you to Novosibirsk in 2½ hours (₽600) and to Biysk in 1½ hours (₽400) but you may have to wait a while for them to fill up.

BUSES FROM BARNAUL

DESTINATION	PRICE	DURATION	FREQUENCY
Biysk	₽300	2½hr	hourly
Chemal	₽865	6½hr	2 daily
Gorno-Altaisk	₽500	4hr	12 daily
Onguday	₽780	8hr	10.45am
Novokuznetsk	₽791	7hr	3 daily
Novosibirsk	₽500	4½hr	hourly
Tomsk	₽850	9hr	2 daily

Getting Around

From pl Pobedy near the train station, buses 19 and 110 head northeast on pr Stroiteley, take a right on pr Lenina and continue to the **river station** (Речной Вокзал) at the terminus of pr Lenina. Buses 17, 57 and 60 link the river station with Demidovskaya pl, then run the length of Krasnoarmeysky pr to pl Pobedy before rejoining pr Lenina at pl Oktyabrya.

Biysk Бийск

3854 / POP 236,000 / MOSCOW +3HR

Friendly Biysk, 160km southeast of Barnaul, is not worth a special detour but its old town merits a wander if you are passing through en route to or from the Altai Mountains, for which it's the nearest railhead.

One of only three cities created on the orders of Peter the Great (the others were Moscow and St Petersburg!), Biysk was founded in 1709 at the junction of the Biya and Katun Rivers, but was quickly burnt down by the Dzhungarian Mongols. Biysk was reestablished 20km to the east in 1718. Unfortunately, nothing remains from this period. Most of the well-preserved architecture of the historic centre dates from the late 1800s.

Sights

Central Biysk is nothing special so if you just have a few hours make a beeline for the **Old Town**. From the train station, buses 6, 10, 17 and 21 are among those that get you there via Krasnoarmeyskaya ul (15 minutes) and return via ul Lenina – the city's parallel central thoroughfares. You'll know you're there when you see the distinctive **Lenin Statue** in front of the City Court at ul Lenina 149. As far as we know it is the only Lenin in Russia dressed in a real Siberian *shanka-ushanka* (winter fur hat with ear flaps).

Start your walking tour at the beautiful 1916 **City Theatre** (Бийский городской драматический театр; www.biyskdrama.ucoz.ru; ul Sovetskaya 25), from which it's about a 30-minute walk northeast along scenic **ul Sovetskaya** to sq Garkavogo via the city's **War Memorial**, with its eternal flame; late-19th-century, silver-domed **Assumption Church** (Успенская церковь; Sovetskaya ul 13) and the **City Garden**. There's an eye-catching **statue of Peter the Great** astride a horse in pl Garkavogo.

Regional Museum MUSEUM

(Краеведческий музей; www.museum.ru/M1345; ul Lenina 134; admission ₽40; 9am-5pm Wed-Sun) Housed in a grand, if dilapidated, 1912 merchant's house with original art nouveau fittings, this fine museum is home to standing stone idols and petroglyphs. It's on

ALTAI BORDER ZONES

The Altai Republic's border zones with China, Kazakhstan and Mongolia have been under the control of the FSB (formerly the KGB) since 2006. Foreigners are required to submit an application for permission to enter these areas. It affects anyone straying off the Chuysky Trakt between Kosh-Agach and the Mongolian border (you do not need the permit in the town or if sticking to the highway); and anyone travelling further south than, and including, Ust-Koksa.

Applications should be made in Russian and must be submitted by fax to the FSB office (p440) in Gorno-Altaisk several weeks before your journey (the entire process can take up to two months). The application should include passport details (everything, including where and when issued and expiry date), planned route, purpose of journey and home address. When the permit is ready, you must swing through Gorno-Altaisk to pick it up before travelling onward.

Needless to say this is infinitely easier if you use the services of a travel agency. Travel agencies outside of Western Siberia are unlikely to be able to do this for you. The tour companies listed in this chapter can usually handle this, but only if you book a tour. The two companies we found that do not require a tour booking (although they prefer one) are Altair-Tur (p442) in Novosibirsk and K2 Adventures (p419) in Omsk.

The likely penalty for travelling in a border zone without a permit is a stiff fine and expulsion from the country.

the east edge of the Old Town, a 5-minute walk north of pl Garkavogo.

Sleeping & Eating

Gostinitsa na Starom Meste HOTEL $$
(Гостиница на Старом Месте; ☎3854-338 788; www.na-starom-meste.ru; ul Sovetskaya 24; s/d incl breakfast from ₽1700/2800;) For those few people who come to Biysk specifically to see the sights, 'Hotel in an Old Place', opposite an 1882 brick building in the middle of the quiet Old Town, is clearly the place to be. Extremely tasteful and the roomy singles are especially good value.

Hotel Tsentralnaya HOTEL $$
(Гостиница Центральная; ☎3854-338 307; ul Lenina 256; s/tw from ₽1500/2200) Of the renovated Soviet ilk, allbeit enlivened by bright pastel wallpaper in the compact rooms. It's centrally placed opposite a pleasant park, a few bus stops southeast of the Old Town.

Kavkazskaya Kukhnya RUSSIAN $
(Кавказская Кухна; ul Lenina 314; meals ₽100-250; 11am-midnight;) Huge portions, cheap Russian beer and shashlyk. It's easy to miss, hidden practically under the tram bridge behind a glistening Sberbank building.

Cafe Randevu RUSSIAN $$
(Кафе Рандеву; Sovetskaya ul 4; mains ₽250-500; 11am-2am) Behind a beautifully renovated Old Town facade, this midrange cafe serves decent food and beer in a pleasant atmosphere.

Information

Post Office (Sovetskaya ul 34; 8am-8pm Mon-Fri, 9am-6pm Sat, 9am-2pm Sun)

Getting There & Away

The 602 train trundles daily to Novosibirsk (*platskart/kupe* ₽700/1770, 9½ hours) via Barnaul. There are also trains to Krasnoyarsk (even-numbered days), Moscow (even-numbered days) and Almaty (odd-numbered days).

Elektrichki to Barnaul depart at 7.26am and 5.34pm (1st-/2nd-class ₽259/197, three hours).

BUSES FROM BIYSK

DESTINATION	PRICE	DURATION	FREQUENCY
Artybash	₽450	4hr	2 daily
Barnaul	₽300	2½hr	hourly
Gorno-Altaisk	₽252	1¾hr	every 90 min
Novokuznetsk	₽484	5¼hr	5 daily
Novosibirsk	₽500 to ₽800	6hr	hourly
Tomsk	₽1400	11hr	3 daily
Ust-Koksa	₽1600	12hr	7.30pm

Gorno-Altaisk
Горно - Алтайск

☎38822 / POP 54,000 / MOSCOW +3HR

Gorno-Altaisk, the capital of the Altai Republic, was founded in 1830 and immediately saw an influx of missionaries eager to convert local pagan tribes. Today it's a somewhat bland mixture of Soviet-era buildings and newer development running through an attractive valley. For travellers, it's a convenient jumping-off point to more far-flung bits of Altai, and it's a required stop for those heading to the Mt Belukha area or other Altai border zones (see boxed text below).

Sights

If you have a day or two to kill in Gorno-Altaisk, why not go for a hike? The city has two single-lift ski slopes that make for nice climbs in the warmer months. Take any bus along the city's seemingly interminable main street, Kommunistichesky pr, and you'll see the them; there's one a couple blocks east of central pl Lenina.

AV Anokhin National Museum of Altai MUSEUM
(Национальный музей Республики Алтай имени А.В. Анохина; ul Choros-Gurkina 46; ₽250; ⏲10am-6pm Wed-Sun) This well-put-together museum offers a good introduction to Altai culture with a range of ethnographic exhibits, wildlife displays and local art and artefacts, including a room dedicated to the Altai landscape painter Grigory Choros-Gurkin. Also houses the mummified 'Siberian Ice Maiden', excavated from southern Altai in the 1990s and thought to date from the 5th century BC.

Svyato-Makarevsky Church CHURCH
(Свято-Макарьевский храм; pr Kommunistichesky 146) Completed in 2006, this attractive wooden church boasts a wonderfully photographic backdrop of rolling lush hills.

Tours

Altai Info TOUR COMPANY
(Алтай Инфо; ☎38822-26 864; Hotel Gorny Altai; ⏲10am-6pm) Can arrange rafting trips.

Sleeping & Eating

There's a good **stolovaya** (mains ₽75-125; ⏲7am-6pm) upstairs in the bus station.

★**Igman** HOTEL $
(Игман; ☎38822-47 242; www.igman04.ru; ul Choros-Gurkina 71; s/d from ₽900/1200; wifi) At the rear of the bus station, Igman is by far the best place to stay in town. Perfect location, good service and spacious rooms at reasonable prices – what's not to like? The cheaper rooms share clean bathrooms. Wi-fi is spotty on the upper floors.

Hotel Gorny Altai HOTEL $
(Гостиница Горный Алтай; ☎38822-284 95; goctaltai@mail.ru; pl Lenina; s/d/tr without bathroom per person ₽750/650/400, d with bathroom ₽1600-2000) This Soviet slab has stubbornly resisted modernization, but it's at least clean and the location is as central as it gets. The shared bathrooms are a bit grubby but do have swanky new shower cabinets.

REGISTERING YOUR VISA IN GORNO-ALTAISK

It's not strictly necessary, but if you are travelling in the Altai Republic you should pay special attention to making sure your visa is properly registered. Technically the rules are the same as elsewhere: you only need to register if you are staying in one district for more than seven business days. But the local authorities tend not to be aware of this, and might demand to see a valid registration and/or a *khodataystsvo* – a document from whoever sponsored your visa, listing where in Altai you'll be visiting (secure one of these before departing).

We advise the following:

- If you'll be staying in Altai for less than seven business days, it should suffice to get one registration in the usual way from a hotel in Gorno-Altaisk or elsewhere.
- If you'll be roaming around more than one district in Altai for *more* than seven business days, then it's a good idea to go to the **Federal Migration Service** (Федеральная Миграционная Служба; ФМС); ☎38822-615 46; top fl, Kommunistichesky pr 109; ⏲9am-12.45pm & 2-6pm Mon-Fri) in Gorno-Altaisk to register your visa for your entire stay in Altai. It's four bus stops west of the bus station, roughly opposite the pretty wooden church at Kommunistichesky pr 146.
- If you'll be staying in Altai for more than seven business days but will be staying in a single district, then it should suffice to register upon arrival in that district – at the local FMS office, the post office or a hotel.

★**Travellers Coffee** CAFE $$
(pr Kommunistichesky 26; mains ₽150-250; ⌚8am-11pm; 📶) This blossoming travel-themed Siberian chain is a welcome addition to Gorno-Altaisk's staid food scene. Well-priced breakfasts, the best coffee in the republic, Russian staples and light bites.

Venetsiya INTERNATIONAL $$
(Венеция; pr Kommunistichesky 68; meals ₽300-700; ⌚noon-2am; 📶) While Italian-themed Venetsiya does have (overpriced) pasta dishes, the menu leans more towards hearty Russian fare, including game dishes such as *maral* (deer meat).

ℹ Information

There's a **post office** (Почта; Kommunistichesky pr 61; ⌚9am-8pm Mon-Sat) next to the bus station. Good city maps are available at street kiosks.

FSB Office (ФСБ; Федеральная служба безопасности); ☎38822-482 48, tel/fax 38822-482 61; pr Kommunistichesky 94) Apply here for border-zone permits. It's two bus stops west of the bus station, just over the Mayma River.

ℹ Getting There & Away

Gorno-Altaisk's airport is out on the Chuysky Trakt in Mayma, 10km west of the centre. S7 has four weekly flights to Moscow, while **Kras Avia** (www.kras-avia.ru) has sporadic flights to Novosibirsk and Krasnoyarsk.

There's no railway but a **booth** (⌚9am-7pm Mon-Fri, 10am-4pm Sat) within the **bus station** (☎38822-224 57; pr Kommunistichesky) sells train tickets.

Buses are the main form of transport around here. In addition to the public buses listed below, private *marshrutky* (in the form of 15-seat Gazelle vans) serve more remote destinations. There are two Gazelle departures every moning to Kosh-Agach (₽500, 7½ hours, 8.30am and 10.30am) from the bus station. Pricier and quicker shared taxis sometimes make morning trips too.

ℹ Getting Around

From central Gorno-Altaisk virtually all eastbound city buses take Kommunistichesky pr past the bus station, FSB building, Federal Migration Service office and market.

Around Gorno-Altaisk

Aya Ая

☎38537

There is a booming tourist scene south of Mayma concentrated around the wobbly, disused wooden bridge at km455 of the Chuysky Trakt. Access is via a new bridge (at km459) over the Katun River – cross this bridge to the other side then backtrack to the old bridge, where you'll find a gaggle of thumping nightclubs in the summer months. If you're stuck in Gorno-Altaisk and looking for a night out, this is where you should head. In the off-season it's pretty much dead.

Many agencies around the wooden bridge offer **rafting trips** (per hour ₽500) and horse rides at short notice; handy if you haven't reserved anything more adventurous. Stalls sell jars of natural honey for around ₽400 and *sera*, a traditional Siberian 'chewing gum' made from cedar tree resin. There are also numerous outdoor cafes serving the usual shashlyk and beer. There are numerous accommodation options along the river here, but unless you want to party we rec-

BUSES FROM GORNO-ALTAISK

DESTINATION	PRICE (₽)	DURATION (HR)	FREQUENCY
Aktash	530	5½	7.15am, 10am
Artybash	400	4	11.55am, 5.20pm
Barnaul	500	4	12 daily
Biysk	252	1¾	every 90min
Chemal	252	2¼	3-4 daily
Novosibirsk	1107	8	4 daily
Onguday	238	3½	2.25pm
Tyungur	800	9	8.20am, 1.45pm (summer)
Ulagan	600	6	7.15am
Ust-Koksa	650-1000	8	8.20am, 1.45pm (summer) & 9.40pm

ommend heading 30km upstream to Manzherok for a more tranquil getaway.

From Gorno-Altaisk, Chemal-bound buses are the best way to get to Aya, or take a taxi (₽500).

Manzherok Манжерок

38844

The riverside lodges in and around peaceful Manzherok, 20km south of Aya, are an outdoorsy alternative to staying in Gorno-Altaisk.

Manzherok also has a burgeoning ski scene on **Mt Sinyukha** near Lake Manzherok in the nearby village of Ozernoe (Озерное). One lift operates year-round (adult/student ₽125/350). The ride up the mountain covers almost 2.5km and takes 25 minutes. If you're feeling spry you can walk up for free. The top of the mountain affords marvelous panoramas of Lake Manzherok and the surrounding countryside from a **viewing platform**. You can also dress up like a Mongolian warrior or pose with an eagle for photos, if that's your thing.

Developers are eying Manzherok as the next Sheregesh, and plan to open hectares of new terrain and install up to 40 lifts over the next few years. Franky, they have a long way to go. When we dropped by there was no sign of new lifts going up and there was only one ski lodge at the base of the hill.

To get to the ski area from the centre of Manzherok, walk 1.5km south on the Chuysky Trakt and take a left at the sign to Ozeroe (at the km473 marker). Proceed 800m to a T-junction in Ozernoe, go left and look for the ski area.

Sleeping

The best accommodation is on the river a few kilometres north or south of town.

Turkomplex Manzherok LODGE $

(Туркомплекс Манжерок; 38844-283 99; www.mangerok-altai.ru; Chuysky Trakt, km469 mark; dm/s/d from ₽500/1000/1500) This well-organised holiday complex just south of Manzherok sits behind a mock-Cossack stockade in a riverbank pine grove. The cheaper rooms have toilets but share showers. There's an artificial beach if you want to splash around in the Katun, mountain bikes for rent (per hour/day ₽150/600) and it has a fleet of whitewater rafts – trips cost ₽500 for two hours or ₽1000 for a full day.

MANZHEROK – THIS IS FRIENDSHIP!

The village of Manzherok found fame in 1966 as the venue for a Soviet–Mongolian youth friendship festival, a big deal for the then-insular USSR. A song was commissioned especially for the occasion and sung by French-born Soviet star Edita Pieha. The result was a catchy pop ditty boasting the chorus 'Manzherok is friendship, our meeting place!' The tune was even accompanied by a video featuring a smiling Pieha and her band dancing around in a snowy forest, which can be found by digging around on Youtube.

Dva Medveda HOTEL $

(Два медведя; 8-913-690 0777; www.dvamedvedya.ru; Chuysky Trakt, km477.5; 2-person tent/d/tr from ₽600/1200/1650) Great-value log cabins set in attractive grounds on the Katun River 6km south of Manzherok. Also offers excursions. The name translates as 'Two Bears' – although you won't see even one.

Vityaz CABINS $$

(Витязь; 8-905-986 8768; Chuysky Trakt, km476.5; log cabins from ₽1500) The idyllic Vityaz, 5km south of Manzherok, has cosy log cabins right on the Katun River. Camping is available for ₽400.

Eating

★Chaynaya Sinyukha UZBEK $$

(Чайная Синюха; Chuysky Trakt, km471.5; meals ₽150-250; 9am-9pm) The freshly prepared Uzbek cusine here is some of the best food in Altai, and well worth stopping for if heading south on the Chuysky Trakt. The *manti* (Uzbek dumplings), dusted with paprika, are partiularly good, and the piping-hot *non* (Uzbek flatbread, or *lavash*) is right out of the *tandir* (clay oven). Healthy salads too.

Information

There's a Sberbank ATM next to the Post Office.

Post Office (Chuysky Trakt, 471km; per hour ₽50; 9am-5pm Mon-Fri)

Getting There & Away

From Gorno-Altaisk, take a Chemal-bound bus to Manzherok or a taxi (₽700). **Vladimir** (8-923-667 5620, 8-913-999 5620) is a charismatic taxi driver who can do local trips or drive you as far as Ust-Koksa (₽4500) or the Mongolian border (₽5000). Pay extra if you make frequent stops en route.

Lake Teletskoe & Artybash

Озеро Телецкое и Артыбаш

☎38843 / POP 4500 / ⏰ MOSCOW +3HR

Deep, delightful Lake Teletskoe is Altai's serene answer to Lake Baikal, a great place simply to relax and catch your breath. It's also Altai's largest lake. Ridge after forested ridge unfolds as you scuttle along on one of the myriad little pleasure boats that buzz out of Artybash village, the lake's charming tourist hub.

Lake Teletskoe drains into the Biya River at its westernmost nose. Artybash is on the right (north) bank, connected by bridge to little Iogach village, the main population centre and bus stop, on the left bank.

Sights & Activities

Boat tours are the main activity, naturally. Besides the popular trip to Korbu Waterfall, you can jump on a hydrofoil to to the **Altyn Tour** camp at the southern end of the lake, some 78km away (per person ₽1800, eight hours return). Most boats leave from the main pier, near the Zamok Hotel. The lake freezes over in winter and the village transforms into a winter wonderland, with snowmobiles the vehicle of choice.

Guesthouses and tour agencies around the bridge also offer **trekking** (per person ₽450), **fishing**, **horse riding** and **rafting** on the Biya River.

Korbu Waterfall WATERFALL

From June to September, there are many daily lake trips (per person ₽800) to Korbu Waterfall. You have a choice between fast, noisy hydrofoils (four hours return) and larger, slower-paced craft (six to eight hours return). The falls are hardly memorable but the journey is very beautiful despite the blaring commentary.

Sleeping & Eating

Many places open in peak season only. Reservations are are highly advisable in July and August. Prices drop by up to 50% off season.

Every second house in Artybash seems to have rooms or huts to rent. Prices start from ₽400 without any facilities but many places demand minimum groups of three or more guests in summer. Look for signs marked 'Сдаю Дом' and 'Сдаётся Дом' (house for rent). Hotel distances given are from the bridge.

TREKKING IN ALTAI

Trekking among Altai's snow-crested mountaintops is one of Western Siberia's main attractions, but it requires considerable preparation: compared to Nepal or New Zealand, hiking here requires a high degree of self-sufficiency. Not even the most popular trails have villages, signs or teahouses. Sadly, guides and packhorses usually aren't easy to arrange quickly in situ, except perhaps in Tyungur or Chemal.

Tour companies can help by prearranging various adventure, hiking, rafting or relaxation packages. Consider using them in July and August to book accommodation as demand very often outstrips supply in summer, especially if you want the luxury of a sit-down toilet.

Travel agencies in Novosibirsk and Barnaul virtually all offer packaged or tailor-made trips to Altai, but only a select few have the English skills to deal with foreigners. A few recommended tour operators follow (additional companies specialising in the Mt Belukha area are listed on p448).

Ak Tur (☎3852-659 407; www.aktour.ru; pr Lenina 10, Barnaul) Offers Altai rafting, road trips and mountain expeditions. Some English spoken.

Altair-Tur (Альтаир-Тур; www.altairtour.ru; ul Sovetskaya 65, Novosibirsk; ⏰10am-7pm Mon-Fri, to 5pm Sat) Good all-around company with many Altai tours; can help with border permits.

Sibir Altai (☎383-299 0403; http://sibalt.ru; ul Chelyuskintsev 36, Novosibirsk; ⏰10am-6pm Mon-Fri, 11am-3pm Sat) Packages Altai trips for local tourists, sold through numerous regional travel agencies.

Tour Academy (☎383-292 8886; http://touracademy.ru; Vokzalnaya magistral 16) Runs tours throughout Altai and in the Sheregesh area too.

There are a few more homestays over the bridge in Iogach (Иогач). We liked the ones at ul Haberezhnaya 27 and 35a (the lakeside road to the left of the bridge).

Elena GUESTHOUSE $
(Елена; ☎8-903-919 8750; ul Teletskaya 53 (900m); d ₽1000) Elena is a cosy complex of self-contained cottages with small beds and kitchenettes. There's an authentic Russian *banya* (per hour ₽500), a boat for hire and a cafe. Open summer and May holidays only.

★**Usadba Stary Zamok** HOTEL $$
(Усадьба Старый замок; ☎38843-276 60; www.zamoktel.ru; km1.4; d ₽1800-3000) This sweetly kitsch little 'castle' has more of a log-cabin feel, with woody, fragrant rooms – some with lake views – opening to shared terraces. The on-site *stolovaya* (open 9am to 9pm in season) is fantastic value and has outdoor seating right on the lake. Jump in the cold lake then hit the *banya* (per hour ₽500).

Hotel Artybash HOTEL $$
(Гостиница Артыбаш; ☎8-961-709 4242; www.artybash.com; d from ₽1800; 📶) The most modern hotel in the area, the good-value Artybash has big, stylish rooms, some with great views of the Biya River, friendly staff, and a good restaurant that offers Altai specialities such as *maral* (wild deer) among a bevvy of Russian staples. It's 300m before the bridge.

Edem HOTEL $$
(Эдем; ☎8-960-961 7688; http://edem-teleckoe.ru; km2.5; d/tw from ₽2300/3000; 📶🏊) Comfy rooms and a host of organised activities make this sprawling complex in the woods east of Artybash a popular choice. It has a decent cafe and a floating *banya* (per hour ₽1000).

Cafe Yevseich RUSSIAN $
(Кафе Евсеич; mains ₽60-100) This modest, friendly cafe serves mostly pre-prepared Central Asia cuisine, with a few Russian entrées thrown in.

Shopping

Souvenir Shops SOUVENIRS
The souvenir shops around the start of the bridge sell all manner of interesting items, such as Altai honey (₽100 a small jar), Altai pop and traditional music, maps, half-litre bottles of deer blood (₽1100 pure, ₽300 if cut with cow blood), Altai T-shirts, and Altai instruments such as jew's harps (*kamys* in the local dialect, *vargan* in Russian; ₽300) and *ocarina* (yurt-shaped flutes).

Information

Sberbank (Сбербанк; ⏰9.30am-noon & 2-3.30pm Mon-Sat) Next to the bridge on the Iogach side. Will change dollars and euros.

Getting There & Away

Buses to Gorno-Altaisk leave from a bus stop in front of the Zolotoe Ozera Cafe at the end of the bridge on the Iogach side of the river at 8.40am and 3.15pm (₽400, four hours). For taxis to Sheregesh (₽5000), ask around at any cafe or tour company.

Chemal Чемал

☎38841 / POP 9000 / ⏰MOSCOW +3HR

At the attractive junction of the Chemal and Katun Rivers, ever-expanding Chemal is heavily touristed in summer but makes a great base for excursions in the surrounding mountains and rivers. It can also be done as a day trip from Gorno-Altaisk, 95km north, or Manzherok. If you want to continue south to Kosh-Agach and the high Altail mountains, you'll first need to backtrack to Ust-Sema on the Chuysky Trakt.

Sights & Activities

In summer tour companies in town and around Varota Sartikpayev Gorge have stalls offering rafting trips on the Katun River from ₽500 per hour.

Varota Sartikpayev Gorge PARK
The tourist action in Chemal revolves around this spectacular canyon near the confluence of the Katun and Chemal rivers. The area occupies an important place in Altai mythology – the white pieces of cloth tied to trees here and elsewhere in the region are part of the Altai people's tradition of honouring their ancestors.

From the Ionno-Bogoslavski Chapel at the northern edge of the gorge, walk about 15 minutes south along a narrow but well-trodden footpath high above the Katun until you emerge behind a small 1935 dam backed by souvenir stalls and open-air cafes selling Uzbek food, beer and traditional Altai tea.

Despite power lines and summer crowds, views remain very pretty. Around the dam you can make 15m bungee jumps (adult/student ₽400/300) into the frothing outpour waters or fly over the waters on a

THE CHUYSKY TRAKT ЧУЙСКИЙ ТРАКТ

The Chuysky Trakt (M52) is a sealed highway that runs 966km from Novosibirsk all the way to the Mongolian border. By far the most interesting stretch – which makes it one of the world's great drives – runs for about 450km south from Mayma to Kosh-Agach in southern Altai. Frothy rivers, harrowing passes, craggy cliffs, rolling steppe, austere desert landscapes and – the coup de grâce – the mighty 4000m mountains of the Chuya range make this one ride you'll never forget.

Plenty of public and private *marshrutky* ply the route between Gorno-Altaisk and Kosh-Agach (approximately seven hours). A ticket costs just ₽500, making this one of life's better cheap thrills. Ask your driver for a seat in the front. If you want to stop (and you *will* want to), you'll have to hire a private car. We recommend hiring a taxi one way, and taking a *marshrutka* the other.

The Route

After following the Katun River north from Aya for about 200km out of Mayma, you'll start climbing up to the **Seminsky Pass**, at 1715m the highest point on the entire Chuysky Trakt. You'll find snack and souvenir kiosks up here along with a winter sports training centre and, rising gradually to the east, bleak and bald **Mt Sarlyk** (2507m). If you're looking for a relatively easy and easy-to-access climb in central Altai, Mt Sarlyk is your answer.

The road descends through Tuekta (km611) and Onguday (km634), then starts climbing again up to the beautiful, serpentine **Chike-Taman Pass** (km663). The pass acquired its name, which means 'flat sole' in Altai, before the Chuysky Trakt was built. The old road was so steep that locals believed you could see the bottom of the shoe of the person walking ahead of you. Today the pass is a more gradual affair, but from near the top (take the path behind the souvenir stands) you can still see the old road, which remains open to off-road vehicles.

The pass descends through **Kupchegen** (km674), with *aily* (yurt-like traditional Altai dwellings) in almost every yard. At km684 you rejoin the Katun River, last seen in Ust-Sema, and at km689 you get your first view of the high Altai mountains as the snow-capped Northern Chuya range comes into view. Next up is **Maly Yaloman** (km696), which sits

zipline (*kanatnaya doroga*, per ride ₽300). Both attractions impose 'fines' on anyone who backs out at the last second!

Cross the Chemal River near the zipline via a footbridge, veer left, and look for a 4WD track heading up the hill directly in front of you to the east. It's a straightforward 45-minute hike to the top of the hill, from where there are fine views of Chemal and its surrounding mountains, valleys and rivers. Descend the way you came and return home via the inconspicuous amusement park near the reservoir at the base of the hill.

Altaysky Tsentr MUSEUM
(ul Beshpekskaya 6; admission ₽200) From the centre of town walk about 500m south along central ul Pchyolkina, past small Park Pobedy, then turn right towards the river at the signpost to find the wonderful Altaysky Tsentr. This comprises three Altai-style wooden *ail*-huts with pointed metal roofs. The centrepiece is the the traditional 'home' *ail*, with traditional clothing, kitchen instruments, furniture and other Altai knick-knacks (check out the cool grass-fueled lighter, ignited with a rock!). The other huts contain a library and some of Choros-Gurkin's ethnographic works.

Adding flavour to a visit here is the eccentric hostess, Tansya Petrovna Bardina, who will regale you with stories of her late husband, the museum's founder, and will insist on taking photos of you from various vantage points within the museum. Good fun even if you don't understand Russian. Opening hours are whenever Tansya Petrovna is around to give you a (mandatory) tour.

Ioanno Bogoslavski Chapel CHURCH
(9am-7pm) On the northern edge of the Varota Sartikpayev Gorge, a wobbly footbridge leads across a stunning canyon to a craggy island in the Katun River on which is perched the tiny wooden Ioanno Bogoslavski Chapel, rebuilt in 2001 to the original 1849 design. Beside it, the rock miraculously shaped like a Madonna and child sculpture is supposedly natural. To get here follow ul Beshpekskaya a few hundred metres beyond the Altaysky Tsentr museum.

in a cliff-ringed curl of river and has a microclimate allowing local villagers to grow pears, cherries and apples. Indeed, Altai is known for its myriad microclimates, and as you drive the length of the Chuysky Trakt you'll be amazed how dramatically the landscape changes with every bend in the road.

When you enter **Inya** (km703), be sure to keep your eyes open for what may be the most dramatically placed and memorable Lenin statue in Russia. At km712.5, picnic tables and prayer flags tempt you to stop for wonderful views of the meeting of the Chuya and Katun Rivers far below. Just beside the slip road for the simple Chuy-Oozy cafe at km714.2, very lightly scored roadside petroglyphs depict little antelope figures. But the big sight here, if you can spot it, is the legendary 'rock face' on the left bank of the Katun. If you can't make out its 'features', pop into the cafe and check out the helpful drawing hanging on a wall. Then go out and have another look. All should now be clear!

There's another petroglyph group at Yalbak Tash crag, a five-minute walk north of km721. There's another petroglyph group at Yalbak Tash crag, a five-minute walk north of km721. The road then snakes scenically through the Chuya Canyon. At km761, look up to the right for a glimpse of a waterfall crashing out of the hills. At km782 you enter Chibit, where there's an enticing yurt camp on the river with awesome views of the snow-capped Mt Aktru (4044m) and Mt Kurkurek (3982m). Some 3km before the tiny settlement of **Iodro**, on the left-hand side, stands a stone idol with a well-preserved and somewhat haunting face.

Clouds permitting, the best views on the whole Chuysky Trakt are between Aktash (km790) and Kosh-Agach (km889). From km801 to km811 the Northern Chuyas are right in your face and you'll want to stop the car as much as possible for photos. Beyond this you begin to traverse the vast and desolate Kuray and Chuy Steppes (km821 to km840 and km870 onwards), with distant panoramas of perennially snow-topped peaks. The Kuray Steppe regularly hosts Russia's paragliding championships.

The road leading to Kosh-Agach sees the greenery start to die out, and the scenery gradually transforms into something resembling a lunar landscape.

Sleeping & Eating

As in the Lake Teletskoe area, locals rent out cottages or their own homes from ₽500 per person – look for the ubiquitous 'Сдаётся Дом' (house for rent) signs. Just north of Chemal, the village of Elekmonar sprawls for 5km along the Katun River and is similarly endowed with myriad basic home- and hut-stays along central ul Sovetskaya – No 107, in an old-school Siberian *izba,* looked attractive.

The food scene in Chemal is extremely limited, as most visitors self-cater from several well-stocked supermarkets on ul Pchyolkina. You'll find plenty of kiosks selling *chebureki* (greasy meat-filled turnovers), *plov* and other Central Asian snacks near the tourist sights.

Altai Voyazh GUESTHOUSE $
(Алтай Вояж; ☎38841-222 68; ul Sovetskaya 4; r per person from ₽400) Opposite the bus station, smack-dab in the middle of town, Altai Voyazh is a simple hostelery that offers very basic rooms upstairs with shared toilets and primitive – but scalding hot! – showers. This may be your only option in the off-season. The hotel offers a range of reasonably priced rafting and hiking trips in summer.

Green House GUESTHOUSE $
(☎8-963-198 7080; ul Beregovaya 8; r per person ₽500) Its location near the river, just north of the centre, makes this a fine option, although facilities are basic. The five double rooms share bathrooms and a kitchen.

Usadba na Altaiskaya GUESTHOUSE $
(☎8-903-967 7813; ul Altaiskaya 13; per person ₽500;) This cosy house has 20 beds with shared bathrooms, a Russian *banya* and a sauna. Ul Altaiskaya is parallel to, and east of, ul Sovetskaya.

Ludmila Usadba GUESTHOUSE $
(Усадьба Людмила; ☎8-903-956 4814; Zelyonaya Rosha 2; s/d ₽500/800) A friendly hostelery just south of Park Pobedy.

WORTH A TRIP

HOLY WATERS & SOUVENIRS

Arzhaan-Su

At km478.7 of the Chuysky Trakt, Arzhaan-Su (Аржан-Су) is a 'holy' cold-water spring at the roadside, shrouded by summer souvenir sellers. Just across the new suspension bridge is Biryuzovaya Katun, a holiday park with a pool, caves and a cafe in a bizarre wooden galleon.

Elekmonar

Five kilometres north of Chemal, Elekmonar is the starting point for multiday hikes or horse rides to the seven attractive Karakol Lakes amid picturesque bald mountaintops. The lakes are approximately 30km beyond Elekmonar – start up ul Sadovaya. A sturdy 4WD could get you most of the way.

Bimtan GUESTHOUSE **$$**
(Вимтан; ☎38841-220 20; ul Beshpekskaya 15; d ₽1500; 📶) Slightly spiffier than most options in town, this small guesthouse roughly opposite the Altaysky Tsentr museum has toilets and showers in its comfortable rooms.

Arafat CENTRAL ASIAN **$**
(Арафат; ul Pyacholkina 62; mains ₽75-150; ⊙10am-10pm) The pre-prepared Uzbek fare here isn't great, but it's about the only place in town that is open year-round. It's just north of the bus station.

ℹ Information

Sberbank (Сбербанк; ul Sovetskaya; ⊙9am-4pm Mon-Fri) Next to the bus station.

ℹ Getting There & Away

There are three or four trips a day to Gorno-Altaisk (₽252, 2¼ hours) via Manzherok, with the 7.40am bus continuing on to Novosibirsk (₽1350, nine hours). Additional trips to Barnaul (3pm) and Novosibirsk (11am) do not stop in Gorno-Altaisk, but do pass by nearby Mayma on the Chuysky Trakt.

If heading south along the Chuysky Trakt, you should arrange in advance to be picked up by private *marshrutka* in Manzherok (km471) or Ust-Sema (km499).

Onguday Онгудай

☎38845 / POP 5100 / ⊙ MOSCOW +3HR

Translating literally as '10 gods' (for the 10 surrounding peaks), this large village isn't especially appealing but it makes a good base for several excursions to the north of town. The basic **Kok Boru Hotel** (Гостиница Кок-бору; ☎38845-211 96; ul Erzumasheva 8; r without bathroom ₽700) is right in the centre of town.

About 22km north of Onguday, the village of Tuekta has several *kurgany* (burial mounds). More *kurgany* can be found in nearby Karakol and Shiba. From Tuekta, a road goes west to the village of Elo, the site for the huge **El-Oiyn** festival, which celebrates Altai culture in even-numbered years on the first weekend of July. The festival attracts up to 60,000 people from all over Russia and beyond. The event, the name of which translates as Folk Games, involves much horse riding, traditional costumes and merrymaking.

A bit south of Tuekta, a dead-end side road to Kulada village passes through **Bichiktu-Boom** (with some traditional Altai *aily*) and an attractive valley which offers hiking and free-camping possibilities. **Kulada** itself is built around a rocky knob and is a holy place in Burkhanism, a curious but almost extinct Altai religion founded in 1904 by shepherd Chet Chelpan, fusing Orthodox Christianity, Buddhism and folk traditions. There is also a small outdoor museum in the village containing a number of well-preserved standing stone idols.

As the first major stop south of Gorno-Altaisk on the Chuysky Trakt, Onguday is relatively well connected, with several bus and *marshrutka* trips daily to Gorno-Altaisk. If heading south, have your hotel pre-book a south-bound *marshrutka*, as most passing vehicles will be full.

Aktash Акташ

☎38846 / POP 3400 / ⊙ MOSCOW +3HR

This rundown and isolated village, whose name means 'white stone' in the Altai language, commands a dramatic area of craggy valleys. It could make a base for mountain adventures in the lovely Northern Chuya range with its challenging mountaineering on **Mt Aktru** (4044m) and **Mt Maashey** (4177m) or for trekking to the **Shavlinsky Lakes** for idyllic mountain views. However, all of these require border permits which, when ready, must be collected in Kosh-

Agach, 100km to the south. Nor will you find qualified guides in Aktash, so arrange those in advance, along with your border permit, from a qualified tour company.

Cyclists taking on the glorious journey east to Tuva via Ulagan might find themselves in Aktash for a night (going beyond Ulagan requires a border permit).

The flashiest hotel in town by a long shot is the often-booked-out **Rasul Hotel** (Гостиница Расул; ☎8-913-992 3344; rasul_ka@mail.ru; Chuysky Trakt; r from ₽1500), easily spotted on the left as you enter town from the north. Other choices are the simple **Uyut Hotel** (☎38846-238 31; ul Pushkina 1; tw ₽800), in a wood house just off central ul Mokhova, and a few cheap unnamed options (ask around). There are cafes, a supermarket and a Sberbank on ul Mokhova near the war monument.

A gas station on the Chuysky Trakt on the south edge of town serves as the bus station. The daily public *marshrutka* to Gorno-Altaisk leaves at 7am (₽530, 5½ hours), or catch the Ulagan-Gorno public *marshrutka* when it passes through at 1pm (pre-booking required). Aktash to Kosh-Agach by taxi costs at least ₽1500.

Kosh-Agach Кош Агач

☎38842 / POP 5500 / ⏲MOSCOW +3HR

Kosh-Agach means 'last tree' in Kazakh, but that tree appears to have died long ago. Some 50km from the Russia–Mongolia border, Kosh-Agach is the driest inhabited place in the Russian Federation, with average rainfalls of under 150mm.

The town has a strange, end-of-the-world feeling about it, with its shanty-type homes petering out into magical flat steppe where free-range camels roam. When the dusty air clears, the nearby mountains appear from nowhere like apparitions. Russians are in the minority here, with Kazakhs and Altai making up something like 90% of the population. Indeed, when the call to prayer sounds from the wooden **Khazret Osman Mosque** (ul Sovetskaya 62), you'll feel every bit like you're in Central Asia.

Sights & Activities

Kosh-Agach is the logical base for climbs in the **Southern Chuya range**, which tops out at 3936m (Mt Iiktu), and there are various other excursions available to those with the proper paperwork.

If you head out of town towards Mongolia, you'll come across Kosh-Agach's large Soviet-era **welcome sign**, which depicts three stern officials (one Slav, one Kazakh and one Altai) standing next to a hammer and sickle. The northern entrance of town is marked by **statues** of a yak, a camel and an eagle. Well worth a look, if only for the great photo ops.

Sleeping & Eating

Along ul Kooperativnaya you'll find several reasonably stocked grocery stores, a *stolovaya* and some simple cafes serving mainly Central Asian fare.

Hotel Tsentralnaya HOTEL $

(☎8-913-690 8428; ul Kooperativnaya 31; s/d/tr without bathroom ₽700/1200/1650; 📶) The rooms here are perfectly comfortable, if time-worn, and it's central and friendly. Wi-fi costs a flat ₽80.

Zarya Hotel GUESTHOUSE $

(☎8-983-582 0170; ul Kommunalnaya 71; s/d ₽350/800; 📶) Popular with bikers on a budget because of its central location just off the Chuysky Trakt and its nice kitchen. The rooms are quite basic, although some do have queen beds for couples.

★**Rasul Hotel** HOTEL $$

(Гостиница Расул; ☎8-913-991 3344; rasul_ka@mail.ru; ul Novochuyskaya 72a; dm ₽1000, d ₽2000, q without/with bathroom ₽2200/4200) This hotel just off the Chuysky Trakt on the north-east side of the river brings a lick of style to down-at-heel Kosh-Agach. Some English is spoken – unheard of in these parts – and it runs great tours for those with the proper permits. Ask staff to point you in the direction of the resident yak herd.

Yulduz CENTRAL ASIAN $

(ul Voyskavaya (Chuysky Trakt) 14; mains ₽100-150; ⏲11am-11pm) South of the centre on the Chuysky Trakt, Kazakh-run Yulduz is reputed to have the best laghman in all of Altai along with *manti* and its specialty Kazan Kebab (lamb), all homemade and fresh. Well worth the longish walk considering the town's other dismal options.

Orientation

Kosh-Agach is divided roughly in half by an often dried-up river. The center of town is southwest of the river, with the two main streets – parallel ul Sovetskaya and ul Kooperativnaya – both intersecting with the Chuysky Trakt near the Khazret Osman Mosque.

Information

Visitors to Kosh-Agach do not need border permits as long as they remain in town. However, you'll need one if you plan to venture off the Chuysky Trakt and into the steppe.

There are several banks with functional ATMs on and around ul Kooperativnaya.

Federal Migration Service (Федеральная Миграционная Служба, ФМС); ul Kooperativnaya 28a; ⌚9am-5pm) No reason to be paranoid but the friendly folks here do check with hotels to make sure foreign guests are registered, and may ask for your *khodataystsvo* if they feel something is amiss.

Post Office (ul Kooperativnaya 50; ⌚9am-6pm Mon-Fri, to 2pm Sat)

Getting There & Away

There are no public *marshrutky* to Gorno-Altaisk but private *marshrutka* (Gazelle) 590 runs at least two daily trips (₽500, 7½ hours, 8.30am and 10.30am), departing from opposite Hotel Tsentralnaya. Book a day in advance through your hotel to ensure a spot.

Shared taxis collect passengers at a stand opposite ul Sovetskaya 55 and head to Gorno-Altaisk (seat/whole taxi ₽700/4000); these can take a while to fill up so if you're in a hurry consider buying any empty seats. A private taxi from here to Aktash costs ₽1500; to the Mongolian border costs ₽700. For the rough ride from the border to Olgii, the nearest Mongolian settlement, you'll have to hire a UAZ (Russian 4WD) on the Mongolian side for a couple of hundred dollars.

Coming in from Mongolia you're unlikely to find transport quickly at the border. One option is to call a hotel in Kosh-Agach to send a taxi for you.

Ust-Koksa, Tyungur & Mt Belukha Усть-Кокса, Тюнгур и Гора Белуха

The holy grail for many mountaineers visiting Altai is **Mt Belukha** (4506m), Siberia's highest peak. This is no peak for amateurs, but recreational hikers can hike around Belukha's base, which has some of the the best scenery Altai has to offer.

The catch, of course, is accessibility. Foreigners need to apply for a border permit to get anywhere near Mt Belukha, a time-consuming and expensive process that puts many visitors off – and indeed prevented us from conducting direct research of the area for this book. If you plan in advance, however, you will not be disappointed.

Activities

The jumping-off point for treks around Mt Belukha is the small village of **Tyungur**, which sits in an appealing valley about 50km south of Ust-Koksa. One popular trek is the two- to three-day hike to stunning **Akkem Lake** at the foot of Mt Belukha. For a shorter trek that will give you a glimpse of the sacred peak, take a long day hike from Tyungur part-way up **Mt Baida**. Full-blown ascents of Belukha (grade 3A to 5A) are only for experienced mountaineers but don't require special permits. Rafting and horse-trekking can also be organised out of Tyungur or Ust-Koksa.

For anything beyond a day hike, be aware that you're heading for real wilderness. Any hiking around Belukha will require a good degree of fitness and a guide and/or back-country navigation experience. Choose only

VERKHNY UYMON

Just 6km from Ust-Koksa, tiny Verkhny Uymon is the unlikely location of not one but two interesting museums that make a side-trip worthwhile if passing through Ust-Koksa. A taxi up here from Ust-Koksa will cost about ₽700 return with wait time.

Nikolai Rerikh House-Museum (www.sibro.ru; Verkhny Uymon; admission ₽40; ⌚9am-7pm) Rerikh stayed in this wood house, owned by a respected Old Believer friend, in 1926 at the tail end of his epic five-year Asian expedition.

Old Believers' Museum (Музей Старообрядчества; Verkhny Uymom; admission ₽40) The Koksa and Uymon Valleys were once a hotbed for Orthodox Old Believers, many of whom fled here in the 1700s to avoid persecution by the official Russian Orthodox Church. In the 1930s the Old Believers offered fierce armed resistance to collectivisation, leading to the almost total destruction of their villages by the Soviet state. This modest museum contains artefacts from their everyday lives.

tour companies with extensive experience in the area. All of the following can organize one- to 12-day hikes in the area, although only Turbaza Vysotnik and K2 are qualified to lead full-blown Belukha ascents. Tour packages include guides, food, acclimatisation climbs if necessary and, in some cases, transport by raft or horseback.

Turbaza Vysotnik (Турбаза Высотник; ☎38848-294 33; www.belukha.ru; dm/d from ₽300/1700, tent space per person ₽150) Almost anything you'll need for mountaineering or treks into the wilderness, including trips to surrounding lakes, is available for hire here, including tents and guides. Associated with St Petersburg tour company LenAlpTours.

K2 (p419) Owner Igor Federov has years of mountaineering experience in the region and can arrange ascents of Belukha as well as peaks in the Northern and Southern Chuya ranges around Aktash.

Uch-Sumer (Уч-Сумер; ☎38822-250 35 in Gorno-Altaisk; www.uch-sumer.ru; ul Zarechnaya 5; yurt space/d ₽500/1400) Locally based operator has many tour options, notably hunting around Lake Kucherla and elsewhere in the mountains where it maintains cabins.

Portal Beluha (http://beluha.net; ul Naberezhnaya 55) Based in Ust-Koksa and has plenty of regional experience.

Sleeping & Eating

The best place to stay in the region is Tyungur's well-organised Turbaza Vysotnik. Staff are friendly and English-speaking and there's a great cafe that is the nearest you'll find to an international traveller hang-out in Altai. It's just across the tiny suspension bridge from the village itself. The other accommodation option in Tyungur is Uch-Sumer, a five-minute walk to the southwest of the bridge. It's popular with an older crowd, many of them hunters.

Much larger Ust-Koksa has several places to stay, ATMs and a few supermarkets – it's a good idea to stock up on supplies here before continuing on to Tyungur, which has a limited food selection.

Getting There & Away

If driving from Gorno-Altaisk, take the Chuysky Trakt as far as Tuekta, just north of Onguday. From Tuekta a sealed road runs due west to Ust-Kan, then south to Ust-Koksa.

From Gorno-Altaisk a daily public *marshrutka* departs to Tyungur at 8.20am, with an additional trip at 1.45pm in the summer (₽800, nine hours). Additionally, there's an overnight trip from Barnaul to Ust-Koksa via Biysk and Gorno-Altaisk.

A taxi along the unsealed road from Ust-Koksa to Tyungur will cost around ₽500.

ALTAI'S STONE IDOLS

Altai is famous for its standing stone idols. Known locally as *kameniy babi* ('stone wenches' – most confusing, given their overwhelmingly masculine forms), the best were carved in human form with moustaches, shown holding a cup that symbolically housed the soul of the dead. Just a few have avoided being carted off to museums. Some examples of varying interest appear beside the Chuysky Trakt and in the depths of Tyungur. There are also many groups of animal-shaped petroglyphs (rock drawings) of debatable origin. These may be fascinating but most are so faint that you might miss the scratches even when you're staring right at them.

Eastern Siberia

Includes ➡

Best Places to Eat

- Rassolnik (p486)
- Kochevnik (p486)
- Figaro (p486)
- Chay Khana (p503)
- Gastropub Tolsty Kray (p470)

Best Places to Stay

- Aldyn Bulak Yurt Hotel (p461)
- Belka Hostel (p489)
- Iris (p467)
- Mergen Bator (p502)
- Nikita's Homestead (p492)

Why Go?

Endless ice-bound winters, kiln-hot summers, a history of imperial exile and Stalinist savagery – Eastern Siberia (Восточная Сибирь) may not sound like everyone's first choice of holiday destination, but there's much more to this vast region than blood-craving mosquitoes and blizzard-lost Gulag camps.

Focus is given to the map by glorious Baikal, the world's deepest lake. Only Siberia could possess such a phenomenon with its crystal waters, mind-boggling stats and a long list of outlandish endemic species. The lake presents a major obstacle to the Trans-Siberian Railway, which cradles Siberia in a string of intriguing cities such as architecturally grand Irkutsk, exotically Asian Ulan-Ude and youthful, oil-rich Krasnoyarsk.

But the trick to enjoying Eastern Siberia is in escaping the cities – hit the Great Baikal Trail, go hunting for Tuvan standing stones or seek out far-flung Buddhist temples in Buryatiya – the possibilities are endless, almost as endless as the immense sweep of geography they occupy.

When to Go

Irkutsk

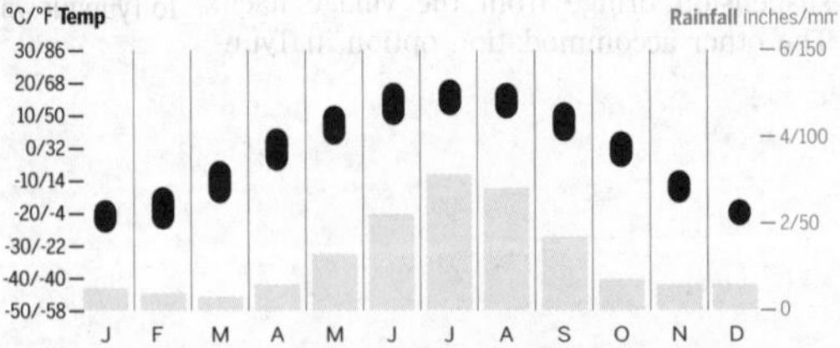

Mar Do a spot of ice fishing on Lake Baikal when the Siberian winter turns its surface hard as steel.

Jul Get on down at Shushenskoe's Mir Sibiri International Music Festival.

Sep Watch larch trees around Lake Baikal turn a fiery yellow during the brief autumn.

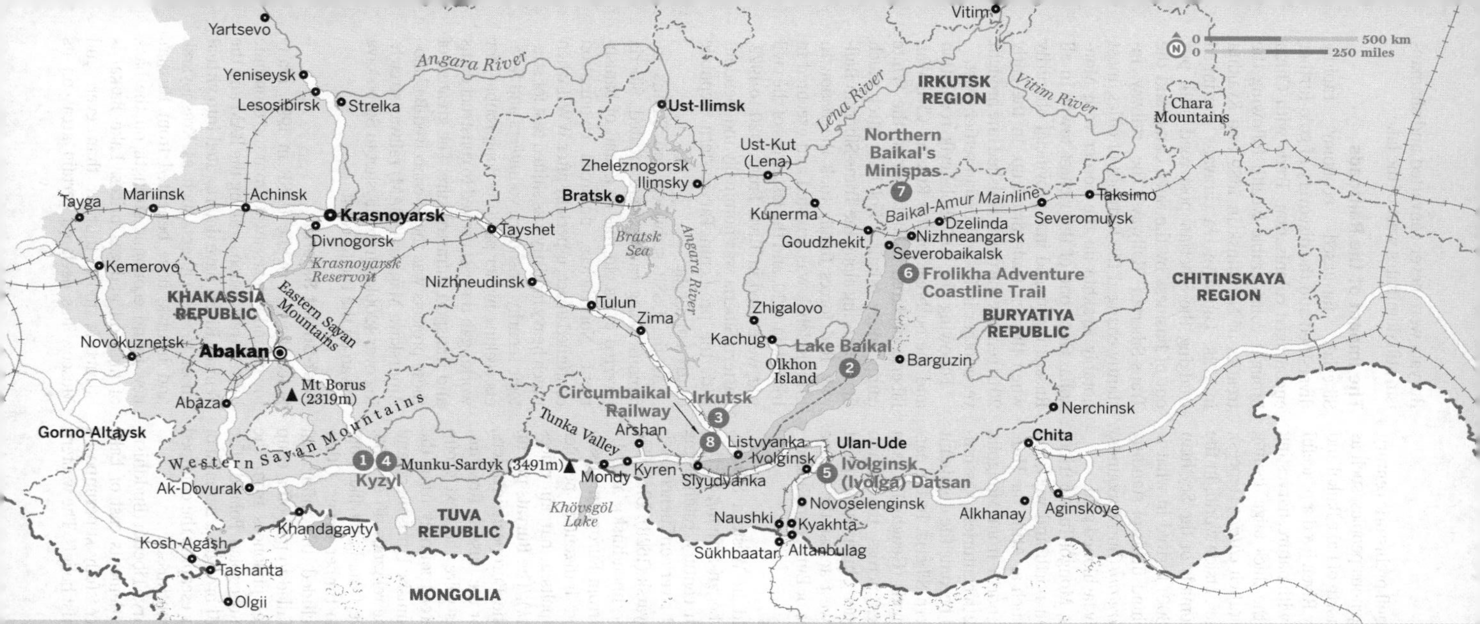

Eastern Siberia Highlights

1 Wonder at the ancient Scythian gold displayed at Kyzyl's **National Museum** (p460).

2 Trek, cycle or hitch a lift across frozen **Lake Baikal** (p478).

3 Wander boulevards of haughty 19th-century architecture in **Irkutsk** (p479).

4 Be amazed at the uncanny sounds a human voice can make during **Tuvan throat singing** (p462).

5 Mooch with the monks at **Ivolginsk (Ivolga) Datsan** (p505) and many other revived Buddhist monasteries.

6 Bag up your boots for the **Frolikha Adventure Coastline Trail** (p476), one of Siberia's most exhilarating long-distance hiking routes.

7 Get into hot water at **northern Baikal's minispas** (p475) for a spot of R'n'R Siberian-style.

8 Take a turn around Baikal's rocky southern shore on the **Circumbaikal Railway** (p494).

History

For century after tranquil prehistoric century, Eastern Siberia's indigenous peoples, such as the Evenki (Tungusi) north of Lake Baikal and the Kets of the Yenisey River, lived a peaceful existence in harmony with nature, harvesting game and berries in the thick taiga, fishing the rivers and building their *chumy* (tepees), largely oblivious of the outside world. In the south, horse-riding nomads of the Scythian culture (700 BC–AD 300) thrived in what is now Tuva, leaving behind fields of standing stones and circular *kurgany* (burial mounds) packed with intricately fashioned gold.

Gradually, however, Mongol-Turkic tribes began their expansion north and west, led by fearsome leaders such as Attila the Hun. The Buryats filtered north from Mongolia during the 11th and 12th centuries to assimilate local peoples and become the dominant ethnic group in Eastern Siberia. In the early 13th century, Chinggis (Genghis) Khaan united Mongol tribes across the region and went on to conquer China. Subsequent khans would sweep west across the steppe to sack the great cities of European Russia.

Enter the Russians

With a firm foothold in Western Siberia, small Cossack units began arriving further east in the early 17th century, establishing an *ostrog* (fortress) at river confluence positions such as Krasnoyarsk (1628), Ulan-Ude (1666, originally Verkhneudinsk) and Irkutsk (1651). Traders from European Russia followed and pressed indigenous peoples into supplying sable pelts at bargain prices (a tax called the *yasak*). The Buryats put up some resistance to the European invaders, but were no match for the Russian firearms.

European peasants were the next group to make the treacherous journey from the west, followed by banished prisoners and Old Believers after the religious rift of 1653; the original defensive forts burst like popcorn into ramshackle timber towns. Other Siberian settlers included the influential Decembrists, who'd failed to pull off a coup in 1825, and political prisoners from the uprisings in Russian-occupied Poland. The end of serfdom in 1861 brought a tsunami of land-hungry peasants escaping the cramped conditions of European Russia.

In the 18th century, Tibetan Buddhism arrived in Buryat settlements east of Lake Baikal and was successfully superimposed onto existing shamanist beliefs. The western Buryats were never converted and shamanism still dominates west of the lake.

The Impact of the Railroads

Siberia's fur-based economy rapidly diversified and the discovery of gold further encouraged colonisation. Trade with China brought considerable wealth following the treaties of Nerchinsk in 1689 and Kyakhta in 1728. Lucrative tea caravans continued trudging the Siberian post road until put out of business by the Suez Canal and the Trans-Siberian Railway. The railway instantly changed the fortunes of cities, most notably Kyakhta on the border with Mongolia. Once one of the richest towns in all Russia, it plunged into provincial obscurity when the tea trade dried up. In the early 20th century the newly finished line brought yet another influx of Russian settlers east.

Following the 1917 Bolshevik revolution and the outbreak of the Russian Civil War, Siberia declared itself firmly in the White camp under Admiral Kolchak. After much fierce fighting along the Trans-Siberian Railway, Red forces finally took the region in 1919. Kolchak was arrested and executed in Irkutsk in 1920, and the last shots of the civil war were fired in Tuva. From 1920 to 1922, Eastern Siberia was nominally independent with the pro-Lenin Far Eastern Republic centred on Chita.

As the USSR stabilised and Stalin's infamous Gulag camps were created, Siberia reverted to its old role as a land of banishment. Nonetheless, unforced colonisation continued apace, especially after WWII when much heavy industry was shifted east for strategic security. Prisoners, volunteers and Soviets seeking higher pay (the 'long rouble') for working in the east arrived to construct dams and transport infrastructure. The greatest of these projects was the ill-conceived Baikalo–Amurskaya Magistral (BAM) railway stretching over 4200km from Tayshet to Sovetskaya Gavan on the Pacific coast.

Post-Soviet Siberia

Since the end of the USSR in 1991, many towns and villages away from the economic beaten track (such as along the BAM and the Yenisey River) have deteriorated into virtual ghost towns. Others, such as Krasnoyarsk and Irkutsk, have benefited from Russia's new-found economic strength on the back of high oil and gas prices. Lake Baikal is attracting more tourists than ever, and Moscow has declared certain areas on its shores special economic zones slated for development. Having weathered the world economic downturn comparatively well, things are better across the region than they have ever been. But with this recent prosperity have come concerns about Siberia's ecologically sensitive habitats and the effects industry and mass tourism may be having on them. Eastern Siberia's Russian cities are firmly behind now confidently authoritarian president Vladimir Putin (who has a soft spot for certain locations in the region), but the self-governing Buryats, Khakass and Tuvans worry about the Kremlin's increasingly centralising tendencies.

KHAKASSIA REPUBLIC & SOUTHERN KRASNOYARSK TERRITORY

Although a mysterious land of lake-dotted taiga (mountain pine) and vast, sparsely populated grasslands, the little-known Khakassia Republic (Хакассия) mostly lacks the show-stopping topography of neighbouring Altai or the cultural attractions of Tuva. Geographically, it is inextricably linked with Southern Krasnoyarsk Territory (Южный Красноярский Край) and the Khakass capital, Abakan, has good transport links to both regions. Until the railway to Tuva is built (if it ever is), Abakan will also remain a stopping-off point en route to Kyzyl.

Like culturally similar Altai, Khakassia was a cradle of Siberian civilisation. Standing stones and *kurgany* pock the landscape; many are more than 3000 years old, though the most visually impressive date from the Turkic period (6th to 12th centuries). The Khyagas (Yenisey Kyrgyz) empire, from which the name Khakassia is derived, ruled much of Central Asia and central Siberia from around AD 840 until its golden age ended abruptly with the arrival of Chinggis Khaan and company.

Most Khyagas later migrated to what is now Kyrgyzstan. Those who remained were picked on by neighbours until joining the Russian Empire in 1701. Compared to neighbouring Tuva, Russian colonisation in relatively fertile Khakassia was comprehensive. Vastly outnumbered, the shamanist Khakass people have been largely Christianised and integrated into Russian society.

Abakan Абакан

3902 / POP 165,200 / MOSCOW +4HR

Founded as a foothold *ostrog* (Cossack fort) in 1675, Abakan remained overshadowed until the 1930s by neighbouring Minusinsk, once the region's centre of European civilisation. With the tables now firmly turned, today the Khakass capital is a leafy, rapidly modernising place with a handful of undemanding sights and a population that will be (perhaps pleasantly) surprised to see you. Probably not worth a special trip on its own, Abakan does serve as a handy base for reaching Shushenskoe and Minusinsk. While the Kuragino–Kyzyl railway remains in limbo, Tuva-bound travellers will spend at least some time here.

Sights & Activities

Khakassia National Museum MUSEUM

(Хакасский национальный краеведческий музей; http://nhkm.ru; ul Pushkina 96; admission ₽100; 10am-6pm) The highlight at the National Museum is the atmospherically low-lit hall containing a striking exhibition dedicated to Khakassia's wealth of standing stones. Curators have erected a kind of mini Stonehenge in the middle of the space, with the walls around lined in 2000-year-old stone fragments – altogether a surprisingly impressive effort. A clearly underfunded collection of random period furniture, shaggy shamanic bric-a-brac and dubious art makes up the rest of the museum.

The foyer still has the best gift shop in town, selling handy Abakan and Minusinsk maps.

Railway Museum MUSEUM

(Музей Истории Красноярской железной дороги; Station concourse; 1-4.45pm Mon-Fri) FREE Worth visiting just to experience a Siberian attraction that doesn't charge admission. Train buffs will find the scale model of Abakan station in 1925, the collection of period railway uniforms and the various oversize chunks of obsolete equipment suitably captivating. Some display cases have been designed to resemble old carriage windows – similar also in that they're bolted firmly shut.

Sleeping

Most places include a breakfast of some kind (though not the kind you may be used to) in their rates. Abakan suffers from high occupancy so book ahead if possible.

Khakassia Republic & Tuva Republic

Chalpan HOTEL $$
(Чалпан; ☎3902-215 302; www.chalpan.ru; proyezd Shchorsa 5a; s/d ₽3650/3850; 📶🏊) By far the best hotel in Khakassia, the purpose-built Chalpan is colourful but not gaudy with imaginatively designed rooms, flashy bathrooms, free tea and coffee in the rooms, a sauna, a pool (!), simple pricing and breakfast. It's well worth enduring the walk along pr Lenina and the staff's slightly indifferent attitude.

Hotel Abakan HOTEL $$
(Гостиница Абакан; ☎3902-203 025; www.abakan-hotel.ru; pr Lenina 59; s ₽600-3100, d ₽1200-3800; 📶) There's a bamboozling array of room categories at what was Abakan's first hotel, from the five unrenovated 'third class' pits to the 19 fully renovated, almost Western standard doubles and beyond. The Soviet past pops up here and there but is slowly being smothered in fluffy white towels and dressing gowns. Truly dire service.

Hotel Khakassia HOTEL $$
(Гостиница Хакассия; ☎3902-223 703; www.hotelkh.nichost.ru; pr Lenina 88; s ₽1900-3800, tw ₽2600-4800; 📶) All rooms at this supercentral hotel have bathrooms and are passably

spruced-up, nevertheless, they remain fundamentally Soviet creations; some suffer from traffic noise and overheat in summer. If they like you, receptionists can cut you a good deal (half-price for 12-hour stays) and as the worst value for money in town, there are often vacancies. Rates include unappetising breakfasts.

Eating & Drinking

Kafe Abakan FAST FOOD $
(Кафе Абакан; pr Lenina 80; mains ₽40-100; ⌚8am-11pm) Prancing petroglyphs and traditional Khakass motifs welcome you to Abakan's best self-service cafeteria and most satisfying cheap eat. Appetising sweet-and-sour chicken meatballs, *plov* (meat and rice), steaks, sausages and many other Russian favourites mean packed tables inside and out at mealtimes. The Russian-only menu is posted at the entrance, so you can decipher at your leisure.

Khoon, Khoorai KHAKASSIAN $
(Хоон, Хоорай; ul Shchetinkina 21; mains ₽200-350; ⌚noon-9pm Sun-Thu, to 2am Fri & Sat) Khakassian culture may be elusive in the republic's capital but sampling traditional food at least just got easier. Traditionally decorated and run by a Khakassian couple, dishes such as *khan* (blood sausage), *khar ta* (horse intestines; yummy!), *khyyma* (horse sausage) and *potkhy* (a kind of porridge made with boiled sour cream) are served at formally laid tables.

Live music Friday and Saturday nights.

Stolichny Supermarket SUPERMARKET $
(Супермаркет Столичный; ul Chertygasheva 108; ⌚8am-11pm) For picnickers and self-caterers, the self-service Stolichny Supermarket is the city centre's best-stocked grocery.

WORTH A TRIP

SALBYK САЛБЫК

This Stonehenge-sized remnant of a 'royal' *kurgan* is Siberia's most impressive ring of **standing stones**. Excavated in 1956, it's in open fields, 5.6km down unsurfaced tracks south of km38 on the Chernogorsk–Sorsk road. About 2km before Salbyk notice the large, grassy dome of the unexcavated **'Princess' kurgan** it once resembled. Taxis from Abakan ask at least ₽1500 return.

★ **Tokana** CAFE
(Токана; ul Chertygasheva 112; ⌚9am-midnight) Green Chesterfield sofas and William Morris-style wallpaper in Abakan? The town's best coffee house would be a superb spot for a caffeine fix anywhere on the planet. Tempting cakes are stacked high, the coffee is expertly barrista-ed and the place is much larger than it looks from outside.

Kotofey CAFE
(Котофей; cnr uls Yarygina & Sovetskaya; ⌚9am-midnight Mon-Fri, from 11am Sat & Sun) Unusually big-windowed corner cafe with frilly lace curtains, proper European-style cafe chairs, the odd leathery bench and decent brews.

Information

Abakan now has ample ATMs, though not all take international cards.

Main Post Office (ul Shchetinkina 20; ⌚8am-10pm Mon-Fri, 9am-6pm Sat & Sun)

ONWARDS TO KYZYL

With the new railroad to Kyzyl on hold, road is the only way to get in and out of Tuva. All transport for the Tuvan capital Kyzyl leaves from the far southeastern corner of the square in front of Abakan's train station. The ticket kiosk for the new official minibus service (₽700, around five hours) is close to the departure point; departures are at 7.50am, 3.30pm and 7pm daily but it's a good idea to buy a ticket at least a day in advance. Shared taxis asking around ₽1000 per seat do the trip slightly faster but drivers are now often hassled at police roadblocks about providing this kind of unsanctioned transport service – this can add hours to the trip. The best time to catch a ride is early morning when train 124 (Krasnoyarsk–Abakan) pulls in. At other times of day you could wait several hours for the vehicle to fill up. **Sayan Ring** (p471) also offers prearranged transfers, but these are only cost-effective for groups.

From Abakan there is no transport to Ak-Dovurak.

MIR SIBIRI MUSIC FESTIVAL

In mid-July around 25,000 music fans make camp in Shushenskoe during the annual **Mir Sibiri** (previously known as the Sayan Ring Festival; www.festmir.ru). The three-day folk-music bash attracts ensembles from across Siberia and the occasional overseas act.

Getting There & Away

AIR

Abakan's old-fashioned little **airport** (www.abakan-airport.ru) is 4km northwest of the city centre. There are flights to Moscow (two daily), Krasnoyarsk (daily) and Irkutsk (three weekly). Buy tickets from the train station **Aviakassa** (3902-239 170; 8am-5pm Mon-Fri) or **TSAVS** (Билетные кассы ЦАВС; www.krascavs.ru; Chertygasheva 106; 8am-8pm).

BUS

Abakan's fairly well-regimented **bus station** (Автовокзал; ul Shevchenko) has connections to the following:

Krasnoyarsk ₽700, 6½ to nine hours, hourly
Minusinsk ₽45, 25 to 40 minutes, very often
Shushenskoe ₽130, 1½ hours, hourly

TRAIN

Abakan has the following rail connections:

Krasnoyarsk *platskart/kupe* ₽1200/1800, 10 hours to 13½ hours, one or two daily
Moscow *platskart/kupe* ₽5500/9400, three days three hours, daily
Novokuznetsk *platskart* ₽900, *kupe* ₽1000 to ₽1300, 10 hours, daily
Novosibirsk *platskart* ₽1420, *kupe* ₽2700 to ₽3000, 22 hours, daily

Getting Around

If you're catching the early-morning S7 Moscow flight, take a taxi (₽100).

Around Abakan

Minusinsk Минусинск

39132 / POP 71,170 / MOSCOW +4HR

Minusinsk's scattering of partly derelict 18th- and 19th-century buildings offers more architectural interest than Abakan, and its grand, crumbling mansions and timber dwellings come as a pleasant surprise. Virtually abandoned during the communist decades, Minusinsk's old town is located across the protoka Minusinskaya waterway from the communist utopia of the new town, 25km east of Abakan.

Jump off *marshrutka* 120 beside the elegant 1803 **Saviour's Cathedral** (Spassky Sobor; ul Komsomolskaya 10) and cross the square to find the superb **Martyanov Museum** (ul Martyanova 6; admission ₽90; 10am-6.30pm). Filling three distinct buildings, the countless halls crammed with local taxidermy, Bronze and Iron Age finds, Tuvan and Khakass standing stones, traditional stringed instruments and shaggy shaman costumes just keep on coming at this admirable repository of the region's past. Away from the obvious prehistoric highlights, more off-beat exhibitions look at the construction of 1970s new Minusinsk and ethnic minorities from Europe that colonised Khakassia in the 19th century. Allow around two hours to see everything and don't even think of veering off from the prescribed tour route.

The museum has two other small branches in town. The **Lenin Museum** (ul Oktyabrskaya 73; admission ₽55; 9am-5pm Mon-Wed & Fri, 10am-5pm Thu) is housed in a complex of wooden buildings just off the original main square, where Lenin often met up with fellow banished comrades (1897–1900). Earlier exiles are the theme of the **Decembrist Museum** (ul Oborony 59; admission ₽50; 9am-6pm Mon-Fri) in a hard-to-find location one block west from the church and three blocks north along ul Oborony.

Sleeping & Eating

Hotel Amyl HOTEL $$

(Гостиница Амыл; 39132-20 106; www.hotelamil.ru; ul Lenina 74; s ₽900-2200, tw & d ₽1100-3000) The town's only decent digs reside in the fading grandeur of a 19th-century palace, half a block southeast of the Martyanov Museum. The 24 rooms range from basic to oddly characterful with comfy sofas, real potted plants and lots of carved wood. There's a tiny weekday-only *zakusochnaya* (pub-cafe) and useful town maps are sold in reception.

Vesna CAFE $

(Весна; ul Lenina 102; mains ₽40-100; 11am-2am) Vesna is a good place for lunch with a central location just off the main square.

Getting There & Away

To get here from Abakan, take bus or *marshrutka* 120 (₽45, 25 to 40 minutes) direct to old-town

Minusinsk. These leave from the left-hand side of the bus station. Buy tickets from the small ticket booth nearby. Catch returning services from opposite the cathedral.

Shushenskoe Шушенское

39139 / POP 17,000 / MOSCOW +4HR

As every Soviet schoolkid was once taught, Shushenskoe played host to Lenin for three years of (relatively comfortable) exile. What textbooks didn't reveal was that in 1898 the young atheist was married in Shushenskoe's **Peter & Paul Church** (Церковь Петра и Павла; ul Novaya; 10am-3pm), much to his later embarrassment.

For the 1970 centenary of Lenin's birth, a two-block area of the village centre was reconstructed to look as it had in 1870. These well-kept 'old' Siberian houses now form the **Shushenskoe Ethnographic Museum** (www.shush.ru; ul Novaya 1; admission ₽150; 10am-6pm). Many are convincingly furnished, and in summer costumed craftsmen sit around carving spoons. It's gently interesting, but as all trips are guided (in Russian) the visit can drag and you're locked into spending over 1½ hours seeing everything. In addition to Lenin's private quarters, other highpoints include the fully stocked late-19th-century shop and a vodka bar, both towards the end of the tour.

Away from the museum, there's not a whole lot to see here other than copious amounts of post-Soviet decay. One odd feature is the sheer number of trees – in places it feels as though the town was built in the middle of a forest without clearing the spot first.

The **post office** (ul Polukoltsevaya 5; 8am-1pm & 2-8pm Mon-Fri, 9am-6pm Sat) offers internet and telephone connection and sells rail and air tickets.

Sleeping & Eating

In the unlikely event you decide to stay over, **Hotel Turist** (Гостиница Турист; 39139-32 841; ul Pushkina 1; s ₽1100-1300, d ₽2000) is a fusty Soviet relic with skin-deep renovation in parts.

The only place in town for a sit-down meal is the unexpectedly bright **Kofeynya Sadko** (Кофейня Садко; 39139-37 199; ul Pervomayskaya 1; mains ₽120-220; 11am-midnight Sun-Thu, to 2am Fri & Sat) opposite the church, where petite portions of flavoursome food arrive on trendy square plates. As virtually the only source of sustenance for visitors, it's often crammed to the gills. The only other options are the kiosks at the bus station offering oily *chebureki* (fried, meat-filled turnovers), chemical-cheese pizza and 3-in-1 coffee. Bring a picnic.

Getting There & Away

Buses serve Abakan (₽130, 1½ hours, hourly), Krasnoyarsk (₽900, 10½ hours, three daily) and Kyzyl (₽650, four to six hours, at least twice daily). While waiting for buses, take time to admire the bus station's spectacular chunk of socialist realism: a gigantic collage celebrating the USSR's achievements, now partially obscured by kiosks.

Usinsky Trakt
Усинский Тракт

Built between 1914 and 1917, the Usinsky Trakt (now the M54 federal highway) is the main road between Minusinsk and Kyzyl in Tuva. Until the Kuragino–Kyzyl railway is completed (if it ever is), this narrow but smooth ribbon of asphalt through the Yergaki Mountains will remain essentially the only route in and out of Tuva for people and goods, most notably Tuva's much-valued coal and other precious minerals. This strategic significance might explain why much of the route is almost Western-standard blacktop.

Around two hours out of Abakan the road skirts the modest historical township of **Yermakovskoe** and passes the fruit-growing villages of **Grigorevka** and **Chyornaya Recha** before climbing into pretty birch-wood foothills. After a shashlyk (kebab) stop in **Tanzybey** (km560) the route climbs more steeply. A truly magnificent view of the crazy, rough-cut Yergaki range knocks you breathless just before km598, and illustrates just why its Turkic name means 'fingers'. Dramatically impressive views continue to km601 and resume between km609 and km612. Expect heavy snowfalls here as late as early June. A **roadside cross** (km603–4) marks the spot where former Krasnoyarsk governor Alexander Lebed (who negotiated an end to the first Chechen War in 1996) died in 2002 when his helicopter snagged power lines. Walk 1.5km up the steep track towards the radar station above for fabulous views from the ridge.

As the track descends, the scenery morphs through wooded river valleys into Tuva's panoramic roller-coaster grasslands. There's a particularly overzealous police checkpoint at **Shivilig** (km703), which almost serves as passport control between Tuva and Russia proper, but the first real settlement the road bisects within Tuva is **Turan**, a ramshackle village of old wooden homes largely inhabited by ethnic Russians. A road barrelling west just before the village heads towards Arzhaan through Tuva's spectacular **Valley of the Kings**. From Turan the road scales one final mountain pass before hurtling down into Kyzyl.

TUVA

Nominally independent before WWII, fascinating Tuva (Тува in Russian, Тыва in Tuvan) is culturally similar to neighbouring Mongolia but with an international cult following all its own. Philatelists remember Tannu Tuva's curiously shaped 1930s postage stamps. World-music aficionados are mesmerised by Tuvan throat singers. And millions of armchair travellers read Ralph Leighton's *Tuva or Bust!*, a nontravel book telling how irrepressible Nobel Prize–winning physicist Richard Feynman failed to reach Soviet-era Kyzyl despite years of trying. Now that visitors are allowed in, Leighton's Friends of Tuva (www.fotuva.org) organisation keeps up the inspirational work with an unsurpassed collection of Tuvan resources on its website. With forests, mountains, lakes and vast undulating waves of beautiful, barely populated steppe, Tuva's a place you'll long remember.

History

Controlled from the 6th century by a succession of Turkic empires, in the 1750s Tuva became an outpost of China, against whose rule the much-celebrated Aldan Maadyr (60 Martyrs) rebelled in 1885. Tibetan Buddhism took root during the 19th century, coexisting with older shamanist beliefs; by the late 1920s one man in 15 in Tuva was a lama.

With the Chinese distracted by a revolution in 1911, Russia stirred up a separatist movement and took Tuva 'under protection' in 1914. The effects of Russia's October Revolution took two years to reach Tuva, climaxing in 1921 when the region was a last bolt-hole of the retreating White Russians, swiftly ejected into Mongolia by 'Red Partisans'. Tuva's prize was renewed independence as the Tuvan Agrarian Republic (Tyva Arat Respublik; TAR), better known to philatelists as Tannu Tuva. However, to communist Russia's chagrin, Prime Minister Donduk's government dared to declare Buddhism the state religion and favoured reunification with Mongolia. Russia's riposte was to install a dependable communist, Solchak Toka, as prime minister, and later to force Tuvans to write their language in the Cyrillic alphabet, creating a cultural divide with Mongolia. Having 'voluntarily' helped Russia during WWII, Tuva's 'reward' was incorporation into the USSR. Russian immigration increased, Buddhism and shamanism were repressed and the seminomadic Tuvans were collectivised; many Tuvans slaughtered their animals in preference to handing them over. When the Soviet Union collapsed in 1991, Tuva was one of only two republics (the other being Chechnya) that looked to secede. Many Russians left for the motherland and most still regard Tuva as a hostile place, with one notable exception – President Putin, who has made several trips to the region, one of which involved his (in) famous bare-chested photo shoot.

Tuvan Culture

Of the republic's 308,000 people, over two-thirds are ethnic Tuvans; they are Buddhist-shamanist by religion, Mongolian by cultural heritage and Turkic by language. Tuvan Cyrillic has a range of exotic extra vowels and most place names have different Russian and Tuvan variants.

Colourful *khuresh* is a form of Tuvan wrestling similar to Japanese sumo but without the ring, the formality or the huge bellies. Multiple heats (rounds) run simultaneously, each judged by a pair of referees, flamboyantly dressed in national costume. They'll occasionally slap the posteriors of fighters who seem not to be making sufficient effort. Tuvans also love Mongolian-style long-distance horse races but are most widely famed for their *khöömei* throat singers. *Khöömei* is both a general term and the name of a specific style in which low and whistling tones, all from a single throat, somehow harmonise with one another. The troll-like *kargyraa* style sounds like singing through a prolonged burp. *Sygyt* is reminiscent of a wine glass being rung by a wet finger: quaintly odd if you hear a recording but truly astonishing when you hear it coming out of a human mouth. Accompanying instruments often include a Jew's harp, a bowed two-stringed *igil* or a three-stringed *doshpular* (Tuvan banjo). Rhythms often remind listeners of horses galloping across the steppe.

The biggest throat-singing ensembles are all-star **Chirgilchin**, inventive **Alash** (www.alashensemble.com), Kaigal-ool's **Huun Huur Tu**, ethno-rock band **Yat-Kha** (www.yat-kha.ru), **Khögzhümchü** and the girl band **Tuva Kyzy** (www.tyvakyzy.com). Many members of the above bands also perform with the **Tuvan National Orchestra**. Until his untimely death in 2013, **Kongar-ol Ondar** was the best-known throat-singer outside Tuva. He collaborated with Frank Zappa and worked on the soundtrack for Oscar-nominated film *Genghis Blues*.

Learning *khöömei* has become surprisingly popular among foreigners in recent years; arranging lessons is now much simpler than it once was.

Tuvan Food

Almost every rural household keeps a vat of *khoitpak* (fermented sour mare's milk), which tastes like ginger beer with a sediment of finely chopped brie. *Khoitpak* is drunk as is or distilled into alcoholic *araka*. Roast *dalgan* (a cereal, similar to Altai's bran-rich *talkan*) can be added to your salted milky tea or eaten with *oreme* (sour cream). Local cheeses include stringy *byshtag* and rock-hard Kazakh-style *kurut* balls.

Tuvans are said to have learnt from Chinggis Khaan a special way to kill their sheep without wasting any of the animal's blood. Collected with miscellaneous offal in a handy intestine, this blood makes up the local delicacy, *khan* sausage. Beyond Kyzyl, truck stops, *pelmeni* (meat ravioli) steamers and temperamental but incredibly cheap village *stolovye* (canteens) are your best hopes for a hot meal unless you're staying with families. Kyzyl residents often take their own supplies when travelling to the provinces.

Festivals & Events

Ask at the Centre for Tuvan Culture (p462) about the following festivals as reliable information is usually impossible to find anywhere else.

Shagaa CULTURAL

(Feb) Tuvan New Year (February) is the biggest festival of the year, with *sangalyr* (purification ceremonies), including a huge spring cleaning, gift giving, visits to relatives and temple rituals.

Khöömei Symposium CULTURAL

(Jun) An erratically held, though possibly now annual event for enthusiasts, anthropologists and musicologists (and anyone else interested) including lectures, talks, demonstrations, competitions and performances, all with a throat singing theme.

Ustuu Khuree MUSIC

(www.ustuhure.ru; Jul) Large world music festival held in and around the Ustuu Khuree temple near Chadan in Western Tuva.

Naadym CULTURAL

(Jul/Aug) Tuva's most dramatic festival is Naadym, usually held in and around Kyzyl in the summer months. Vastly less touristy than the Mongolian equivalent, Naadym is a good opportunity to hear *khöömei* concerts, watch horse races and see *khuresh* wrestling in the flesh.

Dangers & Annoyances

Meeting locals is the key to experiencing Tuva, but be aware that Tuvans are notorious for their reaction to alcohol, becoming disproportionately aggressive, even among friends. Although the situation is improving, travellers should still take extra care wherever they travel in Tuva, making sure to steer well clear of drunks, and avoid

EXPERIENCING KHÖÖMEI

Without doubt, Tuva's great draw is throat singing, aka *khöömei*. If you're interested in seeing a performance, by far the best place to start is the spanking-new Centre for Tuvan Culture (p462), a two-storey timber building opened in late 2011 on the site of the old museum.

Tuvan-speaking Sean Quirk, manager of the Alash ensemble, can usually arrange a short demonstration of the various styles. For a more hands-on experience, take a throat-singing or *doshpular* lesson with National Orchestra member Evgeny Saryglar. Both of these contacts are always in the know about upcoming *khöömei* performances in Kyzyl and beyond.

drinking vodka with local 'friends'. Wandering Kyzyl's streets after dark without local company is also not recommended.

Information

Tuva Online (www.tuvaonline.ru) News from Tuva in English.

VisitTuva (www.visittuva.ru) Official tourism site.

Kyzyl Кызыл

39422 / POP 110,000 / MOSCOW +4HR

Fancifully located at the 'centre of Asia', the Tuvan capital is where the vast majority of travellers begin their exploration of this captivating republic. Although the city's Soviet-era concrete lacks any architectural charm, in recent years the purpose-built National Museum and the superb new Cultural Centre have provided attractive focus for those interested in the country's mesmerising traditions.

The key to enjoying Kyzyl (and all of Tuva) is contacting tour companies and Kyzyl-based English-speaking helpers well in advance – up to two months ahead if you're planning to go anywhere near the Mongolian border, an area for which special permits are needed.

Sights

★National Museum MUSEUM

(Национальный музей; www.museum.tuva.ru; ul Titova 30; admission ₽200, gold exhibition ₽500; 10am-6pm Wed-Sun) One of Tuva's 'must sees', the National Museum's huge modern home contains the usual arrangements of stuffed animals, WWII artefacts and dusty minerals, as well as more impressive halls dedicated to shamanism, Buddhist art and traditional Tuvan sports. However, all of this is just a teasing appetiser before the main course: a single, atmospherically lit and well-guarded room containing kilograms of Scythian gold jewellery, unearthed at Arzhaan I in the Valley of the Kings.

The 3000-year-old gold pieces, which can only be seen on a 40-minute Russian-language guided tour (interpreters available or bring your own), are exquisitely displayed against dark blue felt and seem to illuminate the room with their ancient gleam. Look out for the 1.5kg solid-gold torque, never removed by the Scythian emperor, and thousands of millimetrically fashioned sequins, the likes of which modern-day jewellers claim not to have the skills or tools to reproduce.

Centre of Asia Monument MONUMENT

(Памятник 'Центр Азии'; Yenisey Embankment) If you take a map of the world, cut out Asia and balance the continent on a pin, the centre of gravity would be Kyzyl. Well, only if you've used the utterly obscure Gall's stereographic projection. However, that doesn't stop the city from perpetuating the 'Centre of Asia' idea first posited by a mysterious 19th-century English eccentric and now marked with a brand-new monument by Buryat sculptor, Dashi Namdakov, the man behind the Genghis Khan sculpture at London's Marble Arch.

Tsechenling Datsan BUDDHIST TEMPLE

(Буддийский храм Цеченлинг; ul Shchetinkina-Kravchenko 1) A short walk east along the riverbank from the Centre of Asia Monument stands the white pagoda-style Buddhist temple Tsechenling Datsan. Brightly coloured prayer flags flutter in the breeze outside, but it's disappointingly plain inside. There's a basic canteen and a Buddhist souvenir shop in the grounds.

Museum of Oppression MUSEUM

(Komsomolskaya ul 5; admission ₽50; erratic hours) The tiny and obviously underfunded Museum of Oppression has touching dog-eared photographs of those who disappeared in the Stalin years. Across the grass is the chest-puffing statue of a Nepokorenny ('undefeated') Aldan Maadyr martyr in his pointy slippers.

Tours

Alash Travel TOUR COMPANY

(Алаш-Трэвел; 39422-21 850; alash@tuva.ru; ul Kochetova 60/12) Alash offers full-scale rafting and climbing expeditions and can arrange horse-riding trips between Tuva and Altai. There is, unfortunately, a lack of English speakers in the office.

Tsentr Asii TOUR COMPANY

(Центр Азии; tel/fax 39422-32 326; Hotel Odugen, ul Krasnykh Partizan 36; 9am-6pm) Helpful agency that can arrange air tickets and vehicle transfers.

Sleeping

With a couple of notable exceptions, Kyzyl's limited range of hotels is not much to throat sing about. They're also habitually full, so for a much jollier experience try to arrange a homestay (around ₽1500) through one of

Kyzyl

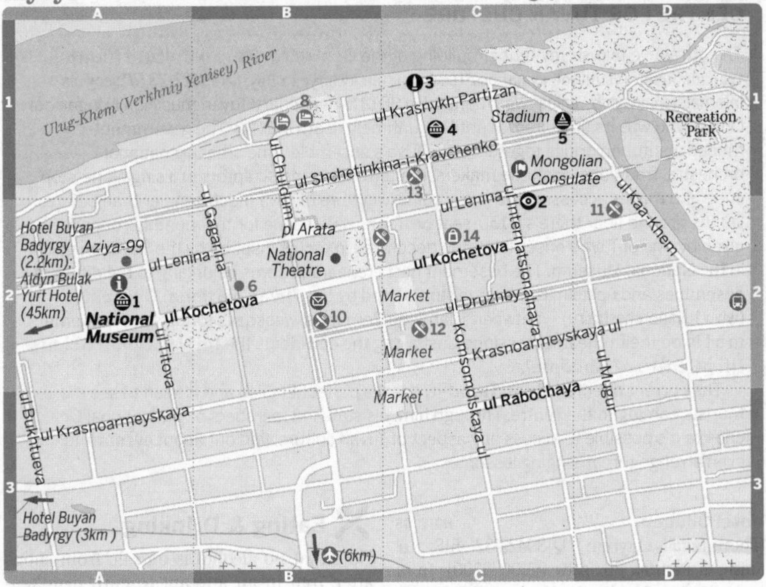

Kyzyl's helpers or tour companies, or stay in an apartment.

★ Aldyn Bulak Yurt Hotel YURT $$
(☎39422-20 628; www.tuvatour.travel; km45 Kyzyl–Ak-Dovurak Rd; per yurt ₽2500-5000, dm tepee/yurt ₽300/650; ❄) Cupped by bare hills at an attractively sacred site by the Yenisey River, the luxury yurts at this upmarket complex have flushing toilets, air-conditioning, hot showers and underfloor heating, while a more authentic experience is provided by basic yurts and tepees. The huge yurt restaurant offers the best Tuvan food you'll taste anywhere in the republic.

Start the day with a climb up to the viewing points for spectacular vistas from the cliffs above the swirling river before paying your respects at the nearby *ovaa* (shamanist holy site) dedicated to *khöömei*. The site is 45km west of Kyzyl, clearly signposted off the main Kyzyl–Ak-Dovurak road. The hotel offers prearranged transfers from Kyzyl for a symbolic ₽100. Due to the remote location there's no wi-fi.

Tuva de Lyuks APARTMENT $$
(☎913 345 5000, 923 375 9999; apt ₽2000) An apartment can be a vastly better deal than a hotel room in Kyzyl, especially if you are travelling in a small group. This new and, it has to be said, sometimes chaotic company offers apartments across Kyzyl, but make sure you ask for their best properties as some can be rough.

Kyzyl

Top Sights
1 National Museum A2

Sights
2 Centre for Tuvan Culture C2
3 Centre of Asia Monument C1
4 Museum of Oppression C1
5 Tsechenling Datsan C1

Activities, Courses & Tours
6 Alash Travel B2
Tsentr Asii .... (see 8)

Sleeping
7 Hotel Kottedzh B1
8 Hotel Odugen B1

Eating
9 Fusion B2
10 Snack Time B2
11 Coffee Man D2
12 Subedey C2
13 Vostorg C1

Shopping
14 Shever C2

DON'T MISS

CENTRE FOR TUVAN CULTURE

The attractive two-storey timber building of the **Centre for Tuvan Culture** (Центр традиционной тувинской культуры/Тыва үндезин культура т□ву; ☎39422-23 571; cnr uls Internatsionalnaya & Lenina) was founded in 2012 by legendary Tuvan musician Kongar-ool Ondar who was its first director until his untimely death in 2013. The government-funded institution brings together all of Tuva's ensembles, the amazing national orchestra, traditional costume makers, metalworkers and sculptors in a single one-stop shop and makes accessing the extraordinary culture of Tuva much simpler than before. On the ground floor there's a 150-seat **concert hall**, venue for the monthly concert given by one of Tuva's ensembles and decorated in motifs inspired by the Scythian gold in the National Museum. The basement hosts rehearsal rooms belonging to the different ensembles and upstairs is the large studio used by the **Tuvan National Orchestra** (www.tuvanorchestra.ru) – between 10am and 2pm most weekdays tourists are welcome to sit in on their rehearsal sessions. Just along the corridor is the **International Scientific Centre of Khöömei**.

The current director **Aldar Tamdyn** speaks perfect English and is keen to see more tourists coming to the centre. Through him, his staff and members of the National Orchestra it's possible to access any aspect of Tuvan culture, find out about events and even arrange throat-singing lessons.

Hotel Odugen HOTEL $$
(Гостиница Одуген; ☎39422-32 518; ul Krasnykh Partizan 36; s/tw ₽2100/3200) In a peaceful location by the Yenisey, this rapidly renovating hotel offers 28 ensuite rooms of varying standards. Whatever you choose, make sure you get one of the rooms with a balcony from where there are spectacular river and mountain views. One of Kyzyl's best bars and a decent terrace cafe are also on the premises.

Hotel Kottedzh HOTEL $$
(Гостиница Коттедж; ☎39422-30 503; ul Krasnykh Partizan 38; s ₽800-4200, tw ₽2400-3800) As well as an illustrious list of former guests including Boris Yeltsin and the 14th Dalai Lama, this 14-room hotel has cosy rooms and acceptable private bathrooms. Breakfast is included and reservations are advised as this place is eternally chock-a-block.

Hotel Buyan Badyrgy HOTEL $$$
(Гостиница Буян Бадыргы; ☎39422-56 420; www.badyrgy.ru; ul Moskovskaya 1; s ₽1800-4000, d ₽4000-6000; ❄📶) Kyzyl's most comfortable sleep is a ₽100 taxi ride from the city centre (or a short trip on airport-bound *marshrutka* 1A). The 37 standard rooms are clean and often smartly fitted out, but some bathrooms could do with an update. The price-to-quality ratio makes this a traveller favourite and a preferable alternative to Kyzyl's hit-and-miss central hotels.

✖ Eating & Drinking

Note that no alcohol is on sale from shops after 7pm in an attempt to curb drunkenness and brawling.

Vostorg FAST FOOD $
(Восторг; ul Shchetinkina-Kravchenko 35; mains ₽40-90; ⊙8am-11pm) Perched above a supermarket of the same name, Kyzyl's best cheap eat is a plasticky no-frills self-service cafeteria where cash-strapped students and office workers fill up for a few roubles on generous platefuls of *pelmeni*, bliny, meatballs, *plov*, pork roast and Ukrainian *holubtsi* (cabbage rolls stuffed with rice and meat). Fresh doughnuts and pastries make this a decent breakfast spot.

Snack Time CANTEEN $
(ul Druzhby 158; mains ₽35-65; ⊙10am-9pm Mon-Sat; 📶) Run by an English-speaking Tuvan this diminutive, brightly hued Russian-style *stolovaya* dishes up tasty pancakes, soups and meatballs as well as some Western additions such as burgers and fries. Located in the rapidly developing market area.

Coffee Man CAFE $
(ul Kochetova 2; mains ₽100-250; ⊙10am-11pm) Once the place to get a cuppa Joe in Kyzyl, Coffee Man is now just another cafe, but one with filling pancakes and an English menu.

Subedey TUVAN $$
(Субедей; ul Druzhby 149; mains ₽200-400; ⊙10am-1am; ❄) If your palette craves gastro-

nomic adventure, head to this oversize Mongolian yurt in the market area for some authentic Tuvan cooking. *Khoorgan khoy edi* is fried mutton, *dalgan usken bydaa* is Tuvan noodle soup and there are milk-based desserts, *khoitpak* (fermented milk) and *araga* (milk vodka) to finish off. The first half of the menu features more European-style mains.

Fusion INTERNATIONAL **$$**
(Кафе Фьюжн; ul Tuvinskykh Dobrovoltsev 13; mains ₽200-400; ⌚noon-midnight Mon-Thu, to 12.45am Fri, 1pm-12.45am Sat, 1pm-midnight Sun; ❄📶📄) If you just wanna hang out with your wireless-enabled device over a brew (of the bean or hop variety) in an unchallengingly stylish, faux-cosmo setting, Fusion is the place to install yourself. The pizza and sushi contain no intestines, the Russian fashion TV no politics and the service is competent if slow.

Shopping

Shever SOUVENIRS
(Шевер; Komsomolskaya 23a; ⌚10am-6pm Mon-Fri, to 4pm Sat) Souvenir and craft shop selling top-quality handmade items such as small pieces of sculpture made from a soft stone called agalmatolite, silver jewellery from Ak-Dovurak, Jew's harps, 'I've-been-to-Tuva' T-shirts and handy city maps.

Information

ATMs are now plentiful in Kyzyl; changing currencies other than euros and dollars could be tricky.

Evgeny Saryglar (ana-saryglar@yandex.ru) Gives throat-singing and *igil* lessons. Have a few introductory sessions via Skype before you arrive.

Post Office (ul Kochetova 53; ⌚8am-10pm Mon-Fri, 9am-6pm Sat & Sun) Has an internet room.

Sean Quirk (alashensemble@gmail.com) US-born manager of the Alash ensemble and member of the National Orchestra. Contact Sean if you're interested in throat-singing performances and demonstrations.

Tourist Office (www.visittuva.ru; National Museum grounds; ⌚Jun-Aug) Summer-only yurt in the grounds of the National Museum. English-speaking staff can assist with accommodation and transport and also distribute free maps and leaflets.

Getting There & Away

Opinions differ on whether the railway line to Kuragino will ever be completed. Even if it is, there's some confusion as to whether passenger services will run on the line. No developments are expected for some years or at least until an investor is found.

AIR

Kyzyl's shockingly up-to-date but sorely underexploited airport handles flights to Krasnoyarsk (daily) and a handy service to Irkutsk (three weekly). Moscow flights were suspended again in 2013 and don't look like making a return any time soon. *Marshrutka* 1A will get you to the airport.

Aziya-99 (Азия-99; ☎39422-22 214; www.asia99.ru; ul Lenina 58; ⌚8am-7pm Mon-Fri, 9am-6pm Sat & Sun) opposite the National Museum sells air tickets for all flights, including services departing from Abakan and Krasnoyarsk.

BUS

For the spectacularly scenic drive to Abakan, unofficial minibuses (₽800, 4½ hours) leave when full from near the bus station but are often targeted by road cops for fines which leads to lengthy waits at road blocks. Infinitely better are the official buses which leave three times a day from within the bus station compound (₽700, five hours), but as these are tiny vehicles, buying a ticket in advance is essential.

Abakan-bound shared taxis and others heading to destinations within Tuva congregate in and around the chaotic car park behind Hotel Mongulek, but you'd be well advised to prearrange private transfers (along with accommodation) to places such as Ak-Dovurak and destinations south along the M54.

Around Kyzyl

On the Yenisey's northern bank, multiple springs gurgle straight from the rocks amid totem poles and trees heavy with prayer flags at cliff-side **Bobry Istochnik** (Beaver Spring). This popular barbecue and picnic spot with picturesque Kyzyl views can only be reached by taxi (at least ₽1000).

The giant **Kadarchy Herder Statue** surveys the city from a bare hill, five minutes' drive from Kyzyl's southernmost edge. Beyond, prayer rags photogenically deck the **Tos Bulak Spring**, which is the closest *arzhaan* (sacred spring) to the capital. To get a taste for the steppe, consider the relatively easy excursion to miragelike **Cheder Salt Lake**, 42km away. The popular but slightly ramshackle lakeside **Cheder Health Spa** (☎39422-20 130) has basic ensuite rooms, but book well ahead as the summer months see hundreds of locals invade this remote location to take mud cures and cool off in the briny waters.

Isolated amid an endless grassy steppe 65km from Kyzyl, **Lake Dus Khol** is crowded with comically mud-blackened vacationers; its waters are so salty that you float Dead Sea style. Larger **Lake Khadyn** nearby is great for summer swimming and camping, though the water is still too salty to drink or use for cooking. To reach both, turn off the M54 at the 840km marker and head 20km along sandy, unsurfaced access tracks; arrange a prepaid private transfer with a Kyzyl agency if you don't fancy putting yourself at the mercy of local taxi drivers.

Following the Ka-Khem (Maly Yenisey) River southeast of Kyzyl, the steppe gives way to agricultural greenery around low-rise **Saryg-Sep**, beyond which an appallingly rutted road continues through woodland to the pretty Old Believers' village of **Erzhey**. Despite the extraordinary inaccessibility, there are several bungalow-hotels and hunting lodges en route and beyond.

From Kyzyl to Erzin

The paved M54 offers a wonderfully varied scenic feast with archetypal Central Asian grassland, then parkland-style rolling woodlands after Balgazyn, thickening to pine forest beyond the food halt at **Shurmak**. Spot shamanic cairns and prayer-rag ticker tape on passes and herders' yurts in picturesque meadows. The landscape gets starkly drier descending past Samagaltay and **Bay Dagh**, a former camel-breeding centre where memorials commemorate the last scuffles of the civil war in 1921. Between km1023 and km1024, radar posts look down on the junction of a smooth, scenic but unpaved road to Mören, 18km away, passing near holy mountain **Ak-Khayyrakan** (1148m). Tour companies and guides in Kyzyl/Krasnoyarsk might be able to show you its revered spring (whose seasonal flow is aided each summer by multiple shamanic ceremonies) and arrange unforgettable yurt stays with nomadic cattle herders in the glorious valleys beyond.

You'll need permits to continue south into the border zone; with plenty of notice, the head office of the **Ubsunur Basin Biosphere Reserve** (☎39422-53 818; ubsunur@tuva.ru) in Kyzyl can arrange these, as can Kyzyl agencies.

Sandy tracks continue 20km south of **Erzin** past Dalí-esque rocky outcrops to **Lake Tore Khol**, a popular local picnic spot. Although it's at the edge of the desert zone, herded horses trotting through the shallows give the area a slight feel of the Camargue in France. Across the water is Mongolia, but the border is closed to foreigners. **Tore Khol yurt camp** on the banks of the lake can be booked through Kyzyl agencies. To the east of Tore Khol the dunes of the **Tsugeer-Els protected landscape** rise high along the left bank of the Tec Khem River.

Western Tuva
Западная Тува

The route looping round to Abakan from Tuva via Askiz is scenically varied, often beautiful and mesmerisingly vast in scale, though the Chinggis Khaan stone near Ak-Dovurak is virtually the only real 'sight'. While independent travel is feasible, you'll see a lot more in Tuva's west in the company of a local or a guide hired in Kyzyl. The Sayan Ring agency in Krasnoyarsk comes this way.

VALLEY OF THE KINGS ДОЛИНА ЦАРЕЙ

This broad grassy vale begins a few kilometres beyond a turning off the M54 highway north of Turan. It's famous in archaeological circles for its pancake-shaped Scythian *kurgany* (burial mounds) named after the village of Arzhaan at the end of the paved road. These have produced the most significant archaeological finds ever made in Tuva, now displayed in Kyzyl's National Museum.

The first roadside *kurgan* is **Arzhaan II**, which lies opposite shimmering Ak Khol (White Lake). During excavations in 2001 archaeologists unearthed some magnificent artefacts in several graves dating from the 7th century BC. Less well-maintained **Arzhaan I**, a little further along the road, is the largest *kurgan* in Tuva. A dig in the early 1970s turned up thousands of gold and silver artefacts plus the graves of two Scythian VIPs, 16 servants and 160 horses, but today only a large disc of clacking stones remains. The valley holds an amazing 700 burial sites and eight large *kurgany* await the archaeologist's trowel. However, digs are unpopular with local villagers and shamans who believe the spirits should be left undisturbed.

WORTH A TRIP

SAY-KHONASH

Located 55km north of Ak-Dovurak, the **Say-Khonash yurt camp** (8-923-542 6566, 8-923-383 7109; www.saixonash.wordpress.com; full board ₽1500) is the quintessential nomadic experience and brings visitors as close to the authentic rural lifestyle as they're ever likely to get without having to acquire Tuvan in-laws first. The six traditionally furnished yurts sleeping 12 are surrounded by real nomads' dwellings and their assorted animals in a jaw-slackeningly remote location few would ever chance upon. The English-speaking owners (Evgeny and Anay-Khaak) and their extended family give masterclasses in felt production, yurt construction, traditional sheep butchery and Tuvan music, as well as organising multiday horse-riding and hiking trips to fantastically off-the-map locations.

No road, never mind public transport, goes anywhere near this place, so transfers from Kyzyl (or Abakan/Krasnoyarsk) must be arranged in advance.

Kyzyl to Ak-Dovurak

The spectacularly picturesque and virtually traffic-free grassland route from Kyzyl to Ak-Dovurak is lined with sacred mountains, nomads' yurts and newly raised stupas. Some 80km out of Kyzyl, dramatic **Mt Khayyrakan** (1148m), a spiky ridge blessed by the 14th Dalai Lama in 1992, comes into view but isn't reached until km107. Climb towards the stupa at the base of the mountain from the roadside cafe where buses make a brief stop. The best place to break the 300km journey is the simple midway **Kafe Aziya** (km145; 8am-11pm), beyond which the conical stand-alone **Mt Syyn-Churee** is scored with almost 200 petroglyphs. The small town of **Chadan** (Chadaana) is attractively dotted with wooden cottages and there's an appealing little **museum** (ul Lenina 33). Apart from being the birthplace of Russia's current minister of defence, Sergey Shoygu, the town is most famous as Tuva's former spiritual centre; the once-great **Ustuu Khuree Temple** 6km south of Chadan was utterly devastated in the Soviet era but has since been rebuilt and now hosts a large annual **music festival** in mid-July, embracing everything from *khöömei* to grunge rock. Participants camp in tents and yurts. Ak-Dovurak and Kyzyl-Mazhalyk are another hour's drive west.

From **Khandagayty**, where the Mongolian border remains closed to foreigners, a glorious but notoriously tough truck track runs to Kosh-Agach in Altai via Mugur-Aksy, passing the glacier-topped **Mt Mongun-Tayga** (3976m). Bring food, a reliable guide, ample extra fuel and spare parts if you plan a truck or jeep convoy. With many deep fords, this route is impassable after rain. It's much more pleasant on horseback; Alash Travel (p460) in Kyzyl can help you organise horses. In ideal conditions it's possible to make the trip by mountain bike in around a week, but getting lost is dangerously easy.

Ak-Dovurak & Kyzyl-Mazhalyk
Ак-Довурак и Кызыл-Мажалык

39441 / MOSCOW +4HR

The world's largest open-pit asbestos mine dominates Ak-Dovurak, Tuva's unlovable second 'city'. Around 10km away, the main attraction is the **Chinggis Khaan stone**, a remarkably well-preserved 1.5m-high moustachioed stone idol. To find it, cross the Shui River to **Kyzyl-Mazhalyk** town then drive 8km towards Ayangalty. About 500m after you pass the turn-off to tiny Bizhiktig Khaya village, the stone figure stands all alone in a field, 400m west of the road. To get close, you may have to pay an admission fee. The surrounding meadows are peppered with less prominent standing stones. Ak-Dovurak taxis want at least ₽600 return.

Long rows of standing stones and Turkic burial sites can be seen by turning onto a dirt track just before the 10km marker on the Teeli road west of Ak-Dovurak. Most still bear fading petroglyphs. Yet more delicately etched ancient stonework is the star attraction at Kyzyl-Mazhalyk's **Regional Museum** (Culture Centre, ul Khomushku Vasily 23; admission by donation; on request), alongside an independence-era newspaper printed in the Tuvan Latin script, a mock-up of a yurt and figures sculpted in a kind of soapstone, a tradition practised in the area since Scythian times.

Ak-Dovurak's **Hotel Cheleesh** (394 332 1255; ul Tsentralnaya 6) has cheap, survivable rooms and staff are friendly. It's upstairs in the rear of the building bearing a giant

Soviet-era mural. However, homestays with local families are infinitely more enjoyable; these can be arranged through Kyzyl agencies and helpers.

From Kyzyl, sporadic *marshrutky* serve Ak-Dovurak (five to seven hours) via Chadan. However, private transfers arranged through Kyzyl agencies allow you to stop along the way and are much safer. Ak-Dovurak city buses run from the centre of town via the bus station (1.5km) to Kyzyl-Mazhalyk.

KRASNOYARSK REGION

Vast and beautiful, the Greenland-shaped Krasnoyarsk region (Красноярский Край) stretches all the way from the Arctic islands of Severnaya Zemlya to a mountainous tip at Mt Borus. Its capital is Krasnoyarsk, a buzzing, forward-looking metropolis and a popular stop for travellers riding the Trans-Siberian Railway.

Krasnoyarsk Красноярск

391 / POP ONE MILLION / MOSCOW +4HR

More orderly and affluent than the average Siberian city, million-strong Krasnoyarsk enjoys an appealing setting amid low hills punctuated by jagged rock formations. While its architecture isn't particularly inspiring, scattered throughout the predominantly unaesthetic concrete of post-WWII industrialisation are a few outstandingly well embellished timber mansions and a sprinkling of unexpected art nouveau curves. Pleasant river trips, the nearby Stolby Nature Reserve and an outstanding regional museum make Krasnoyarsk an agreeable place to break the long journey between Tomsk (612km west) and Lake Baikal.

Sights & Activities

★ **Stolby Nature Reserve** NATURE RESERVE

(www.stolby.ru) Krasnoyarsk's biggest draw are the fingers and towers of volcanic rock called **stolby**. These poke above the woods in the 17,000-hectare Stolby Nature Reserve (Zapovednik Stolby). To reach the main concentration of rock formations, follow the track (7km long) near Hotel Snezhnaya Dolina (bus 50), or take the year-round **chairlift** (Фуникулёр; ₽250) belonging to the ski resort. From the top, walk for two minutes to a great viewpoint or around 40 minutes to reach the impressive **Takmak Stolby**.

New paths and steps mean going it alone is not the dare-devil experience it once was, but English-language tours with SibTourGuide (p471) are a much more pleasant and entertaining affair. Be aware that infected ticks are dangerous between May and July and tick protection or predeparture encephalitis jabs are essential at this time.

Regional Museum MUSEUM

(Краеведческий музей; www.kkkm.ru; ul Dubrovinskogo 84; admission ₽150; 10am-6pm Tue-Wed & Fri-Sun, 1-9pm Thu) Housed in an incongruously attractive 1912 art nouveau Egyptian temple, this is one of Siberia's better museums. Arranged around a Cossack explorer's ship, surprisingly well-presented exhibitions across the two floors examine every facet of the region's past, from Cossacks and gentlemen explorers to the Tunguska explosion and local fauna, prerevolution institutions to religious art.

Highlights include the 20th-century 'nostalgia' section on the upper level and the 4m-tall mammoth skeleton looking like something straight off a Hollywood museum movie set. There are touch-screen games for kids throughout and a decent cafe to look forward to at the end.

Surikov Museum-Estate MUSEUM

(Музей-усадьба Сурикова; www.surikov-dom.com; ul Lenina 98; admission ₽100; 10am-6pm Wed-Sun) The Surikov Museum-Estate preserves the house, sheds and vegetable patch of 19th-century painter Vasily Surikov (1848–1916). The heavy-gated garden forms a refreshing oasis of rural Siberia right in the city centre. More of Surikov's work is on show at the old-school **Surikov Art Museum** (Художественный музей Сурикова; ul Parizhskoy Kommuny 20; admission ₽100; 10am-6pm Tue-Wed & Fri-Sun, 1-9pm Thu).

Resurrection Church CHURCH

(Благовещенская церковь; ul 9 Yanvarya) The top-heavy but elegant Resurrection Church (1804-22) was decapitated in the 1930s but given a new tower in 1998-99. Its icon-filled interior billows with incense.

Literature Museum MUSEUM

(Литературный музей; ul Lenina 66; admission ₽50; 10am-6pm Tue-Sat) This quaint museum within a glorious 1911 merchant's mansion occasionally hosts classical music performances.

Chasovnya Chapel NOTABLE BUILDING

(Часовня; top of Karaulnaya Hill) For some spectacular city views climb Karaulnaya Hill (there's no bus) to the little chapel which features on the Russian 10-rouble banknote (now slowly being replaced with a coin). It was designed in 1855 by Konstantin Thon, the architect behind Moscow's Christ the Saviour Cathedral. At midday a deafening one-gun salute is fired from just below the chapel.

SV Nikolai MUSEUM
(Святой Николай; admission ₽50; ⏲10am-8pm Tue-Sun) Permanently docked below an ugly brown-concrete exhibition centre (formerly the Lenin Museum) is the SV *Nikolai,* the ship that transported future Soviet leader Vladimir Ilych Lenin to exile in Shushenskoe and the future Tsar Nikolai II across the Yenisey in 1891.

Intercession Cathedral CHURCH
(Покровский собор; ul Surikova) This pleasingly small old church dating from 1795 has an interior of unusually glossed and intricately moulded stucco framing haloed saints.

Roev Ruchey Zoo ZOO
(Зоопарк Роев ручей; www.roev.ru; admission ₽200; ⏲9am-9pm) Take bus 50 or 50A to this humane zoo near the Bobrovy Log Ski Resort to see numerous Siberian species.

Bobrovy Log Ski Resort SKI RESORT
(Лыжный курорт Бобровый Лог; www.bobrovylog.ru; ul Sibirskaya 92) Below the Stolby the slap and swish of skis and snowboards can be heard at the Bobrovy Log Ski Resort. Snow cannons keep the slopes going well into May, and in the summer months the Roedelbahn (a kind of downhill forest roller coaster), a pool and regular sports events keep the fun level high. Bus 37 runs from the train station direct to the resort.

Sleeping

Krasnoyarsk has the full range of post-Soviet accommodation options, from unrenovated Soviet dumps to boutique design hotels, vibe-rich hostels to five-star residences.

City Centre

★**SibTourGuide Hostel** HOSTEL $
(☎950 985 8608; www.sibtourguide.com; pr Mira 85, apt 72; dm/d ₽700/900; @📶) Krasnoyarsk's best backpacker halt and one of Eastern Siberia's finest hostels has a great central location with fish-tank views of the bustle on pr Mira. Facilities are spotless, rooms are light and airy and there's a washing machine (₽200) and full service kitchen, plus the full range of SibTourGuide trips can be arranged directly with staff.

Rates include a ₽100 breakfast/meal voucher for the nearby Gastropub Tolsty Kray. Only eight beds, so book well ahead.

Hotel Sever HOTEL $
(Гостиница Север; ☎391-266 2266; www.hotel-sever.net; ul Lenina 121; s/d from ₽500/570; 📶) Take a trip back to the good ol' USS of R at this Soviet armpit of a hotel, a last resort for budget Trans-Sibbers. Most of the rooms are high-ceilinged, overheating, never-been-renovated affairs with the standard monster fridge in the corner, imaginative plumbing solutions and ancient nailed-down lino.

On the upside there's cheap visa registration (₽100) and a decent cafe serving breakfast fare, plus you get to leave at the end of your stay.

Hotel Ogni Yeniseyya HOTEL $
(Гостиница Огни Енисея; ☎391-227 5262; www.oe-hotel.ru; ul Dubrovinskogo 80; s/tw from ₽1275/2200; 📶) One of the last budget options left; there's a vast selection of rooms here, but whatever you plump for, make sure it has Yenisey views.

★**Iris** BOUTIQUE HOTEL $$
(Ирис; ☎391-227 2292; www.iris-apart-hotel.ru; pr Mira 37; s/d ₽3600/4000; 📶) Housed in a 19th-century former religious school for girls, the romantic French theme and impeccable personal service sets the Iris apart from most Siberian hotels. The 10 rooms are done out in soothing beiges and light browns but the *pièce de résistance* here are the two romantic design suites, all period wallpaper, belle époque furniture and mock chateau elements.

Set in a quiet courtyard, well away from the thundering thoroughfares. Breakfast and cheery welcomes included.

Dom Hotel HOTEL $$$
(☎391-290 6666; www.dom-hotel24.ru; ul Krasnoy Armii 16a; r ₽4400-7600; @📶) Centred around a rather characterless courtyard, the 81 light-filled rooms at Krasnoyarsk's top business hotel are immaculately maintained and have become a firm favourite among foreigners looking for Western comforts. Staff are courteous and there is an inexpensive on-site restaurant. Breakfast costs extra.

Soft Hotel HOTEL $$$
(☎391-228 2700; www.softhotel.ru; ul Surikova 16; s/d from ₽5900/6800; ❄📶) With its European

Krasnoyarsk

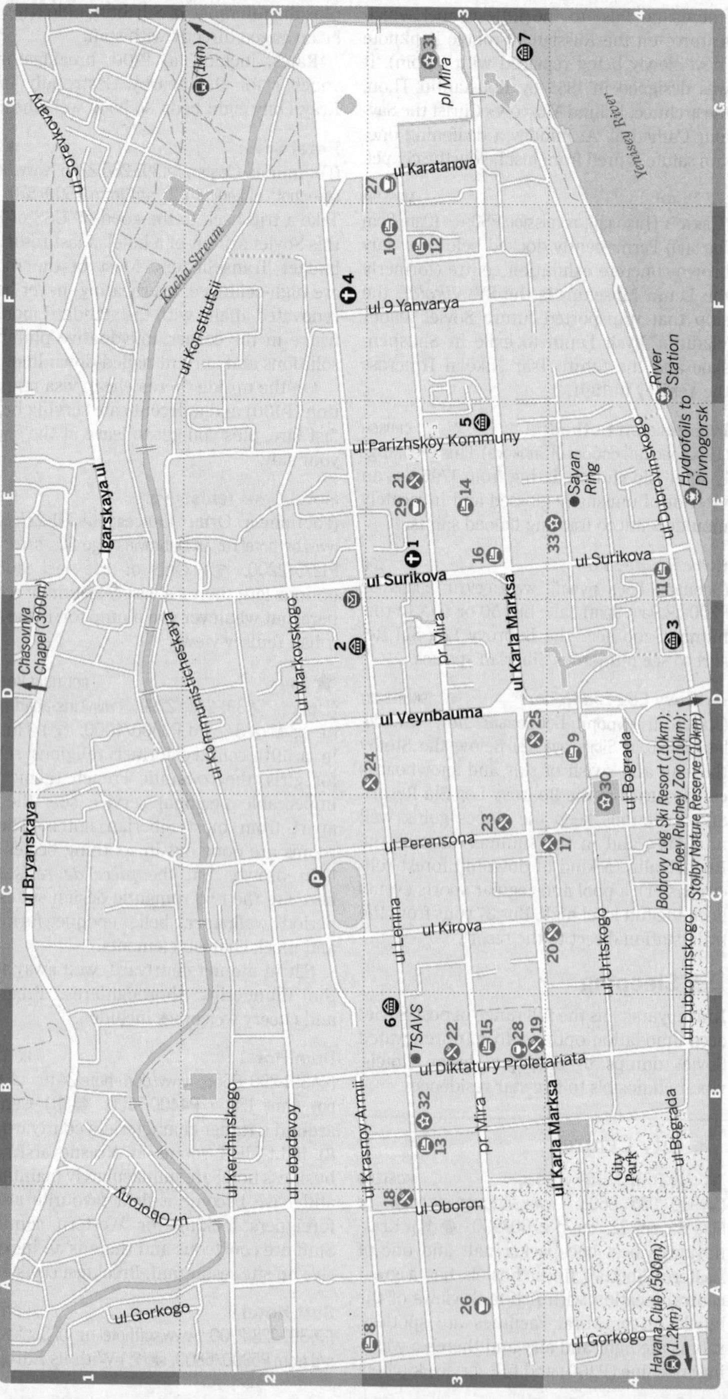
0 500 m
0 0.25 miles
ul Sorevkovany
(1km)
Kacha Stream
ul Konstitutsii
Igarskaya ul
Chasovnya Chapel (300m)
ul Kommunisticheskaya
ul Bryanskaya
ul Markovskogo
ul Kerchinskogo
ul Lebedevoy
ul Oborony
ul Gorkogo
ul Krasnoy Armii
ul Lenina
TSAVS
ul Oboron
pr Mira
pl Mira
ul Karatanova
ul 9 Yanvarya
ul Parizhskoy Kommuny
ul Surikova
ul Veynbauma
ul Perensona
ul Kirova
ul Diktatury Proletariata
ul Karla Marksa
Sayan Ring
ul Uritskogo
ul Bograda
ul Dubrovinskogo
City Park
Yenisey River
River Station
Hydrofoils to Divnogorsk
Bobrovy Log Ski Resort (10km); Roev Ruchey Zoo (10km); Stolby Nature Reserve (10km)
Havana Club (500m); (1.2km)

Krasnoyarsk

Sights

1 Intercession Cathedral E3
2 Literature Museum D2
3 Regional Museum D4
4 Resurrection Church F2
5 Surikov Art Museum E3
6 Surikov Museum-Estate B3
7 SV Nikolai G3

Sleeping

8 Dom Hotel A3
9 Hotel Krasnoyarsk D4
10 Hotel Metelitsa F3
11 Hotel Ogni Yeniseyya E4
12 Hotel Oktyabrskaya F3
13 Hotel Sever B3
14 Iris E3
15 SibTourGuide Hostel B3
16 Soft Hotel E3

Eating

17 Buddha Bar & Lounge C4
18 Gastropub Tolsty Kray A3
19 Kalinka-Malinka Stolovaya No 2 .... B3
20 Krasny Yar Supermarket C4
21 Mama Roma E3
22 Mike & Molly B3
23 Miks Patio C3
24 Rada D3
25 Sem Slona D3

Drinking & Nightlife

26 Kofemolka A3
27 Krem G3
28 Shanti Bar B3
29 Traveller's Coffee E3

Entertainment

30 Opera-Ballet Theatre C4
31 Philharmonia G3
32 Puppet Theatre B3
33 Rock-Jazz Kafe E4

business standard facilities, waxy antique-style furniture, 21st-century bathrooms (with bidets!) and high-flying ceilings, taking the soft option might be the way to go now in Krasnoyarsk. More roubles equals more space though the five *ekonom*-class rooms have lower-standard furniture. Efficient service and good value for money – only the views and the non-buffet breakfast disappoint slightly.

Hotel Krasnoyarsk HOTEL $$$
(Гостиница Красноярск; ☎391-274 9400; www.hotelkrs.ru; ul Uritskogo 94; s/tw from ₽4300/5780; ❄📶) Every Soviet metropolis has one: a concrete lumpen hotel celebrating the city's name in metre-high lettering. But unlike many of these stale relics, the sprawling eight-storey Krasnoyarsk is well kept with bright corridors, totally rebuilt full-service rooms and English-speaking receptionists. Rates are also decidedly 'post-Soviet' but at least breakfast is included.

Hotel Metelitsa HOTEL $$$
(☎391-227 6060; www.hotel-metelica.ru; pr Mira 14; s/d from ₽4300/₽6000; ❄📶🏊) Exclusive minihotel of the type favoured by Russia's oil-stained business elite and the ugliest gallery of pop stars you're ever likely to see. Every room is done out differently, some with design-mag flair, and bathrooms are far from bog standard. Staff speak reluctant English and there's a pool where you can pretend you are by an alpine lake. Breakfast included.

Hotel Oktyabrskaya HOTEL $$$
(Гостиница Октябрьская; ☎391-227 3780; www.hoteloctober.ru; pr Mira 15; s ₽4200-6300, d ₽5600-6300; 📶) Comfortable and professionally run with rooms approximating Western standards, albeit without air-conditioning. Satellite TV includes Western channels and some English is spoken. The trendy lobby area has a stylish juice bar. Includes breakfast.

Stolby Area

Snezhnaya Dolina HOTEL $$
(Снежиая Долина; ☎391-269 8110; www.sneg-dolina.ru; per cottage from ₽5300, s ₽700-3200, d ₽1400-3700; 📶🏊) This accommodation complex has a hotel, a minimotel and rows of cosy cottages meaning lots to choose from. There's a swimming pool, a tennis court and a decent restaurant, but the main draw here is the clean air and the proximity to the stolby and ski slopes.

Eating

Rada VEGETARIAN $
(Рада; ul Lenina 74; mains ₽100-200; ⏰10am-10pm; ❄📶🥗) Krasnoyarsk's sole vegetarian food halt is a cheerfully hip, colourful cafe serving a menu of buckwheat burgers, fish-free paella, veggie *pelmeni* and lots of juice and tea (no coffee). The English-speaking owner tweaks the menu a couple of times a year and Rada is a completely caffeine-free zone.

Buddha Bar & Lounge ASIAN, EUROPEAN $
(ul Karla Marksa 127; mains ₽150-250; noon-midnight;) This low-lit, incense-infused vegetarian cellar lounge is a calming place to escape the city-centre blare. Order a plate of exotic Tibetan food from the English-speaking waitress, then give the bar-top prayer wheel a spin before retreating to the cushioned chill-out lounge where nightly DJs drift chill-out music to a chilled crowd. As if Siberia wasn't chilly enough.

Miks Patio FAST FOOD $
(Микс-Патио; ul Perensona 20; mains ₽30-100; 10am-10pm Mon-Sat, from 11am Sun) With budget-airline decor, a menu heavy with Slavic and Italian comfort food and prompt service, this is the *stolovaya* dragged into the 21st century.

Kalinka-Malinka Stolovaya No 2 CANTEEN $
(pr Mira 100; mains ₽40-80 10am-10pm; 10am-10pm) Celebrating the varied cuisines of former Soviet republics this self-service canteen has a loud, plasticky interior scattered with the odd Soviet nostalgia knick-knack kept well out of punters' reach. The range of dishes extends across a vast swathe of the planet, from unpronounceable Georgian fare to peasanty Ukrainian dishes and Siberian stodge. Some dishes charged per 100g.

Sem Slona CANTEEN $
(ul Karla Marksa 95; mains ₽30-80; 24hr) Got a sudden craving for buckwheat at 3am? Then brave the darkened streets and make your way to this all-hours, no-nonsense canteen plating up solid Russian favourites with a growl. The name translates as 'I could eat an elephant' – this being Siberia, a horse just won't do.

Krasny Yar Supermarket SUPERMARKET $
(Гастроном Красный яр; ul Karla Marksa 133; 24hr) Best supermarket in the city centre with a whole row of ATMs on the right as you enter. Branches across the city.

★ **Gastropub Tolsty Kray** CAFE $$
(Гастропаб Толстый Край; www.esc24.ru; ul Lenina 116; mains ₽200-400; 10am-11pm;) Its English-teacher, expat and traveller clientele, wired castle-themed cellar setting and suitably international menu provide good enough reason to drop in at this Anglophone sanctuary. This great cafe also gives guests a five-minute free (yes free!) call to any number in the world from their table, plus there's free wi-fi and a computer hooked up to the web.

Add to this a globalised beer menu, inventive coffees, real porridge, top-notch cooking and regular live music and you might be looking for ul Lenina 116 sooner rather than later. Used to be known as the English School Cafe.

Mike & Molly ITALIAN $$
(www.mikeandmollycafe.ru; ul D Proletariata 32a; mains ₽200-500; 11am-midnight) The stylishly unassuming interior of this Italian job suggests the focus is firmly on the food and that assumption would be right. Possibly Krasnoyarsk's best lasagnes, pastas, salads and proper starters land promptly on your table as you kick back on the black-cloth wall sofas with a glass of Chianti. Sadly, the sullen service is oh-so Siberioso.

Mama Roma ITALIAN $$
(391-266 1072; pr Mira 50a; pizzas ₽200-470, pasta ₽180-490; 9am-1am;) Herb-infused air wafts temptingly out of this long-established Italian eatery, where chequered tablecloths and admirable attempts at pasta, risotto and pizza may make you feel you're in Rome or Naples – but only if you've never been there.

Drinking & Nightlife

★ **Shanti Bar** BAR
(ul D Proletariata 28; noon-midnight Sun-Thu, to 2am Fri & Sat) Descend the street steps into a cool, low-lit world of Indian food, hookah pipes and herb infusions all enjoyed to a subcontinental soundtrack. Hindu gods wave multi-armed at guests as they enter a transient state on cushion-strewn couches, chilling out with a cocktail or a glass of wine. Located in Krasnoyarsk's safest street – it's bang opposite the regional FSB headquarters.

Traveller's Coffee CAFE
(pr Mira 54; 8am-midnight;) The tempting aroma of newly milled beans lures passers-by into this trendy coffee house where the circular brown-cream leather tub-seats give the impression you're sitting in a cuppa. Friendly service and sensibly priced milkshakes, muffins and pancakes.

Krem CAFE
(391-258 1538; pr Mira 10; 24hr;) Krasnoyarsk's classiest coffee house has black-and-white photography, dark-wood furniture, a belt-stretching dessert menu and reasonably priced lattes and espressos.

WORTH A TRIP

YENISEYSK ЕНИСЕЙСК

Easily reachable by bus, historic Yeniseysk makes an engaging excursion off the Trans-Sib from Krasnoyarsk, 340km away. Founded in 1619, this was once Russia's great fur-trading capital, with world-famous 18th-century August trade fairs (recently revived for tourists), and 10 grand churches punctuating its skyline. Eclipsed by Krasnoyarsk despite a burst of gold-rush prosperity in the 1860s, the town is now a drowsy backwater with an unexpectedly good **Regional Museum** (ul Lenina 106; admission ₽100; ⏲9am-5pm Mon-Sat), some faded commercial grandeur along ul Lenina and many old houses; over 70 are considered architectural monuments. Most appealing of the surviving churches are the walled 1731 **Spaso-Preobrazhensky Monastery** (ul Raboche-Krestyanskaya 105) and the **Assumption Church** (Uspenskaya tserkov; ul Raboche-Krestyanskaya 116) with its unusual metal floor and splendid antique icons.

To reach Yeniseysk, take a bus (₽620, seven hours, 10 daily) from Krasnoyarsk's bus station. The journey time makes a day trip impossible so organise accommodation beforehand through SibTourGuide (p471) in Krasnoyarsk.

Further North along the Yenisey

From mid-June to early October, passenger ships slip along the Yenisey River from Krasnoyarsk to Dudinka in the Arctic Circle (4½ days) via Yeniseysk (17 hours) and Igarka (three days two to seven hours). There are three to four sailings per week, most departing early morning. Returning upstream, journeys take 50% longer so most independent travellers choose to fly back to Krasnoyarsk. Foreigners are not allowed beyond Igarka as Dudinka and nearby Norilsk are 'closed' towns. Contact SibTourGuide in Krasnoyarsk for timetables, tickets and round-trip tours.

Kofemolka CAFE
(Кофемолка; pr Mira 114; ⏲10am-midnight; 📶) Sip roasts from every corner of the bean-growing world amid faux mahogany as dark as the coffees and geometrically patterned screens that divide things up into intimate gossip booths. Long dessert menu.

☆ Entertainment

Opera-Ballet Theatre THEATRE
(Театр оперы и балета; ☎391-227 8697; www.opera.krasnoyarsk.ru; ul Perensona 2) The architecturally nondescript Opera-Ballet Theatre has daily performances of productions such as *Carmen, Swan Lake* and *Romeo and Juliet* starting in the early evening, October to June.

Philharmonia LIVE MUSIC
(Филармония; ☎391-227 4930; www.krasfil.ru; pl Mira 2b) The Philharmonia has three concert halls showcasing folk, jazz and classical music.

Puppet Theatre PUPPET THEATRE
(☎391-211 3000; www.puppet24.ru; ul Lenina 119) Classic Russian puppet shows such as *Chuk i Gek, Doktor Aybolit* and *Goldilocks* for kiddies and adults alike.

Rock-Jazz Kafe LIVE MUSIC
(Рок-Джазз Кафе; ☎391-252 3305; ul Surikova 12; ⏲4pm-6am Tue-Sun) This dark venue showcases live bands around an upturned motorcycle from 10pm most days.

Havana Club CLUB
(Гавана Клуб; www.havanakrk.narod.ru; ul Bograda 134; ⏲ 9pm-1am Mon-Thu, to 3am Fri & Sat) Big nightclub with three dance floors and featuring local DJs.

ℹ Orientation

The city centre's grid layout is easy to navigate, but there's no central square. The zoo, ski resort and Stolby Nature Reserve are over 10km west along the Yenisey's south bank.

ℹ Information

Post Office (ul Lenina 62; ⏲8am-8pm Mon-Fri, 9am-6pm Sat)

Sayan Ring (☎391-245 4646; www.sayanring.com; ul Uritskogo 41; ⏲10am-7pm Mon-Fri) Agency specialising in Tuva and Khakassia tours.

SibTourGuide (☎391-251 654, 950 985 8608; www.sibtourguide.com) Experienced tour guide Anatoly Brewhanov offers personalised hiking trips into the Stolby, imaginative tours around Krasnoyarsk and general travel assistance. He also runs the city's best hostel, provides authentic 'rural experiences' at his dacha, organises cruises along the Yenisey and leads trips to the site of the Tunguska Event, all while maintaining an info-packed website.

Getting There & Away

AIR

From Krasnoyarsk's **Yemelyanovo Airport** (☎391-255 5999; www.yemelyanovo.ru) you can fly to almost anywhere in Russia.

TSAVS (ЦАВС; www.krascavs.ru; ul Lenina 115; ⊙8am-8pm) is a centrally located one-stop shop for all bus, train and air tickets. Krasnoyarsk has the following flight connections:

Irkutsk from ₽7000, twice daily

Kyzyl from ₽4000 to ₽6000, two or three weekly

Moscow from ₽8500, up to seven daily

Novosibirsk from ₽5300, two daily

BOAT

Every few days in summer, passenger boats from Krasnoyarsk's spired **river station** (Речной вокзал) ply the Yenisey to Dudinka (1989km, 4½ to five days) but foreigners may not proceed beyond Igarka. SibTourGuide can arrange tickets.

Summer hydrofoils to Divnogorsk depart up to five times a day, returning an hour later. Buy tickets on board.

BUS

The main **bus station** (Автовокзал; ul Aerovokzalnaya 22) is to the northeast of the city centre and is best reached by buses 49, 24 and 53 from ul Karla Marksa. Destinations include:

Abakan ₽700, five hours, frequent

Divnogorsk ₽70, one hour, frequent

Shushenskoe ₽850, seven hours, three daily

Yeniseysk ₽620, seven hours, 10 daily

TRAIN

TSAVS (p472) is the most central booking office, though the **station** itself is relatively central and often queue-free. Krasnoyarsk has the following rail connections:

Abakan *platskart/kupe* ₽1200/2200, 11½ hours, one daily

Irkutsk *platskart/kupe* ₽1800/3300, 18 hours, up to nine daily

Moscow *platskart* ₽5000, *kupe* ₽10,000 to ₽15,000, two days 16 hours, up to seven daily

Novosibirsk *platskart* ₽1400 to ₽2000, *kupe* ₽2600 to ₽3600, 12 hours, up to 11 daily

Severobaikalsk *platskart* ₽2000 to ₽2200, *kupe* ₽3900 to ₽4300, one day four to 11½ hours, three daily

Tomsk *platskart* ₽1250, 18 hours, every other day

Getting Around

Bus 501 (50 minutes, hourly) runs from the bus station to Yemelyanovo Airport, 46km northwest of the city.

Within the city centre, almost all public transport runs eastbound along ul Karla Marksa or pr Mira, returning westbound on ul Lenina. Frequent, if slow, trolleybus 7 trundles from the train station through the city centre via ul Karla Marksa. Useful bus 50 starts beyond the zoo, passes the Turbaza Yenisey and comes through the centre of town.

From June to September, cycle hire is available near the Rezanov Statue (per hour ₽200).

Divnogorsk Дивногорск

☎39144 / POP 28,300 / ⊙ MOSCOW +4HR

From Krasnoyarsk, a popular day trip by bus or summer hydrofoil follows the Yenisey River 27km to Divnogorsk town through a wide, wooded canyon. Some 5km beyond Divnogorsk's jetty is a vast 90m-high **dam**. Turbine-room visits are not permitted, but if you're lucky you might see ships being lifted by a technologically impressive inclined plane to the huge Krasnoyarsk Sea behind. A few kilometres beyond you can observe ice fishing from December to March or, in the summer, boats and yachts can be hired.

The Krasnoyarsk–Divnogorsk road has a panoramic overlook point at km23 and passes quaint **Ovsyanka** village. From the main road walk 100m (crossing the train tracks) to Ovsyanka's cute wooden **St Inokent Chapel** (ul Shchetinkina) then 50m right to find the **house-museum** (ul Shchetinkina 26; admission ₽100; ⊙10am-6pm Tue-Sun) of famous local writer Victor Astafiev, who died in 2001. Directly opposite in Astafiev's grandma's cottage-compound is the more interesting **Last Bow Museum** (ul Shchetinkina 35; admission ₽100; ⊙10am-6pm Tue-Sun), giving a taste of rural Siberian life.

Hydrofoils (45 minutes, up to five daily) depart from Krasnoyarsk's river station and regular *marshrutky* (₽70) leave from Krasnoyarsk's bus station. Taxis meet boats on arrival in Divnogorsk and want at least ₽1000 return to shuttle you to a point overlooking the dam. However, it's potentially cheaper, safer and more fun to hire a mountain bike from a stand 200m downstream from the quay. SibTourGuide in Krasnoyarsk offers various tailored excursions in English or will include the Divnogorsk loop as part of its 'Ten-Rouble Tour'.

WESTERN BAM

The official start of the 3100km-long Baikal–Amur Mainline (Baikalo–Amurskaya Magistral; BAM) is Tayshet, Siberia's busiest railway junction and a former gulag town. From there the BAM crosses almost virgin territory that is more impressively mountainous than anything along the Trans-Siberian main line. For most travellers the top BAM stop is Severobaikalsk, an almost tourist-ready hub for visiting Baikal's stunning north with thermal mini-spas nestling amid dramatic nameless peaks.

Tayshet Тайшет

☎39563 / POP 35,500 / ⌚MOSCOW +5

All Siberian roads, or railway lines at least, lead to Tayshet, a major rail junction where the Trans-Sib, BAM and Tayshet-Abakan line collide. A child of the Trans-Sib, Tayshet had a difficult childhood as the Gulag capital of Eastern Siberia. Between the late 1930s and the mid-1960s numerous camps and prison colonies occupied bits of town, with everyone from 39,000 Japanese prisoners of war to well-known Moscow intellectuals passing through at various points. Not much remains of the camps today except for a few rows of prisoner-built wooden houses, so to learn more about the town's (dark) past visit the **Regional Museum** (ul Lenina 115; admission ₽20; ⌚10am-6pm Tue-Sat) where easily musterable local historians are desperate to tell foreigners their story. There are also some exhibits belonging to the fascinating Tofalaria, Russia's smallest ethnic group who inhabit excruciatingly remote parts of the Tayshet district.

Tayshet's other main sight is its modernised **railway station** where a huge L series loco stands beached to the right of the building and an Italian-built **water tower** rises in architectural incongruity behind.

Leaving Tayshet's dusty/muddy streets and loco whistles, an interesting excursion is to neighbouring **Biryusinsk**, once a prosperous timber processing town on the Trans-Sib. The local **museum** (ul Kalinina 1; ⌚9am-6pm Mon-Sat) has some interesting rural knick-knacks, old samovars, a mock-up of a Siberian *izba* and a 1950s Soviet nostalgia section. The graves of Lithuanian exiles lie in the cemetery nearby. Biryusinsk is a ₽31 *marshrutka* ride from in front of Tayshet station.

Many rail explorers find themselves changing trains in Tayshet, some spending a whole day at the station waiting for connections. English-speaking **Igor Shalygin** (☎924 716 4004; igor_shaligin@mail.ru) runs a cosy homestay in the old town, can take you out to various beauty spots, romantically lost bits of the Trans-Sib and the old *trakt*, and give you a taste of authentic rural Siberian life.

Bratsk Братск

☎3953 / POP 246,300 / ⌚MOSCOW +5HR

Unless you're a fan of BAM or dam, Bratsk is perhaps not worth leaving the 'comfort' of your carriage bunk, though it does

HERO PROJECT OF THE CENTURY

The BAM is an astonishing victory of belief over adversity. This 'other' trans-Siberian line runs from Tayshet (417km east of Krasnoyarsk) around the top of Lake Baikal to Sovetskaya Gavan on the Pacific coast. It was begun in the 1930s to access the timber and minerals of the Lena Basin, and work stopped during WWII. Indeed, the tracks were stripped altogether and reused to lay a relief line to the besieged city of Stalingrad (now Volgograd).

Work effectively started all over again in 1974 when the existing Trans-Siberian Railway was felt to be vulnerable to attack by a potentially hostile China. The route, cut through nameless landscapes of virgin taiga (mountain pine) and blasted through anonymous mountains, was built by patriotic volunteers and the BAM was labelled 'Hero Project of the Century' to encourage young people from across the Soviet Union to come and do their bit. Despite this source of free labour, building on permafrost pushed the cost of the project to US$25 billion, some 50 times more than the original Trans-Siberian Railway.

New 'BAM towns' grew with the railway, often populated by builders who decided to stay on. However, the line's opening in 1991 coincided with the collapse of the centrally planned USSR and the region's bright Soviet future never materialised. While Bratsk and Severobaikalsk survived, many other smaller, lonely settlements became virtual ghost towns. Today only a handful of passenger trains a day use the line.

neatly break up the journey from both Irkutsk and Krasnoyarsk to Severobaikalsk. The city's raison d'être is a gigantic **dam** (GES), which drowned the original historic town in the 1960s. New Bratsk is an unnavigable necklace of disconnected concrete 'subcities' and belching industrial zones, with the spirit-crushingly dull Tsentralny area at its heart.

Sights & Activities

Bratsk Dam LANDMARK
(Братская ГЭС; www.irkutskenergo.ru) A ferro-concrete symbol of the USSR's efforts to harness the might of Siberia's natural assets, between 1967 and 1971 the Bratsk hydroelectric power station was the world's largest single electricity producer. Slung between high cliffs and somehow holding back the mammoth Bratsk Sea – no one can deny it's a striking spectacle, especially from the window of BAM trains that pass right across the top.

Take any *marshrutka* from Tsentralny to Gidrostroitel, the closest slab of Bratsk to the dam. The only way to access the turbine rooms is through a local tour agency.

Angara Village MUSEUM
(ul Komsomolskaya; admission ₽100; ⏲10am-5pm Wed-Sun) Some 12km from Tsentralny, this impressive open-air ethnographic museum contains a rare 17th-century wooden watchtower and buildings rescued from submerged old Bratsk. A series of shaman sites and Evenki *chumy* (tepee-shaped conical dwellings) lie in the woods behind. Take a taxi or arrange a visit through Taiga Tours.

Sleeping

Hotel Shvedka HOTEL $
(Гостиница Шведка; ☎902 179 0580; www.hotel-shvedka.ru; ul Mira 25; s from ₽1050, d from ₽1400; 📶) Rooms here range from battered and cheap to almost design standard. Ask to see which you're getting before you commit. Breakfast is extra and is taken in the hotel's own cafe.

Hotel Taiga HOTEL $$
(Гостиница Тайга; ☎3953-414 710; www.hotel-taiga.ru; ul Mira 35; s ₽2500, d from ₽2800; 📶) The flashiest show in town is this renovated Soviet hulk where cramped rooms are packed with tasteless furniture but have clean 21st-century bathrooms. Some staff speak English, guest visas are registered and there's a decent hotel restaurant. Breakfast is extra.

Information

Taiga Tours (☎3953-416 513; www.taiga-tours.ru; 2nd fl, Hotel Taiga) Permits and guides to visit the dam's turbine rooms.

Getting There & Away

For Tsentralny, get off BAM trains at the Anzyobi (Анзеби) station and transfer by bus or *elektrichka*. Bratsk has the following rail connections:

Irkutsk *platskart/kupe* ₽1650/3100, 17 to 19½ hours, one or two daily

Krasnoyarsk *platskart/kupe* ₽1400/2600, 13 hours, up to four daily

Moscow *platskart/kupe* ₽5700/11,400, three days four hours, one or two daily

Severobaikalsk *platskart/kupe* ₽1400/2600, 14 to 16 hours, up to four daily

Irkutsk can also be reached by Western-standard coach (₽870, 11 hours) from the Tsentralny **bus station** (ul Yuzhnaya) and summer hydrofoil from a river station in southeast Tsentralny. Check **VSRP** (☎3952-287 115; www.vsrp.ru) for details of the latter.

Severobaikalsk
Северобайкальск

☎30130/30139 / POP 24,900 / ⏲MOSCOW +5HR

Founded as a shack camp for railway workers in the mid-1970s, Severobaikalsk has grown into the most engaging halt on the BAM, where travellers vacate stuffy railway compartments to stretch legs in the taiga or cool off in Lake Baikal. The town itself is a grid of soulless, earthquake-proof apartment blocks with little in between, but the mountainscape and nameless wildernesses backing the lake quickly lure hikers and adventurers away from the concrete. They discover a land more remote, less peopled and generally more spectacular than Baikal's south, a place where lazy bears and reindeer-herding Evenki still rule in timeless peace, despite the best efforts of *Homo sovieticus*.

Sights & Activities

BAM Museum MUSEUM
(Музей БАМа; ul Mira 2; admission ₽50; ⏲10am-1pm & 2-6pm Tue-Sat) The town's friendly little museum has exhibits on BAM railway history (workers' medals, grainy black-and-white photos, 'old' BAM tickets), some Buryat artefacts and a few mammoth bones. Around the corner is a small **art gallery** where local artists display their works.

Railway Station NOTABLE BUILDING

(pr 60 let SSSR; ⏲5am-midnight) The epicentre of SB's world is a striking construction with a nostalgically stranded steam locomotive standing guard to the right. The sweeping architectural design of the brave-new-world station resembles a ski jump – thanks to a previous mayor's love of the sport, it's claimed.

Orthodox Church CHURCH

(Leningradsky pr) SB's newest Orthodox church sports two impressive onion domes in gleaming gold and a monster chandelier inside. It stands just beyond the town's grey-concrete **war memorial**.

Tours

Severobaikalsk has a surprising number of agencies and individuals that can arrange accommodation and backcountry excursions.

Ecoland TOUR COMPANY

(☎30130-36 191; www.ecoland-tour.ru) This award-winning tour agency specialises in horse-riding trips, Baikal boat excursions and trekking.

Maryasov Family TOUR GUIDE

(☎924 391 4514; baikalinfo@gmail.com) The English-speaking Maryasov family (Yevgeny and daughters Alyona and Anna) run Severobaikalsk's hostel, information centre and tourism association as well as organising guided treks to Baikalskoe and Lake Frolikha, seal-spotting trips to Ayaya Bay and Evenki-themed excursions to the village of Kholodnoe.

Rashit Yakhin/BAM Tour TOUR GUIDE

(☎30139-21 560; www.gobaikal.com; ul Oktyabrya 16/2) This experienced full-time travel-fixer, guide and ex-BAM worker suffered an immobilising stroke in the mid-1990s rendering his spoken English somewhat hard to follow. Nonetheless, Rashit is quick to reply to emails and is always keen to please.

NORTHERN BAIKAL'S MINISPAS

Seismic activity in the northern Baikal area shakes free lots of thermal springs around which tiny spas have sprouted. These are great places to soothe aching muscles after days of contortion in your BAM carriage bunk, though facilities are pretty basic. Costs are low for accommodation, food and bathing.

Goudzhekit Гоуджекит

Some 39km northwest of Severobaikalsk, Goudzhekit's lonely BAM station is beautifully situated between bald, high peaks that stay dusted with snow until early June. Five minutes' walk to the right, the tiny timber **spa** has two pools fed by thermal springs whose waters gurgle a soothing 40°C.

There are two basic hotels at the spa, but most visitors just come for the day. Take the *marshrutka* which leaves from in front of Severobaikalsk train station at 9am, noon and 3pm, returning around an hour later.

Dzelinda Дзелинда

Tiny timber Dzelinda 90km east of Severobaikalsk is another hot-springs spa on the BAM railway but with a much more appealing forest location than Goudzhekit. Thermal springs keep the outdoor pools at a toasty 44°C even in winter, and when the surrounding hills are thick with snow and the temperature plunges to -35°C, a warm swim can be exhilarating. Guests stay in timber houses, one of which has an intricately carved gable. All meals are provided. Book transport and accommodation through Severobaikalsk helpers and tour companies.

Khakusy Хакусы

To land at this idyllically isolated hot-spring **turbaza** (holiday camp; www.hakusy.com) requires permits in summer (available through Severobaikalsk tour companies and hotels), but these are waived in February and March, when it takes about an hour to drive across the ice from Severobaikalsk. Bathing is fun in the snow and frozen steam creates curious ice patterns on the wooden spa buildings. In summer, make sure you book the ferry well in advance as it's a popular trip among Russian holidaymakers. An alternative way to reach Khakusy is along the 100km Frolikha Adventure Coastline Trail (see p476).

Sleeping

★ Baikal Trail Hostel HOSTEL $
(☎30130-23 860, 914 834 6802; www.baikaltrail-hostel.com; ul Studencheskaya 12, apt 16; dm ₽600; @📶) Initially set up to house Great Baikal Trail volunteers working in the North Baikal area, this small but spacious apartment-hostel is well equipped with essential backpacker facilities such as kitchen, washing machine and communal climbing frame. It's one of the best places in town to arrange backcountry treks and trips into the wilds around the northern end of Lake Baikal.

Zolotaya Rybka GUESTHOUSE $$
(Золотая Рыбка; ☎30130-21 134; www.baikalgoldenfish.ru; ul Sibirskaya 14; d ₽1200-2500) Well signposted from ul Olkhonskaya, SB's best guesthouse maintains immaculate and imaginatively designed rooms in three buildings providing glimpses of Lake Baikal through the trees. There are spotless toilets and showers throughout, guests have access to kitchens and the cook will prepare a restaurant-standard breakfast on request (₽300 extra).

Hotel Olymp HOTEL $$
(Гостиница Олимп; ☎30130-23 980; www.hotelolymp.ru; ul Poligrafistov 2b; s & d ₽1600-2500; 📶) Severobaikalsk's smartest sleep has spotless, cool, airy rooms though the plumbing could be more professionally screwed down. For this price you might expect breakfast and free wi-fi – you get neither.

Eating & Drinking

For quick eats – *pozi* (dumplings), shashlyk, *plov* and beer – try the **fast food row** east of the station on pr 60 let SSSR or the greasy spoons around the Torgovy Tsentr. Otherwise, pickings are meagre indeed.

TiTs CAFE $
(ТиЦ; Railway Culture Centre, Tsentralny pl; mains ₽40-70; ⏰11am-5pm & 6pm-1am) Climb the gloss-painted stairs for a return to Soviet-style 1980s dining. The food is basic and cheap, the dinner ladies belligerently unsmiling, the alcohol plentiful and the hand-scrawled menu a challenge even to Russian speakers.

Anyuta CAFE $
(Анюта; ul Poligrafistov 3a; mains ₽80-200; ⏰6pm-2am Tue-Sun) Evening dinner nook housed in a red-brick building amid high-rise blocks at the northern end of town.

VIST Supermarket SUPERMARKET
(ВИСТ) **Leningradsky pr 5** (Leningradsky pr 5; ⏰8.30am-9pm); **ul Studencheskaya** (ul Studencheskaya; ⏰8.30am-8pm) The town's VIST supermarkets stock a limited range of groceries.

Information

There are ATMs at the railway station, in the Zheleznodorozhnik Culture Centre and at the Leningradsky pr branch of the VIST Supermarket.

Post Office (Почта; Leningradsky pr 6; ⏰9am-2pm & 3-7pm Mon-Fri, 9am-2pm Sat)

Tourist Office (train station forecourt; ⏰9am-6pm Jun-Aug) Tiny kiosk on the train station forecourt providing information on the North Baikal area.

Warm North of Baikal (www.privet-baikal.ru) English-language website belonging to the local tourism association with tons of information and listings.

Getting There & Away

The **Aviakassa** (Tsentralny pl; ⏰9am-noon & 1-4pm) in the Zheleznodorozhnik Culture Centre sells tickets for flights from Nizhneangarsk Airport, 30km northeast.

FROLIKHA ADVENTURE COASTLINE TRAIL

A part of the Great Baikal Trail, this incredible, relatively demanding 100km adventure trekking route runs between the delta of the Verkhnyaya Angara River and the spa hamlet of Khakusy on Baikal's eastern shore. You'll need a boat to find the start of the trail at the mouth of the river, from where it takes eight days to reach the spa village of Khakusy via countless lonely capes and bays, wild camping by the lake all the way. Exhilarating river crossings (including a biggie – the River Frolikha), deserted beaches and show-stopping Baikal vistas punctuate the trail, and from Ayaya Bay a there-back hike to remote Lake Frolikha beckons.

For more information and trail maps, contact Severobaikalsk tour agencies, the Baikal Trail Hostel or Dresden-based **Baikalplan** (www.baikalplan.de).

BOAT

From late June to late August a hydrofoil service runs the length of Lake Baikal between Nizhneangarsk, Severobaikalsk and Irkutsk via Olkhon Island. Check VSRP (p474) for times and ticket prices.

BUS

Marshrutky cluster outside Severobaikalsk's train station and run to the following destinations:

Baikalskoe ₽70, 45 minutes, two daily

Goudzhekit ₽120, 45 minutes, three daily

Nizhneangarsk Airport ₽50, 50 minutes, half-hourly

TRAIN

Severobaikalsk has the following rail connections:

Bratsk *platskart/kupe* ₽1400/2600, 14 to 16 hours, up to four daily

Irkutsk *platskart/kupe* ₽2600/5000, one day 14 hours, daily

Krasnoyarsk *platskart/kupe* ₽2200/4300, one day four hours, up to four daily

Moscow *platskart* ₽6200, *kupe* ₽8300 to ₽12,500, three days 18 hours, one or two daily

Tynda *platskart/kupe* ₽2000/3800, 26 hours, daily

Around Severobaikalsk

Nizhneangarsk Нижнеангарск

☎30130 / POP 5000 / ⏱MOSCOW +5HR

Until the BAM clunked into town, Nizhneangarsk had led an isolated existence for over 300 years, cobbling together its long streets of wooden houses and harvesting Baikal's rich *omul* (a type of fish) stocks. If truth be told, not much changed when the railway arrived, but despite the appearance of now larger Severobaikalsk 30km away, the 5km-long village remains the administrative centre of northern Baikal.

The **Regional Museum** (ul Pobedy 37; admission ₽100; ⏱10am-6pm Mon-Fri) chases the history of the region back to the 17th century and includes several Evenki exhibits.

To the east of the town a long spit of land known as **Yarki Island** caps the most northerly point of Lake Baikal and keeps powerful currents and waves out of the fragile habitat of the Verkhnyaya Angara delta. You can walk along its length.

Scenic low-altitude flights cross Lake Baikal to Ulan-Ude (six per week) when weather conditions allow.

Marshrutky (₽50, 50 minutes) from Severobaikalsk run every 30 minutes along ul Pobedy then continue along the coast road (ul Rabochaya) to the airport.

Baikalskoe Байкальское

This timeless little fishing village of log-built houses 45km south of Severobaikalsk has a jaw-droppingly picturesque lakeside location backed by wooded hills and snow-dusted peaks. Your first stop should be the small, informal **school museum** (admission ₽100; ⏱10am-4pm) where hands-on exhibits tell the story of the village from the Stone Age to the seal hunts of the 20th century. The only other sight is the wooden **Church of St Inokent**, which strikes a scenic lakeside pose.

Most come to Baikalskoe on a day trip from Severobaikalsk, but if you do want to stay the night, arrange a homestay through tour agencies and fixers in Severobaikalsk. There's no cafe, just a couple of shops selling basic foodstuffs.

Marshrutky (₽90, 45 minutes) leave from outside Severobaikalsk train station every day early in the morning and in the early evening, returning an hour or so later.

A section of the Great Baikal Trail heads north from the fishing port 20 minutes up a cliff-side path towards the radio mast, from which there are particularly superb views looking back towards the village. Beyond that, Baikalskoe's shamanic **petroglyphs** hide in awkward-to-reach cliff-side locations and can only be found with the help of a knowledgeable local. The well-maintained trail continues another 18 scenic kilometres through beautiful cedar and spruce forests and past photogenic **Boguchan Island** to chilly **Lake Slyudyanskoe**, next to which stands the small **Echo turbaza** (holiday camp) – book through the Maryasov family in Severobaikalsk (p475).

The hike makes for a rewarding day trip and, with the path hugging the lake most of the way, there's little chance of getting lost. From the Echo *turbaza* head along a dirt track through the forest to the Severobaikalsk–Baikalskoe road to hitch a lift, or prearrange transport back to Severobaikalsk. Alternatively, some hikers tackle the day the other way round, catching the morning *marshrutka* to Echo *turbaza* then timing the hike to make the evening *marshrutka* back to Severobaikalsk.

LAKE BAIKAL

One of the world's oldest geographical features (formed 25 to 30 million years ago), magnificent Lake Baikal (Озеро Байкал) is the highlight of Eastern Siberia for many. Summer travellers enjoy gob-smacking vistas across waters of the deepest blue to soaring mountain ranges on the opposite shore; rarer winter visitors marvel at its powder-white surface, frozen steel-hard and scored with ice roads. Whether they swim in it, drink its water, skirt its southern tip by train, cycle or dog sled over it in winter or just admire it from 2000km of shoreline, most agree that Siberia doesn't get better than this.

Banana-shaped Baikal is 636km from north to south and up to 1637m deep, making it the world's deepest lake. In fact it's not a lake at all, but the world's future fifth ocean containing nearly one-fifth of the planet's unfrozen fresh water (more than North America's five Great Lakes combined). Despite some environmental concerns, it's pure enough to drink in most places but use common sense. Fed by 300 rivers, it's drained by just one, the Angara near Listvyanka.

Foreign tourists typically visit Baikal from Listvyanka via Irkutsk, but approaching via Ulan-Ude (for eastern Baikal) produces more beach fun and Severobaikalsk (on the BAM railway) is best for accessing wilderness trekking routes. Choosing well is important as there's no round-lake road and the northern reaches are in effect cut off by land from the southern shores. Not even the Great Baikal Trail will create a complete loop as some stretches of shoreline are just too remote. Hydrofoil connections are limited to summer services in the south plus the Irkutsk–Olkhon–Nizhneangarsk run. Inexplicably, there are virtually no scheduled boat services linking the east and west shores.

Baikal

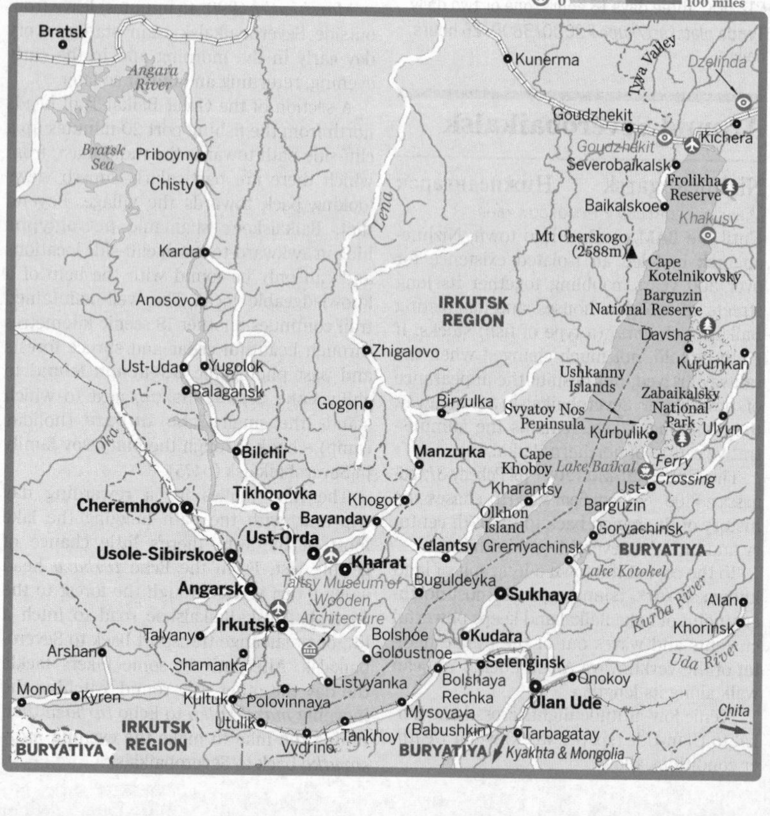

BAIKAL'S ENVIRONMENTAL ISSUES

Home to an estimated 60,000 nerpa seals as well as hundreds of endemic species, Lake Baikal is beautiful, pristine and drinkably pure in most areas. As it holds an astonishing 80% of Russia's fresh water, environmentalists are keen to keep things that way. In the 1960s, despite the pressures of the Soviet system, it was the building of Baikal's first (and only) lakeside industrial plant that galvanised Russia's first major green movement. That plant, the Baikalsk Pulp and Paper Mill, was a major polluter of the lake until it closed in 2013.

But the ecosystem extends beyond the lake itself. Another challenge includes polluted inflows from the Selenga River, which carries much of Mongolia's untreated waste into the lake. The most contentious of recent worries is the US$16 billion Eastern Siberia oil pipeline which runs from Tayshet to the Pacific coast. Completed in 2009, the route deliberately loops north, avoiding the lakeshore itself. But with a potential 1.6 million barrels of oil flowing daily across the lake's northern water catchment area, an area highly prone to seismic activity, environmentalists fear that a quake-cracked pipeline could gush crude into Baikal's feedwaters.

For more information, see the websites of regional ecogroups **Baikal Wave** (http://baikalwave.blogspot.co.uk), **Baikal Watch** (www.earthisland.org/baikal) and the wonderful **Baikal Web World** (www.bww.irk.ru), which has lots about the wildlife, history and legends of the lake.

Note that this section also includes the beautiful inland Tunka and Barguzin Valleys as they're accessed via Baikal towns.

Irkutsk Иркутск

☎3952 / POP 587,900 / ⌚MOSCOW +5HR

The de facto capital of Eastern Siberia, pleasantly historic Irkutsk is by far the most popular stop on the Trans-Siberian Railway between Moscow and all points east. With Lake Baikal a mere 70km away, the city is the best base from which to strike out for the western shoreline. Amid the 19th-century architecture, revived churches, classy eateries and numerous apartment hostels, plentiful English-speaking agencies can help you plan anything from a winter trek across the lake's ice to a short walking tour through the city.

In recent years Irkutsk has seen something of a tourist boom, spawning a municipally funded information centre, detailed city maps planted at strategic points and a handful of freshly conceived museums, as well as the blockbuster 130 Kvartal project, an entire neighbourhood given over to typical Siberian timber buildings housing new restaurants, bars, cafes and the odd museum.

History

Founded in 1661 as a Cossack garrison to extract the fur tax from the indigenous Buryats, Irkutsk was the springboard for 18th-century expeditions to the far north and east, including Alaska – then known as 'Irkutsk's American district'.

As Eastern Siberia's trading and administrative centre, Irkutsk dispatched Siberian furs and ivory to Mongolia, Tibet and China in exchange for silk and tea. Constructed mostly of local timber, three-quarters of the city burnt down in the disastrous blaze of 1879. However, profits from the 1880s Lena Basin gold rush swiftly rebuilt the city's most important edifices in brick and stone.

Known as the 'Paris of Siberia', Irkutsk did not welcome news of the October Revolution. The city's well-to-do merchants only succumbed to the Red tide in 1920, with the capture and execution of White Army commander Admiral Kolchak, whose controversial statue was re-erected in 2004. Soviet-era planning saw Irkutsk develop as the sprawling industrial and scientific centre that it remains today.

Sights

Irkutsk's centre can be easily explored on foot – you'll only need to hop aboard a bus or *marshrutka* to see the Angara Dam and the Znamensky Monastery.

Volkonsky House-Museum MUSEUM

(Дом-музей Волконского; ☎3952-207 532; per Volkonskogo 10; admission ₽200, with Trubetskoy House-Museum ₽300; ⌚10am-6pm Tue-Sun) The duck-egg-blue and white home of

Irkutsk

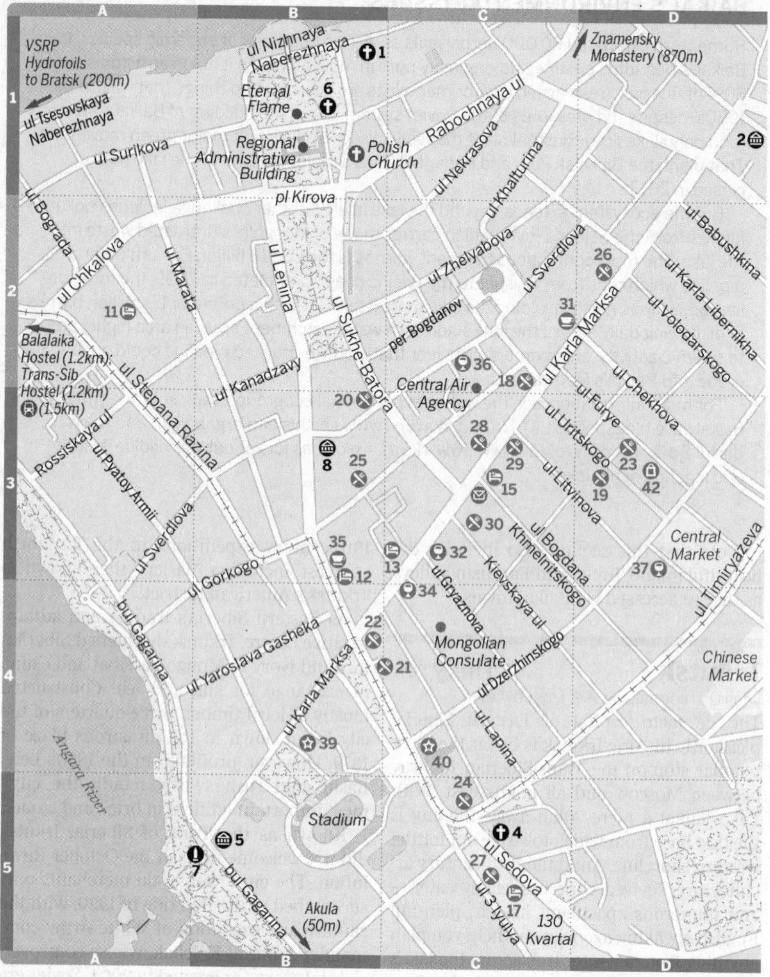

Decembrist Count Sergei Volkonsky, whose wife Maria Volkonskaya cuts the main figure in Christine Sutherland's unputdownable book *The Princess of Siberia*, is a small mansion set in a scruffy courtyard with stables, a barn and servant quarters. Renovated in the late 1980s, the house is now a museum telling the story of the family's exile in Irkutsk.

In the decade leading up to the Volkonskys return to St Petersburg in 1856, the house was the epicentre of Irkutsk cultural life, with balls, musical soirées and parties attended by wealthy merchants and high-ranking local officials. A tour of the building with its big ceramic stoves and orginal staircases takes visitors from the family dining room, where governor Muriev-Amursky once feasted on fruit and veg grown by Volkonsky himself in the garden out back, to the upstairs photo exhibition including portraits of Maria and other women who romantically followed their husbands and lovers into exile.

Emotionally charged items on show include Maria's pyramidal piano, a browsable book of images collected by fellow Decembrist wife, Ekaterina Trubetskaya, of the

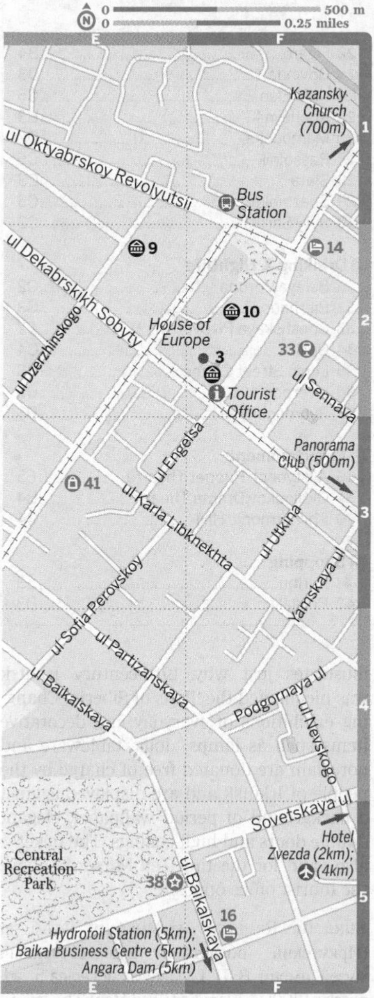

various places the Decembrists were imprisoned, and Maria's music box sent from Italy by her sister-in-law.

Znamensky Monastery MONASTERY

(ul Rabochego Shtaba) FREE Stranded on the wrong side of a thundering roundabout, the 1762 Znamensky Monastery is 1.9km northeast of Skver Kirova. Echoing with mellifluous plainsong, the wonderful interior has muralled vaulting, a towering iconostasis and a gold sarcophagus holding the miraculous relics of Siberian missionary St Inokent. Celebrity graves outside include the nautically themed tomb of Grigory Shelekhov, the man who claimed Alaska for Russia, and a much humbler headstone belonging to Decembrist wife Ekaterina Trubetskaya (directly in front of you as you enter).

White Russian commander Admiral Kolchak was executed by Bolsheviks near the spot where his statue was controversially erected in November 2004 at the entrance to the monastery grounds; the plinth is exaggeratedly high enough to prevent die-hard communists from committing acts of vandalism.

Trolleybus 3 trundles this way.

130 Kvartal NEIGHBOURHOOD

(130th Block; www.130kvartal.irk.ru; btwn uls Sedova & 3 Iyulya; 24hr) FREE What does a city boasting some of Siberia's most impressive original timber architecture do to improve the visitor experience? Yes, that's right, recreate an entire quarter of yet more wooden buildings, some transported here from other locations, some fake. The unromantically-named 130 Kvartal south of the Raising of the Cross Church is nonetheless a pleasant place to stroll, packed with restaurants, cafes and commercial museums, and culminating in Eastern Siberia's only real 21st-century (and quite impressive) shopping mall.

Guarding the entrance to this timber theme park is a monster bronze *babr,* the mythical beast that features on the Irkutsk municipal coat of arms. The spot has become a popular place to have that 'I've been to Irkutsk' photo taken.

Trubetskoy House-Museum MUSEUM

(Дом-музей Трубецкого; ul Dzerzhinskogo 64; admission ₽200, with Volkonsky House-Museum ₽300; 10am-6pm Wed-Mon) Carted off for renovation in 2007, Irkutsk's second Decembrist house-museum made a comeback in 2012 with English-language information, touchscreens and tinkling background music. This pleasingly symmetrical minimansion was actually built for the daughter of Decembrist Sergei Trubetskoy – the original Trubetskoy house near the Znamensky Monastery burnt down in 1908. The lower level tells the Decembrists' story, from failed coup to arrival in Irkutsk, while the upper floor displays personal items belonging toTrubetskaya, Trubetskoy's French wife who died in Irkutsk.

Regional Museum MUSEUM

(Краеведческий музей; 3952-333 449; www.museum.irkutsk.ru; ul Karla Marksa 2; admission ₽200; 10am-7pm Tue-Sun) Irkutsk's rapidly

Irkutsk

Sights

1	Bogoyavlensky Cathedral	B1
2	City History Museum	D1
3	Museum of City Life	F2
4	Raising of the Cross Church	C5
5	Regional Museum	B5
6	Saviour's Church	B1
7	Statue of Tsar Alexander III	B5
8	Sukachev Regional Art Museum	B3
9	Trubetskoy House-Museum	E2
10	Volkonsky House-Museum	F2

Sleeping

11	Admiral Hostel	A2
12	Baikaler Hostel	B3
13	Hotel Sayen	C3
14	Hotel Uzory	F2
15	Hotel Viktoria	C3
16	Hotel Yevropa	F5
17	Kupechesky Dvor	C5
	Marussia	(see 17)

Eating

18	Appetite	C2
19	Arbatski Dvorik	D3
20	Blinnaya Giraffe	B3
21	Domino	C4
22	Figaro	B4
23	Govinda	D3
24	Kafe Elen	C5
25	Kochevnik	B3
26	Mamochka	D2
27	Rassolnik	C5
28	Slata	C3
29	Snezhinka	C3
30	Syty Shmel	C3

Drinking & Nightlife

31	Belaya Vorona	C2
32	Bierhaus	C3
33	Cheshskaya Pivovarnya	F2
34	Chili	C4
35	Lenin Street Coffee	B3
36	Liverpool	C2
37	Ryumochnaya	D3

Entertainment

38	Aystyonok Puppet Theatre	E5
39	Okhlopkov Drama Theatre	B4
40	Philharmonic Hall	C4

Shopping

41	Karibu	E3
42	Prodalit	D3

ageing Regional Museum occupies a fancy 1880s brick building that formerly housed the Siberian Geographical Society, a club of Victorian-style gentlemen explorers. The highlights here are the downstairs ethnographical exhibitions and the nostalgic display of 20th-century junk upstairs, as well as the small gift shop selling birch-bark boxes, jewellery made from Baikal minerals and other interesting souvenirs.

City History Museum MUSEUM
(www.history.irk.ru; ul Frank-Kamenetskogo 16a; admission ₽120; ⏰10am-6pm Thu-Tue) Despite its palatial 19th-century home (built by wealthy merchant Sibiryakov in 1884) what should be Irkutsk's main repository of the past is in fact a rather limited exhibition on the city's history with absolutely nothing in English. Highlights include interesting pre-Russian wooden yurts and tepees, a model of the Kazansky Cathedral, some fascinating blown-up photos of 19th-century Irkutsk and a 20th-century section with bric-a-brac from the Revolution up to the late 1990s.

Museum of City Life MUSEUM
(ul Dekabrskikh Sobyty 77; admission ₽120; ⏰10am-6pm Thu-Tue) This small museum filling six rooms of a former merchant's house illustrates just why 19th-century Irkutsk was nicknamed the 'Paris of Siberia'. Changing exhibitions of everyday and decorative items such as lamps, dolls, tableware and porcelain are donated free of charge by the people of Irkutsk and are displayed against a background of period wallpaper, elegant double doors and high ceilings. The ticket is also valid for the tiny **Tea Museum** above the tourist office opposite.

Sukachev Regional Art Museum ART GALLERY
(Иркутский областной художественный музей имени В. П. Сукачёва; ul Lenina 5; admission ₽100; ⏰10am-6pm Wed-Mon) The grand old art gallery has a valuable though poorly lit collection ranging from Mongolian *thangkas* (Tibetan Buddhist religious paintings) to Russian Impressionist canvases. However, the main reason for coming here may be to see a top-notch temporary show (extra charge).

Raising of the Cross Church CHURCH
(Krestovozdvizhenskaya tserkov; ul Sedova 1) The 1758 baroque Raising of the Cross Church has a fine interior of gilt-edged icons and examples of intricate brickwork in a rounded style that's unique to Irkutsk and the Selenga Delta village of Posolskoe.

Kazansky Church CHURCH

(ul Barrikad) The gigantic Kazansky Church is a theme-park-esque confection of salmon-pink walls and fluoro turquoise domes topped with gold baubled crosses. Get off tram 4 two stops northeast of the bus station.

Angara Dam LANDMARK

Some 6km southeast of the centre, the 1956 Angara Dam is 2km long. Its construction raised Lake Baikal by up to 1m and caused environmental problems, most notably the silencing of the so-called singing sands on Baikal's eastern shore. The dam itself is hardly an attraction but moored nearby is the **Angara icebreaker** (admission ₽150; ⏲10am-8pm).

Originally imported in kit form from Newcastle-upon-Tyne to carry Trans-Siberian Railway passengers across Lake Baikal (the trains went on her bigger sister ship *Baikal,* sunk during the Russian Civil War), it's now a less-than-inspiring museum reached by a permanent gangway. Trolleybuses 3, 5, 7 and 8 head this way.

Statue of Tsar Alexander III MONUMENT

(Памятник Александру III) Adorning the Angara embankment a recast statue of Alexander III (a copy of the 1904 original) has the only tsar ever to visit Siberia looking as though he's holding an invisible balloon on a string.

Saviour's Church CHURCH

(Спасская церковь; Spasskaya tserkov) Constructed in 1706 this is the oldest stone-built church in Eastern Siberia and has remnants of the original murals on its facade. Until the late 1990s it housed a museum, hence the rather bare interior.

Bogoyavlensky Cathedral CHURCH

(Богоявленский собор; ul Nizhnaya Naberezhnaya) This fairy-tale ensemble of mini onion domes atop restored salmon, white and green towers first appeared on the Irkutsk skyline in 1718, but during the Soviet decades served as a dormitory and a bakery. The interior is a fragrant riot of aureoled Byzantine saints with no surface left plain.

☞ Tours

Local tour companies are useful not only for organising excursions but also for booking hotels and most kinds of tickets. All of Irkutsk's hostels can arrange Baikal tours.

Baikaler TOUR COMPANY

(✆3952-336 240; www.baikaler.com) Imaginative Jack Sheremetoff speaks very good English and is well tuned to budget-traveller needs. Original personalised tours, two great hostels and a friendly welcome.

Baikal Adventure TOUR COMPANY

(www.baikal-adventure.com) Energetic agency specialising in adventurous trekking, biking,

THE GREAT BAIKAL TRAIL

Inspired largely by the Tahoe Rim Trail (a hiking path encircling Lake Tahoe in California and Nevada), in summer 2003 a small band of enthusiasts began work on the first section of what was grandly named the Great Baikal Trail (GBT; in Russian, Bolshaya Baikalskaya Tropa, BBT). Every summer since has seen hundreds of volunteers flock to Lake Baikal's pebbly shores to bring the GBT organisation's stated aim – the creation of a 2000km-long network of trails encircling the whole of Lake Baikal – closer to fruition. This lofty ambition may still be a far-off dream, but the GBT is nonetheless the first such trail system in all Russia.

These rudimentary bits of infrastructure, the GBT organisation hopes, will attract more low-impact tourists to the region, thus encouraging ecofriendly businesses to flourish and providing an alternative to industrial and mass tourism development. Volunteers and local activists are also involved in raising awareness of environmental issues among local people, visiting schools and fundraising. Nomination as a finalist in National Geographic's 2008 Geotourism Challenge is arguably the GBT's greatest achievement to date and greatly raised its profile in the world of ecotourism.

Many Baikal explorers simply enjoy trekking the 540km of trails created thus far, but every year young and old from around the world join work crews for a few enjoyable weeks of clearing pathways, cutting steps, creating markers and cobbling together footbridges. Those eager to volunteer should visit the **GBT website** (www.greatbaikaltrail.org) for more details.

THE EASY WAY TO OLKHON ISLAND

To Khuzhir on Olkhon Island, convenient door-to-door transfers (₽800) can be arranged through any of Irkutsk's hostels. Minibuses pick up from any hostel in the morning and drop off passengers at any guesthouse in Khuzhir midafternoon. Hostels sell tickets even to nonguests.

climbing and caving trips and full-blown expeditions.

BaikalComplex TOUR COMPANY
(☎3952-461 557; www.baikalcomplex.com) Well-organised operation offering Lake Baikal accommodation and trips tailored for international travellers.

Baikalinfo TOUR COMPANY
(☎3952-707 012; www.baikalinfo.ru) Baikal tours as well as transfers, hikes and fishing trips.

Green Express TOUR COMPANY
(☎3952-734 400; www.greenexpress.ru) Professional outfit specialising in outdoor activities.

BaikalExplorer TOUR COMPANY
(☎902-560 2440; www.baikalex.com) Baikal cruises, fishing and diving trips.

Sleeping

Irkutsk's accommodation options have been expanding for years, but it's still a good idea to book ahead in the summer months. A handful of hostels have become permanent fixtures but many small apartment hostels still pop up for the hot months only. Despite new arrivals, there's still a noticeable lack of midrange options available.

★ **Baikaler Hostel** HOSTEL $
(☎3952-336 240; www.baikaler.com; apt 11, ul Lenina 9; dm ₽600; ❄@📶) Experienced tour guide Jack Sheremetoff had a super-central apartment hostel in Irkutsk long before the word even entered the Russian language. Despite competition, the city's original backpacker haven is still *the* place to meet travellers and organise trips. The spotless, air-conditioned dorms are spacious, but beds are limited so book ahead. The entrance is at the rear of the building.

Admiral Hostel HOSTEL $
(☎902 560 2440; apt 1, ul Cheremkhovsky 6; dm ₽500-700; @📶) With its Kolchak-inspired name, this cosy 13-bed apartment hostel has become well-established digs for Trans-Siberian wanderers. The lower bunks sport privacy curtains, staff sell bus tickets to Olkhon Island, there's a free (light) breakfast and you can even get your washing done. Enter from the rear of the building.

Trans-Sib Hostel HOSTEL $
(☎904 118 0652; www.irkutsk-hostel.com; per Sportivniy 9a, apt 8; dm/d ₽600/1600; @📶) Well-established, cosy backpacker hostel around a 10-minute walk from the train station offering a kitchen, washing machine, a high bathroom-to-bed ratio and one of the best ranges of owner-led tours in town. Rates include a light breakfast.

Balalaika Hostel HOSTEL $
(☎950 132 0262; www.baikaler.com; per Sportivniy 5a, apt 1; dm ₽600; 📶) Brand-new hostel run by Baikaler for a mixed crowd of Russians and foreign backpackers with lots of communal space. Good location a 10-minute walk from the train station plus the full range of Baikaler tours and transfers available.

Hotel Uzory HOTEL $
(☎3952-209 239; ul Oktyabrskoy Revolyutsii 17; s/tw ₽800/1200) Clean, unpretentious rooms (23) with leopard-skin-patterned blankets but communal bathrooms and toilets. It's popular with independent travellers but maintains a tradition of employing Irkutsk's sourest receptionists.

Hotel Viktoria HOTEL $$
(☎3952-986 808; www.victoryhotel.ru; ul Bogdana Khmelnitskogo 1; s ₽3600-4000, d ₽4200-4600; ❄@📶) Just a few steps off ul Karla Marksa, the 30 rooms at this purpose-built tower hotel remain stylish and unfrumpy despite the antique-style furniture and flowery wall coverings. If you've been in Russia a while, the courteous staff, baths in every room and online booking could feel almost eccentric. Lower rates from September through to May.

Hotel Yevropa HOTEL $$
(Гостиница Европа; ☎3952-291 515; www.europehotel.ru; ul Baikalskaya 69; s/d from ₽3190/3960; ❄📶) Behind nine Doric columns immaculate rooms are realistically priced at this gleaming four-star favour-

ite. Reception staff speak English and the Western-style breakfast is reportedly the best in town.

Hotel Sayen HOTEL $$$
(☎3952-500 000; www.sayen.ru; ul Karla Marksa 13b; r ₽9700-15,500; ❄📶) Described by some as the finest luxury sleep east of the Urals, this very central Japanese hotel gets rave reviews and justifiably so. The 24 rooms enjoy design-mag decor, big baths and gadgets galore, going beyond the standards of many Western hotels. The 24-hour room service, two pricey restaurants and a celebrated Japanese spa provide additional ways to lighten your wallet of roubles.

Kupechesky Dvor HOTEL $$$
(☎3952-797 000; www.kupecheskyhotel.ru; ul Sedova 10; d & tw ₽4600; 📶) Rising high above the 130 Kvartal this professionally run, freshly minted timber hotel mixes traditional wooden architecture with boldly contemporary design features. The 14 rooms come with big colour-swirl carpets, retro light switches, revolving TV towers and some of the best bathrooms in the city. The English-speaking service is top-draw and breakfast in the tiny reception area is included.

Marussia BOUTIQUE HOTEL $$$
(☎3952-500 252; www.marussiahotel.ru; ul Sedova 12; s/d ₽4200/4500; 📶) This spanking-new, timber-built 14-room boutique hotel in the 130 Kvartal has an unpretentious feel with a brown-beige colour scheme, stripped wooden floors sporting rustic rugs but 21st-century bathrooms. Breakfast is taken in the hotel's first-rate cafe and receptionists speak your lingo.

Baikal Business Centre HOTEL $$$
(☎3952-259 120; www.bbc.ru; ul Baikalskaya 279; s ₽4100-6600, tw ₽4900-6600; ❄📶) If you're in Irkutsk on business, this white and blue-glass tower is where you'll want to unsheathe the company credit card. Rooms are just about international standard, there's a business centre and rates are slashed at weekends.

Hotel Zvezda HOTEL $$$
(☎3952-540 000; www.zvezdahotel.ru; ul Yadrintseva 1ж; r from ₽4400; ❄📶) Within a Swiss chalet–style building, the 64 rooms here are modern and comfortable, service is pleasant and English is spoken, though you'd expect little less for these room rates. Its atmospheric restaurant specialises in game and exotic meats.

Eating

Mamochka CAFE $
(Мамочка; ul Karla Marksa 41; mains ₽80-100; ⏲10am-9pm; 📋) With its menu of imaginative salads, filling soups and (almost) healthy mains, this is no ordinary point-and-eat canteen. Swab the decks with a Slovak lager then sit back and admire the interior, a mishmash of old newspapers and Soviet bric-a-brac.

Govinda VEGETARIAN $
(2nd fl, ul Furye 4; mains ₽50-100; ⏲11am-8pm; ❄🌶) Irkutsk's only meat-free restaurant is a small self-service affair with a half-hearted Indian theme and a menu of soya sausages, basmati rice, spicy soups, mild curries, quorn chilli con carne, imaginative desserts and whole plantations of tea.

Syty Shmel CANTEEN $
(Сытый шмель; ul Kievskaya 1; mains ₽60-120; ⏲10am-8pm; 📶) Take your hunger to the 'full-bellied bumble bee' for some tasty Russian dining to a gentle soundtrack. This is the *stolovaya* taken to a classier level with only natural ingredients going into the pizzas, cakes, *plov* and pancakes. There's free coffee at breakfast time, but limited seat numbers mean things get packed out come the lunching hour.

Appetite CANTEEN $
(cnr uls Sukhe-Batora & Karla Marksa; mains ₽60-120; ⏲8am-9pm) When it's midday feeding time in the city centre, this gaudy self-service canteen with red leatherette seating divided into cubicles and a menu of meatballs, pasta, pancakes and the odd healthy option, is the one of the cheapest places to seek out. The Buryat serving staff speak no English so just point at what you want.

Domino FAST FOOD $
(Домино; ul Lenina 13a; pizzas & pancakes ₽40-100; ⏲24hr) Domino may tout itself as a pizza joint but has saved many an early-morning breakfast hunter with its bliny and strong coffee.

Blinnaya Giraffe RUSSIAN $
(ul Sukhe-Batora 8; pancakes ₽50-105; ⏲9am-10pm Mon-Fri, from 10am Sat & Sun) Revamped pancake joint with zany giraffe theme and life-jacket-orange seating. The menu also features pizzas, soups and salads.

Slata SUPERMARKET $

(Слата; ul Karla Marksa 21; 24hr) Supermarkets are surprisingly rare in Irkutsk so this centrally located, open-all-hours store is a godsend. Stocks a lot of ready-to-eat meals (meatballs, steaks, salads), ideal for long train journeys.

★**Kochevnik** MONGOLIAN $$

(Кочевник; 3952-200 459; ul Gorkogo 19; mains ₽300-1200; 11.30am-midnight;) Take your taste buds to the Mongolian steppe for some yurt-size portions of mutton, lamb and steak as well as filling soups and *buuzy* (dumplings), sluiced down with a bottle from the decent foreign wine list. Smiley service, a picture menu, low prices and an exotically curtained summer terrace make this one of the most agreeable places to dine in town.

★**Rassolnik** RUSSIAN $$

(130 Kvartal, ul 3 Iyulya 3; mains ₽300-500; 10am-midnight;) Arguably the best eating addition in the 130. Kvartal, this retro restaurant serves up a 100% Soviet-era menu (think upmarket *pelmeni, okroshka, shchi, kvas* and grandmother's pickles) in a plush Stalinist banqueting hall bedecked in nostalgia-inducing knickknackery. Classic Soviet-era films are projected onto one wall, the menu is designed like a 1960s scrapbook and waiting staff are dressed for the ocassion.

★**Figaro** ITALIAN $$

(www.figaro-resto.com; ul Karla Marksa 22; mains ₽300-700; 10.30am-midnight;) It's pretty obvious from the outside that Figaro is no ordinary Siberian eatery. The glass-fronted dining space peppered with works of art and graced with unpretentiously stylish laid tables fills daily with diners downing award-winning pastas, seafood platters and meat dishes including lamb, wild boar and duck prepared by real Western European chefs.

All bread and pastry is made fresh every day and a friendly, inclusively European ambience dominates.

Snezhinka CAFE $$

(Снежинка; 3952-344 862; Litvinova 2; mains ₽200-500; 10am-midnight) This cosy belle époque–style cafe has attentive English-speaking service and regularly wins local awards for its food. It's been around since 1961, making it the city's longest-serving eatery.

Kafe Elen CAFE $$

(ul Timiryazeva; meals ₽180-350; 9am-10pm Mon-Fri, from 10am Sat & Sun;) Bubbling aquariums, rattan furniture and lots of potted plants make this a tranquil breakfast and lunch spot as you watch the trams trundle past the church opposite.

Arbatski Dvorik RUSSIAN $$$

(Арбатский дворик; 3952-200 633; ul Uritskogo; mains ₽350-1500; noon–last customer;) This upmarket restaurant is all inside-out, the walls lined with imitation facades, doorways and street lamps. However there's nothing topsy-turvy about the impeccable service and well-crafted menu. Oddly, it's accessed via the gaudy Fiesta fast-food place below.

SOMETHING FISHY

No trip to Baikal is complete without tasting **omul**, a distant relative of salmon that's delicious when freshly hot-smoked. There are over 50 other varieties of Baikal fish, including perch, black grayling, ugly frilly-nosed bullheads and tasty *sig* (lake herring). While the lake isn't Russia's greatest place for anglers, from February to April it offers the unusual spectacle of **ice fishing**. There are two forms: individuals with immense patience dangle miniature hooked lines through Inuit-style ice holes; elsewhere, especially in shallow waters, whole teams of villagers string long, thin nets beneath the ice and pull out *omul* by the hundred.

You can get beneath the ice yourself with two professional Irkutsk-based scuba-diving outfits: **Three Dimensions** (3952-587 575; www.dive-baikal.ru) and **SVAL** (3952-295 051; www.svaldiving.ru). But the lake's greatest divers are the unique **nerpa seals**. Indigenous to Lake Baikal, they are the only seal in the world to spend its entire existence in a freshwater environment and thrive in many locations on the lake's shore, but usually (and wisely) away from human populations.

Drinking & Nightlife

★ Belaya Vorona CAFE

(Белая ворона; ul Karla Marksa 37; ⏰9am-10pm Mon-Fri, 10am-11pm Sat & Sun; 📶) Disciples of the bean should definitely head to the 'White Raven', a relaxing cellar-based coffee hang-out on the main drag. A funky soundtrack provides background for caffeine and cakes or a late breakfast as you catch up on emails or wish you could read the Cyrillic paperbacks in the small book exchange. Overheats slightly in winter.

★ Liverpool PUB

(Паб Ливерпуль; ul Sverdlova 28; ⏰noon-3am; 📶) You'll never walk (or drink) alone at Irkutsk's most popular theme pub. Enter through a mocked-up red telephone box to find an interior tiled in Beatles photos and old vinyl LPs and strewn with reminders of northwest England's erstwhile musical prowess. The beer menu is global, the service laid-back and mimicky local bands regularly strum for drinkers.

Bierhaus PUB

(☎3952-550 555; www.bier-haus.ru; ul Gryaznova 1; ⏰noon-2am Mon-Thu, until 4am Fri & Sat, until midnight Sun; 📶) Upmarket Bavarian-style *bierstube* (beer hall with heavy wooden furniture) serving Newcastle Brown and Guinness as well as German beers and sausages. Enter from ul Karla Marksa.

Cheshskaya Pivovarnya PUB

(Чешская пивоварня; ul Krasnogvardeyskaya 29; ⏰5pm-2am Tue-Thu, from 4pm Fri & Sat, to midnight Sun & Mon) You'll smell this place before you see it as Irkutsk's unpretentious micro-brewery-pub creates its own Pilsner Urquell lager, pumping out a pungent hop aroma in the process.

Chili BAR

(Чили; ☎3952-332 190; ul Karla Marksa 26; cocktails from ₽200; ⏰24hr) Aztec-themed nightspot and all-day bar where you can join Irkutsk's moneyed youth on beige couches bathed in flamingo neon for a flashy cocktail or overpriced meal (₽250 to ₽600).

Ryumochnaya BAR

(Рюмочная; ul Litvinova 16; ⏰24hr) If low-cost inebriation is your quest, this no-frills bar is your place.

Lenin Street Coffee CAFE

(ul Lenina 9; ⏰8.30am-9pm; 📶) Simple, no-nonsense coffee place with a Western feel and pricey drinks. Good central place to hang out and surf the web.

Entertainment

Okhlopkov Drama Theatre THEATRE

(Иркутский академический драматический театр имени Н. П. Охлопкова; ☎3952-200 477; www.dramteatr.ru; ul Karla Marksa 14) Shakespeare, Russian classics and local playwright Vampilov staged regularly (in Russian) from September to June.

Aystyonok Puppet Theatre PUPPET THEATRE

(Театр кукол Аистёнок; ☎3952-205 825; www.aistenok-irkutsk.ru; ul Baikalskaya 32) Marionette shows for the kiddies.

Philharmonic Hall LIVE MUSIC

(Филармония; ☎3952-242 968; www.filarmoniya.irk.ru; ul Dzerzhinskogo 2) Historic building staging regular children's shows and musical programs from jazz to classical.

Panorama Club CLUB

(www.clubpanorama.ru; ul Dekabrskikh Sobyty 102) Four dance floors pounding to different music styles and an international DJ guest list.

Akula CLUB

(www.akula-club.ru; bul Gagarina 9; ⏰from 10pm Fri & Sat) Nothing subtle about this place – expect top DJs, litres of ethanol-based beverages and public nudity at some point.

Shopping

Prodalit BOOKSTORE

(Продалить; ul Furye; ⏰10am-7pm Mon-Fri, to 6pm Sat & Sun) This large bookstore on the 2nd floor of a small shopping centre sells regional and city maps, Baikal- and Irkutsk-themed coffee table books and Lonely Planet guides in Russian.

Karibu CLOTHING

(ul Timiryazeva 34; ⏰10am-7pm Mon-Sat, noon-5pm Sun) Tiny shop selling beautifully furry *unty* (traditional deerskin cowboy boots) made on-site and typically costing around ₽10,000. Some English spoken.

Information

Irk.ru (www.irk.ru) Local city info.

Post Office (ul Karla Marksa 28; ⏰8am-8pm Mon-Fri, 9am-6pm Sat & Sun)

Tourist Office (☎3952-205 018; www.irkvisit.info; ul Dekabrskikh Sobyty 77; ⏰9am-6pm Sep-May, to 8pm Jun-Aug; 📶) Municipally funded tourist office with English-speaking staff, free wi-fi, free city maps and lots of well-produced brochures and booklets on Irkutsk and Lake Baikal. Between June and August staff are posted at strategic points around the city handing out info.

WWW Irkutsk (www.irkutsk.org) Bags of information on every aspect of the city.

Getting There & Away

AIR

Irkutsk's antiquated little 'international' **airport** (www.iktport.ru) is handily placed near the city centre. Foreign destinations include Bangkok, Beijing, Seoul and Ulaanbaatar. Direct flights to Germany were scrapped in 2011 but might restart in the coming years.

For Moscow Domodedovo there are direct flights with **S7 Airlines** (from ₽10,500, three daily). Irkutsk also enjoys direct air links to many other domestic destinations, with tickets for all services sold through the convenient **Central Air Agency** (Центральная авиакасса; ☎3952-500 703; http://ikt.moyreys.ru; ul Gorkogo 29; ⏲8am-7pm).

BOAT

In summer hydrofoils buzz along the Angara River to Listvyanka and up Lake Baikal to Bolshie Koty, Olkhon Island, Ust-Barguzin and Nizhneangarsk. Departures are from the Raketa **hydrofoil station** (Речной вокзал) beyond the Angara Dam in Solnechny Mikro-Rayon, two minutes' walk from bus 16 stop 'Raketa'. Timetables are posted by the quay. Services in the other direction to Bratsk leave from a separate jetty in the city centre.

All services are operated by VSRP (p474). Check the English-language website for all times and prices.

BUS

From the partially renovated **bus station** (ul Oktyabrskoy Revolyutsii; ⏲5.30am-8pm) book tickets at least a day ahead in summer for Arshan (₽400, four to five hours, daily), Listvyanka (₽100, 1¼ hours, hourly) via Taltsy (₽80), Bratsk (₽867, 11 hours) and Ust-Kut (on the BAM railway; ₽1570, 12 hours). The station has a left-luggage office.

Minibuses to Ulan-Ude (₽800, seven hours) and Slyudyanka (₽160, two hours) depart throughout the day from the train station forecourt.

TRAIN

Irkutsk has the following rail connections:

Beijing *kupe* ₽14,000, two days 22 hours, twice weekly

Chita *platskart/kupe* ₽1750/3300, 16 to 20 hours, up to six daily

Khabarovsk *platskart/kupe* ₽4500/8900, two days 14 hours, three daily

Krasnoyarsk *platskart/kupe* ₽1750/3300, 18 hours, up to nine daily

Moscow *platskart/kupe* ₽5900/11,800, three days three hours to five days 18 hours, up to seven daily

Severobaikalsk *platskart/kupe* ₽2550/5000, one day 10 hours, daily

Slyudyanka *elektrichka* ₽100, four hours, four daily

Ulaanbaatar *kupe* ₽4800, 27 hours, daily

Ulan-Ude *platskart* ₽1100, *kupe* ₽2000 to ₽2700, 6½ to 8½ hours, up to nine daily

Vladivostok *platskart/kupe* ₽5350/10,700, three days, three daily

Getting Around

Within the central area, walking is usually the best idea as one-way systems make bus routes confusing.

Frequent trolleybus 4 and bus/*marshrutka* 20, 80, 90 and countless others connect the city centre with the airport. A taxi to/from the airport costs around ₽250.

From the train station, trams 1, 2 and 4A run to ul Lenina and ul Timiryazeva, 4A continuing on to the bus station. Tram 4 links the central market with the bus station.

Listvyanka Листвянка

☎3952 / POP 1880 / ⏲ MOSCOW +5HR

As the closest lakeside village to Irkutsk, Listvyanka – aka the 'Baikal Riviera' – is the touristy spot to which most travellers are funnelled to dunk their toes in Baikal's pure waters. Having picked at *omul*, admired the hazy views of the Khamar Daban mountains on the opposite shore and huffed their way from one end of the village to the other, most are on a *marshrutka* back to Irkutsk by late afternoon. But there's more to Listvyanka than this; others stay longer to hike the Great Baikal Trail, discover more about the lake at the Baikal Museum and chill out at one of Siberia's most eco-friendly sleeps.

If you're looking for beach fun, you're at the wrong address – the eastern shore (Buryatiya) is the place to build sandcastles. However, what the Buryat shore doesn't have is Listvyanka's range of activities: anything from short boat trips to diving and jet-skiing in the summer and ice mountain biking to lake treks and ice sculpting in the winter.

Sights & Activities

Sourcing a map at Irkutsk's tourist office before you set off will save a lot of hunting.

Baikal Museum MUSEUM
(ul Akademicheskaya 1, Rogatka; admission ₽300; 9am-7pm) One of only three museums in the world dedicated solely to a lake, this sometimes overly scientific institution examines the science of Baikal from all angles. Pass quickly by the gruesomely discoloured fish samples and seal embryos in formaldehyde to the tanks containing two frolicsome nerpa seals and the various Baikal fish that you may later encounter on restaurant menus. A new attraction is a minisub simulator which takes you deep down into Baikal's nippy waters.

Adjoining the building is a park containing over 400 species of plants, some rare or endangered.

St Nicholas Church CHURCH
(Krestovka) Listvyanka's small mid-19th-century timber church is dedicated to St Nicholas, who supposedly saved its merchant sponsor from a Baikal shipwreck.

Retro Park ART GALLERY
(Krestovka) This garden near the St Nicholas Church is full of wacky sculpture pieces fashioned from old Soviet-era cars and motorbikes.

Nerpinarium AQUARIUM
(www.baikalnerpa.ru; ul Gorkogo 101a; admission ₽300; 11am-5pm Tue-Fri, to 6pm Sat & Sun) Thirty-minute seal shows in a silver building resembling an upturned ship next to the Priboy Hotel.

Baikal Dog Sledding Centre DOG SLEDDING
(908 660 5098; ul Kulikova 136a) From December to March the centre offers thrilling dog sledding on forest tracks. All kinds of tours are available, from 5km tasters to multiday trans-Baikal ice expeditions costing tens of thousands of roubles. Some English spoken. Book through Baikaler.

Sleeping

Many Irkutsk tour agents and even some hostels and hotels have their own guesthouse or homestay in Listvyanka. For turn-up-and-hope homestays the best street to try first is ul Chapaeva.

★ **Belka Hostel** HOSTEL $
(952 626 1251; www.baikaler.com; ul Chapaeva 77a; dm/tw ₽600/1500; @) Previously known as Baikaler Eco-Hostel, this purpose-built hostel located at the far end of ul Chapaeva provides top-notch digs for backpacker prices, leaving Listvyanka's other flat-footed accommodation in its green wake. From the energy-saving light bulbs and basalt-foam insulation to the solar-heated water and solar-generated electricity, owner Jack Sheremetoff has crafted a low-impact haven with lots of personal touches.

Start the day with a bit of sun worship on the yoga deck and breakfast on the forest-facing chill-out area; end it with a scramble up the mini climbing wall and a scrub-down in the *banya* before snuggling up in a hand-made timber bed (no bunks) in an ensuite dorm. Two guest kitchens, 24-hour reception and many other features you won't find anywhere else. Booking well ahead is essential. No wi-fi.

Derevenka HOTEL $$
(914 877 5599; www.baikal-derevenka.ru; ul Gornaya 1; s/d ₽2000/3000, camping pitch ₽180;) On a ridge behind the shore road, cute little wooden huts (named after Baikal's winds) with stove-heaters, private toilets and hot water (but shared showers) offer Listvyanka's most appealing semi-budget choice. Behind the complex is Listvyanka's only official camp site. Rates include breakfast.

Dream of Baikal Hotel HOTEL $$
(3952-496 888; www.dreamofbaikal.ru; ul Gorkogo 105; s ₽2000-2700, d ₽2400-3100;) Set just an endemic species' throw from Baikal's lulling waves/crumbly ice, this brand-new, clumsily named, purpose-built hotel by the market is a step up from Listvyanka's usual timber guesthouses. Rooms bedecked in generous drapery are packed with faux antique furniture. The reception works 24 hours apart from when the receptionist dozes off just after lunch.

U Ozera HOTEL $$
(У Озера; 3952-496 777; www.listvjanka-baikal.ru; Irkutsk Hwy km3; d ₽3300-4300, cottages ₽4000-5000;) Just 10m from the shoreline, it's not surprising that all nine rooms (doubles only) at this small hotel have wonderful lake views. Rooms are a little too intimate but have balconies where you can stretch out. The cottages sleeping two lack the

WORTH A TRIP

TALTSY ТАЛЬЦЫ

About 47km southeast of Irkutsk, 23km before Listvyanka, **Taltsy Museum of Architecture & Ethnography** (Архитектурно-этнографический музей Тальцы; www.talci.ru; 47km from Irkutsk on the Baikalsky trakt; admission ₽200; ⌚10am-5pm) is an impressive outdoor collection of old Siberian buildings set in a delightful riverside forest. Amid the renovated farmsteads are two chapels, a church, a watermill, some Evenki graves and the eye-catching 17th-century Ilim-insk Ostrog watchtower. Listvyanka–Irkutsk buses and *marshrutky* stop on request at Taltsy's entrance (look out for the roadside 'Музей' sign), and the ticket booth is a minute's walk through the forest.

views but offer more space. Located between Krestovka and Rogatka.

Devyaty Val GUESTHOUSE $$
(☎3952-496 814; www.9val.irk.ru; ul Chapaeva 24; d ₽1800-2200; @≋) Friendly, family-run guesthouse where the huge, good-value *lyux* rooms with big beds, TV and private shower and toilet in a long timber extension are a big step up from the *polo-lyux*. There's a small indoor pool and sauna, and rates include breakfast.

Priboy HOTEL $$
(☎3952-496 725; upper fl, ul Gorkogo 101; r from ₽2500) Spitting distance from the lake in the port area, this glass-and-steel hunk of incongruity has seen renovation in recent years, rendering the four lake-view rooms some of the best deals in town. The other 15 chambers are less spectacular but rates include breakfast taken in the downstairs cafe.

Baikal Chalet GUESTHOUSE $$
(☎3952-461 557; www.baikalcomplex.com; ul Gudina 75; tw ₽2000) The 13 comfortable twin rooms in this timber guesthouse around 800m back from the lake are a good deal. Its sister guesthouse in Bolshie Koty offers similar rates and standards. Breakfast included.

Krestovaya pad HOTEL $$$
(☎3952-496 863; www.krestovayapad.ru; ul Gornaya 14a; tw & d ₽4000-7500; 📶) This stylishly upmarket complex of houses with very comfortable international-standard pine-clad rooms dominates the hillside above Krestovka.

Hotel Mayak HOTEL $$$
(Отель Маяк; ☎3952-496 925; www.mayakhotel.ru; ul Gorkogo 85a; s/tw ₽4800/5100; 📶) There were once (now mothballed) plans to transform Listvyanka and other villages on the shores of Lake Baikal into purpose-built resorts with plasticky upmarket hotels like the 'Lighthouse'. The village's most in-your-face hotel has Western-standard rooms, a good restaurant and an unbeatable location near the hydrofoil quay.

Eating

Near the port, the large fish and souvenir market is the best place to buy smoked *omul* and is surrounded by greasy spoons offering cheap *plov* and shashlyk.

Berg House RUSSIAN $
(ul Gorkogo 59; mains ₽250-370; ⌚11am-2am; 📶📋) Between the Mayak Hotel and the post office, this Anglophone-friendly cafe has understatedly laid picnic tables, pleasant service, large portions of fish and meat and Ukrainian Obolon beer on tap.

Cafe Podlemore CAFE $
(ul Gorkogo 31; mains ₽120-160; ⌚9am-midnight; 📋) The Podlemore has porridge and oven-fresh pastries, but rather flummoxed serving staff. Early opening makes it a popular breakfast halt.

Proshly Vek RUSSIAN $$
(Прошлый век; ul Lazlo 1; meals ₽200-450; ⌚noon-midnight; 📋) Listvyanka's most characterful eatery has a nautical theme, a fish-heavy menu and Baikal views. The upper floor is filled with fascinating old junk which you can admire while tucking into *omul* done any which way you please.

Orientation

The village extends 4.5km from Rogatka at the mouth of the Angara to the market area. A single road skirts the shore with three valleys running inland where most of Listvyanka's characterful timber dwellings and accommodation options are located. There's no public transport which can mean some very long walks.

Information

ATMs can be found in the Mayak and Priboy hotels.

Post office (ul Gorkogo 49; ⏲8am-1pm & 2-8pm Mon-Fri, 9am-6pm Sat)

Tourist Office (☎3952-656 099; hydrofoil quay; ⏲10am-6pm) Located at the *marshrutka* terminus (there are several imposters) this surprisingly useful office hands out free maps as well as providing bus, ferry and hydrofoil timetables and offering imaginative Baikal boat trips. Bike rental available.

Getting There & Away

Hourly *marshrutky* (₽100, 1¼ hours) leave for Irkutsk from outside the tourist office (where tickets are bought). The last service departs at 9pm.

From mid-May to late September, hydrofoils stop at Listvyanka between Irkutsk and Bolshie Koty three times a day.

A tiny, battered car ferry lumbers across the never-frozen Angara River mouth to Port Baikal from Rogatka four times a day mid-May to mid-October, just twice a day in the winter months.

See VSRP (p474) for details of all the above boat services.

Port Baikal Порт Байкал

☎3952 / POP 425 / ⏲MOSCOW +5HR

You'd be excused for dismissing Port Baikal as a rusty semi-industrial eyesore when seen from Listvyanka across the unbridged mouth of the Angara River. But the view is misleading. A kilometre southwest of Stanitsa (the port area), Baranchiki is a ramshackle 'real' village with lots of unkempt but authentic Siberian cottages and a couple of handy accommodation options. Awkward ferry connections mean that Port Baikal remains largely uncommercialised, lacking Listvyanka's attractions but also its crowds. It's thus popular with more meditative visitors, but the main draw is that it's both the beginning and terminus of the Circumbaikal Railway.

From 1900 to 1904 the Trans-Siberian Railway tracks from Irkutsk came to an abrupt halt at Port Baikal. They continued on Lake Baikal's far eastern shore at Mysovaya (Babushkin), and the watery gap was plugged by ice-breaking steamships, including the *Angara*, now restored and on view in Irkutsk. Later, the tracks were pushed south and around the lake. This Circumbaikal line required so many impressive tunnels and bridges that it earned the nickname 'The Tsar's Jewelled Buckle'. With the damming of the Angara River in the 1950s, the original Irkutsk–Port Baikal section was submerged and replaced with an Irkutsk–Kultuk shortcut (today's Trans-Siberian). That left poor little Port Baikal to wither away at the dead end of a rarely used but incredibly scenic branch line.

Sleeping & Eating

If the last ferry back to Listvyanka has just left, the Paradis is full and the Yakhont seems too expensive, it's always possible to fall back on several basic homestays in Baranchiki. Ask around or look out for 'сдаются комнаты' signs. If all else fails, the train station has rest rooms and food. Apart from the Yakhont restaurant, a couple of poorly stocked grocery kiosks are the only other sources of sustenance.

Gostevoy Dom Paradis GUESTHOUSE $
(☎3952-607 450; www.baikal.tk; ul Baikalskaya 12; full board ₽1500) This timber guesthouse is set 400m back from the lakeside. Various pine-clad but rather spartan rooms share two Western-style toilets and a shower.

Yakhont HOTEL $$
(☎3952-250 496; www.baikalrest.ru; ul Naberezhnaya 3; s/tw ₽3200/3500) Port Baikal's top digs can be found in a traditionally designed log house decorated with eclectic good taste by the well-travelled English-speaking owners. There's a communal kitchen-dining room, above which rooms have perfect Western bathrooms. The large restaurant below the hotel is the village's sole eatery. Advance bookings are essential.

Getting There & Away

The ferry to Rogatka near Listvyanka's Baikal Museum runs four times daily between mid-May and mid October at 8.15am, 11.15am, 4.15pm and 6.15pm (departures at 6.40am, 10.45am, 3.50pm and 5.15pm from Rogatka) but only twice in winter. Check the schedule beforehand. From mid-June to August there are direct hydrofoils to/from Irkutsk. All services are operated by VSRP (p474).

One or two trains a day come via the slow Circumbaikal route from Slyudyanka.

Bolshie Koty Большие Коты

POP 50 / ⏲MOSCOW +5HR

Tiny and roadless, this serene Baikal village is what the great Siberian escape is all about. But things weren't always this quiet; in the

19th century Koty experienced a mini gold rush and boasted soap and candle factories, a glassworks, churches and a school. Today all that's long since over, leaving Irkutsk's nouveau riche to assemble their lakeside dachas in peace.

A section of the Great Baikal Trail runs between Koty and Listvyanka, a fabulous full- or half-day hike (around 20km). Take plenty of food (drink from the lake) as there's none en route.

Three minutes' walk from the hydrofoil quay, the **Lesnaya 7 Hostel** (☎904 118 7275; www.lesnaya7.com; ul Lesnaya 7; dm ₽700; @) fills a traditional timber house where showers run hot and the 12 beds are all in double rooms. Booking ahead is essential.

The only way to reach Bolshie Koty (unless you hike from Listvyanka) is aboard one of the three hydrofoils a day from Irkutsk (via Listvyanka). Check VSRP (p474) for times and ticket prices. Winter ice roads briefly unite the village with the outside world.

Olkhon Island

Остров Ольхон

POP 1500 / ⏲ MOSCOW +5HR

Halfway up Lake Baikal's western shore and reached by a short ferry journey from Sakhyurta (aka MRS), the serenely beautiful Olkhon Island is a wonderful place from which to view the lake and relax during a tour of Siberia. Considered one of five global poles of shamanic energy by the Buryat people, the 72km-long island's 'capital' is the unlovely village of **Khuzhir** (Хужир), which has seen something of an unlikely tourist boom over the last decade, mainly thanks to the efforts of Nikita's Homestead.

Escaping Khuzhir's dusty, dung-splattered streets is the key to enjoying Olkhon. Every morning tours leave from Khuzhir's guesthouses to the north and south of the island, the most popular a seven-hour bounce in a UAZ minivan to dramatic **Cape Khoboy** at Olkhon's very northern tip, where Baikal seals sometimes bask. Driver-guides cook fish soup for lunch over an open fire, but few speak any English. See the Nikita's Homestead website (www.olkhon.info) for details of this and other excursions. Otherwise, rent a bike and strike out on your own. Maps are available from Nikita's but take all food and water with you as there's none outside Khuzhir.

Some of Olkhon Island falls within the boundaries of the Pribaikalsky National Park. As of summer 2014 there was no charge to enter the park but this might not always be the case (an admission charge of ₽60 was levied for a couple of years).

Sights & Activities

The museum and Shaman Rocks provide minor distraction in Khuzhir.

Museum MUSEUM
(ul Pervomayskaya 24; admission ₽100; ⏲2-8pm Sun-Fri) Khuzhir's small museum displays a random mix of stuffed animals, Soviet-era junk, local art and the personal possessions of its founder, Nikolai Revyakin, a teacher for five decades at the school next door.

Shaman Rocks LANDMARK
A short walk north of Nikita's, the unmistakable Shaman Rocks are neither huge nor spectacular, but they have become the archetypal Baikal vista found on postcards and travel-guide covers. A long strip of sandy beach lines the Maloe More (Little Sea) east of the rocks.

Sleeping & Eating

Khuzhir has an ever-growing range of places to stay, though the vast majority of independent travellers bunk down at Nikita's Homestead. If all 50 rooms at Nikita's are full, staff can arrange homestays costing around ₽850 with meals taken at the Homestead canteen. Booking ahead anywhere in Khuzhir is only necessary during July and August. There's no ATM on the island, so you'll need to bring enough cash to cover your stay.

★ **Nikita's Homestead** GUESTHOUSE $
(☎914 895 7865; www.olkhon.info; ul Kirpichnaya 8; full board per person ₽1000-1500; ⏲reception 8am-11pm) Occupying a sizeable chunk of Khuzhir, this intricately carved timber complex has grown (and continues to grow) into one of Siberia's top traveller hang-outs. The basic rooms in myriad shapes and sizes are attractively decorated with petroglyphs and other ethnic finery and heated by wood-burning stoves – but only a select few have showers (put your name down for the *banya*).

The organic meals are served three times a day in the large canteen near reception and two other (paid) eateries stand behind. There's a small cycle-hire centre and a packed schedule of excursions and activities. Note there is no alcohol for sale at Nikita's and consumption on the premises is frowned upon.

U Olgi GUESTHOUSE $

(908 661 9015; ul Lesnaya 3-1; full board per person ₽1000) This well-liked option has nine rooms, three in a typical village house and six in a purpose-built, pine-fragrant building opposite. New showers and flushing toilets plus scrumptious Siberian fare cooked by Olga herself make this a winner every time. Book through Baikaler (p483) in Irkutsk.

Solnechnaya GUESTHOUSE $

(Солнечная; 3952-683 216; www.olkhon.com; ul Solnechnaya 14; full board per person ₽1100-1450; @) No happening scene like at Nikita's, but it's still a pleasant place to stay offering a good range of activities. Accommodation is in two-storey cabins and tiny single-room shacks with verandahs. Enter from ul Solnechnaya or from near the relay station at the top of the hill.

Getting There & Away

The simplest way to reach Olkhon is aboard the morning *marshrutka* that leaves Irkutsk's hostels around 8.30am. Many other services run in July and August but can be impossible to track down in Irkutsk.

With a little warning, agencies or hostels can usually find you a ride in a private car to/from Irkutsk (5½ hours) for ₽1500 per seat, ₽6000 for the whole car. Prices include the short ferry ride to/from MRS – from mid-January to March an ice road replaces the ferry. When ice is partly formed or partly melted, the island is completely cut off for motor vehicles, though an ad hoc minihovercraft service is sometimes operated by locals.

In summer a hydrofoil service operates from Irkutsk to Olkhon, dropping passengers near the ferry terminal, from where it's possible to hitch a paid lift into Khuzhir. See VSRP (p474) for times and prices.

South Baikal & the Tunka Valley

The windows of trans-Siberian trains passing between Irkutsk and Ulan-Ude frame attractive lake vistas along much of Baikal's south coast. Few travellers are actually tempted off the train along this stretch but if they are, it's usually at Slyudyanka, the starting point for the Circumbaikal train rides and a launch pad into the remotely scenic Tunka Valley.

Slyudyanka Слюдянка

39544 / POP 18,600 / MOSCOW +5HR

The lakeside railway town of Slyudyanka provides a grittier alternative to Listvyanka for those eager to get up close to Lake Baikal's waves/groaning ice and the Trans-Siberian Railway, which hugs the lake's pebbly shore either side of town. Most alight from a train at the glittering, solid-marble **train station**, which is a mere five-minute walk from Lake Baikal. Amid the nearby railway repair sheds and admin buildings you'll also find a fascinating little **museum** (ul Zheleznodorozhnaya 22; admission ₽100; 8am-noon & 1-5pm Wed-Sun) housed in an ornate wooden building set back from ul Zheleznodorozhnaya. There are exhibitions on the Circumbaikal Railway, the history of Slyudyanka and Lake Baikal, plus heaps of railway paraphenalia. Geology buffs should consider heading to the privately run **Baikal Mineral Museum** (ul Slyudyanaya 36; admission ₽150; 10am-7pm), which claims to exhibit every mineral known to man.

A popular picnic excursion is to **Cape Shaman**, an easy 4km stroll north towards Kultuk along Baikal's gravelly shore. A more strenuous trail heads up **Pik Cherskogo** (aka Mt Chersky) along the former post road to Mongolia. Owners of the Slyudyanka Hostel run guided trips there and to the

SELENGA DELTA

Some 300 waterways feed Lake Baikal, but none compare in size and volume to the Selenga River. One of only 80 rivers around the world to form a delta, the Selenga dumps its load of sand (and pollution from Mongolia) on Baikal's eastern shore in a huge fan of islands, reed beds and shallow channels measuring 35km across. Over 200 bird species draw spotters from all over the world; motorboat trips can be arranged through Ulan-Ude agencies. Between birdwatching sessions many bed down in the village of Posolskoe where the Western-standard **Sofiya Hotel** (914 638 9521) shares a lakeside location right beside a beautifully renovated monastery.

WORTH A TRIP

CIRCUMBAIKAL RAILWAY КРУГОБАЙКАЛЬСКАЯ ЖЕЛЕЗНАЯ ДОРОГА

Excruciatingly slow train ride or a great social event? Opinions are mixed, but taking one of the four-per-week Slyudyanka–Port Baikal trains along this scenic, lake-hugging branch line remains a very popular tourist activity. The most picturesque sections of the route are the valley, pebble beach and headland at Polovinnaya (around halfway), and the bridge area at km149. Note that most trains *from* Port Baikal travel by night and so are useless for sightseeing.

The old stone tunnels, cliff cuttings and bridges are an attraction even for non-train-buffs who might drive alongside sections of the route on winter ice roads from **Kultuk**. Hiking the entire route or just sections of the peaceful track is also popular and walking a couple of kilometres from Port Baikal leads to some pleasant, if litter-marred, beaches. Or get off an Irkutsk–Slyudyanka *elektrichka* at Temnaya Pad three hours into the journey and hike down the stream valley for about an hour. You should emerge at km149 on the **Circumbaikal track**, from where you can continue by train to Port Baikal if you time things well.

At the time of research, Matanya trains departed from a side platform at Slyudyanka I station at 1.20pm on Monday, Thursday, Friday and Sunday – check timetables carefully. An additional but more expensive tourist train direct from Irkutsk departs at 8.20am on Wednesday and Saturday, reaching Slyudyanka at 10.30am. Matanya trains arrive in Port Baikal in the evening after the last ferry for Listvyanka has departed, so organising accommodation in advance is advisable.

The wonderfully detailed but now woefully out-of-date website **Circumbaikal Railway** (http://kbzd.irk.ru/Eng/) has photographs of virtually every inch of the route.

Agencies such as **Krugobaikalsky Ekspress** (☎3952-202 973; www.krugobaikalka.ru) run organised Circumbaikal tours from Irkutsk (₽2300) with transfers back to the city at the end of the day.

former marble and mica (*slyud* in Russian, hence the town's name) mines southeast of the town.

Sleeping & Eating

Slyudyanka Hostel HOSTEL $
(☎39544-53 198, 902 576 7344; www.hostel-s.com; ul Shkolnaya 10, apt 7; dm ₽500; @) Six-bed hostel-homestay at the southern end of town providing a great opportunity to experience small-town Siberian family life. A fully equipped kitchen, heaps of outdoorsy tours and hikes and evenings of authentic Baikal hospitality await for those who make the effort to find the place. It's a 20-minute walk, five-minute *marshrutka* ride (No 1) or ₽120 taxi journey along ul Parizhskoy Komuny.

Booking ahead is pretty much essential.

Vsyo budet OK SUPERMARKET $
(Всё будет ОК; ul Lenina 118; ⏲9am-10pm) The 'Everything's Gonna Be OK' supermarket opposite the bus station is the place to stock up on enough noodles, cheese, bread and instant porridge to keep you going all the way to the Urals.

Getting There & Away

Elektrichki (₽100, four daily) from Irkutsk take four hours to arrive at Slyudyanka 1 station; ordinary passenger trains (*platskart* ₽670, up to eight daily) take just two to 2½ hours. Slyudyanka is also the usual starting point for the Circumbaikal Railway trip. From the bus station *marshrutky* run to Arshan (two hours, two daily) and Irkutsk (₽158, two hours, at least hourly).

Arshan Аршан

☎30156 / POP 2460 / ⏲ MOSCOW +5HR

Backed by the dramatic, cloud-wreathed peaks of the Eastern Sayan Mountains, the once drowsy Buryat spa village of Arshan has been rudely awoken from its slumber in recent years. The fast-flowing Kyngarga River still murmurs with ice-cold water from elevated valleys above the village, the prayer wheels still twirl at the tranquil little Buddhist temples and cows still blunder through the streets, but Russian-style tourism has intruded into the idyllic scene, bringing 24-hour *bani*, cut-price vodka, pounding stereos and grisly service in its wake. But despite this Arshan is still the best base in the Tunka Valley from which to strike out into the mountains, with some superb hikes accessible on foot from the village.

Arshan in Buryat means 'natural spring' and it's the pleasantly sweet, health-giving mineral water that most Russians come for. The huge **Sayany Spa** stands at the entrance to the village on the main street (ul Traktovaya), which then fires itself 2km straight towards the mountains.

Opposite the spa grounds, the **Dechen Ravzhalin Datsan** has two sparkling new prayer wheels, a miniature stupa and a dazzlingly colourful interior. From here ul Traktovaya then climbs in a parade of shops, derelict Soviet architecture and plasticky cafes and guesthouses towards the bus station, after which it swerves west to the sprawling **Kurort Arshan** resort where you can sample the water for free (pass through the turnstile near the souvenir kiosks). Head up the stream from here to access the mountain footpaths or cross the river and walk 20 minutes through the forest to the diminutive **Bodkhi Dkharma Datsan**, set in an idyllic mountain-backed glade.

Sleeping

Even late at night locals line the bottom end of ul Traktovaya like hitchhikers, brandishing their 'Жильё' (rooms) signs in hope. These sometimes turn out to be unacceptably basic homestays from ₽300 per bed – check standards before committing. Even if you turn up unannounced you'll have few problems getting a room, even at busy times (July and August). This is probably the way to go in Arshan. Otherwise, try to book ahead at a guesthouse.

Yasnaya Polyana GUESTHOUSE $
(Ясная Поляна; ☎904 114 7808; ul Traktovaya 109; s/d ₽400/800; ⊙Jun-Sep) A friendly local English teacher runs this compound of 10 pine cottages, each containing two beds, a table, a stove ring and sometimes a kettle. Otherwise, things are pretty basic with a sun-heated shower (best in the evenings) and outdoor washing facilities.

To find it, take the second left on entering the village (at ul Traktovaya 99) and keep going until you see a large unmarked green gate on your left.

Pensionat Vershina GUESTHOUSE $
(☎950 388 7590; ul Mikrorayon 22/1; s/d ₽400/800) Located near the Sayany Spa, this purpose-built two-storey guesthouse has cosy timber rooms with shared showers, free *banya* and a small cafe.

Arshansky Bor GUESTHOUSE $
(☎950 050 6481; ul Bratev Domshevikh 44; dm ₽350-450) This unmarked pink building is the best budget place to overnight until the Priyut Alpinista is rebuilt. Rooms are dim and spartan, and facilities display the pressures of mass occupation, but there's a large kitchen, a common room and a barbecue area.

Monetny Dvor GUESTHOUSE $$
(☎904 115 6390; ul Traktovaya 89; d from ₽2000) Timber-built 24-bed guesthouse with rooms in a main building and three two-storey cottages. Cycle hire available.

Priyut Alpinista GUESTHOUSE
(www.iwf.ru; ul Bratev Domshevikh 8) Long a favourite with backpackers, trekkers and climbers, the 'Mountaineer's Refuge' sadly burnt down in 2008. However, there are plans to rebuild it on the same site, three minutes' walk along ul Pavlova from the bus station. In the meantime, contact the owners of the Arshansky Bor for details of the trips into the mountains that used to run from the Priyut Alpinista.

Eating

Eateries are thin on the ground as most Russians prebook full board at the spas. Some of the cafes at the top of ul Traktovaya are truly dire.

Zakusochnaya Khamar Daban CANTEEN $
(Закусочная Хамар Дабан; ul Traktovaya; mains ₽40-100; ⊙10am-1am; ⊛) Located opposite the Sayany Spa, this basic but pleasant canteen serves up a large menu of Buryat and Russian comfort food and cheap beers. The handwritten menu can be a challenge.

Novy Vek RUSSIAN $$
(Новый век; ul Traktovaya 4; ⊙10am-2am) For a proper sit-down meal try this restaurant near the Arshan Spa that has also sprouted a nightclub, entertainment centre and *stolovaya*.

Getting There & Away

The miniature bus station near the top of ul Traktovaya has the village's only ATM, plus left-luggage lockers. Arshan has the following bus and *marshrutka* connections:

Irkutsk ₽400, daily
Slyudyanka ₽200, two hours, one or two daily
Ulan-Ude ₽710, 11 hours, three daily

Beyond Arshan

From the turn-off for Arshan it's just 9km along the Tunka Valley road to the village of **Zhemchug** (Жемчуг) where, for around ₽100, you can wallow in a series of hot pools that leave a chalky-green residue on skin and clothes.

Around 25km further along the road, the valley's unkempt, low-rise little 'capital' **Kyren** (Кырен) is home to the **Tunka National Park HQ** (www.tunkapark.ru; ul Lenina 69). Its small onion-topped **church** (ul Kooperativenaya) adds foreground to the photogenic alpine backdrop.

The valley road ends at **Mondy** (Монды) near **Munku-Sardyk** (3491m), the highest mountain in Eastern Siberia and scene of an annual mass ascent (May) marking the beginning of the climbing season. From the nearby Mongolian border post a road runs 21km to appealing Khövsgöl Lake, Baikal's little sister.

Some 190km west beyond Mondy the dumbfoundingly far-flung **Oka Region** has been dubbed 'Tibet in miniature'. The 'capital' **Orlik** (Орлик) is the obvious place to arrange treks and horse-riding trips into some seriously isolated backcountry.

Eastern Baikal

Sparsely scattered beach villages of old-fashioned log cottages dot the pretty east Baikal coast. Further north is the dramatic Barguzin Valley, from which Chinggis Khaan's mother, Oilun-Ehe, is said to have originated. Some of the area has been slated for mass-tourism development but little has appeared in the intervening years, save for a mirror-smooth shore-hugging road which has cut journey times significantly. Ulan-Ude agencies can book basic accommodation along the east coast where summer *turbazy* (holiday camps) are popular among sand-seeking Russians.

Access to the coast is across a forested pass from Ulan-Ude via tiny **Baturino** village with its elegantly renovated Sretenskaya Church.

After around 2½ hours' drive, the newly paved road first meets Lake Baikal at pretty little **Gremyachinsk** (Гремячинск), a popular trip out of Ulan-Ude for hurried Trans-Siberian travellers with a day to spare. Buses stop at a roadside cafe from which Gremyachinsk's sandy but litter-strewn beach is a 15-minute walk up ul Komsomolskaya. *Marshrutky* back to Ulan-Ude are often full so consider prebooking your return.

Approximately 5km from Gremyachinsk, at least 10 large tourist camps are strung around **Lake Kotokel**, whose thermal springs keep it warm year-round. At the northern end of the lake rises **Monastyrsky Island**, once home to an isolated hermitage and a church.

The main road offers surprisingly few Baikal views until the fishing port of **Turka**, from where there are pleasant walks to several secluded bays in either direction. Bigger **Goryachinsk** (Горячинск), around 3km from the lake, is centred on a typically institutional hot-springs **kurort** (spa) with cheap cottage homestays in the surrounding village.

Further north through the uninhabited taiga lies the quaint little fishing hamlet of **Maksimikha** (Максимиха) where picturesque Baikal beaches stretch northwest. From here the blacktop bends before zipping through the forest to Ust-Barguzin.

Ust-Barguzin Усть - Баргузин

☎30131 / POP 7170 / ⌚MOSCOW +5HR

Low-rise Ust-Barguzin has sandy streets of traditional log homes with blue-and-white carved window frames. These are most attractive towards the northern end of the main street, ul Lenina, where it reaches the Barguzin River **ferry**. From here, views are magical towards the high-ridged peaks of the Svyatoy Nos Peninsula. Other than watching the rusting car ferry being towed by a fume-belching motorboat across the fast-flowing Barguzin River, the only other attraction here is the **Banya Museum** (☎30131-91 574; per Bolnichny 9; ⌚by appointment only), displaying four traditional timber *bani* lovingly fashioned by national park ranger and guide, Alexander Beketov, who also runs a very comfortable **homestay** (☎30131-91 574; full board per person ₽1550, tent pitch ₽100) at the same address. The Beketovs provide a superb base and run tours to the Barguzin Valley and the national park. Their welcome and home-cooked meals make Ust-Barguzin a preferable base to Barguzin.

Daily *marshrutky* to Ulan-Ude (₽435, five hours) run twice a day and will pick you up from your accommodation if you book ahead. In July and August a daily hydrofoil links Ust-Barguzin with Irkutsk and Khuzhir on Olkhon Island; check out VSRP (p474) for details. In February and March the ice drive across Lake Baikal to Severobaikalsk takes around five hours.

Svyatoy Nos (Holy Nose) Peninsula Полуостров Святой Нос

Rising almost vertically out of shimmering waters, dramatic Svyatoy Nos is one of Lake Baikal's most impressive features. It's within the mostly impenetrable **Zabaikalsky National Park** and joined to Ust-Barguzin by a muddy 20km sandbar that's possible but painful to drive along (there's also a toll). Guides can be hired at the **national park offices** (per Bolnichny 9) in Ust-Barguzin for all-day trek-climbs to the top of the peninsula, more than 1800m above Lake Baikal. The views from the summit are truly awe-inspiring.

Nerpa seals are particularly abundant off the peninsula's west coast around the **Ushkanny Islands**, accessible by charter boat from Ust-Barguzin. Contact Alexander Beketov at the national park headquarters. Prices begin at around ₽6000.

Barguzin & the Barguzin Valley Баргузин и Баргузинская долина

30131 / POP 5700 / MOSCOW +5HR

The road north from Ust-Barguzin emerges from thick forests at Barguzin, a low-rise town of wooden cottages that dates back to 1648. Walking from the bus station you can see its handful of dilapidated historic buildings in about 20 minutes by heading along ul Krasnoarmeyskaya past the cursorily renovated old **church** to pl Lenina. Opposite the quaint little post office, the wooden-colonnaded **former Uezdnogo Bank** (ul Krasnoarmeyskaya 54) was once the grand home of Decembrist Mikhail Kyukhelbeker. Other exiles to make a home in Barguzin were Jews from Poland and European Russia who arrived here in the 1830s and 1860s. The last signs of the Jewish community can be seen in the crumbling old **cemetery** (a block northeast of the church) where crooked Hebrew-inscribed graves stand to the left and Orthodox headstones, including that of Kyukhelbeker himself, to the right.

Hidden in the village school and difficult to access, the small **museum** (924 391 3126; www.barguzinmuseum.ru; ul Kalinina 51a; ₽100) has some interesting Decembrist-related exhibits as well as the usual dusty rocks and mammoth bones.

Barguzin's real interest is as a launch pad for visiting the stunningly beautiful **Barguzin Valley** as it opens out into wide lake-dotted grassland, gloriously edged by a vast Toblerone of mountain peaks. These are most accessibly viewed across the meandering river plain from **Uro** village. Similarly inspiring panoramas continue for miles towards the idyllic village of **Suvo**, overshadowed by rock towers of the **Suvo Saxony** (Suvinskaya Saksoniya), so-called for its similarity to rock formations on the Czech–Saxony border. A few kilometres beyond Suvo the roadside **Bukhe Shulun** (Byk), a huge boulder resembling a bull's hoof, is considered to have miraculous powers. Heading north you'll pass through widely scattered, old-fashioned villages where horse carts and sleighs outnumber cars. Way up on the valley's mountainous west side, **Kurumkan** (411km northeast of Ulan-Ude) has a small but photogenic peak-backed *datsan*. The valley tapers to a point 50km north of Kurumkan at **Alla** where a tiny *kurort* (spa) can accommodate guests in the summer months.

Buy tickets ahead for Ulan-Ude-Barguzin *marshrutky* (₽550, seven hours, three daily) and services to Kurumkan (₽660, nine hours, two daily). From Barguzin, public transport to Ust-Barguzin, Uro and Kurumkan is rare, though there's usually at least one service early morning and in the afternoon. Hitchhike or arrange a tour through the Beketovs in Ust-Barguzin.

SOUTHERN BURYATIYA & ZABAIKALSKY TERRITORY

Scenically magnificent, southern Buryatiya crouches on the Mongolian border like a cartographic crab squeezing Lake Baikal with its right pincer. Much of the Baikal region covered earlier also falls within the republic, including Severobaikalsk and the Tunka Valley. For the predeparture lowdown, check out Buryatiya's official English-language **tourism website** (www.visitburyatia.ru) and the **government** website (http://egov-buryatia.ru/eng/), which has English-language tourist information.

The vast, sparsely populated Zabaikalsky Territory (Забайкальский край) stretches as far east as the wild Chara Mountains on the BAM railway, but in its more accessible southern reaches it's most interesting for the capital (Chita), the Buryat Buddhist culture of Aginskoe and Tsugol Buddhist temple.

Buryat Culture

Indigenous ethnic Buryats are a Mongol people who comprise around 30% of Buryatiya's population, as well as 65% of the former Agin-Buryat Autonomous District southeast of Chita. Culturally there are two main Buryat groups. During the 19th century, forest-dwelling western Buryats retained their shamanic animist beliefs, while eastern Buryats from the southern steppes mostly converted to Tibetan Buddhism, maintaining a thick layer of local superstition. Although virtually every Buryat *datsan* was systematically destroyed during the communists' antireligious mania in the 1930s, today Buryat Buddhism is thriving. Many *datsany* have been rebuilt and seminaries for training Buddhist monks now operate at Ivolga and Aginskoe.

The Buryat language is Turkic, though very different from Tuvan and Altai. Dialects vary considerably between regions but almost everyone speaks decent, if heavily accented, Russian. Mongolians claim some Buryat dialects resemble their medieval tongue.

Ulan-Ude Улан-Удэ

☎3012 / POP 404,000 / ⌚MOSCOW +5HR

With its smiley Asian features, cosy city centre and fascinating Mongol-Buddhist culture, the Buryat capital is one of Eastern Siberia's most likeable cities. Quietly busy, welcoming and, after Siberia's Russian cities, refreshingly exotic, it's a pleasant place to base yourself for day trips to Buddhist temples and flits to eastern Lake Baikal's gently shelving beaches, easily reachable by bus. For some travellers UU is also a taster for what's to come in Mongolia.

Founded as a Cossack *ostrog* (fort) called Udinsk (later Verkhneudinsk) in 1666, the city prospered as a major stop on the tea-caravan route from China via Troitskosavsk (now Kyakhta). Renamed Ulan-Ude in 1934, it was a closed city until the 1980s due to its secret military plants (there are still mysterious blank spaces on city maps).

Sights

Lenin Head MONUMENT

(pl Sovetov) Ulan-Ude's main square is entirely dominated by the world's largest Lenin head (where are all the others with which it competes?), which some maintain looks comically cross-eyed. The 7.7m-high bronze bonce was installed in 1970 to celebrate Lenin's 100th birthday. Oddly, UU's bird population never seems to streak Lenin's bald scalp with their offerings – out of respect for the great man's achievements, bark diehard communists (but perhaps due to the barely visible antibird spikes, groan the rest).

Khangalov Museum of Buryat History MUSEUM

(Музее истории Бурятии им. М. Н. Хангалова; Profsoyuznaya ul 29; admission per fl ₽80-120; ⌚10am-6pm Tue-Sun) Housed in a badly ageing Soviet-era structure, the historical museum charges per single-room floor; the best of these is Buddiyskoe Iskustvo (3rd floor), displaying *thangkas*, Buddhas and icons salvaged from Buryatiya's monasteries before their Soviet destruction. Other exhibits include fascinating, gaudy papier mâché models of deities and bodhisattvas rescued from Buryatiya's many prewar *datsany* (temples), home shrine tables and often gory Tibetan medical charts. The less interesting Buryat history floor (2nd) can be spied for free from the balcony above.

Rinpoche Bagsha Datsan BUDDHIST TEMPLE

(ul Dzerzhinskogo) Roosting high above the city's far north, the inside of this new and unexpectedly modern Tibetan temple looks like a kind of Buddhist-themed bus terminal, though the 6m-high gilt Buddha is pretty impressive and if you catch the monks doing their thing with drums, cymbals and chanting the atmosphere can be electric. However the real show-stealer here is the panoramic view of the smog-hazed city ringed by rumpled dust-bare peaks.

A new feature is the circular walk around the temple featuring pavilions with grotesque, man-size representations of the Chinese signs of the zodiac. Take *marshrutka* 97 from outside the Hotel Baikal Plaza on pl Sovetov to the last stop (right by the temple entrance).

Ethnographic Museum MUSEUM
(Verkhnyaya Berezovka; admission ₽150; ⌚9am-5pm Wed-Fri & Sun, 10am-6pm Sat) In a forest clearing 6km from central Ulan-Ude, this outdoor collection of local architecture plus some reconstructed burial mounds and the odd stone totem is worth the trip. It's divided into seven areas, each devoted to a different nationality, tribe or ethnic group. There are Hun-era standing stones, Evenki *chumy*, traditional Buryat yurts, timber European townhouses and a whole strip of Old Believers' homesteads, all brimming with period furniture and inhabited by costumed 'locals' giving craft demonstrations.

Marshrutka 37 from outside the Hotel Baikal Plaza on pl Sovetov passes within 1km and drivers are used to detouring to drop off tourists.

Opera & Ballet Theatre NOTABLE BUILDING
(Бурятский государственный академический театра оперы и балета; ☎3012-213 600; www.uuopera.ru; ul Lenina 51) UU's striking Stalinist-era theatre reopened after lengthy renovation in June 2011 (the first performance was for a group of foreign tourists from the luxury Golden Eagle train). Visitors cannot fail to be impressed by the level of craftsmanship inside, though some might be slightly surprised at the new lick of paint and rub of polish given to all the Soviet symbols, including a couple of smirking Stalins.

Ulan-Ude City Museum MUSEUM
(ul Lenina 26; admission ₽60; ⌚10am-6pm) Occupying the merchant's house where imperial heir Nicholas II stayed in 1891, this small museum has exhibits examining Verkhneudinsk's role in the tea and fur trades, the huge fairs that took place at the trading arches and several other aspects of the city's past.

Odigitria Cathedral CHURCH
(ul Lenina 2) Built between 1741 and 1785, UU's largest church was also the first stone structure to appear in the city. Used as a museum store from 1929 until the fall of communism, its exterior has been renovated in a chalky white and the domes once again tipped with gold, but the interiors are plain whitewash, awaiting their Byzantine decoration.

Nature Museum MUSEUM
(Музей природы Бурятии; ☎3012-214 149; ul Lenina 46; admission ₽100; ⌚10am-6pm Tue-Sun) The Nature Museum has taxidermically stuffed animals and a scale model of Lake Baikal showing just how deep it is.

Geological Museum MUSEUM
(Геологический музей Бурятии; ul Lenina 59; ⌚11am-5pm Mon-Fri) FREE This museum displays rocks, crystals and ores from the shores of Lake Baikal as well as art (for sale) made using multihued grit, sand and pebbles.

Tours

Ulan-Ude has several agencies happy to sell you Buryatiya and Baikal tours. Recommended companies and individuals all speak English and are tuned in to the needs of Western travellers.

★ **Baikal Naran Tour** TOUR COMPANY
(☎3012-215 097; info@baikalnaran.com; Office 105, Hotel Buryatiya, ul Kommunisticheskaya 47a) There's nothing director Sesegma (aka Svetlana) can't arrange for travellers in Buryatiya. An award-winning tour company and by far the best folks to approach if you want to see the republic's more remote corners, Old Believer villages, the Selenga Delta, the Barguzin Valley and the region's Buddhist and Shamanist heritage.

Denis Sobnakov TOUR GUIDE
(☎950 391 6325; www.burtour.com; ul Lenina 63) English-speaking Denis runs the city's best hostel as well as fun-packed walking tours of UU and many other Buryatiya-wide trips.

MorinTur TOUR COMPANY
(☎3012-443 647; www.morintour.com; Hotel Sagaan Morin, ul Gagarina 25) Focuses on east Baikal, offering various ice and fishing adventures, a horse-sledge trip, seal watching, rafting in the Barguzin Valley and climbing on Svyatoy Nos (Holy Nose) Peninsula.

Buryat-Intour TOUR COMPANY
(☎3012-216 954; www.buryatintour.ru; ul Erbanova 12) Can arrange birdwatching in the Selenga Delta, river rafting excursions, visits to Novoseleginsk and city tours. Also sells UU–UB bus tickets.

Sleeping

UU now has hostels and luxury hotels – but little in between. The city doesn't suffer from very high occupancy, except in the summer months when booking ahead is advisable.

Ulan-Ude

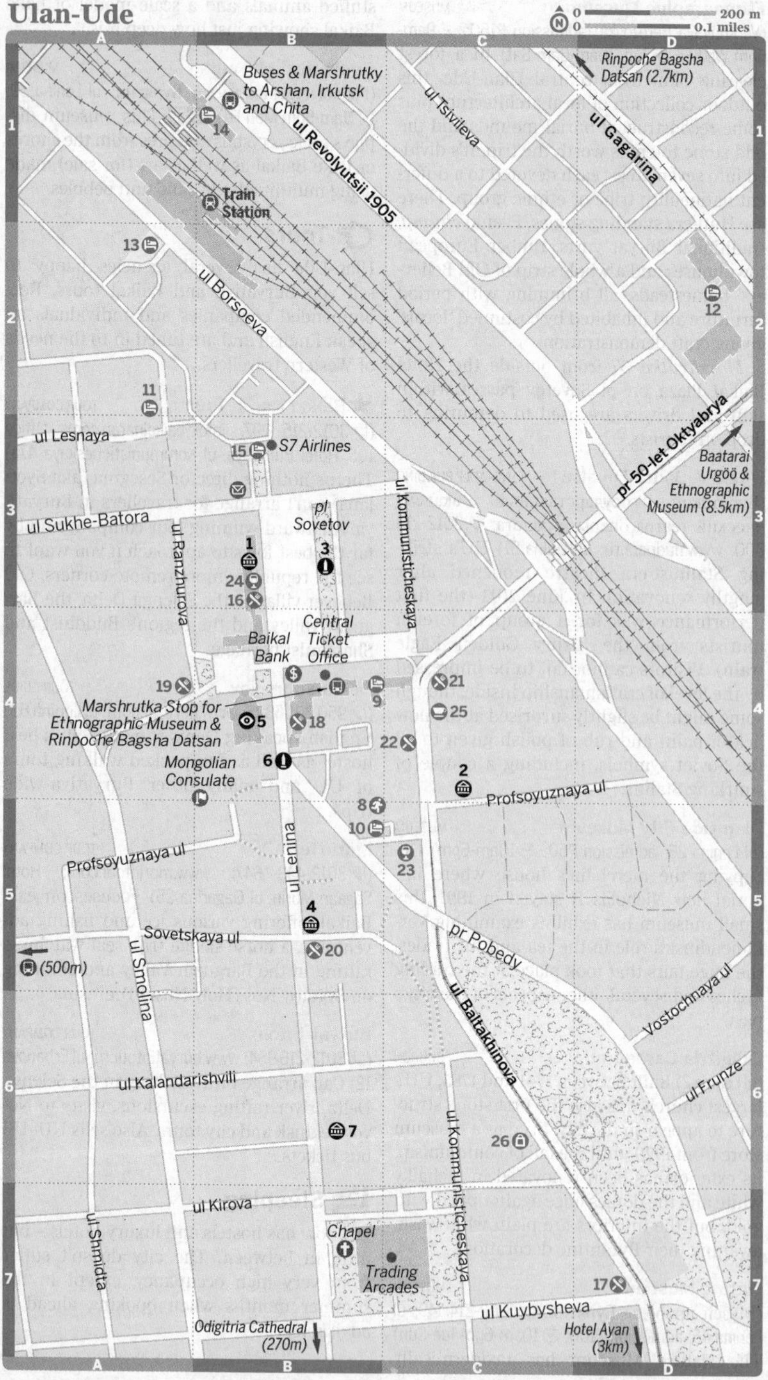
0 200 m
0 0.1 miles
Buses & Marshrutky to Arshan, Irkutsk and Chita
Rinpoche Bagsha Datsan (2.7km)
ul Tsivileva
ul Gagarina
ul Revolyutsii 1905
Train Station
ul Borsoeva
ul Lesnaya
S7 Airlines
pr 50-let Oktyabrya
Baatarai Urgöö & Ethnographic Museum (8.5km)
ul Kommunisticheskaya
pl Sovetov
ul Sukhe-Batora
ul Ranzhurova
Central Ticket Office
Baikal Bank
Marshrutka Stop for Ethnographic Museum & Rinpoche Bagsha Datsan
Mongolian Consulate
Profsoyuznaya ul
ul Lenina
Sovetskaya ul
(500m)
ul Smolina
pr Pobedy
Vostochnaya ul
ul Baltakhinova
ul Kalandarishvili
ul Frunze
ul Kirova
ul Shmidta
Chapel
Trading Arcades
ul Kuybysheva
Odigitria Cathedral (270m)
Hotel Ayan (3km)

Ulan-Ude

★Ulan-Ude Travellers House HOSTEL $
(☎950 391 6325; www.uuhostel.com; ul Lenina 63, apt 18; dm ₽500-650;) So central is this high-ceilinged apartment hostel, you might even catch a glimpse of Lenin's conk from one of the windows. The 14 beds are divided between two spacious, ethnically themed dorms (Russian and Buryat), there's a small kitchen where a free light breakfast is laid out daily, heaps of UU information is pasted on the walls and there's a washing machine for guests to use.

Exceptionally friendly owner Denis is a professional tour guide, fluent English-speaker and guitar demon – bring your six-string for a common-room jam session. He is also planning to open a second branch in the village of Turka on the shores of Baikal itself. A percentage of the hostel's profits go to a local orphanage.

GBT Hostel HOSTEL $
(☎3012-553 470; per Nakhimova 9-2; dm ₽600, d ₽1300; @) An entirely different scene from the Travellers House, this homestay-hostel occupies a suburban house built by Japanese prisoners of war, 2.5km northeast of the city centre. Two dorms sleep 10 and there's one double as well as a fully equipped kitchen. Book ahead and arrange a free station pick-up as it's almost impossible to find on your own.

As the name suggests, the owners are heavily involved in the Great Baikal Trail project and this is one of the best places to get trekking info.

Resting Rooms HOSTEL $
(Комнаты отдыха; ☎3012-282 696; komnaty otdykha, Ulan-Ude train station; 12-/24-hr ₽660/1320) Basic train station dorms good for a couple of hours sleep if arriving in the small hours, but no more.

Hotel Ayan HOTEL $$
(Отель Аян; ☎3012-415 141; www.ayanhotel.ru; ul Babushkina 164; s/d from ₽1000/1600;) The inconvenient location 2km south of the city centre is more than recompensed by pristine international-standard rooms, some with air-conditioning. The cheapest singles are a good deal and every room has its own water heater. There's also a tiny cafe should you get peckish from all the stair climbing you'll do here – incredibly, this six-storey new-build has no lift.

A taxi from the train station costs around ₽170 or arrange a ₽300 private transfer with the hotel.

Hotel Buryatiya HOTEL $$
(Гостиница Бурятия; ☎3012-214 888; www.buryatiahotel.com; ul Kommunisticheskaya 47a; s/d from ₽1950/2700;) The mammoth Buryatiya, the former Intourist hotel, has 220 rooms of wildly differing sizes and standards: from Soviet-era broom cupboards with dodgy plumbing to almost palatial European-standard quarters. One

WORTH A TRIP

NOVOSELENGINSK НОВОСЕЛЕНГИНСК

Stockades and wooden houses on broad dust-blown roads give this small, 19th-century town of ten thousand souls a memorable 'Wild East' feel. The town's top attraction is its **Decembrist Museum** (ul Lenina 53; admission ₽50; ⌚10am-6pm Wed-Sun), which is housed in an unmissable 200-year-old colonnaded mini-mansion in the town's centre. Lower floors are stocked with 19th-century furnishings, while upstairs are maps and photos relating to the Decembrist exiles and their wives.

Walk a couple of kilometres east of the museum through the town towards the Selenga River to see the isolated ruins of the whitewashed **Spassky Church** on the grassy far bank; this is all that remains of Selenginsk, the original settlement, which was abandoned around 1800 due to frequent floods. You'll also find an unremarkable **obelisk** commemorating Martha Cowie, the wife of a Scottish missionary who spent 22 years here translating the Bible into Mongolian and trying (wholly unsuccessfully) to wean the Buryats off Buddhism.

Marshrutky make the scenic trip from Ulan-Ude (1½ hours, six or seven daily).

advantage to staying here is the convenience of extra services (internet room, tour companies, souvenir kiosks, ATMs) on the 1st floor.

Hotel Geser HOTEL **$$**
(Гостиница Гэсэр; ☎3012-216 151; www.geser-hotel.ru; ul Ranzhurova 11; s/tw from ₽3100/4300) Fully modernised, the former Party hang-out is a popular if slightly overpriced option. Most of the 70-plus rooms are of a decent standard – the only Soviet features remaining are clacking parquet floors and the odd clunky fridge. Rates include breakfast and some staff members speak English.

Mergen Bator HOTEL **$$$**
(Отель Мэргэн Батор; ☎3012-200 002; www.mergen-bator.ru; ul Borsoyeva 19b; tw/d ₽5000/7000; ❄📶) UU's only 21st-century hotel is a swish pad indeed and completely on a par with any Western four-star establishment. From the trendy retro-veneered corridors to the commendably equipped fitness centre (₽500 for nonguests), the modern-as-tomorrow bathrooms to the impeccable service, this place is worth splashing out on. Breakfast is included and can be served in your room free of charge.

Hotel Sagaan Morin HOTEL **$$$**
(Отель Сагаан Морин; ☎3012-444 019; www.sagaan-morin.ru; ul Gagarina 25; s/tw ₽3500/4700; 📶) The gleaming 17-storey, 89-room 'White Horse' offers spacious, crisply designed, almost understated rooms, lots of amenities and a 14th-floor restaurant (Panorama) with look-while-you-eat city vistas.

Hotel Baikal Plaza HOTEL **$$$**
(☎3012-210 070; www.baikalplaza.com; ul Erbanova 12; s/tw ₽3500/4200) The 68 modern, if slightly cramped, rooms were arguably UU's finest offering when first renovated a few years ago, and the central location overlooking the Lenin Head is unrivalled. Overtaken by slicker outfits, the Plaza has lowered its prices in recent years.

Eating

Ul Kommunisticheskaya and the surrounding streets are packed with (sometimes very) basic dumpling canteens.

For a fascinating insight into traditional Buryat life, Baikal Naran Tour can arrange dinner in a yurt with a local family out in the suburbs of Ulan-Ude.

Eco Cafe INTERNATIONAL **$**
(ul Tereshkovoy 26a; mains ₽40-80; ⌚9am-11pm; 🖉) Fancifully claiming the city has 'tired of heavy food', the folks behind this subterranean, but bright cafe opposite the UU's drama theatre go against the Buryat grain with light vegetarian and meat dishes, all made using organic ingredients from local suppliers. Take tram 1 or 2 to the Sayany stop.

Shene Buuza BURYAT **$**
(Шэнэ бууза; ul Lenina 44; mains ₽30-60; ⌚9am-9pm) Squeaky-clean, 21st-century version of the traditional Buryat *buuznaya* (dumpling canteen). The decor might be shiny and plastic but the menu of Buryat comfort food is as traditional and cheap as every other *buuznaya* in town.

Appetite CANTEEN $
(ul Lenina 55; mains ₽30-70; ⏰9am-10pm) Join the local office worker lunch crush at this self-service canteen and *buuzy*-free zone where the Russian comfort food is piled high by gruff Buryat servers. Put together a three-course meal for less than ₽200 and consume in the austere privacy of your white MDF booth while admiring the Lenin Head opposite.

Golden Bird FAST FOOD $
(ul Lenina 52; mains ₽40-110; ⏰9am-10pm) Lurid, loud self-service canteen with precisely weighed rations of standard Russian comfort food served on plastic plates and swilled down with Slovak lager.

Sputnik Supermarket SUPERMARKET $
(Супермаркет Спутник; ul Kommunisticheskaya 48; ⏰24hr) A convenient but pricey supermarket stocking foreign groceries.

Chay Khana UZBEK $$
(Чай Хана; Evropa Business Centre, ul Baltakhinova; mains ₽300-400; ⏰11am-midnight Mon-Thu, to 2am Fri, 1pm-2am Sat, to midnight Sun) This high-perched Uzbek restaurant has a triangular cushion-scattered dining space, trendy oriental fabrics and a menu of exotic *plov*, grilled meats and imaginative salads. But it's the spectacular views of UU and the Selenga valley that are the real showstopper here, best enjoyed from the summer terrace. Take the lift to the 9th floor, then the stairs.

The business centre building is nicknamed 'the toilet' – you'll soon see why.

Baatarai Urgöö BURYAT $$
(Barguzinsky Trakt, Verkhnyaya Berezovka; mains ₽200-400; ⏰11am-11pm; 📶) This yurt complex in the Verkhnyaya Berezovka suburb is a great lunch spot after a visit to the Ethnographical Museum. Take a seat in the main tent and give your taste buds the Buryat treatment in the form of *buuzy* (meat-filled dumplings), *bukhuler* (meat broth), *arbin* (raw cow's liver in horse stomach fat) and a glass of *airag* (fermented mare's milk).

The dining space is decorated with suits of Mongol armour, traditional *buryat* furniture and folk costumes, and the serving staff are also dressed for the part. Take *marshrutka* 37 from pl Sovetov to the yurt stop.

Modern Nomads MONGOLIAN $$
(ul Ranzhurova 1; mains ₽200-1000; ⏰11am-11pm; 🗐) Clean-cut and very popular Mongolian place, good for a quick snack and a beer or for a full-blown dinner splurge costing thousands. Meat features heavily on the menu, but there are many veggie-friendly salads and other dishes with a contemporary twist to choose from, too.

Viva Italia ITALIAN $$
(ul Kommunisticheskaya 43; pizzas ₽300-400; ⏰11am-1am Sun-Thu, to 2am Fri & Sat; ❄) A 1980s Italian pop soundtrack, a long, ambitious and slightly overpriced menu of Appenine fare (stick to the pizzas), a European-style lounge and almost every tipple known to Homo-alcoholus – if you must go Italian in Buryatiya, this is the place to do it.

Drinking

Churchill PUB
(Черчилль; www.pubchurchill.ru; ul Lenina 55; ⏰noon-2am) A bekilted Scottish piper (well a bagpiping dummy at least) greets you at the door of this relatively upmarket British-themed pub. The Brit paraphernalia extends throughout the two stylishly finished halls, the food is tasty and there's an international draught beer menu at central London prices.

Bar 12 BAR
(12th fl, Mergen Bator Hotel, Ul Borsoyeva 19b; ⏰24hr) Capping off the Mergen Bator hotel, this bar probably offers the best views of any in Russia, with the entire Buryat capital and the surrounding mountainscape laid out dramatically below you. The bar's party piece is to rotate through 360 degrees every 30 minutes meaning you see the entire panorama without leaving your seat. Drinks and food are pretty pricey.

Bochka BEER HALL
(ul Kommunisticheskaya 52; ⏰11am-1am Sun-Thu, to 2am Fri & Sat) Large timber beer hall serving a range of Russian and international brews to rinse down the succulently smoky shashlyk. The covered terrace is *the* place to do some elbow bending on sultry summer evenings.

Kofeynya Marco Polo CAFE
(Кофейня Marco Polo; ul Kommunisticheskaya 46; ⏰8am-11pm; 📶) This cosy coffee house has a touch of Central European character, great desserts, and wi-fi.

UU TO UB

With flights between the two capitals once again grounded, there are just two ways to travel from the Buryat capital to Ulaanbaatar. The least comfortable way is by Trans-Mongolian **train**, which takes 23 hours to complete the 657km trip and waits a minumum of five hours on the border at Naushki. A much cheaper and convenient way to go is to hop aboard the daily **coach** (₽1300, 10 hours), which leaves from the main bus station. Tickets can be bought from Baikal Naran Tour and the Ulan-Ude Travellers House hostel.

Shopping

Baikal Naran Tour Souvenir Kiosk SOUVENIRS
(room 105, Hotel Buryatiya, ul Kommunisticheskaya 47a) This tiny kiosk in the Baikal Naran Tour office sells authentic Buryat souvenirs such as oriental costumed dolls, shaman drums and colourful felt hats.

Central Market MARKET
(ul Baltakhinova) Tidy, Soviet-era market selling unusual local produce such as pine nuts, reindeer meat, buckthorn juice, *salo* (raw pig fat) and seasonal fruit and veg. At the back of the building are several stores offering *unty*, beautifully decorated reindeer skin boots. Prices start from around ₽9000 a pair.

Orientation

UU's small city centre is easily explored on foot. Divided into two districts, the communist-era upper city is centred around pl Sovetov and the Lenin Head; descend ul Lenina to the partially pedestrianised lower city, the former merchant quarter, half of which still serves as the commercial hub extending from the 19th-century trading rows (pl Revolutsii). Dusty streets of crooked timber dwellings make up the other half. The recently renovated embankment bends round from the new bus station to the Odigitria Cathedral.

Information

Handy ATMs can be found in the Buryatiya hotel and at the train station.

Andriy Suknyov (☎902 564 2678; suknev@gmail.com) Owner of the GBT Hostel, energetic Andriy is the best person to contact for volunteer activities in the region, including work with disabled children in Talovka and trail construction on the GBT.

Baikal Bank (Байкал Банк; pl Sovetov 1; ⏰9am-8pm Mon-Fri, 9am-7pm Sat) Most central place for changing dollars and euros.

Post Office (ul Lenina 61; ⏰8am-10pm Mon-Fri, 9am-6pm Sat & Sun; 📶)

Tourism Portal (www.uutravel.ru) Official tourism website with a smattering of interesting information in English.

Visit Buryatiya (☎3012-210 332; www.visit-buryatia.ru) Official tourist board which runs a summertime-only yurt-based information office on pl Sovetov.

Getting There & Away

AIR

UU's **Baikal Airport** (www.airportbaikal.ru), 11km from the city centre, handles surprisingly few flights. Buy tickets at the **Central Ticket Office** (ul Erbanova 14; ⏰9am-7pm) or **S7 Airlines** (ul Sukhe-Batora 63; ⏰9am-7pm). Ulan-Ude has the following flight connections:

Irkutsk ₽3000, five weekly
Moscow ₽12,000, two daily
Nizhneangarsk ₽5000, three weekly

BUS

Ulan-Ude's main bus station is a tiny but user-friendly affair located to the west of pl Sovetov. Buy all tickets at least a day in advance. The city has the following connections:

Arshan ₽710, 11 hours, three daily
Barguzin ₽550, seven hours, three daily
Ivolga ₽40, 40 minutes, many daily (*marshrutka* 130)
Kurumkan ₽660, nine hours, daily
Kyakhta ₽350, three hours, hourly
Ust-Barguzin ₽435, six hours, twice daily

Additional official/unofficial *marshrutky* to Arshan (₽700, six hours), Irkutsk (₽800, eight hours) and Chita (₽1150, seven hours) run from the train station forecourt, departing throughout the day when full.

TRAIN

When travelling to Irkutsk, take a day train for superb views of Lake Baikal.

Ulan-Ude has the following rail connections:

Beijing *kupe* ₽6000, two days to two days 15 hours, two weekly
Chita *platskart/kupe* ₽1300/2400, 10 to 12 hours, up to six daily
Irkutsk *platskart/kupe* ₽1200/1600, seven to nine hours, up to nine daily
Ulaanbaatar *kupe* ₽3000, 23 hours, daily

ℹ Getting Around

From pl Sovetov *marshrutky* 28, 55 and 77 run a few times hourly to the airport while *marshrutka* 37 passes the hippodrome, Ethnographic Museum and Baatarai Urgöö restaurant. *Marshrutka* 97 climbs to the Rinpoche Bagsha Datsan.

Around Ulan-Ude

You could spend a week making day trips out of Ulan-Ude with Buddhist temples, Old Believer villages and forgotten border settlements to explore. The main routes south are the scenic Ulan-Ude–Kyakhta road, which hugs the Selenga River for much of the way, and the Trans-Mongolian Railway, which crosses the border at the unremarkable railway town of Naushki. Note that both Naushki and Kyakhta are officially off-limits to foreigners as they fall within the border zone. Permits to visit these places should in theory be arranged through UU agencies at least two months before you travel.

Ivolginsk (Ivolga) Datsan
Иволгинский дацан

Possibly the last person you might expect to have backed the building of a Buddhist temple was Stalin, but in 1946 permission came from the Kremlin to erect a *datsan* in Buryatiya, in gratitude to the locals for their sacrifices during WWII it's often claimed. But instead of reviving the erstwhile centre of Buryat Buddhism at Gusinoe Ozero, the authorities granted a plot of marshy land near the village of Ivolga, 35km from central Ulan-Ude, on which the temple was to be built. The first temple was a modest affair, but today the **datsan** has grown large and is expanding fast. The confident epicentre of Russian Buddhism attracts large numbers of the devout as well as tourists on half-day trips from the Buryat capital.

The Ivolginsky *datsan* was one of only two working Buddhist temples in Soviet days (the other was at Aginskoe); most of what you see today has been built in the last two decades. A clockwise walk around the complex takes in countless monastery faculties, administrative buildings, monks' quarters and temples, but the most elaborate of all is the **Itygel Khambin Temple** honouring the 12th Khambo Lama, whose body was exhumed in 2002. To general astonishment, seven decades after his death his flesh had still not decomposed. Some 'experts' have even attested that the corpse's hair is still growing, albeit extraordinarily slowly. The body is displayed six times a year, attracting pilgrims from across the Buddhist world.

To reach the monastery, first take *marshrutka* 130 (₽40, 40 minutes, four hourly) from Ulan-Ude's bus station to the last stop in uninteresting Ivolga. There another *marshrutka* (₽20, no number, just a picture of the monastery or the word Дацан pasted to the front windscreen), waits to shuttle visitors the last few kilometres to the monastery compound. Otherwise contact agencies in Ulan-Ude, which offer private transfers and tours with well-informed guides.

> **OLD BELIEVERS' VILLAGES**
>
> To the south of Ulan-Ude lie several relatively accessible **Old Believers' villages**, most notably Tarbagatay (50km south), with its whitewashed church and small museum, and nearby Desyatnikovo. Turn up unannounced in these places and you'll see precious little; visits involving lots of colourful costumed singing, deliciously hearty homemade food and detailed explanations of the Old Believers' traditions and way of life must be prearranged through Ulan-Ude agencies. Otherwise you could try contacting **Semeyskie** (☎3014-655 958; www.starovery.narod.ru; ul Pushkina 2, Tarbagatay), the old believers' organisation that arranges visits direct.

Tamchinsky Datsan
Тамчинский дацан

First founded in 1741, this was Buryatiya's first Buddhist monastery and the mother ship of Russian Buddhism for two centuries. The original complex, 160km south of Ulan-Ude, was destroyed in the 1930s and the modern reconstruction is small scale and surrounded by the slowly dying village of Gusinoe Ozero (30km south of Gusinoozersk). View the newly renovated former school of philosophy, test out the amazing acoustics of the main temple and chat with the mobile-phone-toting head lama who, for a donation, may let you camp in the grounds and eat in the small refectory.

To get there, take the 7.24am Naushki train from Ulan-Ude (four hours) and alight at Gusinoe Ozero. A train runs back to Ulan-Ude late afternoon or you could hitch a lift to Gusinoozersk at the opposite end of the lake, from where there are regular *marshrutky* back to Ulan-Ude.

Atsagatsky Datsan
Ацагатский дацан

Once the centre of Buryat Buddhist scholarship with an important scriptorium, this *datsan* was completely destroyed in the 1930s, but has crawled back to life since the fall of communism. The tiny on-site **Ayvan Darzhiev Museum** commemorates the Atsagat monk who became a key counsellor to the 13th Dalai Lama. Photogenically gaudy, the little monastery sits on a lonely grassy knoll and is set back from km54 of the old Chita road – unfortunately there is no convenient public transport. A tour from Ulan-Ude will cost around ₽6000 for up to three people.

Kyakhta Кяхта

☎30142 / POP 20,000 / ⏰MOSCOW +5HR

Formerly called Troitskosavsk, the Kyakhta of two centuries ago was a town of tea-trade millionaires whose grandiose cathedral was reputed to have had solid silver doors embedded with diamonds. By the mid-19th century as many as 5000 cases of tea a day were arriving via Mongolia on a stream of horse or camel caravans, which returned loaded with furs.

This gloriously profitable tea trade was brought to a shuddering end with the completion of the Suez Canal and the Trans-Siberian Railway, leaving Kyakhta to wither away into a dust-blown border settlement. Wonderfully preserved by 70 years of communist neglect, the town is dotted with remnants of a wealthier past, which make Kyakhta well worth the trip from Ulan-Ude.

Travellers should be aware that Kyakhta lies well within the Russian border zone and is officially off limits to foreigners without a permit. Ask Ulan-Ude agencies and helpers for the latest situation (travellers do still visit without permits). Foreigners need to apply for a border permit to get anywhere near Kyakhta, a time-consuming and expensive process that puts many visitors off.

Sights

Kyakhta Museum MUSEUM

(ul Lenina 49; admission ₽200; ⏰10am-6pm Tue-Sun) Kyakhta's star attraction is its delightfully eccentric museum, perhaps rather comically dubbed the 'Hermitage of the East' by some overzealous locals. It's certainly one of Siberia's fullest museums with room after musty room of exhibits relating to the tea trade, local plants and animals, Buryat traditions, Asian art and Kyakhta's bit part in WWII. Many of the older exhibits were hauled back to Troitskosavsk by 19th-century Russian gentlemen explorers who launched trans-Asian expeditions from the town. No English signage or information.

Uspenskaya Church CHURCH

(ul Krupskaya) For years Kyakhta's only working church, this beautiful, late-19th-century building was closed twice during the communist decades (1938 and 1962). Leave a donation for its upkeep.

Voskresenskaya Church CHURCH

(Sloboda) Reopened in 2011 following painstaking restoration, the brilliant-white Resurrection Church is the last outpost of European Christianity before Mongolian Buddhism takes over. Take *marshrutka* 1 from ul Lenina.

Trinity Cathedral CHURCH

(ul Lenina) The impressive shell of the 1817 cathedral lies at the heart of the overgrown central park at the end of ul Lenina.

Eating

Letnee Kafe CAFE $

(Летнее кафе; ul Lenina, opposite Hotel Turist; ⏰11am-midnight) No-frills Central Asian shashlyk, *plov* and beer stop on the main drag.

Cafe Sloboda CAFE $

(Кафе Слобода; Sloboda; ⏰11am-11pm) Simple, cheap and clean cafe located 400m along the road from the Voskresenskaya Church, where the road peels off towards the border crossing.

Orientation

Modern Kyakhta is effectively two towns. The main one is centred around ul Lenina, where the bus terminus sits next to the 1853 trading rows *(ryady gostinye)*. The smaller Sloboda district, 4km to the south, is where you'll find the border post.

Getting There & Away

Hourly *marshrutky* (₽350, three hours) leave for Kyakhta from Ulan-Ude's main bus station.

Chita Чита

3022 / POP 324,000 / MOSCOW +6HR

Of all Eastern Siberia's major cities, Chita is the least prepared for visitors. Literally put on the map by the noble-blooded Decembrists, one of whom designed its street-grid layout, today there's nothing aristocratic about this regional capital where Soviet symbols still embellish Stalinist facades, shaven-headed conscripts guard pillared military headquarters and Chinese cross-border peddlers lug monster bales past a well-tended Lenin statue. Non-Chinese foreigners are still a rarity here; tourism is a thing that happens elsewhere.

Echoes of the Decembrist chapter in Chita's history make the city just worth visiting, and a number of attractive old timber merchants' houses grace its arrow-straight streets. It's also the jumping-off point for two of Russia's best Buddhist temples at Aginskoe and Tsugol.

History

Founded in 1653, Chita developed as a rough-and-tumble silver-mining centre until it was force-fed a dose of urban culture in 1827 by the arrival of more than 80 exiled Decembrist gentlemen-rebels – or more precisely, by the arrival of their wives and lovers who followed, setting up homes on what became known as ul Damskaya (Women's St). That's now the southern end of ul Stolyarova, where sadly only a handful of rotting wooden cottages remains amid soulless concrete apartment towers.

As gateway to the new East Chinese Railway, Chita boomed in the early 20th century, despite flirting with socialism. Following the excitement of 1905, socialists set up a 'Chita Republic' which was brutally crushed within a year. After the 'real' revolutions of 1917, history gets even more exciting and complex. Bolsheviks took over, then lost control to Japanese forces who possibly intercepted part of Admiral Kolchak's famous 'gold train' before retreating east. By 1920 Chita was the capital of the short-lived Far Eastern Republic, a nominally independent, pro-Lenin buffer state whose parliament stood at ul Anokhina 63. The republic was absorbed into Soviet Russia in December 1922 once the Japanese had withdrawn from Russia's east coast. Closed and secretive for much of the Soviet era, today Chita is still very much a military city and once again flooded with Chinese traders.

Sights

★Decembrist Museum MUSEUM

(Музей Декабристов; ul Selenginskaya; admission ₽130; 10am-6pm Tue-Sun) If you're on the Decembrist trail through Siberia, this small but comprehensive museum is one of the best, though there's not a word of English anywhere. It's housed in the 18th-century **Archangel Michael log**

THE DECEMBRIST WOMEN

Having patently failed to topple tsarist autocracy in December 1825, many prominent 'Decembrist' gentlemen revolutionaries were exiled to Siberia. They're popularly credited with bringing civilisation to the rough-edged local pioneer-convict population. Yet the real heroes were their womenfolk, who cobbled together the vast sleigh/carriage fares to get themselves to Siberia.

And that was just the start. Pauline Annenkova, the French mistress of one aristocratic prisoner, spent so long awaiting permission to see her lover in Chita that she had time to set up a fashionable dressmakers' shop in Irkutsk. By constantly surveying the prisoners' conditions, the women eventually shamed guards into reducing the brutality of the jail regimes, while their food parcels meant that Decembrists had more hope of surviving the minimal rations of their imprisonment. The Decembrist women came to form a core of civil society and introduced 'European standards of behaviour'. As conditions eventually eased, this formed the basis for a liberal Siberian aristocracy, especially in Chita and Irkutsk where some Decembrists stayed on even after their formal banishment came to an end.

church, an unexpected sight amid the neighbourhood's shambolic apartment blocks. Inextricably linked to the Decembrist story, this was where they came to pray, where Annenkov married his French mistress Pauline and where the Volkonskys buried their daughter Sofia.

The ground-level exhibition begins with the names of all the Decembrists picked out in gold on a green background, followed by interesting items such as the original imperial order sentencing the noble rebels to banishment in Siberia and oils showing their leaders' executions. The 2nd floor looks at the wives who followed their menfolk into the Nerchinsk silver mines and the fates of all the Decembrists once they were allowed to settle where they pleased.

At the time of research the museum building was under threat of confiscation by the Russian Orthodox Church.

Kuznetzov Regional Museum MUSEUM
(Забайкальский краевой краеведческий музей им. А.К. Кузнецова; ☎3022-260 315; ul Babushkina 113; admission ₽140; ⏰10am-5.45pm Tue-Sun) The unexpectedly lively Kuznetzov Regional Museum is housed in an early-20th-century mansion. Here you'll find some pretty interesting local exhibits, including a very thorough examination of the heritage and architectural renaissance of the city and region. There's a decent cafe on the premises.

Datsan BUDDHIST TEMPLE
(ul Bogomyagkova; ⏰24hr) Chita's main Buddhist temple lies just outside the centre, a 15-minute walk or ₽150 taxi ride along Bogomyagkova from where it meets ul Babushkina. It's a recently built affair, but well kept and with all its prayer wheels, butter lamps and yin-yang drums firmly in place. The tranquil grounds are home to a tiny *buuzy* joint.

Cathedral CHURCH
(Кафедральный собор; train station forecourt) The train station reflected in its gilt onion domes, Chita's bright turquoise cathedral is the city's most impressive building, though inside it's lamentably plain. The original pre-Stalin cathedral stood on the main square, right on the spot where Lenin now fingers his lapels.

Sleeping

Chita has little budget accommodation and homestays are nonexistent. Hotels are often full, meaning many travellers who fail to book ahead often have no choice but to check into top-end hotels.

Hotel Arkadia HOTEL $$
(Гостиница Аркадия; ☎3022-352 636; www.arkadiyachita.ru; ul Lenina 120; s ₽1800-2800, tw ₽2500-3800; 📶) Chita's best deal has well-kept rooms, clean bathrooms, online booking, efficient staff and no-fuss visa registration. Often offers very good rates on popular booking websites.

Hotel Zabaikale HOTEL $$
(Гостиница Забайкалье; ☎3022-359 819; www.zabhotel.ru; ul Leningradskaya 36; s from ₽2500, tw from ₽3200; 📶) Unbeatably located overlooking the main square, the cheaper renovated rooms at this huge complex are a fairly good deal. The hotel has a huge range of facilities including an air and rail ticket office, a spa, a children's playroom and a gym.

Grand City Hotel HOTEL $$
(☎3022-212 233; www.hotel-grandcity.ru; ul Amurskaya 96a; dm/s/tw from ₽800/1900/2400; 📶) Chita's newest hotel is situated right opposite the railway station making it a convenient place to zip open the rucksack if arriving by train. That's just about where the positives end as, except for the two-level *lyux* rooms with corner window views of the cathedral, the 64 bedrooms are spartan and cheaply furnished. Breakfast and diabolical service included.

Hotel Vizit HOTEL $$$
(Гостиница Визит; ☎3022-356 945; www.chita-hotelvizit.ru; ul Lenina 93; s/tw ₽3400/6400; ❄📶) Occupying the 5th floor of an ultramodern smoked-glass tower at the busy intersection of ul Lenina and ul Profsoyuznaya, this is Chita's best luxury offering with relaxing ensuite rooms, English-speaking receptionists and sparkling bathrooms. Some doubles have baths and the air-con provides relief from Chita's superheated summers.

Hotel Montblanc HOTEL $$$
(☎3022-357 272; www.eldonet.ru; ul Kostyushko-Grigorovicha 5; s ₽3450-4000, tw ₽4250-4800; ❄📶) A block away from the main square, this purpose-built business hotel has immaculately snazzy rooms, though at these prices the plumbing could be a touch more professional. The buffet breakfast is served

in the Ukraine-themed restaurant and check-out time at reception provides an opportunity to witness just how badly Russian and Chinese businessmen can behave.

Hotel Dauria HOTEL $$$
(Гостиница Даурия; ☎3022-262 350; ul Profsoyuznaya 17; s from ₽2000, d from ₽4000;) Renovated over a decade ago, the ageing but still comfortable rooms here are a last resort. That said, it is possibly Chita's most characterful choice, housed in a historical building. A poor breakfast is included. Reservations are essential.

Eating & Drinking

Eating out ain't high on the list of things to enjoy in Chita, but despite the lack of choice and unimaginative menus, you won't go hungry.

Mama Roma ITALIAN $
(www.mamaroma.ru; ul Lermontova 9; pizzas ₽195-350, other mains around ₽300; 11am-10pm;) Chequered tablecloths, glass divides, an English menu (!) and pleasant staff make this pizzeria an unexpectedly welcoming experience near the train station, probably as it's part of a chain.

Privoz CANTEEN $
(Привозъ; ul Lenina 93; canteen mains ₽20-80; 10am-midnight Sun-Wed, to 1am Thu-Sat) Nautically themed self-service canteen plating up Eurasian staples for prices so low they'll shiver your timbers. There's a fancier restaurant upstairs and look out for the country's first 'monument to the New Russian' in front of the building.

Poznaya Altargana BURYAT $
(Позная Алтаргана; ul Leningradskaya 5; pozi ₽35; 10am-10pm) If *pozi* are your thing, pink-and-flowery Poznaya Altargana is your place, but the tasty *plov* and meatballs are an equally filling alternative. There's a larger branch at ul Babushkina 121.

Khmelnaya Korchma UKRAINIAN $$
(Хмельная корчма; ☎3022-352 134; ul Amurskaya 69; mains ₽150-400; noon-midnight Mon-Thu & Sun, noon-3am Fri & Sat;) Plastic sunflowers, dangling onion strings, folksy embroidered tea towels and a menu of borsch, *salo* (pork fat), *vareniki* (sweet dumplings) and *holubtsi* (cabbage rolls stuffed with rice) teleport you to rural Ukraine. Live music, liberal helpings and a low-priced lunch menu (₽150) possibly make this Chita's best option.

Kafe Traktyr RUSSIAN $$
(Кафе Трактир; ☎3022-352 229; ul Chkalova 93; mains ₽230-500; noon-2am) Russian home-style cooking is served at heavy wooden tables in this rebuilt wooden-lace cottage, with a quietly upmarket Siberian-retro atmosphere. The summer beer-and-shashlyk tent is a popular drinking spot.

Harat's Pub PUB
(ul Leningradskaya 15a; noon-2am) Savour the slightly surreal experience of sipping a pint of Newcastle Brown in an Irish pub in Chita, while pondering just where the owners got all those Celtic flags, old US number plates and imitation Tiffany lamps. Friendly service.

Shokoladnitsa CAFE
(ul Leningradskaya 36; 9am-midnight;) This Europeanly stylish peaceful oasis of a cafe is good for people-watching from the big windows while sipping a beer or coffee and making full use of the free wi-fi.

Shopping

Zabaikalsky Khudozhestvenny Salon SOUVENIRS
(Забайкальский художественный салон; ul Lenina 56; 10am-7pm Mon-Fri, to 6pm Sat, 11am-6pm Sun) This huge shop stocks every perceivable souvenir from across the entire Russian Federation, from Buryat dolls to Kostroma linen, Dzhgel plates to Chita fridge magnets. Local artists' work and the owner's photography also available.

Information

Lanta (Ланта; ☎3022-353 639; www.lanta-chita.ru; ul Leningradskaya 56; 9am-7pm Mon-Fri) Runs limited tours of Chita and Zabaikalsky Region. No English spoken.

Main Post Office (ul Butina 37; 8am-10pm Mon-Fri, 9am-6pm Sat & Sun) Quaintly spired wooden building on pl Lenina.

VTB Bank (ВТБ Банк; ul Amurskaya 41; 9am-6pm Mon-Fri) Has ATMs and currency exchange window.

Getting There & Away

AIR

Kadala Airport (www.aerochita.ru) is 15km west of central Chita. Take bus 40 or *marshrutka* 12 or 14. **AviaEkspress** (АвиаЭкспресс; ☎3022-450 505; www.aviaexpress.ru; ul Lenina 55; 8am-10pm) sells tickets for all flights, including the twice daily service to Moscow (₽12,500).

WORTH A TRIP

NERCHINSK НЕРЧИНСК

Anyone with a knowledge of Russian history will be familiar with the name Nerchinsk. The 1689 Treaty of Nerchinsk recognising Russia's claims to the trans-Baikal region was signed here and 130 years later the Decembrists were sent to work the silver mines around the village. Once one of Eastern Siberia's foremost towns but inexplicably bypassed by the Trans-Siberian Railway just 10km to the south, Nerchinsk leads a forgotten existence with just a few fading reminders of its rich past. If you're looking to break up the long 2200km trip from Chita to Blagoveshchensk, hop off here. Most don't.

The only visitable attraction is the **Butin Palace Museum** (ul Sovetskaya 83; admission ₽100; ⌚10am-1pm & 2-5.30pm Tue-Sat). Mikhail Butin, the local silver baron, built himself this impressive crenellated palace, furnished with what were then claimed to be the world's largest mirrors. He'd bought the mirrors at the 1878 World Fair in Paris and miraculously managed to ship them unscathed all the way to Nerchinsk via the China Sea and up the Amur River. These four mammoth mirrors form the centrepiece of the collection, along with a delightful pair of hobbit-style chairs crafted from polished tangles of birch roots. Three-quarters of the palace, including the grand, triple-arched gateway (demolished in 1970), still stands in ruins.

A block from the museum, the active 1825 **Voskresensky Cathedral** (ul Pogodaeva 85) looks like an opera house from the outside; its interior is plain and whitewashed. Head around the sports pitch with its little silver Lenin to the imposing though now crumbling 1840 **Trading Arches**, desperately in need of renovation. Nearby is a fine colonnaded pharmacy and the very grand facade of the pink former **Kolobovnikov Store** (ul Shilova 3), now a barnlike Torgovy Tsentr filled with some desultory stalls and kiosks.

About 1km south of the museum, just before the post office and bank, a little pink column-fronted building was once the **Dauriya Hotel** (ul Sovetskaya 32). As locals will proudly tell you, Chekhov stayed here in June 1890. Diagonally across the same junction a minuscule bus station is the departure point for services to Priiskovaya.

To reach Nerchinsk, take any train from Chita to Priiskovaya (*platskart/kupe* ₽900/1200, six hours) on the trans-Siberian main line, 10km from Nerchinsk. Change there onto local *marshrutky*.

BUS

The only two services you're likely to need are the *marshrutky* to Aginskoe (₽300, two hours, hourly) and the long-distance minivans to Ulan-Ude (₽800, seven hours). Both leave from a stop on the train station forecourt.

TRAIN

Chita has the following rail connections:

Beijing *kupe* ₽7000, two days five hours, weekly

Blagoveshchensk *platskart/kupe* ₽2600/3700, one day 14 hours, two daily

Khabarovsk *platskart/kupe* ₽3600/6700, one day 15½ to 17½ hours, up to three daily

Tynda *platskart/kupe* ₽2300/3300, 27 hours, every other day

Ulan-Ude *platskart/kupe* ₽1300/2400, 10 to 12 hours, up to six daily

Zabaikalsk *platskart/kupe* ₽1100/1500, 12 hours, daily

Around Chita

Aginskoe Агинское

☎30239 / POP 16,700 / ⌚MOSCOW +6HR

For an intriguing day trip from Chita, take a *marshrutka* (₽300, two hours, hourly) to the spruced-up Buryat town of Aginskoe. Scenery en route transforms from patchily forested hills via river valleys into rolling grassy steppe.

Once in Aginskoe, hop straight into a taxi (₽100) to visit the beautiful old Buddhist **datsan** (6km west of the centre), a large complex of brightly decorated temples and monastery faculties. Back on the central square, the admirably well-curated **Tsybikov Museum** (ul Komsomolskaya 11; admission ₽100; ⌚10am-1pm & 2-5.30pm Mon-Fri) takes an in-depth look at the local Buryat culture. Opposite stands the custard-yellow 1905 **St Nicholas Church** whose reconstruction was bankrolled by former Moscow mayor Yury Luzhkov.

For food, try the greasy spoons around the market where there's also a supermarket and an ATM.

Tsugol Цугол

Set just 2km from the 'holy' Onon River, Tsugol village is not particularly pretty but the perfectly proportioned **Tsugol Datsan** is surely the most memorable Buddhist temple in Russia. Built in 1820, it is just four years younger than Aginskoe Datsan and even more photogenic, with gilded Mongolian script-panels, wooden upper facades and tip-tilted roofs on each of its three storeys. The interior is less colourful than the Ivolginsk temple, but clinging to the front is a unique, colourfully painted wrought-iron staircase.

Getting to/from Tsugol is a pain – it lies 13km from Olovyannaya, reachable by a single morning bus from Chita. From Olovyannaya take a taxi (at least ₽500, more if asked to wait) or hike along the river. On the return journey, you could ask around in Olovyannaya for an unofficial *marshrutka* back to Chita (or Aginskoe) – otherwise it's a long lonely wait for the overnight train (as this leaves at 2am this may be an opportunity to test your hitchhiking skills). Alternatively, ask around at hotels in Chita for excursions to Tsugol.

Russian Far East

Includes ➡

Best Places to Eat

- Gatsby (p522)
- Pyongyang (p530)
- Shinok Pervach (p537)
- Chochur Muran (p543)
- Cafe No 1 (p549)

Best Places to Stay

- Boutique Hotel (p521)
- Optimum Hostel (p529)
- Bed & Breakfast Bravo (p542)
- Hostel 24 (p555)
- Grushanka (p560)

Why Go?

Russia's distant end of the line, the wild wild east, feels likes its own entity. 'Moscow is far' runs the local mantra, and trade and transport connections with Asian neighbours are growing fast.

For those who've not been there, the Russian Far East (Дальний Восток) seems impossibly forbidding and it's often mistaken for Siberia (it was considered part of Siberia in precommunist times). The truth is it's bigger, more remote and, in winter, even colder. Areas of snowcapped mountains and taiga (northern pine), bigger than some European countries, separate former Cossack fort towns, old Gulag camps, decaying Soviet towns along railways heading nowhere special, towns raised on stilts over permafrost and once-closed Soviet ports roaring with new business.

Many travellers skip the Far East entirely, cutting south from Lake Baikal to China – but that's all the better for those who make it. Elbow room is definitely not in short supply.

When to Go

Vladivostok

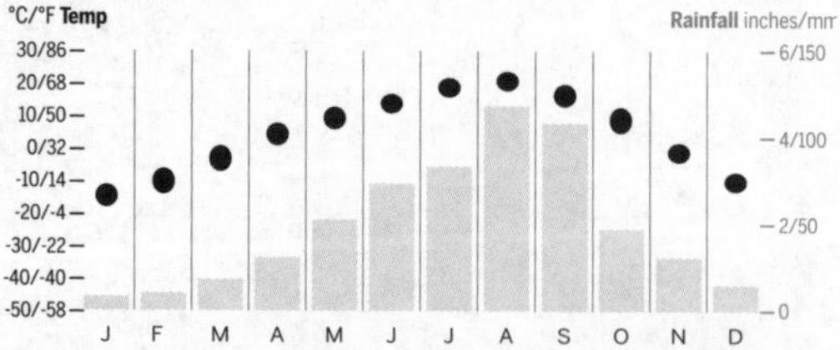

Feb & Mar Still the season for snowy delights, only not dark or slushy.

Jun Essentially midspring, with all the beauty that entails (minus mosquitoes).

Sep & Oct Better weather and more autumn foliage than anywhere else on earth.

History

The Far East is Russia's 'wild east', where hardened Cossacks in the early 17th century – and young Soviets (and Gulag-camp prisoners) in the 20th – came to exploit the region's untapped natural resources, such as gold of the Kolyma, diamonds of Sakha and oil off Sakhalin Island. It was just a big chunk of Siberia until the Soviets anointed it a separate administrative entity in the 1920s. Geographers still consider most of the Far East part of Siberia. Yet it has always felt more distant, more challenging, more godforsaken than points west.

Locally, much ado is made of Anton Chekhov's trip through the Far East to Sakhalin

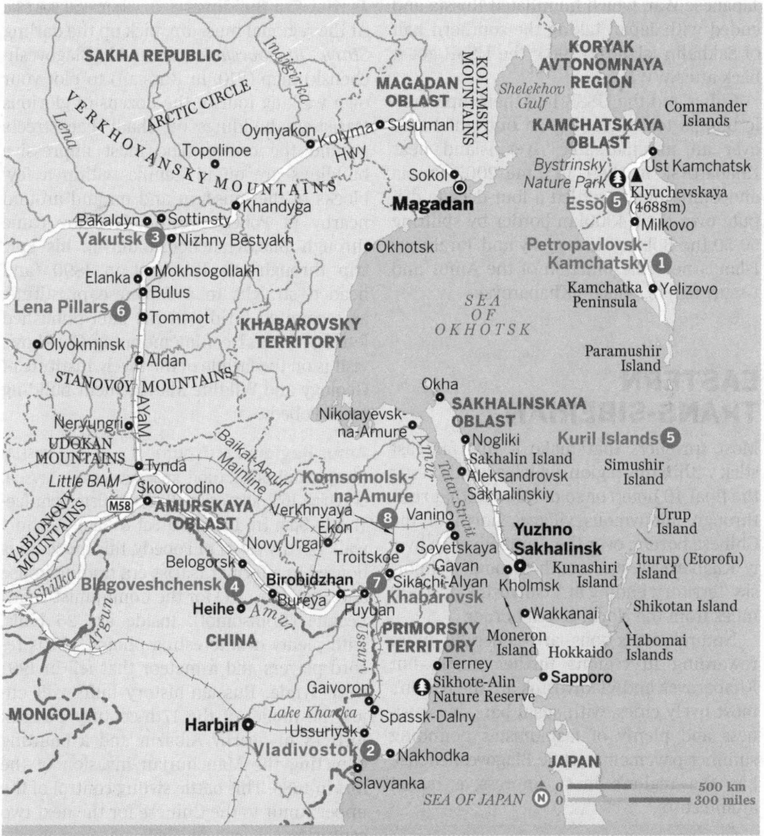

Russian Far East Highlights

1 Climb a volcano around **Petropavlovsk-Kamchatsky** (p551) on the wild Kamchatka Peninsula.

2 View sublime Golden Horn Bay in mountain-spiked **Vladivostok** (p524).

3 Go exotic with horse meat, reindeer and frozen fish meals in fascinating **Yakutsk** (p538).

4 Take in exquisite tsarist-era buildings along the Amur River in **Blagoveshchensk** (p514).

5 Hike amid sublime scenery followed by a soak in a geothermal pool in **Esso** (p559), Kamchatka.

6 Take a cruise to see the magnificent **Lena Pillars** (p541), amid the vast wilderness of the Sakha Republic.

7 Take a scenic riverside stroll, admire grand architecture and enjoy the nightlife in hip **Khabarovsk** (p518).

8 Revisit Soviet power by taking a Gulag-camp tour at **Komsomolsk-na-Amure** (p535).

in 1890; of Bolshevik Marshal Vasily Blyukher's victory in the last major battle of the Russian Civil War at Volochaevka outside Khabarovsk; and of Count Nikolay Muravyov-Amursky, the 19th-century governor of Eastern Siberia who did much to open up the Far East and consolidate Russian control of the Left (north) Bank of the Amur River. Less is made of the Russo-Japanese War, which humiliated Russia and ended with Japan taking the southern half of Sakhalin Island in 1905; the USSR got it back after WWII.

China and the USSR had their diplomatic bumps too, including an outright battle over an unremarkable river island near Khabarovsk in 1969. In June 2005 Russia and China finally settled a four-decade dispute over their 4300km border by splitting 50-50 the Bolshoy Ussurysky and Tarabarov Islands near the junction of the Amur and Ussuri Rivers, outside Khabarovsk.

EASTERN TRANS-SIBERIAN

Most travellers that make it this far east stick within this region, which extends along the final 40 hours or so of railroad that runs through anonymous villages north of the Chinese border, over the Amur River to lively Khabarovsk, and south through Primorsky Territory, ending at Vladivostok, just 100 miles from the North Korea border.

Natural attractions are generally more rewarding in regions further north, but Khabarovsk and Vladivostok are the region's most lively cities, with sushi bars, big business and plenty of fashionistas pounding summer pavements, while Blagoveshchensk has the region's most impressive tsarist architecture.

Blagoveshchensk

Благовещенск

☎4162 / POP 210,000 / ⏰MOSCOW +6HR

It's sometimes easy to forget where you are out here – in deepest Asia – until you find a place like this modest border town, 110km south of the Trans-Siberian and across the Amur River from China. The mix of scattered tsarist-era buildings and Chinese tourists walking past Lenin statues is fascinating. On hot days, locals share the river, jumping in from beaches on opposite shores.

Sights & Activities

A good starting point for a wander around is on the riverfront at pl Lenina, where teen skaters take over the Lenin-statue steps and tots take over the fountains. From here a short walk west along the pleasant riverside promenade, or along parallel ul Lenina, takes you to yawning pl Pobedy.

Tsarist-Era Buildings HISTORICAL BUILDING

At the regional museum, pick up the darling *Stary Blagoveshchensk* (Old Blagoveshchensk) map (₽10, in Russian) to plot your own walking tour of the dozens of glorious tsarist-era buildings on shady backstreets around the centre. The most impressive buildings are on ul Lenina within a few blocks of the museum and on and around nearby pl Pobedy. Anton Chekhov came through Blagoveshchensk during his epic trip through the Far East in 1890 (and headed straight to a Japanese prostitute, as recounted luridly in his later-published letters). A **bust** commemorating Chekhov's visit is on the facade of the lovely Institute of Geology and Wildlife Management building on pl Pobedy.

Amur Regional Museum MUSEUM

(Амурский областной краеведческий музей; ul Lenina 165; admission ₽120; ⏰10am-6pm Tue-Thu, to 9pm Fri, 11am-7pm Sat & Sun) A short walk northwest of pl Pobedy, this museum is housed in a former tsarist-era trading house and Soviet-era HQ for the Communist Youth League (Komsomol). Inside are 26 halls, with plenty of interesting photos, 1940s record players and a meteor that fell in 1991 near Tynda. Russian-history buffs will enjoy the model of the 17th-century Cossack fortress in nearby Albazin and a painting depicting the Manchurian invasion of the fort in 1685. This battle swung control of the upper Amur to the Chinese for the next two centuries.

River Cruises BOAT TRIPS

(per person ₽150) One-hour daytime and evening river cruises leave from a pier at the east end of ul Amurskaya from mid-May through September.

Sleeping & Eating

Green Hostel HOSTEL $

(☎8-924-841 9008; ul Ostrovskaya 65; dm ₽500-700; 📶) This basic, not terribly friendly place has three dorm rooms with lino floors and a shared kitchen. Hard to find, the hos-

INDIGENOUS GROUPS IN THE FAR EAST

Russia's rich cultural melting pot can seem utterly invisible if you only visit the main cities along the Trans-Siberian Railway. For a radically different perspective, it's worth getting off the beaten path, and learning a bit about the Far East's indigenous groups. Following are a few starting points:

Sakha Republic

Inhabiting a vast India-sized republic, the once-marginalised Sakha are today among the nation's most successful indigenous groups. Sakha have rich folk customs, including an oral storytelling tradition of great epic poems (some over 20,000 verses long), unique foods (like raw frozen fish, reindeer meat and fermented mare's milk) and a love for the *khomus* (mouth harp). Yakutsk is the gateway to it all, though if you want to arrange a visit to a shaman or experience traditional life, you'll have to travel well beyond the city.

Kamchatka

The peninsula is home to a number of different groups, including the Even, the Itelmeni and the Koryak. Home to a mix of all three groups, the village of Esso is the best place to learn about the region's cultural diversity, particularly at the excellent Ethnographic Museum. Nomadic Even communities of reindeer herders inhabit hard-to-reach northern regions, though you can join the annual solstice celebration in Anavgay (near Esso) each June. Another Kamchatka event worth planning a trip around is the 1000km-long Beringia dog-sledding race, held in March each year.

Amur River Valley

Numbering around 12,000, the Nanai live on both the Russian and Chinese side of the Amur River. Like many other Far Eastern peoples, the Nanai have a deep respect for nature, and believe the spirit world inhabits most of the physical world around them. The most accessible community to visit is the village of Verkhnyaya Ekon near Komsomolsk-na-Amure.

tel is near the corner of ul Ostrovskaya, one block east of the bus station.

Hotel Armeniya HOTEL $$
(☎4162-230 799; www.armeniablag.ru; ul Krasnoflotskaya 147; s/d incl breakfast from ₽2900/3800; ❄📶) In an ideal location on the riverfront walkway, Armeniya has modern carpeted rooms done up in earthy hues, with flat-screen TVs and flashy, capsule-like showers. The best rooms have river views. There are several restaurants on-site, including a patio pizza spot and an overdecorated dining room serving Armenian fare.

Yubileynaya HOTEL $$
(Гостиница Юбилейная; ☎4162-370 073; www.blghotel.ru; ul Lenina 108; s/d from ₽1800/2600; ❄@📶) This 150-room beast overlooking the river won't win any beauty contests, but the location near pl Lenina is ideal. Rooms are simple spruced-up Soviet fare, while the international restaurant (mains ₽200 to ₽500), festooned with old beer posters, is more 21st century.

Zeya Hotel HOTEL $$
(Гостиница Зея; ☎4162-539 996; www.hotelzeya.ru; ul Kalinina 8; s/d from ₽2040/2520; ❄@📶) Zeya makes a valiant attempt to make Soviet rooms look cheery, but goes a bit over the top with the extrafrilly curtains and bedspreads. Twelve-hour rates available. It's near the river just west of pl Pobedy.

Mega INTERNATIONAL $
(Торгово-развлекательный центр Мега; ul 50 Let Oktyabrya; mains ₽120-350; 📶) Across from the bus station, Mega has a top-floor food court (with free wi-fi).

Kofinya na Bolshoi CAFE $$
(Кофейня на Большой; ul Lenina 159; mains ₽350-700; ⏰8am-1am; 📶) Pleasant cafe with decent cappuccinos and a wide range of fare including eggs and bliny for breakfast, and risotto and pizzas later on. In the same building is a sprawling multilevel eatery and pub serving microbrews and traditional Russian fare.

SharLot Cafe EUROPEAN $$
(ul Lenina 113; mains ₽250-600; 9am-midnight;) One of the best options in the centre for a meal, SharLot has tasty salads, grilled fish and meat dishes, risottos and other eclectic fare. Abstract artwork, young hip waitstaff and groovy tunes draw a stylish crowd.

Getting There & Around

Blagoveshchensk is 110km off the Trans-Siberian, reached via the branch line from Belogorsk. The train station is 4km north of the river on ul 50 Let Oktyabrya, the main north–south artery. Take bus 30 (unless it's heading to 'mikro-rayon') to reach the centre.

Trains heading east backtrack to Belogorsk on their way to Khabarovsk (*kupe/platskartny* from ₽4000/2400, 13 hours, daily). Heading west, trains serve Chita (*kupe/platskartny* ₽5200/2700, 37 hours, odd-numbered days) and Tynda (*kupe/platskartny* ₽4700/2600, 16¼ hours, odd-numbered days).

Additional options are available from Belogorsk to the north or Bureya to the east. *Marshrutky* (fixed-route minibuses) connect Blagoveshchensk's **bus station** (cnr ul 50 let Oktyabrya & ul Krasnoarmeyska) with the train stations in Belogorsk (₽340, two hours, at least hourly from 7.15am to 7.20pm) and Bureya (₽572, 3½ hours, three daily). Don't miss the awesome mosaic of Soviet *sportsmeny* (athletes) opposite the bus station.

The **River Terminal** (Речной вокзал; ul Chaykovskogo 1), 500m east of the Druzhba Hotel, sends eight daily boats to Heihe, China (one way/return ₽1125/1550, 15 minutes), where there's an evening train to Harbin. You'll need a Chinese visa and a multiple-entry Russian visa to return.

Birobidzhan Биробиджан

42622 / POP 80,000 / MOSCOW +7HR

Quiet and shady, Birobidzhan is the capital of the 36,000-sq-km Jewish Autonomous Region and is a couple of hours shy of Khabarovsk on the Trans-Siberian line (if you're heading east). Its concept has always been a bit more interesting than its reality (as evidenced by the quick influx of Jews coming to 'Stalin's Zion' in the 1930s, then leaving the undeveloped swamp just as quickly). Still, its sleepy provincial feel and riverside setting make it worth a half-day visit – more if the weather's good or if you want to explore the city's Jewish heritage.

The town is quite walkable. The main streets ul Lenina and partially pedestrian ul Sholom-Aleykhema parallel the tracks just a five-minute walk south on ul Gorkogo from the train station. The Bira River is another five minutes along, where you'll find a pleas-

LIFE IN A SOVIET EXPERIMENT

'How can anyone live here?' is the nagging question from many outsiders who can't fathom enduring life at –50°C in winter. Another one, some argue, is '*Should* anyone be living here?'

The Soviet experiment – of (forcibly) relocating millions to develop the Far East and Siberia – has yielded a bizarre network of disconnected cities across one of the world's most forbidding regions. Russia gets colder as you move east, yet population density never falters. During the Soviet era, populations of cities such as Yakutsk and Khabarovsk rose 1000%; Komsomolsk, meanwhile, grew from an empty riverside meadow into an industrial city of more than a quarter million.

That'd be impressive if productivity and expenses were on par with European Russia. But during winters that can stretch over half a year, productivity suffers and expenses go way up, requiring bail-out subsidies.

Siberian Curse, by Fiona Hill and Clifford Gaddy, is a fascinating look at Russia's 'temperature per capita'. It suggests that much of Russia is simply too cold and that over-populated areas in the Far East burden the national economy.

If you stop off at purpose-built towns along the Baikal-Amur Mainline (Baikalo-Amurskaya Magistral; BAM), such as Novy Urgal, or make it further north to Magadan (which has lost over a third of its population since the Soviet Union fell), it's tempting to surmise that the whole region is in decline. The truth is far more chequered. Busy Vladivostok saw a ₽600-billion makeover in preparation for the high-profile Asia-Pacific Economic Cooperation (APEC) summit in 2012, and Sakhalin Island is running wild in oil revenue. Even remote Yakutsk is seeing a surge in population, due largely to income from diamonds and gold in the area.

ant sculpture-lined walkway with piped-in music and peaceful views.

History

The Soviet authorities conceived the idea of a homeland for Jews in the Amur region in the late 1920s and founded the Jewish Autonomous Region in 1934 with its capital at Birobidzhan (named for the meeting place of the Bira and Bidzhan Rivers). Most of the Jews came from Belarus and Ukraine, but also from the US, Argentina and even Palestine. The Jewish population never rose above 32,000, and dropped to 17,500 by the end of the 1930s, when growing anti-Semitism led to the ban of Yiddish and synagogues. The Jewish population rose gradually to about 22,000 by 1991, before Russia's Jews began emigrating en masse to Israel. The Jewish population has levelled off at 3000 to 4000 these days.

Sights & Activities

Jewish Birobidzhan CULTURAL HERITAGE

A few vestiges of Birobidzhan's Jewish heritage remain. Note the Hebrew signs on the **train station**, the lively **farmers market** (ul Sholom-Aleykhema) and the **post office** on the riverfront at the southern terminus of ul Gorkogo. On the square in front of the train station a **statue** commemorates Birobidzhan's original Jewish settlers, and on the pedestrian stretch of ul Sholom-Aleykhema is a quirky **statue of Sholem Aleichem** (Памятник Шолом-Алейхему; *Fiddler on the Roof* was based on Aleichem's stories).

A five-minute walk west from the centre on ul Lenina is a complex containing Birobidzhan's Jewish culture centre, **Freid** (Биробиджанская еврейская религиозная община Фрейд; ☎42622-41 531, 8-924-642 8731; ul Lenina 19; ⏰9am-5pm Mon-Fri), and a synagogue with a small Jewish-history **museum** (Музей еврейской истории; ⏰by appointment) inside. Call or ask around for Rabbi Roman Isakovich, who will give you a tour of the complex, talk local history or find you a souvenir *yarmulke* (skullcap).

Regional Museum MUSEUM

(Областной краеведческий музей; ul Lenina 25; admission ₽100; ⏰10am-6pm Wed-Fri, 9am-5pm Sat) Next door to Freid, this museum has an excellent exhibit on the arrival of Jewish settlers to Birobidzhan in the 1930s, plus boars and bears and a minidiorama of the Volochaevka civil-war battle.

Sleeping

Resting rooms HOSTEL $

(komnaty otdykha; ☎42622-91 605; train station; dm per 12/24hr from ₽550/1100, lyux ₽2000) The simple train-station rooms are probably the best option for a quick visit. It's an easy walk from the centre.

Hotel Vostok HOTEL $$

(Гостиница Восток; ☎42622-65 330; ul Sholom-Aleykhema 1; s/d ₽2500/3300; ❄📶) Birobidzhan's central hotel has bright rooms (but saggy beds) in a good location on a pedestrianised street near the market.

Eating & Drinking

Teatralny SHASHLYK $

(Театральный; pr 60 let SSSR 14; mains ₽200-300; ❄) An average indoor Chinese restaurant in winter, in the warm months its outdoor patio near the river is *the* place to eat shashlyki (meat kebabs) and guzzle draught beer. It's behind Birobidzhan's gargantuan Philharmonic Hall.

Felicita CAFE $$

(ul Gorkogo 10; mains ₽250-780; ⏰10am-midnight; 📶) A short stroll from the train station, Felicita is an attractive, Italian-themed cafe, with coffee, salads, light meals and rather mediocre pizzas.

David Trade Centre RUSSIAN $$

(Торговый центр Давид; cnr pr 60 let SSSR & ul Gorkogo; mains ₽250-750; 📶) At this small shopping gallery you'll find a streetside patio for kebabs and casual dining, plus fast-food stalls inside. It's located diagonally across from the Philharmonic.

Information

Library (ul Lenina 25; ⏰9am-7pm Mon-Thu, to 6pm Fri & Sat) Next door to the museum. Sign up for free internet access (but no wi-fi).

Getting There & Away

Coming from the west on the Trans-Siberian, you can easily stop off, have a look and grab a late train or bus for Khabarovsk.

All Trans-Siberian trains stop here, but if you're heading to Khabarovsk, it's cheaper on the *elektrichka* (suburban train; ₽315, three hours, three daily); a *platskartny* seat on other trains starts at ₽530.

You can also catch *marshrutky* to Khabarovsk (₽280, three hours, hourly until 6pm) from beside the train station.

Khabarovsk Хабаровск

☎4212 / POP 590,000 / ⏲ MOSCOW +7HR

The Far East's most pleasant surprise (and a welcome break after days of relentless taiga on the train), Khabarovsk boasts a dreamy riverside setting, vibrant nightlife and broad boulevards lined with pretty tsarist-era buildings. Unlike so many places, the city has developed its riverside in the public interest. It has a great strolling area with multicoloured tiles, parks, monuments and walkways. A one-day stop is easily filled looking around.

It's hot in summer, but winter temperatures give it the unglamorous title of 'world's coldest city of over half a million people.'

History

Khabarovsk was founded in 1858 as a military post by Eastern Siberia's governor general, Count Nikolai Muravyov (later Muravyov-Amursky), during his campaign to take the Amur back from the Manchus. It was named after the man who got the Russians into trouble with the Manchus in the first place, 17th-century Russian explorer Yerofey Khabarov.

Khabarovsk

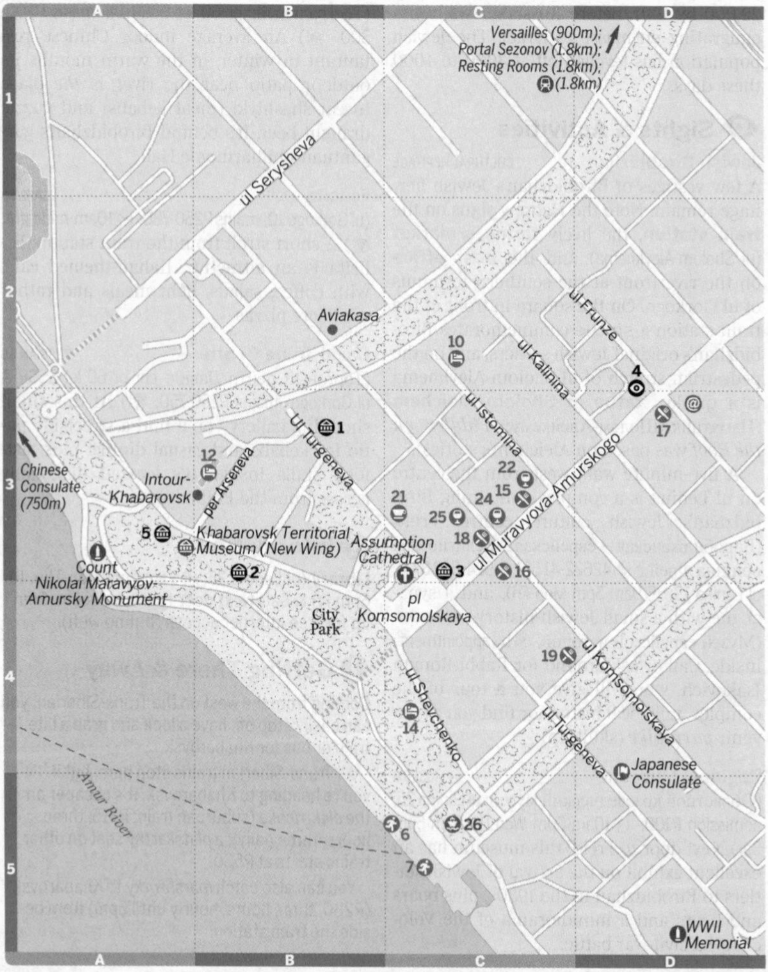

The Trans-Siberian Railway arrived from Vladivostok in 1897. During the Russian Civil War (1920), the town was occupied by Japanese troops. The final Bolshevik victory in the Far East was at Volochaevka, 45km west.

In 1969, Soviet and Chinese soldiers fought a bloody hand-to-hand battle over little Damansky Island in the Ussuri River. Since 1984, tensions have eased. Damansky and several other islands have been handed back to the Chinese.

Sights & Activities

Walking is the main activity in Khabarovsk. Three good spots are the **riverfront**, **Dinamo Park** and **ul Muravyova-Amurskogo** with its impressive turn-of-the-20th-century architecture. Some buildings to look out for on the latter are the striking red-and-black-brick **Far Eastern State Research Library** (Дальневосточная государственная научная библиотека; ul Muravyova-Amurskogo 1), built from 1900 to 1902; the mint-green Style Moderne (Russian take on art nouveau) **Tsentralny Gastronom** (ul Muravyova-Amurskogo 9), built in 1895 and topped by a statue of Mercury; and the former **House of Pioneers** (Дом пионеров; ul Muravyova-Amurskogo 17).

Khabarovsk Territorial Museum MUSEUM

(ul Shevchenko 11; admission ₽350; ⏲10am-6pm, closed Mon & last Fri of month; 📶) Located in an evocative 1894 red-brick building, this museum contains an excellent overview of Russian and Soviet history. Galleries take you decade by decade through the past with fascinating propaganda posters, old film clips, audio snippets, black and white photos (like the sad crowds gathered at the announcement of Stalin's demise) and rooms with period furnishings and accoutrements that give a taste of what life was like.

There's even a small section devoted to the Gulag (fitting, since the nearby prison population was bigger than the city's in the '30s). Another section has garments, sleds and carvings of native peoples. The less intriguing new building has a wing dedicated to the Amur River, with live fish in tanks and more stuffed animals.

Archaeology Museum MUSEUM

(Музей Археологии; ☎4212-24 177; ul Turgeneva 86; admission ₽220; ⏲10am-6pm Tue-Sun) This small five-room gallery displays tools and living essentials from early peoples. Pottery, animal-skin huts, dugout canoes, a tiny model settlement and many early hand tools are here. Don't miss replicas of small 'Paleolithic Madonnas', early carvings (in mammoth tusks) of the female form.

There's also an atmospheric log-lined hut on the main floor, with furs, dried fish, wolf's head and stuffed birds. In front of the museum, check out the reproductions of the petroglyphs found at the ancient Sikachi-Alyan site.

Far Eastern Art Museum ART GALLERY

(Дальневосточный художественный музей; ul Shevchenko 7; admission ₽200; ⏲10am-6pm Tue-Sun) Lots of religious icons, Japanese

Khabarovsk

Sights
1 Archaeology Museum B3
2 Far Eastern Art Museum B3
3 Far Eastern State Research Library C3
4 House of Pioneers D2
5 Khabarovsk Territorial Museum A3
Tsentralny Gastronom .... (see 15)

Activities, Courses & Tours
6 Amur River Cruise C5
7 Amur River Cruise Docks C5
8 Sergey Outfitter F3

Sleeping
9 Amur Hotel F4
10 Boutique Hotel C2
11 Hostel Valencia F3
12 Hotel Intourist B3
13 Hotel Tsentralnaya F1
14 Parus C4

Eating
15 Blin C3
16 Demokratiya C3
17 LaVita D3
18 Maxim C3
19 Russky Restaurant C4
20 Trattoria Semplice F1

Drinking & Nightlife
21 Chocolate C3
22 Gatsby C3
23 Harat's E2
24 Harley Davidson Bar C3
25 Hospital C3

Shopping
Tainy Remesla .... (see 4)

Transport
26 River Terminal C5
Tor .... (see 26)

porcelain and 19th-century Russian paintings are on display here.

Amur River Cruise BOAT TRIPS
(River boat landing; admission from ₽450) Vital to Khabarovsk's rise, the Amur River can be seen on (at times rollicking) party boats. Cruises on the *Moskva-81* depart every two hours from 12.30pm to 12.30am, provided enough customers show up.

Tours

The most popular area tour offered by travel agents is to the interesting Nanai village of **Sikachi-Alyan**, where you can view the Sikachi-Alyan petroglyphs – stone carvings supposedly dating back 12,000 years. Hunting and fishing opportunities abound in the wild and woolly Khabarovsky *kray* (territory).

Portal Sezonov TOUR COMPANY
(Портал Сезонов; ☎4212-398 288; www.dvtravel.ru; ul Leningradskaya 58) Located in the train station, the respected Portal Sezonov runs a wide range of tours, including hiking and fishing trips, as well as city tours. English-speaking guides available.

Sergey Outfitter TOUR GUIDE
(Туристическая компания Вэлком; ☎4212-735 990; www.sergoutfitter.com; ul Dzerzhinskogo 24; ⏰9am-7pm Mon-Sat) Burly Sergey Khromykh is your man if you are looking to do some hunting or fishing in the vast wilderness of Khabarovsk Territory or elsewhere in the Far East.

Festivals & Events

A dazzling display of **ice sculptures** occupies central pl Lenina from January until the spring thaw. Khabarovsk's City Day is a good time to visit; it's 31 May, or the closest Saturday.

Sleeping

Resting rooms HOSTEL $
(komnaty otdykha; ☎4212-383 710; 3rd fl; 4-bed dm 12/24hr ₽800/1200, s 12/24hr ₽1100/1600; wi-fi) The train station's nice resting rooms are a fine option if you're just passing through. Free wi-fi in 15-minute increments.

Kakadu Hostel HOSTEL $
(☎8-914-772 8783; www.kakaduhostel.ru; entrance 1, 7th fl, ul Sheronova 10; dm ₽650-750; air-con wi-fi) This friendly hostel has pleasant four- to eight-bed bunk rooms, which draw a handful of young Russian travellers. There's a kitchen, a tiny verandah in each room and free laundry, but no English is spoken. Get directions before setting out.

★**Hostel Valencia** GUESTHOUSE $$
(☎8-914-172 7262; www.hostelvlc.com; 3rd fl, ul Dzerzhinskogo 21a; r without bathroom from ₽1600) Named after the city where the owners lived for many years, this friendly eight-room guesthouse has bright, attractively designed rooms that are kept sparklingly clean. Span-

ish spoken. Hard to find, the hotel is tucked 75m back from the road (behind a multi-storey hair salon). The owners run two other locations offering similarly good values (on ul Lenina 33 and ul Dikopoltseva 10).

Versailles HOTEL $$
(Версаль; 4212-659 222; http://versal-hotel.net; Amursky bul 46a; s/d incl breakfast from ₽3200/3500;) This cheerful hotel, an easy walk from the train station, has pleasant red-carpeted rooms with fridge and small sitting area. It's set back from the street, fronted with seal lamp posts – just like back in France.

Hotel Tsentralnaya HOTEL $$
(Гостиница Центральная; 4212-303 300; ul Pushkina 52; s/d from ₽1700/1880;) It's been years since the staff would let us see a room (maybe they were burned by Paul Theroux when he stayed here while researching *The Great Railway Bazaar*), but you can expect the standard diet of lightly renovated Soviet fare. Half the 200 rooms look over pl Lenina. A booking fee of 25% applies.

Hotel Intourist HOTEL $$
(Гостиница Интурист; 4212-312 313; http://intour-khabarovsk.ru; Amursky bul 2; s/d from ₽3200/3600;) Teeming with tour groups, this big Bolshevik still breathes as if it's 1975. Service is so-so and the cheaply renovated rooms have thick floral bedspreads and worn carpets (but do have remarkable river views on upper floors). The entrance is on per Arseneva.

★**Boutique Hotel** BOUTIQUE HOTEL $$$
(4212-767 676; www.boutique-hotel.ru; ul Istomina 64; s/d incl breakfast from ₽4600/5500;) Khabarovsk's most foreigner-friendly hotel has large, attractive rooms adorned with black-and-white photos from a bygone era. Throw in gorgeous bathrooms, luxurious white bedspreads and the full complement of mod cons, plus a great location.

Amur Hotel HOTEL $$$
(Гостиница Амур; 4212-221 223; www.amurhotel.ru; ul Lenina 29; s/d incl breakfast from ₽3500/4500;) A solid option, the Amur serves up bright, comfortably furnished rooms that range from small to spacious, and there's a sauna (though it's pricey). It's a long stroll to the riverfront action, but there's a good restaurant on-site (the scallops with black rice is excellent), plus several decent eating and drinking options nearby.

Parus HISTORIC HOTEL $$$
(Парус; 4212-335 555; www.hotel-parus.com; ul Shevchenko 5; r incl breakfast from ₽5700;) Part of a century-old brick building near the water, the 80-room Parus sure makes a grand entrance – with chandeliers, iron staircase and reading room. Rooms are also overdone, but sizeable and with expensive Italian furniture and flat-screen TVs. Friendly, English-speaking service.

Eating

LaVita CAFE $
(ul Maravyova-Amurskogo 26; light dishes ₽130-250; 8.30am-midnight;) A well-situated cafe with comfy chairs, sweet desserts and savoury snacks including quiche (₽130) and pay-by-weight pies filled with meat and cabbage, mushrooms and other ingredients. Decent coffee too.

Stolovaya Lozhka & Tempo Pizza RUSSIAN $
(Столовая Ложка и Темпо Пицца; ul Dikopoltseva 29; meals ₽250-450; stolovaya 9am-9pm, pizzeria 10am-midnight;) One of a host of upmarket *stolovye* (canteens) that have been cropping up all over Russia, this one boasts an outdoor beer patio and is twinned with a pizzeria selling by the slice.

Blin FAST FOOD $
(Блин; Lotus Shopping Centre basement, ul Muravyova-Amurskogo 5; bliny ₽40-100; 10am-11pm) Locals queue up for the bliny here.

Maxim SUPERMARKET $
(Максим; ul Maravyova-Amurskogo 3; 24hr) Good centrally located supermarket.

Trattoria Semplice ITALIAN $$
(4212-206 051; ul Pushkina; pizza small/large around ₽350/520; 11am-11.30pm;) White-painted plank walls, linen curtains and fresh-cut flowers brighten up this downstairs space near pl Lenina. The piping-hot thin-crust pizzas are among the city's best and a small pie can feed two (unless you're famished). One minus: the pounding four-to-the-floor disco beats.

Demokratiya CAFE $$
(Демократия; ul Muravyova-Amurskogo 12; mains ₽350-700; noon-1am;) Join hipsters drinking home brew in this low-lit space. It has good salads and business lunches from ₽180.

Russky Restaurant RUSSIAN $$$
(Ресторан Русский; ☎4212-306 587; Ussuriysky bul 9; mains ₽650-1450; ⊙noon-1am; 📋) The kitsch factor at this Russian-folk-themed restaurant is high but the food is tasty. Feast on Siberian borsch, smoked halibut with pan-seared potatoes or grilled pork loin in one of two dining rooms, one decked out like a wood-lined rustic dwelling, the other evoking imperial pomp.

Drinking & Nightlife

Khabarovsk is most definitely a party town, with arguably the best nightlife east of the Volga.

★**Gatsby** LOUNGE BAR
(☎4212-604 333; ul Istomina 49; ⊙noon-4am Mon-Thu, to 8am Fri & Sat, 5pm-4am Sun; 📶) Handsomely designed Gatsby has a main-level restaurant and lounge (with good food from ₽300 to ₽700). Downstairs is a swanky bar in one room (with big comfy seats around a horseshoe-shaped bar), and a small dance floor with DJ in another room. It draws a young stylish crowd, but the vibe overall is remarkably welcoming. The after parties are legendary here.

Harat's BAR
(ul Maravyova-Amurskogo 44; ⊙5pm-6am) This traditionally decorated Irish-style pub has a good beer selection (with 17 or so on tap) and feels less gloomy than other Khabarovsk drinking spots owing to its upstairs location (with windows!). Live bands play frequently, with occasional cover charges (up to ₽300).

Harley Davidson Bar BAR
(ul Komsomolskaya 88; ⊙24hr) Features nightly shows (rock or country bands, cabaret), 10 brews on tap, tattooed bartenders and a looooong wooden bar. Upstairs is a veran-

TRANSPORT CONNECTIONS FROM KHABAROVSK

DESTINATION	MAIN TRAINS SERVING DESTINATION* & FREQUENCY	RAIL PRICE (₽, PLATSKARTNY/KUPE)	RAIL DURATION	AIRLINES SERVING DESTINATION	AIR PRICE (FROM ₽)	AIR DURATION & FREQUENCY
Beijing	N/A	N/A	N/A	Aeroflot, Aurora	10,300	3hr, 2 weekly
Blagoveshchensk	**35 (daily)**	2300/3800	16hr	Yakutia	4700	2hr, 5 weekly
Irkutsk	1 (even-numbered days), 7 (odd-numbered days), **43 (even-numbered days)**, 99 (odd-numbered days), 133 (odd-numbered days), 207 (even-numbered days)	from 5200/9500	58hr	Aeroflot, Ir-Aero	5800	3¾hr, almost daily
Komsomolsk	351 (daily), **667 (daily)**	from 1100/2000	10hr	N/A	N/A	N/A
Magadan	N/A	N/A	N/A	Aeroflot, Aurora, Ir-Aero, S7, Yakutia Airlines	7700	2¾hr, 3 daily

dah bar with street views. Cover charge runs ₽300 on weekends.

Chocolate CAFE, LOUNGE BAR
(ul Turgeneva 74; mains ₽500-1200; 24hr;) A cafe with a pricey menu of slick international dishes (fajitas, sautéed squid, smoked duck breast) by day, it becomes a prime party spot after hours.

Hospital CLUB
(Клуб Госпиталь; http://hospitalclub.ru; ul Komsomolskaya 79; cover ₽300-1000; Fri & Sat) One of Russia's top clubs, with several packed dance chambers and a consistent line-up of top DJ talent from Russia and abroad. YouTube has highlights.

Entertainment

Platinum Arena SPORTS
(Платинум Арена; 4212-316 140; ul Dikopoltseva 12) This is the home arena for Khabarovsk's ice-hockey team, the Amur Tigers, a hot ticket from October to March.

Lenin Stadium SPORTS
(Стадион Ленина; Riverfront Sports Complex; tickets ₽150) Home to Khabarovsk's first-division football team, SKA-Energiya.

Theatre of Musical Comedy THEATRE
(Хабаровский краевой театр драмы и комедии; 4212-211 196; ul Karla Marksa 64; tickets ₽100-1000) Funny operettas run from November to April; big musical acts run from May to October. There's also the occasional ballet.

Shopping

Tainy Remesla SOUVENIRS
(Тайны ремесла; ul Muravyova-Amurskogo 17; 10am-7pm) This is the best souvenir shop in town, located in the old House of Pioneers building.

DESTINATION	MAIN TRAINS SERVING DESTINATION* & FREQUENCY	RAIL PRICE (₽, PLATSKARTNY/KUPE)	RAIL DURATION	AIRLINES SERVING DESTINATION	AIR PRICE (FROM ₽)	AIR DURATION & FREQUENCY
Moscow	1 (even-numbered days), **43 (even-numbered days)**, 99 (odd-numbered days)	from 9100/16,100	5½ days	Aeroflot, Transaero, VIM Airlines	14,800	8½hr, several daily
Neryungri (via Tynda)	325 (daily)	2700/4800	36hr	N/A	N/A	N/A
Petropavlovsk-Kamchatsky	N/A	N/A	N/A	Aeroflot, Aurora, S7	9800	2½hr, daily
Seoul	N/A	N/A	N/A	Asiana	17,000	3hr, almost daily
Vladivostok	2 (odd-numbered days), **6 (daily)**, 8 (even-numbered days), 100 (even-numbered days), 134 (odd-numbered days), 351 (daily)	from 1700/3000	11-15hr	Aeroflot, Ir-Aero	2200	1¼hr, daily
Yakutsk	N/A	N/A	N/A	Ir-Aero, Yakutia Airlines	13,750	2½hr, daily Mon-Fri
Yuzhno-Sakhalinsk	N/A	N/A	N/A	Aeroflot, Aurora, S7	3500	2hr, 3 daily

*Trains originating in Khabarovsk in bold.

Information

Intour-Khabarovsk (Интур-Хабаровск; ☎ 4212-312 313; www.intour-khabarovsk.com; Hotel Intourist, Amursky bul 2; ⏰ 9am-6pm) This travel agency gives out a free city map.

Knizhny Mir (Книжный мир; ul Karla Marksa 37; ⏰ 9am-8pm) Stock up on Far East maps.

Post office (Почта; ul Muravyova-Amurskogo 28; per hour ₽150; ⏰ internet 8am-8pm Mon-Fri, 9am-6pm Sat & Sun) Get online.

Getting There & Away

Most travel agents book train or air tickets for a modest commission. The best booking agent is **Aviakasa** (Авиакасса; Amursky bul 5; ⏰ 8.30am-8pm Mon-Sat, 9am-6pm Sun) because of its generous opening hours.

AIR

The airport is 7km east of the train station.

BOAT

Many companies at the **river terminal** (Речной вокзал; Ussuriysky bul; ⏰ 8am-7pm) offer morning and evening departures to Fuyuan, China (90 minutes), which cost ₽4000 including tour and overnight lodging. A good company is **Tor** (☎ 4212-584 666). Hydrofoil service to Komsomolsk-na-Amure no longer operates.

BUS

The **bus station** (Автовокзал; ul Voronezhskaya 19), 500m north of the train station (go by tram or bus 4), sends nine buses daily to Komsomolsk (₽500, 6½ hours) and hourly *marshrutky* to Birobidzhan (2¾ hours) until 6pm.

GETTING CHINESE VISAS IN THE FAR EAST

It's best to arrange Chinese visas in your home country, although foreigners with verve can attempt to obtain a Chinese visa on the road. In the Far East, only the consulate in **Khabarovsk** (☎ 4212-302 590; www.chinaconsulate.khb.ru/rus; Southern Bldg, Lenin Stadium 1; ⏰ 11am-1pm Mon, Wed & Fri) provides this service.

A one-month tourist visa for Europeans costs from ₽1200 for five-day processing (expedited visas sometimes possible with a higher fee). Americans pay ₽4800 (10-day processing only). You'll need a letter of invitation, application form and copies of your immigration card, latest hotel registration and Russian visa. All forms are in Russian. Travel agencies in Khabarovsk may be able to assist.

TRAIN

The full-service train station is lovely, with a handy supermarket nearby (to left of station when exiting). Note that almost all trains to Vladivostok are overnight.

Note that the westbound/eastbound 1/2 Rossiya train between Moscow and Vladivostok (*platskart* from ₽14,200) is significantly more expensive than all other trains (*platskart* from ₽9100), and only slightly faster (six days versus six days and 18 hours). The 7/8 train between Novosibirsk and Vladivostok is also relatively expensive.

For Birobidzhan, take any westbound train or a cheaper *elektrichka* (₽320, three hours, three daily).

Getting Around

From the airport, 9km east of the centre, trolleybus 1 goes to pl Komsomolskaya along ul Muravyova-Amurskogo and bus 35 goes to the train station (25 minutes) and bus station. A taxi to the centre from the airport is ₽500; usually ₽300 or ₽400 the other way.

From Khabarovsk's train station, about 3.5km northeast of the waterfront, bus 4 goes to pl Komsomolskaya (board opposite the station and head southeast) and trams 1 and 2 go near pl Lenina.

Trolleybuses and trams cost ₽18.

Vladivostok Владивосток

☎ 4232 / POP 610,000 / ⏰ MOSCOW +7HR

At first look, Vladivostok is something like 'Russia's San Francisco' – a real stunner, with pointed mountains springing up above a network of bays, most strikingly the crooked dock-lined Golden Horn Bay (named for its likeness to Istanbul's). Closer up, it can be a little grey, with Soviet housing blocks squeezed between new condos and century-old mansions. But it's a great place to kick off or finish a trans-Siberian trip – however, be warned: leg muscles not used to the ups and downs of hilly streets will get more sore than a butt on the Trans-Siberian.

Big changes arrived in Vladivostok thanks to the 2012 Asia-Pacific Economic Cooperation (APEC) summit, with billions spent on infrastructure. Timing wise, June can often be grey and wet, while September and October are the nicest, sunniest months (another thing Vladivostok has in common with San Francisco). Vladivostok's City Day is 2 July, or the closest Saturday to it.

History

Founded in 1860, Vladivostok (meaning 'To Rule the East') became a naval base in 1872. *Tsarevitch* Nicholas II turned up in 1891 to inaugurate the new Trans-Siberian rail line. By the early 20th century, Vladivostok teemed with merchants, speculators and sailors of every nation in a manner more akin to Shanghai or Hong Kong than to Moscow. Koreans and Chinese, many of whom had built the city, accounted for four out of every five of its citizens.

After the fall of Port Arthur in the Russo-Japanese War of 1904–05, Vladivostok took on an even more crucial strategic role, and when the Bolsheviks seized power in European Russia, Japanese, Americans, French and English poured ashore here to support the tsarist counterattack. Vladivostok held out until 25 October 1922, when Soviet forces finally marched in and took control – it was the last city to fall.

In the years to follow, Stalin deported or shot most of the city's foreign population. Closed from 1958 to 1992, Vladivostok opened up with a bang – literally (Mafia shoot-outs were a part of early business deals) – in the '90s, and has only started to settle down in recent years.

Vladivostok's infrastructure was torn asunder and rebuilt for the big APEC summit on Russky Island in 2012. The most eye-catching developments include two giant suspension bridges: one across Golden Horn Bay to the previously difficult-to-access Cherkavskogo Peninsula, the other spanning more than 4km to Russky Island across the Eastern Bosphorus Strait. A brand-new university campus opened there in 2012, and officials hope to turn the area into a high-tech research hub in the future – something of a 'Silicon Valley of the East'.

Sights & Activities

Central Vladivostok

On tree-lined streets around the city centre you'll find plenty of tsarist-era buildings from Vladivostok's first crazy incarnation a century past. The main areas for locals to mill about is **pl Bortsov Revolutsii** (on ul Svetlanskaya at the southern end of Okeansky pr) and ul Fokina (aka 'the Arbat'), which is partially pedestrianised and dotted with cafes and shops.

Nearby **Sportivnaya Harbour** has a popular beach and beer and shashlyk stands. You can hire paddle boats and rowboats here, and there's an amusement park just off the waterfront.

Arsenev Regional Museum MUSEUM
(Приморский Государственный Объединенный музей имени В. К. Арсеньева; ☎4232-413 977; ul Svetlanskaya 20; admission ₽200; ⏲10am-7pm Tue-Sun) One of the city's most fascinating museums, the Arsenev Regional Museum, which dates from 1890, recently received a makeover, adding interactive displays to its three floors of galleries.

Exhibits delve into local history, covering early explorers to the region, Vlad's vibrant Chinatown from the early 1900s, and Civil War (with a short silent film playing across a broken screen). In the 'Vremya Dela' room, you can touch and smell the exhibits (the fragrant jar of sea cucumbers is quite powerful). Docents are eager to help, but generally speak Russian only, though occasional English-speaking guides are available for free tours.

Primorsky Picture Gallery ART GALLERY
(Приморская государственная картинная галерея; ☎4232-427 748, 4232-411 162; pr Partizanski 12; admission varies; ⏲11am-7pm Tue-Sun) Vladivostok's bipolar art museum's original locale (ul Aleutskaya 12) has long been under renovation, but may be open by the time you read this. While most of the impressive collection is in storage, bits and pieces rotate through the annexe east of Park Provotsky.

S-56 Submarine MUSEUM
(Подводная лодка С-56; ☎4232-216 757; Korabelnaya nab; admission ₽100; ⏲9am-8pm) Perched near the waterfront, the S-56 submarine is worth a look. The first half is a ho-hum exhibit of badges and photos of men with badges (all in Russian). Keep going: towards the back you walk through an officers' lounge with a framed portrait of Stalin and then onto a bunk room with Christmas-coloured torpedoes. Outside note the '14', marking the WWII sub's 'kills'.

Vladivostok Fortress Museum MUSEUM
(Музей Владивостокская Крепость; ☎4232-400 896; ul Batareynaya 4a; admission ₽200; ⏲10am-6pm) On the site of an old artillery battery overlooking Sportivnaya Harbour, this museum has cannons outside; inside there's a six-room exhibit of photos and many, many guns. English explanations.

Vladivostok

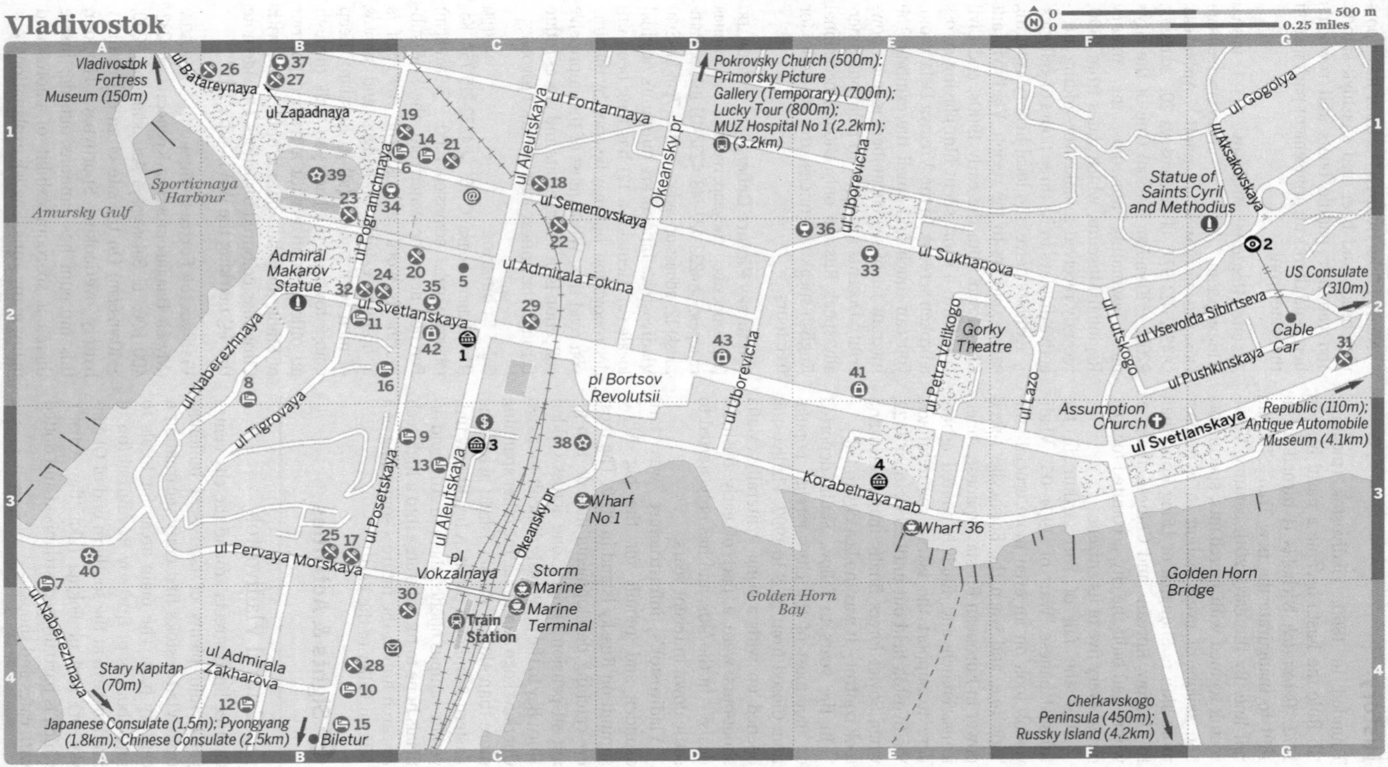
500 m
0.25 miles
Vladivostok Fortress Museum (150m)
ul Batareynaya
ul Zapadnaya
Sportivnaya Harbour
Amursky Gulf
ul Pogranichnaya
ul Aleutskaya
ul Fontannaya
Okeansky pr
Pokrovsky Church (500m); Primorsky Picture Gallery (Temporary) (700m); Lucky Tour (800m); MUZ Hospital No 1 (2.2km); (3.2km)
ul Semenovskaya
ul Uborevicha
ul Gogolya
ul Aksakovskaya
Statue of Saints Cyril and Methodius
Admiral Makarov Statue
ul Admirala Fokina
ul Svetlanskaya
ul Sukhanova
US Consulate (310m)
ul Vsevolda Sibirtseva
Cable Car
ul Pushkinskaya
ul Lutskogo
ul Nabereznaya
pl Bortsov Revolutsii
Gorky Theatre
ul Petra Velikogo
ul Lazo
Assumption Church
Republic (110m); Antique Automobile Museum (4.1km)
ul Tigrovaya
ul Posetskaya
Korabelnaya nab
Wharf No 1
Wharf 36
ul Pervaya Morskaya
pl Vokzalnaya
Storm Marine
Marine Terminal
Train Station
Golden Horn Bay
Golden Horn Bridge
ul Admirala Zakharova
Stary Kapitan (70m)
Japanese Consulate (1.5m); Pyongyang (1.8km); Chinese Consulate (2.5km)
Biletur
Cherkavskogo Peninsula (450m); Russky Island (4.2km)

Vladivostok

Sights

1	Arsenev Regional Museum	C2
2	Funicular Railway	G2
3	Primorsky Picture Gallery	C3
4	S-56 Submarine	E3

Activities, Courses & Tours

5	Dalintourist	C2

Sleeping

6	Antilopa	C1
7	Azimut	A3
8	Equator Hotel	B2
9	Hotel Moryak	C3
10	Hotel Primorye	B4
11	Hotel Versailles	B2
12	Hotel Zhemchuzhina	B4
13	Optimum Hostel	C3
14	Sakura Hostel	C1
15	Teplo	B4
16	Vlad Marine Inn	B2

Eating

17	Belle Bazaar	B3
18	Clover House	C1
19	Dva Gruzina	C1
20	Five O'Clock	C2
21	Korea House	C1
22	Market	C2
23	Mauro Gianvanni	B1
24	München	B2
25	Nostalgiya	B3
26	Oceanarium	B1
27	Paulaner Bräuhaus	B1
28	Pizza M	B4
29	Presto	C2
30	Republic	C4
31	Republic 2	G2
32	Stolovaya No 1	B2

Drinking & Nightlife

33	Moloko & Myod	E2
34	Mumiy Troll	B1
35	Rock's Cocktail Bar	C2
36	Sky Bar	E2
37	Zuma	B1

Entertainment

38	Cukoo	C3
	Philharmonic Hall	(see 29)
39	Stadium Dinamo	B1
40	Yellow Submarine	A3
	Zabriskie Point	(see 40)

Shopping

41	Dom Knigi	E2
42	Flotsky Univermag	C2
43	GUM	D2
	Nostalgiya	(see 25)

Funicular FUNICULAR

(Фуникулёр; ul Pushkinskaya; tickets ₽9; ⏲7am-8pm) Vladivostok's well-oiled **funicular railway** makes a fun 60-second ride up a 100m hill every few minutes. At the top, cross ul Sukhanova via the underpass to a great **lookout** over the bay. It's next to a **statue of Saints Cyril and Methodius** (inventors of the Cyrillic alphabet) on the campus of DVGTU.

The base of the funicular is about a 15-minute walk from the centre.

Outer Vladivostok

Much of the water facing Vladivostok is quite polluted but it gets cleaner as you go north. Sunbathers can get on a northbound *elektrichka* and hop off at any beach that looks good. Try Sedanka, where there are a few resorts with services. You'll find better swimming on Popov or Russky Islands.

Russky Island ISLAND

A fully militarised island for most of the past 150 years, this big island just offshore, which only opened to foreigners in the early 2000s, has been reinvented as a business and academic zone, as home to the sprawling – and off limits to visitors – **Far Eastern Federal University** (www.dvfu.ru) campus. There's great tourism potential here, but at the moment Russky Island is very much a DIY attraction.

Access to the island is by bus over the suspension bridge. Take a northbound bus 29 or bus 15 from Okeansky pr. The more frequent bus 15 takes you to the DVFU campus, from which you can transfer to a minibus 29, which makes a loop, stopping in **Rynda** and other spots on the island. Rynda has a couple of resorts and the best beaches (just hop out when you see one you like). There are many forts on the island, including the **Voroshilov Battery** (Музей Ворошиловская батарея; admission ₽100; ⏲9am-5pm Wed-Sun), where three massive cannons aim roughly at Hokkaido. The battery, now a military museum, was built in 1933–34 and housed 75 soldiers at its peak. Underground you can explore the guts of the battery, while above ground there are great views of the Pacific.

Under construction at time of writing, the massive **Primorsky Aquarium** (http://russian-aquarium.ru) will house an array of sealife exhibits, plus shows of marine mammals.

WORTH A TRIP

AROUND VLADIVOSTOK

The broad, mountainous Primorsky Territory is beloved by locals with cars, who visit the beaches and mountains. You might consider renting a car and doing the same, but note that some areas near the Chinese border require permits. Those without their own wheels lean on pricey tours to get further away. One easy trip to do by public transport is to Nakhodka, where Primorsky's best beaches are a short bus or taxi ride away. Ten daily express buses travel to Nakhodka from Vladivostok's bus station (₽385, three hours); the first is at 8.20am. Less frequent *elektrichki* (suburban trains) make the trip in around five hours (₽258).

Antique Automobile Museum MUSEUM
(Музей автомотостарины; http://automotomuseum.vl.ru; ul Sakhalinskaya 2a; admission ₽100; ⌚10am-6pm Tue-Sun) If you're a bit of a car (or Soviet) nerd, the Antique Automobile Museum is an absolute classic. A room full of Sovietmobiles (motorcycles too) from the 1930s to 1970s includes a 1948 M&M-green GAZ-20 'Pobeda' (Victory). Take bus 31 along ul Svetlanskaya and exit after it reaches ul Borisenko's end.

Fort No 7 FORTRESS
(Форт No 7; admission ₽250; ⌚10am-6pm Tue-Sun) Attention fort fans: Vladivostok teems with sprawling, rather unique subterranean forts built between the late 19th and early 20th centuries to ward off potential Japanese (or American) attacks. Sixteen protective forts (including four on Russky Island) and hundreds of artillery batteries and other military objects encircle Vladivostok. Many buses pass here (like the 107 from the train station); get off at 'Akademicheskaya' stop (one after 'Zarya'), and walk 20 minutes east on the road leading up the hill (you may have to ask directions).

The best to visit is the hilltop Fort No 7, 14km north of the centre. It has 1.5km of tunnels, pretty much untouched since the last 400 soldiers stationed here left in 1923, although the NKVD later used it as an execution chamber. Views are good too. This and other forts can be visited on a tour with Vladivostok Digger Club or with Lotos Co.

Popov Island ISLAND
Just beyond Russky Island, Popov Island is better regarded for its beaches and filled with many guesthouses and dachas (summer country houses). You'll probably need to stay overnight if you head out here, as there is usually only one boat per day (₽100, 1½ hours), departing in the early evening from Vladivostok's first wharf. Ask at a travel agent if they can help with accommodation.

☞ Tours

Vladivostok travel agents run a variety of city and regional tours, but they can get pricey.

Heading outside of Vladivostok into Primorsky Territory, the most interesting tour is probably to **Sikhote-Alin Nature Reserve**, home to the Russian-American Siberian (Amur) Tiger project. It's a short flight or an 11-hour drive to Terney, where the 3440-sq-km forested reserve is headquartered. Chances of seeing a tiger are basically nonexistent, but the reserve is thick with birds, seals and other wildlife, and the scenery is incredible. Dalintourist and Lucky Tour run six-day trips here from about €1300 per person (including guide, transport, accommodation and meals) and can be combined with a stay at Lazovsky Nature Reserve east of Nakhodka, home to a population of about 20 tigers.

The Far East is all about its Amur tigers, and at **Gaivoron**, 235km north of Vladivostok, you can see a couple at the Russian Academy of Sciences biological research reserve, run by Dr Victor Yudin and his daughter. Tours by Vladivostok agents include about 90 minutes of tiger time, lunch and a four-hour ride each way. It's not possible to go independently.

Dalintourist TOUR COMPANY
(☎4232-228 055; www.dalintourist.ru; ul Admirala Fokina 8a; ⌚9am-7pm Mon-Fri, 10am-3pm Sat) Runs area tours and can arrange English-speaking guides.

Lotos Co TOUR COMPANY
(☎4232-414 130; www.lotosco.ru; ul Dalzavodskaya 1, office 303; ⌚10am-6pm Mon-Fri) Offers a comprehensive assortment of tours, including visits to Russky Island, Popov Island and nature trips to the Primorsky Territory (waterfall visits, river rafting).

Lucky Tour TOUR COMPANY
(☎4232-449 944; www.luckytour.com; ul Moskovskaya 1; ⌚9.30am-6pm Mon-Fri) Interesting

tour to Khasan on the North Korea border; requires several weeks' notice.

Vladivostok Digger Club TOUR COMPANY
(Владивостокский диггер-клуб, ВДК; ☎4232-552 086; www.vladdig.org) This outfit leads hour-long to full-day tours of Fort No 7 and other forts, batteries and the tunnels (some 3.5km long) that link them.

Festivals & Events

Vladivostok's big rock festival, **V-Rox** (http://vrox.vladivostok3000.ru), launched in 2013 to much acclaim. Held in mid-August, the four-day fest features some 70 different concerts and DJ sessions around town (including in open-air venues), with performers from Russia, China, Japan, the USA and other corners of the globe.

Sleeping

★Optimum Hostel HOSTEL $
(☎4232-729 111; ul Aleutskaya 17; dm/d ₽750/2100;) In a great central location, Optimum Hostel is the pick of the bunch for value. Clean wood-floored dorm rooms sleep three to six, and there's free laundry and a guest kitchen. Bonus: there's usually someone on hand who speaks a bit of English. It's set in a grand eight-storey 1930s building topped with statues. Head up the steps from street level and look for the 'Optimum' buzzer.

Antilopa HOSTEL $
(☎4232-727 115; 4th fl, ul Pogranichnaya 6; dm ₽450;) This tiny three-room hostel is a friendly, well-priced option in the centre. Noise from the bar next door can be an issue for light sleepers. Russian only spoken. Free laundry.

Teplo HOSTEL $$
(☎4232-909 555; www.teplo-hotel.ru; ul Posetskaya 16; dm/d ₽650/2000;) New in 2014, Teplo brings a dash of style to Vlad's lodging options with a lounge-like lobby (with sofas and table football), and a white-brick corridor leading back to the small but appealing rooms. Each is equipped with TV, fridge and half bath (shower and sink only). There's free laundry and a guest kitchen, and the location on a quiet but central street is excellent.

Vlad Marine Inn HOSTEL $$
(☎4232-208 0280; www.vlad-marine.ru; ul Posetskaya 53; dm ₽500, d with/without bathroom ₽2100/1600;) In a green clapboard building, this appealing new hostel has just five rooms, each with polished wood floors and ample natural light. Dorm beds have small individual flat-screen TVs, and the three doubles are quite nice for the price. The downside: it's hard to find. Look for the tiny shrub-lined lane leading uphill off Posetskaya.

Sakura Hostel GUESTHOUSE $$
(☎4232-773 011; 3rd fl, ul Semenovskaya 5; dm/d/tr ₽810/1620/2300;) A pleasant but simple six-room guesthouse with a great location, Sakura has twittering caged birds, and quirkily furnished rooms full of toy stuffed animals and books. Run by a friendly old soul (who speaks Russian only). Guest kitchen.

Hotel Moryak HOTEL $$
(Гостиница Моряк; ☎4232-499 499; www.hotelm.ru; ul Posetskaya 38; s/d from ₽2100/2600;) This grey-brick yet cheerful place has an endearing lobby with a stuffed version of the hotel namesake – a sea man. The rooms are compact with thin walls (and mattresses) and *tiny* bathrooms. Threadbare econo rooms are quite worn. Laundry is a reasonable ₽250 per bag. No lift.

Equator Hotel HOTEL $$
(Гостиница Экватор; ☎4232-300 110; www.hotelequator.ru; ul Naberezhnaya 20; s/d from ₽3500/3800;) This old-school Soviet hotel has basic midrange rooms that are fairly spacious but minimally equipped. Book an upper-floor even-numbered room for a sea view.

Azimut HOTEL $$
(☎4232-412 808; www.azimuthotels.com; ul Naberezhnaya 9; s/d from ₽2970/3330;) Under renovation at the time of writing, this place has fairly dumpy rooms whose best feature is the excellent sea views. It's in a peaceful location, but a long (uphill) walk to the centre. Check-in is on the 7th floor, where there's also a small terrace bar with fine views.

Hotel Zhemchuzhina HOTEL $$
(Гостиница Жемчужина; ☎4232-414 387; www.gemhotel.ru; ul Bestuzheva 29; s/d from ₽3500/3800;) Formerly the Chayka, this is a well-located but charmless cheapie. Registration costs ₽100. Pay extra for wi-fi.

Hotel Versailles HOTEL $$$
(Гостиница Версаль; ☎4232-264 201; www.hotel-versailles.ru; ul Svetlanskaya 10; s/d incl breakfast ₽5800/6300;) The Versailles does a decent job of recapturing the pre-USSR grace of the century-old hotel that reopened in the '90s, despite enigmatic pairings in the

lobby ('70s lounge seats, tsarist-style chandeliers). Quarters are plenty roomy with exquisite furniture and lovely bathrooms.

Hotel Primorye HOTEL $$$
(Гостиница Приморье; ☎4232-411 422; www.hotelprimorye.ru; ul Posetskaya 20; s/d incl breakfast from ₽4000/4200; @ 📶) In a good location, Primorye has decent rooms with playful details such as funny artwork and a clock, though the design is rather dated and the beds are rock hard. The best rooms are two-room suites with views of the warships in Golden Horn Bay. An enticing bakery adjoins the lobby.

✕ Eating

Eating options coat the town, offering more class and types of cuisine than pretty much anywhere between here and Moscow. Some restaurants offer 'business lunches' from noon to 4pm for ₽200 to ₽350. In good weather, open-air stands sell beer (₽150) and cook up sizzling shashlyki (₽250) and *shawarma* (doner kebab; ₽150) on the waterfront north of Sportivnaya Harbour.

Stolovaya No 1 CAFETERIA $
(Столовая №1; ul Svetlanskaya 1; meals ₽180-250; ⊙7am-1am; 🚭📶🖉) A mix of old-timers and students line up for above-average *stolovaya* fare and appealing ambience – complete with Anglo rock on the stereo, vintage posters (note the giant USSR wall map) and a bar serving espresso drinks and booze. Great central location.

Five O'Clock CAFE $
(ul Admiral Folkina 6; snacks ₽40-100; ⊙8am-9pm Mon-Fri, 9am-9pm Sat, 11am-9pm Sun; 🚭🖉📋) This much-loved local haunt on pedestrianised ul Admirala Folkina serves coffee, muffins, cakes and quiche, all made daily and sold for less than an espresso costs at most other cafes.

Republic CAFETERIA $
(Республика; ul Aleutskaya; meals ₽180-320; ⊙9am-11pm Mon-Fri, 10am-11pm Sat & Sun; 🚭🖉) These perfectly respectable twin *stolovye*, one located on ul Aleutskaya, the other on ul Svetlanskaya, draw more than a couple of cheap dates with their tasty Russian dishes, home brew (from ₽70) and funky interiors. Both have bars on-site.

Clover House FAST FOOD, SUPERMARKET $
(ul Semenovskaya 15; ⊙10am-9pm; 🚭📶🖉) A convenient mall housing a supermarket with a deli, and a top-floor food court with incredible views (and free wi-fi).

Open-air market MARKET
(off ul Semenovskaya & ul Aleutskaya) Stock up on provisions in the open-air market across from Clover House.

★Pyongyang KOREAN $$
(Пхеньян; ul Verkhneportovaya 68b; mains ₽350-750; ⊙noon-midnight; 🖉) Staffed by female newcomers from North Korea who periodically break out in karaoke, this Democratic Republic of Korea–sponsored establishment is just strange enough to be considered a must-visit. You can pick from a photo menu of excellent food such as *bibimbap* (rice mixed with fried egg, sliced meat and other stuff) and spicy fried pork with kimchi.

★Mauro Gianvanni PIZZA $$
(Мауро Джанванни; ☎4232-220 782; ul Fokina 16; mains ₽300-700; ⊙noon-midnight; 🖉📋) This slick little brick-oven pizzeria – run by an Italian – has a modern interior, though most sit out on the deck when weather behaves. The dozen-plus pizzas are crispy and tasty, probably the best east of the Ural Mountains.

Belle Bazaar CAFE $$
(ul Pervaya Morskaya 6/25; mains ₽350-800; ⊙10am-midnight) A pleasant cafe with comfy armchairs amid living-room-like decor (lamps, wallpaper, shelves of knick-knacks). A fine place to linger over decadent desserts, salads or pastas.

Oceanarium INTERNATIONAL $$
(Океанариум; ul Bateryenaya 4; mains ₽400-900; ⊙noon-midnight) Above the oceanarium, this welcoming and handsomely sited eating-and-drinking spot has fine views over the harbour and serves up salads, grilled meats and fish (plus hookahs) to a trendy crowd. Decent beers are on hand (including Guinness and Paulaner on tap).

Nostalgiya RUSSIAN $$
(Ностальгия; ☎4232-410 513; ul Pervaya Morskaya 6/25; mains ₽300-700; ⊙9am-10pm; 📋) This compact, long-running restaurant offers hearty and tasty Russian meals with a little for-the-tsars pomp. Most visitors come for the souvenir shop or a snack at the cafe.

Korea House KOREAN $$
(Semenovskaya 7b; mains ₽400-800; ⊙noon-midnight; 📶📋) A first-rate place for barbecue meat, sushi and the classic *bibimbap.*

It's tucked down a lane, barely visible from Semenovskaya.

Dva Gruzina GEORGIAN $$
(Два Грузина; ul Pogranichnaya 12; mains ₽180-360; ⏲11am-1am;) Sample trademark Georgian *khachapuri* (cheese bread) and juicy plates of *chanakhi* (lamb, eggplant and tomato stew) and barbecued beef.

Presto CAFE $$
(ul Svetlanskaya 15; mains ₽280-720; ⏲9am-11pm;) A good pit stop for coffee, desserts and bistro fare (quiche, mussels, risotto, crêpes) with a jazzy soundtrack and small cafe tables.

Pizza M PIZZA $$
(Пицца М; ☎4232-413 430; ul Posetskaya 20; pizzas ₽270-520; ⏲11am-11pm;) Classier than its name might suggest, the M (next to Hotel Primorye) is one of Vlad's coolest hang-outs, with two unique rooms setting their style sights higher than the humble slice. The pizzas are quite good.

Paulaner Bräuhaus GERMAN $$
(ul Fontannaya 2; mains ₽350-700; ⏲11am-1am) Step into this spacious new beer hall for excellent Paulaner brews made on-site, which go nicely with the roast duck, oven-baked spare ribs, crackling roast pork and other meaty dishes. Waitstaff in lederhosen and Bavarian plaid up the charm factor.

München GERMAN $$
(Мюнхен; ul Svetlanskaya 5; mains ₽400-700; ⏲noon-2am;) More meaty meals and towers of home brew in a basement beer-hall setting.

Drinking & Nightlife

★ **Zuma** LOUNGE BAR
(☎4232-222 666; ul Fontannaya 2; ⏲11am-2am Sun-Thu, 24hr Fri & Sat;) A stylish but welcoming place, this restaurant-lounge is decked out in an elaborate but classy Angkor Wat–themed interior, replete with design surprises (check out the massive black granite bar). Cocktails are pricey (around ₽400), but there's Leffe on tap and mouthwatering pan-Asian cooking (sushi, dumplings, stir-fries), plus creative salads, rack of lamb and more (mains ₽400 to ₽1000).

Stary Kapitan PUB
(Старыий Капитан; ☎4232-771 077; www.old-captainpub.ru; Leitenanta Shmidta 17a; ⏲noon-1am Sun-Thu, to 3am Fri & Sat) Facing the marina, the Old Captain has an excellent selection of draft beers, such as German Weihenstephan (pints around ₽300). Lots of great seafood dishes (pan-seared tiger prawns and scallops) and appetisers (salted herring with black-bread toast) go nicely with the brews (mains ₽435 to ₽900).

Reserve on weekends, when there's live music. In the same complex are two other restaurants, including Parus with outdoor waterfront views.

Mumiy Troll MUSIC BAR
(Мумий Тролль; ul Pogranichnaya 6; ⏲24hr) A fun and lively bar that draws a mix of locals and expats, rock-loving Mumiy Troll has live bands most nights (from 10pm). There's rarely a cover.

Rock's Cocktail Bar BAR
(ul Svetlanskaya) If you prefer a grungier crowd, this basement dive is for you. Cool kids get dancing – and things often get sloppy – late night, as the DJ pays homage to Kurt, Layne, Zack and other '90s icons.

Moloko & Myod LOUNGE BAR
(Молоко и Мёд; ul Sukhanova 6a; mains ₽400-700; ⏲noon-midnight Sun-Thu, to 2am Fri & Sat;) A trendy spot with a streetside terrace, 'Milk & Honey' has a daily brunch plus coffee, pricey cocktails and upscale dishes such as seafood risotto. Blankets warm terrace dwellers on chilly evenings.

Sky Bar LOUNGE BAR
(12th fl, Hotel Hyundai, ul Semenovskaya 29; ⏲6pm-2am) Offers great views.

Yellow Submarine CLUB
(ul Naberezhnaya 9a; cover ₽100-500) Right next to Zabriskie Point, this thumping club draws a younger crowd to hear a mix of live music and techno-spinning DJs.

Cukoo CLUB
(Ку-Ку; Okeansky pr 1a; cover ₽500; ⏲10pm-2am Mon-Thu, to 6am Fri & Sat) One of Vladivostok's poshest clubs, the dance floor here seethes at weekends. Dress to impress to hurdle face control (see boxed text, p106).

Entertainment

Stadium Dinamo SPORTS
(Стадион Динамо; ul Pogranichnaya; tickets ₽180-300) The popular local football team, Luch-Energiya, plays games at this bayside stadium from April to November.

Zabriskie Point LIVE MUSIC
(Забриски Пойнт; ☎4232-215 715; ul Naberezhnaya 9a; cover ₽500-800; ⏲9pm-5am

Tue-Sun) Zabriskie is Vladivostok's main rock and jazz club, drawing an older crowd to view live-music acts such as Blues Line. Pricey, but not without character.

Philharmonic Hall CLASSICAL MUSIC
(Филармония; ☎4232-223 075; ul Svetlanskaya 15) Hosts classical-music and jazz performances.

Shopping

Flotsky Univermag OUTDOOR GEAR
(Флотский универмаг; ul Svetlanskaya 11; ⏰10am-7pm Mon-Fri, to 6pm Sat & Sun) For unusual souvenirs, follow the navy – this outfitter has those cute blue-and-white-striped navy undershirts (₽270) and other navy gear, as well as useful travel gear such as flashlights, knives, maps and toothpaste. Also has an OK map selection.

Nostalgiya SOUVENIRS
(Ностальгия; ul Pervaya Morskaya 6/25; ⏰10am-8pm) Nostalgiya keeps a good range of pricey handicrafts (wood boats from ₽250 and way up) and many art pieces.

GUM SOUVENIRS
(ГУМ; ul Svetlanskaya 35; ⏰10am-8pm Mon-Sat, to 7pm Sun) This Soviet-style department store is the Far East's most elegant art deco building. Some traditional souvenirs on the 1st floor.

Information

There are currency-exchange desks and ATMs all over town.

Dom Knigi (Дом Книги; ul Svetlanskaya 43; ⏰10am-7pm Mon-Sat, 11am-5pm Sun) The best spot for city and regional maps. Though not entirely up to date, the official city website, www.vladivostok-city.com, is useful for pretrip planning. It has loads of restaurant and entertainment listings.

Interface (Интерфейс; ul Semenovskaya 8; per hour ₽70; ⏰9am-2am)

MUZ Hospital No 1 (МУЗ - Больница №1; ☎4232-453 275; ul Sadovaya 22)

Post office (Почта; ul Aleutskaya; per MB ₽5.30; ⏰8am-10pm Mon-Fri, 9am-6pm Sat & Sun) Post, telephone and internet opposite the train station.

Sberbank (Сбербанк; ul Aleutskaya 12; ⏰8.45am-8pm Mon-Sat, 10am-5pm Sun) Accepts travellers cheques (2% commission).

Getting There & Away

Ticket agents all over town sell plane and train tickets, including **Biletur** (Билетур; ☎4232-

TRANSPORT CONNECTIONS FROM VLADIVOSTOK

DESTINATION	MAIN TRAINS SERVING DESTINATION & FREQUENCY	RAIL PRICE (₽, PLATSKARTNY/KUPE)	RAIL DURATION	AIRLINES SERVING DESTINATION	AIR PRICE (FROM ₽)	AIR DURATION & FREQUENCY
Beijing	351 to Ussurinsk (Mon & Thu)	*kupe* 5400 (to Harbin)	40hr (transfer in Harbin)	Aeroflot, China Southern, S7	9500	2½hr, almost daily
Harbin	351 to Ussurinsk (Mon & Thu)	*kupe* 5400	40hr	Aeroflot	6600	1¼hr, 2 weekly
Irkutsk	1 (even-numbered days), 7 (odd-numbered days), 99 (even-numbered days), 133 (even-numbered days)	from 6000/11,900	70hr	S7, Ural Airlines	13,500	4hr, daily

407 700; ul Posetskaya 17; ⏲8am-7pm Mon-Sat, 9am-6pm Sun).

AIR

Vladivostok has a newly renovated airport (www.vvo.aero), located in Artyom (50km from the centre), with convenient rail access to the centre.

BOAT

Storm Marine (☎4232-302 704; www.parom.su; office 124, Marine Terminal; ⏲9am-1pm & 2-6pm Mon-Fri) sends a passenger-only ferry to Donghae, South Korea (from US$205 one way, 20 hours), continuing on to Sakaiminato, Japan (from US$265 one way, 43 hours), every Wednesday at 2pm.

BUS

Buses to Harbin, China, depart daily (except Sunday) around 6.30am (₽2900, eight hours) from the **bus station** (ul Russkaya), 3km north of the centre. There are also frequent departures for Nakhodka (four hours) and other destinations in the Primorsky Territory. Some southbound destinations may be off limits to foreigners without a permit.

TRAIN

Save money by avoiding the Rossiya (1) train to Moscow.

The Harbin train is a headache, with many stops and a long border check. Departures are early evening on Mondays and Thursdays, but the first night you only go as far as Ussurinsk, where they detach your car from the 351. You stay overnight in Ussurinsk and depart the next day for the border and Harbin. It's much quicker and easier to take a bus to Harbin. If you're headed to Beijing by train, you'll need to go to Harbin first and transfer there.

Getting Around

TO/FROM THE AIRPORT

A speedy rail link (the plush Aeroexpress) connects the train station with the airport (43km north in Artyom). There are 10 trains daily, departing every one or two hours between 8am and 8pm (50 minutes, ₽200).

Bus number 107 (₽100) also connects the train station and airport, departing every one to two hours from 8.25am to 8pm.

A taxi booth in the arrivals area charges ₽1500 for trips to the centre (45 minutes to one hour).

LOCAL TRANSPORT

From in front of the train station, buses 23, 31 and 49 run north on ul Aleutskaya then swing east onto ul Svetlanskaya to the head of the bay. For trips of more than 5km, you'll save money ordering a taxi by phone. Try **PrimTaxi** (☎4232-555 255) or the curiously named **Cherepakha** (Turtle; ☎4232-489 948).

Khabarovsk	1 (even-numbered days), 5 (daily), 7 (odd-numbered days), 133 (even-numbered days), 351 (daily)	from 1700/3000	11-15hr	Aeroflot, Ir-Aero	2200	1¼hr, daily
Magadan	N/A	N/A	N/A	S7	13,600	3hr, 2 weekly
Moscow	1 (even-numbered days), 99 (even-numbered days)	from 9600/16,600	6 days	Aeroflot, S7, Transaero,	9900	10hr, frequent
Petropavlovsk-Kamchatsky	N/A	N/A	N/A	Aeroflot, Aurora, S7	10,600	3½hr, daily
Seoul	N/A	N/A	N/A	Aeroflot, Korean Air	11,500	2½hr, daily
Yakutsk	N/A	N/A	N/A	Aurora, Yakutia Airlines	10,600	3hr, 3 weekly
Yuzhno-Sakhalinsk	N/A	N/A	N/A	Aeroflot, S7	7300	2hr, daily

EASTERN BAM

The eastern half of the Baikal-Amur Mainline (Baikalo-Amurskaya Magistral; BAM), covering 2400km from Khani (where the borders of the Sakha Republic, Zabaikalsky Territory and Amurskaya oblast collide) to Sovetskaya Gavan, is perhaps not as visually stimulating as the more mountainous western half, but is still mesmerising.

The highlights of the eastern BAM are the BAM museum in Tynda, the unofficial BAM capital, and the pastel-coloured pseudotsarist architecture of Komsomolsk-na-Amure, where you can also ski, visit Nanai villages or take a Gulag-camp tour. There's not much between Tynda and Komsomolsk besides often-lifeless trees, their roots severed by cruel permafrost below, and a slew of rather uninspired Soviet towns created to finish the railroad. Disembark only if you're searching for ghost towns or gold (prospecting is rife in this region). If you do get off, prepare to wait for up to a day for the next train.

A few links cut down to the Trans-Siberian. From Tynda, you can cut down to Skovorodino on the so-called Little BAM, built long before the BAM proper with slave labour in the 1930s. Other links south are at Novy Urgal and Komsomolsk. The end of the line comes near Vanino, where you can catch a ferry to Sakhalin Island.

Tynda Тында

41656 / POP 35,500 / MOSCOW +6HR

The king of the BAM, Tynda is a nondescript BAM HQ flanked by low-lying pine-covered hills. Many stop here, as it's a hub for trains between Severobaikalsk, Komsomolsk-na-Amure and, on the Little BAM, Blagoveshchensk to the south, or, on the in-progress Amur-Yakutsk Mainline (Amuro-Yakutskaya Magistral; AYaM), Neryungri and Tommot to the north. Don't expect quaint. Tynda's fully Soviet – there was nothing but a few shacks before BAM centralised its efforts here in 1974.

Sights & Activities

Besides the BAM Museum, about the only other thing worth checking out in Tynda is the dramatic sledgehammer-wielding **BAM worker statue** (on ul Mokhortova 10, just south of central ul Krasnaya Presnaya, near its eastern end). **Zarya** is a native Evenki village nearby. Bus 105 from the train station goes eight times daily (30 minutes).

BAM Museum MUSEUM
(Музей истории БАМа; ul Sportivnaya 22; admission with/without guide ₽35/25; 10am-2pm & 3-6pm Tue-Fri, to 7pm Sat) Tynda's pride and joy has four rooms of BAM relics and photos (no English), but also covers native Evenki culture, WWII, local art and regional wildlife. Don't miss the 9m-long 'barrel of Diogenes' parked in the yard, where many later BAM workers lived during the railroad's construction. The museum is hard to find: After crossing the pedestrian bridge from the train station, take the first left, continue 200m and turn right up Sportivnaya, where you'll soon see it on your left.

One section covers the Little BAM and the Gulag prisoners who built it in the 1930s. They lived (and died) in 24 BAM *lagery* ('bamlag', or labour camps) between Tynda and Bamovskaya. Photos chronicle the extreme hardships these prisoners endured. Two rooms are dedicated to the big BAM, sections of which were built in the 1930s, 1940s and 1950s before Stalin died and the project was mothballed. Displays cover the period between its relaunch in 1974 and

WHAM BAM, IT'S THE RED ELVIS!

One of the more bizarre tours of all time rolled through Tynda in August 1979 when the 'Red Elvis' – Dean Reed, an American singer turned Marxist – did a 19-day tour on the Baikal-Amur Mainline (Baikalo-Amurskaya Magistral; BAM), immortalised in his song 'BAM' ('Everybody sing along… the towns are here to stay, it's the future of our day!').

His show at Tynda's Festivalnaya Hill drew 25,000 spectators, but didn't kick off the way he wanted: according to one story, told on the priceless website www.deanreed.de, a local refused to let the American use his horse for a dramatic cowboy entrance.

Reed remains virtually unknown in the West – not surprising with songs like 'Wake Up America' and photos of him chumming around with Central American revolutionaries. He died under mysterious circumstances in East Germany in 1986.

Tip: Hours – and hours – of enjoyment can be had YouTubing Dean's videos. You can read more about him in *Comrade Rockstar* by Reggie Nadelson.

OVERLAND FROM TYNDA TO YAKUTSK

Travellers in Tynda often have their sights on Yakutsk in the Sakha Republic. To get to Yakutsk you must first take a train to **Neryungri**, 5½ hours north. From there you can either fly with Yakutia Airlines (₽10,500, 1¾ hours, daily except Sunday), or embark on one of the Far East's classic overland journeys: 15 to 20 bumpy hours in a Russian UAZ jeep or van to cover 810km on the Amuro-Yakutsk Mainline (Amuro-Yakutskaya Magistral; AYaM) highway.

Daily departures from the Neryungri train station are timed for the 6.22am arrival of the train from Khabarovsk. Most trips are in 11-passenger vans, but if passengers are lacking you may end up in a four-passenger jeep. The price varies with the season, but typically costs around ₽3500 per person. It's a pretty trip that cuts over a mountain pass and through tracts of virgin taiga (mountain pine) before traversing the Lena by *parom* (car ferry) an hour south of Yakutsk. However, it's extremely rough in patches and quite dusty in the warmer months.

Passenger services on the AYaM train line run further north to Aldan (six hours) and Tommot (eight hours), but you'll keep well ahead of the train (and avoid a possible overnight stay in either Aldan or Tommot) by getting a head start from Neryungri.

The AYaM train line actually extends a couple of hundred kilometres beyond Tommot, although passenger services terminate there. The line is being extended to Nizhny Bestyakh (opposite Yakutsk on the Lena River), and there are plans to open the entire route to passenger services. This may happen within the next couple of years, but we're not taking bets.

completion in 1984 (although it wasn't made fully operational until 1991).

Alexey Podprugin OUTDOORS
(☎8-914-552 1455; bamland@mail.ru) Runs kayaking, hiking and cross-country skiing trips.

Festivals & Events

Liven up your visit by arriving during a festival. March sees the **Reindeer Hunter and Herder Festival**. The **Bakaldin Festival** rotates between several nearby Evenki villages in late May or early June, with traditional song, dance, reindeer rides and plenty of reindeer shashlyki and other native delicacies.

Sleeping & Eating

Resting rooms HOSTEL $
(komnaty otdykha; ☎41656-73 297; 6/12/24hr from ₽640/980/1650) Comfy and clean dorm rooms in the train station. Shower available for nonguests (₽150).

Hotel Yunost HOTEL $$
(Гостиница Юность; ☎41656-43 534; ul Krasnaya Presnaya 49; s/d from ₽2000/3700, s/d without bathroom ₽1000/2400) Faded but fine option in centre; Dervla Murphy recuperated here as related in *Through Siberia by Accident*.

Piv Bar Teremok PIZZA $
(Пив Бар Теремок; ul Krasnaya Presnaya; mains around ₽380; noon-midnight; wi-fi) Serves up palatable pizzas, Drakon draught beer (from Khabarovsk) and free wi-fi, with seating on an open-sided verandah. Turn left at the eastern end of Krasnaya Presnaya and walk up 50m.

Information

The train station has an ATM and left luggage office (₽120).

Getting There & Away

The train station – the city's most striking landmark – is across the Tynda River. A pedestrian bridge leads 1km north to ul Krasnaya Presnaya.

Train 75 heads via BAM to Moscow (*kupe/platskartny* ₽14,700/8000, five days) on even-numbered days, stopping in Severobaikalsk (*kupe/platskartny* ₽4200/2400, 27 hours), while train 77 to Novosibirsk (*kupe/platskartny* ₽11,300/6200, 67 hours) takes the Little BAM south on odd-numbered days to connect with the Trans-Siberian line at Skovorodino.

There are several daily departures to Neryungri, including the 325 (from ₽620, 5½ hours), which departs around 1am. Train 364 trundles to Komsomolsk daily at 5.20pm (*kupe/platskartny* ₽4300/2400, 36 hours), and 325 heads daily to Khabarovsk at 2am via Skovorodino (*kupe/platskartny* ₽4300/2400, 28 hours, daily).

Komsomolsk-na-Amure
Комсомольск-на-Амуре

☎4217 / POP 280,000 / MOSCOW +7HR

After days of taiga and grey Soviet towns, Komsomolsk-na-Amure hits the BAM adventurer like a mini St Petersburg.

Komsomolsk-na-Amure

Komsomolsk-na-Amure

Sights
1 Municipal Museum of Regional Studies B4
2 Nauka (Science) Mosaic A2
3 WWII Memorial A4
4 WWII Mosaic B3

Activities, Courses & Tours
5 Nata Tour A2
6 River Cruises A4

Sleeping
7 Biznestsentr B4
8 Dacha Krushcheva B2
9 Hotel Voskhod A2
10 Resting Rooms A1

Eating
11 Bistro B2
12 Kofeynya B2
13 Shinok Pervach A4

Komsomolsk was built virtually from scratch by Stalin in the 1930s as a vital cog in the Soviet Union's military industrial complex.

Set along a few grand boulevards, the city is worth a night or more if you are getting on or off the BAM. Nearby attractions include ski slopes, Nanai villages and rafting.

The location was no accident: the city was far removed from potential prying eyes along the Pacific coast and Chinese border, yet its position along the Amur allowed for relatively easy transport of goods. Imitating the tsars, Stalin erected elaborate neo-Renaissance and neoclassical buildings in the city centre, only festooned with stars, crescents and statues of model Soviet citizens instead of the usual angels and goblins. To build the city he enlisted Communist Youth League (Komsomol – hence the city's name) volunteers as well as Gulag labourers. Around town, factories sprouted up to produce ships, weapons, electricity and, most famously, Sukhoi (Su) fighter jets in a factory that still works today.

Sights & Activities

Just east of the river terminal is a **beach**, which is well attended on nice days.

Soviet Mosaics STREET ART

Komsomolsk has a wealth of wonderful murals. Most were the creation of Khabarovsk-based artist Nikolai Dolbilkin, who lived here in the 1950s and '60s. Among the best are the double triptych **WWII mosaic** (2nd fl, cnr pr Mira & ul Truba) in the central grey *dom kultura* building near Sudostroitel Park (now inside a children's play space); the **nauka (science) mosaic** (pr Lenina) at the Polytechnical Institute, a block east of Hotel Voskhod; and the stunning **electric worker mosaic** (alleya Truda) on the side of the TETs electric station (be mindful of the belligerent security guards at this last one).

Municipal Museum of Regional Studies MUSEUM

(cnr alleya Truda & ul Kirova; admission ₽220; 9.30am-5pm Tue-Fri, 10am-5pm Sat & Sun) In a newly inaugurated building near Sudostroitel Park, several rooms of photos and knick-knacks show how Komsomolsk rose from the tent camps of original pioneers in 1932 to an industrial Soviet city. It also contains some old fish-skin jackets and other Nanai artefacts, plus a space suit not unlike Gagarin wore. A bit pricey for the sure-to-be-quick visit.

Memorials
MONUMENT

Just northwest of the river terminal is the impressive **WWII memorial**, which features stoic faces chipped from stone, with nearby pillars marking the years of WWII. Other memorials include a garbage-strewn sculpture park dedicated to **Gulag victims** (near pr Lenina 1).

River Cruises
BOAT TRIPS

(River Terminal; admission ₽250) On summer weekends, you can hop aboard 90-minute cruises along the Amur River. Boats depart at 3pm Saturday and Sunday as well as 7pm Thursday and Saturday. Buy tickets onboard.

☞ Tours

Nata Tour
TOUR COMPANY

(Ната-Тур; ☑ 4217-201 067; www.komsomolsk-nata.ru; office 110, ul Vasyanina 12; ⊙ 10am-6pm Mon-Fri) Located in the big grey building in back, this experienced travel service arranges three- to five-hour 'Stalin tours' of city communist sites (including a Gulag camp; from ₽1200 per person); adventure tours involving fishing, rafting or skiing; and day trips and/or homestays at Verkhnyaya Ekon. White-water rafting trips involve a train ride to Novy Urgal on the BAM. Slower one- to several-day floats can be done closer to Komsomolsk. Tours of the **Yury Gagarin Aircraft Factory**, where the Su jets are built, can also be arranged.

⌕ Sleeping

Nata Tour can arrange homestays (₽1000 per person including breakfast).

Resting rooms
HOSTEL $

(komnaty otdykha; ☑ 4217-284 193; train station; dm 12/24hr from 640/1100, s 12/24hr without bathroom ₽935/1650) A fine option if you need a break from sleeping on trains.

★ Biznestsentr
HOTEL $$

(Бизнесцентр; ☑ 4217-521 522; bc@etc.kna.ru; ul Dzerzhinskogo 3; s/d incl breakfast from ₽2800/3500; ❋@☎) Komsomolsk's most modern, business-oriented hotel has bright, comfortably furnished rooms with modern bathrooms (including space-shuttle-like shower capsules). English-speaking receptionists are on hand too.

Dacha Krushcheva
GUESTHOUSE $$

(Дача Хрущёва; ☑ 4217-540 659; ul Khabarovska 47; r ₽2100-3400; ❋☎) Built for Nikita Khrushchev, this backstreet dacha is a step

back in time. The suites could fit a Young Pioneers troupe and all six rooms have 1970s furnishings, but big new windows. There's a 25% booking charge.

Hotel Voskhod
HOTEL $$

(Гостиница Восход; ☑ 4217-535 131; pr Pervostroiteley 31; s/d from ₽2850/3300; ❸@☎) A 10-minute walk from the train station, this eight-storey beast has decent recently renovated rooms.

✖ Eating

In the summer you can feast on shashlyk (₽200) and cold drinks along the riverfront overlooking the beach.

Market
MARKET

(Рынок; cnr pr Lenina & pr Mira) Load up on essentials at this small outdoor market.

Kofeynya
CAFE $$

(Кофейня; ul Oktyabrsky 48; snacks ₽60-130; ⊙ 24hr; ❸☎) A fine spot for eggs, blin or *kasha* (porridge) in the morning, set meals at lunchtime (₽170 to ₽250) and light snacks at other times, plus diverse (but weak) coffees.

Bistro
CAFETERIA $

(ul Lenina 19; meals ₽180-300; ⊙ 9am-10pm) Beside pl Lenina, this clean, modern *stolovaya* serves tasty, affordable staples: baked dishes, roast meats, and the usual beet or potato salads are all on offer.

★ Shinok Pervach
UKRAINIAN $$$

(Шинок Первач; ul Dzerzhinskogo 34/5; ul Internatsionalny; mains ₽450-850; ⊙ noon-1am; ☎▣) Among the best restaurants in town, Shinok Pervach serves up tasty grilled fish, roast meats and zingy salads (try the beetroot, walnut and prune for its subtle spice). The chunky wooden tables and circular dining room festooned with ribbons (maypole style) bestow a certain peasant chic to the place. It's pricey, and watch out for hidden charges. Located off ul Internatsionalny, a 15-minute walk northwest of the waterfront.

ⓘ Getting There & Around

Local and long-distance buses leave from the **bus station** (☑ 4217-542 554; ⊙ 6am-10.30pm) near the river. Buses bound for Khabarovsk (from ₽640, six hours) leave every 90 minutes or so from 7am.

For a DIY adventure, head down the Amur River by hydrofoil to its terminus in Nikolayevsk-na-Amure (from ₽4085, 11 hours). The boat departs

BAM ENDS, SAKHALIN BECKONS

Baikal-Amur Mainline (Baikalo-Amurskaya Magistral; BAM) completists will end up in the grey Soviet port town of Vanino (actually the BAM ends 15 minutes beyond Vanino, in Sovetskaya Gavan-Sortirovka). From Vanino, there is a theoretically daily 4pm boat (in reality, it leaves when full when the weather allows) to Kholmsk on Sakhalin Island (tickets ₽1670 to ₽3025, 18 hours). The Russian-only information numbers are ☎42137-74 088 in Vanino and ☎42433-66 098 in Kholmsk. Call the day before to reserve a seat – they should have a reasonable idea of whether the next day's ship will sail. But no guarantees. Or just go and take your chances.

three days a week from the river terminal (currently 7am on Monday, Thursday and Friday).

From Komsomolsk's pink train station the excruciatingly slow 351 leaves daily for Vladivostok (*kupe/platskartny* ₽3700/2100, 24½ hours). There are also services to Khabarovsk (*kupe/platskartny* from ₽2000/1100, 10 hours).

On the BAM, 363 heads west to Tynda (*kupe/platskartny* ₽4300/2400, 37 hours, daily); to reach Severobaikalsk, change in Tynda. The daily train 351 heads east to Vanino (*kupe/platskartny* ₽2200/1200, 11 hours). The BAM's first/last stop, 'Sovetskaya Gavan-Sortirovka', 15 minutes east of Vanino, is not to be confused with the city of Sovetsakaya Gavan, an hour away from Vanino by bus.

Within the city, handy tram 2 runs from the train station along ul Lenina and pr Mira to the river terminal (₽15).

Verkhnyaya Ekon Верхняя Эконь

Tucked between the Amur River and bear-inhabited hills, this village of 500 (of which half are Nanai) makes a fun day trip from Komsomolsk across the river. Its school has a small **Nanai Museum** (Музей Нанай), with old shaman costumes and plenty of Nanai traditional pieces. It's possible to hike up the mountain.

Three daily buses come from Komsomolsk (₽50, one hour), but if you arrange for a taxi you can visit an eerie, unfinished 800m-long BAM tunnel at nearby **Pivan** village (north of the Amur Bridge), including pieces abandoned after WWII broke out.

SAKHA REPUBLIC

Looming like a giant inverted iceberg north of the BAM line, the sprawl of remote Sakha Republic (the country's largest) takes time and effort (or an air ticket) to reach. Life is noticeably different here. The buildings of Yakutsk – a friendly place where Russians are the minority – stand on stilts. Sakha is the correct term for the local ethnic group commonly called by the Evenki name for 'horse people': Yakut. The republic is also known as Yakutia.

The most unrepentant dissidents (including Decembrists and Bolsheviks) were exiled in Sakha. It was a 'jail without doors', as the swamps, mountains, ice and bug-infested forests did a pretty good job of keeping people from going anywhere.

Yakutsk Якутск

☎4112 / POP 215,000 / ⏲ MOSCOW +6HR

Talk about bizarre: the world's coldest city stands on stilts (the shifting permafrost collapses buildings otherwise) and is pretty much cut off from the already remote Far East; a dodgy road to the BAM line takes a ferry ride and 24 hours, and airfares cost over ₽13,000 just to reach Vladivostok! Yet, unlike so many remote Russian cities out here, Yakutsk roars with optimism and gusto. New buildings – some with far more dramatic architecture than you'll see anywhere else in Russia – are popping up all over the city and the population is rising (all the regional gold and diamonds certainly have something to say about why). Brace yourself for extreme weather. It's *hot* in June and July (reaching the upper 30s) and freezing in winter (January averages −40°C).

Yakutsk was founded in 1632 as a Cossack fort and later served as a base for expeditions to the Pacific coast. In the late 19th century, Yakutsk became a boozy, bawdy r'n'r centre for the region's increasing number of goldminers. It reclaimed that reputation somewhat in the wild, anything-goes period following the collapse of the Soviet Union.

Sights & Activities

National Art Museum MUSEUM
(Художественный Музей; ☎4112-335 274; ul Kirova 9; admission ₽300; ⏲10am-6pm Wed-Sun) If time is limited, don't miss this excellent museum, with Sakha-themed exhibits covering local craft-making traditions

(mammoth-tusk carvings, reindeer boots, finely carved urns for *kumiss*, fermented mares milk), landscape paintings and portraits. Don't miss the captivating paintings of village life by Andrey Chikachev (born 1967), the most famous living Sakha artist.

Mammoth Museum and Archaeology & Ethnography Museum MUSEUM
(☎4112-361 647; UGU Bldg, ul Kulakovskogo 48; admission Mammoth/Ethnography museum ₽200/150; ⏰10am-5pm Mon-Fri) All that permafrost in the area has resulted in some

GETTING OUT THERE IN SAKHA (& BEYOND)

Sakha Republic, cut by the 4265km Lena River (which inspired a certain Vladimir to change his name to Lenin), is bigger than France and, as costs are high even in Yakutsk, getting very far is expensive and requires prearranged transport and guides. But if you have the dosh and the will, Sakha and the neighbouring Chukotka offer the chance to journey to some of the world's last great unexplored places. Winter is generally the best time to travel, as *zimniki* (winter roads) open up and there are no bears and mosquitoes to contend with. Websites http://askyakutia.com and http://askmagadan.com are great resources for travel around here. Tour companies in Yakutsk and elsewhere in the Far East can organise tours to any of the following and ensure you have the required permits.

Topolinoe

Topolinoe, 705km northwest of Yakutsk, can be reached by road and is a great place to meet Evenki reindeer herders. Shared taxis go out here sporadically for about ₽5000 one way per person. You will likely have to change cars 295km southwest of Topolinoe in Khandyga, which has accommodation and a Gulag museum.

Tiksi

Found where the Lena drops into the Arctic Ocean, Tiksi (a strategic air-force town in Soviet times, and still a tightly controlled zone) can be reached by air but is best reached on a passenger ferry run by Lena Tur Flot. The four-day trip (one way) from Yakutsk in a shared 3rd-class cabin costs ₽10,500 per person (₽19,000 in a 1st-class cabin) aboard the Mechanic Koulibin. Simple meals are available on board. The ship departs Yakutsk roughly every 10 days from July to early September. You'll need a permit to go, which can take up to two months from a travel agency.

For a bit more luxury, you can take a 14-day cruise from Yakutsk, offered three times a year by US-based Arctic Odysseys between July and early September. The cruise takes in Sottintsy, the Lena Pillars and several other stops – while plenty of birdwatching opportunities loom, particularly at the delta at the Arctic Ocean. A double cabin costs US$3980 per person.

Magadan

A dream for hardened adventurers, the infamous Kolyma Hwy – aka the 'road of bones' due to the countless Gulag labourers who froze to death building it – makes for a tough three- or four-day journey 2200km west to Magadan, the one-time Gulag town known as 'the Gateway to Hell'. It's possible to try to negotiate a ride with a truck for the trip, or to hire 6WD vehicles going in either direction; Visit Yakutia (p541) leads three trips in the summer, for US$2600 per person. The ride on the frozen Indigirka River is quicker after December; things get slushy and often impassable by May.

It's of course much easier to fly to Magadan. Its cruel weather and cruel past aside, Magadan is pretty and pleasant, with a rather European centre in pastels. The rare visitor can camp at a Gulag camp, fish or raft on the Arman River, cross-country ski, see birds, hike – or set off on a reverse journey along the Kolyma Hwy to Yakutsk. Contact the excellent **DVS-Tour** (☎41322-23 296; www.dvs-tour.ru; pr Lenina 3; ⏰ 9am-1pm, 2-6pm Mon-Fri) for help with Magadan trips or to arrange Gulag-camp tours.

Chukotka

'Out there' to a region already considered 'out there', Chukotka Autonomous Region brushes its icy nose with Alaska's and is almost solely inhabited by indigenous peoples and a fair share of whales and walruses. The two main access points are Anadyr and Provideniya, where a number of US-based tours come by charter flight via Nome (June to August). Yakutia Airlines has a weekly flight to Anadyr from Khabarovsk (from ₽30,200 one way).

Yakutsk

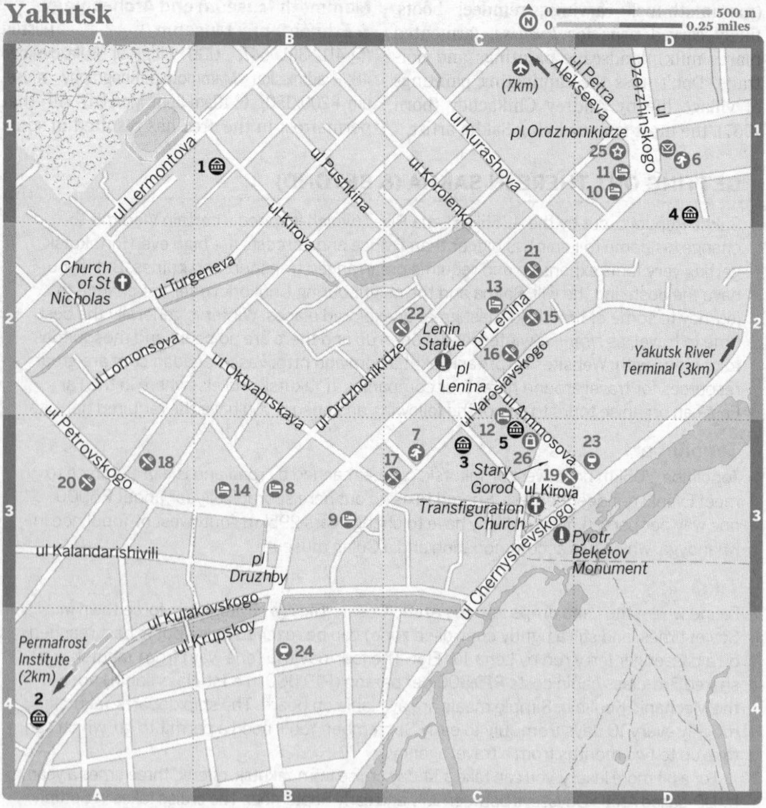

Yakutsk

Sights
1 Khomus Museum........B1
2 Mammoth Museum and Archaeology & Ethnography Museum........A4
3 National Art Museum........C3
4 Regional Museum........D1
5 Treasury of the Sakha Republic........C3

Activities, Courses & Tours
6 Lena Tur Flot........D1
Planet Yakutia........(see 22)
7 Yakutia Travel........C3

Sleeping
8 Bed & Breakfast Bravo........B3
9 Centre Guest House........B3
10 Hotel Lena........D1
11 Hotel Sterkh........D1
12 Hotel Tygyn Darkhan........C2
13 Polar Star Hotel........C2
14 Uyut Mini Hotel........B3

Eating
15 Bar Onegin........C2
16 Bon Ami........C2
17 Jo........C3
18 Kita Gava........A3
19 Makhtal........C3
20 Muus Khaya........A3
21 Stolovka Rublevka........C2
Tamerlyan........(see 11)
22 Tuimaada Torgovy Tsentr........C2
Tygyn Darkhan........(see 12)

Drinking & Nightlife
23 Dikaya Utka........D3
24 Evropa Klub........B4

Entertainment
25 Sakha Theatre........D1

Shopping
Globus........(see 21)
26 Kuday Bakhsy........C3

of the world's best-preserved mammoth skeletons. You can see some at this excellent two-pack of museums. See if they'll let you glimpse into the Mammoth Museum's refrigerated storage room, which is chock-full of mammoth and woolly-rhino bones. The Ethnography Museum (closed on Mondays) has one of the Far East's better displays on indigenous peoples.

Regional Museum MUSEUM

(Якутский государственный объединенный музей истории и культуры народов Севера; ☎4112-425 174; pr Lenina 5/2; admission ₽150; ⏲10am-5pm Tue-Sun) A good place to delve deeper into Sakha culture, it covers local minerals and the region's first Russian settlers along with the standard Soviet natural-history and WWII exhibits. Outside, there's a huge whale skeleton found in 1961.

Khomus Museum MUSEUM

(Музей хомуса; ul Kirova 31; admission ₽200; ⏲10am-1pm & 2-6pm Mon-Sat) *Khomus* (Jew's harps) play a big part in Sakha culture – concerts occur year-round, when performers imitate natural sounds such as a horse neighing. The unexpected (and unfortunately soundtrack-free) Khomus Museum has a collection showcasing international Jew's-harp heroes from present and past. Ask the welcoming staff for a demonstration. You can also buy your own harp here (from ₽3000 to ₽5000) or purchase CDs.

Treasury of the Sakha Republic MUSEUM

(Выставка Сокровищница Республики Саха; www.expo-gx.ru; ul Kirova 12; admission ₽200; ⏲tours 10am-4pm Mon-Fri) Pay a visit to this unique museum for a look at Yakutia's rich mineral wealth combined with fine craft traditions. You'll see exquisite carvings in mammoth tusks, tiny sculptures adorned with precious stones and a radiant 11-carat diamond. Admission is by 40-minute guided **tour**, which departs on the hour (except 1pm).

Tours

Visit Yakutia TOUR COMPANY

(☎8-924-660 9930; www.visityakutia.com) This excellent outfit offers overland trips to Magadan, visits to reindeer herders, winter journeys to Omakhon, Lena Pillar trips, and a range of other outdoor activities – trekking, fishing, rafting, reindeer sledding. It's run by English-speaking Bolot Bochkarev, who runs the excellent information site http://AskYakutia.com.

Planet Yakutia TOUR COMPANY

(☎8-914-270 6565; www.planetyakutia.com; 1st fl, ul Ordzhonikidze 38; ⏲10am-9pm) A remarkably with-it English-speaking tour company, it can answer just about any Sakha-related question you have and find a way to get you where you need to go. Also runs a range of more organised tours, all outlined on its website. It's inside the Tuimaada mall.

Yakutia Travel TOUR COMPANY

(☎4112-351 144, 8-924-662 1144; www.yakutia-travel.com; office 66, ul Yaroslavsky 30/1; ⏲9am-6pm Mon-Fri) Experienced English-speaking staff can prearrange Sakha trips or sell Lena Pillars boat trips. It also offers trips to Sakha villages. An English-speaking guide is ₽1500 per day.

Lena Pillars Ленские Столбы

The area's most popular tour is the boat cruise to the 80km-long Lena Pillars (Lenskie Stolby), a 35-million-year-old stretch of Kimberly limestone on the edge of the Lena River, about 220km south of Yakutsk. Jagged spires and picturesque crumbling fronts (almost bricklike) look like ancient ruins if you squint. Many companies offer one- and two-day tours to the Lena Pillars (including Planet Yakutia and Yakutia Travel. You can also book passage on a comfy 70-cabin ship for a 36- or 48-hour cruise offered by **Lena Tur Flot** (Лена тур флот; ☎4112-263 535; www.lenaturflot.ru; office 100, ul Dzerzhinskogo 2; 36hr cruise s/d cabin ₽9000/14,000). Both tours include about five to eight hours at the pillars, a shaman ceremony and the chance to fish or swim. Meals cost extra (from ₽2400). Boats leave from Yakutsk once or twice weekly from June to September and should be booked ahead through a travel agent or Lena Tur Flot.

Buotama River

Between the Lena Pillars and Yakutsk, cutting west from the Lena, this narrow tree-lined river is popular for kayaking/rafting camping trips, where you can spot bears and fish in the wild. These start at about ₽7500 per person per day not including meals.

Festivals & Events

One of Russia's better-kept secrets, the major Sakha festival of **Ysyakh** (tough to pronounce; try 'ehh-sekhh') is celebrated all over the Sakha Republic each year in June. The biggest event occurs in Us Khatyn field near the village of Zhetai, about 20km north of Yakutsk, on the first Saturday and Sunday after the summer solstice. Don't miss the opening, at noon on Saturday, when hundreds of costumed performers, including Chinggis (Genghis) Khaan–like soldiers, reenact battles and people hand out free skewers of horse meat and offer sips of horse milk.

Stands are filled by Sakha from across the republic, often set up around modern *irasa* (tepees); the rare foreigner is likely to be drawn in for horse meat and *kumiss*. The 'no alcohol' (other than mildly alcoholic *kumiss*) policy keeps things sober during the day, but it can't be guaranteed later on, when many locals come to greet the dawn – an all-night party for young and old. It's well worth planning your Yakutsk detour around this event.

Packed buses head to/from the festival regularly from pr Lenina in Yakutsk (45 minutes).

🛏 Sleeping

Travel agencies can set you up with apartments or homestays with full board from ₽3000 per person per night.

Centre Guest House GUESTHOUSE $
(☑8-924-168 1370; two.mdx@gmail.com; Bldg 2, ul Yaroslavskogo 30; r without bathroom ₽1200-1800; 🛜) This welcoming budget-friendly place has five simple rooms: each with thin mattresses and tile floors that look like reindeer fur. There's just one toilet and one shower/sink. It's the last entrance (before having to stoop down to continue along the footpath), on the 3rd floor, number 56.

Uyut Mini Hotel HOTEL $
(Мини-гостиница Уют; ☑8-984-117 3549; ul Petrovskogo 10; dm/d without bathroom ₽800/1600) Uyut's best feature is its rock-bottom price. All rooms are communal doubles or triples that share a clean bathroom. In other cost-saving news, it provides a kitchen for self-caterers and does laundry for ₽100 per load.

★ Bed & Breakfast Bravo GUESTHOUSE $$
(☑4112-405 111; www.bravo-hotel.ru; 9th fl, ul Ordzhonikidze 49; s/d incl breakfast from ₽1900/2900; 🌐🛜) Bravo offers a winning combination of friendly service and spotless modern rooms outfitted with large flat-screen TVs, big windows, desks and excellent mattresses. The only minus is the paltry breakfast. It's the second entrance in back. Ring buzzer number 64.

Hotel Ontario GUESTHOUSE $$
(☑8-914-222 9030; hotelontario@bk.ru; ul Sergelyakhskoe 13km; s/d from ₽2900/3400; 🌐🛜) Though it's far from the centre, pine-fringed Hotel Ontario lets you wake to singing birds rather than honking horns. Rooms are small, modern and carpeted but cosy with plank walls that smell of cedar. There's a restaurant on-site. It's 13km out of town (a ₽300 taxi ride). Bus 25 stops near here (at Borisovka Pervaya).

Polar Star Hotel HOTEL $$$
(Гостиница Полярная звезда; ☑4112-341 215; pr Lenina 24; s/d incl breakfast from ₽4850/7900; 🌐🌐🛜🌐) Considered the top business hotel in town, Polar Star has fine modern rooms reached by glass elevator. Service can be variable, but there's usually someone on hand who speaks a bit of English. Lots of amenities including a travel agency and a restaurant that serves up European dishes.

Hotel Lena HOTEL $$$
(Гостиница Лена; ☑4112-424 214; www.lena-hotel.ru; pr Lenina 8; s/d incl breakfast from ₽3700/5200; 🛜) A rather pricey but well-located midrange option with upgraded Soviet-style rooms, apart from the worn-out beds.

Hotel Tygyn Darkhan HOTEL $$$
(Гостиница Тыгын Дархан; ☑4112-435 109; www.tygyn.ru; ul Ammosova 9; s/d incl breakfast from ₽5300/6800; 🌐🌐🛜🌐) Just steps from pl Lenina, TD's regular rooms follow a standard Soviet template, but are freshly updated and have modern bathrooms. Rates include use of the indoor pool, sauna and gym.

Hotel Sterkh HOTEL $$$
(Гостиница Стерх; ☑4112-342 701; www.sterkh.biz; pr Lenina 8; s/d incl breakfast from ₽3300/4700; 🌐🌐🛜) This place has bright, pleasantly furnished rooms (with mint green walls), but like other traditional hotels in Yakutsk, it's pricey for what you get. No lift.

🍴 Eating

Stolovka Rublevka CAFETERIA $
(Столовка Рублевка; ul Korolenko 2; meals ₽200-400; ⏱9am-11pm) With leather armchairs and white brick walls, Rublevka is a surprisingly elegant *stolovaya* with a small selection of smoked fish, soups, dumplings, salads and cooked meat and fish plates. Great prices, too.

DON'T MISS

PERMAFROST KINGDOM

Yakutsk's quirkiest attraction allows you to experience the region's famously frosty climes even at the height of the sweltering summer. At **Permafrost Kingdom** (Царство вечной мерзлоты; km7, Vilyusky Trakt; admission ₽400; ⏰9am-7pm) two neon-lit tunnels burrowed into a permanently frozen hill 13km west of Yakutsk's centre have been filled with dozens of fabulous, never-melting ice sculptures of local pagan gods and a host of more recognisable objects and characters – a sitting Buddha, a pharaoh, Ded Moroz (Russia's Santa Claus), a woolly mammoth and an icy interpretation of Picasso's *Guernica*. There's even an ice luge you can slither down wearing the glistening silver coats and woolly boots they hand out to keep you insulated.

Permafrost affects almost every aspect of life in Yakutsk, obstructing drainage, causing unstilted buildings to bow and then collapse, spontaneously chucking up mounds of earth, and emitting enough methane to possibly alter the earth's climate catastrophically. The Permafrost Kingdom is a great way to get up close and personal with this nebulous and omnipresent beast. In this subterranean permafrost zone, the temperature ranges from −7°C in summer to a balmy (relative to outside temperatures) −20°C in winter. Caves adjacent to the kingdom are used for electricity-free cold storage in the warm months.

True permafrost nerds might check out the **Permafrost Institute** (☎4112-334 423; ul Merzlotnaya 36; individual/group per person ₽900/450; ⏰by appointment 9am-5pm), about 2km west of the city centre. It has a lab that stays a constant −6°C, but high prices make this more of a tour-group option.

Bon Ami CAFE $

(ul Yaroslavskogo 22; desserts ₽80-280; ⏰8.30am-8pm Mon-Fri, from 10am Sat & Sun) Pleasant cafe with frothy coffee drinks, buttery croissants and other temptations (cherry Danishes, apple strudel, honeycake, bliny). The takeaway shop is downstairs.

Tuimaada Torgovy Tsentr INTERNATIONAL $

(Торговый центр Туймаада; ul Ordzhonikidze 38; mains ₽150-400; ⏰10am-9pm; 📶) A central mall with a 2nd-floor food court whipping up pizza, noodles, sushi and bubble tea (head to Cafe Shokolodnitsa for free wi-fi). There's also a grocery store on the basement level.

★**Chochur Muran** YAKUT $$

(Чочур Муран; ☎8-924-661 6100; km7, Vilyusky Trakt; meals ₽600-1600; ⏰noon-midnight; 📋) In a wonderful Cossack-style lodge filled with antiques, massive moose heads and a few mammoth artefacts, Chochur Muran is a must-stop if you are heading out to the nearby Permafrost Kingdom. It's the best place around to try Sakha delicacies such as *stroganina* (frozen raw *chyr*, a white fish common in Arctic rivers), *zherebyatiny* (fillet of colt meat) and reindeer. Dog sledding and ice fishing are on offer in winter. Reservations advised.

Tygyn Darkhan YAKUT $$

(Тыгын Дархан Ресторан; ☎4112-343 406; Hotel Tygyn Darkhan, ul Ammosova 9; mains ₽400-800; ⏰noon-3pm & 6-10pm; 📋) Though the atmosphere is lacking, Tygyn Darkhan is *the* place to score Sakha specialities in the centre. Try *indigirka* (frozen raw *chyr* and onions – a bit like eating frozen fish in a ball of snow) and Darkhan *pelmeni* (horse meat dumplings), washed down with a glass of *kumiss* and topped off with whipped cream and foxberries.

Makhtal YAKUT $$

(Махтал; ul Kirova 2; mains ₽350-750; ⏰noon-1am) In the *stary gorod* (old town), Makhtal is one of the Yakutsk's most atmospheric options, with thick log walls adorned with traditional tapestries and handsomely attired waitstaff gliding about in broad-shouldered tunics and long flowing robes. The food is decent but not outstanding. Try *indigirka*, spicy *salat s zherebyatinoy* (horse-meat salad) or *olenina* (venison).

Muus Khaya YAKUT $$

(Муус Хайа; ☎4112-445 508; ul Petrovskogo 13; mains ₽350-800; ⏰noon-2am; 📶📋) A good option for local delicacies, Muus Khaya is a winning combination of restaurant, bar and bowling alley. The ₽300 business lunch is a deal. Ask burly owner Yegor Makarov about his travels around the republic. His photos of frosty landscapes, Yakutian horses and village life adorn the walls.

Kita Gava JAPANESE $$
(Китагава; ul Lermontova 85; meals ₽500-1200; 11am-1am) The best place in town for sushi, Kita Gava is a buzzing place that serves up tasty sashimi platters, noodle soups and plump *gyoza* (dumplings). It's good but not cheap (10-piece platters run ₽680).

Bar Onegin EUROPEAN $$
(Бар Онегин; pr Lenina 23; mains ₽350-650; noon-2am;) Bar Onegin whips up tasty salads, sushi, pastas and grilled-fish dishes. The fettuccine with salmon comes with a dollop of caviar on top. It's a fairly stylish spot, with Pushkin-esque stencils on the wall, and a chatty cocktail-sipping crowd at night.

Jo CAFE $$
(ul Yaroslavskogo 26; mains ₽350-600; 24hr;) An American-style diner with big booths and a hipster vibe, Jo serves up omelettes, burgers, salads and some vegetarian fare (veg lasagna, couscous with vegetables), plus coffees and free wi-fi.

Tamerlyan MONGOLIAN $$
(Тамерлан; 4112-342 802; pl Ordzhonikidze; meals from ₽600; noon-midnight Sun-Wed, to 2am Thu-Sat;) Known for its salad bar (₽89 per 100g) and pick-and-watch-cook (then eat) Mongolian BBQ (₽500 for one trip).

Drinking & Nightlife

Dikaya Utka PUB
(Дикая утка; ul Chernyshevskogo 20; noon-2am Mon-Fri, from 2pm Sat & Sun) A favourite of expats, the spacious wood-lined 'Wild Duck' is the go-to spot for lively conversation and refreshing brews, and there's decent pub grub on hand. There's live music (admission ₽300) on Friday and Saturday nights (from 9pm). It's in the *stary gorod*.

Evropa Klub CLUB
(Европа Клуб; pr Lenina 47; 6pm-6am) The most popular club in the centre, Evropa is a five-storey complex with dance club, sports bar, bowling alley and, uh, strip club.

Galaxy CLUB
(ul Krasilnikova 8) An upscale nightclub experience, 5km out of the centre.

Entertainment

Sakha Theatre THEATRE
(Саха Театр; 4112-341 331; pl Ordzhonikidze) A strikingly modern venue that has theatre and music in the Sakha language; engaging even if you don't get a word of it.

Shopping

Kuday Bakhsy SOUVENIRS
(Кудай Бахсы; ul Ammosova 3a; 10am-7pm Mon-Fri, to 6pm Sat & Sun) In the old city, this is the best place in town to browse for crafts and souvenirs. You'll find mammoth-tusk carvings, leather slippers, reindeer boots and gloves, embroidered dolls, Jew's harps, carved wooden bowls, paintings, knives, bizarre magnets and CDs of traditional music. There's a jewellery shop next door.

Information

There are plenty of ATMs around in the top-end hotels and all along pr Lenina.

Globus (Глобус; ul Korolenko 2; 9am-6pm Mon-Fri, 10am-4pm Sat) Useful topo maps.

Getting There & Away

As of this writing, passenger trains from Neryungri go as far north as Tommot in southern Sakha. The new AYaM passenger train will eventually link Yakutsk with Tommot, Neryungri and Tynda, though work had stalled indefinitely as of 2014.

AIR

The airport, 7km northeast of the town centre, is well connected to most of Russia but tends to have high prices. The following are among the many destinations you can fly to these cities:

Irkutsk From ₽13,000, three hours
Khabarovsk From ₽8000, 2¾ hours
Moscow From ₽15,000, six hours
Novosibirsk From ₽15,200, four hours
Vladivostok From ₽13,000, 3¼ hours

Yakutia Airlines (www.yakutia.aero) flies to all of the above, as well as to Magadan (from ₽12,000, two hours) and serves numerous far-flung destinations in Sakha, including Neryungri (₽10,500, 1¾ hours, daily except Sunday) and Tiksi (from ₽32,000 return, three hours, three weekly). Many air-ticket offices line pr Lenina.

BOAT

The most interesting ferry service is the four-day trip from Yakutsk to Tiksi, departing every 10 days between July and early September offered by Lena Tur Flot (p541). Departures are from the Yakutsk river terminal (Речной вокзал), 2km northeast of the centre.

Also from the river terminal, you can traverse the Lena by *parom* (car ferry) to Nizhny Bestyakh on the opposite bank (₽200, one hour). Departures are every 80 minutes from 7am to 6.20pm. Don't miss the last boat back at 7.40pm.

BUS & TAXI

The rough UAZ journey to Neryungri crosses the Lena an hour south of Yakutsk in industrial Mokhsogollakh. Arrange a ride through a travel agent or call ☎8-914-275 4041.

Getting Around

A handy city bus is line 8 (₽18), which goes past pr Lenina's hotels on its way between the river terminal and bus station. Bus 4 goes to the airport – catch it heading east on pr Lenina. Taxis charge around ₽150 for rides around the centre.

Around Yakutsk

Yakutsk's city limits can get a little grey and grubby at times, but things get natural – and wild – quickly once you leave town. By just hiring a taxi (about ₽600 to ₽800 per hour), you could reach a couple of places; others involve boats.

About 45km south on the road to Pokrovsk, **Orto Doidu** (Орто Дойду; ☎4112-350 373; admission ₽150; ⊙noon-midnight Wed-Sun) is a nature complex with local animals and shady trails, plus an architectural area with Sakha totems and a *balangan* (traditional Yakut winter house).

Sottintsy, about 60km north (on the opposite side of the Amur), is home to the **Druzhba Historical Park**, a collection of traditional dwellings. To get here take a bus to Kangalas and cross the Lena River by *parom* to Sottintsy; it's a 2km walk from the riverbank to the park.

Elanka, a two-hour drive south via Mokhsogollakh, has a few rest houses, a small ethnographic museum and fishing on a peaceful patch of the Lena.

Bulus, a beachside area where ice remains all year, is reached by car ferry from Mokhsogollakh, then a drive south (a three-hour trip).

SAKHALIN ISLAND

El Dorado for oil-struck businessfolk, and 'hell' to Anton Chekhov in 1890 (not to mention the thousands and thousands of prisoners shipped here from the late 19th century), Sakhalin Island (Остров Сахалин) these days is decaying in chunks and booming in others (such as its hub, Yuzhno-Sakhalinsk). It's frequently beautiful too – much of it is filled with a wild terrain of forests, islands of seals, streams full of fish, slopes for skiing and lots and lots of bears – 'much bigger than Kamchatka's', one local assured us. Relatively cheap flights can get you here, but prepare to open the purse strings once you've arrived: Sakhalin is no place for shoestringers.

THE POLE OF COLD

When thermometers dip further below zero than they go above, and as many as two out of three days of your life are spent slipping on snow, you make some adjustments. In many towns around the Far East, hot-water pipes are elevated above the damaging permafrost. Giant fur coats aren't fashion but (an expensive) necessity, and drivers spring for heated garages and keep their cars running wherever they go during the day. 'If your engine goes off,' one local told us, 'that's it – you have to wait till spring.'

But locals swear that this area – which commonly hits −50°C, and reached −66°C in Yakutsk in 2007 – isn't as bad as outsiders think. For one, transport is easier. Rivers freeze over, offering new 'roads' to reach otherwise isolated areas. 'It's not like kids can't go out and play', one local said. 'It's really not as bad as Moscow, because it's dry here. I don't know how they survive the winters there!'

The unofficial 'pole of cold' is **Oymyakon**, a remote village 650km north of Yakutsk that holds the record as the coldest inhabited spot on earth. Temperatures have been recorded as low as −71°C (in the nearby valleys they go down to −82°C). Besides cold, Oymyakon has a breeding station for reindeer, horses and silver foxes. An annual **Pole of Cold Festival**, with reindeer races and (outdoor!) concerts, takes place here or in nearby Tomtor in late March.

Yakutsk travel agencies have discovered a market niche in offering trips to Oymyakon and other places in Sakha where the main attraction is extreme cold. A one-week trip taking in Oymyakon and various other cold places runs to ₽55,000 per person for groups of four to six people, including transport by Russian UAZ jeeps.

CHEKHOV'S SAKHALIN

Perhaps no one will ever really know why, in 1890, Russian literary giant Anton Chekhov left his fame in Moscow and crossed a pre-Trans-Siberian Siberia to come and document the hellish scene of prison life on Sakhalin, which had become a penal colony eight years earlier.

Though cryptic in explaining his move, Chekhov neatly summed up his experiences in the fascinating, if tedious at times, book *Sakhalin Island,* which dryly notes population counts and colourfully describes prisoners chained to wheelbarrows, prisons crawling with cockroaches, freely wandering mass murderers and an overbearing sense of nihilism for many who were banished to the island for life.

Possibly fearing censorship, Chekhov kept a distance from overarching criticism, but wrote to show how a penal system is no way to develop a new region. He summed up, 'If I were a convict, I would try to escape from here, no matter what.'

Chekhov's name now seems forever linked with the island, though many locals seem to shrug their shoulders over the connection. The friendly woman running the Chekhov museum in Aleksandrovsk confessed to us to never having read his work. Another local, fond of the Soviet days, told us, 'He was bourgeoisie! He didn't think about the revolution, only vulgar things like prostitution!'

You'll see more foreigners in Sakhalin than anywhere else in the Far East, but the vast majority are here to do *biznes* (business). If you're in that boat, definitely make a point of getting out of Yuzhno-Sakhalinsk and exploring Sakhalin's wild side. The main 948km-long island is one of 59 (including the Kuril Islands) that make up the Sakhalinskaya Oblast (Sakhalin Region). Sakhalin's weather is despicable. It was practically snowing in mid-June when we last visited. Summer is brief. August and September are the best months, mosquitoes notwithstanding.

History

The first Japanese settlers came across from Hokkaido in the early 1800s, attracted by marine life so rich that one explorer wrote 'the water looked as though it was boiling'. The island – mistakenly named for an early map reference to 'cliffs on the black river' ('Saghalien-Anaghata' in Mongolian) – already had occupants in the form of the Nivkhi, Oroki and Aino peoples but, just as this didn't give pause to the Japanese, the Russians were equally heedless when they claimed Sakhalin in 1853. Japan agreed to recognise Russian sovereignty in exchange for the rights to the Kuril Islands.

Japan restaked its claim on Sakhalin, seizing the island during the Russo-Japanese War, and got to keep the southern half, which it called Karafuto, under the terms of the Treaty of Portsmouth (1905). In the final days of WWII, though, the Soviet Union staged a successful invasion, and Sakhalin became a highly militarised eastern outpost of the Soviet empire, loaded with aircraft, missiles and guns.

In 1990, Muscovite governor Valentin Fyodorov vowed to create capitalism on the island. He privatised retail trade, but most people soon found themselves poorer. Fyodorov left, head down, in 1993. The demise of the USSR and the influx of thousands of oil-industry internationals succeeded where Fyodorov couldn't.

Yuzhno-Sakhalinsk

Южно-Сахалинск

☎4242 / POP 181,700 / ⌚MOSCOW +7HR

There will be budgets broken. New office towers, hotels and apartment buildings (and sushi bars) are rising – along with prices – all over the oil town's streets (which are still named after Lenin, Marx and other communists). It's quite relaxed, with pleasant tree-lined footpaths and looming mountains that you can ride chairlifts up and ski or climb down, and a couple of nods to its distant Japanese history.

Sights & Activities

Sakhalin Regional Museum MUSEUM

(Краеведческий музей; Kommunistichesky pr 29; admission ₽70; ⌚11am-6pm Tue-Sun) The pagoda-roofed Sakhalin Regional Museum has a 21st-century exhibit exploring the Japanese/Soviet overlap of the city's history, typified by the building itself, which served as the home of the Karafuto administration before the Soviets seized the island from the Japanese in 1945. The strong ethnographic section has some unique Aino artefacts and photos from back before the original south Sakhalin inhabitants fled to Japan (check out the photo of the bear ceremony), plus bits on the Nivkhi and the rare Aleuts.

Museum of Sakhalin Island: A Book by AP Chekhov MUSEUM

(Музей книги А. П. Чехова Остров Сахалин; pr Mira 104; admission permanent/temporary collection ₽30/30; ⏲11am-6pm Tue-Sat) Yes, that's really the name of this two-floor showing of Chekhov's few months on Sakhalin. Look for the photo of Chekhov at a picnic with the Japanese consul and his entourage. More interesting than the untranslated Chekhov works are multimedia exhibits and lifesize models that give an idea of life on the island; there's even a re-created sleeping quarters for convicts (though you'll have to imagine the roaches and bedbugs).

A small gallery of temporary artwork is upstairs. The surrounding park has a few sculptures of Chekhov personages.

Art Museum ART GALLERY

(Художественный музей; ☎4242-723 643; ul Lenina 137; admission ₽60; ⏲10am-6pm Tue-Sun) This museum has a modest permanent collection of pre-Soviet Russian oils and Korean and Japanese textiles upstairs, and changing exhibits downstairs. Best is getting inside the unique building, a former Japanese bank built in 1935.

Gorny Vozdukh SKIING

(Горный Воздух; lift ticket summer ₽200, winter all-day pass weekday/weekend ₽1000/1600) 'Mountain Air' ski area looms east of town. A chairlift runs all year (Friday to Sunday only in summer) and leads up the mountain – another heads down the back side. It's about 300m southeast of the 220-acre **Gagarin Park**, named for a cosmonaut and big with rides, shaded walkways and weekend concerts in summer. The jubilant **Gagarin statue** in the northwest portion of the park will thrill lovers of Soviet iconography.

Magazin Stels CYCLING

(☎4242-394 168; pr Pobedy 52; per hour/day ₽300/1000; ⏲10am-7pm Mon-Fri, to 6pm Sat & Sun) Mountain-bike rental.

Tours

The Kuril Islands qualify as trip-of-a-lifetime material. Other tours offered by Yuzhno-Sakhalinsk travel agents include seal-infested Moneron Island off Sakhalin's southwest coast, plus shorter hops to points north, such as Tikhaya Bay, about 140km north of Yuzhno-Sakhalinsk (₽3500 per person); and 1045m Chekhov Peak, a nice one-day climb in the Sakhalin Mountains not far from Yuzhno. Tikhaya Bay is possible as a DIY tour – just jump on any train heading north to Tikhy.

Omega Plus TOUR COMPANY

(☎4242-723 410; www.omega-plus.ru; r 347, ul Kommunistichesky 86; ⏲9am-6pm Mon-Fri, 10am-3pm Sat) The only travel agent in town equipped to handle foreigners, Omega Plus focuses on Japanese heritage tours but also runs various area trips and weeklong trips to the Kurils and Moneron Island. Ask for English-speaking Elena.

Sleeping

In a rare perverse sense of justice, the cheapies have the best location. Don't expect English though. The top-end hotels are excellent, with either a sauna or fitness centre, built-in restaurants and other perks for business travellers.

Moneron HOTEL $

(Монерон; ☎4242-723 453; Kommunistichesky pr 86; s/d/tr from ₽1000/1600/2100; 📶) This sky-blue building facing pl Lenina is the best cheapie and a fun place to revisit Soviet-style arrangements. Rooms share toilets (beware, it's a smoker's den), and each floor has a shared shower (note lack of plural). The *lyux* rooms have private bathrooms, but are poor value. Excellent wi-fi. There's a 25% booking charge.

★ **Lotus Hotel** HOTEL $$

(Гостиница Лотос; ☎4242-430 918; www.lotus-hotel.ru; ul Kurilskaya 41a; s/d from ₽2500/3600; 🚭❄📶) On a peaceful street, the Lotus Hotel has clean and classically furnished rooms, with wood or parquet floors, ample natural light and a small desk. Pricier rooms feature an extra room, a kitchenette and small dining area. Breakfast costs an extra ₽100 per person. Excellent value, but there's no lift.

Yuzhno-Sakhalinsk

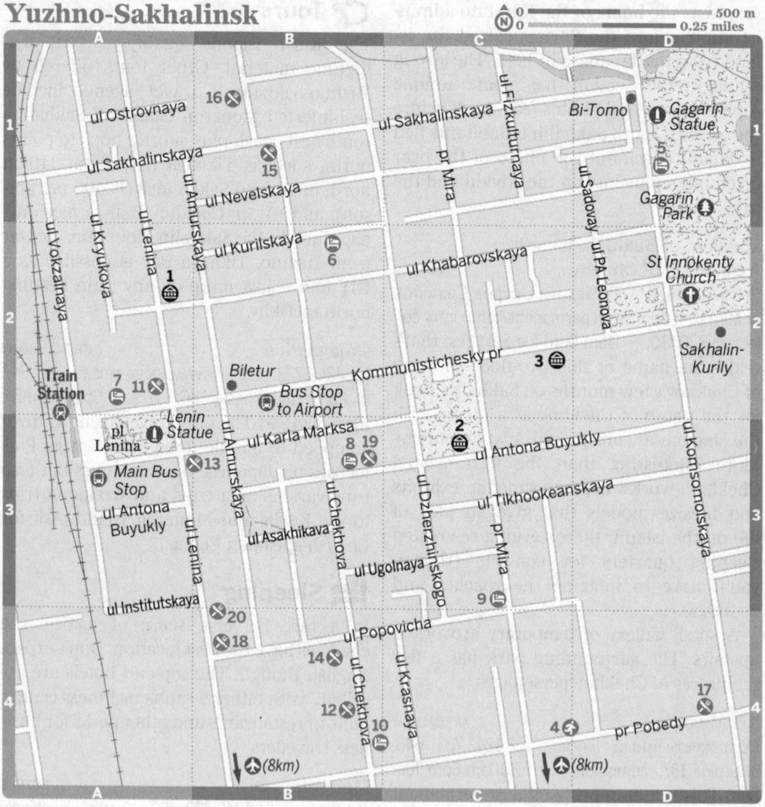

Natalya HOTEL $$

(☎4242-464 949; www.natalyahotel.ru; ul Antona Buyukly 38; s/d incl breakfast from ₽3300/3800; ❄📶) This friendly business hotel offers bright, spacious rooms, with full kitchens (including stove and microwave). Among the homey furnishings, it's like crashing at someone else's apartment. Entrance is in the back.

Rubin Hotel HOTEL $$$

(Гостиница Рубин; ☎4242-424 220; www.rubin-hotel.ru; ul Chekhova 85; s/d incl breakfast from ₽4000/5000; ❄📶) One of Yuzhno's most popular hotels looks like a polished little Scandinavian motor inn – perfectly run, clean and welcoming. All rooms have kitchenettes, and include use of the gym and breakfast in the popular Mishka Pub in the basement.

Pacific Plaza Sakhalin HOTEL $$$

(☎4242-455 000; www.sakhalinpacificplaza.ru; pr Mira 172; s/d incl breakfast from ₽5605/6372; 🚭❄@📶) Inside this eight-floor green-and-grey blob of modernity lurk attractive carpeted rooms with laquered wood furnishings and mod cons. Good service, choice eating spots (restaurant, lobby cafe) and a top-floor bar (with terrace open in summer) add to the appeal.

Gagarin Hotel HOTEL $$$

(☎4242-498 400; www.gagarinhotel.ru; ul Komsomolskaya 133; s/d incl breakfast from ₽3700/4300; 🚭❄@📶) A bit out of the way overlooking the namesake park, this pleasant business hotel capably fills the upper-midrange niche. Rooms are plush, with a modern design and sparkling bathrooms. There's also a sauna. Take the plant-filled stairs past a gurgling fountain up to **Wasabi** (small plates ₽350-450; ⏲6-11pm Mon-Sat, 3-10pm Sun), for good sushi and Japanese fare.

Yuzhno-Sakhalinsk

Sights

1 Art Museum ... A2
2 Museum of Sakhalin Island: A Book by AP Chekhov ... C3
3 Sakhalin Regional Museum ... C2

Activities, Courses & Tours

4 Magazin Stels ... C4
Omega Plus ... (see 7)

Sleeping

5 Gagarin Hotel ... D1
6 Lotus Hotel ... B2
7 Moneron ... A2
8 Natalya ... B3
9 Pacific Plaza Sakhalin ... C3
10 Rubin Hotel ... B4

Eating

11 Cafe No 1 ... A2
12 Cippolini ... B4
13 Fursato ... B3
14 Melnitsa ... B4
15 Melnitsa 2 ... B1
16 Moosehead ... B1
17 Nihon Mitai ... D4
18 Supermarket Pervy ... B4
19 Taj Mahal ... B3
20 Veranda ... B4
Wasabi ... (see 5)

Drinking & Nightlife

Mishka Pub ... (see 10)

Eating & Drinking

Business lunches are naturally popular here – think ₽300 to ₽350. For shashlyk and beer tents head to Gagarin Park.

Veranda CAFETERIA $
(Веранда; ul Lenina 219; meals ₽300-400; 8am-10pm Mon-Fri, 11am-10pm Sat & Sun;) This good, affordable *stolovaya* has excellent choices, and you can eat well for under ₽350. Free wi-fi.

Melnitsa CAFE $
(Мельница; ul Popovicha 73b; pastries ₽50-80; 8am-8pm Mon-Fri, from 10am Sat & Sun;) One of Sakhalin's best bakeries with sticky Danishes, rich eclairs and other sweet temptations. Decent coffees and loose teas too. Not easy to spot from the road. There's a second **Melnitsa** (ul Sakhalinskaya 45;) 10 blocks north.

Supermarket Pervy SUPERMARKET $
(Первый супермаркет; ul Lenina 219; 7am-midnight) Good supermarket, with tempting bakery items and hot prepared dishes.

★ **Cafe No 1** EUROPEAN $$
(Кафе №1; ul Lenina 218; mains ₽400-1200) A fashion-minded crowd gathers at this stylish but welcoming eating and drinking spot near pl Lenina. The sizeable menu features excellent dishes such as rack of lamb, Sakhalin scallops with eggplant caviar, and risotto with porcini mushrooms. Good beer selection and ambient grooves.

Nihon Mitai JAPANESE $$
(4242-720 550; pr Pobedy 28b; small plates ₽180-620; 11am-11pm;) Yuzhno's favourite sushi spot is a bit out of the centre, but the stylish bamboo 2nd-floor dining room is good for soba noodles and ramen (₽410 to ₽550) and picking from the sushi conveyor belt after 7pm (from ₽180 à la carte). The ground floor has a small grocer with some Japanese products.

Fursato JAPANESE $$
(Фурсато; ul Lenina 179; mains ₽300-800; noon-11pm) Across from pl Lenina, this casual Japanese spot serves up good but pricey sushi and sashimi platters, belly-filling *tonkatsu* (breaded pork cutlet), plus silky rich bowls of ramen, udon and soba noodles. The disco music is a minus.

Cippolini ITALIAN $$
(SFERA Business Centre, ul Chekhova 78; mains ₽300-1000; 11.30am-2.30pm & 6pm-midnight;) This slick basement restaurant-bar has an extensive pub menu (including pizzas, pastas, seafood, steaks). Upstairs, stop in the cafe (open 8.30am to 5pm weekdays) for a coffee on the go. An expat fave.

Moosehead PUB FOOD $$
(www.sakhwest.ru; ul Militseyskaya 8b; mains ₽300-1000; 5pm-late Mon-Fri, from noon Sat, from 3pm Sun;) Expats in the know head to this big dark-wood bar for cold beer and pub grub, famous seafood chowder and themed party nights.

Taj Mahal INDIAN $$
(4242-499 488; ul Antona Buyukly 38; veg/meat mains around ₽350/680; 11.30am-10pm;) Heavy inlaid wooden furniture and red tapestries set the stage for tasty chicken tikka masala, rich curries and fluffy naan bread.

Mishka Pub PUB
(4242-424 220; ul Chekhova 85; mains ₽280-580; 6.30am-midnight) In the Rubin Hotel's basement, this tiny expat haven is popular for its huge Russian business lunch (noon to 3pm, ₽280). Later on, stop in for pub grub

> **MOVING ON?**
>
> For tips, recommendations and reviews, head to shop.lonelyplanet.com to purchase a downloadable PDF of the Sapporo & Hokkaido chapter from Lonely Planet's *Japan* guide.

(cheeseburgers, pizzas, chicken wings) and beer (with Leffe and Hoegarden on tap).

Getting There & Away

AIR

The airport is 8km south of the centre. Several airlines, including Sakhalin's flagship carrier Aeroflot and S7 fly regularly to Khabarovsk (from ₽6500), Vladivostok (from ₽7300), Moscow (from ₽15,600) and elsewhere.

Aeroflot and Asiana alternate daily flights to Seoul, while Aurora has flights to Tokyo and Sapporo (two weekly).

You can buy domestic or international tickets at **Biletur** (Билетур; ☎4242-437 474; Kommunistichesky pr 74; ⏲9am-7pm).

BOAT

From June to September, once- or twice-weekly ferries run from Korsakov, 40km south of Yuzhno-Sakhalinsk, to Wakkanai on Hokkaido (from ₽8875, four hours). Book tickets at **Bi-Tomo** (Би-томо; ☎4242-726 889; bitomo@isle.ru; ul Sakhalinskaya 1/1; ⏲9am-6pm Mon-Fri) or Omega Plus (p547).

Boats also run to the Kuril Islands and from the southern Sakhalin port of Kholmsk to Vanino on the mainland.

BUS

From the main bus stop outside the train station you can catch bus 56 for Kholmsk (₽300, about 45 minutes) hourly from 8.45am to 9pm, bus 115 to Korsakov (₽135, one hour, frequent) half-hourly or bus 111 to Aniva (about one hour).

TRAIN

From the train station, facing pl Lenina, the fastest train is the 1, which heads north at 8.30pm daily, stopping at Tymovsk (*kupe/platskartny* ₽2900/1500, 9½ hours) and the end of the line, Nogliki (*kupe/platskartny* ₽3400/1800, 12 hours). The 2 train back from Nogliki is a night train. *Elektrichki* go to Bykov (daily, 1¾ hours) and Novoderevenskya (two daily, 30 minutes).

Getting Around

Bus 63 leaves for the airport, going east, from the bus stop on Kommunistichesky pr near ul Amurskaya (₽15, 30 minutes). A taxi to/from the airport costs about ₽350.

Kholmsk Холмск

There's really no reason to visit this grotty port, 40km west of Yuzhno, unless you are getting on or off the boat to Vanino. If you get stuck here waiting for the ferry, kill time on the waterfront promenade and, if need be, shack up at **Hotel Kholmsk** (Гостиница Холмск; ☎42433-52 854; ul Sovetskaya 60; s/d ₽1400/2000). Bus 56 connects Yuzhno with Kholmsk (₽300, 45 minutes, hourly).

KAMCHATKA

There are few places in the world that can simultaneously enthral and disappoint quite like Kamchatka (Камчатка). A fickle temptress, it tends to hide its primal beauty behind a veil of thick clouds and fog.

But when the skies finally clear and the powdered snouts of several dozen volcanoes appear through the clouds, all else melts away and you understand that you're in a special place. No matter what you went through to get here, no matter how long you've spent grounded, it was all worth it.

Visitors to Kamchatka are an intriguing mix of outdoorsy types and package tourists. The former have back-country adventure on their mind; the latter want to see Kamchatka's otherworldly geysers, fuming volcanoes and bears the easy way – by helicopter. They're united by deep pockets.

Yet against all odds, Kamchatka has suddenly become viable for independent, relatively budget-conscious travellers. The permit situation has relaxed, allowing visitors to take public transport north to Esso in the heart of the peninsula, where a slick nature-park office is busy mapping trails in English and guesthouses hawk beds for less than ₽1000. Here hot springs abound and you are not far from several volcanoes, including tempestuous Mt Klyuchevskaya (4688m), the tallest active volcano in Eurasia.

The capital, Petropavlovsk-Kamchatsky, may be gritty, but it's in an incredible setting and also has its share of easily accessible activities, including lift skiing into late May and some very doable volcano climbs. Kamchatka may not be a budget destination yet, but no longer is it strictly the domain of tycoons.

History

The man credited with the discovery of Kamchatka, in 1696, was the half-Cossack, half-Sakha adventurer Vladimir Atlasov, who, like

most explorers of the time, was out to find new lands to plunder. He established two forts on the Kamchatka River that became bases for the Russian traders who followed.

The native Koryaks, Chukchi and Itelmeni warred with their new self-appointed overlords, but fared badly and their numbers were greatly diminished. Today, the remnants of the Chukchi nation inhabit the isolated northeast of Kamchatka, while the Koryaks live on the west coast of the peninsula with their territorial capital at Palana.

Kamchatka was long regarded as the least hospitable and most remote place in the Russian Empire. In the 19th century, the peninsula became a useful base for exploring Alaska. When Alaska was sold off in 1867, Kamchatka might also have been up for grabs if the Americans had shown enough interest.

During the Cold War, Kamchatka was closed to all outsiders (Russians too) and took on a new strategic importance; foreign interest was definitely no longer welcome. It became a base for military airfields and early-warning radar systems, while the coastline sheltered parts of the Soviet Pacific Fleet.

Getting Around

Locals are fond of repeating that on Kamchatka 'there are no roads, only directions'. You will have a hard time getting 'out there', where the bulk of Kamchatka's glory is (volcano bases, rivers, geysers), without an arranged 6WD truck or helicopter (or several-day hike) – though longer hikes are a possibility too. Regular bus connections go as far north as Esso and Ust-Kamchatsk. The cold months see *zimniki* (winter roads) open up that go further still.

Used by vulcanologists and travellers alike, Mi-2 (capacity: six or eight people) and Mi-8 (capacity: 20 people) helicopters charge by time travelled in the air. The price is high (about ₽70,000 to ₽125,000 per hour) and it's risen astronomically over the past several years. Rides are exciting (and loud), with unbelievable views, windows you can open and room to roam about.

Kamchatka also has its own airline, **Petropavlovsk Kamchatsky Air Enterprise** (www.airport-pkc.ru), which does both scheduled and chartered forays to remote hamlets in the north part of the peninsula, such as Ossora, Palana and Tilichiki on the peninsula, and to Nikolskoye in the Commander Islands, known for its abundant wildlife and seal rookeries. Download the schedule from the website.

> **NORTHERN KAMCHATKA**
>
> Esso and Ust-Kamchatsk are easily reached by public transport. Much of the rest of the north, however, requires a helicopter, plane, 4WD or 6WD.

Petropavlovsk-Kamchatsky

Петропавловск-Камчатский

4152 / POP 195,000 / MOSCOW +8HR

Some see Petropavlovsk as a necessary evil, a hub to Russia's most beautiful scenery, while others focus on the city's sublime setting, which faces Avacha Bay and is overlooked by two giant volcanoes and surrounded by a long line of snowcapped mountains.

Though it's one of the oldest towns in the Far East, Petropavlovsk's seemingly endless main avenue is lined with mostly grim Soviet block housing, but there are enough attractions to fill a day or two, and the people are quite nice – more outdoorsy and less of that Russian gruffness than elsewhere.

During the Soviet era the town became a sizeable Pacific Fleet submarine base, but its present prosperity is owed completely to the fishing industry, especially its most famous delicacies, salmon and the gargantuan Kamchatka crab (king crab).

Sights & Activities

Historic Centre NEIGHBOURHOOD

It's worth a wander around the de facto centre of town, where **Lenin** stares out at the bay from pl Lenina. Along the bay is a stone **beach** with great views of Mt Vilyuchinsky, and nearby some cafes serving beer. Looming over the downtown area to the north is **Mt Mishennaya** (382m), an easy climb. Diminutive **Nikolskaya Hill** is to the south near a quaint **wooden chapel** (ul Krasintsev).

Petropavlovsk-Kamchatsky

0 — 1 km
0 — 0.5 miles

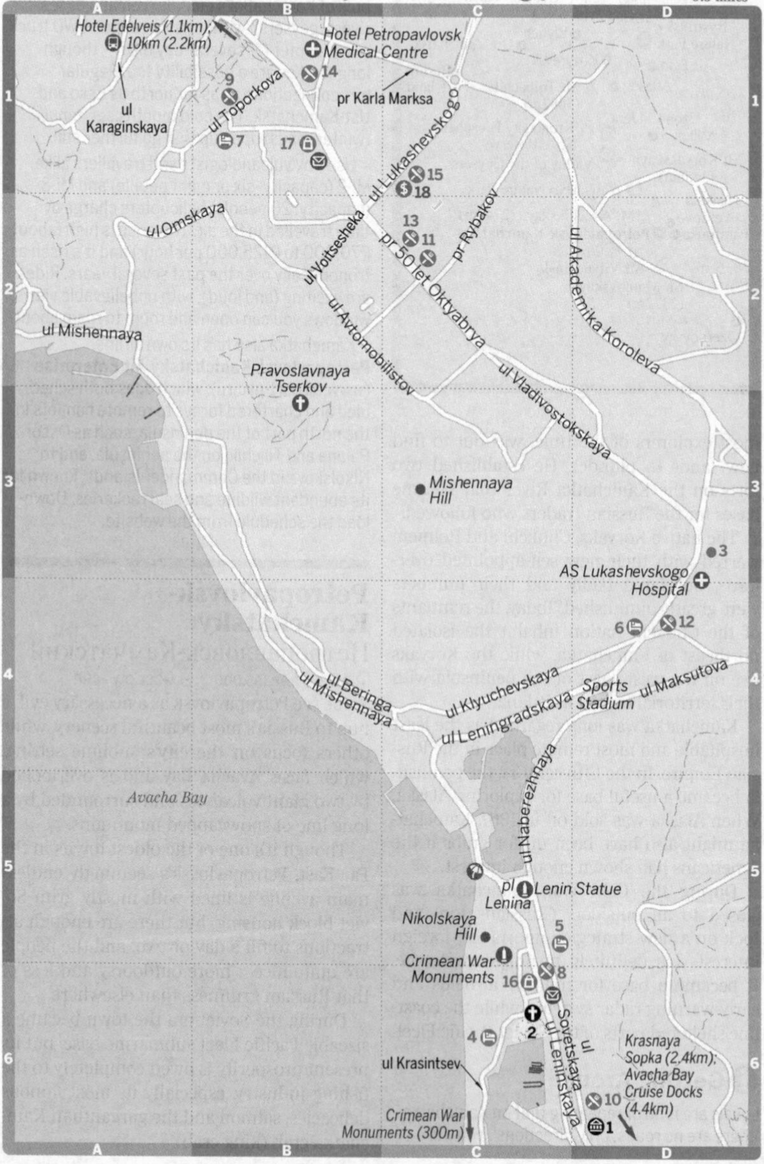

Petropavlovsk-Kamchatsky

Sights
1 Kamchatka Regional Unified Museum D6
2 Wooden Chapel C6

Activities, Courses & Tours
3 Kamchatintour D3

Sleeping
4 Baza Po Priyomu Turistov C6
5 Hostel 24 .... C5
6 Hotel Avacha D4
7 Hotel Geyser B1

Eating
8 Bistro C6
9 Cucaracha B1
10 Korea House D6
11 Market C2
12 Milk Café D4
13 Molino C2
14 San Marino B1
15 Yamato C1

Drinking & Nightlife
Barraka .... (see 13)

Shopping
16 Ethno-Salon Shaman C6
17 Planeta Knig B1

Information
Galant City .... (see 12)
Parus .... (see 13)
18 Planeta Shopping Centre C1

Kamchatka Regional Unified Museum MUSEUM
(Камчатский краевой объединенный музей; ul Leninskaya 20; admission ₽120; ⏲10.30am-6pm Wed-Sun) Housed in an attractive half-timbered building overlooking the bay, this museum features an imaginative mix of relics and murals that outline Kamchatka's history, including dioramas of nomadic herders, old cannonballs and flags, photos of the 1975 Tolbachik eruption and maps showing Alaskan expansion.

Avacha Bay BOAT TRIPS
Petropavlovsk's stunningly beautiful bay, with volcanic **Mt Vilyuchinsky** (2173m) visible across the way on most days, is best appreciated on an **Avacha Bay cruise.** Standard three-hour cruises (per person ₽1700) take place most days in summer; book through any travel agency. Better are the more sporadic six-hour tours that reach **Starichkov Island**, a haven for bird life (from ₽3500 per person, including lunch).

Krasnaya Sopka SKIING
(Красная Сопка; ⏲Nov-May) One of several ski areas within the city limits, this one is noteworthy for incredible views of Avacha Bay. T-bars take you up for ₽60 per run.

Tours

Explore Kamchatka, Kamchatintour and Lost World can all do the main tours (and many more), offer visa support and help you charter helicopters, planes or 6WD vehicles. They are all run out of Petropavlovsk or Yelizovo, where the helicopter pad is. Petropavlovsk has dozens of tour companies, so by all means shop around – but these have shown consistently good service over the years.

Other popular tour activities include rafting and combo rafting/fishing trips, horse riding, dog sledding, snowmobiling, diving and fly fishing for salmon.

Explore Kamchatka TOUR COMPANY
(☎8-962-280 7840; www.explorekamchatka.com; ul Bolshokova 41, Yelizovo) This place in Yelizovo is run by an Alaskan who promotes alternative destinations and frequently helps visitors with unique requests (eg film crews seeking unique surfing spots). She's a mine of information for independent travellers and runs a great little B&B (p558).

Kamchatintour TOUR COMPANY
(☎4152-427 071; www.kamchatintour.ru; ul Leningradskaya 61; ⏲9am-7pm Mon-Fri, daily in summer) This is the most helpful Petropavlovsk agency we've found in terms of preplanning help and responsiveness, although much of its business is with Japanese groups. It can get you to its camp at Mt Avachinskaya on short notice.

Lost World TOUR COMPANY
(☎4152-498 328; www.travelkamchatka.com; room 4, ul Frolova 4/1, Petropavlovsk; ⏲9am-6pm Mon-Fri, daily in summer) This long-running operation has experienced guides (including outdoorsy vulcanologist vets) that specialise in somewhat smaller groups.

Valley of the Geysers
Долина Гейзеров

Kamchatka's most famous attractions lie 200km northeast of Petropavlovsk in the spectacular Valley of the Geysers (Dolina Geyzerov). Discovered in 1941, the 8km-long valley of a few-dozen geysers cut through by the Geysernaya River is part of the protected **Kronotsky Biosphere State Reserve**. A 2007 earthquake, contrary to some outside reports, did not destroy the valley, though a few areas were lost.

Around 200 geothermal pressure valves sporadically blast steam, mud and water heavenward. The setting is exquisite and walking tours along a boardwalk take you past some of the more colourful and active geysers.

To get there you must travel by helicopter with a group on a day trip. Arrange through any travel agent. Rising petrol prices only

HOW TO SEE KAMCHATKA

While it's getting easier than ever to visit Kamchatka on your own, limited infrastructure, permit requirements and risks like bear attacks and avalanches make preplanned tours mandatory for many places and highly advisable for others.

Tours

Many of Kamchatka's main sights, such as the Valley of the Geysers and Lake Kurilskoe, are only available by organised tour. To do a tour doesn't mean packing onto a busload of 50 camera-toting tourists. Some groups are private, just two to four people, and most groups are fewer than 20 people.

Tours range from simple day trips to one- to two-week all-inclusive odysseys taking in several sights or activities. Plan ahead, especially in July and August. Otherwise days can be wasted waiting for a guide to return from a trip or transport to be arranged from Petropavlovsk.

Tours usually include everything: guides, transport, permits, hotels or tents to sleep in, sleeping bags and food. Most of the high-profile tours involve helicopter rides or 6WD/4WD transport.

Prices for the big day trips – Valley of the Geysers, Lake Kurilskoe and Mt Mutnovskaya – are set by the helicopter companies and tend to cost the same no matter which travel agency you use. Travel agencies pool clients for these tours. A day trip to the Valley of the Geysers costs ₽27,000 per person, including a one-hour helicopter ride each way, lunch and stops at Uzon Caldera and Zhupanova River.

Prices for longer tours vary wildly depending on how much time is spent in helicopters. A weeklong tour involving some camping and taking in several key sights might cost €2500 to €3500, including a few helicopter rides.

DIY Without Guides

DIY travel is more difficult and comes with serious risks. Especially if you're looking to venture into the back country, any misstep can be dangerous, and you're best off having an experienced guide. A couple of local geologists were eaten by bears in 2008, by no means the first bear mauling in these parts. Winter travel eliminates the risk of bear attacks but creates new risks, such as days-long white-outs. This ain't Disneyworld.

With those caveats established, the easiest fully DIY trips around Petropavlovsk include the hike up Mt Avachinskaya and trekking along the well-marked trails from Mt Avachinskaya to Nalychevo Valley. Another option is to head up to Esso, 10 hours north of Petropavlovsk by bus, where Bystrinsky Nature Park has an extensive network of well-marked and well-mapped trails.

DIY with Guides

If you're wanting to get more 'out there' than Nalychevo or Esso, another option is simply hiring a local guide and going on a weeklong or longer trek. Some travellers have done so to explore huge pockets of wilderness not featured here.

The Visitor Centre in Yelizovo is the best place to get a freelance guide.

partially explain the gigantic boom in price – from US$250 per person in 2004 to nearly US$1000 in 2014. Many visitors feel it's simply too much for what you get.

For an extra ₽6000 per person, the four- or five-hour trip can be extended with stops at **Zhupanova River** and **Uzon Caldera**, the remains of a 40,000-year-old volcano, now a 10km crater with steamy lakes.

Lake Kurilskoe
Озеро Курильское

Kamchatka's 'bear lake' – reached by helicopter – is so popular with the area's bears that, in August and September (when up to three million red salmon come to spawn), visitors can almost get tired of looking at them. The huge lake, formed by an eruption nearly 9000 years ago, is rimmed by volcanoes and home to a couple of lodges. The only trails in the area are bear trails. Don't wander alone: a Japanese photographer was eaten by a bear here in 2000.

Travel agents can set you up with a group flying out here on a day trip for ₽35,000 per person. Lost World has a 10-day bear/volcano trip that includes a few days around Lake Kurilskoe and a few days around Mt Mutnovskaya for €3350 per person.

Mt Mutnovskaya
Гора Мутновская

Walking down into an active 4km-wide cone, past boiling mud pools and ice crevices cut by hot vapours of volcanic fumes is like Frodo and Sam's last trek in *The Lord of the Rings*. Kamchatka vulcanologists, who love all of Kamchatka's volcanoes, seem to hold Mt Mutnovskaya (2322m) in special regard – for studying, climbing or simply observing.

A wild road – handled by 6WD or good 4WD vehicles – reaches the base, but only after snows melt in mid-August (when some Petropavlovsk agencies offer day trips here). Otherwise, it's an expensive helicopter ride or an 8km to 15km hike (up to four hours one way, though not a difficult climb), depending on accessibility, to reach the cone, where you can hike (or ski) down past boiling mud pools.

It's particularly important to have a guide here. Weather can turn suddenly, and it's easy to get lost. Many tours climb the oval-shaped caldera of nearby **Gorely** (1829m). Base camps here are tent only.

Heliskiing & Back-Country Skiing

Heliskiing tours of the mountains and volcanoes that make an arc around Petropavlovsk include unreal experiences such as skiing onto Pacific beaches or into Mt Mutnovskaya's fuming crater. Sky-high prices, however, deter most travellers.

Tours typically guarantee four days of skiing in a 10-day period to allow for weather inconsistencies – any wind or fog grounds the birds. If the weather cooperates, you can pay (a lot) for extra days of heliskiing. Otherwise, the buffer days are spent snowcat skiing at the base of Mt Avachinskaya or at one of several small ski areas around town, trying out the hot springs, cruising around Avacha Bay or touring wild Pacific beaches. Conditions are most reliable in February and March.

The three main operators are **Vertikalny Mir** (www.vertikalny-mir.com), **Russian Heliboarding Club** (www.helipro.ru) and Explore Kamchatka (p553). Keep in mind that a massive avalanche swept away a helicopter and killed 10 people on a trip in 2010.

Back-country skiing, such as trips into Nalychevo Valley, where there are also hot springs to splash in, is a cheaper alternative.

Sleeping

Petro's hotels are, on balance, poor value. Staff are friendly enough but you're paying an awful lot for cramped rooms that can't hide from their Soviet past.

Any wi-fi usually costs extra. Rates generally include breakfast.

★ Hostel 24 HOSTEL **$**
(Хостел 24; ☎4152-420 001; hostel24.kamchatka@gmail.com; ul Sovetskaya 48; dm/d ₽750/2500; wi-fi) A welcome addition to Kamchatka, Hostel 24 has clean rooms with wood floors and simple colour schemes, with four to 12 beds in each. There's also laundry, a guest kitchen and free wi-fi (a rarity in this region). It's well located near the historic centre.

Baza Po Priyomu Turistov PENSION **$$**
(База по приему туристов; ☎4152-420 591; ul Krasintsev 1; s/d ₽2250/2500) In an ideal downtown location, this place offers much better value than most of Petropavlovsk's 'top-end' hotels. Rooms are small and cosy, but adequately furnished with area rugs, TV and minifridge (although some bathrooms lack sinks, so you must brush your teeth in the shower). There's an 11pm curfew.

Hotel Edelveis HOTEL $$
(Гостиница Эдельвейс; ☎4152-295 000; www.idelveis.com; pr Pobedy 27; dm ₽1000, s/d without bathroom ₽3000/4000, with bathroom ₽3600/5200;) Although the location isn't ideal, Edelveis deserves high marks for friendliness (some staff speak English) and its old-fashioned but comfy economy rooms and slicker standard rooms.

Hotel Avacha HOTEL $$$
(Гостиница Авача; ☎4152-427 331; www.avacha-hotel.ru; ul Leningradskaya 61; s/d from ₽4900/6500; @) Across from a lively shopping centre, the rooms here are attractive enough but retain Soviet dimensions, especially the bathrooms. There's a sauna, gym, ATM and air-ticket agency downstairs. The very Russian breakfast is filling.

Hotel Geyser HOTEL $$
(Гостиница Гейзер; ☎4152-419 570; www.geyser-hotel.ru; ul Toporkova 10; s/d from ₽2900/4000; @) Rooms here have views of Avacha Bay and are decently outfitted (flat-screen TV, desk, minifridge, renovated bathroom), but the pale-green colour scheme might make you queasy. Thin walls.

Eating & Drinking

It's a shame the city doesn't have a better selection of restaurants and bars, given how much time tour groups spend waiting around for bad weather to clear.

Market RUSSIAN $
(Рынок; pr 50 let Oktyabrya 16; 9am-8pm) This sprawling market is a great spot for smoked fish, bread, cheeses, vegetables and other fare. There's also a small *stolovaya* next door (Kafe Lite), with inexpensive cooked dishes.

Cucaracha MEXICAN $
(☎4152-320 200; ul Toporkova; mains ₽220-410; 11am-11pm;) On the 2nd floor of the 'rollerdrom' (a kids' amusement centre), Cucaracha serves burritos, quesadillas and other Mexican fare. The dishes are nothing special but it's one of the only places in town with free wi-fi. No alcohol.

Bistro CAFETERIA $
(Бистро; ul Sovetskaya 49; meals ₽150-250; 10am-8pm) Simple cafeteria.

★**San Marino** RUSSIAN $$
(Сан Марино; ☎4152-252 481; pr Karla Marksa 29/1; mains ₽350-950; noon-1am;) San Marino is Petropavlovsk's best place for an excellent, exotic meal of Kamchatka crab, scallops, halibut and other delicacies. It all goes nicely with a frosty mug of Kamchatka beer (₽120). Entrance off pr Pobedy.

Milk Cafe CAFE $$
(Милк Кафе; 3rd fl, Galant City Mall, ul Leningradskaya; mains ₽280-650; 11am-10pm;) The town's best pizzas are at this bright cafe, which also has some healthy soups, salads (and fondue!), plus a fine coffee selection. The menu has pictures in lieu of English.

Yamato JAPANESE $$
(Ямато; ☎4152-267 700; ul Lukashevskogo 5; meals ₽400-800; noon-midnight;) Inside the Planeta Shopping Centre, Yamato serves surprisingly tasty sushi in a low-lit setting with a dash of style (and a long fish-filled aquarium).

Molino ITALIAN $$
(Молино; Parus Shopping Centre, pr 50 let Oktyabrya 16/1; mains ₽250-600; 10am-1am) It doesn't have the best pizza in town but it's well located on the central avenue and has reasonably priced beer and good people watching.

Korea House KOREAN $$
(ul Leninskaya 26; meals ₽400-1000; 11am-11pm;) An upscale pan-Asian eatery with local seafood on the menu, and you can also cook up your own meats tableside.

Barraka LOUNGE BAR
(Барака; 4th fl, Parus Shopping Centre, pr 50 let Oktyabrya 16/1; noon-5am) This swanky rooftop lounge in the Parus Shopping Centre has excellent if pricey sushi, a ₽300 business lunch and notable after-hours parties.

Shopping

Prepurchase Petropavlovsk maps in Vladivostok or Khabarovsk if you can. Local malls carry them for double the price (about ₽350).

Ethno-Salon Shaman SOUVENIRS
(Этно-салон Шаман; ul Leninskaya 57; 10am-7pm Mon-Fri, 11am-5pm Sat & Sun) The city's best souvenir shop has a selection of carvings in ivory and wood, fur hats, reindeer leather boots and other crafty items.

Planeta Knig SOUVENIRS
(Планета книг; ul Tushkanova; 10am-6pm Mon-Sat) Has some OK souvenirs and a regional map.

WORTH A TRIP

THE KURILS

Spreading northeast of Japan, like stepping stones to Kamchatka, this gorgeous and rugged 56-island chain of 49 active volcanoes, azure-blue lagoons, steaming rivers and boiling lakes is one of the world's great adventures. The Kurils are part of the Pacific 'Ring of Fire' – the islands being the visible tips of an underwater volcanic mountain range. The rare visitors here are treated to dramatic landscapes, isolated coastal communities a world apart from the rest of Russia, and seas and skies brimming with marine and bird life.

The three most populous islands, accessible by public boat and/or plane, are Kunashir, Iturup and Shikotan. You can attempt to visit these islands on your own, but secure permits first through a travel agent or from the border control office in Yuzhno-Sakhalinsk. Be prepared to get stuck for a few days because of storms and heavy fog. Late summer and early autumn provide the best chance of stable weather.

Aurora (www.flyaurora.ru) flies to Yuzhno-Kurilsk on Kunashir Island five times per week, and to Buravestnik, Iturup, four times per week. On the seas, **Sakhalin-Kurily** (Сахалин-Курилы; ☎in Yuzhno-Sakhalinsk 4242-762 524; 'Fregat' office, 3rd fl, ul Kommunistichesky 21; ⏰10am-4pm) has a ferry that departs twice a week from Sakhalin to Kunashir, Shikotan, Iturup and back to Sakhalin. The entire loop takes up to two days. Omega Plus in Yuzhno-Sakhalinsk offers groups of four or more a seven-/eight-day tour to Kunashir or Iturup Island for ₽45,000 to ₽60,000 per person, including visa support. Transport is by public boat. Individuals can piggyback on these trips.

More northern islands, many of them uninhabited, can only be visited by private sea craft or on upmarket expeditions such as several 12- to 13-day cruises by **Heritage Expeditions** (www.heritage-expeditions.com). It offers a trip between Kamchatka and Sakhalin, and another from Sakhalin Island to Magadan; these typically happen in May and June (from US$6700 per person).

Information

You can find ATMs at the main post office and in most hotels and shopping centres, including **Parus** (Парус; pr 50 let Oktyabrya) and **Galant City** (Галант; ul Leningradskaya) across from Hotel Avacha.

AS Lukashevskogo Hospital (Больница им. А.С. Лукашевского; ☎4152-120 610; ul Leningradskaya 114)

Hotel Petropavlovsk Medical Centre (☎4152-252 075; 2nd fl, pr Karla Marksa 31a; ⏰9am-8pm Mon-Fri)

Main post office (Главпочтамт; ul Leninskaya 60; per hour ₽100; ⏰internet 10am-7pm Mon-Fri, post 8am-8pm Mon-Fri, 9am-6pm Sat, to 4pm Sun)

Post office (Почта; ul Tushkanova 9; per hour ₽100; ⏰8am-8pm Mon-Fri, 9am-6pm Sat)

Rescue Service (☎4152-410 395)

Getting There & Away

From the Petropavlovsk airport in Yelizovo, 30km northwest, there are at least daily flights to the following destinations:

Khabarovsk From ₽7000, 2½ hours

Moscow From ₽16,000, nine hours

Novosibirsk From ₽13,600, seven hours

Vladivostok From ₽9500, 3½ hours

The major hotels and the main post office have ticketing agents. Flights during the peak July/August period sell out months in advance so book ahead.

In the summer, Yakutia Airlines flies between Anchorage, Alaska and Petropavlovsk (US$930/1620 one way/return). The 4½-hour flight runs on Saturdays between mid-July and mid-September. For more details visit www.airrussia.us.

From the **10km bus station** (Автовокзал, avtovokzal desyaty kilometr; pr Pobedy), buses depart daily at 9am to Esso (₽1560, nine to 10 hours), and at 8am to Ust-Kamchatsk (₽2150, 13 hours) via Klyuchi (₽1700, 11 hours).

Getting Around

Kamchatka's 25km central avenue enters the city limits near the 10km bus station as pr Pobedy and changes its name 11 times as it snakes around bayside hills. Dozens of buses (₽16) and *marshrutky* (₽30) run along its length.

Buses for the airport (₽30, 35 minutes) depart from the 10km bus station; take bus 104 marked 'Aeroport'. From the airport, take any bus signboarded '10km' from the 'Petropavlovsk' stop across from the terminal. Taxis are about ₽700.

Call ☎460 160 for the best taxi rates around town or to Paratunka/Yelizovo.

Around Petropavlovsk-Kamchatsky

Mt Avachinskaya & Mt Koryakskaya

Two volcanoes near Petropavlovsk stand side by side 20km north of town (about 35km by road). The bigger and more forbidding one is Mt Koryakskaya (3456m), which takes experienced climbers two days to climb. The smaller one on the east is Mt Avachinskaya, generally included on tours and one of Kamchatka's 'easier' volcanoes to summit (about four to six hours up). Avachinskaya last erupted in 1991, but you can see it smoking daily.

A base-camp complex serves both volcanoes and sees a lot of action, including skiers and snowmobiles into early July; it gets quieter as you climb up. Just below Avachinskaya, the aptly named Camel Mountain is an easy one-hour climb, with lots of Siberian marmots on top and great views of Mt Koryakskaya.

Getting here is problematic. Snow blocks the final few kilometres of the rough access road through mid-July, which means you'll have to walk (or better yet, cross-country ski) the last bit, or hire Kamchatintour's snowcat. After mid-July you can get all the way to the base camp in a 4WD. The Visitor Centre in Yelizovo is the best place to find a driver. Freelance drivers charge ₽2800 to ₽3800 per car one way (₽4500 to ₽5500 for round trip with wait time) to the base camp from Yelizovo; some can guide you up the mountain for an extra ₽2500 per group. Travel agencies might charge ₽6000 per car.

Kamchatintour (p553) has its own camp at the foot of Avachinskaya and offers a day trip out here for about ₽7000 per person including lunch and snacks at the camp and a guide.

No permits are required to hike up Avachinskaya.

Nalychevo Nature Park

One of Kamchatka's most accessible attractions for hearty independent travellers is this nature park encompassing lovely Nalychevo Valley and the 12 volcanoes (four active) that surround it. A trail extends about 40km north from Mt Avachinskaya to the park's main base area, where there are many huts, camping spots, an information centre and, in summer, a handful of rangers who can point out hiking trails leading to hidden hot springs.

Camping is in designated areas or huts that vary wildly in quality. Before heading out, secure a park permit (₽500), pick up a crude trail map and reserve a hut (per person ₽150 to ₽800) at the **park office** (☎4152-411 710; ul Zaivoko 19) in Yelizovo. GPS coordinates are also available. You might encounter foraging bears from June to September; the park office can brief you on proper precautions.

To get here, follow the instructions to Mt Avachinskaya, then walk. It's about a two-day hike from the Avachinskaya base camp to the park's main base area. You can exit the park via Pinachevo on the park's western boundary, but arrange to be picked up beforehand.

Yelizovo Елизово

☎41531 / ⏱MOSCOW +8HR

With an efficient new visitor centre and some reasonable accommodation, this low-key town near the airport is positioning itself as an alternative to Petropavlovsk for independent travellers.

The main attractions are hikes in the surrounding wilderness and the hot springs of nearby Paratunka.

Yelizovo's small **Regional Museum** (Краеведческий Музей; ul Kruchiny 13; admission ₽100; ⏱10am-6pm Tue-Sat) has ethnographic exhibits, Russian weavings, local art and the requisite stuffed sables and marmots.

The Visitor Centre can arrange apartment rentals in the area for ₽1500 and up. **Yelizovo B&B** (☎41531-66 601, 8-962-280 7840; www.explorekamchatka.com; 41 Bolshakova ul; r incl breakfast per person ₽1700), run by an American woman who operates Explore Kamchatka (p553), has three inviting rooms in a bright house, one of the best deals in the Far East. The **Art Hotel** (Арт Гостиница; ☎41531-71 443; www.artotel-kamchatka.ru; ul Kruchiniy 3; r ₽3650) is a cheerful place on the main drag in town; some rooms have a private sauna. The **Villa Hostel** (☎41531-332 232; ul Uralskaya 2) has tidy, wood-panelled rooms in a battered-looking concrete building.

The **Visitor Centre** (☎8-962-282 5265, weekends 8-961-961 8558; www.welcometokamchatka.ru; ul Ryabikov 1a; ⌚10am-5pm Mon-Fri, to 7pm Jul & Aug), on the 2nd floor of the bus station, can point you in the direction of good hikes in the area, find you a trekking guide or help you join an organised tour.

Across from the bus station, the 3rd floor of the Meridian Torgoviy Centre has free (slow) wi-fi. Frequent buses link Yelizovo's bus station with the airport.

Paratunka Паратунка

Sprawled-out Paratunka (25km south of Yelizovo) is a leafy network of spa resorts set up around hot-spring-fed swimming pools. One of many, **Lesnaya** (☎4152-469 081; admission ₽250; ⌚10am-midnight) is surrounded by wood and has a sizeable pool and a decent (but pricey restaurant). It's on the left before reaching Paratunka (inform the driver where you're going).

One worthwhile night out around here is a vodka-downing **Exotic Picnic with a Farmer** (☎8-924-792 3468) aka 'dinner with Sasha', an engaging Muscovite transplant who makes vegetarian meals from wild plants by his dacha, sings folk songs and makes many toasts. For some, it gets too drunken. It's ₽1000 to 1600 per person. Most travel agents can arrange this.

Paratunka is served by bus 111 from Petropavlovsk or 110 from Yelizovo (₽45 to ₽60).

Esso Эссо

☎41542 / POP 3000 / ⌚MOSCOW +8HR

The totally independent travellers' best destination in Kamchatka, Esso is set snug in a valley of green mountains, with a network of well-mapped hiking trails extending into surrounding Bystrinsky Nature Park, plus hot-spring pools in town and rafting and horse-riding options nearby. It's a quiet, lovely place with the scent of pine, and locals who live in picturesque wooden cottages.

Evenki people migrated here 150 years ago from what is now the Sakha Republic, becoming the distinct Even people in the process. Here they met the local Itelmeni and Koryak people as well as Russians. Although Esso remains a mixed community, the nearby village of Anavgay is mostly Even.

Sights & Activities

Ethnographic Museum MUSEUM

(ul Naberezhnaya 14a; admission ₽150; ⌚10am-6pm Wed-Sun) You can find out much about the history of the area's peoples in this well-kept museum in a charming Cossack-style *izba* (wooden house) set beside the burbling river that flows through Esso. The museum contains some truly memorable old photos. There's a souvenir shop in a separate building.

Reindeer Herds WILDLIFE

A few reindeer herds of 1000 to 2000 heads, managed by nomadic Evens, can be tracked down around Esso and Anavgay. They are reachable by helicopter in the warm months, and possibly by snowmobile during winter. An hour in a helicopter costs ₽130,000 in these parts.

Bystrinsky Nature Park HIKING

A nature reserve in Russia with trail maps in English and a fully Westernised visitor centre? You'd better believe it. Bystrinsky is a shining exception to the rule of neglected regional and national parks in Russia. Outside the **Esso Visit Centre** (☎8-909-836 8383; www.visitkamchatka.ru; ul Lenina 8; ⌚8.30am-12.30pm & 2-6pm Mon-Fri), a glossy sign in English describes 11 spectacular hikes of 2km to 42km. Inside you'll find extensive trail maps, brochures on this and other protected areas in Kamchatka, helpful English-speaking staff and even some German interns (it's funded by a German foundation). It gives away a town map as well.

It doesn't have guides but can help you find one and also arrange helicopter or 6WD charters should you wish to venture further to see reindeer herds or climb area volcanoes not in the park.

Before you set off anywhere on your own, have the staff brief you on bear precautions and keep them apprised of your itinerary. And be warned: the easy-sounding 2km hike is a difficult grunt straight up steep Pionerskaya Sopka (Pioneer Hill) just north of town.

Attached to the visit centre is a small **museum** (admission ₽50), where you can learn about the locally famous Beringia dogsled race.

The Visit Centre also has info about traditional crafts in the area, and workshops where you can visit the artists.

Hot Springs HOT SPRINGS

FREE Esso is proud of its hot *istochniki* (springs). Most hotels have a simple one, and there's a big, popular public pool in town (admission free). Ask at the Visit Centre about other appealing hot pools in the area.

Rafting RAFTING

Ask about rafting opportunities on the swift **Bystraya River** (its name means 'fast') at Altai guesthouse. One of the first operators in Esso, it offers tours ranging from one day to one week, camping and salmon fishing along the way. The price is ₽3000 per person per day including all equipment. July to September is the best time to go.

Festivals & Events

Neighbouring Anavgay holds a rollicking **Even New Year** festival during summer solstice, with plenty of dancing and singing into the wee hours.

Sleeping & Eating

Esso is the biggest bargain in the Far East for accommodation. Most guesthouses arrange meals.

★ **Grushanka** GUESTHOUSE $

(Грушанка; ☎8-962-281 0101; Medvezhiy Ugol 5; r per person incl breakfast ₽850) Run by a friendly older couple, Grushanka gives a warm welcome. All-wood rooms have a cabin-like feel with pretty views of the countryside. There's a small hot pool facing the mountains in back.

Altai GUESTHOUSE $

(Алтай; ☎8-914-622 5454; www.essotur.com; ul Mostovaya 12a; s/d/tr from ₽1500/2000/2500;) Near the bus stop, Altai is a gingerbread-like house with cozy but worn rooms and a small hot pool. Many excursions offered, including rafting trips, ski tours and visits to reindeer camps. Bicycle hire. English spoken.

Sychey GUESTHOUSE $

(Отель Домик Сычей; ☎8-914-622 9682; Naberezhnaya 5a; r per person ₽750) Natalya runs this appealing little guesthouse on the well-manicured grounds of her house. It's right next to the public pool.

Tri Medvedya LODGE $

(Три Медведя; ☎8-902-461 5563; r per person ₽1200) This two-storey wooden house has a mountain-lodge feel, with a fireplace, bear-skin rugs and cocoon-like beds.

Paramushir Tur HOTEL $$

(Парамушир Тур; ☎41542-21 442; www.paramushir.ru; ul 40 Let Pobedy 11; s/d incl breakfast from ₽2000/3600;) This slightly gaudy offering at the base of Pionerskaya Hill is your choice if you need mod cons. Pricey wi-fi available.

Minutka CAFE $

(Минутка; mains ₽80-130; 10am-8pm) Simple cafe near the museum.

Shardi CAFE $

(Шарди; ul Sovetskaya 14; mains ₽100-300) A basic eating/drinking spot.

Zarya GROCERIES $

(Заря; ul Sovetskaya; 9am-10pm) You can self-cater at this small food shop.

Information

Library (Библиотека; ul 50 Let Oktyabrya 11; per minute ₽2; noon-7pm Mon-Sat) Computers for getting online (but no wi-fi).

Sberbank (ul Sovetskaya 8; 9.30am-4pm Mon-Fri) ATM.

Getting There & Around

The daily bus to Petropavlovsk departs at 7am from in front of the green plank-wood **ticket office** (ul Mostovaya 9). You can hire mountain bikes at Altai guesthouse (per hour/day ₽200/600).

Understand Russia

Russia Today

The controversies surrounding the jailing of Pussy Riot members, the Sochi Winter Olympics, the annexation of Crimea and the shooting down of the Malaysia Airlines flight MH-17 have meant that recently Russia has seldom been far from international headlines. And the face most readily associated with the country is that of Vladimir Putin, who polarises opinion between those who see him as the leader of a party of 'crooks and thieves', and those who hail him as the president of an economically and politically resurgent Russia.

Best on Film

Pussy Riot: A Punk Prayer Directed by Mike Lerner and Maxim Pozdorovkin, this documentary is about the trial of the Pussy Riot trio.

My Perestroika (www.myperestroika.com) Robin Hessman's film focuses on five Russians and the effects on their lives of the past 20 turbulent years.

A Winter Journey Sergei Taramaev and Lubov Lvova direct this art-house feature. It has scooped awards at film festivals abroad but been shunned in Russia because of its gay love theme.

Best in Print

Russia – A Journey with Jonathan Dimbleby Also a BBC series, this is a revealing snapshot of a multifaceted country by one of the UK's top broadcasters.

The Last Man in Russia Oliver Bullough's spot-on portrait of modern Russia, told through the tumultuous and tragic life of an Orthodox priest.

Lost Cosmonaut and **Strange Telescopes** Daniel Kalder's books explore some of Russia's quirkiest and least-visited locations.

Releasing the Prisoners

For thrashing out a couple of lines of their 'Punk Prayer' in Moscow's Cathedral of Christ the Saviour, three members of the female punk group Pussy Riot were jailed for two years in August 2012. The trial hit headlines around the world and brought condemnation on Russia for its approach to freedom of speech and human rights. In their 2013 report on the country, Human Rights Watch noted the 'unprecedented crackdown against civic activism' since the re-election of Vladimir Putin.

Six weeks later, one of the trio changed her lawyer and managed to get her sentence suspended. The other two – Maria Alyokhina and Nadezhda Tolokonnikova – remained in jail until December 2013 when they were released in an amnesty celebrating the 20th anniversary of Russia's constitution. Putin granted freedom to 25,000 people under the amnsesty, including the former oligarch Mikhail Khordokovsky, who had been incarcerated for a decade, and 30 people arrested on a Greenpeace ship protesting oil exploration in the Arctic.

Controversial Olympics

Shortly after her release, Tolokonnikova stated that she had been released only because of the approaching Olympics Games, which Putin did not want ruined. Indeed, as the most expensive Olympics ever with a budget of more than US$51 billion, the sporting event was hyped as Russia's chance to turn around world opinion on the country, often still seen in the harsh light of the Soviet and Yeltsin years of decline. Was it money well spent? Well, Russia did top the medals table and the event was mostly hailed an organisational success.

However, the Olympics also acted as a lightning rod for disaffected Russians. The LGBT community protested the introduction of a controversial law banning the distribution of 'propaganda of nontraditional sexual relationships' and increased homophobia in the country. Environmentalists were angered by the detrimental effects of construction for the event. Tolokonnikova and fellow Pussy Rioters showed up in Sochi to make another guerilla video – and were attacked by Cossack guards wielding whips.

Bolotnaya Square

Graft associated with the Olympics, the tip of an iceberg of corruption that is commonly believed to riddle Russian society, was just one of the many reasons why citizens, mainly in Moscow and St Petersburg, began to openly protest against the ruling party United Russia and its leader Putin during 2011 and 2012. The biggest protest involved upwards of 50,000 people and centred on Moscow's Bolotnaya Sq. Leading opposition figure Alexey Navalny and others, including popular novelist Boris Akunin, spoke in favour of fair elections.

A proposed 'March of Millions' to Bolotnaya on 6 May 2012, the eve of Putin's presidential inauguration, led to criminal charges being laid against 28 people for mass riots, and the eventual sentencing in February 2014 of seven of the accused to prison terms of up to four years. Amnesty International called it a hideous injustice at the end of what they believed to be a show trial. However, attention was shifting rapidly away from Moscow to revolutionary events 850 kilometres southwest in Kyiv.

Taking Back Khrushchev's Gift

Months of street protests in Ukraine devolved into violent clashes, resulting in more than 100 deaths in late 2013 and early 2014. On 21 February 2014, Ukrainian President Viktor Yanukovych fled Kyiv for Moscow. With his administration deposed, and an interim government yet to establish its legitimacy across the country, Russian special troops aided by local riot police began taking over government buildings and military facilities in Crimea. This peninsula on the north coast of the Black Sea had been transferred to Ukraine in 1954 by the Supreme Soviet as a symbolic gesture of the country's 300-year union with Russia. However, nearly 60% of its population are ethnic Russians and Russia's Black Sea Fleet had been based at Sevastapol since the 18th century, underlining the peninsula's key strategic value.

Only Crimean Tatars and a handful of Ukrainian activists voiced their disagreement at what was happening in Crimea, as the region's new Russia-backed government organised a 'referendum' on 16 March. The new leaders claimed that 97% 'voted' in favour of Crimea joining Russia; a few days later Moscow rubber-stamped the decision by incorporating the region into the Russian Federation. State Duma representative and Putin supporter Vyacheslav Nikonov justified the annexation by comparing it with the Cuban Missile Crisis in reverse, with Russia forced to

POPULATION: **143.8 MILLION**

AREA: **17,098,242 SQ KM**

GDP: **US$2.092 TRILLION**

GDP GROWTH: **0.5% (FORECAST FOR 2014)**

INFLATION: **7.2% (FORECAST)**

UNEMPLOYMENT: **4.9% (MAY 2014)**

if Russia were 100 people

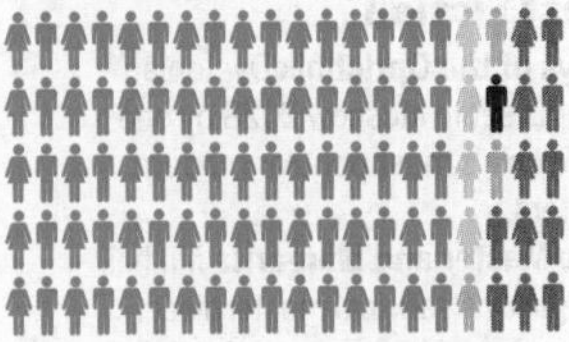

80 would be Russian
4 would be Tatar
2 would be Ukrainian
1 would be Bashkir
1 would be Chuvash
12 would be other

belief systems

(% of population)

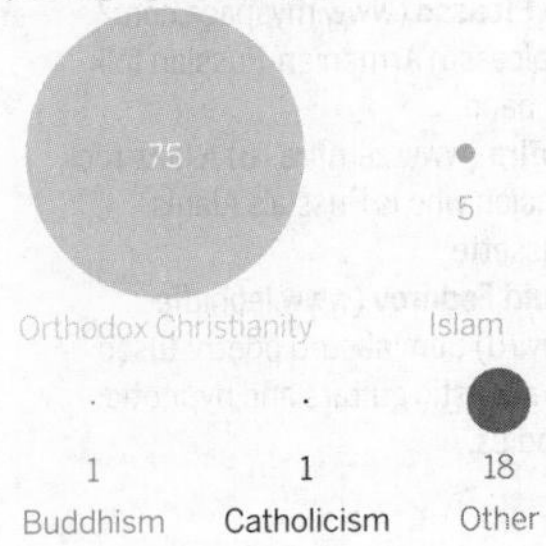

population per sq km

Best on the Internet

Calvert Journal (www.calvertjournal.com) Best online guide to the creative and progressive side of Russia.

Russia! (www.readrussia.com) Sparky cultural and political features on all things Russian.

Russia in Global Affairs (http://eng.globalaffairs.ru) Features relating to Russian politics, economy and culture.

Russia Beyond the Headlines (www.rbth.com) News, views and cultural features sponsored by the government-backed *Rossiyskaya Gazeta.*

Best Fiction

Days of the Oprichnik Dystopian drama set in Moscow 2028 by one of Russia's most popular modern writers.

The Master and Margarita Mikhail Bulgakov's satirical masterpiece.

Snowdrops An edgy morality tale by AD Miller set in contemporary Russia.

Top Playlist

Leningrad (www.sosimc.ru) Punk rock, Latino, polka and Tom Waits with a strong brass section.

Markscheider Kunst (www.mkunst.ru) Afro-beat-infused music.

Deti Picasso (www.myspace.com/detipicasso) Armenian-Russian folk-rock band.

Zemfira (www.zemfira.ru) A jazz-rock musician who is Russia's Alanis Morissette.

Leonid Fedorov (www.leonidfedorov.ru) Semiabsurd poetry fused with acoustic guitars and hypnotic melodies.

defend its interests against an overly aggressive West. Detractors instead compared it with Hitler's move into the Sudetenland in 1938.

Putin's Endgame

While the takeover of Crimea was largely peaceful, subsequent events in ethnic Russian–dominated areas of southern Ukraine have been the opposite. International sanctions have been imposed on Russia following the MH-17 disaster, prompting Russia to issue its own sanctions against the West. No wonder many are labelling this the start of a new cold war.

None of this has dented Putin's popularity ratings. A poll conducted in August 2014 by the Levada Center found that the Russian President had an approval rating of 87%, a six-year high and an increase of more than a third since the beginning of 2014. This is against a background where Russia's opposition media is finding it tougher than ever to get its message heard above pro-Kremlin views.

However, there is ample evidence of how damaging the crisis has been to Russia's economy, which has been hit by capital flight (thought to exceed $60 billion in the first three months of 2014), a depressed stockmarket and a devalued rouble. In May, the IMF reported that Russia is in recession, slashing its growth forecast for 2014 for the country to 0.2%. Laws have been introduced to regulate the use of public wi-fi hotspots and popular blogs on the internet.

History

How Russia became the largest country on earth and modern-day superpower, is an epic tale that puts *War & Peace* to shame for its cast of characters and dramatic events. The birth of the Russian state is usually identified with the founding of Novgorod in AD 862, although from the early 13th century until 1480 Russia was effectively a colony of the Mongols. The following six hundred years have seen an ever-expanding nation ruled by tsars, commissars and presidents.

Formation of the Country

Russian Ancestors: Slavs & Vikings

There is some disagreement about where the Slavs originated, but in the first few centuries AD they expanded rapidly to the east, west and south from the vicinity of present-day northern Ukraine and southern Belarus. These Eastern Slavs were the ancestors of the Russians; they were still spreading eastward across the central-Russian woodland belt in the 9th century. From the Western Slavs came the Poles, Czechs, Slovaks and others. The Southern Slavs became the Serbs, Croats, Slovenes and Bulgarians.

The Slavs' conversion to Christianity in the 9th and 10th centuries was accompanied by the introduction of an alphabet devised by Cyril, a Greek missionary (later St Cyril), which was simplified a few decades later by a fellow missionary, Methodius. The forerunner of Cyrillic, it was based on the Greek alphabet, with a dozen or so additional characters. The Bible was translated into the Southern Slav dialect, which became known as Church Slavonic and is the language of the Russian Orthodox Church's liturgy to this day.

The first Russian state developed out of the trade on river routes across Eastern Slavic areas – between the Baltic and Black Seas and, to a lesser extent, between the Baltic Sea and the Volga River. Vikings from Scandinavia – the Varangians, also called Varyagi by the Slavs – had been nosing east from the Baltic since the 6th century AD, trading and raiding for furs, slaves and amber, and coming into conflict with the Khazars and with Byzantium, the eastern centre of Christianity. To secure their hold on the trade routes, the Vikings made themselves masters of settlements

In line with common usage, we use directly transliterated names for pre-1700 rulers, anglicised names from Peter the Great until 1917, and again transliterated after that – thus Andrei Bogolyubov not Andrew, Vasily III not Basil; but Peter the Great not Pyotr, Catherine the Great not Yekaterina etc.

TIMELINE

c 30,000 BC

Humans settle in many locations across what would become Russia's vast territory, including Sunghir near Vladimir and along the Aldan River in the Sakha Republic in the Russian Far East.

c AD 300

The Huns, a nomadic people from the Altai region, move into eastern Europe. Under their leader Attila their empire stretches from the Ural River to the Rhine.

AD 862

The legendary Varangian (Scandinavian) Rurik of Jutland gains control of Staraya Ladoga and builds the Holmgard settlement near Novgorod. The infant version of Russia is born.

in key areas – places such as Novgorod, Smolensk, Staraya Ladoga and Kyiv (Kiev) in Ukraine. Though by no means united themselves, they created a loose confederation of city-states in the Eastern Slavic areas.

Old Russia Fortresses

- Staraya Ladoga
- Smolensk
- Pskov
- Stary Izborsk
- Rostov kremlin

Kyivan Rus

In the 9th century, Rurik of Jutland founded the Rurik dynasty, the ruling family of the embryonic Russian state of Kyivan Rus and the dominant rulers in Eastern Slavic areas until the end of the 16th century. Kyivan Rus became a Christian state under Vladimir I, who also introduced the beginnings of a feudal structure to replace clan allegiances. However, some principalities – including Novgorod, Pskov and Vyatka (north of Kazan) – were ruled democratically by popular *vechi* (assemblies).

Kyiv's supremacy was broken by new invaders from the east – first the Pechenegs, then in 1093 the Polovtsy sacked the city – and by the effects of European crusades from the late 11th century onward, which broke the Arab hold on southern Europe and the Mediterranean, reviving west-east trade routes and making Rus a commercial backwater.

THE RUSSIAN ORTHODOX CHURCH

In AD 988 Vladimir I adopted Christianity from Constantinople (Istanbul today), the eastern centre of Christianity in the Middle Ages, effectively starting the Russian Orthodox Church. The church flourished until 1653 when it was split by the reforms of Patriarch Nikon who insisted, among other things, that the translation of the Bible be altered to conform with the Greek original and that the sign of the cross be made with three fingers, not two.

Even though Nikon was subsequently sacked by Tsar Alexey, his reforms went through and those who refused to accept them became known as Starovery (Old Believers) and were persecuted. Some fled to Siberia or remote parts of Central Asia, where in the 1980s one group was found who had never heard of Vladimir Lenin, electricity or the revolution. Only from 1771 to 1827, from 1905 to 1918, and again recently have Old Believers had real freedom of worship.

Peter the Great replaced the self-governing patriarchate with a holy synod subordinate to the tsar, who effectively became head of the church. When the Bolsheviks came to power Russia had over 50,000 churches. Atheism was vigorously promoted and Josef Stalin attempted to wipe out religion altogether until 1941, when he decided the war effort needed the patriotism that the church could stir up. Nikita Khrushchev renewed the attack in the 1950s, closing about 12,000 churches. By 1988 fewer than 7000 churches were active and many of the priests allowed still to practise were in the pay of the KGB.

Since the end of the Soviet Union, the church has seen a huge revival, with around 90% of Russians identifying themselves as Russian Orthodox. New churches are being built and many old churches and monasteries – which had been turned into museums, archive stores and even prisons – have been returned to church hands and are being restored.

AD 945

Start of the reign of Svyatoslav I, who makes Kyiv the dominant regional power by campaigning against quarrelling Varangian princes and dealing the Khazars a series of fatal blows.

1093–1108

Vladimir Monomakh takes control of territory bounded by the Volga, Oka and Dvina Rivers, moves his capital to Suzdal and, in 1108, founds Vladimir, thus creating the Vladimir-Suzdal principality.

1147

Vladimir's son, Yury Dolgoruky, builds a wooden fort, the forerunner of Moscow's Kremlin, and invites his allies to a banquet there; he's later considered the city's founder.

1169

Yury's son, Andrei Bogolyubov, sacks Kyiv and moves his court to Vladimir, where he houses the Vladimir *Icon of the Mother of God* in the newly built Assumption Cathedral.

The Rise of Rostov-Suzdal

The northern Rus principalities began breaking from Kyiv after about 1050. As Kyiv declined, the Russian population shifted northward and the fertile Rostov-Suzdal region northeast of Moscow began to be developed. Vladimir Monomakh of Kyiv founded the town of Vladimir there in 1108 and gave the Rostov-Suzdal principality to his son Yury Dolgoruky, who is credited with founding the little settlement of Moscow in 1147.

Rostov-Suzdal grew so rich and strong that Yury's son Andrei Bogolyubov tried to use his power to unite the Rus principalities. His troops took Kyiv in 1169, after which he declared Vladimir his capital, even though the church's headquarters remained in Kyiv until 1300. Next, Rostov-Suzdal began to gear up for a challenge against the Bulgars' hold on the Volga–Ural Mountains region. The Bulgar people had originated further east several centuries before and had since converted to Islam. Their capital, Bolgar, was near modern Kazan, on the Volga.

Rus was the name of the dominant Kyivan Viking clan, but it wasn't until the 18th century that the term Russian or Great Russian came to be used exclusively for Eastern Slavs in the north, while those to the south or west were identified as Ukrainians or Belarusians.

The Golden Horde

Meanwhile, over in the east, a confederation of armies headed by the Mongolian warlord Chinggis (Genghis) Khaan (1167–1227) was busy subduing most of Asia, eventually crossing Russia into Europe to create history's largest land empire. In 1223 Chinggis' forces met the armies of the Russian princes and thrashed them at the Battle of Kalka River. This push into European Russia was cut short by the death of the warlord, but his grandson Batu Khaan returned in 1236 to finish the job, laying waste to Bolgar and Rostov-Suzdal, and annihilating most of the other Russian principalities, including Kyiv, within four years. Novgorod was saved only by spring floods that prevented the invaders from crossing the marshes around the city.

Batu and his successors ruled the Golden Horde (one of the khanates into which Chinggis' empire had broken) from Saray on the Volga, near modern Volgograd. At its peak the Golden Horde's territory included most of eastern Europe stretching from the banks of the Dnieper River in the west to deep into Siberia in the east and south to the Caucasus. The Horde's control over its subjects was indirect: although its armies raided them in traditional fashion if they grew uppity, it mainly used collaborative local princes to keep order, provide soldiers and collect taxes.

Ex-diplomat Sir Fitzroy Maclean wrote several entertaining, intelligent books on the country. *Holy Russia* is a good, short Russian history, while *All the Russias: The End of an Empire* covers the whole of the former USSR.

Alexander Nevsky & the Rise of Moscow

One such 'collaborator' was the Prince of Novgorod, Alexander Nevsky, a Russian hero (and later a saint of the Russian Church) for his resistance to German crusaders and Swedish invaders. In 1252, Batu Khaan put him on the throne as Grand Prince of Vladimir.

Nevsky and his successors acted as intermediaries between the Mongols and other Russian princes. With shrewd diplomacy, the princes of

13th century

Novgorod joins the emerging Hanseatic League, a federation of city-states that controlled Baltic and North Sea trade, and becomes the League's gateway to the lands east and southeast.

1240

Aged 19, Alexander, Prince of Novgorod, defeats the Swedes on the Neva River near present-day St Petersburg, thus earning himself the title 'Nevsky'.

1300

As Kyiv loses its political and economic significance, the headquarters of the Russian Orthodox Church moves to Vladimir. In 1325 Metropolitan Peter moves the episcopal see to Moscow.

1328

The Khan of the Golden Horde appoints Ivan I (Ivan the Moneybags) as Grand Prince of Vladimir with rights to collect taxes from other Russian principalities.

NOBLE TITLES

The title 'tsar', from the Latin *caesar*, was sometimes used by Ivan III in his diplomatic relations with the West. Ivan IV was the first ruler to be formally crowned 'Tsar of All Russia'. Peter the Great preferred emperor, though tsar remained in use. We usually use empress for a female ruler; a tsar's wife who does not become ruler is a *tsaritsa* (in English, tsarina). A tsar's son is a *tsarevitch* and his daughter a *tsarevna*. Boyars were feudal landholders who formed the early Russian aristocracy.

Russians often refer to the Mongol invaders as Tatars, when in fact the Tatars were simply one particularly powerful tribe that joined the Mongol bandwagon. The Tatars of Tatarstan actually descended from the Bulgars who are distantly related to the Bulgarians of the Balkans.

Masha Holl's Russian History (http://history.mashaholl.com) abounds with intriguing details, such as the fact that surnames didn't exist in Russia for most of the Middle Ages.

Moscow obtained and hung on to the title of grand prince from the early 14th century while other princes resumed their feuding. The church provided backing to Moscow by moving there from Vladimir in the 1320s and was in turn favoured with exemption from Mongol taxation.

With a new-found Russian confidence, Grand Prince Dmitry put Moscow at the head of a coalition of princes and took on the Mongols, defeating them in the battle of Kulikovo Pole on the Don River in 1380. The Mongols crushed this uprising in a three-year campaign but their days were numbered. Weakened by internal dissension, they fell at the end of the 14th century to the Turkic empire of Timur (Tamerlane), which was based in Samarkand (in present-day Uzbekistan). Yet the Russians, themselves divided as usual, remained vassals until 1480.

Ivan the Great

In 1478 Novgorod was first of the Great Russian principalities to be brought to heel by Ivan III. To secure his power in the city he installed a governor, deported the city's most influential families (thus pioneering a strategy that would be used with increasing severity by Russian rulers right up to Stalin) and ejected the Hanseatic merchants.

The exiles were replaced with Ivan's administrators, whose good performance was rewarded with temporary title to confiscated lands. This new approach to land tenure, called *pomestie* (estate), characterised Ivan's rule. Previously, the boyars (high-ranking nobles) had held land under a *votchina* (system of patrimony) giving them unlimited control and inheritance rights over their lands and the people on them. The freedom to shift allegiance to other princes had given them political clout, too. Now, with few alternative princes left, the influence of the boyars declined in favour of the new landholding civil servants. This increased central control spread to the lower levels of society with the growth of serfdom.

1382

Led by the Khan Tokhtamysh, the Mongols invade again, slaughtering half of Moscow's population but allowing a supplicant Dmitry to remain Grand Prince of Vladimir.

1389

Vasily I takes over his father Dmitry's titles on his death, without the weakened Khan's approval. He continues unifying the Russian lands and makes an alliance with Lithuania.

1425–62

The 10-year-old Vasily II becomes Prince of Moscow. His long rule is plagued by civil war but also sees the collapse of the Golden Horde into smaller khanates.

1462

Ivan III (Ivan the Great) succeeds his father, Vasily II. He is the first ruler to adopt the title 'tsar' and goes on to reign for 43 years.

Ivan IV (the Terrible)

Ivan IV's marriage to Anastasia, from the Romanov boyar family, was a happy one – unlike the five that followed her death in 1560, a turning point in his life. Believing her to have been poisoned, Ivan instituted a reign of terror that earned him the sobriquet *grozny* (literally 'awesome' but commonly translated as 'terrible') and nearly destroyed all his earlier good works.

His subsequent career was indeed terrible, though he was admired for upholding Russian interests and tradition. His military victories helped transform Russian into the multi-ethnic, multireligious state it is today. However, his campaign against the Crimean Tatars nearly ended with the loss of Moscow, and a 24-year war with the Lithuanians, Poles, Swedes and Teutonic Knights to the west also failed to gain any territory for Russia.

Ivan's growing paranoia led him to launch a savage attack on Novgorod in 1570 that finally snuffed out that city's golden age. An argument about Ivan beating his son's wife (possibly causing her miscarriage) ended with the tsar accidentally killing his heir in 1581 with a blow to the head. Ivan himself died three years later during a game of chess in 1584. The later discovery of high amounts of mercury in his remains indicated that he died from poisoning – possibly by his own hand, as he had habitually used mercury to ease the pain of a fused spine.

Read all about Moscow's Kremlin – both the building and the notion of it as the seat of Russian power – in *Red Fortress; The Secret Heart of Russia's History* by Catherine Merridale, joint winner of the 2014 Wolfson History Prize.

The Time of Troubles

Ivan IV's official successor was his mentally enfeebled son Fyodor, who left the actual business of government to his brother-in-law, Boris Godunov, a skilled 'prime minister' who repaired much of the damage done by Ivan. Fyodor died childless in 1598, ending the 700-year Rurikid dynasty, and Boris ruled as tsar for seven more years.

Shortly after Boris' death, a Polish-backed Catholic pretender arrived on the scene claiming to be Dmitry, another son of Ivan the Terrible (Dmitry had in fact died in obscure circumstances in Uglich in 1591, possibly murdered on Boris Godunov's orders). This 'False Dmitry' gathered a huge ragtag army as he advanced on Moscow. Boris Godunov's son was lynched and the boyars acclaimed the pretender tsar.

Thus began the Time of Troubles (the Smuta), a spell of anarchy, dynastic chaos and foreign invasions. At its heart was a struggle between the boyars and central government (the tsar). Peace was restored in 1613 when 16-year-old Mikhail Romanov, a relative of Ivan IV's first wife, became tsar, the first of a new dynasty that was to rule until 1917.

The story of Boris Godunov inspired both a play by Alexander Pushkin in 1831 and an opera by Modest Mussorgsky in 1869.

1480

Ivan's armies face down those of the Tatars who come to extract tributes withheld by Muscovy for four years; this ends the Golden Horde's dominance of Russia.

1505–33

Vasily III annexes the autonomous Russian provinces of Pskov and Ryazan, captures Smolensk from Lithuania and extends Moscow's influence south along the Volga towards Kazan.

1533

Aged three, Ivan IV is proclaimed Grand Prince of Moscow when his father, Vasily III, dies. His mother acts as regent until she dies – possibly poisoned – in 1538.

1547

The coronation of Ivan IV (whose military victories and fearsome temper later earn him the name Ivan the Terrible) sees the 16-year-old become 'Tsar of all the Russias'.

The Empire Expands

Peter the Great

Peter I, known as 'the Great' for his commanding 2.24m frame and his equally commanding victory over the Swedes, dragged Russia kicking and screaming into Europe and made the country a major world power.

In 2008 in a telephone poll conducted by the TV station Rossiya that involved over 50 million people, the medieval prince Alexander Nevsky took top place as the most famous Russian, followed by reformist Prime Minister Pyotr Stolypin, who was assassinated in 1911, and Stalin.

Born to Tsar Alexey's second wife, Natalia, in 1672, Peter was an energetic and inquisitive youth who often visited Moscow's European district to learn about the West. Dutch and British ship captains in Arkhangelsk gave him navigation lessons on the White Sea.

Following his mother's death in 1694 and his half-brother Ivan's in 1696, Peter became Russia's sole ruler and embarked on a modernisation campaign, symbolised by his fact-finding mission to Europe in 1697–98. Travelling incognito under the name Peter Mikhailov, Peter learned about shipbuilding in Holland and met with fellow rulers in Prussia, the Netherlands, England, Austria and Poland. He also hired a thousand experts for service in Russia.

Peter's alliance with Prussia and Denmark led to the Great Northern War against Sweden (1700–21). The rout of Charles XII's forces at the Battle of Poltava (1709) heralded Russia's power and the collapse of the Swedish empire. The Treaty of Nystadt (1721) gave Peter control of the Gulf of Finland and the eastern shores of the Baltic Sea. In the midst of all this (in 1707) he put down another peasant rebellion, led by Don Cossack Kondraty Bulavin, and founded his new capital of St Petersburg in 1703.

Peter's Reforms

Peter's lasting legacy was mobilising Russian resources to compete on equal terms with the West. His territorial gains were small, but the strategic Baltic territories added ethnic variety, including a new upper class of German traders and administrators who formed the backbone of Russia's commercial and military expansion.

Right up to the turn of the 20th century, Russia had serfs: peasants and servants who were tied to their master's estates. The value of those estates was determined not by their size or output but by the number of such indentured souls.

Vast sums of money were needed to build St Petersburg, pay a growing civil service, modernise the army and launch naval and commercial fleets. But money was scarce in an economy based on serf labour, so Peter slapped taxes on everything from coffins to beards, including an infamous 'Soul Tax' on all lower-class adult males. The lot of serfs worsened, as they bore the main tax burden.

Even the upper classes had to chip in: aristocrats could serve in either the army or the civil service, or lose their titles and land. Birth counted for little, with state servants being subject to Peter's Table of Ranks, a performance-based ladder of promotion, in which the upper grades conferred hereditary nobility. Some aristocrats lost all they had, while capable state employees of humble origin and thousands of foreigners became Russian nobles.

1552
Ivan IV defeats the surviving Tatar khanates of Kazan and, four years later, Astrakhan, thus acquiring for Russia the entire Volga region and a chunk of the Caspian Sea coast.

1580
Yermak Timofeevich and his band of Cossack brigands capture Tyumen from the Turkic khanate Sibir and, two years later, take the capital, Isker, initiating Russia's expansion into Siberia.

1598
Fyodor I dies without producing an heir, ending the 700-year-old Rurikid dynasty. Boris Godunov seizes the throne and proves a capable tsar, instituting educational and social reforms.

1605
Boris' son Fyodor II lasts just three months as tsar before he and his mother are assassinated on the arrival in Moscow of the first False Dmitry.

Female Rulers

Peter died in 1725 without naming a successor. His wife Catherine, a former servant and one-time mistress of the tsar's right-hand man Alexander Menshikov, became the first woman to rule imperial Russia. In doing so, she blazed a path for other women, including her daughter Elizabeth and, later, Catherine the Great, who, between them, held on to the top job for the better part of 70 years.

Catherine left day-to-day administration of Russia to a governing body called the Supreme Privy Council, staffed by many of Peter's leading administrators. When the council elected Peter's niece Anna of Courland (a small principality in present-day Latvia) to the throne, with a contract stating that the council had the final say in policy decisions, Anna reacted by disbanding the council.

Anna ruled from 1730 to 1740, appointing a Baltic German baron, Ernst Johann von Bühren, to handle affairs of state. His name was Russified to Biron, but his heavy-handed, corrupt style came to symbolise the German influence on the royal family that had begun with Peter the Great.

During the reign of Peter's daughter, Elizabeth (1741–61), German influence waned and restrictions on the nobility were loosened. Some aristocrats began to dabble in manufacture and trade.

Benson Bobrick's book *East of the Sun* is a rollicking history of the conquest and settlement of Siberia and the Russian Far East, and is packed with gory details.

THE COSSACKS

The word 'Cossack' (from the Turkic *kazak*, meaning free man, adventurer or horseman) was originally applied to residual Tatar groups and later to serfs, paupers and dropouts who fled south from Russia, Poland and Lithuania in the 15th century. They organised themselves into self-governing communities in the Don Basin, on the Dnepr River in Ukraine and in the southern Urals. Those in a given region (eg the Don Cossacks) were not just a tribe; the men constituted a *voysko* (army), within which each *stanitsa* (village-regiment) elected an *ataman* (leader).

Mindful of their skill as fighters, the Russian government treated the Cossacks carefully, offering autonomy in return for military service. Cossacks such as Yermak Timofeevich were the wedge that opened Siberia in the 17th century. By the 19th century there were a dozen Cossack armies from Ukraine to the Russian Far East and, as a group, they numbered 2.5 million people.

The Cossacks were not always cooperative with the Russian state. Three peasant uprisings in the Volga-Don region – 1670, 1707 and 1773 – were Cossack-led. After 1917 the Bolsheviks abolished Cossack institutions, though some cavalry units were revived in WWII. Since 1991 there has been a Cossack revival particularly in the Don region. Cossack regiments have been officially recognised, there is a presidential adviser on Cossacks and some Cossacks demand that the state recognise them as an ethnic group.

1606

Vasily Shuysky plots against the False Dmitry, has him killed and becomes tsar until 1610, when he is, in turn, deposed and exiled to Warsaw.

1612

A Russian militia, led by Prince Dmitry Pozharsky, retakes Moscow after three years of occupation by the Poles, a victory commemorated every 4 November by the Day of Unity.

1613

Sixteen-year-old Mikhail Romanov, a relative of Ivan IV's first wife, is elected tsar by the Assembly of the Land (Zemsky Sobor), starting the Romanov dynasty.

1645

Under the careful watch of boyar Boris Morozov, 16-year-old Aleksey I becomes tsar. During his reign Russia's territory expands to over 800 million hectares as the conquest of Siberia continues.

RUSSIANS IN AMERICA

In 1648 the Cossack Semyon Dezhnev sailed round the northeastern corner of Asia, from the Pacific Ocean into the Arctic. Eighty years later Peter the Great commissioned Vitus Bering, a Danish officer in the Russian navy, to head the Great Northern Expedition, which was ostensibly a scientific survey of Kamchatka (claimed for the tsar in 1697 by the explorer Vladimir Atlasov) and the eastern seaboard. In reality the survey's aim was to expand Russia's Pacific sphere of influence as far south as Japan and across to North America.

On his second expedition Bering succeeded in discovering Alaska, landing in 1741. The Bering Strait separating Alaska from the Russian mainland is named after him. Unfortunately, on the return voyage his ship was wrecked off an island just 250km east of the Kamchatka coast. Bering died on the island and it, too, now carries his name.

Survivors of Bering's crew brought back reports of an abundance of foxes, fur seals and otters inhabiting the islands off the mainland, triggering a fresh wave of fur-inspired expansion. An Irkutsk trader, Grigory Shelekhov, landed on Kodiak Island (in present-day Alaska) in 1784 and, 15 years later, his successor founded Sitka (originally called New Archangel), the capital of Alaska until 1900.

Russia's early-19th-century attempts to gain more of a foothold on the west coast of America, which included visits by the imperial emissary Nikolai Rezanov to Spanish-controlled California in 1806, are documented with verve in *Glorious Misadventures* by Owen Matthews. It all came to naught and in 1867 Russia opted to sell all 1,518,800 sq km of its Alaskan territory to the US for $7.2 million – worth $119 million today.

Catherine II (the Great)

Daughter of a German prince, Catherine came to Russia at the age of 15 to marry Empress Elizabeth's heir apparent, her nephew Peter III. Intelligent and ambitious, Catherine learned Russian, embraced the Orthodox Church and devoured the writings of European political philosophers.

Robert K Massie's *Peter the Great – His Life and World* is a good read about one of Russia's most influential rulers, and provides much detail about how he created St Petersburg.

Once empress, she embarked on a program of reforms, though she made it clear that she had no intention of limiting her own authority. A new legal code was drafted, the use of torture limited and religious tolerance supported. But any ideas she might have had of improving the lot of serfs went overboard with the violent peasant rebellion of 1773–74, led by the Don Cossack Yemelyan Pugachev, which spread from the Ural Mountains to the Caspian Sea and along the Volga. Hundreds of thousands of serfs responded to Pugachev's promises to end serfdom and taxation, but were beaten by famine and government armies. Pugachev was executed and Catherine put an end to Cossack autonomy.

In the cultural sphere, Catherine increased the number of schools and colleges and expanded publishing. Her vast collection of paintings forms

1667

The war between Russia and Poland over modern-day Ukraine and Belarus ends with the Treaty of Andrusovo; Kyiv, Smolensk and lands east of the Dnepr remain under Russian control.

1670–71

Cossack Stepan (Stenka) Razin leads an uprising in the Volga-Don region. His army of 200,000 seizes the entire lower Volga Basin before he is captured and executed in Red Square.

1676–82

Fyodor III's keen intelligence lays the foundations for a more liberal attitude in the Russian court. Civil and military appointments start to be determined by merit rather than nobility.

1682

Aleksey I's 10-year-old son Peter I becomes joint tsar with his chronically ill half-brother Ivan V. Ivan's elder sister, Sophia, acting as regent, holds the real power.

the core of the present-day Hermitage collection. A critical elite gradually developed, alienated from most uneducated Russians, but also increasingly at odds with central authority – a 'split personality' common among future Russian radicals.

Territorial Gains

Catherine's reign saw major expansion at the expense of the weakened Ottoman Turks and Poles, engineered by her 'prime minister' and foremost lover, Grigory Potemkin (Potyomkin). War with the Turks began in 1768, peaked with the naval victory at Çesme and ended with a 1774 treaty giving Russia control of the north coast of the Black Sea, freedom of shipping through the Dardanelles to the Mediterranean and 'protectorship' of Christian interests in the Ottoman Empire – a pretext for later incursions into the Balkans. Crimea was annexed in 1783.

Poland had spent the previous century collapsing into a set of semi-independent units with a figurehead king in Warsaw. Catherine manipulated events with divide-and-rule tactics and even had another former lover, Stanislas Poniatowski, installed as king. Austria and Prussia proposed sharing Poland among the three powers, and in 1772, 1793 and 1795 the country was carved up, ceasing to exist as an independent state until 1918. Eastern Poland and the Grand Duchy of Lithuania – roughly, present-day Lithuania, Belarus and western Ukraine – came under Russian rule.

Alexander I

Catherine was succeeded by her son, Paul I. A mysterious figure in Russian history (often called the Russian Hamlet by Western scholars), he antagonised the gentry with attempts to reimpose compulsory state service and was killed in a coup in 1801.

Paul's son and successor was Catherine's favourite grandson, Alexander I, who had been trained by the best European tutors. He kicked off his reign with several reforms, including an expansion of the school system that brought education within reach of the lower middle classes. But he was soon preoccupied with the wars against Napoleon.

Under the Treaty of Tilsit in 1807, Alexander agreed to be Emperor of the East while Napoleon was declared Emperor of the West. This alliance, however, lasted only until 1810, when Russia's resumption of trade with England provoked the French leader to raise an army of 600,000 for an ill-fated march on Moscow.

Meanwhile Russia was expanding its territory on other fronts. The kingdom of Georgia united with Russia in 1801. After a war with Sweden (1807–09), Alexander became Grand Duke of Finland. Russia argued with Turkey over the Danube principalities of Bessarabia (covering modern Moldova and part of Ukraine) and Wallachia (now in Romania),

Documents in Russian History (http://academic.shu.edu/russian-history/index.php/Main_Page) is an online source of primary documents on Russia, including proclamations by the tsars and speeches by Lenin and Stalin.

Read about the fascinating life of Grigory Potemkin, lover of Catherine the Great and mover and shaker in 18th-century Russia, in Simon Sebag Montefiore's *Prince of Princes: The Life of Potemkin.*

1689

Following a botched coup, Sophia enters a convent. Peter's mother, Natalia, becomes the power behind the throne. Her death in 1694 leaves her son as effective sole ruler.

1695

Peter sends Russia's first navy down the Don River and captures the Black Sea port of Azov from the Crimean Tatars, vassals of the Ottoman Turks.

1700–21

Russia battles Sweden for control of the Baltic in the Great Northern War. Sweden, fighting on several fronts, eventually cedes much territory, including Estonia and part of Karelia.

1703

Peter I establishes the Peter and Paul Fortress on Zayachy Island in the Neva River, thus founding Sankt Pieter Burkh (St Petersburg), named after his patron saint.

taking Bessarabia in 1812. Persia ceded northern Azerbaijan a year later and Yerevan (in Armenia) in 1828.

The Road to Revolution

The Decembrists

The hit rock opera *Juno and Avos*, running on stage in Moscow since 1981, is a Madame Butterfly-esque drama based on the tragic, real-life romance between Russian noble and adventurer Nikolai Rezanov and Conchita Arguello, the teenage daughter of the head of the Spanish mission in San Francisco.

Named after the month of their ill-fated and disorganised attempt to overthrow the new tsar, Nicholas I, the Decembrists were a secret society of reform-minded young army officers and upper class nobles. Alexander Herzen, the 'father of Russian socialism', called them 'a perfect galaxy of brilliant talent, independent character and chivalrous valour'.

The war against Napoleon and the subsequent four-month occupation of Paris exposed these officers to far more liberal ideas than existed in their homeland. On their return to Russia, they formed a couple of secret societies with the general aims of emancipating the serfs and introducing a constitutional monarchy. The officers' chance for action came with the unexpected death of Alexander on 19 November 1825.

Alexander's youngest brother, the militaristic Nicholas, was due to be crowned on 26 December. On 14 December a group of officers led 3000 troops into St Petersburg's Senate Square, proclaiming their loyalty instead to Constantine, Alexander's elder brother. However, their leader, Prince Trubetskoy, suffering a last-minute change of heart, was a no-show along with other key figures. The revolt was quickly squashed by troops loyal to Nicholas.

Five of the Decembrists were executed and over 100 – mostly aristocrats and officers – were exiled to Siberia along with their families for terms of hard labour, mostly in rural parts of the Chita region. Pardoned by Tsar Alexander II in 1856, many of these exiles chose to stay on in Siberia, their presence having a marked effect on the educational and cultural life in their adopted towns.

Vincent Cronin's book, *Catherine, Empress of all the Russias*, paints a more sympathetic portrait than usual of a woman traditionally seen as a scheming, power-crazed sexpot.

The Crimean War

Nicholas I's reign (1825–55) was a time of stagnation and repression under a tsar who claimed: 'I do not rule Russia; 10,000 clerks do.' There were positive developments, however. The economy grew and grain exports increased. Nicholas detested serfdom, if only because he detested the serf-owning class. As a result, peasants on state lands, nearly half the total, were given title to the land and, in effect, freed.

In foreign policy, Nicholas' meddling in the Balkans was eventually to destroy Russian credibility in Europe. In 1854, Russian troops marched into the Ottoman provinces of Moldavia and Wallachia – ostensibly to protect Christian communities there. This was the spark for the Crimean War with the Ottoman Empire, Britain and France. At Sevastopol an

1712–14

At the behest of Peter I, government institutions begin to move from Moscow, and St Petersburg assumes the administrative and ceremonial role as the Russian capital.

1724

Catherine I (born Martha Elena Scowronska to lowly Latvian peasants), secretly betrothed to Peter I in 1707 and publicly married in 1712, is officially announced as Russia's coruler.

1728

After the death of Peter I and two years of rule by his wife, Catherine, his grandson Peter II shifts the Russian capital back to Moscow.

1730

The direct male line of the Romanov dynasty ends with Peter II's death. His successor is Anna, Duchess of Courland, daughter of Peter the Great's half-brother and coruler, Ivan V.

Anglo-French-Turkish force besieged the Russian naval headquarters. Inept command on both sides led to a bloody, stalemated war.

In 1856, Alexander II, Nicholas' successor, accepted peace in Crimea on unfavourable terms. The war had revealed the backwardness behind the post-1812 imperial glory and the time for reform had come.

Revolutionary Movements

Abolition of serfdom in 1861 opened the way for a market economy and industrialisation. Railways and factories were built, and cities expanded as peasants left the land. Foreign investment in Russia grew during the 1880s and 1890s, but nothing was done to modernise farming, and very little to help peasants. By 1914, 85% of the Russian population was still rural, but their lot had barely improved in 50 years.

Peasants were angry at having to pay for land they considered theirs by right. Radical students, known as *narodniki* (populists), took to the countryside in the 1870s to rouse the peasants, but the students and the peasants were worlds apart and the campaign failed.

Other populists saw more value in cultivating revolution among the growing urban working class (the proletariat), while yet others turned to

Adam Zamoyski's book *1812: Napoleon's Fatal March on Moscow* is packed with graphic detail and individual stories that bring the famous defeat to life.

THE IMPACT OF 1812

The inspiration most memorably for Tchaikovsky's *1812 Overture* and a plot point in Leo Tolstoy's epic novel *War and Peace,* the cultural impact of Napoleon's failed bid to conquer Russia endures today. But, according to Stephen Talty, author of the *The Illustrious Dead: The Terrifying Story of How Typhus Killed Napoleon's Greatest Army,* if it hadn't been for a disease spread by lice, Napoleon's forces might have stood a far better chance of achieving their goal.

Vastly outnumbered, Russia's army retreated throughout the summer of 1812, scorching the earth in an attempt to deny the French sustenance and fighting some successful rearguard actions. However, it was the general filthiness of Poland and Lithuania that undermined the unwashed French troops who began to succumb to typhus. By the time Napoleon reached Borodino, 130km outside Moscow, his army was down to around 100,000 men. The battle here was extremely bloody but inconclusive, with the Russians withdrawing in good order.

Before the month was out, Napoleon entered a deserted Moscow; the same day, the city began to burn down around him (by whose hand has never been established). Alexander ignored his overtures to negotiate. With winter coming and his supply lines overstretched, Napoleon was forced to retreat. His starving troops were picked off by Russian partisans. Only one in 20 made it back to the relative safety of Poland, and the Russians pursued them all the way to Paris.

1732

Empress Anna reverses the decision of Peter II and moves the capital to St Petersburg, presiding over the recommencement of the city's construction and development.

1740

Twelve days before her death, Empress Anna adopts a two-month-old baby. He becomes Tsar Ivan VI, with his natural mother, Anna Leopoldovna of Mecklenburg, as regent.

1741

Elizabeth, second-oldest daughter of Peter I and Catherine I, seizes power in a bloodless coup. She creates the most luxurious court in Europe.

1756

Russia takes on Prussia in the Seven Years' War that engulfs Europe; her armies are victorious at Battle of Gross-Jägersdorf in 1757, but hold off invading Königsberg.

terrorism: one secret society, the People's Will, fatally attacked Alexander II with a bomb in 1881.

Not all opponents of tsarism were radical revolutionaries. Some moderates, well off and with much to lose from a revolution, called themselves liberals and advocated constitutional reform along Western European lines, with universal suffrage and a *duma* (national parliament). However, Alexander II refused to set up a representative assembly.

Discontent was sometimes directed at Jews and took the form of violent mass attacks (pogroms). At their height in the 1880s, these were often fanned by the authorities to divert social tension onto a convenient scapegoat.

The publication of nobleman Aleksandr Radishchev's *A Journey from St Petersburg to Moscow* (1790), a passionate attack on the institution of serfdom, enraged Catherine the Great; Radishchev's beliefs later inspired the Decembrist revolutionaries.

Rise of Marxism

The more radical revolutionaries were genuinely surprised that there was no uprising after Alexander II's assassination. Most were rounded up and executed or exiled, and the reign of his son Alexander III was marked by repression of revolutionaries and liberals alike. Many revolutionaries fled abroad – including Georgy Plekhanov and Pavel Axelrod, founders of the Russian Social-Democratic Workers Party in 1883, and, in 1899, Vladimir Ulyanov, better known by his later pseudonym, Lenin.

Social democrats in Europe were being elected to parliaments and developing Marxism into 'parliamentary socialism', improving the lot of workers through legislation. But in Russia there was no parliament – and there was an active secret police, to boot. At a meeting of the Socialist International movement in London in 1903, Lenin stood for violent overthrow of the government by a small, committed, well-organised party, while Plekhanov stood for mass membership and cooperation with other political forces.

Lenin won the vote through clever manoeuvring, and his faction came to be known as the Bolsheviks (meaning members of the majority); Plekhanov's faction became the Mensheviks (members of the minority). The Mensheviks actually outnumbered the Bolsheviks in the party, but Lenin clung to the name, for obvious reasons.

Russo-Japanese War

Nicholas II, who succeeded his father, Alexander III, in 1894, was a weak man who commanded less respect than his father, but was equally opposed to representative government.

The most serious blow to his position was a humiliating defeat by Japan when the two countries clashed over their respective 'spheres of influence' in the Far East – Russia's in Manchuria and Japan's in Korea. As in Crimea 50 years before, poor diplomacy led to war. In 1904 Japan attacked the Russian naval base at Port Arthur (near Dalian in present-day China).

1761
With Russian troops occupying Berlin, Prussia is saved only by Elizabeth's death in 1761 and the ascension to the throne of her pro-German nephew, Peter III.

1762
A coup led by a lover of Catherine II (Catherine the Great) ousts her husband Peter III. Catherine becomes empress and Peter is murdered shortly after.

1768–74
Victories in the Russo-Turkish War, including the decisive Battle of Chesma, expand Russian control in southern Ukraine and give access to two ports on the Black Sea.

1773
Emilian Pugachev, a Don Cossack, claims to be the overthrown Peter III and begins a violent peasant uprising, which is subsequently quelled by brute force.

The war continued on land and sea, with the ultimate disaster for Russia coming in May 1905, when the entire Baltic fleet, which had sailed halfway around the world to relieve Port Arthur, was sunk in the Tsushima Straits off Japan. In September 1905 Russia signed the Treaty of Portsmouth (New Hampshire), under the terms of which it gave up Port Arthur, Dalny and southern Sakhalin as well as any claims to Korea – but retained its preeminent position in Manchuria.

Despite all this, Siberia and the Russian Far East were prospering. From 1886 to 1911, the immigrant population leapt above eight million, thanks partly to ease of access via the new Trans-Siberian Railway. Most immigrants were peasants, who put Siberian agriculture at the head of the class in grain, stock and dairy farming. (Before the October Revolution, Europeans had Siberian butter on their tables.)

Geoffrey Hosking's *Russia and the Russians* is a definitive one-volume trot through 1000 years of Russian history by a top scholar.

1905 Revolution

Unrest across Russia became widespread after the fall of Port Arthur. On 9 January 1905 a priest named Georgy Gapon led a crowd of some 200,000 people to the Winter Palace in St Petersburg to petition the tsar for better working conditions. Singing 'God Save the Tsar', they were met by imperial guards, who opened fire and killed several hundred. This was Bloody Sunday.

Social democrat activists formed soviets (workers' councils) in St Petersburg and Moscow, which proved remarkably successful: the St Petersburg Soviet, led by Mensheviks under Leon Trotsky, declared a general strike, which brought the country to a standstill in October.

In 1909 Sergei Prokudin-Gorsky set out to shoot all of the 'lands and people living on Russian land' using his own colour photographic technique. View the stunning results at www.prokudin-gorsky.ru/collection.htm.

The tsar gave in and general elections were held in April 1906 that created a *duma* with a leftist majority that demanded further reforms. The tsar disbanded it. New elections in 1907 pushed the *duma* further to the left. It was again disbanded, and a new electoral law, limiting the vote to the upper classes and Orthodox Christians, ensured that the third and fourth *duma* were more cooperative with the tsar, who continued to choose the prime minister and cabinet.

The capable prime minister, Pyotr Stolypin, abolished the hated redemption payments in the countryside. Enterprising peasants were now able to buy decent parcels of land, which could be worked efficiently; this led to the creation of a new class of *kulak* (wealthier peasant) and to a series of good harvests. It also made it easier for peasants to leave their villages, providing a mobile labour force for industry. Russia enjoyed unprecedented economic growth and radical activists lost their following.

Still, Stolypin was assassinated in 1911 and the tsarist regime again lost touch with the people. Nicholas became a puppet of his strong-willed, eccentric wife, Alexandra, who herself fell under the spell of the Siberian mystic Rasputin.

1796
Upon Catherine the Great's death, her son Paul I ascends the throne. One of his first acts as tsar is to decree that women can never again rule Russia.

1801
Tsar Paul is murdered in his bedroom in the fortress-like Mikhaylovsky Castle. The coup places on the throne Alexander I, who vows to continue the reformist policies of his grandmother.

1807
Following defeats at Austerlitz, north of Vienna, and then at Friedland, in Prussia, Alexander I signs the Treaty of Tilsit with Napoleon, uniting the two sides (in theory) against England.

1810
Napoleon's armies make their ill-fated march on Moscow. Muscovites burn two-thirds of the capital rather than see it occupied by the French who are forced to retreat.

THE PRIEST OF SEX

Grigory Rasputin was born in the Siberian village of Pokrovskoe in 1869. Never a monk as is sometimes supposed, Rasputin experienced a vision of the Virgin while working in the fields in his mid-20s and left Pokrovskoe to seek enlightenment. On his wanderings he came to believe, as did the contemporary Khlyst (Whip) sect, that sinning (especially through sex), then repenting, could bring people close to God.

In St Petersburg Rasputin's racy brand of redemption, along with his soothing talk, compassion and generosity, made him very popular with some aristocratic women. Eventually, he was summoned by Tsaritsa Alexandra and seemed able, thanks to some kind of hypnotic power, to halt the uncontrollable bleeding of her haemophiliac son, Tsarevitch Alexey, the heir to the throne. As he continued his dissolute life, Rasputin's influence on the imperial family grew to the point where he could make or break the careers of ministers and generals. He became increasingly unpopular and many scapegoated him for Russia's disastrous performance in WWI.

In 1916 Prince Felix Yusupov and others hatched an assassination plot. According to Yusupov's own account of the murderous affair, this proved to be easier said than done: Rasputin survived poisoning, several shots and a beating, all in one evening at St Petersburg's Yusupov Palace. Apparently he died only when drowned in a nearby river. However, a 2004 BBC documentary uncovered evidence that Rasputin actually died from his bullet wounds, one of which was delivered by a British secret agent working in conjunction with the Russian plotters. For the fascinating background to this version of events read Andrew Cook's *To Kill Rasputin*.

WWI & February Revolution

Russia's involvement with the Balkans made it a main player in the world war that began there in 1914. The Russian campaign went badly from the start. Between 1915 and 1918 the theatre of war was mostly around Russia's western border and often on enemy territory. Much, if not most, of the fighting was with Austro-Hungarians in Galitsia (Halichina in Ukrainian), rather than with the Germans. The latter didn't make major advances into Russian territory until 1918, by which time an estimated two million Russian troops had been killed and Germany controlled Poland and much of the Baltic coast, Belarus and Ukraine.

The tsar responded to antiwar protests by disbanding the *duma* and assuming personal command in the field. At home, the disorganised government failed to introduce rationing, and in February 1917 in Petrograd (the new, 'less German' name for St Petersburg), discontent in the food queues turned to riots, kicking off the February Revolution. Soldiers and police mutinied, refusing to fire on demonstrators. A new Petrograd Soviet of Workers' and Soldiers' Deputies was formed on the 1905 model,

1814

Russian troops briefly occupy Paris after driving Napoleon back across Europe. A 'Holy Alliance' between Russia, Austria and Prussia is the outcome of the Congress of Vienna in 1815.

1817

Alexander I's appointment of the brutal general Alexey Yermelov to subdue the fractious tribes of the Caucasus sows seeds of discontent that continue to have repercussions today.

1825

Alexander I dies suddenly; reformers assemble in St Petersburg to protest the succession of Nicholas I. The new tsar brutally crushes the Decembrist Revolt, killing hundreds in the process.

1853–56

Russia takes on an alliance of the British, French and the Ottoman Empire in the Crimean War, a conflict that includes the infamous Charge of the Light Brigade.

and more sprang up elsewhere. The reconvened *duma* ignored an order to disband itself and set up a committee to assume government.

Now there were two alternative power bases in the capital. The soviet was a rallying and debating point for factory workers and soldiers; the *duma* committee attracted the educated and commercial elite. In February the two reached agreement on a provisional government that would demand the tsar's abdication. The tsar tried to return to Petrograd but was blocked by his own troops. On 1 March he abdicated.

By turns anecdotal and specific, *A People's Tragedy: The Russian Revolution, 1891–1924* by erudite scholar Orlando Figes paints a vivid picture of this tumultuous period in Russian history.

October Revolution

The provisional government announced general elections for November 1917 and continued the war despite a collapse of discipline in the army and popular demands for peace. On 3 April Lenin and other exiled Bolsheviks returned to Petrograd. Though in the minority in the soviets, the Bolsheviks were organised and committed. They won over many with a demand for immediate 'peace, land and bread', and believed the soviets should seize power at once. But a series of violent mass demonstrations in July, inspired by the Bolsheviks, was in the end not fully backed by the soviets and was quelled. Lenin fled to Finland and Alexander Kerensky, a moderate Social Revolutionary, became prime minister.

In September the Russian military chief of staff, General Kornilov, sent cavalry to Petrograd to crush the soviets. Kerensky turned to the left for support against this insubordination, even courting the Bolsheviks, and defeated the counter-revolution. After this, public opinion favoured the Bolsheviks, who took control of the Petrograd Soviet (chaired by Trotsky, who had joined them) and, by extension, all the soviets in the land. Lenin decided it was time to seize power and returned from Finland in October.

During the night of 24 October 1917, Bolshevik workers and soldiers in Petrograd seized government buildings and communication centres, and arrested the provisional government, which was meeting in the Winter Palace. (Kerensky escaped, eventually dying in the USA in 1970.) Soon after, a provisional government was formed, headed by Lenin, with Trotsky as commissar for foreign affairs and the Georgian Josef Stalin as commissar for nationalities, in charge of policy for all non-Russians in the former empire.

Local soviets elsewhere in Russia seized power relatively easily, but the coup in Moscow took six days of fighting. The general elections scheduled for November went ahead with half of Russia's male population voting. Even though 55% chose Kerensky's rural socialist party and only 25% voted for the Bolsheviks, when the Founding Assembly met in January the Bolsheviks disbanded it after its first day in session, thus setting the antidemocratic tone for the coming decades.

1855

Nicholas I's successor, Alexander II, starts negotiations to end the Crimean War and realises reform is necessary if Russia is to remain a major European power.

1860

The Treaty of Peking sees China cede to Japan all territory east of the Ussuri and as far south as the Korea border, including the newly established port of Vladivostok.

1861

The emancipation of the serfs frees labour to feed the Russian industrial revolution. Workers flood into the capital, leading to overcrowding, poor sanitation, epidemics and societal discontent.

1866

The revolutionary Dmitry Karakozov makes an unsuccessful attempt on the life of Alexander II, the first of several assassination bids; all student groups are banned at St Petersburg University.

Soviet Russia

Civil War

The Soviet government immediately redistributed land to those who worked it, signed an armistice with the Germans in December 1917 and set up its own secret police force, the Cheka. Trotsky, now military commissar, founded the Red Army in January 1918. In March the Bolshevik Party renamed itself the Communist Party and moved the capital to Moscow.

Seventeen Moments in Soviet History (http://soviethistory.macalester.edu) is a well-designed site that covers all the major events and social movements during the life of the USSR in fascinating detail.

The murder of Nicholas II and his family in July 1918 was the prelude to a systematic program of arrest, torture and execution of anyone opposed to Soviet rule. Those hostile to the Bolsheviks, collectively termed 'Whites', had developed strongholds in the south and east of the country. But they lacked unity, including as they did tsarist stalwarts, landlord-killing social revolutionaries, Czech prisoners of war, Finnish partisans and Japanese troops. The Bolsheviks had the advantage of controlling the heart of Russia, including its war industry and communications. Full-scale civil war broke out in early 1918 and lasted until 1922 when the Red Army was victorious at Volochaevka, west of Khabarovsk.

By 1921 the Communist Party had firmly established one-party rule, thanks to the Red Army and the Cheka, which continued to eliminate opponents. Some opponents escaped, joining an estimated 1.5 million citizens in exile.

War Communism

During the civil war, a system called War Communism subjected every aspect of society to the aim of victory. This meant sweeping nationalisation in all economic sectors and strict administrative control by the Soviet government, which in turn was controlled by the Communist Party.

The Party itself was restructured to reflect Lenin's creed of 'democratic centralism', which held that Party decisions should be obeyed all the way down the line. A new political bureau, the Politburo, was created for

THE SWITCH IN CALENDARS

Until 1918 Russian dates followed the Julian calendar, which lagged behind the Gregorian calendar (used by pretty much every other country in the world) by 13 days. The new Soviet regime brought Russia into line by following 31 January 1918 with 14 February (skipping 1 to 13 February). This explains why, in Russian history, the revolution was on 25 October 1917 while in the West it occurred on 7 November 1917. The Julian calendar is still used in Russia by the Orthodox Church, which is why Christmas Day is celebrated on 7 January instead of 25 December.

1867

Debts from the Crimean War force Russia to sell gold-rich Alaska and the Aleutian Islands to the USA – their only supporter during the conflict – for US$7.2 million.

1877–78

War against the Ottoman Empire results in the liberation of Bulgaria and annulment of the conditions of the Treaty of Paris of 1856 that ended the Crimean War.

1881

Terrorists finally kill Alexander II. St Petersburg's Church of the Saviour on Spilled Blood is built on the site of the assassination. Alexander III undoes many of his father's reforms.

1882

Jews are subject to harsh legal restrictions in retribution for their alleged role in the assassination of Alexander II. A series of pogroms provokes Jewish migration from Russia.

Party decision-making, and a new secretariat supervised Party appointments, ensuring that only loyal members were given responsibility.

War Communism was also a form of social engineering to create a classless society. Many 'class enemies' were eliminated by execution or exile, with disastrous economic consequences. Forced food requisitions and hostility towards larger, more efficient farmers, combined with drought and a breakdown of infrastructure, led to the enormous famine of 1920–21, when between four and five million people died.

Edmund Wilson's magnum opus, *To the Finland Station* (1940), is the most authoritative account of the development of socialism and communism in Russia.

The New Economic Policy

Under the New Economic Policy (NEP) adopted in 1921, the state continued to own the 'commanding heights' of the economy – large-scale industry, banks, transport – but allowed private enterprise to reemerge. Farm output improved as the kulaks consolidated their holdings and employed landless peasants as wage earners. Farm surplus was sold to the cities in return for industrial products, giving rise to a new class of traders and small-scale industrialists called nepmen. By the late 1920s, agricultural and industrial production had reached prewar levels.

But the political tide was set the other way. At the 1921 Party congress, Lenin outlawed debate within the Party as 'factionalism', launching the first systematic purge among Party members. The Cheka was reorganised as the GPU (State Political Administration) in 1922, gaining much greater powers to operate outside the law.

Stalin vs Trotsky

In May 1922 Lenin suffered the first of a series of paralysing strokes. After his 1924 death, his embalmed remains were put on display in Moscow and a personality cult was built around him – all orchestrated by Stalin.

But Lenin had failed to name a successor and had expressed a low opinion of 'too rude' Stalin. The charismatic Trotsky, hero of the civil war and second only to Lenin as an architect of the revolution, wanted collectivisation of agriculture – an extension of War Communism – and worldwide revolution. He attacked Party 'bureaucrats' who wished to concentrate on socialism in the Soviet Union.

But even before Lenin's death, the powers that mattered in the Party and soviets had backed a three-man leadership of Zinoviev, Kamenev and Stalin, in which Stalin already pulled the strings. As Party general secretary, he controlled all appointments and had installed his supporters wherever it mattered. In 1927 he succeeded in getting Trotsky, his main rival, expelled.

1883

The revolutionaries Georgy Plekhanov and Pavel Axelrod flee to Switzerland, adopt Marxism and found the Russian Social-Democratic Workers Party. One of their converts is Vladimir Lenin.

1886

Alexander III authorises the building of 7500km of railroad across Siberia between Chelyabinsk and Vladivostok, laying the foundations for the Trans-Siberian Railway.

1895

Lenin commands Russia's first Marxist cell in St Petersburg. He's arrested and sentenced to three years of exile in Shushenskoe where he marries Nadezhda Krupskaya in a church wedding.

1896

Nicholas II's reign is marked by tragedy from the start when a stampede by crowds assembled in Moscow for his coronation results in over 1300 being trampled to death.

Five-Year Plans & Farm Collectivisation

The first of Stalin's Five-Year Plans, announced in 1928, called for quadrupling the output of heavy industry, such as power stations, mines, steelworks and railways. Agriculture was to be collectivised to get the peasants to fulfil production quotas, which would feed the growing cities and provide food exports to pay for imported heavy machinery.

Simon Sebag Montefiore has penned two highly revealing and entertaining books about Russia's most notorious 20th-century leader: *Stalin: The Court of the Red Czar* and *Young Stalin*.

The forced collectivisation of agriculture destroyed the country's peasantry (still 80% of the population) as a class and as a way of life. Farmers were required to pool their land and resources into *kolkhozy* (collective farms), usually consisting of about 75 households and dozens of square kilometres in area, which became their collective property, in return for compulsory quotas of produce. These *kolkhozy* covered two-thirds of all farmland, supported by a network of Machine Tractor Stations that dispensed machinery and advice (political or otherwise).

Farmers who resisted – and most *kulaks* did, especially in Ukraine and the Volga and Don regions, which had the biggest grain surpluses – were killed or deported to labour camps in the millions. Farmers slaughtered their animals rather than hand them over, leading to the loss of half the national livestock. A drought and continued grain requisitions led to famine in the same three regions in 1932–33, in which millions more people perished. Ukrainians consider this famine, known as *golodomor*, a deliberate act of genocide against them while others say Stalin deliberately orchestrated this tragedy to wipe out opposition.

The Gulag

The Whisperers: Private Life in Stalin's Russia by Orlando Figes is an engrossing account of how ordinary people coped with the daily harsh realities of Soviet life.

Many new mines and factories were built in Central Asia or Siberia, which was resource-rich but thinly populated. A key labour force was provided by the network of concentration camps begun under Lenin and now called the Gulag, from the initial letters of Glavnoe Upravlenie Lagerey (Main Administration for Camps), which stretched from the north of European Russia through Siberia and Central Asia to Russia's Far East.

The Gulag's inmates – some of whose only 'offence' was to joke about Stalin or steal two spikelets of wheat from a *kolkhoz* field – cut trees, dug canals, laid railway tracks and worked in factories in remote areas, especially Siberia and the Russian Far East. A huge slice of the northeast was set aside exclusively for labour camps, and whole cities such as Komsomolsk-na-Amure and Magadan were developed as Gulag centres.

The Gulag population grew from 30,000 in 1928 to eight million in 1938. The average life expectancy after being sentenced to the Gulag was two years: 90% of inmates died. The Gulag continued well after WWII; Boris Yeltsin announced the release of Russia's 'last 10' political prisoners from a camp near Perm in 1992.

1903

The Russian Social-Democratic Workers Party splits into the radical Bolsheviks and the more conservative Mensheviks. The two factions coexist until 1912, when the Bolsheviks set up their own party.

1904–05

In the Russo-Japanese War the Russians lose Port Arthur and see their fleet virtually annihilated. When Japan occupies Sakhalin Island, Russia is forced to sue for peace.

1905

Hundreds of people are killed when troops fire on peaceful protestors presenting a petition to the tsar. Nicholas II is held responsible for the tragedy, dubbed Bloody Sunday.

1906–07

Nicholas II allows elections for a parliament *(duma)* in 1906 and 1907. Both *duma* prove to be too left-wing for the tsar so he promptly dissolves them.

Anne Applebaum, author of the Pulitzer Prize–winning *Gulag: A History,* reckons that at least 18 million people passed through the camp system. Many more suffered, though. Nadezhda Mandelstam, whose husband Osip Mandelstam, a highly regarded poet, was exiled to Siberia in 1934, wrote that a wife considered herself a widow from the moment of her husband's arrest. She was almost right – Osip lasted four years before dying at the Vtoraya Rechka transit camp in Vladivostok.

The Purges

Early camp inmates were often farmers caught up in the collectivisation, but in the 1930s the terror shifted to Party members and other influential people not enthusiastic enough about Stalin. A series of show trials were held in Moscow, in which the charges ranged from murder plots and capitalist sympathies to Trotskyist conspiracies. The biggest such trial was in 1938 against 21 leading Bolsheviks, including Party theoretician Bukharin.

Throughout 1937 and 1938, the secret police (now called the NKVD, the People's Commissariat of Internal Affairs) took victims from their homes at night; most were never heard of again. In the non-Russian republics of the USSR, virtually the whole Party apparatus was eliminated on charges of 'bourgeois nationalism'. The bloody purge clawed its way into all sectors and levels of society – even 400 of the Red Army's 700 generals were shot. Its victims are thought to have totalled 8.5 million.

Stalin once remarked that the death of one person was tragic, the death of a million 'a statistic': historians conservatively estimate that some 20 million Soviet citizens died as a result of his policies, purges and paranoia.

The German–Soviet Pact

In 1939 Russian offers of a security deal with the UK and France to counter Germany's possible invasion of Poland were met with a lukewarm reception. Under no illusions about Hitler's ultimate intentions, Stalin needed to buy time to prepare his country for war and saw a deal with the Germans as a route to making territorial gains in Poland.

On 23 August 1939 the Soviet and German foreign ministers, Molotov and Ribbentrop, signed a nonaggression pact. A secret protocol stated that any future rearrangement would divide Poland between them; Germany would have a free hand in Lithuania and the Soviet Union in Estonia, Latvia, Finland and Bessarabia, which had been lost to Romania in 1918.

Germany invaded Poland on 1 September; the UK and France declared war on Germany on 3 September. Stalin traded the Polish provinces of Warsaw and Lublin with Hitler for most of Lithuania and the Red Army marched into these territories less than three weeks later. The Soviet gains in Poland, many of which were areas inhabited by non-Polish speakers and had been under Russian control before WWI, were quickly incorporated into the Belarusian and Ukrainian republics of the USSR.

1911

Having survived court intrigues, including the wrath of Tsaritsa Alexandra for ordering Rasputin's expulsion from St Petersburg, reforming prime minister Pyotr Stolypin is assassinated while at the theatre in Kyiv.

1912

The election of a fourth *duma* coincides with worker strikes. Even so, an exiled Lenin tells an audience in Switzerland that there will be no revolution in his lifetime.

1914

WWI kicks off with an unprepared Russia invading Austrian Galicia and German Prussia and immediately suffering defeats. St Petersburg becomes the less Germanic-sounding Petrograd.

Feb 1917

The February Revolution in Petrograd results in a soviet of Workers' and Soldiers' Deputies as well as a reconvened *duma;* Nicholas II abdicates on 1 March.

The Great Patriotic War

'Operation Barbarossa', Hitler's secret plan for an invasion of the Soviet Union, began on 22 June 1941. Russia was better prepared, but the disorganised Red Army was no match for the German war machine, which advanced on three fronts. Within four months the Germans had overrun Minsk and Smolensk and were just outside Moscow. They had marched through the Baltic states and most of Ukraine and laid siege to Leningrad. Only an early, severe winter halted the advance.

Stalingrad by Antony Beevor is a superb book based on new access to long-secret archives and concentrates on the human cost of WWII.

The Soviet commander, General Zhukov, used the winter to push the Germans back from Moscow. Leningrad held out – and continued to do so for 2¼ years, during which over half a million of its civilians died, mainly from hunger.

German atrocities against the local population stiffened resistance. Stalin appealed to old-fashioned patriotism and eased restrictions on the Church, ensuring that the whole country rallied to the cause with incredible endurance. Military goods supplied by the Allies through the northern ports of Murmansk and Arkhangelsk were invaluable in the early days of the war. All Soviet military industry was packed up, moved east of the Ural Mountains and worked by women and Gulag labour.

Stalingrad & the End of WWII

Lasting 199 days and claiming something in the order of 1.5 million lives, the Battle for Stalingrad was the longest, deadliest and strategically most decisive of WWII. By the end of 1943 the Red Army had driven the Germans out of most of the Soviet Union; it reached Berlin in April 1945.

Harrison Salisbury's *The 900 Days: The Siege of Leningrad* is the most thorough and harrowing account of the city's sufferings in WWII.

The USSR's total losses, civilian and military, in WWII are thought to have numbered between 25 and 27 million. This compares to wartime deaths of between five and seven million for Germany, 400,000 for Britain and 330,000 for the USA.

Such sacrifices meant that the US and British leaders, Roosevelt and Churchill, were obliged to observe Stalin's wishes in the postwar settlement. At Tehran (November 1943) and Yalta (February 1945) the three agreed each to govern the areas they liberated until free elections could be held.

Soviet troops liberating Eastern Europe propped up local communist movements, which formed 'action committees' that either manipulated the elections or simply seized power when the election results were unfavourable.

The Cold War

Control over Eastern Europe and postwar modernisation of industry, with the aid of German factories and engineers seized as war booty, made the Soviet Union one of the two major world powers. The first

Oct 1917
Lenin returns from Finland to lead the Bolshevik coup. Alexander Kerensky's moderate Socialist Party wins the November election, a result ignored by the Bolsheviks.

Mar 1918
The Treaty of Brest-Litovsk marks Russia's formal exit from WWI and confirms the independence of Belarus, Finland, Ukraine and the Baltic states. The capital is moved to Moscow.

Jul 1918
Having first been exiled to Tobolsk, Nicholas II, his immediate family and servants are murdered in Yekaterinburg as nationwide civil war between White and Red forces ensues.

1920
Admiral Alexander Kolchak's White Army is defeated by the Red Army at Omsk. Kolchak retreats to Irkutsk where he's captured and shot. The civil war is over two years later.

postwar Five-Year Plan was military and strategic (more heavy industry); consumer goods and agriculture remained low priorities.

A cold war was shaping up between the communist and capitalist worlds, and in the USSR the new demon became 'cosmopolitanism' – warm feelings towards the West. The first victims were the estimated two million Soviet citizens repatriated by the Allies in 1945 and 1946. Some were former prisoners of war or forced labourers taken by the Germans; others were refugees or people who had taken the chance of war to escape the USSR. They were sent straight to the Gulag in case their stay abroad had contaminated them. Party and government purges continued as Stalin's reign came to resemble that of Ivan the Terrible.

The Khrushchev Thaw

With Stalin's death in 1953, power passed to a combined leadership of five Politburo members. One, Lavrenty Beria, the NKVD boss responsible under Stalin for millions of deaths, was secretly tried and shot (and the NKVD was reorganised as the KGB, the Committee for State Security, which was to remain firmly under Party control). In 1954 another of the Politburo members, Nikita Khrushchev, a pragmatic Ukrainian who had helped carry out 1930s purges, launched the Virgin Lands campaign, bringing vast tracts of Kazakhstan and Central Asia under cultivation. A series of good harvests did his reputation no harm.

During the 20th Party congress in 1956, Khrushchev made a 'secret speech' about crimes committed under Stalin. It was the beginning of de-Stalinisation (also known as the Thaw), marked by the release of millions of Gulag prisoners and a slightly more liberal political and intellectual climate. The congress also approved peaceful coexistence between communist and noncommunist regimes. The Soviet Union, Khrushchev argued, would soon triumph over the 'imperialists' by economic means. Despite the setback of the 1956 Hungarian rebellion, which was put down by Soviet troops, in 1957 he emerged the unchallenged leader of the USSR.

International Crises

A cautious détente between the USSR and the US in the late 1950s was undermined by a series of international crises. In 1961 Berlin was divided by the Wall to stop an exodus from East Germany. In 1962, the USSR supplied its Caribbean ally Cuba with defensive weapons, effectively stationing medium-range missiles with nuclear capability on the doorstep of the US. After some tense calling of bluff that brought the world to the brink of nuclear war, it withdrew the missiles.

A rift also opened between the Soviet Union and China, lasting roughly from the 1960, when Khrushchev withdrew Soviet advisers and

Mar 1921

Sailors and soldiers at Kronshtadt rebel against the Communists' increasingly dictatorial regime. The rebellion is brutally suppressed as debate with the Communist Party is outlawed.

Mar 1921

The New Economic Policy (NEP), allowing limited private enterprise alongside state control of large-scale industry and infrastructure, is adopted by the 10th Party Congress and remains until 1927.

1922

Josef Stalin is appointed Communist Party general secretary. The Union of Soviet Socialist Republics (USSR) is founded.

1924

Lenin dies at 53 without designating a successor. Petrograd changes its name to Leningrad in his honour. Power is assumed by a triumvirate of Stalin, Lev Kamenev and Grigory Zinoviev.

economic assistance from the neighbouring country, to the death of Chairman Mao in 1976. During this period the two communist superpowers competed for the allegiance of newly independent Third World nations and came into conflict over areas in Central Asia and the Russian Far East that had been conquered by the tsars.

Red Plenty by Francis Spufford is an ingenious piece of writing – part novel, part social history – that focuses on real people and events from the 1950s to the late 1960s, when it briefly looked like the Soviet economic system was besting that of capitalist economies.

Khrushchev might have weathered such international problems if his domestic policies had been more successful. His chaotic attempts to reform the Communist system inevitably drew a backlash from more conservative members of the party. In 1964, the Central Committee relieved Khrushchev of his posts because of 'advanced age and poor health'. He lived on in obscurity until dying of a heart attack in 1971.

The Brezhnev Stagnation

The new 'collective' leadership of Leonid Brezhnev (general secretary) and Alexey Kosygin (premier) soon devolved into a one-man show under conservative Brezhnev. Khrushchev's administrative reforms were rolled back and the economy stagnated, propped up only by the exploitation of huge Siberian oil and gas reserves.

As repression increased, the 'dissident' movement grew, along with *samizdat* (underground publications). Prison terms and forced labour did not seem to have the desired effect and, in 1972, the KGB chief, Yury Andropov, introduced new measures that included forced emigration and imprisonment in 'psychiatric institutions'.

WINNING THE SPACE RACE

The Space Race was the phrase used to sum up the Cold War rivalry between the US and the USSR to be the first to send rockets, satellites and people into outer space. Starting with both sides' efforts to develop rocket-delivered weapons during the 1940s, the competition really got going with Soviet advances in the late 1950s. The successful launch of satellite Sputnik I into orbit in 1957 was followed by Yury Gagarin's historic trip in 1961. Two years later Valentina Tereshkova became the first woman in space, and, in 1965, Alexey Leonov was the first person to perform a spacewalk.

NASA, the US space agency, was desperate to regain the initiative. By spending the equivalent of $150 billion in 2010 dollars (18 times the cost of digging the Panama Canal) on its Apollo project, the US managed to put men on the moon by the end of the 1960s. Some 40-odd years later, with the retirement of the US space shuttle Atlantis, the initiative is back with Russia's federal space agency Roscosmos (www.federalspace.ru), the only body now transferring space travellers – be they astronauts or cosmonauts – out to the International Space Station.

For more about the Space Race read *Red Moon Rising: Sputnik and the Rivalries that Ignited the Space Age* by Matthew Brzezinski.

1928

Stalin introduces the first Five-Year Plan, a program of centralised economic measures, including farm collectivisation and investment in heavy industry, designed to make the Soviet Union into a superpower.

1929

Expelled from the Communist Party in 1927, Leon Trotsky goes into exile, ending up in Mexico, where an agent of Stalin wielding an ice pick finishes him off in 1940.

1932–33

Famine kills millions as the forced collectivisation of farms slashes grain output and almost halves livestock. Agriculture does not reach precollectivisation levels until 1940.

1934

Leningrad party boss Sergei Kirov is murdered as he leaves his office at the Smolny Institute. The assassination kicks off the Great Purges, ushering in Stalin's reign of terror.

Government and Party elites, known as *nomenklatura* (literally, 'list of nominees'), enjoyed lavish lifestyles, with access to goods that were unavailable to the average citizen. The ponderous, overcentralised economy, with its suffocating bureaucracy, was providing fewer and fewer improvements in general living standards. Corruption spread in the Party and a cynical malaise seeped through society. Brezhnev was rarely seen in public after his health declined in 1979.

Glasnost

Brezhnev's successor Yury Andropov replaced some officials with young technocrats and proposed campaigns against alcoholism (which was costing the economy dearly) and corruption, later carried out under Gorbachev. He also clamped down on dissidents and increased defence spending.

But the economy continued to decline and Andropov died in February 1984, only 15 months after coming to power. Frail, 72-year-old Konstantin Chernenko, his successor, didn't even last that long. Mikhail Gorbachev, the next incumbent of the top job, understood that radically different policies were needed if the moribund Soviet Union was to survive.

Night of Stone: Death and Memory in Twentieth-Century Russia by Catherine Merridale is an enthralling read, viewing the country's bleak recent history through the prisms of psychology and philosophy.

The energetic 54-year-old launched an immediate turnover in the Politburo, bureaucracy and military, replacing many of the Brezhnevite 'old guard' with his own, younger supporters. 'Acceleration' in the economy and *glasnost* (openness) – first manifested in press criticism of poor economic management and past Party failings – were his initial slogans. Management initiative was encouraged, efficiency rewarded and bad practices allowed to be criticised.

At his first meeting with Ronald Reagan in Geneva in 1985, Gorbachev suggested a 50% cut in long-range nuclear weaponry. By 1987 the two superpowers had agreed to remove all medium-range missiles from Europe, with other significant cuts in arms and troop numbers following. The 'new thinking' also put an end to Russia's military involvement in Afghanistan and led to improved relations with China.

Perestroika & Political Reform

In an effort to tackle the ingrained corruption of the Communist Party, *perestroika* (restructuring) combined limited private enterprise and private property, not unlike Lenin's NEP, with efforts to push decision-making and responsibility out towards the grass roots. New laws were enacted in both these fields in 1988, but their application met resistance from the centralised bureaucracy.

The release at the end of 1986 of a famous dissident, Nobel Peace Prize winner Andrei Sakharov, from internal exile was the start of a general

1936–38
At the Moscow show trials former senior Communist Party leaders are accused of conspiring to assassinate Stalin and other Soviet leaders, dismember the Soviet Union and restore capitalism.

1939
When talks with Britain and France on a mutual defence treaty fail, Stalin signs a nonaggression pact with Germany, thus laying the ground for Poland's invasion and WWII.

1940
Lithuania, Latvia and Estonia are incorporated into the USSR; along with Moldavia, they bring the total of SSRs up to its final number of 15.

1941
Hitler invades Russia, beginning what is referred to in Russia as the Great Patriotic War. The Red Army is unprepared, and German forces advance rapidly across the country.

freeing of political prisoners. Religions were allowed to operate more and more freely.

In 1988 Gorbachev announced a new 'parliament', the Congress of People's Deputies, with two-thirds of its members to be elected directly by the people. A year later, the first elections for decades were held and the congress convened, to outspoken debate and national fascination. Though dominated by Party *apparatchiki* (members), the parliament also contained outspoken critics of the government such as Sakharov and Boris Yeltsin.

Sinatra Doctrine

Gorbachev sprang repeated surprises, including sudden purges of difficult opponents (such as the populist reformer Yeltsin), but the forces unleashed by his opening-up of society grew impossible to control. From 1988 onward the reduced threat of repression and the experience of electing even semi-representative assemblies spurred a growing clamour for independence in the Soviet satellite states.

Twenty years after the explosion at the Chornobyl nuclear station in Ukraine, Gorbachev wrote 'even more than my launch of *perestroika*, [Chornobyl] was perhaps the real cause of the collapse of the Soviet Union'.

One by one, the Eastern European countries threw off their Soviet puppet regimes in the autumn of 1989; the Berlin Wall fell on 9 November. The Brezhnev Doctrine, Gorbachev's spokesperson said, had given way to the 'Sinatra Doctrine': letting them do it *their* way. The formal reunification of Germany on 3 October 1990 marked the effective end of the Cold War.

In 1990 the three Baltic states of the USSR also declared (or, as they would have it, reaffirmed) their independence – an independence that, for the present, remained more theoretical than real. Before long, most other Soviet republics either followed suit or declared 'sovereignty' – the precedence of their own laws over the Soviet Union's. Gorbachev's proposal for an ill-defined new federal system for the Soviet Union won few friends.

Rise of Yeltsin

Also in 1990, Yeltsin won chairmanship of the parliament of the giant Russian Republic, which covered three-quarters of the USSR's area and contained more than half its population. Soon after coming to power, Gorbachev had promoted Yeltsin to head the Communist Party in Moscow, but had then dumped him in 1987–88 in the face of opposition to his reforms there from the Party's old guard. By that time, Yeltsin had already declared *perestroika* a failure, and these events produced a lasting personal enmity between the two men. Gorbachev increasingly struggled to hold together the radical reformers and the conservative old guard in the Party.

Once chosen as chairman of the Russian parliament, Yeltsin proceeded to jockey for power with Gorbachev. He seemed already to have con-

1942

Time magazine names Stalin Man of the Year, an accolade he'd previously received in 1939. Russia wins the Battle of Stalingrad at a cost of more than a million lives.

1944

In January the 872-day blockade of Leningrad by the Germans is broken. Leningrad has suffered over a million casualties and is proclaimed a hero city.

1945

In the closing days of WWII, with Japan on its knees, the Soviet Union occupies the Japanese territories of southern Sakhalin Island and the Kuril Islands.

1945

The end of WWII sees Soviet forces occupy much of Eastern Europe, leaving Berlin and Vienna divided cities. Winston Churchill refers to an 'iron curtain' coming down across Europe.

cluded that real change was impossible not only under the Communist Party but also within a centrally controlled Soviet Union, the members of which were in any case showing severe centrifugal tendencies. Yeltsin resigned from the Communist Party and his parliament proclaimed the sovereignty of the Russian Republic.

Economic Collapse

In early 1990 Gorbachev persuaded the Communist Party to vote away its own constitutional monopoly on power, and parliament chose him for the newly created post of executive president, which further distanced the organs of government from the Party. But these events made little difference to the crisis into which the USSR was sliding, as what was left of the economy broke down and organised crime and black-marketeering boomed, profiting from a slackening of Soviet law and order.

Gorbachev's Nobel Peace Prize, awarded in the bleak winter of 1990–91 when fuel and food were disappearing from many shops, left the average Soviet citizen literally cold. The army, the security forces and the Party hardliners called with growing confidence for the restoration of law and order to save the country. Foreign Minister Eduard Shevardnadze, long one of Gorbachev's staunchest partners but now under constant old-guard sniping for 'losing Eastern Europe', resigned, warning of impending hardline dictatorship.

The August Coup

In June 1991 Yeltsin was voted president of the Russian Republic in the country's first-ever direct presidential elections. He demanded devolution of power from the Soviet Union to the republics and banned Communist Party cells from government offices and workplaces in Russia.

On 18 August 1991 the communist old guard attempted a coup but, in Moscow, Yeltsin escaped arrest and went to the White House, seat of the Russian parliament, to rally opposition. Crowds gathered outside the White House, persuaded some of the tank crews (who had been sent to disperse them) to switch sides, and started to build barricades. Yeltsin climbed on a tank to declare the coup illegal and call for a general strike. Troops disobeyed orders and refused to storm the White House.

The following day huge crowds opposed to the coup gathered in Moscow and Leningrad. Kazakhstan rejected the coup and Estonia declared full independence from the Soviet Union. On 21 August the tanks withdrew; the remaining coup leaders fled and were arrested.

End of the Soviet Union

Yeltsin responded by demanding control of all state property and banning the Communist Party in Russia. Gorbachev resigned as the USSR

1947

US president Harry Truman initiates a policy of 'containment' of Soviet influence; a Cold War breaks out between the two rival superpowers that lasts until 1990.

1948

Allied forces occupying western zones of Germany unify their areas, leading to a year-long Soviet blockade of western Berlin. The result is the split of Germany into two states.

1949

Having used espionage to kick-start its nuclear research program, the Soviet Union conducts its first nuclear weapon test (code name First Lightning) in August.

1950

Following a two-month visit to Moscow, Mao and Stalin sign the Sino-Soviet Treaty of Friendship and Alliance, which includes a US$300 million low-interest loan from Russia to China.

Party's leader the following day, ordering that the Party's property be transferred to the Soviet parliament.

Even before the coup, Gorbachev had been negotiating a last-ditch bid to save the Soviet Union with proposals for a looser union of independent states. In September the Soviet parliament abolished the centralised Soviet state, vesting power in three temporary governing bodies until a new union treaty could be signed. In the meantime Yeltsin was steadily transferring control over everything that mattered in Russia from Soviet hands into Russian ones.

On 8 December Yeltsin and the leaders of Ukraine and Belarus, meeting near Brest in Belarus, announced that the USSR no longer existed. They proclaimed a new Commonwealth of Independent States (CIS), a vague alliance of fully independent states with no central authority. Russia kicked the Soviet government out of the Kremlin on 19 December. Two days later eight more republics joined the CIS.

Robert Service has written celebrated biographies of Lenin, Stalin and Trotsky, as well as the *Penguin History of Modern Russia*, charting the country's history from Nicholas II to Putin.

With the USSR dead, Gorbachev was a president without a country. He formally resigned on 25 December, the day the white, blue and red Russian flag replaced the Soviet red flag over the Kremlin.

The Yeltsin Years

Economic Reform & Regional Tensions

Even before Gorbachev's resignation, Yeltsin had announced plans to move to a free-market economy, appointing in November 1991 a reforming government to carry this out. State subsidies were to be phased out, prices freed, government spending cut and state businesses, housing, land and agriculture privatised. Yeltsin became prime minister and defence minister, as well as president as an emergency measure.

With the economy already in chaos, all of Russia's nominally autonomous ethnic regions, some of them rich in natural resources, declared themselves independent republics, leading to fears that Russia might disintegrate as the USSR had just done. These worries were eventually defused, however, by three things: a 1992 treaty between the central government and the republics; a new constitution in 1993, which handed the other regions increased rights; and by changes in the tax system.

Some benefits of economic reform took hold during 1994 in a few big cities, notably Moscow and St Petersburg (the name to which Leningrad had reverted in 1991), where a market economy was taking root and an enterprise culture was developing among the younger generations. At the same time crime and corruption seemed to be spiralling out of control.

1953
In March Stalin suffers a fatal stroke. Lavrenty Beria takes charge, but in June is arrested, tried for treason and executed. Nikita Khrushchev becomes first secretary.

1955
In response to the US and Western Europe forming NATO, the Soviet Union gathers together the communist states of Central and Eastern Europe to sign the Warsaw Pact.

1956
Soviet troops crush a Hungarian uprising. Khrushchev makes a 'secret speech' denouncing Stalin, thus commencing the de-Stalinisation of the Soviet Union, a period of economic reform and cultural thaw.

1959
US vice-president Richard Nixon's visit to Moscow is followed with a trip by Khrushchev to the US; he brings the idea of the self-service cafeteria back to the USSR.

Conflict with the Old Guard

Yeltsin's 'shock therapy' of economic reforms and plummeting international status put him on a collision course with the parliament, which was dominated by communists and nationalists, both opposed to the course events were taking. Organised crime was also steadily rising and corruption at all levels seemed more prevalent than before.

Yeltsin sacrificed key ministers and compromised on the pace of reform, but the parliament continued to issue resolutions contradicting his presidential decrees. In April 1993 a national referendum gave Yeltsin a big vote of confidence, both in his presidency and in his policies. He began framing a new constitution that would abolish the existing parliament and define more clearly the roles of president and legislature.

Finally, it came down to a trial of strength. In September 1993 Yeltsin dissolved the parliament, which in turn stripped him of all his powers. Yeltsin sent troops to blockade the White House, ordering the members to leave by 4 October. Many did, but on 2 and 3 October the National Salvation Front, an aggressive communist-nationalist group, attempted an insurrection, overwhelming the troops around the White House and attacking Moscow's Ostankino TV centre, where 62 people died. The next day troops stormed the White House, leaving at least 70 members of the public dead.

Reforming the Constitution

Russia's constitution was adopted by a national referendum in December 1993, the same month elections were held for a new two-house form of parliament. The name of the more influential lower house, the State Duma (Gosudarstvennaya Duma), consciously echoed that of tsarist Russia's parliaments.

The new constitution established a complex federal system of government, currently made up of 46 *oblasti* (regions), 22 semiautonomous *respubliki* (republics), nine *kraya* (territories), four autonomous *okruga* (districts), one autonomous region (the Jewish Autonomous Oblast) and the federal cities of Moscow, St Petersburg and Sevastopol. The republics have their own constitution and legislation; territories, regions, the federal cities and the autonomous districts and region have their own charter and legislation.

This structure is partly a hangover from the old Soviet system of nominally autonomous republics for many minority ethnic groups. Yeltsin struck deals with the republics, which largely pacified their demands for more autonomy, and in the new constitution awarded regions and territories much the same status as republics but declared that federal laws always took precedence over local ones.

1962

US–Soviet relations take a turn for the worse during the Cuban Missile Crisis. Russia's climb-down in the Caribbean standoff deals a blow to Khrushchev's authority at home.

1964

A coup against Khrushchev brings Leonid Brezhnev to power. Poet and future Nobel laureate Joseph Brodsky is labelled a 'social parasite' and sent into exile.

1965

Oil begins to flow in Siberia as Prime Minister Alexey Kosygin tries to shift the Soviet economy over to light industry and producing consumer goods. His reforms are stymied by Brezhnev.

1972

President Richard Nixon visits Moscow to sign the first Strategic Arms Limitation Treaty, restricting nuclear ballistic weapons and ushering in a period of détente between the two superpowers.

One flaw of the constitution is that the president and the parliament can both make laws and effectively block each other's actions. In practice, the president can usually get his way through issuing presidential decrees. During Yeltsin's turbulent rule this happened often.

Yeltsin: A Life by Timothy J Colton casts a favourable light on the much maligned former president, who led the destruction of Soviet Communism and the establishment of the Russian Federation.

War in Chechnya

Yeltsin's foreign policy reflected the growing mood of conservative nationalism at home. The sudden demise of the Soviet Union had left many Russian citizens stranded in now potentially hostile countries. As the political tide turned against them, some of these Russians returned to the motherland. Under such circumstances the perceived need for a buffer zone between Russia and the outside world became a chief concern – and remains so.

Russian troops intervened in fighting in Tajikistan, Georgia and Moldova as UN-sanctioned peacekeepers, but also with the aim of strengthening Russia's hand in those regions, and by early 1995 Russian forces were stationed in all the other former republics except Estonia and Lithuania.

However, in the Muslim republic of Chechnya, which had declared independence from Russia in 1991, this policy proved particularly disastrous. Attempts to negotiate a settlement or have Chechnya's truculent leader Dzhokhar Dudayev deposed had stalled by the end of 1994.

Yeltsin ordered troops into Chechnya for what was meant to be a quick operation to restore Russian control. But the Chechens fought bitterly and by mid-1995 at least 25,000 people, mostly civilians, were dead, and the Russians had only just gained full control of the destroyed Chechen capital, Grozny. Dudayev was still holding out in southern Chechnya and guerrilla warfare continued unabated. Yeltsin's popularity plummeted and, in the December 1995 elections, communists and nationalists won control of 45% of the Duma.

Russia: A 1,000-Year Chronicle of the Wild East by Martin Sixsmith presents an epic and very readable sweep of Russia's history. It is also a 50-part radio series for BBC Radio 4.

Rise of the Oligarchs

By early 1996, with presidential elections pending, Yeltsin was spending much time hidden away, suffering frequent bouts of various ill-defined sicknesses. When he was seen in public he often appeared to be confused and unstable. However, with the help of oligarchs such as media barons Boris Berezovsky and Vladimir Gusinsky, the communists led by Gennady Zyuganov were kept off TV, ensuring that the only message the Russian voters received was Yeltsin's.

In the June elections, Zyuganov and a tough-talking ex-general, Alexander Lebed, split the opposition vote, and Yeltsin easily defeated Zyuganov in a run-off in early July. The communists and other opposition parties returned to their grousing in the Duma, while Lebed was handed the poisoned chalice of negotiating an end to the messy Chechen war. Russian troops began withdrawing from Chechnya in late 1996.

1979

Russia invades Afghanistan to support its Marxist-Leninist regime against US-backed Islamic militants. The conflict drags on for nine years and is considered the Soviet Union's 'Vietnam'.

1980

Because of the invasion of Afghanistan, the US and 61 other nations boycott the Olympic Games held in Moscow. Four years later Soviet teams boycott the Los Angeles Olympics.

1982–84

KGB supremo Yury Andropov is president for 15 months until his death in 1984. His successor, the doddering 72-year-old Konstantin Chernenko, hardly makes an impact before dying 13 months later.

1985

Mikhail Gorbachev, 54, is elected general secretary of the Communist Party, the first Soviet leader to be born after the revolution. He institutes policies of *perestroika* and *glasnost*.

In November Yeltsin underwent quintuple heart-bypass surgery. While he recuperated, much of 1997 saw a series of financial shenanigans and deals that were power grabs by the various Russian billionaires and members of Yeltsin's inner circle known as 'the Family'. (Yeltsin himself would later come under investigation by Swiss and Russian authorities. However, following his resignation in 1999, Yeltsin was granted immunity from legal prosecution by his successor, Vladimir Putin.)

Economic Collapse & Recovery

By the spring of 1998 Russia was effectively bankrupt. Yeltsin tried to exert his authority by sacking the government for its bad economic management, but it was too late as foreign investors who had propped up Russia's economy withdrew their capital. On 17 August the rouble was devalued, and in a repeat of scenes that had shaken the West during the Depression of 1929, many Russian banks faltered, leaving their depositors with nothing.

However, following the initial shock, the growing Russian middle class, mostly paid in untaxed cash dollars, suddenly realised that their salaries had increased threefold overnight (if counted in roubles) while prices largely remained the same. This led to a huge boom in consumer goods and services. Luxuries such as restaurants and fitness clubs, previously only for the rich, suddenly became available to many more people. The situation also provided a great opportunity for Russian producers of consumer goods: in 1999 imported products were rapidly being replaced by high-quality local ones.

LAYING THE LAST TSAR TO REST

The disposal of bodies of the Romanovs at Ganina Yama in 1918 had been a bungled mess, leaving the bones to be uncovered in 1976, a discovery that was kept secret until the remains were finally fully excavated in 1991. A year later the remains were conclusively identified as Tsar Nicholas II, his wife Tsaritsa Alexandra, three of their four daughters, the imperial doctor and three servants.

Missing were the remains of the imperial couple's only son, Tsarevitch Alexey, and one of their daughters, giving a new lease of life to theories that the youngest daughter, Anastasia, had somehow escaped. In 1994 an official Russian inquiry team managed to piece together the skulls found in the pit, badly damaged by rifle butts, hand grenades and acid. Using plaster models of the faces, DNA tests and dental records, they determined that the three daughters found were Olga, Tatyana – and Anastasia. The missing daughter was Maria, whose remains were unearthed in 2007 and formally identified along with those of her brother Alexey in 2008.

In mid-1998 the imperial remains were given a proper funeral at St Petersburg's SS Peter and Paul Cathedral, to lie alongside their predecessors dating back to Peter the Great. The Orthodox Church later canonised the tsar and his family as martyrs.

1989–90

Gorbachev pulls Soviet troops from Afghanistan. He wins the Nobel Peace Prize in 1990, as Germany is reunited and Moscow relinquishes its increasingly enfeebled grip on Eastern European satellites.

1991

A failed coup in August against Gorbachev seals the end of the USSR. On Christmas Day, Gorbachev resigns and Boris Yeltsin takes charge as president of the Russian Federation.

1993

In a clash of wills with the Russian parliament, Yeltsin sends in troops to deal with dissenters at Moscow's White House and Ostankino TV tower.

1994

Russian troops invade the breakaway republic of Chechnya in December. In a brutal two-year campaign the Chechen capital, Grozny, is reduced to rubble and 300,000 people flee their homes.

Moscow Bombings

In September 1999 a series of explosions rocked Moscow, virtually demolishing three apartment blocks and killing nearly 300 people. This unprecedented terrorism in the nation's capital fuelled unease and xenophobia, particularly against Chechens, who were popularly perceived as being responsible. An FSB (Federal Security Service; successor to the KGB) investigation concluded in 2002 that the bombings were masterminded by two non-Chechen Islamists – a view disputed by some, including the FSB operative Alexander Litvinenko, who would later be assassinated by lethal radiation poisoning in London in 2006.

The discovery of similar bombs in the city of Ryazan in September 1999, on top of Chechen incursions into Dagestan, was used by the Kremlin as a justification for launching air attacks on Grozny, sparking the second Chechen war. Amnesty International and the Council of Europe criticised both sides in the conflict for 'blatant and sustained' violations of international humanitarian law. Today, the conflict has eased to a controllable simmer under the watch of the Kremlin-friendly Chechen president Ramzan Kadyrov.

Among the many rights enshrined in Russia's constitution are those to free trade and competition, private ownership of land and property, freedom of conscience and free movement in and out of the country. It also bans censorship, torture and the establishment of any official ideology.

GOVERNING RUSSIA IN THE 21ST CENTURY

Russia's president is the head of state and has broad powers. He or she appoints the key government ministers, including the prime minister (who is effectively the deputy president), interior and defence ministers. The Duma has to approve the president's appointees. Presidential elections are held every six years.

The Duma's upper house, the Federation Council (Sovet Federatsii), has 166 seats occupied by two unelected representatives from each of Russia's administrative districts. Its primary purpose is to approve or reject laws proposed by the lower house, the State Duma, which oversees all legislation. Its 450 members are equally divided between representatives elected from single-member districts and those elected from party lists. This gives extra clout to the major parties and efforts to replace this system of representation with a purely proportional system have been shunned. Duma elections are held every four years in the December preceding the presidential elections.

In 2000, Putin started to recentralise power in the Kremlin by creating eight large federal districts each with an appointed envoy. He also saw to it that the regions would have federally appointed governors. In March 2014, the Crimean Federal District was added following Russia's annexation of this area that for the previous 23 years had been part of Ukraine.

1996

Poor health doesn't stop Yeltsin from running for, and winning, a second term as president. His election is ensured by assistance from influential business oligarchs.

1999

On New Year's Eve, in a move that catches everyone on the hop, Yeltsin resigns and entrusts the caretaker duties of president to his prime minister, Vladimir Putin.

2002

In October a 700-strong audience at Moscow's Palace of Culture Theatre is taken hostage by around 50 Chechen terrorists. Security forces storm the theatre, resulting in over 100 casualties.

2004

Putin is reelected. Russia's economy booms off the back of buoyant oil and gas prices. In September Chechen terrorists hold 1200 hostages at a school in Beslan, North Ossetia; there are 344 casualties.

The Putin Years

Rise of the Siloviki

Yeltsin's appointed successor, Vladimir Putin, swept to victory in the March 2000 presidential elections. The one-time KGB operative and FSB chief boosted military spending, reestablished Kremlin control over the regions and cracked down on the critical media. Despite the increasingly bloody Chechen war, support for Putin remained solid, bearing out the president's own view – one that is frequently endorsed by a cross-section of Russians – that 'Russia needs a strong state power'.

Putin's cooperation with and support for the US-led assault on Afghanistan in the wake of 9/11 initially won him respect in the West. But doubts about the president's tough stance began to mount with the substantial death tolls of hostages that followed sieges at a Moscow theatre in October 2002 and at a school in Beslan in 2004.

Reelected in 2004, Putin's power was consolidated as Russia's global status grew, in direct correlation to the money the country earned off natural gas and oil sales and a booming economy. Behind the scenes an alliance of ex-KGB/FSB operatives, law enforcers and bureaucrats, known as *siloviki* (power people), appeared to be taking control. The most prominent victims were oligarchs who either fled the country or, as in the case of one-time oil billionaire Mikhail Khordorkovsky, had their assets seized and, following trials widely regarded as unfair, sentenced to long stretches in prison.

The Oligarchs: Wealth and Power in the New Russia by David Hoffman gives a blow-by-blow account of the rise and sometimes fall of the 'robber barons' of modern Russia.

Stoking Russian Nationalism

In 2005 the Kremlin, worried at the prospect of a Ukrainian-style Orange Revolution, supported the founding of the ultranationalist youth group Nashi (meaning Ours), a band of ardent Putin and United Russia supporters who have been compared both to Komsomol (the Soviet youth brigade) and the Hitler Youth.

One of Nashi's stated aims was 'elimination of the regime of oligarchic capitalism'. However, the group has become best known for its aggressive protests against perceived enemies of the Russian state (which have included foreign missions in Russia, such as the UK embassy, and opposition politicians) and for its summer camp held in the forests around Lake Seliger attended by upward of 10,000 youths.

Russian nationalism also came to the fore in relations with neighbouring Georgia and Ukraine. A six-day war broke out in August 2008 between Russia and Georgia over the breakaway regions of South Ossetia and Abkhazia, which Russia later recognised as independent countries. Russian Foreign Minister Sergei Lavrov was quoted in a radio interview

A History of Russia, by Nicholas Riasanovsky, is one of the best single-volume versions of the whole Russian story through to the end of the Soviet Union.

Jun 2005

China and Russia settle a post-WWII dispute over 2% of their 4300km common border. For the first time, the whole border between the two countries is legally defined.

2007

The assassination of former FSB spy Alexander Litvinenko in London and closure of the British Council offices in St Petersburg and Yekaterinburg see UK–Russia relations reach a new low.

May 2008

Former chairman of Gazprom Dmitry Medvedev succeeds Putin as Russia's third elected president. One of his first acts is to install his predecessor as prime minister.

Aug 2008

Georgia makes military moves on the autonomous regions of South Ossetia and Abkhazia. A brief war with Russia follows and Georgia is forced to back down.

on Ekho Moskvy as saying 'We will do anything not to allow Georgia and Ukraine to join NATO.'

Threats by Russia's largest company, Gazprom, to cut off gas supplies to Ukraine in 2006 and 2008 because of unpaid bills also sent shudders through much of Europe – a quarter of its gas comes from Gazprom and is piped through Ukraine.

Medvedev's Presidency

With no credible opponent, the March 2008 election of Dmitry Medvedev, a former chairman of Gazprom, as president was a forgone conclusion. Loyal to Putin ever since they worked together in the early 1990s for the St Petersburg government, 42-year-old Medvedev (the youngest Russian president so far) carried through his election promise of making Putin his prime minister.

At times during his presidency, Medvedev appeared to come out of the shadow of his predecessor. He sacked Moscow's long-serving mayor Yury Luzhkov in September 2010 and, a month later, struck a truce with NATO over a European missile defence shield. However, in August 2011, Putin said that he would run again for the presidency in 2012 and that Medvedev would be his chosen prime minister. Such political manoeuvering confirmed in the eyes of many that Putin had been pulling the strings behind a pliant Medvedev, biding his time until he could run again for the top job.

Kicking the Kremlin by Marc Bennetts, a Moscow-based contributor to this guide, offers a pacy, eyewitness account of Russia's 2011–2012 protest movement.

The Return of Putin

Russia's constitution has a two-consecutive term limit for presidents, but before the 2012 election changes were made to boost that term from four to six years. Hence when Putin was re-elected in March 2012 with over 60% of the vote many people feared that they could conceivably be stuck with him for another 12 years.

There's no doubting Putin's popularity; however, he and his party United Russia are far from universally loved, as proved by the tens of thousands who took to the streets of Moscow to protest the results of the national legislative elections of December 2011. The victory of United Russia was dogged by widespread allegations of vote-rigging and corruption. In Chechnya, the former *bete noir* of Kremlin leaders, United Russia received 99.5% of the vote – a figure matched by votes cast in favour of the ruling party in a Moscow psychiatric hospital.

United Russia's eventual tally was just under 50% of the vote, down from 64% in 2007, enough to give it a majority in parliament but no longer the two-thirds it needs to alter the constitution.

2009

The global financial crisis hits Russia as the price of crude oil plummets. The economy begins to recover later in the year. US President Obama visits Moscow in July.

2010

The FBI uncovers a spy ring of 10 Russian agents in the US, including the sultry redhead Anna Chapman; they are swapped in Vienna for four US agents.

2012

Putin is elected president for the third time with over 60% of the vote, for an extended term of six years. Medvedev becomes the prime minister.

The Russian People

Among the diverse people you might encounter in the world's biggest country are a Nenets reindeer herder in Siberia, a marketing executive in Moscow, an imam in Kazan or a Buddhist Buryat taxi driver in Ulan-Ude. Within the Russian Federation, one's 'nationality' refers to one's ethnicity rather than one's passport – and Russia has dozens of nationalities. Despite such enormous ethnic and cultural variation, there is much that Russian citizens have in common.

Demographic Trends

Over the last century Russia has gone from a country of peasants living in villages to a highly urban one with close to three-quarters of its 143.8 million population living in cities and towns. Rural communities are left to wither, with thousands of villages deserted or dying.

Russia is facing an alarming natural decline in its population, around 0.5% per year. Results of the October 2010 census put the country's population at 142.9 million, down 2.3 million since the last census in 2002 and by nearly 3.4 million from a decade ago.

In April 2011 the government announced it would spend ₽1.5 trillion (US$53 billion) on demographic projects that would raise the birth rate by an ambitious 30% in the next five years. Adding to an existing policy of making cash payouts of ₽250,000 (US$8725) to women who have more than two children is a scheme to provide free land to families with three children or more, as well as increased child benefits and more affordable housing for young people. Harking back to a post-WWII Soviet policy, the government will also resume dishing out medals to 'heroic mothers' who have babies for Russia.

According to the Russian Health Ministry, in 2008 there were 1.7 million births in Russia and 1.2 million abortions. In 1920 Russia became the first country in the world to legalise abortion and, since then, it has remained the most popular form of birth control, with women allowed to terminate up to the 12th week of pregnancy. According to Russian news agency RIA Novosti, 1.2 million Russian women choose to terminate their pregnancies each year and 30,000 of them become sterile, many from the estimated 180,000 abortions performed outside the law. In its investigation the news agency also found several Moscow clinics offering discounts for abortions on International Women's Day.

Russkiy Mir (www.russkiymir.ru) was created by the Russian government in 2007 as an organisation to preserve and promote the Russian language and culture throughout the world.

Moscow is Europe's largest city with a population of 11.5 million. Add in the city's unregistered residents and the real figure is likely as high as 17 million, according to experts. In contrast 6400 villages disappeared between the 2002 and 2010 censuses, as their populations dwindled to zero.

Lifestyle

There can be a vast difference in the quality of life of urban and rural Russians. Sochi-style redevelopments are far from the norm, with many areas of Russia seemingly unchanged from the days of the USSR – as witnessed in any of the preserved-in-Soviet-formaldehyde towns along the Baikal-Amur Mainline (Baikalo-Amurskaya Magistral; BAM).

That said, some common features of contemporary life across Russia stand out, such as Soviet-era flats, dachas (summer country homes), education and weekly visits to the *banya* (bathhouse). Cohabitation remains

INTERACTING WITH LOCALS

While it's true that some Russians can be miserable, uncooperative and guarded in their initial approach to strangers, once you've earned a small crumb of friendship, hospitality typically flows with extraordinary generosity. Visitors can find themselves regaled with stories, drowned in vodka and stuffed full of food. An invitation to a Russian home will typically result in all of this being repeated several times, even when the family can ill afford the expense. This can be especially true outside the big cities, where you'll meet locals determined to share everything they have with you, however meagre their resources.

There's a similar bipolarity in the Russian sense of humour. Unsmiling gloom and fatalistic melancholy remain archetypically Russian, but, as in Britain, this is often used as a foil to a deadpan, sarcastic humour. You'll also see this contradiction in Russians' attitudes towards their country. They love it deeply and will sing the praises of Mother Russia's great contributions to the arts and sciences, its long history and abundant physical attributes, then just as loudly point out its many failures.

The extreme side of this patriotism can manifest itself in an unpleasant streak of racism. Don't let it put you off, and take heart in the knowledge that as much as foreigners may be perplexed about the true nature of the Russian soul, the locals themselves still haven't got it figured out either. As the poet Fyodor Tyutchev said, 'You can't understand Russia with reason...you can only believe in her.'

less common than in the West, so when young couples get together, they get married just as often as not.

As the economy has improved so too has the average Russian's lifestyle, with more people than ever before owning a car, a computer and a mobile phone, and taking holidays abroad. The lives of Russian teenagers today couldn't be more different from those of their parents, who just a generation ago had to endure shortages of all kinds of goods on top of the ideology of Soviet communism. It's not uncommon to come across young adults who have only the vaguest, if any, idea about Lenin or Stalin.

This is balanced against the memories of those who knew the former Soviet leaders only too well and are now suffering as the social safety net that the state once provided for them has been largely withdrawn.

Apartments & Dachas

For the vast majority of urban Russians, home is within a Soviet-vintage, drab, ugly housing complex. Many of these were built during the late 1950s and early 1960s when Khrushchev was in power, so are known as Khrushchevkas (or sometimes *khrushchoby,* for Khrushchev, and *trushchoby,* or slums). Meant to last just a couple of decades, they are very dilapidated on the outside, while the insides, though cramped, are invariably cosy and prettily decorated.

A scene in a *banya* kicks off the comedy *Irony of Fate* (*Ironiya Sudby ili s Legkim Parom*, 1975) directed by Eldar Ryazanov, a much-loved movie screened on TV every New Year's Eve.

While there's usually a play area for kids in the middle of apartment blocks, they don't typically come with attached gardens. Instead, something like a third of Russian families have a dacha. Often little more than a bare-bones hut (but sometimes quite luxurious), these retreats offer Russians refuge from city life, and as such figure prominently in the national psyche. On half-warm weekends, the major cities begin to empty out early on Friday as people head to the country.

One of the most important aspects of dacha life is gardening. Families use this opportunity to grow all manner of vegetables and fruits to eat over the winter. Flowers also play an important part in creating the proper dacha ambience, and even among people who have no need to grow food, the contact with the soil provides an important balm for the Russian soul.

The Banya

For centuries, travellers to Russia have commented on the particular (and in many people's eyes, peculiar) traditions of the *banya;* the closest English equivalents – bathhouse and sauna – don't quite sum it up. To this day, Russians make it an important part of their week, and you can't say you've really been to Russia unless you've visited one.

The main element of the *banya* is the *parilka* (steam room). Here, rocks are heated by a furnace, with water poured onto them using a long-handled ladle. Often a few drops of eucalyptus or pine oil (and sometimes even beer) are added to the water, creating a scent in the burst of scalding steam released into the room. After this, some people grab hold of a *venik* (a tied bundle of birch branches) and lightly beat themselves, or each other, with it. It does appear sadomasochistic, and there are theories tying the practice to other masochistic elements of Russian culture. Despite the mild sting, the effect is pleasant and cleansing: apparently, the birch leaves (or sometimes oak or, agonisingly, juniper branches) and their secretions help rid the skin of toxins.

The *banya* tradition is deeply ingrained in the Russian culture that emerged from the ancient Viking settlement of Novgorod, with the Kyivan Slavs making fun of their northern brothers for all that steamy whipping. In folk traditions, it has been customary for the bride and groom to take separate *bani* with their friends the night before the wedding, with the *banya* itself the bridge to marriage. Husband and wife would also customarily bathe together after the ceremony, and midwives used to administer a steam bath to women during delivery. (It was not uncommon to give a hot birch minimassage to the newborn.) The *banya*, in short, is a place for physical and moral purification. For more about the design and health benefits of the *banya* see www.rusbanya.com/eng.htm.

Best Bani

- *Sanduny Baths, Moscow*
- *Kruglye Bani, St Petersburg*
- *Helio Spa, Suzdal*
- *Skazka Banya, Aya*
- *Banya Museum, Ust-Barguzin*

Education

From its beginning as an agrarian society in which literacy was limited to the few in the upper classes, the USSR achieved a literacy rate of 98% – among the best in the world. Russia continues to benefit from this legacy. Russian schools emphasise basics such as reading and mathematics, and the high literacy rate has been maintained. Many students go on to university and men can delay or avoid the compulsory national service by doing so.

BANYA RITUALS

Follow these tips to blend in with the locals at the *banya:*

- Bring a thermos of tea mixed with jam, spices and heaps of sugar. A few bottles of beer and some dried fish also do nicely, although at the better *bani,* food and drink are available.
- Strip down in the sex-segregated changing room, wishing '*Lyogkogo* (pronounced *lyokh*-ka-va) *para!*' to other bathers (meaning something like 'May your steam be easy!'), then head off into the *parilka*.
- After the birch-branch thrashing (best experienced lying down on a bench, with someone else administering the 'beating'), run outside and either plunge into the *basseyn* (ice-cold pool) or take a cold shower.
- Stagger back into the changing room, wishing fellow bathers '*S lyogkim parom!*' (Hope your steam was easy!).
- Wrap yourself in a sheet and discuss world issues before repeating the process – most *banya* aficionados go through the motions about five to 10 times over a two-hour period.

Technical subjects such as science and mathematics are valued and bright students are encouraged to specialise in a particular area from a young age. A June 2011 report by the Russian public opinion foundation FOM found that teachers are among the country's worst bribe-takers. Higher education is the most corrupt sphere, with bribes taken for admission to universities, exams and degrees. Corruption in preschools and kindergartens in 2010 grew fourfold to ₽13,838 billion (US$495 million), with the average bribe paid for admission being ₽8025 (US$287).

Weddings

The results of studies carried out by the UN Development Programme in Russia (www.undp.ru/?iso=RU) covers issues such as poverty reduction, HIV/AIDS and democratic governance.

During any trip to Russia you can't help but notice the number of people getting hitched, particularly on Friday and Saturday when the registry offices (Zapis Aktov Grazhdanskogo Sostoyaniya, shortened to ZAGS) are open for business. Wedding parties are particularly conspicuous, as they tear around town in convoys of cars making lots of noise and having their photos taken at the official beauty and historical spots. A relatively new tradition (imported from Italy) is for a couple to place a lock inscribed with their names on a bridge and throw away the key into the river below.

Church weddings are fairly common; the Russian Orthodox variety go on for ages, especially for the best friends who have to hold crowns above the heads of the bride and the groom during the whole ceremony. For a marriage to be officially registered, though, all couples need to get a stamp in their passports at a ZAGS. Most ZAGS offices are drab Soviet buildings with a ceremonial hall designed like a modern Protestant church less the crucifix. There are also *dvortsy brakosochetaniy* (purpose-built wedding palaces) – a few are in actual old palaces of extraordinary elegance.

After the couple and two witnesses from both sides sign some papers, the bride and the groom exchange rings (which in the Orthodox tradition are worn on the right hand) and the registrar pronounces them husband and wife. The witnesses each wear a red sash around their shoulders with the word 'witness' written on it in golden letters. The groom's best man takes care of all tips and other payments since it's traditional for the groom not to spend a single *kopek* (smallest unit of Russian currency) during the wedding. Another tradition is that the bride's mother does not attend the wedding ceremony, although she does go to the party.

Multiethnic Russia

According to the UN 'Demographic Yearbook', Russia has the highest rate of divorce of any country in the world: in In 2012 about 650,000 couples divorced. More than half of those got married in the same year.

Over 195 different ethnic groups are designated as nationalities in Russia – a result of the country's development through imperial expansion, forced movements and migration over many hundreds of years. On paper, the USSR's divide-and-rule politics promoted awareness of ethnic 'national' identities. However, according to Professor Aviel Roshwald of Georgetown University, the drawing of ethnic boundaries was often arbitrary and designed to make each of the designated groups dependent on the Soviet state for their very identity.

With Sovietisation came a heavy dose of Slavic influence. Most native peoples have adopted Russian dress and diet, particularly those who live in the bigger towns and cities.

Tatars

Russia's biggest minority is the Tatars (3.9% of the population according to the 2010 census), who are descended from the Mongol-Tatar armies of Chinggis (Genghis) Khaan and his successors, and from earlier Hunnic, Turkic and Finno-Ugric settlers on the middle Volga. From around the 13th century, the Tatars started moving out of Siberia towards the European side of Russia, a process that sped up as Cossack forces conquered their way eastwards from the 16th century.

Today the Tatars are mostly Muslim, and about 2 million of them form nearly half the population of the Tatarstan Republic, the capital of which is Kazan. A couple more million or so Tatars live in other parts of Russia and the Commonwealth of Independent States (CIS).

The Moscow-based human-rights group SOVA Center (www.sova-center.ru) issues regular reports on racism and xenophobia in Russia. In 2013 they found 21 people died and 178 were injured as a result of racist and neo-Nazi violence, and nine people received credible murder threats.

Chuvash & Bashkirs

You'll encounter the Chuvash and Baskhir minority groups in the middle Volga region. The Chuvash, descendants of Turkic pre-Mongol settlers in the region, are mainly Orthodox Christian and form a majority (around 68% of the population) in the Chuvash Republic, immediately west of the Tatarstan Republic. The capital is Cheboksary (also known as Shupashkar).

The Muslim Bashkirs have Turkic roots. About half of them live in the Republic of Bashkortostan (capital: Ufa), where they are outnumbered by both Russians and Tatars. After the fall of Kazan in 1555, the Bashkirs 'voluntarily' aligned themselves with Russia. But various conflicts and rebellions subsequently broke out and it wasn't until the mid-18th century that Russian troops achieved full pacification of the area.

Finno-Ugric Peoples

In central and Northern European Russia, there are several major groups of Finno-Ugric peoples, distant relatives of the Estonians, Hungarians and Finns:

- Orthodox or Muslim Mordvins, a quarter of whom live in the Republic of Mordovia (capital Saransk)
- Udmurts or Votyaks, predominantly Orthodox, two-thirds of whom live in Udmurtia (capital Izhevsk)
- Mari, with an animist/shamanist religion, nearly half of whom live in Mary-El (capital Yoshkar-Ola)

RACISM IN RUSSIA

Russia's constitution gives courts the power to ban groups inciting hatred or intolerant behaviour. Unfortunately, racist abuse and xenophobia remain a fact of life in this multiethnic nation. It's not uncommon to hear Central Asians and Caucasians referred to by the derogatory *churki* and *khachi*, Ukrainians *khokhly* and Jews *zhidy*. Even supposedly 'liberal' elements of Russian society can come out with shockingly racist remarks: anti-corruption activist and opposition politician Alexey Navalny has frequently stated that half of all violent crimes in Russia are committed by immigrants – even though this figure is disputed.

Racial abuse of black African players in the nation's professional soccer leagues refuses to go away, with incidents such as in 2012 when a petition from the largest fan group of Zenit, a St Petersburg-based team, demanded that the club exclude black players.

To their credit Zenit enlisted a local ad agency to help change fans' attitudes. A clever cartoon video (www.en.fc-zenit.ru/main/video/gl2397) was created featurig the national Russian icon Pushkin – who had an Ethiopian great-grandfather and was notably swarthy in skin colour.

In Russia's favour, attitudes are broadening among younger and more affluent Russians as, for first time in the nation's history, large numbers of people are being exposed to life outside the country. Under communism people were rarely allowed to venture abroad – now they are doing so in droves. Today over 20 million Russians travel abroad each year compared to 2.6 million in 1995. The result, apart from a fad for the exotic – whether it's Turkish pop music or *qalyan*s (hookahs) in restaurants – is a greater tolerance and better understanding of other cultures.

- ➡ Komi, who are Orthodox, most of whom live in the Komi Republic (capital Syktyvkar)
- ➡ Karelians, found in the Republic of Karelia, north of St Petersburg
- ➡ Sami, also known as Laps or Laplanders, mainly in the Kola Peninsula.

Finno-Ugric people are also found in Asian Russia. The Khanty, also known as the Ostyak, were the first indigenous people encountered by 11th-century Novgorodian explorers as they came across the Ural Mountains. Along with the related Mansi or Voguls, many live in the swampy Khanty-Mansisk Autonomous District on the middle Ob River, north of Tobolsk.

Both the Unrepresented Nations and Peoples Organization (www.unpo.org; UNPO) and the Red Book of the Peoples of the Russian Empire (www.eki.ee/books/redbook) contain profiles of more than 80 different ethnic groups found in the lands currently or once ruled by Russia.

Peoples of the Caucasus

The Russian northern Caucasus is a real ethnic jigsaw of at least 19 local nationalities including the Abaza and Adygeya (both also known as the Circassians), Chechens, Kabardians, Lezgians and Ossetians. Several of these peoples have been involved in ethnic conflicts in recent years.

Dagestan, which means 'mountain country' in Turkish, is an ethnographic wonder, populated by no fewer than 81 ethnic groups of different origins speaking 30 mostly endemic languages.

Together with the Dagestani, Ingush and other groups in the northwest Caucasus, Chechens are known in Russia by the common name *gortsy* (highlanders). Academic experts on the highly independent *gortsy* note how they continue to live by strict codes of honour and revenge, with clan-oriented blood feuds not uncommon even today. Most of the *gortsy* are Sunni Muslims, although the Salafist version of Islam has become popular in recent years.

The Smithsonian National Museum of Natural History in Washington, DC, provides a virtual exhibition on the native peoples of Siberia and Alaska (www.mnh.si.edu/arctic/features/croads).

Turkic peoples in the region include the Kumyk and Nogay in Dagestan, and the Karachay and Balkar in the western and central Caucasus.

Peoples of Siberia & the Russian Far East

More than 30 indigenous Siberian and Russian Far East peoples now make up less than 5% of the region's total population. The most numerous groups are the ethnic Mongol Buryats, the Yakuts or Sakha, Tuvans, Khakass and Altai. While each of these has a distinct Turkic-rooted language and their 'own' republic within the Russian Federation, only the Tuvans form a local majority.

Among the smaller groups are the Evenki, also called the Tungusi, spread widely but very thinly throughout Siberia. Related tribes include the Evens, scattered around the northeast but found mainly in Kamchatka, and the Nanai in the lower Amur River Basin; it's possible to visit some Nanai villages near Khabarovsk.

Anna Reid's *The Shaman's Coat* is both a fascinating history of the major native peoples of Siberia and the Russian Far East and a lively travelogue.

The Arctic hunter-herder Nenets (numbering around 35,000) are the most numerous of the 25 'Peoples of the North'. Together with three smaller groups they are called the Samoyed, though the name is not very popular because it means 'self-eater' in Russian – a person who wears himself out physically and psychologically.

The Chukchi and Koryaks are the most numerous of six Palaeo-Siberian peoples of the far northeast, with languages that don't belong in any larger category. Their Stone Age forebears, who crossed the Bering Strait ice to the USA and Greenland, may also be remote ancestors of the Native Americans, Eskimos, Aleuts and the Oroks of Sakhalin Island.

Religion

Russia adopted Christianity under Prince Vladimir of Kyiv in 988 after centuries of following animist beliefs. Since 1997 the Russian Orthodox Church (Russkaya Pravoslavnaya Tserkov; www.mospat.ru) has been legally recognised as the leading faith and has resumed its prolific role in public life, just as it had in tsarist days. However, Russia is also a multiconfessional state with sizeable communities of Muslims, Buddhists and Jews and a constitution enshrining religious freedom.

Russian Orthodox Church

This highly traditional religion is so central to Russian life that understanding something about its history and practices will enhance any of the inevitable visits you'll make to a Russian Orthodox church.

Patriarch Kirill I of Moscow and All Russia is head of the Church. The patriarch's residence is Moscow's Danilovsky Monastery while the city's senior church is the Cathedral of Christ the Saviour. The Church's senior bishops bear the title metropolitan.

Decor & Services

Churches are decorated with frescoes, mosaics and icons with the aim of conveying Christian teachings and assisting veneration. Different subjects are assigned traditional places in the church (the Last Judgement, for instance, appears on the western wall). The central focus is always an iconostasis (icon stand), often elaborately decorated. The iconostasis divides the main body of the church from the sanctuary, or altar area, at the eastern end, which is off limits to all but the priest.

Apart from some benches to the sides, there are no chairs or pews in Orthodox churches; people stand during services such as the Divine Liturgy (Bozhestvennaya Liturgia), lasting about two hours, which is held daily any time between 7am and 10am. Most churches also hold services at 5pm or 6pm daily. Some services include an *akafist*, a series of chants to the Virgin or saints.

Services are conducted not in Russian but 'Church Slavonic', the Southern Slavic dialect into which the Bible was first translated for Slavs. Paskha (Easter) is the focus of the Church year, with festive midnight services launching Easter Day.

Monastery Beauty

Trinity Monastery of St Sergius, Sergiev Posad

Pechory Monastery, Pechory

Solovetsky Transfiguration Monastery, Solovetsky Islands

Tikhvin Monastery of the Mother of God, Tikhvin

Valaam Transfiguration Monastery, Valaam

Other Christian Churches

Russia has small numbers of Roman Catholics, and Lutheran and Baptist Protestants, mostly among the German, Polish and other non-Russian

CHURCH-VISITING RULES

- Working churches are open to everyone.
- As a visitor you should take care not to disturb any devotions or offend sensibilities.
- On entering a church, men bare their heads and women cover theirs.
- Shorts on men and miniskirts on women are considered inappropriate.
- Hands in pockets or crossed legs or arms may attract frowns.
- Photography is usually banned, especially during services; if in doubt, ask permission first.

ethnic groups. Communities of Old Believers still survive in Siberia, where you may also encounter followers of Vissarion (www.vissarion.eu), considered by his followers to be a living, modern-day Jesus.

According to a 2007 US government report on religious freedom, Russian courts have tried to use the 1997 religion law (asserting the Orthodox Church's leading role) to ban or impose restrictions on the Pentecostal Church, Jehovah's Witnesses and other minority Christian faiths.

In its 'freedom of conscience' report for 2007 the SOVA Center found that 'nontraditional' religious organisations in Russia faced 'serious difficulties' in relation to the construction of buildings or leasing of facilities.

Just as in Catholic countries, children are traditionally named after saints as well as having a given name. Each saint has a 'saint's day' set in the Orthodox calendar. The day of one's namesake saint is celebrated like a second birthday.

Islam

Islam is Russia's second-most widely professed religion and experts believe it is practised by between seven million and nine million people. There are many more millions who are Muslims by ethnicity. They are mainly found among the Tatar and Bashkir peoples east of Moscow and a few dozen of the Caucasian ethnic groups. Nearly all are Sunni Muslims, except for some Shi'a in Dagestan. Muslim Kazakhs, a small minority in southeast Altai, are the only long-term Islamic group east of Bashkortostan.

Muslim history in Russia goes back more than 1000 years. In the dying days of tsarist Russia, Muslims even had their own faction in the *duma* (parliament). The Islamic Cultural Centre of Russia, which includes a *madrasa* (college for Islamic learning), opened in Moscow in 1991.

Some Muslim peoples – notably the Chechens and Tatars – have been resistant to being brought within the Russian national fold since the fall of the Soviet Union, but this has been due as much to nationalism as to religion. In an apparent effort to ease tensions between the state and Muslim communities following the war in Chechnya, Russia became a member of the influential Organisation of Islamic Conferences in 2003.

Islam in Russia is fairly secularised – in predominantly Muslim areas you'll find women who are not veiled, for example, although many will wear headscarves; also, the Friday holy day is not a commercial holiday. Few local Muslims seriously abide by Islam's ban on drinking alcohol.

In response to the Pussy Riot incident at Moscow's Cathedral of Christ the Saviour, the Russian parliament in 2013 passed a law making it a crime to insult people's religious feelings in public, punishable by up to three years in prison.

CHURCH NAMES

chasovnaya	chapel	часовня
khram	church or temple	храм
monastyr	convent or monastery	монастырь
sobor	cathedral	собор
svyatoi	saint	святой
tserkov	church	церковь
Blagoveshchenskaya	Annunciation	Благовещенская
Borisoglebskaya	Boris & Gleb	Борисоглебская
Nikolskaya	Nicholas	Никольская
Petropavlovskaya	Peter & Paul	Петропавловская
Pokrovskaya	Intercession	Покровская
Preobrazhenswkaya	Transfiguration	Преображенская
Rizopolozhenskaya	Deposition of the Robe	Ризоположенская
Rozhdestvenskaya	Nativity	Рождественская
Troitskaya	Trinity	Троицкая
Uspenskaya	Assumption or Dormition	Успенская
Vladimirskaya	Vladimir	Владимирская
Voskresenskaya	Resurrection	Воскресенская
Voznesenskaya	Ascension	Вознесенская
Znamenskaya	Holy Sign	Знаменская

Buddhism

There are around 1.5 million Buddhists in Russia, a figure that has been growing steadily in the years since *glasnost* (openness), when Buddhist organisations became free to reopen temples and monasteries.

The Kalmyks – the largest ethnic group in the Republic of Kalmykia, northwest of the Caspian Sea – are traditionally members of the Gelugpa or 'Yellow Hat' sect of Tibetan Buddhism, whose spiritual leader is the Dalai Lama. They fled from wars in western Mongolia, where Buddhism had reached them not long before, to their present region in the 17th century.

The Gelugpa sect reached eastern Buryatiya and Tuva via Mongolia in the 18th century, but only really took root in the 19th century. As with other religions, Stalin did his best to wipe out Buddhism in the 1930s, destroying hundreds of *datsans* (Buddhist temples) and monasteries and executing or exiling thousands of peaceable *lamas* (Buddhist priests).

Since 1950, Buddhism has been organised under a Buddhist Religious Board based at Ivolginsk. The Dalai Lama has visited Buryatiya, Tuva and Elista, the capital of the Republic of Kalmykia, despite Chinese pressure on the Russian government to not grant the Tibetan leader a visa, as reported by the BBC. For more about Buddhism in Russia see www.buddhist.ru/eng.

If you are allowed into a working mosque, take off your shoes (and your socks, if they are dirty). Women should wear headscarves and dress modestly; men should also have their legs covered.

Buddhist Temples

Ivolginsk Datsan, Buryatiya

Aginskoe Datsan, Zaibaikalsky Territory

Tsugol Datsan, Zaibaikalsky Territory

Buddhist Temple, St Petersburg

Judaism

Jews, who are estimated to number around 200,000 people, are considered an ethnicity within Russia, as well as a religion. Most have been assimilated into Russian culture.

The largest communities are found in Moscow and St Petersburg, both of which have several historic, working synagogues. There's also a small, conservative community of several thousand 'Mountain Jews' (Gorskie Yevrei) living mostly in the Caucasian cities of Nalchik, Pyatigorsk and Derbent. Siberia was once home to large numbers of Jews but now you'll only find noticeable communities in Yekaterinburg and the Jewish Autonomous Region – created during Stalin's era – centred on Birobidzhan.

There are two umbrella organisations of Russian Jewry:

Federation of Jewish Communities of the CIS (www.fjc.ru) supports the Italian-born Berl Lazar as chief rabbi – he is also a member of the Public Chamber of Russia, an oversight committee for government.

Russian-Jewish Congress (www.rjc.ru) recognises Russian-born Adolf Shayevich as their chief rabbi.

Beyond the Pale: The History of Jews in Russia (www.friends-partners.org/partners/beyond-the-pale/index.html) is an online version of an exhibition on Jewish history that has toured the country.

Animism & Shamanism

Many cultures, from the Finno-Ugric Mari and Udmurts to the nominally Buddhist Mongol Buryats, retain varying degrees of animism. This is often submerged beneath, or accepted in parallel with, other religions. Animism is a primal belief in the presence of spirits or spiritual qualities in objects of the natural world. Peaks and springs are especially revered and their spirits are thanked with token offerings. This explains (especially in Tuva and Altai) the coins, stone cairns, vodka bottles and abundant prayer ribbons that you'll commonly find around holy trees and mountain passes.

Spiritual guidance is through a medium or shaman: a high priest, prophet and doctor in one. Animal skins, trance dances and a special type of drum are typical shamanic tools, though different shamans have different spiritual and medical gifts. Siberian museums exhibit many shamanic outfits. Krasnoyarsk's regional museum shows examples from many different tribal groups. Tuva is the most likely place to encounter practising shamans.

Popular among a few New Age groups, another form of religious shamanism emphasises the core philosophical beliefs of ecological balance and respect for nature. Buryat shaman Sarangerel's book, *Riding Windhorses,* is a great general introduction to shamanism.

There are three shamanic school-clinics in Kyzyl, Tuva, but, like visiting a doctor, you'll be expected to have a specific need and there will be fees for the consultation.

Performing Arts & Music

By late tsarist Russia the performing arts had evolved into grand and refined spectacles of ballet and opera created to entertain the nobility of St Petersburg and Moscow. These still delight audiences of all means around the world. But it's not all about the classical in Russian performing arts – rock and pop music are just as popular here as they are elsewhere, Chekhov's plays are staged alongside experimental theatre and circus is revered as a great night's entertainment.

Dance

Birth of Russian Ballet

First brought to Russia under Tsar Alexey Mikhailovich in the 17th century, ballet in Russia evolved as an offshoot of French dance combined with Russian folk and peasant dance techniques. The result stunned Western Europeans when it was first taken on tour during the late 19th century.

The official beginnings of Russian ballet date to 1738 and the establishment of a school of dance in St Petersburg's Winter Palace, the precursor to the famed Vaganova School of Choreography, by French dance master Jean-Baptiste Landé. Moscow's Bolshoi Theatre dates from 1776. However, the true father of Russian ballet is considered to be Marius Petipa (1818–1910), the French dancer and choreographer who acted first as principal dancer, then premier ballet master, of the Imperial Theatre in St Petersburg. All told, he produced more than 60 full ballets (including Tchaikovsky's *Sleeping Beauty* and *Swan Lake*).

For Ballet Lovers Only (www.for-ballet-lovers-only.com) has biographies of leading Bolshoi and Mariinsky dancers, both past and present, as well as a good links section if you want to learn more about Russian ballet.

At the turn of the 20th century – Russian ballet's heyday – St Petersburg's Imperial School of Ballet rose to world prominence, producing a wealth of superstars including Vaslav Nijinsky, Anna Pavlova, Mathilda Kshesinskaya, George Balanchine and Michel Fokine. Sergei Diaghilev's Ballets Russes, formed in Paris in 1909 (with most of its members coming from the Imperial School of Ballet), took Europe by storm. The stage decor was painted by artists such as Alexander Benois.

Soviet Era to Modern Day

During Soviet rule, ballet enjoyed a privileged status, which allowed schools such as the Vaganova and companies like St Petersburg's Kirov (now the Mariinsky) and Moscow's Bolshoi to maintain lavish productions and high performance standards. At the Bolshoi, Yury Grigorovich emerged as the leading choreographer, with *Spartacus, Ivan the Terrible* and other successes that espoused Soviet moral and artistic values. Meanwhile, many of Soviet ballet's biggest stars emigrated or defected, including Rudolf Nureyev, Mikhail Baryshnikov and Natalia Makarova.

As the Soviet Union collapsed, artistic feuds at the Bolshoi between Grigorovich and his dancers, combined with a loss of state subsidies and the continued financial lure of the West to principal dancers, led to a crisis in the Russian ballet world. Grigorovich resigned in 1995, prompting dancers loyal to him to stage the Bolshoi's first-ever strike. The company ran through a series of artistic directors before finding stability and renewed acclaim under the dynamic direction of Alexey Ratmansky from 2004 to 2008. *Dreams of Japan,* one of the 20-plus ballets that Alexey Ratmansky has choreographed, was awarded a prestigious Golden Mask award in 1998. Under his direction the Bolshoi won Best Foreign Company in 2005 and 2007 from the prestigious Critics' Circle in London.

Scandals have dogged the Bolshoi in recent years. In 2011 the troupe's director Gennady Yanin was forced to step down following the release on the internet of erotic photos of him. In 2013 the former prima ballerina Anastasia Volochkova claimed that the Bolshoi was a 'giant brothel' with dancers forced to sleep with wealthy patrons. The same year Sergei Filin, the Bolshoi's artistic director, suffered damaged eyesight and a burned face in an acid attack orchestrated by Pavel Dmitrichenko, a dancer in the company.

Meanwhile in St Petersburg, charismatic Valery Gergiev is secure in his position at the Mariinsky, where he has been artistic director since 1988 and overall director since 1996. The ballet troupe reports to Yury Fateyev, who has pushed the dancers to embrace more than the classical repertoire for which they are most famous, staging ballets by George Balanchine and Jerome Robbins as well as Ratmansky, whose *Anna Karenina* (based on the Tolstoy novel) premiered in 2010.

Natasha's Dance: A Cultural History of Russia by Orlando Figes is an excellent book offering plenty of colourful anecdotes about great Russian writers, artists, composers and architects.

Native Folk Dancing & Music

Traditional Russian folk dancing and music is still practised across the country, although your best chance of seeing it as a visitor is in cheesy shows in restaurants or at tourist-orientated extravaganzas such as Feel Yourself Russian (www.folkshow.ru) in St Petersburg. Companies with solid reputations to watch out for include Igor Moiseyev Ballet (www.moiseyev.ru), the Ossipov Balalaika Orchestra (www.ossipovorchestra.ru/en) and the Pyatnitsky State Academic Russian Folk Choir, all offering repertoires with roots as old as Kyivan Rus, including heroic ballads and the familiar Slavic *trepak* (stamping folk dances).

In Siberia and the Russian Far East, it's also possible to occasionally catch dance and music performances by native peoples. In the Altai, minstrels sing epic ballads, while in Tuva *khöömei* (throat singing) ranges from the ultradeep troll-warbling of *kargyraa* to the superhuman self-harmonising of *sygyt.*

The roots of Russian music lie in folk song and dance, and Orthodox Church chants. *Byliny* (epic folk songs of Russia's peasantry) preserved folk culture and lore through celebration of particular events such as great battles or harvests.

Music

Classical, 19th Century

Mikhail Glinka (1804–57) is considered the father of Russian classical music: he was born in Smolensk, where an annual festival is held in his honour. As Russian composers (and other artists) struggled to find a national identity, several influential schools formed, from which some of Russia's most famous composers emerged. The Group of Five – Modest Mussorgsky, Nikolai Rimsky-Korsakov, Alexander Borodin, Cesar Kui and Mily Balakirev – believed a radical departure from traditional Western European composition necessary, and looked to *byliny* (epic folk songs) and folk music for themes. Their main opponent was Anton Rubinstein's conservatively rooted Russian Musical Society, which became the St Petersburg Conservatory in 1861, the first conservatory in Russia.

Triumphing in the middle ground was Pyotr Tchaikovsky (1840–93), who embraced Russian folklore and music as well as the disciplines of the Western European composers. The former lawyer first studied music at the St Petersburg Conservatory, but he later moved to Moscow to teach at the conservatory there. This was where all his major works were composed, including, in 1880, the magnificent *1812 Overture.*

Among his other famous pieces are the ballets *Swan Lake* (Lebedinoye Ozero), *Sleeping Beauty* (Spyashchaya Krasavitsa) and *The Nutcracker*

(Shchelkunchik); the operas *Eugene Onegin* (Yevgeny Onegin) and *Queen of Spades* (Pikovaya Dama), both inspired by the works of Alexander Pushkin; and his final work, the *Pathétique* Symphony No 6. The romantic beauty of these pieces belies a tragic side to the composer, who led a tortured life as a closeted homosexual. The rumour mill has it that rather than dying of cholera, as reported, he committed suicide by poisoning himself following a 'trial' by his peers about his sexual behaviour.

Ken Russell's *The Music Lovers* is a feverishly sensational and at times hysterical biopic about Tchaikovsky. Richard Chamberlain plays the famously closeted composer and Glenda Jackson his entirely unsuitable wife, Nina.

Classical, 20th Century

Following in Tchaikovsky's romantic footsteps were Sergei Rachmaninov (1873–1943) and Igor Stravinsky (1882–1971) – both fled Russia after the revolution. Stravinsky's *The Rite of Spring* – which created a furore at its first performance in Paris – and *The Firebird* were influenced by Russian folk music. Sergei Prokofiev (1891–1953), who also left Soviet Russia but returned in 1933, wrote the scores for Sergei Eisenstein's films *Alexander Nevsky* and *Ivan the Terrible*, the ballet *Romeo and Juliet*, and *Peter and the Wolf*, beloved of those who teach music to young children. He fell foul of the fickle Soviet authorities towards the end of his life and died on the same day as Stalin.

Dmitry Shostakovich (1906–75), who wrote brooding, bizarrely dissonant works, as well as accessible traditional classical music, was also alternately praised and condemned by the Soviet government. Despite initially not to Stalin's liking, Shostakovich's Symphony No 7 – the *Leningrad* – brought him honour and international standing when it was performed by the Leningrad Philharmonic during the Siege of Leningrad. The authorities changed their minds again and banned his music in 1948, then 'rehabilitated' him after Stalin's death.

Progressive new music surfaced slowly in the post-Stalin era, with limited outside contact. Symphony No 1 by Alfred Schnittke (1934–98), probably the most important work of this major experimental modern Russian composer, had to be premiered by its champion, conductor Gennady Rozhdestvensky, in the provincial city of Gorky (now Nizhny Novgorod) in 1974. It was not played in Moscow until 1986.

Opera

Russian opera was born in St Petersburg when Mikhail Glinka's *A Life for the Tsar*, which merged traditional and Western influences, premiered on 9 December 1836. It told the story of peasant Ivan Susanin, who sacrifices himself to save Tsar Mikhail Romanov. He followed this with another

BUYING TICKETS FOR PERFORMANCES & EVENTS

Teatralnye kassy (theatre ticket offices, sometimes kiosks) are found across all sizeable cities, although it's not difficult to buy face-value tickets from the *kassa* (ticket office) at the venue itself, typically open for advance or same-day sales from early afternoon until the start of the evening show. Outside the major cities tickets can start as low as ₽100. Only the most popular shows tend to sell out completely, so there's usually hope for obtaining same-day seats. In Moscow and St Petersburg, however, competition is much greater and the top venues have 'foreigner pricing'. It can be worth falling back on a hotel service bureau or concierge to get the best tickets, even though that can mean paying a huge premium over face value.

Tickets for both Moscow's Bolshoi and St Petersburg's Mariinsky Theatres can be booked online – this is the best way to ensure that you get the seat you want. For Moscow events, consider booking using a web-based service such as www.parter.ru.

If all else fails, there are usually touts (scalpers): not only professionals but also people with spares. It's standard practice to sell tickets outside the main entrance before starting time. Remember that prices are a free-for-all and you run the risk of obstructed views. Before handing over any money make sure that the ticket actually has the date, performance and section you want.

folk-based opera, *Ruslan and Lyudmila* (1842), thus inaugurating the 'New Russian School' of composition.

Another pivotal moment in Russian opera was the 5 December 1890 premiere of Tchaikovsky's *Queen of Spades* at the Mariinsky. Adapted from a tale by Alexander Pushkin, it surprised and invigorated the artistic community by successfully merging opera with topical social comment.

In March 2005 the Bolshoi premiered its first new opera in 26 years, *Rosenthal's Children* – with music by Leonid Desyatnikov and words by Vladimir Sorokin – to a hail of protests over its controversial plot about cloning. In 2006, the unconventional production of Tchaikovsky's *Eugene Onegin* by the Bolshoi opera company's director Dmitry Tcherniakov split public opinion in Russia but wowed critics abroad.

Even so, contemporary opera in Russia continues to gain popularity. In 2012, Vasily Barkhatov produced four new operas written by Russian composers, in collaboration with the Laboratory of Contemporary Opera, an initiative of the Ministry of Culture. Sorokin is working on a new series of operas and *Marevo* (Mirage in English), the first opera from Provmyza, a Nizhny Novgorod–based art collective, was nominated for 2014's Innovation award in the visual-art category.

Russian opera has produced many singing stars, from Fyodor Chaliapin in the early years of the 20th century to the current diva, soprano Anna Netrebko, who started as a cleaner at the Mariinsky and now commands the stages of top opera houses around the world.

Rock & Pop

The Communist Party was no fan of pop music. Back in the 1960s, the gravel-voiced Vladimir Vysotsky (1938–80) was the dissident voice of the USSR, becoming a star despite being banned from TV, radio and major stages. Denied the chance to record or perform to big audiences, Russian rock groups were forced underground. By the 1970s – the Soviet hippie era – this genre of music had developed a huge following among a disaffected, distrustful youth. One of the most famous groups of this era is Mashina Vremeni (Time Machine; www.mashina.ru), who formed in 1969 and are still going strong with the original lead vocalist Andrey Makarevich.

Although bands initially imitated their Western counterparts, by the 1980s there was a home-grown sound emerging. In Moscow, Leningrad (St Petersburg) and Yekaterinburg, in particular, many influential bands sprung up. Boris Grebenshikov and his band Akvarium (Aquarium; www.aquariumband.com) from Yekaterinburg caused a sensation wherever they performed; his folk rock and introspective lyrics became the emotional cry of a generation. At first, all of their music was circulated by illegal tapes known as *magizdat,* passed from listener to listener; concerts – known as *tusovka* (informal parties) – were held in remote halls or people's apartments in city suburbs, and just attending them could be risky. Other top bands of this era include DDT, Nautilus Pompilius and Bravo, whose lead singer Zhanna Aguzarova became Soviet rock's first female star.

Late-Soviet rock's shining star, though, was Viktor Tsoy, an ethnic Korean born in Leningrad, frontman of the group Kino; the band's classic album is 1988's *Gruppa Krovi* (Blood Group). Tsoy's early death in a 1990 car crash sealed his legendary status. Fans gather on the anniversary of his death (15 August) to this day and play his music. His grave, at the Bogoslovskogo Cemetery in St Petersburg, has been turned into a shrine, much like Jim Morrison's in Paris. There is also the 'Tsoy Wall', covered with Tsoy-related graffiti, on ul Arbat in Moscow.

Contemporary stars of the Russian rock scene include Mumiy Troll (http://mumiytroll.co), formed by Vladivostok-born Ilya Lagutenko. The band regularly plays international festivals, such as SXSW. In 2013, Lagutenko kick-started the similar V-ROX music festival in Vladivostok, a city that a quarter of a century before had been closed to foreigners. Also gaining traction outside Russia is Tesla Boy (www.teslaboy.com), a synth-pop band led by Anton Sevidov. Roma Litvinov, aka Mujuice, is considered one of Russia's most innovative electronic musicians; his composition includes elements of jazz.

Music Festivals

Afisha Picnic (http://picnic.afisha.ru), Moscow

Sergei Kuryokhin International Festival (SKIF; www.kuryokhin.net/en/skif/about.html), St Petersburg

Usadba Jazz (www.usadba-jazz.ru), Moscow, St Petersburg

V-ROX (www.vrox.vladivostok3000.ru/en), Vladivostok

Still going strong are girl duo t.A.T.u, who represented Russia in the 2003 Eurovision Song Contest and performed at the 2014 Sochi Olympics opening ceremony, and Dima Bilan (www.bilandima.ru/eng), who won Russia the Eurovision contest in 2008.

Directed by Alexey Uchitel in 1988, *Rock* is a revealing documentary about the Leningrad rock scene of the 1980s, featuring legends such as Boris Grebenshikov and Viktor Tsoy.

Theatre

Drama lover Catherine the Great set up the Imperial Theatre Administration and authorised the construction of Moscow's Bolshoi Theatre. During her reign Denis Fonvizin wrote *The Brigadier* (1769) and *The Minor* (1781), satirical comedies that are still performed today.

Nineteenth-century dramatists included Alexander Pushkin, whose drama *Boris Godunov* (1830) was later used as the libretto for the Mussorgsky Opera; Nikolai Gogol, whose tragic farce *The Government Inspector* (1836) was said to be a favourite play of Nicholas I; Alexander Griboedov, whose comedy satire *Woe from Wit* was a compulsory work in Russian literature lessons during the Soviet period; and Ivan Turgenev, whose languid *A Month in the Country* (1849) laid the way for the most famous Russian playwright of all: Anton Chekhov (1860–1904).

Chekhov's *The Seagull* (1896), *The Three Sisters* (1901), *The Cherry Orchard* (1904) and *Uncle Vanya* (1899), all of which take the angst of the provincial middle class as their theme, owed much of their success to their 'realist' productions at the Moscow Art Theatre by Konstantin Stanislavsky, which aimed to show life as it really was.

Theatre remained popular through the Soviet period, not least because it was one of the few areas of artistic life where a modicum of freedom of expression was permitted. Stalin famously said that although Mikhail Bulgakov's *White Guard* (1926) had been written by an enemy, it still deserved to be staged because of the author's outstanding talent. Bulgakov is perhaps the only person dubbed an enemy by Stalin and never persecuted. The avant-garde actor-director Vsevolod Meyerhold was not so fortunate (see the boxed text, p614).

Oleg and Vladimir Presnyakov write plays and direct together under the joint name Presnyakov Brothers; they've been praised for their dramas' natural-sounding dialogue and sardonic wit. *Terrorism*, their best-known work, has been performed around the world.

Today both Moscow's and St Petersburg's theatre scene are as lively as those in London and New York. Notable directors include Kama Gingkas, who works with the Moscow Art Theatre, Pyotr Fomenko, who heads up Moscow's Pyotr Fomenko Workshop Theatre, and Lev Dodin at the Maly Drama Theatre in St Petersburg. Dmitry Krymov, who began his career as a stage designer, heads up the Krymov Lab at Moscow's School of Dramatic Arts where he crafts incredible, visually dramatic productions that have toured internationally. These include a version of Shakespeare's *A Midsummer Night's Dream* and *Opus No 7*, which in its two acts pays homage to the Jews lost in the Holocaust and the classical composer Shostakovich.

Circus

While Western circuses grow smaller and become scarce, the Russian versions are still like those from childhood stories – prancing horses with acrobats on their backs, snarling lions and tigers, heart-stopping high-wire artists and hilarious clowns. They remain a highly popular form of entertainment.

The Russian circus tradition has roots in medieval travelling minstrels called *skomorokhi,* although the first modern-style circus (a performance within a ring) dates to the reign of Catherine the Great. The country's first permanent circus was established in St Petersburg in 1877 and, in 1927, Moscow's School for Circus Arts became the world's first such training institution. Many cities still have their own troupes and most at least have an arena for visiting companies. Best known is Moscow's Nikulin Circus.

In recent years, most major troupes have cleaned up their act with regard to the treatment of animals. In Moscow and St Petersburg circuses it is unlikely you will see animals treated cruelly or forced to perform degrading acts.

Literature & Cinema

Some of the most vivid impressions of Russia have been shaped by the creative works of the country's writers and movie-makers. Although they really only got going in the 19th century, Russian writers wasted little time in carving out a prime place in the world of letters, producing towering classics in the fields of poetry and prose. In the process they have bagged five Nobel Prizes and frequently found themselves in conflict with the Russian establishment.

Literature

The Golden Age

The great collection of works produced during the 19th century has led to it being known as the 'Golden Age' of Russian literature. This was the time of the precocious and brilliant Alexander Pushkin (1799–1837), who penned the verse *The Bronze Horseman* and *Eugene Onegin,* and Mikhail Lermontov (1814–41), author of *A Hero of Our Time.* Both were sent into exile by the authorities for their seditious writings; and both died young in duels, securing their romantic reputations for a country enthralled by doomed young heroes.

Continuing the tradition of literary criticism of the powers that be was the novelist and playwright Nikolai Gogol (1809–52), whose novel *Dead Souls* exposed the widespread corruption in Russian society. Gogol created some of Russian literature's most memorable characters, including Akaky Akakievich, the tragicomic hero of *The Overcoat,* and Major Kovalyov, who chases his errant nose around St Petersburg when the shnozzle makes a break for it in the absurdist short story *The Nose.* His love of the surreal established a pattern in Russian literature that echoes through the works of Daniil Kharms, Mikhail Bulgakov and Viktor Pelevin in the next century.

More radical writers figured in the second half of the 19th century. In *Fathers and Sons,* by Ivan Turgenev (1818–83), the antihero Bazarov became a symbol for the anti-tsarist nihilist movement of the time. Before penning classics such as *Crime and Punishment* and *The Brothers Karamazov,* which deals with questions of morality, faith and salvation, Fyodor Dostoevsky (1821–81) fell foul of the authorities and was exiled for a decade from St Petersburg, first in Siberia and later in what is now Kazakhstan.

Leo Tolstoy (1828–1910) sealed his reputation as one of Russia's greatest writers with his Napoleonic War saga *War and Peace,* and *Anna Karenina,* a tragedy about a woman who violates the rigid sexual code of her time. Such was his popularity that his unorthodox beliefs in Christian anarchy and pacifism protected him from reprisals by the government.

The Silver Age

From the end of the 19th century until the early 1930s, the 'Silver Age' of Russian literature produced more towering talents. First came the rise of the symbolist movement in the Russian arts world. The outstanding figures of this time were philosopher Vladimir Solovyov (1853–1900);

Some notable Silver Age wordsmiths were the poet Velimir Khlebnikov and the poet and playwright Vladimir Mayakovsky, who, together with other futurists, issued the 1913 'Slap in the Face of Public Taste' manifesto urging fellow writers 'to throw Pushkin out of the steamship of modernity'.

The Last Station (2009), based on the novel by Jay Parini, is about the last year of Tolstoy's life. Christopher Plummer, who plays the writer, and Helen Mirren, playing his wife Sofya, were both nominated for Oscars.

PUSHKIN IS OUR EVERYTHING

The phrase 'Pushkin is our everything', uttered by cultured Russians, provides the title for an insightful 2014 documentary (www.pushkinfilm.com) about the national bard by American writer/director Michael Beckelhimer. Today, it is rare to meet a Russian who cannot quote some Pushkin. However, for several years after the writer's untimely death in 1837 at age 38, following a duel fought over the honour of his wife, his works languished in relative obscurity.

Beckelhimer's documentary reveals how Pushkin's reputation was revived by 1880, when the first of what would be many statues of the nation's poet across Russia was unveiled in Moscow by the likes of Ivan Turgenev and Fyodor Dostoevsky. That status was enhanced and solidified in Russian consciousness during the Soviet era when, in 1937, Stalin orchestrated major centennial celebrations of the poet's death, emphasising his alleged atheism and his proto-communist politics (neither of which was entirely true).

Flat English translations of Pushkin's lyrical, witty and imaginative works, which range from classical odes and sonnets to short stories, plays and fairy tales, can often leave non-Russian speakers wondering what all the fuss is about. It is clear that Pushkin has had a strong influence on language spoken by Russians today. The enraptured Russians interviewed in the documentary talk of the lightness and beauty of Pushkin's words, and how they continue to resonate for them today, nine generations after they were first written.

writer Andrei Bely (1880–1934), author of *Petersburg,* regarded by Vladimir Nabokov as one of the four greatest novels of the 20th century; and Maxim Gorky (1868–1936), who is considered to be the founder of socialist realism with his 1907 novel *Mother,* written during a Bolshevik Party fundraising trip in the USA.

For a riveting account of Pushkin's fatal duel with French nobleman Georges d'Anthès and the events that preceded it, read Serena Vitale's *Pushkin's Button.*

Alexander Blok (1880–1921) was a poet whose sympathy with the revolutions of 1905 and 1917 was praised by the Bolsheviks as an example of an established writer who had seen the light. His tragic poem 'The Twelve', published in 1918, shortly before his death, likens the Bolsheviks to the 12 Apostles who herald the new world. However, Blok soon grew deeply disenchanted with the revolution and in one of his last letters wrote that his Russia was devouring him.

Banned Writers & Nobel Prize Winners

The life of poet Anna Akhmatova (1889–1966) was filled with sorrow and loss – her family was imprisoned and killed, her friends exiled, tortured and arrested, her colleagues constantly hounded – but she refused to leave her beloved St Petersburg. Her verses depict the city with realism and monumentalism, particularly her epic *Poem Without a Hero.*

Another key poet of this age who also suffered for his art was Osip Mandelstam (1891–1938), who died in a Stalinist transit camp near Vladivostok. Akhmatova's and Mandelstam's lives are painfully recorded by Nadezhda Mandelstam in her autobiographical *Hope Against Hope.*

If you don't have the time or stamina for Tolstoy's *War and Peace,* then sample the master's work in his celebrated novellas *The Death of Ivan Ilyich* and *The Devil.*

The work of the great satirist Mikhail Bulgakov (1891–1940), including *The Master and Margarita* and *Heart of a Dog,* was banned for years, as was the dark genius absurdist work of Daniil Kharms (1905–42). Kharms starved to death during the Siege of Leningrad in 1942; it would be two decades later that his surreal stories and poems started to see the light of day and began to be circulated in the Soviet underground press.

Although best known abroad for his epic novel *Doctor Zhivago,* Boris Pasternak (1890–1960) is most celebrated in Russia for his poetry. *My Sister Life,* published in 1921, inspired many Russian poets thereafter. *Doctor Zhivago,* first published in an Italian translation in 1957, secured him the Nobel Prize for Literature in 1958, but Pasternak turned it down, fearing that if he left Russia to accept the award he would not be allowed to return.

One writer who managed to keep in favour with the communist authorities was Mikhail Sholokhov (1905–84), with his sagas of revolution and war among the Don Cossacks – *And Quiet Flows the Don* and *The Don Flows Home to the Sea*. He won the Nobel Prize for Literature in 1965.

Made into a movie by David Lean, Boris Pasternak's *Doctor Zhivago* is a richly philosophical novel spanning events from the dying days of tsarist Russia to the birth of the Soviet Union, offering personal insights into the revolution and the Russian Civil War along the way.

Late Soviet Period Literature

The relaxing of state control over the arts during Khrushchev's time saw the emergence of poets such as Yevgeny Yevtushenko, who gained international fame in 1961 with *Babi Yar* (which denounced both Nazi and Russian anti-Semitism), as well as another Nobel Prize winner, Aleksandr Solzhenitsyn (1918–2008), who wrote mainly about life in the Gulag system.

Some believe the camp experience as related in *Kolyma Tales* by the great literary talent Varlam Shalamov (1907–82) is even more harrowing than that depicted by Solzhenitsyn. Also gaining critical praise was another former Kolyma inmate Eugenia Ginzburg (1904–77) for her memoir *Into the Whirlwind,* initially published abroad in 1967.

The fiercely talented poet Josef Brodsky (1940–96), also a Nobel Prize winner, hailed from St Petersburg and was a protégé of poet Anna Akhmatova. In 1964 he was tried for 'social parasitism' and exiled to the north of Russia. However, after concerted international protests led by Jean-Paul Sartre, he returned to Leningrad in 1965, only to continue to be a thorn in the side of the authorities. Like Solzhenitsyn, Brodsky was exiled to the US in 1972.

Preceding *glasnost* (openness) was native Siberian writer Valentin Rasputin, who is best known for his stories decrying the destruction of the land, spirit and traditions of the Russian people. His 1979 novel *Farewell to Matyora* is about a Siberian village flooded when a hydroelectric dam is built.

RUSSIA'S CONSCIENCE

Few writers' lives sum up the fickle nature of their relationship with the Russian state better than that of Aleksandr Solzhenitsyn (1918–2008). Born just before the emergence of the Soviet Union, he was persecuted and exiled by that regime, only to return to a country that considered him, in his latter years, both a crank and its conscience. Embraced by Vladimir Putin (whom Solzhenitsyn praised as 'a good dictator') for his nationalism, staunch belief in Russian Orthodoxy and hatred of the decadent West, the one-time dissident was given what amounted to a state funeral.

Decorated twice with medals for bravery during WWII, the young Solzhenitsyn first fell foul of the authorities in 1945 when he was arrested for anti-Stalin remarks found in letters to a friend. He subsequently served eight years in various camps and three more in enforced exile in Kazakhstan.

Khrushchev allowed the publication in 1962 of Solzhenitsyn's first novel, *One Day in the Life of Ivan Denisovich,* a short tale of Gulag life. The book sealed the writer's reputation and in 1970 he was awarded the Nobel Prize for Literature, although, like Boris Pasternak before him, he did not go to Sweden to receive it for fear that he would not be allowed to re-enter the USSR. Even so, he was exiled in 1974, when he went to the USA. He finally returned to Russia in 1994.

To the end Solzhenitsyn remained a controversial figure. He was detested by many Gulag survivors, who accused him of collaborating with prison authorities. They looked suspiciously on Solzhenitsyn's ability to gain sole access to the archives that allowed him to write his best-known work, *The Gulag Archipelago,* which describes conditions at the camps on the Solovetsky Islands, even though he was never imprisoned there himself. In his final book, *200 Years Together,* about the history of Jews in Russia, he laid himself open to accusations of anti-Semitism.

Post-Soviet Writers

Recent years have witnessed a publishing boom, with the traditional Russian love of books as strong as ever. One of the most popular novelists is Boris Akunin, whose series of historical detective novels, including *The Winter Queen* and *Turkish Gambit,* feature the foppish Russian Sherlock Holmes, Erast Fandorin.

To find out more about contemporary Russian literature go to Read Russia (www.readrussia.org) which has various online resources and organises events to promote Russian writing.

Among the more challenging contemporary Russian writers who have made their mark are Viktor Yerofeyev, whose erotic novel *Russian Beauty* has been translated into 27 languages, and Tatyana Tolstaya, whose *On the Golden Porch,* a collection of stories about big souls in little Moscow flats, made her an international name when it was published in the West in 1989. Her 2007 novel *The Slynx* is a dystopian fantasy set in a post-nuclear-holocaust world of mutant people, fearsome beasts and totalitarian rulers.

The prolific science-fiction and pop-culture writer Viktor Pelevin has been compared to the great Mikhail Bulgakov. Several of his novels, including *The Yellow Arrow* and *The Sacred Book of the Werewolf,* have also been widely translated. Vladimir Sorokin established his literary reputation abroad with his novels *The Queue* and *Ice*. In *Day of the Oprichnik,* he describes Russia in the year 2028 as a nationalist country ruled with an iron fist that has shut itself off from the West by building a wall.

The anthology *Today I Wrote Nothing: The Selected Writings of Daniil Kharms,* translated by Matvei Yankelevich, is worth dipping into to discover the bizarre works of this eccentric absurdist writer.

Dmitry Bykov is one of the biggest names currently in Russian literary circles; he published a well-regarded biography of Boris Pasternak in 2007. His 2006 novel, *ZhD* (entitled *Living Souls* in its English translation), a satirical, anti-utopian, conspiracy-theory-laden tale of civil war set in near-future Russia, caused furious debate because of its Russophobic and anti-Semitic themes. Mikhail Shishkin has won all Russia's major literary awards. His books, including *Maidenhair* (2006), are being translated into English.

Cinema

The Propaganda Years

Even though there were a few Russian films made at the start of the 20th century, it was really under the Soviet system that this modern form of storytelling began to flourish. Lenin believed cinema to be the most important of all the arts and along with his Bolshevik colleagues saw the value of movies as propaganda.

THE IMPACT OF SOCIALIST REALISM

In 1932 the Communist Party demanded socialist realism: the 'concrete representation of reality in its revolutionary development...in accordance with...ideological training of the workers in the spirit of Socialism'. Henceforth, artists had the all-but-impossible task of conveying the Party line in their works and not falling foul of the notoriously fickle tastes of Stalin in the process.

The composer Dmitry Shostakovich, for example, was officially denounced twice (in 1936 and 1948) and suffered the banning of his compositions. Strongly opposed to socialist realism, theatre director Vsevolod Meyerhold had his theatre closed down; in 1939 he was imprisoned and later tortured and executed as a traitor. He was cleared of all charges in 1955.

Writers were particularly affected, including Vladimir Mayakovsky, who committed suicide, and the poet Anna Akhmatova, whose life was blighted by persecution and tragedy. Many, including Daniil Kharms, had their work driven underground, or were forced to smuggle their manuscripts out to the West for publication, as Boris Pasternak did for *Doctor Zhivago*.

Vast resources were pumped into studios to make historical dramas about Soviet and Russian victories such as Sergei Eisenstein's *Battleship Potemkin* (1925), a landmark of world cinema, and his *Alexander Nevsky* (1938), which contains one of cinema's great battle scenes. However, Eisenstein's *Ivan the Terrible* (1945), a discreet commentary on Stalinism, fell foul of state sponsors and was banned for many years.

The 1936 hit musical *Circus* was typical of the kind of propaganda movies were forced to carry at the height of Stalinism. The plot concerns an American circus artist hounded out of the US because she has a black baby; she finds both refuge and love, of course, in the Soviet Union. The lead actress, Lyubov Orlova, became the Soviet Union's biggest star of the time. She also headlined *Volga, Volga* (1938), another feel-good movie said to be Stalin's favourite film.

Rossica is a glossy journal published by Academia Rossica (www.academia-rossica.org). It features the works of top Russian contemporary writers and artists.

Taking Cinematic Risks

Of later Soviet directors, the dominant figure was Andrei Tarkovsky, whose films include *Andrei Rublyov* (1966), *Solaris* (1972) – the Russian answer to *2001: A Space Odyssey* – and *Stalker* (1979), which summed up the Leonid Brezhnev era pretty well, with its characters wandering, puzzled, through a landscape of clanking trains, rusting metal and overgrown concrete. Tarkovsky died in exile in 1986.

Winning an Academy Award for best foreign-language film, *Moscow Doesn't Believe in Tears* (1980), directed by Vladimir Menshov, charts the course of three provincial gals who make Moscow their home from the 1950s to the 1970s. It's said that Ronald Reagan watched this kitchen-sink drama to get an idea of the Russian soul before his meetings with Gorbachev.

Glasnost brought new excitement in the film industry as film-makers were allowed to reassess Soviet life with unprecedented freedom and as audiences flocked to see previously banned films or the latest exposure of youth culture or Stalinism. Notable were Sergei Solovyov's avant-garde *ASSA* (1987), staring rock-god Viktor Tsoy and the artist Afrika (Sergei Bugaev), and Vasily Pichul's *Little Vera* (1989), for its frank portrayal of a family in chaos (exhausted wife, drunken husband, rebellious daughter) and its sexual content – mild by Western standards but startling to the Soviet audience.

Soviet cinema wasn't all doom, gloom and heavy propaganda. The romantic comedy *Irony of Fate* (1975) has a special place in all Russians' hearts, while a whole genre of 'Easterns' are epitomised by *White Sun of the Desert* (1969), a rollicking adventure set in Turkmenistan during the Russian Civil War of the 1920s. This cult movie, still one of the top-selling DVDs in Russia, is traditionally watched by cosmonauts before blast-off.

T@ke Two (http://d2.rg.ru) is an annual online festival of notable Russian films – features, documentaries and animations – released the previous year.

Post-Soviet Cinema

By the time Nikita Mikhalkov's *Burnt by the Sun* won the best foreign-language movie Oscar in 1994, Russian film production was suffering. Funding had dried up during the early 1990s, and audiences couldn't afford to go to the cinema anyway. The industry was back on track by the end of the decade though, with hits such as Alexy Balabanov's gangster drama *Brother* (1997) and Alexander Sokurov's *Molokh* (1999). Sokurov's ambitious *Russian Ark* was an international success in 2002, as was Andrei Zvyaginstev's moody thriller *The Return* the following year.

The glossy vampire thriller *Night Watch* (2004) struck box-office gold both at home and abroad, leading to an equally successful sequel, *Day Watch* (2006), and to Kazakhstan-born director Timur Bekmambetov being lured to Hollywood. An audience favourite at various film festivals has been *Stilyagi* (2008; entitled *Hipsters* for its international release), a musical that casts a romantic eye on fashion-obsessed youths in 1950s

Russia. Another international success, *How I Ended This Summer* (2010), is a tense thriller about the deadly clash of temperaments between an older and a younger scientist working on an isolated meteorological station off the coast of Chukotka.

Return to Censorship

Leviathan, a bleak tale of one man's struggle against corruption in northern Russia, directed by Andrei Zvyagintsev, received the Best Screenplay award at the Cannes Film Festival in 2014. However, at the time of research, it was struggling to be shown in Russia due to a recent law banning the use of expletives in films and all other media (as well as stage performances).

Although Putin has said he does not favour censorship, he has also said he is interested in Russian films that promote patriotism, and values such as a healthy lifestyle, spirituality, kindness and responsibility, along with meeting the strategic goals of Russia. Such propaganda movies include the 3D war epic *Stalingrad,* a 2013 box-office smash in Russia. And with the Kremlin investing some ₽6.7 billion in movie production in 2013, it can afford to call the shots.

Mikhail Kalatozov's tragic WWII drama *The Cranes Are Flying* (1957), judged best film at Cannes in 1958, illuminates the sacrifices made by Russians during the Great Patriotic War.

Russian Animation

Little known outside Russia is the country's great contribution to the art of animation. Two years before Disney's *Snow White,* stop-motion animation was used for *New Gulliver* (1935), a communist retelling of *Gulliver's Travels* featuring more than 3000 puppets. And rather than Disney's films, it was actually Lev Atamanov's beautiful *The Snow Queen* (1957), based on the Hans Christian Andersen story, that inspired young Hayao Miyazaki to become the master Japanese animator that he is today.

One of Russia's most respected animators today is Yury Norshteyn, whose masterpiece, *Hedgehog in the Mist* (1975), is philosophical and full of references to art and literature. The current master of the medium is Alexander Petrov, who paints in oil on glass sheets using his fingertips instead of brushes. He photographs one frame, modifies the picture with his fingers and photographs the next; this painstaking approach takes around a year of work to create just 10 minutes of film. *The Cow* (1989), his first solo work, displays Petrov's trademark montage sequences, in which objects, people and landscapes converge in a psychedelic swirl. Petrov won an Academy Award for *The Old Man and the Sea* (1999), based on the Hemingway novella. He was also nominated in 2007 for the dazzling *My Love,* an animated short set in prerevolutionary Russia.

The excellent blog Animatsiya (www.niffiwan.livejournal.com) includes many clips from Russian animation films.

Architecture & Visual Art

From heavily detailed religious icons and onion-domed churches to statues of heroic workers and soaring Stalinist towers, Russian art and architecture has a distinctive style. In the post-Soviet world, architects and artists are pretty much free to do as they please. Visual artists, in particular, have done so with relish, both thumbing their noses at the past and present and embracing and rediscovering traditional Russian crafts and artistic inspiration.

Architecture

Until Soviet times most Russians lived in homes made of wood. The *izba* (single-storey log cottage) is still fairly common in the countryside, while some Siberian cities, notably Tomsk, retain fine timber town houses intricately decorated with 'wooden lace'. Stone and brick were usually the preserves of the Church, royalty and nobility.

Wooden Buildings

- Tomsk
- Kizhi Museum Reserve
- Vitoslavlitsy, Veliky Novgorod
- Nizhnyaya Sinyachikha, Sverdlovsk Region
- Museum of Volga People's Architecture & Culture, Nizhny Novgorod

Early Russian Churches

Early Russian architecture is best viewed in the country's most historic churches, in places such as Veliky Novgorod, Smolensk, Pskov and Vladimir-Suzdal. At their simplest, churches consisted of three aisles, each with an eastern apse (semicircular end), a dome or cupola over the central aisle next to the apse, and high vaulted roofs forming a crucifix shape centred on the dome.

Church architects developed the three-aisle pattern in the 11th and 12th centuries. Roofs then grew steeper to prevent the heavy northern snows collecting and crushing them, and windows grew narrower to keep the cold out. Pskov builders invented the little *kokoshnik* gable, which was semicircular or spade-shaped and usually found in rows supporting a dome or drum.

Where stone replaced brick, as in Vladimir's Assumption Cathedral, it was often carved into a glorious kaleidoscope of decorative images. Another Vladimir-Suzdal hallmark was the 'blind arcade', a wall decoration resembling a row of arches. The early church-citadel complexes required protection, and thus developed sturdy, fortress-style walls replete with fairy-tale towers – Russia's archetypal kremlins.

In the 16th century, the translation of the northern Russian wooden church features, such as the tent roof and the onion dome on a tall drum, into brick added up to a new, uniquely Russian architecture. St Basil's Cathedral, the Ivan the Great Bell Tower in the Moscow Kremlin and the Ascension Church at Kolomenskoe are three high points of this era.

In the 17th century builders in Moscow added tiers of *kokoshniki*, colourful tiles and brick patterning, to create jolly, merchant-financed churches. Mid-century, Patriarch Nikon outlawed such frippery, but elaboration returned later in the century with Western-influenced Moscow baroque, featuring ornate white detailing on red-brick walls.

Baroque to Classicism

Mainstream baroque reached Russia as Peter the Great opened up the country to Western influences. As the focus was on his new capital, St Petersburg, he banned new stone construction elsewhere to ensure stone supplies. The great Italian architect Bartolomeo Rastrelli created an inspired series of rococo-style buildings for Empress Elizabeth. Three of the most brilliant were the Winter Palace and Smolny Cathedral, both in St Petersburg, and Catherine Palace at nearby Tsarskoe Selo.

Later in the 18th century, Catherine the Great turned away from rococo 'excess' towards Europe's new wave of classicism. This was an attempt to re-create the ambience of an idealised ancient Rome and Greece, with their mathematical proportions and rows of columns, pediments and domes. Catherine and her successors built waves of grand classical edifices in a bid to make St Petersburg the continent's most imposing capital. The simple classicism of Catherine's reign was exemplified by the Great Palace at Pavlovsk.

The grandiose Russian Empire–style was developed under Alexander I, highlighted in buildings such as the Admiralty and Kazan Cathedral in St Petersburg. St Isaac's Cathedral, built for Nicholas I, was the last big project of this wave of classicism in St Petersburg. Moscow abounds with Russian Empire–style buildings, as much of the city had to be rebuilt after the fire of 1812.

Style Moderne

- *Yaroslavsky vokzal, Moscow*
- *Vitebsky vokzal, St Petersburg*
- *Singer Building, St Petersburg*
- *Kupetz Eliseevs, St Petersburg*
- *Vyborg*

Revivals & Style Moderne

A series of architectural revivals, notably of early Russian styles, began in the late 19th century. The first pseudo-Russian phase produced the state department store GUM, the State History Museum and the Leningradsky vokzal (train station) in Moscow, and the Moskovsky vokzal and the Church of the Saviour on Spilled Blood in St Petersburg.

The early-20th-century neo-Russian movement brought a sturdy classical elegance to architecture across the nation, culminating in the extraordinary Kazansky vokzal in Moscow, which imitates no fewer than seven earlier styles. About the same time, Style Moderne, Russia's take on art nouveau, added wonderful curvaceous flourishes to many buildings right across Russia.

Soviet Constructivism

The revolution gave rein to young constructivist architects, who rejected superficial decoration in favour of buildings whose appearance was a

FIGHTING TO PRESERVE THE PAST

In Russia it's down to national and local governments to decide what pieces of architecture warrant preservation. St Petersburg in particular spends millions of roubles on maintaining and renovating its stock of historic buildings. However, the pressure group Zhivoi Gorod (Living City; www.save-spb.ru) claims that the city is more interested in destruction, citing the demolition of hundreds of historically important buildings in recent years. However, citizen action in the city did manage to put the dampers on the controversial Okhta Tower, the planned headquarters of Gazprom.

The Moscow Architecture Preservation Society (MAPS; www.maps-moscow.com), a pressure group founded by architects, historians, heritage managers and journalists of various nationalities, has been fighting for several years to preserve the capital's architectural heritage. Its research shows more than 400 of the city's listed buildings have been demolished since 1989. Under threat at the time of research were several of the capital's key 20th-century pieces of architecture including the constructivist apartment block Narkomfin, the Shukhov radio tower and Melnikov House.

direct function of their uses and materials – a new architecture for a new society. They used glass and concrete in uncompromising geometric forms.

Konstantin Melnikov was probably the most famous constructivist and his own house off ul Arbat in Moscow is one of the most interesting examples of the style; the offices of Moscow news agencies *Pravda* and *Izvestia* are others. In the 1930s, the constructivists were denounced, and a 400m-high design by perpetrators of yet another revival – monumental classicism – was chosen for Stalin's pet project, a Palace of Soviets in Moscow, which mercifully never got off the ground.

Stalin favoured neoclassical architecture as it echoed ancient Athens; 'the only culture of the past to approach the ideal', according to Anatoly Lunacharsky, the first Soviet commissar of education. The dictator also liked architecture on a gigantic scale, underlining the might of the Soviet state. This style reached its apogee in the 'Seven Sisters', seven Gothic-style skyscrapers that sprouted around Moscow soon after WWII.

In 1955, Khrushchev condemned the 'excesses' of Stalin (who had died two years earlier) and disbanded the Soviet Academy of Architecture. After this, architects favoured a bland international modern style – constructivism without the spark, you might say – for prestigious buildings, while no style at all was evident in the drab blocks of cramped flats that sprouted countrywide.

Contemporary Architecture

Following the demise of the Soviet Union, architectural energies and civic funds initially went into the restoration of decayed churches and monasteries, as well as the rebuilding of structures such as Moscow's Cathedral of Christ the Saviour.

As far as contemporary domestic, commercial and cultural buildings are concerned, post-Soviet architects have not been kind to Russia. Featuring bright metals and mirrored glass, these buildings tend to be plopped down in the midst of otherwise unassuming vintage buildings, particularly in Moscow. The oil-rich economy is producing some changes for the better and helping to fund interesting projects in the capital and elsewhere, such as the Garage Museum of Contemporary Art in Gorky Park being designed by Rem Koolhaas' OMA.

Archi.ru (www.archi.ru) is an online resource that includes a daily digest of what's happening in the world of Russian architecture.

Visual Art

Icons

Originally painted by monks as a spiritual exercise, icons are images intended to aid the veneration of the holy subjects they depict. Some believe that there are some icons that can grant luck and wishes, or even cause miracles.

The beginning of a distinct Russian icon tradition came when artists in Veliky Novgorod started to be influenced by local folk art in their representation of people, producing sharply outlined figures with softer faces and introducing lighter colours, including pale yellows and greens. The earliest outstanding painter was Theophanes the Greek (Feofan Grek in Russian). He lived between 1340 and 1405, working in Byzantium, Novgorod and Moscow, and bringing a new delicacy and grace to the form. His finest works are in the Annunciation Cathedral of the Moscow Kremlin.

Andrei Rublyov, a monk at Sergiev Posad's Trinity Monastery of St Sergius and Moscow's Andronikov Monastery, was 20 years Theophanes' junior and the greatest Russian icon painter. His most famous work is the dreamy *Holy Trinity,* on display in Moscow's Tretyakov Gallery.

Moscow's Federation Tower (www.federationtower.ru) is set to be the tallest building in Europe when it opens in 2016 as part of the huge Moskva-City development.

The layman Dionysius, the leading late-15th-century icon painter, elongated his figures and refined the use of colour. In the 16th century icons grew smaller and more crowded, their figures more realistic and Russian looking. In 17th-century Moscow, Simon Ushakov moved towards Western religious painting with the use of perspective and architectural backgrounds.

Peredvizhniki

The major artistic force of the 19th century were the Peredvizhniki (Wanderers), who saw art as a force for national awareness and social change. The movement gained its name from the touring exhibitions with which the artists widened their audience. It was patronised by the industrialists Savva Mamontov – whose Abramtsevo estate near Moscow became an artists colony – and brothers Pavel and Sergei Tretyakov (after whom the Tretyakov Gallery is named). The Peredvizhniki included Vasily Surikov, who painted vivid Russian historical scenes; Nicholas Ghe, with his biblical and historical scenes; the landscape painter Ivan Shishkin; and Ilya Repin, perhaps the best loved of all Russian artists. Repin's work ranged from social criticism *(Barge Haulers on the Volga)* through history *(Zaporizhsky Cossacks Writing a Letter to the Turkish Sultan)* to portraits of the famous.

The propaganda magazine *USSR in Construction* (1930–41) featured stunning design and photography by Nikolai Troshin, El Lisstsky, Alexander Rodchenko and Varvara Stepanova.

Isaac Levitan, who revealed the beauty of the Russian landscape, was one of many others associated with the Peredvizhniki. The end-of-century genius Mikhail Vrubel, inspired by sparkling Byzantine and Venetian mosaics, also showed traces of Western influence.

Modernism

Around the turn of the 20th century, the Mir Iskusstva (World of Art) movement in St Petersburg, led by Alexander Benois and Sergei Diaghilev under the motto 'art pure and unfettered', opened Russia to Western innovations such as Impressionism, art nouveau and symbolism. From about 1905, Russian art became a maelstrom of groups, styles and 'isms' as it absorbed decades of European change in just a few years, before it gave birth to its own avant-garde futurist movements.

Natalia Goncharova and Mikhail Larionov were at the centre of the Cézanne-influenced Jack of Diamonds group (with which Vasily Kandinsky was also associated) before developing neoprimitivism, based on popular arts and primitive icons.

In 1915 Kasimir Malevich announced the arrival of suprematism, declaring that his utterly abstract geometrical shapes – with the black square representing the ultimate 'zero form' – finally freed art from having to depict the material world and made it a doorway to higher realities.

Churches

- *Cathedral of St Sophia, Veliky Novgorod*
- *Trinity Cathedral, Pskov*
- *St Basil's Cathedral, Moscow*
- *Church of the Intercession on the Nerl, Bogolyubovo*

Soviet-Era Art

Futurists turned to the needs of the revolution – education, posters, banners – with enthusiasm, relishing the chance to act on their theories of how art shapes society. But at the end of the 1920s, formalist (abstract) art fell out of favour; the Communist Party wanted socialist realism. Images of striving workers, heroic soldiers and inspiring leaders took over. Malevich ended up painting portraits (penetrating ones) and doing designs for Red Square parades.

After Stalin, an avant-garde 'conceptualist' underground was allowed to form. Ilya Kabakov painted, or sometimes just arranged, the debris of everyday life to show the gap between the promises and realities of Soviet existence. Erik Bulatov's 'Sots art' pointed to the devaluation of language by ironically reproducing Soviet slogans or depicting words disappearing over the horizon. In 1962 the authorities set up a show of

PROTEST ART

Say what you like about contemporary artists in Russia, but don't accuse them of shying away from controversial subjects or putting their own safety, not to mention liberty, on the line for their art.

The feminist punk-rock collective Pussy Riot became a cause celeb when their attempt to video their guerilla-style performance in Moscow's Cathedral of Christ the Saviour saw three of their members – Nadezhda Tolokonnikova, Maria Alyokhina and Yekaterina Samutsevich – sentenced to two years jail. Tolokonnikova was also a member, along with her husband Pyotr Verzilov, of the radical art collective Voina (War), infamous for such in-the-name-of-art events as filming live sex acts at Timiryazev State Biology Museum in Moscow and painting a 64m-tall penis on a drawbridge in St Petersburg in 2010; for that last stunt Voina won a ₽400,000 government-sponsored Innovatzia contemporary-art prize the following year.

Then there's performance artist Petr Pavlensky who, on 10 November 2013, Russia's annual Police Day, strode onto Red Square, undressed, sat down on the cobblestones near Lenin's Mausoleum and hammered a 20cm nail through his scrotum. The St Petersburg-trained artist issued a statement saying this action, entitled *Fixation*, was 'a metaphor for the apathy, political indifference and fatalism of modern Russian society'. In past performances Pavlensky had stitched up his mouth in support of Pussy Riot and stood in front of St Petersburg's Kazan Cathedral. In another naked performance entitled *Carcass Pavlensky*, he lay in front of the entrance to St Petersburg's Legislative Assembly wrapped in barbed wire.

such 'unofficial' art at the Moscow Manezh; Khrushchev called it 'dog shit' and sent it back underground. In the mid-1970s it resurfaced in the Moscow suburbs, only to be literally bulldozed back down.

Contemporary Art

In the immediate post-Soviet years, a lot of contemporary painters of note abandoned Russia for the West. Today, with increased economic prosperity, many of the most promising young artists are choosing to stay put. At specialist art galleries in Moscow and St Petersburg, you can find the latest works by Russians in and out of the motherland.

One of the best-known Russian painters today is the religious artist Ilya Glazunov (www.glazunov.ru), a staunch defender of the Russian Orthodox cultural tradition. Creating more iconoclastic works are the Siberian collective Blue Noses, Voina, Aleksandr Kosolapov, Mikhail Roginskii and the artist group AES+F (www.aes-group.org), whose multimedia work, such as *The Feast of Trimalchio*, reflects the lust for luxury in contemporary Russia.

Contemporary art galleries are booming from St Petersburg across to Perm. Prestigious events to mark on your calendar include the Moscow Biennale of Contemporary Art (www.moscowbiennale.ru), the annual commercial gallery show, Art Moscow (www.art-moscow.ru), and the Kandinsky Prize (www.kandinsky-prize.ru), an exhibition of up-and-coming Russian artists.

A couple of good online resources for Russia's contemporary art scene are GIF.RU (www.gif.ru/rusart) and Art Guide (www.artguide.ru), which includes details of galleries and art shows in Moscow and St Petersburg.

Folk & Native Art

An amazing spectrum of richly decorated folk art has evolved in Russia. Perhaps most familiar are the intricately painted, enamelled wood boxes called *palekh*, after the village east of Moscow that's famous for them; and *finift*, luminous enamelled metal miniatures from Rostov-Veliky.

From Gzhel, also east of Moscow, came glazed earthenware in the 18th century and its trademark blue-and-white porcelain in the 19th century. Gus-Khrustalny, south of Vladimir, maintains a glass-making tradition as old as Russia. Every region also has its own style of embroidery and some specialise in knitted and other fine fabrics.

The classic and comprehensive *A History of Russian Architecture*, by William Craft Brumfield, covers all the major epochs from the stone churches of Kyivan Rus to post-Stalinist industrial buildings.

The most common craft is woodcarving, represented by toys, distaffs (tools for hand-spinning flax) and gingerbread moulds in the museums, and in its most clichéd form by the nested *matryoshka* dolls. Surely the most familiar symbol of Russia, they actually only date from 1890 (see www.russian-crafts.com/crafts-history/nesting-dolls-history.html for the history of the *matryoshki* and other crafts). You'll also find the red, black and gold lacquered pine bowls called *khokhloma* overflowing from souvenir shops. Most uniquely Slavic are the 'gingerbread' houses of western and northern Russia and Siberia, with their carved window frames, lintels and trim. The art of carpentry flourished in 17th- and 18th-century houses and churches.

A revived interest in national traditions has recently brought good-quality craftwork into the open, and the process has been boosted by the restoration of churches and mosques and their artwork. There has also been a minor resurgence of woodcarving and bone carving. An even more popular craft is *beresta*, using birch bark to make containers and decorative objects, with colours varying according to the age and season of peeling. In Tuva, soapstone carving and traditional leather forming are also being rediscovered.

Food & Drink

Russia's glorious culinary heritage is enriched by influences from the Baltic to the Far East. The country's rich black soil provides an abundance of grains and vegetables used in a wonderful range of breads, salads, appetisers and soups that are the highlight of any Russian meal. Its waterways yield a unique range of fish and, as with any cold-climate country, there's a great love of fat-loaded dishes – Russia is no place to go on a diet!

Staples & Specialities

Breakfast

Typical *zavtrak* (breakfast) dishes include bliny (pancakes) with sweet or savoury fillings, various types of *kasha* (porridge) made from buckwheat or other grains, and *syrniki* (cottage-cheese fritters), delicious with jam, sugar and the universal Russian condiment, *smetana* (sour cream). *Khleb* (bread) is freshly baked and comes in a multitude of delicious varieties.

Local Tastes

- *Horsemeat fillets, Sakha Republic*
- *Dried elk noses and lips, Sakha Republic*
- *Chewy reindeer cartilage, Kamchatka*
- *Khoitpak (fermented sour milk), Tuva*

Appetisers & Salads

Whether as the preamble to a meal or something to nibble on between shots of vodka, *zakuski* (appetisers) are a big feature of Russian cuisine. They range from olives to bliny with mushrooms and from *tvorog* (cheese curd) to caviar, and include a multitude of inventive salads. Among the most popular recipes that you'll find on restaurant menus are *salat olivye* (chopped chicken or ham, potatoes, eggs, canned peas and other vegetables mixed with mayonnaise) and *selyodka pod shuboi* (literally 'herrings in fur coats'), a classic from the Soviet era that has slices of herring, beetroot and pickles covered in a creamy sauce.

Soups

No Russian meal is complete without soup, even in the summer when there are several refreshing cold varieties. The main ones to sample include the following:

➡ borsch – this beetroot soup hails from Ukraine but is now synonymous with Russia throughout the world. It can be served hot or cold and usually with *smetana*

CAVIAR – IF BUYING, BUY CAREFULLY

While nothing is as evocative of Russian imperial luxury as Beluga caviar, be aware that the sturgeon of the Caspian Sea are facing extinction due to the unsustainable and illegal plunder of their roe. If you do buy some black caviar, make a responsible purchase. Buy caviar only from shops (not on the street or at markets), in sealed jars (not loose) and, most importantly, make sure the jar or tin is sealed with a CITES (Convention on International Trade in Endangered Species) label, an international trade-control measure set up to reduce sturgeon poaching. Under international law, tourists are only permitted to bring home 250g of caviar per person.

For more information read *The Philosopher Fish* by ecojournalist Richard Adams Carey, a lively investigation into the life of the endangered sturgeon and the prized caviar it provides, and Vanora Bennett's lyrical *The Taste of Dreams*.

poured on top of it. Some borsch is vegetarian (ask for *postny* borsch), although most is made with beef stock

- *okroshka* – a cold soup, made with chopped cucumber, potatoes, eggs, meat and herbs in a base of either *kvas*, fermented rye-bread water, or *kefir*, drinking yoghurt
- *shchi* – there are vegetarian versions and ones with chicken, beef or lamb, but the base of this soup is always plenty of cabbage
- *solyanka* – a sometimes flavoursome concoction of pickled vegetables, meat and potato that used to be the staple winter food for the peasantry
- *ukha* – this classic recipe has four types of fish, herbs and a few vegetables in a transparent bouillon.

Main Courses

Traditional Russian cuisine tends to be meaty and quite heavy. Popular dishes include the following:

- *bef stroganov* – a beef, mushrooms and sour-cream dish said to have been invented in the mid 19th century by a French cook employed by the St Petersburg noble Alexander Stroganov
- *zharkoye* – hot pot; a meat stew served piping hot in a little jug
- *kotleta po kievsky* – chicken Kiev
- shashlyk – meat or fish kebabs
- *myaso po monastirsky* – beef topped with cheese is often relabelled *myaso po Sibirski* (Siberian meat)
- *pelmeni* – pasta dumplings generally stuffed with pork or beef that are served either heaped on a plate with sour cream, vinegar and butter, or in a stock soup. Variations such as salmon or mushroom *pelmeni* are found on the menus of more chic restaurants.

Russian chocolate and *konfetki* (sweets) are excellent and, with their colourful wrappings, make great presents. Local producers typically use more cocoa, so their chocolate is not as sweet as some non-Russian brands. Reputable manufacturers include Krasny Oktyabr (Red October) and Krupskoi.

Central Asian–style dishes are also common, notably *plov* (fried rice with lamb and carrot) and *lagman* (noodles and meat in a soupy broth that gets spicier the further south you go). The range of fish and seafood is enormous, but common staples include *osyetrina* (sturgeon), *shchuka* (pike), *losos* or *syomga* (salmon), *treska* (chub) and *kalmar* (squid).

Desserts

The Russian sweet tooth is seriously sweet. Russians love *morozhenoye* (ice cream) with a passion: it's not unusual to see people gobbling dishfuls, even in the freezing weather. Gooey *torty* (cream cakes), often decorated in lurid colours, are also popular. *Pecheniye* (pastries) are eaten at tea time, in the traditional English style.

Regional Specialities

From the *koryushki* (freshwater smelt) that feature on menus in St Petersburg in late April to the mammoth king crabs of Kamchatka, Russia abounds with regional food specialities. As these two examples illustrate, different varieties of fish and seafood are always worth sampling. Try dried, salty *oblyoma* fish, found in the Volga, or Lake Baikal's delicious *omul*, a cousin of salmon and trout. Russia's Far East doesn't yield many specialist dishes but in the port of Vladivostok you can be sure of the freshness of seafood such as *kalmary* (calamari) and *grebeshki* (scallops).

Honey is used as an ingredient in several dishes and drinks in Western European Russia such as *vzbiten*, the decorated gingerbread made in Tula, a tea with herbs and the alcoholic drink *medovukha*. Cowberries, reindeer and elk meat are ingredients that figure in the cuisine of Northern European Russia. From this region, *lokhikeytto* is a deliciously creamy Karelian salmon and potato soup, ideally served with crispy croutons.

VEGETARIANS & VEGANS

Unless you're in one of the big cities or visiting during Lent, when many restaurants have special nonmeat menus, Russia can be tough on vegetarians. Main dishes are heavy on meat and poultry, vegetables are often boiled to death and even the good vegetable and fish soups are usually made from meat stock.

If you're vegetarian, say so, early and often. You'll see a lot of cucumber and tomato salads, and – if so inclined – will develop an eagle eye for spotting *baklazhan* (eggplant) and dairy dishes. *Zakuski* (appetisers) include quite a lot of meatless ingredients such as eggs and mushrooms. Potatoes *(kartoshka, kartofel, pure)* are usually filed under 'garnish' not 'vegetable'.

Vegabar.ru (www.vegabar.ru) lists information about vegetarian restaurants and cafes in Moscow and St Petersburg.

The tapestry of peoples and cultures along the Volga River yields several other specialities, such as the Finno-Ugric clear dumpling soup *sup s klyutskami*. The dried-horsemeat sausage *kasylyk* and *zur balish* meat pie are both from Tatarstan, where *chek chek* (honey-drenched macaroni-shaped pieces of fried dough) are an essential part of any celebration.

In the Altai region of southern Siberia you can masticate on *sera*, a chewing gum made from cedar oil. While around the ski resort of Sheregesh, sample the wild leek with a distinctive garlicky taste known as *kabla* in the local language and *cheremsha* in Russian.

The Buddhist-influenced culinary traditions of the Republic of Kalmykia have brought the Tibetan-style buttery tea known as *dzhomba* to Europe. Further east in Buryatiya, and throughout the Russian Far East, you'll often encounter the steamed, palm-sized dumplings known as *manti, buuzy* and *pyan-se* (a peppery version). Two or three make a good, greasy meal. Siberia is most famous for its *pelmeni* (small ravioli dumplings) and you'll find local variations in all the major cities across the region.

Among the many Caucasus dishes you may come across are *sokhta* (a mammoth sausage stuffed with minced liver and rice), eaten around Dombay, and Kabardian food such as *zharuma* (fiery sausage stuffed with minced lamb, onion and spices), *gedlibzhe* (a spicy chicken dish) and *geshlubzhe,* a saucy bean dish that can be sampled around Nalchik. The sinfully delicious Ossetian *pirozhki* are pizza-like pies that come in *olibakh* (cheese), *sakharadzhin* (cheese and beet leaves) and *fidzhin* (meat) varieties.

Please to the Table by Anya von Bremzen and John Welchman is nothing if not comprehensive, with more than 400 recipes from the Baltics, Central Asia and all points between, plus a wealth of background detail on Russian cuisine.

Georgian Cuisine

Russian cuisine also borrows enormously from neighbouring countries, most obviously from those around the Caucasus, where shashlyk originated. Described by writer Darra Goldstein as 'heaven's table scraps', the rich, spicy cuisine of the former Soviet republic of Georgia must be sampled while in Russia. Georgian meat and vegetable dishes use ground walnuts or walnut oil as an integral ingredient, yielding a distinctive rich, nutty flavour. Also characteristic of Georgian cuisine is the spice mixture *khmeli-suneli,* which combines coriander, garlic, chillies, pepper and savoury with a saffron substitute made from dried marigold petals.

Grilled meats are among the most beloved items on any Georgian menu. Herbs such as coriander, dill and parsley, and other ingredients such as scallions are often served fresh, with no preparation or sauce, as a palate-cleansing counterpoint to rich dishes. Grapes and pomegranates show up not only as desserts, but also as tart complements to roasted meats.

Russian Cookbooks

A Taste of Russia (Darra Goldstein)

Culinaria Russia (ed. Marion Trutter)

The Russian Heritage Cookbook (Lynn Visson)

For vegetarians, Georgian eggplant dishes (notably garlic-laced *badrizhani nivrit*), *lobiyo* (spicy beans) and *khachapuri* (cheese bread) are a great blessing. *Khachapuri* comes in three main forms:

- flaky pastry squares (snack versions sold at markets)
- *khachapuri po-imeretinsk* – circles of fresh dough cooked with sour, salty *suluguni* cheese (sold in restaurants)
- *khachapuri po-adzharski* – topped with a raw egg in the crater (mix it rapidly into the melted cheese; sold in restaurants)

The Food and Cooking of Russia by Lesley Chamberlain (www.lesleychamberlain.co.uk), based on the author's research in the country during the late 1970s, is full of recipes as well as insights into what shaped Russian dining habits in the 20th century.

Here are a few more Georgian favourites to get you started when faced with an incomprehensible menu:

- *basturma* – marinated, grilled meat; usually beef or lamb
- *bkhali* or *phkali* – a vegetable puree with herbs and walnuts, most often made with beetroot or spinach
- *buglama* – beef or veal stew with tomatoes, dill and garlic
- *chakhokhbili* – chicken slow-cooked with herbs and vegetables
- *chikhirtmi* – lemony chicken soup
- dolmas – vegetables (often tomatoes, eggplant or grape leaves) stuffed with beef
- *kharcho* – thick, spicy rice and beef or lamb soup
- *khinkali* – dumplings stuffed with lamb or a mixture of beef and pork
- *lavash* – flat bread used to wrap cheese, tomatoes, herbs or meat
- *pakhlava* – a walnut pastry similar to baklava, but made with sour-cream dough
- *satsivi* – walnut, garlic and pomegranate paste, usually used as a chicken stuffing in cold starters
- *shilaplavi* – rice pilaf, often with potatoes.

Drinks

Alcoholic Drinks

Spirits

Vodka, distilled from wheat, rye or, occasionally, potatoes, is the quintessential Russian alcohol. The word comes from *voda* (pronounced va-*da*, meaning 'water'). The classic recipe for vodka (a 40% alcohol-to-water mixture) was patented in 1894 by Dmitry Mendeleyev, the inventor of the periodic table. The drink's flavour derives from what's added after distillation, so as well as 'plain' vodka you'll find *klyukovka* (cranberry vodka, one of the most popular kinds), *pertsovka* (pepper vodka), *starka* (vodka flavoured with apple and pear leaves), *limonnaya* (lemon vodka) and *okhotnichya* (meaning 'hunter's vodka', with about a dozen ingredients, including peppers, juniper berries, ginger and cloves).

'Drinking is the joy of the Rus. We cannot live without it.' With these words, Vladimir of Kyiv, the father of the Russian state, is said to have rejected abstinent Islam on his people's behalf in the 10th century.

Among the hundreds of different brands for sale are famous ones, such as Stolichnaya and Smirnoff, as well as those named after presidents (Putinka, the country's top seller) and banks (Russian Standard). Better labels are Moskovskaya, Flagman, Gzhelka and Zelonaya Marka (meaning 'Green Mark'), which was named after the Stalin-era government agency that regulated vodka quality. For more brands see www.russianvodka.com.

Russian brandy is called *konyak* – the finest come from the Caucasus. Winston Churchill reputedly preferred Armenian *konyak* over French Cognac, and although standards vary enormously, local five-star brandies are generally good.

Homemade moonshine is known as *samogon;* if you're at all in doubt about the alcohol's provenance, don't drink it – some of this stuff is highly poisonous.

Beer

Russians categorise beer by colour rather than fermentation process: light, red or semidark and dark. Light is more or less equivalent to lager and the last two are close to ales. The alcohol content of some stronger beers can be as high as 10%.

The local market leader is Baltika, based in St Petersburg and with 11 other breweries across the country, but there are scores of other palatable local brands and a growing sector of microbreweries.

Russian Beers

- *Klinskoye Svetloe, lager*
- *Nevskoe Imperial, lager*
- *Yarpivo, pilsner*
- *Stary Melnik, lager*
- *Sibirskaya Korona, witbier*

Wine

The local wine industry is notable mainly for its saccharine *polusladkoe* (semisweet) or *sladkoe* (sweet) dessert wines. Good *bryut* (very dry and only for sparkling wine), *sukhoe* (dry) and *polusukhoe* (semidry) reds are readily found; however, finding a palatable Russian dry white can be pretty tough. Locally produced sparkling wine Shampanskoye is cheap (around ₽300 a bottle) and popular even though it tastes nothing like champagne.

For more information about Russian wines see Russian Wine Country (www.russianwinecountry.com).

Drinking Etiquette

➡ Breaking open a can or bottle of beer and drinking it while walking down the street or sitting in a park is pretty common.

➡ If you find yourself sharing a table at a bar or restaurant with locals, it's odds-on they'll press you to drink with them. Even people from distant tables, spotting foreigners, may be seized with hospitable urges.

➡ Vodka is drunk one shot at a time, neat of course, not sipped. This can be fun as you toast international friendship and so on, but vodka has a knack of creeping up on you from behind and the consequences can be appalling.

➡ It's traditional (and good sense) to eat a little something after each shot.

➡ Don't place an empty bottle on the table – it's considered polite to leave it on the floor.

➡ Refusing a drink can be very difficult, and Russians may continue to insist until they win you over. If you can't quite stand firm, take it in small gulps with copious thanks, while saying how you'd love to indulge but you have to be up early in the morning (or something similar).

➡ If you're really not in the mood, one sure-fire method of warding off all offers (as well as making people feel quite awful) is to say *'Ya alkogolik'* (*'Ya alkogolichka'* for women): 'I'm an alcoholic.'

DRINKING WATER

Dodgy tap water has caused sales of bottled water to proliferate to the point where almost half the water drunk in Russia comes from a bottle. Since 2004, more than 2000 licences have been issued to producers of bottled water; not all of it is as pure as it may seem. The Bottled Water Producers Union claim you're likely to be safer drinking water labelled *stolovaya* (purified tap water, which accounts for the vast majority of what's available) rather than *mineralnaya voda* (mineral water), which doesn't have to meet so many legal requirements for purity. One reliable brand of mineral water is *Narzan*. For those concerned about both the environment and their health, boiling water and using a decent filter are sufficient if you want to drink what comes out of the tap.

Nonalcoholic Drinks

Russians make tea by brewing an extremely strong pot, pouring small shots of it into glasses, and topping the glasses up with hot water. This was traditionally done from the samovar, a metal urn with an inner tube filled with hot charcoal. Modern samovars have electric elements, like a kettle, which is actually what most Russians use to boil water for tea these days. Putting jam in tea instead of sugar is quite common for those who like it a little sweeter.

Starbucks-style cafes serving barista-style coffee are found all across Russia's bigger cities – cappuccino, espresso, latte and mocha are now as much a part of the average Russian lexicon as elsewhere.

The popular nonalcoholic beer *kvas* is made from bread and flavoured with ingredients that can include honey and horseradish. In summer, it's often dispensed on the street from big, wheeled tanks and is highly refreshing.

Sok can mean anything from fruit juice (usually in cartons rather than fresh) to heavily diluted fruit squash. *Mors,* made from all types of red berries, is a popular *sok*. *Napitok* means 'drink' – it's often a cheaper and weaker version of *sok,* maybe with some real fruit thrown in.

If you're buying milk away from big supermarkets check whether it's pasteurised. *Kefir* (yoghurt-like sour milk) is served as a breakfast drink – and is also recommended as a hangover cure. The Bashkirs, the Kazakhs of southernmost Altai and the Sakha people drink *kumiss* (fermented mare's milk).

Restaurant.ru (http://en.restoran.ru) carries listings and reviews for places to eat in Moscow and St Petersburg. It also has a section with recipes.

Where to Eat & Drink

In general, a *kafe* is likely to be cheaper yet often more atmospherically cosy than a *restoran,* many of which are aimed at hosting weddings and banquets more than individual diners. A *kofeynya* is generally an upmarket cafe, though they often serve great meals too, as will a *pab* (upmarket pub with pricey imported beers) or *traktir* (a tavern, often with 'traditional' Russian decor). A *zakusochnaya* can be anything from a pleasant cafe to a disreputable bar, but they usually sell cheap beer and have a limited food menu. Occasionally you'll come across *ryumochnaya,* dive bars specialising in vodka or *konyak* shots.

Increasingly common as you head east, a *buzznaya* is an unpretentious eatery serving Central Asian food and, most notably, *buuzy*. These are meat dumplings that you need to eat very carefully in order to avoid

A GIFT TO YOUNG HOUSEWIVES *Mara Vorhees*

The most popular cookbook in 19th-century Russia was called *A Gift to Young Housewives,* a collection of favourite recipes and household-management tips. The author, Elena Molokhovets, a housewife herself, was dedicated to her 10 children, to the Orthodox Church and to her inexperienced 'female compatriots' who might need some assistance in keeping their homes running smoothly.

Reprinted 28 times between 1861 and 1914, Molokhovets' bestseller had new recipes and helpful hints added to each new edition. The last edition included literally thousands of recipes, as well as pointers on how to organise an efficient kitchen, set a proper table and clean a cast-iron pot.

Having gone out of print during the Soviet era, Molokhovets' 'gift' was bestowed upon contemporary readers when Joyce Toomre, a culinary historian, translated and reprinted this historical masterpiece. The 1992 version, *Classic Russian Cooking: Elena Molokhovets' A Gift to Young Housewives,* includes Toomre's detailed analysis of mealtimes, menus, ingredients and cooking techniques.

spraying yourself with boiling juices, as an embarrassed Mikhail Gorbachev famously did when visiting Ulan-Ude.

In old Soviet-era hotels and stations the *bufet* serves a range of simple snacks including *buterbrod* (open sandwiches). The *stolovaya* (canteen) is the common person's eatery, often located near stations or in public institutions such as universities. They are invariably cheap. Slide your tray along the counter and point to the food, and the staff will ladle it out. While unappealing, Soviet-style *stolovaya* remain, newer 'chic' versions with very palatable food are also common in cities and towns.

In smaller towns the choice will be far narrower, perhaps limited to standard Russian meals such as *pelmeni* and *kotlety* (cutlets); in villages there may be no hot food available at all (though there's almost always do-it-yourself pot noodles available from kiosks and shops). The choice is particularly abysmal in Tuva (beyond Kyzyl).

Ordering Food

It's always worth asking if a restaurant has an English-language menu. If not, even armed with a dictionary and a good guidebook, it can be difficult to decipher Russian menus (the different styles of printed Cyrillic are a challenge). Russian menus typically follow a standard form: first come *zakuski* (appetisers, often grouped into cold and hot dishes) followed by soups, sometimes listed under *pervye blyuda* (first courses). *Vtorye blyuda* (second courses; mains) are also known as *goryachiye blyuda* (hot courses). They can be divided into *firmenniye blyuda* (house specials, often listed at the front of the menu), *myasniye blyuda* (meat dishes), *ribniye blyuda* (fish dishes), *ptitsa blyuda* (poultry dishes) and *ovoshchniye blyuda* (vegetable dishes).

If the menu leaves you flummoxed, look at what the other diners are eating and point out what takes your fancy to the staff. Service charges are uncommon, except in the ritziest restaurants, but cover charges are frequent after 7pm, especially when there's live music (one would often gladly pay to stop the music). Check if there's a charge by asking, '*Vkhod platny?*' Leave around a 10% tip if the service has been good.

There is no charge for using the *garderob* (cloakroom) so do check in your coat before entering. Not doing so is considered extremely bad form.

In *A Year of Russian Feasts*, Catherine Cheremeteff Jones recounts how Russia's finest dishes have been preserved and passed down through the feast days of the Russian Orthodox Church.

Celebrating with Food

Food and drink have long played a central role in many Russian celebrations from birthdays to religious holidays. It's traditional, for example, for wedding feasts to stretch on for hours (if not days in some villages) with all the participants generally getting legless.

The most important holiday for the Russian Orthodox Church is Paskha (Easter). Coming after the six-week fast of Lent, when meat and dairy products are forsworn, Easter dishes are rich, exemplified by the traditional cheesecake (also known as *paskha*) and the saffron-flavoured buttery loaf *kulich*. Together with brightly decorated boiled eggs, these are taken in baskets to church to be blessed during the Easter service.

Bliny are the food of choice during the week-long Maslenitsa (Butter Festival), which precedes Lent – it is the equivalent of Mardi Gras elsewhere.

Christmas (which is celebrated on 7 January in the Russian Orthodox calendar) is not as big a festival as New Year's Eve, which is celebrated with a huge feast of *zakuski* and other traditonal foods such as tangerines, Russian salads and *kholodets* (meat jelly). However, it is traditional to eat a sweet rice pudding called *kutya* at Christmas. The same dish is also left as an offering on graves during funerals.

Quick Eats

There's plenty of fast food available from both local and international operations, supplemented by street kiosks, vans and cafes with tables. *Pitstsa* (pizza, often microwaved) and shashlyk are common fare, as are bliny and *pelmeni*.

All large cities have Western-style supermarkets and food stores with a large range of Russian and imported goods. You'll generally have to leave all bags in a locker before entering. Many places are open 24 hours.

As well as supermarkets, there are smaller food stores, called *kulinariya*, which sell ready-made food. There are also the ubiquitous food-and-drink kiosks, generally located around parks and markets, on main streets and near train and bus stations – their products are usually poor, but the kiosks are handy and reasonably cheap.

It's common to find restaurants serving a set three-course menu *(biznes lunch)* from noon to 4pm, Monday to Friday, costing as little as ₽150 (up to ₽500 in Moscow and St Petersburg).

Every sizeable town has a *rynok* (market), where locals sell spare produce from their dacha (country house) plots (check the market fringes), while bigger traders offload trucks full of fruit, vegetables, meat, dried goods and dairy products. Take your own shopping bag and go early in the morning for the liveliest scene and best selection; a certain amount of bargaining is acceptable, and it's a good idea to check prices with a trustworthy local first.

Homes, roadside vendors and well-stocked markets are your best bet for tasting the great range of wild mushrooms, *paporotniki* (fern tips), *shishki* (cedar nuts) and various soft fruits (red currants, raspberries) laboriously gathered by locals from the forest.

Habits & Customs

It's traditional for Russians to eat a fairly heavy early-afternoon meal *(obed)* and a lighter evening meal *(uzhin)*. Entering some restaurants, you might feel like you're crashing a big party. Here, the purpose of eating out is less to taste exquisite food than to enjoy a whole evening of socialising and entertainment, with multiple courses, drinking and dancing. Dress is informal in all but top-end places.

Most restaurant menus give the weight of portions as well as the price. In most cases, you'll be expected to choose an accompanying 'garnish' (priced separately) of *ris* (rice), potato or *grechka* (split buckwheat).

While restaurants and cafes are common, dining out for the average Russian is not as common as it is in many other countries – don't be surprised if the choice of places to dine is limited outside the main cities. If you really want to experience Russia's famous hospitality – not to mention the best cuisine – never pass up the opportunity to eat at a Russian home. Be prepared to find tables groaning with food and hosts who will never be satisfied that you're full, no matter how much you eat or drink.

Eating with Kids

In all but the fanciest of restaurants children will be greeted with the warmest of welcomes. Some restaurants also have special children's rooms with toys. Kids' menus are uncommon, but you shouldn't have much problem getting the little ones to guzzle bliny or *bifshteks* – a Russian-style hamburger served without bread, and often topped with a fried egg. Also, make sure you check whether the milk is pasteurised – outside major cities it often isn't.

Landscape & Wildlife

As you'd expect for the world's largest country, spanning 13% of the globe, there's an enormous variety of terrain and wildlife in Russia. Mountains include Mt Elbrus (5642m), Europe's highest peak, and the highly active volcanoes of Kamchatka. Vegetative zones range from the frozen tundra in northern Siberia around the Arctic Circle to seemingly endless taiga (forest) and the fecund steppe (grasslands). Fauna boasts the rare Asian black bear and Amur tiger.

Lay of the Land

Urban development is concentrated mainly across western European Russia and along the iron ribbon of tracks that constitute the Trans-Siberian Railway, thinning out in the frozen north and southern steppe.

Northern Russia is washed by the Barents, Kara, Laptev and East Siberian Seas. South of Finland, Russia opens on the Gulf of Finland, an inlet of the Baltic Sea; St Petersburg stands at the eastern end of this gulf.

East of Ukraine, the Russian Caucasus region commands stretches of the Black Sea and rugged, mountainous borders with Georgia and Azerbaijan. East of the Caucasus, Russia has an oil-rich stretch of Caspian Sea coast, north of which the Kazakhstan border runs up to the Ural Mountains.

Beyond the Urals, Asian Russia covers nearly 14 million sq km. Contrary to popular conception, only the western section of Asian Russia is actually called Siberia (Sibir). From the Amur regions in the south and the Sakha Republic (Yakutia) in the north, it becomes officially known as the Russian Far East (Dalny Vostok). The eastern seaboard is 15,500km long, giving Russia more 'Pacific Rim' than any other country.

The Wild Russia website (www.wild-russia.org) belongs to the US-based Center for Russian Nature Conservation, which assists and promotes nature conservation across Russia and publishes the English-language journal *Russian Conservation News*.

Rivers & Lakes

Though none has the fame of the Nile or the Amazon, six of the world's 20 longest rivers are in Russia. Forming the China–Russia border, the east-flowing Amur (4416km) is nominally longest, along with the Lena (4400km), Yenisey (4090km), Irtysh (4245km) and Ob (3680km), all of which flow north across Siberia, ending up in the Arctic Ocean. In fact, if one were to measure the longest stretch including tributaries (as is frequently done with the Mississippi–Missouri in North America), the Ob–Irtysh would clock up 5410km, and the Angara–Yenisey a phenomenal 5550km. The latter may in fact be the world's longest river if Lake Baikal and the Selenga River (992km) are included, which directly feed into it. Lake Baikal itself is the world's deepest, holding nearly one-fifth of all the world's unfrozen fresh water.

Europe's longest river, the Volga (3690km), rises northwest of Moscow and flows via Kazan and Astrakhan into the Caspian Sea, the world's largest lake (371,800 sq km). Lake Onega (9600 sq km) and Lake Ladoga (18,390 sq km), both northeast of St Petersburg, are the biggest lakes in Europe.

Until the 20th century, boats on Russia's rivers offered the most important form of transport. Today, rivers are still economically important, but mostly as sources of hydroelectric power, with dozens of major dams creating vast reservoirs. It's possible to visit Russia's largest hydroelectric dam at Sayano-Shushenskaya on the Yenisey near Sayanogorsk.

Novaya Zemlya, two islands that together cover 90,650 sq km, are a far northern extension of the Ural Mountains in the Barents Sea. In October 1961 the USSR exploded the most powerful nuclear weapon ever tested here.

Vegetation & Wildlife

To grasp the full extent of Russia's enormous diversity of wildlife, it is useful to understand the country's major vegetative zones.

Tundra

Falling almost completely within the Arctic Circle, and extending from 60km to 420km south from the coast, the tundra is the most inhospitable of Russia's terrains. The ground is permanently frozen (in places recorded to a depth of 1450m) with whole strata of solid ice and just a thin, fragile carpet of delicate lichens, mosses, grasses and flowers lying on top. The few trees and bushes that manage to cling tenaciously to existence are stunted dwarfs, the permafrost refusing to yield to their roots. For nine months of the year the beleaguered greenery is also buried beneath thick snow. When the brief, warming summer comes, the permafrost prevents drainage and the tundra becomes a spongy wetland, pocked with lakes, pools and puddles.

The BBC website Nature Places (www.bbc.co.uk/nature/places/Russia) has a series of short videos highlighting different aspects of Russia's amazing landscape and biodiversity.

Not surprisingly, wildlife has it hard on the tundra and there are few species that can survive its climate and desolation. Reindeer, however, have few problems and there are thought to be around four million in Russia's tundra regions. They can endure temperatures as low as –50°C and, like the camel, can store food reserves. Reindeer sustain themselves on lichen and grasses, in winter sniffing them out and pawing away the snow cover.

A similar diet sustains the lemming, a small, round, fat rodent fixed in the popular consciousness for its proclivity for launching itself en masse from cliff tops. More amazing is its rate of reproduction. Lemmings can produce five or six litters annually, each comprising five or six young. The young in turn begin reproducing after only two months. With the lemming three-week gestation period, one pair could spawn close to 10,000 lemmings in a 12-month period. In reality, predators and insufficient food keep numbers down.

Beautiful Lakes

- *Baikal, Eastern Siberia*
- *Seliger, Tver Region*
- *Onega, Karelia*

Other tundra mammals include the Arctic fox, a smaller, furrier cousin of the European fox and a big lemming fan, and the wolf, which, although it prefers the taiga, will range far and wide, drawn by the lure of reindeer meat. Make it as far as the Arctic coast and you could encounter seals, walruses (notably around Chukotka), polar bears and whales.

Taiga

Russia's taiga is the world's largest forest, covering about 5 million sq km (an area big enough to blanket the whole of India) and accounting for about 25% of the world's wood reserves. Officially the taiga is the dense, moist subarctic coniferous forest that begins where the tundra ends and which is dominated by spruces and firs. Travelling on the Baikal-Amur Mainline (BAM) through the depths of Siberia, two or three days can go by with nothing but the impenetrable and foreboding dark wall of the forest visible outside the train: 'Where it ends,' wrote Chekhov, 'only the migrating birds know.'

Roger Took's *Running with Reindeer* is a vivid account of his travels in Russia's Kola Peninsula and the wildlife found there.

Though the conditions are less severe than in the Arctic region, it's still harsh and bitterly cold in winter. The trees commonly found here are pine, larch, spruce and fir. In the coldest (eastern) regions the deciduous larch predominates; by shedding its leaves it cuts down on water loss, and its shallow roots give it the best chance of survival in permafrost conditions.

Due to the permanent shade, the forest-floor vegetation isn't particularly dense (though it is wiry and spring-loaded, making it difficult for humans to move through), but there are a great variety of grasses, moss, lichens, berries and mushrooms. These provide ample nourishment for the animals at the lower end of the food chain that, in turn, become food for others.

Among the wildlife that flourishes here are squirrels, chipmunks (which dine well on pine-cone seeds), voles, lemmings, polecats, foxes, wolverines and, less commonly now, the sable – a weasel-like creature whose luxuriant pelt played such a great role in the early exploration of Siberia.

The most common species of large mammal in the taiga is the elk, a large deer that can measure over 2m at the shoulder and weighs almost as much as a bear. The brown bear itself is also a Siberian inhabitant that you may come across, despite the Russian penchant for hunting it. Other taiga-abiding animals include deer, wolves, lynx and foxes.

Steppe

From the latitudes of Voronezh and Saratov down into the Kuban area north of the Caucasus and all the way across southwestern Siberia stretch vast areas of flat or gently undulating grasslands know as steppe. Since much of this is on humus-rich *chernozem* (black earth), a large proportion is used to cultivate grain. Where soil is poorer, as in Tuva, the grasslands offer vast open expanses of sheep-mown wilderness, encouraging wildflowers and hikers.

The delta through which the Volga River enters the Caspian is, in contrast to the surrounding area, very rich in flora and fauna. Huge carpets of the pink or white Caspian lotus flower spread across the waters in summer, attracting over 200 species of birds in their millions. Wild boar and 30 other mammal species also roam the land.

The small saygak (a type of antelope), an ancient animal that once grazed all the way from Britain to Alaska, still roams the more arid steppe regions around the northern Caspian Sea. However, the species is under threat of extinction from hunting and the eradication of its traditional habitat.

Forest.ru (http://old.forest.ru/eng), a site about Russian forests, their conservation and sustainable usage, has a lot of background and current information in English.

Caucasus

The steppe gives way to alpine regions in the Caucasus, a botanist's wonderland with 6000 highly varied plant species, including glorious wildflowers in summer. Among the animals of the Caucasus are the tur (a mountain goat), bezoar (wild goat), endangered mouflon (mountain sheep), chamois (an antelope), brown bear and reintroduced European bison. The lammergeier (bearded vulture), endangered griffon vulture, imperial eagle, peregrine falcon, goshawk and snowcock are among the Caucasus' most spectacular birds. Both types of vulture have been known to attack a live tur.

The Russian Far East, A Reference Guide for Conservation and Development, edited by Josh Newell, gathers work by 90 specialists from Russia, the UK and the US on this fascinating chunk of the country.

Kamchatka

The fantastic array of vegetation and wildlife in Kamchatka is a result of the geothermal bubbling, brewing and rumbling that goes on below the peninsula's surface, which manifests itself periodically in the eruption of one of around 30 active volcanoes. The minerals deposited by these eruptions have produced some incredibly fertile earth, which is capable of nurturing giant plants with accelerated growth rates. John Massey Stewart, in his book *The Nature of Russia,* gives the example of the dropwort, normally just a small, unremarkable plant, which in Kamchatka can grow by as much as 10cm in 24 hours and reach a height of up to 4m. In the calderas (craters) of collapsed volcanoes, hot springs and thermal vents maintain a high temperature year-round, creating almost greenhouselike conditions for plants. Waterfowl and all manner of animals make their way here to shelter from the worst of winter.

The volcanic ash also enriches the peninsula's rivers, leading to far greater spawnings of salmon than experienced anywhere else. And in

PUTIN & THE TIGERS

It's no secret that Vladimir Putin has a thing for tigers. In a publicity stunt in 2008, he was pictured fixing a tracking collar to a fully grown female Siberian tiger (also known as Amur tigers) after having shot her with a tranquilising dart. The same year, for his 56th birthday, Putin was presented with a two-month-old tiger cub: he later donated it to a zoo in Krasnodar Territory.

In November 2010, Putin hosted the International Tiger Conservation Forum in St Petersburg with the aim of doubling the number of tigers in the wild from 3200 to 7000 by 2022, the next Chinese Year of the Tiger. And in 2014, Putin was at it again, releasing three orphaned tigers into a remote part of the Amur Region.

thermally warmed pools the salmon also gain weight at a much increased rate. All of which is good news for the region's predatory mammals and large seabirds (and for local fisherfolk). The bears, in particular, benefit and the numerous Kamchatkan brown bears are the biggest of their species in Russia: a fully grown male stands at over 3m and weighs close to a tonne. Other well-fed fish-eaters are the peninsula's sea otters (a protected species), seals and the great sea eagle, one of the world's largest birds of prey, with a 2.5m wingspan. The coastline is particularly favoured by birds, with over 200 recognised species including auks, tufted puffins and swans.

WCS Russia (www.wcsrussia.org) estimates that of the 400 Siberian tigers left in the wild, 95% of them live in the Russian Far East.

Ussuriland

Completely unique, Ussuriland is largely covered by a monsoon forest filled with an exotic array of flora and fauna, many species of which are found nowhere else in Russia. The topography here is dominated by the Sikhote-Alin Range, which runs for more than 1000km in a spine parallel to the coast. Unlike the sparsely vegetated woodland floor of the taiga, the forests of Ussuriland have a lush undergrowth, with lianas and vines twined around trunks and draped from branches.

However, it's Ussuriland's animal life that arouses the most interest – not so much the wolves, sables or Asian black bears (tree-climbing, herbivorous cousins to the more common brown bears, also found here), as the Siberian or Amur tiger. The largest of all wild cats, the Siberian tiger can measure up to 3.5m in length. They prey on boar, though they've been observed to hunt and kill bears, livestock and even humans.

Ussuriland is also home to the Amur leopard, a big cat significantly rarer than the tiger, though less impressive and consequently less often mentioned. Around 30 of these leopards roam the lands bordering China and North Korea. Sadly, both the leopard and tiger are under threat from constant poaching by both Chinese and Russian hunters. For more about this beautiful animal see ALTA Amur Leopard Conservation (www.amur-leopard.org).

World Heritage Sites

- *Virgin Komi Forests, the Ural Mountains*
- *Lake Baikal*
- *Kamchatka's volcanoes*
- *Altai Mountains*
- *Western Caucasus*
- *Curonian Spit*
- *Central Sikhote-Alin Range*
- *Uvs Nuur Basin*
- *Wrangel Island Reserve*

Environmental Issues

Oil & Gas Exploration

Environmental groups including Greenpeace Russia (www.greenpeace.org/russia/en) and the Norway-based NGO Bellona (www.bellona.org) are highly critical of Russia's oil and gas industry expanding their operations in the country's delicate Arctic regions. In September 2013, the Russian navy intercepted Greenpeace's icebreaker *Arctic Sunrise*, towed it 320km to Murmansk where the crew of 28 and two journalists onboard were jailed for over two months on charges of piracy and hooliganism: they had been protesting oil exploration in the Barents Sea.

TOP PARKS & RESERVES

PARK	FEATURES	BEST TIME TO VISIT
Bystrinsky Nature Park	mountain hikes, volcanoes, reindeer herds	Jul & Aug
Kronotsky Biosphere State Reserve	volcanoes (11 active cones), geysers, bears, caribou, seals, otters	Jul & Aug
Kurshskaya Kosa National Park	giant sand dunes, ornithological station, 'dancing forest' of twisted pines	year-round
Prielbruse National Park	Mt Elbrus, glaciers, waterfalls, bears, chamois, wild goats, enormous range of plant life	skiing year-round; climbing & hiking Jun-Sep
Samara Bend National Park	Zhiguli Hills, hiking along rocky ledges, grand Volga vistas	Jun–Aug
Sikhote-Alin Nature Reserve	Manchurian red deer, wild boar, subtropical forests, tigers	Jul & Aug
Stolby Nature Reserve	volcanic rock pillars	Aug–Apr
Taganay National Park	some of the southern Ural Mountains' notable ridges (Small, Middle & Big Taganay, Itsyl)	Jul–Sep
Teberdinsky State Natural Biosphere Reserve	European bison, lynx, bears, chamois, boar & deer in a near-pristine temperate ecosystem	skiing Dec–Apr; climbing & hiking May–Sep
Zyuratkul National Park	forested ridges, heart-shaped lake	Jul–Sep

Few would dispute that Russia's delicate tundra and arctic ecosystems have been destabilised by the construction of buildings, roads and railways and the extraction of underground resources. Of particular concern is the impact on the low-lying Yamal Peninsula at the mouth of the Ob, which contains some of the world's biggest gas reserves; parts of the peninsula have been crumbling into the sea as the permafrost melts near gas installations. However, Russian gas monopoly Gazprom claims continued development of the on- and offshore Yamal fields is 'crucial for securing Russia's gas production build-up' into the 21st century (see www.gazprom.com/about/production/projects/mega-yamal).

It's not just in the Arctic that new oil and gas fields are being developed: the Caspian and Baltic Seas and the Sea of Japan around Sakhalin and Kamchatka are also being drilled. Yet, according to Greenpeace Russia, there are almost no sea oil-spill and toxic-pollution prevention and response programs in the country – as demonstrated when an oil tanker sank in the Azov Sea in November 2007, spilling 1300 tonnes of fuel oil and 6100 tonnes of sulphur into the sea, affecting at least 20km of coastline.

Russia has around 101 official nature reserves (*zapovedniki*) and 37 national parks (*natsionalniye parki*), ranging from the relatively tiny Bryansk Forest (122 sq km) on the border with Ukraine to the enormous 41,692 sq km Great Arctic Nature Reserve in the Taymyr Peninsula, the nation's largest such reserve.

Sochi, Khimki & Beyond

Campaign groups such as Bellona claimed that environmental law was rewritten to accommodate illegal construction and waste dumping on previously protected lands during the construction phase of the Sochi Winter Olympics, and that the area's drinking water was poisoned. When locals attempted to protest, they were harassed and jailed, such as environmentalist Evgeny Vitishko who is serving three years in a penal colony for his activism (http://freevitishko.org) and is recognised as a prisoner of conscience by Amnesty International.

Another battle between environmentalists and the government has been over the Khimki Forest, covering around 1000 hectares northwest of Moscow where it forms part of the city's green belt. A Kremlin-backed proposal to build a motorway through this ancient woodland sparked a grassroots campaign against the project that managed to get it suspended (but not halted) in 2010.

Yet another flash point is likely to be the Stolby Nature Reserve, the location for the Winter Universiades Games in 2019. To facilitate development for the games, the reserve may be demoted to a national park, thus easing its environmental protection status and perhaps leading to similar problems as experienced in Sochi.

Survival Guide

Directory A–Z

Accommodation

B&Bs, Homestays & Serviced Apartments

For an insight into how Russians really live, book a room in a private home (usually a flat) sharing with the owners. These 'bed and breakfast' (B&B) or 'homestay' operations are usually clean and respectable, though rarely large! In the major cities it's also possible to rent serviced apartments by the day or longer.

Moscow and St Petersburg have organisations specifically geared to accommodate foreign visitors in private flats at around €30 to €40 per person, normally with English-speaking hosts, breakfast and other services, such as excursions and extra meals.

Many travel agencies and tourism firms in these and other cities, as well as overseas, also offer homestays. The price will depend on things like how far the flat is from the city centre, whether the hosts speak English and whether any meals are provided. Also check whether a homestay or serviced-apartment agency can provide visa support and registration and what the costs of this might be.

Camping

Camping in the wild is allowed, except in those areas signposted 'Не разбивать палатку' (No putting up of tents) and/or 'Не разжигать костры' (No campfires). Check with locals if you're in doubt.

Kempingi (organised camp sites) are rare and usually only open from June to September. Unlike Western camp sites, small wooden cabins often take up much of the space, leaving little room for tents. Some *kempingi* are in quite attractive woodland settings, but communal toilets and washrooms are often in poor condition and other facilities few.

Hostels

Increasingly common across Russia, particularly along the main trans-Siberian route from St Peterburg to Vladivostok, Western-style hostels are a boon for budget (and other travellers) as they not only offer affordable accom-

SLEEPING PRICE RANGES

Russia offers everything from cosy homestays to luxury hotels. The following price ranges are for high season and usually include private bathroom.

€ <₽1500 (₽3000 in Moscow and St Petersburg)

€€ ₽1500 to ₽4000 (₽3000 to ₽8000 in Moscow and St Petersburg)

€€€ >₽4000 (₽8000 in Moscow and St Petersburg)

Make bookings by email or fax rather than telephone so you get a written copy of your reservation. A few hotels, usually old Soviet-style ones without online booking, add a *bron* (booking surcharge) which can be up to 50% of the first night's accommodation rate.

If you're looking for cheaper places to stay, head for the smaller towns or consider a homestay or serviced apartment; many travel agencies can arrange these. Occasionally, *potselenye* (twin rooms) are cheaper than singles, but you may end up sharing with a stranger unless you make it clear that you'd prefer single occupancy.

HOMESTAY AGENCIES

The following agencies can arrange homestays, mainly in Moscow and St Petersburg (as can some travel agencies), from as little as US$15 a day, but more commonly it's €30 to €60 depending on location and quality of accommodation.

Host Families Association (HOFA; ☎7-911 766 5464; www.hofa.ru)

International Homestay Agency (www.homestayagency.com/homestay/russia.html)

Worldwide Homestay (www.worldwidehomestay.com/Russia.htm)

AirBnB (www.airbnb.com) and **Couchsurfing** (www.couchsurfing.org) also have many major cities and towns in Russia covered.

modation but also friendly and clued-up English-speaking staff. A dorm bed in a Moscow or St Petersburg hostel runs from ₽500 to ₽800.

Hotels

A few hotels (usually budget ones) aren't registered for foreign guests or will only take you if you've already registered your visa, though these are fairly rare. Also rare are hotels charging a higher price for foreigners – this is against Russian law, but in practical terms there is little you can do about it, even if you arrive with Russian friends.

Most hotels have a range of rooms at widely differing prices – there's always a price list displayed (on the wall or in a menu-style booklet on the counter) listing the price for every category. Staff are generally obliging about allowing guests to look around before checking in: ask '*Mozhno li posmotret nomer?*' (May I see the room?).

Not all hotels have genuine single rooms and 'single' prices often refer to single occupancy of a double or twin room. Some hotels, mainly in the bottom and lower-middle ranges, have rooms for three or four people where the price per person is less than a single or double would be. Beds are typically single and where there is a double bed you'll generally pay somewhat more than for a similarly sized twin room.

Hot-water supplies are fairly reliable, but since hot water is supplied on a district basis, whole neighbourhoods can be without it for a month or more in summer when the system is shut down for maintenance (the best hotels have their own hot-water systems).

A *lyux* room equates to a suite with a sitting room in addition to the bedroom and bathroom. A *polu-lyux* room is somewhat less spacious.

In cities and towns, many midrange and top-end hotels catering to businesspeople drop their prices at weekends. There can also be significant seasonal variations, with top prices kicking in over holiday periods such as the first nine days of January and May.

PROCEDURES

When you check in practically all hotels will ask to see your passport – they may then keep it for anywhere up to 24 hours in order to register you with the authorities. Some budget and midrange hotels still operate a system where on each floor a *dezhurnaya* (floor lady) guards the keys for all the rooms in her little kingdom, and from whom you can arrange things like hot water to make tea.

Modern hotels generally have a check-out time (usually noon). However, some places charge by *sutki*, ie for a stay of 24 hours. Check which you've paid for before rushing to pack your bags. If you want to store your luggage somewhere safe for a late departure, arrange it with the *dezhurnaya* or front-desk staff.

Resting Rooms

Resting rooms *(komnaty otdykha)* are found at all major train stations and several of the smaller ones as well as at a few larger bus stations. Generally, they have basic (but often quite clean) shared accommodation with communal sink and toilet. Some have showers but you'll often pay an extra fee to use them. Sometimes there are single and double rooms and, rarely, more luxurious ones with private bathrooms. The beds generally can be rented by the half-day (around ₽1000) or 24-hour (around ₽1700) period. Some will ask to see your train ticket before allowing you to stay.

BOOK YOUR STAY ONLINE

For more accommodation reviews by Lonely Planet authors, check out http://lonelyplanet.com/russia/hotels/. You'll find independent reviews, as well as recommendations on the best places to stay. Best of all, you can book online.

PRACTICALITIES

Weights & Measures Russia uses the metric system. Menus often list food and drink servings in grams: a teacup is about 200g, a shot glass 50g. The unit for items sold by the piece, such as eggs, is *shtuka* ('thing' or 'piece') or *sht*.

TV Channels include **Channel 1** (Pervy Kanal; www.1tv.ru), **NTV** (www.ntv.ru), **Rossiya** (http://rutv.ru), **Kultura** (http://tvkultura.ru), **Sport 1** (http://sportodin.ru), **RenTV** (www.ren-tv.com) and the English-language **Russia Today** (http://rt.com). Each region has a number of local channels, while in many hotels you'll have access to CNN and BBC World, plus several more satellite channels in English and other languages.

Radio Broken into three bands: AM, UKV (66MHz to 77MHz) and FM (100MHz to 107MHz). A Western-made FM radio usually won't go lower than 85MHz.

DVDs Russian DVDs are region code 5.

Discount Cards Always flash your student card or International Student Identity Card (ISIC) before paying for admission to museums etc – you may get the student rate.

Turbazy, Rest Houses & Sanatoriums

A *turbaza* is typically a no-frills holiday camp aimed at outdoor types. Basic accommodation is usually in spartan multiroom wooden bungalows or *domiky* (small huts). Don't expect indoor plumbing. In the Soviet era, *turbazy* were often owned by a factory or large company for use by its employees. Many became somewhat decrepit, but these days more and more are privatised and have been spruced up. At some, you can arrange boating, skiing, hiking or mountaineering.

Doma otdykha (rest houses) are similar to *turbazy*, although usually more luxurious. In peak seasons it's often essential to book through travel agencies in regional cities as demand can be very high.

Sanatory (sanatoriums) have professional medical staff on hand to treat any illnesses you may have, design your diet and advise on correct rest. Most are ugly concrete eyesores in otherwise attractive rural or coastal settings. Sanatoriums can be spas, sea resorts (there are several good ones in Sochi and the Kaliningrad Region) or resorts where you can get some kind of non-traditional treatment (with *kumiss*, fermented mare's milk, for instance).

Children

Families planning to travel to Russia with their kids should have few fears.

Baby changing rooms are uncommon and you wouldn't want to use many public toilets yourself, let alone change your baby's nappy in them. Head back to your hotel or to a modern cafe or fast-food outlet where the toilets, while typically small, should be clean. Nappies, powdered milk and baby food are widely available except in very rural areas.

There's no shortage of toy shops, but don't expect to find many, if any, English-language kids' publications. In Moscow and St Petersburg there several restaurants with play sections for kids.

Lonely Planet's *Travel with Children* contains useful advice on how to cope with kids on the road and what to bring to make things go more smoothly.

Customs Regulations

- Searches beyond the perfunctory are quite rare, but clearing customs when you leave Russia by a land border can be lengthy.
- Visitors are allowed to bring in and take out up to US$10,000 (or its equivalent) in currency, and goods up to the value of €10,000, weighing less than 50kg, without making a customs declaration.
- Fill in a customs declaration form if you're bringing into Russia major equipment, antiques, artworks or musical instruments (including a guitar) that you plan to take out with you – get the form stamped in the red channel of customs to avoid any problems leaving with the same goods.
- If you plan to export anything vaguely 'arty' – instruments, coins, jewellery, antiques, antiquarian manuscripts and books (older than 50 years) or art (also older than 50 years) – it should first be assessed by the **Ministry of Culture** (Коллегия экспертизы; Map p64; 499-391 4212; ul Akademika Korolyova 21 bldg 1, office 505, 5th fl; price ₽350; 11am-5pm Mon-Fri; M VDNKh); it is very difficult to export anything over 100 years old. Bring your item (or a photograph, if the item is large) and your receipt.

If export is allowed, you'll be issued a receipt for tax paid, which you show to customs officers on your way out of the country.

Electricity

Access electricity (220V, 50Hz AC) with a European plug with two round pins. A few places still have the old 127V system. Some trains and hotel bathrooms have 110V and 220V shaver plugs.

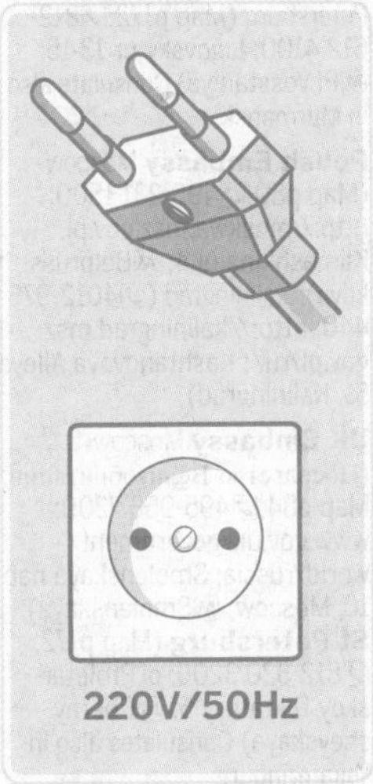

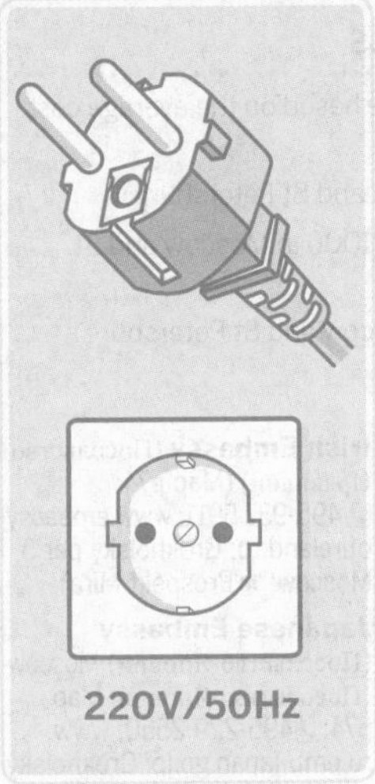

Embassies & Consulates

See www.russianembassy.net for a list of Russian embassies and consulates overseas. If you will be travelling in Russia for a long period of time (say a month or more), and particularly if you're heading to remote locations, it's wise to register with your embassy. This can be done over the telephone or by email.

Australian Embassy (Посольство Австралии) Moscow; Map p74; ☎495-956 6070; www.russia.embassy.gov.au; Podkolokolny per 10a/2, Moscow; Ⓜ Kitay-Gorod); St Petersburg (Map p162; ☎812-325 7334; www.russia.embassy.gov.au; 14 Petrovsky pr; Ⓜ Sportivnaya).

Belarusian Embassy (Консульство Белорусии) **Moscow** (Посольство Белорусии; Map p74; ☎495-777 6644; www.embassybel.ru; ul Maroseyka 17/6, Moscow; Ⓜ Kitay-Gorod); Kaliningrad (☎4012-214 412; ul Dm Donskogo 35a); St Petersburg (Map p172; ☎812-274 7212; ul Bonch-Bruevicha 3a; Ⓜ Chernyshevskaya) Consulates also in Kazan, Khabarovsk, Krasnoyarsk, Nizhny Novgorod, Novosibirsk, Rostov-on-Don, Smolensk, Ufa and Yekaterinburg.

Canadian Embassy (Посольство Канады) Map p84; ☎495-925 6000; http://russia.gc.ca; Starokonyushenny per 23, Moscow; Ⓜ Kropotkinskaya

Chinese Embassy (Посольство Китая) Moscow (Посольство Китая; Map p64; ☎consular 499-951 8435; http://ru.chinese embassy.org/rus; ul Druzhby

ABOUT MUSEUMS (& OTHER TOURIST ATTRACTIONS)

Some major Moscow attractions, such as the Kremlin, State History Museum and St Basil's, have ditched foreigner prices. All adults pay whatever the foreigner price used to be; all students, children and pensioners pay the low price. However, in St Petersburg foreigner prices rule, as they do generally across the country. Higher foreigner fees are said to go towards preserving works of art and cultural treasures that might otherwise receive minimal state funding.

Moscow and St Petersburg apart, non-Russian labels, guides or catalogues in museums are fairly uncommon. If good English labelling at a museum is not mentioned in our reviews, assume that you'll need a dictionary to work out the precise details of what you're seeing – or be prepared to pay an additional fee for a guided tour.

Here are a few more working practices of Russian museums to keep in mind:

- Admittance typically stops one hour before the official closing time.
- If you wish to take photos or film a video there will be a separate fee for this, typically an extra ₽100 for a still camera and ₽200 for video camera.
- Once a month many places close for a 'sanitary day', in theory to allow the place to be thoroughly cleaned. If you specially want to see a museum, it's always best to call ahead to check when it's open.

EATING PRICE RANGES

The following price ranges are based on the average cost of a restaurant's main dish:

€ <₽300 (<₽500 in Moscow and St Petersburg)

€€ ₽300 to ₽800 (₽500 to ₽1000 in Moscow and St Petersburg)

€€€ >₽800 (> ₽1000 in Moscow and St Petersburg)

6, Moscow; MUniversitet); **Khabarovsk** (☎4212-302 590; www.chinaconsulate.khb.ru/rus; Southern Bldg, Lenin Stadium 1; ⏱11am-1pm Mon, Wed & Fri); St Petersburg (Посольство Китая; Map p176; ☎812-713 7605; http://saint-petersburg.chineseconsulate.org/rus/; nab kanala Griboyedova 134; MSadovaya, Sennaya Ploshchad). Consulates also in Irkutsk and Yekaterinburg.

Finnish Embassy (Посольство Финляндии) Moscow (Посольство Финляндии; Map p84; ☎495-787 4174; www.finland.org.ru; Kropotkinsky per 15/17; MPark Kultury); **St Petersburg** (Map p172; ☎812-331 7600; www.finland.org.ru; Preobrazhenskaya pl 4; MChernyshevskaya).

French Embassy Moscow (Посольство Франции; Map p90; ☎495-937 1500; www.ambafrance-ru.org; ul Bolshaya Yakimanka 45, Moscow; MOktyabrskaya); St Petersburg (Map p166; ☎812-332 2270; www.ambafrance-ru.org/-Consulat-Saint-Petersbourg; 5th fl, Nevsky pr 12; MAdmiralteyskaya). Consulate also in Yekaterinburg.

German Embassy (Посольство Германии) Moscow (Посольство Германии; Map p64; ☎495-937 9500; www.germania.diplo.de; Mosfilmovskaya ul 56, Moscow; 🚌119, MUniversitet); St Petersburg (Map p172; ☎812-320 2400; www.germania.diplo.de; Furshtatskaya ul 39; MChernyshevskaya) Consulates also in Kaliningrad, Novosibirsk and Yekaterinburg.

Irish Embassy (Посольство Ирландии) (Map p74; ☎495-937 5911; www.embassy-ofireland.ru; Grokholsky per 5, Moscow; MProspekt Mira)

Japanese Embassy (Посольство Японии) Moscow (Посольство Японии; Map p74; ☎495-229 2550; www.ru.emb-japan.go.jp; Grokholsky per 27; MArbatskaya); St Petersburg (Посольство Японии; Map p166; ☎812-314 1434; nab reki Moyki 29; MNevsky Prospekt) Consulates also in Khabarovsk, Vladivostok and Yuzhno-Sakhalinsk.

Latvian Embassy Moscow (☎495-232 9760; www.am.gov.lv/en/moscow; ul Chapligina 3; MChistye Prudy); Kaliningrad (☎4012-706 755; Englesa ul 52a)

Lithuanian Embassy Moscow (☎495-785 8605; http://ru.urm.lt; Borisoglebsky per 10; MArbatskaya); St Petersburg (Map p172; ☎812-327 2681; ul Ryleyeva 37; MChernyshevskaya); Kaliningrad (Map p266; ☎4012-957 688; www.consulate-kaliningrad.mfa.lt; Proleterskaya ul 133)

Mongolian Embassy (Посольство Монголии) Moscow (Посольство Монголии; Map p80; ☎495-690 6792; Borisoglebsky per 11, Moscow; MArbartskaya); Moscow Consular Section (Посольство Монголии (Визовый отдел); Map p84; ☎499-241 1548; Spasopeskovsky per 7/1; MSmolenskaya); Irkutsk (Посольство Монголии; ☎3952-342 145; www.irconsul.angara.ru; ul Lapina 11); Ulan-Ude (Посольство Монголии; ☎3012-215 275; ul Profsoyuznaya 6).

Netherlands Embassy (Посольство Королевства Нидерландов) (Map p80; ☎495-797 2900; www.netherlands-embassy.ru; Kalashny per 6, Moscow; MArbatskaya)

New Zealand Embassy (Map p80; ☎495-956 3579; www.nzembassy.com; Povarskaya ul 44, Moscow; MArbatskaya)

Norwegian Embassy (Посольство Норвегии; Map p80; ☎495-951 1000; www.norvegia.ru; ul Povarskaya 7, Moscow; MArbatskaya) St Petersburg (Map p172; ☎812-612 4100; Ligovsky pr 13-15; MPl Vosstaniya) Consulate also in Murmansk.

Polish Embassy Moscow (Map p80; ☎495-231 1500; http://moskwa.msz.gov.pl; Klimashkina ul 4; MBelorusskaya); Kaliningrad (☎4012-976 440; http://kaliningrad.msz.gov.pl/ru/; Kashtanovaya Alleya 51, Kaliningrad)

UK Embassy Moscow (Посольство Великобритании; Map p84; ☎495-956 7200; www.gov.uk/government/world/russia; Smolenskaya nab 10, Moscow; MSmolenskaya); **St Petersburg** (Map p172; ☎812-320 3200; pl Proletarskoy Diktatury 5; MChernyshevskaya) Consulates also in Yekaterinburg

Ukrainian Embassy (Посольство Украины) (Map p80; ☎495-629 9742; http://russia.mfa.gov.ua; Leontevsky per 18, Moscow; MPushkinskaya)

US Embassy Moscow (Посольство США; Map p80; ☎495-728 5000; http://moscow.usembassy.gov; Bol Devyatinsky per 8, Moscow; MBarrikadnaya); St Petersburg (☎812-331 2600; ul Furshtatskaya 15; MChernyshevskaya) Consulate also in Yekaterinburg and Vladivostok

Food

For more information, see the Food & Drink chapter (p623).

Gay & Lesbian Travellers

- Russia is a conservative country and being gay is generally frowned upon. LGBT people face stigma, harassment and violence in their everyday lives.
- Homosexuality isn't illegal, but promoting it (and other LGBT lifestyles) is. What constitutes promotion is at the discretion of the authorities.
- There are active and relatively open gay and lesbian scenes in both Moscow and St Petersburg. Elsewhere, the gay scene tends to be underground.
- For a good overview, visit http://english.gay.ru, which has up-to-date information, good links and a resource for putting you in touch with personal guides for Moscow and St Petersburg; and http://comingoutspb.ru/en/en-home, the site of a St Petersburg–based support organisation.

Health

- **Insurance** Good emergency medical treatment is not cheap in Russia, so take out a policy that covers you for the worst possible scenario, such as an accident requiring an emergency flight home.
- **Recommended vaccinations** No vaccinations are required for travel to Russia, but the World Health Organization (WHO) recommends that all travellers should be covered for diphtheria, tetanus, measles, mumps, rubella and polio, regardless of their destination. Since most vaccines don't produce immunity until at least two weeks after they're given, visit a physician at least six weeks before departure.
- **Availability and cost of health care** Medical care is readily available across Russia but the quality can vary enormously. The biggest cities and towns have the widest choice of places, with Moscow and St Petersburg well served by sparkling international-style clinics that charge handsomely for their generally excellent and professional service: expect to pay around US$100 for an initial consultation. In remote areas doctors won't usually charge travellers, although it's recommended to give them a present – such as chocolate, fancy alcohol or just money. In some cases, medical supplies required in a hospital may need to be bought from a pharmacy and nursing care may be limited. Note that there can be an increased risk of hepatitis B and HIV transmission via poorly sterilised equipment.
- **Infectious diseases** These include rabies, tick-borne encephalitis (a serious risk in rural Russia from May to July), HIV and AIDS, typhoid and hepatitis A. Consider having vaccinations before departure.
- **Environmental hazards** These include altitude sickness in the high mountains of the Caucasus, the Altai and Kamchatka; depending on the season, heat exhaustion and heat stroke or hypothermia and frostbite; stings or bites from insects, leeches and snakes.
- **Water safety** While brushing your teeth with it is OK, assume that tap water isn't safe to drink. Stick to bottled water, boil water for 10 minutes or use water-purification tablets or a filter. Do not drink water from rivers or lakes as it may contain bacteria or viruses that can cause diarrhoea or vomiting.

Insurance

We strongly recommend taking out travel insurance. Check the small print to see if the policy covers potentially dangerous sporting activities, such as diving or trekking. For medical treatment, some policies pay doctors or hospitals directly but most require you to pay on the spot and claim later (keep all receipts and documentation). Check that the policy covers ambulances or an emergency flight home. Worldwide travel insurance is available at www.lonelyplanet.com/travel-insurance. You can buy, extend and claim online anytime – even if you're already on the road.

Internet Access

Although main post or telephone offices have internet terminals, in our experience, few actually appear to be working. If you don't have your own wireless-internet-enabled (wi-fi) devices then it's likely easiest to get online in the business centres of hotels.

Wi-fi is common, particularly in Moscow and St Petersburg and other large cities, and often access is free (you may have to ask for a password, or *parol*, to get online) or available for the cost of a cup of coffee or via a prepaid card that allows you a set amount of time online.

A few hotels have a high-speed link via broadband cables; if so, they can usually provide the connection cords for your laptop, if you don't have one.

Legal Matters

Avoid contact with the myriad types of police. It's not uncommon for them to bolster their incomes by extracting 'fines' from the unaware; you always have the right to insist to be taken to a police station (we don't recommend this) or that the 'fine' be paid the legal way, through Sberbank. If you need police assistance (ie you've been the victim of a robbery or an assault) go to a station with a local for both language and moral support. Be persistent and patient.

Note anyone caught smoking in a public place, which includes bars, public areas of hotels, restaurants, children's playgrounds, station platforms or at the end of carriages on long-distance trains, will be eligible for fines of up to ₽1500, according to a new law that came into force in 2014.

If you are arrested, the police are obliged to inform your embassy or consulate immediately and allow you to communicate with it without delay. You can't count on the rules being followed, so be polite and respectful towards officials and hopefully things will go far more smoothly for you. In Russian, the phrase 'I'd like to call my embassy' is '*Pozhaluysta, ya khotel by pozvonit v posolstvo moyey strany*'.

Money

The Russian currency is the rouble (рубль), abbreviated as 'py' or 'p'. There are 100 *kopeks* in a rouble and these come in coin denominations of one (rarely seen), five, 10 and 50. Also issued in coins, roubles come in amounts of one, two, five and 10, with banknotes in values of 10, 50, 100, 500, 1000 and 5000 roubles.

ATMs

Using a credit card or the debit card you use in ATMs at home, you can obtain cash as you need it. You're rarely a block or so from an ATM: look for signs that say *bankomat* (БАНКОМАТ).

Credit Cards

These are commonly accepted, but don't rely on them outside of the major cities and towns. Most sizeable cities have banks or exchange bureaux that will give you a cash advance on your credit card, but be prepared for paperwork in Russian.

Exchanging Money

You'll usually get the best exchange rates for US dollars, though euros are increasingly widely accepted and will get good rates, for instance, in Moscow and St Petersburg. British pounds are sometimes accepted in big cities, but the exchange rates are not so good; other currencies incur abysmal rates and are often virtually unchangeable.

Any currency you bring should be pristine: banks and exchange bureaux do not accept old, tatty bills with rips or tears. For US dollars, make certain they are the post-2006 designs printed with large offset portraits.

Carrying around wads of cash isn't the security problem you might imagine – nowadays, there are a lot of Russians with plenty more money on them than you. For security, though, divide your money into three or four stashes hidden out of view about your person.

Every town of any size will have at least one bank (most often Sberbank; www.sberbank.ru) or exchange office – be prepared to fill out a lengthy form and show your passport. Rates can vary from one establishment to the next (and are linked to how much cash you want to change – larger amounts get better rates) so it's always worth shopping around.

International Transfers

Larger towns and cities will have at least one bank or exchange office that can handle Western Union money wires. Ask at any bank for this information.

Travellers Cheques

These can be difficult to exchange outside the largest cities and the process can be lengthy. Expect to pay 1% to 2% commission. Not all travellers cheques are treated equally by those Russian establishments willing to handle them. In descending order of acceptance, the favourites are American Express (Amex), Thomas Cook and Visa; you'll have little or no luck with other brands. The most likely bank to cash travellers cheques is Sberbank, with branches in all the major cities.

For information on tipping, see p23.

RUSSIAN STREET NAMES

We use the Russian names of all streets and squares to help you when deciphering Cyrillic signs and asking locals the way. To save space, we use the following abbreviations.

bul	bulvar	бульвар	boulevard
nab	naberezhnaya	набережная	embankment
per	pereulok	переулок	side street
pl	ploshchad	площадь	square
pr	prospekt	проспект	avenue
sh	shosse	шоссе	road
ul	ulitsa	улица	street

Opening Hours

Shops 10am-8pm

Banks 9am-6pm Monday to Friday

Restaurants noon-midnight

Bars noon-midnight (until 5am Friday and Saturday)

Photography

Any town or city will have several photographic shops where you can download digital snaps to CD and buy memory cards and major brands of print film. Slide film is not widely sold, so bring plenty of rolls with you. The same rare specialist shops that sell slide film will also have a smattering of camera gear by leading brands such as Nikon and Canon.

Photographing People

Use judgement and discretion when taking photos of people. It's always better to ask first, and if the person doesn't want to be photographed, respect their privacy; older people can be uneasy about being photographed, but a genuine offer to send on a copy can loosen your subject up.

In Russian, 'May I take a photograph of you?' is '*Mozhno vas sfotografirovat?*'. And 'I'll send you a copy' is Я пришлю вам копию (*Ya prishlyu vam kopiyu*).

Restrictions

Be very careful about photographing stations, official-looking buildings and any type of military-security structure – if in doubt, don't snap! Travellers, including a Lonely Planet author, have been arrested and fined for such innocent behaviour.

Some museums and galleries forbid flash pictures, some ban all photography and most will charge you extra to snap away (typically ₽100). Some caretakers in historical buildings and churches will also charge you for the privilege of using a still or video camera.

Post

The Russian post service is **Pochta Rossia** (www.russianpost.ru). *Pochta* (ПОЧТАМТ) refers to any post office, *glavpochtamt* to a main post office and *mezhdunarodny glavpochtamt* to an international one. The main offices are open from 8am to 8pm or 9pm Monday to Friday, with shorter hours on Saturday and Sunday; in big cities one office will possibly stay open 24 hours a day.

Outward post is slow but fairly reliable; if you want to be certain, use registered post (*zakaznaya pochta*). Airmail letters take two to three weeks from Moscow and St Petersburg to the UK, longer from other cities and three to four weeks to the USA or Australasia. To send a postcard or letter up to 20g anywhere in the world by air costs ₽26.

In major cities you can usually find the services of at least one of the international express carriers, such as FedEx or DHL.

Incoming mail is so unreliable that many companies, hotels and individuals use private services with addresses in Germany or Finland (a private carrier completes the mail's journey to its Russian destination). Other than this, your *reliable* options for receiving mail in Russia are nil: there's no poste restante, and embassies and consulates won't hold mail for transient visitors.

If sending mail to Russia or trying to receive it, note that addresses should be in reverse order: Russia (Россия), postal code (if known), city, street address, then name.

Public Holidays

New Year's Day 1 January

Russian Orthodox Christmas Day 7 January

Defender of the Fatherland Day 23 February

International Women's Day 8 March

International Labour Day/ Spring Festival 1 May

Victory Day 9 May (marks the WWII victory over the Germans in 1945)

Russian Independence Day 12 June (marks the day the Russian republic of the USSR proclaimed its sovereignty in June 1991)

Unity Day 4 November

Many businesses are also closed from 1 January to 7 January. Easter Monday is also widely celebrated across Russia.

Safe Travel

Crime

SCAMS

Be wary of officials, such as police (or people posing as police), asking to see your papers or tickets at stations – there's a chance they're on the lookout for a bribe and will try to find anything wrong with your

GOVERNMENT TRAVEL ADVICE

The following government websites offer travel advisories and information on current hot spots.

Australian Department of Foreign Affairs (www.smarttraveller.gov.au)

British Foreign Office (www.gov.uk/government/organisations/foreign-commonwealth-office)

Canadian Department of Foreign Affairs (www.dfait-maeci.gc.ca)

US State Department (http://travel.state.gov)

documents, or basically hold them ransom. The only course of action is to remain calm and polite and stand your ground. Try to enlist the help of a passer-by to translate (or at least witness what is going on).

STREET CRIME

The streets of big cities such as Moscow and St Petersburg are as safe (or as dangerous) as those of New York and London: there are pickpockets, purse-snatchers and all the other crimes (and criminals) endemic to big cities anywhere. The key is to be neither paranoid nor unconcerned – use common sense and try to fit in: shun clothes and accessories that show you're a tourist.

THEFT

Don't leave anything of worth in a car, including sunglasses, CDs and cigarettes. Valuables lying around hotel rooms also tempt fate. At camp sites, watch for items on clothes lines and in cabins. If you stay in a flat, make sure it has a well-bolted steel door.

It's generally safe to leave your belongings unguarded when using the toilets on trains, but you'd be wise to get to know your fellow passengers first.

Dangerous Regions

Check with your government's foreign-affairs ministry at home or your embassy in Russia for the latest danger zones. Heading to Dagestan, for example, or other areas of civil unrest and general lawlessness, is not recommended. Terrorism is also something to be aware of as the suicide bomb attacks in Volgograd in December 2013 showed – security measures are in place at all major train and bus stations, as well as airports but they are not always strictly followed.

Certain very isolated villages suffer from the unpredictable side effects of chronic alcoholism, especially in western Tuva where locals are frequently drunk and armed with knives.

In more remote areas of the country specific natural hazards include bears and, in late May to July, potentially fatal tick-borne encephalitis (particularly in Siberia and Ussuriland in the Russian Far East). And if trekking in Kamchatka, remember that many of those volcanoes are volatile.

Border Zones & Restricted Areas

Other areas to be careful of approaching are Russia's borders which, official border crossings aside, are usually off-limits. Being caught near borders could result in a large fine at best and deportation at worst. The same goes for Russia's closed cities (usually associated with the military in some way).

Then there are regulated areas (Зоны с регламентированным посещением для иностранных граждан), mainly wilderness zones scattered across the country, for which you need official permission from the Federalnaya Sluzhba Bezopasnosti (FSB) to enter. These are not obvious and rarely marked – if you are planning any serious back-country exploration it's worth checking first what official permits you may need to avoid incurring fines or deportation.

Racism & Discrimination

Racism is a problem. Russian neo-Nazi and skinhead groups are violent and have been linked to many murders.

Attacks on Africans and Asians on city streets are not uncommon. Visitors of African, Middle Eastern and Asian descent should be aware that they may not always receive the warmest of welcomes, though Russian racism seems particularly focused towards Caucasian peoples (ie people from the Caucasus, not white-skinned Europeans).

Racist attitudes or statements can also come from highly educated Russians. Anti-Semitism, which was state-sponsored during Soviet times, is still easily stirred up by right-wing political parties.

It's a good idea to be vigilant on the streets around Hitler's birthday (20 April), when bands of right-wing thugs have been known to roam around spoiling for a fight with anyone who doesn't look Russian.

Transport & Road Safety

Take care when crossing the road in large cities: some crazy drivers completely ignore traffic lights, while others tear off immediately when the lights change (which can be suddenly), leaving you stranded in the middle of the road.

Telephone

The country code for Russia is ☎7.

Local calls from homes and most hotels are free. To make a long-distance call or to call a mobile from most phones, first dial 8, wait for a second dial tone, then dial the area code and phone number. To make an international call dial ☎8, wait for a second dial tone, then dial ☎10, then the country code etc. Some phones are for local calls only and won't give you that second dial tone.

From mobile phones, dial ☎+ and then the country code to place an international call.

Mobile Phones

There are several major networks, all offering pay-as-you-go deals.

Beeline (http://moskva.beeline.ru)

Megafon (http://moscow.megafon.ru)

MTS (www.mts.ru)

Skylink (http://skylink.ru)

Reception is available right along the Trans-Siberian Railway and increasingly in rural areas. MTS probably has the widest network, but also the worst reputation for customer service. Our researchers found Beeline to be pretty reliable.

To call a mobile phone from a landline, the line must be enabled to make paid (ie nonlocal) calls. SIMs and phone-call-credit top-up cards, available at mobile-phone shops and kiosks across cities and towns (you'll usually find them in the airport arrival areas and train stations) and costing as little as ₽300, can be slotted into your regular mobile-phone handset during your stay. Call prices are very low within local networks, but charges for roaming larger regions can mount up; cost-conscious locals switch SIM cards when crossing regional boundaries.

Topping up your credit can be done either via prepaid credit cards bought from kiosks or mobile-phone shops or, more commonly, via certain ATMs (look for phone logos on the options panel; note the instructions are in Russian but a Russian speaker would be able to help you) and the brightly coloured QIWI Cash-in pay-point machines found in all shopping centres, metro and train stations and the like. Choose your network, input your telephone number and the amount of credit you'd like, insert the cash and it's done, minus a small fee for the transaction. Confirmation of the top-up comes via a text message (in Russian) to your phone.

Pay Phones

Taksofon (ТАКСОФОН, pay phones) are located throughout most cities. They're usually in working order, but don't rely on them. Most take prepaid phonecards. There are several types of card-only phones, and not all cards are interchangeable. Card phones can be used for either domestic or international calls.

Phonecards & Call Centres

Local phonecards (Телефонная карта) come in a variety of units and are available from shops and kiosks; they can be used to make local, national and international calls.

Sometimes a call centre is better value for international calls: you give the clerk the number you want to call, pay a deposit and then go to the booth you are assigned to make the call; afterwards, you either pay the difference or collect your change. Such call centres are common in Russian cities and towns – ask for *mezhdunarodny telefon* (Международный телефон).

Time

There are 11 time zones in Russia; the standard time is calculated from Moscow, which is GMT/UTC plus four hours year-round.

Moscow & St Petersburg	noon
Samara	1pm
Yekaterinburg & Tyumen	2pm
Novosibirsk	3pm
Krasnoyarsk & Tuva	4pm
Irkutsk & Ulan-Ude	5pm
Chita	6pm
Vladivostok & Sydney	7pm
Sakhalin region	8pm
Kamchatka	9pm
San Francisco	1am
New York	4am
London	9am
Paris & Berlin	10am
Kaliningrad, Helsinki & Minsk	11am

TRAIN TIME

Right across Russia, timetables for long-distance trains are written according to Moscow time. The only exceptions are those for suburban services that run on local time – but not always, so double-check. Station clocks in most places are also set to Moscow time. We list how far ahead cities and towns are of Moscow time, eg Moscow +5hr, meaning five hours ahead of Moscow.

Toilets

Pay toilets are identified by the words платный туалет *(platny tualet)*. In any toilet, Ж *(zhensky)* stands for women's, while M *(muzhskoy)* stands for men's.

Public toilets are rare and often dingy and uninviting. Toilets in major hotels, cafes or shopping centres are preferable.

In all public toilets, the babushka you pay your ₽20 to can also provide miserly rations of toilet paper; it's always a good idea to carry your own.

Tourist Information

Tourist offices remain a rarity in Russia. We've located ones in Arkhangelsk, Yelizovo, Esso, Irkutsk, Kaliningrad, Kazan, Kyzyl, Perm, Petrozavodsk, Pskov, St Petersburg, Svetlogorsk, Uglich and

Veliky Novgorod. Along the main trans-Siberian route, Western-style hostels are good sources of local information.

You're mainly dependent on the moods of hotel receptionists and administrators, service bureaux and travel firms for information. The latter two exist primarily to sell accommodation, excursions and transport – if you don't look like you want to book something, staff may or may not answer questions.

Overseas, travel agencies specialising in Russian travel are your best bet.

Travellers with Disabilities

Disabled travellers are not well catered for in Russia. Many footpaths are in poor condition, hazardous even for the mobile. There is a lack of access ramps and lifts for wheelchairs. However, attitudes are enlightened and things are slowly changing. Major museums such as the Hermitage offer good disabled access. **Liberty** (Map p182; ☎812-232 8163; www.libertytour.ru; ul Polozova 12, Office 1; Ⓜ Petrogradskaya) is a tour agency specialising in wheelchair-accessible tours in St Petersburg.

Before setting off, get in touch with your national support organisation (preferably with the travel officer, if there is one). A number of organisations offer general travel advice.

Accessible Journeys (☎800-846 4537; www.disabilitytravel.com; 35 West Sellers Ave, Ridley Park, PA 19078) USA

Mare Nostrum (☎030-4502 6454; www.mare-nostrum.de; Oudenarder Strasse 7, Berlin 13347) Germany

Mobility International USA (☎541-343 1284; www.miusa.org; ste 343, 132 East Broadway, Eugene, Oregon 97401) USA

Nican (☎02-6241 1220, 1800-806 769; www.nican.com.au; Unit 5, 48 Brookes St, Mitchell, ACT 2911) Australia

Tourism For All (☎0845-124 9971; www.tourismforall.org.uk; 7A Pixel Mill, 44 Appleby Rd, Kendal, Cumbria LA9 6ES)

Visas

If your trip into or out of Russia involves transit through, or a stay in, another country, such as Belarus, China, Mongolia or Kazakhstan, our advice is to arrange any necessary visa or visas in your home country *before* you enter Russia. For comprehensive information about visas, see our Getting Your Visa chapter (p24).

Volunteering

Local enterprises, environmental groups and charities that are trying to improve Russia's environmental and social scorecard are usually on the lookout for volunteers. A good example is the Great Baikal Trail project helping to construct a hiking trail around Lake Baikal. The US-based School of Russian & Asian Studies (SRAS) has complied an online list of volunteer opportunities in Russia (www.sras.org/volunteer_opportunities_in_russia). Other possibilities:

CCUSA (www.ccusa.com/Programs/CampCounselorsRussia.aspx) This US-based organisation runs programs for those wanting to volunteer on Russian youth summer camps.

Ecologica Youth Trust (www.ecologia.org.uk) Runs no-profit community centres for fostering children in Kitezh and Orion in the rural Kaluga region south of Moscow.

Go Overseas (www.gooverseas.com/volunteer-abroad/russia) Lists a range of opportunities from working in hospitals to summer youth camps.

International Cultural Youth Exchange (www.icye.org) Offers a variety of volunteer projects, mostly in Samara.

Language Link Russia (www.jobs.languagelink.ru) Volunteer to work at language centres across the country.

World 4U (www.world4u.ru/english.html) Russian volunteer association.

Women Travellers

Russian women are very independent and, in general, you won't attract attention by travelling alone. That said, it's not uncommon for a woman dining or drinking alone to be mistaken for a prostitute. Sexual harassment on the streets is rare, but a woman alone should certainly avoid ad-hoc taxis at night – have one called for you from a reputable company.

Stereotyping of gender roles remains strong. Russian men will also typically rush to open doors for you, help you put on your coat, and, on a date, act like a 'traditional' gentleman. (In return, they may be expecting you to act like a traditional lady.)

Russian women tend to dress up and wear lots of make-up on nights out. If you wear casual gear, you might feel uncomfortable at a restaurant, a theatre or the ballet; in rural areas, wearing revealing clothing will probably attract unwanted attention.

Work

Bureaucracy makes getting a job or starting a business in Russia a hassle, but it's certainly not impossible. It is wise to use a professional relocation firm to navigate the country's thicket of rules and regulations surrounding employment of foreigners. Good websites for expats are www.expat.ru and www.redtape.ru/forum.

Transport

GETTING THERE & AWAY

Flights, cars and tours can be booked online at lonelyplanet.com/bookings.

Entering the Country

Unless you have a transit visa, you can enter the country on a one-way ticket (even if your visa is only good for one day, it's unlikely anyone will ask to see your outgoing ticket), so you have a great deal of flexibility once inside Russia to determine the best way of getting out again.

Air

Airports

Moscow's **Sheremetyevo** (Шереметьево, SVO; ☎495-578 6565; www.svo.aero) and **Domodedovo** (Домодедово; www.domodedovo.ru) airports, and St Peterburg's **Pulkovo** (LED; www.pulkovoairport.ru) airport host the bulk of Russia's international flights.

Plenty of other cities have direct international connections, including Arkhangelsk, Irkutsk, Kaliningrad, Kazan, Khabarovsk, Krasnodar, Mineralnye Vody, Murmansk, Nizhny Novgorod, Novosibirsk, Perm, Yekaterinburg and Yuzhno-Sakhalinsk.

Land

Border Crossings

Russia shares borders with Azerbaijan, Belarus, China, Estonia, Finland, Georgia, Kazakhstan, Latvia, Lithuania, Mongolia, North Korea, Norway, Poland and Ukraine; all except Azerbaijan, Georgia and North Korea are open to non-Russian travellers. Before planning a journey into or out of Russia from any of these countries, check out the visa situation for your nationality. See p24 for more information.

Popular land approaches include trains and buses from Central and Baltic European countries or on either the trans-Manchurian or trans-Mongolian train routes from China and Mongolia.

On trains, border crossings are a straightforward but drawn-out affair, with a steady stream of customs and ticket personnel scrutinising your passport and visa. If you're arriving by car or motorcycle, you'll need to show your vehicle registration and insurance papers, and your driving licence, passport and visa. These formalities are usually minimal for Western European citizens.

On the Russian side, chances are your vehicle will be subjected to a cursory inspection by border guards (things will go faster if you open all doors and the boot yourself, and shine a torch for the guards at night). You pass through customs separately from your car, walking through a metal

CLIMATE CHANGE & TRAVEL

Every form of transport that relies on carbon-based fuel generates CO_2, the main cause of human-induced climate change. Modern travel is dependent on aeroplanes, which might use less fuel per kilometre per person than most cars but travel much greater distances. The altitude at which aircraft emit gases (including CO_2) and particles also contributes to their climate change impact. Many websites offer 'carbon calculators' that allow people to estimate the carbon emissions generated by their journey and, for those who wish to do so, to offset the impact of the greenhouse gases emitted with contributions to portfolios of climate-friendly initiatives throughout the world. Lonely Planet offsets the carbon footprint of all staff and author travel.

detector and possibly having hand luggage X-rayed.

Train fares quoted for trips to/from Russia are for a *kupe* (compartment) in a four-berth compartment unless otherwise mentioned. Certain routes also offer cheaper *platskartny* (3rd-class open carriage) fares.

Belarus

BUS

There are at least two buses a week from Minsk to Moscow and one a week to St Petersburg.

CAR & MOTORCYCLE

Long queues at border crossings are common. There are six main road routes into Russia from Belarus, the recommended one being the E30 highway that connects Brest and Minsk with Smolensk and finishes up in Moscow.

TRAIN

Minsk is well connected by train with Kaliningrad (₽3860, 11 hours, two to three daily), Moscow (₽3500, eight to 12 hours, eight daily), Smolensk (₽2500, four hours, 11 daily) and St Petersburg (₽4670, 13–14 hours, three daily).

China

BUS

The road from Manzhouli to Zabaikalsk in the Chitinskaya Region is open to traffic; it's also possible to cross from Heihe to Blagoveshchensk using a ferry across the Amur River. It's possible to take a bus between Manzhouli and Zabaikalsk, but asking Russians for a ride is usually faster.

TRAIN

The classic way into Russia from China is along the trans-Mongolian and trans-Manchurian rail routes. Vladivostok and Khabarovsk have other options for travelling overland to China.

Estonia

The nearest border crossing from Tallinn is at Narva. There are daily trains between Tallinn and Moscow (₽8680, 15 hours) and St Petersburg (₽1720 *platskartny;* six hours 20 minutes). By bus you can connect to/from Tallinn with St Petersburg (from €20, 7½ hours, seven daily) and Kaliningrad (€32, 16 hours, two daily).

Finland

BUS

There are many daily buses between Helsinki and St Petersburg and Helsinki and Petrozavodsk, as well as three buses a week from Murmansk to Rovaniemi.

CAR & MOTORCYCLE

Highways cross at the Finnish border posts of Nuijamaa and Vaalimaa (Brusnichnoe and Torfyanovka, respectively, on the Russian side). Fill up with petrol on the Finnish side (preferably before you get to the border petrol station, which is more expensive than others and closes early). Watch carefully for all road signs; a few roads involve tricky curves and signposting is not all it should be. It's best to make this drive during daylight hours.

TRAIN

High-speed Allegro trains (from ₽2300, 3½ hours, four daily) connect St Petersburg and Helsinki. The daily Leo Tolstoy (31/34) service between Moscow and Helsinki (₽6000, 14 hours) also passes through St Petersburg (₽4000, seven hours).

Kazakhstan

CAR & MOTORCYCLE

Roads into Kazakhstan head east from Astrakhan and south from Samara, Chelyabinsk, Orenburg and Omsk.

TRAIN

There are trains on even days between Moscow and Almaty (₽11,500, three days and seven hours) and a few times a week from Astrakhan to Atyrau (₽17,300, 12 hours) in addition to several services from Siberia.

Latvia

BUS

Rīga is connected by bus to St Petersburg (€33, 11 hours, six–11 daily) and Kaliningrad (€14, nine hours, two daily).

CAR & MOTORCYCLE

The M9 Rīga–Moscow road crosses the border east of Rezekne (Latvia). The A212 road from Rīga leads to Pskov, crossing a corner of Estonia en route.

TRAIN

Overnight trains run daily between Rīga and Moscow (₽7000, 15 hours, 40 minutes) and St Petersburg (₽5200, 15 hours).

Lithuania

BUS

From Kaliningrad there are services to Klaipėda (₽445, four hours, two daily) and Vilnius (₽920, six hours, one daily).

CAR & MOTORCYCLE

The border-crossing points from Kaliningrad into Lithuania are Chernyshevskoe/Kibartay, Sovetsk/Panemune, Pogranichnoe/Ramonishkyay and Morskoe/Nida.

TRAIN

Services link Vilnius with Kaliningrad (from ₽1900 *platskartny,* six hours, three daily) Moscow (from ₽4000, 14–15 hours, three daily) and St Petersburg (from ₽5900, 13 hours, 30 minutes, two daily). The St Petersburg trains cross Latvia and the Moscow ones cross Belarus, for which you'll need a Belarus visa or transit visa.

Mongolia

BUS

There are direct daily buses between Ulaanbaatar and Ulan-Ude.

CAR & MOTORCYCLE

It's possible to drive between Mongolia and Russia at the Tsagaanuur–Tashanta and Altanbulag–Kyakhta borders. Getting through these borders can be a very slow process; it helps to have written permission from a Mongolian embassy if you wish to bring a vehicle through.

TRAIN

Apart from the trans-Mongolian train connecting Moscow and Beijing, there's a direct train twice a week from Ulaanbaatar to Moscow (₽15,200, four days and five hours) as well as a daily service to and from Irkutsk (₽4500, 27 hours).

Norway

BUS

There are bus connections between Murmansk and Kirkenes; see p308.

CAR & MOTORCYCLE

The border crossing is at Storskog/Borisoglebsk on the Kirkenes–Murmansk road. As this is a sensitive border region, no stopping is allowed along the Russian side of this road. Also non-Russian registered vehicles are barred from the Nikel–Zapolyarnye section of the M18 highway between 11pm and 7am and any time on Tuesday, Thursday or Saturday. On those days you will be diverted via Prirechniy, a longer drive involving a rough, unpaved section.

Poland

BUS

There are two daily buses between both Gdansk and Oltshyn and Kaliningrad as well as daily buses to/from Warsaw; see p273.

CAR & MOTORCYCLE

The main border crossing to/from Kaliningrad is at Bezledy/Bagrationovsk on the A195 highway. Queues here can be very long.

TRAIN

Warsaw is connected with Moscow (from ₽5400, 17–18 hours, two daily). The Moscow trains enter Belarus near Brest, so you'll need a Belarus visa or transit visa.

United Kingdom & Western Europe

Travelling overland by train from the UK or Western Europe takes a minimum of two days and nights.

There are no direct trains from the UK to Russia. The cheapest route you can take is on the **Eurostar** (www.eurostar.com) to Brussels, and then via Cologne and Warsaw to Moscow, a journey that also passes through Minsk (Belarus). The total cost can be as low as £207 one way. See www.seat61.com/Russia.htm for details of this and other train services to Moscow.

Crossing the Poland–Belarus border at Brest takes several hours while the wheels are changed for the Russian track. All foreigners visiting Belarus need a visa, including those transiting by train – sort this out before arriving in Belarus. To avoid this hassle consider taking the train to St Petersburg from Vilnius in Lithuania, which runs several times a week via Latvia. There are daily connections between Vilnius and Warsaw.

From Moscow and St Petersburg there are also regular international services to European cities including Amsterdam, Berlin, Budapest, Nice, Paris, Prague and Vienna.

For European rail timetables check www.railfaneurope.net, which has links to all of Europe's national railways.

Ukraine

At the time of writing parts of southeastern Ukraine were dangerously volatile – most border crossings are closed and transportation services to and from Russia suspended in this region.

BUS

A handful of weekly buses travel from Kharkiv across the border into Russia on the E95 (M2) road. The official frontier crossing is 40km north of Kharkiv and is near the Russian border town of Zhuravlevka. Check the security situation carefully before arranging to cross into or out of Russia on this route.

CAR & MOTORCYCLE

The main auto route between Kyiv and Moscow starts as the E93 (M20) north of Kyiv, but becomes the M3 when it branches off to the east some 50km south of Chernihiv. At the time of writing this was the main safe border crossing for vehicles between Ukraine and Russia.

TRAIN

Trains from Kyiv to Moscow cross at the Ukrainian border town of Seredyna-Buda. Trains on this route are as follows (specific numbers are for the best southbound/northbound services):

Moscow–Kyiv *firmeny* (premium class) ₽4200, 9½ hours, daily, 1/2

Moscow–Kyiv ₽3700, 12–14 hours, nine daily

Moscow–Lviv ₽5000, 23 hours, two daily via Kyiv

Moscow–Odesa ₽5200, 23 hours, daily via Kyiv, 23/24

St Petersburg–Kyiv ₽6500, 22 hours, 30 minutes, one daily, 53/54

St Petersburg–Lviv ₽7000, 37½ hours, daily, 47/48

St Petersburg–Odesa ₽7300, 35 hours, one daily, 19/20

There are also many trains on the Moscow–Kharkiv line,

all of which pass through Kharkiv (from ₽3800, 12 hours) and proceed to southern Ukrainian destinations such as Donetsk (from ₽4670; 18 hours). While the situation in southeastern Ukraine and Crimea remains unstable it's advisable to make enquiries about safety before proceeding into or out of the country in this direction.

Sea

Passenger ferries:

- Batumi (Georgia) to Sochi
- Donghae (Korea) to Vladivostok
- Helsinki (Finland) to St Petersburg
- Lappeenranta (Finland) to Vyborg
- Sakaiminato (Japan) to Vladivostok
- Stockholm (Sweden) to St Petersburg
- Tallinn (Estonia) to St Petersburg
- Trabzon (Turkey) to Sochi
- Wakkanai (Japan) to Korsakov on Sakhalin

Tours

Trips to Moscow and St Petersburg are easily organised on your own. But for more complex itineraries, having an agency assist in booking transport and accommodation, securing guides and helping with the visa paperwork is a good idea. For many outdoor activities, such as hiking or rafting, the services of an expert agency or guide are almost always required. Or you may choose to go the whole hog and have everything taken care of on a fully organised tour.

Agencies and tour companies can provide a range of travel services; most can help arrange visas and transport tickets within Russia. Numerous, more locally based agencies can provide tours once you're in Russia. Many work in conjunction with overseas agencies, so if you go to them directly you'll usually pay less.

Australia

Eastern Europe/Russian Travel Centre (☎02-9262 1144; www.eetbtravel.com)

Passport Travel (☎03-9500 0444; www.travelcentre.com.au)

Russian Gateway Tours (☎02-9745 3333; www.russian-gateway.com.au)

Sundowners (☎1300 133 457; www.sundownersoverland.com) Specialises in trans-Siberian packages and tours.

Travel Directors (☎08-9242 4200; www.travel-directors.com.au) Upmarket trans-Siberian and Russian river-cruise tour operator.

China

Monkey Business (☎8610-6591 6519; www.monkeyshrine.com) Tours on the trans-Siberian, trans-Manchurian and trans-Mongolian trains. Its Hong Kong branch is Moonsky Star Ltd (☎852-2723 1376).

Germany

Lernidee Reisen (☎030-786 0000; www.lernidee-reisen.de)

Japan

MO Tourist CIS Russian Centre (☎03-3432 7239; www.mo-tourist.co.jp) Can help arrange ferries and flights to Russia.

United Kingdom

Go Russia (☎020-3355 7717; www.justgorussia.co.uk) Cultural and adventure holiday specialist.

GW Travel Ltd (☎0161-928 9410; www.goldeneagle-luxurytrains.com) Offers luxury trans-Siberian tours on the Golden Eagle.

Into Russia (☎0844-875 4026; www.into-russia.co.uk)

Real Russia (☎020-7100 7370; www.realrussia.co.uk)

Regent Holidays (☎020-7666 1244; www.regent-holidays.co.uk)

Russia Experience (☎0845-521 2910; www.trans-siberian.co.uk) Experienced and reliable operator that has adventurous programs across the country.

Russia House (☎020-7403 9922; www.therussiahouse.co.uk) Agency experienced at dealing with corporate and business travel needs.

Russian National Tourist Office (☎020-985 1234; www.visitrussia.org.uk) Offers tours across the country.

United States of America

Exeter International (☎813-251 5355; www.exeter-international.com) Specialises in luxury tours to Moscow and St Petersburg.

Go To Russia Travel (☎404-827 0099; www.gotorussia.com) Has offices in Atlanta, San Francisco and Moscow; offers tours and a full range of travel services.

Mir Corporation (☎206-624 7289; www.mircorp.com) Award-winning operation with many different tours.

Ouzel Expeditions (☎907-783 2216; www.ouzel.com) Specialises in Kamchatka fishing trips.

Sokol Tours (☎724-935 5373; www.sokoltours.com) Tour options include train trips, Tuva and Kamchatka.

VisitRussia (☎1886-787 7420; www.visitrussia.com) Can arrange package and customised tours; offices in New York, Moscow and St Petersburg.

GETTING AROUND

Getting around Russia is a breeze thanks to a splendid train network and a packed schedule of flights between all major and many minor towns and cities. In the summer months many rivers and lakes are navigable and have cruises and ferry operations. For hops between towns there are buses, most often *marshrutky* (fixed-route minibuses).

Don't underestimate the distances involved: Russia is huge. From Yekaterinburg at the western limits of Siberia to Vladivostok on the Pacific coast is about the same distance as from Berlin to New York, while even a relatively short overland hop, such as the one from Irkutsk to its near neighbour Khabarovsk, is still roughly equivalent to the distance from London to Cairo.

Air

Major Russian airlines, including **Aeroflot** (www.aeroflot.com), **Rossiya** (www.rossiya-airlines.com), **S7** (www.s7.ru), **Sky Express** (www.skyexpress.ru/en), **Transaero** (www.transaero.com) and **UTAir** (www.utair.ru) have online booking, with the usual discounts for advance purchases. Otherwise, it's no problem buying a ticket at ubiquitous *aviakassa* (ticket offices), which may be able to tell you about flights that you can't easily find out about online overseas. Online agencies specialising in Russian air tickets with English interfaces include **Anywayanyday** (☎495-363 6164; www.anywayanyday.com) and **Pososhok.ru** (☎495-234 8000; www.pososhok.ru).

Whenever you book airline tickets in Russia you'll need to show your passport and visa. Tickets can also be purchased at the airport right up to the departure of the flight and sometimes even if the city-centre office says that the plane is full. Return fares are usually double the one-way fares.

It's a good idea to reconfirm your flight at least 24 hours before take-off, and check on the day of departure too as flights can be delayed, often for hours and with no or little explanation.

Airlines may bump you if you don't check in at least 60 minutes before departure and can be very strict about charging for checked bags that are overweight, which generally means anything over 20kg.

Have your passport and ticket handy throughout the various security and ticket checks that can occur, right up until you find a seat. Some flights have assigned seats, others do not. On the latter, seating is a free-for-all.

Most internal flights in Moscow use either Domodedovo or Vnukovo airports; if you're connecting to Moscow's Sheremetyevo international airport, allow a few hours to cross town. Small town airports offer facilities similar to the average bus shelter.

Boat

One of the most pleasant ways of travelling around Russia is by river. You can do this either by taking a

AIRLINE SAFETY IN RUSSIA

Deadly lapses in Russian airline safety are frighteningly common. A string of accidents involving Tupolevs – including one near Smolensk (April 2010) which killed 96 people, including the Polish president, and near Petrozavodsk (June 2011) which killed 44 – has raised particular concerns about the continued use of these vintage planes. Then there was the November 2013 crash of a Boeing 737 Tatarstan Airlines flight at Kazan, which killed all 50 people on board.

If you're worried about airline safety, the good news is that for many destinations in Russia, getting there by train or bus is practical and often preferable (if you have the time). But in some cases – where you're short of time or where your intended destination doesn't have reliable rail or road connections – you will have no choice but to take a flight.

Industry experts recommend taking the following factors into account when deciding whether an airline is safe to fly with in Russia:

- Where there's a choice stick to airlines that are member of the International Air Transport Association; these include Aeroflot, Transaero, S7 and UTAir.
- A Class 1 Russian airport, which has more than seven million passengers per year, is much more likely to be safe to fly in and out of than a Class 5 airport, which serves less than 100,000 passengers a year.
- Fly an airline with regularly scheduled flights, not a charter. The accident rate for charter flights is about three times higher than for regular flights.
- Fly off season. Accidents in Russia tend to peak in busy travel season, when pilots and ground crews are more likely to be overworked and excessively tired.
- Check http://aviation-safety.net or http:// airport.airlines-inform.ru to see the number of accidents and incidents at an airport and read traveller reviews.

cruise, which you can book directly with an operator or also through agencies in Russia and overseas, or by using scheduled river passenger services. The season runs from late May through mid-October, but is shorter on some routes.

Moscow, St Petersburg & the Volga

There are numerous cruise boats plying the routes between Moscow and St Petersburg, many stopping at some of the Golden Ring cities on the way. Longer cruises to Northern European Russia and south along the Volga also originate in either of these cities. Some cruises are specifically aimed at foreign tourists.

Generally, for lower prices you can also sail on a boat aimed at Russian holidaymakers; note that it was one of these cruises that sank on the Volga near Kazan in July 2011, drowning over 120 people. Other boat operators and agencies:

Cruise Company Orthodox (499-943 8560; www.cruise.ru) Offices in Moscow and Rostov-on-Don.

Infoflot (921-341 5282; www.infoflot.com) The market leader, with offices in Moscow, St Petersburg, Samara, Nizhny Novgorod, Kazan and Rostov-on-Don.

Mosturflot (495-221 7222; www.mosturflot.ru)

Rechflot (495-981 4555; www.rechflot.ru)

Rechturflot (495-646 8700; www.rtflot.ru)

Solnechny Parus (812-327 3525; www.solpar.ru) St Petersburg agency with its own fleet of yachts and motorboats for charter.

Viking Rivers Cruises (0800-319 6660; www.vikingrivercruises.com)

Vodohod (495-223 9604; www.bestrussiancruises.com)

Northern European Russia

Northern European Russia (including St Petersburg) is well served by various waterborne transport options. Apart from hydrofoil services along the Neva River and the Gulf of Finland from St Petersburg to Petrodvorets, there are also very popular cruises from St Petersburg to Valaam in Lake Ladoga, some continuing on to Lake Onega, Petrozavodsk and Kizhi. Also, from Rabocheostrovsk you can take boats to the Solovetsky Islands.

Black Sea

Between June and September frequent hydrofoils connect the Black Sea ports of Novorossiysk and Sochi.

Siberia & the Russian Far East

Siberia and the Russian Far East have a short navigation season (mid-June to September), with long-distance river transport limited to the Ob and Irtysh Rivers (Omsk–Tara–Tobolsk–Salekhard), the Lena (Ust-Kut–Lensk–Yakutsk) and the Yenisey (Krasnoyarsk–Yeniseysk–Igarka–Dudinka). You can also make one-day hops by hydrofoil along several sections of these rivers, along the Amur River (Komsomolsk–Nikolaevsk) and across Lake Baikal (Irkutsk–Olkhon–Severobaikalsk–Nizhneangarsk). Other Baikal services are limited to short hops around Irkutsk/Listvyanka and from Sakhyurta to Olkhon unless you charter a boat, most conveniently done in Listvyanka, Nizhneangarsk, Severobaikalsk or Ust-Barguzin. Irkutsk agencies can help.

Ferries from Vanino cross the Tatar Strait to Sakhalin, but it can be murder trying to buy a ticket in the sum-

USEFUL RUSSIAN TERMS FOR BOAT TRAVEL

When buying tickets for a hydrofoil, avoid *ryad* (rows) one to three – spray will obscure your view, and, although enclosed, you'll often get damp.

речной вокзал	*rechnoy vokzal*	river station
ракета, комета, заря	*raketa, kometa, zarya*	river-going hydrofoil
метеор	*meteor*	sea-going hydrofoil
теплоход	*teplokhod*	large passenger boat
катер	*kater*	smaller river or sea boat
корабль	*korabl*	generic word for large ship
лодка	*lodka*	small rowing boat
паром	*parom*	ferry
вверх	*vverkh*	upstream
вниз	*vniz*	downstream
туда	*tuda*	one way
туда и обратно	*tuda i obratno*	return

mer months. Although sailings are supposed to take place daily, in reality there is no set schedule. There are also irregular sailings from Korsakov, on Sakhalin, across to Yuzhno-Kurilsk in the Kuril Island chain (and you'll need a permit for the visiting the Kurils to make this voyage).

Out of Vladivostok there is a range of ferries to nearby islands and to beach resorts further south along the coast. For the truly adventurous with a month or so to spare, it may be possible to hitch a lift on one of the supply ships that sail out of Nakhodka and Vladivostok up to the Arctic Circle towns of Anadyr and Provideniya.

Beware that boat schedules can change radically from year to year (especially on Lake Baikal) and are only published infuriatingly near to the first sailing of each season.

Bus & Marshrutky

Long-distance buses tend to complement rather than compete with the rail network. They generally serve areas with no railway or routes on which trains are slow, infrequent or overloaded.

Most cities have an intercity *avtovokzal* (автовокзал, bus station). Tickets are sold at the station or on the bus. Fares are normally listed on the timetable and posted on a wall. As often as not you'll get a ticket with a seat assignment, either printed or scribbled on a till receipt. If you have luggage that needs to be stored in the bus baggage compartment then you'll have to pay an extra fare, typically around 10% of the bus fare. Some bus stations may also apply a small fee for security measures.

Marshrutky (a Russian diminutive form of *marshrutnoye taksi*, meaning a fixed-route taxi) are minibuses that are sometimes quicker than larger buses and rarely cost much more. Where roads are good and villages frequent, *marshrutky* can be twice as fast as buses and are well worth paying extra for.

Car & Motorcycle

Bearing in mind erratic road quality, lack of adequate signposting, fine-seeking highway police and, in remote areas, the difficulty of obtaining petrol (not to mention spare parts), driving in Russia can be a challenge. But if you've a sense of humour, patience and a decent vehicle, it's an adventurous way to go.

Motorbikes will undergo vigorous scrutiny by border officials and highway police, especially if you're riding anything vaguely flashy. Motorcyclists should also note that while foreign automobile companies now have an established presence in Moscow, St Petersburg and other major cities, you shouldn't count on being able to access any necessary spare parts across the country. A useful general site for motorcyclists, with some information on Russian road conditions, is www.horizons-unlimited.com; for car drivers also see http://expat.ru/s_driving.php.

Bringing Your Own Vehicle

You'll need the following if bringing in your own vehicle:

- your licence
- the vehicle's registration papers
- third-party insurance valid in Russia
- a customs declaration promising that you will take your vehicle with you when you leave.

To minimise hassles, make sure you have all your documents translated into Russian. For more details see www.waytorussia.net/Transport/International/Car.html.

Driving Licence

To legally drive your own or a rented car or motorcycle in Russia you'll need the following:

- to be over 18 years of age
- have a full driving licence
- have an International Driving Permit with a Russian translation of your licence, or a certified Russian translation of your full licence (you can certify translations at a Russian embassy or consulate).

Fuel & Spare Parts

Western-style petrol (gas) stations are common. Petrol comes in four main grades and ranges from ₽25 to ₽30 per litre. Unleaded petrol is available in major cities. *Dizel* (diesel) is also available (around ₽26 a litre). In the countryside, petrol stations are usually not more than 100km apart, but you shouldn't rely on this.

Rental & Hire Cars

Self-drive cars can be rented in all major Russian cities. Depending on where you're going, consider renting a car with a driver – they will at least know the state of local roads and be able to negotiate with traffic police should you be stopped.

Private cars sometimes operate as cabs over long distances and can be a great deal if there's a group of you to share the cost. Since they take the most direct route between cities, the savings in time can be considerable over slow trains and meandering buses. Typically you will find drivers offering this service outside bus terminals. Someone in your party must speak Russian to negotiate a price with the driver.

Select your driver carefully, look over their car and try to assess their sobriety before setting off. Note that you'll always have to pay return mileage if renting 'one way' and that many local drivers want to get home the same night, even if that's at 3am.

Road Conditions

Russian roads are a mixed bag – sometimes smooth, straight dual carriageways, sometimes pot-holed, narrow, winding and choked with the diesel fumes of slow, heavy vehicles. Driving much more than 300km in a day is pretty tiring.

Russian drivers use indicators far less than they should and like to overtake everything on the road – on the inside. They rarely switch on anything more than sidelights – and often not even those – until it's pitch black at night. Some say this is to avoid dazzling others, as, for some reason, dipping headlights is not common practice.

If an oncoming driver is flashing his headlights at you, this usually means to watch out for traffic police ahead.

Road Rules

- Drive on the right.
- Traffic coming from the right generally (but not always) has the right of way.
- Speed limits are generally 60km/h in towns and between 80km/h and 110km/h on highways.
- There may be a 90km/h zone, enforced by speed traps, as you leave a city.
- Children under 12 may not travel in the front seat; seatbelt use is mandatory.
- Motorcycle riders (and passengers) must wear crash helmets.
- The maximum legal blood-alcohol content is 0.03%, a rule that is strictly enforced. Police will first use a breathalyser test to check blood-alcohol levels. You have the legal right to insist on a blood test (which involves the police taking you to a hospital).
- Traffic lights that flicker green are about to change to yellow, then red. You will be pulled over if the police see you going through a yellow light, so drive cautiously.

The GIBDD

Russia's traffic police are officially called the GIBDD (ГИБДД, standing for Государственная инспекция безопасности дорожного движения; www.gibdd.ru) but still commonly known by its previous acronym: the GAI. The traffic cops are authorised to stop you, issue on-the-spot fines and, worst of all, shoot at your car if you refuse to pull over.

The GIBDD are notorious for hosting speed traps and finding way to stop cars and collect 'fines' on the spot. Russian drivers often mount dashboard cameras in their cars to record what is going on, in a bid to stop corrupt police faking evidence or unfairly prosecuting them – you might want to do likewise!

There are permanent police checkpoints at the boundary of many Russian regions, cities and towns – make sure your car is clean and in good condition to avoid being pulled over. For serious infractions, the GIBDD can confiscate your licence, which you'll have to retrieve from the main station. If your car is taken to a police parking lot, you should try to get it back as soon as possible, since you'll be charged a huge amount for each day that it's kept there.

Get the shield number of the arresting officer. By law, GIBDD officers are not allowed to take any money at all – fines should be paid via Sberbank. However, in reality Russian drivers normally pay the police approximately half the official fine, thus saving money and the time eaten up by Russian bureaucracy, both at the police station and the bank.

Hitching

Hitching is never entirely safe and Lonely Planet doesn't recommend it. Travellers who hitch should understand that they are taking a small but potentially serious risk.

That said, hitching in Russia is a common method of getting around, particularly in the countryside and remote areas not well served by public transport. In cities, hitching rides is called hailing a taxi.

Rides are hailed by standing at the side of the road and flagging passing vehicles with a low, up-and-down wave (not an extended thumb). You are expected to pitch in for petrol; paying what would be the normal bus fare for a long-haul ride is considered appropriate.

Use common sense to keep safe. Avoid hitching at night. Women should exercise extreme caution. Avoid hitching alone and let someone know where you are planning to go.

Local Transport

Most cities have good public-transport systems combining bus, trolleybus and tram; the biggest cities also have metro systems. Public transport is very cheap and easy to use, but you'll need to be able to decipher some Cyrillic. Taxis are plentiful.

Boat

In St Petersburg, Moscow and several other cities located on rivers, coasts, lakes or reservoirs, public ferries and water excursions give a different perspective.

Bus, Marshrutky, Trolleybus & Tram

Services are frequent in city centres but more erratic as you move out towards the edges. They can get jam-packed in the late afternoon or on poorly served routes.

A stop is usually marked by a roadside 'A' sign for buses, 'T' for trolleybuses, and ТРАМВАЙ or a 'T' hanging over the road for trams. The fare (₽10 to ₽20) is usually paid to the conductor; if there is no conductor, pass the money to the driver. You will be charged extra if you have a large bag that takes up space.

Within most cities, *marshrutky* double up official bus routes but are more frequent. They will also stop between official bus stops, which can save quite a walk.

Metro

The metro systems of Moscow and St Petersburg are excellent. There are smaller ones in Kazan, Nizhny Novgorod, Novosibirsk, Samara, Vologda and Yekaterinburg.

Taxi

There are two main types of taxi in Russia: the official ones you order by phone and 'private' taxis (ie any other vehicle on the road).

Check with locals to determine the average taxi fare in that city at the time of your visit; taxi prices around the country vary widely. Practice saying your destination and the amount you want to pay so that it comes out properly. The better your Russian, the lower the fare (generally). If possible, let a Russian friend negotiate for you: they'll do better than you will.

OFFICIAL TAXIS

Official taxis have a meter that they sometimes use, though you can always negotiate an off-the-meter price. There's a flag fall, and the number on the meter must be multiplied by the multiplier listed on a sign that *should* be on the dashboard or somewhere visible. Extra charges are incurred for radio calls and some night-time calls. Taxis outside of luxury hotels often demand usurious rates although, on the whole, official taxis are around 25% more expensive than private taxis.

PRIVATE TAXIS

To hail a private taxi, stand at the side of the road, extend your arm and wait until something stops. When someone stops for you, state your destination and be prepared to negotiate the fare – fix this before getting in. If the driver's game, they'll ask you to get in *(sadites)*. Consider your safety before doing this.

RISKS & PRECAUTIONS

- Avoid taxis lurking outside foreign-run establishments, luxury hotels, railway stations and airports – they often charge far too much.
- Know your route: be familiar with how to get there and how long it should take.
- Never get into a taxi that has more than one person already in it, especially after dark.
- Keep your fare money in a separate pocket to avoid flashing large wads of cash.
- If you're staying at a private residence, have the taxi stop at the corner nearest your destination, not the exact address.
- Trust your instincts – if a driver looks creepy, take the next car.

Tours

Once in Russia, you'll find many travel agencies specialising in city tours and excursions. Sometimes these are the best way to visit out-of-the-way sights.

Trains

The trains of **Russian Railways** (RZD, РЖД; http://rzd.ru) are generally comfortable and, depending on the class of travel, relatively inexpensive for the distances covered. Every train in Russia has two numbers – one for the eastbound train (even-numbered trains) and one for the westbound (odd-numbered trains).

A handful of high-speed services aside, trains are rarely speedy but have a remarkable record for punctuality – if you're a minute late for your train, the chances are you'll be left standing on the platform. The fact that RZD managers have a large portion of their pay determined by the timeliness of their trains not only inspires promptness, but also results in the creation of generous schedules. You'll notice this when you find your train stationary for hours in the middle of nowhere only to suddenly start up and roll into the next station right on time.

Buying Tickets

There are a number of options on where to buy, including online from RZD. Bookings open 45 days before the date of departure. You'd be wise to buy well in advance over the busy summer months and holiday periods such as New Year and early May, when securing berths at short notice on certain trains can be difficult. Tickets for key trains on the busy Moscow–St Petersburg route can also be difficult to come by; keep your options flexible and you should be able to find something.

Even if you're told a particular service is sold out, it still may be possible to get on the train by speaking with the chief *provodnitsa* (carriage attendant). Tell her your destination, offer the face ticket price first and move slowly upwards from there. You can usually come to some sort of agreement.

AT THE STATION

You'll be confronted by several ticket windows. Some are special windows reserved exclusively for use by the elderly or infirm, heroes of the Great Patriotic War or members of the armed forces. All will have different operating hours and generally non-English-speaking staff.

READING A TRAIN TIMETABLE

Russian train timetables vary from place to place but generally list a destination; number and category of train; frequency of service; and time of departure and arrival, in Moscow time unless otherwise noted. For services that originate somewhere else, you'll see a starting point and the final destination on the timetable. For example, when catching a train from Yekaterinburg to Irkutsk, the timetable may list Moscow as the point of origin and Irkutsk as the destination. The following are the key points to look out for.

Number

- Номер *(nomer)* The higher the number of a train, the slower it is; anything over 900 is likely to be a mail train.

Category

- Скорый (*Skory*, fast trains)
- Пассажирский (*Passazhirsky*, passenger trains)
- Почтово – багажный (*Pochtovo-bagazhny*, post-cargo trains)
- Пригородный (*Prigorodny*, suburban trains)

There may also be the name of the train, usually in quotation marks, eg 'Россия' ('Rossiya').

Frequency

- ежедневно (*yezhednevno*, daily; abbreviated еж)
- чётные (*chyotnye*, even-numbered dates; abbreviated ч)
- нечётные (*nechyotnye*, odd-numbered dates; abbreviated не)
- отменён (*otmenyon*, cancelled; abbreviated отмен)

Days of the week are listed usually as numbers (where 1 is Monday and 7 Sunday) or as abbreviations of the name of the day (Пон, Вт, Ср, Чт, Пт, С and Вск are, respectively, Monday to Sunday). Remember that time-zone differences can affect these days. So in Chita (Moscow +6hr) a train timetabled at 23.20 on Tuesday actually leaves 5.20am on Wednes-

The sensible option, especially if there are long queues, is to avail yourself of the service centre (сервис центр) found at most major stations. Here you'll encounter helpful staff who, for a small fee (typically around ₽200), can book your ticket. They sometimes speak English.

Tickets for suburban trains are often sold at separate windows or from an automatic ticket machine (автомат). A table beside the machine tells you which price zone your destination is in.

AT TRAVEL AGENCIES & TICKET BUREAUX

In big cities and towns it's possible to buy tickets at special offices and some travel agencies away from the station.

ONLINE

You can buy tickets online directly from RZD. During the booking process, when asked to fill in 'Document Type' you should pick 'Foreign document' and then enter your passport number. RZD has two types of electronic tickets:

- **e-tickets** – these are coupons detailing your your 14-digit order and 14-digit e-ticket numbers. Print them out and exchange for paper tickets at stations in Russia. Some stations have dedicated exchange points and/or self-service terminals; at all others you go to the regular booking windows.
- **e-registration** – only available for trains where you board at the initial station of the service, these are 'paperless' tickets; you'll still be sent an email confirmation but there's no need to exchange this for a regular ticket. You show the confirmation email and your passport to the *provodnitsa* on boarding the train. Note when booking these trains on RZD's site, when asked to fill in 'Document Type' you should pick 'Foreign document' and then enter your passport number.

Other online travel sites also allow you to book tickets and have the ticket delivered to your home or hotel, or pick it up at an agency or at the train station.

Long Distances

The regular long-distance service is a *skory poezd*

day. In months with an odd number of days, two odd days follow one another (eg 31 May, 1 June). This throws out trains working on an alternate-day cycle so if travelling near month's end pay special attention to the hard-to-decipher footnotes on a timetable. For example, '27/V – 3/VI ч' means that from 27 May to 3 June the train runs on even dates. On some trains, frequency depends on the time of year, in which case details are usually given in similar abbreviated small print: eg '27/VI – 31/VIII ч; 1/IX – 25/VI 2, 5' means that from 27 June to 31 August the train runs on even dates, while from 1 September to 25 June it runs on Tuesday and Friday.

Arrival & Departure Times

Corresponding trains running in opposite directions on the same route may appear on the same line of the timetable. In this case you may find route entries like время отправления с конечного пункта *(vremya otpravlenia s konechnogo punkta),* or the time the return train leaves its station of origin. Train times are given in a 24-hour time format, and almost always in Moscow time (Московское время, *Moskovskoye vremya*). But suburban trains are usually marked in local time (местное время, *mestnoe vremya*). From here on it gets tricky (as though the rest wasn't), so don't confuse the following:

- время отправления *(vremya otpravleniya)* Time of departure
- время отправления с начального пункта *(vremya otpravleniya s nachalnogo punkta)* Time of departure from the train's starting point
- время прибытия *(vremya pribytiya)* Time of arrival at the station you're in
- время прибытия на конечный пункт *(vremya pribytiya v konechny punkt)* Time of arrival at the destination
- время в пути *(vremya v puti)* Duration of the journey

Distance

You may sometimes see the расстояние *(rastoyaniye)* – distance in kilometres from the point of departure – on the timetable as well. These are rarely accurate and usually refer to the kilometre distance used to calculate the fare.

(fast train). It rarely gets up enough speed to really merit the 'fast' label. The best *skory* trains often have names, eg the Rossiya (the Moscow to Vladivostok service). These *firmeny poezda* (name trains), generally have cleaner cars and more convenient arrival and departure hours; they sometimes also have fewer stops, more first-class accommodation and restaurant cars.

A *passazhirsky poezd* (passenger train) is an intercity train, found mostly on routes of 1000km or less. Journeys on these can take longer, as the trains clank from one small town to the next. However, they are inexpensive and often well timed to allow an overnight sleep between neighbouring cities. Avoid trains numbered over 900. These are primarily baggage or postal services and are appallingly slow.

Short Distances

A *prigorodny poezd* (suburban train), commonly nicknamed an *elektrichka,* is a local service linking a city with its suburbs or nearby towns, or groups of adjacent towns; they are often useful for day trips, but can be fearfully crowded. There's no need to book ahead for these – just buy your ticket and go. In bigger stations there may be separate timetables, in addition to *prigorodny zal* (the usual name for ticket halls) and platforms for these trains.

Timetables

Timetables are posted in stations and are revised twice a year. It's vital to note that the whole Russian rail network runs mostly on Moscow time, so timetables and station clocks from Kaliningrad to Vladivostok will be written in and set to Moscow time. Suburban rail services are the only general exception, which are usually listed in local time; it's best to check this.

Most stations have an information window; expect the attendant to speak only Russian and to give a bare minimum of information. Bigger stations will also have computerised terminals where you can check the timetable.

HOW TO BUY & READ YOUR TICKET

When buying a ticket in Russia, it's a good idea to arrive at the station or travel agency prepared. If you don't speak Russian, have someone who does write down the following information for you in Cyrillic:

- How many tickets you require.
- Your destination.
- What class of ticket.
- The preferred date of travel and time of day for departure. Use ordinary (Arabic) numerals for the day and Roman numerals for the month.

Departure time
Always in Moscow time

Train number
The lower the number, the higher the standard and the price; the best trains are under 100. Odd-numbered trains head towards Moscow; even ones head east, away from the capital.

Train type

Carriage number and class
Л = two-bed SV
М = four-bed SV
К = *kupe*
П = *platskartny*
О = *obshchiy*

Departure date
Day and month

From/to

Bed number
If this is blank, the provodnitsa will allocate a bed on boarding

Passport number
With two-digit prefix for passport type and name of passenger

Total cost of ticket

Service charges
eg с бельём (with bed linen)

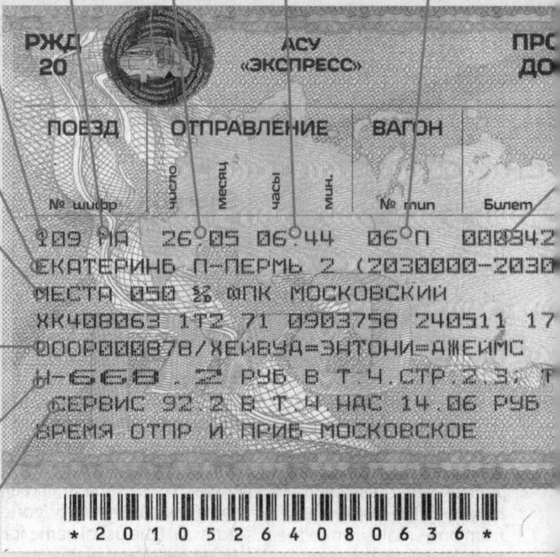
РЖД
20
АСУ «ЭКСПРЕСС»
ПОЕЗД
ОТПРАВЛЕНИЕ
ВАГОН
№ шифр
число
месяц
часы
мин.
№ тип
Билет
109 МА 26.05 06.44 06 П 000342
ЕКАТЕРИНБ П-ПЕРМЬ 2 (2030000-2030
МЕСТА 050 % ФПК МОСКОВСКИЙ
ХК408063 1Т2 71 0903758 240511 17
000Р000878/ХЕЙВУД=ЭНТОНИ=ДЖЕЙМС
И-668.2 РУБ В Т.Ч.СТР.2.3;
СЕРВИС 92.2 В Т.Ч.НАС 14.06 РУБ
ВРЕМЯ ОТПР И ПРИБ МОСКОВСКОЕ
* 2 0 1 0 5 2 6 4 0 8 0 6 3 6 *

Also bring your passport; you'll be asked for it so that its number and your name can be printed on your ticket. The ticket and passport will be matched up by the *provodnitsa* (female carriage attendant) before you're allowed on the train – make sure the ticket-seller gets these details correct.

Tickets are printed by computer and come with a duplicate. Shortly after you've boarded the train the *provodnitsa* will come around and collect the tickets: sometimes they will take both copies and give you one back just before your final destination; often they will leave you with the copy. It will have been ripped slightly to show it's been used. Hang on to this ticket, especially if you're hopping on and off trains, since it provides evidence of how long you've been in a particular place if you're stopped by police.

Sometimes tickets are also sold with separate chits for insurance in the event of a fatal accident, or for bed linen and meals, but usually these prices appear on the ticket itself. The following is a guide for deciphering your Russian train ticket.

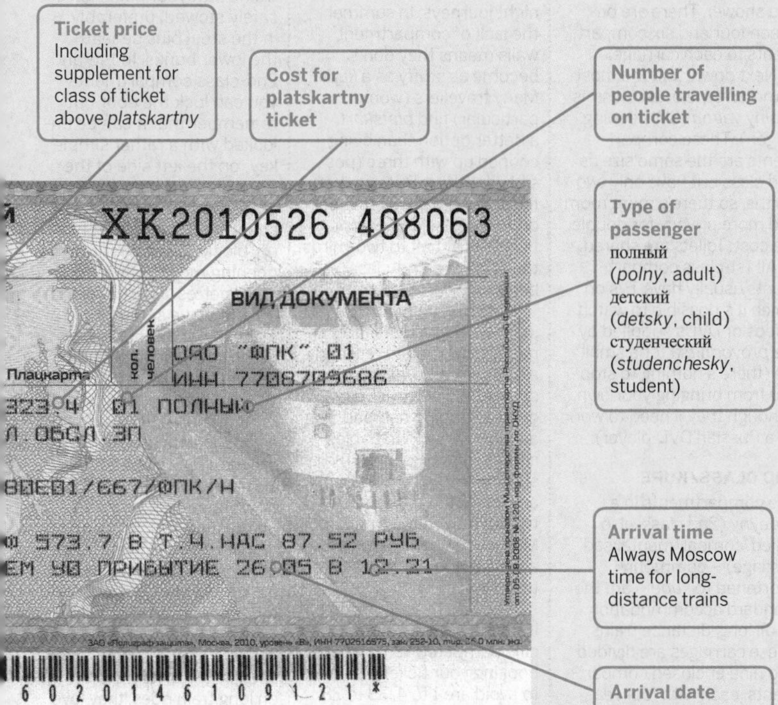

Online timetables are available on RZD's website (http://rzd.ru) and www.poezda.net.

Classes

In all classes of carriage with sleeping accommodation, if you've not already paid for a pack of bed linen and face towels (called *pastil*) in your ticket price, the *provodnik/provodnitsa* will offer it to you for a small charge, typically around ₽110. In 1st class the bed is usually made up already.

1ST CLASS – MYAGKY & SPALNY VAGON

The very top class (*myagky* – soft class – or *lyux*), only available on certain premium long-distance services, offers a compartment sleeping up to two with an attached toilet and shower. There are between four and six compartments to each carriage.

Next down, and the most common type of 1st class, is *spalny vagon* (SV, sleeping wagon). These compartments are the same size as 2nd class but have only two berths, so there's more room and more privacy for double the cost. Toilets are shared.

All 1st-class compartments usually have TVs on which it's possible to watch videos or DVDs supplied by the *provodnitsa* for a small fee (there's nothing to stop you from bringing your own, although they'll need to work on a Russian DVD player).

2ND CLASS/KUPE

The compartments in a *kupeyny* (2nd class, also called 'compartmentalised' carriage) – commonly shortened to *kupe* – are the standard accommodation on all long-distance trains. These carriages are divided into nine enclosed compartments, each with four reasonably comfortable berths, a fold-down table and just enough room between the bunks to turn around.

In every carriage there's also one half-sized compartment with just two berths. This is usually occupied by the *provodnitsa* or reserved for railway employees; it's where you may end up if you do a deal directly with a *provodnitsa* for a train ticket.

3RD CLASS/ PLATSKARTNY

A reserved-place *platskartny* carriage, sometimes also called *zhyostky* (hard class) and usually abbreviated to *platskart*, is a dorm carriage sleeping 54. The bunks are uncompartmentalised and are arranged in blocks of four down one side of the corridor and in twos on the other, with the lower bunk on the latter side converting to a table and chairs during the day.

Despite the lack of privacy, *platskart* is a deal for one-night journeys. In summer the lack of compartment walls means they don't become as stuffy as a *kupe*. Many travellers (women in particular) find *platskart* a better option than being cooped up with three (possibly drunken) Russian men. It's also a great way to meet ordinary Russians. *Platskart* tickets cost half to two-thirds the price of a 2nd-class berth.

However, on multiday journeys some *platskart* carriages can begin to resemble a refugee camp, with clothing strung between bunks, a great swapping of bread, fish and jars of tea, and babies sitting on potties while their snot-nosed siblings tear up and down the corridor. Only the hardy would want to do Moscow to Vladivostok or a similar nonstop journey this way.

If you do travel *platskart*, it's worth requesting specific numbered seats when booking your ticket. The ones to avoid are 1 to 4, 33 to 38, and 53 and 54, found at each end of the carriage close to the samovar and toilets, where people are constantly coming and going. Also note that 39 to 52 are the doubles with the bunk that converts to a table.

4TH CLASS/OBSHCHIY

Obshchiy (general) is unreserved. On long-distance trains the *obshchiy* carriage looks the same as a *platskartny* one but, when full, eight people are squeezed into each unenclosed compartment, so there's no room to lie down. Suburban trains normally have only *obshchiy* class, which in this case means bench-type seating. On a few daytime-only intercity trains there are higher grade *obshchiy* carriages with more comfortable, reserved chairs.

Dangers & Annoyances

Make certain on all sleeper trains that your baggage is safely stowed, preferably in the steel bins beneath the lower bunks. In 1st- and 2nd-class compartments you can lock the door but remember that it can be unlocked with a rather simple key; on the left side of the door, about three-quarters of the way up, there's a small steel switch that flips up, blocking the door from opening more than a few centimetres. Flip this switch up and make sure to stuff a piece of cork or equivalent in the cavity so it can't be flipped back down by a bent coat hanger.

At station halts it's also a good idea to ask the *provodnitsa* to lock your compartment while you go down to stretch your legs on the platform. In cheaper *platskartny* carriages your unguarded possessions are often safer as there are more people around to keep watch.

Generally, Russians love speaking with foreigners; on long train rides, they love drinking with them as well. Avoiding this is not always as easy as it would seem. Choose your drinking partners very carefully on trains and only drink from new bottles when you can watch the seal being broken.

Left Luggage

Many train stations have a left-luggage room (камера хранения, *kamera khranenia*) or left-luggage lockers (автоматические камеры хранения, *avtomaticheskiye kamery khranenia*). These are generally secure, but make sure you note down the room's opening and closing hours and, if in doubt, establish how long you can leave your stuff. Typical costs are around ₽120 per bag per day (according to size) or ₽120 per locker.

Here is how to work the left-luggage lockers (they're generally the same everywhere). Be suspicious of people who offer to help you work them, above all when it comes to selecting your combination.

➡ Put your stuff in an empty locker.

➡ Decide on a combination of one Russian letter and three numbers and write it down or remember it.

➡ Set the combination on the inside of the locker door.

➡ Close the locker.

➡ Pay the attendant the fee.

To open the locker, set your combination on the outside of your locker door. Note that even though it seems as if the knobs on the outside of the door should correspond directly with those on the inside, the letter is always the left-most knob, followed by three numbers, on both the inside and the outside. After you've set your combination, wait a second or two for the electrical humming sound and then pull open the locker.

Language

Russian belongs to the Slavonic language family and is closely related to Belarusian and Ukrainian. It has more than 150 million speakers within the Russian Federation and is used as a second language in the former republics of the USSR, with a total number of speakers of more than 270 million people.

Russian is written in the Cyrillic alphabet (see the next page), and it's well worth the effort familiarising yourself with it so that you can read maps, timetables, menus and street signs. Otherwise, just read the coloured pronunciation guides given next to each Russian phrase in this chapter as if they were English, and you'll be understood. Most sounds are the same as in English, and the few differences in pronunciation are explained in the alphabet table. The stressed syllables are indicated with italics.

BASICS

Hello.	Здравствуйте.	*zdrast*·vuy·tye
Goodbye.	До свидания.	da svi·*da*·nya
Excuse me.	Простите.	pras·*ti*·tye
Sorry.	Извините.	iz·vi·*ni*·tye
Please.	Пожалуйста.	pa·*zhal*·sta
Thank you.	Спасибо.	spa·*si*·ba
You're welcome.	Пожалуйста.	pa·*zhal*·sta
Yes./No.	Да./Нет.	da/nyet

WANT MORE?

For in-depth language information and handy phrases, check out Lonely Planet's *Russian Phrasebook*. You'll find it at **shop.lonelyplanet.com**, or you can buy Lonely Planet's iPhone phrasebooks at the Apple App Store.

How are you?	
Как дела?	kak di·*la*
Fine. And you?	
Хорошо. А у вас?	kha·ra·*sho* a u vas
What's your name?	
Как вас зовут?	kak vas za·*vut*
My name is ...	
Меня зовут ...	mi·*nya za*·vut ...
Do you speak English?	
Вы говорите по-английски?	vi ga·va·*ri*·tye pa·an·*gli*·ski
I don't understand.	
Я не понимаю.	ya nye pa·ni·*ma*·yu

ACCOMMODATION

Where's a ...?	Где ...?	gdye ...
boarding house	пансионат	pan·si·a·*nat*
campsite	кемпинг	*kyem*·ping
hotel	гостиница	ga·*sti*·ni·tsa
youth hostel	общежитие	ap·shi·*zhih*·ti·ye
Do you have a ... room?	У вас есть ...?	u vas yest' ...
single	одноместный номер	ad·na·*myest*·nih *no*·mir
double	номер с двуспальней кроватью	*no*·mir z dvu·*spal'*·nyey kra·*va*·tyu
How much is it for ...?	Сколько стоит за ...?	*skol'*·ka *sto*·it za ...
a night	ночь	noch'
two people	двоих	dva·*ikh*
The ... isn't working.	... не работает.	... ne ra·*bo*·ta·yit
heating	Отопление	a·ta·*plye*·ni·ye

hot water	Горячая вода	ga·*rya*·cha·ya va·*da*
light	Свет	svyet

DIRECTIONS

Where is ...?
Где ...? gdye ...

What's the address?
Какой адрес? ka·*koy* a·dris

Could you write it down, please?
Запишите, пожалуйста. za·pi·*shih*·tye pa·*zhal*·sta

Can you show me (on the map)?
Покажите мне, пожалуйста (на карте). pa·ka·*zhih*·tye mnye pa·*zhal*·sta (na *kar*·tye)

Turn ...	Поверните ...	pa·vir·*ni*·tye ...
at the corner	за угол	za *u*·gal
at the traffic lights	на светофоре	na svi·ta·*fo*·rye
left	налево	na·*lye*·va
right	направо	na·*pra*·va

behind ...	за ...	za ...
far	далеко	da·li·*ko*
in front of ...	перед ...	*pye*·rit ...
near	близко	*blis*·ka
next to ...	рядом с ...	*rya*·dam s ...
opposite ...	напротив ...	na·*pro*·tif ...
straight ahead	прямо	*prya*·ma

EATING & DRINKING

I'd like to reserve a table for ...	Я бы хотел/хотела заказать столик на ... (m/f)	ya bih khat·*yel*/khat·*ye*·la za·ka·*zat'* *sto*·lik na ...
two people	двоих	dva·*ikh*
eight o'clock	восемь часов	*vo*·sim' chi·*sof*

What would you recommend?
Что вы рекомендуете? shto vih ri·ka·min·*du*·it·ye

What's in that dish?
Что входит в это блюдо? shto *fkho*·dit v *e*·ta *blyu*·da

That was delicious!
Было очень вкусно! *bih*·la o·chin' *fkus*·na

Please bring the bill.
Принесите, пожалуйста счёт. pri·ni·*sit*·ye pa·*zhal*·sta shot

CYRILLIC ALPHABET

Cyrillic		Sound
А, а	a	as in 'father' (in a stressed syllable); as in 'ago' (in an unstressed syllable)
Б, б	b	as in 'but'
В, в	v	as in 'van'
Г, г	g	as in 'god'
Д, д	d	as in 'dog'
Е, е	ye	as in 'yet' (in a stressed syllable and at the end of a word);
	i	as in 'tin' (in an unstressed syllable)
Ё, ё	yo	as in 'yore' (often printed without dots)
Ж, ж	zh	as the 's' in 'measure'
З, з	z	as in 'zoo'
И, и	i	as the 'ee' in 'meet'
Й, й	y	as in 'boy' (not transliterated after **ы** or **и**)
К, к	k	as in 'kind'
Л, л	l	as in 'lamp'
М, м	m	as in 'mad'
Н, н	n	as in 'not'
О, о	o	as in 'more' (in a stressed syllable);
	a	as in 'hard' (in an unstressed syllable)
П, п	p	as in 'pig'
Р, р	r	as in 'rub' (rolled)
С, с	s	as in 'sing'
Т, т	t	as in 'ten'
У, у	u	as the 'oo' in 'fool'
Ф, ф	f	as in 'fan'
Х, х	kh	as the 'ch' in 'Bach'
Ц, ц	ts	as in 'bits'
Ч, ч	ch	as in 'chin'
Ш, ш	sh	as in 'shop'
Щ, щ	shch	as 'sh-ch' in 'fresh chips'
Ъ, ъ	–	'hard sign' meaning the preceding consonant is pronounced as it's written
Ы, ы	ih	as the 'y' in 'any'
Ь, ь	'	'soft sign' meaning the preceding consonant is pronounced like a faint y
Э, э	e	as in 'end'
Ю, ю	yu	as the 'u' in 'use'
Я, я	ya	as in 'yard' (in a stressed syllable);
	ye	as in 'yearn' (in an unstressed syllable)

I don't eat ...	Я не ем ...	ya nye yem ...
eggs	яиц	*ya*·its
fish	рыбы	*rih*·bih
poultry	птицы	*ptit*·sih
red meat	мяса	*mya*·sa

Signs

Вход	Entrance
Выход	Exit
Открыт	Open
Закрыт	Closed
Справки	Information
Запрещено	Prohibited
Туалет	Toilets
Мужской (М)	Men
Женский (Ж)	Women

Key Words

bottle	бутылка	bu·*tihl*·ka
bowl	миска	*mis*·ka
breakfast	завтрак	*zaf*·trak
cold	холодный	kha·*lod*·nih
dinner	ужин	*u*·zhihn
dish	блюдо	*blyu*·da
fork	вилка	*vil*·ka
glass	стакан	sta·*kan*
hot (warm)	жаркий	*zhar*·ki
knife	нож	nosh
lunch	обед	ab·*yet*
menu	меню	min·*yu*
plate	тарелка	tar·*yel*·ka
restaurant	ресторан	ris·ta·*ran*
spoon	ложка	*losh*·ka
with/without	с/без	s/byez

Meat & Fish

beef	говядина	gav·*ya*·di·na
caviar	икра	i·*kra*
chicken	курица	*ku*·rit·sa
duck	утка	*ut*·ka
fish	рыба	*rih*·ba
herring	сельдь	syelt'
lamb	баранина	ba·*ra*·ni·na
meat	мясо	*mya*·sa
oyster	устрица	*ust*·rit·sa
pork	свинина	svi·*ni*·na
prawn	креветка	kriv·*yet*·ka
salmon	лососина	la·sa·*si*·na
turkey	индейка	ind·*yey*·ka
veal	телятина	til·*ya*·ti·na

KEY PATTERNS

To get by in Russian, mix and match these simple patterns with words of your choice:

When's (the next bus)?	
Когда (будет следующий автобус)?	kag·*da* (*bu*·dit *slye*·du·yu·shi af·*to*·bus)
Where's (the station)?	
Где (станция)?	gdye (*stant*·sih·ya)
Where can I (buy a padlock)?	
Где можно (купить нависной замок)?	gdye *mozh*·na (ku·*pit'* na·vis·*noy* za·*mok*)
Do you have (a map)?	
Здесь есть (карте)?	zdyes' yest' (*kart*·ye)
I'd like (the menu).	
Я бы хотел/хотела (меню). (m/f)	ya bih khat·*yel*/khat·*ye*·la (min·*yu*)
I'd like to (hire a car).	
Я бы хотел/хотела (взять машину). (m/f)	ya bih khat·*yel*/khat·*ye*·la (vzyat' ma·*shih*·nu)
Can I (come in)?	
Можно (войти)?	*mozh*·na (vey·*ti*)
Could you please (write it down)?	
(Запишите), пожалуйста.	(za·pi·*shiht*·ye) pa·*zhal*·sta
Do I need (a visa)?	
Нужна ли (виза)?	nuzh·*na* li (*vi*·za)
I need (assistance).	
Мне нужна (помощь).	mnye nuzh·*na* (*po*·mash)

Fruit & Vegetables

apple	яблоко	*yab*·la·ka
bean	фасоль	fa·*sol*
cabbage	капуста	ka·*pu*·sta
capsicum	перец	*pye*·rits
carrot	морковь	mar·*kof'*
cauliflower	цветная капуста	tsvit·*na*·ya ka·*pu*·sta
cucumber	огурец	a·gur·*yets*
fruit	фрукты	*fruk*·tih
mushroom	гриб	grip
nut	орех	ar·*yekh*
onion	лук	luk
orange	апельсин	a·pil'·*sin*
peach	персик	*pyer*·sik
pear	груша	*gru*·sha
plum	слива	*sli*·va
potato	картошка	kar·*tosh*·ka
spinach	шпинат	shpi·*nat*
tomato	помидор	pa·mi·*dor*
vegetable	овощ	*o*·vash

Other

bread	хлеб	khlyep
cheese	сыр	sihr
egg	яйцо	yeyt·*so*
honey	мёд	myot
oil	масло	*mas*·la
pasta	паста	*pa*·sta
pepper	перец	*pye*·rits
rice	рис	ris
salt	соль	sol'
sugar	сахар	*sa*·khar
vinegar	уксус	*uk*·sus

Drinks

beer	пиво	*pi*·va
coffee	кофе	*kof*·ye
(orange) juice	(апельсиновый) сок	(a·pil'·*si*·na·vih) sok
milk	молоко	ma·la·*ko*
tea	чай	chey
(mineral) water	(минеральная) вода	(mi·ni·*ral'*·na·ya) va·*da*
wine	вино	vi·*no*

EMERGENCIES

Help!	Помогите!	pa·ma·*gi*·tye
Call ...!	Вызовите ...!	*vih*·za·vi·tye ...
a doctor	врача	vra·*cha*
the police	милицию	mi·*li*·tsih·yu

Leave me alone!
Приваливай! pri·*va*·li·vai

There's been an accident.
Произошёл несчастный случай. pra·i·za·*shol* ne·*shas*·nih *slu*·chai

I'm lost.
Я заблудился/заблудилась. (m/f) ya za·blu·*dil*·sa/za·blu·*di*·las'

Where are the toilets?
Где здесь туалет? gdye zdyes' tu·al·*yet*

I'm ill.
Я болен/больна. (m/f) ya *bo*·lin/bal'·*na*

It hurts here.
Здесь болит. zdyes' ba·*lit*

I'm allergic to (antibiotics).
У меня алергия на (антибиотики). u min·*ya* a·lir·*gi*·ya na (an·ti·bi·*o*·ti·ki)

SHOPPING & SERVICES

I need ...
Мне нужно ... mnye *nuzh*·na ...

I'm just looking.
Я просто смотрю. ya *pros*·ta smat·*ryu*

Can I look at it?
Покажите, пожалуйста. pa·ka·*zhih*·tye pa·*zhal*·sta

How much is it?
Сколько стоит? *skol'*·ka *sto*·it

That's too expensive.
Это очень дорого. e·ta *o*·chen' *do*·ra·ga

There's a mistake in the bill.
Меня обсчитали. min·*ya* ap·shi·*ta*·li

bank	банк	bank
market	рынок	*rih*·nak
post office	почта	*poch*·ta
telephone office	телефонный пункт	ti·li·*fo*·nih punkt

TIME, DATES & NUMBERS

What time is it?
Который час? ka·*to*·rih chas

It's (10) o'clock.
(Десять) часов. (*dye*·sit') chi·*sof*

morning	утро	*ut*·ra
afternoon	после обеда	*pos*·lye ab·*ye*·da
evening	вечер	*vye*·chir
yesterday	вчера	vchi·*ra*
today	сегодня	si·*vod*·nya
tomorrow	завтра	*zaft*·ra

Monday	понедельник	pa·ni·*dyel'*·nik
Tuesday	вторник	*ftor*·nik
Wednesday	среда	sri·*da*
Thursday	четверг	chit·*vyerk*
Friday	пятница	*pyat*·ni·tsa
Saturday	суббота	su·*bo*·ta
Sunday	воскресенье	vas·kri·*syen*·ye

Question Words

What?	Что?	shto
When?	Когда?	kag·*da*
Where?	Где?	gdye
Which?	Какой?	ka·*koy*
Who?	Кто?	kto
Why?	Почему?	pa·chi·*mu*

January	январь	yan·*var'*
February	февраль	fiv·*ral'*
March	март	mart
April	апрель	ap·*ryel'*
May	май	mai
June	июнь	i·*yun'*
July	июль	i·*yul'*
August	август	*av*·gust
September	сентябрь	sin·*tyabr*
October	октябрь	ak·*tyabr'*
November	ноябрь	na·*yabr'*
December	декабрь	di·*kabr'*

1	один	a·*din*
2	два	dva
3	три	tri
4	четыре	chi·*tih*·ri
5	пять	pyat'
6	шесть	shest'
7	семь	syem'
8	восемь	*vo*·sim'
9	девять	*dye*·vyat'
10	десять	*dye*·syat'
20	двадцать	*dva*·tsat'
30	тридцать	*tri*·tsat'
40	сорок	*so*·rak
50	пятьдесят	pi·dis·*yat*
60	шестдесят	shihs·dis·*yat*
70	семьдесят	*syem'*·dis·yat
80	восемьдесят	*vo*·sim'·di·sit
90	девяносто	di·vi·*no*·sta
100	сто	sto
1000	тысяча	*tih*·si·cha

TRANSPORT

Public Transport

A ... ticket (to Novgorod).	Билет ... (на Новгород).	bil·*yet* ... (na *nov*·ga·rat)
one-way	в один конец	v a·*din* kan·*yets*
return	в оба конца	v o·ba kan·*tsa*

bus	автобус	af·*to*·bus
train	поезд	*po*·ist
tram	трамвай	tram·*vai*
trolleybus	троллейбус	tra·*lyey*·bus
first	первый	*pyer*·vih
last	последний	pas·*lyed*·ni
metro token	жетон	zhi·*ton*
platform	платформа	plat·*for*·ma
(bus) stop	остановка	a·sta·*nof*·ka
ticket	билет	bil·*yet*
ticket office	билетная касса	bil·*yet*·na·ya *ka*·sa
timetable	расписание	ras·pi·*sa*·ni·ye

When does it leave?
Когда отправляется? kag·*da* at·prav·*lya*·it·sa

How long does it take to get to ...?
Сколько времени нужно ехать до ...? *skol'*·ka *vrye*·mi·ni *nuzh*·na *ye*·khat' da ...

Does it stop at ...?
Поезд останавливается в ...? *po*·yist a·sta·*nav*·li·va·yit·sa v ...

Please stop here.
Остановитесь здесь, пожалуйста! a·sta·na·*vit*·yes' zdyes' pa·*zhal*·sta

Driving & Cycling

I'd like to hire a ...	Я бы хотел/хотела взять ... на прокат. (m/f)	ya bih kha·*tyel*/kha·*tye*·la vzyat' ... na pra·*kat*
4WD	машину с полным приводом	ma·*shih*·nu s *pol*·nihm pri·*vo*·dam
bicycle	велосипед	vi·la·si·*pyet*
car	машину	ma·*shih*·nu
motorbike	мотоцикл	ma·ta·*tsikl*
diesel	дизельное топливо	*di*·zil'·na·ye *to*·pli·va
regular	бензин номер 93	ben·*zin no*·mir di·vi·*no*·sta tri
unleaded	очищенный бензин	a·*chi*·shi·nih bin·*zin*

Is this the road to ...?
Эта дорога ведёт в ...? e·ta da·*ro*·ga vid·*yot* f ...

Where's a petrol station?
Где заправка? gdye za·*praf*·ka

Can I park here?
Здесь можно стоять? zdyes' *mozh*·na sta·*yat'*

I need a mechanic.
Мне нужен автомеханик. mnye *nu*·zhihn af·ta·mi·*kha*·nik

The car has broken down.
Машина сломалась. ma·*shih*·na sla·*ma*·las'

I have a flat tyre.
У меня лопнула шина. u min·*ya* lop·*nu*·la *shih*·na

I've run out of petrol.
У меня кончился бензин. u min·*ya kon*·chil·sa bin·*zin*

GLOSSARY

You may encounter some of the following terms and abbreviations during your travels in Russia.

aeroport – airport
ail – hexagonal or tepee-shaped yurt
apteka – pharmacy
arzhaan – Tuvan sacred spring
ataman – Cossack leader
aviakassa – air ticket office
avtobus – bus
avtostantsiya – bus stop
avtovokzal – bus terminal
AYaM – Amuro-Yakutskaya Magistral or Amur-Yakutsk Mainline

babushka – literally, 'grandmother', but used generally in Russian society for all old women
BAM – Baikalo-Amurskaya Magistral or Baikal-Amur Mainline, a trans-Siberian rail route
bankomat – automated teller machine (ATM)
banya – bathhouse
bashnya – tower
biblioteka – library
bifshteks – Russian-style hamburger
bilet – ticket
bolnitsa – hospital
bolshoy – big
boyar – high-ranking noble
bufet – snack bar selling cheap cold meats, boiled eggs, salads, bread, pastries etc
bukhta – bay
bulvar – boulevard
buterbrod – open sandwich
byliny – epic songs

chebureki – fried, meat-filled turnovers
chum – tepee-shaped tent made of birch bark
CIS (Commonwealth of Independent States) – an alliance (proclaimed in 1991) of independent states comprising the former USSR republics (less the three Baltic states); Sodruzhestvo Nezavisimykh Gosudarstv (SNG)

dacha – country cottage, summer house
datsan – Buddhist monastery
detsky – child's, children's
dezhurnaya – woman looking after a particular floor of a hotel
dolina – valley
dom – house
duma – parliament
dvorets – palace
dvorets kultury – literally, 'culture palace'; a meeting, social, entertainment, education centre, usually for a group such as railway workers, children etc

elektrichka – suburban train
etazh – floor (storey)

finift – luminous enamelled metal miniatures
firmeny poezda – trains with names (eg Rossiya); these are generally nicer trains
FSB (Federalnaya Sluzhba Bezopasnosti) – the Federal Security Service, the successor to the KGB

garderob – cloakroom
gastronom – speciality food shop
gavan – harbour
gazeta – newspaper
GIBDD (Gosudarsvennaya Inspektsiya po bezopasnosti dorozhnogo dvizheniya) – the State Automobile Inspectorate, aka the traffic police, still commonly known by their previous acronym GAI
glasnost – literally, 'openness'; the free-expression aspect of the Gorbachev reforms
glavpochtamt – main post office
gora – mountain
gorod – city, town
gostinitsa – hotel
gostiny dvor – trading arcade
Gulag (Glavnoe Upravlenie Lagerey) – Main Administration for Camps; the Soviet network of concentration camps
GUM (Gosudarstvenny Univermag) – State Department Store

igil – bowed, two-stringed Tuvan instrument
Intourist – old Soviet State Committee for Tourism, now privatised, split up and in competition with hundreds of other travel agencies
istochnik – mineral spring
izba – traditional, single-storey wooden cottage

kafe – café
kameny baba – standing stone idol
kamera khranenia – left-luggage office
kanal – canal
karta – map
kartofel, kartoshka – potatoes
kassa – ticket office, cashier's desk
kater – small ferry
kazak – Cossack
kempingi – organised camp sites; often have small cabins as well as tent sites
KGB (Komitet Gosudarstvennoy Bezopasnosti) – Committee of State Security
khachapuri – Georgian cheese bread
khleb – bread
khokhloma – red, black and gold lacquered pine bowls
khöömei – Tuvan throat singing
khram – church
khuresh – Tuvan style of wrestling
kino – cinema
kleshchi – ticks
kniga – book
kokoshniki – colourful gables and tiles laid in patterns
kolkhoz – collective farm
komnaty otdykha – resting rooms found at all major train stations and several smaller ones
kompot – fruit squash
Komsomol – Communist Youth League

kopek – the smallest, worthless unit of Russian currency
kordony – forest lodges, often found in national parks
korpus – building (ie one of several in a complex)
kray – territory
kremlin – a town's fortified stronghold
kulak – a peasant wealthy enough to own a farm, hire labour and engage in money lending
kupeyny, kupe – 2nd-class compartment on a train
kurgan – burial mound
kurort – spa
kvartira – flat, apartment
kvas – fermented rye bread water

lavra – senior monastery
lyux – a kind of hotel suite, with a sitting room in addition to bedroom and bathroom; a *polu-lyux* suite is the less spacious version

Mafia – anyone who has anything to do with crime, from genuine gangsters to victims of their protection rackets
magazin – shop
maly – small
manezh – riding school
marka – postage stamp or brand, trademark
marshrutka, marshrutnoye taksi – minibus that runs along a fixed route
matryoshka – set of painted wooden dolls within dolls
medovukha – honey ale (mead)
mestnoe vremya – local time
mezhdunarodny – international
mineralnaya voda – mineral water
monastyr – monastery
more – sea
morskoy vokzal – sea terminal
Moskovskoye vremya – Moscow time
most – bridge
muzey – museum; also some palaces, art galleries and non-working churches
muzhskoy – men's (toilet)
myagky – 1st-class train compartment

naberezhnaya – embankment
Nashi – Ours; ultranationalist youth group
nizhny – lower
nomenklatura – literally, 'list of nominees'; the old government and Communist Party elite
novy – new
novy russky – New Russians

obed – lunch
oblast – region
obshchiy – 4th-class place on a train
okruga – districts
omul – a cousin of salmon and trout, endemic to Lake Baikal
ostrog – fortress
ostrov – island
OVIR (Otdel Viz i Registratsii) – Department of Visas and Registration; now known under the acronym PVU, although outside Moscow OVIR is still likely to be in use
ozero – lake

palekh – enamelled wood boxes
parnyatnik – statue, monument
Paskha – Easter
passazhirsky poezd – intercity stopping train
pelmeni – Russian-style ravioli stuffed with meat
perekhod – underground walkway
perestroika – literally, 're-structuring'; Mikhail Gorbachev's efforts to revive the Soviet economy
pereulok – lane, side street
pirozhki – savoury pies
platskartny, platskart – 3rd-class place on a train
ploshchad – square
pochta – post office
poezd – train
poliklinika – medical centre
polu-lyux – less spacious version of a *lyux*, a hotel suite with a sitting room in addition to the bedroom and bathroom
polyana – glade, clearing
posolstvo – embassy
prichal – landing, pier
prigorodny poezd – suburban train
prigorodny zal – ticket hall
produkty – food store
proezd – passage
prokat – rental
propusk – permit, pass
prospekt – avenue
provodnik (m), provodnitsa (f) – carriage attendant on a train
PVU (Passportno-Vizovoye Upravleniye) – passport and visa department, formerly OVIR (an acronym which is still likely to be in use outside Moscow)

raketa – hydrofoil
rayon – district
rechnoy vokzal – river station
reka – river
remont, na remont – closed for repairs (a sign you see all too often)
restoran – restaurant
Rozhdestvo – Russian Orthodox Christmas
rynok – market

sad – garden
samovar – an urn used to heat water for tea
selo – village
sever – north
shawarma – grilled meat and salad wrapped in flat bread
shashlyk – meat kebab
shosse – highway
shtuka – piece (many items of produce are sold by the piece)
skory poezd – literally, 'fast train'; a long-distance train
sobor – cathedral

soviet – council
sovok – a contraction of *sovokopniy*, meaning communal person and referring to those who were born and lived during the Soviet period
spalny vagon – SV; 1st-class place on a train
spusk – descent, slope
Sputnik – former youth-travel arm of Komsomol; now just one of the bigger tourism agencies
stanitsa – Cossack village
stary – old
stolovaya – canteen, cafeteria
suvenir – souvenir

taiga – northern pine, fir, spruce and larch forest
taksofon – pay telephone
teatr – theatre
teatralnaya kassa – theatre ticket office
thangka – Buddhist religious paintings
traktir – tavern
tramvay – tram
tserkov – church
TsUM (Tsentralny Univermag) – name of a department store
tualet – toilet
tuda i obratno – literally, 'there and back'; return ticket
turbaza – tourist camp

ulitsa – street
univermag, universalny magazin – department store
ushchelie – gorge or valley
uzhin – supper

val – rampart
vareniki – dumplings with a variety of possible fillings
venik – tied bundle of birch branches
verkhny – upper
vkhod – way in, entrance
voda – water
vodny vokzal – ferry terminal
vokzal – station
vostok – east
vykhodnoy den – day off (Saturday, Sunday and holidays)

yantar – amber
yezhednevno – every day, daily
yug – south
yurt – nomad's portable, round tent-house made of felt or skins stretched over a collapsible frame of wood slats

zakaznaya – registered post
zakuski – appetisers
zal – hall, room
zaliv – gulf, bay
zamok – castle, fortress
zapad – west
zapovednik – special purpose (nature) reserve
zavtrak – breakfast
zhensky – women's (toilet)
zhetony – tokens (for metro etc)

Behind the Scenes

SEND US YOUR FEEDBACK

We love to hear from travellers – your comments keep us on our toes and help make our books better. Our well-travelled team reads every word on what you loved or loathed about this book. Although we cannot reply individually to postal submissions, we always guarantee that your feedback goes straight to the appropriate authors, in time for the next edition. Each person who sends us information is thanked in the next edition – the most useful submissions are rewarded with a selection of digital PDF chapters.

Visit **lonelyplanet.com/contact** to submit your updates and suggestions or to ask for help. Our award-winning website also features inspirational travel stories, news and discussions.

Note: We may edit, reproduce and incorporate your comments in Lonely Planet products such as guidebooks, websites and digital products, so let us know if you don't want your comments reproduced or your name acknowledged. For a copy of our privacy policy visit lonelyplanet.com/privacy.

OUR READERS

Many thanks to the travellers who used the last edition and wrote to us with helpful hints, useful advice and interesting anecdotes:
Nick Botham, Katerina Canyon, Nicolas Combremont, Christophe Cozien, Jonathan Dickinson, Kennet Fischer Föh, Erik Futtrup, Basia Jóźwiak, Helene Karson, Leslye Korvola, Tim McCready, Marie-Louise Miginiac, Patricia O'Donnell, Karin Ratschbacher, Naomi Rose, Natalia Snezhnaya, Caroline Swain, Jiri Varadinek, Michael von Külmer

AUTHOR THANKS

Simon Richmond

Many thanks to my fellow authors and Brana at HQ; Sasha & Andrey for a lovely place to stay, the ever knowledgeable Peter Kozyrev, Chris Hamilton, Adelya Dayanova, Polina Adrianova, Dimitri Ozerkov, Vladimir Stolyarov, Yegor Churakov, Oksana, Maxim Pinigin, Alexander Kim, Maria Isserlis, Yevgenia Semenoff and Polina at the Street Art Museum.

Marc Bennetts

Thanks to Tanya and Masha for a warm welcome when I arrived home from this research trip. Thanks also to Brana Vladisavljevic and Simon Richmond for steering me through the new system. Thanks also to everyone who helped me out during my travels.

Greg Bloom

Thanks to Dima for the hospitality in Sheregesh. Thanks to Rita for the Altai advice and for hooking me up with several contacts. Thanks to Vladimir, my crazy cab driver, for the colourful language and Chuysky Trakt anecdotes. Thanks to Russian Railways for being so damn punctual. Thanks to Transaero for the upgrade to business class. Thanks to *kalyan*. Thanks to the peeps of Western Siberia for being good souls.

Marc Di Duca

Huge *dyakuyu* goes to Kyiv parents-in-law Mykola and Vira for looking after sons Taras and Kirill while I was in Siberia. Big thanks to Alex in Chita, Denis and Marina in Ulan-Ude, Andriy and Anya in Slyudyanka, Zhenya in Irkutsk, Igor, Lena and Georgy in Tayshet, the Maryasovs of Severobaikalsk, Anatoliy and Alex in Krasnoyarsk, Aldar and everyone at the Tuvan Cultural Centre, Evgeniy, Anay-Khaak, Sean and Enrique in Kyzyl, Real Russia in London for their hassle-free visa service and of course my wife Tanya, for suffering my long absences from our home in Sandwich, Kent.

Anthony Haywood

Thanks to those who helped out with local knowledge, mostly anonymously, along the way, but especially to Katya Y. in Kazan and Katya P. in Perm. In Yekaterinburg I'd like to thank Konstantin and Olga Brylyakov for sharing their knowledge (and delicious cream cake!), and Luba Suslyakova for her expert opinions and good company over dinner. Thanks also to the staff at LP, especially Anna Tyler and Brana Vladisavljevic.

Anna Kaminski

I would like to thank everyone who'd helped me along the way, not least Brana, Simon for all the advice and encouragement, Tamara and Mark, my predecessors, and the rest of the Russia team. An *ogromnoye spasibo* to friends old and new, particularly Dmitrii Babenko and Svetlana Tsybendorzhieva in Murmansk, as well as Aleksanr, Ksenia, Aleksei, Andrei, Vadim and Natalia, Igor and Anna in Kirovsk – the chapter wouldn't have been the same without your help! I'm also much obliged to my parents for fuelling my wanderlust with their own tales of the Russian north…and for everything else.

Tom Masters

Huge thanks to my many friends in St Petersburg, but especially Anatoliy Buzinskiy at Dozhd, Biblioteka Gogolya and Letovpitere for making such huge efforts to help me with contacts and introductions. Thanks to my old friend and tireless Petersburger Simon Patterson, his wife Olga Dmitrieva and their amazing children for making me feel at home during my stay, and also for organising my accommodation. Thanks also to such reliable comrades as Nikita Yumanov, Gena Bogolepov, Alexei Dmitriev, Alexei Chernov, Nikita Slavich, Dima Dzhafarov, Sasha & Andrey, Peter Kozyrev and Nastya Makarova. At Lonely Planet big thanks to Simon Richmond, Anna Tyler, Brana Vladisavljevic and all the in-house eds and cartos for their hard work on this title.

Leonid Ragozin

Many thanks to my wife Masha Makeeva for bearing with my absences and for accompanying me on the Yaroslavl section of this trip. Huge thanks to my LP colleague Branislava Vladisavljevic for her patience and helping with numerous issues that were coming up in the course of research. It was also great to catch up with fellow authors – Simon Richmond, Anthony Haywood and Mara Vorhees – in Moscow. Good to see you again!

Tamara Sheward

Huge thanks go out to Dasha, Vasily, Danil, Olga and Katerina, the brilliant tourist info folks in Kaliningrad and Veliky Novgorod, the eternally-helpful Anton and (the other!) Tamara, the countless babushki who helped with (and spoiled) bubba Masha on the road, and to the incomparably amazing Baba Ritik. All the love in the universe and beyond to Dusan and Masha. Durak adventure forever!

Regis St Louis

Thanks go to Anna Kaminski and Greg Bloom for helpful tips on the Far East; Martha Madsen for her hospitality and many tips in Yelizovo; Irina and Sasha for a warm welcome in Esso; Yelena for loads of info at Omega Plus in Yuzhno-Sakhalinsk; Anastasia for Vladivostok insight; Sasha for the Russky Island excursion; Yegor Makarov for Sakha lore, and Aita, Illary, Elena and expats for all the help in Yakutsk. Hugs to Cassandra and daughters Magdalena and Genevieve for a warm homecoming.

Mara Vorhees

Самое болшое спасибо to my friend and co-author, Leonid Ragozin, who is a pleasure to work with and *fontanka* of information about his hometown. Thanks to Tim O'Brien (of course), Marc Bennetts, Simon Richmond and Andrei Muchnik for lots of ideas. And finally, what a treat to spend time (not enough) with two dear friends from my past: `Nasha Pasha' Yesin and Lyonya Klyuev. As always, thanks to my little guys S&V, for challenging me to see familiar destinations from new perspectives, and to Daddio, for, well, everything.

ACKNOWLEDGMENTS

Climate map data adapted from Peel MC, Finlayson BL & McMahon TA (2007) 'Updated World Map of the Köppen-Geiger Climate Classification', *Hydrology and Earth System Sciences*, 11, 163344.

Moscow metro map: © Art. Lebedev Studio

Illustrations p58-9 and p156-7 by Javier Zarracina

Cover photograph: Transfiguration Cathedral, Kizhi, Republic of Karelia, Russia, Johanna Huber / 4Corners ©

THIS BOOK

This 7th edition of Lonely Planet's *Russia* guidebook was researched and written by Simon Richmond, Marc Bennetts, Greg Bloom, Marc Di Duca, Anthony Haywood, Anna Kaminski, Tom Masters, Leonid Ragozin, Tamara Sheward, Regis St Louis and Mara Vorhees. The same authors worked on the previous edition. Mark Elliott and Robert Reid worked on the 5th edition. This guidebook was commissioned in Lonely Planet's London office and produced by the following:

Commissioning Editor
Anna Tyler

Destination Editor
Branislava Vladisavljevic

Product Editor
Elizabeth Jones

Regional Senior Cartographer
Valentina Kremenchutskaya

Book Designer
Jessica Rose

Assisting Editors
Andrew Bain, Kellie Langdon, Anne Mulvaney, Charlotte Orr, Jeanette Wall

Assisting Cartographers
Julie Dodkins, Michael Garrett, James Leversha

Assisting Book Designer
Virginia Moreno

Cover Research
Naomi Parker

Thanks to Sasha Baskett, Kate Chapman, Penny Cordner, Pete Cruttenden, Brendan Dempsey, Bruce Evans, Ryan Evans, Justin Flynn, Larissa Frost, Anna Harris, Jouve India, Kate James, Andi Jones, Wayne Murphy, Claire Naylor, Karyn Noble, Dianne Schallmeiner, Ellie Simpson, John Taufa, Samantha Tyson, Lauren Wellicome, Juan Winata

Index

Map Pages **000**
Photo Pages **000**

B

Map Pages **000**
Photo Pages **000**

I

J

K

L

Map Pages **000**
Photo Pages **000**

R

Map Pages **000**
Photo Pages **000**

Map Pages **000**
Photo Pages **000**

Map Legend

Sights
- Beach
- Bird Sanctuary
- Buddhist
- Castle/Palace
- Christian
- Confucian
- Hindu
- Islamic
- Jain
- Jewish
- Monument
- Museum/Gallery/Historic Building
- Ruin
- Shinto
- Sikh
- Taoist
- Winery/Vineyard
- Zoo/Wildlife Sanctuary
- Other Sight

Activities, Courses & Tours
- Bodysurfing
- Diving
- Canoeing/Kayaking
- Course/Tour
- Sento Hot Baths/Onsen
- Skiing
- Snorkelling
- Surfing
- Swimming/Pool
- Walking
- Windsurfing
- Other Activity

Sleeping
- Sleeping
- Camping

Eating
- Eating

Drinking & Nightlife
- Drinking & Nightlife
- Cafe

Entertainment
- Entertainment

Shopping
- Shopping

Information
- Bank
- Embassy/Consulate
- Hospital/Medical
- Internet
- Police
- Post Office
- Telephone
- Toilet
- Tourist Information
- Other Information

Geographic
- Beach
- Hut/Shelter
- Lighthouse
- Lookout
- Mountain/Volcano
- Oasis
- Park
- Pass
- Picnic Area
- Waterfall

Population
- Capital (National)
- Capital (State/Province)
- City/Large Town
- Town/Village

Transport
- Airport
- Border crossing
- Bus
- Cable car/Funicular
- Cycling
- Ferry
- Metro station
- Monorail
- Parking
- Petrol station
- S-Bahn/S-train/Subway station
- Taxi
- T-bane/Tunnelbana station
- Train station/Railway
- Tram
- Tube station
- U-Bahn/Underground station
- Other Transport

Note: Not all symbols displayed above appear on the maps in this book

Routes
- Tollway
- Freeway
- Primary
- Secondary
- Tertiary
- Lane
- Unsealed road
- Road under construction
- Plaza/Mall
- Steps
- Tunnel
- Pedestrian overpass
- Walking Tour
- Walking Tour detour
- Path/Walking Trail

Boundaries
- International
- State/Province
- Disputed
- Regional/Suburb
- Marine Park
- Cliff
- Wall

Hydrography
- River, Creek
- Intermittent River
- Canal
- Water
- Dry/Salt/Intermittent Lake
- Reef

Areas
- Airport/Runway
- Beach/Desert
- Cemetery (Christian)
- Cemetery (Other)
- Glacier
- Mudflat
- Park/Forest
- Sight (Building)
- Sportsground
- Swamp/Mangrove